Lecture Notes in Computer Science 4742

Commenced Publication in 1973
Founding and Former Series Editors:
Gerhard Goos, Juris Hartmanis, and Jan van Leeuwen

Ivan Stojmenovic   Ruppa K. Thulasiram
Laurence T. Yang   Weijia Jia
Minyi Guo   Rodrigo Fernandes de Mello (Eds.)

Parallel and Distributed Processing and Applications

5th International Symposium, ISPA 2007
Niagara Falls, Canada, August 29-31, 2007
Proceedings

Volume Editors

Ivan Stojmenovic
University of Ottawa, Ottawa, ON, Canada
E-mail: ivan@site.uottawa.ca

Ruppa K. Thulasiram
University of Manitoba, Winnipeg, MB, Canada
E-mail: tulsi@cs.umanitoba.ca

Laurence T. Yang
St. Francis Xavier University, Antigonish, NS, Canada
E-mail: ltyang@stfx.ca

Weijia Jia
City University of Hong Kong, Hong Kong, China
E-mail: itjia@cityu.edu.hk

Minyi Guo
Aizu University, Aizu-Wakamatsu, Fukushima-ken, Japan
E-mail: minyi@u-aizu.ac.jp

Rodrigo Fernandes de Mello
University of São Paulo, São Carlos, SP, Brazil
E-mail: mello@icmc.usp.br

Library of Congress Control Number: 2007933582

CR Subject Classification (1998): F.1, F.2, D.1, D.2, D.4, C.2, C.4, H.4, K.6

LNCS Sublibrary: SL 1 – Theoretical Computer Science and General Issues

ISSN 0302-9743
ISBN-10 3-540-74741-9 Springer Berlin Heidelberg New York
ISBN-13 978-3-540-74741-3 Springer Berlin Heidelberg New York

Springer is a part of Springer Science+Business Media

springer.com

Printed in Germany

Typesetting: Camera-ready by author, data conversion by Scientific Publishing Services, Chennai, India
Printed on acid-free paper SPIN: 12117895 06/3180 5 4 3 2 1 0

Preface

We are very proud and honored to have been entrusted to be Program and General Chairs of the Fifth International Symposium on Parallel and Distributed Processing and Applications (ISPA07) in Niagara Falls (Canada), August 29-31, 2007. We received 244 submissions, showing by quantity and quality that ISPA is a popular and respected conference in the area. Submissions were first screened for their relevance and general submission requirements, and 226 of them were kept for evaluation. All these manuscripts underwent a rigorous peer-review process. At the end, 83 articles were accepted for presentation and inclusion in the proceedings, comprising 34% of original submissions. Many individuals contributed to the success of this conference. We take this opportunity to thank all authors for their submissions, many of whom traveled great distances to participate in this symposium and make their valuable contributions. Our Program Vice Chairs helped enormously by putting together a Program Committee, assigning and tracking reviews for each paper, and making summary recommendations. Lei Pan (Software and Languages Track), Xiaoming Li (Architectures and Systems), Mohamed Ould-Khaoua (Networks), Cheng-Zhong Xu (Middleware and Cooperative Computing), M. Cristina Pinoti (Algorithms and Applications), Dan A Simovici (Datamining and Databases), Amiya Nayak (Fault Tolerance and Security) made an outstanding contribution to the fair selection of the best articles for the conference. We are also indebted to a small army of Program Committee members who put hard work and long hours into reviewing each paper in a timely and professional way! Thanks to all the Program Committee members for their valuable time and effort in reviewing the papers. Without their help and advice this program would not have been possible. We also appreciate the support from the invited speakers, Sitharama Iyengar, Pradip Srimani, and Hai Jin. Their keynote speeches greatly benefited the audience. We would like to also thank Tony Li Xu for his help with the submission system, which facilitated our work. Last but not the least, we are indebted to Steering Chairs Minyi Guo and Laurence T. Yang for offering us this opportunity.

August 2007

Ivan Stojmenovic
Ruppa K. Thulasiram
Laurence T. Yang
Weijia Jia
Minyi Guo
Rodrigo Fernandes de Mello

Organization

Executive Committee

General Chairs	Jie Wu, Florida Atlantic University, USA Ruppa K. Thulasiram, University of Manitoba, Canada
General Vice Chair	Mieso Denko, University of Guelph, Canada
Program Chairs	Ivan Stojmenovic, University of Ottawa, Canada Weijia Jia, City University of Hong Kong, China
Program Vice Chairs	Lei Pan, JPL, California Institute of Technology, USA Xiaoming Li, Peking University, China Mohamed Ould-Khaoua, University of Glasgow, UK Cheng-Zhong Xu, Wayne State University, USA M. Cristina Pinoti, Università degli Studi di Perugia, Italy Dan A Simovici, University of Massachusetts, USA Amiya Nayak, University of Ottawa, Canada
Steering Chairs	Minyi Guo, University of Aizu, Japan Laurence T. Yang, St. Francis Xavier University, Canada
Publicity Chairs	Guoing Cong, IBM T.J. Watson Research Center, USA Rasit Eskicioglu, University of Manitoba, Canada Jong-Hyuk Park, Hanwha S&C, Korea
Publication Chairs	Rodrigo Fernandes de Mello, University of São Paulo, Brazil Tony Li Xu, St. Francis Xavier University, Canada
Workshop Chairs	Parimala Thulasiraman, University of Manitoba, Canada Xubin (Ben) He, Tennessee Technological University, USA
Web Chairs	Rodrigo Fernandes de Mello, University of São Paulo, Brazil Tony Li Xu, St. Francis Xavier University, Canada Liu Yang, St. Francis Xavier University, Canada
Local Organizing Chair	Mieso Denko, University of Guelph, Canada

Program Committee

Kamel Adi	University of Quebec, Canada
Jesus S. Aguilar-Ruiz	Pablo de Olavide University, Seville, Spain
Ahmad Al-Dubai	Napier University, UK
Paul von Allmen	JPL, California Institute of Technology, USA
Irfan Awan	Bradford University, UK
Mark Baker	University of Reading, UK
Alan A. Bertossi	University of Bologna, Italy
Lubomir Bic	University of California at Irvine, USA
Azzedine Boukerche	Univeristy of Ottawa, Canada
Anu Bourgeois	Georgia State University, USA
Monica Brockmeyer	Wayne State University, USA
Gerth Brodal	University of Aarhus, Denmark
Wentong Cai	Nanyang Technological University, Singapore
Toon Calders	Eindhoven University of Technology, The Netherlands
Jiannong Cao	Hong Kong Polytechnic University, Hong Kong
Eddy Caron	Parallel Computing Lab, ENS Lyon, France
Vipin Chaudhary	State University of New York at Buffalo, USA
Daoxu Chen	Nanjing University, China
Michele Colajanni	University of Modena e Reggio Emilia, Italy
Guojing Cong	IBM T.J. Watson Research Center, USA
Yafei Dai	Peking University, China
Qianni Deng	Shanghai Jiaotong University, China
Michael Dillencourt	University of California at Irvine, USA
Karim Djemame	Leeds University, UK
Chabane Djeraba	University of Lille I, France
Mourad Elhadef	University of Ottawa, Canada
Robert Elsaesser	University of Paderborn, Germany
Mohamed Eltoweissy	Virginia Tech, USA
Rod Fatoohi	San Jose State University, USA
Michele Flammini	University of L'Aquila, Italy
Satoshi Fujita	Hiroshima University, Japan
Leszek Gasieniec	University of Liverpool, UK
Aristides Gionis	University of Helsinki, Finland
Mourad Gueroui	University of Cergy-Pontoise, France
Fabrice Guillet	University of Nantes, France
Yanbo Han	Institute of Computing Technology, China
Yanxiang He	Wuhan University, China
Yasushi Inoguchi	Japan Advanced Institute of Science and Technology, Japan
Szymon Jaroszewicz	Technical University Szczecin, Poland
Song Jiang	Wayne State University, USA

Xiaohong Jiang	Tohoku University, Japan
Yuming Jiang	Norwegian University of Science and Technology, Norway
Hai Jin	Huazhong University of Science and Technology, China
Elias Duarte Jr.	Federal University of Parana, Brazil
Hirotsugu Kakugawa	Osaka University, Japan
Vana Kalogeraki	University of California at Riverside, USA
Helen Karatza	Aristotle University of Thessaloniki, Greece
Ahmad Khonsari	Institute for Studies in Theoretical Physics and Mathematics, Iran
Chung-Ta King	National Tsing Hua University, Taiwan
Leila Kloul	University of Versailles, France
Hiroaki Kobayashi	Tohoku University, Japan
Evangelos Kranakis	Carleton University, Ottawa, Canada
Adlen Ksentini	University of Rennes 1, France
Mohan Kumar	Unveirsity of Texas at Arlington, USA
Francis Lau	University of Hong Kong, Hong Kong
Christian Lavault	Universite Paris 13, France
Seungwon Lee	JPL, California Institute of Technology, USA
Rogerio De Lemos	University of Kent, UK
Xiaoming Li	Peking University, China
Hai Liu	City University of Hong Kong, Hong Kong
Errol Lloyd	Univerity of Delaware, USA
Pedro Lopez	Universidad Politecnica de Valencia, Spain
Samia Loucif	UAE University, UAE
Jianguo Lu	University of Windsor, Canada
Junzhou Luo	South Eastern University of China, China
Lewis M. Mackenzie	University of Glasgow, UK
Subhamoy Maitra	Indian Statistical Institute, India
Soumen Maity	Indian Institute of Technology, India
Florent Masseglia	INRIA, Sophia Antipolis, France
Susumu Matsumae	Tottori University of Environmental Studies, Japan
Ingo Mierswa	University of Dortmund, Germany
Geyong Min	Bradford University, UK
Marine Minier	INSA Lyon, France
Ali Miri	University of Ottawa, Canada
Eiji Miyano	Kyushu Institute of Technology, Japan
Mohamed Naimi	Université Cergy-Pontoise, France
Koji Nakano	Hiroshima University, Japan
Takashi Nanya	University of Tokyo, Japan
Alfredo Navarra	University of Bordeaux, France
Amiya Nayak	University of Ottawa, Canada
Sotiris Nikoletseas	Patras University, Greece
Lucila Ohno-Machado	Harvard University, USA

Stephan Olariu	Old Dominion University, USA
Beng Chin Ooi	National University of Singapore, Singapore
Mohamed Ould-Khaoua	University of Glasgow, UK
Benno Overeinder	Vrije Universiteit, The Netherlands
Linda Pagli	University of Pisa, Italy
Lei Pan	JPL, California Institute of Technology, USA
Andrzej Pelc	University of Quebec, Canada
M. Cristina Pinoti	Università degli Studi di Perugia, Italy
Jan F. Prins	University of North Carolina, Chapel Hill, USA
Omar F. Rana	Cardiff University, UK
Shangping Ren	Illinois Institute of Technology, USA
Romeo Rizzi	University of Udine, Italy
Jose Rolim	University of Geneva, Switzerland
Bimal Roy	Indian Statistical Institute, India
Stephan Ruhrup	University of Paderborn, Germany
Pedro M. Ruiz	University of Murcia, Spain
Subash Saini	NASA Ames Research Center, USA
Hamid Sarbazi-Azad	Sharif University, IPM, Iran
Alireza Shahrabi	Glasgow Caledonian University, UK
Anil Shende	Roanoke College, VA, USA
Dan A. Simovici	University of Massachusetts, USA
Henk Sips	Technische Universiteit Delft, The Netherlands
Neeraj Suri	TU Darmstadt, Germany
Alan Sussman	University of Maryland, USA
Mineo Takai	University of California at Los Angeles, USA
Michela Taufer	University of Texas at El Paso, USA
Nigel Thomas	Newcastle University, UK
Doru E. Tiliute	University of Suceava, Romania
Abderezak Touzene	Sultan Qaboos University, Oman
Damla Turgut	Unversity of Central Florida, USA
Michalis Vazirgiannis	Athens University of Economics, Greece
Marion Videau	INRIA, France
Cho-Li Wang	University of Hong Kong, Hong Kong
Dajin Wang	MontClair State University, USA
Dongsheng Wang	Tsinghua University, China
Zhiying Wang	National University of Defense Technology, China
Jianbin Wei	South Dakota School of Mines and Technology, USA
Prudence W.H. Wong	The University of Liverpool, UK
Yongwei Wu	Tsinghua University, China
Cheng-Zhong Xu	Wayne State University, USA
Jingling Xue	University of New South Wales, Australia
Mohammed J. Zaki	Rensselaer Polytechnic Institute, USA
Jingyuan Zhang	University of Alabama, USA
Jianjun Zhao	Shanghai Jiao Tong University, China
Si Qing Zheng	University of Texas at Dallas, USA

Bingbing Zhou	University of Sydney, Australia
Shujia Zhou	NASA Goddard Space Flight Center, USA
Xiaobo Zhou	University of Colorado at Colorado Springs, USA
Hans Zima	JPL, California Institute of Technology, USA
Albert Zomaya	Univesity of Sydney, Australia

Additional Reviewers

Mohammad Zubair Ahmad
Michele Albano
Abdelkader Amar
Christoph Ambuhl
Kiran Anna
Matthew Badin
Idzam Baharudin
Carlos D. Barranco
Georg Birkenheuer
Julien Blanchard
Luis C. E. Bona
Vineet Chaoji
Hanhua Chen
Pedro Cuenca
Jérôme David
Francisco M. Delicado
Benjamin Depardon
Ryusuke Egawa
Yuhong Feng
Jean-Michel Fourneau
Song Fu
Olac Fuentes
Samuel Galice
Mat Grove
Abdelhak Guéroui
Mohammad Hasan
Jan Hidders
Kashif Iqbal
Mahavir Jhawar
Wei Jie
Jik-Soo Kim
Ming Kin Lai
Rahim Lakhoo
Laurent Lefevre
Fabrizio Luccio
Panagis Magdalinos
Pietro Manzoni
Russell Martin
Henning Meyerhenke
Luca Moscardelli
Leonardo Mostarda
Akihiro Musa
Beomseok Nam
Sukumar Nandi
Juan A. Nepomuceno
Isabel A. Nepomuceno-Chamorro
Fukuhito Ooshita
Stefan-Gheorghe Pentiuc
Benjarath Phoophakdee
Beatriz Pontes
Francesco Potort
Fasheng Qiu
San Ratanasanya
Abdelmounaam Rezgui
Domingo Rodriguez-Baena
Sushmita Ruj
Vipin Sachdeva
Leonardo Salayandia
Iman Saleh
Saeed Salem
Seetharami Seelam
Ali Shahrabi
Ke Shi
Julia Sidirova
Charuka Silva
Ken-ichi Suzuki
Hiroyuki Takizawa
Yoshinobu Tamura
Ana Varbanescu
Hong Wang
Xue Wang
Griffin Weber
Joe Shang-Chieh Wu
Qin Xin

Linhao Xu
Xiaoyan Yang
Il-Chul Yoon
Zhibin Yu
Pingpeng Yuan
Wenhui Zhang
Zhenjie Zhang
Xiliang Zhong
Yu Zhou

Table of Contents

Keynote Speech

Algorithms and Applications

Architectures and Systems

Datamining and Databases

Fault Tolerance and Security

Middleware and Cooperative Computing

Networks

Software and Languages

Self-stabilizing Distributed Algorithms for Networks

Pradip K. Srimani

Department of Computer Science
Clemson University, South Carolina, USA
srimani@cs.clemson.edu

Abstract. Many essential fundamental services for networked distributed systems (ad hoc, wireless or sensor) involve maintaining a global predicate over the entire network (defined by some invariance relation on the global state of the network) by using local knowledge at each of the participating nodes. The participating nodes can no longer keep track of even a small fraction of the knowledge about the global network due to limited storage. We need a new paradigm of localized distributed algorithms, where a node takes simple actions based on local knowledge of only its immediate neighbors and yet the system achieves a global objective. Self-stabilization is a relatively new paradigm for designing such localized distributed algorithms for networks; it is an optimistic way of looking at system fault tolerance and scalable coordination; it provides a cost effective built-in safeguard against transient failures that might corrupt data in a distributed system. We introduce self-stabilizing protocol design with the example of a total dominating set in a network graph and discuss some open problems.

Brief Biography

Pradip K. Srimani is a professor of computer science at Clemson University, South Carolina (he was department chair between August 2000 and December 2006). He had previously served the faculty of Indian Statistical Institute, Calcutta, Gesselschaft fuer Mathematik und Datenverarbeitung, Bonn, West Germany, Indian Institute of Management, Calcutta, India, Southern Illinois University, Carbondale, Illinois, Colorado State University in Ft. Collins, Colorado and University of Technology, Compiegne, France. He received his Ph. D. degree in Radio Physics & Electronics from University of Calcutta, Calcutta, India in 1978.

He has authored/co-authored more than 200 papers in journals and conferences and edited two books for IEEE Computer Society Press. He had served in the past as Editor-in-Chief for IEEE Computer Society Press and as a member of the Editorial Boards of IEEE Software, IEEE Transactions on Knowledge and Data Engineering, and Parallel Computing. He has served as a Distinguished Visiting Speaker and Chapter Tutorial Speaker for IEEE Computer Society for the past several years. He has guest edited special issues for IEEE Trans.

I. Stojmenovic et al. (Eds.): ISPA 2007, LNCS 4742, pp. 1–2, 2007.

Comput., IEEE Trans. Software Eng., Parallel Computing, IEEE Computer, Software, Journal of Computer & Software Engineering, Journal of Systems Software, VLSI Design, International Journal of Systems Science etc. He has served on the national IEEECS/ACM task force on curriculum design for computer science and computer engineering He has also served many conferences in various capacities as program chair, general chair and tutorial speaker. Currently, he serves as a Commissioner of Computing Accreditation Commission of ABET and the editorial boards of IEEE Trans. Parallel & Distributed Systems and International Journal of Sensor Networks. He is a Fellow of IEEE.

Feature Extraction and Coverage Problems in Distributed Sensor Networks

Sitharama S. Iyengar

Department of Computer Science
Louisiana State University
Baton Rouge, USA
iyengar@bit.csc.lsu.edu

Abstract. Distributed Sensor Network is a classical area of multidisciplinary science. This needs a special type of computing, communication and sensing. This talk presents some new results on the following topics: 1) An optimization framework based on mathematical programming for maximizing the coverage probability of a sensor field under the constraints of investment limit; 2) Feature extraction using sensor networks.

Brief Biography

Prof. Sitharama S. Iyengar is the Chairman and Roy Paul Daniels Chaired Professor of Computer Science at Louisiana State University, Baton Rouge, and is also the Satish Dhawan Chaired Professor at the Indian Institute of Science, Bangalore. His publications include 6 textbooks and over 400 research papers. His research interests include high-performance algorithms, data structures, sensor fusion, data mining, and intelligent systems. He is a fellow of IEEE, ACM, AAAS and IPDS. He is a recipient of the Distinguished Alumnus award of the Indian Institute of Science, Bangalore. He has served as the editor of several IEEE journals and is the founding editor-in-chief of the International Journal of Distributed Sensor Networks.

I. Stojmenovic et al. (Eds.): ISPA 2007, LNCS 4742, p. 3, 2007.

Peer-to-Peer Computing: From Applications to Platform

Hai Jin

School of Computer Science and Technology
Huazhong University of Science and Technology
Wuhan, China
hjin@hust.edu.cn

Abstract. In the last several years, we have made great efforts on prototype development and deployments of real systems about peer-to-peer computing. We have released many famous systems in CERNET of China, including: 1) a live streaming system based on P2P computing, named AnySee, in 2004; 2) a P2P VoD system, named GridCast, a P2P based E-Learning system, named APPLE, in 2005; 3) a P2P based gaming platform, named PKTown, and a P2P-based high performance computing platform, named P2HP, in 2006; 4) a P2P live streaming system for wireless environment, named MoSee, in 2007. All these deployed systems have attracted more attention on innovative P2P applications. In the last several years, there are about more than 100,000 users, which have enjoyed the services provided by these applications and we also have collected many data sets about users behaviors in different applications. Based on these logs from real systems, there is one finding: single platform, which includes many typical P2P applications, is a promising system for users, developers and researchers. For users, they can enjoy different services in one software, not many dazzling applications. For developers, they can deploy new P2P services quickly based on the functions and support by platform. For researchers, they can model the complex network and make statistic analysis and physical evolvement based on the traces provided by the platform. In the future, we will focus on P2P based platform, named Ripple, which is to construct a Reliable independent P2P layered engine with manageability to support services, including scientific research, streaming services, game services and etc.

Brief Biography

Hai Jin received his BS, MA and Ph.D. degree in computer engineering from Huazhong University of Science and Technology (HUST) in 1988, 1991 and 1994, respectively. He is a Professor of Computer Science and Engineering at HUST in China. He is now the Dean of School of Computer Science and Technology at HUST. In 1996, he was awarded German Academic Exchange Service (DAAD) fellowship for visiting the Technical University of Chemnitz in Germany. He

I. Stojmenovic et al. (Eds.): ISPA 2007, LNCS 4742, pp. 4–5, 2007.

worked for the University of Hong Kong between 1998 and 2000 and participated in the HKU Cluster project. He worked as a visiting scholar at the University of Southern California between 1999 and 2000. He is the chief scientist of the largest grid computing project, ChinaGrid, in China.

A Self-stabilizing Algorithm For 3-Edge-Connectivity

Abusayeed M. Saifullah[1] and Yung H. Tsin[2,3]

[1] Computer and Inf. Science and Engineering, University of Florida, Gainesville, Florida, USA
asms@cise.ufl.edu
[2] School of Computer Science, University of Windsor, Windsor, Ontario, Canada
peter@uwindsor.ca
[3] Research partially supported by **NSERC** under grant NSERC-781103

Abstract. The adoption of self-stabilization as an approach to fault-tolerant behavior has received considerable research interest over the last decade. In this paper, we propose a self-stabilizing algorithm for 3-edge-connectivity of an asynchronous distributed model of computation. The self-stabilizing depth-first search algorithm of Collin and Dolev [4] is run concurrently to build a depth-first search spanning tree of the system. Once such a tree of height h is constructed, the detection of all 3-edge-connected components of the system requires $O(h)$ rounds. The result of computation is kept in a distributed fashion in the sense that, upon stabilization of another phase of the algorithm, each processor knows all other processors that are 3-edge-connected to it. *Until now, this is the only algorithm to compute all the 3-edge-connected components in the context of self-stabilization.* Assuming that every processor requires m bits for the depth-first search algorithm, the space complexity of our algorithm is $O(hm)$ bits per processor.

1 Introduction

The concept of self-stabilization pertains to a theoretical framework of non-masking fault-tolerant distributed systems. A *self-stabilizing system* is capable of tolerating any unexpected transient fault without being assisted by any external agent. Regardless of the initial state, it can reach a legitimate global state in finite time and can remain so thereafter unless it experiences any subsequent fault. Many fundamental as well as some advanced graph theoretic problems in computer network have been studied in the context of self-stabilization over the last decade.

Several algorithms for 2-edge-connectivity and 2-vertex-connectivity are available in the literature of self-stabilization. The algorithm in [3] can find the bridge-connected components by assuming the existence of a depth-first search spanning tree of the system. This algorithm stabilizes in two phases and, for a system with n processors, each phase requires $O(n^2)$ moves to reach a legitimate configuration by assuming that the preceding phase has stabilized. If a breadth-first search tree of the network is known, then the algorithm in [11] can detect the bridges in $O(n^3)$ moves and that in [9] can detect the articulation points in $O(n^3)$ moves. The algorithm in [10] finds the biconnected components in $O(n^2)$ moves if a breadth-first search tree and all the bridges of the network are known. Each of the algorithms [3,9,10,11] mentioned above requires $O(n\Delta \lg \Delta)$ bits

I. Stojmenovic et al. (Eds.): ISPA 2007, LNCS 4742, pp. 6–19, 2007.

per processor, where Δ is an upper bound on the degree of a processor. The algorithm proposed by Devismes [5] uses a weaker model (one that does not require every node to have a distinct identifier) and can detect the cut-nodes and bridges in $O(n^2)$ moves if a depth-first search tree of the network is known. This algorithm is memory efficient ($O(n \lg \Delta + \lg n)$ bits per processor) but does not find the bridge-connected or biconnected components. The complications induced by the 3-edge-connectivity problem are higher than those induced by the 2-edge-connectivity or 2-vertex-connectivity and, to the best of our knowledge, no self-stabilizing algorithm for this problem is available.

The algorithm, proposed in this paper is a self-stabilizing algorithm which computes all the 3-edge-connected components of a distributed system of computers. In a distributed system modeled as an undirected connected graph $G = (V, E)$, a *3-edge-connected component* is a maximal subset $X \subseteq V$ such that the *local edge-connectivity* is at least 3 for any $x, y \in X$, where *local edge-connectivity* for two nodes x, y of G is the minimum number of edges in $F \subseteq E$ such that x and y are disconnected in $G - F$ (the resulting graph after removing the edge set F from G). The property of edge-connectivity calls for considerable attention in graph theory since it measures the extent to which a graph is connected. In telecommunication systems and transportation networks, this property represents the reliability of the network in presence of link failures. Moreover, when communication links are expensive, edge-connectivity plays a vital role to minimize the communication cost. For distributed computer model, efficient algorithms have been proposed for 3-edge-connectivity [8,14]. The algorithm by Jennings et al. [8] is a direct implementation of the sequential algorithm of Taoka et al. [12]. It, therefore, follows the idea of the latter closely by performing multiple depth-first searches over the network, partitioning the network, and classifying the cut-pairs into two different types and determining them separately. In the worst case, the algorithm requires $O(n^3)$ time and messages. Tsin [14] has proposed another algorithm for 3-edge-connectivity for the distributed model which requires only $O(n^2)$ time and messages in the worst-case. Furthermore, it is different from [8] and [12] in the sense that it does not classify cut-pairs into different types and that it makes no attempt to partition the network and performs the depth-first search only once. Since these algorithms [8,14] are not self-stabilizing, they cannot start execution from arbitrary configuration and are not capable of tolerating the transient faults.

Like all the existing self-stabilizing algorithms for graph connectivity [2,3,5,9,10,11], a self-stabilizing depth-first search algorithm, such as that of Collin and Dolev [4], is run concurrently with our algorithm to construct a depth-first search spanning tree of the network. Once such a tree of the system is constructed, our algorithm, in the first phase, computes a set of ordered pairs of nodes at each node. This is done by propagating the set towards the root of the tree. The time and space complexities of our algorithm are equivalent to those of the aforementioned self-stabilizing algorithms for 2-edge-connectivity and biconnectivity. For a system of n processors, the first phase stabilizes after $O(nh)$ moves, where h is the height of the depth-first search spanning tree. At this stage, each 3-edge-connected component C is detected by a node $p \in C$ such that all nodes in C belong to $T(p)$, the subtree rooted at p. To keep the results in a distributed fashion, the second phase of the algorithm is devoted to the propagation of the results of the first phase to all processors. Assuming that every processor requires m

bits for the depth-first search algorithm of Collin and Dolev [4], the space complexity of our algorithm is $O(hm)$ bits per processor.

2 Background Knowledge

2.1 Distributed System, Fault Tolerance, and Self-stabilization

A *distributed system* is generally defined as a set of processing elements or state machines interconnected by a network of some fixed topology. Each machine maintains a set of local variables whose contents specify its *local state*. The *global state* of the system is expressed in terms of the local states of all processors. Distributed systems are exposed to constant changes of their environment and are subject to transient faults. A *transient fault* is an event that may change the state of a system by corrupting the local states of the machines. *Fault tolerance* is the ability of a system to regain its state even in the presence of internal faults. The property of self-stabilization represents a departure from the previous approaches to fault tolerance. The notion was introduced by Dijkstra in 1974 in his classic paper [6]. Since a self-stabilizing system regains correct global state regardless of initial state, the complicated task of initializing the system is no longer needed. The global state of the system is defined by a *predicate*, a boolean function over the whole system. When the system satisfies the predicate, it is said that the system is in a *legitimate state*. The state of the system is said to be *illegitimate* when it does not satisfy the predicate. A self-stabilizing algorithm can be encoded as a set of rules. Each rule has two parts: the *privilege* and the *move* as shown below:

$$\textbf{if} < privilege > \textbf{then} < move >$$

A *privilege* of a processor is a boolean function of its own state and the states of its neighbors. A processor that satisfies its privilege can make a move. A *move* is an action taken by a processor that changes the local state of the processor.

2.2 Some Definitions from Graph Theory

For ease of explanation of the proposed algorithm, some definitions from graph theory are in order. A *connected undirected graph* is denoted by $G = (V, E)$, where V is the *set of nodes* and E is the *set of edges* of G. Two nodes are *neighboring* if they are connected by an edge. For a node $p \in V$, the *set of neighboring nodes* of p is denoted by $Neig_p$. In G, $F \subseteq E$ is a *cut* or *edge-separator* if $F \neq \emptyset$ and the total number of components in $G - F$ is greater than that in G and no proper subset of F has this property, where $G - F$ represents the graph after removing F from G. If $|F| = k$ i.e. the number of edges in F is k, then F is called a *k-cut*. The only edge in 1-cut is called a *bridge*. A cut with two edges is called a *cut-pair* or *separation-pair*. A graph G is *k-edge-connected* if every edge-separator (cut) of G has at least k edges. The *local edge-connectivity*, $\lambda(x, y; G)$, for two nodes x, y of G is the minimum number of edges in $F \subseteq E$ such that x and y are disconnected in $G - F$. A maximal subset $X \subseteq V$ such that $\lambda(x, y; G) \geq k$ for any $x, y \in X$ is called a *k-edge-connected component* of G.

A *depth-first search* over an undirected connected graph G generates a *spanning tree* of G and every edge becomes either a *tree edge* or a *non-tree edge*. In the self-stabilizing depth-first search algorithm of Collin and Dolev [4], every node p orders its edges by some arbitrary ordering α_p. For any edge $e = (p, q)$, $\alpha_p(q)$ ($\alpha_q(p)$, respectively) is the edge index of e according to α_p (α_q, respectively). Let the depth-first search tree, generated from this algorithm, of G be denoted by T. The *root* of T is a predesignated node and is always denoted by r. Every node p maintains a variable called $Path_p$ which is a sequence of edge indices from r to p. The algorithm uses a *lexicographic order relation* $\prec$ on the path representation and the *concatenation* of any edge index with a path is denoted by the operator $\oplus$. If there exists a unique $q \in Neig_p$ such that $Path_p = Path_q \oplus \alpha_q(p)$, then q is called the *parent* of p and is denoted by Par_p. For a node p, *the set of children* $Ch(p) = \{q \in Neig_p | p = Par_q\}$. A node p is a *leaf node* if $Ch(p) = \emptyset$, otherwise it is a *non-leaf node*. A *u-v tree path* is a path in T connecting nodes u and v. A *root-to-leaf* path in T is a path that connects r and a leaf node. In the spanning tree T, the height of a node $p \in V$ is equal to $|Path_p| - 1$, where $|Path_p|$ is the number of edge indices in the value $Path_p$. A node q is an *ancestor* of p in T if $Path_q$ is a prefix of $Path_p$ while p is called a *descendant* of q. The *set of ancestors* and the *set of descendants* of p are denoted by $Anc(p)$ and $Des(p)$, respectively. The sets $Anc(p) - \{p\}$ and $Des(p) - \{p\}$ are called the *set of proper ancestors* of p and *the set of proper descendants* of p, respectively. The *set of tree edges* in T is denoted by E_T while $E - E_T$ is the *set of all non-tree edges*. A *subtree* rooted at p, denoted by $T(p)$, in T is the subgraph of T induced by $Des(p)$. For a tree edge (p, q), we shall assume that p is the parent of q, while for a non-tree edge (s, t), we shall assume that t is an ancestor of s in T. A tree edge (p, q) is called the *parent link* of q and a *child link* of p. An *outgoing* non-tree edge of p connects p to one of its proper ancestors while an *incoming* non-tree edge of p connects p to one of its proper descendants. $Out(p)$ and $In(p)$ represent the *set of outgoing non-tree edges* of p and the *set of incoming non-tree edges* of p, respectively. If two edges, e and e', form a cut-pair in G, then either both edges are tree edges or exactly one of them is a non-tree edge. In the former case, the cut-pair is said to be of *type-2* while in the latter case, it is of *type-1* [12].

3 Model of Computation

The distributed system is represented by an undirected connected graph $G = (V, E)$. The set of nodes V in G represents the set of processors $\{p_1, p_2, \cdots, p_n\}$, where n is the total number of processors in the system, and E represents the set of bidirectional communication links between two processors. We shall use the terms *node* and *processor* interchangeably throughout this paper. We assume that the graph is bridgeless. (Any graph with bridges can be handled by first dividing the graph into bridge-connected components using the algorithm from [3], and then by applying our algorithm for every such component.) There is a predesignated processor r, called the *root*, and for the remaining processors there are no distinct identities. The network is asynchronous and the communication facilities are limited only between the neighboring processors. The program of each processor consists of a set of shared variables and a finite set of rules. Each processor executes the same program with different values. A processor can both read and write to its own variables. It can also read the variables owned by the neighboring processors but cannot write to their variables.

Let X_i be the set of possible states of processor p_i. A *configuration* $c \in (X_1 \times X_2 \times \cdots X_n)$ of the system is a *vector* of states and is referred to the *global state* or *configuration*. An *execution* of a distributed protocol is a finite or infinite sequence of configurations $Y = (c_0, c_1, \cdots, c_i, c_{i+1}, \cdots)$ such that for $i \geq 0$, $c_i \rightarrow c_{i+1}$ (called a *single computation step* or *move*), if c_{i+1} exists, else c_i is a *terminal configuration*, where $c_i \rightarrow c_{i+1}$ denotes the transition from c_i to c_{i+1}. At any given configuration a *central daemon* activates a single processor which executes a single computation step or move. However, following Burns et al. [1], a *distributed daemon* that can select more than one processor to move simultaneously will work as well. Every move takes the system into a new global state. The time complexity of the algorithm is expressed in terms of the number of *rounds* [7] or the number of moves needed to reach a legitimate state.

4 Basis of the Proposed Algorithm

Let, from a set of nodes, function ***min*** returns the node which is the ancestor of all nodes in the set. For each node $v \in V$, we define two terms: $Low1(v)$ and $Low2(v)$ which were introduced in [13] and [14], respectively.

Definition 1. $Low1(v) := min(\{v\} \cup \{Low1(x) | x \in Ch(v)\} \cup \{s | (v, s) \in Out(v)\})$;

Definition 2. $$Low2(v) := \begin{cases} min(\{Low1(w) | w \in Ch(v) \wedge w \neq w'\} \cup \{s | (v, s) \in Out(v)\} \cup \{v\}), \text{ if } \exists w' \in Ch(v) \text{ such that } Low1(v) = Low1(w'); \\ min(\{Low1(w) | w \in Ch(v)\} \cup \{s | (v, s) \in Out(v) \wedge s \neq Low1(v)\} \cup \{v\}), \text{ otherwise}; \end{cases}$$

Let (x, y) be a non-tree edge which forms a type-1 cut-pair with an edge (u, v). It is pointed out in [14] that if we consider that (x, y) is split into a child link (x, y') of x and a non-tree edge (y', y), then we can replace the type-1 cut-pair $\{(x, y), (u, v)\}$ with the type-2 cut-pair $\{(x, y'), (u, v)\}$, where y' is considered as a fictitious child of x. Based on this, we build the data structure for our algorithm in a way such that type-1 and type-2 cut-pairs can be treated exactly alike. As a result, we may assume without loss of generality that all the cut-pairs are type-2 cut-pairs. Theorem 1 due to Tsin [14] gives a sufficient and necessary condition for determining type-2 cut-pairs.

Theorem 1. *In T, let $e, e' \in E_T$ be such that $e = (u, v)$ and $e' = (x, y)$, where v is an ancestor of x. Then $\{e, e'\}$ is a (type-2) cut-pair in G if and only if there does not exist a non-tree edge (s, t) such that either $s \in Des(v)$ but $s \notin Des(y)$ and $t \in Anc(u)$, or $s \in Des(y)$ and $t \in Anc(x)$ but $t \notin Anc(u)$.*

The idea underlying the algorithm is as follows: for each edge (x, y) (note that if (x, y) is a non-tree edge, then we are talking about the fictitious edge (x, y')), if no cut-pair containing the edge has been determined and if $Low1(x)$ is a proper ancestor of $Low2(x)$, then, by Theorem 1, (x, y) is a possible cut-edge that is capable of generating cut-pairs with edges lying on the tree-path $Low1(x) - Low2(x)$. An ordered pair $(x, Low2(x))$ is thus created to convey such information. This ordered pair is then routed towards the root. On its way up, the ordered pair could be eliminated, or replaced by an ordered pair $(x, Low2(x'))$, where x' is an ancestor of x. Suppose at an ancestor v of x, the ordered pair becomes (x, v), then it indicates that the parent link of v and (x, y) form a cut-pair. Based on these cut-pairs, we determine all the 3-edge-connected components.

5 The Algorithm

The depth-first search algorithm of Collin and Dolev [4] runs concurrently with our algorithm and let the depth-first search spanning tree of graph $G = (V, E)$ be denoted by T. For ease of explanation, we assume that T is already generated. This type of assumption was also made by Chaudhuri [2,3], Karaata [9,10], Devismes [5], and Karaata et al. [11]. The algorithm detects the cut-pairs and the 3-edge-connected components by computing a set of ordered pairs of nodes for each processor in the first phase. This phase is encoded as a single rule for each processor which helps every processor determine the nodes from its descendants which are 3-edge-connected to the node. The second phase is also encoded as a single rule for each processor. In this phase, the results of the first phase are propagated to all the processors so that, upon stabilization, every processor knows all the processors that are 3-edge-connected to it. The algorithm is self-stabilizing since the variables calculated by the rules for each processor need not be initialized and hence the algorithm can start with any arbitrary initial values for these variables of each processor. In the description of the algorithm, the function ***min*** returns the ancestor of all nodes from a set of nodes, or returns the minimum number from a set of numbers. A similar function $\boldsymbol{min}_{lex}$ returns the node whose *path* value is lexicographically minimum.

5.1 Description of the Algorithm

Phase *I* (Calculation of the Set of Ordered Pairs by Each $v \in V$). At every node v, a set, $S(v)$, is maintained. The structure of $S(v)$ is as follows: Each element of the set is an ordered pair of nodes representing a non-tree edge or a virtual edge. The nodes of the ordered pairs all lie on the same root-to-leaf path in T. Moreover, the ordered pairs have a *nested ordering*, $(x_1, q_1), (x_2, q_2), \cdots, (x_{k'}, q_{k'})$, such that x_{i+1} is an ancestor of x_i while q_{i+1} is a descendant of q_i. The node v is an ancestor of $x_i, 1 \leq i \leq k'$, and a descendant of $q_i, 1 \leq i \leq k'$. The ordered pairs indicate that, for $2 \leq i \leq k'$, there may be an edge on the $x_i - x_{i-1}$ tree-path that can generate new cut-pairs with some edges lying on the $q_i - q_{i-1}$ tree-path, and the non-tree edge $(x_1, Low1(x_1))$ can generate new cut-pairs with some edges lying on the $Low1(x_1) - q_1$ tree-path. Every node v also maintains a set of nodes, $3Set(v)$, such that the set contains a subset of the 3-edge-connected component containing v with v being an ancestor of all the nodes in that set. In the set $S(v)$, for every pair of nodes $(x_i, q_i) \in S(v), 1 \leq i \leq k'$, the node x_i is represented by its $3Set$-value. If node x_1 is such that $(x_1, Low1(x_1))$ is an outgoing non-tree edge of x_1 and $Low1(x_1) \neq Low1(x)$, for every $x \in Ch(x_1)$, then the non-tree edge, or more precisely the fictitious tree-link, $(x_1, Low1(x_1))$ can generate cut-pairs with some of the edges lying on the path $Low1(x_1) - q_1$. Since $path_v$ is unique for each v, it can be used as an identifier for node v. As a result, all the ancestors of node v can be identified if only v is known.

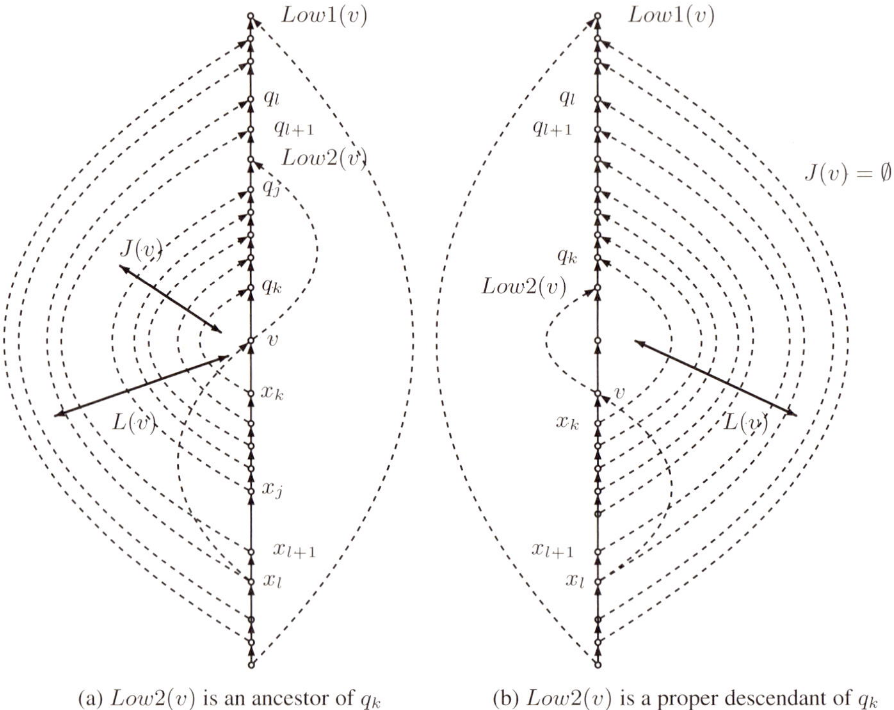

(a) $Low2(v)$ is an ancestor of q_k (b) $Low2(v)$ is a proper descendant of q_k

Fig. 1. The sets $J(v)$ and $L(v)$ for node v

During the execution of the algorithm, at each leaf node v in T, node v creates $S(v)$ with one element $(v, Low2(v))$ indicating that only the edges on the path $Low1(v) - Low2(v)$ could form a cut-pair with the non-tree edge $(v, Low1(v))$. At each non-leaf node v, the node computes $Low1(v)$ and $Low2(v)$ based on the $Low1$ values it reads from its children and the *path* values it reads from its outgoing non-tree edges, and creates $S(v)$ based on the sets $S'(w), \forall w \in Ch(v)$, where $S'(w)$ is a subset of $S(w)$ that node v reads from the child w. For each processor u, the subset $S'(u)$ is determined as follows. Let $S(u)$ be $\{(x_1, q_1), (x_2, q_2), \cdots, (x_{k'}, q_{k'})\}$ in nested order. Then $S'(u)$ is $S(u) - \{(x_{k'}, q_{k'})\}$ if $u = q_{k'}$ meaning that there is an edge on the $x_{k'} - x_{k'-1}$ tree-path which forms a cut-pair with the parent link of u and all the nodes in $3Set(x_{k'})$ form a 3-edge-connected component. Otherwise, $S'(u)$ is simply equal to $S(u)$.

Let node w_v be a child of v such that $Low1(w_v) = Low1(v)$. If w_v is non-unique, then node v picks one whose $path$ value is lexicographically minimum. For a node v, if w_v does not exist, then w_v is denoted by $null$. Then node v reads in $S(w_v)$ and disregards the S sets of the remaining children. However, for each child s whose S set is rejected by node v, v absorbs *3Set(x)*, $\forall (x, q) \in S'(s)$, into $3Set(v)$. This is because, by Theorem 1, no new cut-pairs can be generated by any edge within the subtrees of those children. If $w_v = null$ because $Low1(v)$ is defined by an outgoing non-tree edge of v, then $S(w_v)$ is $\emptyset$. If $w_v = null$, then v simply creates its own $S(v)$ with the element $(v, Low2(v))$. Otherwise, Let $(x_1, q_1), (x_2, q_2), ..., (x_k, q_k)$ $(k \geq 0)$ be the set $S'(w_v)$ in nested order. Then v modifies $S'(w_v)$ to calculate $S(v)$, in the following ways:

(i) Let j $(1 \leq j \leq k)$ = $min(\{i|(x_i, q_i) \in S'(w_v)$ and $Low2(v)$ is an ancestor of $q_i\} \cup \{\infty\})$. Then, by Theorem 1, every edge lying on the $v - x_j$ tree-path can no longer generate new cut-pair (Figure 1(a)). Let $J(v)$ denotes the set $\{(x_i, q_i) \in S'(w_v)|j \leq i \leq k\}$. Each x_i such that $(x_i, q_i) \in J(v)$ is 3-edge-connected to v (Figure 1(a)). If $j = \infty$, then $J(v)$ is $\emptyset$.

(ii) Let $l = min(\{i|$ there exists an incoming non-tree edge of v, (s, v), such that s is a descendant of $x_i\} \cup \{\infty\})$. By Theorem 1, every edge lying on the $v - x_l$ tree-path can no longer generate new cut-pair (Figures 1(a), 1(b)). Let $L(v)$ denotes the set $\{(x_i, q_i) \in S'(w_v)|l \leq i \leq k\}$. Each x_i such that $(x_i, q_i) \in L(v)$, is 3-edge-connected to v (Figures 1(a), 1(b)). If $l = \infty$, then $L(v)$ is $\emptyset$.

(iii) Now v absorbs *3Set*(x_i), $\forall(x_i, q_i) \in J(v) \cup L(v)$ into $3Set(v)$ since these x_i's are 3-edge-connected to v. Then the ordered pairs in $J(v) \cup L(v)$ are deleted from $S'(w_v)$. Let $q(v) = Low2(v)$ if $l = \infty$ and $q(v) = min(Low2(v), q_l)$ otherwise. Finally, $(v, q(v))$ is added to $S'(w_v) - (J(v) \cup L(v))$. Therefore, $S(v)$ can be defined as follows:

$S(v) := (S'(w_v) - (J(v) \cup L(v))) \cup \{(v, q(v))\};$

The legitimate state of phase *I* is defined by the following predicate:

$$\textbf{\textit{PREDICATE 1}} \equiv (\forall v \in V)S(v) := \begin{cases} (v, Low2(v)), \text{ if } w_v = null; \\ (S'(w_v) - (J(v) \cup L(v))) \cup \{(v, q(v))\}, \\ \text{otherwise;} \end{cases}$$

Algorithm 1 shows the pseudo code for phase *I*. [Any value defined by macro will be replaced by the corresponding macro definition in the rule during the execution. Recall that for $v \in V$, $Ch(v)$, $In(v)$, $Out(v)$, $Anc(v)$, and $Des(v)$ represent the sets of children, incoming non-tree edges, outgoing non-tree edges, ancestors, and descendants, respectively.]

Lemma 1. *Regardless of the initial state and regardless of the privileges selected, phase* I *(Algorithm 1) stabilizes to* $PREDICATE\ 1$ *if* T *is already constructed and remains unchanged.*

Proof. For each node v in T, let $d(v)$ be the distance between v and the leaf with maximum height in $T(v)$, the subtree rooted at v. For any node v in T, $0 \leq d(v) \leq h$, where h is the height of T. We prove the lemma by induction on $d(v)$, where $v \in V$. Any $u \in V$ with $d(u) = 0$ is a leaf node and $w_u = null$. Therefore, $S(u) = \{(u, Low2(u))\}$. Now we assume that for each node $x \in V$ with $d(x) \leq k(k \geq 0)$, we have $S(x) = \{(x, Low2(x))\}$ if $w_x = null$, and $S(x) = (S'(w_x) - (J(x) \cup L(x))) \cup \{(x, q(x))\}$ if $w_x \neq null$. Each $q \in V$ with $d(q) = k + 1$ reads the S' sets of its children. For each $z \in Ch(q)$, $d(z) = k$. By the induction hypothesis, each $S(z)$ is correctly calculated. Since T remains unchanged during the execution of phase *I*, $J(q)$, $L(q)$, and w_q are known to q. Therefore, q must calculate $S(q)$ correctly. That is, $\forall v \in V$ such that $d(v) = k + 1$, $S(v) = \{(v, Low2(v))\}$ if $w_v = null$, and $S(v) = (S'(w_v) - (J(v) \cup L(v))) \cup \{(v, q(v))\}$ otherwise. Hence the property is true for each processor p with $d(p) \leq k + 1$. With $k = h$ the lemma holds. □

Algorithm 1. Phase I: Set $S(v)$ calculation for each $v \in V$

Macros:

$Low1(v) := min(\{v\} \cup \{Low1(x) | x \in Ch(v)\} \cup \{s | (v,s) \in Out(v)\})$;

$$Low2(v) := \begin{cases} min(\{Low1(w) | w \in Ch(v) \wedge w \neq w'\} \cup \{s|(v,s) \in Out(v)\} \cup \{v\}), \text{ if} \\ \exists w' \in Ch(v) \text{ such that } Low1(v) = Low1(w'); \\ min(\{Low1(w)|w \in Ch(v)\} \cup \{s|(v,s) \in Out(v) \wedge s \neq Low1(v)\} \cup \\ \{v\}), \text{ otherwise;} \end{cases}$$

$w_v := min_{lex}(\{w' \in Ch(v) | Low1(v) = Low1(w')\})$ if w' exists, and $w_v = null$ otherwise;

/* The set $S(v) := \{(x_1, q_1), \cdots, (x_{k'}, q_{k'})\}$*/

$S'(v) := S(v) - \{(x_{k'}, q_{k'})\}$ if $v = q_{k'}$, and $S'(v) = S(v)$ otherwise;

/* The set $S'(v) := \{(x_1, q_1), \cdots, (x_k, q_k)\}$*/

$J(v) := \{(x_i, q_i) \in S'(w_v) | j \leq i \leq k\}$, where $j := min(\{i | Low2(v) \in Anc(q_i)\} \cup \{\infty\})$;

$L(v) := \{(x_i, q_i) \in S'(w_v) | l \leq i \leq k\}$, where $l := min(\{i | \exists (s,v) \in In(v) \wedge s \in Des(x_i)\} \cup \{\infty\})$;

$q(v) := Low2(v)$ if $l = \infty$, and $q(v) = min(Low2(v), q_l)$, otherwise;

Rules:

For each $v \in V$,

$(w_v = null) \wedge S(v) \neq \{(v, Low2(v))\} \Rightarrow$
  $\{ S(v) := \{(v, Low2(v))\}$;
  $3Set(v) := \{v\} \cup 3Set(x_i), \forall (x_i, q_i) \in S'(u), \forall u \in Ch(v); \}$

$(w_v \neq null) \wedge S(v) \neq (S'(w_v) - (J(v) \cup L(v))) \cup \{(v, q(v))\} \Rightarrow$
  $\{ S(v) := (S'(w_v) - (J(v) \cup L(v))) \cup \{(v, q(v))\}$;
  $3Set(v) := \{v\} \cup 3Set(x_i), \forall (x_i, q_i) \in J(v) \cup L(v) \cup S'(u), \forall u \in Ch(v) - \{w_v\}; \}$

Lemma 2. *During the execution of phase* I *(Algorithm 1), in each illegitimate state, at least one processor enjoys the privilege.*

Proof. Suppose to the contrary that, during Phase I of computation, the system is in an illegitimate state and no processor enjoys the privilege. Since no processor enjoys the privilege, for each $v \in V$ with $w_v = null$, $S(v) = \{(v, Low2(v))\}$ and for each $v \in V$ with $w_v \neq null$, $S(v) = (S'(w_v) - (J(v) \cup L(v))) \cup \{(v, q(v))\}$. By the definition of $PREDICATE$ 1, this is the legitimate state of phase *I* which contradicts our assumption. Hence the lemma follows. □

Lemma 3. *During the execution of phase I of computation (Algorithm 1) no illegitimate state can reappear, provided T remains unchanged during the entire period of execution.*

Proof. Suppose to the contrary that there are two identical illegitimate states, say L_1 and L_2, and the number of moves required to reach L_2 from L_1 is m ($m \geq 1$) in phase *I*. Since, in phase *I*, a move made by a node $v \in V - \{r\}$ may only cause its parent to make a move, this move can never be the cause of its own move. Therefore, there must be at least one node $u \in V$ for which $S(u)$ in L_1 is different from $S(u)$ in L_2 which contradicts that L_1 and L_2 are identical. □

Lemma 4. *For any node $v \in V - \{r\}$, let $(x_1, q_1) \cdots (x_k, q_k)$ be $S(v)$ in nested order and $v = q_k$ in the legitimate state of phase* I. *Then there exists a link lying on the*

$x_k - x_{k-1}$ tree-path which forms a cut-pair with the parent link of v if $k > 1$, or there exists a non-tree link (x, y) such that x is a descendant of v which forms a cut-pair with the parent link of v if $k = 1$.

Proof. For the computation of the set $S(v)$, node v absorbs *3Set*(x_i), $\forall (x_i, q_i) \in J(v) \cup L(v)$ into $3Set(v)$ since these x_i's are 3-edge-connected to v, and the ordered pairs in $J(v) \cup L(v)$ are deleted from $S'(w_v)$. This means that there exists no node x_b, for $b \leq k-1$, in $S(v)$ which is 3-edge-connected to v. Again, in the computation of $S(v)$, the value of q_k is set to either $Low2(v)$ or q_l, where $l := min(\{i | \exists (s, v) \in In(v) \wedge s \in Des(x_i)\} \cup \{\infty\})$, which indicates the farthest (from v) node 3-edge-connected to v in the ancestors of v. Therefore, $q_k = v$ implies that no proper ancestor of v is 3-edge-connected to v. Hence there must exist a link lying on the $x_k - x_{k-1}$ tree-path which forms a cut-pair with the parent link of v if $k > 1$. When $k = 1$ i.e. $S(v)$ consists of only one pair, all the nodes absorbed into $3Set(v)$ are 3-edge-connected to v and no descendant of v is 3-edge-connected to any proper ancestor of v. Since $q_k = v$ means that no proper ancestor of v is 3-edge-connected to v, there must be a non-tree link (x, y) such that x is a descendant of v which forms a cut-pair with the parent link of v. □

Lemma 5. *For any node $v \in V$, let $(x_1, q_1) \cdots (x_k, q_k)$ be $S(v)$ in nested order in the legitimate state of phase* I. *If $v = q_k$, then $3Set(v)$ is a 3-edge-connected component in G.*

Proof. All nodes descendant of v which are 3-edge-connected to v are absorbed into $3Set(v)$ and, by Lemma 4, no proper ancestor of v is 3-edge-connected to v if $v = q_k$. Hence the lemma follows. □

Lemma 6. *Let $C_1, C_2, \cdots, C_m$ be all the 3-edge-connected components of G and, for each C_i ($1 \leq i \leq m$), $v_i \in C_i$ be such that all the nodes of C_i belong to $T(v_i)$. Then, in the legitimate state of phase* I, *each C_i must be detected by v_i.*

Proof. Suppose to the contrary, the system is in a legitimate state but a 3-edge-connected component C_b, $1 \leq b \leq m$, has not been detected by v_b. This implies that $3Set(v_b)$ did not absorb all the nodes from the descendants of v_b which are 3-edge-connected to v_b and that $S(v_b)$ has not been calculated. By Lemma 1, the system is still in an illegitimate state which contradicts our initial assumption about the state of the system. □

Phase *II* (Propagating the 3-Edge-Connected Components to all the Processors) In phase *I*, after stabilization, all the 3-edge-connected components of G are detected but the information is available at only one processor of each component. This information is propagated downward in T to let every processor p know the 3-edge-connected component containing p. For every node v, let $\sigma_v = 3Set(v)$ if $3Set(v)$ is a 3-edge-connected component, and $\sigma_v = \emptyset$ otherwise. The information passed through a processor p, in phase *II*, is a set D_p (Definition 4 below) consisting of σ_p and zero or more σ_t, where $t \in Anc(p) - \{p\}$. Every processor p calculates its own D_p based on the D set of its parent, D_{Par_p}, as follows: the processor p reads in each $\sigma_s \in D_{Par_p}$ such that σ_s contains at least one node $x \in Des(p)$. These σ_s's form the set D'_p.

Definition 3. $D'_p := \{C | C \in D_{Par_p} \wedge C \cap Des(p) \neq \emptyset\}$

For every processor p, the set D_p can be calculated recursively.

Definition 4.

$$D_p := \begin{cases} D'_p \cup \{\sigma_p\}, & \text{if } \sigma_p \neq \emptyset; \\ D'_p, & \text{otherwise}; \end{cases}$$

Remark 1. For the root r, $D'_r = \emptyset$ since r has no parent. Therefore, $D_r = \{\sigma_r\}$.

The rule defined for each $p \in V$ is:
$\sigma_p \neq \emptyset \wedge D_p \neq D'_p \cup \{\sigma_p\} \Rightarrow D_p := D'_p \cup \{\sigma_p\}$;
$\sigma_p = \emptyset \wedge D_p \neq D'_p \Rightarrow D_p := D'_p$;
The following predicate defines the legitimate state for this phase:

$$\textit{PREDICATE 2} \equiv (\forall p \in V) D_p := \begin{cases} D'_p \cup \{\sigma_p\}, & \text{if } \sigma_p \neq \emptyset; \\ D'_p, & \text{otherwise}; \end{cases}$$

The pseudo code of the algorithm for phase *II* is shown in Algorithm 2.

Algorithm 2. Phase II: Propagating 3-edge-connected Component (for $p \in V$)

Macro:
$D'_p := \{C | C \in D_{Par_p} \wedge C \cap Des(p) \neq \emptyset\}$;
Rule:
For each $p \in V$:
$\sigma_p \neq \emptyset \wedge D_p \neq D'_p \cup \{\sigma_p\} \Rightarrow D_p := D'_p \cup \{\sigma_p\}$;
$\sigma_p = \emptyset \wedge D_p \neq D'_p \Rightarrow D_p := D'_p$;

Lemma 7. *Regardless of the initial state and regardless of the privileges selected, phase* II *(Algorithm 1) stabilizes to $PREDICATE$ 2 if $PREDICATE$ 1 holds.*

Proof. By applying induction on the distance of a node from the root, the proof is similar to that of Lemma 1. □

Lemma 8. *During the execution of phase* II *(Algorithm 2), in each illegitimate state, at least one processor enjoys the privilege.*

Proof. Similar to Lemma 2. □

Lemma 9. *During the execution of phase* II *of computation (Algorithm 2) no illegitimate state can reappear provided phase* I *remains stabilized during the entire period of execution.*

Proof. Similar to Lemma 3. □

Lemma 10. *In the legitimate state of phase II, for every $p \in V$, there must be one and only one $C \in D_p$ such that $p \in C$.*

Proof. Each σ_u $(u \in V)$ is an equivalence class of V w.r.t. the 3-edge-connectivity relation. Hence there is no σ_u such that $u \neq p$ and $\sigma_u \cap \sigma_p \neq \emptyset$. Let us consider the case when $\sigma_p \neq \emptyset$. If $\sigma_p \neq \emptyset$, then $p \in \sigma_p$ and $\sigma_p \in D_p$ and no $v \in Anc(p) - \{p\}$ has a σ_v such that $p \in \sigma_v$. If $\sigma_p = \emptyset$, then there is a unique $v \in Anc(p) - \{p\}$ such that $p \in \sigma_v$. This σ_v will propagate downward to each $u \in \sigma_v$. Therefore, p must have this σ_v in D_p. Again, there is no y such that $y \neq v$ and $p \in \sigma_y$. Therefore, σ_v is the only $C \in D_p$ such that $p \in C$. □

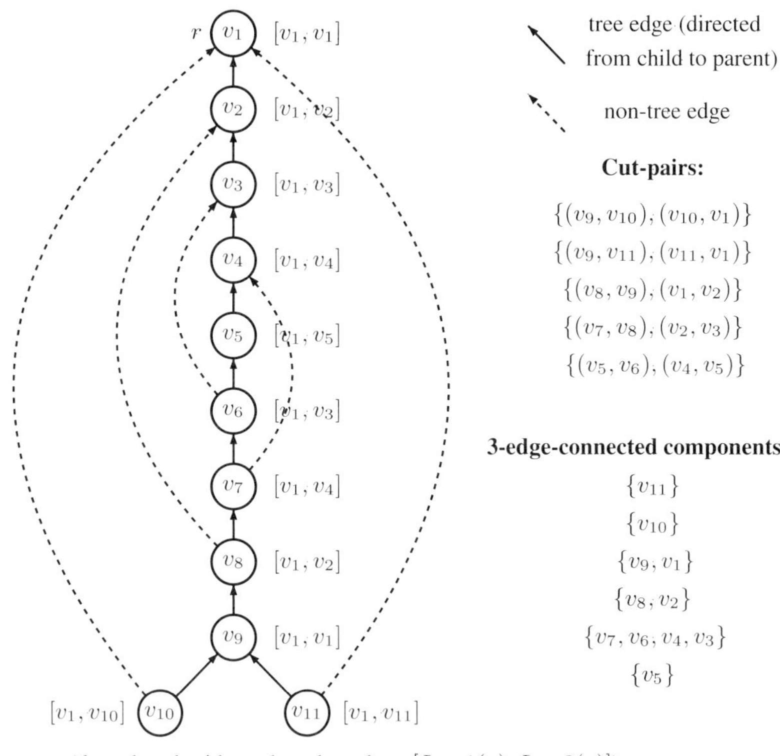

Fig. 2. A Depth-First Search Spanning Tree T

Lemma 11. *In the legitimate state of phase II, let C be the only element of D_p such that $p \in C$, then C is the 3-edge-connected component containing p.*

Proof. Let, $\sigma_p \neq \emptyset$. Then, by Lemma 10, C is σ_p which is the 3-edge-connected component containing p. Again, $\sigma_p = \emptyset$ implies that there is a unique $v \in Anc(p) - \{p\}$ such that $p \in \sigma_v$ and this σ_v must propagate to p in phase *II*. Therefore, C must be σ_v which is the 3-edge-connected component containing p. □

Lemma 12. *When the system reaches the legitimate state for the 3-edge-connectivity algorithm (Algorithm 1 and Algorithm 2), every processor $p \in V$ knows all other processors in G which are 3-edge-connected to p.*

Proof. Follows from Lemma 6 and Lemma 11. □

Figure 2 shows a depth-first search spanning tree of the corresponding undirected graph. When Phase *I* statbilizes, every node $v \in \{v_1, v_2, v_3, v_5, v_{10}, v_{11}\}$ satisfies the condition $v = q_k$, and the 3-edge-connected components of G are determined as $\{v_1, v_9\}$, $\{v_2, v_8\}$, $\{v_3, v_4, v_6, v_7\}$, $\{v_5\}$, $\{v_{10}\}$, $\{v_{11}\}$ at v_1, v_2, v_3, v_5, v_{10}, v_{11}, respectively.

6 Complexity Analysis

Lemma 13. *Phase I of the algorithm (Algorithm 1) needs $O(nh)$ moves to reach a legitimate configuration after the depth-first search algorithm stabilizes.*

Proof. Any move made by a node v can cause a sequence of moves by all the nodes on the $r - v$ tree-path. Therefore, the number of moves caused by an initial move is bounded by $h-1$. Since there can be at most n initial moves in the system during phase *I*, the total number of moves is bounded by nh i.e. $O(nh)$. □

Lemma 14. *Phase II of the algorithm (Algorithm 2) needs $O(nh)$ moves to reach a legitimate configuration after phase I stabilizes.*

Proof. Similar to Lemma 13. □

Lemma 15. *Phase I of the algorithm (Algorithm 1) needs $O(h)$ rounds to reach a legitimate configuration after the depth-first search algorithm stabilizes.*

Proof. For each node v in T, let us use the term $d(v)$ (d-value) used in the proof of Lemma 1. In the first round of phase *I*, all the processors with d-value=0 make moves. These processors will never make any move after 1st round. Then the processors with d-value=1 make the moves in the second round and make no moves after this. Since for any node v in T, $0 \leq d(v) \leq h$, where h is the height of T, phase *I* of the algorithm stabilizes after $O(h)$ rounds. □

Lemma 16. *Phase II of the algorithm (Algorithm 2) needs $O(h)$ rounds to reach a legitimate configuration after phase I stabilizes.*

Proof. Similar to Lemma 15. □

Lemma 17. *Assuming that every processor requires m bits for the depth-first search algorithm, the space complexity of the self-stabilizing algorithm for 3-edge-connectivity is O(hm) bits per processor.*

7 Conclusion

Self-stabilization has emerged as a promising paradigm for the design, control, and maintenance of fault-tolerant distributed systems. A distributed system lacking the property of self-stabilization may stay in an illegitimate state forever. Until now, the algorithm proposed in this paper is the only self-stabilizing algorithm to address the 3-edge-connectivity problem. We have analyzed that the time and space requirements for our 3-edge-connectivity algorithm are equivalent to those of the available self-stabilizing algorithms for 2-edge-connectivity or biconnectivity, although the level of difficulty for the former is higher.

References

1. Burns, J.E., Gouda, M., Miller, R.: On relaxing interleaving assumptions. In: Proceedings of the MCC Workshop on Self-stabilizing Systems, MCC technical Report No. STP-379-89 (1989)
2. Chaudhuri, P.: A self-stabilizing algorithm for detecting fundamental cycles in a graph. Journal of Computer and System Science 59(1), 84–93 (1999)
3. Chaudhuri, P.: An $\mathbf{O}(n^2)$ self-stabilizing algorithm for computing bridge-connected components. Computing 62(1), 55–67 (1999)
4. Collin, Z., Dolev, S.: Self-stabilizing depth-first search. Information Processing Letters 49(6), 297–301 (1994)
5. Devismes, S.: A silent self-stabilizing algorithm for finding cut-nodes and bridges. Parallel Processing Letters 15(1&2), 183–198 (2005)
6. Dijkstra, E.W.: Self-stabilizing systems in spite of distributed control. Communications of the ACM 17(1), 643–644 (1974)
7. Dolev, S., Israeli, A., Moran, S.: Uniform dynamic self-stabilizing leader election. IEEE Trans. on Parallel and Distributed Systems 8(4), 424–440 (1997)
8. Jennings, E., Motyckova, L.: Distributed computations and maintenace of 3-edge-connected components during edge insertions. In: Proceedings of the 3rd Colloquium SIROCCO 1996, Certosa di Pontignano, Siena, pp. 224–240 (June 1996)
9. Karaata, M.H.: A self-stabilizing algorithm for finding articulation points. International Journal of Foundations of Computer Sciences 10(1), 33–46 (1999)
10. Karaata, M.H.: A stabilizing algorithm for finding biconnected components. Journal of Parallel and Distributed Computing 62(5), 982–999 (2002)
11. Karaata, M.H., Chaudhuri, P.: A self-stabilizing algorithm for bridge finding. Distributed Computing 12(1), 47–53 (1999)
12. Taoka, S., Watanabe, T., Onaga, K.: A linear time algorithm for computing all 3-edge-connected components of a multigraph. IEICE Trans. Fundamentals E75(3), 410–424 (1992)
13. Tarjan, R.E.: Depth-first search and linear graph algorithms. SIAM J. Computing IV, 146–160 (1972)
14. Tsin, Y.H.: An efficient distributed algorithm for 3-edge-connectivity. International Journal of Foundations of Computer Science 17(3), 677–701 (2006)

Number of Processors with Partitioning Strategy and EDF-Schedulability Test: Upper and Lower Bounds with Comparison*

Arezou Mohammadi and Selim G. Akl

School of Computing, Queen's University,
Kingston, Ontario, Canada K7L 3N6
{arezoum,akl}@cs.queensu.ca

Abstract. In this paper, we study the problem of scheduling a set of n periodic preemptive independent hard real-time tasks on the minimum number of processors. We assume that the partitioning strategy is used to allocate the tasks to the processors and the EDF method is used to schedule the tasks on each processor. It is known that this scenario is NP-hard; thus, it is unlikely to find a polynomial time algorithm to schedule the tasks on the minimum number of processors. In this work, we derive a lower and an upper bound for the number of processors required to satisfy the constraints of our problem. We also compare a number of heuristic algorithms with each other and with the bounds derived in this paper. Numerical results demonstrate that our lower bound is very tight and it is very close to the optimal solution.

1 Introduction

The purpose of a real-time system is to produce a response within a specified time-frame. In other words, for a real-time system not only the logical correctness of the system should be satisfied, but also it is required to fulfill the temporal constraints of the system. A real-time application is normally composed of multiple tasks with different levels of criticality. *Hard real-time tasks*, which are the type of real-time tasks that we consider in this paper, cannot miss any deadlines. Otherwise, undesirable or fatal results will be produced in the system [8,11,16,17]. Typically, a real-time system consists of a controlling system (e.g. a computer) and a controlled system (e.g. an environment). If a number of events occur close together, the computer will need to schedule the computations so that each response is provided within the required time bounds. It may be that, even so, the system is unable to meet all possible unexpected demands. In order to prevent failure of the system, one should increase the number of the processors. Having a sufficient number of processors, one is able to schedule the tasks without missing any deadlines. Multiprocessor scheduling algorithms are categorized into either Partitioning or Global strategy. In this paper, we focus our attention

* This work was supported by the Natural Sciences and Engineering Research Council (NSERC) of Canada.

I. Stojmenovic et al. (Eds.): ISPA 2007, LNCS 4742, pp. 20–31, 2007.

on algorithms that use a partitioning strategy. Partitioning strategies reduce a multiprocessor scheduling problem to a set of uniprocessor ones, thereby allowing well-known uniprocessor scheduling algorithms to be applied to each processor. Using the partitioning approach, we need to consider both an allocation algorithm to determine the processor that should be assigned to each task and a scheduling algorithm to schedule the tasks assigned on each processor. One of the main concerns in designing a partitioning strategy is finding an algorithm to allocate the tasks to the minimum number of processors that are required. Many methods have been devised to make a good combination of the pair of (allocation, scheduling) algorithms. The most popular scheduling algorithms are the Rate Monotonic (RM) and the Earliest Deadline First (EDF) algorithms, since both of them are optimal scheduling algorithms on uni-processor systems [10]. By optimality, we mean that if an optimal algorithm cannot schedule a task set on a processor such that deadlines are met, there is no other scheduling algorithm that can do so. Some researchers have focused on the problem when RM scheduling is used on each processor (see, for example, [12,13]). However, our concern is solving the problem by employing a partitioning method, when the EDF scheduling algorithm is used on each processor and the allocation algorithm fits into the following frame. In this paper we generally talk about any allocation algorithm which picks up tasks one by one and assigns each task to one of the existing processors and if there is not enough room on them for the new task, then we add a new processor. It is proved in [1,7] that the problem is reducible to the Bin Packing problem (BPP), and consequently the problem is NP-hard. Therefore, the most efficient known algorithms use heuristics, which may not be the optimal solution, to accomplish very good results in most cases (See Section 3) [4,5,9,14]. In [2], it is proved that the worst-case achievable utilization (see Section 2) on M processors for all of the above-mentioned heuristics (and also for an optimal partitioning algorithm) is only $(M+1)/2$, even when an optimal uniprocessor scheduling algorithm such as EDF is used. In other words, there exist task systems with utilization slightly greater than $(M+1)/2$ that cannot be correctly scheduled by any partitioning approach. Let an *implementation* consist of a hardware platform and the scheduler under which the program is executed. An implementation is said to be *feasible* if every execution of the program meets all its deadlines. Based on the properties of the real-time system, the parameters of the system, and the algorithm applied for scheduling, we may determine sufficient conditions for feasibility of the scheduling algorithm. In what follows, by *schedulability test*, we mean checking whether the sufficient conditions of a given scheduling algorithm hold for a set of real-time tasks. For instance, for a set of periodic hard real-time tasks, there exist simple schedulability tests corresponding to the case where the relative deadlines are all equal to the periods. In such a case, if all tasks are periodic and have relative deadlines equal to their periods, they can be feasibly scheduled by the EDF algorithm *if and only if* the utilization factor of the set of the tasks is smaller than or equal to 1. In this paper, we use EDF scheduling on each processor. Therefore, we should look for an appropriate allocation algorithm to assign the tasks to the minimum number of processors while the EDF-schedulability condition is satisfied on each processor. The problem is reducible to the BPP, and therefore, we take advantage of the existing heuristic algorithms for BPP. We derive upper and lower bounds for the number of processors required by any allocation algorithm with the EDF schedulability test for each processor. We compare our bounds with a number of heuristic algorithms using simulations. As expected, the number of processors as determined by the heuristic algorithms is bounded by our upper and lower bounds. The upper bound derived here is for the number of processors achieved by any allocation algorithm in our framework and with EDF-schedulability test on each processor. Therefore, the number of processors required by the allocation algorithms should not exceed the upper bound derived in the paper. The lower bound that is obtained in this paper is very tight and its results are very close to the results of the FFDU and BFDU algorithms discussed in Section 3. The minimum number of the processors required for scheduling is equal to or larger than the proposed lower bound for the number of processors and smaller than the best heuristic algorithm. Since we look for the algorithm with the minimum number of processors, the best heuristic algorithm amongst the above heuristic algorithms is the one with the least guaranteed performance. Simulation results lead us to the fact that the difference between the number of processors achieved by the FFDU and BFDU algorithm and the results of an optimal algorithm is negligible.

The remainder of this paper is organized as follows. We introduce terminology in Section 2. Then, in Sections 3, the Bin Packing problem and a number of its approximation algorithms are discussed. In Section 4, we formally define the problem under study. In Section 5, we derive the upper and lower bounds for the number of processors. In Section 6, we present simulation results and compare the performance of the heuristic algorithms with the upper and lower bounds derived in this paper. Section 7 contains the conclusions.

2 Terminology

A number of the timing properties of a given task $\tau_j \in T = \{\tau_1, \tau_2, ..., \tau_n\}$ are as follow [8,11,17].

- *Deadline* (d_j): Time by which execution of the task should be completed.
- *Execution time* (e_j): Time taken without interruption to complete the task, after the task is started.
- *Priority* (ρ_j): Relative urgency of the task.
- *Period* (P_j): In the case of a periodic task τ_j, a period means once per a time interval of P_j or exactly P_j time units apart.
- *Utilization factor* (u_j): The utilization factor of a periodic task τ_j is defined by e_j/P_j. The utilization factor of a set of n periodic tasks is defined by $\sum_{i=1}^{n} e_i/P_i$.

Other issues to be considered in real-time scheduling are as follows.

- *Multiprocessor/Single-processor systems:* The number of available processors is one of the main factors in deciding how to schedule a real-time system. In multiprocessor real-time systems, the scheduling algorithms should prevent simultaneous access to shared resources and devices. Moreover, the best strategy to reduce the communication cost should be provided [10]. Multiprocessor scheduling techniques fall into two general categories: *Global scheduling algorithms* and *Partitioning scheduling algorithms*. Global scheduling algorithms store the tasks that have arrived, but not finished their execution, in one queue which is shared among all processors. Suppose there exist m processors. At every moment, the m highest priority tasks of the queue are selected for execution on the m processors using preemption and migration if necessary [10]. On the other hand, partitioning scheduling algorithms partition the set of tasks such that all tasks in a partition are assigned to the same processor. Tasks are not allowed to migrate, hence the multiprocessor scheduling problem is transformed to many uniprocessor scheduling problems [10]. Generally, for systems that contain more than one processor, we not only should decide about the appropriate scheduling algorithm, but also we have to specify the *allocation algorithm* which assigns the tasks to the available processors. For multiprocessor real-time systems, calculating the utilization bounds associated with *(scheduling, allocation)* algorithm pairs leads us to achieving the sufficient conditions for feasibly scheduling, analogous to those known for uniprocessors. This approach allows us to carry out fast schedulability tests and to qualify the influence of certain parameters, such as the number of processors, on scheduling. For some algorithms, this bound considers not only the number of processors, but also the number of the tasks and their sizes [8,10].

- *EDF scheduling algorithm:* The EDF scheduling algorithm is a dynamic-priority scheduling algorithm in which a higher priority is assigned to the request that has an earlier deadline, and a higher priority request always preempts a lower priority one [8,10]. Suppose each time a new ready task arrives, it is inserted into a queue of ready tasks which is sorted by the deadlines. The following assumptions are made for the EDF algorithm: No task has any nonpreemptable section and the cost of preemption is negligible. Only processing requirements are significant and other resource requirements are negligible. All tasks are independent. The tasks do not have to be periodic. EDF is an optimal uniprocessor scheduling algorithm [10]. It is shown in [10] that a set of periodic hard real-time tasks with relative deadlines equal to their periods, can be feasibly scheduled by the EDF scheduling algorithm on a uniprocessor system *if and only if* $\sum_{i=1}^{n} e_i/P_i \leq 1$ [10].

3 The Bin Packing Problem (BPP)

The Bin Packing problem can be defined as follows. Given N objects to be placed in bins of capacity V each, it is required to determine the minimum number of bins to accommodate all N objects. More formally, we are asked to find a partition and assignment of a set of objects such that a constraint is satisfied or an objective function is minimized. In computational complexity theory, the bin packing problem is a combinatorial NP-hard problem, as observed in [1,7]. The Best Fit Decreasing (BFD) and First Fit Decreasing (FFD) algorithms are two approximation algorithms for the problem that use no more than $(11/9)OPT+1$ bins, where OPT is the number of bins given by the optimal solution [3]. The simpler of these, the FFD strategy, operates by first sorting the items to be inserted in decreasing order by volume, and then by inserting each item into the first bin in the list with sufficient remaining space. The sorting step is relatively expensive, but without it for the BF and FF algorithms, we only achieve the looser bound of $(17/10)OPT + 2$. A more efficient version of FFD uses no more than $(71/60)OPT+1$ bins [6,15]. In this paper, we take advantage of the heuristic algorithms provided for one-dimensional BPP. We simulate the heuristic algorithms in Table 1 for the Bin Packing problem, which can be categorized into two types of algorithms: the FF algorithm with EDF-schedulability and the BF algorithm with EDF-schedulability. In this paper, we sort the tasks in increasing or decreasing order of execution time, period, or utilization of tasks. The FF algorithm with EDF-schedulability and the BF algorithm with EDF-schedulability are descibed as follows.

Table 1. A number of heuristic algorithms for the Bin Packing problem

Algorithm	Method	Sorting Order	Sorting Criterion
FFIE	FF algorithm with EDF-schedulability	ascending	execution times
FFIP	FF algorithm with EDF-schedulability	ascending	periods
FFIU	FF algorithm with EDF-schedulability	ascending	utilization factors
FFDE	FF algorithm with EDF-schedulability	descending	execution times
FFDP	FF algorithm with EDF-schedulability	descending	periods
FFDU	FF algorithm with EDF-schedulability	descending	utilization factors
BFIE	BF algorithm with EDF-schedulability	ascending	execution times
BFIP	BF algorithm with EDF-schedulability	ascending	periods
BFIU	BF algorithm with EDF-schedulability	ascending	utilization factors
BFDE	BF algorithm with EDF-schedulability	descending	execution times
BFDP	BF algorithm with EDF-schedulability	descending	periods
BFDU	BF algorithm with EDF-schedulability	descending	utilization factors

- *BF Algorithm with EDF-schedulability:* In the algorithm, we pick the tasks one by one from the sorted array of the tasks, and then find the processor amongst the existing processors which has the largest remaining capacity. We then check whether the selected processor has enough room for the task in hand, namely τ_j. In other word, we check if $\sum_{i=1}^{j} e_i/P_i \leq 1$, where $\{\tau_1, \tau_2, ..., \tau_{j-1}\}$ are the tasks that have already been assigned to the processor. If the chosen processor has enough room, we assign the task to the processor. Otherwise, none of the other existing processors have enough space, and we should add a new processor and assign the task to the new processor. We repeat the above procedure for all of the tasks one by one. We have provided six various algorithms of this type which are distinguishable by the order used to sort the tasks. The running time of the BF algorithms is $O(n\log n)$, where n is the number of hard real-time tasks.

- *FF Algorithm with EDF-schedulability:* The algorithm works as follows. Similar to the previous algorithm, we sort the tasks based on one of the above criteria into an array. We start with one processor. We pick the tasks one by one from the sorted array and assign them to the recently added processor as long as the utilization factor of the set of the tasks assigned to the processor does not exceed 1. Once it exceeds unity, we add another processor and assign the last task, which could not be assigned to the previous processor, to the new processor. We use the round robin method to pick the tasks. As the previous algorithm, we have provided six various of algorithms of this type which are distinguishable by the order used to sort the tasks. The running time of the FF algorithms are $O(n\log n)$, where n is the number of hard real-time tasks. In the following algorithm, V_j is the number of tasks that so far have verified if they can be assigned to processor j. Using V_j, we want to check if all of the unassigned tasks have been verified for possibility of assigning them to the jth processor. TA is the total number of tasks that are assigned during the program. The tasks and processors are indexed by parameters i and j, respectively, in the following algorithm.

4 Problem Definition

Consider a set of n hard real-time tasks $T = \{\tau_1, \tau_2, ..., \tau_n\}$. The tasks are periodic, independent and preemptive. Their deadlines are equal to their periods. Multiprocessing is acceptable. The processors are identical. Migration is not allowed. Except for the processors, there are no other shared resources in the system. The objective is finding lower and upper bounds for the number of processors required by the following class of algorithms:

1 A partitioning strategy is used. Therefore we consider a combination of (allocation algorithm, scheduling algorithm) for any algorithm in this class.
2 The EDF scheduling algorithm is used on each processor.
3 Various allocation algorithms that are considered in this paper share the following common properties: Start with one processor. Take tasks one by one and decide which of the existing processors should be assigned to the task, while sufficient conditions of EDF-schedulability should be satisfied for each processor. Each allocation algorithm adds a new processor to the system, only if there is not enough spare capacity for the new task on the existing processors to guarantee the feasibility of EDF-scheduling.
4 Considering items 1 and 2 above, it is guaranteed that all of the deadlines are met by any algorithm in this class. We prove this by contradiction as follows. Given an algorithm in the class, we assume that there exists at least one task that can not meet its deadline. In this case, there exists at least one processor which has been assigned to a set of tasks, including the task that can not meet its deadline, where the EDF algorithm has not feasibly scheduled the set of tasks on the processor. But this is not possible, because,

while assigning the processors to the tasks, the sufficient condition of feasibly scheduling by EDF is satisfied.

5 Lower and Upper Bounds

Using the partitioning strategy, it is required to have an algorithm to allocate a processor to each task and a scheduling algorithm to schedule the tasks on each processor. In this paper, we use either the BF or FF algorithm to determine the processor which should be assigned to each task. As mentioned earlier, we use the EDF scheduling algorithm for each processor, because employing the EDF algorithm allows the problem to be reducible to BPP with fixed size bins with capacity equal to one. Our problem will be reduced to finding an appropriate efficient algorithm that allocates the tasks to the minimum number of processors while meeting their deadlines is guaranteed. We know that so long as the sum of the utilizations of the tasks assigned to a processor is no greater than 1, the task set is EDF-schedulable on the processor. Therefore, the problem reduces to making task assignments with the property that the sum of the utilizations of the tasks assigned to a processor does not exceed 1. In this paper, we find and prove a lower bound for the minimum number of processors for any allocation algorithm that has the properties discussed in Section 4. The lower bound that is obtained in this paper is very tight and its results are very close to the results of the FFDU and BFDU algorithms discussed in Section 3. Considering the lower bound, simulation results lead us to the fact that the difference between the number of processors achieved by the FFDU algorithm and the results of an optimal algorithm is negligible. We also find an upper bound for the number of processors required by any allocation algorithms in our framework and with EDF-schedulability test on each processor. In this paper, we try a bunch of heuristic algorithm with an EDF schedulability test, compare them with each other and the upper and lower bounds provided in this paper.

5.1 A Lower Bound

Theorem 1: Consider a set of n periodic, independent, preemptive and hard real-time tasks $T = \{\tau_1, \tau_2, ..., \tau_n\}$, *where their deadlines are equal to their periods. Multiprocessing is acceptable. The processors are identical. Migration is not allowed. Except for the processors, there are no other shared resources in the system. We have* $m \leq h$, *where h is the number of the processors which are required to guarantee that the tasks can meet their deadlines by any algorithm, which belongs to the class of algorithms defined in Section 4, and* $m = \lceil \sum_{i=1}^{n} (e_i/P_i) \rceil$, *with* e_i *and* P_i *being the execution time and period of task* τ_i.

Proof: We prove this theorem by contradiction. Assume that to the contrary the expression $m > h$ is true. In other words,

$$h < m \tag{1}$$

We consider any arbitrary set T_h of the tasks that are EDF-schedulable on h processors, when we use the partitioning strategy. Therefore, $T_h \subseteq T$, and since

$$\sum_{\tau_j \text{is a task on the first processor}} (e_j/P_j) \leq 1$$
$$\sum_{\tau_j \text{is a task on the second processor}} (e_j/P_j) \leq 1$$
$$\vdots$$
$$\sum_{\tau_j \text{is a task on the } h^{\text{th}} \text{ processor}} (e_j/P_j) \leq 1,$$

we have

$$\sum_{\tau_j \in T_h} (e_j/P_j) \leq h \tag{2}$$

On the other hand, from the fact that h is a natural number and from (2), we conclude that

$$\left\lceil \sum_{\tau_j \in T_h} (e_j/P_j) \right\rceil \leq h \tag{3}$$

Considering $m = \lceil \sum_{i=1}^{n} (e_i/P_i) \rceil$ and from (1) and (3), we conclude that

$$\left\lceil \sum_{\tau_j \in T_h} (e_j/P_j) \right\rceil < \left\lceil \sum_{i=1}^{n} (e_i/P_i) \right\rceil \tag{4}$$

Therefore,

$$T_h \neq T. \tag{5}$$

From (5) and $T_h \subseteq T$, we conclude that $T_h \subset T$. Therefore, all of the tasks in T are not EDF-schedulable on h processors. Hence, $m \leq h$.

5.2 An Upper Bound

Theorem 2: Consider a set of n periodic, independent, preemptive and hard real-time tasks $T = \{\tau_1, \tau_2, ..., \tau_n\}$, where their deadlines are equal to their periods. Multiprocessing is acceptable. The processors are identical. Migration is not allowed. Except for the processors, there are no other shared resources in the system. We have $h < 2m$, where h is the number of the processors which are required to guarantee that the tasks can meet their deadlines by the algorithm, which belongs to the class of algorithms defined in Section 4, and $m = \lceil \sum_{i=1}^{n} (e_i/P_i) \rceil$, where e_i and P_i are the execution time and period of a task τ_i, respectively.

Proof: Suppose that the tasks have been assigned on h processors via one of the algorithms that satisfy the assumptions of the problem.

The occupied portion of the kth processor is given by

$$U_k = \sum_{\tau_j \text{is a task on the } k^{\text{th}} \text{ processor}} \frac{e_j}{P_j} \tag{6}$$

and the unoccupied portion of the kth processor is therefore

$$R_k = 1 - U_k. \tag{7}$$

We define R and U as follows.

$$R = \sum_{\tau_j \text{is a task assigned on one of the } h \text{ processors}} R_j \tag{8}$$

$$U = \sum_{\tau_j \text{is a task assigned on one of the } h \text{ processors}} U_j \tag{9}$$

From (6) and (9), we obtain

$$U = \sum_{i=1}^{n} (e_i/P_i). \tag{10}$$

From the assumptions of the theorem, we have $m = \lceil \sum_{i=1}^{n} (e_i/P_i) \rceil$. Therefore, from (10), we obtain

$$m = \lceil U \rceil. \tag{11}$$

Having $U \leq \lceil U \rceil$ and from (11), we have the following inequality:

$$U \leq m. \tag{12}$$

On the other hand, from (7), (8) and (9), we conclude

$$R + U = h. \tag{13}$$

For any combination of (allocation algorithm, scheduling algorithm) of the class of algorithms considered in this paper (refer to Section 5), we have

$$U_j > R_i, \tag{14}$$

where $j > i$. Otherwise, there was enough space for the tasks, which are currently assigned to the jth processor, on the ith processor and it was not required to add the jth processor to the system. From (14), we can say that $U_h > R_1$. Therefore, we have

$$1 - U_h < 1 - R_1. \tag{15}$$

From (15) and (7), we obtain that $R_h < U_1$ which, together with (14), results in the following set of inequalities

$$\begin{cases} U_1 > R_h \\ U_2 > R_1 \\ \vdots \\ U_h > R_{h-1} \end{cases} \tag{16}$$

From (16), we conclude that

$$R_1 + R_2 + \cdots + R_h < U_1 + U_2 + \cdots + U_h. \tag{17}$$

Considering (8), (9) and (17), we have

$$R < U \tag{18}$$

From (18), (12), and (13), we conclude that $h < 2m$.

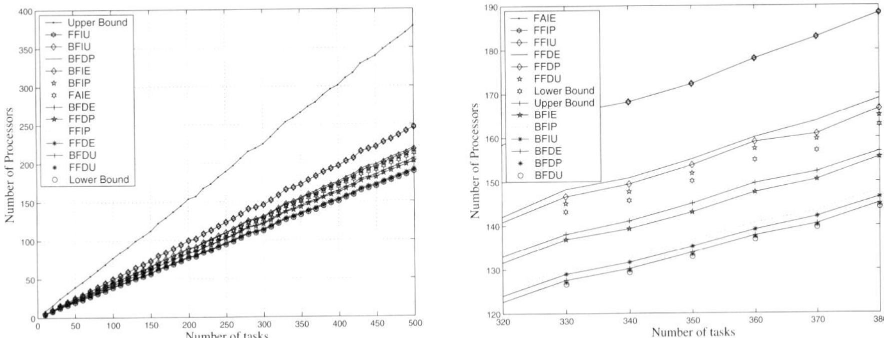

Fig. 1. Left: Number of processors required for scheduling n real-time tasks by various EDF-based partitioning algorithms Right: Enlarged version of the figure on the left

6 Simulation Results

We have implemented the 12 algorithms discussed in Section 3 to compare them with the upper and lower bounds provided in this paper. Simulation conditions are as follows. Each set of data includes n hard real-time tasks. For each task, we randomly generate e_i and p_i, which are the execution time and period, respectively. While generating the data sets, we have considered the relation $e_i < p_i$ for each task. Then, we generate 20 different data sets with size n. We next execute each of the aforementioned algorithms, namely the 12 heuristic algorithms and lower and upper bounds, on each data set. We compute the average of the aggregations of the number of the processors of the 20 simulations for data set with size n. The simulation is done for the algorithms for $n = 1$ to 500, with step 10. Each heuristic algorithm allocates and schedules the tasks on a number of processors and computes the number of processors required by the algorithm. Lower and upper bounds are computed based on Theorem 1 and Theorem 2 derived in this paper. Simulation results are provided in the left hand side of Figure 1. As expected, the results of the heuristic algorithms are between the upper and the lower bounds. We observe in the left hand side of Figure 1 that the FFDU and then BFDU algorithms have the closest outputs to the lower bound. The optimal solution lies between the lower bound and the FFDU. We also observe that the lower bound is very tight and the results of both of the FFDU and FDBU algorithms are very close to the optimal solution. For instance, it is shown in the right hand side Figure 1 that for 20 sets of $n = 350$ tasks, the average of the lower bound for the required processors is equal to 133, where the FFDU and BFDU algorithms return 133.5 and 134 processors on the average, respectively. The optimal value is in the range of 133 to 134 processors. As we observe, the difference is negligible. In fact, the number of processors that are found by the lower bound are very close to the numbers found by the optimal algorithm. The running time of the lower bound is $O(n)$. Moreover, the FFDU algorithm has polynomial, as opposed to exponential, growth in the number of tasks. In other words, it assigns a set of hard real-time tasks to a set of processors in polynomial time and the number of processors, which is required by this algorithm, is almost equal to minimum. As already stated, an efficient version of FFD uses no more than $(71/60)OPT + 1$ bins in BPP [6,15]. This ratio states the guaranteed performance of the approximation algorithm. Comparing the numerical results of lower bound and the number of processors required by FFDU algorithm and considering the tightness of the lower bound, we observe that, on the average, the difference of performance of FFDU and the optimal algorithm is negligible. Calculating the upper bound, we find out that by a combination of any allocation algorithm (according to the definition given in this paper) and the EDF scheduling algorithm, we require no more than $2\lceil\sum_{i=1}^{n}(e_i/P_i)\rceil$ processors to schedule the set of hard real-time tasks.

7 Conclusions

In this paper, we studied the problem of scheduling a set of independent periodic hard real-time tasks on the minimum number of identical processors such that the timing constraints of the events are satisfied. We focused on the partitioning strategy and when the EDF scheduling algorithm schedules the tasks assigned to each processor. Therefore, we looked for an appropriate allocation algorithm to assign the tasks to as few processors as possible, while the EDF-schedulablity test is satisfied on each processor. The problem is reducible to the BPP problem. Considering the fact that the problem is NP-hard, there is not any known polynomial algorithm to solve the problem. Since there exists some approximation heuristic algorithms for BPP, we can take advantage of the existing theorems for our problem. In this paper, we have derived an upper and a lower bound for the number of processors of any combination of (allocation, EDF scheduling) algorithm, where allocation algorithms are fit into the frame we have defined in Section 4. We implemented 12 heuristic algorithms and as we expected, the number of processors required by the heuristic algorithms lie between the bounds. Since we are looking for the algorithm that uses the minimum number of processors required, the optimal algorithm should be between the lower bound and the best approximation algorithm (the best algorithm among the 12 heuristic algorithms discussed in Section 3 are enough for our purposes). Among the 12 algorithms, the FFDU algorithm is the best and therefore, the optimal solution should be placed between the lower bound and the number of processors given by the FFDU algorithm. The lower bound is tight and the FFDU algorithm has a small guaranteed performance as compared with the optimal algorithm. As noted in the numerical results, the difference between the average number of processors from the FFDU algorithm and the lower bound is minimal. In fact, since the lower bound is tight, the difference between the results of the optimal algorithm and FFDU algorithm is negligible. We have also derived an upper bound for the number of processors. This upper bound is observed to satisfy the properties described in Theorem 2.

References

1. Alvim, A.C.F., Glover, F., Ribeiro, C.C., Aloise, D.J.: Local search for the bin packing problem. In: Hansen, P., Ribeiro, C.C. (eds.) MIC99. Extended Abstracts of the III Metaheuristics International Conference, Angra dos Reis, Brazil, pp. 7–12 (1999)
2. Carpenter, J., Funk, S., Holman, P., Srinivasan, A., Anderson, J., Baruah, S.: A Categorization of Real-time Multiprocessor Scheduling Problems and Algorithms. In: Leung, J.Y. (ed.) Handbook of Scheduling: Algorithms, Models, and Performance Analysis, CRC Press, Boca Raton, FL, USA (2004)
3. Chekuri, C., Motwani, R., Natarajan, B., Stein, C.: Approximation techniques for average completion time scheduling. SIAM Journal on Computing 31(1), 146–166 (2001)
4. Coffman Jr., Galambos, G., Martello, S., Vigo, D.: Bin Packing Approximation Algorithms: Combinatorial Analysis. In: Du, D., Pardalos, P. (eds.) Handbook of Combinatorial Optimization, Kluwer, Amsterdam (1998)
5. Coffman, E.G., Garey Jr., M.R., Johnson, D.S.: Approximation algorithms for NP-hard problems. In: Chapter Approximation algorithm for bin packing: A survey, pp. 46–93. PWS, Boston, MA, USA (1996)
6. Garey, M.R., Johnson, D.S.: A 71/60 theorem for bin packing. Journal of Complexity 1, 65–106 (1985)
7. Garey, M.R., Johnson, D.S.: Computers and Intractability: A Guide to the Theory of NP-Completeness. W. H. Freeman, New York (January 15, 1979)
8. Joseph, M.: Real-time Systems: Specification, Verification and Analysis. NATO ASI Series, Series F: Computer and Systems Sciences. Prentice Hall, NJ (1996)
9. Kao, C.-Y., Lin, F.-T.: A Stochastic Approach for the One-Dimensional Bin-Packing Problems. In: Proceedings of 1992 IEEE International Conference on System, Man, and Cyberbetics, Chicago, Illinois, October 18-21, 1992, IEEE Computer Society Press, Los Alamitos (1992)
10. Krishna, C.M., Shin, K.G.: Real-Time Systems. MIT Press and McGraw-Hill, Cambridge (1997)
11. Laplante, P.A.: Real-time Systems Design and Analysis, An Engineer Handbook. IEEE Computer Society, IEEE Press, Los Alamitos (1993)
12. Lopez, J.M., Garcýa, M., Dýaz, J.L., Garcýa, D.F.: Utilization Bounds for Multiprocessor Rate-Monotonic Scheduling. Real Time Systems 24(1) (January 2003)
13. Lopez, J.M., Dýaz, J.L., Garcýa, D.F.: Minimum and Maximum Utilization Bounds for Multiprocessor Rate Monotonic Scheduling. IEEE Transaction on Parallel and Distributed Systems 15(7), 642–653 (2004)
14. Martello, S., Toth, P.: Knapsack problems. John Wiley and Sons, Chichester (1990)
15. Minyi, Y., Lei, Z.: A simple proof of the inequality MFFD$(L) = 71/60OPT(L)+1$, L for the MFFD bin-packing algorithm. Acta Mathematicae Applicatae Sinica 11, 318–330 (1995)
16. Mohammadi, A., Akl, S.: Scheduling algorithms for real-time systems. Technical Report No.2005-499 School of Computing Queen's University (2005)
17. Stankovic, J.A., Ramamritham, K.: Tutorial Hard Real-Time Systems. IEEE Computer Society Press, Los Alamitos (1988)

Architecture-Based Optimization for Mapping Scientific Applications to Imagine

Jing Du, Xuejun Yang, Guibin Wang, Tao Tang, and Kun Zeng

National Laboratory for Paralleling and Distributed Processing, School of Computer, National University of Defense Technology, Changsha 410073, China
jingdu@nudt.edu.cn

Abstract. It is a challenging issue whether scientific applications are suitable for Imagine architecture. To address this problem, this paper presents a novel architecture-based optimization for the key techniques of mapping scientific applications to Imagine. Our specific contributions include that we achieve fine kernel granularity and choose necessary arrays to organize appropriate streams. Specially, we develop a new stream program generation algorithm based on the architecture-based optimization. We implement our algorithm to some representative scientific applications on ISIM simulation of Imagine, compared the corresponding FORTRAN programs running on Itanium 2. The experimental results show that the optimizing stream programs can efficiently improve computational intensiveness, enhance locality of LRF and SRF, avoid index stream overhead and enable parallelism to utilize ALUs. It is certain that Imagine is efficient for many scientific applications.

Keywords: scientific application, Imagine, kernel partition, stream forming.

1 Introduction

Imagine is a programmable stream processor aiming at media applications [1, 2]. However the research whether scientific applications are suitable for Imagine is open. Therefore we focus on exploring the key techniques for mapping scientific applications to Imagine.

Imagine consists of eight SIMD clusters and three level memory hierarchy. Each cluster contains six arithmetic functional units, a communication unit and a 256-word scratchpad unit (SP) used for local arrays. The three level memory hierarchy includes several local register files (LRFs), a 128 KB stream register file (SRF) and off-chip DRAM to keep the functional units saturated during stream processing [3-5]. Fig. 1 diagrams the Imagine stream architecture. The applications on Imagine are structured as some computation kernels that operate on sequences of data records called streams [6-8]. Imagine can achieve high computational ability compared with common processors for computational intensive applications, which present the fine locality in LRF and SRF and fully utilize so many ALUs in multilevel parallel. However, most scientific applications consist of loop nests that iterate over the same large array. It is a simple streaming method to look upon each inner loop as a separate kernel and each

I. Stojmenovic et al. (Eds.): ISPA 2007, LNCS 4742, pp. 32–43, 2007.

array as a stream. But this method can't exploit the superiority of Imagine owing to small kernel granularity and overfull streams [9], and results in very poor performance. Furthermore, the stream compiler can perform limited program optimizations. These limitations make it necessary to research the programming optimization on Imagine for better resource utilization.

The major challenges in mapping scientific applications to Imagine are to implement appropriate kernel partition and stream forming techniques that fully utilize the superiority of the underlying architecture. To solve this problem, we present a novel architecture-based programming optimization on Imagine. Our specific contributions include that we can not only achieve fine kernel granularity to increase instruction level parallelism (ILP) and computational intensiveness, but also choose necessary arrays to organize appropriate streams in order to enhance data locality and avoid index stream overhead. Specially, we develop a new stream program generation algorithm based on the architecture-based optimization. To evaluate the effectiveness of our algorithm, we implement some representative scientific applications on ISIM simulation of Imagine, compared the corresponding FORTRAN programs running on Itanium 2. The experimental results show that the optimizing stream programs can effectively improve computational intensiveness, enhance locality of LRF and SRF, avoid index stream overhead and enable parallelism to utilize ALUs. It is certain that Imagine is effective for many scientific applications.

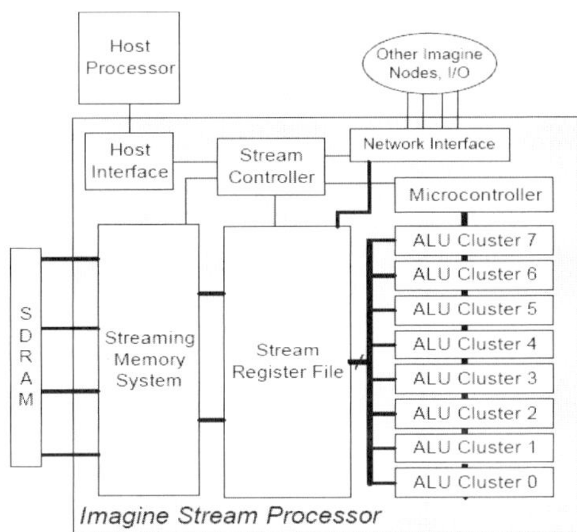

Fig. 1. The Imagine stream architecture

2 Related Work

Though media applications are becoming the main consumers of stream processors [10, 11], there is an important effort to research whether scientific applications are suitable for stream processors. Examples including efficient fluid flow simulation [12, 13] and iterative solvers for sparse linear systems [14, 15] have been demonstrated to run on GPU, which is a graphic stream processor. Many linear algebra routines and scientific applications have been mapped to the Merrimac supercomputer that is also stream architecture [16, 17]. Some dense and sparse matrix applications and some mathematic algorithms such as transitive closure have been implemented on Imagine [18]. However the prior studies focus on how these idiographic applications are expressed as stream programs, there is little research on general automatic generation of stream programs on stream architectures. Paper [19, 20] developed some programming optimizations for mapping scientific programs to Imagine, while it did not present a systemic automatic streaming algorithm for performance enhancement. Our work is a further effort to research the optimal programming approach to improve the underlying hardware utilization in stream processor.

3 Architecture-Based Programming Optimization

The major challenges in mapping scientific applications to Imagine are to implement appropriate kernel partition and stream forming techniques that fully utilize the superiority of the underlying architecture [21, 22].

3.1 Kernel Partition

To improve computational intensiveness, high ILP parallelism and fine data locality between kernels, we restructure all the loops that need be mapped to Imagine through loop transformations [23] as follows.

- Loop Distribution

Loop distribution can be used to convert a loop to multiple streaming loops. We can distribute loops according to data-centric analysis, and form several blocks relate to different arrays. This transformation decreases the kernel granularity and creates extra communication overhead. Thus it is worth attempting other transformations that can achieve fine kernel granularity before performing loop distribution.

- Loop Fusion

Loop fusion can restructure existing loops for computational intensiveness and kernel granularity by using transformations including array expansion, privatization, alignment, and replication. We merge different regions on the same array into a large loop to form a kernel to increase the computational intensiveness. Besides, we need to combine loops to enlarge the kernel granularity by changing iteration ranges, and thus parallelism in kernels can be increased via fully utilizing multi-ALUs on Imagine.

- Loop Scheduling

To enhance data locality between kernels, we need use loop scheduling to schedule the loops that exist data dependency in different kernels successively. There are two aspects of loop scheduling. Primarily we schedule the kernels operate on the same array successively to make SRF reuse possibly. Another aspect is we can transfer some loops in the previous kernel to the next kernel, if these loops exist data dependency with partial loops in the next kernel. This idea can reduce the producing of intermediate results to guarantee SRF capacity enough and enhance SRF reuse. The essence of this transformation is to distribute the loops in different kernels and then to fuse partial loops to a kernel based on data-centric analysis.

- Instruction Scheduling

When the above factors are satisfied, on the premise of accuracy being ensured, this method may reduce the number of write times to the same record, and prepare for combining single instruction operations.

3.2 Stream Forming

Aiming at exploiting parallelism according to the number of clusters and reducing inter-cluster communication, programmers distribute parallelizable data among the clusters and put the data that dependence can't be eliminated on the same cluster for improving data locality in kernels and reducing memory access overhead via loop analysis. So it is necessary to reform the original stream so that the new stream can exploit the underlining hardware performance. Stream forming involves stream select, record structure and stream organization.

3.2.1 Stream Select

Stream select focuses on choosing appropriate arrays operations as streams. To reduce DRAM access overhead and avoid maintaining storage consistency, we need select successive basic streams as operation objects of kernels. Though an array may be referenced many times in different access pattern, its corresponding basic stream will be generated as one copy. And then we must collect statistics of access pattern and access region of all arrays at the beginning of the program, and select the basic streams according to the least common array region of high access frequency. For example, Fig. 2(a) gives an example program and Fig. 2(b) presents the corresponding data layout of array A. After performing basic stream selecting on the program, three data access pattern will generate a same basic stream shown in Fig. 2(c), which will avoid unnecessary stream loading and storage overhead.

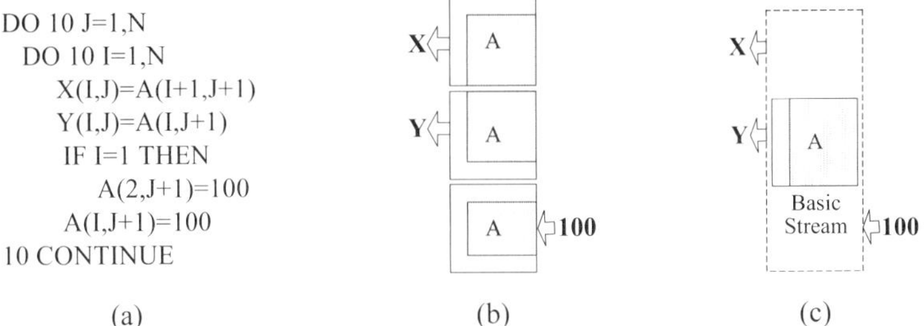

Fig. 2. An example of selecting basic stream

3.2.2 Record Structure

All items of a record are placed on a cluster to perform the same computations, so the key issue of record structure is which elements need to be combined as a record [19]. Firstly, there are limited parameters allowed in a kernel due to the restriction of the architecture. Therefore we take statistics of the array elements that perform the same computations, and then combine these data as a record. This idea can reduce the number of streams so that the kernel can be bigger by loop fusion. Secondly, to avoid assigning dependent data within an iteration to different clusters, we combine the dependent record into a big record according to the capacity of LRF. This method can make full use of LRF to enhance LRF locality. Besides, combining record will also lighten SRF's storage burden, so as to improve the locality in SRF level.

3.2.3 Stream Organization

After selecting required streams and constructing suited record structure, we need to consider how to distribute these arrays on clusters, that is stream organization. This process reorders the arrays with supplementing and updating the variant boundary by using dependence analysis and program transformation techniques. Stream organization aims at enhancing data locality in kernels, reducing DRAM reorder overhead caused by index stream and exploiting cluster parallelism for making full use of arithmetic units per cluster. We describe our methods of stream organization as follows, aiming at developing these techniques for handling arbitrary loop nests. In our work, we look upon loop iteration spaces unrolling as stream organization pattern, so our methods can be described by appropriate loop transformations.

1. Perfect Loop Nests

The stream organization for perfect loop nests aims at developing techniques for improving computational intensiveness, enhancing LRF locality, reducing index streams and achieving parallelism on clusters.

- Improve computational intensiveness

Different references to an array form different derived streams on the only basic stream. We perform three optimizations to improve computational intensiveness. First, unifying different derived streams by stream enlarging can combine the streams referenced by same computations as a long stream. Then if there are diversiform access pattern of a stream in a kernel and different access region can be overlapped each other, we need consider reusing the common block to meet the diversiform access pattern denoted stream reusing. Last, to enhance data reusing for long stream between kernels we perform stripmining optimization to partition steam. So we can reuse the small strip of long stream in SRF to improve computational intensiveness.

We explicate stream enlarging and stream reusing in detail according to an example modified from a scientific application Swim in SPEC 2000. Fig. 3(a) shows the example that is a perfect loop nest and performs multiform access pattern on data A. Fig. 3(b) presents the data layout of A in original loop. After stream enlarging, the access overhead of A is reduced by 26% (5/19) shown in Fig. 3(c). Go on performing stream reusing on data linked by the same curve in Fig. 3(c), the access overhead is reduced by 57% (8/14) again and the number of input parameters is reduced from 19 to 6 shown in Fig. 3(d).

- Enhance LRF locality

Exploiting locality in clusters relates to not only a high degree of record reuse and the spatial reuse on a cluster but also the number of SPs and the capability of LRF.

Firstly, the dependences tell that two references point to the same LRF location, thus the LRF reuse is highest when records are accessed sequentially, that is we must eliminate the loop-carried dependence [24] through array expansion, alignment etc. transformations and avoid assigning dependent data to different clusters.

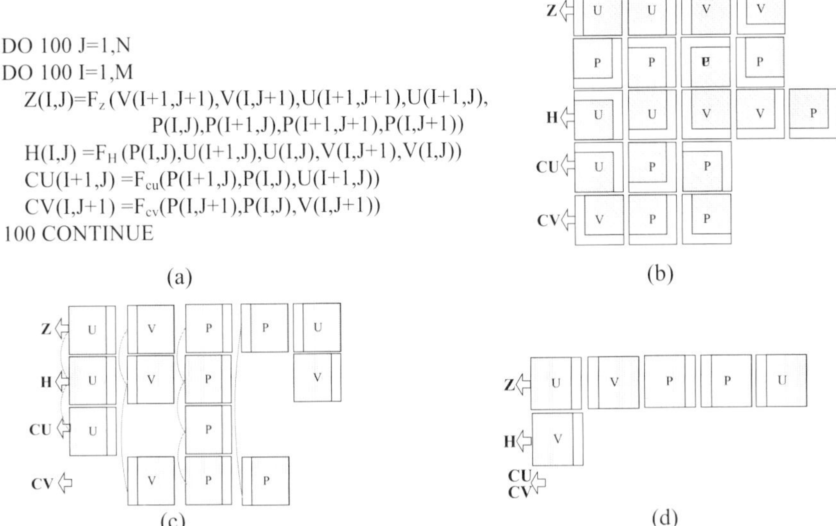

DO 100 J=1,N
DO 100 I=1,M
Z(I,J)=F_Z (V(I+1,J+1),V(I,J+1),U(I+1,J+1),U(I+1,J),
P(I,J),P(I+1,J),P(I+1,J+1),P(I,J+1))
H(I,J) =F_H (P(I,J),U(I+1,J),U(I,J),V(I,J+1),V(I,J))
CU(I+1,J) =F_cu(P(I+1,J),P(I,J),U(I+1,J))
CV(I,J+1) =F_cv(P(I,J+1),P(I,J),V(I,J+1))
100 CONTINUE
(a)
Z
H
CU
CV
(b)
(c)
(d)

Fig. 3. Stream enlarging and stream reusing

Secondly, consider reducing the overhead caused by SPs. The spatial locality in LRF occurs when each iteration accesses a LRF location that is adjacent to the location used in the previous iteration, thus the variables are assigned to SPs for the latter iteration using. So the utilization of SPs is important for enhancing LRF locality. Up to this point, we must reduce the dependent threshold of inner loop which denotes how many SPs would be allocated to reduce SP overhead.

Thirdly, to avoid the problems of overfull SPs and limited LRF capability caused by long streams, we must perform two transformations: first, the loop-carried dependence need be converted into loop-independent dependence [24] for eliminating the LRF reuse between loops; second, LRF locality with limited capability can be improved by stripmining the inner loop so that a strip length fits in LRF and then moving the loop that iterates over the strips to the outermost position.

- Avoid index streams

The usage of index stream makes stream organization flexibly, but it also brings too much extra overhead of stream reordering and reloading. So we must avoid using index streams. Above all, we must choose appropriate basic streams and then structure streams according to the basic stream by diverse loop transformations as follows, aiming at shortening the length and stride of index stream.

Firstly, use loop interchange [23] to restructure the stream according to the basic stream for shortening the index stride. For example, suppose the basic stream are stored in column-major order so if the loop iterating over a row is at the innermost position, we must perform loop interchange to avoid the use of index stream, so the innermost loop is striding over the contiguous dimension.

Secondly, perform unroll-and-jam [23] to reduce the length of index stream by improving computations per record. As an example, consider the loop in Fig. 4. By

DO I= 1, N*2
  DO J = 1, M
    A(I) = A(I) + B(J)
 	
Original program
	DO I = 1, N*2, 2
	  DO J= 1, M
	    A(I) = A(I) + B(J)
	    A(I+1) = A(I+1) + B(J)
	Unroll-and-jam

K=0
DO J = 1, M
  K=K + B(J)
DO I = 1, N*2
  A(I) = A(I) + K
Data-centric loop splitting
	DO M =1, N*2/8
	  DO I=1,N
	    DO K□1, 8
	      J=M*8 + K
	    A(I) = A(I) + B(J)
	Stripmining

Fig. 4. Example program

performing this transformation, the index stream length of B is shortened from N*2 to N to reduce the overhead of index stream loading.

Thirdly, we bring forward a new transformation to avoid the utilization of index streams for higher performance compared with unroll-and-jam, which is data-centric loop splitting shown in Fig. 4. We can distill the computations that reuse data with large temporal span as self-governed loop. As the previous example, the multiple loop can be split into two loops with computations on B and A respectively due to the discontinuous temporal reuse of B(J), thus the kernel can use the basic streams of B and A without indexing overhead.

- Enable parallelism according to the number of clusters

Performance can be improved by converting the available parallelism into a form more suitable for Imagine. Consider parallelizing the outer loop so that the inner loops that have the most dependence can be assigned to the same cluster.

Firstly, select the proper parallel algorithm to parallelize the outer loop [25]. Consider using existing transformations like loop interchange, loop reversal, and loop skewing to uncover parallelism and move it to the outermost position possible.

Secondly, enabling parallelism for optimal performance need concern for architectural issues such as the number of clusters by loop tiling [26]. For example, performance can be improved by stripmining the outer loop shown in Fig. 4.

2 Imperfectly Nested Loops

When loops are imperfectly nested loops and the loops can't be mapped to kernels directly, consider maximal loop distribution to produce a collection of loops each of which may be perfectly nested. Then we can perform the techniques of perfect loop nests. But if an imperfectly nested loop is produced due to too much spatial overhead or other factors, we consider executing the outer loop in serial and move on.

3.3 A Stream Program Generation Algorithm

Firstly, **SGA** algorithm applies **KernelPartition** algorithm for kernel partition. Then it employs the routine **StreamingLoop** to explore suited streams on each loop of all kernels.

```
ALGORITHM: SGA
INPUT: The program P
OUTPUT: A stream program
KernelPartition(P)
for each k_i
  for each loop l_j in k_i
     StreamingLoop(l_j)

ALGORITHM: KernelPartition(P)
INPUT: program P
OUTPUT: code sections {k_i} as kernels
get the most time-consuming {k_i} by profiling
form the basic streams{BS_i } by profiling
// data(k_i)=input(k_i) ∪ output(k_i)
for each k_i and k_j
    if data(k_i) ∩ data(k_j) ≠ Φ
        k_i=merge(k_i, k_j)
distribut {k_i} to {nk_i} based on the arrays in k_i
for each nk_i and nk_j  do begin
    if data(nk_i) ∩ data(nk_j) ≠ Φ  then begin
        ki=merge(nk_i,nk_j)
        if input(k_i) ∩ output(k_i-1) ≠ Φ
            schedule some loops in k_i-1 to k_i
            // enhance SRF resuse
    end // form new data-centic sections{k_i}
end
```

```
ALGORITHM: StreamingLoop(l)
INPUT: l is loop nests to be mapped to stream code
OUTPUT: the streams of l
StreamingLoopNest(l,success)
if success  then begin
     if l can be distributed then begin
          distribute l into loop nests l_1,l_2,...,l_n
          for each l_i
               StreamingLoop(l_i)
     end
     else begin
          for each outer loop l' nested in l
               StreamingLoop(l')
     end
end

ALGORITHM: StreamingLoopNest(l,success)
INPUT: l is a perfect loop nests to be mapped to stream code
OUTPUT: the streams of l
// {l_i} are loops in l
success:=false
if success then begin
     select arrays that must be transferred to streams  //stream select
     select a loop l' as outermost loop to parallelize
     eliminate the loop-carried dependence between loops nested in l'
     //enhance special reuse according to the LRF capability
     shorten the dependent threshold in each inner loops //reduce SPs
     organize streams based on BS_i by diverse transformations
     //avoid index stream
     perform loop tiling on l' for eight clusters
     choose suited record elements  // Record Structure
     success:=true
end
```

Fig. 5. The SGA algorithm

KernelPartition first find the most time-consuming parts and form the basic streams. Then restructure the program based on data-centric analysis, aiming at improving computational intensiveness, kernel granularity and SRF locality.

StreamingLoop first invokes **StreamingLoopNest** to attempt perfect-nest strategies discussed in Section 3.2.3. If this fails, it tries distributing the loop into a collection of sub-nests, mapping each one to stream code recursively. If the loop cannot be distributed, it sequentializes the outermost loop and calls itself recursively nested in that loop.

4 Experimental Results and Analysis

To evaluate the effectiveness of our optimization, we select 7 scientific applications listed in Table 1. Dfft and Transp are the most time-consuming subroutines in Capao that is an optics application. We use three versions for each application: the serial FORTRAN version (Seri), the original stream version (Orig) and the optimizing stream version (SGA). The FORTRAN programs compiled with Intel's compiler (-O3) are tested on an Itanium 2 based server configured with a 1.6GHz Itanium 2 processor with 16KB L1-cache, 256KB L2-cache, 6MB L3-cache and 4GB memory. Note that only one core of Itanium 2 is used in our test. And the other two stream versions run on ISIM that is a cycle-accurate simulator of Imagine [7].

Table 1. Specifications of applications

Name	Swim	Transp	Vpenta	Dfft	Laplace	Jacobi	GEMM
Source	Spec2000	-	NASA	-	NCSA	-	BLAS
Arrays	14	5	8	1	1	4	2
Size	513×513	512×512	920×920	4096	256×256	128×128	256×256

Table 2 illustrates the performance results of the optimizing programs compared with the original stream programs and the serial programs. It is obvious that our optimization provides high speedup of Transp, Dfft, Laplace, Jacobi and GEMM compared with Itanium 2 system, and other 2 applications (Swim, Vpenta) perform comparably. This is because Imagine has more simple control logic, higher memory bandwidth and higher computational performance, while Itanium 2 is highly sensitive to memory latency. Table 2 also shows our optimization has achieved high speedup of all the applications compared with the original stream versions, because our optimization can efficiently exploit the tremendous potential of Imagine for scientific applications.

Table 2. Comparison of different implementation for the scientific applications

Applications	Swim	Transp	Vpenta	Dfft	Laplace	Jacobi	GEMM
Speedup(SGA vs. Seri)	1.36	2.15	1.72	15.01	3.41	2.04	3.17
Speedup(SGA vs. Orig)	4.21	2.53	3.81	5.22	2.65	3.57	5.39

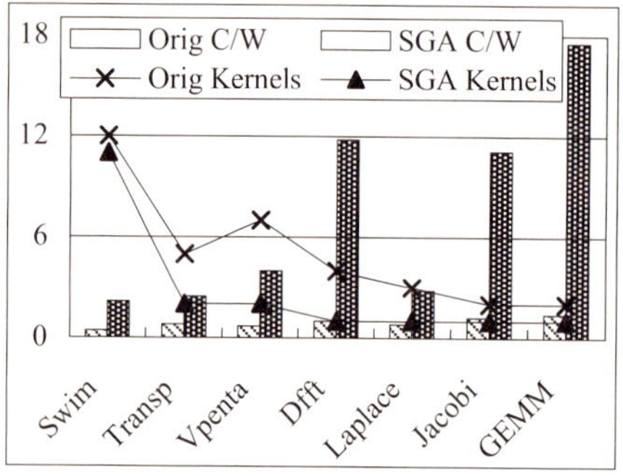

Fig. 6. The effect on kernel size

Fig. 7. The reduction of index streams

Fig. 6 shows the effect on kernel size by applying our optimization compared with the original stream programs, as well as the computations per word (C/W) and the number of kernels (Kernels). We can observe our optimization improves the kernel granularity of all the programs. But the granularity of Swim achieves a little varying, because it has huge data amount and irregular access pattern so that the loops are difficult to be distributed or combined, resulting in low computational density. The other applications can enlarge the code amount of kernels obviously (loop fusion, loop scheduling and instruction scheduling are used here), and computational intensiveness is enhanced accordingly (steam reusing, reducing index streams, eliminating the loop-carried dependence and stripmining are used here) except Transp. Transp that involves two imperfectly loop nests applies loop distribution and loop fusion by array expanding effectively, however all the arrays in Transp are referenced rarely leading a little variety of computational intensiveness.

Fig. 7 shows the reduction of index streams by applying our SGA algorithm. We can observe the index streams of all the optimizing applications are reduced observably, which is owing to changing the original basic streams at the beginning of the programs and using stream reusing. Specially, the index stream can be eliminated in Vpenta when streams are short due to regular data access pattern.

Fig. 8 shows the SRF to memory and LRF to memory bandwidth utilization ratios respectively when applications are running on Imagine. The LRF to memory bandwidth ratio are over 67:1, 53:1 and 34:1 across GEMM, Jacobi and Dfft, due to our optimization enhancing the computational intensiveness and therefore the abundant memory access of these three applications focusing on LRF. While Swim present low LRF to memory ratio for its long streams can't be partitioned due to dependence. Additionally, the SRF bandwidth utilization of Swim, Transp and Laplace respectively is just twice as the memory bandwidth utilization, which shows SRF just transfers the data from memory to LRF resulting in low SRF reusing.

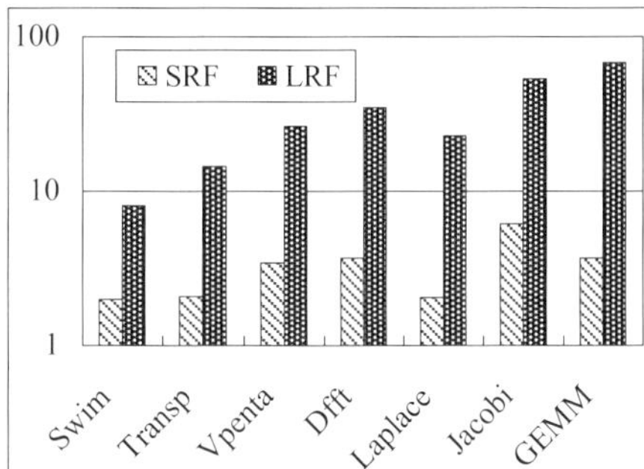

Fig. 8. The bandwidth utilization optimized by SGA

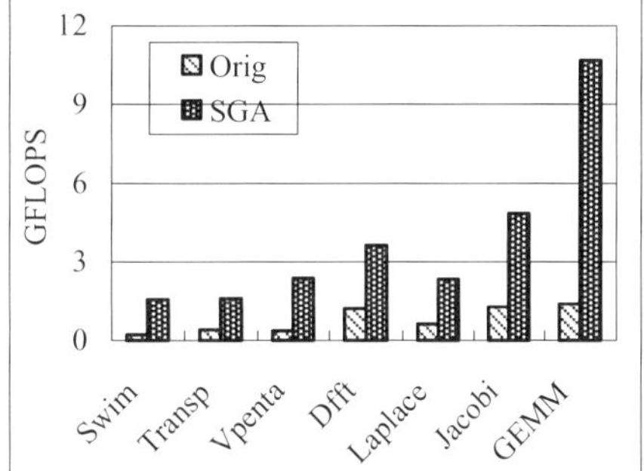

Fig. 9. Computation rate of applications

Fig. 9 presents the computation rate of the stream applications measured in GFLOPS. Imagine' peak performance can achieve 16GFLOPS. The results show that the sustained performance of all the optimizing stream programs has reached 10% to 67% of the peak performance, but the original stream programs just reach 2% to 9% of the peak performance. This is because our SGA algorithm can efficiently exploit Imagine's potentials from multiple ALUs through optimizations like select appropriate basic streams, reduce index streams, stream reusing, stripming et. al, which have increased kernel's computational intensiveness to exploit cluster's ILP, avoided communication latency and reduced overhead in memory access. However Swim and Transp optimized by SGA still achieve a little performance improvement owing to these programs still exist overfull index streams so that memory delay can't be overlapped and the ALUs can't be saturated at all time.

5 Conclusion and Future Work

In this paper, we have presented a novel stream program generation algorithm based on our architecture-based optimization for mapping scientific applications to Imagine. The key techniques are to implement appropriate kernel partition and stream forming that fully utilize the superiority of the underlying architecture, by means of data-centric program transformations. Our approach is simple and generates stream programs for scientific applications in our experiment. The experimental evaluation shows that the performance of our algorithm scales well with effectively improving computational density, enhancing locality of LRF and SRF, avoiding index stream overhead and enabling parallelism to utilize ALUs. It is certain that Imagine is efficient for many scientific applications.

One future work is to research more program transformations in our algorithm to exploit more architectural features of Imagine so that our algorithm can achieve higher performance and much wider applicability. Another is to search more scientific applications suitable for stream architecture by applying our algorithm. We would like to exploit common programming model to improve coding efficiency, due to existing program model exposing so many controls to programmers.

Acknowledgements. We gratefully thank the Stanford Imagine team for the use of their compilers and simulators and their generous help. We specifically thank lab 610 of School of Computer Science in National University of Defense Technology for helpful discussions and comments on this work. We also acknowledge the reviewers for their insightful comments. The work of this paper was supported by the Natural Science Foundation of China under the Grant No. 60621003 and 60633050.

References

1. Amarasinghe, S., William: Stream Architectures. In: Proceedings of the International Conference on Parallel Architectures and Compilation Techniques (2003)
2. Khailany, B., et al.: Imagine: Media Processing with Streams. IEEE Micro, 35–46 (2001)
3. Kapasi, U.J., et al.: Programmable Stream Processors. IEEE Computer, 54–62 (2003)
4. Khailany, B.: The VLSI Implementation and Evaluation of Area-and Energy-Effcient Streaming Media Processors. Ph.D. thesis, Stanford University (2003)
5. Kapasi, U.J., Dally, W.J., et al.: The Imagine Stream Processor. In: Processings of the International Conference on Computer Design (2002)
6. Das, A., et al.: Imagine Programming System User's Guide 2.0 (2004)
7. Mattson, P.R.: A Programming System for the Imagine Media Processor. Dept. of Electrical Engineering. Ph.D. thesis, Stanford University (2002)
8. Amarasinghe, S., et al.: Stream Languages and Programming Models. In: Proceedings of the International Conference on Parallel Architectures and Compilation Techniques (2003)
9. Jayasena, N.S.: Memory Hierarchy Design for Stream Computing. Ph.D. thesis, Stanford University (2005)
10. Andrew, A.L., William, T., Saman, A.: Linear Analysis and Optimization of Stream Programs. In: Proceedings of the SIGPLAN '03 Conference on Programming Language Design and Implementation, San Diego, CA (2003)

11. Owens, J.D., Rixner, S., et al.: Media Processing Applications on the Imagine Stream Processor. In: Proceedings of the 2002 International Conference on Computer Design (2002)
12. Fan, Z., Qiu, F., Kaufman, A., Yoakum-Stover, S.: Gpu Cluster for High Performance Computing. In: ACM / IEEE Supercomputing Conference (2004)
13. Harris, M.J., Baxter, W.V., Scheuermann, T., Lastera, A.: Simulation of Cloud Dynamics on Graphics Hardware. In: Proceedings of the ACM SIGGRAPH/EUROGRAPHICS conference on Graphics hardware, Aire-la-Ville, Switzerland, pp. 92–101. ACM Press, New York (2003)
14. Bolz, J., Farmer, I., Grinspun, E., SchrÖder, P.: Sparse Matrix Solvers on the Gpu: Conjugate Gradients and Multigrid. ACM Transactions on Graph, 917–924 (2003)
15. Göddeke, D.: Gpgpu Performance Tuning. Tech. rep. University of Dortmund, Germany (2005), http://www.mathematik.uni-dortmund.de/ goeddeke/gpgpu/
16. Dally, W.J., et al: Merrimac: Supercomputing with Streams. In: ACM / IEEE Supercomputing Conference (2003)
17. Erez, M., Ahn, J., Garg, A., et al: Analysis and Performance Results of a Molecular Modeling Application on Merrimac. In: ACM / IEEE Supercomputing Conference (2004)
18. Griem, G., Oliker, L.: Transitive Closure on the Imagine Stream Processor. In: The 5th Workshop on Media and Streaming Processors, SanDiego, CA (2003)
19. Du, J., Yang, X., et al: Scientific Computing Applications on the Imagine Stream Processor. In: Proceedings of the 11th Asia-Pacific Computer Systems Architecture Conference, Shanghai, China (2006)
20. Yang, X., Du, J., et al: Matrix-Based Programming Optimization for Improving Memory Hierarchy Performance on Imagine. In: Proceedings of the 4th International Symposium on Parallel and Distributed Processing and Applications (ISPA), Sorrento, Italy (2006)
21. Suh, J., et al.: A Performance Analysis of PIM, Stream Processing, and Tiled Processing on Memory-Intensive Signal Processing Kernels. In: Proceedings of the annual international symposium on Computer Architecture (2003)
22. Ahn, J.H., et al.: Evaluating the Imagine Stream Architecture. In: Proceedings of the annual international symposium on Computer Architecture (2004)
23. Wolfe, M.J.: High Performance Compilers for Parallel Computing. Addison-Wesley, Reading (1996)
24. Kuck, et al: Dependence Graphs and Compiler Optimizations. In: The 8th ACM Symposium on the Principles of Programming Languages, Williamsburg, VA (1981)
25. Wolf, M.E., et al.: A Loop Transformation Theory and an Algorithm to Maximize Parallelism. IEEE Transactions on Parallel and Distributed Systems 2(4), 452–471 (1991)
26. Xue, J.: Loop Tiling for Parallelism. Kluwer Academic Publishers, Boston (2000)

Implementation and Optimization of Sparse Matrix-Vector Multiplication on Imagine Stream Processor

Li Wang, Xue Jun Yang, Gui Bin Wang, Xiao Bo Yan, Yu Deng, Jing Du, Ying Zhang, Tao Tang, and Kun Zeng

National Labotary for Parelleling and Distributed Processing,
School of Computer,
National University of Defense Technology,
Changsha 410073, Hunan P.R. of China
dragonfly@linux-vs.org,
{xjyang,xbyan,yudeng,zhangying}@nudt.edu.cn

Abstract. Sparse matrix-vector multiplication (shortly SpMV) dominates the performance of many scientific and engineering applications. However, it tends to run much more slowly than its dense counterpart because the algorithms have poor temporal and spatial locality, the memory access patterns are irregular. Its performance depends heavily on both the nonzero structure of the sparse matrix and on the machine architecture. In this paper, we address the problem of implementing and optimizing SpMV on Imagine stream processor. We present three classes of implementation algorithms based on different key ideas, first two of which highlight different aspects of underlying stream architecture, and the third algorithm is inspired by the SpMV vector implementation. Then we discuss some critical optimizations. The experimental results over same benchmarks show we achieve up to an average 67 percent relative improvement over published evaluation.

Keywords: Sparse Matrix-Vector Multiplication, Imagine, stream processor.

1 Introduction and Motivation

Sparse matrix operations dominate the performance of many scientific and engineering applications. In particular, iterative methods are commonly used in algorithms for linear systems, least square problems, and eigenvalue problems, which involve a sparse matrix-vector product in the inner loop. In these solvers, a multiplication y := Ax has to be carried out repeatedly, often thousands of times, for the same m×n sparse matrix A, each time for a updated value of dense vector x. However, Sparse Matrix-vector multiplication is a particularly challenging algorithmic kernel, the performance of sparse matrix algorithms is often disappointing on modern cache-based machines. Because the algorithms have poor temporal and spatial locality, the memory access patterns are irregular, and there is more overhead for manipulating the data structure

I. Stojmenovic et al. (Eds.): ISPA 2007, LNCS 4742, pp.44–55,2007.

representation. Performance is highly dependent on the nonzero structure of the sparse matrix, the organization of the data and its computation, and the hierarchy and exact parameters of the hardware memory system. Considerable researches of SpMV implementation and optimization have been conducted on scalar, vector, shared memory and distributed memory parallel architectures [21, 22, 23, 24, 25], but we are not aware of any research on stream architecture. We only notice that [1, 2] published SpMV evaluations on Cell, VIRAM and Imagine, but they did not describe their implementation and tuning in detail. In this paper, we focus on the implementation and optimization of SpMV on Imagine stream processor. We present three classes of algorithms for solving SpMV, and explore some performance-dependent optimizations, most of which are not mentioned by [1, 2]. Experimental results show we obtain an average 1.67x speedup over the evaluations on Imagine published in [2] for same benchmarks, which is even competitive with an IA64 implementation with skimming through the results published in [1].

The rest of this paper is organized as follows. Section 2 introduces the Imagine architecture and its programming model. Section 3 presents our methodology for solving SpMV on Imagine. In Section 4, we explore some optimizations. In Section 5, we present experimental results obtained over benchmarks used in [2], demonstrating the improvement of our methodology. In Section 6, we conclude the paper.

2 Background

2.1 Imagine Architecture

Stream processors are designed for computationally intensive applications characterized by high data parallelism and producer-consumer locality with little global data reuse. Stream processors have demonstrated significant performance advantages in domains such as signal processing, multimedia and graphics. Yet, it has not been sufficiently validated whether stream processor is efficient for scientific computing. Imagine is a programmable streaming microprocessor developed by Stanford University [3, 4, 5, 6]. The general layout diagram of Imagine is presented [7] in Figure 1. Imagine contains 48 arithmetic units, and a unique three level memory hierarchy designed to keep the functional units saturated during stream processing. The memory hierarchy consists of off-chip SDRAM (2.1GB/s), a 128KB stream register file(SRF) (25.6GB/s), and direct forwarding of results among arithmetic units via 528 local register files (LRF) (435GB/s) of which 256 per cluster are indirectly addressable. The architecture is centered around the SRF, which reads data from off-chip DRAM through a memory system interface and sequentially feeds the 8 arithmetic clusters. The local storage of the SRF can effectively reuse intermediate results (producer-consumer locality), allowing for the amortization of off-chip memory accesses. In addition, the SRF can be used to overlap computations with memory traffic, by simultaneously reading from main-memory while writing to the arithmetic clusters (double-buffering). Each of Imagine's 8 arithmetic clusters consists of 6 functional units containing 3 adders, 2 multipliers, and a divide/square root. A single microcontroller broadcasts VLIW instructions in SIMD fashion to all of the arithmetic clusters. This is in contrast to traditional vector architecture which issues a single instruction per cycle, counting on

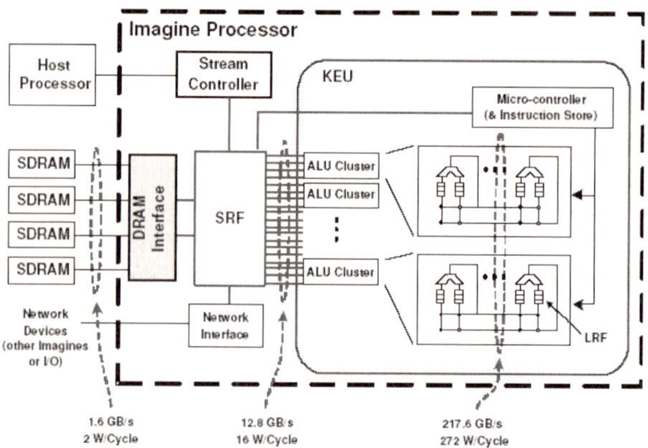

Fig. 1. Diagram of Imagine architecture with bandwidth hierarchy numbers

parallelism within each vector instruction to achieve high performance. The Imagine architecture emphasizes raw processing power.

2.2 Programming Models

The programming model of Imagine represents applications as a set of computation kernels that consume and produce data streams. Each data stream is a sequence of data records of the same type, and each kernel is a program that performs the same set of operation on each input stream element, and produces one or more output streams. The programming model is described in two languages: the stream level and the kernel level [8, 9, 10, 11]. A stream level program is written in StreamC language, which is derived from C++ language. A kernel level program is written in KernelC language, which is C-like expression syntax. The StreamC program executed for the host thread represents the data communication between the kernels that perform computations. However, programmers must consider the stream organization and communication using this explicit stream model, which increases the programming complexity[12]. So the optimization for stream programming is important to achieve significant performance improvements on the Imagine architecture.

3 Methodology

3.1 Conditional Stream Solution

To implement SpMV on Imagine efficiently, there are some challenges. Imagine's 8 SIMD-controlled clusters are ideal for processing long streams of independent data elements. However, this simple model is not true in SpMV. Since the length of nonzeros in each matrix line is random and unequal, SpMV requires data-dependent control. Fortunately conditional streams mechanism [15] is presented to address this problem by introducing two new primitives: conditional input and conditional output. With a conditional input operation, a new data element is fetched from the input stream into a cluster only if a local condition code corresponding to that data element is true. Conditional outputs work in a similar fashion: they append data elements to an output stream only if a local condition code corresponding to that data element is true. These condition codes are typically calculated along with the data elements. The conditional stream primitives are conceptually simple for the programmer but are powerful enough to handle complex data-dependent behavior.

We present CS (Conditional Stream) algorithm version 1 in figure 2. The computational kernel receives three input streams, str_a is matrix nonzeros, str_x is the indexed elements of the source dense vector, and the third stream (str_rowlen) indicates the amount of nonzeros in each line. The algorithm loops every matrix line (outer loop, line 1), first obtains the amount of nonzeros in current line from str_rowlen (line 3), and divides it by 8 (line 4). Let's assume the quotient is p, remainder is q. Then performs p iterations to consume 8*p elements from str_a and str_x respectively, does the required multiply-adds (line 5-9). Then only flows out q elements by using conditional stream (line 11-12), doing the remaining multiply-adds (line 13). Finally algorithm sums the partial sums on eight clusters (line 14-16), and stores the dot product to str_y (line 17).

```
1   for (i = 0; i < rownum; i++) {  // loop every matrix line
2     result = 0;
3     str_rowlen >> rowlen;// obtain number of nonzeros in current line
4     quotient = rowlen / 8;  // obtain quotient of rowlen divided by eight
      // 8-way SIMD, all clusters processing simultaneously
5     for (i = 0; i < quotient; i++) {
6       str_a >> a;
7       str_x >> x;
8       result = result + a * x;
9     }
10    remainder = rowlen % 8;  // obtain remainder of rowlen divided by eight
      // only remainder clusters take part in valid computation
11    str_a(cluster_id() < remainder) >> a;
12    str_x(cluster_id() < remainder) >> x;
13    result = result + cluster_id() < remainder?a * x:0;
      // sum the partial sums on eight clusters
14    result = result + commucperm(0x67452301, result);
15    result = result + commucperm(0x44660022, result);
16    result = result + commucperm(0x00004444, result);
17    str_y << result;   // store the dot product
18  }
```

Fig. 2. Pseudocode for CS algorithm V1 solving SpMV

Since conditional stream has more overhead than regular stream, we try to reduce the usage of conditional stream. We note that in SpMV the multiplication is done unconditionally, so we consider to change the computational order. We present CS algorithm version 2, the detail is omitted. The algorithm consists of two kernels. One kernel does the multiplication, which can be done unconditionally, leading to a very simple and fast kernel. The other kernel applies the similar algorithm to V1 to do the sum. In CS algorithm V2, the bottleneck lies in the sum. In Imagine, each cluster contains three adders and two multipliers, the sum and multiplication can be done simultaneously. Separating the two operations degrades the performance. Furthermore, an additional stream is needed to hold the intermediate result. Experimental results show that V2 achieves poorer performance than V1, so we don't discuss V2 further.

We also note that V1 uses eight clusters to process a line per iteration, using intercluster communication to sum partial sums (line 14-16), the overhead is considerable. We present algorithm version 3 to assign each cluster to sum a line. But as mentioned in [2], the lock-step execution of the SIMD architecture would limit performance to the longest computation. So performance is highly dependent on the nonzero structure of the sparse matrix. In most cases, it produces poorer performance than V1. As a result, we recommend V1 as the candidate to the conditional stream solution and only present the experimental results for V1.

3.2 ScratchPad Solution

Each arithmetic cluster of Imagine contains a 256-word scratchpad unit (SP). The scratchpad is a small word-addressable memory used for small indexed addressing operations within a cluster. The scratchpad register file allows for coefficient storage, short arrays, small look-up tables, and some local register spilling.

The key idea behind SP (ScratchPad) solution is using SP as the indexed addressing temporary storage. We present SP algorithm version 1 in figure 3. The computational kernel receives three input streams, str_a is matrix nonzeros, str_x is the indexed elements of the source dense vector, the third stream (str_rownum) indicates the row number in sparse matrix of each element in str_a. SP is used as an indexed addressing temporary storage. It stores the latest partial sums of each line (not more than 256 lines). The algorithm includes three parts. Part one (line 2-4) clears all SP items. In the main body (line 5-12), kernel performs the core computation, Once kernel fetches three input elements: a, x and rownum from str_a, str_x and str_rownum respectively, it reads the latest partial sum from SP using the line information as index, performs a multiply-add, then stores the updated result back to corresponding SP item. Part three (line 13-19) sums the partial sums on eight clusters, obtains 256 dot products per kernel run. If the matrix contains more than 256 lines, the kernel needs multi-runs. The row number information is also needed some tiny pre-processing, i.e. modulo by 256.

The scratchpad register file has slower access speed than local register file (LRF). The SP algorithm V1 has total 512+ N/4 SP accesses per cluster, assuming N is the number of nonzeros. To improve the performance, we try lazy algorithm to reduce the access frequency to SP. We tried the SP algorithm version 2. The difference between SP algorithm V1 lies in part two. We use a LRF temporary variable to record last line number. If current line number equal with last line number holds on all clusters, which indicates no element from new line emergences, the intermediate result needs not be stored back. Otherwise stores the intermediate result back to SP, and clears the intermediate result selectively. By this way, we reduce the SP accesses to [512+M, 512+N/8], assuming M is the matrix dimension. Thus, this improvement cancels all SP read and some SP write. But experiments show that SP algorithm V2 achieves poorer performance than V1. It is because although V2 has fewer SP accesses, the main loop in V2 adopts 'while' loop, the iteration number is not known at compile time. So the compiler can hardly benefit from static optimizations such as loop unroll, software pipeline, which degrades the performance instead.

```
array<float> sum(256); // declare a 256-item array reside in SP
for (i = 0; i < 256; i++) { // clear the array items
    sum[i] = 0;
}
for (i = 0; i < strlen/8; i++) {
    str_a >> a;
    str_x >> x;
    str_rownum >> rownum;
    result = sum[rownum]; // read the latest partial sum of line rownum
    result = result + a * x;
    sum[rownum] = result; // store the updated partial sum
}
for (i = 0; i < 256; i++) {
    result = sum[i]; // read the partial sums of line i
    // sum the partial sums on the eight clusters
    result = result + commucperm(0x67452301, result);
    result = result + commucperm(0x44660022, result);
    result = result + commucperm(0x00004444, result);
    str_y << result; // store the dot product
}
```

Fig. 3. Pseudocode for SP algorithm V1 solving SpMV

We present SP algorithm version 3 as the tradeoff. In this algorithm, for each iteration of the main loop, we write back the intermediate result to SP unconditionally, and clear the temporary selectively according to the line information. The number of SP accesses is 512+N/8, to be the upper bound of the V2. But since it adopts 'for' loop, which is more regular than 'while', brings more compile time optimizations adoptable. Experiments shows V3 has the best performance in SP algorithms. As a result, we recommend V3 as the candidate to the scratchpad solution and only present the experimental results adopting V3.

3.3 Zero Padding Solution

Inspired by the ITPACK format [16] presented for solving SpMV on vector machine, we present zero padding solution. The key idea behind this solution is padding the sparse matrix with zeroes to make it more regular. We pad the sparse matrix such that each row has the amount of nonzeros to be multiple of eight, which is the number of clusters in Imagine. All clusters process one row at a time together, using intercluster communication to sum the partial sums. Since the amount of nonzeros is always be multiple of eight, it is adaptive to run on 8-way SIMD, which leads to a very simple kernel, as shown in figure 4. But its performance is dependent on the original amount of nonzeros of each row. Fortunately the useless computations introduced are easy to evaluate. Assuming the average amount of nozeros is M, then the upper bound of useless computations is 7/M. Since at the worst cases, 7 zeros are introduced in each line.

```
loop_count(rownum) { // loop per matrix line
  result = 0;
  str_rowlen >> rowlen;
  // obtain number of nonzeros in current line
  loop_count(rowlen/8) {
    str_a >> a;
    str_x >> x;
    result = result + a * x;
  }
  // sum the partial sums on eight clusters
  result = result + commucperm(0x67452301, result);
  result = result + commucperm(0x44660022, result);
  result = result + commucperm(0x00004444, result);
  str_y << result;
}
```

Fig. 4. Pseudocode for ZP algorithm solving SpMV

We also tried another padding method. We force per eight rows to be the same length and to be multiple of 8, thus we can cancel the intercluster communications, and assign a unique row to a cluster by organizing streams across rows, which leads to an even simpler kernel. But the overhead to padding and organizing stream is high, so we don't discuss it further.

4 Optimization

4.1 Stream Level Optimization

4.1.1 Avoid Usage of Index Stream

Imagine uses index stream mechanism to support scatter/gather operation. The usage of index stream makes stream organization flexibly from programmer, but it achieves poor performance owing to too much extra overhead of DRAM reordering on the current implementation. [17] appears to be a promising solution from hardware. Here we expand the indexed source vector stream to as many elements as in the sparse matrix, so we can organize the indexed source vector elements as a regular basic stream, avoid the usage of index stream, which is performance-dependent.

4.1.2 Strip Mining, Avoid Usage of Double Buffering

Double-buffering cycles portions of a large stream through two halves of a smaller buffer in SRF. By using this mechanism, Imagine can support arbitrary large stream whose size exceeds the SRF. But double buffering is inefficient. Strip mining applies the series of stream operations to a small portion of the initial input to produce a small portion of the final output, such that the output of every stream operation fits in the

SRF. It then applies the series to another small portion of the initial input to produce another small portion of the final output, and so on until all of the initial input has been processed. It is more efficient than double buffering. Since in most cases, SpMV programs operate on inputs that are larger than the SRF, this optimization is essential for good performance.For SpMV, we can split stream by matrix rows.

4.1.3 Organize Smaller Streams, Call kernel Multiple Times

Since Imagine supports overlapping of computation and memory access, we could exploit the potential by organizing smaller streams and calling kernel multiple times to hide the memory access latency. Of course, the precondition is application correctness semantics must be guaranteed. Here for SpMV, we can split the stream by matrix rows which is described in 4.1.2.

4.2 Kernel Level Optimization

4.2.1 Introduce More Computations in a Kernel

Since Image has massive computation units which bring tremendous computational potential, the key idea behind this optimization is introducing as many computations as possible to exploit the potential. There are two methods taking aim at this target: (1) Introduce more stream arguments; (2) Loop unroll to consume more stream elements in an iteration. For example we list the inner loop code in CS algorithm V1 in figure 5, In each iteration, only one multiply-add operation is performed. If we double the arguments of the kernel, we obtain the new loop as in figure 6. Also we can arrive at the target by loop unroll, the code is in figure 7.

```
for (i=0; i<quotient;i++) {
    str_a >> a;
    str_x >> x;
    result = result+a*x;
}
```

Fig. 5. Initial code

```
for (i=0;i<quotient;i++) {
    str_a1 >> a1; str_a2 >> a2;
    str_x1 >> x1; str_x2 >> x2;
    result1 = result1 + a1 * x1;
    result2 = result2 + a2 * x2;
}
```

Fig. 6. More stream arguments

```
for (i=0;i<quotient/2;i++) {
    str_a >> a1; str_a >> a2;
    str_x >> x1; str_x >> x2;
    result1 = result1 + a1 * x1;
    result2 = result2 + a2 * x2;
}
```

Fig. 7. Loop unroll

4.2.2 Loop Software Pipelining

Software pipelining is a technique in which a loop is divided into multiple stages and different stages of n iterations are executed at once. Modulo software pipelining is an algorithm for producing a software pipelined loop that relies on determining the shortest possible schedule length for the loop, called the minimum iteration interval or minII, then attempting to construct a software pipelined loop with that length. If the attempt fails, an attempt is made to construct a loop of length minII + 1, and so on until a valid iteration interval (loop length) is found. Software pipelining is an efficient way to improve performance. Imagine compiler [18] supplies the 'pipeline' hint to modulo software pipeline any nonnested loop.

5 Experimental Results

We evaluate SpMV performance over the benchmarks used in [2]. Two matrices are used for this experiment, each with different characteristics that enable us to explore how architectural and programming differences affect performance. They are very representative. The first matrix LSHAPE is from Harwell-Boeing collection [19] and represents a finite matrix problem. It is a 1008x1009 matrix with an average of 6.8 nonzeros and a maximum of 7 nonzeros per row. The second matrix LARGEDIS contains a pseudo-random pattern of non-zeros using a construction algorithm from the DIS specification [20], parameterized by the matrix dimension, and the number of nonzeros. The input matrix size is 10000x10000 with an average of 18 nonzeros and a maximum of 82 nonzeros per row.

We implement the algorithms mentioned above on ISIM which is a cycle accurate simulator of Imagine [18]. To evaluate performance we measure the number (in millions) of float operations per second (MFLOPS). We call raw MFLOPS as the total number of operations (including redundant ops), and corrected MFLOPS as only those operations generating new information. The experimental results are in figure 8. We tested three classes of algorithms respectively which are CS algorithm V1, SP algorithm V3 and ZP algorithm. The data we list in our experiments are corrected MFLOPS. The data we referenced from [2] are not known whether be corrected MFLOPS or raw MFLOPS, not mentioned by them. As the results show, we achieve 0.87x, 1.8x and 2.22x speedup respectively on LSHAPE, 1.189x, 1.6x and 1.52x speedup respectively on LARGEDIS. For LSHAPE has a maximum of 7 nonzeros per row, the CS algorithm V1 can be greatly simplified. Since the quotient variable in CS algorithm V1 is always zero, the codes of 4th to 9th lines can be deleted, which leads to a maxium 2.52x speedup as shown as CS Tuned in figure 8. The average performance we obtain is about 327 MFLOPS. We note that it is competitive with an IA64 or AMD64 implementation with skimming through the results published in [1]. Although the conclusion is imprecise due to the different benchmarks, it is referable. From the results, we can also conclude that CS algorithm has relatively poor performance compared with SP and ZP algorithm, but it is highly tunable according to the nonzero structure of the sparse matrix.

The overlapping degree between computation and memory access on an application is an important factor that decides the performance of that application on a stream processor. Figure 9 demonstrates the distribution of memory access time, kernel execution time and microcode loading time, i.e. what percent they take up as to the total program run time. As the results show, memory access time takes a majority of the program run time, the sum of memory access percentage and kernel execution percentage greatly exceeds 100%, which means computation is well hidden by memory access. It is good for memory-intensive applications, such as SpMV.

SRF (or LRF) -to-memory throughput ratio is the ratio of the data throughput in the SRF (or LRF) to that in the off-chip memory, assuming the frequency of the off-chip memory is 200M. Figure 10 shows the SRF/LRF-to-memory throughput ratios of running SpMV on LSHAPE. Figure 11 shows the ratios of running SpMV on LARGEDIS. It can be observed that all algorithms achieve the same SRF-to-memory throughput ratio, which is 5:1. That means SpMV can hardly exploit SRF locality. SRF

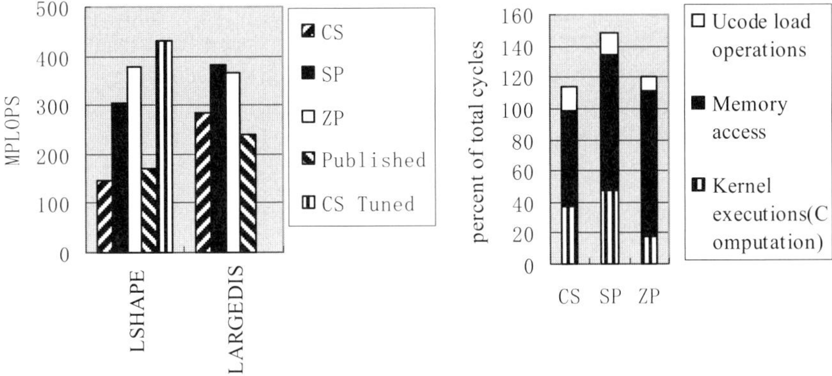

Fig. 8. SpMV performance

Fig. 9. Percent of total cycles

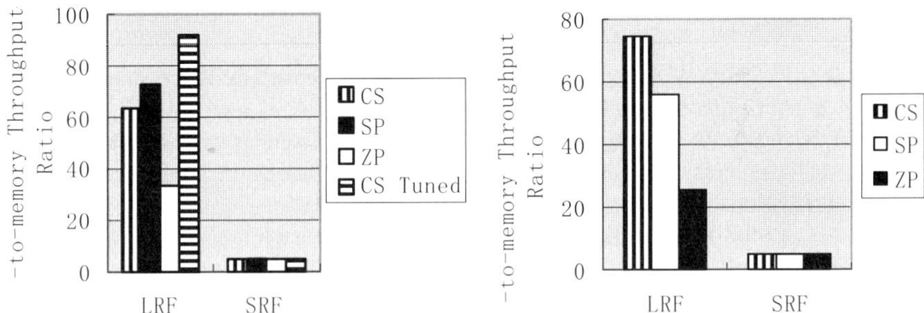

Fig. 10. S RF- and LRF-to-memory throughput ratios of LSHAPE

Fig. 11. SRF- and LRF-to-memory throughput ratios of LARGEDIS

only serves as the hierarchy through which data must go between off-chip memory and LRF. But high LRF-to-memory throughput ratios can be achieved, so we can conclude that exploiting LRF locality is an efficient way to improve the SpMV performance.

6 Conclusion

This paper examined implementation and optimization of SpMV on the Imagine stream processor. We presented three classes of algorithms, first two of which highlights different aspects of underlying architecture, they are conditional stream, scratchpad. The third algorithm is inspired by the SpMV vector implementation, using zero padding technique. Furthermore, we discuss some performance-dependent optimizations. The experiments show we achieve 1.67x average speedup over same benchmark over published evaluation, which is even competitive with an IA64 implementation with skimming through the results published in [1]. These demonstrate that stream processor is a promising alternative to accelerate SpMV.

Acknowledgements. The authors would like to gratefully thank Stanford's Imagine group for providing access to the Imagine simulator. We specifically thank lab 620 of School of Computer in National University of Defense Technology for helpful discussions and comments on this work. We also acknowledge the reviewers for their insightful comments. This work was supported by NSFC (60621003 and 60633050).

References

1. Williams, S., Shalf, J., Oliker, L., Husbands, P., Kamil, S., Yelick, K.: The Potential of the Cell Processor for Scientific Computing. Paper LBNL-59071 (2005)
2. Narayanan, M., Oliker, L., Janin, A., Husbands, P., Li, X.S.: Scientific kernels on VIRAM and imagine media processors. Paper LBNL-54908 (2002)
3. Khailany, B., et al.: Imagine: Media processing with streams. IEEE Micro 21(2), 35–46 (2001)
4. Kapasi, U.J., Rixner, S., Dally, W.J., Khailany, B., Ahn, J.H., Mattson, P., Owens, J.D.: Programmable Stream Processors, pp. 54–62. IEEE Computer Society Press, Los Alamitos (2003)
5. Kapasi, U.J., Dally, W.J., et al.: The Imagine Stream Processor. In: Processings of the 2002 International Conference on Computer Design (2002)
6. Rixner, S., Dally, W., Kapasi, U.J., Khailany, B., Lopez-Lagunas, A., Mattson, P., Owens, J.D.: Media processing applications on Imagine media processor. In: Proceedings of the 2002 International Conference on Computer design (2002)
7. Ahn, J.H., Dally, W.J., et al.: Evaluating the Imagine Stream Architecture. In: ISCA 2004 (2004)
8. Mattson, P., et al.: Imagine Programming System Developer's Guide (2002), http://cva.stanford.edu
9. Mattson, P.R.: A Programming System for the Imagine Media Processor. Dept. of Electrical Engineering. Ph.D. thesis, Stanford University (2002)
10. Amarasinghe, S., et al.: Stream Languages and Programming Models. In: PACT 2003 (2003)
11. Das, A., Mattson, P., et al.: Imagine Programming System User's Guide 2.0 (2004)
12. Johnsson, O., Stenemo, M., ul-Abdin, Z.: Programming & Implementation of Streaming Applications. Master's thesis, Computer and Electrical Engineering Halmstad University (2005)
13. Toledo, S.: Improving the memory-system performance of sparse-matrix vector multiplication. IBM Journal of Research and Development (1997)
14. Rixner, S., Dally, W.J., Kapasi, U.J., Mattson, P., Owens, J.D.: Memory Access Scheduling. In: Proceedings of the 27th Annual International Symposium on Computer Architecture, pp. 128–138 (2000)
15. Kapasi, U., Dally, W., Rixner, S., Mattson, P., Owens, J., Khailany, B.: Efficient Conditional Operations for Data-parallel Architectures. In: Proceedings of the 33rd Annual International Symposium on Microarchitecture (2000)
16. Kincaid, D., Oppe, T., Young, D.: ITPACKV: 2D user's guide. Tech. Rep. CAN-232, Univ. of Texas, Austin (1989)
17. Jayasena, N., Erez, M., Ahn, J.H., Dally, W.J.: Stream Register Files with Indexed Access. In: HPCA 2004 (2004)
18. Das, A., Mattson, P., et al.: Imagine Programming System User's Guide 2.0 (2004)

19. Market, M.: Harwell-Boeing Sparse Matrix Collection. At http://math.nist.gov/MatrixMarket/collections/hb.html
20. DIS Stressmark Suite: v 1.0. Titan Systems Corp. (2000), At http://www.aaec.com/projectweb/dis/
21. Im, E.J.: Optimizing the performance of sparse matrix-vector multiplication. Ph.D. thesis, University of California (2000)
22. Im, E.J., Yelick, K.: Optimizing sparse matrix vector multiplication on SMPs. In: 9th SIAM Conference on Parallel Processing for Scientific Computing, San Antonio, TX (1999)
23. Pinar, A., Heath, M.: Improving performance of sparse matrix–vector multiplication. In: Proceedings of Supercomputing Portland (1999)
24. Toledo, S.: Improving memory-system performance of sparse matrix–vector multiplication. In: Proceedings of the 8th SIAM Conference on Parallel Processing for Scientific Computing Minneapolis, MN (1997)
25. Vuduc, R., Moon, H.-J.: Fast sparse matrix-vector multiplication by exploiting variable blocks. In: Proceedings of the International Conference on High-Performance Computing and Communications, Sorrento, Italy (2005)

A Mutual Exclusion Algorithm for Mobile Agents-Based Applications*

Chun Cao[1], Jiannong Cao[2], Xiaoxing Ma[1], and Jian Lü[1]

[1] State Key Laboratory of Novel Software Technology, Nanjing University, China
{caochun,xxm,lj}@ics.nju.edu.cn

[2] Department of Computing, Hong Kong Polytechnic University, Hong Kong SAR
csjcao@comp.polyu.edu.hk

Abstract. The mobile agent (MA) technology has been widely applied in distributed applications. However, since mobile agents are highly autonomous, coordinating the their behaviours is hard. We concentrate on the mutual exclusion issue in this paper and propose an algorithm for achieving mutex among mobile agents. In contrast to the existing algorithms for traditional distributed processes, the proposed algorithm does not require MAs to have a pre-knowledge about other competitors, nor the total number of them. MAs can join/leave the competition session freely. The algorithm performance is also evaluated through simulations.

1 Introduction

The mobile agent (MA) computing paradigm has several advantages, including bandwidth saving, autonomous working and environment adapting, and so on [1]. Motivated by its features, many distributed applications have been developed based on mobile agents. When working for some specific application, the autonomous MAs need to be coordinated to ensure that their individual actions will aggregately achieve the ultimate objective of the application. All the issues involved in coordination from traditional distributed applications, such as synchronization, mutual exclusion, leader selection, etc., also need to be considered in MA-based ones. In this paper, we concentrate on the mutual exclusion problem in MA-based distributed applications.

Though the problem of mutual exclusion had been studied intensively in distributed systems, new challenges are still met during the design of a mutual exclusion algorithm for MA-based applications. Existing works, such as [3], [4], [5], [9] and [8], etc., are for *stationary* processes and are based on some restrictive assumptions: competing processes for the CS are predetermined, and each has certain pre-knowledge of other competitors as well. On the contrary, in a MA-based application, MAs, being processes that can migrate from site to site, may come from different users with no knowledge about others, nor the total number of the concurrent competitors for the same CS. They can join/leave the

* The work in this paper is supported by NSFC (60403014), 863 Program (2006AA01Z159), 973 Program of China (2002CB312002), JSNFC (BK2006712).

I. Stojmenovic et al. (Eds.): ISPA 2007, LNCS 4742, pp. 56–67, 2007.

competition freely. On another hand, in many application scenarios, the set of competitors is defined with other notions indirectly. A typical situation is that the mutual exclusion are enforced among MAs on a fixed set of MA sites, which are the running platforms for MAs.

We have designed an algorithm for MAs to realize distributed mutual exclusion. The mobility, as a unique characteristic of mobile agents against stationary ones, is the fundamental on which our design is based. By the algorithm in this paper, mutual exclusion can be achieved among arbitrary number of MAs on a fixed set of MA sites. Different from existing mutex algorithms for traditional distributed processes, the proposed algorithm is carried by MAs themselves, and it does not require MAs to have a pre-knowledge about other competitors, nor the total number of them. MAs can join/leave the competition session freely. The algorithm imposes no constraints upon the agents to limit their dynamicism.

The rest of this paper is organized as the following: Section 2 discusses related work about distributed mutual exclusion algorithms. Section 3 describes the design of the algorithm. In section 4, we present the correctness proof of the algorithm. Result of performance evaluation through simulations will be shown in Section 5. The last section concludes the paper.

2 Related Work

Mutual exclusion algorithms can be classified as either centralized or distributed. A centralized algorithms that employs a central decision-maker suffers from both the inefficiency and single point of failure [6]. Almost all of the distributed ones fall into two schemes: permission-based and token-based.

For the first scheme, a process that wants to enter the CS asks for permissions from the others and waits until all permissions have arrived. Upon receiving a request, a process sends the permission out if it is not interested in the CS; otherwise, the conflicting requests have to be served according to some priority (usually the logical timestamp and process id). Lamport proposed such an algorithm in [3] and Ricart made an optimization on the algorithm to minimize the number of control messages [7]. Improvements concerning the management and the size of the site set that a process must send requests to have also been proposed. Majority consensus and quorum-based algorithms allow the process to collect only *enough* permissions to enter the CS [9]. Maekawa reduced the quorum size to $\sqrt{N}$ [4]. For token-based algorithms, the right to enter the CS is materialized by a *token*. Only the process possessing this unique token can enter the CS. The main problems for this approach are managing the circulation and ensuring the liveness the token. Sites, on which the processes locate, are always structured with some special topology, such as a ring [8] or a tree [5].

In both permission-based and token-based distributed algorithms above, the processes competing for entering the CS are predetermined and dispersed over several sites statically. With partial or total knowledge about the participating processes, a process knows whom it should send the requests to and gain permissions from in order to enter the CS. However, as mentioned in the first part of this paper, the above assumptions can hardly be satisfied in MA-based applications, which lead us to design a new algorithm described in this paper.

3 Description of the Algorithm

3.1 System Model

Taking the highly dynamic nature of MA-based applications into consideration, sharing the global application structure which is constantly changing among all the competing MAs will be too costly to be practical. Passing a token in an ad-hoc way also leads to inefficient solutions, especially within a large area. We design our algorithm based on the system model as shown in Figure 1. Each CS is associated with a set of sites S. A *site* here refers to a general MA platform. Any mobile agent that wants to enter the CS has to travel and work over the sites in the set. Each site in the set has an ID, ranged from 1 to N (N is the size of the set). Every MA also has an unique ID. A "blackboard" is setup on each site to facilitate information exchanging by allowing MAs to reading/writing from/onto it.

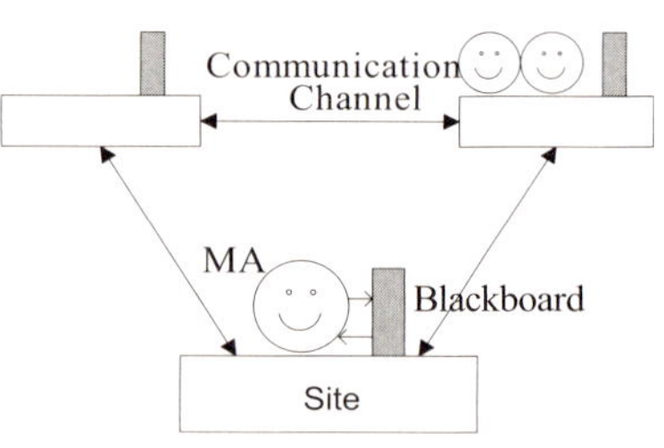

Fig. 1. System Model

Basically, this model is a general mobile agent system model with an additional "blackboard" that enables the indirect interaction between the MAs. Each site provides the services for MA transportation, messaging, and local resource accessing. MAs can carry out their tasks on the sites and migrate from one site to another autonomously. We assume that the inter-agent message passing mechanism is implemented in MA platforms. Given the id of the peer, one agent can send a message to it without caring about its location.

3.2 Algorithm Overview

The basic idea of our algorithm originates from the majority consensus voting scheme in distributed database management proposed by Thomas [2]. We let the MAs gather permissions from the sites and the one who get permissions from a majority of those sites can enter the CS. On intending to enter the CS, a mobile agent will travel around the sites in S and try to acquire permission from the visiting site by adding its request to a queue on the blackboard of that site. Once the agent's request stands at the head of the queue, we say that the agent gains the permission from the site. If the agent currently gets more permissions than any other agent and no other agent has a potential to exceed this one (that means the majority of the sites reaches a consensus on the MA to enter the CS), we say that the request of this agent (or simply this agent) gets ***ordered***. Once ordered, the agent stops migration and prepares for executing the CS. Otherwise, it needs to go on to obtain more permissions from other sites until it gets ordered. During the migration, the agent will also propagate the status of the queues of previously visited sites to those on its migrating path. As all the participators are trying to keep the information both on the sites and in themselves up-to-date, all of them will reach a consistent global view of the sequence of entering the CS.

3.3 Data Structure and Messages

Three data structures are defined in the algorithm as follows.

Request (R). *Request* is a tuple denoting the intention of an agent to enter the CS. It is defined by a 3-tuple: $R =< ID_A, ID_S, SEQ >$, where ID_A is the unique ID of the agent who issued this request, ID_S is the ID of the site on which the agent issued this request and SEQ is a number used to distinguish the requests issued by the same agent respectively.

Ordered List (OL). OL is a sequence of the requests which have already been ordered: $OL = [R_1, R_2, \ldots, R_n]$

Request Table (RT). A request table is a table with three columns. The first column SID is the id of the sites. For a row that $SID = i$, it records the status for site i (S_i). The second column TS is the time stamp of that site, which will be increased monotonously only when agent enqueues its request on that site or the request that originates from that site is remove by the agent after it finishes the execution of CS. So it represents how recent the information about site i is in this RT. The last column *Queue* is the requests enqueued at that site. The whole tables keeps the status of the site set S.

Messages. Mobile agents will send two types of messages, $ENTER$ messages and $WAIT$ ones, when executing the algorithm. An $ENTER$ message has the parameter R which identifies the request that can be fulfilled immediately. The receiver of an ENTER message is informed of its turn to enter the CS. In addition to the same parameter R in an $ENTER$ message, a $WAIT$ message has one more parameter R_{next}. Upon receiving a $WAIT$ message, an agent is told that its request R has been ordered and the next request following R to be fulfilled is R_{next}. Here, sending a message $ENTER(R)$ or $WAIT(R, R_{next})$ means to send the message to the agent with id=$R.ID_A$.

3.4 Algorithm Details

On the blackboard of each site k, there is a copy of OL and RT, denoted as SOL_k and SRT_k respectively. Each agent i also carries its own OL and RT, written as AOL_i and ART_i. In addition, it has a data item $NextR_i$ to keep the request that can be fulfill after its own.

On requesting the CS. When an agent i requests the CS on site k(see Figure 2), it will first initialize its AOL_i and ART_i(Step 1,2), increase the sequence number (Seq) and generate a new request (Step 3). Then it will start its trip for permission-gathering until it becomes ***ordered*** ($beOrdered = true$) (Step 5). To enter the CS,

1. let $AOL_i = null$
2. for each $ART_i[j] \in ART$, let $ART_i[j] =< j, 0, null > (j = 1 \ldots N)$
3. if it's the first time requesting the CS, let Seq=0, else let $Seq = Seq + 1$; $R_i =< i, k, Seq >$
4. let $n = k$, $beOrdered = false$,
5. while($beOrdered = false$) do the following repeatedly
   (a) migrate to site n
   (b) initialize SRT_n and SOL_n if current site has not the two structures
   (c) call *UPDATE* procedure
   (d) append R_i to $SRT_n[n].Queue$ and $ART_i[n].Queue$, $SRT_n[n].TS{+}{+}, ART_i[n].TS{+}{+}$
   (e) call *ORDER* procedure
   (f) if $R_i \in AOL_i$ the set $beOrdered = true$, else set n to be an unvisited site's id
6. if R_i is on top of AOL_i then enter CS immediately, otherwise, wait on the current site to be informed to enter CS.

Fig. 2. Agent i begins requesting CS on Site k

it still has to wait until its request reaches the top of AOL_i or some other agent sends it an *ENTER* message(Step 6).

On arriving at site n during the execution of this algorithm, the agent will initialize the data structure SOL_n and SRT_n if they do not exist yet (Step 5.(b)). Then it will try to synchronize its AOL_i and ART_i with SOL_n and SRT_n stored on current site (Step 5.(c), see *UPDATE* procedure). After that, the agent will append its request to the queue of current site (Step 5.(d)) and check if any agent can get ordered (Step 5.(e), see *ORDER* procedure). The agent will continue its journey until itself gets ordered (Step 5.(f)).

UPDATE* procedure.** The *UPDATE* procedure is the key for the mobile agents to reach an agreement on the executing sequence of the CS. The main objective of this procedure is to remove those outdated requests from both the agent and current site and to synchronize the information in the two entities. The ***outdated requests, which refer to those satisfied requests, are deleted from AOL, ART, SOL and SRT. An outdated request, say R, can be made out by the difference of $ART_i[R.ID_S]$ against $SRT_n[R.ID_S]$. The goal of the UPDATE procedure is achieved in the following four steps:

1. For each R in SOL_n, if $ART_i[R.ID_S].TS > SRT_n[R.ID_S].TS$, that means the request table carried by the agent maintains newer information about the queue of site $R.ID_S$. So if this request R is in neither AOL_i nor $ART_i[R.ID_S].Queue$ but still exists in SOL_n, according to the post-processing (to be describe later), it must be an outdated one and have to be deleted from both SOL_n and SRT_n. Because those requests that precede this one must have been fulfilled before it, they should also be removed (Figure 3, Step 1). In the same way, outdated request are removed from AOL_i (Step 2).

2. After outdated requests are removed from OLs, AOL_i (SOL_n) is replaced by SOL_n (AOL_i) if the latter is longer (Step 3).
3. For each row r in ART_i and SRT_n, if any request R, where $R.ID_S = r$, is in $ART_i[r].Queue$ but not in $SRT_n[r].Queue$ and $ART_i[r].TS < SRT_n[r].TS$, then this R must also be an outdated one and can be removed from ART_i safely (Step4). In the same way, all this kind of request in SRT_i can be cleaned up (Step 5).
4. Finally, each row in ART_i (SRT_n) is replaced by the corresponding one of SRT_n (ART_i), if the latter has a larger time stamp (Step 6).

1. if $\exists R, (R \in AOL_i) \wedge (R \notin SOL_n) \wedge (R \notin SRT_n[R.ID_S].Queue) \wedge (SRT_n[R.ID_S].TS > ART_i[R.ID_S].TS)$
   for all R' precedes R in AOL_i, delete R' from AOL_i and ART_i
2. if $\exists R, (R \in SOL_n) \wedge (R \notin AOL_i) \wedge (R \notin ART_i[R.ID_S].Queue) \wedge (ART_i[R.ID_S].TS > SRT_n[R.ID_S].TS)$
   for all R' precedes R, delete R' from SOL_n and SRT_n
3. let $AOL_i = SOL_n$ if $length(AOL_i) < length(SOL_n)$, otherwise, let $SOL_n = AOL_i$
4. for each R that $(R \in ART_i[R.ID_S].Queue) \wedge (R \notin SRT_n[R.ID_S].Queue) \wedge (ART_i[R.ID_S].TS < SRT_n[Q.ID_S].TS)$, remove R from ART_i
5. for each R that $(R \in SRT_n[R.ID_S].Queue) \wedge (R \notin ART_i[R.ID_S].Queue) \wedge (SRT_n[R.ID_S].TS < ART_i[Q.ID_S].TS)$, remove R from SRT_n
6. let $ART_i[j] = SRT_n[j]$ if $ART_i[j].TS < SRT_n[j].TS$, otherwise, let $SRT_n[j] = ART_i[j]$. $(j = 1 \ldots N)$

Fig. 3. The *UPDATE* procedure for agent i on site n

***ORDER* procedure.** In the *ORDER* procedure, the agent checks which mobile agent can be ordered so far. If more than one request obtains the most number of permissions, the one with a smallest id gets ordered. The permissions ($P(R_i)$) that agent $R_i.ID_A$ got are calculated as $P(R_i) = \sum_{r=1}^{N} V(SRT[r], R_i)$, where $V(SRT[r], R_i)$ is set to 1 (if $SRT[r].Queue[0] = R_i$) or 0 (otherwise).

The ordered one will be appended to AOL_i and SOL_n and removed from ART_i and SRT_n. Then the agent tries to calculate again for another one. The process ends until no request can be ordered. Agents issued those ordered request are informed to switch to *ordered* status and the $NextR$ is also told. If the first ordered request locates at the top of AOL_i, the corresponding agent is informed to enter the CS directly.

Message processing. On receiving a message $ENTER(R)$, if the agent currently is not requesting the CS or the sequence number in R is smaller than the one maintained by itself (in both cases, it means that the agent has finished the CS), the agent will inform the agent in $NextR$ (if not null) to enter the CS. Otherwise, it enters the CS directly (see Figure 2, Step 6). Upon receiving a message $WAIT(R, R_{next})$, if the agent currently is not requesting the CS or the

1. let $continue = true, chain = null$
2. loop while $Continue = true$
   (a) construct the sequence of requests $[R_1, R_2, \ldots, R_M](1 \leq M \leq N)$ that
      – $R_m \in SRT_n[j].Queue(j = 1 \ldots N)$ and $P(R_m) > 0$
      – for $(g < h, 0 \leq g \leq h \leq M)$, $P(R_g) > P(R_h)$ or $(P(R_g) = P(R_h)$ and $R_g.ID_A < R_h.ID_A)$
   (b) if $(P(R_1) - P(R_2) > N - \sum_{m=1}^{M} P(R_m)) \vee (P(R_1) - P(R_2) = N - \sum_{m=1}^{M} P(R_m) \wedge (R_1.ID_A < R_2.ID_A)$, append R_1 to AOL_i, SOL_n and $chain$, delete R_1 from ART_i and SRT_n, else let $continue = false$
3. if $chain \neq null$
   (a) send messages $WAIT(chain[i], chain[i+1])$, $1 \leq i \leq length(chain)$
   (b) if $chain[0] = AOL_i.Queue[0]$, send message $ENTER(chain[0])$, else send message $WAIT(chain[0], chain[1])$

Fig. 4. The *ORDER* procedure by agent i on site n

sequence number in R is smaller than the current sequence number maintained by itself, the agent will tell the $NextR$ (if not null) to enter the CS. Otherwise, it change its state to *Ordered* (let $beOrdered = true$) and set $NextR$ to R_{next}.

Post processing. When an agent has finished its executing of CS, it will migrate to the original site where it issued the request. After having updated the site's status, it removes the request from SOL and SRT and increases the timestamp of site's queue so that others can recognize its request as an outdated one. If its following request has been identified, it will tell the agent to enter the CS. These cleaning up steps are described in Figure 5.

1. if not on the site $k(= R.ID_S)$, migrate to that site k
2. call *UPDATE* procedure
3. if $R_i \in SOL_k$, for all R' precedes R_i, delete R' from SOL_k and $SRT_k[i].Queue(i = 1 \ldots N)$
4. remove R_i from $SRT_k[k].Queue$, $SRT_k[k].TS{+}{+}$
5. if $NextR \neq null$, send message $ENTER(NextR)$

Fig. 5. On releasing the *CS* by agent i

3.5 An Example

Suppose for some MA-based application, the action of accessing some resource (the entering of CS) has to be sequenced among the MAs on three sites, $S1$, $S2$ and $S3$. Two agents, $Agent1$ and $Agent2$, are requesting the resource simultaneously at moment 1 on $S1$ and $S2$ respectively.

As described in the algorithm, $Agent1$ will add its request R_1 to site $S1$ while $Agent2$ will add its R_2 to $S2$. Neither of the two agents can get ordered so far. So they start to migrate to another site. Suppose $Agent1$ moves quicker than $Agent2$ so it arrived at $S3$ at moment 2. After appending its request on $S3$, $Agent1$ finds itself ordered and is at the top position of AOL_1.

So it enter the CS immediately. $Agent2$ migrated to $S1$ at moment 3 and still cannot be ordered, so it has to travel to the last site $S3$ and arrived there at moment 4. Here, $Agent2$'s request get ordered, following R_1 in SOL_3. Messages $WAIT(R_1, R_2)$ and $ENTER(R_1)$ are sent out in sequence. $Agent1$ receives the $WAIT$ message and set the $NextR$ to R_2. The ENTER message is ignored because it has already in CS. At moment 5, $Agent1$ finishes its CS and returns to $S1$ for cleaning up jobs. An $ENTER$ message is sent to $Agent2$. After $Agent2$ finishes the CS, the cleaning steps is also carried out at site $S2$ by it. The changes of the information in the sites and the agents at those moments are illustrated in Figure 7.

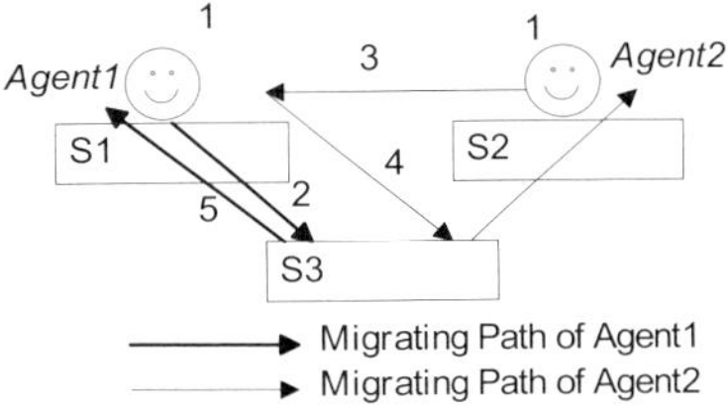

Fig. 6. An example

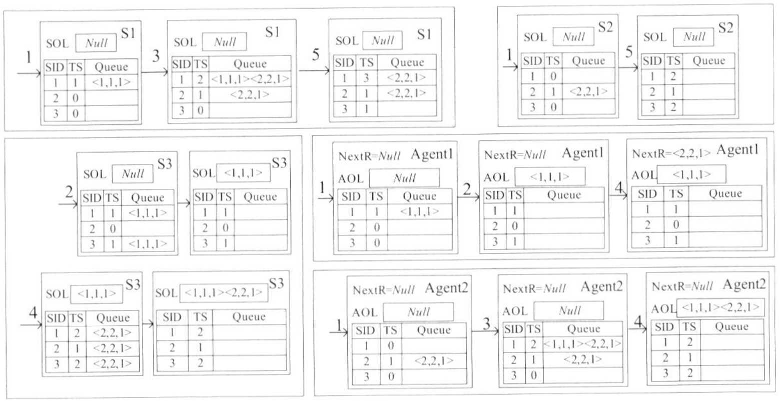

Fig. 7. State changes in the sites and agents

4 Correctness Proof

In this section, we argue the correctness of the algorithm by showing that this algorithm guarantees mutual exclusion as well as ensures deadlock and starvation freedom.

Lemma 1. *An agent can determine its request's order after no more than N-1 hops.*

Proof. After agent i hopped N-1 times, each queue in SRT of the site last visited must not be empty. According to the $ORDER$ procedure, there must be one request that can be ordered. If the ordered request doesn't belong to agent i, there must still be at least one request in each queue. So another request can get ordered and the $ORDER$ procedure will not stop until the agent i get ordered. Thus the lemma is true.

Lemma 2. *When R_i get ordered at site k, any outdated request cannot exist at top of the queue of any row in SRT_k.*

Proof. We do this proof on induction of the nth ordered request during the whole running process of the algorithm. For $n = 1$, there is no outdated request and the first one, say R_1, got ordered one site S_1. For $n = 2$, R_1 may become outdated. So when R_2 get ordered on site S_2, those rows R_1 occupies the first rank must be still be R_1 or $null$(if R_2 never visited the corresponding site, and suppose the number of such rows equals to $B_1^{'}$, $B_1^{'} \geq 0$). At the time when R_1 ordered on S_1, $P(R_1) - P(R_2) \geq N - \sum P(R_m)$ (if $P(R_1) - P(R_2) = N - \sum P(R_m)$, $R_1.ID_A < R_2.ID_A$). When R_2 ordered on S_2, $P^{'}(R_2) - P^{'}(R_1) \geq N - \sum P^{'}(R_m^{'})$ (if $P^{'}(R_2) - P^{'}(R_1) = N - \sum P^{'}(R_m^{'})$, $R_2.ID_A < R_1.ID_A$). Because $P^{'}(R_2) \leq P(R_2) + (N - \sum P(R_m))$, we get $P^{'}(R_2) \leq P(R_1)$, and thus $P^{'}(R_2) \leq R^{'}(R_1) + B_1^{'}$. If $P^{'}(R_2) = P^{'}(R_1) + B_1^{'}$, then $P^{'}(R_2) - P^{'}(R_1) = N - \sum P^{'}(R_m^{'})$ and $P(R_1) - P(R_2) = N - \sum P(R_m)$, which leads to a contradiction that $R_1.ID_A < R_2.ID_A$ and $R_2.ID_A < R_1.ID_A$. So $P^{'}(R_2) < P^{'}(R_1) + B_1^{'}$. Thus, R_2 cannot be ordered. Suppose when kth request get ordered on S_k, there is no outdated request at head of any row. Then on $(k+1)$th request ordered on S_{k+1}, if there exists any outdated requests $\{R_m\}(1 \leq m \leq k)$, then at lease R_k must be there, otherwise, R_{k+1} will know all the outdated requests because when R_k get ordered there is no outdated request, as the inductive assumption. So R_{k+1} cannot occupy those rows where R_k stands on top. So again, we can proof that R_{k+1} cannot get ordered as for n=2. And this concludes the proof.

Lemma 3. *When some request R_i gets ordered on site l, if there is some request R_j which get ordered before R_i and has not been satisfied, R_j must exist in SOL_l.*

Proof. According to the algorithm, if $Agent_j$ has been ordered but not finished its CS, then its request R_j must be in either SOL_k or $SRT_k[k].Queue$ ($R_j.ID_S = k$). So when R_i get ordered, because R_j has not finished its CS, R_j will not be removed from any OL. If $R_j \notin SOL_l$, then for each row r where $SRT_m[r].Queue[0] = R_j$ at the time when R_j got ordered on site m, $SRT_l[r].Queue[0] = R_j$ or $SRT_l[r].Queue = null$ (no outdated request can be there, according to Lemma 2). So when R_j ordered on S_m, $P(R_j) - P(R_i) \geq N - \sum P(R_n)$ (if $P(R_j) - P(R_i) = N - \sum R(R_n), ID_j < ID_i$). When R_i ordered on S_l, $P^{'}(R_i) - P^{'}(R_j) \geq N - \sum R^{'}(R_n^{'})$(if $P^{'}(R_i) - P^{'}(R_j) = N - \sum P^{'}(R_p^{'}), ID_i < ID_j$). Because $P^{'}(R_i) \leq P(R_i) + (N - \sum P(R_n))$, so $P^{'}(R_i) \leq P(R_j)$, which means $P^{'}(R_i) \leq P^{'}(R_j) + B_j^{'}$. If $P^{'}(R_i) = P^{'}(R_j) + B_j^{'}$, then $P^{'}(R_i) - P^{'}(R_j) = N - \sum P^{'}(P_n^{'})$ and $P(R_j) - P(R_i) = N - \sum P(R_n)$ which leads to contradiction that $ID_i > ID_j$ and $ID_j > ID_i$. So $P^{'}(R_i) < P^{'}(R_j) + B_j^{'}$. Thus, R_i cannot be ordered. Thus the lemma must be true.

Lemma 4. *Two different requests cannot get ordered simultaneously.*

Proof. Assume R_i and R_j get ordered at the same time. They when R_i get ordered, $P(R_i) > P(R_j)$ or $P(R_i) = P(R_j)$ and $R_i.ID_A < R_j.ID_A$. When R_j get ordered, $P^{'}(R_j) > P^{'}(R_i)$ or $P^{'}(R_j) = P^{'}(R_i)$ and $R_j.ID_A < R_i.ID_A$

(Lemma 2). This means either request gets more permission than the other or either request has a smaller agent id than the other. This is a contrary and the lemma is proved.

Lemma 5. *The order of those requests in any OL are same.*

Proof. This can be proved in two parts: for any not outdated request R_j, if there exists R_i that $R_i \prec R_j$ in some OL then $R_i \prec R_j$ in any OL or R_j is outdated and removed; if there exists R_i and R_m that $R_i \prec R_m \prec R_j$ in some OL, then if $R_i \prec R_j$ in any other OL, R_m will still be between that two requests in that OL. From Lemma 4 and 3, we know the requests are ordered one by one and each ordered request must know the previous ones which are not outdated. Assume for some request R_j, if in some OL, a request R_i which precedes R_j ($R_i \prec R_j$) and in some other OL, $R_j \prec R_i$. R_j is not outdated and R_i must also be not outdated. So there will still be a R_i before R_j (Lemma 3). Because one request will appear no more than once in any OL according the the algorithm, the assumption cannot be true. For any outdated request R_o, if R_o is removed from any OL, all the requests that precedes R_o will also be deleted. So if $R_i \prec R_j$, for each R_m that $R_i \prec R_m \prec R_j$, in any OL, R_m will exist between R_i and R_j. Otherwise, if R_m is removed as an outdated request, R_i will also be removed. So the requests are in the same order for any OL.

Theorem 1. *Mutual exclusion is achieved.*

Proof. Assume the contrary that two agents, say A and B, get into CS at the same time. For any one can enter the CS, it may either order itself or receive and ENTER message from the preceding one. Because two agents cannot got ordered simultaneously (Lemma 4), So there two cases here. The first case is that A is ordered and find itself on top of AOL_A, B receives an ENTER message. Then B must be ordered somewhere before the A get order, and according to Lemma 3, B must exist in AOL_A when A get ordered. So A cannot stand of top of AOL_A. The other case is that Both receive an ENTER message. Suppose A receives ENTER message from SA while B from SB. If SA=SB, that means the same agent send ENTER message to A and B. Because in each OL, requests are sequenced in the same order. So for any agent, the $NextR$ will not be change from one unsatisfied request to another unsatisfied one. If SA≠SB, because either A precedes B or B precedes A and in any OL the order is the same (Lemma 5) and neither of this two request is outdated, so this is also not possible. Thus the theorem is proved.

Theorem 2. *Neither deadlock nor starvation is impossible.*

Proof. The deadlock happens when no agent can be in the CS while there do exist some one requesting for it. Assume the contrary, the deadlock is possible. And this may result in two case. First one, no agent can get permission to enter the CS, this is impossible because of Lemma 1. In the second case, there may exist two agents A and B, where A is waiting for the ENTER message from B and B waiting for the ENTER message from A which indicates $R_A \prec R_B$ and $R_B \prec R_A$. This is contradiction to Lemma 5.

Starvation occurs when one agent must wait infinitely to enter its CS even though other agents are entering and exiting their own critical section. Assume the contrary, that starvation is possible. In our algorithm, an agent's migration and execution time, the duration in the CS, the message's passing time and the joining speed of new competitors are all finite. So the agent will be migrating over all the sites with finite request in any queue. Thus the agent will get ordered ultimately. If an agent is starvation, it must be waiting for preceding priority agent message infinitely. Because there can only be finite number of agents which precede this agent and they will exit the CS in finite time, so this agent will not wait for infinite time. And this concludes the proof.

5 Performance Evaluation

A simulation is conducted for performance evaluation. MA environments with variable number of sites are simulated via Java concurrent programming. Each active mobile agent is simulated by a thread. Mobile agents initialize request for the CS on a random site concurrently. After the execution of the algorithm on its visiting site, the agent is suspended for up to 10 time units before migrating to the next site. The duration in CS is 100 time units.

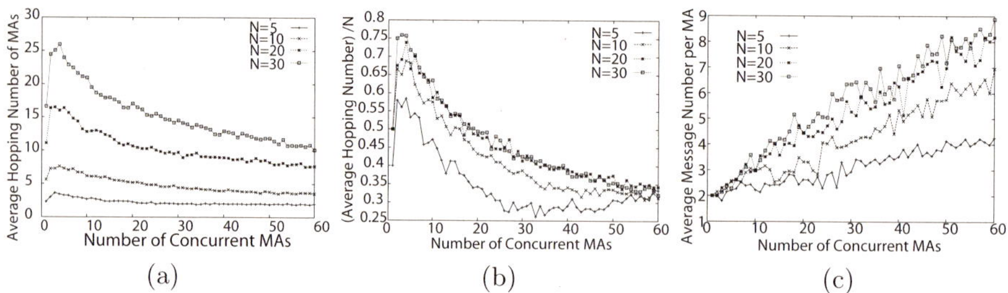

Fig. 8. Simulation results

For N=5, 10, 20 and 30 respectively, we count the average hopping number of single MA before it gets ordered (see (a)) with up to sixty MAs requesting for the CS simultaneously. And from (b), we can see that for all the four configuration, the proportion of the sites which agents have to navigate over to get ordered is almost the same. This two metrics increase dramatically as the number of competitors augment from one to about four and then decrease gradually. The cause of such curves is obvious. When just one MA is requesting for CS, it has only to travel more than half of the sites to get ordered. While there are some competitors added into the system, some site may vote to others but the queue status are not propagated quickly enough. So the sites that should be visited get more than the half. As the system gets more and more congested, because of MAs' random hopping, the sites vote averagely. Meantime, the queue status is updated more frequently. This makes the MAs get ordered with fewer hops. And as the load get heavier, we can see in (b), the proportion tends towards less than 1/3 finally. We also counted the messages that one MA sends during the execution of this algorithm (see (c)).

6 Conclusions

We have introduced the design of a distributed mutual exclusion algorithm for MA-based application. Compared with those existing distributed mutex algorithms, the participators need not be be pre-organized and mutual knowledge is also not necessary. And this algorithm fits for MA-based applications. We also present the proof with respect to guaranteed mutual exclusion, deadlock freedom and starvation freedom. The simulation result shows this algorithm's efficiency especially in heavy load condition.

References

1. Lange, D.B., Oshima, M.: Seven good reasons for mobile agents. Commun. ACM 42(3), 88–89 (1999)
2. Thomas, R.H.: A majority consensus approach to concurrency control for multiple copy databases. ACM Trans. Database Syst. 4(2), 180–209 (1979)
3. Lamport, L.: Time, clocks, and the ordering of events in a distributed system. Commun. ACM 21(7), 558–565 (1978)
4. Maekawa, L.: A sqr(n) algorithm for mutual exclusion in decentralized systems. ACM Trans. Comput. Syst. 3(2), 145–159 (1985)
5. Helary, J.M., Mostefaoui, A., Raynal, M.: A general scheme for token- and tree-based distributed mutual exclusion algorithms. IEEE Trans. Parallel Distrib. Syst. 5(11), 1185–1196 (1994)
6. Singhal, M.: A taxonomy of distributed mutual exclusion. J. Parallel Distrib. Comput. 18(1), 94–101 (1993)
7. Ricart, G., Agrawala, A.K.: An optimal algorithm for mutual exclusion in computer networks. Commun. ACM 24(1), 9–17 (1981)
8. Maddi, A.: Token based solutions to m resources allocation problem. In: Proceedings of the 1997 ACM symposium on Applied computing, pp. 340–344. ACM Press, New York (1997)
9. Gifford, D.K.: Weighted voting for replicated data. In: Proceedings of the seventh ACM symposium on Operating systems principles, pp. 150–162. ACM Press, New York (1979)

A Distributed Metaheuristic for Solving a Real-World Scheduling-Routing-Loading Problem*

Laura Cruz Reyes, Juan Javier González Barbosa, David Romero Vargas, Hector Joaquin Fraire Huacuja, Nelson Rangel Valdez, Juan Arturo Herrera Ortiz, Bárbara Abigail Arrañaga Cruz, and José Francisco Delgado Orta

Instituto Tecnológico de Ciudad Madero, México
lcruzreyes@prodigy.net.mx, jjgonzalezbarbosa@hotmail.com, davidr@matcuer.unam.mx, hfraire@prodigy.net.mx, {ia32_,juanarturo_,aralia38,axl_136}@hotmail.com

Abstract. In this paper a real and complex transportation problem including routing, scheduling and loading tasks is presented. Most of the related works only involve the solution of routing and scheduling, as a combination of up to five different types of VRPs (Rich VRP), leaving away the loading task, which are not enough to define more complex real-world cases. We propose a solution methodology for transportation instances that involve six types of VRPs, a new constraint that limits the number of vehicles that can be attended simultaneously and the loading tasks. They are solved using an Ant Colony System algorithm, which is a distributed metaheuristic. Results from a computational test using real-world instances show that the proposed approach outperforms the transportation planning related to manual designs. Besides a well-known VRP benchmark was solved to validate the approach.

1 Introduction

A company that transports goods to supply customers usually needs to plan the routes that the fleet must follow, since the transportation means a high percentage of the value added to goods, 5% to 20% of the total cost [1], therefore it is necessary to find efficient ways to plan it.

Nowadays, the solution of real-life world transportation problems requires the development of robust methods that support the hard inherited complexity of this kind of problems. A methodology to give solution was proposed, in an integrated way, to three tasks included in a generic transportation problem (RoSLoP): Routing, Scheduling and Loading. The routing task focused in is a generic VRP known as Rich VRP, and includes six important types of VRPs. To test the approach a Transportation System based on two heuristic algorithms (TSHA) was built.

* This research was supported in part by CONACYT and DGEST.

I. Stojmenovic et al. (Eds.): ISPA 2007, LNCS 4742, pp. 68–77, 2007.

The paper is structured as follows: section two defines the vehicle routing problem and gives a short review of the related works. Section three describes the tasks of a real bottled products transportation problem. Section four describes the solution methodology using and Ant Colony System algorithm (ACS), which is a distributed metaheuristic that combines an adaptive memory with a local heuristic function to repeatedly construct solutions of hard combinatorial optimization problems, and the DiPro algorithm, a new heuristic that solves load distribution. Section five resumes the experimental results obtained. The last section shows the conclusions and future works.

2 Vehicle Routing Problem (VRP) and Related Works

The classical problem of VRP is defined on a graph with a differentiated vertex (depot) that has travel costs or times associated with each arc. A set of m vehicles routes starting and ending at the depot, with minimal total cost, have to be designed in such a way that each of the remaining vertices is visited by exactly one vehicle. The value of m can be part of the data or the decision variables.

The types of VRPs are built by adding new restrictions such as capacity in the vehicles (CVRP, [2]), time windows for the customers and depots (VRPTW, [3]), several depots to supply the demands (MDVRP, [4]), split deliveries (SDVRP, [5],), multiple use of vehicles (VRPM, [6]), vehicles with a heterogeneous capacity (HVRP, [7]), and others.

In the revised literature, most of scientific papers target a specific VRP problem. Only a few papers like [8] presents approaches to solve several types of VRPs. In order to overcome these limitations a methodology to solve several types of VRP problems that are involved in the definition of real-world transportations instances is proposed.

3 Scheduling-Routing-Loading Problem (RoSLoP)

The transportation of bottle products, described in this section, was specified by our industrial partner. This problem has three main sub-problems which are: Routing, Loading and Scheduling.

The objective of the routing task is to assign routes to vehicles with the minimum total cost. The restrictions are based on six VRP variants (CVRP, VRPM, HVRP, VRPTW, sdVRP and SDVRP) and the new one CCVRP (Customer Capacity VRP) that limits the number of vehicles that can be in a location at the same time.

In the Loading task, the distribution of the goods in the vehicles is planned by satisfying a set of restrictions that depend on the company conditions. This problem is known as Bin-Packing Problem (BPP) few BPP variants related to VRP have been studied.

In the companies of our industrial partner, the manual procedure to distribute the load is threefold: first, the demand given by our customer is transformed into

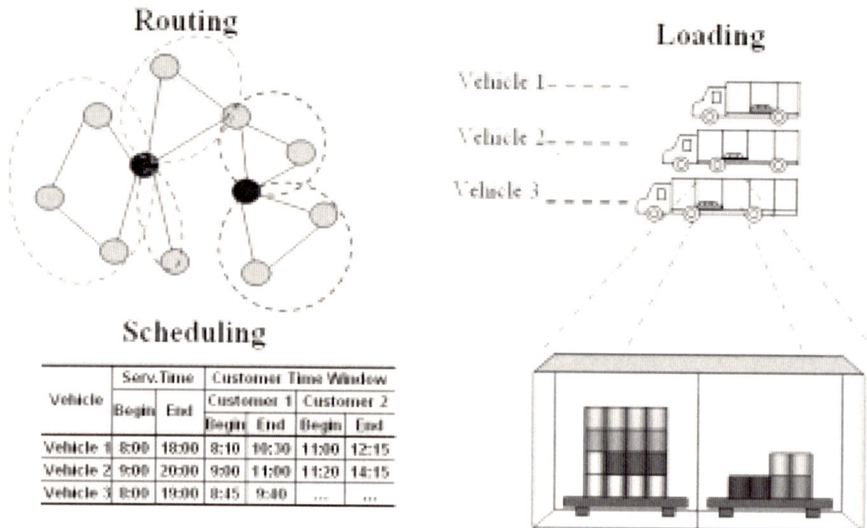

Fig. 1. RoSLoP subproblems

product beds; second, the beds are used to build the platforms; and third, the platforms are assigned into the pallets of the vehicles. For the assignment, all sides of the vehicles must be balanced in weight.

During the scheduling, programs containing the arrival time of each vehicle to the customers are elaborated.

In order to generalize the transportation problem of this research, the Routing-Scheduling-Loading Problem (RoSLoP) is formulated as follows: "Given a set of customers with a demand to be satisfied, a set of depots that are able to supply them and a set of BPP and VRP variants that restrict them, the Routing, Scheduling and Loading for vehicles needs to be designed such as: customer demands are completely satisfied; the total cost is minimized; and the constraints are satisfied".

4 Methodology

The methodology of solution consists of two steps; the first solves the Routing and Loading tasks with the heuristics algorithms ACS and DiPro. The ACS algorithm uses DiPro to distribute the products in the vehicle during the construction of the routes. The second step solves the scheduling task.

4.1 Ant Colony System (ACS) Algorithm

The ACS algorithm designed to solve the Routing task is a distributed meta-heuristic based on the approach shown in [3] and its goal is to find the minimum number of vehicles needed to satisfy all the customer demands in a RoSLoP instance.

In order to build a solution, the proposed ACS algorithm uses two measures known as closeness η and the pheromone trail τ. These measures can be associated with two customers (η_{ij},τ_{ij}) or with a vehicle (η_c,τ_c). They are calculated according with [3] for customers, while for a vehicle the equations (1 to 3) are proposed in this paper.

In the vehicle closeness, equation (1), three vehicle properties are combined: the truck size, velocity and remained time for service. The vehicle which has the better balanced between these properties will be the best.

$$\eta_c = \frac{1}{nv_c * (\overline{TM_c} + \overline{TR_c}) * \frac{tr_c}{tt_c}} \tag{1}$$

where η_c is the closeness of vehicle c; nv_c are the trips needed by the vehicle c to supply all the demands; $\overline{TM_c}$ is the average load/unload time of a vehicle c; $\overline{TR_c}$ is the average travel time of a vehicle c; tr_c is the available service time of the vehicle c; and tt_c is the total service time of the vehicle c.

The pheromone trail τ measures how attractiveness is to include a certain element into a solution. This value is modified by the ants during the construction of the solutions. The global updating of the pheromone trail for vehicles is shown in the equation (2) while the local updating is in the equation (3).

$$\tau_c = (1 - \rho) * \tau_c + \frac{\rho}{J_\psi^{gb}} \tag{2}$$

$$\tau_c = (1 - \rho) * \tau_c + \rho * \tau_0 \tag{3}$$

where $\rho \in [0, 1]$ is a pheromone evaporation parameter and J_ψ^{gb} is the length of the best global known solution ψ^{gb} achieved by the ACS algorithm at the moment of the updating; τ_0 is the initial value of the trail.

The ACS algorithm shown in Figure 2 is mainly regulated by three parameters: ρ, β (relative importance of the closeness η); and q_0 (probability of chose among exploitation and exploration). In the algorithm, an initial feasible solution is created using a Nearest Neighborhood algorithm (line 1). After that it creates an ant colony whose purpose is to minimize the number of vehicles used (lines 4 to 18). In this process, a improved global solution is searched building a fixed number of ants per colony and updating the pheromone trail for vehicles and customers locally and globally (lines 13-14 and 16-17 respectively). When a local solution has been improved (line 9), the current colony ends (line 12), the local solution is compared with respect to the best global solution (line 19) and the updates have done (line 20-21), to continue with the execution of the algorithm. The stop conditions of lines 18 and 22 are specified with respect to the number of iterations and time of execution respectively.

In the ACS algorithm the functions *#active_vehicles* and *#visited_customers* determine the number of vehicles used in a solution and the number of customers visited in the solution, respectively. The function *#depot* tells which depot is the owner of a specific vehicle. The integer vector IN_j stores the number of times a customer j hasn't been inserted in a solution. IN is used by the construction

```
ACS_Algorithm (β, ρ, q0)
ψ^gb ← Initial_Solution                                  /*initialize global best solution*/
t ← #active_vehicles(ψ^gb ) − 1                        /* number of vehicles for a new solution*/
repeat                                                    /* start ACS algorithm*/
  repeat                                                  /* start minimization of number of vehicle*/
    ψ^lb ← Initial _Solution                              /*initial local best solution*/
    for each ant k ∈ K                 /*start ant colony system optimization with k ants*/
      ψ^k ← new_ant_solution (k, t, IN )                  /* new solution with t vehicles*/
      ∀j ∉ψ^k: IN_j ← IN_j+ 1                  /* Customer has not been visited in IN times*/
      If #visited_customers (ψ^k) > #visited_customers(ψ^lb) then
        ψ^lb ← ψ^k
        ∀j : IN_j ← 0
        end_repeat                                        /*colony ends if solution is improved*/
    ∀c ∈ ψ^lb : τ_c = (1 − ρ) ∗ τ_c + ρ/J_ψ^lb            /*vehicle pheromone local update*/
    ∀(i, j) ∈ ψ^lb : τ_ij = (1 − ρ) ∗ τ_ij + ρ/J_ψ^lb    /*customer pheromone local update*/
    end for each
    ∀c ∈ ψ^gb : τ_c = (1 − ρ) ∗ τ_c + ρ/J_ψ^gb            /* vehicle pheromone global update*/
    ∀(i, j) ∈ ψ^gb : τ_ij = (1 − ρ) ∗ τ_ij + ρ/J_ψ^gb    /*customer pheromone global update*/
  until stop criterion is reached
  if ψ^lb is feasible and ψ^lb improves ψ^gb then        /* if global best is improved*/
    ψ^gb ← ψ^lb
    t ← #active_vehicles(ψ^gb ) − 1
until stop criterion is reached
```

Fig. 2. ACS Algorithm used to solve RoSLop Instances

procedure to favor the customers that are less frequently included in a solution Ψ. The constructive procedure *new_ant_solution* builds the new solution with the ant k. It consists in building routes using t vehicles to satisfy customer demands.

4.2 DiPro Algorithm

Figure 3 shows a graphical description of DiPro Algorithm. In order to distribute a customer demand in a vehicle, the products are ordered by its supported weight. After that, the goods are organized in homogeneous beds and homogeneous platforms. Then, the remaining product boxes of each product are used to form heterogeneous beds with different products that have the same category and belong to the same area.

The rest of homogeneous beds that could not form homogeneous platforms in the previous process are combined with heterogeneous beds to form heterogeneous platforms by area. The heterogeneous platforms are created by following the Round Robin mechanism used in processor scheduling. A round robin is an arrangement of choosing all elements in a group equally in some rational order, usually from the top to the bottom of a list and then starting again at the top of the list and so on. In DiPro, the arrangement is the remaining beds of products

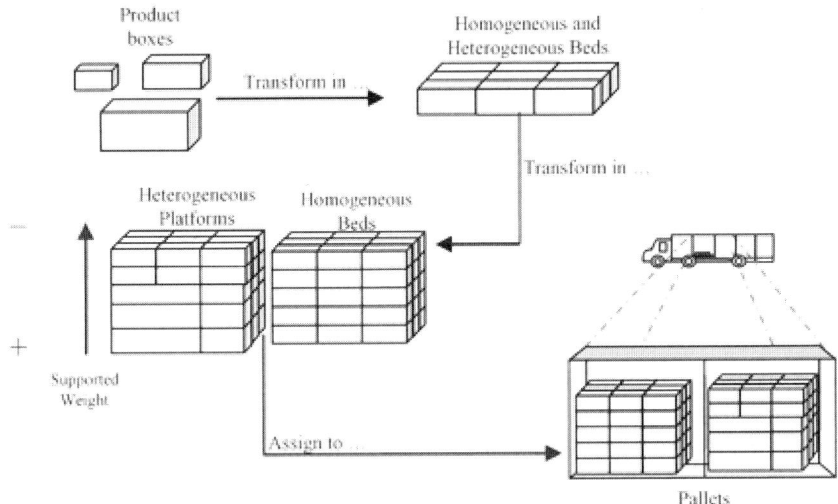

Fig. 3. DiPro Algorithm

that could not be allocated in homogeneous platforms; the order is given by their supported weight.

Once all the platforms have been built, all the created platforms are ordered by weight and then assigned to the pallets. It is necessary to take into account that the left and the right side of the vehicle must be weighed balanced and that the heaviest platforms go in the front and the lightest in the back.

5 Experimental Results

5.1 Evaluation of a Basic ACS Algorithm

In this experiment, a version of the ACS Algorithm that solves VRPTW with other scientific community heuristics that solve the same variant was compared. During the experiment, 56 VRPTW instances of the Solomon's benchmark were solved. The cases were composed by the six different problem types (which are R1, R2, C1, C2, RC1, and RC2). Each instance contains 100 locations.

The basic algorithm was implemented in C#, and each instance was solved 30 times. The experiments were executed under the next conditions: Xeon Processor at 3.06 GHz, with 3.87 Gb of RAM Memory and Windows Server 2003 as Operative System. The values for the parameters of the ACS algorithm for VRPTW were: ants used = 10, colonies = 5; generations = 40; $q_0 = 0.9$; $\beta = 1$; $\rho = 0.1$.

Table 1 shows the comparison between the ACS Algorithm and four of the best known algorithms that have solved VRPTW. Columns two to six show the average number of vehicles used in the solutions by each kind of instance. The last column is the combination of the average number of vehicles shown in the results

Table 1. Four of the best known algorithms compared with ACS VRPTW with respect to vehicles

Algorithm	Number of Vehicles needed						Average
	R1	R2	C1	C2	RC1	RC2	
[9]	11.92	2.73	10.00	3.00	11.50	3.25	7.06
[10]	11.92	2.73	10.00	3.00	11.50	3.25	7.06
[11]	11.92	2.73	10.00	3.00	11.63	3.25	7.08
[3]	12.00	2.73	10.00	3.00	11.63	3.25	7.10
ACS Algorithm	**12.58**	**3.09**	**10.00**	**3.00**	**12.25**	**3.38**	**7.38**

Table 2. Four of the best known algorithms compared with ACS VRPTW with respect to distance

Algorithm	Total of Distance traveled						Average
	R1	R2	C1	C2	RC1	RC2	
ACS Algorithm	**1221.9**	**954.6**	**828.7**	**594.1**	**1383**	**1128.8**	**1018.57**
[3]	1217.73	967.75	828.4	589.86	1382.4	1129.19	1019.225
[9]	1222	975.12	828.4	589.86	1390	1128.38	1022.2933
[11]	1228.06	969.95	828.38	589.86	1392.6	1144.43	1025.5417
[10]	1251.4	1056.6	828.5	590.06	1414.9	1258.15	1066.5933

of a whole set of instances. The considered algorithms were: Reactive Variable Neighborhood Search [9], Hybrid Genetic Algorithm [10], Genetic Algorithm [11], Multi-Objective Ant Colony System [3].

The results reported by the ACS algorithm in Table 1 and 2 are based on an average taken from cases that were runned 30 times, while the rest of the values shown by the other algorithms belong to the best results found in all their runnings. The other researchers experiments are different in some aspects like: the number of times that a case is runned, the running time, the equipment where the instances were executed and the way that the results are reported. The researchers report their results based in a sample which experimental designs do not show the real behavior of an algorithm [12]. Due to this, it is not possible to compare the actual results of the ACS algorithm; however, it could be appreciated that the implementation used in this research is efficient [13]. Due to this performance it was decided to implement the ACS algorithm in such a way that it could be used to solve more complex real-world instances, like the RoSLoP instances.

5.2 Solving Real-World RoSLoP Instances

Our industrial partner defines an efficient system as the one that can solve a real-world instance in 10 minutes or less, satisfying 100% of the demands and minimizing the number of vehicles used.

The instances used in this experiment are real-world cases presented in a bottled product transportation company. Table 3 shows the description of such

Table 3. Real-world RoSLoP instance description

Instance	Description of the real-world RoSLoP Instances						
	Customers	Vehicles	Depots	Arcs	Customer capacity	Depot capacity	Customer demands
Case 01	7	8	1	10	1	2	12681
Case 02	6	8	1	10	1	2	10953
Case 03	7	8	1	10	1	2	15040
Case 04	7	8	1	10	1	2	12624
Case 05	7	8	1	10	1	2	14262

Table 4. Experimental Results

Instances	Metrics							
	Vehicles used in the solution				Supplied products			
	NNH	TSHA[1]	TSHA[2]	Manual	NNH	TSHA[1]	TSHA[2]	Manual
Case 01	8	7	7	7	11077	12681	12681	12681
Case 02	8	5	5	6	10953	10953	10953	10953
Case 03	8	7	6	6	8019	15040	15040	15040
Case 04	8	6	5	5	11302	12624	12624	12624
Case 05	8	8	7	7	11283	14262	14262	14262

[1] Execution time of five seconds.
[2] Execution time of ten minutes.

cases. The column five is the number of arcs in the connection matrix. Columns six and seven mean the number of vehicles that can be simultaneously loaded or unloaded in a location. The last column is the amount of product boxes demanded by the whole set of customers of a real-world RoSLoP instance.

The VRP variants used to describe the routing task of the RoSLoP instances are: CVRP, VRPM, HVRP, VRPTW, VRPSD, VRPsd and CCVRP a new restriction in which the customer has a limited attention capacity for vehicles.

The algorithm was implemented in C#. The conditions of this experiment given by our industrial partner were: AMD Athlon XP, 1.3 GHz, 192 Mb in RAM, Windows XP Operative System. The values for the parameters of the ACS algorithm for VRPTW were: ants used = 15, colonies = 5; $q_0 = 0.9$; $\beta = 2$; $\rho = 0.1$.

The results obtained were compared with a Nearest Neighborhood Heuristic (NNH) and with the manual solution given by the procedure used in the bottle product transportation company. In Table 4 the solutions gotten by our system TSHA are compared with the manual procedure and the NNH. It is important to say that the NNH gets a solution in one second and the manual procedure takes around sixteen hours.

As it is shown in Table 4, the performance of TSHA in comparison with the manual procedure, improves the consumed time in all the cases. It also improves the number of vehicles in 20% of the cases. In all cases, TSHA satisfies the demands and does it better than NNH algorithm which was the quickest.

6 Conclusions and Future Work

This paper shows the feasibility of solving real-world instances of the transportation problem named RoSLoP because it includes routing, scheduling and loading tasks. The proposed solution methodology is based on a distributed metaheuristic (ACS algorithm) and a deterministic heuristic (DiPro algorithm).

In comparison with the manual procedure, Transportation System based on Heuristic algorithms (TSHA) reduced the time needed to find a solution from 16 hours to 10 minutes. It also reduced, in a 20% of the cases, the number of vehicles needed to supply the customer. In general, the solutions given by TSHA can be considered efficient solutions according with the standard given by our industrial partner.

Besides, a well-known benchmark of the vehicle routing problem (VRP)was solved.

For future works we are planning to manage more than six VRP variants and solve instances of very large scale. We also plan to solve the load distribution task by using a Bin-Packing approach.

References

1. Toth, P., Vigo, D.: The Vehicle Routing Problem. Monographs on Discrete Mathematics and Applications. SIAM, Philadelphia (2001)
2. Blasum, U., Hochstätter, W.: Application of the Branch and Cut Method to the Vehicle Routing Problem. Universität zu Köln, BTU Cotbus (May15, 2002)
3. Gambardella, L., Taillar, E., Agazzi, G.: MACS-VRPTW: A Multiple Ant Colony System for Vehicle Routing Problems with Time Windows. Technical Report IDSIA. IDSIA-06-99. Lugano, Switzerland (1999)
4. Mingozzi, A., Vallet, A.: An exact Algorithm for Period and Multi-Depot Vehicle Routing Problems. Department of Mathematics, University of Bologna, Bolonga, Italy (2003)
5. Archetti, C., Mansini, R., Speranza, M.: The Vehicle Routing Problem with capacity 2 and 3, General Distances and Multiple Customer visits. In: ORP 2001, Paris (September 26-29, 2001)
6. Taillard, E., Laport, G., Gendreau, M.: Vehicle Routing Problem with Multiple Use of Vehicles. Centre de Recherche sur les transports. Publicacin CRT-95-19 (March 1995)
7. Taillard, E.: A Heuristic Column Generation Method For the Heterogeneous Fleet VRP. Istituto Dalle Moli di Studi sull Inteligenza Artificiale, Switzerland. CRI-96-03 (May 1996)
8. Psinger, D., Ropke, S.: A general Heuristic for Vehicle Routing Problems. DIKU, University of Copenhagen (February 25, 2005)
9. Bräysy, O.: A Reactive Variable Neighborhood Search Algorithm for the Vehicle Routing Problem with Time Windows. Working paper, SINTEF Applied Mathematics, Department of Optimization, Norway (2001)

10. Berger, J., Barkaoui, M., Bräysy, O.: A Parallel Hybrid Genetic Algorithm for the Vehicle Routing Problem with Time Windows. Working Paper, Defense Research Establishment Valcartier, Canada (2001)
11. Homberger, J., Gehring, H.: Two Evolutionary Meta-heuristics for the Vehicle Routing Problem with Time Windows. Infor. 37, 297–318 (1999)

Cellular ANTomata
(Extended Abstract)

Arnold L. Rosenberg

Dept. of Computer Science, Univ. of Massachusetts, Amherst, MA 01003, USA
rsnbrg@cs.umass.edu

Abstract. Cellular automata can form the basis of a practical model for a broad range of tasks that require the coordination of many simple computing devices. We propose using "semi-synchronous" cellular automata as a platform for efficiently realizing ant-inspired algorithms that coordinate robots within a fixed, geographically constrained environment. We present an appropriate formalization of the resulting *Cellular ANTomaton* model, illustrated via "proof-of-concept" problems that have ant-robots move and aggregate in various ways.

Keywords: Ant-inspired Robotics; Cellular automata; Mini-factories.

1 Introduction

As we encounter novel computing environments that offer new opportunities while posing new challenges, it is natural to seek inspiration from natural analogues of these environments. Thus, empowered with technology that enables mobile intercommunicating robotic computers, it is compelling to seek inspiration from social insects—in 2-dimensional settings, mainly ants—when contemplating how to use the computers effectively and efficiently in environments that defy centralized control; many sources (cf. [3,4,6]) have done precisely that. After considering the strengths and the weaknesses of the robot-as-ant metaphor in the light of current computer technology, we propose a variant of cellular automata [2,13]—that we name *Cellular ANTomata*—as a platform for developing the algorithmics of robotic mobile computers within constrained geographic environments. We specify the proposed model in detail and illustrate it via "proof-of-concept" problems that have ant-robots move and aggregate in various ways.

1.1 Motivating Cellular ANTomata

Our use of cellular automata as a conceptual/algorithmic platform arises from the following considerations. While nature is a valuable source of inspiration in domains where it operates successfully—such as the functioning of social insects—one must not follow nature too literally. Some features and behaviors observed in social insects retain useless remnants of evolutionary cul-de-sacs. Others depend on realities in nature, such as the availability of multitudes of expendable individual agents, that differ sharply from the realities in the world

I. Stojmenovic et al. (Eds.): ISPA 2007, LNCS 4742, pp. 78–90, 2007.

of robotic mobile computers. We therefore strive for a conceptual algorithmic platform that adapts features inspired by the former world to the exigencies of the latter—at least within constrained environments.

1.2 Ant-Robots in a Factory

We focus on situations wherein robotic mobile computers (henceforth, *"ants"*) function within a fixed geographically constrained environment. We expect ants to be able to:

- navigate the environment, avoiding collisions with obstacles and one another;
- communicate with and sense one another, by "direct contact" (as when real ants meet) and by "timestamped message passing" (as when real ants deposit volatile pheromones);
- discover goal objects (*"food"*) and convey food from one location to another;
- assemble in desired locations, in desired physical configurations.

A standard approach. A natural approach to achieving artificial ants is to enhance electro-mechanical robots that have both mobility and grasping/conveying capability with additional "machinery" that enables computation and both direct and "timestamped" communication. Indeed, researchers (cf. [6]) have equipped robots with small transceivers that function as generators and receptors of "virtual" pheromones. Such an avenue to artificial ants may be inevitable when robots must navigate unbounded (e.g., external) environments. But when robots are to function as, say, manufacturing aids in a geographically constrained environment such as a factory floor, two features of this approach call out for emendation.

1. The likely level of use of each ant's computing and communicating "machinery" will tax any battery technology that powers the "machinery."

2. The potential for accidents such as unintended impacts will greatly increase the cost of each ant, via either the extra weight needed to insulate electronics or the frequent replacement of incapacitated/damaged ants.

An alternative approach. Our model revisits the relationship of ants to their environment (henceforth, the *"(factory) floor"*). In the "standard" approach, all intelligence and initiative resides in the ants; the factory floor is a brainless, passive environment which is just a physical platform upon which ants sit and move. While such an organization of the "world" is unavoidable when ants operate outdoors in unconstrained, uncontrollable environments, it is eminently avoidable on a factory floor. We propose to invert the active-passive relationship between ants and the floor, by tesselating the floor with tiles that are identical in size and shape, embedding within each tile a copy of some standard computer of modest capability. We posit that each computer has:

- a number of I/O ports that is sufficient for necessary communications;
- c registers that record levels of c types of virtual pheromones (cf. [6]) whose volatility is modeled by a scheduled decrementing of the associated register.

In a single "step," each tile/computer is capable of:

1. detecting whether or not it has upon it: • an obstacle or a portion thereof (e.g., a wall covering many tiles); • an ant; • a food item that an ant can pick up and/or move and/or manipulate; • both an ant and a food item.

2. communicating with neighboring tiles—those it shares an edge or corner with—by receiving one message from each and transmitting one message to each in each "step;" sample messages could be: "I DO (NOT) HAVE AN ANT;" "I DO (NOT) HAVE FOOD;" "I DO (NOT) CONTAIN AN OBSTACLE;" "I HAVE LEVEL ℓ_i OF PHEROMONE i." (Note that we use "King's-move" adjacencies.)

3. communicating with an ant that resides on the tile, via messages such as: "PICK UP THE FOOD;" "MOVE TO THE NEIGHBORING TILE IN DIRECTION D" (D is a compass direction).

Now, ants never collide with obstacles or other ants: they move only by command of the tile they reside on—which communicates constantly with its neighbors. Moreover, ants are now much simpler, containing little electronics except as needed to receive commands from the tile they reside on; consequently, malfunctions/accidents are much rarer and less expensive than with "smart" ants.

1.3 Two Basic Model Features

(a) Factory floors must be *scalable* in structure and efficiency; e.g., computers may not exploit information about the size of the floor (number of tiles). **(b)** Our model is "synchronous," in that computers assemble inputs from all neighbors before committing to any action. This does *not* mean that all computers hear the tick of the same clock, but, rather, that variations in clocking between neighboring computers are small (since they come from geographical neighbors). That said, it is easy to implement our algorithms in a *completely distributed manner*, with all coordination among computers being via explicit messages, rather than shared "clock ticks."

Space constraints limit us to high-level sketches of algorithms and analyses.

1.4 Related Work

Our use of *Cellular automata* (*CA*, for short) to realize ant-inspired algorithms and behavior is not original. In [4], CA underlie an ant-inspired algorithm for a genre of flow problem; in [3], CA implement an ant-inspired clustering algorithm. Most closely related to our model is the *DFMS* model of [1], an iterative array of minicomputers that can be programmed to compute source-target paths for microscopic droplets that co-reside on the array with obstacles and other special features. All of these sources depart from our goal by focusing on a single computational problem and by positing centrally programmed models, with, e.g., global name spaces for tiles/computers. Also closely related to our model, but with a specialized focus, are the many papers on the "firing squad" synchronization problem for CA, [10], especially the 2-dimensional variant [8]. Finally, "numerical pheromones" appear in, e.g., [6].

2 Cellular ANTomata

CA are a natural candidate for realizing intelligent factory floors, being composed of *finite-state machines* (*FSMs*) arranged in simply structured arrays. Studied since the 1960s [5,10,12], CA remain of interest to this day [7,8,14], providing a formal model of computers [13,14] that combines mathematical simplicity with levels of efficiency that make them feasible for many real computational tasks. Indeed, CA are remarkably efficient for a broad range of tasks that require the tight coordination of many simple agents [3,4,5,8,10]. Our variant of CA, *Cellular ANTomata*, is tailored to the algorithmics of ants on a factory floor.

2.1 Basics

As with CAs, Cellular ANTomata place a copy of a single FSM at each node of a *square mesh*. (One easily restricts our *2-dimensional* model to one dimension or extends it to three. We define our model in great detail, to facilitate implementation of our model ("hardware") and algorithms ("software").

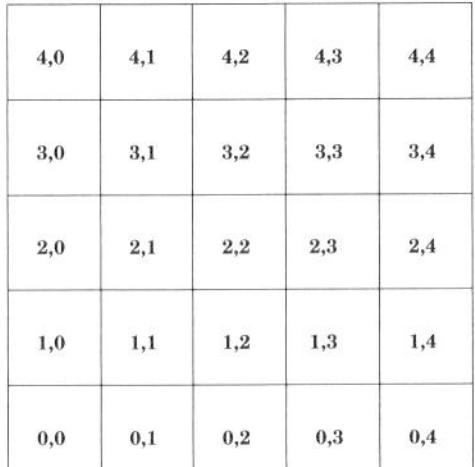

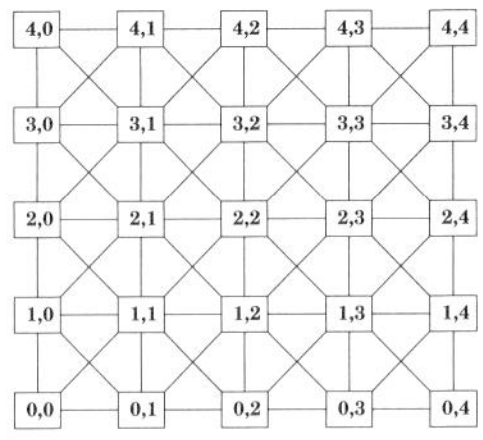

Fig. 1. A 5×5 tiled floor; its associated graph (edges represent mated opposing arcs)

Tiled floors and meshes (Fig. 1). We tesselate a square floor with identical tiles[1] and abstract the floor as a *side-n 2-dimensional mesh*, $\mathcal{M}_n$. The nodes of $\mathcal{M}_n$ are the tiles, formally, the set[2] $[0, n-1] \times [0, n-1]$. $\mathcal{M}_n$'s *King's-move* arcs are tiles' adjacencies, labeled by the compass directions: E, SE, S, SW, W, NW, N, NE; cf. Fig. 2(left) and Table 1. Each node $v = \langle i, j \rangle$ of $\mathcal{M}_n$ is connected by a mated in-arc and out-arc to each of its (≤ 8) neighboring nodes (see Table 2).

- If $i, j \in \{0, n-1\}$ then v is a *corner* node and has 3 neighbors.
- If $i = 0$ (resp., $i = n-1$) and $j \in [1, n-2]$, then v is a *bottom* (resp., *top*) node. If $j = 0$ (resp., $j = n-1$) and $i \in [1, n-2]$, then v is a *left* (resp., *right*) node. These four are collectively *edge* nodes; each has 5 neighbors.
- If $i, j \in [1, n-2]$, then v is an *internal* node and has 8 neighbors.

FSMs: Finite-State Machines. An FSM $\mathcal{F}$ in a cellular ANTomaton is given by:

[1] We discuss only square tiles; simple modifications allow, say, hexagonal tiles.

[2] $\mathbb{N}$ is the nonnegative integers. For $i \in \mathbb{N}$ and $j \geq i$, $[i, j] \stackrel{\text{def}}{=} \{i, i+1, \ldots, j\}$.

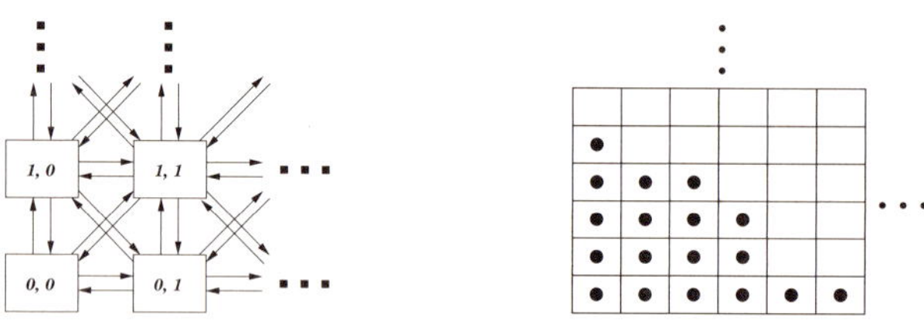

Fig. 2. (Left) The 2×2 corner of a mesh, with all incident arcs. (Right) The 6×6 "prefix" of $\mathcal{Q}_{SW}$, with 18 optimally parked ants (denoted by dots); cf. Section 3.

Table 1. The NEWS and diagonal arc-labels, and their actions

Arc label	Arc action	Leads node $\langle i, j \rangle$	to node ...
E	move to *East*	$(i \in [0, n-1],\ j \in [0, n-2])$	$\langle i, j+1 \rangle$
W	move to *West*	$(i \in [0, n-1],\ j \in [1, n-1])$	$\langle i, j-1 \rangle$
N	move to *North*	$(i \in [0, n-2],\ j \in [0, n-1])$	$\langle i+1, j \rangle$
S	move to *South*	$(i \in [1, n-1],\ j \in [0, n-1])$	$\langle i-1, j \rangle$
NE	move to *Northeast*	$(i \in [0, n-2],\ j \in [0, n-2])$	$\langle i+1, j+1 \rangle$
SW	move to *Southwest*	$(i \in [1, n-1],\ j \in [1, n-1])$	$\langle i-1, j-1 \rangle$
NW	move to *Northwest*	$(i \in [0, n-2],\ j \in [1, n-1])$	$\langle i+1, j-1 \rangle$
SE	move to *Southeast*	$(i \in [1, n-1],\ j \in [0, n-2])$	$\langle i-1, j+1 \rangle$.

- a finite set Q of *states*. $Q = K \times [0, I_1] \times [0, I_2] \times \cdots \times [0, I_\ell]$, where K is a set of "control" variables, and each $I_j \in \mathbb{N}$. This endows ants with ℓ types of pheromones, the kth of which can exist at any intensity $i \in [0, I_k]$.
- an *input "alphabet"* IN, which is the union of:
  —the set of all messages that $\mathcal{F}$ can receive from neighboring FSMs,
  —$\{0, 1\}^3$: binary indicators of the presence of an ant, an obstacle, food;
- an *output "alphabet"* OUT, which is the union of:
  —the set of all messages that $\mathcal{F}$ can send to neighboring FSMs,
  —the set O: possible orders to the resident ant (if it exists).
- a state-transition function $\delta : Q \times IN \rightarrow Q \times OUT$, associating a state $\langle k, i_1, \ldots, i_\ell \rangle$ and input $e_{IN} \in IN$ with an output $e_{OUT} \in OUT$ and a new state $\langle k', i'_1, \ldots, i'_\ell \rangle$. Each $i'_j - i_j \in \{0, -1, 1\}$: a pheromone level stays stable (0 change) or evaporates (-1 change) or is reinforced *by an ant* ($+1$ change).

2.2 Cellular ANTomata

Given $n \in \mathbb{N}$ and FSM $\mathcal{F}$, the *FSM-array* $\mathbf{F}_n(\mathcal{F})$ is constructed by: **(a)** *populating* $\mathcal{M}_n$ *with copies of* $\mathcal{F}$. One assigns each copy of $\mathcal{F}$ a unique *index* from $[0, n-1] \times [0, n-1]$ and places each $\mathcal{F}_{i,j}$ at node $\langle i, j \rangle$ of $\mathcal{M}_n$. (We then speak of "an internal," "a corner," or "an edge" FSM.) **(b)** *endowing each FSM with sensors for ants, obstacles, and food, and with a unidirectional communication channel that a resident ant will respond to.* **(c)** *connecting each FSM with a bidirectional communication channel to each of its King's-move neighbors.* Thus, the input

Table 2. The communication links of mesh nodes

Corner node	talks to node:	via out-arc:	via in-arc:
$\langle 0,0\rangle$	$\langle 1,0\rangle$	N	S
	$\langle 1,1\rangle$	NE	SW
	$\langle 0,1\rangle$	E	W
$\langle n-1,0\rangle$	$\langle n-2,0\rangle$	S	N
	$\langle n-2,1\rangle$	SE	NW
	$\langle n-1,1\rangle$	E	W
$\langle n-1,n-1\rangle$	$\langle n-2,n-1\rangle$	S	N
	$\langle n-2,n-2\rangle$	SW	NE
	$\langle n-1,n-2\rangle$	W	E
$\langle 0,n-1\rangle$	$\langle 0,n-2\rangle$	W	E
	$\langle 1,n-2\rangle$	NW	SE
	$\langle 1,n-1\rangle$	N	S

Node	talks to node:	via out-arc:	via in-arc:
$\langle i,j\rangle$	$\langle i,j-1\rangle$	W	E
	$\langle i+1,j-1\rangle$	NW	SE
	$\langle i+1,j\rangle$	N	S
	$\langle i+1,j+1\rangle$	NE	SW
	$\langle i,j+1\rangle$	E	W
	$\langle i-1,j+1\rangle$	SE	NW
	$\langle i-1,j\rangle$	S	N
	$\langle i-1,j-1\rangle$	SW	NE

Node-type	talks to node:	via out-arc:	via in-arc:
Bottom node $\langle 0,j\rangle$	$\langle 0,j-1\rangle$	W	E
	$\langle 1,j-1\rangle$	NW	SE
	$\langle 1,j\rangle$	N	S
	$\langle 1,j+1\rangle$	NE	SW
	$\langle 0,j+1\rangle$	E	W
Top node $\langle n-1,j\rangle$	$\langle n-1,j-1\rangle$	W	W
	$\langle n-2,j-1\rangle$	SW	NW
	$\langle n-2,j\rangle$	S	N
	$\langle n-2,j+1\rangle$	SE	NE
	$\langle n-1,j+1\rangle$	E	E
Left node $\langle i,0\rangle$	$\langle i-1,0\rangle$	S	N
	$\langle i-1,1\rangle$	SE	NW
	$\langle i,1\rangle$	E	W
	$\langle i+1,1\rangle$	NE	SW
	$\langle i+1,0\rangle$	N	S
Right node $\langle i,n-1\rangle$	$\langle i-1,n-1\rangle$	S	N
	$\langle i-1,n-2\rangle$	SW	NE
	$\langle i,n-2\rangle$	W	E
	$\langle i+1,n-2\rangle$	NW	SE
	$\langle i+1,n-1\rangle$	N	E

and output alphabets of each internal FSM include the set of directional messages $S = \Sigma_N \times \Sigma_{NE} \times \Sigma_E \times \Sigma_{SE} \times \Sigma_S \times \Sigma_{SW} \times \Sigma_W \times \Sigma_{NW}$. S is suitably edited for corner and edge FSMs by replacing inputs from/outputs to nonexistent neighbors by "NIL;" e.g., the message-set for $\mathcal{F}_{0,j}$ is: $\Sigma_N \times \Sigma_{NE} \times \Sigma_E \times \{\text{NIL}\} \times \{\text{NIL}\} \times \{\text{NIL}\} \times \Sigma_W \times \Sigma_{NW}$.

Note 1. **(a)** Because we "invert" Nature, messages flow "below the surface" that entities reside on. Hence: *Obstacles atop FSMs do not impede the flow of messages.* **(b)** Choosing between King's- vs. NEWS-move arrays is a matter of cost allocation. The former are architecturally more complicated but algorithmically simpler and more efficient; the latter are architecturally simpler but require a longer state-change cycle. **(c)** To achieve *scalability* (cf. Section 1.3), we insist that algorithms treat n as an *unknown*, never exploiting its specific value.

$\mathcal{F}_{0,0}$ is the *general* of $\mathbf{F}_n(\mathcal{F})$, the only FSM that accepts inputs (usually commands) from the "outside world"—say, for definiteness, via its western input port (so that Σ_W must contain all external commands). We expect the "outside world" to tell the general when to initiate activities.

3 "Parking" the Ants

We now have an FSM-array "park" its ants "compactly:" each ant moves as close as possible to the corner cell of the quadrant that it resides in when parking is initiated. This activity is easily achieved within our model; *it is not achievable at all within the standard setting of "smart" ants navigating a passive earth.*

3.1 The Formal Parking Problem

A *quadrant* of $\mathcal{M}_n$ is the induced subgraph[3] on the following node-set.

Quadrant	Node-set	Quadrant	Node-set
$\mathcal{Q}_{SW}$	$[0, \lceil n/2\rceil - 1] \times [0, \lceil n/2\rceil - 1]$	$\mathcal{Q}_{NW}$	$[\lceil n/2\rceil, n-1] \times [0, \lceil n/2\rceil - 1]$
$\mathcal{Q}_{SE}$	$[0, \lceil n/2\rceil - 1] \times [\lceil n/2\rceil, n-1]$	$\mathcal{Q}_{NE}$	$[\lceil n/2\rceil, n-1] \times [\lceil n/2\rceil, n-1]$

$\mathcal{M}_n$'s kth *diagonal* ($k \in [0, 2n-2]$) is: $\Delta_k = \{\langle i,j\rangle \in [0,n-1]\times[0,n-1] \mid i+j = k\}$. For $d \in [1, 2n-1]$, $\mathcal{Q}_{SW}$'s *radius-d L_1-quarter-sphere* is $\bigcup_{k=0}^{d-1} \Delta_k$. Other quadrants' quarter-spheres are defined analogously.

The *parking problem for* $\mathcal{Q}_{SW}$ requires the ants in $\mathcal{Q}_{SW}$ to cluster within the most compact L_1-quarter-sphere "centered" at $\langle 0,0\rangle$; cf. Fig. 2(right).[4] Formally, one must minimize the *parking potential function:* $\Pi(t) = \sum_{k=0}^{2n-2} (k+1) \times$ (the number of ants residing on Δ_k at step t). Thus, if parking begins with $m(m-1)/2 + p$ ants in $\mathcal{Q}_{SW}$, where $p \le m$, then for all sufficiently large t, $\Pi(t) = \sum_{i=1}^{m-1} i^2 + mp = m(m-1)(2m-1)/6 + mp$.

3.2 Initiating Parking

We begin to park ants by partitioning the parking problem into independent quadrant-specific subproblems (that are solved in parallel). A central subproblem is to let ants know which quadrant they reside in.

3.2.1 Sketch: Algorithm Activate_Center_Cells

$\mathcal{F}_{0,0}$ activates the center FSM(s) via two messages. A northward message (eventually[5]) enlists $\mathcal{F}_{n-1,0}$ in the activation. A northeasterly message "semi-activates"

[3] The *induced subgraph* of $\mathcal{G} = (N, A)$ on $N' \subseteq N$ has all arcs from A both of whose endpoints are in N'.

[4] One easily adapts the problem definition and algorithm to $\mathcal{M}_n$'s other quadrants.

[5] Since messages proceed from neighbor to neighbor, this process takes $\Theta(n)$ steps.

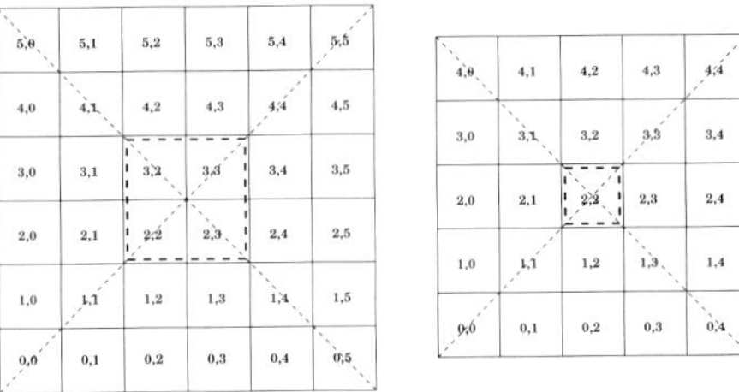

Fig. 3. Illustrating the "centers" of even- and odd-sided meshes

all FSMs along the SW-NE diagonal. Once activated, $\mathcal{F}_{n-1,0}$ sends a southeasterly message, which "semi-activates" all FSMs along the NW-SE diagonal. For even n, activation is achieved when both $\mathcal{F}_{n/2-1,n/2-1}$ and $\mathcal{F}_{n/2,n/2}$ become "semi-activated" along the SW-NE diagonal and both $\mathcal{F}_{n/2-1,n/2}$ and $\mathcal{F}_{n/2,n/2-1}$ become "semi-activated" along the NW-SE diagonal. A center cell identifies its quadrant from the directions of its fellow center cells. For odd n, activation is achieved when $\mathcal{F}_{\lceil n/2 \rceil, \lceil n/2 \rceil}$ becomes "semi-activated" along both the SW-NE and NW-SE diagonals. See Fig. 3.

3.2.2 Sketch: Algorithm Initiate_Parking_SW

Once activated, $\mathcal{M}_n$'s center cell(s) each broadcast a message into its quadrant that tells ant-holding FSMs to initiate the parking process appropriate to that quadrant. (When n is odd, the unique center cell broadcasts distinct messages into each quadrant.)

3.3 Parking Within $\mathcal{Q}_{SW}$

Table 3 specifies the permissible local ant-moving rules used in our parking algorithm. For brevity, we word rules as though every $\mathcal{F}_{i,j}$ is internal; trivial modifications accommodate extremal FSMs. Note that each ant-move may create "holes" that enable further ant-moves.

3.3.1 Sketch: Algorithm Park_in_$\mathcal{Q}_{SW}$

FSMs that hold ants continually broadcast "I HAVE AN ANT" toward $\langle 0, 0 \rangle$; antless FSMs continually broadcast "I HAVE A HOLE" away from $\langle 0, 0 \rangle$. Ant-holding FSMs move their ants closer to the desired configuration *while honoring the priorities implicit in the ordering of moves in Table 3.* Thus:

At each step, Rule SW has precedence over Rule S, which, in turn has precedence over Rule W. In-diagonal rules (NW and SE) destabilize configurations in which no diagonal-lowering move applies.

Termination. Simultaneously with parking: FSMs continually check if their diagonals are full of ants or of holes. When a diagonal Δ_k is found to be full of ants (resp., holes), that fact is broadcast to Δ_{k+1} (resp., Δ_{k-1}). Parking terminates when at most one diagonal contains both ants and holes, and no diagonal with holes is closer to $\langle 0, 0 \rangle$ than any diagonal with ants. Fig. 4 illustrates Algorithm Park_in_$\mathcal{Q}_{SW}$ (without the termination phase).

Table 3. The repertoire of local ant-moves, in decreasing order of priority

Rule SW. A southwesterly ant-move: $\mathcal{F}_{i,j}$ sends its ant to $\mathcal{F}_{i-1,j-1}$ (along arc SW).
Trigger. $\mathcal{F}_{i,j}$ has an ant; $\mathcal{F}_{i-1,j-1}$ has no ant.
Effect. Rule SW decreases the parking potential Π by 2.

↑↑↑ Rule SW is not needed for correctness, but it enhances efficiency ↑↑↑

Rule S. A southerly ant-move: $\mathcal{F}_{i,j}$ sends its ant to $\mathcal{F}_{i-1,j}$ (along arc S).
Trigger. $\mathcal{F}_{i,j}$, $\mathcal{F}_{i-1,j-1}$ have ants; $\mathcal{F}_{i-1,j}$ has no ant.
Effect. Rule S decreases Π by 1.

Rule W. A westerly ant-move: $\mathcal{F}_{i,j}$ sends its ant to $\mathcal{F}_{i,j-1}$ (along arc W).
Trigger. $\mathcal{F}_{i,j}$, $\mathcal{F}_{i-1,j-1}$, $\mathcal{F}_{i-1,j}$ have ants; $\mathcal{F}_{i,j-1}$ has no ant.
Effect. Rule W decreases Π by 1.

Rule NW. A northwesterly ant-move: $\mathcal{F}_{i,j}$ sends its ant to $\mathcal{F}_{i+1,j-1}$ (along arc NW).
Trigger. $\mathcal{F}_{i,j}$, $\mathcal{F}_{i-1,j-1}$, $\mathcal{F}_{i,j-1}$, $\mathcal{F}_{i-1,j}$ have ants; $\mathcal{F}_{i+1,j-1}$ has no ant.
Effect. Rule NW does not change Π; it helps search for holes in lower diagonals.

Rule SE. A southeasterly ant-move: $\mathcal{F}_{i,j}$ sends its ant to $\mathcal{F}_{i-1,j+1}$ (along arc SE).
Trigger. $\mathcal{F}_{i,j}$, $\mathcal{F}_{i-1,j-1}$, $\mathcal{F}_{i,j-1}$, $\mathcal{F}_{i-1,j}$, $\mathcal{F}_{i+1,j-1}$ have ants; $\mathcal{F}_{i-1,j+1}$ has no ant.
Effect. Rule SE does not change Π; it helps search for holes in lower diagonals.

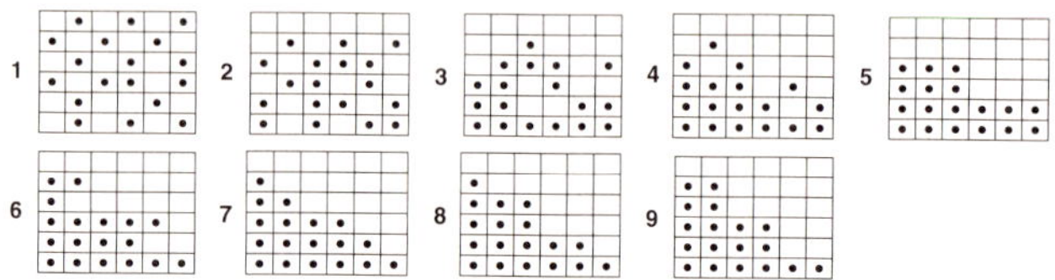

Fig. 4. Nine steps of our parking algorithm

Note 2. The “systolic” strategy of moving ants in phases by direction facilitates the orchestration of ants for many computational problems.

3.3.2 Algorithm Verification and Analysis

Theorem 1. (a) *When Algorithm* Park_in_$\mathcal{Q}_{SW}$ *terminates, all ants reside in a configuration that minimizes $\Pi(t)$.* **(b)** *Each ant in $\mathcal{Q}_{SW}$ when the parking process is initiated reaches its final parking position in $O(n^2)$ FSM cycles.*

Proof (Sketch). Because Algorithm Park_in_$\mathcal{Q}_{SW}$ executes all rules continually: **(a)** Our rules preclude each way that ants can fail to end up properly parked. Specifically: • *Ants end up “left justified” in each row and “bottom justified” in each column.* • *If row i (resp., column j) contains c ants, and row $i+1$ (resp., column $j+1$) contains d ants, then $c-2 \leq d \leq c$.* • *At most one diagonal contains both an ant and a hole.* Thus, the ants end up in a potential-minimizing configuration, then halt. **(b)** The (very conservative) bound on timing follows because each application of Rule SW (resp., S or W) decreases $\Pi(t)$ by 2 (resp., by 1). Some ant follows one of these rules at least every n steps, since ants that cannot follow either rule wander along their current diagonals searching for a hole in the next lower diagonal. Since $\mathcal{Q}_{SW}$ has $\approx n/2$ diagonals, the bound would follow even if only one ant were to move per cycle (which is very unlikely).

4 Having Ants Find Food Quickly

We consider now a problem in which $r \geq 1$ cells of $\mathcal{M}_n$ each contain a single ant and $s \geq 1$ cells each contain a single food item; a cell can contain both an ant and food. Our goal is to ensure that: if $r \leq s$, then each ant gets food; if $r > s$, then every food item is taken by some ant. We consider two variants of this problem. In Section 4.1, each cell of $\mathcal{M}_n$ can contain an ant or a food item; in Section 4.2, a cell can contain an obstacle that precludes the presence of both food and ants, thereby inhibiting the movement of ants (*but not of messages!*). It is simple to allow many kinds of food, even endowed with different priorities.

4.1 Finding Food with No Obstacles

Our algorithm proceeds greedily.

4.1.1 Sketch: Algorithm Find_Food

Food finding begins with $\mathcal{F}_{0,0}$ broadcasting an INITIATE message. Let $\mathcal{F}_{i,j}$ be a generic FSM in $\mathbf{F}_n(\mathcal{F})$. **(a)** If $\mathcal{F}_{i,j}$ contains food, then it broadcasts a food-announcement, with an indication of the direction toward it; e.g., it sends the message "I HAVE FOOD_S" to its northen neighbor, $\mathcal{F}_{i+1,j}$. **(b)** $\mathcal{F}_{i,j}$ relays each food-announcement that it receives into the quadrant "opposite" to the one the message came from, as illustrated in Fig. 5. **(c)** If $\mathcal{F}_{i,j}$ possesses both food and

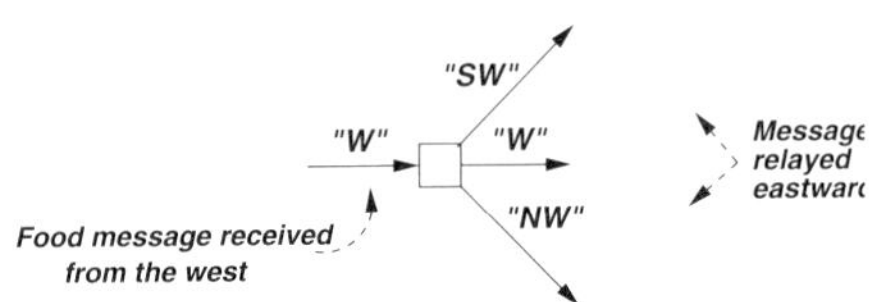

Fig. 5. The regimen for relaying food-announcing messages, for direction W

an ant, then it matches the two and does not announce that food item (though it continues to relay announcements about other food). **(d)** If $\mathcal{F}_{i,j}$ possesses an ant but no food, then it sends "I HAVE AN UNMATCHED ANT" in the direction of $\mathcal{F}_{0,0}$. If it receives any food-announcements, then it selects one (say, for definiteness, in clockwise priority from the north) and moves its ant in the direction of that food. It continues to relay that food-announcement in case it combines multiple collinear messages. **(e)** Food finding is terminated by $\mathcal{F}_{0,0}$ when it ceases to receive either "I HAVE FOOD" or "I HAVE AN UNMATCHED ANT" messages.

4.1.2 Algorithm Verification and Analysis

Theorem 2. *Say that there are r ants and s food items on $\mathcal{M}_n$ when Algorithm* Find_Food *is initiated. If $r \geq s$, then some ant will reach every food item; if $s \geq r$, then every ant will get food.*

Proof (Sketch). A food-announcement is broadcast until an ant reaches the food. Hence, if $s \geq r$, every ant will eventually get food, since competition diminishes with every food-ant match. Conversely, foodless ants keep moving in response to food-announcements; hence, if $r \geq s$, some ant will eventually reach every food item. Termination is guaranteed by the two "unmatched-item" messages. When $\mathcal{F}_{0,0}$ stops hearing either message, it knows that either food or ants have run out. "Eventual" is hard to quantify, but the process is "locally efficient:" each step by a food-announcing message and a food-pursuing ant follows a shortest path to/from food.

An enhancement. By endowing each food-announcing message with a pheromone whose level decreases with each relay, one can have ants pursue the closest food item—at least to within the resolution of the pheromone-level "counter."

4.2 Finding Food with Obstacles

We now allow some nonempty cells of $\mathcal{M}_n$ contain food and/or an ant (as before) while others contain (portions of) obstacles; see Fig. 6. Our goal is to adapt Algorithm Find_Food to accommodate obstacles that inhibit the passage of ants—but, recall, *not* of messages.

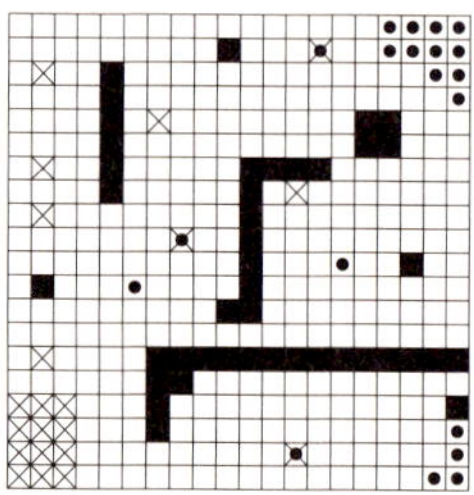

Fig. 6. A mesh some of whose cells contain ants (dots), food (X-es) and obstacles (filled cells); three ants have food

4.2.1 Sketch: Algorithm Find_Food-Avoid_Obstacles

Each FSM $\mathcal{F}$ functions as in Algorithm Find_Food, with the following exceptions. **(a)** If $\mathcal{F}$ contains an obstacle, then it informs its neighbors of that fact. **(b)** If $\mathcal{F}$ contains an ant A *and* receives a food-announcement from an obstacle-containing neighbor, then $\mathcal{F}$ sends A on a clockwise circuit of the obstacle. A proceeds until it either finds a food trail to follow or receives the termination signal. If A's circuit is interrupted by: *(i)* an edge of $\mathcal{M}_n$ for the first time, then A reverses direction; *(ii)* an edge of $\mathcal{M}_n$ for the second time, then A halts and announces "FOOD INACCESSIBLE;" *(iii)* an ant B that has food or is proceeding clockwise around another obstacle, then A switches roles with B; *(iv)* an ant that is proceeding counterclockwise around this obstacle, then A reverses direction.

4.2.2 Algorithm Verification and Analysis

Theorem 3. *Say that there are r ants and s food items that are mutually accessible on $\mathcal{M}_n$ when Algorithm* Find_Food-Avoid_Obstacles *is initiated. If $r \geq s$,* *then one of these ants will reach every food item; if $s \geq r$, then every one of these ants will get food.*

Proof (Sketch). One of the following happens when ant A attempts a clockwise circuit of an obstacle. (**1**) *A finds a food trail that is unblocked by an obstacle.* A follows that trail away from the current obstacle. (Of course, competition may cause it to return later.) (**2**) *A encounters an edge of $\mathcal{M}_n$.* Reversing direction allows A to continue pursuing food, unless all available food is cut off by the obstacle—which causes A to encounter a second edge. (**3**) *A encounters another ant, B, that blocks its path.* If B is following a food trail, then A would recognize that trail also—so we know that B is either sitting on food or skirting an obstacle also. If B's obstacle is distinct from A's, then B, too, is proceeding in a clockwise sense; in this case and when B is sitting on food, having A and B switch roles avoids an impasse. If B is skirting the same obstacle as A, then B has encountered an edge of $\mathcal{M}_n$, so A reverses direction immediately, thereby avoiding an impasse. (**4**) *A keeps circling the obstacle, never encountering an edge of $\mathcal{M}_n$, a food trail, or another ant.* A's journey then ends eventually because of Algorithm Find_Food's termination signal. This occurs, e.g., if other ants reach food item(s), so that all trails are terminated. In all cases, A eventually either is free to pursue food or is told to terminate its search because no unmatched food is accessible.

5 Conclusion

Progress. Our goal has been to motivate and illustrate a conceptual/algorithmic framework that inverts the "natural" relationship between mobile robots and the environment that they navigate. Our adapted "semi-synchronous" cellular automata create a world in which the "factory floor" contains the intelligence, while the identical "ants" are simple devices that respond to commands from the "floor." We have formalized *Cellular ANTomata* and presented two "proof-of-concept" problems that illustrate different aspects of the model's capabilities. *Plans.* Ongoing work focuses on extended algorithmics—e.g., having ants move obstacles, assemble food to specified locations, thread mazes, deal with faults—and on high-level ant-orchestration via, e.g., the "systolic" phasing in Algorithm Park_in_$\mathcal{Q}_{SW}$ and other mechanisms inspired by sources such as [11].

Thanks to: O. Brock, R. Grupen, H. Lee for helpful comments and pointers.

References

1. Böhringer, K.F.: Modeling and controlling parallel tasks in droplet-based microfluidic systems. IEEE Trans. Computer-Aided Design of Integrated Ccts. and Systs. 25, 329–339 (2006)
2. Burks, A.W. (ed.): Essays on Cellular Automata. Univ. Illinois Press, Urbana-Champaign, IL (1970)

3. Chen, L., Xu, X., Chen, Y., He, P.: A novel ant clustering algorithm based on cellular automata. In: IEEE/WIC/ACM Intl. Conf. Intelligent Agent Technology (2004)
4. Chowdhury, D., Guttal, V., Nishinari, K., Schadschneider, A.: A cellular-automata model of flow in ant trails: non-monotonic variation of speed with density. J. Phys. A: Math. Gen. 35, L573–L577 (2002)
5. Cole, S.N.: Real-time computation by n-dimensional iterative arrays of finite-state machines. In: 7th IEEE Symp. on Foundations of Computer Science, pp. 53–77 (1966)
6. Geer, D.: Small robots team up to tackle large tasks. IEEE Distr. Systs. Online 6(12) (2005)
7. Goles, E., Martinez, S. (eds.): Cellular Automata and Complex Systems. Kluwer, Amsterdam (1999)
8. Gruska, J., La Torre, S., Parente, M.: Optimal time and communication solutions of firing squad synchronization problems on square arrays, toruses and rings. In: Calude, C.S., Calude, E., Dinneen, M.J. (eds.) DLT 2004. LNCS, vol. 3340, pp. 200–211. Springer, Heidelberg (2004)
9. `http://www.kivasystems.com/`
10. Moore, E.F. (ed.): The firing squad synchronization problem. Sequential Machines, Selected Papers, pp. 213–214. Addison-Wesley, Reading, MA (1962)
11. Spezzano, G., Talia, D.: The CARPET programming environment for solving scientific problems on parallel computers. Parallel and Distributed Computing Practices 1, 49–61 (1998)
12. von Neumann, J.: The Theory of Self-reproducing Automata. In: Burks, A.W. (ed.) Univ. of Illinois Press, Urbana-Champaign, IL (1966)
13. Wolfram, S. (ed.): Theory and Application of Cellular Automata. Addison-Wesley, Reading, MA (1986)
14. Wolfram, S.: Cellular Automata and Complexity: Collected Papers. Addison-Wesley, Reading, MA (1994)

Key-Attributes Based Optimistic Data Consistency Maintenance Method

Jing Zhou, Yijie Wang, and Sikun Li

National Key Laboratory for Parallel and Distributed Processing,
Institute of Computer, National University of Defense Technology,
Changsha, China, 410073
jingle77@126.com, wwyyjj1971@vip.sina.com, lisikun@263.net.cn

Abstract. Peer-to-peer distributed storage systems usually replicate data objects on multi-node to improve the performance and availability. However, updates may be delayed for P2P systems are generally large-scale and strong distributed, and then the performance of resource location in Internet would be depressed. According to that, an optimistic data consistency maintenance method based on key-attributes is proposed. In the method, updates about key-attributes are separated from user request. Key-updates are propagated by latency-overlay update propagation model, that is, updates are always propagated to nodes having maximum or minimal latency, and assured and uncertain propagation paths of updates are all taken into account. Based on classifying key-update conflicts, a double-level reconciling mechanism including the preprocessing of buffer and the processing of update-log is applied to detect and reconcile conflicts, and then conflicts are solved by policies of last-writer-win and divide-and-rule. Lastly, the technique of managing and maintaining update-log is discussed for the above is deployed based on the information storied in update-log. Delaying key-attributes updates cannot occur by the optimistic disposal method, and then it cannot depress efficiency of resource location based on key-attributes, which adapts well to P2P systems in Internet. The simulation results show it is an effective optimistic consistency maintenance method, achieves good consistency overhead, resource location and access overhead, and has strong robustness.

1 Introduction

WWW has become a ubiquitous media for content sharing and distribution. Applications using the Web spans from small business applications to large scientific calculations. P2P distributed storage system [1, 2, 3] has been widely acknowledged as the fastest growing Internet application ever. By utilizing immense storage resources distributed in Internet, it can adapt dynamic environment of Internet to provide data sharing and storage services for massive users and massive data. It has strong scalability and self-organization, and the popular P2P data sharing systems mostly adopt unstructured topology [4, 5, 6]. Unstructured topology is simple to be constructed and to be maintained, and is prone to support flexible search criteria.

P2P systems replicate data objects on multiple nodes to improve availability and performance [7, 8, 9]. Data replication has many advantages such as avoiding single

I. Stojmenovic et al. (Eds.): ISPA 2007, LNCS 4742, pp. 91–103, 2007.

server failure, reducing access response time and balancing load, but it unavoidably introduces well-known consistency issues. Consistency issue in presence of update requests is one of the major challenges in replicated systems in the Internet [10].

P2P systems are usually large-scale, wide area distributed and strongly dynamic, therefore design deficiency of replication algorithm may bring on updates to be delayed timelessly. The delay of updates would depress the performance of resource search if deferred updates are oriented to key descriptions about data object, which are often used as search criteria.

The method *KBOC* (Key-attributes Based Optimistic data Consistency maintenance method) is proposed to improve the performance of resource location in presence of update issue in P2P distributed storage system. It separates updates on key-attributes from user request, and then propagates key-updates by latency-overlay update propagation model. It divides update conflicts into congruence, coverage, and intersection types, and applies a double-level mechanism to detect and reconcile conflicts, and then resolves conflicts by last-writer-win and divide-and-rule policies.

The remainder of this paper is organized as follows. Section 2 gives correlative conceptions and definitions. Section 3 describes our optimistic method. We evaluate the design from several aspects in Section 4 and conclude in Section 5.

2 Key-Update and Update-Log

2.1 Conceptions and Definitions

P2P distributed storage systems usually store several data resources oriented to specific applications. Each resource has its own features and is described, managed and located according to certain criterions.

***Definition* 1. Key-Attribute Set.** Key-attribute is the data to describe resource attributes, to locate and manage resource and to conduce to data retrieval in P2P systems. Key-attribute Set is the group of key-attributes that belong to homogeneous resource in P2P system, and $KS(Re_s)$ represents the Key-attribute Set of resource Re_s .

According to the above definition, metadata information and search criteria frequently used in search engineer can be regarded as key-attributes of data objects. P2P systems in Internet generally offer resource retrieval based on key-attributes. Each node saves object descriptors used for resource location. The issuer forwards original search requests to other nodes, and then local node accomplishes match operation on search criteria. The update on key-attributes has following features:

- Key-attributes usually fall into some resource attributes. Attributes of data objects are simple to be described, and cannot bring on discrepancy or alter along with the alteration of data objects but attribute value.
- It needs little storage space to record values of key-attributes, so updates on key-attributes are little too.
- Key-attributes are not mutually dependent on each other, and it need not take causality between updates into account.

An update on data object submitted by user consists of several separate modifications to different data segments. After respectively described for each one in semantic, the update converts into a set of modifications semantic descriptions. *KBOC* uses semantic information to represent an update, which is denoted as $Update_{i,j}(DE)$. Here, DE is the logical identifier of updated data object, i is node identifier of issuer, and j is the sequence number of update.

$Update_{i,j}(DE)$ is a group of two-tuple $\langle I_{i,j,k}(DE), U_{i,j,k}(DE)\rangle$, where $I_{i,j,k}(DE)$ is the description about updated data information, $U_{i,j,k}(DE)$ is the corresponding information after being updated, and k is the serial number of update item. We give the following definition based on above semantic description.

***Definition* 2. Key-Update.** An update $Update_{i,j}(DE)$ is the key-update about data object DE if it meets the following expression:

$$\left\{I_{i,j,k}(DE) \middle| (DE \in Re_s) \wedge \left(\langle I_{i,j,k}(DE), U_{i,j,k}(DE)\rangle \in Update_{i,j}(DE)\right)\right\} \subseteq KS(Re_s)$$

Updates submitted by users may contain operations about key or un-key information. Our method only studies propagation and conflict of key-updates. After updates are described in semantic, it is easy to extract key-updates from user requests.

2.2 Key-Update Conflict

Suppose u_1 and u_2 are updates on the same data object and there are no causality between them, the key-attributes they refer to are $\{k_1,k_2,k_3\}$ and $\{k_1,k_2,k_4,k_5\}$ respectively, and update u_1 is issued before update u_2 and replica A receives update u_2 firstly. So, update u_2 would be really accepted by replica A until it receives update u_1.
However, the followings are noticeable.

① *Pseudo-conflict* updates. There are no conflict between update u_1 and update u_2 about key-attributes $\{k_4,k_5\}$, and simple order preserving between updates would prevent the propagation of pseudo-conflict updates.

② *Insignificant* updates. Even if updates were applied by the order of u_1u_2, final values of key-attributes $\{k_1,k_2,k_3,k_4,k_5\}$ would be $\{k_1(u_2),k_2(u_2),k_3(u_1),k_4(u_2),k_5(u_2)\}$. The operation that u_1 points to $\{k_1,k_2\}$ is covered with u_2.

③ *Losing* updates. If updates were applied without keeping the order, update that has early issue-clock would be refused when it was received after updates with later issue-clock had been received. So, key-attribute k_3 would not be updated.

***Definition* 3. Key-Update Conflict.** Two updates $Update_{i,j}(DE)$ and $Update_{l,m}(DE)$ are conflictive if and only if $KS_{i,j}(DE) \cap KS_{l,m}(DE) \neq \varnothing$.

Here, $KS_{i,j}(DE) = \left\{I_{i,j,k}(DE) \middle| (DE \in Re_s) \wedge \left(\langle I_{i,j,k}(DE), U_{i,j,k}(DE)\rangle \in Update_{i,j}(DE)\right)\right\}$ and

$KS_{l,m}(DE) = \left\{I_{l,m,n}(DE) \middle| (DE \in Re_s) \wedge \left(\langle I_{l,m,n}(DE), U_{l,m,n}(DE)\rangle \in Update_{l,m}(DE)\right)\right\}$.

$\boldsymbol{Rlist(p)}$	// **Replica index table**, node p uses it to record local known replicas information.
DE : Logical identifier of data object	
$S(p)$: A group of replica identifiers that node p has known about data object DE	
$\boldsymbol{Kupda(p, Re_s)}$	// **Key-update table**, node p extracts key-updates about resource Re_s and records them in it.
DE : Logical identifier of data object	$U\_body_{i,j} : Update_{i,j}(DE)$
$T_{i,j}$: Wall-clock when update is issued	$Tag_{i,j}$: Update tag with defaulting 0
$P_{i,j}$: Set $\langle N \rangle$	// Node N has received update $Update_{i,j}(DE)$ and $P_{i,j}[0]$ is the issuer of the update.
$UP_{i,j}$: Set $\langle N \rangle$	// The field of $UP_{i,j}$ is a group of nodes that have indefinitely received the update.

Fig. 1. Data Structures

In order to make the causation of conflict explicit, key-update conflict is divided into three types as follows.

- *Congruence* type (*I* type): $KS_{i,j}(DE) = KS_{l,m}(DE)$
- *Coverage* type (*II* type): $(KS_{i,j}(DE) \subset KS_{l,m}(DE)) \vee (KS_{i,j}(DE) \supset KS_{l,m}(DE))$
- *Intersection* type (*III* type): $(KS_{i,j}(DE) - KS_{l,m}(DE) \neq \varnothing) \wedge (KS_{l,m}(DE) - KS_{i,j}(DE) \neq \varnothing)$
  and $(KS_{l,m}(DE) \cap KS_{i,j}(DE) \neq \varnothing)$

2.3 Data Structures in Update-Log

Update-log is organized by following the states of replicas and recording propagation paths. It is not only used for communications during update propagations, but helping to achieving eventual consistency when node failure or network partition arises. The update-log in each node has two data structures, as are shown in Figure 1.

With not misconceiving, all expressions would omit data object information for concisely expressing. For example, $Update_{i,j}(DE)$ would be abbreviated to $Update_{i,j}$, and $KS_{i,j}(DE)$ would be abbreviated to $KS_{i,j}$.

3 Key-Attributes Based Optimistic Consistency Maintenance

The occurrence of *KBOC* is to meet the requirement of rapidly updating on key-attributes in P2P distributed storage systems. *KBOC* is based on decentralized and unstructured P2P system, including three modules: key-update propagation model, detecting and reconciling key-update conflict, and maintenance of update-log.

The following process maintains consistency of key-attributes: ① The issue node receives updates from the user. ② Key-updates are extracted, and then assigned serial number in the domain of updates about the same data object. ③Key-updates are written into the key-update table. ④ Network latency among nodes recorded in replica index table is gotten, and then update propagation objects are selected. ⑤ Propagating key-updates by update propagation model introduced in Section 3.1. ⑥ One replica may synchronously receive several key-updates from other nodes and records them into update buffer, and then deals them with preprocessing. ⑦ The remainder updates after being preprocessed are processed to detect conflict with updates in key-update table, and outdated updates are removed and new updates are added. Then updates are continually propagated from step ④ to step ⑦.

3.1 Key-Update Propagation Model

P2P systems have strongly dynamic behavior, and the information of replica is not full or same for each node, which is brought by the failure of network connection or node and network latency. It is trustless to transfer updates by multicast in such environment, and the replica would continue to disperse updates in the form of multicast just after it receives them, which can bring on redundant messages.

Blindness and redundancy should be avoided as possible during update propagation. *KBOC* utilizes two mechanisms to propagate key-updates.

Double-delay-biased: Node N sorts other known replicas according to network latency. Then it selects nodes having minimal (min) or maximal (max) network latency with node N to transmit updates. It can assure that updates are received by other replicas, offer updates wide-area scattering, and avoid local converge of updates.

Double-path-overlay: *KBOC* records two groups of nodes that are $P_{i,j}$ and $UP_{i,j}$ shown in Figure 1, and takes them into account for propagating updates. For nodes min and max , it could not ensure that they can all receive the propagated update though it may be transmitted to them from the same node at one time. Therefore, min is regarded as dubious node and is recorded in $UP_{i,j}$ of node max , as same to max . $P_{i,j}$ can avoid transferring redundant message, and $UP_{i,j}$ can solve the problem of unreliable information propagation.

3.2 Detecting and Reconciling Updates Conflicts

KBOC utilizes two rules to reconcile key-update conflicts.

- Last-writer-win (*LWW*): It aims at conflicts of *congruence* type. It is used for solving problems of *insignificant* updates, and the update that has later issue-clock would prevail over others for updates on the same group of key-attributes.
- Divide-and-rule (*DAR*): It aims at conflicts of *coverage* type and *intersection* type, which is used for solving problems of *pseudo-conflict* updates or *losing* updates. It assures that the former rule is valid, does not lose significant updates, and avoids the delay of key-update propagation that is brought by pseudo-conflict.

KBOC detects and reconciles key-update conflicts by utilizing double-level mechanism as follows.

- Preprocessing key-update buffer: For any replica r , all the updates propagated from other replicas are firstly recorded in local key-update buffer. The setting of buffer preprocessing has following advantages: ①Several propagation paths of duplicate updates are united and the redundancy is removed, where replica r may receive duplicate updates from different replica because updates are transferred along several paths. ②The conflict of *congruence* type can be detected and solved ahead of time, which would depress computation overhead of handling key-update table. Figure 3 shows the preprocess algorithm.

- Detecting and reconciling conflicts in key-update table: Updates in buffer after being preprocessed are compared with that in key-update table, where *KBOC* would distinguish types of key-update conflict, analyze causations, and introduce corresponding solving scheme. Figure 4 shows the relevant algorithm.

After the algorithm, key-update table meets followings.

① Though updates may be separated in order to simplify latter comparisons during the algorithm, there is not more than one item for an update lastly. It is because that *KBOC* unites such updates before the end of algorithm, which can reduce the number of propagated updates and then depress computation overhead for replicas that would receive updates next.

```
Procedure ProcessBuffer ( Peer $p$, Resource $Re_s$ )
  Get the set of data objects from the buffer in node $p$, and put it to $DS$ ;
  for each $DE \in DS$
    if $Size(Buffer(p), DE) > 1$                                   // There are several updates on $DE$ in buffer.
    then if $\exists_{Update_{i,j}, Update_{l,m} \in Buffer(p)} (P_{i,j}[0] = P_{l,m}[0] \wedge T_{i,j} = T_{l,m})$   //Judge if there are duplicate updates.
      then $P_{i,j} \leftarrow P_{i,j} \cup P_{l,m}$ ; $UP_{i,j} \leftarrow (UP_{i,j} \cup UP_{l,m}) - P_{i,j} - P_{l,m}$ ;   // Unite propagation paths.
           Delete the item of duplicate update from buffer.
      if $\exists_{Update_{i,j}, Update_{l,m} \in Buffer(p)} (KS_{i,j} = KS_{l,m})$   //Judge if there are conflicts of $I$ type.
      then Compare $T_{i,j}$ with $T_{l,m}$ , and suppose $T_{i,j} \geq T_{l,m}$ ;
           Delete the item of update $Update_{l,m}$ from buffer because it has early issue-clock.
  Get the information of key-updates in buffer, and put it into $L(DE)$ ;
  $ProcessKupda(p, Re_s, L(DE))$ ; return;    // Call the algorithm of detecting and reconciling conflicts.
```

Fig. 2. The preprocess algorithm

② It is impossible that there are same key-attributes for any two items, namely $\forall_{Update_{i,j}(D_{s,d}), Update_{l,m}(D_{s,d}) \in Kupda(p, Re_s)} (KS_{i,j}(D_{s,d}) \cap KS_{l,m}(D_{s,d}) = \varnothing)$.

③ Suppose the number of key-attributes for any data resource is k , the number of items for any data object of the resource in key-update table is no more than k .

3.3 Update-Log Maintenance

Key-updates are forwarded based on replica information recorded in replica index table, and key-update conflicts are detected and reconciled based on information in key-update table. Next, we show how to maintain them.

(1) Maintenance of replica index table

Replica information in replica index table is maintained to keep consistency when replica addition or removal arises, which can avoid transmitting redundant information and accelerate the convergence of update propagation.

KBOC takes a replica addition or removal as an update to replica index table. For the message of describing replica addition or removal is small, multicast is utilized to issue it by the added or removed replica. The replica receiving it firstly updates local replica index table, and then forwards it to replicas besides the sender by multicast. If a replica receives a duplicate message, it would put the message on one side.

There is the contextual sequence between the addition and the removal of the same replica, so the rule of "first add then removal" must be observed. If replica r receives a message about removing replica r', while replica r' is not recorded in local replica index table of replica r, consistency maintenance for network partition is called, as is introduced next. Replica addition or removal is decided according to the global replication strategy, and it cannot occur that one replica is immediately removed after it is added. Therefore, we can conclude that replica r may be in network partition for a previous period and it lost communication with some replicas.

(2) Maintenance of key-update table

Key-update table records the information of updates received by local replica. If receiving updates that are unseen or have later issue-clock than the existing updates of the same object, the replica records them in local key-update table and then forwards them to others.

If the set of replicas of data object DE recorded in replica index table comprises the union of $P_{i,j}$ and $UP_{i,j}$ of update $Update_{i,j}(DE)$, in order to avoid the incompletion of propagation, $Update_{i,j}(DE)$ is transmitted to the replicas in $UP_{i,j}$ until $UP_{i,j}$ is null. Incompletion of propagation is brought by uncertainty of multicast.

- Replica r recovers from failure. For each local data object DE, replica r orders latency with all the replicas of DE that are listed in local replica index table and gets replica r' that has minimum latency. Then, it compares the latest issue-clock between replica r and r'. If replica r is lesser, it replicates records of DE in key-update table in replica r', and replicates relevant information in replica index table in replica r' to substitute local records.
- Replica r recovers from network partition.
  ① Get replica r' to reconcile. For each local data object DE, replica r gets update $Update_{i,j}(DE)$, the issue-clock of which is latest and the interval between that and current clock does not exceed threshold T_0. Then, it gets a set of nodes SS by uniting $P_{i,j}$ and $UP_{i,j}$ of $Update_{i,j}(DE)$. A set of nodes S is got by uniting SS of all local data object, and then we deem that replica r and the nodes in set S were in the same partition previously. For each data object DE in replica r, replica r gets set S' and selects replica r' to reconcile. Here, $S'=(S(r)-S)|\langle DE,S(r)\rangle\in Rlist(r)$, and r' is a member of set S' and the latency between it and replica r is minimal.
  ② Reconcile with replica r'. Replica r reads information of key-updates in replica r' and writes them into local buffer, and then calls the algorithm of detecting and reconciling key-update conflicts in Section 3.2. Then, replica r' replicates information of key-updates in replica r, and two replicas achieve consistency. Additionally, two replicas compare and reconcile replica index tables.

Procedure ProcessKupda (Peer p, Resource Re_s , *UpdateList L(DE)*)
for each $Update_{l,m} \in L(DE)$ $tag = 0$; $E_{ks} \leftarrow \varnothing$; $N_{ks} \leftarrow \varnothing$; $G_{ks} \leftarrow \varnothing$;
for each $Update_{i,j} \in Kupda(p, Re_s)$ //Detect conflicts between updates in buffer and key-update table.
if $(KS_{l,m} \cap KS_{i,j} \neq \varnothing)$ **then** $tag = 1$; //There is conflict, and then judge the type of conflict.
if $KS_{i,j} = KS_{l,m}$ // The conflict is of *I* type.
then if $T_{l,m} < T_{i,j}$ **then break**; //According to *LWW*, if update in buffer has early issue-clock, it is omitted.
if $(T_{l,m} = T_{i,j}) \wedge (P_{l,m}[0] = P_{i,j}[0])$ // The update in buffer is a duplicate.
then $P_{i,j} \leftarrow P_{i,j} \cup P_{l,m}$; $UP_{i,j} \leftarrow (UP_{i,j} \cup UP_{l,m}) - P_{i,j} - P_{l,m}$;**break**; // Unite propagation paths.
else Delete the item of update $Update_{i,j}$ from key-update table because it has early issue-clock;
Add new item $(p, Re_s, DE, U\_body_{l,m}, T_{l,m}, P_{l,m} \cup \{p\}, UP_{l,m}, 1)$ to key-update table; **break**;
if $KS_{i,j} \supset KS_{l,m}$ // The conflict is of *II* type.
then if $T_{l,m} < T_{i,j}$ **then break**;//According to *LWW*, if update in buffer has early issue-clock, it is omitted.
else Alter the item of update $Update_{i,j}$, where the value of attribute $U\_body_{i,j}$ is modified to $\{\langle I_{i,j,k}, U_{i,j,k}\rangle | \langle I_{i,j,k}, U_{i,j,k}\rangle \in Update_{i,j} \wedge I_{i,j,k} \in KS_{i,j} \wedge I_{i,j,k} \notin KS_{l,m}\}$ and others are unaltered;
// According to *DAR* rule.
Add new item $(p, Re_s, DE, U\_body_{l,m}, T_{l,m}, P_{l,m} \cup \{p\}, UP_{l,m}, 1)$ to key-update table; **break**;
if $KS_{i,j} \subset KS_{l,m}$ // The conflict is of *II* type.
then if $T_{l,m} < T_{i,j}$ **then** $E_{ks} \leftarrow E_{ks} \cup \{KS_{i,j}\}$;
// E_{ks} records key-attributes that are referred by winners in key-update table
else $N_{ks} \leftarrow N_{ks} \cup \{KS_{i,j}\}$; // N_{ks} records key-attributes that are referred by winners in buffer
Delete the item of update $Update_{i,j}$ from key-update table because it has early issue-clock;
Add new item $(p, Re_s, DE, U\_body'_{l,m}, T_{l,m}, P_{l,m} \cup \{p\}, UP_{l,m}, 1)$ to key-update table, where $U\_body'_{l,m} = \{\langle I_{l,m,n}, U_{l,m,n}\rangle | \langle I_{l,m,n}, U_{l,m,n}\rangle \in Update_{l,m} \wedge I_{l,m,n} \in KS_{i,j}\}$; // *DAR* rule.
if $(KS_{i,j} - KS_{l,m} \neq \varnothing) \wedge (KS_{l,m} - KS_{i,j} \neq \varnothing) \wedge (KS_{l,m} \cap KS_{i,j} \neq \varnothing)$ // The conflict is of *III* type.
then if $T_{l,m} < T_{i,j}$ **then** $G_{ks} \leftarrow KS_{l,m} - E_{ks} - N_{ks} - (KS_{i,j} \cap KS_{l,m})$; $E_{ks} \leftarrow E_{ks} \cup \{KS_{i,j} \cap KS_{l,m}\}$;
// G_{ks} records key-attributes that would be referred by new separated updates and not referred by any one in key-update table.
else $G_{ks} \leftarrow KS_{l,m} - E_{ks} - N_{ks}$; $N_{ks} \leftarrow N_{ks} \cup \{KS_{i,j} \cap KS_{l,m}\}$;
Alter the item of update $Update_{i,j}$, where the value of attribute $U\_body_{i,j}$ is modified to $\{\langle I_{i,j,k}, U_{i,j,k}\rangle | \langle I_{i,j,k}, U_{i,j,k}\rangle \in Update_{i,j} \wedge I_{i,j,k} \in KS_{i,j} \wedge I_{i,j,k} \notin KS_{l,m}\}$ and others are unaltered;
if $G_{ks} \neq \varnothing$ **then** Add new item $(p, Re_s, DE, U\_body'_{l,m}, T_{l,m}, P_{l,m} \cup \{p\}, UP_{l,m}, 1)$ to key-update table, where $U\_body'_{l,m} = \{\langle I_{l,m,n}, U_{l,m,n}\rangle | \langle I_{l,m,n}, U_{l,m,n}\rangle \in Update_{l,m} \wedge I_{l,m,n} \in G_{ks}\}$;
if $tag = 0$ **then** Add new item $(p, Re_s, DE, U\_body_{l,m}, T_{l,m}, P_{l,m} \cup \{p\}, UP_{l,m}, 1)$ to key-update table;
if $\exists_{Update_{i,j}, Update_{l,m} \in Kupda} (T_{i,j} = T_{l,m} \wedge P_{i,j}[0] = P_{l,m}[0])$
then Unite items of updates that are issued by the same replica at the same time; **return**;

Fig. 3. The algorithm of detecting and reconciling key-update conflicts

4 Simulation

Anti-entropy [11] is a reconciliation mechanism, in which each node periodically reconciles with another node. According to partner selection policy for session, we choose three representative methods to compare with ours. The *uniform* policy assigns every replica an equal probability of being selected as partner. For *latency-biased* policy, nearby replicas have a greater probability than more distant replicas of being randomly selected. For *tree* policy, replicas are organized into a tree, and messages are propagated randomly along the arcs in the tree.

OptorSim [12] was developed to evaluate the effectiveness of replica optimization algorithms. In our simulations, we utilize OptorSim to construct a P2P distributed environment with 1,000 nodes. The system storages 10 types data resources. The number of key-attributes is 300, and each resource randomly selects 50 to compose its key-attribute set. There are 100 data objects for each resource, each data object is 1GB, and key-attributes of each data object are randomly assigned when it is created. Each node records information of key-attributes for local data objects.

According to the range of the number of key-attributes that an update would refer to, we divide update into six types shown in Table 1. For any update of resource Re_s, the update of T_x type covers k key-attributes randomly chosen from $KS(Re_s)$, where k falls into the range of the number of key-attributes that corresponds to T_x type.

(1) Consistency Overhead

The results comparing *KBOC* with other methods in consistency overhead for fixed and dynamically altered number of replicas are shown in Figure 5 and 6. The simulator creates fixed number of replicas for each data object at initialization, and distributes them to randomly chosen nodes. It is run until 5,000 updates have been processed. For the latter, 10,000 random accesses to data object are additionally disposed, and replica addition or removal is done according to frequency of access.

Table 1. Update types

Type identifier	The number of key-attributes	Probability
T_1	$[1,5]$	25%
T_2	$(5,10]$	40%
T_3	$(10,20]$	25%
T_4	$(20,30]$	6%
T_5	$(30,40]$	3%
T_6	$(40,50]$	1%

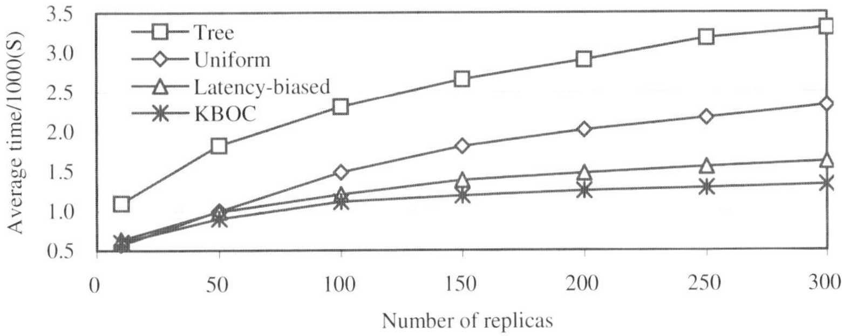

Fig. 4. Relation between the number of replicas and average update propagation time

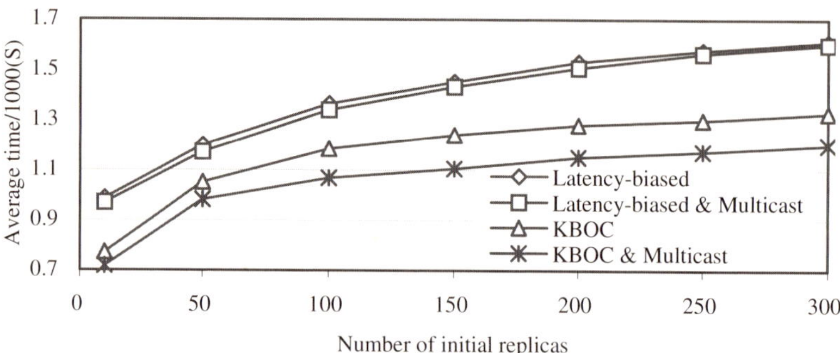

Fig. 5. Relation between the number of initial replicas and average update propagation time

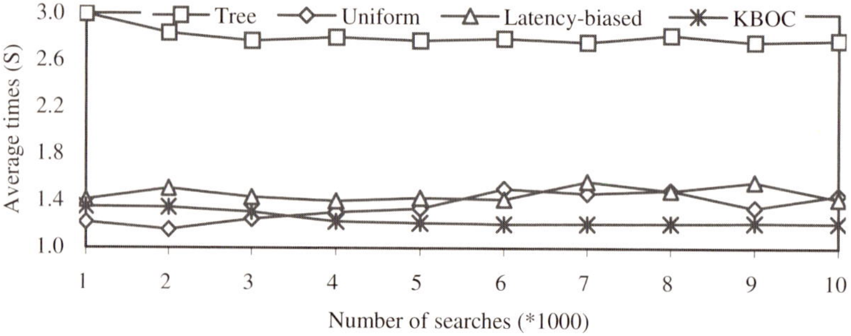

Fig. 6. Relation between the number of searches and average resource location time

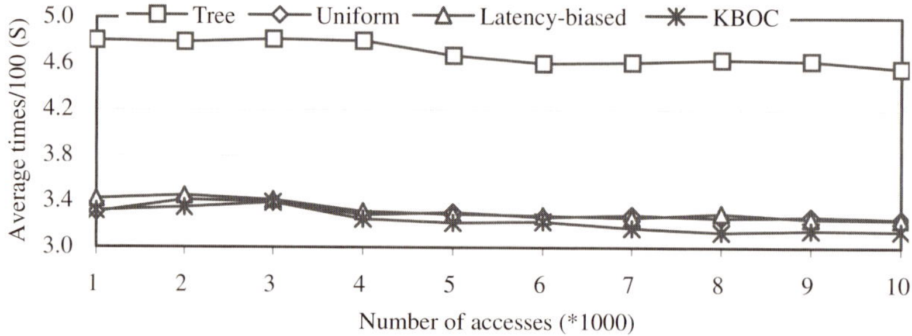

Fig. 7. Relation between the number of accesses and average resource access time

The result in Figure 5 shows that the tree method has worst performance because of restricting to the hierarchy among nodes, the uniform method performs quite well for small numbers of replicas, and the update propagation overhead of our method is less than latency-biased. The main reason is that *KBOC* always propagates updates to nodes with maximal and minimal communication latency without other restriction.

The result in Figure 6 shows that multicast can improve performance of *KBOC*. Replicas early learn the existence of new added replicas, and then updates can be

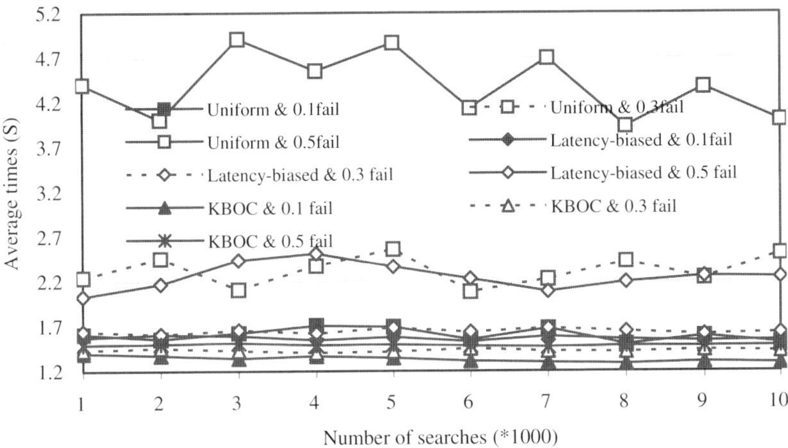

Fig. 8. Relation between the number of searches and average resource location time in node failure

propagated in wider area. However, for latency-biased method, one best replica is replicated to create new replica and replicas always reconcile with the least latency one. Therefore, it is indifferent to the addition of remote replica and multicast has little effect on performance.

(2) Resource Location and Resource Access Overhead

The distinction between resource location and resource access is that the former only needs to search data object, but the latter need read located data object from remote node to local node. Here, two-way random forwarding method is used to locate data.

The results comparing *KBOC* with other methods in resource location overhead and resource access overhead are shown in Figure 7 and 8. The simulator is run until 5,000 updates had been processed, and at the same time, it disposes 10,000 random processes (search or access) to data objects. The process latency is averaged over 200 latest processes for each interval of 1000. At simulator initialization, each node stores 100 randomly chosen data objects. Each search is issued from a random node, and it randomly chooses 10 key-attributes in its own key-attribute set to search.

The results in Figure 7 show that *KBOC* has better performance of resource location. The main reason is that it emphases on solving conflicts of key-updates, and the rapid propagation of key-update helps to reducing the time of resource location.

The results in Figure 8 show that located replica is near to access node with update propagation accelerated, and then remote data transmission can be avoided. Additionally, the system creates new data replicas with the increasing of accesses, and more replicas can decrease access overhead in a little range.

(3) Robustness

The results comparing *KBOC* with other methods in node failure are shown in Figure 9. Each node stores 100 randomly chosen data objects at initialization, randomly chosen $1000\times node\ failure\ ratio$ nodes are scattered in failure during simulation, and failure nodes would recover after random time.

The results show that node failure has furthest effect to uniform method because nodes blindly deliver updates to others without considering their states, and *KBOC* has stronger robustness. The main reason is that updates are forwarded according to latency, so they can be always propagated to active replicas.

5 Conclusions

The optimistic method *KBOC* is proposed according to the requirement of rapidly updating key information in distributed system in Internet, which is not referred in traditional replication algorithms. In *KBOC*, key-updates are separated from user update request firstly, and then propagated by latency-overlay update propagation model. Double-level mechanism is applied to detect and reconcile key-update conflicts, and key-update conflicts are solved by last-writer-win and divide-and-rule rules. Maintenance of update-log after node failure or network partition is discussed.

KBOC has following features: ①It solves uncertainty, blindness and redundancy of update propagation, and improves the performance. ②Key-update conflicts are divided into *congruence*, *coverage*, and *intersection* three types, which are defined with different cause. The dividing of conflicts could make a concrete analysis of concrete problems. ③The optimistic disposal on key-updates accommodates well to the requirement of P2P systems in Internet. It cannot occur that the performance of resource location based on key-attributes is depressed because of delaying key-updates. ④The consistency of key-updates can be achieved after node failure or network partition.

The simulation results show that it is an effective data consistency maintenance method to dispose key-updates for P2P distributed storage system in Internet. It can achieve good consistency overhead and cannot affect the performance of resource location based on updated key-attributes. It has good access overhead and strong robustness, and is applicable to P2P systems with strongly dynamic behavior.

References

1. Dahlin, M., Gao, L., Nayate, A., Venkataramani, A., Yalagandula, P., Zheng, J.: PRACTI: Replication for Large-scale Systems. Technical Report, TR-04-28, University of Texas at Austin, Austin (2004)
2. Saito, Y., Karamanoli, C., Karlsson, M., Mahalingam, M.: Taming Aggressive Replication in the Pangaea Wide-area File System. In: Proceedings of the fifth symposium on Operating systems design and implementation, pp. 15–30. ACM Press, New York (2002)
3. Byung, B., Kang, H.: S2D2: A framework for scalable and secure optimistic replication [Ph.D. Thesis]. University of California, Berkeley (2004)
4. van Renesse, R., Schneider, F.B.: Chain replication for supporting high throughout and availability. In: Proceedings of sixth symposium on operating systems design & implementation (OSDI'04), San Francisco, CA (2004)
5. Wang, Z., Das, S.K., Kumar, M., Shen, H.: Update Propagation through Replica Chain in Decentralized and Unstructured P2P Systems. In: Proceedings of the 4th IEEE International Conference on Peer-to-Peer Computing (P2P 2004), pp. 64–71. IEEE Computer Society, Washington (2004)

6. Leontiadis, E., Dimakopoulos, V.V., Pitoura, E.: Creating and Maintaining Replicas in Unstructured Peer-to-Peer Systems. Technical Report, TR2006 -01, Department of Computer Science, University of Ioannina, Ioannina, Greece (2006)
7. Yu, H., Vahdat, A.: Consistent and Automatic Replica Regeneration. ACM Transactions on Storage 1(1), 3–37 (2005)
8. Vecchio, D.D., Son, S.H.: Flexible Update Management in Peer-to-Peer Database Systems. In: Proceedings of the 9th International Database Engineering & Application Symposium (IDEAS 05), pp. 435–444. IEEE Computer Society, Washington (2005)
9. Wang, Z., Kumar, M., Das, S.K., Shen, H.: File Consistency Maintenance through Virtual Servers in P2P Systems. In: Proceedings of the 11th IEEE Symposium on Computers and Communications (ISCC 2006), pp. 435–441. IEEE Computer Society, Washington (2006)
10. Loukopoulos, T., Ahmad, I., Papadias, D.: An Overview of Data Replication on the Internet. In: Proceedings of the International Symposium on Parallel Architectures, Algorithms and Networks (ISPAN), pp. 694–711. IEEE Computer Society, Los Alamitos (2002)
11. Petersen, K., Spreitzer, M.J., Terry, D.B.: Flexible update propagation for weakly consistent replication. In: 16th ACM Symposium on Operating Systems Principles, pp. 288–301. ACM Press, New York (1997)
12. Bell, W.H., Cameron, D.G., Capozza, L., Millar, P., Stockinger, K., Zini, F.: Optorsim: a grid simulator for studying dynamic data replication strategies. International Journal of High Performance Computing Applications 17(4), 403–416 (2003)

Parallelization Strategies for the Points of Interests Algorithm on the Cell Processor

Tarik Saidani, Lionel Lacassagne, Samir Bouaziz, and Taj Muhammad Khan

Université de Paris-Sud, Institut d'Electronique Fondamentale, Bâtiment 220, F-91405 Orsay Cedex, France
firstname.name@ief.u-psud.fr

Abstract. The Cell processor is a typical example of a heterogeneous multiprocessor-on-chip architecture that uses several levels of parallelism to deliver high performance. Closing the gap between peak performance and sustained performance is the challenge for software tool developers and the application developers. Image processing and media applications are typical "main stream" applications. In this paper, we use the Harris algorithm for detection of points of interest (PoI) in an image as a benchmark to compare the performance of several parallel schemes on a Cell processor. The impact of the DMA controlled data transfers and the synchronizations between SPEs explains the differences between the performance of the different parallelization schemes. These results will be used to design a tool for an efficient mapping of image processing applications on multi-core architectures.

1 Introduction

Recent trends in designing general purpose processors have focused on increasing Thread Level Parallelism - for example through Chip Multiprocessing architectures - rather than improving clock frequencies of single-task scalar systems which posed computing and energy efficiency problems. One way of facing these problems was found in SIMD architectures, either by duplicating complete processing units (according to Flynn's definition), or by inserting dedicated SIMD instructions inside existing CPUs (aka SWAR for SIMD Within A Register) - like Altivec or SSE. A good example can be found in the IBM Cell Processor[1]. However, developers are now faced with implementation problems, such as efficiently distributing code among the processing elements and generating DMA (Direct Memory Access) requests required by data flows. This paper is organized as follows. A presentation of the Cell Broadband Engine and applications that have already been benchmarked on the Cell are given, followed by a description of the Harris points of interest algorithms and its different implementation models. The influence of transfers on performance is then discussed. Finally, effective performance results are provided and discussed. The final part gives conclusions about our experiments and gives perspectives for future works.

2 The Cell Processor

The Cell processor is a heterogeneous, multi-core chip consisting of one 64-bit power processor element (PPE), eight specialized units called synergistic processors (SPE) [2],

I. Stojmenovic et al. (Eds.): ISPA 2007, LNCS 4742, pp. 104–112, 2007.

other interfacing units and a high bandwidth bus called Element Interconnect Bus (EIB), that allows communications between the different components. Assuming a clock speed of 3.2 Ghz, the Cell processor has a theoretical peak performance of 204.8 Gflops/s in single precision and 14.6 Gflops in double precision. The EIB supports a peak bandwidth of 204.8 Gbytes/s for internal transfers (when performing 8 simultaneous non-colliding 25GB/s transfers). The PPE unit is a traditional 64-bit PowerPC Processor with a vector multimedia extension (VMX). This Cell's main processor is in charge of running the OS, and coordinating the SPEs. Each SPE consists in a synergistic processor unit (SPU) and a Memory Flow Controller (MFC). The SPE holds a local storage of 256 KB, and a 128-bit SWAR (very close to Altivec) unit dedicated to high-performance data-intensive computation. The MFC holds a 1D DMA controller, that is in charge of transferring data from external devices to the local store, or writing back computation results to main memory. One of the main characteristics of the Cell processor is its distributed memory hierarchy. The main drawback of this kind of memory, is that the software must handle the limited size of the local storage of each SPE, by issuing DMA transfers from or toward main storage.

3 Related Work

The different examples of implementations on the Cell processor ([3], [4], [5] and [6]) consider a SPMD (Single Program Multiple Data) parallelization model on micro-benchmarks (few operators with a reduced amount of transfers), and do not explore other models. This implementation strategy is the most obvious one, and does not require any complex synchronization mechanism to work. In our paper, we present the Harris points of interest (POI) algorithm which is representative of several image processing algorithms, since it includes multiplication, thresholding and convolution kernels. It is also an interesting case study because its data flow graph allows different mapping strategies on the Cell processor. By exploring different parallelization schemes, we can show different aspects of the influence of DMA transfers on the performance, and compare practical results with the expectations.

4 The Harris Points of Interests Algorithm

In our paper we use a common image processing algorithm known as Harris points of interest. This application was chosen because its operator graph allows different implementation models. The Harris algorithm 4 is a mix of operators on pixels and convolution kernels. It is composed of four steps of basic operators, with up to three parallel operations, and many transfers with or without borders, in details we have:

1. a gradient computation (usually a Sobel X & Y operators),
2. three parallel multiplications, to combine first derivatives together,
3. three parallel Smoothing operations (usually a 3×3 Gauss Kernel),
4. a coarsity computation (Harris point operator) : $K = S_{xx}S_{yy} - S_{xy}^2$

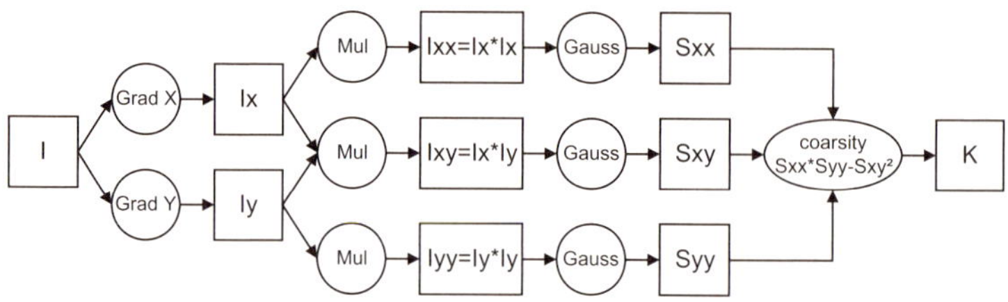

Fig. 1. Harris algorithm

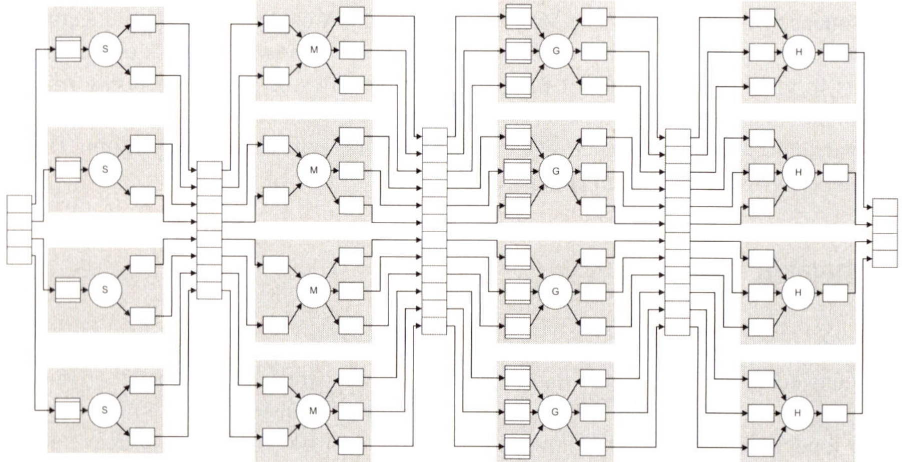

Fig. 2. POI SPMD model

5 Implementation Models for the POI Algorithm

5.1 SPMD Model

In all the following figures, S stands for the Sobel operator, M for the multiplication, G for Gauss and H for Harris. The gray rectangles represents and SPE. The SPMD programming model (Fig. 2) equally divides the image into eight regions of processing (RoPs) blocks, mapped on the SPUs (in the figure, only 4 SPEs are drawn to get a smaller figure, but 8 SPEs are actually used). All SPUs execute the same program/code.The PPU lets the SPUs run one operator on the whole image before proceeding with the next operator. For example, it will not issue the command for Multiplication operator until all the SPUs have finished performing the Sobel operator and the whole of the image has been transfered back into the XDR.

5.2 Conventionnal Pipeline Model

This implementation of the POI algorithm (Fig. 3) consists in mapping the graph in pipeline fashion, where the RoP consist in the entire image. This way, we considerably

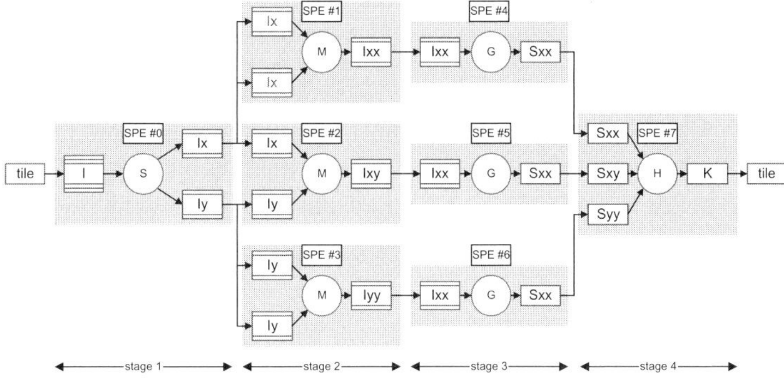

Fig. 3. POI simple pipeline model

serialize the algorithm, and maximize the amount of transfers between SPEs. Assuming that most of the transfers are performed serially, the contention rate on the bus is minimized. The transfers in this version are characterized by top and bottom borders, added for the convolution kernels. Left and right borders where removed by performing registers renaming.

5.3 Half Pipeline Model

In this version (Fig. 4), we rely on the TLP offered by the Cell processor by merging two successive operators in pairs, the Sobel with the Multiplication, and Gauss with Harris. Thus, we divide the graph into two threads, that can be duplicated four times to fill in the entire set of SPEs. Unlike the previous version, and considering that there are four threads running concurrently in each step, the EIB bandwidth can be considerably affected because of the important amount of concurrent transfers.

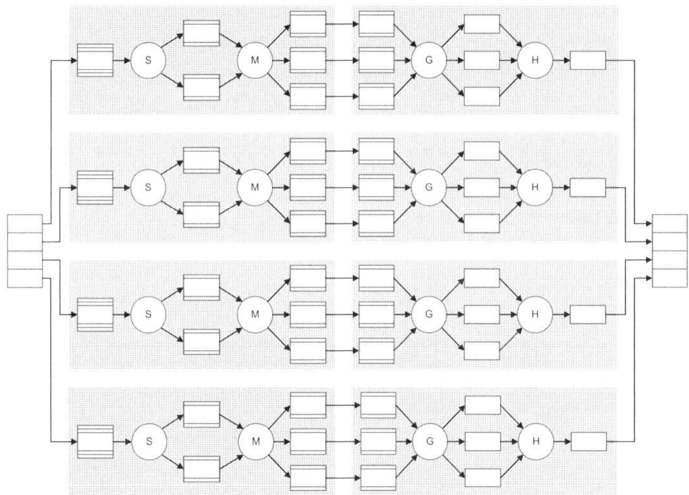

Fig. 4. Half Pipeline model

5.4 Models Comparison

The SPMD model is the easiest one to implement. Since every SPE performs the same computations on different input data, a single piece of code is developed and sent to each processing element. However, doing so implies storing the intermediate results either in the processor local memory (thus drastically restraining the size of the processed tile), or in the central memory, which leads to many transfers and thus communication bus contentions. However, if the simple pipeline model fully benefits from inter-SPEs communication facilities, it implies many transfers per computation and does not take advantage from the TLP offered by the Cell processor. The half pipeline model which can be considered as a compromise between the two precedent versions, exploits the fast communications between SPEs and the TLP. In the next section, we will verify if implementation results agree with our expectations.

5.5 Considerations on the DMA Transfers

DMA transfers are the main issue when developing image processing applications on the Cell processor. The size of computation tiles is the first parameter to consider. On the one hand, these pieces of data must be as large as possible (up to the LS). Transferring large tiles, reduces the amount of reloads when performing convolution kernels. On the other hand DMA requests must be performed in 16 KB chunks. Otherwise EIB bandwidth is seriously affected [7]. The internal bus bandwidth is also related to the number of concurrent transfers, as that the EIB can handle up to 12 non-colliding parallel transfers (3 per node). The last constraint on DMA requests concerns inter-SPE transfers, that needs a synchronization mechanism (Fig. 5). This process aims to ensure data coherence, but can causes SPE stalls when signaling is quite slow.

5.6 Benchmark Results

In this part of the paper, we present some preliminary results of our different models. In our experiments, we considered different image sizes. Pixels are coded in single precision floats format in order to have a simplified transfer management, and also because of the limitations of the SPU instruction set. We measured the execution time (CPP) with 4KB, 8KB and 16KB tiles to evaluate the impact of the tile size on it. The metric used is *cpp*, which is the number of clock cycles per pixel.

$$cpp = \frac{\text{cpu cycles}}{N^2} \tag{1}$$

Image size is N $\times$ N pixels.The *cpp* is more representative than *cpi* (cycles per instruction) to compare the complexity per pixel of different algorithms. It also shows the influence of memory transfers on computation and allows a fair comparison between the architectures,as this measure is independent from the clock frequency. According to the curves in Fig. 6, Fig. 7 and Fig. 8, one can note that *cpp* decreases when tile size increases for all versions. This is due to the difference in the amount of transferred data. One can also note that 16KB is the optimal value of DMA message, that guarantees a maximum bandwidth on the EIB [7]. This is why we obtain an optimal cpp with a 16KB tile. Although it is theoretically the best one, the half pipeline does not reach satisfying

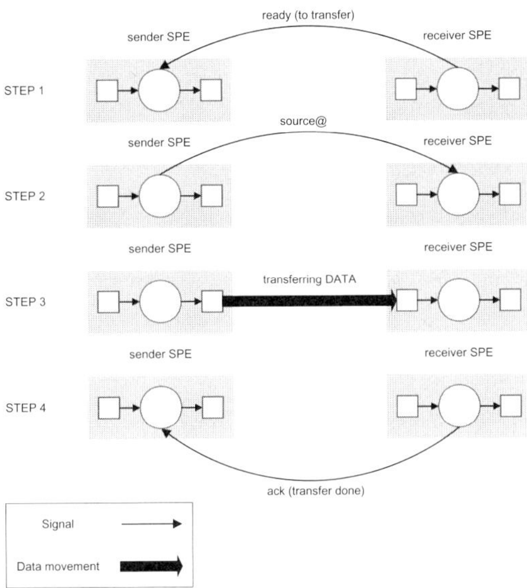

Fig. 5. Example of synchronization steps between two SPEs when transferring Data from one SPE to another SPE

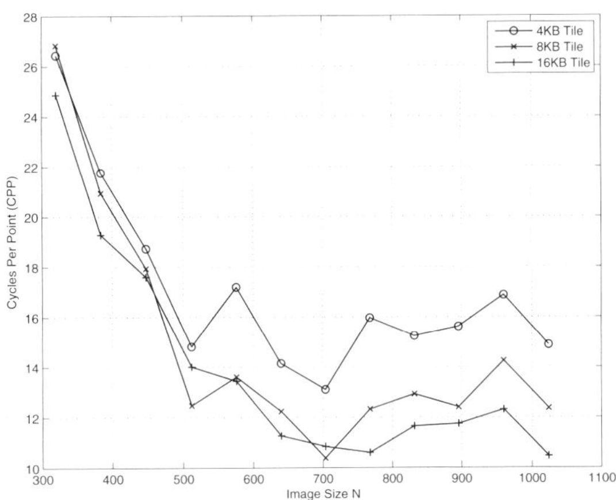

Fig. 6. Cycles per pixel for the SPMD Implementation

performances. This comes from the big contention on the bus caused by the collision of the numerous transfers running concurrently, and the effect of synchronizations that causes SPE stalls. The comparison between different implementations (Fig. 9) shows that the SPMD version has the best *cpp*.

Comparison with a single core Implementation. To get a better idea of the gain provided by the Cell processor, we compare the SPMD version with an equivalent implementation on a mono-core PowerPC G5 using the Altivec ISA (Instruction Set

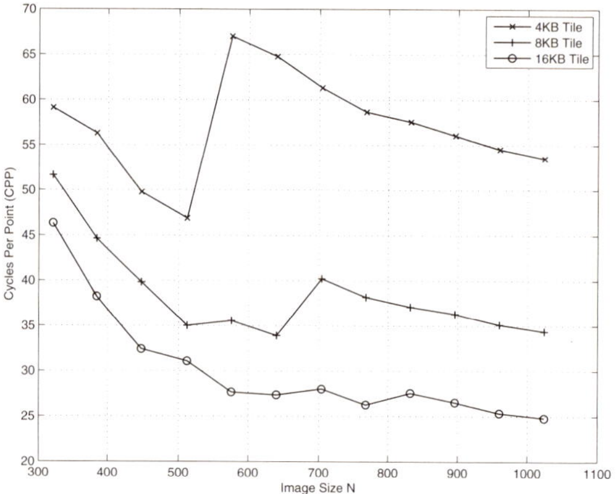

Fig. 7. Cycles per pixel for the Pipeline Implementation

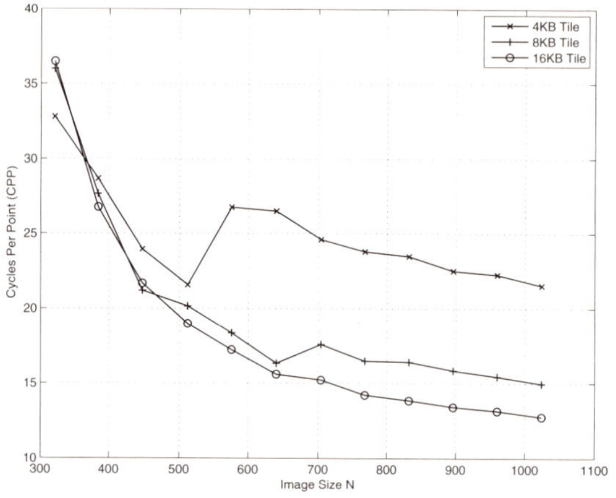

Fig. 8. Cycles per pixel for the Half Pipeline Implementation

Architecture), knowing that both of the Altivec and SPU units are in-order processors, and all of the instructions used to code the POI algorithm on the SPU have their corresponding instructions on the Altivec extension. The main characteristic of the G5, is that performance is limited by the cache size, which is used to minimize the bottleneck due to memory transfers : the *cpp* increases dramatically when the processed data do not fit in the cache. This handover is amplified by the cache misses, and can not be avoided but just deferred by increasing the cache size. Unlike the G5 processor, the SPU does not use the cache mechanism to improve memory transfers. The size of processed data (tile) is fixed by the user with taking into account the size of the local storage. The *cpp* decreases while the data size increases and reaches a constant value for large image sizes. With the SPMD version using 8 SPUs and large image sizes, the speed-up is approximately x7, which is close to the x8 maximum speed-up.

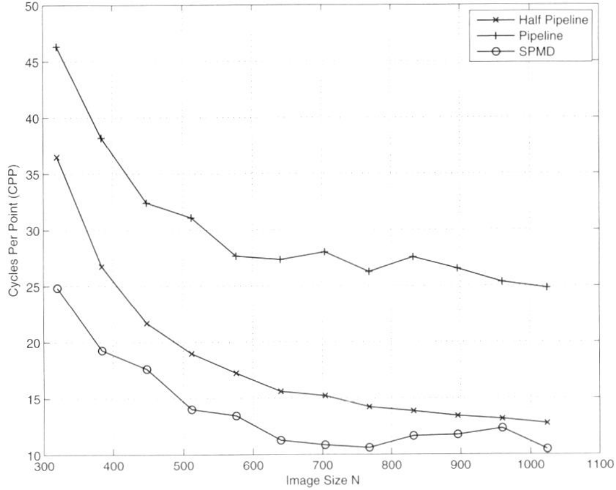

Fig. 9. Comparison between implementations for 16KB Tiles

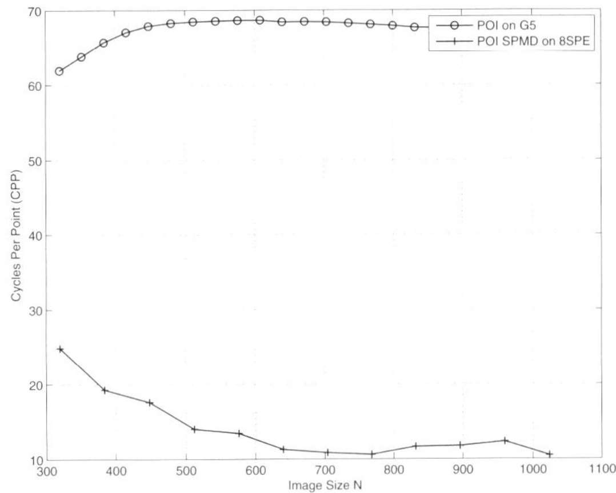

Fig. 10. Comparison Between G5 and Cell SPMD version

6 Conclusion and Future Work

We introduced different distribution models for the Harris POI algorithm on the Cell processor. This application was chosen for its variant schemes of parallelization and also because it includes different kinds of computation kernels. The influence of the size of memory transfers and the number of concurrent ones on the performance decrease is noted. The performances reached by pipeline versions do not match our expectations. This is due to costly synchronizations between SPEs that increases the number of stalls in the threads and numerous concurrent transfers that causes contention on the EIB. Better handling of synchronizations is one of the projected improvements. The obtained results will be exploited to design a tool for efficient image processing code distribution on the Cell processor and other multi-core platforms. Examples of parallelization methods can be found in [5], [8] and [9]. Tiling is the better strategy for distributing code on such architectures, since memory transfers are the bottleneck that limits performance.

References

1. Pham, D., Aipperspach, T., Boerstler, D., Bolliger, M., Chaudhry, R., Cox, D., Harvey, P., Harvey, P., Hofstee, H., Johns, C., Kahle, J., Kameyama, A., Keaty, J., Masubuchi, Y., Pham, M., Pille, J., Posluszny, S., Riley, M., Stasiak, D., Suzuoki, M., Takahashi, O., Warnock, J., Weitzel, S., Wendel, D., Yazawa, K.: Overview of the Architecture, Circuit Design, and Physical Implementation of a First-generation Cell Processor. IEEE Journal of Solid-State Circuits 41, 179–196 (2006)
2. IBM: Cell Broadband Engine Programming Handbook. Version 1.0 edn. IBM (2006)
3. Petrini, F., Fossum, G., Fernández, J., Varbanescu, A.L., Kistler, M., Perrone, M.: Multicore Surprises: Lessons Learned from Optimizing Sweep3D on the Cell Broadband Engine. In: IEEE/ACM International Parallel and Distributed Processing Symposium (2007)
4. Greene, J., Cooper, R.: A Parallel 64k Complex fft Algorithm for the IBM/Sony/Toshiba Cell Broadband Engine Processor. In: Global Signal Processing Expo. (2005)
5. Eichenberger, A.E., O'Brien, J.K., O'Brien, K.M., Wu, P., Chen, T., Oden, P.H., Prener, D.A., Shepherd, J.C., So, B., Sura, Z., Zhang, A.W.T., Zhao, P., Gschwind, M.K., Archambault, R., Gao, Y., Koo, R.: Using Advanced Compiler Technology to Exploit the Performance of the Cell Broadband Engine Architecture. IBM Ssystems Journal 45 (2006)
6. Benthin, C., Wald, I., Scherbaum, M., Friedrich, H.: Ray Tracing on the CELL Processor. In: IEEE Symposium on Interactive Ray Tracing (2006)
7. Kistler, M., Perrone, M., Petrini, F.: Cell Multiprocessor Communication Network: Built for Speed. IEEE Micro 26, 10–23 (2006)
8. Fatahalian, K., Knight, T.J., Houston, M., Erez, M., Horn, D.R., Leem, L., Park, J.Y., Ren, M., Aiken, A., Dally, W.J., Hanrahan, P.: Sequoia: Programming the Memory Hierarchy. In: Proceedings of the 2006 ACM/IEEE Conference on Supercomputing (2006)
9. Knight, T.J., Park, J.Y., Ren, M., Houston, M., Erez, M., Fatahalian, K., Aiken, A., Dally, W.J., Hanrahan, P.: Compilation for Explicitly Managed Memory Hierarchies. In: Proceedings of the 2007 ACM SIGPLAN Symposium on Principles and Practice of Parallel Programming (2007)

RWA Algorithm for Scheduled Lightpath Demands in WDM Networks

Sooyeon Park[1], Jong S. Yang[2], Moonseong Kim[3], and Young-Cheol Bang[1,*]

[1] Dep. of Computer Engineering, Korea Polytechnic University, Korea
{anisoo,ybang}@kpu.ac.kr
[2] Korea Institute of Industrial Technology Evaluation and Planning, Korea
yjs@mail.itep.re.kr
[3] School of Info. and Comm. Engineering, Sungkyunkwan University, Korea
moonseong@ece.skku.ac.kr

Abstract. We have proposed and evaluated a novel heuristic algorithm of routing and wavelength assignment (RWA) for scheduled lightpath demands (SLD). Our algorithm is shown here to have a performance gain in terms of the number of wavelengths up to 65.8% compared with the most recently introduced method, TDP_RWA, and works on directed and undirected optical networks. Also, we show the execution time of our proposed method is feasible.

1 Introduction

Emerging real-time multimedia communication applications and increasing traffic demands in networks cannot be supported by the current Internet architecture. The wavelength division multiplexing (WDM) technology employed in optical networks is developed to support such services that require the electronic processing speeds, and will replace Internet backbone in near future. To send a message from a source to a destination, WDM optical network should setup a connection between optical layers of each end node such as the one in circuit-switched networks. This connection process can be done by determining a path between the two end nodes, and such a path is referred as a lightpath. Once a connection is setup the entire bandwidth on the lightpath is reserved until it is terminated.

As mentioned above, a message is supposed to be sent though a lightpath that requires a route and a wavelength for each connection so that it should be effective to select lightpaths for request demands to utilize bandwidths of optical networks efficiently. This is known as the problem of routing and wavelength assignment (RWA). Especially in the case of no wavelength converter, given a physical optical network and the requested demands, the RWA problem is to select a suitable route and wavelength among the many possible choices for each connection so that no two paths sharing a link are assigned the same wavelength [2].

In the most common way, RWA deals separately with route and wavelength assignment such that at first a route of the light path is selected and then a wavelength is

* Corresponding author.

I. Stojmenovic et al. (Eds.): ISPA 2007, LNCS 4742, pp.113–124,2007.

assigned on the selected route in efficient way. RWA problem on the optical networks is known to be NP-complete [12], and many heuristic approaches have been proposed in [2][4][5][6]. Also more mechanisms are intensively surveyed in [3].

The optical transport network (OTN) provides the optical virtual private network (OVPN) as the key service network, where there exist three types of lightpath demands; static, scheduled, and dynamic. Static lightpath demands are given by OVPN clients to minimize connectivity and bandwidth requirements, and dynamic lightpath demands are to establish and release connection in time. At releasing time, reserved resources are also released. In the case of the scheduled lightpath demand (SLD), request demands are based on specific time. This type of demand is to increase the capacity of network at specific times on certain links. For example, periodical data backup performed at specific time can use SLD.

In real world OTN, most of demands will be static and scheduled as explained in [7][10]. This is because traffic load in a transport network is fairly predictable for its periodic nature. Fig. 1 shows the traffic on the New York-Washington link of the Abilene backbone network during a typical week. A similar periodic pattern was observed on all the other links of the network in the same period. Fig.1 is a clear evidence of the link between the intensity of communication among humans using the network, and the network traffic load [7].

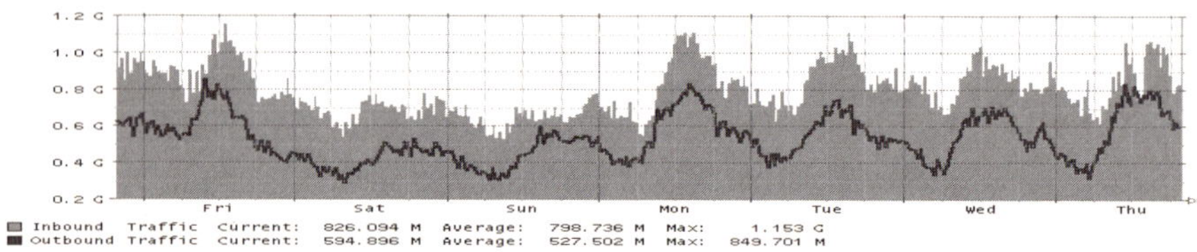

Fig. 1. Traffic on the New York-Washington link of the Abilene backbone network form October 13, 2005 to October 20, 2005

One of characteristics of RWA is to reuse wavelength [8][9] such that if there are two paths between arbitrary nodes without sharing links, two paths can use same wavelength at the same time [8][9]. For example in Fig. 2, consider two paths from 1 to 3 (path A) and from 3 to 5 (path B). Since these two paths do not share any link, there will be no problem for A and B to use the same wavelength at any time. Thus, it is clear that if we find more link-disjoint paths in a given network then the number of wavelength may be decreased. In the case that two paths are sharing any link, if service times of two paths are not overlapped then it is also clear only single wavelength is enough for both paths.

Using these simple notions of an link-disjoint path and usage-time, we consider an optical network, $G = (V, E)$, where V and E are the set of vertices and the set of links, respectively. $\Delta = \{\delta_1, \delta_2, \ldots\ldots, \delta_n\}$ is a set of SLDs, and each SLD can be represented by 4 tuples (s, t, u, w), $\delta = \{s, t, u, w\}$, where s and t are source and destination nodes of a demand, u and w are setup and teardown times of a demand. λ is a wavelength assigned at lightpath. Let $\Delta_T = \{\Delta_{T1}, \Delta_{T2}, \ldots\ldots, \Delta_{Tk}\}$ be a set of groups such that each Δ_{Ti}, $1 \le i \le k$, consists of δ which does not share usage-time. Then our objective is to propose a new algorithm to reduce the number of wavelengths and give the feasible computation time for SLD.

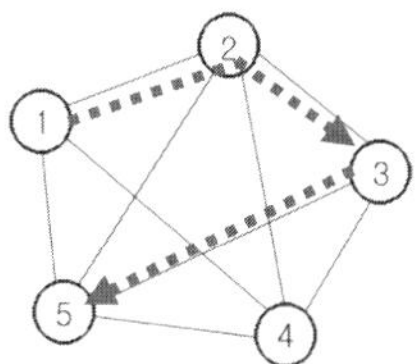

Fig. 2. Wavelength Routing Network

The paper is organized as follows. We discuss related works on RWA in Section 2. We propose a new RWA algorithm regarding to SLD in Section 3. Performance evaluation of the proposed algorithm is presented in Section 4. Finally, we conclude in Section 5.

2 Related Work

RWA algorithms have been intensively studied in the literature [2][3][4][5][6] because of its importance for the efficiency of optical networks. Among those algorithms, BGAforEDP [3][4] is known to be one of the simplest and most efficient algorithms introduced so far.

BGAforEDP is to find link-disjoint paths based on the shortest path algorithm to assign a route and a wavelength to a lightpath. It is shown that BGAforEDP is suitable for static demands but not appropriate for SLD because of characteristics such that starting time and teardown time are not considered for each static request [6]. For SLD, the Combinatorial Optimal Solution (COS) has been introduced [10], but it is complex and impractical for the computational time [5]. Using COS, time-complexity increases exponentially as the number of demands increase. For this reason, Steven [8] and Stern [9] considered the bound and branch (B&B) search algorithm to reduce the computational time, but B&B still does not give feasible computational time [8][9]. So Chlamtac [1] introduced the meta-heuristic TABU search algorithm. In the case of TABU, the performance is somewhat low with high complexity. The method called sRWA, based on FF [3], was introduced [10], but usage-time of each connection was not considered.

TDP-RWA [6], recently new method, was proposed to take both the computational time and the number of wavelength into consideration. TDP-RWA separates SLDs into several groups such that usage-time of connection for each SLD cannot be overlapped in the same group but can be overlapped between different groups. That is, SLDs in same group can have same wavelength. Also, SLDs in other groups may have a same wavelength if lightpaths are link-disjoint each other with paths that a wavelength has already been assigned. Due to simplicity of algorithm, computational time decreases dramatically but more number of wavelength are required than other algorithms [6]. In this paper we propose a new RWA algorithm for SLDs that is feasible in terms of the computational time and outperforms any other heuristic algorithms in terms of wavelengths.

3 Proposed Algorithm

RWA problems on optical network focus on minimizing the number of wavelengths as well as selecting appropriate routes to minimize the end-to-end delay to support request demands. In this section, we describe our proposed algorithm named SP_TDP_RWA that takes following two observations into account for SLD.

(1) Link-disjoint lightpaths can use the same wavelength
(2) If the usage-times of lightpaths with sharing links are different each other, the same wavelength can be assigned to those lightpaths

Based on observation (1) and (2), it is clear that if there are enough link-disjoint lightpaths we may reduce the number of wavelengths as many as possible. So, a mechanism to select routes can decide the number of wavelengths. To derive an efficient algorithm, we first divide request demands into several groups such that request demands in the same group have the different service time each other, and sort groups in non-decreasing order based on number of request demands included. Then SP_TDP_RWA has following five steps.

Step1. Select routes that use the minimum number of links for group to be considered and then delete links selected from a given network to compute link-disjoint paths for other groups.
Step2. Repeat step 1 until all groups are considered.
Step3. Assign the same wavelength to all routes computed in step 1 and 2.
Step4. Restore a given graph to consider request demands of which wavelength are not assigned.
Step 5.Repeat step 1 through 5 until all request demands are considered.

Especially, step 1 should be carefully treated. To minimize the number of links to constitute a lightpath, a new path *P'* can be selected by concatenating minimum number of links to any previously selected lightpath *P* if *P'* satisfies the delay bound, $\max(diam(G), \sqrt{|E|})$. Otherwise, the shortest path is used as a lightpath *P'*. In this manner, we minimize the number of links used for a group to be considered so that probability of finding link-disjoint paths for other group can be increased. Also, our mechanism is working well with both undirected and directed networks.

Consider $\Delta_T = \{\Delta_{T1} = \{\delta_{11}, \delta_{12}, \ldots\ldots, \delta_{1|\Delta_{T1}|}\}, \Delta_{T2} = \{\delta_{21}, \delta_{22}, \ldots\ldots, \delta_{2|\Delta_{T2}|}\}, \ldots\ldots \Delta_{Tk} = \{\delta_{k1}, \delta_{k2}, \ldots\ldots, \delta_{2|\Delta_{T2}|}\}\}$ and NSFNET in Fig. 3, where Δ_T is sorted in non-decreasing order based on number of δ included. Then Fig.4 shows how to compute routes and assign wavelength for arbitrary Δ_{Ti} with $1 \le i \le k$ in Table.1, where $\max(diam(G), \sqrt{|E|})$ is 4.

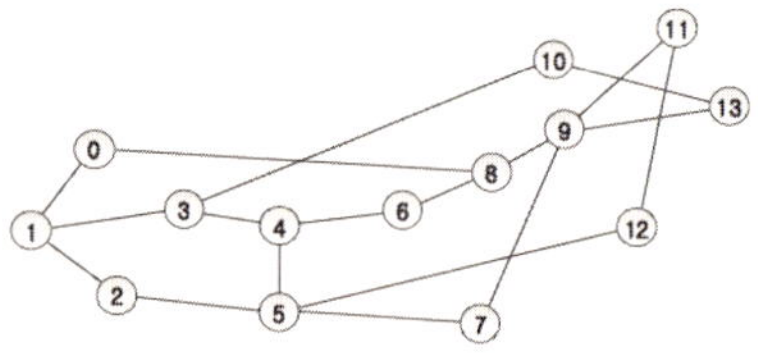

Fig. 3. NFSNET Topology

Table 1. Set of SLDs for Δ_{Ti}

SLD	SLD = (s, t, u, w)				Number of Links
	Source	Destination	Setup time	Teardown time	
δ_{i1}	3	8	2:00	3:00	3
δ_{i2}	4	6	3:00	5:00	1
δ_{i3}	6	10	13:00	14:00	3
δ_{i4}	1	9	19:00	21:00	3

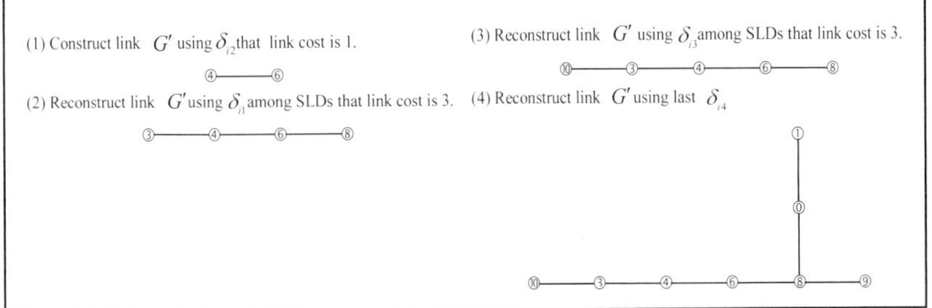

Fig. 4. Path Selection and G' construction using Δ_{Ti}

In number (1), since the number of links for the shortest path $P_{\delta_{i2}}$ for δ_{i2} is one that is minimum among the computed shortest paths for all $\delta \in \Delta_{Ti}$, we choose $P_{\delta_{i2}}$ and construct G' by adding links on $P_{\delta_{i2}}$, where G' is initially empty. In number (2), since the number of links on the computed shortest path for δ_{i1} is minimum among the computed shortest paths for $\delta \in \Delta_{Ti} = \Delta_{Ti} - \{\delta_{12}\}$, $P_{\delta_{i1}}$ is considered. The computed shortest path of G is 3-1-0-8 and a path reusing $P_{\delta_{i2}}$ (4-6) is 3-④-⑥-8, where both paths are satisfying the delay bound, $\max(diam(G), \sqrt{|E|}) = 4$. Thus, we select path (3-④-⑥-8) for δ_{i1}, since only two more links are used by sharing links on $P_{\delta_{i2}}$ instead of using three links for the shortest path 3-1-0-8. After then links (3, 4) and (6, 8) are added to G'. In this manner, ⑥-④-③-10 and 1-0-⑧-9 are selected for $P_{\delta_{i3}}$ and $P_{\delta_{i4}}$ in number (3)-(4), respectively. Suppose G'' is G - G'. Then repeat to find a lightpath for any $\delta \in \Delta_T - \{\Delta_{Ti}\}$ if a path is available. After check every SLDs in Δ_T, the same λ_i is assigned to lightpaths selected. Fig. 5 shows the entire process to assign routes and wavelengths.

The function, SP_TDP_RWA() in Fig. 6, consists of three functions. TDP-Selector( ), ADD_SLD( ), and Other_Group( ). TDP-Selector() groups service-time disjoint SLDs, $\Delta_T = \{\Delta_{T1}, \Delta_{T2}, \ldots, \Delta_{Tk}\}$. ADD_SLD() assigns wavelength to set of SLDs in the checked Δ_{Tk}. Other_Group() is to find link-disjoint paths of SLDs in $\Delta_T - \{\Delta_{Ti}\}$ and assigns the wavelength to them. At line 02, λ is wavelength to be assigned to SLDs that are selected at each process, and k is number of elements in set Δ_T with $\Delta_T = \{\Delta_{T1}, \Delta_{T2}, \ldots\ldots, \Delta_{Tk}\}$. The line 03-08 are repeated until all groups of Δ_T are checked. At line 05, links of G' are deleted from G to find link-disjoint paths for SLDs in $\Delta_T - \{\Delta_{Ti}\}$. Once all SLDs for a certain wavelength are checked and there are SLDs of which a wavelength is not assigned, the other wavelength is considered for them with G.

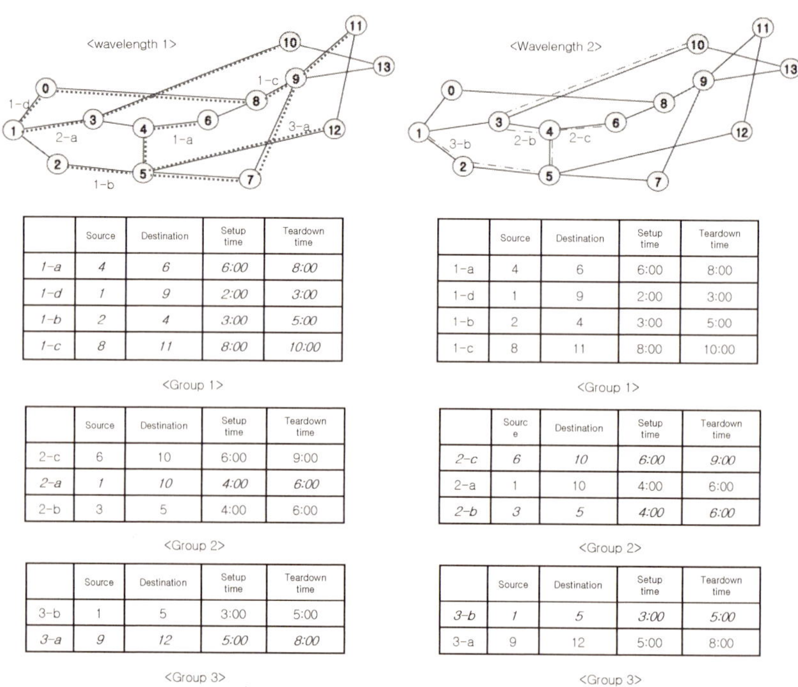

Wavelength 1:

	Source	Destination	Setup time	Teardown time
1-a	4	6	6:00	8:00
1-d	1	9	2:00	3:00
1-b	2	4	3:00	5:00
1-c	8	11	8:00	10:00

<Group 1>

	Source	Destination	Setup time	Teardown time
2-c	6	10	6:00	9:00
2-a	1	10	4:00	6:00
2-b	3	5	4:00	6:00

<Group 2>

	Source	Destination	Setup time	Teardown time
3-b	1	5	3:00	5:00
3-a	9	12	5:00	8:00

<Group 3>

Wavelength 2:

	Source	Destination	Setup time	Teardown time
1-a	4	6	6:00	8:00
1-d	1	9	2:00	3:00
1-b	2	4	3:00	5:00
1-c	8	11	8:00	10:00

<Group 1>

	Source	Destination	Setup time	Teardown time
2-c	6	10	6:00	9:00
2-a	1	10	4:00	6:00
2-b	3	5	4:00	6:00

<Group 2>

	Source	Destination	Setup time	Teardown time
3-b	1	5	3:00	5:00
3-a	9	12	5:00	8:00

<Group 3>

Fig. 5. Example of wavelength assignment: Bold type font is SLD that is selected for a certain wavelength, where a, b, c and d are selected order. For example, selected order in Group 1 is 1-a, 1-b, 1-c and 1-d

```
SP_TDP_RWA (G, Δ)
01 Δ_T = TDP − Selector(G, Δ)
02 λ = 1, k = 0
03 while( |Δ_T| ≠ k)
04     G′ = ADD_SLD (Δ_Tk, λ, G)
05     G″ = G - G′
06     G′ = Other_Grou p( Δ_T - {Δ_Tk}, G″) ∪ G′
07     λ = λ + 1
08     k = k + 1
```

Fig. 6. Proposed new SP_TDP_RWA Algorithm

```
ADD_SLD(Δ_Tk, λ, G)
01  for j = 1 to |Δ_Tk|
02      Find δ_kn = (s_n, t_n, u_n, w_n) with the smallest cost at Δ_Tk
03      Find shortest path P(s_n, t_n) in G
04      new_path_distance = Find_New_Path(δ_n, G)
05      if new_path_distance ≤ d
06          if new_path_distance ≤ (distance of (s_n, t_n) in G)
07              Assign λ to new path of (s_n, t_n)
08              G′(V′, E′) = G′(V′, E′) ∪ link of new paht of (s_n, t_n)
10          else
11              Assign λ to path of (s_n, t_n) in G
12              G′(V′, E′) = G′(V′, E′) ∪ path of (s_n, t_n) in G
13      else
14          Assign λ to path of (s_n, t_n) in G.
15          G′(V′, E′) = G′(V′, E′) ∪ path of (s_n, t_n) in G
```

Fig. 7. ADD_SLD Algorithm

ADD_SLD( ) in Fig. 7 is the function to assign wavelength for $\Delta_{kj} = \{\delta_{k1}, \delta_{k2}, \ldots\ldots, \delta_{k|\Delta_{kj}|}\}$. The line 01-15 are repeated until all $\delta_k \in \Delta_{kj}$ are checked. At line 02, we find $\delta_{kn} = (s_n, t_n, u_n, w_n)$ with the smallest number of links, and shortest path of (s_n, t_n) is computed at line 03 from *G*. Find_New_Path( ) at line 04 is the function to find new path reusing links of previously selected paths. Line 05-12 are executed if the cost of new path is less than or equal to $\mathbf{max}(\mathbf{dim}(G), \sqrt{|E|})$. Line 06-08 are executed when cost of new path is less than that of the shortest path in network *G*. At line 07, we assign λ to a new path, and add new links to G'. If the cost of new path is longer than that of shortest path in network *G*, line 10-11 assign a wavelength to the shortest path, and add links of shortest path G'.

```
δ_n = {s_n, t_n, u_n, w_n}
end_node = {E_1, E_2, E_3, ......, E_l}
Find_New_Path(δ_n, G)
k = 1
while( k ≠ |end_node|)
    m = 1
    while(m ≠ |end_node|)
        Findshorestpath P_1(s_n, E_k) in G
        Findshorestpath P_2(E_k, E_m) in G'
        Findshorestpath P_3(E_m, t_n) in G
        if new_path_distance > distance of P_1 + distance of P_2 + distance of P_3
            new_path_distance = P_1 + P_2 + P_3
            new_path = s_n → E_k → E_m → t_n
```

Fig. 8. Find_New_Path algorithm that find new path

The function, Find_New_Path( ), in Fig. 8 is to find new path reusing links of G' which means new path shares the links of paths previously selected. To concatenate new source and destination to previously selected paths, line 02-10 are repeated until checking all end nodes of which degree of node is 1 in link G'. Line 05-07 are to find a path that is from s_n to t_n via any end-node. Fig. 9 shows an example to find a new path of (5, 6). Path of (5, 6) in (c) is shortest, so this can be used as a new path.

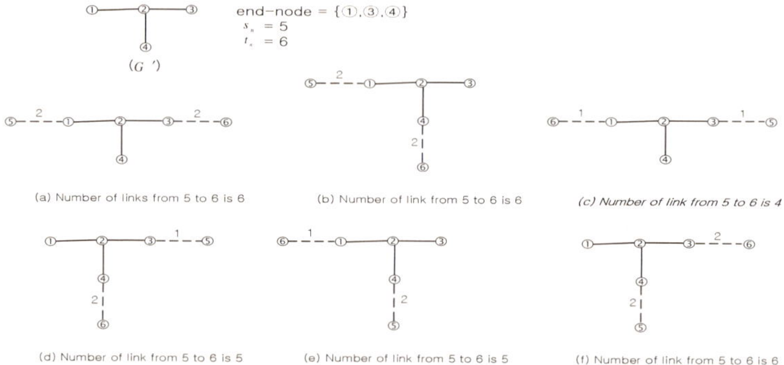

Fig. 9. Example to find new path as share links of G'. Number on link represents the number of links between two nodes. If not represented, it means 1.

```
Other_Grou p(Δ_T - {Δ_Tk}, G″)
01    i = 1
02    while (i ≠ |Δ_T - {Δ_Tk}|)
03       Find shortest path of P(s_i, t_i) in G″
04       if P(s_i, t_i) exists in G″
05          G' = G′ ∪ P(s_i, t_i)
06          G″ = G″ - P(s_i, t_i)
```

Fig. 10. Algorithm to find path to assign wavelength to SLD in other groups

Other_Group( ), in Fig. 10 is the function to find link-disjoint paths that do not share link with Δ_{Tk}, and assign the same wavelength to SLDs in $\Delta_T - \{\Delta_{Tk}\}$. We repeat the line 02-06 until all SLDs in $\Delta_T - \{\Delta_{Tk}\}$ are checked. At line 3, we check to know whether a path from s to t is in G''. If disjoint path exists, add links of path to G', and then delete G' from G''. And then, we repeat SP_TDP_RWA() to assign new wavelength to SLDs that are not assigned starting from Δ_{Tk+1} again. In this manner, we can assign wavelengths to all SLDs.

4 Performance Evaluation

We compare the performance of SP_TDP_RWA with those of BGAforEDP[4], TDP_RWA[6] and sRWA[10] in terms of the number of wavelengths. Network topologies used for performance evaluation are randomly generated directed networks [11]. In this evaluation, *Pe* is the probability of links in a network, therefore if *Pe* is 1, this means complete graph. *Pl* is the probability of SLDs in a network. If *Pl* is 1, this means that every request occurs between every two node pairs. If *Pl* is 0.3, then requests are used only 30% among every request that occurs between every two node pairs. Because several requests between two nodes are possible to occur, we evaluated performance when several requests occurred. If *Nc* is 3, this means that request occurs between two node pairs. *Tservice* means average service-time of requests. If *Tservice* is 4, this means that each service-time is 4 hours. In this paper, we supposed that network has 20 nodes. We implemented evaluations 1000 times for each evaluation condition and obtain the average number of wavelengths assigned.

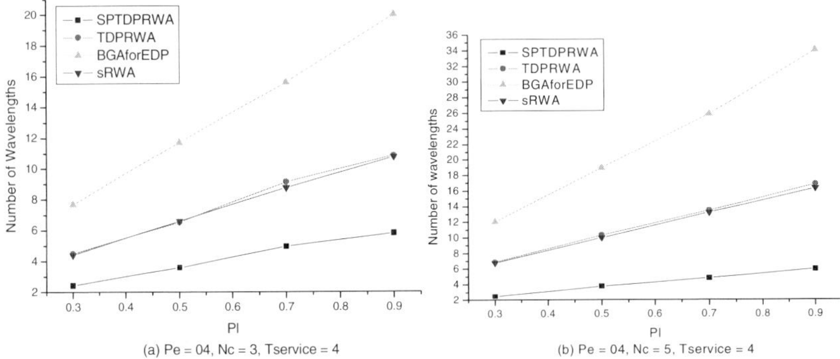

Fig. 11. Number of wavelengths as *Pl* increases (*Pe* = 0.4, *Nc* = 3 or 5, *Tservice* = 4)

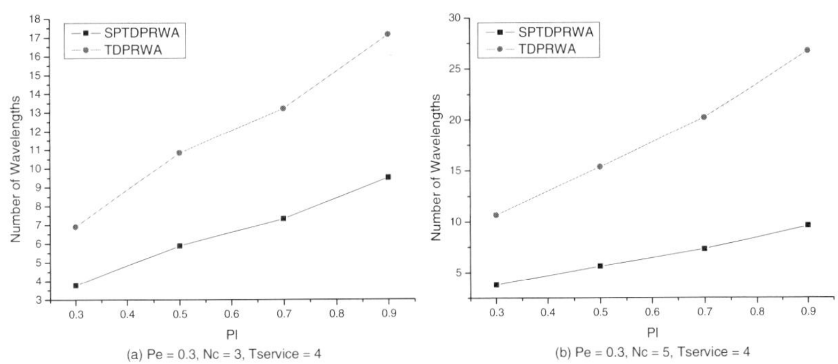

Fig. 12. Number of wavelengths as *Pl* increases (*Pe* = 0.3, *Nc* = 3 or 5, *Tservice* 4)

Fig. 11 shows number of wavelength as *Pl* increases in random networks with 20 nodes when *Nc* is 3 or 5, *Pe* is 0.4 and *Tservice* is 4 hours. And Fig. 12 shows number of wavelength as *Pl* increases when *Nc* is 3 or 5, *Pe* is 0.3 and *Tservice* is 4. As shown in Fig. 11 and 12, SP_TDP_RWA, our proposed algorithm, outperforms any other algorithm in terms of wavelength at any condition with fixed *Tservice*.

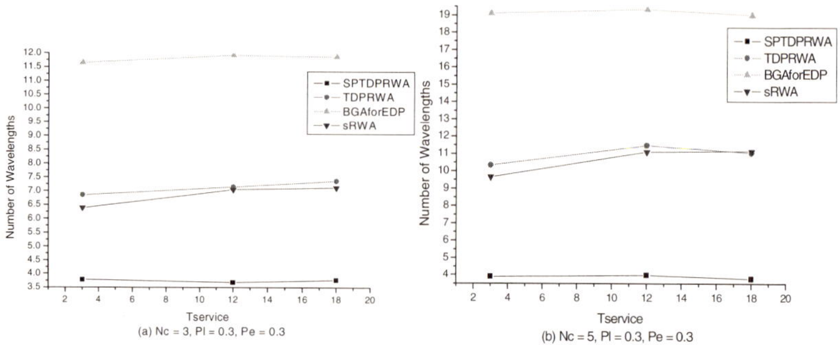

Fig. 13. Number of wavelengths as Tservice increases (Nc = 3 or 5, Pl = 0.3, Pe = 0.3)

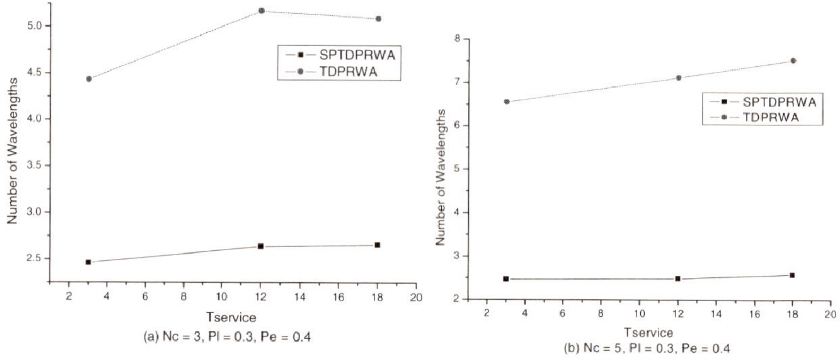

Fig. 14. Number of wavelengths as Tservice increases (Nc = 3 or 5, Pl = 0.3, Pe = 0.4)

Fig. 13 shows number of wavelength as *Tservice* increases in random networks with 20 nodes when *Nc* is 3 or 5, *Pl* is 0.3 and *Pe* is 0.3. And Fig. 14 shows number of wavelength as *Tservice* increases when *Nc* is 3 or 5, *Pl* is 0.3 and Pe is 0.4. From Fig. 13 and 14, we may also conclude that SP_TDP_RWA outperforms TDP_RWA as *Tservice* is increased. Also, the number of wavelength using SP_TDP_RWA is very steady.

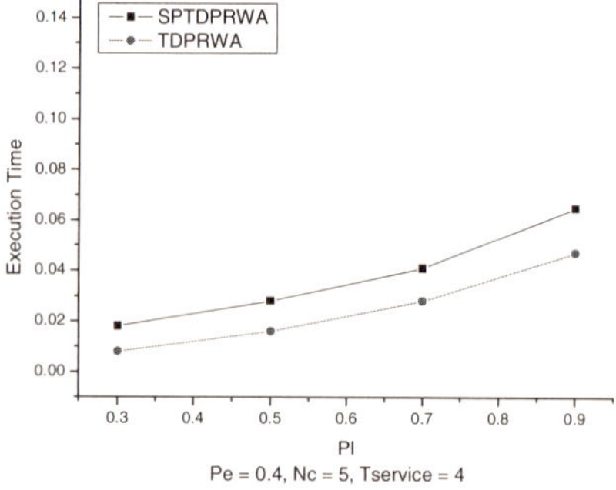

Fig. 15. Average execution time as Pl increases (Pe = 0.4, Nc = 5, Tservice = 4)

In Fig. 15, we illustrate average execution time as *Pl* increases in random directed networks when *Nc* is 5, *Pe* is 0.4, and *Tservice* is 4 hours. SP_TDP_RWA requires some more execution time than TDP_RWA, but this is small enough to ignore for whole performance.

SP_TDP_RWA is to minimize the number of links for selecting paths using single wavelength for a certain group so that probability of finding link-disjoint paths using the same wavelength is increased for SLDs in other groups. For this reason, SP_TDP_RWA outperforms TDP_RWA[6] from 44.4% to 65.8% in terms of wavelength with feasible execution time.

5 Conclusion

In this paper, we proposed new wavelength assignment algorithm, SP_TDP_RWA, for Scheduled Lightpath Demand (SLD) in OVPN. Using characteristics of the RWA of SLD, we made time-disjoint SLDs in the same group, and then we found paths sharing links of previously selected paths for SLDs in the same group to increase number of link-disjoint paths available for SLDs in other groups. As a result, SP_TDP_RWA dramatically decreased the number of wavelength. Also execution time is feasible when comparing TDA_RWA of which execution time is best among mechanisms introduced so far.

References

1. Chlamtac, I., Ganz, A., Karmi, G.: Lightpath Communications: An Approach to High-Bandwidth Optical WAN's. Transactions on Communications 40(7), 1171–1182 (1992)
2. Ramaswami, R., Sivarajan, K.: Routing and wavelength assignment in all-optical networks. Transactions on Networking 3, 489–500 (1995)
3. Zang, H., Jue, J.P., Mukherjee, B.: A Review of Routing and Wavelength Assignment Approaches for Wavelength-routed Optical WDM Networks. Optical Networks Magazine 1(1), 47–60 (2000)
4. Manohar, P., Manjunath, D., Shevgaonkar, R.K.: Routing and Wavelength Assignment in Optical Networks from Edge Disjoint Path Algorithms. Communications Letter 5, 211–213 (2002)
5. Kirovski, D., Potkonjak, M.: Efficient Coloring of a Large Spectrum of Graphs. In: Proceeding of Design Automation Conference, pp. 427–432. IEEE Computer Society Press, Los Alamitos (1998)
6. Ahn, H.G., Lee, T.-J., Chung, M.Y., Choo, H.: RWA on Scheduled Lightpath Demands in WDM Optical Transport Networks with Time Disjoint Paths. In: Kim, C. (ed.) ICOIN 2005. LNCS, vol. 3391, pp. 342–351. Springer, Heidelberg (2005)
7. Advanced Networking for Research and Education [Online]. Available: http://abilene.internet2.edu
8. Finn, S.G., Barry, R.A.: Optical Services in Future Broadband Networks. Network 10(6), 7–13 (1996)
9. Stern, T.E., Bala, K., Jiang, S., Sharony, J.: Linear lightwave networks: performance issues. Journal of Lightwave Technology 11(5), 937–950 (1993)

10. Kuri, J., Puech, N., Gagnaire, M., Dotaro, E., Douville, R.: Routing and Wavelength Assignment of Scheduled Lightpath Demands. Journal on Selected Areas in Communications 21(8), 1231–1240 (2003)
11. Rodionov, A.S., Choo, H.: On Generating Random Network Structures: Connected Graphs. In: Kahng, H.-K., Goto, S. (eds.) ICOIN 2004. LNCS, vol. 3090, pp. 483–491. Springer, Heidelberg (2004)
12. Choi, J.S., Golmie, N., Lapeyrere, F., Mouveaux, F., Su, D.: A functional classification of routing and wavelength assignment schemes in DWDM networks: Static case. In: Proceeding of International Conference on Optical Communication and Networks (2000)

Optimizing Distributed Data Access in Grid Environments by Using Artificial Intelligence Techniques

Rodrigo F. de Mello[1], Jose Augusto Andrade Filho[1], Evgueni Dodonov[1], Renato Porfirio Ishii[2], and Laurence T. Yang[3]

[1] University of São Paulo, ICMC - Department of Computer Science, São Carlos, SP, Brazil
{mello,augustoa,eugeni}@icmc.usp.br
[2] Federal University of Mato Grosso do Sul, Department of Computer and Statistics Campo Grande, MS, Brazil
renato@dct.ufms.br
[3] St. Francis Xavier University Antigonish, NS, Canada
lyang@stfx.ca

Abstract. This work evaluates two artificial intelligence techniques for file distribution in Grid environments. These techniques are used to access data on independent servers in parallel, in order to improve the performance and maximize the throughput rate. In this work, genetic algorithms and Hopfield neural networks are the techniques used to solve the problem. Both techniques are evaluated for efficiency and performance. Experiments were conduced in environments composed of 32, 256 and 1024 distributed nodes. The results allow to confirm the decreasing in the file access time and that Hopfield neural network offered the best performance, being possible to be applied on Grid environments.

1 Introduction

The evolution of the processors and network technologies had motivated the development of distributed systems. Such systems require the access and transfer of huge amounts of data, offering the best possible throughput combined with the low latency values. Different works were oriented to solve this problem [1,2].

Motivated by these works, this paper presents a study and evaluation of artificial intelligence techniques in order to find out an efficient data distribution solution over heterogeneous computing environments. The main goal is to maximize the data access rate (throughput) in distributed environments. The distributed data access techniques use parallel data access, having the logical file divided in chunks (data units) in order to increase the global I/O operations performance. The data access sequence is automatically determined depending on the system configurations such the network delays, chunk size and the number of chunks accessed in parallel.

This work uses and evaluates two data distribution techniques: the first based on genetic algorithms [3] and the second on Hopfield artificial neural networks [4]. The performance and the efficiency of both techniques are evaluated and compared.

I. Stojmenovic et al. (Eds.): ISPA 2007, LNCS 4742, pp. 125–136, 2007.

Genetic Algorithms (GA) [3] are used as search and optimization technique in several domains. These algorithms are based on nature select mechanisms focusing at survival of the most capable individuals. GA does not always give the best possible solution, however provides good local solutions for NP-complete problems.

The problem solution using genetic algorithms involves two different aspects: solution encoding into the form of chromosomes, where each chromosome represents a possible solution, and a fitness function applied to find the best solution.

The Hopfield artificial neural network [5] was introduced as an associative memory between input and output data. This network realizes association of inputs and outputs using an energy function which is based on a Lyapunov energy function. This function is applied in dynamic systems theory in order to evaluate the existence of stable states. The goal of such systems is to prove that modifications in the system state results in an energy function decreasing, up to a minimum value. The usage of this energy function motivated the adoption of the Hopfield network for solving optimization problems. In such problems the goal is to obtain the global minimum of the energy function, what represents the best solution for a certain situation. The energy function surface is stored in the network weight values.

This paper is divided in the following sections: 2) related work in distributed filesystem area; 3) the problem of file distribution in Grids; 4) presentation and evaluation of the presented model; 5) results and analysis 6) conclusions.

2 Related Work

Several works have addressed the data distribution in distributed environments. The first solutions were based on parallel file systems such as PFS [6] and PPFS [7]. They rely on the underline hardware and are mostly used in parallel machines and supercomputers.

The network technology had evolved to the usage of network workstations for data distribution and access, such as NPFS [8] and PVFS [9]. These technologies explore the parallel file concepts, dividing a file into several segments (named chunks or stripes) localized on independent servers. Thus, a logical file was accessed in a parallel way, offering high throughput and low latency values. The usage of specific optimization techniques, such as data caching, prefetching [10], optimized timeouts and retransmission mechanisms has increased the performance of I/O operations.

NPFS and PVFS use a centralized managing process for global operation coordinations, such as file open, close, rename and deletion requests.

Afterwards, the technique of global file mapping was introduced in AFS and OpenAFS filesystems [11]. It offers transparent access to files localized on distinct networks, having each network represented as a different cell. The filesystem maps all requires network cells into a local directory (usually */afs/*) offering transparent distributed data access, supporting multiple authentication and data distribution techniques.

With the introduction of Grid computing concept [12], the need of specific filesystems to deal with features of heterogeneous environments such as network delays, computer capacities and architectures were evidenced. Some questions must be considered such as the support for large number of clients, disconnected operations, variable latencies and client heterogeneity. In this new approach of distributed filesystems are GridFTP [1], GFARM [13], GSI-SFS [14] and GridNFS [2].

GridFTP system was introduced in order to provide distributed data access for Grid environments and it is part of the Globus Toolkit [15]. It is based on the FTP protocol with several extensions such as concurrent file access, partial data transfer, server-to-server transfers and command queuing.

GFAM and GridNFS filesystems offer transparent access to data located in Grids extending existent network filesystems. While GFARM project intends to use currently available network filesystems such as SMBFS, GridFTP and NFS, GridNFS uses the NFSv4 filesystem as the base software.

Another approach is offered by GSI-SFS [14] technology. This filesystem intends to offer a single system image, exclusive and on-demand data access, data integrity, security and transparency.

Special cases of distributed filesystems are the peer-to-peer (P2P) systems, such as Gnutella [16], Kazaa [17], E-Donkey [18], BitTorrent [19] and Overnet [20].

The P2P systems use direct connections among clients for data transfer. The support for parallel data transfers and mechanisms for automated search for the closest and available clients provide an efficient network usage. However, the dependency on centralized servers and data trackers for peer coordination makes these systems inadequate for most Grid environments.

3 The Problem of File Distribution in Grids

Making a file available anywhere in a Grid computing environment is not an ordinary problem. There are many aspects to consider, such as: from where the file is being accessed; who is accessing the file; the network usage; network delays; how many and which computers are using the file and others.

Let a Grid computing environment as presented in figure 1. The problem is to split and distribute files over this environment minimizing the average time to read and write them from any computer.

Consider the time needed to send a message composed of n packets between computers of the same network α ($M_{R\alpha \to \alpha}$) is defined by the equation 1, where d_p is the communication cost for a packet and np is the number of packets which compose the message. The packet size is defined during a negotiation phase between the sender and receiver. This depends on the network characteristics such as the number of nodes (switches, routers etc) between both.

$$M_{R_\alpha \to \alpha} = d_p \times np \tag{1}$$

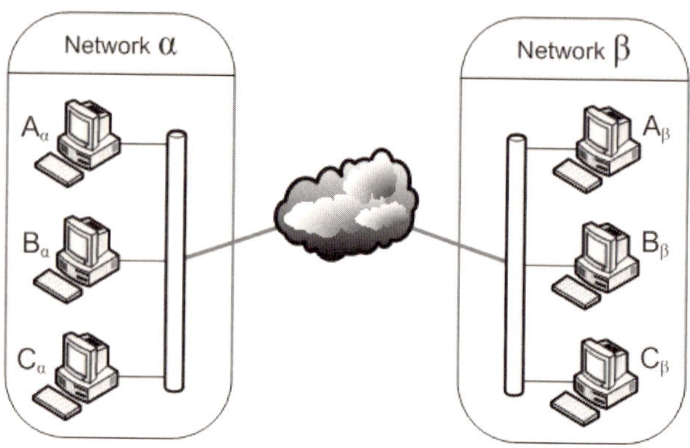

Fig. 1. Networks α and β, connected via Internet

Consider the time needed to read n bytes from a hard disk ($HD_{R,i}$) by the equation 2, where T_{HD} is the hard disk throughput for reading at the computer i.

$$HD_{R,i} = \frac{n}{T_{HD}} \tag{2}$$

A complete file is divided into chunks (file data units) which can be distributed over the Grid environment. For this distribution each data unit has to be converted into a network message. The number of packets to distribute this data unit depends on its size and the network packet size. If the chunk is larger than the packet size then the message to send the chunk will be composed of several packets.

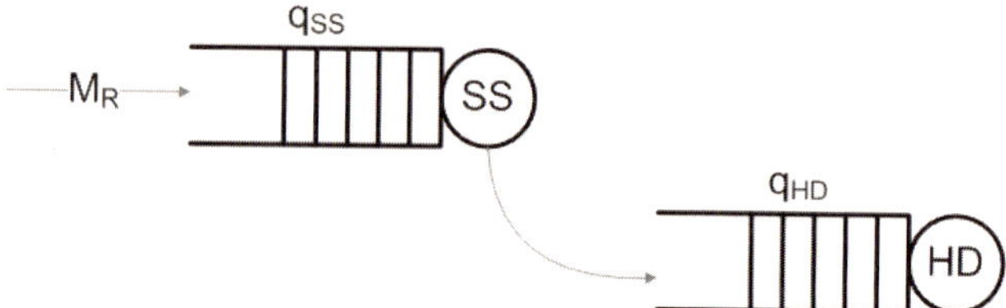

Fig. 2. A sample of queuing network for message transmission

At first, these chunks will be distributed over the local network – in this case α – once the delay is smaller. When the time needed to access the file from the local network (a computer of the network α) is higher than the delay to communicate to a computer of network β, we have to consider to send some chunks to be stored in the computers of network β. For this, the equation presented in 3 is evaluated where: $M_{R_{\alpha\to\alpha}}$ is the average communication delay among computers in the network α, $M_{R_{\alpha\to\beta}}$ is the communication delay between networks α and β, $q_{HD_{i,j}}$ and $q_{HD_{x,y}}$ are the hard disk queue length (in seconds) for the computer i and x of the network j and y, respectively.

$$HD_{i,\alpha} + M_{R_{\alpha\to\alpha}} + q_{HD_{i,\alpha}} > HD_{x,\beta} + M_{R_{\alpha\to\beta}} + q_{HD_{x,\beta}} \tag{3}$$

However, when the condition expressed in equation 3 is false, there is no advantage in sending file chunks to be stored in computers of β.

Although this condition (equation 3) is defined only for two networks, it can be easily extended to larger environments. As the environment grows, the amount of computational power needed to analyze this condition also grows.

In order to obtain an answer for this problem in an affordable time, this work adopts two different techniques: genetic algorithms and Hopfield neural networks. The solutions are presented in the following section.

4 Proposal and Evaluation of File Distribution Techniques

In order to obtain high throughput in the file access over Grid environments, this paper presents and evaluates two techniques for the data distribution in distributed filesystems.

4.1 Model Architecture

The first proposed technique uses genetic algorithms to define the best distribution of file chunks in Grid environments, the second one uses a Hopfield artificial neural network. The proposed solution considers that a file f is composed of n chunks c of a fixed size s ($f = \{c_0, c_1, c_2, ..., c_{n-1}\}$). These chunks are distributed among computers.

The main goal of this work is to maximize the data reading and writing throughput for each Grid computer. As each computer may access an arbitrary subset of data, this list of chunks is constantly modified for each computer. As the latency of routes among Grid machines dynamically changes, it is necessary to provide an efficient way to determine the best data access sequence.

The genetic algorithm solution creates individuals (chromosomes) composed of n genes, where each gene represents a chunk. Individuals are evaluated through a fitness function for generations. After the fitness evaluation, the best individuals are crossed and mutated with a pre-defined probability. The section 4.2 presents a more detailed analysis on fitness function and other aspects of genetic algorithms.

The solution with Hopfield artificial neural network uses the same equation of the genetic algorithm solution to define the energy function. This network runs until it reaches a solution (the global energy function minimum). This method is explained in the section 4.3.

The main objective of both techniques was the evaluation of the reading and writing cost in a file with 100 MBytes of size, distributed in chunks of 64 KBytes. To evaluate the throughput capacity, the number of chunks accessed in parallel was modified during the execution of experiments. This allowed the evaluation of different parallelism levels for accessing the file. For example, letting a ncp value equal to 3, the access simultaneously occurs in blocks of three chunks. If the first chunk is stored in the computer a, the second in b and the third in c, the read time in parallel will be calculated by the equation 4, where: L_a, L_b and L_c are the latencies to retrieve the chunks, in order, a, b e c.

$$T = MAX(L_a, L_b, L_c) \tag{4}$$

The more chunks read in parallel, the smaller is the time needed to read the file, and the same process happens with data writing. However, there is a limitation in this approach as large number of parallel I/O requests consume system resources, such as sockets, communication channels, allocated memory among others. Besides the computational cost factors, another relevant aspect is that the chunk retrieved may not be needed at that time. For example, an application may request a huge file needing just some chunks at the beginning and at the end of it. In this case, the computer does not need to read many sequential chunks in parallel, since not all of then would be necessary. The best option would be to read some initial chunks in parallel and then read the others, avoiding unnecessary data accesses.

4.2 Genetic Algorithm Model Implementation

The genetic algorithm was based on the implementation by *Jeff Smith* [1]. This version was designed with genes composed of float numbers, strings and sequential lists. It is also supports operators such as selection, crossover and mutation.

The original version includes an implementation for float numbers which could be extended to integers. In the original implementation, the mutation and individual creation numbers were not generated in pre-defined intervals and this was necessary to deal with the distribution of chunks, since these numbers refer to computers where chunks are stored. In order to fix this problem, a set of classes (*GAInteger* and *ChromInteger*) based on integer numbers, and allowing selection in an interval, was implemented.

Each chromosome, formed by genes, is a vector of non-unique integers where the ith element represents where – in which computer – the chunk i is stored. When a file has n chunks (or genes), the chromosome dimension would be n. The fitness function used in this context has a complexity of $O(n \times m)$, where n is the number of chunks, i.e. the chromosome dimension, and m is the number of computers. A pseudo-code of the fitness function is shown on the algorithm 3, where:

- i - computer in the environment which needs to access a file;
- p - computer in the environment which has an specific chunk of the file;
- $L[i][p]$ - matrix containing the network delays between computers i and p;
- $RttTable$ - function used to calculate the network delay based on [21];
- $delay$ - stores the amount of time needed to access k chunks in parallel;
- nc - number of computers in the environment;
- j - identifier of a new chunk group to be accessed in parallel;
- k - combined with j $(j + k)$, it represents the gene to be accessed;

[1] http://sourceforge.net/projects/java-galib/

- $gene[i]$ - feature vector which represents where the ith chunk is stored;
- cd - the chromosome dimension, i.e., the number of genes;
- ncp - the amount of chunks to be read in parallel;
- $lat[i]$ - latency vector which represents the time needed to access the chunks from the computer i;
- $Max(lat[], nc)$ - it returns the time needed to access the chunks in parallel, this function is based on equation 4;
- $delay$ - the time needed to access ncp chunks in parallel.

```
L[][] = RttTable()
fitTotal ← 0
for (i = 0; i < nc; i++) do
  for (intj = 0; j < cd; j += ncp) do
    doublelat[] ← newdouble[nc]
    for (intk = 0; k < ncp; k++) do
      if (j + k < cd) then
        p ← gene[j + k]
        lat[p] += L[i][p]
      end if
    end for
    delay += Max(lat, nc)
  end for
end for
return ← 1.0 / (delay / nc)
```

Fig. 3. Fitness function

A two-point crossover was used in the experiments, and the selection was performed by ranking. The two fittest chromosomes are taken into the next generation. The experiment was conduced with a population of 1,000 individuals evolving for 10,000 generations.

In the initialization, the algorithm received the distributed environment data as input (number of computers, file size, chunk size, RTT etc) through a configuration file. Next, the initial population was defined and evolved until it reached the maximum number of generations. The chromosome of the last generation with best fitness function value is chosen as result. This process was repeated for different number of chunks accessed in parallel.

4.3 Hopfield Neural Network Model Implementation

The Hopfield neural network solution was developed in C language. The main objective of this technique was to minimize the cost involved in accessing a distributed file. Each solution for the problem was expressed by a matrix, where the lines represented the chunk number and the columns the amount of computers in the environment. An energy function was applied over this matrix.

The energy function used in this work is defined in the equation 5, where $tanh$ is the hyperbolic tangent function, $computer$ is a computer in the environment, $process$ is a chunk, λ is the gain parameter and u is the voltage vector or synaptic weight.

$$E = \frac{((1.0 + tanh(u[computer][process] * \lambda))}{2} \quad (5)$$

The Hopfield network runs until it reaches the function minimum. The algorithm also computes the maximum RTT (*Round Trip Time*), adding the costs involved in the communication by using the equation 6 where: *ncomps* is the total number of computers in the environment, *nchunks* is the number of chunks in the distributed file, *rtt* is the communication cost to access a chunk i in the computer *comp*.

$$\sum_{comp=0}^{ncomps} \sum_{i=0}^{nchunks} rtt[comp][i] \tag{6}$$

The central property of an energy function is that it always decreases (or hold on a value) when a system evolves in accordance with its dynamics [4]. In this way, the attractors (machines with lower communication cost) are the energy surface local minimum.

The algorithm is initialized with the example input pattern, in this case, the distributed environment characteristics (number of computers, $fsize$, $csize$, rtt, etc). In the next step, it is used the product rule, i.e., the Hebb learning postulate [4] to compute the network synaptic weights (equation 7) where: u is the synaptic weight vector (voltages), τ is the weight update speed, A and B are constants which represent the importance of the terms, *logmaxrtt* is a logistic function applied to the maximum RTT and *logvariance* is a logistic function of the statistical RTT variance.

$$\begin{aligned}\sum_{i=0}^{nchunks} \sum_{j=0}^{ncomps} u[i][j] += (-(\frac{u[i][j]}{\tau}) - (A * logmaxrtt) \\ - (B * logvariance)) * TIME\_STEP\end{aligned} \tag{7}$$

The state vector elements are updated in an asynchronous way, i.e., randomly and one at a time, according to equation 7. The iteration is repeated until the state vectors remain unchanged. The output is a vector with the response times for reading *ncp* parallel chunks.

5 Results

The figure 4 presents the mean response time (y-axis) for reading or writing data in distributed files using the solutions obtained with the genetic algorithm and the Hopfield neural network. The x-axis represents the number of chunks read or written in parallel. Experiments were conduced until reaching a minimum sample size following the central limit theorem [22]. It is possible to observe that results of the genetic algorithm distributing file chunks over 32 computers and Hopfield for the same configuration are similar, with the first technique presenting a slightly better performance. The results for the genetic algorithm distributing over 256 computers and Hopfield in the same situation show a small performance advantage for the second technique, since it presents a lower mean response time for data access.

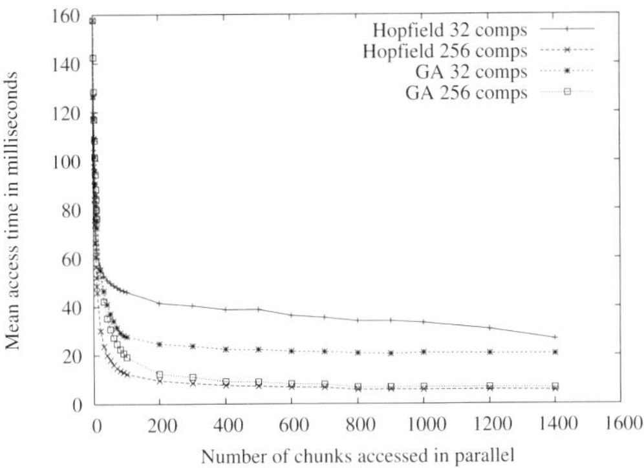

Fig. 4. Results in response time for reading or writing

The evaluation of the mean time to access data is relevant. However, it is also important to evaluate the cost to find data distribution solutions in an environment (figure 5). The figure 6 presents the same results from figure 5 in a scale which allows a better comparison (in time) required to find solutions of file chunk distributions.

The time used to find the distribution solution is close to zero in Hopfield with 32 computers. Hopfield with 256 computers and the genetic algorithm with 32 computers show similar response times, around 2, 000 milliseconds, i. e., 2 seconds. The genetic algorithm with 256 computers presents larger execution times, thus making difficult the observation of the data presented in figure 5 and requiring a zoom, resulting in the figure 6.

The obtained results confirmed that the data distribution quality of genetic algorithm and Hopfield are similar, although the processing time of the former is prohibitive and less interesting for the considered problem. The genetic algorithm approach may lead to a processing overload in a system, making unfeasible the distribution of file chunks.

The figure 7 presents the speedup (equation 8, where: T_s is execution time in the slowest system and T_f the execution time in the fastest one) in order to compare

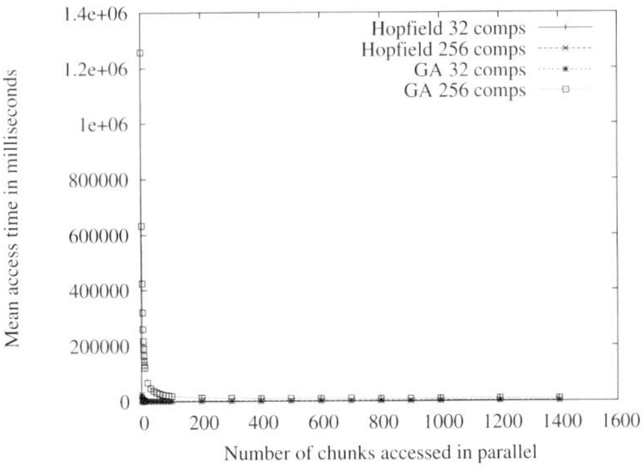

Fig. 5. Time consumed to find out a solution of data distribution

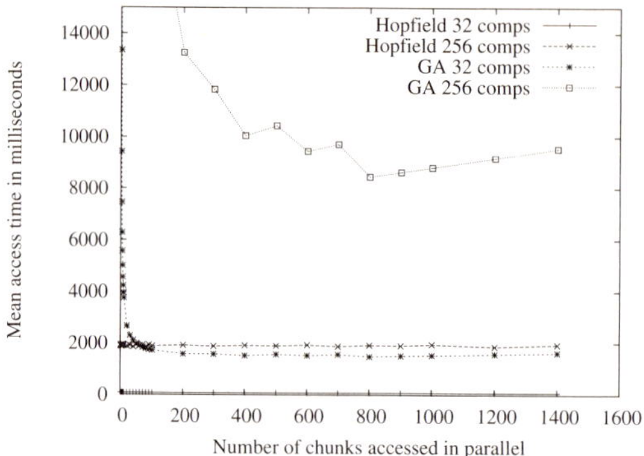

Fig. 6. Time consumed to find out a solution of data distribution – Zoom

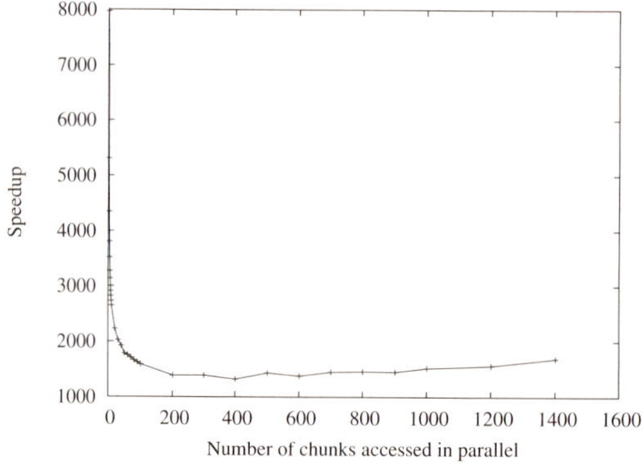

Fig. 7. Speedup of genetic algorithm compared to Hopfield – data distributed over 256 computers

the processing time of genetic algorithms to Hopfield. The Speedup compares the execution speed improvements from one application to another. It was observed that, in the worst case, where 1 chunk is being accessed at a time, Hopfield was 7,968.54 times faster than the genetic algorithm. In all cases the processing cost of the genetic solution is at least 1,300 times larger than Hopfield. Even when using a small number of generations, around 1,000, Hopfield has shown better result than the genetic approach.

$$S = \frac{T_s}{T_f} \tag{8}$$

6 Conclusion

This paper evaluated optimization techniques for distributing file chunks in distributed environments. Two techniques were evaluated, the first based on genetic algorithms and the second on Hopfield neural networks. Both approaches presented good results for data distribution, although the time needed to find out solutions with Hopfield was significantly better. This improvement is due to the fact that genetic algorithms use probabilistic and extensive searches when defining and evaluating individuals, while Hopfield uses the descendent gradient in order to change network weights and identify the global minimum of the energy function. For environments with a large number of computers, Hopfield networks are indicated for data distribution and optimization.

Acknowledgments

This paper is based upon work supported by CAPES, Brazil under grant no. 032506-6. Any opinions, findings, and conclusions or recommendations expressed in this material are those of the authors and do not necessarily reflect the views of CAPES.

References

1. Stockinger, H., Samar, A., Allcock, B., Foster, I., Holtman, K., Tierney, B.: File and object replication in data grids (2001)
2. GridNFS: `http://www.mgrid.umich.edu/projects/gridnfs.html`
3. Semenov, M.A., Terkel, D.A.: Analysis of convergence of an evolutionary algorithm with self-adaptation using a stochastic lyapunov function. Evol. Comput. 11, 363–379 (2003)
4. Haykin, S.: Neural Networks - A Compreensive Foundation. Prentice-Hall, Englewood Cliffs (1994)
5. Hopfield, J.J.: Neural networks and physical systems with emergent collective computational abilities. Neurocomputing: foundations of research, 457–464 (1988)
6. Freedman, C.S., Burger, J., Dewitt, D.J.: SPIFFI — a scalable parallel file system for the Intel Paragon. IEEE Transactions on Parallel and Distributed Systems 7, 1185–1200 (1996)
7. Huber Jr., J.V., Elford, C.L., Reed, D.A., Chien, A.A, Blumenthal, D.S.: PPFS: A high performance portable parallel file system. In: Jin, H., Cortes, T., Buyya, R. (eds.) High Performance Mass Storage and Parallel I/O: Technologies and Applications, pp. 330–343. IEEE Computer Society Press and Wiley, New York (2001)
8. Guardia, H.C.: Considerações sobre as estratégias de um Sistema de Arquivos Paralelos integrado ao processamento distribuído. PhD thesis, EPUSP (1999)
9. Carns, P.H., Ligon III, W.B., Ross, R.B., Thakur, R.: PVFS: A parallel file system for linux clusters. In: Proceedings of the 4th Annual Linux Showcase and Conference, Atlanta, GA, USENIX Association, pp. 317–327 (2000)
10. Dodonov, E.: Um mecanismo integrado de Cache e Prefetching para sistemas de entrada e saída de alto desempenho. Master's thesis, DC/UFSCar (2004)
11. OpenAfs: `http://www.openafs.org/`
12. Foster, I., Kesselman, C., Tuecke, S.: The anatomy of the Grid: Enabling scalable virtual organizations. In: Sakellariou, R., Keane, J.A., Gurd, J.R., Freeman, L. (eds.) Euro-Par 2001. LNCS, vol. 2150, p. 1. Springer, Heidelberg (2001)
13. Datafarm, U.G.: Building a high performance parallel file system
14. GSI-SFS: `http://www.biogrid.jp/e/research_work/gro1/gsi_sfs/`
15. Foster, I., Kesselman, C.: Globus: A metacomputing infrastructure toolkit. The International Journal of Supercomputer Applications and High Performance Computing 11, 115–128 (1997)

16. Gnutella protocol: http://rfc-gnutella.sourceforge.net/
17. FastTrack protocol: http://en.wikipedia.org/wiki/FastTrack
18. eDonkey protocol: http://wiki.tcl.tk/11094
19. BitTorrent protocol: http://www.bittorrent.com/protocol.html
20. Overnet network: http://en.wikipedia.org/wiki/Overnet
21. E., D., F., M.R., T., Y.L.: A network evaluation for lan, man and wan grid environments. In: Yang, L.T., Amamiya, M., Liu, Z., Guo, M., Rammig, F.J. (eds.) EUC 2005. LNCS, vol. 3824, Springer, Heidelberg (2005)
22. Shefler, W.C.: Statistics: Concepts and Applications. Benjamin, Cummings (1988)

Techniques for Designing Efficient Parallel Graph Algorithms for SMPs and Multicore Processors

Guojing Cong[1] and David A. Bader[2,*]

[1] IBM TJ Watson Research Center, Yorktown Heights, NY, 10598
gcong@us.ibm.com

[2] College of Computing, Georgia Institute of Technology, Atlanta, GA, 30332
bader@cc.gatech.edu

Abstract. Graph problems are finding increasing applications in high performance computing disciplines. Although many regular problems can be solved efficiently in parallel, obtaining efficient implementations for irregular graph problems remains a challenge. We propose techniques for designing and implementing efficient parallel algorithms for graph problems on symmetric multiprocessors and chip multiprocessors with a case study of parallel tree and connectivity algorithms. The problems we study represent a wide range of irregular problems that have fast theoretic parallel algorithms but no known efficient parallel implementations that achieve speedup without serious restricting assumptions about the inputs. We believe our techniques will be of practical impact in solving large-scale graph problems.

Keywords: Spanning Tree, Minimum Spanning Tree, Biconnected Components, Shared Memory.

1 Introduction

Graph theoretic problems arise in several traditional and emerging scientific disciplines such as VLSI design, optimization, databases, and computational biology. There are plenty of theoretically fast parallel algorithms, for example, optimal PRAM algorithms, for graph problems; however, in practice few parallel implementations beat the best sequential implementations for arbitrary, sparse graphs. Much previous algorithm design effort aimed at reducing the complexity factors with work-time optimality as the ultimate goal. In practice this often yields complicated algorithms with large hidden constant factors that frustrate attempt of implementation on real parallel machines [1,2].

Modern symmetric multiprocessors (SMPs) and chip multiprocessors (CMPs) are becoming very powerful and common place. Most of the high performance computers are clusters of SMPs and/or CMPs. PRAM algorithms for graph problems can be emulated much easier and more efficiently on SMPs than on distributed memory platforms because shared memory allows for fast, concurrent access to an irregular datastructure that is often difficult to partition well for distributed memory systems. Unfortunately,

* This work is supported in part by NSF Grants CAREER CCF-0611589, NSF DBI-0420513, ITR EF/BIO 03-31654, IBM Faculty Fellowship and Microsoft Research grants, and DARPA Contract NBCH30390004.

I. Stojmenovic et al. (Eds.): ISPA 2007, LNCS 4742, pp. 137–147, 2007.

emulation – even with aggressive algorithm engineering efforts – oftentimes does not produce parallel implementations that beat the best sequential implementation. There remains a big gap between the algorithmic model and SMPs. Architectural factors including memory hierarchy and synchronization cost are hard to encompass into a parallel model, yet they greatly affect the performance of a parallel algorithm. For many parallel models, it is hard to predict for a given problem whether an $O(\log n)$ algorithm runs faster than an $O(\log^2 n)$ algorithm on any real architecture. New design paradigm that considers these factors are called for.

We have conducted extensive study on the design of practical parallel algorithms for graph problems that run fast on SMPs. Our parallel implementations for the spanning tree, minimum spanning tree (MST), biconnected components, and other problems, achieved for the first time good parallel speedups for sparse, arbitrary inputs on SMPs [3,4,5]. In this paper we present techniques that are proven to be effective either by our experimental study or by theoretic analysis on realistic models for fast graph algorithm design. These techniques address factors of modern architectures that are transparent to most parallel models but crucial to performance. For example, we propose asynchronous algorithms for reducing the synchronization overhead and I/O efficient PRAM simulation for designing cache-friendly parallel algorithms with irregular graph inputs. The problems we study are fundamental in graph theory. We believe our techniques can help build efficient parallel implementations for a wide range of graph algorithms on SMPs, and future manycore systems.

The rest of the paper is organized as follows. The remainder of Section 1 summarizes previous studies of experimental results and our new results. Sections 2, 3 and 4 discuss the impact of limited number of processors, synchronization and multiple levels of memory hierarchy on performance, respectively, and present parallel techniques for the corresponding scenarios. Section 5 presents an example for reducing the constants in algorithmic overhead. In Section 6 we conclude and give future work. Throughout the paper, we use n and m to denote the number of vertices and the number of edges of an input graph $G = (V, E)$, respectively.

1.1 Previous Studies and Results

Different variations of the spanning tree and connected components algorithms based on the "graft-and-shortcut" approach have been implemented (see, e.g., [6,7,8,9]) on a number of platforms including Cray Y-MP/C90, TMC CM-2 and CM-5, and Maspar MP-1. These implementations achieve moderate speedups for regular inputs, and are slower than the best sequential implementation for irregular inputs.

Chung and Condon [10] implemented parallel Borůvka's algorithm on the CM-5. Dehne and Götz [11] studied practical parallel algorithms for MST using the BSP model. The parallel implementations either do not beat the sequential implementation, or are not appropriate for handling large, sparse graphs.

Woo and Sahni [12] presented an experimental study of computing biconnected components on a hypercube. They use an adjacency matrix as the input representation that wastes a huge amount of memory for sparse graphs.

1.2 Our Results

We have developed a number of practical parallel algorithms [3,4,5]. Our methodology for designing these parallel algorithms is based upon an in-depth study of available PRAM approaches and techniques as discussed in this paper. Our spanning tree algorithm is the first to achieve good parallel speedups for the notoriously hard arbitrary, sparse instances [3]; our MST algorithm is the only one known that achieves parallel speedups for all test inputs [4]; our biconnected components algorithm filters out edges that are not essential in computing the components, and runs fast with relatively low memory consumption compared with previous implementations [5]. Table 1 summarizes our performance results on SUN Enterprise 4500 with 10 processors. All the input graphs have $1M$ vertices but different number of edges. Comparing against the best sequential implementation, the "prior speedup" column shows the speedups we achieve for our implementation of the best performing algorithms published prior to our study, and the "our speedup" column shows the speedups we achieve for algorithms designed with techniques presented in this paper. We see that prior algorithms run slower than the best sequential implementation with a moderate number of processors, while our new algorithms achieve good parallel speedups.

Table 1. Performance comparison of our algorithms and best performing previously published algorithms. Here $1M = 1048576$, $n = 1M$, and m is the number of edges.

Problem	Input Type	Edges(m)	Prior speedup	Our speedup
Spanning Tree	random graph	$20M$	0.36	3.1
	Torus	$4M$	0.5	2.6
Minimum Spanning Tree	random graph	$20M$	0.46	4.5
	Torus	$4M$	2.2	3.7
Biconnected Components	random graph	$20M$	0.72	3.8

2 Adapting to the Available Parallelism

Nick's Class ($\mathcal{NC}$) is defined as the set of all problems that run in polylog-time with a polynomial number of processors. Whether a problem P is in $\mathcal{NC}$ is a fundamental question. The PRAM model assumes an unlimited number of processors, and explores the maximum inherent parallelism of P. Although several massively parallel supercomputers now have thousands of processors, the number of processors available to a parallel program is still nowhere near the size of the problem. Acknowledging the practical restriction of limited parallelism provided by real computers, Kruskal *et al.* [13] argued that non poly-logarithmic time algorithms (e.g., sublinear time algorithms) could be more suitable than polylog algorithms for implementation with practically large input size. We observe this is still true for current problems and parallel machines. In practice if an $\mathcal{NC}$ algorithm does not perform well, it is worthwhile to consider $\mathcal{EP}$ (short for *efficient parallel*) algorithms which by the definition in [13] is the class of algorithms that achieve a polynomial reduction in running time with a poly-logarithmic inefficiency. More formally, let $T(n)$ and $P(n)$ be the running time of a parallel algorithm and the number of processors employed, and $t(n)$ be the running time of the best sequential algorithm, then $\mathcal{EP}$ is the class of algorithms that satisfies

$$T(n) \leq t(n) \text{ and } T(n) \cdot P(n) = O(t(n)).$$

We refer to $\mathcal{EP}$ as a class of algorithms where the design focus is shifted from reducing the complexity factors to solving problems of realistic sizes efficiently with a limited number of processors.

Many $\mathcal{NC}$ algorithms take drastically different approaches than their respective sequential algorithms and incur significant parallel overhead. For many algorithms it could take impractically large problem sizes to show any performance advantage. The $\mathcal{EP}$ algorithms, on the other hand, can have advantages coming from limited parallelism, i.e., larger granularity of parallelism, and hence less synchronization. $\mathcal{EP}$ algorithms also tend to work better with distributed-memory environments (e.g., many practical LogP and BSP algorithms [14,15]).

We propose a technique that blends the $\mathcal{EP}$ and $\mathcal{NC}$ approaches so that an algorithm adapts to the number of available processors. The implementation is efficient when there are few processors such as in a multicore chip or a small SMP, and provides enough parallelism when scaling to a larger number of processors. As a case study next we present the design of our MST algorithm – MST-BC.

Many parallel MST algorithms in the literature are based on Borůvka's approach [16,4]. These algorithms run in $O(\log^k n)$ (k is a constant) time with $O(n)$ processors. Performance in general is not good on current SMPs. MST-BC uses multiple, coordinated instances of Prim's sequential algorithm running on the graph's shared data structure. In fact, it marries Prim's algorithm with that of the naturally parallel Borůvka approach. The basic idea of MST-BC is to let each processor simultaneously run Prim's algorithm from different starting vertices. Each processor keeps growing its subtree when there exists a lightweight edge that connects the tree to a vertex not yet in another tree, and the subtree matures when it can grow no further. The lightest incident edges are then found for the isolated vertices (the Borůvka step). Special care is taken to ensure the isolation of mature subtrees that is crucial to the correctness of the algorithm. When all of the vertices have been incorporated into mature subtrees, each subtree is contracted into a supervertex, and the approach is called recursively until only one supervertex remains. We refer interested readers to [4] for details of the algorithm and proof of correctness.

MST-BC is adaptive to the available number of processors. When there are n processors available, each processor can grow only a subtree of one edge in an iteration, MST-BC behaves exactly as parallel Borůvka's algorithm; when there is only one processor available, MST-BC degenerates to Prim's algorithm. The interesting case is that when p ($p \ll n$) processors are available, multiple instances of Prim's algorithm runs in each iteration alternated with Borůvka steps. MST-BC performs well when the graph is large and sparse and the number of processors is small compared with the input size. The technique of adapting to the number of available processors is also applicable in the case of parallel spanning tree.

3 Reducing Synchronization Cost

Synchronization is achieved by using barriers or locks. Synchronization is crucial to correctness and performance. In Section 3.1 we present a technique called lazy synchronization that aggressively reduces the amount of synchronization primitives in an algorithm. Section 3.2 shows how to trade a large number of expensive locking operations with a small number of barrier operations.

3.1 Lazy Synchronization

Barriers can be placed after each statement of the program to ensure PRAM-like synchronous execution. For many algorithms, however, this practice will seriously degrade the performance. Barriers are only needed at steps where events should be observed globally.

When adapting a PRAM algorithm to SMPs, a thorough understanding of the algorithm usually suffices to eliminate unnecessary barriers. Reducing synchronization is a pure implementation issue. Lazy synchronization, on the other hand, is an algorithm design technique. Lazy synchronization means much more than inserting a minimum number of synchronization primitives. More importantly, we design algorithms that are as asynchronous as possible. Reduced level of synchronization in general yields greater granularity of parallelism. Lazy synchronization also allows nondeterministic intermediate results but deterministic solutions. For example, in MST-BC, the selection of a light edge is nondeterministic, while we are guaranteed that the answer is one of the possible spanning trees of minimum weight. In a parallel environment, to ensure correct final results oftentimes we do not need to define a total ordering on all the events occurred, and a partial ordering in general suffices. Relaxed constraints on ordering reduce the number of synchronization primitives in the algorithm. Application of lazy synchronization generally involves a careful arrangement of read/write operations to reach consensus with proofs of correctness.

Here we take the spanning tree problem as a case study. Our parallel spanning tree algorithm for shared-memory multicores and multiprocessors has two main steps: 1) stub spanning tree, and 2) work-stealing graph traversal. In the first step, one processor generates a stub spanning tree, that is, a small portion of the spanning tree by randomly walking the graph for $O(p)$ steps. The vertices of the stub spanning tree are evenly distributed into each processor's queue, and each processor in the next step will traverse from the first element in its queue. After the traversals in step 2, the spanning subtrees are connected to each other by this stub spanning tree. In the graph traversal step, each processor traverses the graph (by coloring the nodes) similar to the sequential algorithm in such a way that each processor finds a subgraph of the final spanning tree. Work-stealing is used to balance the load for graph traversal (We refer interested readers to [3] for details of work-stealing).

One problem related to synchronization that we have to address is that there could be portions of the graph traversed by multiple processors and be in different subgraphs of the spanning tree. The immediate remedy is to synchronize using either locks or barriers. With locks, coloring the vertex becomes a critical section, and a processor can only enter the critical section when it gets the lock. Although the nondeterministic behavior is now prevented, it does not perform well on large graphs due to an excessive number of locking and unlocking operations.

In our algorithm there are no barriers introduced in graph traversal. As we will show the algorithm runs correctly without barriers even when two or more processors color the same vertex. In this situation, each processor will color the vertex and set as its parent the vertex it has just colored. Only one processor succeeds at setting the vertex's parent to a final value. For example, using Fig. 1, processor P_1 colored vertex u, and processor P_2 colored vertex v, at a certain time they both find w unvisited and are now in a race to color vertex w. It makes no difference which processor colored w last because w's parent will be set to either u or v (and it is legal to set w's parent to either of them; this will not change the validity of the spanning tree, only its shape). Further, this event does not create cycles in the spanning tree. Both P_1 and P_2 record that w is connected to each processor's own tree. When each of w's unvisited children are visited by various processors, its parent will be set to w, independent of w's parent.

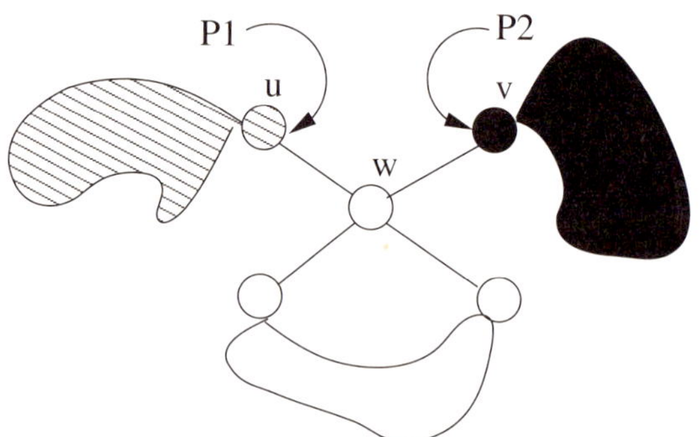

Fig. 1. Two processors P_1 and P_2 see vertex w as unvisited, so each is in a race to color w and set w's parent pointer. The shaded area represents vertices colored by P_1, the black area represents those marked by P_2, and the white area contains unvisited vertices.

Lemma 1. *On a shared-memory parallel computer with sequential memory consistency, the spanning tree algorithm does not create any cycles.*

We refer interested readers to [3] for details of the proof. Note that different runs of the algorithm may produce trees of different topologies, yet each is a correct spanning tree.

3.2 Barriers and Locks

Locks and barriers are meant for different types of synchronizations. In practice, the choice of using locks or barriers may not be very clear. Take the "graft and shortcut" spanning tree algorithm for example. For graph $G = (V, E)$ represented as an edge list, we start with n isolated vertices and $2m$ processors. For edge $e_i = \langle u, v \rangle$, processor P_i $(1 \leq i \leq m)$ inspects u and v, and if $v < u$, it grafts vertex u to v and labels e_i to be a spanning tree edge. The problem here is that for a certain vertex v, its multiple incident edges could cause grafting v to different neighbors, and the resulting tree may not be valid (note that Shiloach-Vishkin's original algorithm is based on priority CRCW [17]). To ensure that v is only grafted to one of the neighbors, locks can be used. Associated with each vertex v is a flag variable protected by a lock that shows whether v has been grafted. In order to graft v a processor has to obtain the lock and check the flag, thus race conditions are prevented. A different solution uses barriers [18] in a two-phase election. No checking is needed when a processor grafts a vertex, but after all processors are done (ensured with barriers), a check is performed to determine which one succeeds and the corresponding edge is labeled as a tree edge. There is no clear winner between the two synchronization scheme for performance. Whether to use a barrier or lock is dependent on the algorithm design as well as the barrier and lock implementations. Locking typically introduces large memory overhead. When contention among processors is intense, the performance degrades seriously.

4 Cache Friendly Design

The increasing speed difference between processor and main memory makes cache and memory access patterns important factors for performance. The number (and pattern) of memory accesses could be the dominating factor of performance instead of computational complexities. For sequential algorithms, there have emerged quite a number of cache-aware and cache-oblivious algorithms that are shown to have good cache performance (see, e.g.[19,20]).

The fact that modern processors have multiple levels of memory hierarchy is generally not reflected by most of the parallel models. As a result, few parallel algorithm studies have touched on the cache performance issue. The SMP model proposed by Helman and JáJá is the first effort to model the impact of memory access and cache over an algorithm's performance [21]. The model forces an algorithm designer to reduce the number of non-contiguous memory accesses. However, it does not give hints to the design of cache-friendly parallel algorithms. Park *et al.* [22] proposed adjacency array representation of graphs that is more cache-friendly than adjacency list, and the access pattern can still be erratic. Simultaneous memory accesses to "random" memory locations determined by the irregular structure of the input make it hard to come up with cache friendly designs.

Chiang *et al.* [23] presented a *PRAM simulation* technique for designing and analyzing efficient external-memory (sequential) algorithms for graph problems. This technique simulates the PRAM memory by keeping a task array of $O(N)$ on disk in $O(scan(N))$ blocks. For each PRAM step, the simulation sorts a copy of the contents of the PRAM memory based on the indices of the processors for which they will be operands, and then scans this copy and performs the computation for each processor being simulated. The following can be easily shown:

Theorem 1. *Let A be a PRAM algorithm that uses N processors and* $O(N)$ *space and runs in time T. Then A can be simulated in* $O(T \cdot sort(N))$ *I/Os [23].*

Here $sort(N)$ represents the optimal number of I/Os needed to sort N items striped across the disks, and $scan(N)$ represents the number of I/Os needed to read N items striped across the disks. Specifically,

$$sort(x) = \frac{x}{DB} \log_{\frac{M}{B}} \frac{x}{B}$$

$$scan(x) = \frac{x}{DB}$$

where M = # of items that can fit into main memory, B = # of items per disk block, and D = # of disks in the system.

We observe that a similar technique can be applied to the cache-friendly parallel implementation of PRAM algorithms. I/O efficient algorithms exhibit good spatial locality behavior that is critical to good cache performance. We apply the *PRAM simulation* technique to the efficient parallel implementation. Instead of having one processor simulate the PRAM step, we have $p \ll n$ processors perform the simulation concurrently. The simulated PRAM implementation is expected to incur few cache block transfers between different levels. For small input sizes it would not be worthwhile to apply this technique as most of the data structures can fit into cache. As the input size increases, the cost to access memory becomes more significant, and applying the technique becomes beneficial.

Our experimental studies show that on current SMPs oftentimes memory writes have larger impact than reads on the performance of the algorithm [4]. This is because with the snoopy-cache consistency protocol for current SMPs, memory writes tend to generate more protocol transactions than memory reads and concurrent writes also create consistency issues of memory management for the operating system and the corresponding memory management is of higher cost than reads. We could have incorporated this fact into a parallel model by separating the number of memory reads and writes as different parameters, but then other questions like how to weigh their different importance would emerge. Here the message is that for graph problems that are generally irregular in nature, when standard techniques of optimizing the algorithm for cache performance do not apply, trading memory reads for writes might be an option. For a detailed example, we refer interested readers to the parallel Borůvka's implementation described in [4].

5 Algorithmic Optimizations

For most problems, parallel algorithms are inherently more complicated than the sequential counterparts, incurring large overheads with many algorithm steps. Instead of lowering the asymptotic complexities, in many cases we can reduce the constant factors and improve performance. Algorithmic optimizations are problem specific. We demonstrate the benefit of such optimizations with our biconnected components algorithm [5].

We developed a new algorithm that eliminates edges that are not essential in computing the biconnected components. For any input graph, edges are first eliminated before the computation of biconnected components is done so that at most $min(m, 2n)$ edges are considered. Although applying the filtering algorithm does not improve the asymptotic complexity, in practice, the performance of the biconnected components algorithm can be significantly improved.

We say an edge e is *non-essential* for biconnectivity if removing e does not change the biconnectivity of the component to which it belongs. Filtering out *non-essential* edges when computing biconnected components (of course we will place these edges back in later) may produce performance advantages. Recall that the Tarjan-Vishkin algorithm (TV) is all about finding the equivalence relation $R_c'^*$ [18,16]. Of the three conditions for R_c', it is trivial to check for condition 1 which is for a tree edge and a non-tree edge. Conditions 2 and 3, however, are for two tree edges and checking involves the computation of *high* and *low* values. To compute *high* and *low*, we need to inspect every nontree edge of the graph, which is very time consuming when the graph is not extremely sparse. The fewer edges the graph has, the faster the *Low-high* step. Also when we build the auxiliary graph, the fewer edges in the original graph means the smaller the auxiliary graph and the faster the *Label-edge* and *connected-components* steps.

Suppose T is a BFS tree, then we have

Theorem 2. *The edges of each connected component of* $G-T$ *are in one biconnected component [5].*

Combining our algorithm for eliminating *non-essential* edges and TV, the new biconnected components algorithm runs in $max(O(d), O(\log n))$ time with $O(n)$ processors on CRCW PRAM, where d is the diameter of the graph. Asymptotically the new algorithm is not faster than TV. In practice, however, we achieve parallel speedups upto 4 with 12 processors on SUN Enterprise 4500 using the filtering technique. This is remarkable, given that the sequential algorithm runs in linear time with a very small hidden constant in the asymptotic complexity.

6 Conclusion and Future Work

We present algorithm design and engineering techniques for running parallel algorithms on SMPs, multicore, and manycore processors, with case studies taken from tree and connectivity problems. Our implementations are the first that achieve good speedups over a wide range of inputs. PRAM algorithms provide a good resource of reference when solving problems with parallel computers, yet with real machines, modifications to PRAM algorithms or new designs are necessary for high performance. We discussed the impact of limited number of processors, synchronization and multiple level of memory hierarchies on algorithm designs, and presented techniques that deal with these factors. As these factors we discussed will continue to be crucial to an algorithm's performance on multiprocessor systems, we expect our studies have significant impact on the experimental studies of parallel computing. We are also investigating running parallel graph algorithms on systems with transactional memory.

References

1. Bader, D.A., Cong, G.: Efficient parallel algorithms for multi-core and multiprocessors. In: Rajasekaran, S., Reif, J. (eds.) Handbook of Parallel Computing: Models, Algorithms, and Applications, CRC press, Boca Raton, USA (2007)
2. Bader, D.A., Cong, G., Madduri, K.: Design of multithreaded algorithms for combinatorial problems. In: Rajasekaran, S., Reif, J. (eds.) Handbook of Parallel Computing: Models, Algorithms, and Applications, CRC press, Boca Raton, USA (2007)
3. Bader, D.A., Cong, G.: A fast, parallel spanning tree algorithm for symmetric multiprocessors (SMPs). In: IPDPS 2004. Proceedings of the 18th International Parallel and Distributed Processing Symposium, Santa Fe, New Mexico (2004)

4. Bader, D.A., Cong, G.: Fast shared-memory algorithms for computing the minimum spanning forest of sparse graphs. In: IPDPS 2004. Proc. 18th Int'l Parallel and Distributed Processing Symp., Santa Fe, New Mexico (2004)
5. Cong, G., Bader, D.: An experimental study of parallel biconnected components algorithms on symmetric multiprocessors (SMPs). In: IPDPS 2005. Proceedings of the 19th International Parallel and Distributed Processing Symposium, Denver, Colorado (2005)
6. Greiner, J.: A comparison of data-parallel algorithms for connected components. In: SPAA-94. Proc. 6th Ann. Symp. Parallel Algorithms and Architectures, Cape May, NJ, pp. 16–25 (1994)
7. Hsu, T.S., Ramachandran, V., Dean, N.: Parallel implementation of algorithms for finding connected components in graphs. In: Bhatt, S.N. (ed.) Parallel Algorithms: 3rd DIMACS Implementation Challenge, October 17-19, 1994. DIMACS Series in Discrete Mathematics and Theoretical Computer Science, vol. 30, pp. 23–41 (1997)
8. Krishnamurthy, A., Lumetta, S.S., Culler, D.E., Yelick, K.: Connected components on distributed memory machines. In: Bhatt, S.N. (ed.) Parallel Algorithms: 3rd DIMACS Implementation Challenge, October 17-19, 1994. DIMACS Series in Discrete Mathematics and Theoretical Computer Science, vol. 30, pp. 1–21. American Mathematical Society, Providence, RI (1997)
9. Goddard, S., Kumar, S., Prins, J.: Connected components algorithms for mesh-connected parallel computers. In: Bhatt, S.N. (ed.) Parallel Algorithms: 3rd DIMACS Implementation Challenge, October 17-19, 1994. DIMACS Series in Discrete Mathematics and Theoretical Computer Science, vol. 30, pp. 43–58 (1997)
10. Chung, S., Condon, A.: Parallel implementation of Borůvka's minimum spanning tree algorithm. In: IPPS'96. Proc. 10th Int'l Parallel Processing Symp., pp. 302–315 (1996)
11. Dehne, F., Götz, S.: Practical parallel algorithms for minimum spanning trees. In: Workshop on Advances in Parallel and Distributed Systems, West Lafayette, IN, pp. 366–371 (1998)
12. Woo, J., Sahni, S.: Load balancing on a hypercube. In: Proc. 5th Int'l Parallel Processing Symp., Anaheim, CA, pp. 525–530. IEEE Computer Society Press, Los Alamitos (1991)
13. Kruskal, C., Rudolph, L., Snir, M.: Efficient parallel algorithms for graph problems. Algorithmica 5, 43–64 (1990)
14. Culler, D.E., Karp, R.M., Patterson, D.A., Sahay, A., Schauser, K.E., Santos, E., Subramonian, R., von Eicken, T.: LogP: Towards a realistic model of parallel computation. In: 4th Symp. Principles and Practice of Parallel Programming, ACM SIGPLAN, pp. 1–12. ACM Press, New York (1993)
15. Valiant, L.G.: A bridging model for parallel computation. Commun. ACM 33, 103–111 (1990)
16. JáJá, J.: An Introduction to Parallel Algorithms. Addison-Wesley Publishing Company, New York (1992)
17. Shiloach, Y., Vishkin, U.: An $O(\log n)$ parallel connectivity algorithm. J. Algs. 3, 57–67 (1982)
18. Tarjan, R., Vishkin, U.: An efficient parallel biconnectivity algorithm. SIAM J. Computing 14, 862–874 (1985)
19. Arge, L., Bender, M., Demaine, E., Holland-Minkley, B., Munro, J.: Cache-oblivious priority queue and graph algorithm applications. In: Proceedings of the 34th Annual ACM Symposium on Theory of Computing, Montreal, Canada, pp. 268–276. ACM Press, New York (2002)
20. Bender, M., Demaine, E., Farach-Colton, M.: Cache-oblivious search trees. In: FOCS-00. Proc. 41st Ann. IEEE Symp. Foundations of Computer Science, Redondo Beach, CA, pp. 399–409. IEEE Press, Los Alamitos (2000)

21. Helman, D.R., JáJá, J.: Designing practical efficient algorithms for symmetric multiprocessors. In: Goodrich, M.T., McGeoch, C.C. (eds.) ALENEX 1999. LNCS, vol. 1619, pp. 37–56. Springer, Heidelberg (1999)
22. Park, J., Penner, M., Prasanna, V.: Optimizing graph algorithms for improved cache performance. In: IPDPS 2002. Proc. Int'l Parallel and Distributed Processing Symp., Fort Lauderdale, FL (2002)
23. Chiang, Y.J., Goodrich, M., Grove, E., Tamassia, R., Vengroff, D., Vitter, J.: External-memory graph algorithms. In: Proceedings of the 1995 Symposium on Discrete Algorithms, pp. 139–149 (1995)

Distributed Memorization for the k-Vertex Cover Problem

Peter J. Taillon

School of Computer Science, Carleton University,
1125 Colonel By Drive, Ottawa, Ontario, K1S 5B6, Canada
ptaillon@scs.carleton.ca

Abstract. We present the first investigation of the well-known memorization technique for solving the k-Vertex Cover problem in a distributed setting. Memorization was introduced by Robson [15] in his paper on solving the Maximum Independent Set problem. The idea is to augment a recursive algorithm with the capability to store subproblem instances and solutions of bounded size in a table that can be quickly referenced, so that subproblems are guaranteed to be solved exactly once. This approach has recently been applied with success to improve the complexity of the fixed-parameter tractable algorithms for solving the k-Vertex Cover problem [12,5]. We present a general parallel approach for using memorization to solve the k-Vertex Cover problem where the subgraphs are precomputed [12]. In this case, the subgraphs and corresponding solutions are generated in a preprocessing step, rather than during the recursion. Our technique makes efficient use of the processors generating the lookup table, while at the same time requiring less space. We describe a distributed algorithm using this technique, well-suited to cluster or grid computing platforms.

1 Introduction and Background

The objective of this work is to combine the advances in FPT k-vertex cover algorithms with the promise of large-scale cluster architectures that are becoming the *de facto* parallel environment. This paper is a natural extension of the work presented in [6] that presented the first parallel k-vertex cover algorithm. Recent results have shown the applicability of parallel FPT k-vertex cover for solving large-scale problems from computational biology in grid or cluster-based computing environments [4,1]. In grid computing, potentially heterogeneous machines are networked to form a virtual parallel machine. This aggregation of computational power is ideally suited to large real-world problems that scale beyond current dedicated parallel hardware. For example, typical instances that arise in problems in computational biology are beyond feasibility even for polynomial time algorithms. In an attempt to tackle such problems, there are instances of computational consortia, e.g., university research centres, confederating their resources using wide-area networking for a short-term, common experiment (e.g., see [13,14]). This type of massive-scale, cooperative computational endeavour is likely the prototype for future experiments that require

I. Stojmenovic et al. (Eds.): ISPA 2007, LNCS 4742, pp. 148–159, 2007.

resources beyond those available at a single site. With an ever-growing number of consortia, it is likely this approach will witness greater acceptance.

This paper is organized as follows. We begin with an overview of fixed-parameter tractability, and the memorization technique for solving the k-VERTEX COVER problem. Next we describe a generic parallel algorithm for efficiently generating the memorization lookup table. We then propose a distributed adaptation of the algorithm for a grid framework to take advantage of more extensive, possibly heterogeneous, computational resources.

1.1 Parameterized Complexity

The problem of deciding if a graph, $G = (V, E)$, has a *vertex cover*, i.e., a subset of vertices $VC \subseteq V$, $|VC| \leq K$, such that every edge is adjacent to one of the vertices in VC, is one of the original six problems shown to be NP-complete by Karp [11]. A closely-related problem is to determine an *independent set*, that is to say a subset of vertices, $I \subseteq V$, such that no two vertices in I are adjacent. Downey and Fellows [10] developed parameterized tractability as a framework for studying classes of problems that are NP-complete and yet for which there exist algorithms that decide the problem in time bounded by an exponential function of some fixed parameter, k. Thus the parameterized version of VERTEX COVER, known as the k-VERTEX COVER problem, asks whether the graph G has a vertex cover of size at most k, where k is fixed. Algorithms for problems that are *fixed-parameter tractable*, or FPT, have a complexity described by $O(n^{O(1)} + f(k))$, where n is the size of the problem instance, f is an arbitrary function, and k is a constant.

1.2 FPT Techniques

Essentially all FPT k-vertex cover algorithms consist of two phases: a series of *kernelization* operations followed by an exhaustive *bounded tree search*.

Kernelization is a polynomial-time process in which a problem instance, $\langle G = (V, E), k\rangle$, is reduced to an instance, $\langle G' = (V', E'), k'\rangle$, where the size of V' is bounded by a function of the parameter k and $k' \leq k$. The graph G has a k-vertex cover if and only if the graph G' has a k'-vertex cover. The current best kernelization algorithms generate linear kernels, i.e., the graph G' consists of at most $2k'$ vertices. For a survey of kernelization techniques see [2].

Bounded tree search [10] is a combinatorial search method in which a kernelized problem instance, $\langle G', k'\rangle$, can be exhaustively analyzed and where the associated recursion tree is bounded in size by a function, $f(k')$. For this phase the focus is on formulating branching rules that identify small vertex-adjacency patterns. These branching rules infer the possible local minimum vertex covers for these patterns. For example, let x be the root node in the search tree with an associated instance $\langle G' = (V', E'), k'\rangle$ and let $VC \subseteq V'$ denote a set of vertices thought to be in the k'-vertex cover. Now consider some vertex v in V'. We can create two subproblems under node x, each of which can be solved recursively: (i) we add vertex v to VC, generating subproblem

$\langle G'' = G' \setminus \{v\}, k'' = k' - 1\rangle$; or (ii) we add the vertices $N(v)$ to VC, generating subproblem $\langle G'' = G' \setminus N[v], k'' = k' - \deg(v)\rangle$.[1] This straightforward branching rule yields an algorithm with complexity $O(kn + 2^k k^2)$. The current best algorithms, employing more intricate branching rules, have complexity $O(kn + c^k)$, where $c < 2$.

1.3 Parallel FPT

Algorithms for solving the k-Vertex Cover problem that combine parallelism with FPT techniques have been investigated with notable success [6,1]. We describe a simplified version of the parallel framework introduced in [6] and subsequently used in [1]. We assume there are p processors, each labelled P_i, $0 \le i \le p-1$, connected with some network mechanism. Let $\langle G', k'\rangle$ be a kernelized instance at the root of the search tree. The processors generate in parallel a breadth-first search tree of some depth, j, with $O(p)$ leaves, using the branching rule described above in Subsection 1.2. To create a proper tree the processors, once at depth $O(\log p)$, must each have a unique subproblem and it must be the case that no subproblem is left unassigned. After executing $O(\log p)$ branching operations, each processor P_i, $0 \le i \le p-1$, recursively searches its subproblem $\langle G'_i, k'_i\rangle$ located at leaf i.

1.4 Memorization

Robson [15,16] uses a technique similar to dynamic programming, called *memorization* or *memoization*, to solve the Maximum Independent Set problem. Given an n-vertex graph, $G = (V, E)$, the main idea is to maintain a lookup table, T, of small subgraphs of bounded size derived from G, and their corresponding maximum independent sets. The algorithm uses a recursive search tree to find a maximum independent set, $I \subseteq V$, through a series of complex branching rules similar in structure to those derived for k-vertex cover algorithms. Let $G_i = (V_i, E_i)$ denote a subproblem where $|V_i| \le \alpha n$ and $0 < \alpha < 1$ is a constant. When G_i is generated during recursion, the subproblem is solved exactly for some maximum independent set, I_i. The pair $\langle G_i, I_i\rangle$ is then stored in a lookup table. If instance G_i is generated later as a subproblem in another branch of the tree, then the maximum independent set I_i associated with G_i can be extracted in polynomial time. A value for α can be determined that balances the cost of building the table with subgraphs of size at most αn and the cost of the initial search tree to some depth $n - \alpha n$. Robson's algorithm has complexity $O(1.211^n)$ requiring exponential space [15] and was recently improved to $O(1.189^n)$ [16].

Memorization can be adapted to the k-Vertex Cover problem but only if the underlying algorithm is *standard*, that is to say it uses vertex-deletion operations during the tree search. Algorithms that use vertex-folding, and as a result introduce new vertices during the tree search, can not be used in conjunction with memorization (e.g., [8]). In the case of the parameterized k-Vertex

[1] $N(v)$ denotes the set of vertices adjacent to vertex v and $N[v] = N(v) \cup \{v\}$.

COVER problem, the parameter can be used to bound the size of the subgraphs. Niedermeier and Rossmanith [12] show how to reduce the complexity of their k-VERTEX COVER algorithm, with running time $O(kn + 1.29175^k k)$ using polynomial space, to one with complexity $O(kn + 1.2832^k k)$ and exponential space. Unlike Robson, their idea is to precompute the subgraphs and solutions in a preprocessing phase.

Recall from Subsection 1.2 the relationship between a graph and the size of the minimum vertex cover given a problem with a linear kernel: the input to the tree search phase is a instance, $\langle G', k' \rangle$, where G' consists of at most $2k'$ vertices. In the first phase, the algorithm generates all induced subgraphs of G' of size up to some $s = \alpha k'$, and stores all precomputed solutions in the table, each of which has a cover size at most $\alpha k'/2$. In the second phase, the recursive search proceeds as usual on instance $\langle G', k' \rangle$ with the following change: when the value of the parameter at some level i in the tree drops below the threshold, $k'_i \leq \alpha k'/2$, the precomputed solution corresponding to the subgraph is extracted in polynomial time from the lookup table.

We denote by $T(k')$ the size of a search tree of depth k'. Let $T(k' - \alpha k'/2)) \cdot O(k)$ be the cost to generate a search tree to some intermediate depth $k' - \alpha k'/2$ and look up a solution, and let $T(\alpha k'/2) \cdot 2\binom{2k'}{\alpha k'}$ denote the cost of building the table of precomputed solutions for induced subgraphs of size up to $\alpha k'$. The time complexity of the algorithm is bounded by, $T(k') \leq T(k' - \alpha k'/2) \cdot O(k) + O\Big(T(\alpha k'/2) \cdot \binom{2k'}{\alpha k'}\Big)$. Computing a value of $\alpha = 0.05245457$ minimizes the overall running time by equating of $T(k' - \alpha k'/2)$ and $T(\alpha k'/2) \cdot \left(4/\alpha^{\alpha}(2-\alpha)^{2-\alpha}\right)^{k'}$ to within constant factors, where the last term is a bound using Stirling's formula. Substituting α into $T(k - \alpha k/2)$, which in this case describes the current best standard algorithm for k-VERTEX COVER of [12], gives a running time $O(kn + (1.29175^{k-\alpha k/2})k)$. This yields an overall complexity of $O(kn + 1.2831^k k)$.

The recently-published algorithm of Chandran and Grandoni [5] combines the idea of Robson, whereby subproblems of bounded size are solved exactly once and stored for future lookup, with the parameter bounding approach of Niedermeier and Rossmanith. The initial branching in the tree consists of processing vertices of high degree, in this case degree greater than 6. They reduce the size of the lookup table by only storing induced, connected subgraphs of order at most 6, and derive a careful strategy for branching on small components by deducing a lower bound on the size of the minimum vertex cover for each component. The algorithm solves the k-VERTEX COVER problem with complexity $O(kn + 1.2745^k k^4)$.

The memorization approach of Niedermeier and Rossmanith can be seen to be effectively the same technique as that used by Robson, and Chandran and Grandoni, except the cost of initially processing a small subgraph instance is extracted from the complexity of the search tree phase, and done in an explicit preprocessing step.

2 Parallel Memorization

In what follows, we use as a basis the algorithm of Niedermeier and Rossmanith [12] that relies on the precomputation of small subgraphs and corresponding solutions. We first describe adapting memorization to this framework in a straightforward manner, with the branching described in Subsection 1.2. This would entail each processor, P_i, $0 \leq i \leq p-1$, following a unique path to an intermediate depth, and then generating a local lookup table, T_i. Assuming an initial input $\langle G = (V, E), k \rangle$, and some α determined *a priori*, we sketch the algorithm as follows:

1. In parallel, the processors calculate a kernelized graph instance, $\langle G' = (V', E'), k' \rangle$.
2. The processors build a search tree of depth $O(\log p)$, by branching on the vertices in V', such that each processor, $P_0, P_1, \ldots, P_{p-1}$, has a unique subproblem at a given leaf, i, $0 \leq i \leq p-1$.
3. Using the vertex set at leaf i, $0 \leq i \leq p-1$, a processor P_i generates all induced, connected subgraphs up to some bounded size, $s = \alpha k$, and their corresponding minimum vertex covers, and stores them locally in table, T_i.
4. Each processor P_i, $0 \leq i \leq p-1$, then processes its local subproblem as per some standard memorization algorithm, while referring locally to lookup table T_i.

2.1 Asymptotic Analysis

Without loss of generality, let the table T_0, generated at P_0, be the largest lookup table generated over all processors, P_i, $0 \leq i \leq p-1$. Let t_0 be its size, with $T(t_0)$ being the time required to generate the table. This complexity includes the cost of generating all induced, connected subgraphs, and determining their minimum vertex covers.

3 Refined Parallel Memorization

In the sections that follow, we focus our attention on the complexity of building the lookup table in a parallel environment. We now describe a refinement to the lookup table generation phase that enables us to reduce its time and space complexity requirements. The refinement is based on a key observation that many subgraphs in the lookup table will be generated unnecessarily, i.e., they, in effect, will never be used later to lookup a solution. Although we refer to the algorithm of Niedermeier and Rossmanith, this framework can serve to adapt any future standard memorization algorithm to a parallel environment.

3.1 Effective Table Generation

We begin with a simple illustration from which we derive a more general theorem. This initial exposition pertains to a sequential model, and in the next section we show how this leads to the improved parallel algorithm. Consider the stage in the algorithm at which we generate the lookup table, T, containing all induced, connected subgraphs up to some bounded size, s, derived from kernelized instance $\langle G' = (V', E'), k' \rangle$. Along with each subgraph entry we store an associated minimum cover. In what follows, let VC be a set of vertices representing the partial k-vertex cover at some step in the tree search. Having generated T, we begin search tree branching as per the steps of some standard algorithm. Assume the first processing rule we apply is the binary branching rule described in Subsection 1.2, i.e., given a node in the search tree and some vertex v, we create two subproblems each of which can be solved recursively: (i) we add vertex v to VC, generating subproblem $\langle G'' = G' \setminus \{v\}, k'' = k' - 1 \rangle$; or (ii) we add the vertices $N(v)$ to VC, generating subproblem $\langle G'' = G' \setminus N[v], k'' = k' - \deg(v) \rangle$. We now consider all the possible induced, connected subgraphs that can be derived from the remaining vertices in the subgraphs G'' located at these two children. We require three important lemmas:

Lemma 1. *Consider the subset of all subgraphs, $\mathcal{G}$, stored in T, that contain at vertex v. The subset $\mathcal{G}$ will never be accessed by any lookup during subsequent steps of the algorithm.*

Proof. After the algorithm generates the lookup table T the search tree phase begins. The search tree is generated by removing combinations of vertices that are hypothesized to be in the vertex cover. After the first application of the branching rule, the vertex v has been removed from G'. Any subsequent remaining subgraph derived from G' can not contain the vertex v, and so no future lookup will ever access any of the subgraphs in $\mathcal{G}$. □

Following the exposition in Subsection 1.4, let $s = \alpha k$, $0 < \alpha < 1/2$, such that the number of induced, connected subgraphs in table T is at most $O\left(\binom{2k}{\alpha k}\right)$.

Lemma 2. *If we postpone the generation of table T by one level of the tree search, T will contain fewer induced, connected subgraphs, $O\left(\binom{2(k-1)}{\alpha(k-1)}\right)$.*

Proof. Follows directly from Lemma 1. □

The next lemma describes the relationship described in Lemma 2 between the tables located at each child in the tree.

Lemma 3. *Let V' be a set of vertices, $v \in V'$, and let T_v represent a lookup table created by generating all induced, connected subgraphs from the set $V' \setminus \{v\}$. After branching on $\{v\}$, $N(v)$ as described above, the contents of the lookup table in the leftmost child, T_v, is a superset of the induced, connected subgraphs in the rightmost child, $T_{N(v)}$. This implies the following relationship: $T \supset T_v \supset T_{N(v)}$.*

Proof. Let $G' = (V', E')$ be a graph with $2k$-vertices and let $s > 2$. Recall that we only want to store induced, connected subgraphs. Given the set of vertices, V', we can generate all induced, connected subgraphs of size at most s by enumerating all subsets of vertices and checking whether a given subset forms an induced, connected subgraph of G' in time complexity $\sum_{i=2}^{s}\binom{2k}{i} \in O\Big(\binom{2k}{s}\Big)$. Consider two sets of vertices, $S_1 = V'$ and $S_2 = V' \setminus \{v\}$, and again consider enumerating all subsets of S_1 and of S_2 of sizes $2, 3, \ldots, s$. The subsets generated by S_1 and S_2 will only differ in the subsets that contain vertex v. If the subsets form an induced, connected subgraph of G, then clearly the subgraphs generated by sequences from S_1 form a superset of the subgraphs generated by the sequences in S_2. □

Lemmata 1, 2, 3 imply we can generate a smaller lookup table if we postpone its generation during the search tree phase. More importantly, although we branched and created two children at the root, we still need only generate one lookup table, and this table is in fact smaller than one that would have been built prior to the branching phase. This refinement can be generalized as follows:

Lemma 4. *Let $G = (V, E)$ be a graph and let $S = (v_1, v_2, \ldots, v_m)$ be a sequence of vertices drawn from V. Given an initial search tree, associate with each level, i, $1 \leq i \leq m$, a distinct branching rule that generates two children, $v_i \cup VC$ and $N(v_i) \cup VC$. We call set S a* branching sequence. *(Note that S forms an independent set.) The relationship between the lookup tables at each leaf of the search tree at depth m can be described as follows:*

$$T_{v_1,v_2,\ldots,v_m} \supset T_{v_1,v_2,\ldots,v_{m-1},N(v_m)} \supset \cdots \supset T_{N(v_1),N(v_2),\ldots,N(v_{m-1}),N(v_m)}$$

Proof. Follows from Lemmata 1, 2, 3. □

Lemma 4 argues that if you can find a branching sequence of vertices, the size of the lookup table can be reduced even further. These four lemmata indicate that it is possible to improve any k-vertex cover algorithm that uses memorization by determining a branching sequence, and branching on them appropriately at the beginning of the search tree phase. We can now state a more general theorem as follows:

Theorem 1. *Given a kernelized graph, $G' = (V', E')$, and a branching set S with m vertices, we can build a lookup table, T, of induced, connected subgraphs of size at most $\alpha(k-m)$, with corresponding minimum vertex covers, in time, $O\Big(T(\alpha(k-m)/2) \cdot \binom{2(k-m)}{\alpha(k-m)}\Big)$, where $T(\alpha(k-m)/2)$ is the time complexity to find a minimum cover in a subgraph of size at most $\alpha(k-m)$.*

Proof. Follows directly from Lemmata 1, 2, 3, 4. □

3.2 Improved Parallel Memorization

The refinement described in Section 3.1 can be used to develop an efficient parallel algorithm based on memorization. We assume p processors are available, and an initial instance $\langle G = (V, E), k\rangle$. We describe the algorithm as follows:

1. In parallel, processors, P_i, $0 \leq i \leq p-1$, calculate a kernelized graph instance, $\langle G' = (V', E'), k'\rangle$.

2. The processors calculate a branching sequence, $S = (v_1, v_2, \ldots, v_m)$, drawn from V', where $\log_2 p \leq m$.
3. The processors build a search tree of depth $\log p$, by branching on the vertices in $S = (v_1, v_2, \ldots, v_{\log_2 p})$, such that each processor, P_i, has a unique subproblem at a given leaf, i, $0 \leq i \leq p-1$:
   (a) without loss of generality, assume the path from the root of the tree to processor P_0 consisted of applying the rules that added vertices to the partial cover as follows: $v_1 \cup VC, v_2 \cup VC, \ldots, v_m \cup VC$;
   (b) in parallel, the processors, P_i, $0 \leq i \leq p-1$, generate all induced, connected subgraphs in size up to some bound, s, and their solutions, based on the vertex set of the instance at processor P_0, and store these in a table, T_0.
4. Each processor P_i, $0 \leq i \leq p-1$, then processes its local subproblem as per a standard memorization algorithm, referencing a copy of T_0 stored locally.

The current best sequential k-vertex cover algorithms initially process vertices with high degree, e.g., degree greater than 6, using the binary branching rule. In Step (2), after $\log_2 p$ vertices have been added to the sequence, we can enforce that only candidate vertices with degree > 6 are added to S. In Step (4), each processor begins its own local branching using the remaining sequence vertices, $v_{\log_2 p+1}, \ldots, v_m$. This maximizes the number of vertices excluded from the table, while ensuring that local sequential branching complexity is not affected by the choice of sequence vertices.

Asymptotic Analysis. Without loss of generality, again let T_0 be the largest lookup table generated over all processors, $P_i, 0 \leq i \leq p-1$, with size t_0 and let $T(t_0)$ be the time required to generate the table. The improved table generation algorithm has space complexity $O(t_0)$ and time complexity $O(T(t_0)/p)$.

Determining a Branching Sequence. An important step in the algorithm is the determination of the set S, of size $m \geq \log_2 p$, with which we initially built the search tree. It is not sufficient to branch on some arbitrary set, $S \subseteq V$, as this will not guarantee the property described in Lemma 4. Let $G = (V, E)$ be a graph for which we want to determine a branching sequence, S. We can determine S by iterating through V, selecting a vertex $v \in V$, adding v to S, and removing vertices $N[v]$ and adjacent edges from V. A branching sequence can be thus generated in $O(|E|)$. After $\log_2 p$ vertices have been added to S, selection can be restricted to vertices with degree greater than 6: these vertices can be the initial branching vertices at each processor during the local computation phase. In this way, the complexity of the local sequential branching at each processor is unaffected and the table generated can be reduced further in size.

Generating Subgraphs in Parallel. Step (3)b of the algorithm, wherein the induced, connected subgraphs are generated, can be performed efficiently in parallel. There has been extensive research in developing adaptive parallel algorithms for generating combinatorial objects [3,17], where adaptive means the algorithm can run on a parallel model assuming some arbitrary number of processors.

4 Distributed Memorization Algorithm

In this section we describe a Coarse-Grained Multicomputer (CGM) style algorithm for managing the lookup table data structure, where we require the table, of size t_0, to be distributed evenly across the processors. This model is well-suited to distributed computation in that is assumes commodity compute nodes that typically have large amounts of memory and storage.

4.1 Distributed Lookup Table

The CGM model [9] comprises p processors, P_i, $0 \leq i \leq p-1$ with local memory storage such that $n/p \geq p^{\epsilon}$, $\epsilon > 0$, and interconnected with an arbitrary communication fabric. Computation and communication are separated into synchronous super-steps. In a communication round, each processor can send or receive $O(n/p)$ data words. The running time of a CGM algorithm is the sum of the time required for each computation and communication round. In the coarse-grained model, we assume a single copy of the lookup table data structure for T_0, generated as described in Subsection 3.2, is evenly distributed across the memory of the processors, requiring $O(t_0/p)$ space per node.

In our distributed model, a table lookup is replaced with a query sent to a remote processor. The processors execute a fixed number of local computations steps, $O(q)$, during which they can generate at most q queries. The queries are stored in a queue and later processed during a synchronized bulk communication step. Because the queries are independent within a given tree search, a processor can simply backtrack and continue searching instead of waiting for each query to be resolved. This also eliminates the possibility of a single processor being overwhelmed with query requests, and not being able to advance with its own tree search, by restricting query processing to a discrete phase rather than having the processors issue requests asynchronously. Finally, by randomizing the local search phase at each processor, we reduce the likelihood that processors eventually generate subgraphs that map to table entries stored on the same processor.

In what follows, we make the following assumptions. First, the lookup table data structure has been created and indexed, so that each processor knows the ranges of the subgraphs stored at a given processor. This means the processors executed the algorithm described in Subsection 3.2, and processors exchanged table indexing information. Secondly, initial branching has taken place, i.e., each processor, P_i, $0 \leq i \leq p-1$, has a unique subproblem instance, $\langle G'_i, k'_i \rangle$. Thirdly, each processor begins its local search from a randomly selected vertex in its own subproblem, $v_i \in V'_i$.

The algorithm consists of a repetition of the following phases, until either a processor determines the input is a yes-instance, or all processors determine a no-instance:

1. **Local computation:** each processor, P_i, $0 \leq i \leq p-1$, executes the standard memorization algorithm, for some fixed number of steps on its local

subproblem instance $\langle G_i', k_i' \rangle$. When a processor P_i requires a lookup table access, it places its request, q_i^j, in a local queue, to a maximum of q queries.
2. **Communication:** each processor P_i traverses its query queue and forwards query, q_i^j, $1 \leq j \leq q$, to the processor that stores the appropriate segment of the lookup table. When possible, a processor will satisfy a query locally if there exists a local segment satisfying the range for that query.
3. **Local computation:** each processor P_i satisfies any query request received in the previous step by performing a local table lookup.
4. **Communication:** each processor P_i forwards the query responses to the originating processors.
5. **Local computation:** each processor P_i verifies the responses to its queries, q_i^j, by combining the value in the response with its current partial cover, to determine if a cover of size k_i' has been found. If a cover has been found, P_i notifies all other processors to terminate. Otherwise P_i resumes its suspended tree search at Step (1).

Asymptotic Analysis. We assume the number of local tree-search computation operations in Step (1) is bounded by some fixed constant, $O(q)$. The communication in Step (2) requires time $O(q(\alpha k'))$. Similarly, the computation in Step (5) would have complexity $O(q(\alpha k'))$.

Once the table is generated, segments of size $O(q^\epsilon)$, $\epsilon > 1$, can be distributed across the processors using some randomizing hash function. Scattering the segments, coupled with the randomized nature of the tree search, reduces the probability that all processors will forward all of their queries to a common node during a specific communication step. At the start of Step (1) each processor P_i randomly selects a vertex from its unique subproblem $\langle G_i', k_i' \rangle$, on which it initiates a randomized, depth-first search. With some probability each processor in Step (3) receives at most $O(q(\alpha k'))$ queries, hence, Step (3) and Step (4) would require at most $O(q(\alpha k'))$ time. This leads us to the following conjecture:

Theorem 2. *Let $O(T(k) \cdot k)$ be the sequential time for a memorization-based tree-search algorithm. We assume a CGM model, comprising p processors, P_i, $0 \leq i \leq p-1$, interconnected with an arbitrary communication fabric. The CGM-based memorization algorithm requires $O(T(k) \cdot k/p)$ local computation steps and $O((T(k)/p)/q)$ communication rounds using $O(q(\alpha k'))$-relations with high probability.*

Unfortunately, formulating a precise determination of the probability that all queries are sent to the same processor during the same time step is an extremely technical endeavour, requiring a characterization of the input graph and a distribution of its bounded-size subgraphs. Heretofore we have assumed arbitrary input for the algorithm, and so a complete analysis remains an open problem.

Bounding Computation Steps. We now consider the number of computation steps, $O(q)$, that bounds the number of queries generated. Recall that the objective of the CGM model is to minimize the impact of communication on the algorithm while maximizing local computation. During a CGM communication round, a processor P_i packs as much data as possible into a single message destined for a processor P_j in order to minimize both communication overhead and the number of communication rounds overall. This contrasts with the PRAM model for example, where unitary data is exchanged assuming negligible communication cost.

Let q be some fixed integer. Consider a processor P_i and let $T(\hat{k})$ be the size of some intermediate search tree explored by P_i, such that the $O(c^{\hat{k}})$ leaves of $T(\hat{k})$ would correspond to queries, $q_1, q_2, \ldots, q_q$, that would be sent during a communication round. Recall that the lookup table is divided into segments, each in lexicographic order, and evenly distributed across the processors. For sufficiently small q the subgraph associated with query q_1 differs from the subgraph associated with query q_q by a small, bounded number of vertices. Relative to the size of the lookup table segment at each processor, with high probability, the subgraphs associated with queries, $q_1, q_2, \ldots, q_q$, will have their solutions stored at the same processor. This implies the queries can in fact be packed into a single message destined for a specific processor during a communication round. Let h be the optimal size for a message assuming a particular underlying communication fabric. Choosing q such that $\alpha k \cdot q \leq h$ we can optimize the number of queries for a given communication round as a function of the message size. In the worst case, the subgraphs span a lexicographic boundary between segments stored on different processors, entailing a message be sent to two processors.

From our algorithm recall that a processor performs a search in random, depth-first fashion through its search tree. The property of lexicographic "closeness" between subgraphs in the queries is a natural byproduct of the fact that a processor searches the subtree $T(\hat{k})$ in its entirety before backtracking to the rest of the search tree. The height of $T(\hat{k})$ can be determined as follows. Assuming c is the base of the exponent in the complexity of the underlying k-vertex cover algorithm then $\hat{k} = \log_c q$. During the initial stages of its search, when the parameter reaches $(k - \alpha k/2) - \hat{k}$, the subtree rooted at that depth is explored exhaustively.

5 Conclusion and Future Work

We presented the first investigation of the well-known memorization technique to solve the k-Vertex Cover problem posited in what has become the standard parameterized parallel framework [6,1]. This framework can serve to adapt any future standard k-vertex cover algorithm to a parallel environment.

The objective of this work is to combine the advances in FPT k-vertex cover algorithms ([6,7,1]) with the promise of large-scale cluster architectures that are becoming the *de facto* parallel environment. Our next step is to extend this work to an experimental setting in order to better understand the impact of the massive memory resources available in large-scale commodity clusters, similar in architecture to the *Canadian Internetworked Scientific Supercomputer*, or CISS, experiments [14].

Referenccs

1. Abu-Khzam, F.N., Langston, M.A., Shanbhag, P., Symons, C.T.: Scalable parallel algorithms for FPT problems. Algorithmica 45, 269–284 (2006)
2. Abu-Khzam, F.N., Collins, R.L., Fellows, M.R., Langston, M.A., Suters, W.H., Symons, C.T.: Kernelization algorithms for the vertex cover problem: Theory and experiments. In: ALENEX. Proceedings of the ACM-SIAM Workshop on Algorithm Engineering and Experiments, pp. 62–69. ACM Press, New York (2004)
3. Akl, S.G., Gries, D.R., Stojmenović, I.: An optimal parallel algorithm for generating combinations. Information Processing Letters 33, 135–139 (1990)
4. Baldwin, N.E., Collins, R.L., Leuze, M.R., Langston, M.A., Symons, C.T., Voy, B.H.: High-performance computational tools for motif discovery. In: Proceedings of the IEEE International Workshop on High Performance Computational Biology, pp. 192–199. IEEE Computer Society Press, Los Alamitos (2004)
5. Chandran, L.S., Grandoni, F.F.: Refined memorization for vertex cover. Information Processing Letters 93, 125–131 (2005)
6. Cheetham, J., Dehne, F., Rau-Chaplin, A., Stege, U., Taillon, P.J.: Solving large FPT problems on coarse grained parallel machines. Journal of Computer and System Sciences 67, 691–706 (2003)
7. Cheetham, J., Dehne, F., Rau-Chaplin, A., Stege, U., Taillon, P.J.: A parallel FPT application for clusters. In: Proceedings of the IEEE-ACM International Symposium on Cluster Computing and the Grid (CCGrid), pp. 70–77. IEEE Computer Society Press, Los Alamitos (2003)
8. Chen, J., Kanj, I.A., Xia, G.: Improved parameterized upper bounds for VERTEX COVER. In: The 31st International Symposium on Mathematical Foundations of Computer Science (MFC), pp. 238–249 (2006)
9. Dehne, F.: Guest editor's introduction. Algorithmica Special Issue on Coarse Grained Parallel Algorithms 24, 173–176 (1999)
10. Downey, R.G., Fellows, M.R.: Parameterized Complexity. Springer, Heidelberg (1998)
11. Karp, R.: Reducibility among combinatorial problems. Complexity of Computer Computations, pp. 85–104. Plenum Press, New York (1972)
12. Niedermeier, R., Rossmanith, P.: On efficient fixed-parameter algorithms for weighted vertex cover. Journal of Algorithms 47, 63–77 (2003)
13. Pinchak, C., Lu, P., Schaeffer, J., Goldenberg, M.: Practical heterogeneous placeholder scheduling in overlay metacomputers: Early experiences. In: Feitelson, D.G., Rudolph, L., Schwiegelshohn, U. (eds.) JSSPP 2002. LNCS, vol. 2537, pp. 85–105. Springer, Heidelberg (2002)
14. Pinchak, C., Lu, P., Schaeffer, J., Goldenberg, M.: The Canadian Internetworked Scientific Supercomputer. In: Proceedings of the 17th Annual International Symposium on High Performance Computing Systems and Applications (HPCS), pp. 193–199 (2003)
15. Robson, J.M.: Algorithms for maximum independent sets. Journal of Algorithms 7, 425–440 (1986)
16. Robson, J.M.: Finding a maximum independent set in time $O(2^{n/4})$. Technical Report LaBRI Université Bordeaux I 1251-01 (2001)
17. Stojmenović, I.I.: Listing combinatorial objects in parallel. International Journal of Parallel, Emergent and Distributed Systems 21, 127–146 (2006)

MADARP: A Distributed Agent-Based System for On-Line DARP

Claudio Cubillos, Broderick Crawford, and Nibaldo Rodríguez

Pontificia Universidad Católica de Valparaíso,
Escuela de Ingeniería Informática,
Av. Brasil 2241, Valparaíso,
Chile
{claudio.cubillos,broderick.crawford,
nibaldo.rodriguez}@ucv.cl

Abstract. The present work describes the design of a distributed agent system devoted to the Dial-a-Ride Problem. This routing and scheduling problem consists in finding a set of routes and schedules for each vehicle that satisfies a set of trip requests comming from users. The agent system distributes an improved insertion heuristic for the scheduling of passengers' trip requests over a fleet of vehicles. Agents make use of the contract-net protocol as base coordination mechanism for the planning and scheduling of passenger trips.

1 Introduction

The field of passenger transport systems has received an increasing attention during last years due to different factors: contamination, high traffic and congestion problems. In addition, citizens require more flexible transportation alternatives in the cities according to their needs. The requirement of covering more diffuse travel patterns, varying periods of low demand, city-peripheral journeys, as well as commuting trips often make conventional public transport systems unable to guarantee the level of service required to address the user needs.

As response, new alternatives to satisfy de transport demands of the citizens are being conceived [1], with planning methodologies capable of considering dynamic and distributed information in the routing and scheduling process.

The present work has been focused into taking a greedy insertion heuristic for the planning and scheduling of trip requests and embedding it on a software architecture that adopts the agent paradigm as a way to provide the required distribution by means of using the contract-net protocol for coordinating the agents through the planning procedure.

The work is structured as follows. Section 2 starts presenting other works in the field for then at section 3 detailing the main actors of the Dial-a-Ride problem considered in this work. Section 4 outlines the considered dynamic variant of DARP and the agent architecture is depicted in Section 5. Section 6 explains the routing algorithm to be distributed for then drawing some conclusions at Section 7.

I. Stojmenovic et al. (Eds.): ISPA 2007, LNCS 4742, pp. 160–169, 2007.

2 Related Work

Agent technology applied to transportation has been widely researched in literature [6],[11],[13] most of them focused in the transportation of goods (e.g. vehicle routing problem, pickup & delivery problem). Although the multiagent paradigm [15] appears as a promising technology, capable of providing a flexible assignment and service, it is hard to find in literature agent architectures devoted to the transportation of passengers (e.g. dial-a-ride problem, demand-responsive transport). [11] and [13] present agent-based systems for goods transportation. [11] uses the Contract-Net Protocol (CNP) plus a stochastic post-optimization phase to improve the result initially obtained. In [13] is presented the Provisional Agreement Protocol (PAP), based on the Extended CNP and de-commitment.

In the soft computing field, we can find the use of an ant-colony based system [12], genetic algorithms (GA) for the optimization of the assignment ([9][4]) and the use of fuzzy logic for the travel times ([10] [14])

Within non-agent approaches, Coslovich et al. [3] have addressed a dynamic dial-a-ride where people might unexpectedly ask a driver for a trip at a given stop by using a two-phase method and a neighborhood of solutions generated off-line. A software system for D-DARP was proposed by Horn [7]. The optimization capabilities of the system are based on least-cost insertions of new requests and periodic re-optimization of the planned routes.

3 Main Actors

In a complex service system like the passenger transportation, there are many possible users or actors who have a direct interest in the commercial, social and infrastructural impacts of the services. These are described in the following.

3.1 End-Users

Passengers prefer to have access to a wide range of destinations and extensive coverage of the public transport services. Easy access to services both in terms of suitable vehicles and appropriate time-tables is also important to them. Suitable vehicles are easy to board and have space for luggage and personal devices. Other important requirements are an easy-to-use booking procedure, a reasonable pricing, to have sufficient and correct information on the transportation service (e.g. time-tables providing maximum operating hours) and a deliver transportation in a reasonable time period from the travel decision.

Other ordinary-passenger requirements are to have: 1) minimum number of deviations and delays on the tour, 2) access to other modes, but minimum number of transfers and 3) last-minute booking possibility. These requirements, associated with efficiency of the service are not ranked so highly amongst the special user groups, who have more time for traveling.

3.2 Operators

Transport operators' requirements for trasportation systems may vary considerably depending on the current transport market and the role of trasportation services in it. As with any other enterprise, operators aim to create viable and sustainable services for their customers. They may also want to expand their market share or develop totally new markets.

Trasportation services may be expected to increase cost efficiencies in service provision, maximize patronage, maximize occupancy and minimize dead running. To gain an increase in efficiency suitable technical support systems are needed. Special attention must be paid to the operations of the Travel Dispatch Center. The transportation market should also provide suitable easy-access vehicles for both bus and taxi operators.

Considering the trasportation service as a whole, operators are obliged to fairly allocate work, costs and revenues especially in the multi-modal trasportation environment. Integration with other modes and transport services may also be in their interest despite the natural competition between the operators and even between the different modes of transport. Freedom to continue to develop their own business and the ability to expand their coverage area may also be on the list of operators' requirements despite their interest in co-operation.

4 The On-Line DARP

From the Operational Research (OR) perspective, the transportation of passengers has traditionally been mentioned in literature under the name of Dial-a-Ride Problem (DARP). In the DARP problem, users formulate requests for transportation from a specific origin (pickup point) to a specific destination (drop-off/delivery point). Transportation is carried out by vehicles that provide a shared service in the sense that several users may be in the vehicle at the same time. The aim is to design a minimum-cost set of vehicle routes serving all requests.

The process of routing is a process of finding routes i.e. a sequence of stops, for each vehicle. The process of scheduling is a process of finding time schedules for a given set of routes. Finding an optimal schedule for a fixed route can be solved in O(n) time. A customer is a person that has a transportation request. A trip is a journey between one pickup location and its corresponding delivery location. A stop location is a common term for either pickup or delivery location.

Hence, a DARP problem solution consists of a set of routes and schedules for each vehicle. At any given time, a vehicle will be either in a slack period (i.e. idling) or in an active period. A schedule block is a continuous period of active vehicle time between any two successive slack periods. In recent literature a schedule block is referred by the term mini-cluster. A route is a sequence of vehicle stop locations. Route is sometimes called schedule sequence. A time schedule, or just schedule, is the list of times when the vehicle has to be at each stop location.

DARPs are equivalent to VRPs (Vehicle Routing Problem) with the addition of precedence and pairing constraints between pickup and drop-off locations. Our present implementation of DARP has included the following modelling assumptions:

Time Windows: In the problem variant with Time Windows (DARPTW) customers impose earliest/latest possible service time intervals. There are different models for constructing the time windows. The majority of real-life pickup and delivery problems are time restricted in a tight or loose way.

The model considers a *pickup time window [ept, lpt]* and a *delivery time window [*edt_i*, ldt]* (see Figure 1). It is considered the specification of a *delivery time* for each customer. This time is assigned to the upper bound of the delivery time window (*ldt*). The parameter *WS* sets the width of all the delivery time windows. In this a way, a vehicle serving the customer *i* must reach the destination node nd_i, neither not before the edt_i time, nor after the ldt_i time.

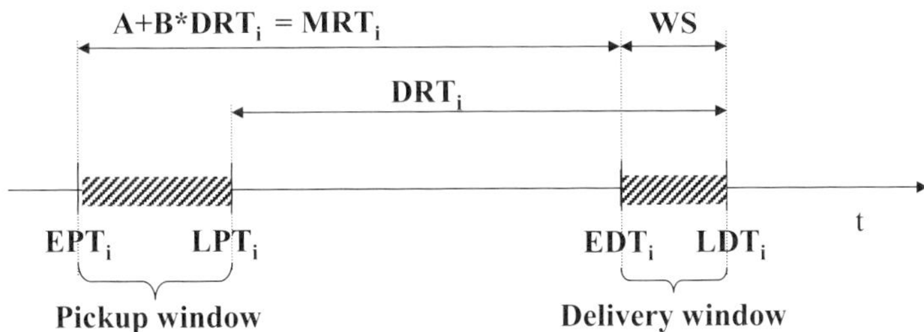

Fig. 1. Time-Windows model for clients pickup and delivery interva

Capacitated Vehicles: When servicing a customer/location involves picking up or delivering people, vehicle capacities restrict the number of customers/allocations or the number of demands that can be serviced by a given vehicle.

Multiple Vehicles: If the service will be done by one vehicle, the corresponding problem is called the single-vehicle variant of the problem (1-DARP). If there is a fleet of vehicles available for the service, the problem is known as the multi-vehicle variant of the problem (m-DARP) which corresponds in our case.

Multiple Depots: In a number of environments, not all vehicle routes start from and end on the same depot, especially when dealing with multiple vehicles. In the most general case, vehicles can have diverse depots for departing at the beginning and for arriving at the end of the journey.

Passenger Trip Duration: When dealing with passenger transportation is usual to add a limit to the length of the client's journey aboard a given vehicle. This restriction is often mentioned in literature under the name of Maximum Ride Time (MRT) and is usually proportional to Direct Ride Time (DRT), the time needed for the trip but without any deviations (shortest path). Therefore, the MRT has an specific value for each client.

In our implementation, the Delivery times (see Figure 1) define a *time window for pick-up*, the pair (ept_i, lpt_f), where $ept_i=edt_i-MRT(Ns_i,Nd_i) \wedge lpt_i=edt_i-DRTe(Ns_i,Nd_i)$.

Vehicle Route Duration: This formulation allows for constraints on the lengths and/or durations of vehicle tours. For example, such considerations arise from constraints on the geographic coverage of a given vehicle, its refueling requirements and restrictions on the drivers' duty day (e.g. different shifts or time-blocks, lunch breaks) among others.

Dynamic Model: Static formulations assume that customer demand is known ahead in time (e.g. models assuming "advance reservations"). In contrast, in dynamic models DARP (D-DARP), new customer requests are eligible for immediate consideration, requiring revisions of already established routes and schedules. In addition, dynamicity can include delays or cancellations due to traffic-jams, accidents, vehicle breakdowns or simply a client no-show situation, all of which imply a re-planning of the original routes.

5 The Agent Architecture

The agent architecture used for distributing the algorithm is presented in Figure 2. The diagram corresponds to the second step in the agent oriented software engineering (AOSE) methodology called PASSI, namelly the Agent Identification model. In [5] more details are given on the agent architecture. For further information on the PASSI methodology please refer to [2].

The main actors of the agent architecture are the Client and Vehicle GUIs, which are interface agents for communicating with the involved human actors.

The Broker's main role is to provide a publish/subscribe infrastructure that allows vehicles to enter or leave the system freely and allows clients to query the system for available transport services. Hence, it knows which transportation services are available and their characteristics. The Map is wrapping the underlying Geographical Information System (GIS) providing the routes, distances and times between points within the zone under service coverage.

The Trip-Request agent is responsible of having the client's request fulfilled and of communicating him about the result and possible changes in the original plan (e.g. delays, trip cancellations).

The Planner agent is the agent in charge of executing a mediation role in the layer. It processes all the client's requests coming through the Trip-request agents. For this, it uses the contract-net protocol (CNP) to contact all the Schedules (agents) of the available vehicles and ask them for trip proposals for a given client.

Schedule agents manage the trip plans (work-schedule) of their corresponding vehicles. In practical terms, the agent will have to make proposals upon request and in case of winning will have to include the trip into its actual plan. Upon changes informed either by the Vehicle agent or Planner agent, the Schedule agent will update the plan and reschedule the remaining requests. The schedule agent implements a greedy insertion heuristic for routing and scheduling which is further explained in the next section.

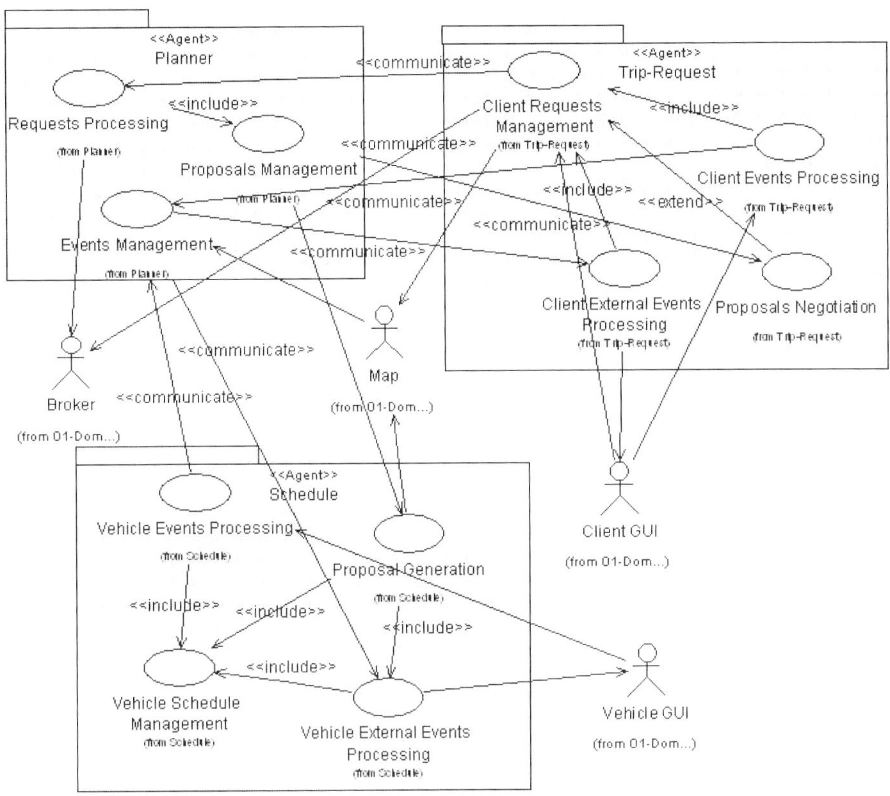

Fig. 2. The agent architecture for DARP shows the diverse agents involved, all over the Jade agent platform

6 Routing Algorithm

As stated before, during the planning process schedule agents make proposals of trip insertions which are managed by the planner. Therefore, each of these agents contains a scheduling heuristic to search in the state space for suitable alternatives.

The routing algorithm used by vehicles (schedule agents) for finding the "optimal" sequence of pickups and deliveries is based on the ADARTW algorithm [8], a constructive greedy heuristic. ADARTW finds all the feasible ways in which a new customer can be inserted into the actual work schedule of a vehicle, choosing the one that offers the maximum additional utility according to a certain objective function.

Figure 3 shows a schedule block that serves 3 customers (h, i, j) while evaluating the insertion of a fourth one (customer x). Each of them has their pick-up (+) and delivery (-) stops respectively.

The search must include all the schedule blocks contained in the vehicle's work-schedule. In a block with already d stops (2 per customer) there are (d+1)(d+2)/2 possible insertions, considering that the customer's pickup must always precede his

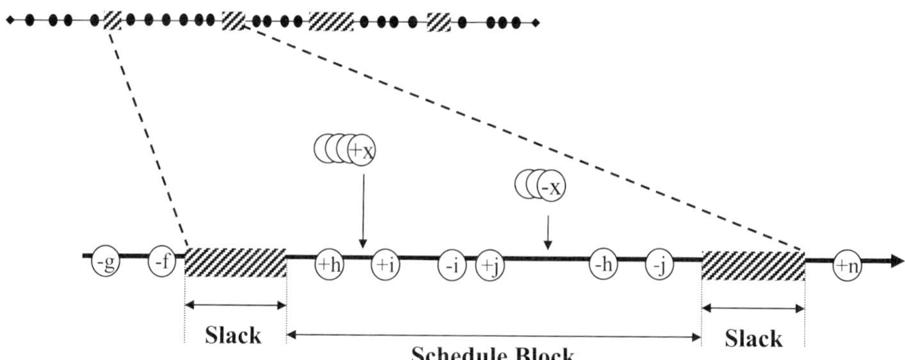

Fig. 3. Work-schedule used by vehicles, consisting in sequences of schedule blocks and slacks

delivery and that is not possible to pickup a client in one block and deliver him in another (because of the block's definition).

Once we have found that a possibility of insertion is feasible, it is necessary to define the actual times for those events, that is, the Actual Pick-up Time and the Actual Delivery Time. This problem is often mentioned in literature as the scheduling problem, as once the sequence of trips (route) has been fixed the following step is to define the exact position where the sequence will be placed in time.

Commonly, there will be a time interval in which can be inserted, meaning that the sequence can be scheduled more early or late in time within that interval. Several authors program the actual times as soon as possible for reducing the travel and waiting times of the customers, reason why our implementation does it in this way.

6.1 Work-Schedule

The model used for the vehicles' work-schedules considers that along the day a vehicle can be in any of these three states: at a depot, in travel or inactive. When the vehicle is at a depot means that it has not started its service period or has just finished it. When the vehicle is in travel, means that it is actually going to pickup or delivery passengers generating schedule blocks. As [8] shows, a schedule block corresponds to a sequence of pickups and deliveries for serving one or more trip requests. A schedule block always begins with the vehicle starting on its way to pick-up a customer and ends when the last on-board customer is discharged.

The third state is when the vehicle is inactive or idle generating a slack time. In this case the vehicle is parked and waiting to serve a next customer and then begin another schedule block.

Therefore, a complete vehicle's work-schedule will have periods of vehicle's utilization (schedule blocks) and inactive periods (slacks times) in which the vehicle is available and waiting.

6.2 Time-Windows Feasibility

The time-windoews feasibility processing is tightly coupled to the work-schedule model. Within the checking algorithm, different restrictions need to be checked for a given potential solution. The most important ones are the time windows, the capacity constraints (on number and type) and the bounds on the duration of clients' ride and of vehicle route.

This represented a challenging aspect of the work, as in general is difficult to find in literature the used mechanism for tackling this point. In Jaw et al. [8] is described only in general terms and most research papers state a change from the previous work but not its specific implementation.

For a block X with *w* events representing either a pickup or a delivery of passengers, Jaw's work presents the following calculations representing how much the events can be anticipated/posticipated in time.

$BUP(X_i) = Min\ (\ Min\ (AT(X_i) - ET(X_i)\ ),\ SLK_0)$

$BDOWN(X_i) = Min\ (LT(X_i) - AT(X_i)\ )$

$AUP(X_i) = Min\ (AT(X_i) - ET(X_i)\ )$

$ADOWN(X_i) = Min\ (Min\ (LT\ (X_i) - AT(X_i)\ ),\ SLK_{w+1})$

With $0 < i < w+1$, SLK_0 and SLK_{w+1} being the (possible) slack periods immediately preceding and following the block respectively. $ET(X_i)$, $AT(X_i)$ and $LT(X_i)$ represent the early, actual and late times of the event X_i respectively.

Our developed model is based on the Jaw's calculations on BUP and ADOWN but adds the important idea of intersecting the time windows restrictions along a piece of route, allowing to simplify the processing of the time windows feasibility check and making it possible to evaluate the insertion of the whole client (pickup and delivery) at the same time.

Therefore, in the case of the implemented insertion heuristic the starting point is the schedule block under which to evaluate the insertion of the new client. The Fig. 4 (a) shows a detailed view when evaluating the insertion of the pickup (X^+) and delivery (X^-) of a client. Between the pickup and the delivery are one or more events separating them and at the beginning (or ending) of the block is a slack or the bus depot. The approach is to divide the schedule block in three sub-blocks A, B and C for the events before the pickup, in between and after the delivery respectively. A special case is when both events are consecutive meaning that the block B includes only the distance from the pickup to the delivery of the new client.

The Fig. 4 (b) shows the time windows and distances needed for the evaluation and intersection. The interval $[ET^A, LT^A]$ represents the earliest and latest times to which the event A_M can be shifted (anticipated / posticipated) without violating the time window constraints of all the events within its block. A similar thing happens with intervals $[ET^B, LT^B]$ and $[ET^C, LT^C]$ on the events B_1 and C_1 for the blocks B and C respectively. Therefore, is needed to identify the feasible shift up and shift down for each of the three blocks. For the block A are used the BUP and BDOWN of the event A_M as they consider the previous events, while for the block C the AUP and ADOWN of C_1 are needed. For block B is needed the AUP and ADOWN for B_1 but considering only until B_N and not the events on block C as the normal calculations would. Then, for interval $[ET^A, LT^A]$ we have: $ET^A = AT(A_M) - BUP(A_M)$ and $LT^A = AT(A_M) + BDOWN(A_M)$.

A similar thing happens with $[ET^B, LT^B]$ and $[ET^C, LT^C]$. Distance $D1^+$, $D2^+$, $D1^-$ and $D2^-$ correspond to the distances between the nodes indicated by the respective arrows in the figure. The next step is intersecting the time intervals of the three blocks and the two time windows coming from the new client's pickup and delivery events.

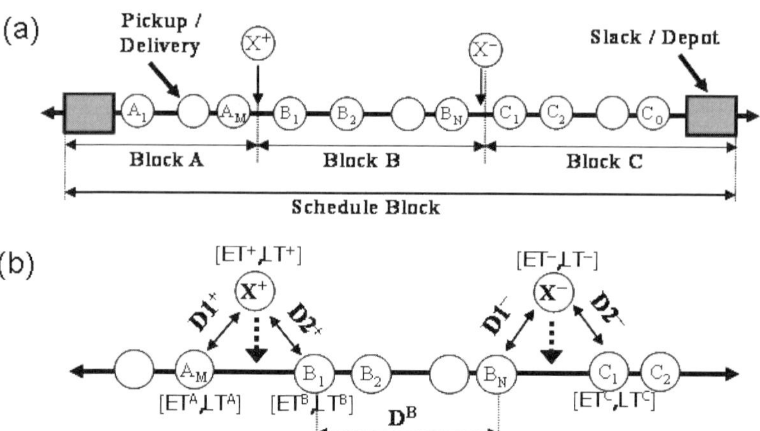

Fig. 4. Time-windows feasibility-check procedure

This intersection needs to consider the distances separating each of the five intervals. For this reason, a point in the schedule is used as reference and all the intervals are translated to that reference obtaining a single time interval [ET, LT]. By using the pickup event (X^+) of the new client as reference point and following Fig. 4 (b) are obtained:

$ET = Max (ET^A + D1^+ ; ET^+ ; ET^B - D2^+ ; ET^- - D1^- - D^B - D2^+ ; ET^C - D2^- - D1^- - D^B - D2^+)$

$LT = Min (LT^A + D1^+ ; LT^+ ; LT^B - D2^+ ; LT^- - D1^- - D^B - D2^+ ; LT^C - D2^- - D1^- - D^B - D2^+)$

This [ET, LT] interval represents the feasibility area in which to set the new schedule with respect to the reference point. The actual time for the reference point (X^+ in this case) must be set and hence the actual times for the whole schedule block can be calculated as they depend on the fixed distances between one event and another. Defining the optimal place within this interval corresponds to the scheduling problem mentioned before.

7 Conclusions

A distributed planning of trip requests based on a greedy insertion heuristic has been presented. The agent architecture makes use of the contract net protocol for the coordination of the agent society while schedule agents encapsulate the insertion heuristic, allowing a transparent parallelization of the searching procedure.

Further work considers the inclusion of probability distributions for other events such as delays, no-show of clients and vehicles breakdowns, all of which imply a re-planning process and further parallelization tests.

Acknowledgement

This work is part of Project No. 209.746/2007 entitled "Coordinación en una sociedad multiagente dedicada a la programación y control bajo ambiente dinámico", funded by the Pontifical Catholic University of Valparaíso (www.pucv.cl).

Rcferences

[1] Ambrosino, G., et al.: EBusiness Applications to Flexible Transport and Mobility Services (2001), available online at: http://citeseer.nj.nec.com/ ambrosino01ebusiness.html
[2] Burrafato, P., Cossentino, M.: Designing a multiagent solution for a bookstore with the passi methodology. In: 4th Fourth International Bi-Conference Workshop on AgentOriented Information Systems (2002)
[3] Coslovich, L., Pesenti, R., Ukovich, W.: A Two-Phase Insertion Technique of Unexpected Customers for a Dynamic Dial-a-Ride Problem. Technical Report Working paper, Universita di Trieste, Italy (2003)
[4] Cubillos, C., Rodríguez, N., Crawford, B.: A Study on Genetic Algorithms for the DARP Problem. J. In: Mira, J., Alvarez, J.R. (eds.) IWINAC 2007, Part I. LNCS, vol. 4527, pp. 498–507. Springer, Heidelberg (2007)
[5] Cubillos, C., Gaete, S.: Design of an Agent-Based System for Passenger Transportation using PASSI. In: Mira, J., Alvarez, J.R. (eds.) IWINAC 2007, Part II. LNCS, vol. 4528, pp. 531–540. Springer, Heidelberg (2007)
[6] Fischer, K., Müller, J.P., Pischel, M.: Cooperative Transportation Scheduling: An application Domain for DAI. Journal of Applied Artificial Intelligence 10 (1996)
[7] Horn, M.E.T.: Fleet Scheduling and Dispatching for Demand-Responsive Passenger Services. Transportation Research C 10C, 35–63 (2002)
[8] Jaw, J., et al.: A heuristic algorithm for the multiple-vehicle advance request dial-a-ride problem with time windows. Transportation Research 20B(3), 243–257 (1986)
[9] Jih, W., Hsu, J.: Dynamic Vehicle Routing using Hybrid Genetic Algorithms. In: IEEE Int. Conf. on robotics & Automation. Detroit (1999)
[10] Kikuchi, S., Donnelly, R.A.: Scheduling Demand-Responsive Transportation Vehicles using Fuzzy-Set Theory. Journal of Transportation Engineering 118(3), 391–409 (1992)
[11] Kohout, R., Erol, K., Robert, C.: In-Time Agent-Based Vehicle Routing with a Stochastic Improvement Heuristic. In: AAAI/IAAI Int. Conf., Orlando, Florida, pp. 864–869 (1999)
[12] Montemanni, R., Gambardella, et al.: A new algorithm for a dynamic vehicle routing problem based on ant colony system. In: 2nd Int. Workshop on Freight Transportation and Logistics (2003)
[13] Perugini, D., Lambert, D., et al.: A distributed agent approach to global transportation scheduling. In: IEEE/ WIC Int. Conf. on Intelligent Agent Technology, pp. 18–24. IEEE Computer Society Press, Los Alamitos (2003)
[14] Teodorovic, D., Radivojevic, G.: A Fuzzy Logic Approach to Dynamic Dial-A-Ride Problem. Fuzzy Sets and Systems 116, 23–33 (2000)
[15] Weiss, G.: Multiagent Systems: A Modern Approach to Distributed Artificial Intelligence. MIT Press, Massachusetts, USA (1999)

An Incremental Distributed Algorithm for a Partial Grundy Coloring of Graphs

Lyes Dekar[1], Brice Effantin[2], and Hamamache Kheddouci[2]

[1] Université de Lyon, Lyon, F-69003, France
Laboratoire LIESP, Université Lyon1, IUTA, Département Informatique,
71 rue Peter Fink, F-01000 Bourg en Bresse, France
ldekar@bat710.univ-lyon1.fr
[2] Université de Lyon, Lyon, F-69003, France
Laboratoire LIESP, Université Lyon1,
Bâtiment Nautibus (ex.710), 43 bd du 11 Novembre 1918,
69622 Villeurbanne Cedex, France
{beffanti,hkheddou}@bat710.univ-lyon1.fr

Abstract. A coloring of a graph $G=(V,E)$ is a partition of $\{V_1, V_2 \ldots V_k\}$ of V into k independent sets called color classes. A vertex $v \in V_i$ is called a Grundy vertex if it is adjacent to at least one vertex in color class V_j, for every $j<i$. In the partial Grundy coloring, every color class contains at least one Grundy vertex. Such a coloring gives a partitioning of the graph into clusters for which every cluster has a clusterhead (the Grundy vertex) adjacent to some other clusters. Such a decomposition is very interesting for large distributed systems and networks. In this paper, we propose a distributed algorithm to maintain the partial Grundy coloring of any graph G when an edge is added

1 Introduction

We consider graphs without loops or multiple edges. Let $G=(V,E)$ be a graph where $|V|=n$ and $|E|=m$. A *k-coloring* of G is a function c defined on $V(G)$ into a set of colors $C=\{1,2,\ldots,k\}$ such that for each vertex $x \in V(G)$, $c(x) \in C$. A *proper k-coloring* is a k-coloring verifying the condition $c(x) \neq c(y)$ for any pair of adjacent vertices $x,y \in V(G)$. Then, we define a *Grundy vertex* as a vertex v of G, adjacent to vertices colored by every color 1 to $c(v)-1$. A *Grundy coloring* is then defined as a proper coloring where every vertex is a Grundy vertex. In 1979, Christen and Selkow [3] introduced a parameter, the *Grundy number*, which maximizes the number of colors such that a graph admits a Grundy coloring. This parameter was very studied for different classes of graphs (trees [11, 17], power graphs [10], cartesian product of graphs [5],...). It was also compared to several other parameters (ochromatic number [7], achromatic number [11], Grundy number of the complement graph [4],...). Moreover, many algorithms were proposed to determine the Grundy coloring of a graph ([12, 13]).

More recently, Erdös et al. [8] presented the concept of *partial Grundy coloring*, which is a refinement of a Grundy coloring. A *partial Grundy k-coloring* is a proper k-coloring where any color has at least one Grundy vertex. Then the *partial Grundy*

I. Stojmenovic et al. (Eds.): ISPA 2007, LNCS 4742, pp.170–181,2007.

number of a graph G, denoted $\delta\Gamma(G)$, is the maximum integer k such that G admits a partial Grundy k-coloring. In [8], Erdös et al. related the partial Grundy number to the upper ochromatic number. More recently, Shi et al. [14] showed that the problem of determining the partial Grundy number of a graph is NP-complete even for chordal graphs and bipartite graphs. They also proposed a linear-time algorithm to determine the partial Grundy number of trees and graphs with girth larger than 8.

Although a minimal coloring is a partial Grundy coloring, in our paper we try to maximize as possible the number of colors in the graph. It is very important to note that the coloring constraint in partial Grundy coloring is not only on the neighborhood of each vertex, but on the entire graph, contrary to the Grundy coloring.

In this paper, we propose an incremental distributed algorithm to maintain a partial Grundy coloring of a graph when edges are added (to avoid to compute a new coloring for the entire graph). In addition, our algorithm aims to maximize (as possible) the number of colors in the graph. A general motivation of our work is that coloring problems are very efficient tools to model conflicts in networks for example. Moreover, a vertex coloring of a graph gives a particular partitioning (or clustering) of this graph. Thus, the studied coloring allows us to partition the graph into color classes and in each class, we determine a clusterhead able to join directly some other classes (those with less colors). Such a clustering can have many interests for example in the routing of information where it is very useful to join particular sets of vertices or to limit the length of a path. Furthermore, such an algorithm can be used to compute a partial Grundy coloring of any graph since an algorithm proposed in [14] enables to compute this coloring for a spanning tree of the graph and our method maintains the coloring when remaining edges are added (a lot of polynomial algorithms exist to determine a spanning tree [1, 2, 9]).

We first start by some definitions and notations used in the remainder of the paper. For a vertex v, we denote its neighborhood by $N(v)$ (note that the set of colors of $N(v)$ is denoted $N_c(v)$). We let $d(v)=|N(v)|$, the number of neighbors of vertex v, or its *degree*, and we let $\Delta=\max\{d(i)|i\in V\}$. In a partial Grundy coloring, we denote the Grundy vertex in each color class i by g_i. Note that, if several vertices can be Grundy vertices for color i, only one is considered. The set of Grundy vertices $\{g_1,g_2,\ldots,g_k\}$ forms the Grundy sequence $(g_1,g_2,\ldots,g_k)$ of the graph. A Grundy vertex g_i is said *satisfied* if for any $q\in[1, i-1]$, there exists at least one vertex $x\in N(g_i)$ such that $c(x)=q$. Then, in our algorithm, vertices can have different states. Thus, we define the *status* of a vertex to precise the state of each vertex. A vertex v can have three different states:

- *Grundy*: a Grundy vertex is adjacent to all colors from 1 to $c(v)-1$. Note that $v.status=Grundy$ means $g_{c(v)}\equiv v$.
- *satisfaction*: a satisfaction vertex is used by a Grundy vertex to be satisfied. It is so a neighbor of a Grundy vertex. Note that if several neighbors of a Grundy vertex has the same color, only one will be a satisfaction vertex.
- *normal*: a vertex is normal if it is neither a Grundy nor a satisfaction vertex.

The remainder of the paper is organized as follows. In Section 2 we present a first procedure used in our distributed algorithm, to evaluate the color for which a vertex can become a Grundy vertex. This procedure is important to maximize the total number of colors. Then, in Section 3 we propose a distributed approach to determine a partial Grundy coloring of a graph.

2 The Possible Grundy Color Set

In this section, we propose a procedure to determine the possible colors for which a vertex v can become a Grundy vertex. This step is important in our algorithm since it allows a vertex to determine if it can be a Grundy vertex for a color.

Let G be a graph with a partial Grundy k-coloring. Each vertex x of the graph can easily maintain the list of colors it can get, denoted by $L(x)=\{1,2,\ldots,k\}\backslash c(w)$ for any $w\in N(x)$ such that *w.status=Grundy* or *w.status=satisfaction*. In other terms, $L(x)$ contains all the colors not appearing on a Grundy or satisfaction neighbor of x. Let v be the vertex of G we want to evaluate. We define by $P(v)$, all the possible colors that v can take to become a Grundy vertex. Note that $\forall c\in P(v)$, we have $c \leq d(v)+1$. To become a Grundy vertex, v must put each color c, with $c<c(v)$, on one of its neighbors. In order to find $P(v)$, we generate a bipartite graph $H=(V_1,V_2,E')$ where the two vertices sets are $V_1=\{x_1,x_2,\ldots,x_{|L|}\}$ with $L=\bigcup_{x\in N(v)} L(x)$ and $V_2=\{y_1,y_2,\ldots,y_{|N(v)|}\}=N(v)$. Thus, V_2 is the set of neighbors of v, and V_1 is the set of colors that can get the vertices of V_2. These two sets are initially colored as follows: $c(x_i)=c$ such that $c\in L$ and $c(x_i) \neq c(x_j)$ for $1 \leq i \neq j \leq |L|$, and for any $y_i\in V_2$ we have $c(y_i)=\Delta+2$. Then, an edge $(x_i,y_i)\in E'$ exists if $c(x_i)\in L(y_i)$.

Then, we provide a procedure to find an optimal repartition of consecutive colors on the neighbors of v, represented by the vertices of V_2. The aim of this procedure is to place a maximum number of consecutive colors of V_1 on vertices of V_2 starting from the lowest one to determine the colors for which v can be a Grundy vertex. Let q be the smallest color not on a vertex of V_2. Vertex v can be a Grundy vertex of all other colors from 1 to q which does not appear on a Grundy or satisfaction neighbor of v.

```
Procedure 1: Possible_Grundy_color (v)
BEGIN
Let H=(V1,V2,E') be the bipartite graph defined by V1={x1,
x2,..., x|L|} where L=⋃_{x∈N(v)} L(x), V2={y1,y2,...,y|N(v)|}=N(v),
where each vertex xi has a different color of L and for
any yi∈V2 we have c(yi)=Δ+2. Finally, (xi,yi)∈E' exists if
c(xi)∈L(yi).
While V1≠∅ do
  Let x be the vertex of V1 such that
                                c(x)=min{c(u)|u∈V1}.
  While x∈V1 do
    Let y be a vertex of V2 such that
              d(y)=min{d(u)|u∈N(x) and c(u)>c(x)}.
    If y exists then c(y)=c(x). Endif
    Remove x from V1(H).
    If y exists and N(y)≠∅ then
          Let x be the vertex such that
          c(x)=min{c(u)|u∈N(y)}.
    Endif
   Endwhile
```

```
Endwhile
Let q=min{c|c≥1 and for any yi, c(yi)≠c}.
   If q>c(v) and v.status=satisfaction  then Q=c(v)
   Else Let Q be the set of colors {1,2,…,q}\c(yi) for
   any yi such that yi.status=Grundy or
                                  yi.status=satisfaction.
   EndIf
Return Q.
END
```

In the following, we prove that the set of colors returned by Procedure 1 contains colors for which the vertex v can be a Grundy vertex.

Lemma 1. *Procedure 1 determines a set of colors for which the vertex v can be a Grundy vertex with a $O(\Delta)$ complexity.*

Proof. Let $H=(V_1,V_2,E')$ be the bipartite graph defined in Procedure 1. Then this procedure affects colors to vertices of $V_2(H)$. The procedure returns a set of consecutive colors not appearing on a Grundy or a satisfaction neighbor of v. Then, vertex v can be a Grundy vertex for any of these colors. Moreover, each color of V_1 is assigned to a vertex of V_2 only once. As $|V_1|=\Delta$, then the complexity of Procedure 1 is $O(\Delta)$. ■

We associate to this procedure, a second $O(\Delta)$ procedure, denoted *Put_Grundy(v,c)*, used to color the vertex v and some of its neighbors according to the colors affectation performed by Procedure 1, in order to make v a Grundy vertex for color c and its neighbors satisfaction vertices for colors $1,\ldots, c-1$.

3 Distributed Approach for a Partial Grundy Coloring

In this section we study the following question: if G is a graph with a partial Grundy coloring, can such a coloring be maintained (and improved) when new edges are added to G? Thus we first prove that when an edge is added to a graph G, a partial Grundy coloring can always be found. If an edge is added between two vertices with different colors, every vertex does not need to change neither its color nor its state.

Lemma 2. *Let $G=(V,E)$ be a graph with a partial Grundy coloring. For a graph $G'=(V,E')$ where $E'=E\cup\{(x,y)\}$, if $c(x)\neq c(y)$ then G' has a partial Grundy coloring.*

Proof. Since $c(x)\neq c(y)$, the added edge does not influence the coloring of G. Then this coloring is a partial Grundy coloring for G'. ■

A conflict appears only if a new edge joins two vertices with the same color. Then, if an endpoint of a new edge is a normal vertex, only this vertex needs to change its color.

Lemma 3. *Let $G=(V,E)$ be a graph with a partial Grundy coloring. Let x and y be two non adjacent vertices of G such that $c(x)=c(y)$ and x is a normal vertex. Let $G'=(V,E')$ be a graph such that $E'=E\cup\{(x,y)\}$. Then, the graph G' admits a partial Grundy coloring.*

Proof. Since $c(x)=c(y)$ then the coloring of G' is not proper. Since the vertex x is a normal vertex, it can change its color without influencing the Grundy vertices of the graph. The vertex x takes the minimum color $c \notin N_c(x)$. The Grundy vertices of the graph G stay Grundy vertices for G'. Then, the coloring of G' is a partial Grundy coloring. ■

Grundy and satisfaction vertices have less possibilities to change their colors. However, the removal of at most one color provides a partial Grundy coloring of the graph.

Lemma 4. *Let $G=(V,E)$ be a graph with a partial Grundy k-coloring. Suppose that a color j, with $1 \leq j \leq k$ is removed from the coloring of G. Then, there exists a partial Grundy k'-coloring of G where $k' \geq k-1$.*

Proof. Let $(g_1, g_2, \ldots, g_k)$ be a Grundy sequence of G. Let S be the set of vertices colored with color j. If we put $c(s)=\varnothing$ for any $s \in S$, then the color j is removed and is not represented in the Grundy sequence. Thus, each vertex g_i, with $i>j$, is not any more a Grundy vertex. By decreasing the coloring of every vertex v of G such that $c(v)>j$, the subgraph G\S is colored with $k-1$ colors. Since any Grundy vertex g_i could be a Grundy vertex for colors 1 to $i-1$, a Grundy sequence $(g_1, g_2, \ldots, g_{k-1})$ is deduced. To complete the coloring of G, each vertex $s \in S$ is colored by $c(s)=\min\{q | q \notin N_c(s)\}$. Thus, if a vertex s is adjacent to the $k-1$ existing colors, it introduces a new color and it becomes its Grundy vertex. Therefore $k' \geq k-1$. ■

Lemma 5. *Let $G=(V,E)$ be a graph with a partial Grundy k-coloring. Let x and y be two non adjacent vertices such that x and y are not normal vertices and $c(x)=c(y)$. Let $G'=(V,E')$ be a graph such that $E'=E \cup \{(x,y)\}$. Then, the graph G' admits a partial Grundy coloring.*

Proof. The new edge makes the coloring not proper. Since x and y are not normal vertices, they cannot change their color. Therefore, if we remove the color $c(x)$ from the graph, then Lemma 4 shows that there exists a partial Grundy coloring for G'. ■

Thus, the following theorem proves that from any graph G, a partial Grundy coloring can be found for any graph $G \cup \{(i,j)\}$, where $i,j \in V(G)$.

Theorem 6. *Let $G=(V,E)$ be a graph with a partial Grundy k-coloring. Let x and y be two non adjacent vertices of G. Let $G'=(V,E')$ be a graph such that $E'=E \cup \{(x,y)\}$. Then, G' admits a partial Grundy k'-coloring with $k' \geq \max\{\chi(G), k-1\}$.*

Proof. Lemmas 2,3,4 and 5 enumerate any possible case of edge adding and prove that such a coloring exists. By definition, if a coloring is proper, it has at least $\chi(G)$ colors. Thus, G' admits a partial Grundy k'-coloring where $k' \geq \max\{\chi(G), k-1\}$. ■

Since it is always possible to find a partial Grundy coloring of a graph when an edge is added, then we study a distributed method to determine such a coloring.

3.1 Distributed Algorithm

In a distributed system, a vertex exchanges information only with its neighborhood. Every vertex has a set of local variables to determine the local state of the vertex. Distributed algorithms are a very attractive topic for a lot of fields and several graph problems arise naturally in distributed systems. For example, distributed algorithms for finding spanning trees, matchings, independent sets or particular colorings have been studied [6,15,16]. Such algorithms are so very interesting and efficient for dynamic networks.

We propose in this section a distributed algorithm to maintain a partial Grundy coloring when an edge is added to the graph. Thus, we suppose that the graph is initialized by a partial Grundy coloring. Since each vertex is autonomous, then any event or change in its neighborhood can imply a local processing that can be extended to other vertices in the graph. The edge adding is a change for which the two endvertices can react. This reaction consists to execute a set of actions according to the state of the vertex. So, both the vertices check if the edge causes a color conflict or if it can use the new edge to introduce a new color in the graph in order to increase the total number of colors. In the case where a color conflict is detected then the vertex tries to solve the problem locally by changing its state. This change can make the coloring not partial Grundy because Grundy vertices become not satisfied and thus the Grundy sequence not complete. Since the vertices are independent, Grundy vertices are able to detect that the coloring is not partial Grundy since they can verify if they are Grundy vertices. If they are not, they start a set of procedures to re-establish a partial Grundy coloring.

In our study we assume a synchronized model. Our algorithm is based on an exchange of messages between the vertices. Thus, in one communication round, every vertex checks its messages, executes some actions to react to them, and sends new messages. Then, two or more processes can be in conflict (for example, two adjacent processes colored with the same color). Then, a central daemon is used to select among all these processes, the next process to compute. Thus, if two or more processes are in conflict, we cannot predict which process will be computed next. Since each vertex is independent, it needs some local variables:

x.status: the status of the vertex *x* (*Grundy*, *satisfaction*, *Normal*)
x.t[j]: defines the sequence number of the vertex *j*.
x.k: defines the number of colors of the graph.
x.request: represents the set of colors for which a Grundy vertex is searched.
x.response: represents the set of colors for which at least one Grundy vertex has been found.
x.search: similar to *x.request* and defined for the needs of our algorithm.
x.wait: indicates if a vertex is in a waiting state (1: waiting state, 0: not waiting state).
x.del: indicates the color to delete from the graph to re-establish a partial Grundy coloring.

Some actions of our algorithm consist to broadcast a message to all the vertices in the graph. The reception of a message by a vertex causes the execution of a procedure linked to this message. To avoid the multiple execution of a procedure by a vertex, we use a sequence number. We assume that each vertex maintains a sequence number of each vertex in the graph. A vertex increases by one its sequence number and joins it every time it initiates a message. A vertex that receives this message executes the procedure only if the sequence number associated to the message sender is different to the sequence number received in the message (this means the vertex considers this message once).

Next we describe all the procedures used during the execution of our algorithm. The main procedure is *Processing()* which initiates the appropriate actions according to the graph changes (adding of edges and not proper coloring). The *Processing()* procedure is executed continuously at each vertex. It enables to reestablish a proper coloring and/or to perform the adequate actions when the graph coloring is not anymore a partial Grundy coloring.

```
Procedure 2: Processing ()
BEGIN
If c(x)=Null and ∀z∈N(x),
z.wait=0 then
 c(x)=min{l>0|∀j∈N(x),
                    c(j)≠l}.
 Maximize_colors().
Endif
If x.status=normal and
           c(x)≠Null then
 If c(x)∈N_c(x) then
  c(x)=min{l>0|∀j∈N(x),
       c(j)≠l}.
 Endif
Maximize_colors ().
Endif.
If x.status=satisfaction and
∃y∈N(x)|y.status=satisfaction
or Grundy and c(y)=c(x) then
x.status= normal.
Endif.
If x.status=Grundy and
 ∃q∈{1,2,…,c(x)-1} such
 that ¬∃y∈N(x) / c(y)=q
 and y.status=satisfaction
 then
 If
∃z∈N(x)|z.status=normal
 and q∈L(z) then c(z)=q.
 Else
  x.t[x]=x.t[x]+1.
  x.request=
         x.request∪{c(x)}.
  x.wait=1.
  Send to each z∈N(x):
  Search_Substitute(x,
            j.t[x],c(x),q).
  Start Waiting ().
 Endif
Endif
END
```

As we saw, one of the main objectives is to maximize the number of colors. The Procedure 3 is then used to check if a vertex can take a new color ($k+1$) to increase the number of colors of the graph. If it can do it then it declares itself a Grundy vertex for this color and informs the other vertices in the graph.

Moreover, during the process, if a vertex takes a new color in the graph then it informs all the other vertices by sending an *Update* (c, t_0, i) message. Every vertex x that receives this message (initiated by vertex i) updates its number of colors (Procedure 4). If many Grundy vertices have this color then only one among them stays Grundy. The selected vertex, to stay Grundy for this new color c, is the vertex with the smallest value in the set returned by *Possible_GrundyColor(x)* procedure. The other Grundy vertices (and their satisfaction vertices) for this color become normal.

In the *processing()* procedure, a vertex sends a *Search_Substitute*(j, t_0, c, q) message to find a Grundy vertex to a color. Then, when a vertex x receives a *Search_Substitute*(j, t_0, c, q) message (initiated by vertex j), it checks if it can be the Grundy vertex for the color c (Procedure 5). In order to become a Grundy vertex for c, the vertex must be a normal or satisfaction vertex and the color c must belong to the set of Grundy colors computed by the *Possible_GrundyColor* procedure. Note that a satisfaction vertex can be Grundy for its color only. If the two conditions are satisfied then x becomes a new Grundy vertex for the color c and it informs the remaining vertices by sending a *Substitute_Found* message. Otherwise it propagates the received message and notes that color q will be the removed color if no Grundy vertex is found for color c.

```
Procedure 3:Maximize_Colors()
BEGIN
If x.status=normal and
x.k+1∈Possible_GrundyColor(x)
then
   c(x)=x.k+1.
   x.k=x.k+1.
   x.status=Grundy.
   Put_Grundy(x,k+1).
   x.t[x]=x.t[x]+1.
   Send to each v∈N(x):
   Update (x.k, x.t[x], x).
Endif
END
```

```
Procedure 4:Update(c,t0,i)
BEGIN
If t0> x.t[i] then
 x.t[i]=t0.
 x.k=c.
 If c(x)=c and
      x.status=Grundy then
 If x>i then Vertex x and
every satisfaction vertex
which satisfies only x be-
come normal
  Endif
 Endif
 Send to each v∈N(x): Up-
date (c, t0, i).
Endif
END
```

```
Procedure 5:
Search_Substitute(j,t0,c,q)
BEGIN
  If t0 > x.t[j] then
     x.t[j]=t0
     x.del=q.
     if |x.request|=0 then
      waiting().
      x.wait=1.
     Endif
  x.request=x.request ∪{c}
If c∈Possi-
ble_GrundyColor(x) and
x.status=normal or satis-
faction  then
     x.status= Grundy.
     c(x)= c.
     Put_Grundy(x,c).
     x.t[x]=x.t[x]+1.
     x.response=x.response
                       ∪{c}.
     Send to each z∈N(x):
     Substitute_Found (x,
              x.t[x],c,j).
    Else
     Send to each z∈N(x):
Search_Substitute(j,t0,c,q)
      Endif
  Endif
END
```

```
Procedure 6:Substitute_Found
             (p, t0, c, j)
BEGIN
 If t0>x.t[p] then
  x.response=x.response∪{c}.
   If (c(x)=c,
x.status=Grundy and
Max{Possible_GrundyColor(x)}>
Max{Possible_GrundyColor(p)})
or (x=j)  then
   Vertex x and every satis-
faction vertex which satis-
fies only x become normal.
     If ∃c'∈ x.search , c'
is the closest to
Max{Possible_GrundyColor(x)}
     then
      x.status= Grundy.
      c(x)= c'.
      Put_Grundy(x,c').
      x.t[x]=x.t[x]+1.
x.response=x.response∪{c'}
Send to each z∈N(x):
Substitute_Found(x,
            x.t[x],c',j).
     Endif
   Endif
   Send to each z∈N(q):
Substitute_Found (p,t0,c,j).
 Endif
END
```

Then, when the Grundy vertex j to replace receives a *Substitute_Found* (p, t_0, c, j) message, it puts its status and the status of its satisfaction vertices to normal (Procedure 6). Since several substitutes can appear, only the substitute with the smallest value in the set returned by *Possible_GrundyColor(x)* procedure is selected. This allows the others to be Grundy vertices for larger colors. These substitutes and their satisfaction vertices become then normal.

Finally, when a vertex is waiting for a response from the remainder of the graph, it uses the following procedure. Indeed, a vertex receives a message for any color without Grundy vertices. Then, if a new Grundy vertex is found for these colors, another message is received. Thus, after a delay $2.diam(G)+1$, a vertex received a first message from any ex-Grundy vertices and a second message from any new Grundy vertices. If some colors have no Grundy vertices, the coloring must be modified and a color can be removed.

```
Procedure 7: Waiting ()
BEGIN
After a time 2diam(G)+1 do
   If |x.response|< |x.request| then
     x.k=x.k-1.
     If c(x)=x.del then c(x)=Null. x.state=normal. Endif
      If c(x)>x.del then c(x)=c(x)-1.   Endif
      x.request=∅.   x.response=∅.   x.wait=0.
   Endif
Enddo
END
```

Next, we prove that this algorithm gives a partial Grundy coloring of G when an edge is added.

Theorem 7: *Let G be a graph with a partial Grundy coloring. If an edge is added to G, then a partial Grundy coloring is re-established with O(nm) exchanged messages and O(n) color changes, when n is the order of G and m its edge number.*

Proof. First note that the propagation of a message in all the graph is done in $O(m)$ messages. Then, not satisfied Grundy vertices send a *Search_Substitute* message in the graph to find Grundy vertices for their colors. And at most $(n-\Delta)$ vertices can become Grundy vertices for one of these colors. Thus, the search of Grundy vertices needs $O(nm)$ messages. Since the update message is propagated once for each new color found, the number of exchanged messages to re-establish a partial Grundy coloring is then $O(nm)$. Moreover, each vertex can change its color at most once when a color is removed and once when a Grundy vertex is searched. The determined coloring needs then $O(n)$ changes of colors. ■

Theorem 8: *The time complexity to reach a partial Grundy coloring is O(diam (G)).*

Proof. Each vertex waits for a delay $2.diam(G)+1$ to decide to remove a color (if necessary). Moreover, the time lag between the start of the waiting procedure for two vertices is at most $diam(G)$. Thus, such a coloring is determined in time $O(diam(G))$. ■

3.2 Execution of the Algorithm

In this subsection we provide an example of the execution of our algorithm where an edge is added between two non normal vertices with the same color.

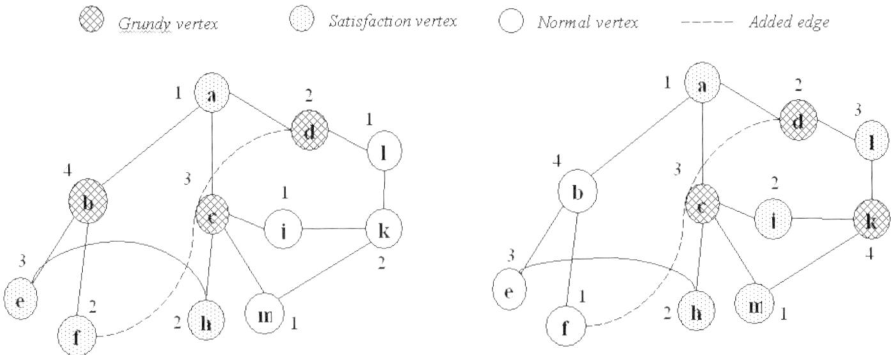

Fig. 1. an edge (d,f) is added to a graph with a partial Grundy coloring

Let G be graph with a partial Grundy coloring, as described in Figure 3(a).

1 The edge (d,f) is added to the graph.
2 The resulting coloring is not proper and then is not partial Grundy.
3 The vertex f becomes a normal vertex.
4 The Grundy vertex b is not anymore adjacent to a satisfaction vertex with color 2. Then, it does not satisfy the Grundy condition.
5 The vertex b sends the Search_ Substitute(b , $j.t[x]$, 4, 2) message in all the graph and becomes in a waiting state.
6 Every vertex that receives the Search_Substitute message checks if it can be a Grundy vertex for the color 4 (it calls the *Possible_GrundyColor(x)* procedure) and becomes in a waiting state.
7 The vertex k can be a Grundy vertex for the colors {1, 2, 3, 4}. Then, it takes the color 4 and put the colors 1, 2 and 3 in its neighborhood by calling the *Put_Grundy(k,4)* procedure.
8 The vertex k sends the *Substitute_Found(k, t_0, 4, b)* message to all the vertices in the graph.
9 By receiving the *Substitute_Found* message sent by k, the vertex b and all its satisfaction vertices become normal.
10 The vertex f takes the smallest color not appearing in its neighborhood and calls the *Maximize_colors()* procedure.
11 A partial Grundy coloring is reestablished in the graph, as shown in Figure 3(b).

4 Conclusion

In this paper we proposed an incremental distributed algorithm to maintain a partial Grundy coloring. This algorithm is based on exchanges of messages between the vertices to share information. Moreover, although a minimal coloring is a partial Grundy coloring, our algorithm tries to maximize the total number of colors. Thus, this algorithm computes a partial Grundy coloring of a graph G (n vertices and m edges) in time $O(diam(G))$, where $diam(G)$ is the diameter of the graph, and it needs $O(nm)$ messages and $O(n)$ changes of colors. A question comes then naturally: can we maintain this coloring if edges are removed ? And what happens about vertices ? Currently, a fully dynamic view of the problem is studied where the add and the removal of edges and vertices are considered. Since systems are more and more large, the aim is to go to a completely independent solution to maintain properties of graphs when their topologies evolve.

References

1. Antonoiu, G., Srimani, P.K.: A self-stabilizing distributed algorithm for minimal spanning tree problem in a symmetric graph. Computer & Mathematics with Application 35(10), 15–23 (1998)
2. Bui, M., Butelle, F., Lavault, C.: A distributed algorithm for constructing a minimum diameter spanning tree. Journal of Parallel and Distributed Computing 64, 571–577 (2004)
3. Christen, C.A., Selkow, S.M.: Some perfect coloring properties of graphs. Journal of Combinatorial Theory B27, 49–59 (1979)
4. Cockayne, E.J., Thommason, A.G.: Ordered Colourings of graphs. Journal of Combinatorial Theory B32, 286–292 (1982)
5. Effantin, B., Kheddouci, H.: Grundy number of graphs. Discussiones Mathematicae Graph Theory 27(1), 5–18 (2007)
6. Effantin, B., Kheddouci, H.: A Distributed Algorithm for a b-Coloring of a Graph. In: Guo, M., Yang, L.T., Di Martino, B., Zima, H.P., Dongarra, J., Tang, F. (eds.) ISPA 2006. LNCS, vol. 4330, pp. 430–438. Springer, Heidelberg (2006)
7. Erdös, P., Hare, W.R., Hedetniemi, S.T., Laskar, R.: On the equality of the Grundy and ochromatic numbers of a graph. Journal of Graph Theory 11(2), 157–159 (1987)
8. Erdös, P., Hedetniemi, S.T., Laskar, R.C., Prins, G.C.E.: On the equality of the partial Grundy and upper ochromatic numbers of graphs. Discrete Mathematics 272, 53–64 (2003)
9. Fujie, T.: An exact algorithm for the maximum leaf spanning tree problem. Computers & Operations Research 30, 1931–1944 (2003)
10. Germain, C., Kheddouci, H.: Grundy numbers of powers of graphs. Discrete Mathematics (to appear)
11. Hedetniemi, S.M., Hedetniemi, S.T., Beyer, T.: A linear algorithm for the Grundy (coloring) number of a tree. Congressus Numerantium 36, 351–363 (1982)
12. Hedetniemi, S.T., Jacobs, D.P., Srimani, P.K.: Linear time self-stabilizing colorings. Information Processing Letters 87, 251–255 (2003)
13. Huang, S.-T., Hung, S.-S., Tzeng, C.-H.: Self-stabilizing coloration in anonymous planar networks. Information Processing Letters 95, 307–312 (2005)

14. Shi, Z., Goddard, W., Hedetniemi, S.T., Kennedy, K., Laskar, R., MacRae, A.: An algorithm for partial Grundy number on trees. Discrete Mathematics 304, 108–116 (2005)
15. Shi, Z., Goddard, W., Hedetniemi, S.T.: An anonymous self-stabilizing algorithm for 1-maximal independent set in trees. Information Processing Letters 91, 77–83 (2004)
16. Šparl, P., Žerovnik, J.: 2-local distributed algorithms for generalized coloring of hexagonal graphs. Electronic notes in Discrete Mathematics 22, 321–325 (2005)
17. Telle, J.A., Proskurowski, A.: Algorithms for vertex partitioning problems on partial k-trees. SIAM Journal on Discrete Mathematics 10(4), 529–550 (1997)

Efficient Multidimensional Data Redistribution for Resizable Parallel Computations

Rajesh Sudarsan and Calvin J. Ribbens

Department of Computer Science
Virginia Tech, Blacksburg, VA 24061-0106
{sudarsar,ribbens}@vt.edu

Abstract. Traditional parallel schedulers running on cluster supercomputers support only static scheduling, where the number of processors allocated to an application remains fixed throughout the execution of the job. This results in under-utilization of idle system resources thereby decreasing overall system throughput. In our research, we have developed a prototype framework called ReSHAPE, which supports dynamic resizing of parallel MPI applications executing on distributed memory platforms. The resizing library in ReSHAPE includes support for releasing and acquiring processors and efficiently redistributing application state to a new set of processors. In this paper, we derive an algorithm for redistributing two-dimensional block-cyclic arrays from P to Q processors, organized as 2-D processor grids. The algorithm ensures a contention-free communication schedule for data redistribution if $P_r \leq Q_r$ and $P_c \leq Q_c$. In other cases, the algorithm implements circular row and column shifts on the communication schedule to minimize node contention.

Keywords: Dynamic scheduling, Dynamic resizing, Data redistribution, Dynamic resource management, process remapping, resizable applications.

1 Introduction

As terascale supercomputers become more common and as the high-performance computing (HPC) community turns its attention to petascale machines, the challenge of providing effective resource management for high-end machines grows in both importance and difficulty. A fundamental problem is that conventional parallel schedulers are static, i.e., once a job is allocated a set of resources, they remain fixed throughout the life of an application's execution. It is worth asking whether a dynamic resource manager, which has the ability to modify resources allocated to jobs at runtime, would allow more effective resource management. The focus of our research is on dynamically reconfiguring parallel applications to use a different number of processes, i.e., on *dynamic resizing* of applications.[1]

In order to explore the potential benefits and challenges of dynamic resizing, we are developing ReSHAPE, a framework for dynamic **Re**sizing and **S**cheduling of **H**omogeneous **A**pplications in a **P**arallel **E**nvironment. The ReSHAPE framework includes a

[1] An extended version of this paper is available as Computing Research Repository (CoRR) Technical Report, http://arxiv.org/abs/0706.2146v1

I. Stojmenovic et al. (Eds.): ISPA 2007, LNCS 4742, pp. 182–194, 2007.

programming model and an API, data redistribution algorithms and a runtime library, and a parallel scheduling and resource management system framework. ReSHAPE allows the number of processors allocated to a parallel message-passing application to be changed at run time. It targets long-running iterative computations, i.e., homogeneous computations that perform similar computational steps over and over again. By monitoring the performance of such computations on various processor sizes, the ReSHAPE scheduler can take advantage of idle processors on large clusters to improve the turnaround time of high-priority jobs, or shrink low-priority jobs to meet quality-of-service or advanced reservation commitments.

Dynamic resizing necessiates runtime application data redistribution. Many high performance computing applications and mathematical libraries like ScaLAPACK [1] require block-cyclic data redistribution to achieve computational efficiency. Data redistribution involves four main stages — data identification and index computation, communication schedule generation, message packing and unpacking and finally, data transfer. Each processor identifies its part of the data to redistribute and transfers the data in the message passing step according to the order specified in the communication schedule. A node contention occurs when one or more processors sends messages to a single processor. A redistribution *communication schedule* aims to minimize these node contentions and maximiz network bandwidth utilization. Data is packed or marshalled on the source processor to form a message and is unmarshalled on the destination processor.

In this paper, we present an algorithm for redistributing two-dimensional block-cyclic data from P (P_r rows $\times P_c$ columns) to Q (Q_r rows $\times Q_c$ columns) processors, organized as 2-D processor grids. We evaluate the algorithm's performance by measuring the redistribution time for different block-cyclic matrices. If $P_r \leq Q_r$ and $P_c \leq Q_c$, the algorithm ensures a contention-free communication schedule. In other cases the algorithm minimizes node contentions by performing row or column circular shifts on the communication schedule. The algorithm discussed in this paper supports 2-D block cyclic data redistribution for only one- and two-dimensional processor topology.

The rest of the paper is organized as follows. Section 2 discusses prior work in the area of data redistribution. Section 3 briefly reviews the architecture of the ReSHAPE framework and discusses in detail the two-dimensional redistribution algorithm. Section 4 reports our experimental results of the redistribution algorithm with the ReSHAPE framework tested on the System X cluster at Virginia Tech. We conclude in Section 5 discussing future directions to this research.

2 Related Work

Data redistribution within a cluster using message passing approach has been extensively studied in literature. Many of the past research efforts were targeted towards redistributing one-dimensional cyclic arrays between the same set of processors within a cluster on a 1-D processor topology. To reduce the redistribution overhead cost, Walker and Otto [12] and Kaushik [7] proposed a K-step communication schedule based on modulo arithmetic and tensor products repectively. Ramaswamy and Banerjee [9] proposed PITFALLS which uses line segments to map array elements to processors. The algorithm does not usecommunication schedules for data transfer. Thakur et al. [11,10] use *gcd* and *lcm* methods for redistributing cyclically distributed one dimensional arrays. The technique proposed by Kalns and Ni [6] assigns logical ranks to map source data to target processors. Hsu et al. [5] further extended this work and proposed a generalized processor mapping technique for redistributing data from cyclic(kx) to cyclic(x), and vice versa. Chung et al. [2] propose an efficient method for index computation using basic-cycle calculation (BCC) technique for redistributing data from cyclic(x) to cyclic(y) on the same processor set. Hsu et al. [13] extended the work by Chung et al. [2] by using generalized basic-cyclic calculation method to redistribute data. The redistribution framework proposed by Lim et al. [8] uses a generalized circulant matrix formalised communication schedule for data redistribution.

Prylli et al. [14], Desprez et al. [3] and Lim et al. [15] have proposed efficient algorithms for redistributing two dimensional block cyclic arrays. Prylli et al. [14] proposed a simple scheduling algorithm, called Caterpillar, for redistributing data across one- and two-dimensional processor grids. The Caterpillar algorithm does not have a global knowledge of the communication schedule and redistributes the data using the local knowledge of the communications at every step. As a result, this algorithm is not efficient for data redistribution using "non-all-to-all" communication. Desprez et al. [3] propose a general solution for redistributing block-cyclic data from P processors to Q processors. The algorithm is based upon a bipartite matching technique and fails to ensure a contention-free communication schedule. The redistribution algorithm proposed by Lim et al. [15] can redistribute two-dimensional arrays across a 2-D processor grid topology on the same set of processors with a different topology. Park et al. [16] proposed their algorithm as an extension to this idea for efficiently redistributing one-dimensional block-cyclic arrays with cyclic(x) distribution on P processors to cyclic(kx) on Q processors where P and Q can be any arbitrary positive value.

The Caterpillar algorithm by Prylli et al. [14] is the closest related work to our algorithm in that it supports data redistribution across a checkerboard processor topology. In our research, we extend the ideas in [15] and [16] to develop an algorithm to redistribute two-dimensional block-cyclic data distributed across a 2-D processor grid topology. Unlike Desprez et al. [3], we allow overlap among processors in the source and destination processor set. Our algorithm builds an efficient communication schedule and uses non-all-to-all communication for data redistribution. We apply row and column transformations using the circulant matrix formalism to minimize node contentions in the communication schedule.

3 System Overview

The ReSHAPE framework, shown in Figure 1(a), consists of two main components. The first component is the application scheduling and monitoring module which schedules and monitors jobs and gathers performance data in order to make resizing decisions based on application performance, available system resources, resources allocated to other jobs in the system and jobs waiting in the queue. The second component of the framework consists of a programming model for resizing applications. This includes a resizing library and an API for applications to communicate with the scheduler to

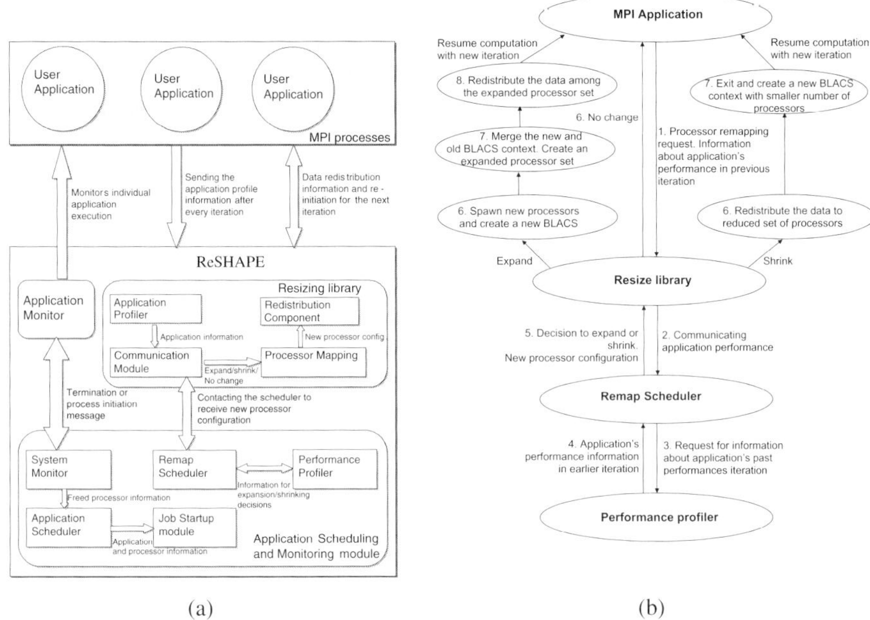

(a) (b)

Fig. 1. (a) Architecture of ReSHAPE (b) State diagram for application expansion and shrinking

send performance data and actuate resizing decisions. The resizing library includes algorithms for mapping processor topologies and redistributing data from one processor topology to another. The individual components in these modules are explained in detail in [17].

3.1 Resizing Library

The resizing library provides routines for changing the size of the processor set assigned to an application and for mapping processors and data from one processor set to another. An application needs to be re-compiled with the resize library to enable the scheduler dynamically to add or remove processors to/from the application. During resizing, rather than suspending the job, the application execution control is transferred to the resize library which maps the new set of processors to the application and redistributes the data (if required). Once mapping is completed, the resizing library returns control back to the application and the application continues with its next iteration. The application user needs to indicate the global data structures and variables so that they can be redistributed to the new processor set after resizing. Figure 1(b) shows the different stages of execution required for changing the size of the processor set for an application.

Our API gives programmers a simple way to indicate *resize points* in the application, typically at the end of each iteration of the outer loop. At resize points, the application contacts the scheduler and provides performance data to the scheduler. The metric used to measure performance is the time taken to compute each iteration. The scheduler's decision to expand or shrink the application is passed as a return value. If an application is allowed to expand to more processors, the response from the Remap Scheduler includes the size and the list of processors to which an application should expand. A call to the redistribution routine remaps the global data to the new processor set. If the Scheduler asks an application to shrink, then the application first redistributes its global data across a smaller processor set, retrieves its previously stored MPI communicator, and creates a new BLACS [18] context for the new processor set. The additional processes are terminated when the old BLACS context is exited. The resizing library notifies the Remap Scheduler about the number of nodes relinquished by the application.

3.2 Data Redistribution

The data redistribution library in ReSHAPE uses an efficient algorithm for redistributing block-cyclic arrays between processor sets organized in a 1-D (row or column format) or checkerboard processor topology. The algorithm for redistributing a 1-D block-cyclic array over a one-dimensional processor topology was first proposed by Park et al. [16]. We extend this idea to develop an algorithm to redistribute both one- and two-dimensional block-cyclic data across a two-dimensional processor grid of processors. In our redistribution algorithm, we assume the following:

- Source processor configuration: $P_r \times P_c$ $(rows \times columns)$, P_r, $P_c > 0$.
- Destination processor configuration: $Q_r \times Q_c$ $(rows \times columns)$, Q_r, $Q_c > 0$.
- The data granularity is set at the block level, i.e., a block is the smallest data that will be transferred which cannot be further subdivided. This block size is specified by the user.
- The data matrix, *data*, which needs to be redistributed, is of dimension $n \times n$.
- Let the block size be *NB*. Therefore total number of data blocks = $(n/NB) * (n/NB) = N \times N$, represented using matrix *Mat*.
- We use $Mat(x, y)$ to refer $block(x, y)$, $0 \leq x, y < N$.
- The data that can be equally divided among the source and destination processors P and Q respectively, i.e., N is evenly divisible by P_r, P_c, Q_r, and Q_c. Each processor has an integer number of data blocks.
- The source processors are numbered $P_{(i,j)}$, $0 \leq i < P_r$, $0 \leq j < P_c$ and the destination processors are numbered as $Q_{(i,j)}$, $0 \leq i < Q_r$, $0 \leq j < Q_c$

Problem Definition. We define 2D block-cyclic distribution as follows. Given a two dimensional array of $n \times n$ elements with block size *NB* and a set of P processors arranged in checkerboard topology, the data is partitioned into $N \times N$ blocks and distributed across P processors, where $N = n/NB$. Using this distribution a matrix block, $Mat(x, y)$, is assigned to the source processor $P_c * (x\%P_r) + y\%P_c$, $0 \leq x < N$, $0 \leq y < N$. Here we study the problem of redistributing a two-dimensional block-cyclic matrix from P processors to Q processors arranged in checkerboard topology, where $P \neq Q$ and NB is fixed. After redistribution, the block $Mat(x, y)$ will belong to the destination processor $Q_c * (x\%Q_r) + y\%Q_c$, $0 \leq x < N, 0 \leq y < N$.

Redistribution Terminologies

(a) Superblock: A superblock is defined as the smallest set of data blocks whose mapping pattern from source to destination processor can be uniquely identified. For a

2-D processor topology data distribution, each superblock is represented as a table of R rows and C columns, where

$R = lcm(P_r, Q_r) \qquad C = lcm(P_c, Q_c)$

The entire data is divided into multiple superblocks and the mapping pattern of the data in each superblock is identical to the first superblock, i.e., the data blocks located at the same relative position in all the superblocks are transferred to the destination processor. A 2-D block matrix with Sup elements is used to represent the entire data where each element is a Superblock. The dimensions of this block matrix are Sup_R and Sup_C where,

$Sup_R = N/R \qquad Sup_C = N/C \qquad Sup = (N/R * N/C)$

(b) **Layout:** Layout is an 1-D array of $Sup_R * Sup_C$ elements where each element is a 2-D table which stores the block ids present in that superblock. There are Sup 2-D tables in the Layout array where each table has the dimension $R \times C$.

(c) **Initial Data-Processor Configuration (IDPC):** This table represents the initial processor layout for the data before redistribution for a single superblock. Since the data-processor mapping is identical over all the superblocks, only one instance of this table is created. The table has R rows $\times C$ columns. *IDPC(i, j)* contains the processor id $P_{(i,j)}$ that owns the block $Mat(i, j)$ located at the same relative position in all the superblocks, ($0 \leq i <, R, 0 \leq j < C$).

(d) **Final Data-Processor Configuration (FDPC):** The table represents the final processor configuration for the data layout after redistribution for a single superblock. Like *IDPC*, only one instance of this table is created and used for all the data superblocks. The dimensions of this table is $R \times C$. *FDPC(i, j)* contains the processor id $Q_{(i,j)}$ that owns the block $Mat(i, j)$ after redistribution located at the same relative position in all the superblocks, ($0 \leq i < R, 0 \leq j < C$).

(e) The source processor for any data block *Mat(i, j)* in the data matrix can be computed using the formula

$$Source(i, j) = P_c * (i\%P_r) + (j\%P_c)$$

(f) **Communication schedule send table ($C_{Transfer}$):** This table contains the final communication schedule for redistributing data from source to destination layout. This table is created by re-ordering the *FDPC* table. The columns of $C_{Transfer}$ correspond to P source processors and the rows correspond to individual communication steps in the schedule. The number of rows in this table is determined by $(R*C)/P$. The network bandwidth is completely utilized in every communication step as the schedule involves all the source processors in data transfer. A positive entry in the $C_{Transfer}$ table indicates that in the ith communication step, processor j will send data to $C_{Transfer}(i, j), 0 \leq i < (R * C)/P, 0 \leq j < (P_r * P_c)$.

(g) **Communication schedule receive table (C_{Recv}):** This table is derived from the $C_{Transfer}$ table where the columns correspond to the destination processors. The table has the same number of rows as the $C_{Transfer}$ table. A positive entry at $C_{Recv}(i, j)$ indicates that processor j will receive data from source processor at $C_{Recv}(i, j)$ in the ith communication step, $0 \leq i < (R*C)/P, 0 \leq j < (Q_r*Q_c)$. If $(Q_r * Q_c) \geq (P_r * P_c)$, then the additional entries in the C_{Recv} table are filled with -1.

Algorithm

Step 1: *Create Layout table*

The Layout array of tables are created by traversing through all the data blocks in matrix $Mat(i,j)$, where $0 \leq i, j < N, 0 \leq j < N$. The superblocks in $Mat(i,j)$ is traversed in row-major format.

Pseudocode:

for $superblockcount \leftarrow 0$ **to** $Sup - 1$ **do**
  for $i \leftarrow 0$ **to** $R/P_r - 1$ **do**
    for $j \leftarrow 0$ **to** $C/P_c - 1$ **do**
      for $k \leftarrow 0$ **to** $P_r - 1$ **do**
        for $l \leftarrow 0$ **to** $P_c - 1$ **do**
          $Layout[superblockcount](i * C/P_c + k, j * R/P_r + l) =$
            $Mat(superblockid_{row} * R + i * P_c + k,$
            $superblockid_{col} * C + j * P_r + l)$
  if$(reached\ end\ of\ column)$ **then**
    $increment\ Sup_R$
    $Sup_C \leftarrow 0$
  else
    $increment\ Sup_C$

Step 2: *Creating IDPC and FDPC tables*

An entry at $IDPC(i, j)$ is calculated using the index i and j of the table and the size of the source processor set P, $0 \leq i < R, 0 \leq j < C$. The Source function returns the processor id of the owner of the data before redistribution stored in that location.

Similarly, an entry $FDPC(i, j)$ is computed using the i and j coordinates of the table and the size of the destination processor set Q, $0 \leq i < R, 0 \leq j < C$. The Source function returns the processor id of the owner of the redistributed data stored in that location.

Pseudocode:

for $i \leftarrow 0$ **to** $R - 1$ **do**
  for $j \leftarrow 0$ **to** $C - 1$ **do**
    $IDPC(i,j) \leftarrow Source(i,j) \leftarrow P_c * (i\%P_r, j\%P_c)$

for $i \leftarrow 0$ **to** $R - 1$ **do**
  for $j \leftarrow 0$ **to** $C - 1$ **do**
    $FDPC(i,j) \leftarrow Source(i,j) \leftarrow Q_c * (i\%Q_r, j\%Q_c)$

Step 3: *Communication schedule tables($C_{Transfer}$ and C_{Recv})*

The $C_{Transfer}$ table stores the final communication schedule for transferring data between the source and the destination processors. The columns in $C_{Transfer}$ correspond to source processor $P_{(i,j)}$. The table has $C_{TransferRows}$ rows and $(P_r * P_c)$ columns, where

$$C_{TransferRows} = (R * C)/(P_r * P_c)$$

Each entry in the $C_{Transfer}$ table is filled by sequentially traversing the *FDPC* table in row-major format. The data corresponding to each processor inserted at the appropriate column at the next available location. An integer counter updates itself and keeps track of the next available location (next row) for each processor.

Pseudocode:

$$processor\_id = IDPC(i, j)$$
$$C_{Transfer}(counter_j, processor\_id) \leftarrow FDPC(i, j)$$
$$Update\ counter_j$$

where $0 \leq i < R$ and $0 \leq j < C$. Each row in the $C_{Transfer}$ table forms a single communication step where all the source processors send the data to a unique destination processor. The C_{Recv} table is used by the destination processors to know the source of their data in a particular communication step.

$$C_{Recv}(i, C_{Transfer}(i, j)) = j$$

where $0 \leq i < C_{TransferRows}$ and $0 \leq j < (Q_r \times Q_c)$.

Node contention can occur in the $C_{Transfer}$ communication schedule if any one of the following conditions are true

(i) $P_r \geq Q_r$

(ii) $P_c \geq Q_c$

(iii) $P_r \geq Q_r$ and $P_c \geq Q_c$

If there are node contentions in the communication schedule, create a *Processor Mapping* (PM) table of dimension $R \times C$ and initialize it with the values from FDPC table. To reduce node contentions, the *PM* tables are circularly shifted in row or columns. To maintain data consistency, the same operations are performed on the IDPC table and the superblock tables within the Layout array. The $C_{Transfer}$ table is created from the modified PM table. We identify 3 situations where node contentions can occur. Case 1 and case 2 are applicable during both expansion and shrinking of an application while Case 3 can occur only when an application is shrinking to a smaller destination processor set.

Do the following operation on IDPC, PM and on each 2-D table in the Layout array.

Case 1: If $P_r > Q_r$ and $P_c < Q_c$ then

1. Create (R/P_r) groups with P_r rows in each group.
2. For $1 \leq i < P_r$, perform a circular right shift on each row i by $P_c * i$ elements in each group.
3. Create the $C_{Transfer}$ table from the resulting *PM* table.

Case 2: If $P_r < Q_r$ and $P_c > Q_c$ then

1. Create (C/P_c) groups with P_c columns in each group.
2. For $1 \leq j < P_c$, perform a circular down shift on each column j by $P_r * j$ elements in each group.
3. Create the $C_{Transfer}$ table from the resulting *PM* table.

Case 3: If $P_r > Q_r$ and $P_c > Q_c$ then

1. Create (C/P_c) groups with P_c columns in each group.
2. For $1 \leq j < P_c$, perform a circular down shift each column j by $P_r * j$ elements in each group.
3. Create (R/P_r) groups with P_r rows in each group.
4. For $1 \leq i < P_r$, perform a circular right shift each row i by $P_c * i$ elements in each group
5. Create the $C_{Transfer}$ table from the resulting *PM* table.

The C_{Recv} table is not used when the schedule is not contention-free. Node contention results in overlapping entries in the C_{Recv} table thus rendering it as unusable.

Step 4: *Data marshalling and unmarshalling*

If a processor's rank equals the value at $IDPC(i, j)$, then the processor collects the data from the relative indexes of all the superblocks in the Layout array. Each collection of data over all the superblocks forms a single message for communication for processor j.

If there are no node contentions in the schedule, each source processor stores $(R * C)/(P_r * P_c)$ messages, each of size $(N * N/(R * C))$ in the original order of the data layout. The messages received on the destination processor are unpacked into individual blocks and stored at an offset of $(R/Q_r) * (C/Q_c)$ elements from the previous data block in the local array. The first data block is stored at the $zero^{th}$ location of the local array. If the communication schedule has node contentions, the order of the messages are shuffled according to row or column transformations. In such cases, the destination processor performs reverse index computation and stores the data at the correct offset.

Step 5: *Data Transfer*

The message size in each send communication is equal to $(N * N)/(R * C)$ data blocks. Each row in the $C_{Transfer}$ table corresponds to a single communication step. In each communication step, the total volume of messages exchanged between the processors is $P * (N * N/(R * C))$ data blocks. This volume includes cases where data is locally copied to a processor without performing a MPI_Send and MPI_Recv operation. In a single communication step j, a source processor P_i sends the marshalled message to the destination processor given by $C_{Transfer}(j, i)$, where $0 \leq j < C_{TransferRows}$, $0 \leq i < (P_r * P_c)$,

Data Transfer Cost. The total redistribution cost includes index and schedule computation cost, message packing/unpacking cost, and the data transfer cost. Of these, the data transfer cost constitutes a significant percentage of the total redistribution overhead. The data transfer cost for each communication step includes message start-up (latency) cost and the transmission cost. For every communication call using MPI_Send and MPI_Recv, there is a latency overhead associated with it. Let us denote this time to initiate a message by λ. Let τ denote the time taken to transmit a unit size of message from source to destination processor. Thus, the time taken to send a message from a source processor in a single communication step is $((N * N)/(R * C)) \ * \tau$. The total data transfer cost for redistributing the data across destination processors is $C_{TransferRows} * (\lambda + ((N * N)/(R * C)) * \tau)$.

4 Experiments and Results

This section presents experimental results which demonstrate the performance of our two-dimensional block-cyclic redistribution algorithm. The experiments were conducted on 50 nodes of a large homogeneous cluster (System X). Each node is a dual 2.3 GHz PowerPC 970 processor with 4GB of main memory. Message passing was done using MPICH2 [19] over a Gigabit Ethernet interconnection network. We integrated the redistribution algorithm into the resizing library and evaluated its performance by measuring the total time taken by the algorithm to redistribute block-cyclic matrices from P to Q processors. We present results from two sets of experiments. The first set of experiments evaluates the performance of the algorithm for resizing and compares it with the Caterpillar algorithm. The second set of experiments focuses on the effects of processor topology on the redistribution cost. Table 1 shows all the possible processor configurations for various processor topologies. Processor configurations for the one-dimensional processor topology ($1 \times Q_r * Q_c$ or $Q_r * Q_c \times 1$) are not shown in the table. For the two sets of experiments described in this section, we have used the following matrix sizes - $2000 \times 2000, 4000 \times 4000, 6000 \times 6000, 8000 \times 8000, 12000 \times 12000, 16000 \times 16000, 20000 \times 20000$ and 24000×24000. A problem size of 8000 indicates the matrix 8000×8000. The processor configurations listed in Table 1 evenly divide the problem sizes listed above.

Table 1. Processor configuration for various topologies

Topology	Processor configurations
Nearly-square	$1 \times 2, 2 \times 2, 2 \times 3, 2 \times 4, 3 \times 3, 3 \times 4, 4 \times 4, 4 \times 5, 5 \times 5, 5 \times 6, 6 \times 6, 5 \times 8, 6 \times 8$
Skewed-rectangular	$1 \times 2, 2 \times 2, 2 \times 3, 2 \times 4, 3 \times 3, 2 \times 6, 2 \times 8, 2 \times 10, 5 \times 5, 3 \times 10, 2 \times 18, 2 \times 20, 2 \times 24, 2 \times 1, 3 \times 2, 4 \times 2, 6 \times 2, 8 \times 2, 10 \times 2, 10 \times 3, 18 \times 2, 20 \times 2, 24 \times 2$

4.1 Overall Redistribution Time

Every time an application acquires or releases processors, the globally distributed data has to be redistributed to the new processor topology. Thus, the application incurs a redistribution overhead each time it expands or shrinks. We assume a nearly-square processor topology for all the processor sizes used in this experiment. The matrix stores data as double precision floating point numbers. Figure 2(a) shows the overhead for redistributing large dense matrices for different matrix sizes using the our redistribution algorithm. Each data point in the graph represents the data redistribution cost incurred when increasing the size of the processor configuration from the previous (smaller) configuration. Problem size 8000 and 12000 start execution with 2 processors, problem size 16000 and 20000 start with 4 processors, and the 24000 case starts with 6 processors. The starting processor size is the smallest size which can accommodate the data. The trend shows that the redistribution cost increases with matrix size, but for a fixed matrix size the cost decreases as we increase the number of processors. This makes sense because for small processor size, the amount of data per processor that must be transferred is large. Also the communication schedule developed by our redistribution algorithm is independent of the problem size and depends only on the source and destination processor set size.

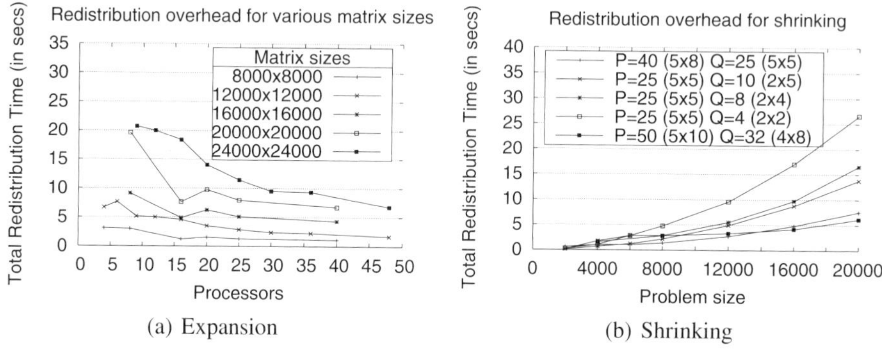

(a) Expansion (b) Shrinking

Fig. 2. Redistribution overhead incurred while resizing using ReSHAPE

Figure 2(b) shows the overhead cost incurred while shrinking large matrices from P processors to Q processors. In this experiment, we assign the values for P from the set 25, 40, 50 and Q from the set 4, 8, 10, 25 and 32. Each data point in the graph represents the redistribution overhead incurred while shrinking at that problem size. From the graph, it is evident that the redistribution cost increases as we increase the problem size. Typically, a large difference between the source and destination processor set results in higher redistribution cost. The rate at which the redistribution cost increases depends on the size of source and destination processor set. But we note that smaller destination processor set size has a greater impact on the redistribution cost compared to the difference between the processor set sizes. This is shown in the graph where the redistribution cost for shrinking from $P = 50$ to $Q = 32$ is lower compared to the cost when shrinking from $P = 25$ to $Q = 10$ or $P = 25$ to $Q = 8$.

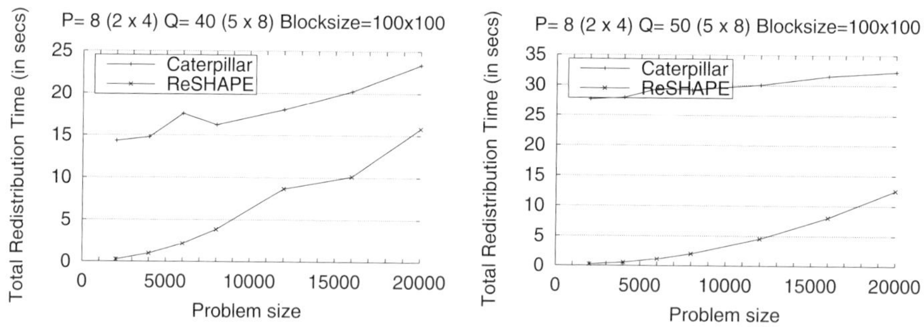

(a) Redistribution overhead while resizing from 8 to 40 processors (b) Redistribution overhead while resizing from 8 to 50 processors

Fig. 3. Comparing the total redistribution time for data redistribution in our algorithm with Caterpillar algorithm

Figure 3(a) and 3(b) compares the total redistribution cost of our algorithm and the Caterpillar algorithm. We have not compared the redistribution costs with the bipartite redistribution algorithm as our algorithm assumes that data redistribution from P to Q processors includes an overlapping set processors from the source and destination processor set. The total redistribution time is the sum total of schedule computation time, index computation time, packing and unpacking the data and the data transfer time. In each communication step, each sender packs a message before sending it and the receiver unpacks the message after receiving it. The Caterpillar algorithm does not attempt to schedule communication operations and send equal sized messages in each step. Figure 3(a) shows experimental results for redistributing block-cyclic two-dimensional arrays from a 2×4 processor grid to a 5×8 processor grid. On average, the total redistribution time of our algorithm is 12.7 times less than the Caterpillar algorithm. In Figure 3(b), the total redistribution time of our algorithm is about 32 times less than of the Caterpillar algorithm. In our algorithm, the total number of communication calls for redistributing from 8 to 40 processors is 80 whereas in Caterpillar the number is 160. Similarly, the number of MPI communication calls in our algorithm for redistributing 2D block-cyclic array from 8 processors to 50 processors is 196 as compared to 392 calls in the Caterpillar algorithm.

5 Discussion and Future Work

In this paper we have introduced a framework, ReSHAPE, that enables parallel message passing applications to be resized during execution. We have extended the functionality of the resizing library in ReSHAPE to support redistribution of 2-D block-cyclic matrices distributed across a 2-D processor topology. We build upon the work by Park et al. [16] to derive an efficient 2-D redistribution algorithm. Our algorithm redistributes a two-dimensional block-cyclic data distribution on a 2-D grid of P ($P_r \times P_c$) processors to two-dimensional block-cyclic data distribution on a 2-D grid with Q ($Q_r \times Q_c$) processors, where P and Q can be any arbitrary positive value. The algorithm ensures a contention-free communication schedule if $P_r \leq Q_r, P_c \leq Q_c$. For all other conditions involving P_r, P_c, Q_r, Q_c, the algorithm minimizes node contention in the communication schedule by performing a sequence of row or column circular shifts. Currently the algorithm can redistribute $N \times N$ blocks of data on P processors to Q processors only if Q_r and Q_c evenly divide N so that all the processors have equal number of integer blocks. We plan to generalize this assumption so that the algorithm can redistribute data between P and Q processors for any arbitrary value of P and Q.

Acknowledgement

This work was supported in part by NSF ITR grant CNS-0325534.

References

1. Blackford, L.S., Choi, J., Cleary, A., D'Azevedo, E., Demmel, J., Dhillon, I., Dongarra, J., Hammerling, S., Henry, G., Petitet, A., Stanley, K., Walker, D., Whaley, R.C.: ScaLAPACK User's Guide, SIAM, Philadelphia (1997)
2. Chung, Y.C., Hsu, C.H., Bai, S.W.: A Basic-Cycle Calculation Technique for Efficient Dynamic Data Redistribution. IEEE Trans. Parallel Distrib. Syst. 9, 359–377 (1998)

3. Desprez, F., Dongarra, J., Petitet, A., Randriamaro, C., Robert, Y.: Scheduling Block-Cyclic Array Redistribution. In: Proceedings of the Conference ParCo'97, vol. 12, pp. 227–234 (1998)
4. Guo, M., Pan, Y.: Improving communication scheduling for array redistribution. J. Parallel Distrib. Comput. 65, 553–563 (2005)
5. Hsu, C.H., Chung, Y.C., Yang, D.L., Dow, C.R.: A Generalized Processor Mapping Technique for Array Redistribution. IEEE Trans. Parallel Distrib. Syst. 12, 743–757 (2001)
6. Kalns, E.T., Ni, L.M.: Processor Mapping Techniques Toward Efficient Data Redistribution. IEEE Trans. Parallel Distrib. Syst. 6, 1234–1247 (1995)
7. Kaushik, S.D., Huang, C.H., Johnson, R.W., Sadayappan, P.: An approach to communication-efficient data redistribution. In: ICS '94: Proceedings of the 8th international conference on Supercomputing, pp. 364–373 (1994)
8. Lim, Y.W., Bhat, P.B., Prasanna, V.K.: Efficient Algorithms for Block-Cyclic Redistribution of Arrays. In: SPDP '96: Proceedings of the 8th IEEE Symposium on Parallel and Distributed Processing, p. 74. IEEE Computer Society Press, Los Alamitos (1996)
9. Ramaswamy, S., Simons, B., Banerjee, P.: Optimizations for efficient array redistribution on distributed memory multicomputers. Journal of Parallel Distributed Computing 38, 217–228 (1996)
10. Thakur, R., Choudhary, A., Fox, G.: Runtime Array Redistribution in HPF Programs. In: Scalable High Performance Computing Conference, Knoxville, Tenn., pp. 309–316 (1994)
11. Thakur, R., Choudhary, A., Ramanujam, J.: Efficient Algorithms for Array Redistribution. IEEE Trans. Parallel Distrib. Syst. 7, 587–594 (1996)
12. Walker, D.W., Otto, S.W.: Redistribution of block-cyclic data distributions using MPI. Concurrency: Practice and Experience 8, 707–728 (1996)
13. Hsu, C.H., Bai, S.W., Chung, Y.C., Yang, C.S.: A Generalized Basic-Cycle Calculation Method for Efficient Array Redistribution. IEEE Trans. Parallel Distrib. Syst. 11, 1201–1216 (2000)
14. Prylli, L., Tourancheau, B.: Efficient Block-Cyclic Data Redistribution. In: Fraigniaud, P., Mignotte, A., Bougé, L., Robert, Y. (eds.) Euro-Par 1996. LNCS, vol. 1123, pp. 155–164. Springer, Heidelberg (1996)
15. Lim, Y.W., Park, N., Prasanna, V.K.: Efficient Algorithms for Multi-dimensional Block-Cyclic Redistribution of Arrays. In: ICPP '97: Proceedings of the international Conference on Parallel Processing, pp. 234–241 (1997)
16. Park, N., Prasanna, V.K., Raghavendra, C.S.: Efficient Algorithms for Block-Cyclic Array Redistribution Between Processor Sets. IEEE Transactions on Parallel and Distributed Systems 10, 1217–1240 (1999)
17. Sudarsan, R., Ribbens, C.J.: ReSHAPE: A Framework for Dynamic Resizing and Scheduling of Homogeneous Applications in a Parallel Environment. Technical Report cs.DC/0703137, Computing Research Repository(CoRR) (2007)
18. Dongarra, J., Whaley, R.C.: A user's guide to the BLACS v1.1. Technical Report CS-95-281, Computer Science Department, University of Tennesse, Knoxville, TN (also LAPACK Working Note #94) (1997)
19. MPICH2 v1.03 (2005), available from: http://www-unix.mcs.anl.gov/mpi/mpich

Distributed Local 2-Connectivity Test of Graphs and Applications

Brahim Hamid, Bertrand Le Saëc, and Mohamed Mosbah

LaBRI-University of Bordeaux-1
351, cours de la libération
Talence, 33405, France
{hamid,lesaec,mosbah}@labri.fr

Abstract. The vertex connectivity of a graph is the smallest number of vertices whose deletion separates the graph or makes it trivial. This work is devoted to the problem of vertex connectivity test of graphs in a distributed environment based on a constructive approach. The contribution of this paper is threefold. First, using a pre-constructed spanning tree of the considered graph, we present a protocol to test whether a given graph is 2-connected using only local knowledge. Second, we present an encoding of this protocol using graph relabeling systems. The last contribution is the implementation of this protocol in the message passing model. For a given graph G, where M is the number of its edges, N the number of its nodes and Δ is its degree, our algorithms need the following requirements: The first one uses $O(\Delta \times N^2)$ steps and $O(\Delta \times \log \Delta)$ bits per node. The second one uses $O(\Delta \times N^2)$ messages and $O(N^2)$ time and $O(\Delta \times \log \Delta)$ bits per node. Furthermore, the studied network is *semi-anonymous*: Only the root of the pre-constructed spanning tree needs to be identified. Moreover, we investigate some applications that can use our protocol as a pre-processing task for initial configurations.

1 Introduction

Graphs offer a suitable abstraction for problems in many areas. An undirected graph is connected if there is a path between every pair of nodes. For instance, when a communication network is represented as a connected graph, the quality of the reachability of any couple of nodes in such a network, and hence their communication, will depend on the number of paths between these nodes. The number of disjoint paths is the connectivity. This information can be used to design distributed applications on unreliable networks [2,3,12,13]. For example, testing and then preserving k-connectivity of a wireless network is a desirable property to tolerate failures and avoid network partition [2]. In this paper, we propose a general and a constructive approach based on local knowledge to test whether a given graph is 2 connected in a distributed environment. Therefore, our work may be used as a core of protocols using the connectivity as input information. A network is represented as a connected, undirected graph denoted by $G = (V, E)$ where a node in V represents a process and an edge in E represents bidirectional communication link.

I. Stojmenovic et al. (Eds.): ISPA 2007, LNCS 4742, pp. 195–207, 2007.

Previous Works. In the late 1920s, Menger [13] studied the connectivity problem and some related properties. Since then many results have been obtained in this area. The best known works about the k-vertex connectivity test problem may be summarized in [13,11,5,4,7,6]. In [11] an algorithm to test the 2-connectivity of graphs is given. This is a *depth first search* based algorithm with a time complexity of $O(M + N)$. Thereafter, the computation of the vertex connectivity is reduced to solve a number of max-flow problems. For the first time this approach was applied in [5]. The computation of the maximum flow is used as a basic procedure to test the vertex connectivity. The remaining works try to reduce the number of calls to max-flow procedure using some knowledge about the structure of the graph. The time complexity of the presented algorithms is bounded by $O(k \times N \times M)$. All of these works are presented in a centralized setting assuming global knowledge about the graph to be examined.

Our Model. To encode distributed algorithms we will use two general models: The graph relabeling systems [8] and the asynchronous message passing system [1,12]. In the local computations model, and particularly graph relabeling systems (GRS), the local state of a process is encoded by labels associated with the corresponding node. At each step of the computation on a node, labels are modified in a ball of neighbors around this node. These relabeling can be applied in any order or even concurrently on disjoint subgraphs. This model is asynchronous since several relabeling steps may be applied at the same time and since it does not require that all of them have to be performed. In this work, we consider only relabeling between two neighbors. The execution time of a computation is the length of the corresponding relabeling sequence.

In the asynchronous message passing model (MPS), each process has its own local memory, with no shared global memory. Processes communicate by sending and receiving messages through existing communication links. Networks are asynchronous in the sense that processes operate at arbitrary rates and messages transfer delay are unbounded, unpredictable but finite. However, we assume that messages order are preserved. An algorithm in such a system consists of a local program at each node. The program encodes the local actions that processor may make. The actions of the program include modification of local variables, send messages to and receive messages from each of its neighbors in the corresponding graph topology.

Our Contribution. Let G be a graph with a distinguished node v_0 and let T be a spanning tree of G rooted at v_0. The vertex connectivity test algorithms presented here have the following characteristics: Each of them is based on a pre-constructed spanning tree [9] and uses only local knowledge. That is, to perform a computing step, only information related to the states of the neighbors is required. Especially, each node knows its neighbors in G and in the current spanning tree T the "position" of a node is done by its $father$ except for the root, and a set of ordered $sons$. The algorithms make a traversal of the tree starting from the root. Each visited node v computes the set of its sons not reached by the root in the graph G deprived of v. So each node checks if all its sons are reached by the root in the subgraph induced by its deletion. The graph is 2 connected iff all the checks are positive. In the opposite case, the graph is not 2-connected. Moreover, this protocol does not need a completely identified network. Only the root needs to be identified: The network is *semi-anonymous*. Then, we give two possible implementation of our protocol in the two previous models. To our knowledge, there is no distributed algorithm in the literature to deal with the k-vertex connectivity test of graphs. As we shall see, our protocol may be used as a brick to deal with such a problem.

The rest of the paper is organized as follows. In Section 2, we introduce the notion of procedure using an example of the distributed spanning tree computation. In Section 3, we present our protocol to deal with the problem of the 2-vertex connectivity test of graphs. In the following section, we show an encoding of this protocol in the local computations model. The proofs of its correctness and some complexity results are also given. We discuss in Section 5 the implementation of this protocol in the asynchronous message passing model. We introduce in Section 6 possible applications of our protocol. Finally, Section 7 concludes the paper with short discussion about future works.

2 Spanning Tree Procedure

A tree $T = (V_T, E_T)$ is a connected graph that have no cycle and an elected node v_0 called the root. We denote by $Sons(v)$ the set of the sons of v. In the sequel, we assume that the list "Sons" of v is ordered. A node $u \in V_T$ with no son is called a leaf of T. Then, a spanning tree $T = (V_T, E_T)$ of a graph $G = (V_G, E_G)$ is a tree such that $V_T = V_G$ and $E_T \subseteq E_G$. The tree can be defined also by $T(Father, Sons)$. We denote by T_v a tree with root v. We denote by $T(u) \setminus v$ the maximal subtree of T that contains the node u, but not v.

In the sequel, we will need to define some "procedures"with parameters to encode our algorithms. This notion of procedure is similar to the "interacting components" used in [10]. For a sake of uniformity, procedures will use the following standard header format:

$$\mathbf{name}\,(\mathbf{struct_0}, \cdots \mathbf{struct_i}; \mathbf{node_0}, \cdots \mathbf{node_j}; \mathbf{lab_0}, \mathbf{val_0}, \mathbf{val'_0}; \cdots ; \mathbf{lab_l}, \mathbf{val_l}, \mathbf{val'_l})$$

The header of the procedure is composed of its name and a set of optional parameters. Each of the sets is separated using the character ";". The first set of parameters is the structures of the manipulated graphs, the second is the set of the distinguished nodes. The rest is related to used labels, their required initialization values and their expected values. The following graph relabeling system describes an encoding of the *spanning tree procedure*.

Here, $Father(v) = \perp$ means that v has no defined father. First, v_0 the root of T applies the rule $STR1$ to initialize the computation. At any computation step based on the application of the rule $STR2$, when a node w not yet in the tree, finds a neighbor v in T labeled $Stage(v) = WA$, this node (w) includes itself in the tree by changing its $Stage$ to WA. Moreover, at the same time, $Father(w)$ is set to v and w is added to the sons list of v. So at each execution of the rule $STR2$, the number of nodes not yet in the tree decreases by 1. When

Algorithm 1. $STP\_GRS(G, T; v_0; Stage, X, Y; Father; Sons)$

- **Input :** A graph $G = (V, E)$ and v_0 the chosen root.
  - **Labels:**
    - $B(v)$: the set of (locally) ordered immediate neighbors of v which is an initial data,
    - $Stage(v)$: the state of v can take many values. The only used in this procedure is: "X" as the initial value, "WA" to mean that v has been included in the tree and "Y" to mean that v finished locally its computation.
    - $Father(v)$: is the father of v in the on-building spanning tree.
    - $Sons(v)$: an ordered list of the sons of v in the previous tree.
    - $Included(v)$: the set of v's neighbors included for the first time in the on-building spanning tree.
    - $Terminated(v)$: the set of v's neighbors that finished locally the computation of the spanning tree.
  - **Initialization:**
    - $\forall v \in V$, $Stage(v) = X$.
- **Results:** A spanning tree $T = (V, E_T)$ of G with root v_0 such that $\forall v \in V$, $Stage(v) = Y$.
- **Rules:**

$STR1$: **The node v_0 starts the computation**
Precondition :
- $Stage(v_0) = X$

Relabeling :
- $Stage(v_0) := WA$
- $Father(v_0) := \perp$
- $Sons(v_0) := \emptyset$
- $Included(v_0) := \emptyset$
- $Terminated(v_0) := \emptyset$

$STR2$: **Spanning rule acting on 2 nodes v, w where w is not yet in the on-building tree**
Precondition :
- $Stage(w) = X$
- $v \in B(w)$ and $Stage(v) = WA$

Relabeling :
- $Stage(w) := WA$
- $Father(w) := v$
- $Sons(w) := \emptyset$
- $Terminated(w) := \emptyset$
- $Sons(v) := Sons(v) \cup \{w\}$
- $Included(v) := Included(v) \cup \{w\}$
- $Included(w) := \{v\}$

$STR3$: **Node v discovers its neighbors already included in the tree**
Precondition :
- $Stage(v) = WA$
- $w \in B(v)$, $Stage(w) = WA$ and $w \notin Included(v)$

Relabeling :
- $Included(v) := Included(v) \cup \{w\}$
- $Included(w) := Included(w) \cup \{v\}$

$STR4$: **Node v finishes locally the computation of a spanning tree**
Precondition :
- $Stage(v) = WA$
- $Included(v) = B(v)$ and $Terminated(v) = Sons(v)$

Relabeling :
- $Stage(v) := Y$
- **if** $(Father(v) \neq \perp)$ $Terminated(Father(v)) := Terminated(Father(v)) \cup \{v\}$

v finds all its neighbors already included in the tree (rule $STR3$), it applies the rule $STR4$. This means that v has locally terminated its computation, then it informs its father. Note that this rule is executed firstly by the leaves. The computation finishes when $Stage(v_0) = Y$. In this case, all the nodes v also satisfy $Stage(v) = Y$. Obviously we have a spanning tree of G rooted at v_0 defined by the third components and the fourth components of the labels of the nodes. The root of the spanning tree is then the unique node with its father equals to $\perp$. We denote by $\#M$ the size of the set M. Therefore, we claim the following:

Property 1. *Given a graph $G = (V, E)$ and a distinguished node v_0. The STP_GRS builds a spanning tree of G rooted at v_0 using $(\#E + \#V + 1)$ rules.*

3 2-Vertex Connectivity Test of Graphs

In this section we present a protocol to test whether a given graph G is 2-connected. A vertex v of a connected graph G is a "cut-node" iff $G \setminus v$ is not connected. Since a 2-connected graph is a graph without any cut-node, we explore all the nodes of G, each visited node is tested to know if it is or not a cut-node. We introduce the notion of "succorer son" as follows.

Definition 2. *Let $G = (V, E)$ be a connected graph and $T(Father, Sons)$ be a spanning tree of G rooted at v_0. For each pair of nodes u, v in G, we say that u is reached by v in G iff there is a path in G linking v to u. Thus, we say that v is a succorer son of v_d iff the following holds:*

1. *$v \in Sons(v_d)$,*
2. *if $v \neq v_0$ then v is not reached by v_0 in $G \setminus v_d$,*
3. *$\neg \exists\, u \in Sons(v_d)$ such that $u < v$ and v is reached by u in $G \setminus v_d$.*

The following is an immediate application of this definition:

Proposition 3. *Let $G = (V, E)$ be a connected graph. Then G is 2-connected iff $\forall\, T$ a spanning tree of G rooted at some node v_0 then only v_0 admits a succorer son.*

3.1 Our Protocol

We now present an overview of our distributed test protocol. Along this description, we will give the main keys to understand why our protocol is based on a general and a constructive approach. It consists of the following phases: (1) the computation of the spanning tree called *Investigation tree*, denoted by Inv_T, of G with root v_0, (2) exploration of Inv_T to compute the succorer sons of each node of G.

In phase one, we use an algorithm as described in the previous section. This procedure constructs a spanning tree Inv_T of a given graph G rooted at v_0 with local detection of the global termination. It means that v_0 detects the end of the spanning tree computation of G. In phase two, the tree Inv_T is explored using "depth-first trip" [12]. When the trip reaches a node v_d, v_d does the following:

1. *disconnects.* Node v_d disconnects itself.
2. *disconnected node v_d is the root.*
   (a) *configures.* An auxiliary spanning tree T of G, where v_0 is disconnected, is built.
   (b) *computes the first succorer son.* Node v_0 chooses its first son as its first succorer son. Let r be such a son. It will become the chosen root.
   (c) *maximal tree construction.* Node r is in charge to build a spanning tree T' of $G \setminus v_d$ rooted at itself.
3. *disconnected node v_d is not the root.*
   (a) *propagates.* Node v_d informs the root v_0 of the Inv_T about its disconnection.
   (b) *configures.* An auxiliary tree T of G, where v_d is disconnected, is built.
   (c) *maximal tree construction.* The root of T starts the computation of its maximal tree T' of $G \setminus v_d$.
   (d) *responds.* Eventually, v_0 constructs its maximal tree, so it responds to v_d.
4. *succorer sons computation.* Node v_d looks in its sons if there is some node not included in the maximal tree.
   i. If there exists such a son, and $v_d = v_0$: Node v_0 stops the treatment and states that G is not 2-connected.
   ii. If there exists such a son, and $v_d \neq v_0$: Node v_d stops the exploration informing the root v_0 which states that G is not 2-connected.
   iii. Otherwise, node v_d continues the exploration on Inv_T.

The algorithm terminates according to the following cases: (*i*) if the root admits more than one succorer son, (*ii*) if some node admits a succorer son, (*iii*) after the exploration of all nodes of G without the two previous cases. In the last case, there is only one succorer son which is the first son of v_0 the root of the chosen spanning tree Inv_T. Then, v_0 states that G is 2-connected. As we shall see, the aim of the configuration step represented above as *configures* is to prepare the application of the succorer sons computation of some node v_d.

The *maximal tree construction procedure* is applied on the node r which is in charge to build and to mark its maximal tree of $G \setminus v_d$. Let T be a spanning tree of G. We denote by T' the "on-building" tree of $G \setminus v_d$. This procedure is composed of the following steps:

1. *computes the base of the tree.* This base of T' is the subtree of $T \setminus v_d$ rooted at r. It is identified using a marking procedure (see below).
2. *search extension.* Using a "depth-first trip" [12] on T' each node v is visited until one of the neighbor of v is not yet included in the current tree T'.
3. *connection is found.* The visited node v finds a neighbor u that is not in the "on-building" tree. Such a node is called a *connection entry* and v is named a *connection node*. Therefore, the edge (u, v) is added to T'. The subtree of T containing u is reorganized in such a way that u becomes its root using the *root changing procedure* (see below). Then, this subtree is included in T' and its nodes are marked as nodes of T'. Now, the search of isolated subtrees is restarted on the extended T'.

Finally, r detects that it had extended as much as possible its tree and the procedure is terminated.

4 Encoding of Our Protocol

In this section, we propose an encoding of our protocol using graph relabeling systems. We start by describing its main procedure: The *maximal tree construction procedure.* This procedure is composed of *five* rules and uses *two* procedures: The *marking procedure* and the *root changing procedure.* In the sequel we present a short description of these two procedures. The *maximal tree construction procedure* is more detailed.

Marking Procedure ($MP\_GRS(T; v_0; Stage, X, Y)$). The goal of this procedure is to transform the labels of each node v from $Stage(v) = X$ into $Stage(v) = Y$. Therefore, if the MP_GRS is applied to a tree $T = (V, E)$ rooted at v_0, v_0 will detect that all the nodes of T are marked Y after the application of $2\#V$ steps.

Root Changing Procedure ($RCP\_GRS(T; r; Treated)$). If a node r requests to replace the root v_0 of T, the nodes "between" [1] v_0 and r have to reorganize their lists of sons and their fathers. Hence, after the application, in the worst case, of $2\#V$ steps node r becomes the new root of T.

[1] The nodes on the simple path linking v_0 and v.

Maximal Tree Construction Procedure ($MTCP\_GRS(G, T, T'; v_d, r)$). Given a node v_d of a spanning tree T of a graph G, this procedure builds a maximal tree T' of $G \setminus v_d$ rooted at r. We propose an encoding of this procedure using means of local computations, then we present an example of its run and its analysis.

Algorithm 2. $MTCP\_GRS(G, T, T'; v_d, r)$

- **Input:** A graph $G = (V, E)$ with a spanning tree $T = (V, E_T)$, and a chosen node r.
  - **Labels:**
    - $Stage(v) \in \{A, D, Ended, F, SC, W\}$, $Father(v)$, $Sons(v)$, $B(v)$,
    - $To\_Explore(v)$, $Potential(v)$, $To\_Ignore(v)$.
  - **Initialization:**
    - $\forall v \in V \setminus \{v_d\}$, $Stage(v) = A$,
    - $\forall v \in Sons(v_d)$, $Father(v) = \perp$,
    - $\forall v \in V$, $To\_Explore(v) = Sons(v)$,
    - $\forall v \in V$, $Potential(v) = \emptyset$,
    - $\forall v \in V$, $To\_Ignore(v) = \emptyset$.
- **Result:** A maximal tree T' of $G \setminus v_d$ with root r. In this case, r is labeled $Ended$.
- **Rules:**

$MTR1$: **Node r labels the nodes of its subtree to F and starts the attempt of reconnection**
  Precondition :
  - $Stage(r) = A$
  Relabeling :
  - $Potential(r) := B(r) \setminus (Sons(r) \cup To\_Ignore(r))$
  - **MP_GRS(T_r; r; Stage, A, F)**
  - $Stage(r) := SC$

$MTR2$: **Node v is a connection node**
  Precondition :
  - $Stage(v) = SC$
  - $u \in Potential(v)$
  - $Stage(u) = A$
  Relabeling :
  - **RCP_GRS(T(u) $\setminus$ v_d; u)**
  - **MP_GRS(T_u; u; Stage, A, F)**
  - $Father(u) := v$
  - $Sons(v) := Sons(v) \cup \{u\}$
  - $To\_Explore(v) := To\_Explore(v) \cup \{u\}$

$MTR3$: **Node u is labeled F**
  Precondition :
  - $Stage(u) = F$
  - $u \in B(v)$ and $u \in Potential(v)$
  Relabeling :
  - $Potential(v) := Potential(v) \setminus \{u\}$
  - $To\_Ignore(u) := To\_Ignore(u) \cup \{v\}$

$MTR4$: **Node v is not a connection node, it delegates the reconnection search to one of its sons u**
  Precondition :
  - $Stage(v) = SC$
  - $Potential(v) = \emptyset$
  - $u \in To\_Explore(v)$
  Relabeling :
  - $To\_Explore(v) := To\_Explore(v) \setminus \{u\}$
  - $Potential(u) := B(u) \setminus (Son(u) \cup \{v\} \cup To\_Ignore(u))$
  - $Stage(u) := SC$
  - $Stage(v) := W$

$MTR5$: **The subtree with root v does not contain connection node**
  Precondition :
  - $Stage(v) = SC$
  - $Stage(Father(v)) = W$ /* This condition is not necessary, but clarifies the rule. */
  - $Potential(v) = \emptyset$
  - $To\_Explore(v) = \emptyset$
  Relabeling :
  - $Stage(v) := Ended$
  - **if** ($Father(v) \neq \perp$) $Stage(Father(v)) := SC$

After the initialization $\forall v \in V \setminus v_d$, $Stage(v) = A$. The chosen node r initiates the computation: It is the only one that executes the rule $MTR1$. So r executes the *marking procedure*. When r finishes the execution of this procedure, its subtree T_r in T is labeled F. It means that this subtree is included in the on-building tree. Node r switches to the "searching connection" phase ($Stage(r) = SC$). Then, step by step, a tree T_r rooted at r is extended. At any time there is only one node labeled SC and this node is in charge to extend the tree it belongs to.

If a node v labeled SC finds a neighbor u labeled A (a connection entry) in its "Potential" set, it executes the rule $MTR2$ to extend T_r : The subtree containing u is reorganized in such a way that u becomes its root and then this subtree is added to T_r using the edge (v, u). Let $T(u) \setminus v_d$ be the tree that contains the connection entry u. Node u starts the execution of the *root changing procedure*. The *marking procedure* is then applied to the tree rooted at u in order to relabel its nodes to F. Now, u is added to T_r, label *Father* of u is set to v and u is added in both $Sons(v)$ and $To\_Explore(v)$.

In parallel, the rule $MTR3$ is used by a node w to update the lists "Potential" and to prepare their computations using the lists "To_Ignore". If a node w is labeled F, then it cannot be a candidate for reconnection. Since it is yet in the tree, it must be avoided from the lists "Potential" of its neighbors. Moreover, the neighbors of w yet in the tree (they are labeled F, W , or SC) have to be ignored in its "Potential". When a node v labeled SC has an empty list "Potential", v executes the rule $MTR4$ to indicate that it does not succeed to find an extension for T_r. So it transfers the label SC to one of its sons that restarts the process of reconnection.

Eventually, node v in T_r has extended as much as possible T_r. Then, it informs with rule $MTR5$ its father ($Stage(v) = Ended$). Now, this last node can proceed with the extension search from one of its other sons. When $Stage(r) = Ended$, one of the largest tree rooted at r of $G \setminus v_d$ has been computed. Thus, r detects the end of the *maximal tree construction procedure*. The following Lemma shows the tasks invoked by the execution of this procedure when applied to a graph G about one of its node v_d.

Lemma 4. *After the application of the* $MTCP\_GRS$ *to a graph* $G = (V, E)$, *node* r *constructs a maximal tree including all the nodes reached by* r *in* $G \setminus v_d$ *using, in the worst case,* $\#E + 4\#V$ *rules.*

4.1 2-Vertex Connectivity Test Algorithm

In this part, we present an encoding of our protocol referred to in the following as $2\mathcal{VCT}\_\mathcal{GRS}$ algorithm. We use the label Suc to encode the succorer sons. So $Suc(v)[v_d]$ is set to *true* to denote that v is the succorer son of v_d. The $2\mathcal{VCT}\_\mathcal{GRS}$ algorithm uses *nine* rules and *three* procedures: The *spanning tree construction procedure* to construct the investigation tree, the *simple path propagator procedure* to encode phase $3(a)$ and its reversible version to encode phase $3(d)$ and the *configuration procedure* to encode both phases $2(a)$ and $3(b)$. Phases $2(c)$ and $3(c)$ are achieved using the *maximal tree construction procedure* presented above. Now, we present a short description of the two new procedures. Then, we give a full description of the algorithm and an example of its run.

Simple Path Propagator Procedure ($SPPP\_GRS(T; v; Traversed, X, Y)$). The aim of this procedure is to propagate an information along a simple path linking some node v to the root of the tree $T = (V, E_T)$. Hence, the application of the $SPPP\_GRS$ to T involves, in the worst case, the application of $\#V$ steps.

Configuration Procedure ($CP\_GRS(Inv\_T, T; v_0, v_d; Stage, X, Y; Required)$). This procedure allows to do the required initializations of the *maximal tree construction procedure* in order to compute the succorer sons. Moreover, v_d prepares its disconnection: Each of its sons sets its label "Father" to $\perp$. To encode efficiently our protocol, we collect the states of the sons of v_d during the application of the *root changing procedure* using the label $Treated$[2]. We denote by $Required\_CP$ the required initializations [3]. Thus, the cost of the *configuration procedure* is only $O(\#V)$ time when applied to a graph $G = (V, E)$.

Algorithm 3. 2-Vertex connectivity test algorithm ($2\mathcal{VCT}\_\mathcal{GRS}$)

- **Input:** A graph $G = (V, E)$ and a node $v_0 \in V$.
- **Labels:**
  - $Stage(v)$, $B(v)$, $Treated(v)$,
  - $InvStage(v) \in \{A, D, KO, N, OK, Over, W\}$,
  - $Traversed(v) \in \{O, 1\}$,
  - $InvFather(v)$, $InvSons(v)$.
- **Initialization:**
  - $\forall v \in V$, $InvStage(v) = N$, $Treated(v) = \emptyset$ and $Traversed(v) = 0$,
  - $\forall v \in V, \forall u \in B(v)\ SUC(v)[u] = false$.
- **Result:** Two possible results :
  - $InvStage(v_0) = Over$ to mean that the graph G is 2-connected.
  - $InvStage(v_0) = KO$ to mean that the graph G is not 2-connected.
- **Rules:**

$VCTR1$: **Node v_0 starts to build the tree** $Inv\_T(InvFather, InvSons)$
Precondition :
- $InvStage(v_0) = N$

Relabeling :
- **STP_GRS(G, Inv_T; v_0; InvStage, N, A; InvFather; InvSons)** /*all the nodes v satisfy : $InvStage(v) = A$.*/

$VCTR2$: **Node v_0 initializes the test** $Inv\_T(InvFather, InvSons)$ **/*v_0 is the only node such that** $InvFather(v_0) = \perp$ [4]***/**
Precondition :
- $InvStage(v_0) = A$
- $InvFather(v_0) = \perp$
- $r \in Sons(v_d)$

Relabeling :
- $InvStage(v_0) := D$
- **CP_GRS(Inv_T, T; v_0, v_0; Stage, N, A; Required_CP)**
- **Suc(r)[v_0] := true**
- **MTCP_GRS(G, T, T_r; v_0, r)**

$VCTR3$: **Node v_d has not found a succorer son**
Precondition :
- $InvStage(v_d) = D$
- $Traversed(v_d) = 0$
- $Treated(v_d) = Sons(v_d)$

Relabeling :
- $InvStage(v_d) := OK$

$VCTR4$: **Node v_d finds a succorer son**
Precondition :
- $InvStage(v_d) = D$
- $Traversed(v_d) = 0$
- $v \in Sons(v_d)$
- $Stage(v) = A$

Relabeling :
- $InvStage(v_d) := KO$

$VCTR5$: **Node v ends the computation of its succorers sons, one of its son will become activated**
Precondition :
- $InvStage(v) = OK$
- $v_d \in InvSons(v)$

Relabeling :
- $InvSon(v) := InvSon(v) \setminus \{v_d\}$
- $InvStage(v) := W$
- $InvStage(v_d) := D$
- $Traversed(v_d) := 1$
- **SPPP_GRS(Inv_T; v_d; Traversed, 0, 1)**

$VCTR6$: **Node v_0 is informed about the activation of some node v_d, it computes its maximal tree and then informs v_d.**
Precondition :
- $InvFather(v_0) = \perp$
- $Traversed = 1$

Relabeling :
- **CP_GRS(Inv_T, T; v_0, v_d; Stage, Ended, A; Required_CP)**
- **MTCP_GRS(G, T, T_{v_0}; v_0)**
- **SPPP_GRS^{-}1(Inv_T; v_0;Traversed,1,0)**

$VCTR7$: **Node v ends the examination of its subtree**
Precondition :
- $InvStage(v) = OK$
- $InvSons(v) = \emptyset$
- $InvFather(v) \neq \perp$

Relabeling :
- $InvStage(v) := Over$
- $InvSons(InvFather(v)) := InvSons(InvFather(v)) \setminus \{v\}$
- $InvStage(InvFather(v)) := OK$

$VCTR8$: **Node v_0 detects the end and the success of the test algorithm**
Precondition :
- $InvStage(v) = OK$
- $InvSons(v) = \emptyset$
- $InvFather(v) = \perp$

Relabeling :
- $InvStage(v) := Over$

$VCTR9$: **The information about the failure of the test is transferred to the root v_0**
Precondition :
- $InvStage(v_d) = KO$
- $InvFather(v_d) \neq \perp$

Relabeling :
- $InvStage(v_d) := Over$
- $InvStage(Father(v_d)) := KO$

$2\mathcal{VCT}\_\mathcal{GRS}$ **Algorithm.** As depicted in Algorithm 3, let $G = (V, E)$ be a graph and $v_0 \in V$ be a node to launch the test algorithm. We have $\forall v \in$

[2] Treated(InvFather(v)):=Treated(InvFather(v)) ∪ {v}.

[3] Father, Sons, Potential, To_Ignore, To_Explore, Treated, Traversed.

V, $InvStage(v) = N$. The node v_0 starts the computation: It builds a spanning tree Inv_T of G rooted at v_0 ($VCTR1$). Subsequently, all the vertices of G are such that $InvStage = A$.

Since the test scheme is based on the use of a "depth-first trip" exploration on the tree Inv_T, the root v_0 is the only one able to start the trip with the rule $VCTR2$. Except the particular case of v_0, when a node is ready to be examined it switches its label to D ($VCTR5$). The examination phase of the node v_d consists on the test if for a given spanning tree T of G deprived of v_d, v_0 is able to build a maximal tree T' of $G \setminus v_d$ including the sons of v_d in T. It proceeds as follows: The node v_d informs v_0 about its attention to compute its succorer sons applying the $SPPP\_GRS$ ($VCTR5$). Then v_0 configures the labels using the CP_GRS which cleans the spanning tree T' of G rooted at v_0 and disconnecting v_d. At the end of the *configuration procedure*, v_0 starts to build its maximal tree T' of $G \setminus v_d$ using the $MTCP\_GRS$ presented above ($VCTR6$).

Eventually v_0 constructs such a tree and responds to v_d using a reversible version of the $SPPP\_GRS$. When v_d receives the information from v_0, it looks in the set "Treated" if all its sons in T are included in T'. If v_d finds at least one son v labeled $Stage(v) = A$: The test fails ($VCTR4$) and then stops. The current node v_d will be labeled $InvStage(v_d) = KO$. Then it informs its father in Inv_T applying the rule $VCTR9$ until the root v_0 which states that the graph G is not 2-connected. In the other case("Treated=Sons"), v_d continues the exploration ($VCTR3$, $VCTR5$) choosing one of its not yet observed son. It transfers the label D to such a son.

Eventually a node v_d finishes the exploration of all the nodes in its sub-tree ($InvSons(v_d) = \emptyset$). So it informs its father that the computation is over ($VCTR7$). Now v_d is removed from the list $InvSons$ of its father which then can continue the exploration choosing one of its not yet observed son. Furthermore, only the root v_0 detects the end of the "trip" when all its sons are over. It means that all the nodes are examined and succeeded. So v_0 applies the rule $VCTR8$ to state that the graph G is 2-connected.

For the time complexity, the worst case corresponds to the case when the *maximal tree construction procedure* succeeds for every node. For the space requirements, every node needs to maintain subsets of its neighbors as descendants. We use $\log x$ to denote $\log_2 x$. Thus, the following result completes the analysis.

Theorem 5. *The 2VCT_GRS algorithm encodes a distributed computation of the 2-vertex connectivity test of a graph. When the 2VCT_GRS is applied to a graph* $G = (V, E)$, *its time complexity is in* $O(\Delta \times \#V^2)$ *and its space complexity is in* $O(\Delta \times \log \Delta)$ *bits per node.*

5 Asynchronous Message Passing Model

The proposed protocol is implemented in the asynchronous message passing model. Since, computations are based on local information, the implementation is achieved using a transformation adding simple changes. The proofs of correctness and the complexity analysis are based on those of the local computations model. Here we give an example of an implementation of the *spanning tree procedure* to illustrate such a transformation (see Algorithm 4). Then, the following property holds:

Algorithm 4. $STP\_MPS(G,T;v_0;Stage,X,Y;Father;Sons)$

```
– Input : A graph G = (V, E) and v0 the chosen root.
  • Variables:
      * The set of labels used to encode the spanning tree procedure in the local computations model,
      * i, p, q : integer;
  • Initialization:
      * ∀v ∈ V, Stage(v) = X.
– Results: A spanning tree T = (V, E_T) of G with root v0 such that ∀v ∈ V, Stage(v) = A.
– Actions:

STA1 : {For the initiator v0 only, execute once:}
       Stage(v0) := WA;
       Father(v0) := ⊥;
       Sons(v0) := ∅;
       Included(v0) := ∅;
       Terminated(v0) := ∅;
       for i := 1 to deg(v0) do send<st_tok> via port i;

STA2 : {A message <st_tok> has arrived at v from port q}
1:       if (Stage(v) = X)
           Stage(v) := WA;
           Father(v) := q;
           Sons(v) := ∅;
           Included(v) := {q};
           Terminated(v) := ∅;
           send<st_son> via port q;
2:           if (deg(v) = 1)
               Stage(v) := Y;
               send<st_back> via port q;
3:           else
               for i := 1 to deg(v) do
4:                     if (i ≠ q) send<st_tok> via port i;
5:       else
           Included(v) := Included(v) ∪ {q};
6:         if (Included(v) = B(v) and Sons(v) = ∅) send<st_back> via port Father(v);

STA3 : {A message <st_son> has arrived at v from port q}
       Sons(v) := Sons(v) ∪ {q};
       Included(v) := Included(v) ∪ {q};

STA4 : {A message <st_back> has arrived at v from port q}
       Terminated(v) := Terminated(v) ∪ {q};
1:       if (Included(v) = B(v) and Terminated(v) = Sons(v))
           Stage(v) := Y
2:         if (Father(v) ≠⊥)
             send<st_back> via port Father;
```

Property 6. *Given a graph* $G = (V,E)$ *with diameter* $D(G)$ *and a chosen node* v_0. *The* STM_MPS *builds a spanning tree of* G *rooted at* v_0 *in* $O(D(G))$ *time using* $O(\#E + \#V)$ *messages.*

6 Applications

Our work may be used as a core of algorithms to preserve control structures while crash or disconnection of certain nodes occur. A useful particular example is the distributed maintenance of spanning trees.

6.1 Maintenance of a Spanning Tree of k-Connected Graphs

We consider a network modeled by a graph $G = (V,E)$. Let $T = (V,E_T)$ be a spanning tree of G rooted at a distinguished node v_0. After the crash of a node v, we have to rebuild another spanning tree of G deprived of v

with a minimum of changes. Our protocol may be adapted to deal with the problem of the maintenance of a spanning tree of k-connected graphs with $k-1$ consecutive failures. This is an application of the succorer sons computations and the *maximal tree construction procedure*. As presented in this work, in the 2-connected graph, only the root admits a succorer son. So, if v [5] is not the root of the actual tree, the root will succeed to build such a spanning tree. In the case of the root, its succorer son will assure this task. For the k-connected graphs, also only the root of the given tree admits a succorer son. It means that after the deletion of any set of $k-1$ nodes the resulted graph admits only one succorer son: It's a succorer son of the resulted tree. So, to maintain a spanning tree of such a graph in the presence of at most $k-1$ failures it suffices to update the succorer son after each failure occurrence and then to apply the same algorithm as the case of one failure.

6.2 Maintenance of a Forest of Spanning Trees

As the connectivity of a network might change over time, the graph modeling it may be disconnected. In fact, after the deletion of some nodes, results of failures, the network may become splitted and partitioned into many components. It would be desirable to maintain a dynamic structure of trees of such networks. So we propose an application of our algorithm to deal with the maintenance of a forest of trees. That is, each component computes its spanning tree. We add an extension of our test algorithm to complete the computation of the succorer sons of each node. After the failure of some node, its succorer sons are able to construct a spanning tree of each of the disconnected component using the *maximal tree construction procedure*. Thus, such knowledge increases the degree of the parallelism during the computation.

7 Conclusion and Future Works

This work deals with the test of the 2-vertex connectivity of graphs in a distributed setting using local knowledge. We present a new formalization of such a problem using the notion of succorer sons. This notion is defined under an arbitrary pre-constructed spanning tree of the graph to be tested. So using a constructive approach we compute the set of succorer sons of all the nodes. Therefore, to check whether a given graph is 2-connected it suffices that the only node which admits a succorer son is the root of the pre-constructed spanning tree.

The protocol is encoded in the local computations model and implemented in the message passing model using a set of procedures. Given a graph $G = (V, E)$ with degree Δ and N nodes: The first algorithm requires $O(\Delta \times N^2)$ steps and $O(\Delta \times \log \Delta)$ bits per node. The second one achieves correctly the test of the 2-vertex connectivity of G in $O(N^2)$ time using $O(\Delta \times N^2)$ messages and $O(\Delta \times \log \Delta)$ bits per node.

[5] The crashed node.

Furthermore, our work has an extra benefit: Algorithms encoded in the used version of local computations model may be implemented in the asynchronous message passing model with a transformation including simple changes. Furthermore, the transformation guarantees the following: (1) the proofs used in the first one allows to deduce the proofs for the second one, (2) the complexity measures may be also deduced.

For the k-vertex connectivity test, we conjecture that we can use the previous procedures to generalize our algorithm to test the k-vertex connectivity of graphs in polynomial time. Intuitively, we can reduce this problem to the case of $k = 2$ followed by an incremental test procedure.

References

1. Attiya, H., Welch, J.: Distributed computing, fundamentals, simulations and advanced topics. McGraw-hill international (UK) limited, New York (1998)
2. Bahramgiri, M., Hajiaghayi, M.T., Mirrokni, V.S.: Fault-tolerant and 3-dimensional distributed topology control algorithms in wireless multi-hop networks. In: IEEE Int. Conf. on Computer Communications and Networks (ICCCN02), pp. 392–397. IEEE Computer Society Press, Los Alamitos (2002)
3. Chen, W., Wada, K.: Optimal fault-tolerant routings with small routing tables for k-connected graphs. J. Discrete Algorithms 2(4), 517–530 (2004)
4. Esfahanian, A.H., Hakimi, S.L.: On computing the connectivities of graphs and digraphs. Networks, 355–366 (1984)
5. Even, S., Tarjan, R.E.: Network flow and testing graph connectivity. SIAM Journal on Computing 4(4), 507–518 (1975)
6. Gabow, H.N.: Using expander graphs to find vertex connectivity. In: 41st Annual Symposium on Foundations of Computer Science, pp. 410–420 (2000)
7. Henzinger, M.R., Rao, S., Gabow, H.N.: Computing vertex connectivity: new bounds from old techniques. J. Algorithms 34(2), 222–250 (2000)
8. Litovsky, I., Métivier, Y., Sopena, E.: Graph relabeling systems and distributed algorithms. In: Ehrig, H., Kreowski, H.J., Montanari, U., Rozenberg, G. (eds.) Handbook of graph grammars and computing by graph transformation, vol. III, pp. 1–56. World Scientific Publishing, Singapore (1999)
9. Métivier, Y., Mosbah, M., Sellami, A.: Proving distributed algorithms by graph relabeling systems: Example of tree in networks with processor identities. In: Applied Graph Transformations (AGT2002), Grenoble (2002)
10. De Prisco, R., Lampson, B., Lynch, N.: Revisiting the paxos algorithm. In: Mavronicolas, M. (ed.) WDAG 1997. LNCS, vol. 1320, pp. 111–125. Springer, Heidelberg (1997)
11. Tarjan, R.E.: Depth-first search and linear graph algorithms. SIAM Journal on Computing 1, 146–160 (1972)
12. Tel, G.: Introduction to distributed algorithms, 2nd edn. Cambridge University Press, Cambridge (2000)
13. West, D.: Introduction to graph theory, 2nd edn. Prentice-Hall, Englewood Cliffs (2001)

Comparing Direct-to-Cache Transfer Policies to TCP/IP and M-VIA During Receive Operations in MPI Environments

Farshad Khunjush and Nikitas J. Dimopoulos

Department of Electrical and Computer Engineering
University of Victoria, Victoria, B.C., Canada,
{fkhunjus,nikitas}@ece.uvic.ca

Abstract. The main contributors to message delivery latency in message passing environments are the copying operations needed to transfer and bind a received message to the consuming process/thread. To reduce this copying overhead, we introduce architectural extensions comprising a specialized network cache and instructions. In this work, we study the possible overhead and cache pollution introduced through the operating system and the communications stack as exemplified by Linux, TCP/IP and M-VIA. We introduce this overhead in our simulation environment and study its effects on our proposed extensions. Ultimately, we have been able to compare the performance achieved by an application running on a system incorporating our extensions with the performance of the same application running on a standard system. The results show that our proposed approach can improve the performance of MPI applications by 10% to 20%.

1 Introduction

The main contributors to message delivery latency in message passing environments are the copying operations needed to transfer and bind a received message to the consuming process/thread. Reducing the communications latency will allow the decrease of the computation grain with potential increases to the parallelization of an application. To reduce this copying overhead and reach a finer granularity, architectural extensions comprising of a specialized *network cache* and instructions to manage the operations of this *cache* [1,2,3,4] have been introduced and implemented. The results show that adding this extension has no adverse effect on the normal operation of the processor caching system. The results also show reduced message delivery latency and consequently, increased potential parallelism in parallel applications.

The present study compares the benefits of the network cache environment introduced earlier to two common communication protocols (i.e., TCP/IP and VIA [5]). We also present new metrics that better characterize the behavior of an application and the messaging environment under the protocols being considered.

Specifically, we compare two proposed policies, which determine when a message is to be bound and sent to the data cache, to the above-mentioned communication protocols. We call these policies *DTCT* (Direct to Cache Transfer)

I. Stojmenovic et al. (Eds.): ISPA 2007, LNCS 4742, pp. 208–222, 2007.

and *lazy DTCT*. Under the *DTCT* policy, a message is transferred to the data cache upon binding, while under the *lazy DTCT* policy, a message remains in the network cache (even after it is bound) and it is transferred to the data cache only if it is bound and scheduled to be evicted from the network cache.

For this part of our study we use the Virtutec Simics environment, a full system simulator, including processor core, peripheral devices, memories, and network connections [6]. We evaluate the receive operations overhead in TCP/IP and VIA implementation of MPICH [7] and explore the cache behavior during those operations. We use MVICH [8] as the VIA implementation of MPICH. The CG benchmark, from the NAS [9] Parallel benchmark suite, and PSTSWM [10] benchmark are used for this purpose.

We have used the system simulation environment described above to obtain cache and network traffic parameters in a complete system environment. We used the achieved data within the SimpleScalar [11] simulation environment of our extensions to obtain a realistic evaluation of the behavior of our proposed extensions in a system environment.

This paper is organized as follows. Section 2 discusses related work; section 3 summarizes the architectural extensions introduced to support the efficient processing of the sending and receiving of messages in a parallel processing environment. Section 4 describes briefly the TCP/IP and VIA protocols. Section 5 discusses the simulation environment and our assumptions; section 6 discusses the obtained results, and finally our conclusions are discussed in section 7.

2 Motivation and Related Work

High performance computing is increasingly concerned with efficient communication across the interconnect. System Area Networks (SANs), such as Myrinet [12] and InfiniBand [13], provide high bandwidth and low latency while several user-level messaging techniques have removed the operating system kernel and protocol stack from the critical path of communications [14,15]. A significant portion of the software communication overhead is attributed to message copying. Traditional software messaging layers employ four message copying operations involving the send and receive buffers, as shown in Fig. 1.

At the send side, user-level messaging layers use programmed I/O or DMA to avoid system buffer copying. Address translation can be accomplished using a kernel module, or by caching a limited number of address translations as in U-Net/MM [16]. Some network interfaces also permit writing directly into the network.

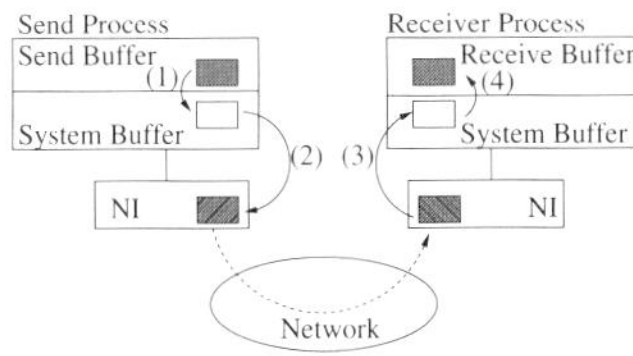

Fig. 1. Message copying operations from the send buffer to the receive buffer

Contrary to the send side, bypassing the system buffer copying at the receiving side may not be achievable. Processes at the sending side do not know the destination buffer address. Therefore, when a message arrives at the receiving side it is buffered, if the receive call has not been posted yet.

Several techniques have been developed that attempt to alleviate the latency introduced by this buffering. These include VMMC-2 [14], Fast Sockets [15], MPI-LAPI [17] or re-mapping, copy-on-write techniques [18], and offloading TCP/IP processing onto the NIC [19]. All of these solutions try to overcome the communication overhead at the network interface to CPU connection. However, the overhead remains due to multiple data accesses to the memory, interrupt, and resource scheduling. The Virtual Interface Architecture (VIA) specification was introduced to standardize the available user-level network interfaces [5]. A major concern with all page remapping techniques is their poor performance for short messages, which are very common in parallel computing.

In addition to the above-mentioned methods that try to alleviate the software communication bottleneck at the NIC to CPU connection, there are other methods that try to reduce the bottleneck at the hardware level in TCP/IP environments. One method is the integration of NIC on the CPU die [20] to reduce the high-overhead communication between the CPU and NIC. Direct Cache Access (DCA) [21,22] transfers the I/O data directly into the CPU's data cache. However, this cannot be achieved before the target address is resolved. The resolution of the target address imposes serialization and cannot be hidden. Our architectural solution [1,2,3,4] hides the resolution of the target address by storing the received message in a special *network cache*.

Remote direct memory access (RDMA) [23] was introduced to improve data movements at the receiver, but this requires the modification of applications in order to be RDMA-aware.

Techniques have also been proposed that predict future accesses in distributed shared memory [24] and other techniques that predict message destinations in message-passing systems [25,26]. The work in predicting the message to be consumed next allows us to manage the received messages efficiently [26].

3 Architectural Extensions

In previous work [1,2,3,4], we introduced and studied several aspects of a network processor extension. In this section, we include a brief description of our proposed extension relevant to the discussion in the remainder of this paper. For a more complete discussion, we refer the reader to references [1,2,3,4]. As stated, our aim is to introduce architectural extensions [4] that will facilitate the placement of the message payload in a cache, bound and ready to be consumed by the consuming thread/process. We accomplish this through the introduction of a special network cache, shown in Fig. 2, and extensions to the ISA. We consider that a message includes, in addition to the payload, a message ID which may be part of, or the total MPI message envelope. The message ID is used to identify the message and bind it to its target address. We consider two memory spaces:

- *Network memory space*: This is where network buffers are allocated and where received messages remain while waiting to be bound to the process address space.
- *Process memory space*: This is the process memory address space where process objects, including bound messages, live.

The overall architecture of a network-extended node is shown in Fig. 3.

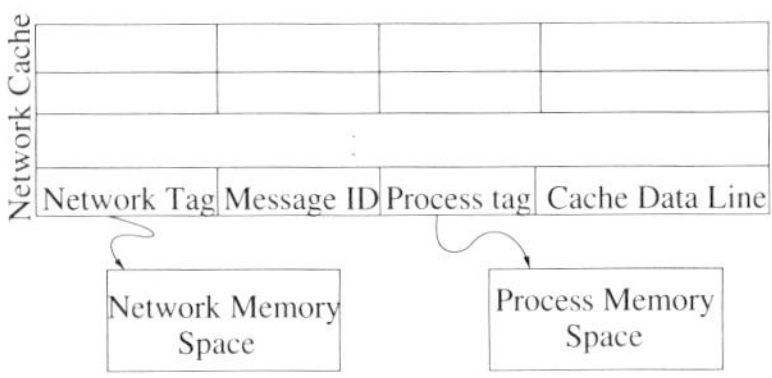

Fig. 2. *process* and *network* memories and their relation through the network cache

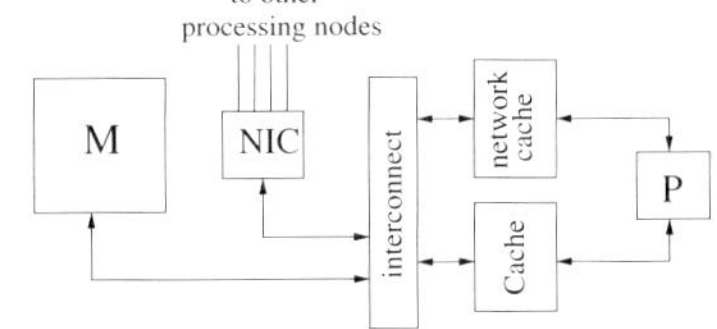

Fig. 3. The overall architecture of a network-extended node

3.1 Operation

We assume messages of length identical to or less than that of a network cache line (i.e., *Short Messages*). The network cache incorporates three separate tags. The *network tag* is associated with the Network Memory Space, while the *process tag* is associated with the Process Memory Space. A separate *message ID tag* holds the message ID. All three tags can be searched associatively and the process tag is set when the message is bound to the destination process.

Upon its arrival, a message is cached in the network cache. The message remains in the network cache and migrates to the Network Memory Space according to a cache replacement policy, which may utilize the prediction heuristics discussed in [26], to replace the message that is least likely to be consumed next.

3.2 Late Binding

A *receive call* targeting a message in the network cache will invalidate the *message ID* and *network tag* and will set the *process tag* to point to the address of the object destined to receive the message in Process Memory Space. From this point onward, the cache line is associated with the Process Memory Space. On cache replacement, the message is written back to its targeted object in Process Memory Space and eventually to the data cache. Both the data cache and the network cache are searched for cached objects, and the aforementioned binding process ensures that the object is not replicated in the *network* and *data* caches.

3.3 Early Binding

While late binding binds an early arriving message to a subsequent receive, an earlier posted receive could prepare and reserve a cache line in the network cache and set the corresponding *process_tag* and *message ID_tag* in anticipation of a subsequent message. When the message arrives, it is placed directly into the reserved cache line and immediately becomes available to the process.

3.4 ISA Extensions

A set of specialized instructions is used to manage the network cache and to also facilitate the binding operation. We call this set of instructions and the associated *network cache* a *network processor extension.* These specialized instructions are: *network_load* ,*network_store*, and *network_store* [4].

In subsequent sections, we briefly describe the TCP/IP and VIA protocols; then, we discuss the simulation infrastructure we are developing to evaluate the impact of the above-mentioned extensions on performance.

4 TCP/IP and VIA Overview

4.1 TCP/IP Protocol

The TCP/IP protocol uses *sockets* as the user interface to send and receive data to and from the NIC. To send a message, the sender copies the data into a transmit buffer and pushes a descriptor into the corresponding send queue of the socket. Then, the sender transmits a request to the NIC which transfers the data already copied into the socket's buffers into the NIC's transmit FIFO queue, and finally into the network.

At the receiver, the arrived data is transferred into the NIC's receive FIFO queue. Then, using DMA, it transfers the arrived data into the socket buffer in the kernel space. After the arrival of the data packet, NIC notifies the processor of the arrival of new data. The operating system copies the newly arrived data into the user buffer.

4.2 VIA Protocol

In this study we use M-VIA (ver1.2) [27], which is a modular implementation of the Virtual Interface Architecture (VIA) Specification. Each VI instance, which is a communication endpoint, includes send and receive queues as shown in Fig. 4. VIA provides two types of data transfer. The first is a traditional send/receive messaging method, and the second is Remote Direct Memory Access (RDMA). In this work, we are concerned with the message passing environment of VIA, that is, the traditional send/receive messaging method. With the send/receive method, the receiver has to post the corresponding receive descriptor before the arrival of a message. When receiving a packet before posting the corresponding receive descriptor, the receiver discards the arrived message. Therefore, the discarded packet has to be resent by the sender.

When sending a message, the sender application creates a descriptor, including the virtual address and the length of the send buffer, in the registered memory region [27]. The descriptor is posted, and the NIC is informed through the doorbell mechanism, which is used to notify the VI NIC that work has been placed in a work queue. The NIC obtains the address and length of the user buffer from the descriptor and transfers the data from the user buffer to the NIC via DMA. Thereafter, the NIC injects the data into the network.

At the receiver side, the application creates a receiver descriptor in the registered memory, including the virtual address of the receive buffer. The descriptor is posted and the NIC is informed through the doorbell mechanism. Having received the information from the network, the NIC stores the incoming message in staging buffers in NIC and the message header is checked to find the VI ID at the receiving side. Then, the NIC transfers the message from the staging memory to the user space using DMA.

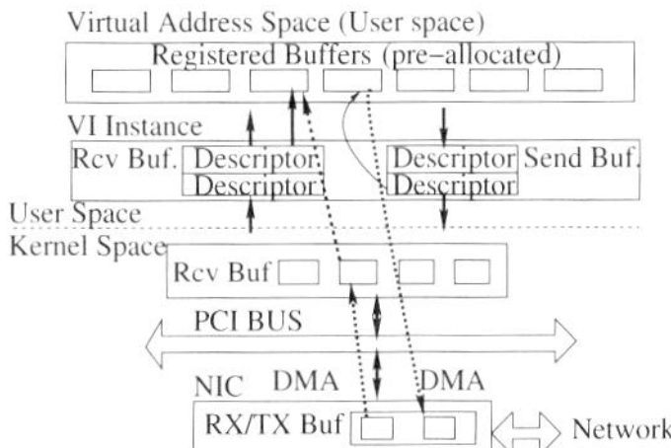

Fig. 4. VIA Comm. Protocol

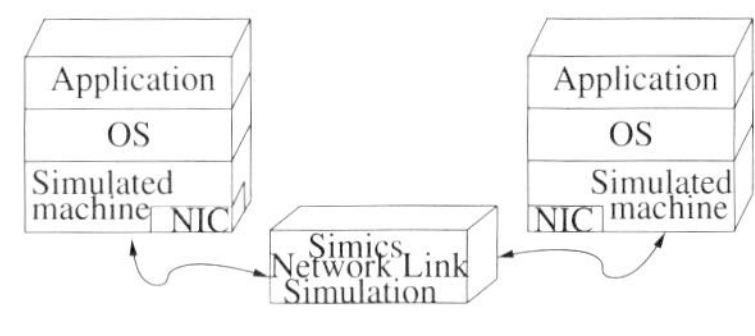

Fig. 5. A multi-computer config. in Simics

To transfer the received data to its final destination, legacy protocols such as TCP/IP have a layered and deep stack architecture that introduces extra overhead. However, user-level communication protocols such as VIA have access to the user's application memory and employ smaller stack architecture which results in less overhead. It is worth mentioning that VIA still transfers the received data into the main memory; therefore, the processor experiences a data cache miss at least in its first access to the received data. In contrast, our proposed extensions transfer the received data into a network cache which can be accessed quickly.

The following describes the methodology and simulation environment used to obtain the overhead of the MPI_Receive function for all protocols.

5 Methodology and Simulation Environment

As explained earlier, the aim of this work is to evaluate the effectiveness of our proposed Direct-to-Cache transfer policies compared to well-established communication protocols such as TCP/IP and VIA. In order to establish a sound comparison, and to consider the overhead that an operating system inevitably introduces, we proceed in two phases. The first involves the study of the communication and memory requirements of MPI applications over established protocols , TCP/IP and VIA. The second uses the parameters established in phase one to study the effect of our proposed extensions.

It was necessary to use this phased approach because it was not possible to establish a complete environment (simulation or otherwise) that incorporates the proposed extensions, networking stack, operating system and application environment.

5.1 Overhead Measurement During MPI_Receive Operation

To evaluate the overhead incurred by TCP/IP and VIA protocols and to explore the data cache behavior during receive operations, we use the Virtutec Simics, which simulates network nodes and all their software, from network device drivers to operating systems as well as communication stacks and application programs.

In this study, we use the enterprise-multi configuration of the predefined and preconfigured platforms. This setting is based on the enterprise system configuration, which simulates x86-p4 processors running RedHat Linux 7.3 with kernel version 2.4.18-3[1].

In the enterprise-multi configuration two x86-p4 based PCs are connected through an Ethernet link, as shown in Fig. 5. The network interface model has been changed to DEC21140A, a Fast Ethernet NIC, because it is able to transfer data to and from the host memory via DMA; furthermore, its driver exists in the communication protocol's implementation of M-VIA. We also added a 32KB ICache and a 512KB L2 unified cache to each processor model. The size of L1 DCache is varied for the simulation experimentation.

To investigate the overhead incurred by the TCP/IP protocol, we instrumented the Linux kernel version 2.4.18-3 to collect the necessary information without interfering with the normal execution of the simulated processors. For this, we use the *magic* instruction facility provided in Simics. We added this instruction at appropriate locations in the TCP/IP and M-VIA protocols inside the kernel as well as the M-VIA implementation and compiled them.

Having prepared the environment for evaluating the receive function's overhead, we ran several ping-pong micro-benchmarks and used the K-best measure algorithm [28] to find the incurred overhead in each protocol. Fig. 6 shows the overhead of the MPI_Receive function in a message passing environment in TCP/IP and M-VIA implementations. Because we are concerned with short messages this statistic represents each protocol's overhead, and consists of context switching and memory copying operations as well as communication processing, to receive one byte messages in different cache configurations[2].

As shown in Fig. 6, the overhead in TCP/IP is almost 1.5 times more than that in VIA during receive operations, which is consistent with the fact that the TCP/IP protocol has a deeper protocol stack. For the remaining of this work, we shall compare the performance of our proposed extensions to the more efficient VIA environment.

---

[1] Kernel version 2.4.18-3 is not the latest version of Linux distributions. Newer kernel implementations such as 2.6 have better stack management in the TCP/IP protocol. However, the last distribution of M-VIA supports kernel version 2.4.18-3; therefore, it was necessary to use it as a matter of support by the available VIA implementation. The same statement holds for DEC21140A, which is a 100Mbps in comparison to available Gbps NICs.

[2] In Fig. 6 to 10, we use the notation s-l-i to denote the organization of the cache. s represents the total number of sets regardless of the way, l represents the length of the cache line and i represents the interleaving factor and . Thus 32-16-4 means a cache of 32 sets (regardless of the interleaving factor) each having lines of 16B for a

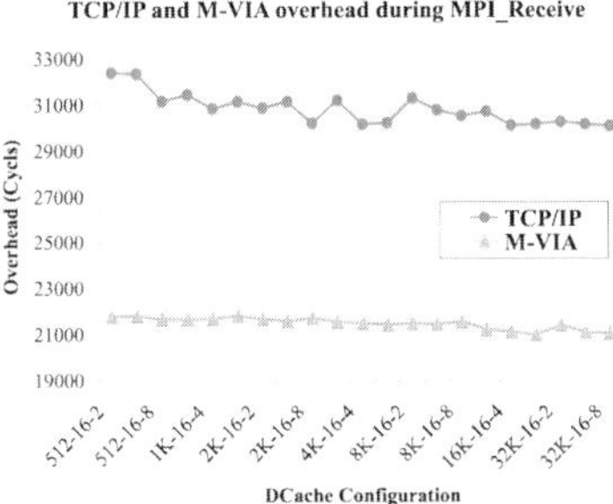

Fig. 6. TCP/IP and M-VIA overhead during MPI_Receive

5.2 Cache Behavior during and after MPI_Receive

The cache state is an important factor in analyzing discussed earlier protocols. Because the communication protocols execute on the same processor during receive operations, the caching system is affected by activities such as context switching and the execution of communication protocols.

Moreover, a micro-architectural simulation environment (e.g., SimpleScalr) has to take into account all the execution details, such as interference incurred by communication protocols and context switching during the receive function, in order to evaluate the proposed architectures accurately. This interference can affect not only the execution of communication protocols but also the behavior of applications after returning from the MPI_Receive function. For example, if the communication protocol pollutes the data cache due to its large working set during the receive function, the useful and valid data, which are needed after returning from that function, would be evicted from the data cache. For

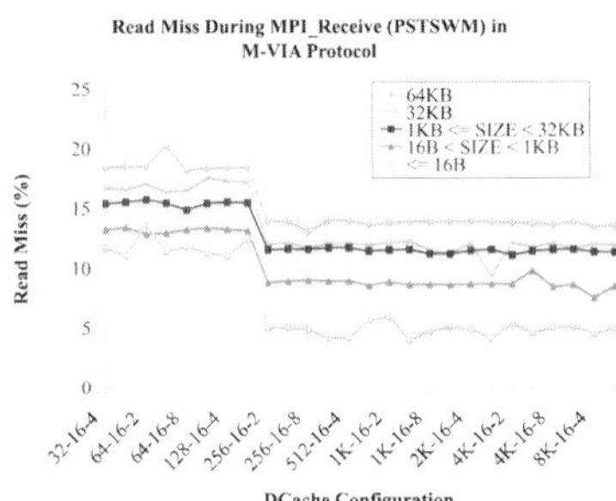

Fig. 7. Read Miss Rate during MPI_Receive in PSTSWM

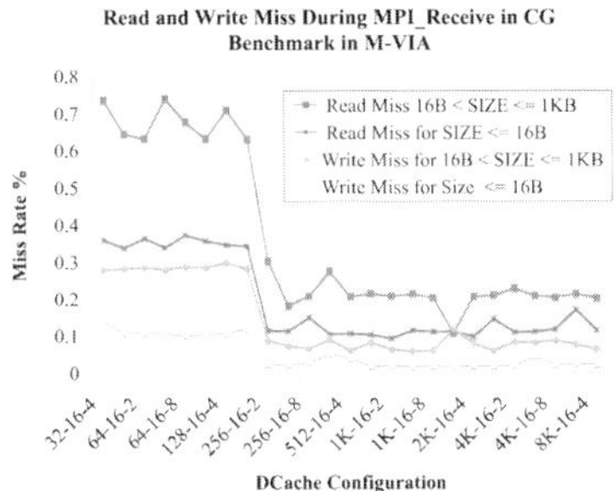

Fig. 8. Miss Rate (R/W) during MPI_Receive in CG

this, we ran the CG benchmark from the NAS parallel benchmark suite and the PSTSWM benchmark on the Simics simulator and explored their cache behavior.

total size of 32 * 16 = 512B. Changing the interleaving factor affects the number of sets in each cache configuration.

We measured the miss rates of the data cache during and after the receive operation by executing the above-mentioned MPI applications in different cache configurations. These miss rates will be used in the simulation environment that implements our proposed extension (i.e., SimpleScalar). As mentioned above,

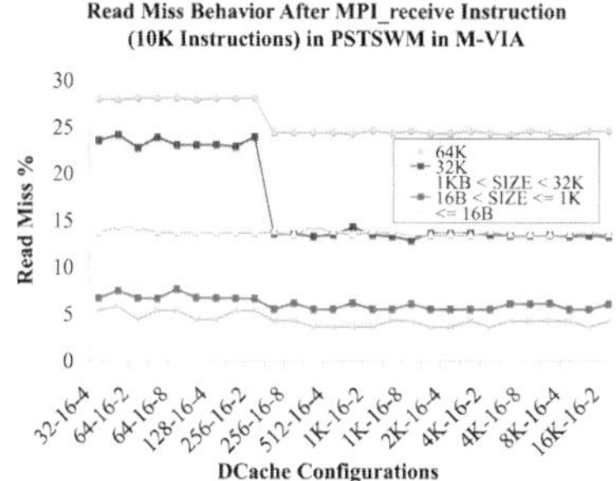

Fig. 9. Read Miss Rate after MPI_Receive in PSTSWM

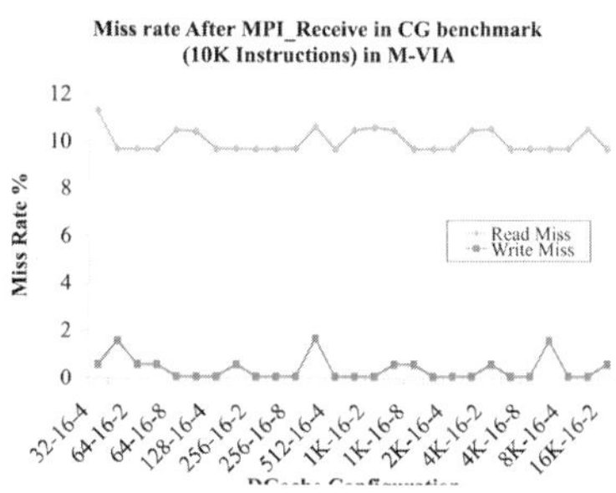

Fig. 10. Miss Rate (R/W) after MPI_Receive in CG

the communication protocol for this part of the study was M-VIA. Fig. 7 to 10 illustrate the data cache miss rates versus different cache configurations in CG, and PSTSWM benchmarks for different payload sizes (from <=16B to 64KB). As can be seen, the data cache miss rate during the receive function in CG is less than that in PSTSWM. This phenomenon is explained by considering the working set of each benchmark. Because the CG benchmark's working set is smaller in comparison to that of the PSTSWM, the data cache miss rates in CG are considerably less than those in PSTSWM. Also, the cache miss rates show similar behavior (i.e., diminish at about 32KB). This behavior is observed for both benchmarks and for both during and after an MPI_Receive. We shall use this cache configuration (i.e., 32KB - 256 sets, 8-way, 16B cache lines) in the subsequent experiments.

6 Results

After preparing the environment and importing the information from the previous section into our simulator, we implemented our *Network Processor* extension and tested the effectiveness of this extension in handling short messages.

Our simulator is a modified version of Sim-outorder from SimpleScalar suite and is installed on a dual Xeon processor running at 2.4 GHz. As we are concerned with short messages (of a length identical to or less than that of a network cache line), we used the CG and PSTSWM benchmarks, which have numerous short messages in point-to-point communication. We ran 1M instructions in fast forward mode and then to the completion of each benchmark in performance simulation mode. The simulator parameters are shown in Table 1. In 64 processes case, the total number of received messages by the master process for the CG, including short (<= 16B) and long ones (> 16B), is 4208. For the PSTSWM,

Table 1. Simulator configuration

DL1 (Data Cache L1) Size	32KB (256 sets, 8-way, 16B blk.)
DL1 Access Latency	2 Cycles
L2 Cache Access Latency	15 Cycles
IL1 (Instruction Cache) Size	16KB (512sets, 1-way, 32B blk.)
IL1 Access Latency	2 Cycles
Memory Access Latency	200 Cycles <first_chunk>
Memory Access Latency	4 Cycles <inter_chunk>
Memory Access Bus Width	16B
Network Section	2KB (64 sets, 2-way, 16 B blk.)
Message Section	256B (32 sets ,8-way, 1B blk.)
Process Section	256B (64 sets, 4-way,1B blk.)

the total number of received messages by the master process, including short and long messages, is 10463 for the 64 processor case.

In this work, we focus our investigation on the effectiveness of our extension compared to VIA. Specifically, we want to establish how the proposed network extension speeds up the delivery of the payload to the consuming process as compared to a processor that does not employ our extension and uses standard protocols (i.e., VIA).

6.1 Network Cache Organization

The network cache mechanism presented in section 3 (and in Fig. 2) calls for searches based on a network tag, as long as the received message has not been bound to the receiving process. During binding, the message is identified through the *message ID*, while after the message is bound it is identified through its *process tag*. These identifiers (the *network tag*, *message tag* and *process tag*) need to be searched. However, a fully associative organization is not practical. Therefore, a set-associative organization has been introduced as described in Fig. 11. The network cache is divided into three sections: *network*, *message* and *process*. The *network* section stores message payloads indexed by the *network tag* that links the payload to the buffer in network space where the received message is located. The *message section* stores pointers to the message payload which exists in the *network section*, while the *message ID* is used as a tag. Similarly, the *process section* also stores a pointer to the message payload, while the process address (which is determined after a receive call is issued) forms the tag that identifies the said pointer. The associativity of each section is determined

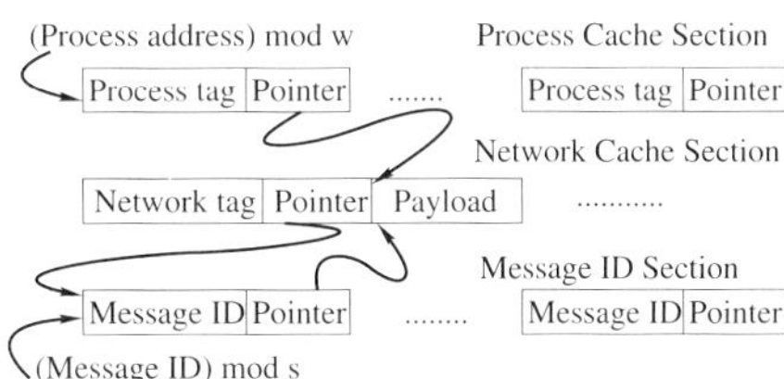

Fig. 11. Set-associative implementation of the network cache

independently and is set to ensure a minimum number of replacements (because of conflicts in any of the three tags).

The impact of varying the size and associativity of the network cache has been studied in [1,3]. Those studies proved that a small network cache section is sufficient to accommodate all the messages. Therefore, the size of network cache is customized to 2KB (e.g., 64 sets, 2-way, 16B blocks) onward.

Simulation results for the two policies referred to earlier (DTCT and lazy DTCT) are presented here. Both policies affect short messages only (i.e., having payloads of <=16B), while longer messages are transferred directly to the main memory bypassing the *network cache*.

In order to compare the impact of our methods on the access time, and eventually on the execution time of MPI applications, we simulated the following environments.

- The NIC uses DMA to transfer the data into the receive buffers in the kernel space. Then the processor transfers the message into its final destination using the copy operation. This mechanism is the same as the VIA protocol. We call this policy *VIA*.
- The processor uses our extension to transfer data into the data cache (short messages) or the processor memory (long messages). We have already introduced this policy as *DTCT*.
- The bound message (short message) is left in the network cache or is transferred into the process memory (long messages). We have already introduced this policy as *lazy DTCT*.

As explained, we have established two alternative policies to handle the message during binding. The first (DTCT) dictates that a bound message is transferred immediately to the data cache after it is bound. The second (lazy DTCT) leaves the bound message in the network cache and the processor obtains it based on the *process tag*. The first method (DTCT) allows the processor to access the message at the data cache speed; however, it incurs the overhead of physically transferring the bound message to the data cache and of managing the data cache itself. The second method is devoid of the transfer overhead, but because of indirection each access costs twice as much compared to the data cache access. In subsequent sections, we study the impact of the proposed network cache and determine its speed-up in comparison to M-VIA and TCP/IP protocols.

6.2 Message Access-Time Behavior

In this section, we compare the message access time characteristics of the above-mentioned policies. We define *first access time* as the time needed between the issue of a receive call and the first access of the message by the computation. This includes both the miss penalty and the hit access times that are necessary to access the data. *Message last-access-time* defines the time needed between the issue of a receive call and the access of the message is last accessed by the computation before the arrival of the next message. *Message last-access-time* includes both the miss penalty and the hit access times that are inevitable in order to

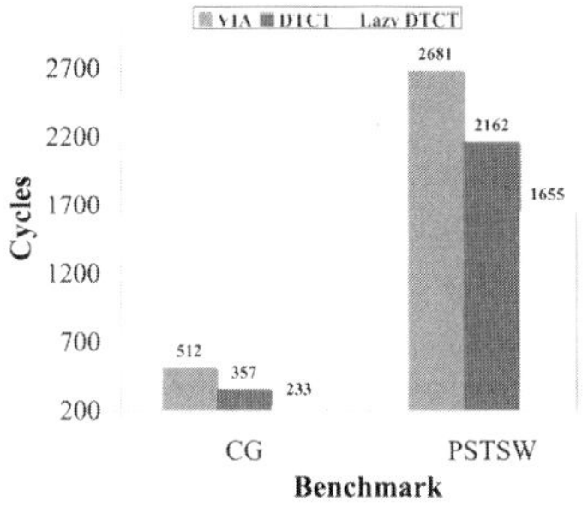

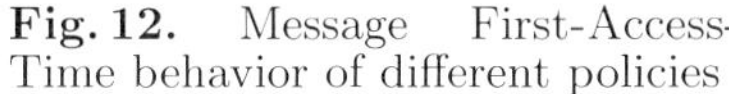
Fig. 12. Message First-Access-Time behavior of different policies

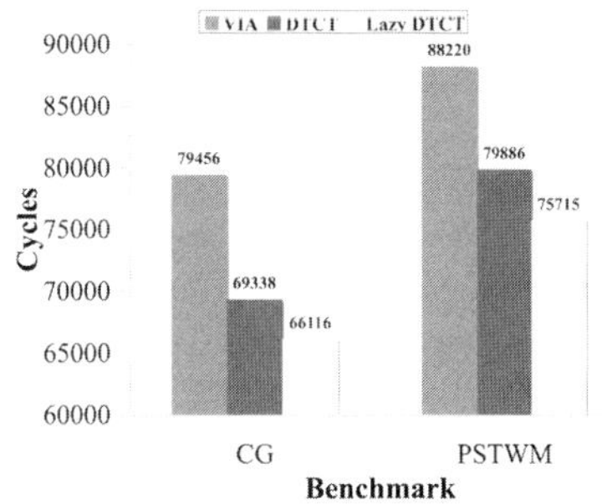

Fig. 13. Message Last-Access-Time behavior of different policies

access the data. Fig. 12 and 13 show the results of our experiments. The results confirm that the DTCT policies access the data for the first and last times faster than M-VIA and the data can be consumed sooner by the consuming processor. This promises that DTCT policies in high-bandwidth SANs can provide data to a CPU in such a way that it can be consumed quickly, which in turn reduces the message delivery latency, and consequently increases the potential parallelism in parallel applications.

It is also obvious that the Lazy DTCT outperforms DTCT in terms of accessing and consuming the data. The reason for this behavior is the use of a different area (Network cache) to keep the arrived data separate from the working set of the running application, which resides inside the data cache. Therefore, this policy prevents the pollution of the data cache. Moreover, it is possible that in the DTCT the received data evicted from the data cache means longer access time in subsequent accesses.

6.3 Speed Up

In this section, we compared the execution time and speed up of DTCT policies to M-VIA. *Speed up* defines the ratio of the execution time of the M-VIA implementation to the ones using DTCT policies.

Fig. 14 shows the result of our experiment, that DTCT and Lazy DTCT both outperform M-VIA by 10% to 20%. Therefore, our proposed extensions would result in clusters with efficient receive side communications, thus allowing finer granularity and improved parallelism. We also investigated whether the achieved speed up is as the result of having two cache spaces (i.e., Data and Network caches) for DTCT approaches or not. For this, we used a data cache size twice as large as the baseline cache size (32KB) for the VIA approach to show the effect of having more cache spaces in comparison to DTCT and Lazy DTCT, which have more cache spaces as the result of adding network cache. As can be observed form Fig. 15, both the lazy DTCT and DTCT still outperform VIA, although VIA has more data cache in comparison to the DTCT and Lazy DTCT approaches.

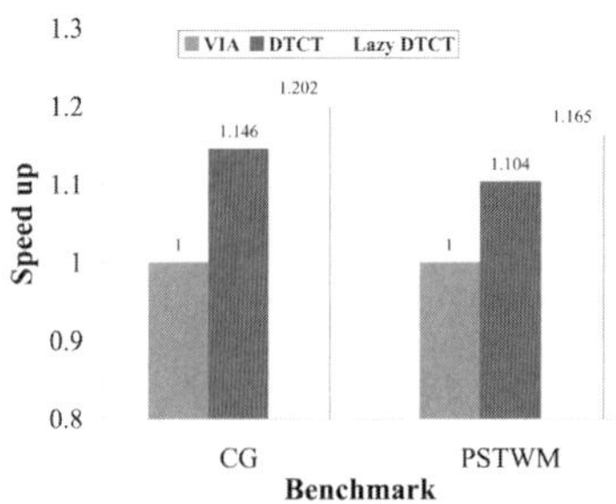

Fig. 14. DTCT Policies speed up in Comparison to VIA

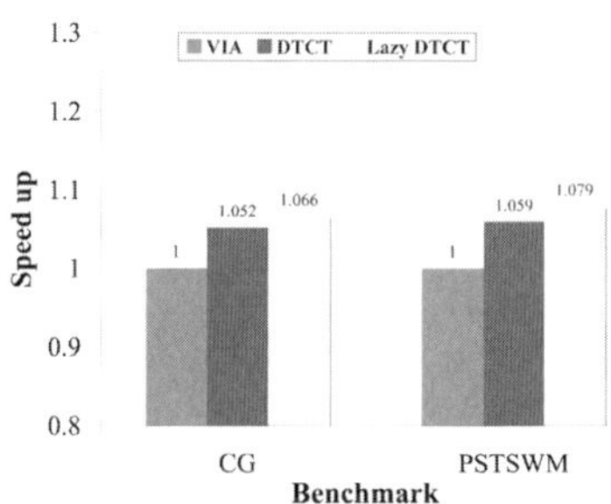

Fig. 15. The effect of Data cache size increase (i.e., 64KB) in VIA with respect to DTCT policies

7 Discussion and Conclusions

In this work we have presented the results of the evaluation of a network processor extension specifically targeted at decreasing the message reception latency in an MPI environment. Our aim has been to study the comparison of DTCT approaches to TCP/IP and VIA protocols.

Our simulations have shown that by using the proposed network extension together with DTCT approaches we improve the execution of MPI applications by 10% to 20%.

The observed *speed up* is attributed to improved communication efficiency afforded by our methods. It is well known [29] that the CG (class A) and PSTSWM benchmarks show poor scalability beyond 16 processors signifying that, on average, the communication portion becomes larger than the computation portion. At these scales, the computation portion is not long enough to completely hide the communication and thus inefficiencies and poor scalability result. Since our extensions result in more efficient communications, our environment can hide the communications portion more efficiently, and thus yield better *speed up* at finer granularities.

We also demonstrate that DTCT methods provide significant reductions in the access latency for the arrived messages in I/O intensive environments (such as message passing configurations and SMPs) without polluting the data cache because the arrived data is kept inside a separate cache.

The statistics also show that the bound messages persisted long enough in the process cache to actually be used by the intended recipient. Moreover, we show that a small process cache is sufficient to overcome costly replacements. In addition, the size of the network cache and the message cache are small. We have established that, indeed, our proposed extension improves the communication by enabling the delivery of the message payload to the consuming process earlier than otherwise possible. Therefore, it is our thesis that our proposed extensions result in clusters with efficient receive side communications, thus allowing a finer granularity and improved parallelism. We also plan to apply the proposed DTCT techniques at the L2 cache level for long messages, which can be compared to the Intel IO/AT technique supported by its latest processors.

References

1. Khunjush, F., Dimopoulos, N.J.: Lazy Direct-To-Cache Transfer during Receive Operations in a Message Passing Environment. In: Proceedings, the 3rd ACM International Conference on Computing Frontiers, CF'06, pp. 331–340 (2006)
2. Khunjush, F., Dimopoulos, N.J.: Evaluation of Direct-To-Cache Transfer during Receive Operations in a Message Passing Environment. In: Proceedings, the Second International Workshop on Advanced Networking and Communications Hardware, ANCHOR2005, in conjunction with ISCA-32, pp. 22–29 (2005)
3. Khunjush, F., Dimopoulos, N.J.: Hiding Message Delivery and Reducing Memory Access Latency by providing Direct-to-Cache Transfer during Receive Operations in a Message Passing Environment. ACM SIGARCH Computer Architecture News 34(1), 41–48 (2006)
4. Afsahi, A., Dimopoulos, N.J.: Architectural Extensions to Support Efficient Communication Using Message Prediction. In: Proceedings, HPCS2002, pp. 20–27 (2002)
5. Dubunicki, S., et al.: The Virtual Interface Architecture. IEEE Micro, 66–76 (March-April 1998)
6. Engblom, J., et al.: Developing Embedded Networked Products using the Simics Full-System Simulator. In: Proceedings PIMRC 2005 (2005)
7. MPICH-A Portable Implementation of MPI: Available at `http://www-unix.mcs.anl.gov/mpi/mpich1/`
8. MVICH: MPI for Virtual Interface Architecture, `http://www.nersc.gov/research/FTG/mvich/index.html`
9. Bailey, D., et al.: The NAS Parallel Benchmarks 2.0: Report NAS-95-020. Nasa Ames Research Center (1995)
10. Worley, P., Foster, I.: Parallel Spectral Transform Shallow Water Model: A Runtime-tunable parallel benchmark code. In: Proceedings of the Scalable High Performance Computing Conference, pp. 207–214 (1994)
11. Austin, T., et al.: SimpleScalar: an infrastructure for computer system modeling. IEEE Computer 35(2), 59–67 (2002)
12. Boden, N., et al.: Myrinet: A Gigabit-per-Second Local Area Network. IEEE Micro (1995)
13. InfiniBand Trade Association: InfiniBand Architecture Specification, `http://www.infinibandta.org`
14. Dubnicki, C., et al.: VMMC-2: Efficient Support for Reliable, Connection-Oriented Communication. In: Proceedings of the Hot Interconnect'97 (1997)
15. Rodrigues, S., et al.: High-Performance Local Area Communication with Fast Sockets. In: USENIX 1997 (1997)
16. Basu, A., Welsh, M., Eicken, T.V.: Incorporating Memory Management into User-Level Network Interface. Hot Interconnects V (1997)
17. Banikazemi, M., et al.: MPI-LAPI: An Efficient Implementation of MPI for IBM RS/6000 SP Systems. IEEE Trans. Parallel Distri. Systems 12(10), 1081–1093 (2001)
18. Chu, H.: Zero-copy TCP in Solaris. In: Proceedings of the USENIX Annual Technical Conference, pp. 253–263 (1996)

19. Alacritech, Inc.: Allacritech / SLIC technology overview, http://www.alacritech.com/html/tech_review.html
20. Binkert, N.L., et al.: Performance Analysis of System Overheads in TCP/IP Workloads. In: Proceedings, PACT 2005 (2005)
21. Huggahalli, R., Iyer, R., Tetrick, S.: Direct Cache Access for High Bandwidth Network I/O. In: Proceedings, ISCA-32, pp. 50–59 (2005)
22. Lauritzen, K., et al.: Intel I/O acceleration technology improves network performance, reliability and efficiently. Technology@Intel magazine (2005), http://www.intel.com/technology/magazine/communications/Intel-IOAT-0305.pdf
23. RDMA Consortium: http://www.rdmaconsortium.org/
24. Acacio, M.E., et al.: Owner Prediction for Accelerating Cache-to-Cache Transfers in a cc-NUMA Architecture. In: Proceedings, SC2002 (2002)
25. Kim, J., Lilja, D.J.: Characterization of Communication Patterns in Message-Passing Parallel Scientific Application Programs. In: Proceedings of the Workshop on Communication, Architecture, and Applications for Network-based Parallel Computing, HPCA-4, pp. 202–216 (1998)
26. Afsahi, A., Dimopoulos, N.J.: Efficient Communication Using Message Prediction for Cluster of Multiprocessors. In: Falsafi, B. (ed.) CANPC 2000. LNCS, vol. 1797, pp. 162–178. Springer, Heidelberg (2000)
27. M-VIA: Virtual Interface Architecture for Linux (2001), Was available at http://www.nserc.gov/research/FTG/via/
28. Bryant, R.E., O'Hallaron, D.R.: Computer Systems: A Programmer's Perspective. Prentice-Hall, Englewood Cliffs (2003)
29. Cappelo, F., Etiemble, D.: MPI versus MPI+OpenMP on the IBM SP for the NAS Benchmarks. In: Reich, S., Anderson, K.M. (eds.) Open Hypermedia Systems and Structural Computing. LNCS, vol. 1903, Springer, Heidelberg (2000)

Virtual Distro Dispatcher: A Costless Distributed Virtual Environment from Trashware

Flavio Bertini, D. Davide Lamanna, and Roberto Baldoni

Dipartimento di Informatica e Sistemistica "Antonio Ruberti"
Università degli studi di Roma "La Sapienza", Italy
{flavio.bertini,davide.lamanna,roberto.baldoni}@dis.uniroma1.it

Abstract. Obsolete hardware can be effectively reused through intelligent software optimization, which is possible only when source code is available. Virtual Distro Dispatcher (VDD) is a system that produces virtual machines on a central server and projects them on a number of costless physical terminals. VDD is the result of an extreme software optimisation based on virtualization and terminal servers. VDD creates and projects Linux distros that are completely customizable and different from each other. They are virtual desktop machines that can be used for testing or developing and are completely controllable directly from each terminal. Memory consumption has been strongly reduced without sacrificing performances. Test results are encouraging to proceed with the research towards clustering.

Keywords: Trashware, LTSP, User Mode Linux, Clustering, Virtualization.

1 Introduction

The massive diffusion of Information and Communication Technologies (ICTs) has as a consequence that a huge quantity of obsolete computers are widespread around the world. The main reason why hardware needs to have higher and higher performance is that software is, often uselessly, more and more resource consuming and not accessible. Software development relies on hardware development and vice versa. Such a vicious circle causes a damage for users, who are obliged to buy new hardware even if they could use the old one in a much more efficient way. In this scenario, Trashware movement [8] is spreading worldwide to give to computers the correct time of obsolescence, thus facing the ecological problem related to e-waste from its very roots. Doing Trashware means working on a sustainable adoption of hardware resources which are still effectively usable and are instead destined to dumps. Trashware is deeply related to Open Source and Free Software movements. Open Source software represents an indispensable tool, as it enables full control on hardware/software optimisation, whereas the sadly common practice of not distributing software source-code prevents users

I. Stojmenovic et al. (Eds.): ISPA 2007, LNCS 4742, pp. 223–234, 2007.

from almost any possibility of optimising their systems. The optimisation we propose in this article is based on two main concepts: virtualization and terminal server. Virtualization is normally used to supply for servers (e.g., FTP or HTTP servers), which guarantee security and protection as they are virtual. Instead of this, we propose to run proper virtual desktop machines and then project them to scarce and old computers (working as terminals), which are literally costless thanks to Trashware. Such a distributed virtual environment is excellent for testing Linux distributions. The Linux Terminal Server Project (LTSP) [3] is a very cheap solution for building computer labs by just buying one good PC and using a number of old machines as terminals. Virtual Distro Dispatcher (VDD), which is based on it, supplies for several Linux distros that are completely customizable and different from each other. They are virtual machines that can be used for testing or whatever purpose, as they are completely controllable from each terminal, whereas LTSP provides terminals that are all identical, lacking in control, and only configurable *una tantum* by the server administrator. VDD can dramatically reduce the cost of hardware for such a complex development environment and it is licensed as GPL software. The virtualization system used by VDD implies five main constraints to be respected:

- **C1** - Open Source software (for integration with other systems and maximum optimisation);
- **C2** - Modularity and file-based structure;
- **C3** - Easy and quick restore;
- **C4** - User level kernel execution;
- **C5** - Linux only emulation (no need for emulating other operating systems).

The choice is among five popular virtualization systems: VMWare [9], Xen [10], Qemu [11], User Mode Linux [1],[4] and Bochs [12].

	C1	**C2**	**C3**	**C4**	**C5**
VMWare		$\surd$			
Xen	$\surd$	$\surd$	$\surd$		$\surd *$
QEMU	$\surd$	$\surd$	$\surd$		
UML	$\surd$	$\surd$	$\surd$	$\surd$	$\surd$
Bochs	$\surd$		$\surd$	$\surd$	

$*$ Microsoft Windows® license does not allow modifications to the operating system. In the future, hopefully, it could be that we will be able to emulate that operating system too

UML is very easy to manage, because we only need three files: an executable guest kernel image, a root filesystem and a swap filesystem. Also for this reason, we chose to start our research with UML, that is the only one satisfying all the five constraints. That is also the main reason why our final choice was UML (see the table above). The aim of the paper is to present an innovative system which allows users and developers to approach Free Software in a secure and inexpensive way. We use LTSP as a mean for distributing virtual sessions, as it is quite stable and provides an easy and fast bootstrap for a large number of thin clients. User Mode Linux is also very fast in starting and it is quite efficient performance-wise. In section 2, we present some of the related works that are the starting point of our piece of research. Section 3 explains what virtualization is and how to get a virtual system working, focusing particularly on UML. In section 4, we talk about the opportunity for joining UML and LTSP and in section 5 we explain how to do it. Section 6 describes security and performance issues that are relevant for a virtual laboratory made through VDD. Section 7 presents performance tests in a number of cases and section 8 deals with future directions of our work, especially in order to speed up the whole system.

2 Related Work

In Italy, there are several research groups doing Trashware, like Binario Etico[1]. Their work is strictly focused on Free Software. For this reason, they provide an excellent technical support, both on software solutions and configuration, without which our research work would have not been possible. We were able to set up a quite sophisticated testbed without any significant charge, except from the purchase of two new machines, being able to support the working charge coming from a network of obsolete computers (12 terminals). An important contribution to Trashware was given by [5], describing how to integrate clustering with LTSP. An extensive performance analysis shows how clustering can be useful, especially in a distributed environment. This is the starting point for the present work, which take into account virtualization as a new direction to be explored and integrated. About virtualization, User Mode Linux (UML) [1],[4] appears appropriate for integration with other technologies, in particular the ones we are interested with. This is mainly due to its filesystem based structure, which allows for easy managing its components as separate modules [1]. Our piece of research is tightly based on UML, through which we have been able to obtain a fast and easy to use virtual distribution. Many research groups [1],[4], and individuals [6] are contributing to UML development[2]. Main contribution in [6] is the introduction of skas0 mode (see section 6), as an alternative to tt-mode, which presents strongly reduced security risks. Linux Terminal Server Project [3], is also a good idea when Trashware is concerned. LTSP is already helping in several circumstances. For example, schools can benefit of what Trashware and LTSP does [7], when licenses and new hardware are not affordable. As the use of LTSP and Trashware is growing everyday, this piece of research intends to take to the extreme their possibilities. HPC clustering is an effective way to increase

[1] Further informations at: http://trashware.linux.it/wiki/TrashWiki - http://www.binarioetico.org - http://www.isf-roma.org

[2] On [6], it is possible to get host and guest kernel-patches maintained by Paolo Giarrusso.

performance [5],[8]. Our model of LTSP/UML based laboratory would benefit a lot from clustering in order to reduce the physiologic slow-down caused by intense use of several virtual machines. An HPC system like OpenMosix has been already used with LTSP, as described in [5]. We now need to join clustering with Terminal Server concept and Virtualization. Another important contribution to this effort has been brought by a research study on cluster solutions, aiming at scalability and high availability, based on OpenSSI, which we acknowledge in section 9. In order to get into details of what VDD is and what is based on, we need to have a look on what LTSP and UML are.

3 Virtualization

The present piece of research is strongly based on virtualization. The system we set up is able to run a number of real and complete GNU/Linux virtual distributions. Designing a virtualization system involves the evaluation of a number of issues concerning the use it is called for. There is a fair amount of software available which supports the emulation of an operating system. Among to most famous, one can cite: VMWare, Bochs, Qemu and Xen. Our first requirement was to implement an Open Source system under GNU/GPL License[3]. The choice of User Mode Linux (UML) as the engine for VDD appeared to us to be the most appropriate. "User Mode Linux is a safe, secure way of running Linux versions and Linux processes"[4]. UML is composed of well-defined basic parts, including an user-mode kernel image, which is executable in a command line shell, a root filesystem (i.e. a single file fits all) and a swap file. UML is normally used to run buggy software, including new kernels and distros, and to hack around without exposing the physical Linux box. The fact of being based on filesystem images is particularly suitable in a distributed environment like ours, where failover can not be disregarded. Recovery is easy and fast. Other virtualization systems work in such a way[5], but do not offer opportunities for integration with the rest of our system, which is completely Open Source. Also, the possibility of setting up very easily a highly configurable development system is particularly attractive when different virtual workstations needs to be created and distributed in the same environment. Besides, thanks to its modular structure, one can recover or substitute all its parts separately. If a different filesystem becomes necessary, for instance, one can just operate on it, without influencing, e.g., the executable kernel file. Another important aspect we took into account in our choice is that it is possible not only to shape the host kernel, as we already highlighted, but also the guest (UML) kernel. In such a way it is possible to supply for a huge quantity of virtual hardware, much more than what real hardware can do. The possibility to specify, inside the UML kernel configuration file, options like the CPU architecture used by the host system, makes UML flexible and adaptable pretty much in any circumstance.

[3] General Public License is a Free Software license.

[4] Directly from http://user-mode-linux.sourceforge.net/

[5] For example, VMWare works using image files containing the full installation of an operating system.

4 UML and LTSP: Virtual Machines and Physical Terminals

UML is often being used to create operating systems that are entirely dedicated to accomplish only one task. For example, it is possible to dedicate a Linux machine entirely to a FTP Server or a Web Server. This is particularly useful when it is necessary for security reasons to limit the number of services managed by a server at the same time. Apart from preventing attacks, such a feature is attractive for us because a stable version of a machine is fully recoverable in any time, which makes it ideal for a development workstation. UML allows to consider guest systems as real workstations. If one looks the machine from outside, within the LAN topology it is part of, she will be able to see all UML machines as normal PCs belonging to a computer network. If one is using a PC in the same LAN, she will never know if she is communicating with a real machine or a virtual one. Normally, all the virtual machines are physically run and used on a single machine. Remote login to a particular virtual machine is of course possible, but this is not at all what we mean by dispatching machines on nodes of a LAN. We are indeed interested in projecting the whole machine to a different node as opposed to just gain access to it from outside. For this reason, we considered the integration of LTSP in our system. LTSP allows to connect several diskless thin clients to a Linux Server. LTSP is based on four-services: TFTP (Trivial File Transfer Protocol), DHCP (Dynamic Host Configuration Protocol), XDMCP (X Display Manager Control Protocol) and NFS (Network File System). These four services, together, allow for file transferring between nodes, remote login, managing IP addresses without conflicts, and sharing the minimal filesystem used by all nodes to work. The best way to join LTSP with UML seemed to us to be through the Xorg[6] Server support. As we said before, we need to project virtual sessions to all the LAN thin clients. Xorg is actually a server, even if it runs on a thin client. For this reason, we used it to show graphical virtual sessions (i.e. KDE executed in a virtual terminal by an UML session). Our approach is to put all thin-client Xorg servers in listening mode on a specific socket using a minimal shell. Once UML virtual machines are up and running, one is able to project their KDE sessions by simply doing an environmental variable export. The previous value of `DISPLAY` variable needs to be overridden in order to indicate what is its new X server address and socket. Finally, our window manager can be run by launching `startkde` command.

5 Dispatching on Terminals: Virtual Distro Dispatcher

As we said, the purpose of this piece of research is to find the contact point to unify virtualization to Terminal Server concept. The basic idea is to project every virtual session (possibly completely different from each other) on every thin client, in a perfectly transparent way. Virtual Distro Dispatcher provides

[6] The X.Org Foundation Open Source Public Implementation of X11.

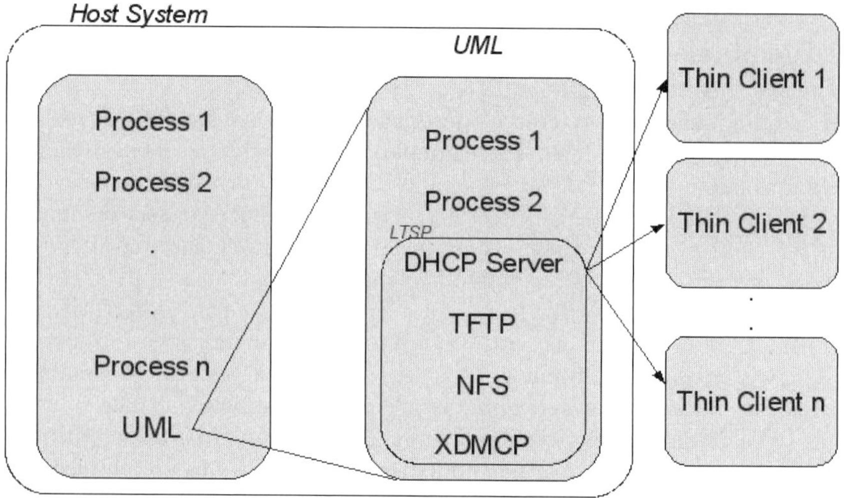

Fig. 1. The first approach

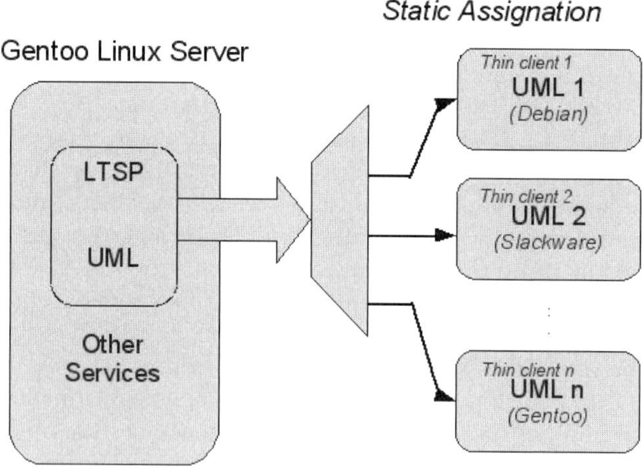

Fig. 2. The second approach in *Static Assignation* case

the possibility to obtain several different environments, one for each terminal. In such an effort, there are two main approaches to consider: the first one is quite easy to understand and to implement and consists of installing UML and setting up LTSP inside it. VDD logic is a simple solution to realize a join between these two technologies, but it has driven us to a fundamental issue: using a virtual distro in order to supply for a needed service[7], i.e. LTSP itself. Figure 1 shows the architecture for this first approach.

[7] In §4, e.g., we talk about installing a FTP server into a virtual machine.

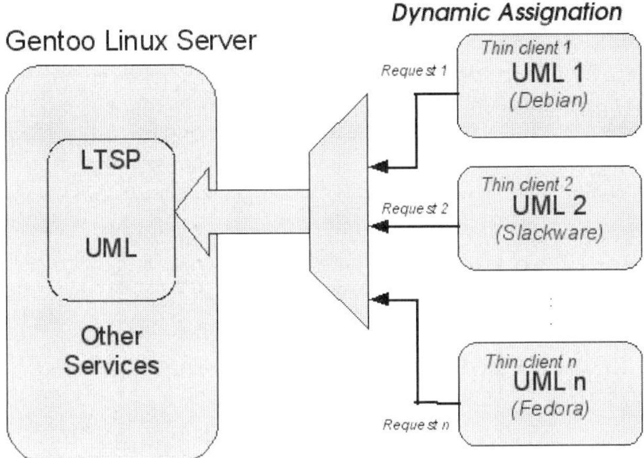

Fig. 3. The second approach in *Dynamic Assignation* case

As it appears clear at a glance, this is a restrictive methodology. It does not allow neither to obtain satisfying performances, nor to get a scalable and customizable system. The reason why we do not like this approach is that it is not possible for developers to have a choice. Our work is mainly oriented to developers and debuggers necessities. What we intend for customizable, in this context, is to give to developers the possibility to choose what distribution to use for their tests or works. The other approach is certainly more effective and proposes the opposite of what we have just described: UML inside LTSP. In this case, LTSP plays the role of an intermediate mean, which allows all terminals to use a virtual session. This approach is implementable in two ways: Dynamic Assignation and Static Assignation (Figure 2 and 3). In the first mode, Server decides what is the distribution to send to a thin client. In the second mode, instead, the generic thin-client user chooses what to use herself.

In our laboratory, we used the Static Assignation. This choice is based only on a practical reason. The laboratory is used also by inexperienced people (e.g. students) and we thought it was better to decide ourself what distribution to send on a thin client. The strong point of the last methodology (UML inside LTSP) is that it is possible to switch easily among two assignation modes. The second mode is recommended in a development environment in which node users are expert system administrators. In fact, if some developer would like to do a new kernel testing or try buggy software, she will decide what distribution is better to use. Practically speaking, all what we need is to start UML on the host, directly from the Terminal Server and, once a thin client has logged in, we can get access to its minimal shell. From there, we can open an X Server socket. Next step is to start a windows manager (e.g. KDE) from the Terminal Server (into UML) after specifying the `DISPLAY` environment variable in order to tell UML where its display is and to run the graphical session. The final result is that it will be possible to use Linux by KDE on a thin client screen, all in a virtual session.

6 Performance and Security Issues

UML development has pursued both memory usage efficiency and protection. There are currently three working modes available, each of which presents different performance and security issues: TT-Mode, SKAS3-Mode, SKAS0-Mode.

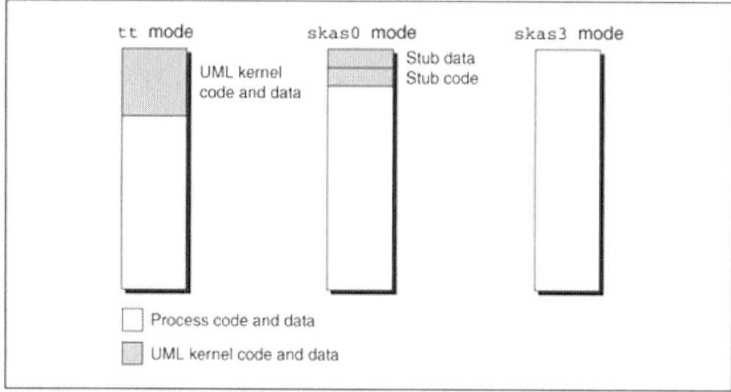

Fig. 4. Address space division in each situation: tt, skas0 and skas3 modes

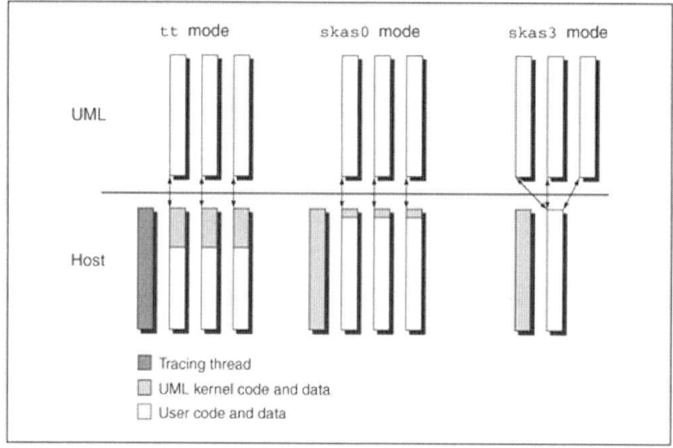

Fig. 5. Processes behaviour in guest and host system for each mode

TT-Mode: A first way of working of UML is based on a tracing thread mode (tt-mode), whose job is to listen guest System Calls and to forward them to the host system. Besides, in this mode, memory is basically shared between processes and UML kernel. Typically, the guest kernel is allocated in the upper bound of the address space. Processes instead, are allocated in the following 5 GB of memory. This causes a serious security problem, because the memory is shared between processes and kernel code. In fact, due to this situation, a false process can easily execute code in kernel mode and prevent the guest kernel to be a real (good) process. It is sufficient for someone to know the UML internal structure and she can get into the host system directly.

SKAS3-Mode: Problems encountered in tt-mode can be solved by using a patch, whose aim is to modify the host kernel as well as to manage the address space in a different way. Skas3, or *Separate Kernel Address Space*, has now got to the third version. When applied to the host kernel, it adds a new file in `/proc` (`/proc/mm`) and creates a new address space to hold the guest kernel. Regarding performance aspects, there is a big amount of wasted memory working in this mode. We can say that a lot of slow-downs can occur because, for every process on the guest system, the host creates a new one straight away. The reason why such a waste of memory occurs is that every process can live in a separate address space. Every process has got a separate address space, which it shares with kernel code and data. Skas3 prevents false processes to deliver an attack. This is possible because of the isolation between guest kernel and processes. In this case, we do not have memory sharing. There are no tracing threads and system calls are intercepted by the guest kernel itself. For every guest process, there is only one host process. There are two advantages doing so: no waste of memory and no risk for UML crashes, resulting in a strongly reduced possibility to compromise the host system integrity. As a matter of fact, what happen inside UML is confined in itself. The only Skas3 con is that it is not always supported. It depends on an old UML version and the host CPU architecture is not already supported.

Skas0-Mode: This mode can be used when Skas3 mode is not supported. For example, if we had an X86_64 host machine, skas3 would not be able to work.

As explained in [1],[6], it is possible to make something between Skas3 and tt-mode. In fact, like the tt-mode, for every guest process, there is an host process and, as for the Skas3 mode, the guest kernel will be executed in a separate address space without a tracing thread. In this way, we can take advantage of Skas3 performances even though there is an amount of wasted memory like the tt-mode. Skas0 mode is less efficient than Skas3 but it is certainly better than tt-mode. The Skas0 basic idea is to insert a little quantity of kernel code in the shared memory in order to reduce opportunities for attacks. The system we developed has been built upon two of three previously described modes: Skas3 for the x86 CPU architecture and the Skas0 for the x86_64 CPU (only for performance tests). Mainly, we have to consider the Skas3 mode. We do not use UML versions which are not supporting Skas3 mode. Regarding the filesystem image, which contains the GNU/Linux distribution, we chose to create a new one by means of *debootstrap* utility. Our UML distribution is Debian GNU/Linux. We got kernel sources from the official website[8]. After configuring the Debian base system, we could start to use User Mode Linux.

7 Performance Analysis

Our testbed has got the following characteristics:

- 1 Intel Pentium 4 3000 MHz
- 1024 Mbytes RAM

[8] http://www.kernel.org

- 4 SATA 80Gb Hard Disks
- 13 100Mbps Ethernet cards
- 12 diskless thin clients[9]
- 1 100Mbps Ethernet switch

After several tests, the final system resulted to be quite usable, without significant slow-downs. In order to analyse system performance, we chose to evaluate computational time of a CPU bound process. The right test for us, seemed to be a kernel compilation on its *defconfig*[10]. Our tests, whose results are shown in Figure 6, consist of a vanilla kernel compilation in three cases: firstly on the host system (A), then on a thin client (B) and finally on a thin client inside UML (C). This test has been repeated ten times for each case in order to estimate a mean value for any measurement.

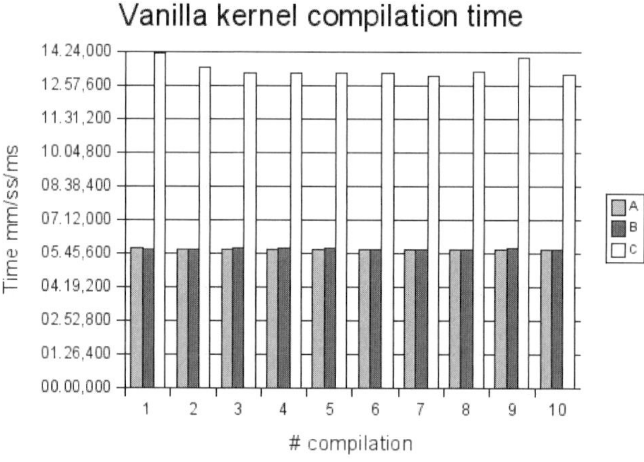

Fig. 6. Benchmark results

The most significant case is C. As it is shown in Figure 6, the compilation time in this third case is higher with respect to case A and B. These results confirm the actual benefit that one would get by integrating a clustering system, in order to increase performance (see section 8). The whole system could be part of a bigger one, in which it is possible to integrate further technologies to get a fully functional and faster final system. Although UML is host-CPU optimized, the aim of who is writing is to go ahead. We are trying to find out further techniques to improve the whole service. As a matter of fact, results persuaded us to use Clustering HPC systems in order to improve performance hits, even if we obtained a fully usable system with no significant slow-downs. HPC Clustering oriented technologies we are considering are OpenMosix[13] or

[9] Generally we used many different architectures for thin clients, but the typical one is a Pentium II@233 MHz with 64 Mbytes RAM, floppy disk, CD-ROM reader and an Ethernet card.

[10] For each test, we did `make defconfig` on the kernel tree.

OpenSSI[14]. Another possibility is to use an alternative virtualization system. The next step can be to experiment Xen.

8 Conclusion and Future Works

The combination of different technologies makes it possible to realize new systems, aiming at incrementing supplied services and/or their performance. Open Source paradigm is essential in such an effort. The main innovation we presented here is the fusion between a distributed system and virtualization. LTSP already allows us to distribute login and GNU/Linux sessions to a thin-client LAN. But systems showed on the screens are not virtual machines. They are the remote execution of a single physical machine. Whereas we succeeded in distributing virtualization on to a diskless node of a LAN. Virtualization dispatching allows users to use their own distros and developers to do their real work in a costless, secure and comfortable virtual environment. Performances analysis is an important aspect to be considered when joining LTSP and UML. Virtual Distro Dispatcher could be much lighter if supported by a distributed server instead of a central one. In fact, if we consider large scale service distribution, the central server could be lagged. Since we would like to enlarge VDD environments, we think is absolutely necessary to boost up our system by using HPC clustering. Figure 7 shows a prototype of a full VDD based laboratory, which is also supported by an HPC Clustering system.

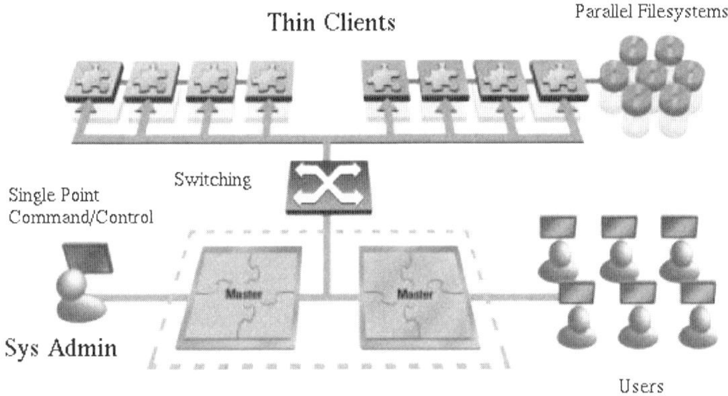

Fig. 7. Future laboratory prototype

In this case, we have two clusters and two possible LANs: one for virtual-distro based thin-clients, and another one for LTSP based thin-client network. We are hence proposing something scalable, accommodating different necessities. This is a multiple sections example, whose aim is to show how one can easily change and personalize the global system as needed. We intend now to set up an HPC Clustering system, in order to enlarge virtualization dispatching without any lag, so that more users can access our system.

Acknowledgements

We wish to thank Andrea Leone. His work on scalable and high-available clusters on a distributed platform is the presupposition and the natural course of our piece of research. The support of our colleagues Daniele Carcasole and Alessandro Di Stefano has been essential to mastering LTSP, a system on which they conducted in-depth studies and research. Finally, we are grateful to Binario Etico that provided hardware resources, expertise and a laboratory to conduct research and tests.

References

1. Dike, J.: User Mode Linux® (Bruce Perens Open Source)
2. Stallings, W.: Operating Systems: Internals and Design
3. Linux Terminal Server Project: http://www.ltsp.org
4. The User-Mode-Linux Kernel Home Page: http://user-mode-linux.sourceforge.net/
5. Russo, R., Lamanna, D., Baldoni, R.: Distributed software platforms for rehabilitating obsolete hardware
6. Giarrusso, P.: Skas and Guest patches: http://www.user-mode-linux.org/blaisorblade/
7. Gasperson, T.: Old school cuts ties with Windows, http://business.newsforge.com/business/05/09/28/1843234.shtml?tid=37
8. http://trashware.linux.it/wiki/TrashWiki
9. VMWare: http://www.vmware.com/
10. Xen: http://www.xensource.com/
11. Qemu: http://fabrice.bellard.free.fr/qemu/
12. Bochs: http://bochs.sourceforge.net/
13. OpenMosix: http://openmosix.sourceforge.net/
14. OpenSSI: http://openssi.org/

A Parallel Infrastructure on Dynamic EPIC SMT and Its Speculation Optimization

Qingying Deng[1], Minxuan Zhang[2], and Jiang Jiang[3]

[1] PDL, College Of Computer, National University Of Defense Technology, Changsha 410073, Hunan, P.R. China
freesunnybird@gmail.com,
[2] mxzhang@nudt.edu.cn,
[3] jiang_jiang@nudt.edu.cn

Abstract. SMT(simultaneous multithreading) processors execute instructions from different threads in the same cycle, which has the unique ability to exploit ILP(instruction-level parallelism) and TLP(thread-level parallelism) simultaneously. EPIC(explicitly parallel instruction computing) emphasizes importance of the synergy between compiler and hardware. Compiler optimizations are often driven by specific assumptions about the underlying architecture and implementation of the target machine. Control and data speculations are effective ways to improve instruction level parallelism. In this paper, we present our efforts to design and implement a parallel environment, which includes an optimizing, portable parallel compiler OpenUH and SMT architecture EDSMT based on IA-64. Meanwhile, its speculation is also reexamined.[1]

1 Introduction

The combination of limited instruction parallelism suitable for superscalar issue, practical limits to pipelining, and a "power ceiling" limited by practical cooling limitations has limited future speed increases within conventional processor cores to the basic Moore's law improvement rate of the underlying transistors. Processor designers must find new ways to effectively utilize the increasing transistor budgets in high-end silicon chips to improve performance in ways that minimize both additional power usage and design complexity. And it is also useful to examine the problem from the point of view of different performance requirements.

SMT [1] and CMP(chip multiprocessing) [2] are two architectural approaches to exploit thread-level parallelism using available on-chip resources. SMT allows instructions from multiple threads to share several critical processor resources, thus increasing their utilization. The advantage of SMT is area-efficient throughput [3]. CMPs, on the other hand, improve system throughput by replicating

[1] This work was supported by "863" project No. 2002AA110020, Chinese NSF No. 60376018, No. 60273069 and No. 90207011.

I. Stojmenovic et al. (Eds.): ISPA 2007, LNCS 4742, pp. 235–244, 2007.

processor cores on a single die. As both these paradigms are targeted toward multithreaded workloads, comparing their efficiency in terms of performance, power, and thermal metrics has drawn the attention of several researchers [4][5][6].

DSMT (Dynamic SMT) integrates dynamic threads extracting and threads switching mechanism into SMT architecture, which further improves the ability to exploit TLP parallelism. Based on the software-hardware cooperation, EPIC can effectively exploit ILP with relatively low hardware complexity. A new microarchitecture called EDSMT was proposed to expand EPIC with simultaneous multithreading execution.

Compiler optimizations are typically driven by specific assumptions about the underlying architecture and implementation of the target machine. When new processing paradigms change these architectural assumptions, however, we must reevaluate machine dependent compiler optimizations in order to maximize performance on the new machines[7]. EDSMT presents to the compiler a different model for hiding operation latencies and sharing code and data.

As a result, in order to have a deep research on parallel compilation SMT and CMP architecture, and hardware-software cooperation, construct a basic platform is very important. We studied EDSMT Microarchitecture and developed its simulator EDSMTSIM, which adopted the trace-driven simulation methodology. OpenUH(based on Pro64 and OpenMP) developed by University of Houston was used to construct our parallel compiler with some modifications. We investigated the extent to which simultaneous multithreading affects the use of speculation compiler optimization which can hide memory latencies and expose instruction-level parallelism but may incur additional instruction overhead in EDSMTSIM.

We introduce our parallel Infrastructure in section 2, which includes the introduction of parallel compiler , EDSMT architecture and EDSMTSIM simulator. In section 3 we present speculation in IA-64. In section 4 shows EDSMT 's speculation and the simulation results. Conclusions and future work are given in section 5.

2 Parallel Infrastructure

2.1 Parallel Compilation Structure

The goal of parallel compilation is narrow the gap between the peak speed of HPC and the actual performance which end user can get. Multi-source Multi-target, Multilevel, and Multigrid became the trend of parallel compilation[8], OpenUH is one of that kind.

OpenUH is available as stand-alone software or with the Eclipse integrated development environment. It is based on SGI's open source Pro64 compiler, which targets the IA-64 Linux platform. OpenUH merges work from the two major branches of Open64 (ORC and Pathscale) to exploit all upgrades and bug fixes. It is a portable OpenMP compiler, which translates OpenMP 2.5 directives in conjunction with C, C++, and FORTRAN 77/90 (and some FORTRAN 95). It has a full set of optimization modules, including an interprocedural analysis (IPA) module, a loop nest optimizer (LNO), and global optimizer. A variety of state-of-the-art analyses and transformations are available, sometimes at multiple levels[9].

The OpenUH consists of the frontends, optimization modules, OpenMP transformation module, a portable OpenMP runtime library, a code generator and IR-to-source tools. Fig. 1 shows the structure. Most of these modules are derived from the corresponding original Open64 module. It is a complete compiler for Itanium platforms, for which object code is produced, and may be used as a source-to-source compiler for non-Itanium machines using the IR-to-source tools.

The OpenMP program is parsed by the appropriate extended language frontend and translated into WHIRL IR(tree-based intermediate representations) with OpenMP pragmas. Then the interprocedural analyzer (IPA), is enabled if desired to carry out interprocedural alias analysis, array section analysis, inlining, dead function and variable elimination, interprocedural constant propagation and more. After that, the loop nest optimizer (LNO) will perform many standard loop analyses and optimizations, such as dependence analysis, register/cache blocking (tiling), loop fission and fusion, unrolling, automatic prefetching, and array padding. The transformation of OpenMP, which lowers WHIRL with OpenMP pragmas into WHIRL representing multithreaded code with OpenMP runtime library calls, is performed after LNO. Subsequently the global scalar optimizer (WOPT) is invoked. It transforms WHIRL into an SSA form for more efficient analysis and optimizations and converts the SSA form back to WHIRL after the work has been done. In WOPT phase , a lot of standard compiler passes out including control flow analysis (computing dominance, detecting loops in the flowgraph), data flow analysis, alias classification and pointer analysis, dead code elimination, copy propagation, partial redundancy elimination and strength reduction are carried.

The CG(code generation) phase depends on the target machine: for Itanium platforms, CG in Open64 can be directly used to generate object files. For a non-Itanium platform, the whirl2c or whirl2f translator will be invoked instead; in this case, code represented by Mid WHIRL is translated back to compilable, multithreaded C or Fortran code with OpenMP runtime calls. To complete the translation by compiling the output from OpenUH into object files a native C or Fortran compiler must be invoked on the target platform.

The last phase is the linking of object files with the portable OpenMP runtime library and final generation of executables for the target machine.

2.2 Microarchitecture of EDSMT

Simultaneous Multithreading (SMT) processors improve performance by allowing running instructions from several threads simultaneously at a single cycle. Co-scheduled threads share some resources, such as issue queues, physical registers, and functional units.

Explicitly Parallel Instruction Computing(EPIC) architectures developed by HP and Intel allow the compiler to express program instruction level parallelism directly to the hardware to deal with increasing memory latencies and penalties. Specifically, the Itanium architecture deploys a number of EPIC techniques which enable the compiler to represent control speculation, data dependence speculation, and predication to enhance performance. These techniques have individually been shown to be very effective in dealing with memory penalties. In addition to these techniques, the Itanium architecture provides a virtual register stack to reduce the penalty of memory accesses associated with procedure calls and to leverage the performance advantages of a large register file. Predication converts control dependencies to data dependencies, software pipelining enables the compiler to interleave the execution of several loop iterations without having to unroll a loop, and Branch Prediction Hints give accurate predication.

DSMT(Dynamic SMT) [10]and EPIC[11] design philosophy became the two basic points of our EDSMT research. There are two levels of parallelism in EDSMT .

- (1) Vertical parallelism-ILP: Depends on the Pro64 compiler, while EDSMT hardware only provides the executive environment.
- (2) Horizontal parallelism-TLP: Depends on the parallel compiler and dynamic thread extractor, EDSMT hardware supports its execution.

There are two kinds of DSMT implementations. One modifies superscalar structure slightly. With few hardware changes,it can shorten the development time (SMT in Intel's Xeon added only 5% die area). In this case hardware designer only need to focus on construction of a high speed superscalar processor and appliance of the multithreading switching and dynamic thread extraction. Threads share the hardware except fetch, context switch, instruction retirement, tracecache, and speculation multithreading control. The other changes hardware a lot in order to dissociate the thread's instruction window and simplify the fetch and retire stage in the pipeline. Each thread has its own instruction window, decoder, register file and retirement logic to issue instructions at the same time.To fully use the die area and share resources,we choose the latter.

By adopting EPIC, instruction window exploited by software is much larger than by hardware, parallelism can be achieved; because the parallelism is mainly developed by compiler, the hardware design was simplified which can save a lot of resources,and the chip speed can also be improved.

Based on DSMT and EPIC, EDSMT should fully use the resources in Itanium, but a few modifications must be considered. Fig.2 shows the Microarchitecture of EDSMT. Instruction bundles from different threads dispatched by the dispatch logic which works as the Multithreading scheduler. It is carefully designed to reduce dependency and get more parallelism.

2.3 EDSMTSIM Design

Simulator is important in architecture design. As EDSMT is a new Microarchitecture, We developed a simulator–EDSMTSIM for our research.

EDSMTSIM is a trace-driven microprocessor simulator which adopts some technologies in the Multithreading simulator-SMTSIM. In order to reduce complexity, the actual execution of instructions is separated from the pipeline control, that means the pipeline only processes dependency detection, branch, and

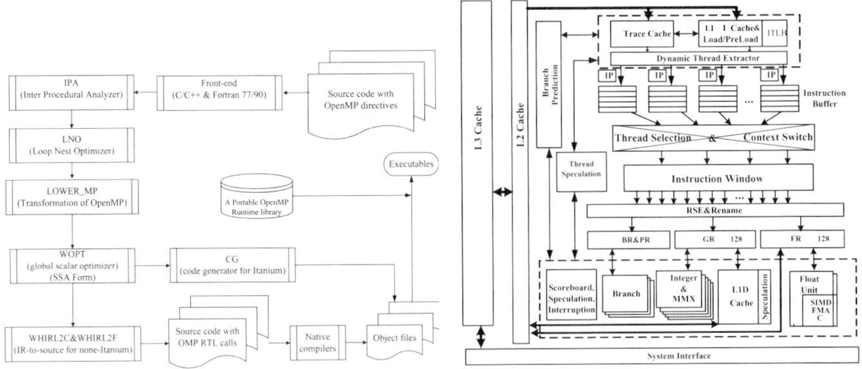

Fig. 1. OpenUH Infrastructure

Fig. 2. Microarchitecture of EDSMT

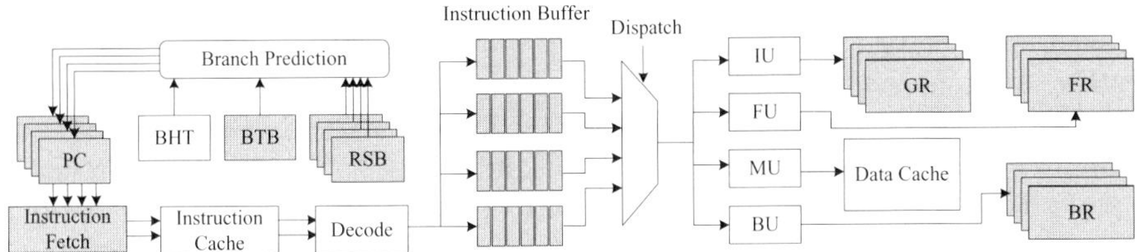

Fig. 3. EDSMTSIM Structure

exception, while actual execution is emulated by specific module which can be called by pipeline. Instruction is executed right after the fetch stage, then we record its control information(trace) and modify the CPU states. Following the instruction trace, in the backend of the pipeline stages, activities such as dependency control, cache miss, branch misprediction, and modification of the scoreboard are simulated in a way of counting pipeline stall cycles.

Fig.3 depicts the structure of EDSMTSIM. IU, FU, MU, and BU represent Integer Unit, Float Unit, Memory Unit and Branch Unit respectively. It has 11 Function Units including 4 IU, 3 FU, 3 BU, and 2 MU. Every thread has its own PC, RSB, Register Files and Instruction Bundle Queue. Instruction Cache, Data Cache, BHT and Function Units are shared by all the threads. Pipeline is divided to 8 stages as in the Itanium2 structure.

3 Speculation in IA-64

Data speculation refers to the execution of instructions on most likely correct (but potentially incorrect) operand values. Control speculation refers to the execution of instructions before it has been determined that they would be executed in the normal flow of execution. Both types of speculation are effective techniques to improve program performance.

Despite the large register file in IA-64[12], many instructions will need to load data from memory. If a load misses the primary cache, a hit in the second-level cache takes several cycles to complete. If the data is needed by a subsequent instruction, the entire processor might grind to a halt until the cache access is completed. Out-of-order processors handle this situation by executing nondependent instructions while the load is being processed, dynamically reordering the instruction flow. This mechanism requires extensive and complex circuitry that consumes die space and is difficult to debug.

The IA-64 solution is for the compiler to insert nondependent instructions between a load and the first instruction that uses the data, which can eliminate this complex out-of-order logic and hide the load latency. This code transformation is difficult, however, when a conditional branch is in the way, as Fig. 4 shows. If the load is put before the branch, it would get executed even if the branch goes the other way. While this mistake could simply waste some of the processor's time, the situation becomes intolerable if the load generates an exception that never would have occurred if the load had been executed in the correct program sequence.

The solution, as implemented in IA-64, is a speculative, or nonfaulting, load. A speculative load, indicated by the .S suffix, will not trigger an exception; instead, if an exception occurs, the target register will be marked invalid. This is a fairly simple mechanism, requiring only that each register have a valid bit. As Fig. 4 shows, a CHK.S instruction is later used to check whether the register contents are valid; if not, an exception occurs. The CHK.S instruction is typically placed before the first usage of the loaded data. Using this mechanism, the load can be placed as early as possible in the code, as long as the address can be computed. Speculative loads thus provide the compiler with maximum flexibility to hide cache latency.

4 EDSMT 's Speculation Consideration

Today's optimizing compilers rely on aggressive code scheduling to hide instruction latencies. In global scheduling techniques, such as trace scheduling or hyperblock scheduling, instructions from a predicted branch path may be moved above a conditional branch, so that their execution becomes speculative. If at runtime, the other branch path is taken, then the speculative instructions are useless and potentially waste processor resources.

On in-order superscalars or VLIW machines, software speculation is necessary, because the hardware provides no scheduling assistance. On an EDSMT processor, multithreading is also used to hide latencies. (As the number of SMT threads is increased, instruction throughput also increases.) Therefore, the latency-hiding benefits of software speculative execution may be needed less, or even be unnecessary, and the additional instruction overhead introduced by incorrect speculations may degrade performance.

Our experiments were designed to evaluate the appropriateness of software speculative execution on SPECint2000 programs for EDSMT. EDSMTSIM is used as

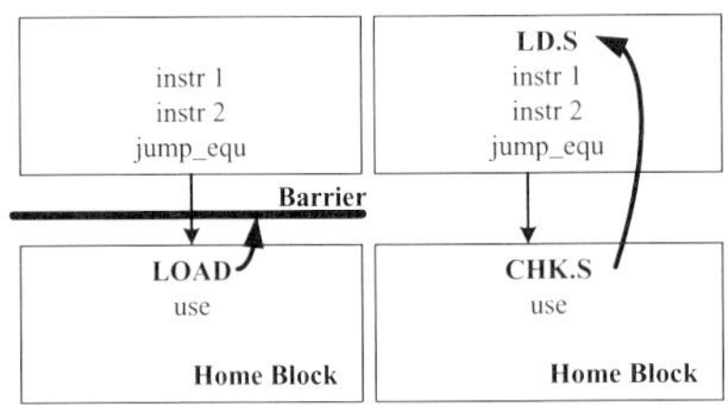

Fig. 4. IA-64's speculative load can be moved further up, providing more instructions to fill the hardware latency between the load and the use of its data

Parameter	EDSMTSIM Value
Fetch Width	2 bundles ,6 instructions per cycle
Basic Fetch Policy	ICOUNT2.2
Instruction Queues	16 for each separated Queues
Functional Units	2 IU, 4 MU, 2 FU, 3 BU
Physical Registers	128 GR, 128 FR, 64 PR, 8 BR per thread
L1I cache, L1D cache	16KB, 4-way, 64-bytes lines, 1 cycle access
L2 cache	256KB, 8-way, 64-bytes lines, 10 cycles latency
L3 cache	3MB, 12-way, 64-bytes lines, 50 cycles latency
Main Memory Latency	100 cycles

Fig. 5. Baseline Configuration of Simulator

simulator and configuration details are provided in Fig.5. For a compiler we use the OpenUH which affords a greater degree of flexibility and more aggressive utilization of EPIC features than would be available in commercial production compilers or GCC. The results highlight two factors that determine its effectiveness for EDSMT: static branch prediction accuracy and instruction throughput.

Correctly-speculated instructions have no instruction overhead; incorrectly-speculated instructions, however, add to the dynamic instruction count. Therefore, speculative execution is more beneficial for applications that have high speculation accuracy, e.g., loop-based programs with either profile-driven or state-of-the-art static branch prediction.

Fig. 6 compares the dynamic instruction counts between (profile-driven) speculative and nonspeculative versions of our applications. Small increases in the dynamic instruction count indicate that the compiler has been able to accurately predict which paths will be executed. Consequently, speculation may incur no penalties. Higher increases in dynamic instruction count, on the other hand, mean wrong-path speculations, and a probable loss in performance.

While instruction overhead influences the effectiveness of speculation, it is not the only factor. The level of instruction throughput in programs without speculation is also important, because it determines how easily speculative overhead can be absorbed. With sufficient instruction issue bandwidth (low IPC), incorrect speculations may cause no harm; with higher per-thread ILP or more threads, software speculation should be less profitable, because incorrectly-speculated instructions are more likely to compete with useful instructions for processor resources (in particular, fetch bandwidth and functional unit issue). Fig.7 contains the instruction throughput for each of the applications. For some programs IPC is higher with software speculation, indicating some degree of absorption of the speculation overhead. In others, it is lower, because of additional hardware resource conflicts, most notably L1 cache misses.

Speculative instruction overhead (related to static branch prediction accuracy) and instruction throughput together explain the speedups illustrated in

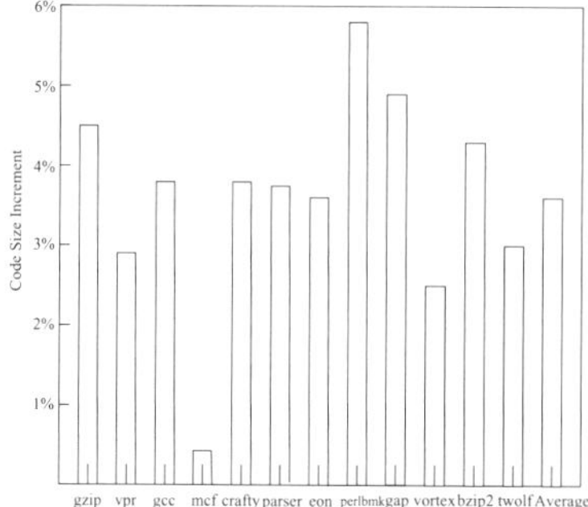

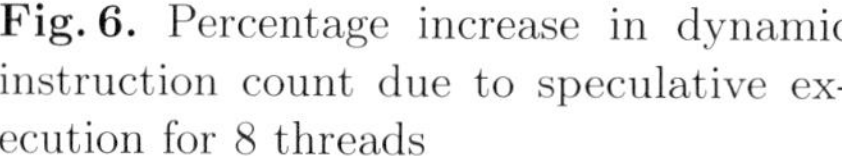
Fig. 6. Percentage increase in dynamic instruction count due to speculative execution for 8 threads

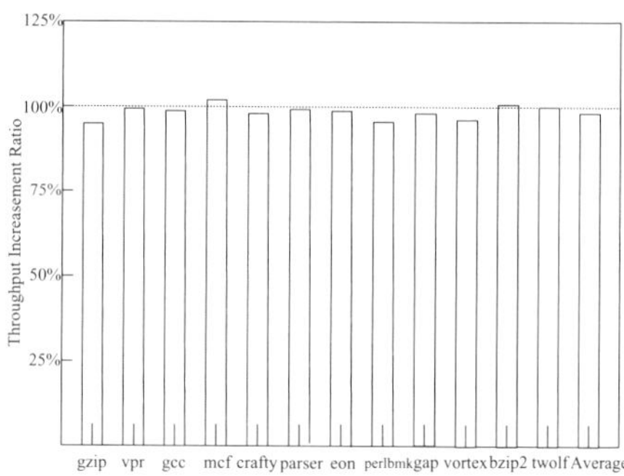

Fig. 7. Throughput without over with profile-driven software speculation for 8 threads

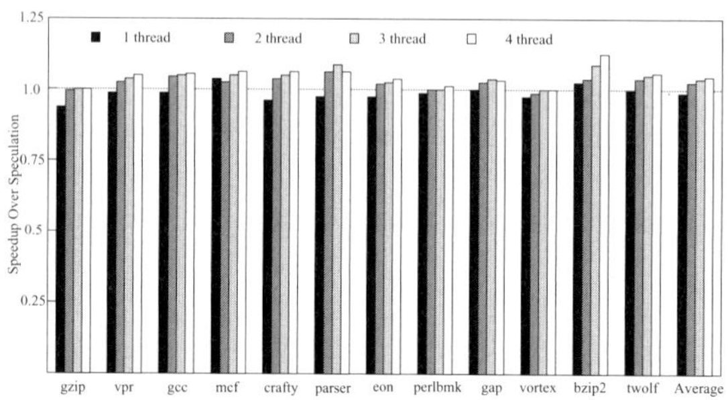

Fig. 8. Speedups of applications executing without software speculation over with speculation (speculative execution cycles / no speculation execution cycles)

Fig.8. When both factors were high (bizp2), speedups without software speculation were greatest. If one factor was low or only moderate, speedups were minimal or nonexistent (perlbmk had only speculation overhead). Without either factor (vortex), software speculation helped performance, and for the same reasons it benefits other architectures – it hid latencies and executed the speculative instructions in otherwise idle functional units.For these applications (and a few others as well), as more threads are used, the advantage of turning off speculation generally becomes even larger. Additional threads provide more parallelism, and therefore, speculative instructions are more likely to compete with useful instructions for processor resources.

The bottom line is that, while loop-based applications should be compiled with software speculative execution, non-loop applications should be compiled without it. Doing so either improves EDSMT program performance or maintains its current level –performance is never hurt.

5 Conclusions and Future Work

Because typical server workloads have very low amounts of instruction-level parallelism and many memory stalls, most of the hardware associated with superscalar instruction issue is essentially wasted for these applications. SMT and chip multiprocessors are making significant inroads into the marketplace.

Viewed another way, the transition to SMT and CMP is inevitable because past efforts to speed up processor architectures with techniques that do not modify the basic von Neumann computing model, such as pipelining and superscalar issue, are encountering hard limits. As a result, the microprocessor industry is leading the way to multicore architectures; however, the full benefit of these architectures will not be harnessed until the software industry fully embraces parallel programming.

We proposed a parallel infrastructure, including an optimizing, portable parallel compiler OpenUH and SMT architecture EDSMT based on IA-64. The experiment results also demonstrate that our infrastructure is a very good choice for parallel compiler and architecture research, especially for the structure of EPIC which combined compiler and architecture tightly. We also examined speculation optimization in the context of EDSMT architecture. Our results show that software speculative execution can be bad for an EDSMT, because it decreases useful instruction throughput. In our EDSMT design, with the reduction of speculation optimization, we can simplify compiler design and construct a more compact EDSMT core.

In the future, we will focus on other optimizations such as register allocation and RSE constitution, fetch policy, resource organization and allocation, cache structure, thread scheduling and so on. Meanwhile, we are considering a compact EDSMT to construct homogeneous and heterogeneous CMP systems.

References

1. Tullsen, D., Eggers, S., Levy, H.: Simultaneous Multithreading: Maximizing On-Chip Parallelism. In: The 22rd Annual International Symposium on Computer Architecture (ISCA), pp. 392–403 (1995)
2. Olukotun, K., Nayfeh, B.A., Hammond, L., Wilson, K., Chang, K.: The Case for a Single-Chip Multiprocessor. SIGOPS Oper. Syst. Rev. 30(5), 2–11 (1996)
3. Li, Y., Brooks, D., Hu, Z., Skadron, K., Bose, P.: Understanding the Energy Efficiency of Simultaneous Multithreading. In: The 2004 International Symposium on Low Power Electronics and Design, pp. 44–49 (2004)
4. Sasanka, R., Adve, S.V., Chen, Y.-K., Debes, E.: The Energy Efficiency of CMP vs. SMT for Multimedia Workloads. In: The 18th Annual International Conference on Supercomputing, pp. 196–206 (2004)
5. Kaxiras, S., Narlikar, G., Berenbaum, A.D., Hu, Z.: Comparing Power Consumption of an SMT and a CMP DSP for Mobile Phone Workloads. In: The 2001 International Conference on Compilers, Architecture,and Synthesis for Embedded Systems, pp. 211–220 (2001)

6. Li, Y., Skadron, K., Hu, Z., Brooks, D.: Performance, Energy, and Thermal Considerations for SMT and CMP Architectures. In: The Eleventh IEEE International Symposium on High Performance Computer Architecture (HPCA), pp. 71–82 (2005)
7. Lo, J.L., Eggers, S.J., Levy, H.M., Parekh, S.S., Tullsen, D.M.: Tuning Compiler Optimizations for Simultaneous Multithreading. In: The 30th Micro, pp. 114–124 (1997)
8. Jianhua, Y., Hongmei, W.: Actuality and Trend of Parallel Language and Compilation. Computer Engineering, pp. 97–98 (December 2004)
9. OpenUH: An Optimizing, Portable OpenMP Compiler (2006), http://www2.cs.uh.edu/copper/pubs.html
10. Akkary, H., Driscoll, M.A.: A dynamic multithreading processor. In: The 31st annual ACM/IEEE international symposium on Microarchitecture, pp. 226–236 (1998)
11. Schlansker, M.S., Rau, B.R.: EPIC: Explicitly Parallel Instruction Computing. IEEE Computer 32(2), 37–45 (2000)
12. Itanium Processor Microarchitecture Reference: for Software Optimization 05 (2002), http://www.developer.intel.com/design/ia64/itanium.htm

An SRP Target Mode to Improve Read Performance of SRP-Based IB-SANs

Zhiying Jiang[1,2], Jin He[1], Jizhong Han[1], Xigui Wang[1,2], Yonghao Zhou[1,2], and Xubin He[3]

[1] Institute of Computing Technology, Chinese Academy of Sciences, 100080 Beijing, China
[2] Graduate University, Chinese Academy of Sciences, 100039 Beijing, China
{ianjiang,hejin,hjz, wxg,zhouyonghao}@ict.ac.cn
[3] Department of Electrical & Computer Engineering, Tennessee Technological University, Cookeville, TN 38505, USA
hexb@tntech.edu

Abstract. SCSI RDMA Protocol (SRP) is used to build high performance Storage Area Networks (SANs) over InfiniBand, or SRP-based IB-SANs for short. The I/O read performance is critical for many read dominant applications, such as multimedia, remote sensing, data backup, etc. However, if I/O accesses focus on a specific storage device of an IB-SAN, the local I/O performance of single device could become the bottleneck, leaving the network performance under utilized. In this paper, we propose an SRP target mode called Target Disk Cache Assisted (tDCA) mode, which explores the file read-ahead feature and page cache of Linux to tackle the performance gap between storage devices and network. Experimental results show that this strategy improves the read performance in terms of throughput which is increased significantly for both random read with good locality and sequential read.

1 Introduction

InfiniBand Architecture (IBA) [1] offers some features such as low latency, high throughput and low CPU overhead. It utilizes Remote Direct Memory Access (RDMA) mechanism and dedicated protocol offload engines, and is widely used in high performance computing and database systems [2,3]. Meanwhile, more Storage Area Networks (SANs) are built over InfiniBand based on dedicated protocols, known as IB-SANs. Such protocols which transfer SCSI data using RDMA include SCSI RDMA Protocol (SRP) [4], an ANSI standard, and iSCSI Extensions for RDMA Specification (iSER) [5], an IETF draft. There are many controversies over their respective merits at present, but iSER has the advantage of compatibility with iSCSI, while SRP has better performance due to directly mapping SCSI over InfiniBand. This paper focuses on SRP-based IB-SANs.

I. Stojmenovic et al. (Eds.): ISPA 2007, LNCS 4742, pp. 245–255, 2007.

Although utilizing a high speed network, an IB-SAN may not demonstrate superior overall performance in some cases because of the access pattern of storage applications and the performance constraints of storage devices [6]. Consequently, under certain access pattern such as that all accesses are directed to a specific device, its performance is likely to limit the overall system performance, leaving the high speed network under utilized.

In addition, for many read dominant applications, such as multimedia, remote sensing, data backup, etc, the I/O read performance is critical. For storage applications with certain access patterns, specific mechanisms are used to make up the performance gap between the storage devices and network interfaces. For instance, read-ahead could be applied to applications with continuous data access, such as multimedia services. Cache could be applied to applications with certain data reuse, such as database systems. Therefore, we propose an SRP target mode called Target Disk Cache Assisted (tDCA) mode, where read-ahead and cache are used together to reduce the number of disk accesses, thereby improving the overall performance available to applications.

In order to verify the effectiveness of above mechanisms, we implemented a prototype tDCA module using Linux file read-ahead and page cache. Experimental results show that the overall performance in terms of throughput is increased by 7% ~ 137% for sequential read, and by a factor of 5 ~ 20 for random read with good locality. Although our efforts focus on SRP, some of our conclusions are also applicable to iSER.

The rest of this paper is organized as follows. The background is presented in Section 2. We discuss the performance limitation of storage devices in Section 3. Section 4 describes the tDCA mode in details followed by our preliminary performance evaluation in Section 5. We briefly discuss the related work in Section 6 and draw our conclusions in Section 7.

2 Background

SRP is a client/server protocol where the client, or SRP initiator, establishes a session over one or more RDMA channels with the server or SRP target. This section gives an overview of InfiniBand, followed by an introduction to the architecture of SRP initiator and target, and a brief description of the transfer of SCSI commands and data read/write.

2.1 InfiniBand Overview

InfiniBand Architecture (IBA) [1] is an interconnect technology primarily used in high performance computing. The IBA specification defines an interconnection between processor nodes and I/O nodes such as storage devices. It is independent of hardware and software environments. IBA has many advantages such as high bandwidth, reliability and scalability features for I/O. It has extremely low latency and low CPU overhead. With IBA, applications directly access the IBA network hardware, without the interaction of operating systems (OS), which makes message passing operation more efficient.

Two types of channel adapters are defined in IBA: Host Channel Adapter (HCA) and Target Channel Adapter (TCA). HCA offers an interface through which the consumer can use the functions specified by IBA verbs. TCA is a programmable DMA engine that initiates DMA operations locally and remotely.

Two useful communications are provided by IBA: channel semantics and memory semantics. The former, also called Send/Receive, is a classic communication style that one side pushes the data and the other receives the data. The memory semantics, also known as RDMA, provides a way for an initiating node to directly read or write the virtual address space of a remote node. When the initiating node sends a read or write request, data are retrieved from or placed to the remote memory without involving the remote applications or OS. This is especially useful in massively parallel computing clusters.

2.2 Architecture of SRP Initiator and Target

The architecture of SRP initiator and target is shown in Figure 1. On the initiator side, the SCSI disk driver, SCSI unifying layer and SRP initiator driver belong to the three layers of Linux SCSI subsystem, respectively. The upper layer SCSI disk driver provides a generic block device read/write interface to applications such as file systems and database systems, and also converts the read/write requests into SCSI requests. The SCSI unifying layer converts the SCSI requests into SCSI commands and data transfer sequences, and sets the status of SCSI requests according to the SCSI responses returned by the SRP initiator driver. The lower layer SRP initiator driver is a Host Bus Adapter (HBA) driver that controls the delivery of the SCSI commands and data and collects the SCSI responses. All these SCSI information are encapsulated into the particular transport protocol SRP, and then transferred over InfiniBand, rather than over a SCSI bus in a traditional HBA. Among the three layers, only the SRP initiator driver needs to be specially designed and implemented, as the others are existing components in Linux kernel.

On the target side, the SRP driver consists of two components: a generic SCSI target mid-level (STML) and a front-end target driver (FETD). The FETD handles all details of the transport protocol, which includes receiving SCSI commands from the SRP initiator, exchanging SCSI data and returning SCSI responses. The STML is responsible for storing data to or retrieving from specific storage devices and also handles SCSI errors and maintains SCSI state information. STML is totally independent of the transport protocol used in the FETD. In the two-layered architecture, the FETD is compatible with different implementations of STML.

Currently two different implementations of the STML are available, according to what type of storage device is used. The DISKIO, as shown in Figure 1, is based on SCSI/SATA disks, and the MEMORYIO is based on the main memory of the target. With DISKIO, all SCSI commands received from the FETD are simply delivered to the local SCSI subsystem of the target, which is responsible for command processes and data storing to or retrieving from local disks, and is responsible for returning status information to the STML. With MEMORYIO, SCSI data are not stored. What the STML returns to the initiator in processing a SCSI read command are random data in the target main memory, and data received from the initiator in processing a SCSI

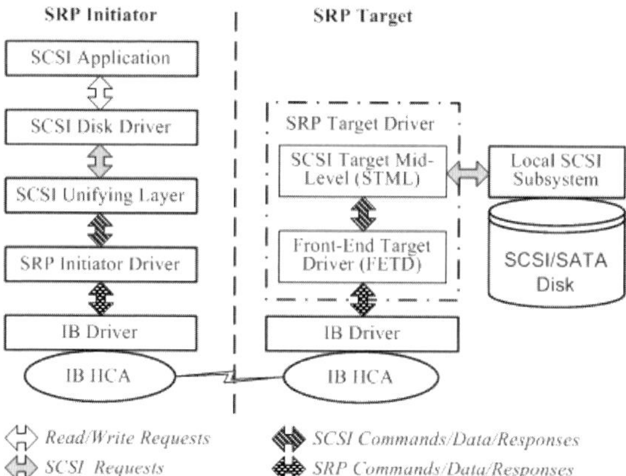

Fig. 1. Architecture of SRP initiator and target (DISKIO)

write command are simply discarded. DISKIO is for practical use while MEMORYIO is used for performance analysis of a SCSI transport protocol.

2.3 SCSI Read/Write: Command and Data Transfer

Figure 2 (a) illustrates the command and data transfer for a typical SCSI read. First, an SRP command (containing the SCSI read command) is sent from the SRP initiator to the target with one Send/Receive operation. Second, data are retrieved from local storage devices by the target. Third, data are transferred to the initiator with one or more RDMA write operations. Finally, an SRP response (containing a SCSI response) is returned to the initiator via one Send/Receive operation.

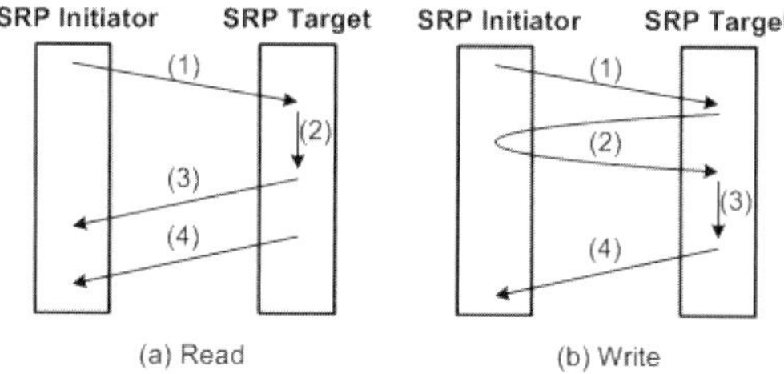

Fig. 2. SCSI read/write: command and data transfer

Similarly, the process for a SCSI write is as shown in Figure 2 (b): First, an SRP command (containing the SCSI write command) is sent with one Send/Receive operation; Second, data are transferred from the initiator to the target with one or more RDMA read operations; Third, data are stored to local storage devices; Finally, an SRP response is returned via one Send/Receive operation.

3 Performance Limitation of Storage Devices

Three key factors affect the overall performance of a network storage system: the access pattern of storage applications, the network performance and the storage device performance. In an SRP-based IB-SAN, network performance is usually not the bottleneck, because SRP directly maps the SCSI protocol over the InfiniBand transport layer, taking advantage of the high performance, low cost RDMA. However, this may bring the performance gap between storage devices and network interfaces.

Let's take the sequential read for example. We measured the throughput of sequential reads of the SRP block device on the initiator side, with the target in MEMORYIO and DISKIO respectively. The SRP block device is mapped to a single SATA disk in DISKIO (See Section 5.1 for the experimental environment). For request size of 16KB, the throughput with MEMORYIO and DISKIO is about 198MB/s and 48MB/s, respectively.

The only difference between MEMORYIO and DISKIO is the characteristics of the storage device: With MEMORYIO, the cost of accessing the storage device could be ignored because no real disk I/O is involved; With DISKIO, however, each SCSI read command causes one disk read. The performance limitation of disk read and the software overhead of the local SCSI subsystem make the overall throughput for 16KB sequential read with DISKIO much lower than that with MEMORYIO. Similar conclusions could be drawn by comparing the throughput with the two modes for random read, sequential write or random write.

The performance of MEMORYIO sets out the capability of RDMA to support a high performance SAN, while that of DISKIO shows the insufficiency of practical storage devices. This does not matter much when multiple storage devices are accessed by multiple applications at the same time, because the network could be fully utilized with aggregate I/O of all storage devices. When most accesses are directed to a specific device due to locality for some applications, however, the overall performance is limited by the performance of storage devices on the target side, leaving the network performance under utilized.

4 Design and Implementation

4.1 Basic Idea

For storage applications with certain access patterns, specific mechanisms could be used to smooth the performance gap between storage devices and network interfaces, thus improving the overall system performance. In this paper, we use both read-ahead and cache to reduce the disk I/O overhead for an SRP-based IB-SAN.

Read-ahead means reading several adjacent blocks of data before they are actually requested, which returns the related data immediately for several subsequent read commands without waiting for disk access, because they are already available in memory. For applications with continuous data access, such as multimedia services, when the STML gets one SCSI read command, it is possible to predict the data referred by the subsequent SCSI read commands. Read-ahead will help reduce the latency in this scenario.

Cache is used to speedup the data access of the SRP target, which could reduce disk access for SCSI read commands and minimize or postpone disk writes for SCSI write commands, if the referred data are cached. For applications with certain data reuse, such as database systems, repeated accesses to the same data are quite common.

Both read-ahead and cache could reduce the average time to store or retrieve data in STML by reducing direct disk access, and therefore could improve the overall performance of an SRP-based IB-SAN.

4.2 Design and Implementation

Mechanisms existing in Linux kernel are utilized to verify the effectiveness of read-head and cache, which simplifies our design and implementation. Read-ahead of regular files and block device in Linux consists of reading several adjacent pages of data before they are actually requested, and disk cache allows the system to keep some data in memory that is normally stored in a disk. Both of them could make further access to that data be satisfied quickly without accessing the disk, thus enhance disk I/O performance.

There are generally several types of disk cache in Linux [9], including buffer cache and page cache. The buffer cache stores data of disk blocks. And the page cache stores page frames that contain data belonging to specific files. Starting from the Linux kernels 2.4, the buffer cache and the page cache are merged, which we call page cache hereafter.

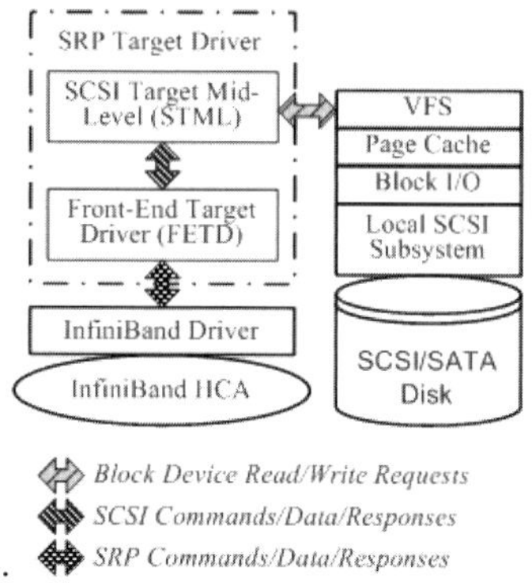

Fig. 3. Architecture of SRP target (tDCA)

There are two interfaces through which applications could utilize the page cache: regular files and block device files. Typically for an SRP target using a SATA disk,

1. Utilizing the regular file interface means simulating a storage device with a regular file. A file system should be established on the disk and regular files should be created first. Then each SCSI read/write command is translated into one or more read/write access to the regular files. This is similar to the UNH iSCSI FILEIO [10]. In this case, file read-ahead could be utilized, but not all of the disk space could be used for storing data.

2. Utilizing the block device file interface means translating each SCSI read/write command into one or more read/write access to the block device file related to the disk. In this case, file read-ahead could be utilized and all disk space could be used for storing data.

We use the block device file interface to implement our Target Disk Cache Assisted (tDCA) mode for SRP. Its architecture is shown in Figure 3, where VFS stands for the Virtual File system of Linux, which provides the block device file interface.

5 Performance Experiment and Evaluation

To verify the effectiveness of tDCA, we conduct preliminary experiments to measure and evaluate the performance of an SRP-based IB-SAN with target DISKIO and tDCA.

5.1 Experiment Setup

As shown in Figure 4, three computers are used in our experiments. Two Dell PowerEdge 430 nodes act as the SRP initiator and target, respectively. Each node is configured with Intel(R) Xeon(TM) CPU 2.80GHz, 1MB L2 cache, 2GB memory, 133MHz PCI-X bus and a Mellanox MT25204 InfiniBand HCA . The two HCAs are connected through a Mellanox MT47396 InfiniBand switch. One Seagate ST380013AS 80GB SATA disk is used on the target as the storage device.

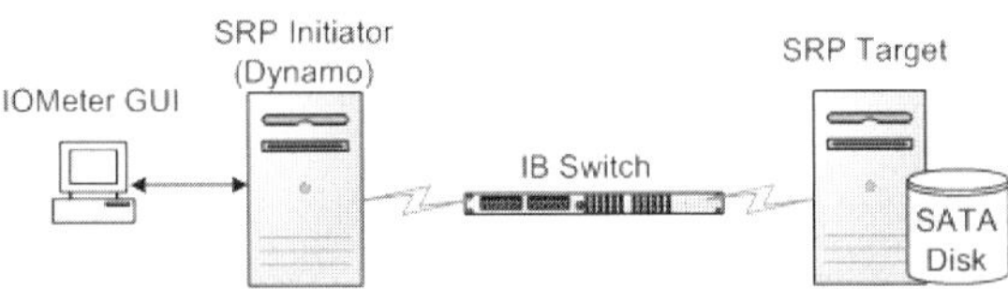

Fig. 4. Experiment setup

The initiator is running Linux vanilla kernel 2.6.20 which has built-in drivers for InfiniBand and SRP initiator. The target is running Linux kernel 2.4.21-4.EL of Redhat AS 3, and the InfiniBand driver is IBGD-1.8.0 [7] including the SRP target.

The IOMeter benchmarking tool (version 20060627) [8] is used for performance measurement. It consists of two parts: a client and a controller. The Linux-based client called dynamo runs on the initiator and the Windows-based controller with graphical user interface (GUI) runs on a separate PC as shown in Figure 4.

5.2 Methodology

In order to evaluate the impact of read-ahead, the throughput of tDCA for sequential read is measured under different I/O request sizes. Different typical read-ahead sizes at the target are used to check the impact on the overall performance. Two parameters of the Linux kernel 2.4.21-4.EL, *vm.max-readahead* and *vm.min-readahed*, define the minimal and maximum size of each read-ahead and they are used to adjust the read-ahead size at the target. In addition, the page cache at the target is cold at the beginning of each test and the total data set accessed in each test is much smaller than the size of the SATA disk 80GB, therefore, the data reuse rate is zero for each sequential read test, and the page cache at the target does not take any effect.

In order to evaluate the impact of cache, the throughput of tDCA for random read of good locality is measured under different I/O request sizes. The locality of each test is also adjusted to check its impact on the overall performance. The random I/O requests are limited in a small range of the data set, and the size of data set is dynamically tuned to get different locality. The page cache at the target is warm at the beginning of each test. In addition, the read-ahead size is set to zero so the file read-ahead at the target does not take any effect.

5.3 Results

Figures 5-7 shows our measurement results. It is obvious that read-ahead at the target dramatically improves the performance for sequential read. As shown in Figure 5, for different I/O request sizes, the throughput of tDCA is increased by 7% ~ 37% compared to that of DISKIO. In addition, the larger each read-ahead is, as shown in Figure 6, the better performance could be achieved.

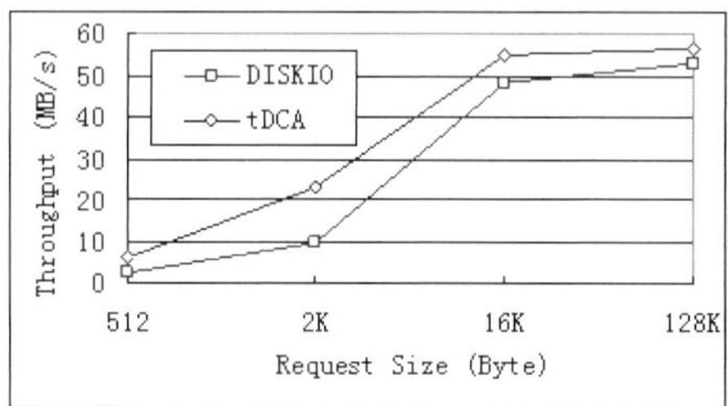

Fig. 5. Sequential read throughput for different I/O request sizes. For tDCA, the read-ahead size at the target is 24KB.

In addition, cache at the target improves the performance for random read with good locality. As shown in Figure 7, for different I/O request sizes, the throughput of tDCA is increased by a factor of 5 ~ 20 compared to that of DISKIO. In addition, the better locality the random read is, the better performance could be acquired.

For some access patterns the read performance of tDCA is close to MEMORYIO. For instance, when the I/O request size is under 1KB for sequential read with a 24KB read-ahead size at the target, or when the I/O request size is under 2KB for random read within a 256MB data set size and without read-ahead at the target, the throughput of DISKIO is approximately 84% of MEMORYIO.

Additionally, the performance of tDCA for random write with good locality and sequential write is also evaluated. It is observed that, the throughput of tDCA for random write within a 320MB data set size is increased by from 37% to a factor of 14 compared to that of DISKIO for different I/O request sizes. For sequential write of small I/O request sizes (512B ~ 16KB), the throughput of tDCA is increased by 67% ~ 165% compared to that of DISKIO. For large I/O request sizes (32KB ~ 128KB), however, the throughput of tDCA is lower than that of DISKIO.

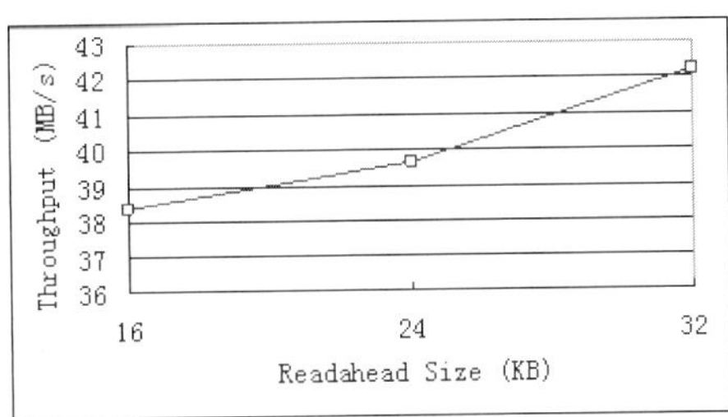

Fig. 6. Sequential read throughput for different read-ahead sizes at the target. The I/O request size is 4KB.

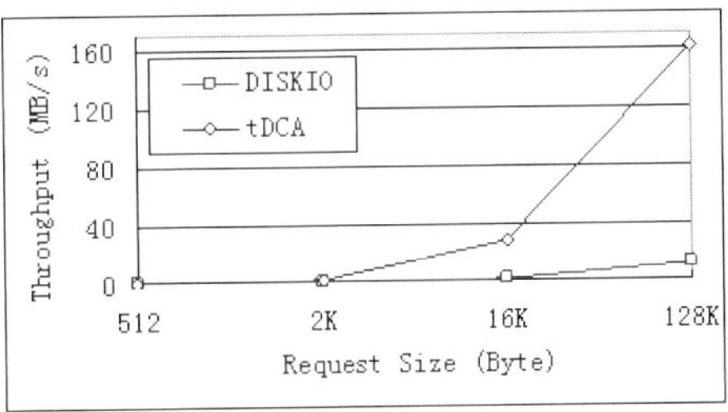

Fig. 7. Random read throughput for different I/O request sizes. The data set size of each test is 384MB.

6 Related Work

Cache is used widely to improve the performance of IP-SANs. In STICS [11] and iCache [12], caches were added between IP network interfaces and application nodes, or between IP network interfaces and storage nodes, to store SCSI commands and data. These caches took effect because the performance of IP network is usually the bottleneck of an IP-SAN, and these caches reduced the amount of data and controlling messages transferred over the network. As a result the overload of network decreased to a certain extent, and the overall performance of IP-SANs was improved. However, the performance of network is usually not the bottleneck of an IB-SAN and the performance limitation of storage devices is what we concern about in this paper.

Storage over InfiniBand has been studied recently. In RDMA Assisted iSCSI [13], RDMA support for SCSI data transfer was added in the traditional iSCSI system, in order to evaluate the impact of RDMA on storage over InfiniBand. Our study is based on SRP, which is a complete and mature standard. In RiCache [14], cache on the iSCSI initiator side was introduced. The idea in RiCache is that the memory used as cache is partially on the iSCSI target side. Our tDCA is different in that memory on the SRP target side is used as cache for the target directly.

In the new generation of SRP Target [15], the STML is replaced by an independent "Generic SCSI Target Mid-level for Linux" (SCST) [16]. The SCST has the same idea as our tDCA, i.e. utilizing the file read-ahead and page cache of Linux to achieve or store data for a SCSI Read or Write command through the block file device interface. But no similar research work on the new SRP target has been found.

7 Conclusions

In this paper we investigated the performance limitation of storage devices in an SRP-based IB-SAN in the case that most accesses focus on a specific device, and then proposed an SRP target mode called tDCA, which utilizes file read-ahead and page cache of Linux to smooth the performance gap between storage devices and network interfaces, thus improving the overall read performance. Experimental results show that with tDCA the throughput is increased by 7% ~ 137% for sequential read and by 5 ~ 20 times for random read with good locality. These improvements are valuable to many read dominant applications such as multimedia services and database systems.

Acknowledgements

This work is supported in part by the National Basic Research Program of China (973 Program) 2004CB318202. It is also sponsored by Tennessee Tech University Research Office under a faculty research grant and the Center for Manufacturing Research. We would also like to thank the anonymous reviewers for their valuable comments.

References

1. InfiniBand Trade Association: InfiniBand Architecture Specification vol. 1, 2 (Release 1.2) (2004), http://www.infinibandta.org/specs
2. Liu, J., Wu, J., Panda, D.K.: High Performance RDMA-Based MPI Implementation over InfiniBand. International Journal of Parallel Programming. 32, 167–198 (2004)
3. Oracle: Achieving Mainframe-Class Performance on Intel Servers Using InfiniBand Building Blocks (2003), http://www.oracle.com/technology/deploy/availability/pdf/oracle_IB.pdf
4. Cris Simpson: SCSI RDMA Protocol - 2 (SRP-2) (2003), http://www.t10.org/ftp/t10/drafts/srp2/srp2r00a.pdf
5. Mike Ko: iSCSI Extensions for RDMA Specification (2006), http://www.ietf.org/internet-drafts/draft-ietf-ips-iser-06.txt
6. Qiang, C., Changsheng, X.: The Study of the I/O Request Response Time in Network Storage System. Journal of Computer Research & Development. 40, 1271–1276 (2003)
7. Mellanox: InfiniBand Gold Collection for Linux (Gen1) version 1.8.x (2006), https://docs.mellanox.com/dm/ibgold/ReadMe.html
8. The IOMeter Project (2006), http://www.iometer.org
9. Bovet, D.P., Cesati, M.: Understanding the Linux Kernel, 1st edn. O'Reilly (2000) ISBN: 0-596-00002-2
10. The UNH-iSCSI Project (2006), http://sourceforge.net/projects/unh-iscsi
11. He, X., Zhang, M., Yang, Q.: STICS: SCSI-to-IP cache for storage area networks. Journal of Parallel and Distributed Computing 64, 1069–1085 (2004)

12. He, X., Yang, Q., Zhang, M.: A caching strategy to improve iSCSI performance. In: The IEEE Annual Conference on Local Computer Networks, pp. 6–8 (2002)
13. Liu, J., Panda, D.K., Banikazemi, M.: Evaluating the Impact of RDMA on Storage I/O over InfiniBand. In: SAN-3 Workshop (2004)
14. Liu, X., Wang, N., Sun, G., Han, J., Han, C.: Remote iSCSI Cache on InfiniBand: An Approach to Optimize iSCSI System. In: ICPPW'06, pp. 527–534 (2006)
15. OpenFabrics Alliance: SRP Target Development Git Tree (2007), http://www.openfabrics.org/git/?p= vu/srpt.git;a=summary
16. Bolkhovitin, V.: Generic SCSI Target Mid-level for Linux (2007), http://scst.sourceforge.net

An FPGA Design to Achieve Fast and Accurate Results for Molecular Dynamics Simulations

Eunjung Cho, Anu G. Bourgeois, and Feng Tan

Computer Science Department of Georgia State University
echo@student.gsu.edu, anu@cs.gsu.edu, fengtan@gmail.com

Abstract. A Molecular Dynamics (MD) system is defined by the position and momentum of particles and their interactions. The dynamics of a system can be evaluated by an N-body problem and the simulation is continued until the energy reaches equilibrium. Thus, solving the dynamics numerically and evaluating the interaction is computationally expensive even for a small number of particles in the system. We are focusing on long-ranged interactions, since the calculation time is $O(N^2)$ for an N particle system. There are many existing algorithms aimed at reducing the calculation time of MD simulations. Multigrid (MG) method [1] reduces $O(N^2)$ calculation time to $O(N)$ time while still achieving reasonable accuracy. Another movement to achieve much faster calculation time is running MD simulation on special purpose processors and customized hardware with ASICs or FPGAs. In this paper, we design and implement an FPGA-based MD simulator with an efficient MG method.

1 Introduction

Extensive research has been focused on the field of Molecular Dynamics (MD) over the past 20 years. MD describes a classical particle molecular system as a function of time and has been successfully applied to understand and explain macro phenomena from micro structures, since it is in many respects similar to real experiments. An MD system is defined by the position and momentum of particles and their interactions (potential). The dynamics of a system can be evaluated by solving Newton's equation of motion, which is an N-body problem [3]. The classical N-body problem requires a numerical solution because general analytical solutions are not enough to prove it.

Solving the dynamics numerically and evaluating the interactions is computationally expensive even for a small number of particles in the system. The interactions of particles to be evaluated are short-ranged interactions and long-ranged interactions. It takes $O(N)$ time to calculate short-ranged interactions and $O(N^2)$ for long-ranged interactions with the number of particles N. So we are focusing on long-ranged interactions due to the intensive computational time.

Many approaches have been proposed to improve the performance of MD simulation. These approaches are divided into two categories by focusing on either the software or on the hardware. The software approach involves developing efficient algorithms to calculate the forces. For current study, many algorithms have been introduced and large scale parallel computers are used to achieve reasonable

I. Stojmenovic et al. (Eds.): ISPA 2007, LNCS 4742, pp. 256–267, 2007.

computational time. Ewald's method [7] runs in $O(N^{3/2})$ time and PM[1][3]method applies discrete fast Fourier transforms (FFT) to compute long-range interactions (reciprocal force) and reduce $O(N^{3/2})$ to $O(N\log N)$. Multigrid (MG) [2] method requires $O(N)$ time complexity for a given accuracy. Sagui and Darden [6] describe two techniques (LGM and LDM) based on MD method for classical MD simulations of biomolecules. We proposed an efficient *Multi-level Charge assignment method (MCA)* [22] that reduces calculation time and achieves better accuracy in LGM and LDM.

The hardware approach has focused on running MD simulation in special purpose processors or developed Application-Specific Integrated Circuit (ASIC) to achieve much faster calculation time. RASTRUN[15] and GRAPE-2A[16] has pipelines of digital signal processors. MODEL [17] is an ASIC machine for evaluating Lennard Jones (LJ) potential and Coulombic potential. Although the special purpose processors are very powerful, it is much more expensive than microprocessor-based software solutions. ASIC is another powerful way but the development of customized circuits is a very complicated process and the development span is very long. In addition, it is hard to modify the circuit if the solution is changed later.

To overcome these disadvantages of previous works for MD simulation, we are proposing a project that exploits *reconfigurable models* to run MD simulations in a flexible and efficient manner. This allows efficient communication and faster computation than conventional *non-reconfigurable* models. Field programmable gate arrays (FPGAs) is one of the most widely studied reconfigurable model. Since FPGAs recently has more functions that can be used for large problems such as MD simulation, many researches are designing circuits with FPGA for large scale applications. Navid Azizi et al. [18] show the feasibility of using FPGA to implement large-scale application-specific computations by implementing MD simulation. Youngfeng Gu et al.[19] provide an FPGA implementation for Coulombic force as well as Lennard Jones force.

In this paper, we describe an efficient method, Multi-level charge assignment (MCA) for MD simulation and provide experimental results to show its improved accuracy. We design FPGA-based MD simulator based on MCA method and provide preliminary FPGA implementation of the method in detail.

We organize this paper as follows. In Section 2, we provide background of MD simulations. Section 3 describes the background for Multigrid method and our proposed version, MCA method. In Section 4, current hardware-based approaches of MD simulation are introduced. In Section 5, we explain our proposed architecture and FPGA implementation. Finally Section 6 provides concluding remarks and proposes additional research lines for the future.

2 Background of Molecular Dynamics Simulation

In Molecular Dynamics (MD) simulation, dynamics are calculated by Newtonian mechanics [1]. MD simulation integrates acceleration to obtain position and velocity changes of atoms in the system. This process is continued every 1 femtosecond or other time scale.

There are other approaches to describe forces of an MD system. Newton's equation of motion describes nature conserving the energy but other approaches modify the forces to achieve equilibrium states satisfying certain specified requirements, such as constant temperature, constant pressure or rigid molecules.

The force $\vec{F}_i$ can be described by the potential energy (U)

$$\vec{F}_i = -\nabla_i U(\vec{x}_1, \vec{x}_2, \ldots, \vec{x}_N) + \vec{F}_i^{extended}$$

where U is the potential, N is the number of atoms in the system and $\vec{F}_i^{extended}$ is an extended force like velocity-based friction.

The *potential U* consists of bonded potentials and non-bonded potentials. It takes O(N) time to calculate the bonded potentials and O(N^2) for non-bonded potentials. So many researchers focus on the non-bonded interactions due to the intensive computational time. Non-bonded interactions can be divided as electrostatic potential ($U^{electrostatic}$) and Lennard-Jones ($U^{Lennard\text{-}Jones}$) potential. $U^{electrostatic}$ represents Coulomb potential and $U^{Lennard\text{-}Jones}$ represents a van der Waals attraction and a hard-core repulsion.

These potentials are pair-wise interactions and the formulation is given by

$$U_{ij}^{electrostatic} = \frac{1}{4\pi\varepsilon_0} \frac{q_i q_j}{\left\|\vec{x}_{ij}\right\|^2}. \quad (1)$$

where π, ε_0 is constant and q_i, q_j are the charges of atoms i and j.

$$U_{ij}^{Lennard-Jones} = \frac{A_{ij}}{\left\|\vec{x}_{ij}\right\|^{12}} - \frac{B_{ij}}{\left\|\vec{x}_{ij}\right\|^{6}}. \quad (2)$$

where $A_{ij} \geq 0$ and $B_{ij} \geq 0$ are the Lennard-Jones (LJ) parameters for atoms i and j. They define the energy minimum and the cross-over point, where the LJ function is zero. The $U^{Lennard\text{-}Jones}$ can be calculated in O(N) time, since the LJ function decays very fast. But $U^{electrostatic}$ takes O(N^2) time by Equation 1. Many methods try to reduce the time while still achieving reasonable accuracy. We also proposed a method, Multi-level Charge assignment [22] to reduce the O(N^2) time to O(N) time, however with improved accuracy as compared to existing techniques.

3 Multigrid Method

As mentioned above, there are many methods which reduce the calculation time of electrostatic force. In this section, we will explain the methods based on Multigrid (MG) to evaluate the electrostatic force in O(N) time.

3.1 Multigrid Method Background

The Multigrid (MG) method was introduced in the 1960's to solve partial differential equations (PDE). Recently it has been applied and implemented for N-body problems and achieve O(N) time complexity at given accuracy.

The basic idea of MG is to hierarchically separate the force potential into a *short range part* plus a *smooth part (slowly varying part of energy)*. MG method uses gridded interpolation for both the charges (source) and the potentials (destination) to represent its smooth(coarse) part.[2] The splitting and coarsening are applied recursively and define a grid hierarchy (Refer to Figure 1).

MG method is faster for a given error rate, but cannot provide better accuracy than other methods such as Ewald's method [7] and Multipole method [4]. In order to use MG method, we need to map an arbitrary distribution of discrete particles onto a grid space. There are several mapping schemes, *charge assignment* scheme, and those schemes play an important part in MD simulation, since both accuracy and efficiency depend on the *charge assignment* scheme. That is, the charges must be spread over a fairly large number of grid points, which can become the most time-consuming part of the algorithm. Beckers et al. [8] presented a new implementation of P3M method by solving Poisson's equation in real space with a Successive OverRelaxation (SOR) method, but the accuracy is not good enough. So Sagui and Darden [6] proposed modified Lattice Diffusion Multigrid (LDM) method that improved accuracy and speeds up the algorithm. In addition, they proposed another method, Lattice Gaussian Multigrid (LGM) [6] method, which is more accurate, but more time consuming.

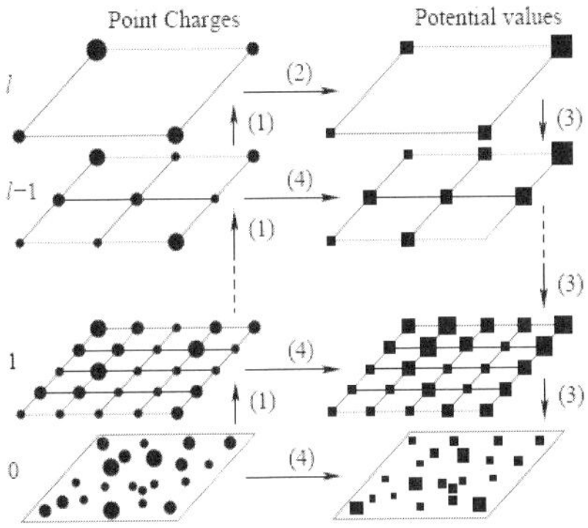

Fig. 1. The multilevel scheme of MG algorithm [2]. (1) Aggregate to coarser grids (2) Compute potential induced by the coarsest grid (3) Interpolate potential values from coarser grids (4) Local corrections.

3.2 Multi-level Charge Assignment Method

Many techniques for Molecular Dynamics (MD) simulation are based on MG method since this method is efficient and can be used in parallel machine. However, most applications using MG method provide inconsistent accuracy by the structure of molecules to be simulated and adjust the parameters in an unsystematic way. Since particle charges are interpolated onto the grid, the grid charge or charge distribution on a grid point could not represent well the particle charges when the particles of molecule are not spread evenly.

We proposed a method to provide consistent accuracy and reduce errors even if the distribution of particles is not balanced. In MG method, charge assignment and back interpolation are very important steps since accuracy and efficiency depend on these steps. We proposed Multi-level Charge Assignment method (MCA) [22] which provides better accuracy with little additional cost. The main idea of MCA is two fold; 1) the size of the finest grid is a factor to improve the accuracy, but the efficiency is decreased; 2) many molecules have different structures so grid points represent different number of particles. MCA uses different sizes of finest grid when the finest grid represents more particles than a particular threshold value and interpolates the particle charges to the grids.

The method consists of four steps: (1) calculate the density of particles for each grid point; (2) apply multi-level charge assignment if the density of grid x is greater than threshold, k. Then interpolate and smooth the charges onto a grid; (3) calculate the electrostatic potential on the grid via Multigrid (MG) methods; (4) back interpolate the forces and energy from the grid to the particle space.

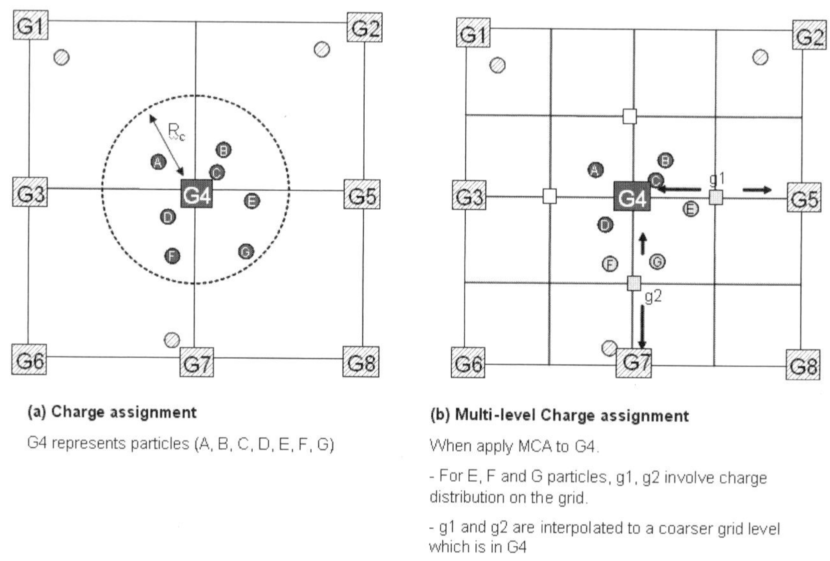

Fig. 2. Multi-level Charge Assignment example

Figure 2 shows an example that applies MCA on grid G4. Figure 2 (a) shows the charge assignment for the original MG method. The charges of particles (solid circle; A, B, C, D, E, F and G) are interpolated to G4 since the particles are located within R_c (cutoff distance). Figure 2 (b) shows an example when MCA is applied to interpolate those particles (solid circle). We would consider that the charges for particles E, F and G are interpolated to g1 and g2 which are smaller grids and have smaller cutoff distance ($R_c/2$) since particle E is closer to g1 than G4 and particle F and G is closer to g2 than G4, therefore MCA is applied. Then, g1 and g2 are interpolated to a coarser grid level G4.

Table 1. Total execution time and accuracy for LDM [6] and Multi-level method (MCA) on Calcium molecule and Bpti molecule

	Calcium Molecule			Bpti Molecule		
	LDM	MCA		LDM	MCA	
Time(sec)	62.78	63.90	1.78% slower	118.14	119.16	0.8% slower
Accuracy	0.0217	0.0204	6% better accuracy	0.0022	0.0018	19.5% better accuracy

Table 1 shows simulation results and compares the proposed method with LDM [6]. As can be seen, experiments on Calcium Molecule and Bpti Molecule show improved accuracy for the proposed method and particularly, the experiments on BPTI shows much better improvement (19.5%). The reason that BPTI displays better results than the Calcium molecule is that more atoms in BPTI molecule are applied to MCA method. As we mentioned, if the molecule is not spread evenly in grid, MCA method provides efficient charge assignment and back interpolation.

4 Related Work - Hardware Approaches

The number of atoms in a Molecular Dynamics (MD) system is typically large and the MD simulation must continue until the forces reach equilibrium. Therefore, the total time required is significantly large, even if efficient algorithms are applied to the simulation. Many hardware approaches provide rapid and accurate MD simulation of biomolecules, but these are very expensive compared to use the microprocessor. In this section, we present current techniques that apply customized hardware rather than microprocessor-based software solutions for MD simulation.

4.1 Special Purpose Machines and Application-Specific Integrated Circuit (ASIC)

Shinjiro Toyoda et al. [17] developed a custom processor called MODEL (MOlecular Dynamics processing ELement) for calculating *Lennard Jones force* and *Coulombic force* and a scalable plug-in machine to a workstation. The processors work in parallel and have pipeline architecture. Their MD engine system consists of 76 MODELs and is approximately 50 times faster than the equivalent software implementation on a 200 MHz Sun Ultra 2. The magnitude of forces was determined through table lookup since computation of these forces required greater than 99% of the CPU time in software-based simulations. The MD engine system using MODEL chips apply Ewald method [7] to calculate Coulombic forces and the method allows precise calculation of Coulombic forces. Although MODEL achieves highly improved simulation results, developing an ASIC such as MODEL not only takes much time, but also is very expensive. Most of all, it is hard to modify the circuits when the solution needs to be changed. GRAPE(GRAvity PipE) [15][16] is one of the ASIC machines which are originally developed for gravitational problems and currently many GRAPEs have been developed for N-body problem such as MD simulation. Yuto Komeiji et al. [15] developed MD-GRAPE. MD-GRAPE is one of the GRAPEs and computes force and potential efficiently. The architecture of GRAPE is simple and easy to develop. They did not use floating point arithmetic throughout as was done in MODEL. Instead, position is stored as a 40-bit fixed-point number and the force is accumulated onto an 80-bit fixed-point number. The switch to fixed-point reduces the hardware requirements substantially. However, floating-point was still used for the calculation of the forces. MD-GRAPE divides the force calculation into two. Only the $O(N^2)$ operations were off-loaded to the hardware in this system and $O(N)$ operations were performed on a host computer. Thus, the communication time with host limits the performance of the system if the number of particles is not large enough.

4.2 FPGA-Based ASP (Application Specific Processor)

Due to lack of flexibility in their dedicated hardware circuits, it is hard for ASIC machines to be altered or upgraded. Recently, reconfigurable computing has emerged as an alternative to ASIC. It allows hardware circuits to be configured to perform the target task. Field Programmable Gate Arrays (FPGAs) are semiconductor devices that processes digital information and can be reprogrammed without slowing performance. FPGA boards are cheap compared to ASIC and are very flexible due to its reprogrammable feature. Navid Azizi et al. [18] exploit FPGA technology for simulating Molecular Dynamics (MD). They show that FPGAs is a feasible technology to develop large-scale application specific computation, such as MD simulation and developed FPGA-based ASP (Application Specific processor) to calculate Lennard Jones force of MD simulation. Their platform is TM3 [23], which contains multiple interconnected FPGAs and consists of four Virtex-E 2000 devices connected to each other via 98-bit bidirectional buses. They propose effective organization (two arrays for position) of the memory and FPGA speed (100 MHz) to improve the performance 20 times better than software implementation (2.4 GHz P4). In longer simulations, the error in potential energy remained below 1% while kinetic energy differences between hardware and software were less than 5%.

Even if Navid Azizi et al. introduce FPGA-based ASP in MD simulation, they calculate only Lennard Jones force. Youngfeng Gu et al. [19] explore FPGA implementation for MD simulation and complete the calculation for non-bonded forces (Coulombic force and Lennard Jones force) of MD simulation. They apply the direct method [1] to calculate those forces and used Annapolis Microsystem Wildstar board Virtex-II XC2VP70-5 FPGA and simulate VP100, Xilinx Virtex-II Pro XC2VP100 -6 FPGA. They compare their FPGA implementation with 2.GHz Xeon CPU and shows it can be accelerated from 31 times to 88 times with respect to a software implementation, depending on the size of the FPGA and the simulation accuracy.

5 Implementation of Multigrid Method in FPGA

Since MG method is efficient and can be parallelized, many approaches for MD simulation are based on MG method. As we mentioned, most applications using MG method provide inconsistent accuracy by distribution of particles in molecules to be simulated and adjust the parameters unsystematically to get better accuracy. Multi-level Charge Assignment (MCA) method applies multi-level interpolation that adjusts the grid charge and charge distribution and achieves a simulation that is more accurate without much increasing calculation time.

In this section, we present our proposed architecture for FPGA based MD simulation with an efficient MG method, MCA.

5.1 Molecular Dynamics Simulation Architecture Design

We describe 7 steps to design FPGA-based MD simulator (Figure 3). Step 0 in Figure 3 is preprocessing density of fine grid in order to apply MCA to the grids which represent too many particles. Step 1 in Figure 3 is *MCA_Anterpolate* process that maps particle charges to the finest grid level. Step 2-Step 6 in Figure 3 is similar with the procedure of original MG method.

```
Step 0 : Preprocessing density of fine grid
Step 1 : MCA_ANTERPOLATE particle charges → C_Grid(1)
Step 2: WHILE K = 1 ..Max-1
        ANTERPOLATE C_Grid(K) → C_Grid (K+1)
Step 3 : COMPUTE energy values on C_Grid(Max)
Step 4 : WHILE K = Max .. 2
        INTERPOLATE E_Grid(K+1) → E_Grid(K)
        CORRECT E_Grid(K)
Step 5 : INTERPOLATE E_Grid(1) → particles energies
        CORRECT particles energies
Step 6 : COMPUTE forces and total energy
-----------------------------------------------------------------
* K level Charge Grid : C_Grid(K)   * K level Energy Grid : E_Grid(K)
* Finest charge grid : C_Grid(1)    * Finest Energy grid : E_Grid(1)
```

Fig. 3. MCA Algorithm for MCA method on FPGA

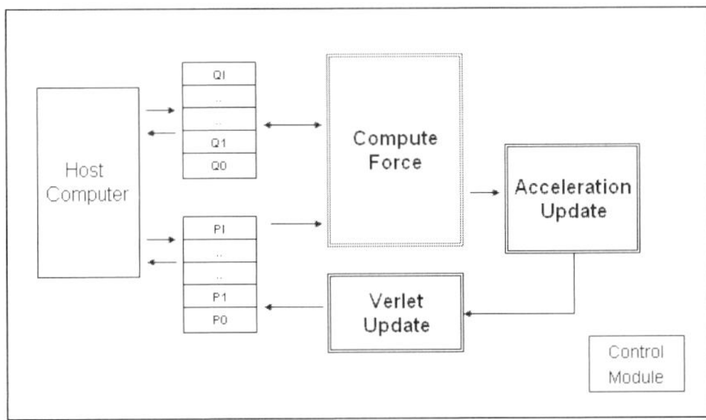

Fig. 4. Block diagram of MD simulator

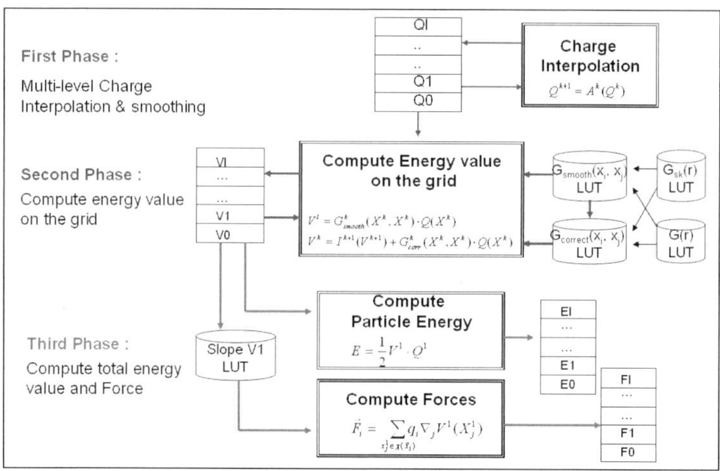

Fig. 5. *Compute Force* Block diagram of MD simulator

We consider the precision of proposed architecture since the precision of system affects arithmetic accuracy of MD simulation which is calculated by designed circuits. T. Amisaki et al. [25] examined many factors that affect the arithmetic accuracy of a dedicated accelerator that calculated non-bonded interactions. They found that the pair-wise force should be calculated with at least 29 bits of precision using coordinates that, in turn, should have at least 25. Our system is using 29 bits for the pair-wise force and 25 bits of precision for coordinates of particles.

Our system communicates with a host computer to update coordinates of particles during MD simulation. Figure 4 shows the top level of block diagram of the proposed architecture. The host computer stores coordinates and charges of particles in memory P0 and Q0 respectively. Also, it calculates density of the finest grid as a preprocessing step of MCA method. *Compute Force* block diagram is a main module to evaluate the forces and potentials using a Multigrid method. Once the forces are evaluated, *Acceleration Update* block accumulates the forces and *Verlet Update* block updates position and velocity of particles. We are using Verlet algorithm [24] to update the velocity.

Figure 5 shows the block diagram of *Compute force* module shown in Figure 4. It performs three phases; first phase is interpolation and smoothing which interpolate charge of particles to charge of finest grids and interpolate charge of grids to charge of coarser grid (steps 1 and 2 in Figure 3); second phase is computing energy value on the grids (steps 3, 4 and 5 in Figure 3); third phase is computing total energy value and force (step 6 in Figure 3).

Now having described the process for MD simulation, we will present its implementation for FPGAs.

5.2 FPGA Implementation for MD Simulation

We design an FPGA model using *SysGen* and *Simulink* on *Matlab* so that the model applies the Multigrid method to calculate non-bonded interactions. The target FPGA is Virtex-IV of Xilink Inc.

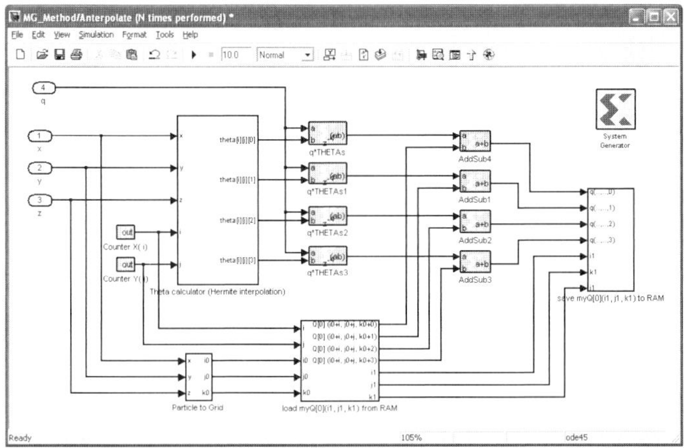

Fig. 6. *Anterpolate* module of Multigrid Model

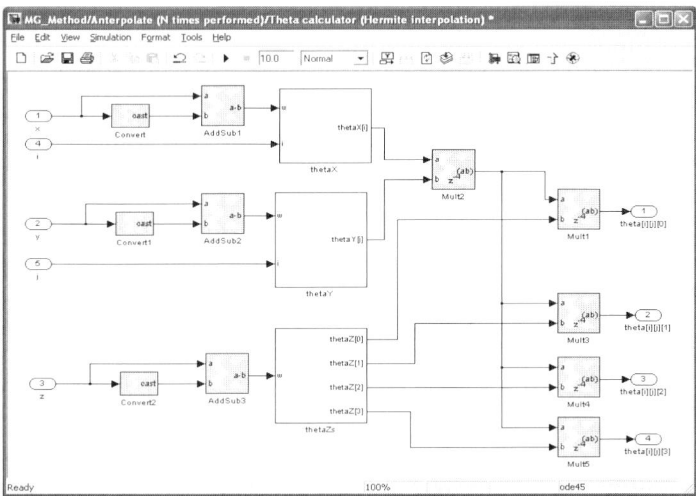

Fig. 7. *Theta calculator* module in *Anterpolate* module of MG Model

Figure 6 presents an *Anterpolate* module that assigns charges of particles to charges of the finest grids. Anterpolate step is the most time consuming part of Multigrid method and it takes $O(K{\cdot}N)$ calculation time, where N is the number of atoms in the MD simulation and K is a large constant that depends on the order of the interpolation function. *Anterpolate* module simulates 4th order Hermite interpolation and 3 grid levels. For each iteration of MD simulation, the module consumes 128 * N clock counts (each loop cycle consumes 128 sample periods). In Figure 6, we are using two counters (Counter X, Counter Y) instead of three for x, y, and z axis in order to reduce the sample periods. This results in an increase of logic units required, specifically 3 multiplier in *Theta calculator* module, but it improves the performance.

Figure 7 shows the *Theta calculator* module and the module provides all thetas for z axis in a subsystem (*thetaZs*) and reduces the sample period, but adds three multipliers. We could reduce theta calculation time to 32 * N clock counts (each loop cycle consumes 32 sample periods) by removing one counter and add 15 more multipliers.

The real calculation time of the MD simulation system depends on the speed of the processor. However, we reduce the floating point operations using table look-ups to calculate the interpolation functions and MCA method itself improves the performance and accuracy as Table 1 shows.

6 Conclusion

In this paper, we designed the architecture of FPGA-based MD simulation with an efficient MG method, MCA and implement an FPGA-based MD simulator. MCA provide an O(N) calculation time for accurate and efficient calculation of the electrostatic forces for MD simulation and gives consistent accuracy and reduces errors even if the distribution of particle is not balanced. Since FPGA is cheap and flexible compared to ASICs, this simulator based on MCA provide much faster calculation time and better accuracy. Currently, we have completed the design of the whole MD simulator, but have only implemented the *Compute Force Block* shown on Figure 4. As future work, we will complete implementations of other blocks in the proposed MD simulator. This will help provide the real calculation time to evaluate electrostatic forces with the FPGA implementation.

References

1. Rapaport, D.C.: The Art of Molecular Dynamics Simulation. Cambridge Univ. Press, Cambridge (1995)
2. Skeel, R.D., Texcan, I.: Multiple Grid methods for Classical molecular Dynamics. J. Comput. Chem. (2002)
3. Izaguirre, J.A., Matthey, T.: Parallel multigrid summation of the N-body problem (2004)
4. Rankin, W., Board, J.: A Portable Distributed Implementation of the Parallel Multipole Tree Algorithm. In: Proceedings, IEEE Symposium on High Performance Distributed Computing (1995)
5. Banerjee, S., Board Jr., J.A.: Efficient charge assignment and back interpolation in multigrid methods for molecular dynamics. Journal of Computational Chemistry, 26–29 (2005)
6. Sagui, C., Darden, T.: Multigrid methods for classical molecular dynamics simulations of biomolecules. Journal of Chemical Physics (2006)
7. Ewald, P.P.: Ann. Phys. Leipzig IV, 253 (1920)
8. Beckers, J., Lowe, C.P, De Leeuw, S.W.: Mol. Simul. 20, 369 (1998)
9. York, D., Yang, W.: The fast fourier poisson method for calculating ewald sums. J. Chem. Phys. (1994)
10. Briggs, E.L., Sullivan, D.J., Bernholc: Real-space multigrid-based approach to large-scale electronic structure calculations. Physical Review B 54(20) (1996)

11. Matthey, T., Izaquirre, J.: ProtoMol: A molecular dynamics framework with incremental parallelization. In: Proc. 10th SIAM Conference on Parallel Processing for Scientific Computing (2001)
12. Bernard, P., Gautier, T.: Large scale simulation of parallel molecular dynamics, Parallel and Distributed Processing. In: 13th International and 10th Symposium on Parallel and Distributed Processing (1999)
13. Sagui, C., Darden, T.A.: MOLECULAR DYNAMICS SIMULATIONS OF BIOMOLECULES: Long-Range Electrostatic Effects. Annual Review of Biophysics and Biomolecular Structure (1999)
14. Kaviani, A., Rown, S.: Hybrid FPGA architecture. In: Fourth International ACM Symposium on Field-Programmable Gate Arrays, pp. 3–9 (1996)
15. Komeiji, Y., Yokoyama, H., Uebayasi, M., Taiji, M., et al.: A high performance system for molecular dynamics simulation of biomolecules using a special-purpose computer. Journal of Computational Chemistry 20(2), 185–199 (1999)
16. Komeiji, Y., Uebayasi, M., Takata, R., Shimizu, A., Itsukashi, K., Taiji, M.: Fast and accurate molecular dynamics simulation of a protein using a special-purpose computer. Journal of Computational Chemistry 18(12) (1998)
17. Toyoda, S., Miyagawa, H., kitamura, K.: Development of MD Engine: High-Speed Accelerator with Parallel Processor Design for Molecuclar Dynamics Simulations. Journal of Computational Chemistry 20(2), 185–199 (1999)
18. Azizi, N., Kuon, I., Egier, A., Darabiha, A., Chow, P.: Reconfigurable Molecular Dynamics Simlator. In: 12th Annual IEEE Symposium on Field-Programmable Custom Computing Machines (FCCM'04), pp. 197–206 (2004)
19. Gu,Y., Tom, V., Martin, C.: Herbordt: Accelerating Molecular Dynamics Simulations with Configurable Circuits. IEE Proceedings on Computers & Digital Techniques (2006)
20. Amisaki, T., Fujiwara, T., Kusumi, A., Miyagawa, H., Kiamura, K.: Error evaluation in the design of a special-purpose processor that calculates nonbonded forces in molecular dynamics simulation. Journal of computational chemistry 16(9), 1120–1130 (1995)
21. Vaidyanathan, R., Trahan, J.L.: Dynamic Reconfiguration. Springer, Heidelberg (2004)
22. Cho, E., Bourgeois, A.G.: Multi-level Charge Assignment for Accurate and Efficient Molecular Dynamics (MD) Simulation. In: International Modeling and Simulation Multiconference (2007)
23. TM – 3 documentation: http://www.eecg.utoronto.ca/ tm3/
24. Allen, M.P., Tildesleley, D.J.: Computer Simulation of Liquids. Oxford University Press, Oxford (1987)
25. Amisaki, T., Fujiwara, T., Kusumi, A., et al.: Error evaluation in the design of a special-purpose processor that calculates nonbonded forces in molecular. Journal of computational chemistry 16(9), 1120–1130 (1995)

Performance and Complexity Analysis of Credit-Based End-to-End Flow Control in Network-on-Chip

Seongmin Noh, Daehyun Kim, Vu-Duc Ngo, and Hae-Wook Choi

System VLSI Lab, SITI Research Center, School of Engineering
Information and Communications University (ICU)
Yusong P.O. Box 77, Taejon 305-714, Korea
{noci1004,daehyunleft,duc75,hwchoi}@icu.ac.kr

Abstract. Network-on-Chip is an alternative paradigm to improve communication bandwidth compared to bus-based communication, and its performance degrades if there is no effective flow control method., Heterogeneous networks with very slow processing elements (PEs) especially need a flow control mechanism at the transport layer to prevent too much packet injection. In this paper, a credit-based end-to-end flow control (CB-EEFC) is implemented to control the network latency at high traffic loads. Simulation in mesh networks shows improved performance in latency and 0.5% up to 3% saturated throughput decrease with the CB-EEFC method. RTL gate level simulation shows that a network interface using CB-EEFC brings about a 31.4% increase in complexity compared to a network interface without CB-EEFC.

1 Introduction

Development in silicon technology will soon allow a single chip to integrate billions of transistors, functioning many processing units (such as CPU, DSP, other processors). In spite of this advance, bus has become a communication bottleneck for future SoCs. To solve this problem, Network-on-Chip (NoC) has been proposed [1]-[3] as a solution to provide better scalability, reliability and higher bandwidth compared to bus-based communication architecture. Fig. 1 shows a 4×4 mesh-based NoC that consists of sixteen processing units. These processing elements (PEs) communicate with each other through routers by packet-based communication. While the NoC architecture provides substantial bandwidth and concurrent communication capability; its performance can significantly degrade in the absence of an effective flow control mechanism as its traffic increases. Such flow control endeavors to avoid resource starvation and congestion in the network by controlling the flow of the packets which are competing for resources, such as links and buffers. In the NoC domain, the term flow control has been used in the context of switch-to-switch [3], [4], [5] or end-to-end [6] transport protocols. These protocols provide a smooth traffic flow by preventing buffer overflow and packet drops.

I. Stojmenovic et al. (Eds.): ISPA 2007, LNCS 4742, pp. 268–277, 2007.

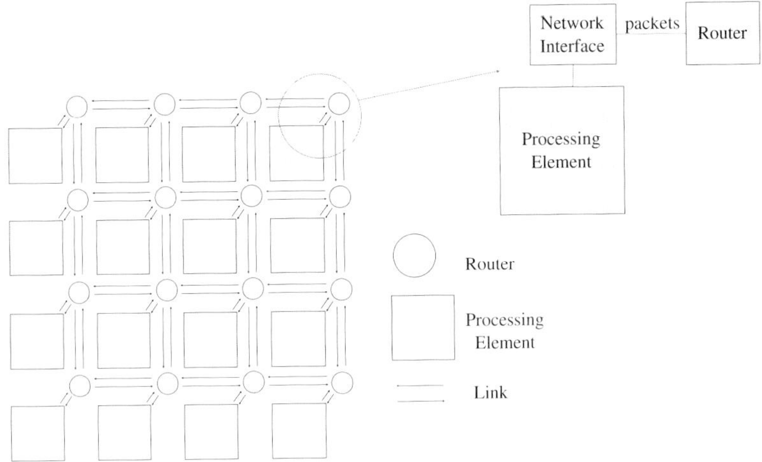

Fig. 1. NoC Block diagram: 4×4 mesh topology

This paper presents details of the use of the credit-based end-to-end flow control (CB-EEFC) method as one of the flow control mechanisms, and analysis of the performance and complexity of CB-EEFC in NoC is performed. The CB-EEFC between any two nodes in a NoC environment is implemented with network interfaces of two nodes and intermediate routers. In addition, their latency and throughput performance are examined together with the complexity of the network interface (NI). The rest of the paper is organized as follows. CB-EEFC is briefly reviewed in Section 2. Section 3 describes the router and network interface architecture used in the simulation. Performance analysis is presented in Section 4, and in Section 5, complexity analysis is made. Finally Section 6 presents the conclusion.

2 Credit-Based End-to-End Flow Control

In the transport layer, flow control is defined as any scheme by which the transport sender limits the rate at which data is sent over the network [7]. Two techniques are widely used in current transport layers, either alone or together, and they are credit- or window-based flow control and rate control. In credit-based flow control, the transport sender continues sending new data as long as space remains in the sending credit. In general, this credit may be fixed or variable in size. In fixed size credit control, ACKs from the transport receiver are used to get the transport sender's credit. CB-EEFC is widely used for computer networks, especially by TCP on Ethernet, and its theoretical performance has been analyzed in [8]. However, for network-on-chip architecture, this flow control is applied rarely [6] because of the large number of dedicated buffers for each peer-to-peer communication and the high complexity of the NI [9]. In credit-based flow control for each channel, as shown in Fig. 2, there is a counter (called 'space') that tracks the empty buffer space of the remote destination buffer. This counter is initialized with the remote buffer size. When data is sent from the source NI, the counter is decremented. When data is consumed by the destination PE at the other side, credits are produced in the remote NI (credit) to indicate that more empty space is available. These credits are sent to the producer of data to be added to its space counter.

Credit is piggybacked in the packet headers to improve efficiency, so credit is sent back to source when a response exists. If there is no response to the source and some amount (defined as 'threshold') of credit is accumulated, then a packet with only credit information is generated. This is called an 'empty credit packet'.

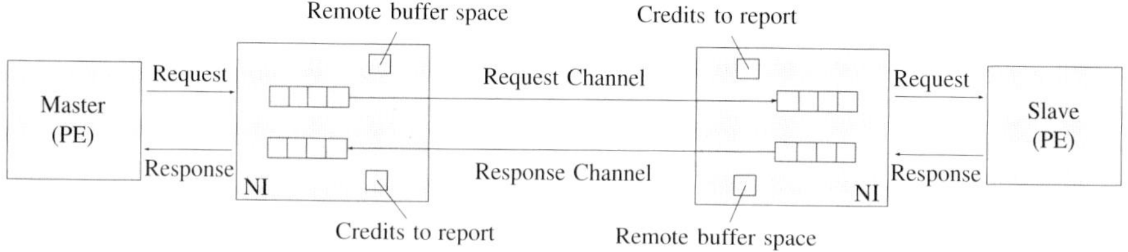

Fig. 2. CB-EEFC implementation

3 Implementation of CB-EEFC on NOC Architecture

To measure the performance and complexity of CB-EEFC flow control in NoC architecture, a NoC environment was employed, which used a hardware description language (HDL). The implementation architecture of the router and NI is described in 2 followings subsections.

3.1 Router Implementation

Fig. 3 illustrates a generic NoC router used in this work. The router has P input ports and P output ports, and its components are an input unit, routing computation unit, crossbar switch, and switch allocator. This router uses the wormhole switching method and an XY deterministic routing algorithm. Switch-to-switch flow control is also performed by credit-based flow control in the data link layer, which is in a different level than the transport layer CB-EEFC.

3.2 NI Implementation

Implementation of the network interface mainly followed Aethereal NI architecture [6] with CB-EEFC, but a different packet format was used. This NI converts Open Core Protocol (OCP) [10] messages of PEs to packets for the network. The NI also supports Guaranteed Throughput (GT) as well as Best Effort (BE) service, but details of its implementation are omitted since they are outside of the scope of this paper.

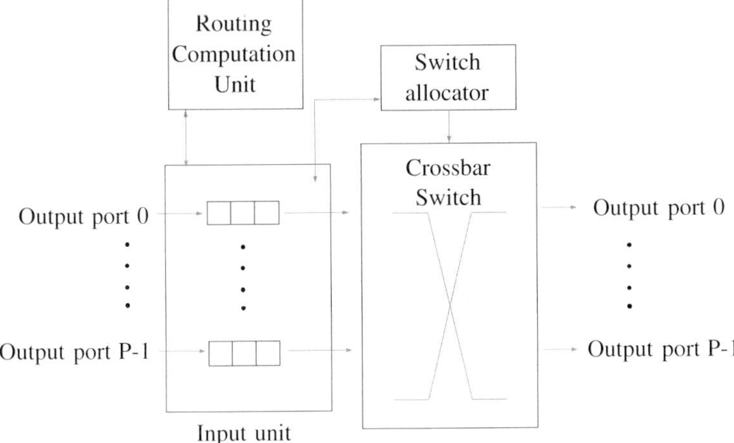

Fig. 3. Block diagram of generic router

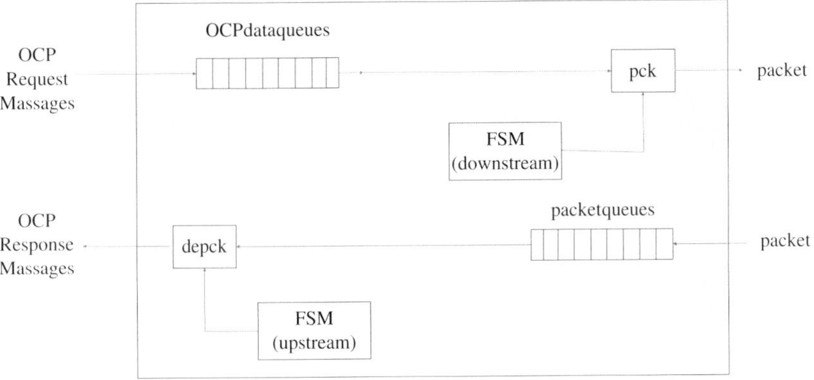

Fig. 4. Block diagram of NI without CB-EEFC

Fig. 4 shows the overall NI architecture without CB-EEFC. The components include two buffers for each stream (downstream and upstream), a packetizer, a depacketizer, and a Finite State Machine (FSM) for control. The FSM has several states, such as single read request, burst read request, single write request, and burst write request states according to the OCP data message or flit in the buffer. The information about states controls the packetization and depacketization functions in order to make proper flits or OCP data messages. A block diagram of an NI with CB-EEFC is displayed in Fig. 5, and credit-related data or control signal flow is indicated by the dotted lines. Following are some different aspects of an NI without CB-EEFC. Firstly, this NI architecture has buffers for each connection and an arbiter for selection of the processing buffer. For arbitration of queues, a matrix arbiter [11] is utilized to guarantee fair arbitration. The second point is regarding 'space' information in the

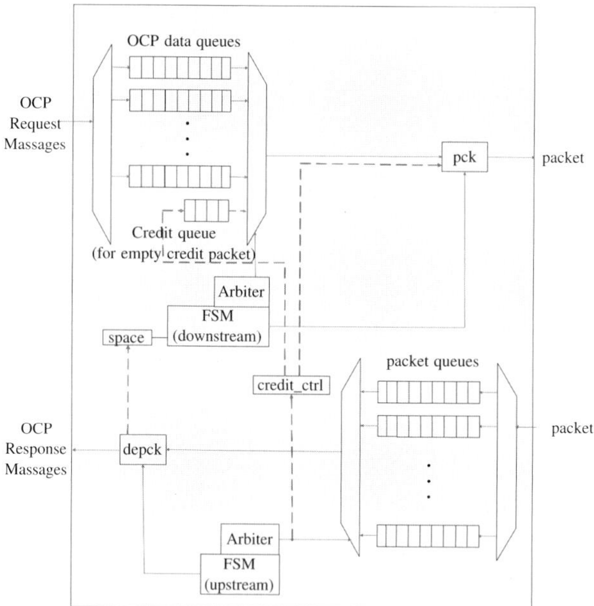

Fig. 5. Block diagram of NI with CB-EEFC

downstream FSM. As explained in Section. 2, this space information tracks the empty buffer size on the destination NI. When one flit is generated, then space value is decremented and it is recovered when credit is received. If value of space is smaller than the number of flits which will be made, then the FSM prevents the buffer from generating the packet in order to control traffic injection. Another important implementation is the credit_ctrl block for credit generation going upstream. Whenever a packet is processed (depacketized), the credit information is generated and accumulated in the credit_ctrl block. Then, this credit information is piggybacked to the source or transported by empty credit packets if the accumulated credit is greater than the threshold. A credit queue is used for buffering these empty credit packets. In addition, the FSMs, packetizer and depacketizer are revised to support generation and acceptance of empty credit packets. The FSM downstream is shown by Fig. 6. It displays the separated states according to the type of transfer (read/write, single/burst) and type of flit to make (head, body and tail flits). For readability of the state diagram, only the main arcs are drawn. Starting from the initial state, the state can change to four kinds of macro states (single or burst read/single write/burst write/empty credit packet) based on OCP data of the selected buffer after arbitration. Once the head flit is generated, consecutive body and tail flits are produced with positive edge of clock. Finally, after all data in the buffer are emptied, then the state returns to the initial state. All state transitions occur only when related space has a sufficient value to make packets. In this article, only the slave NI attached to a master PE is presented and a master NI attached to a slave PE are just counterparts of the slave NI which follows the same architecture.

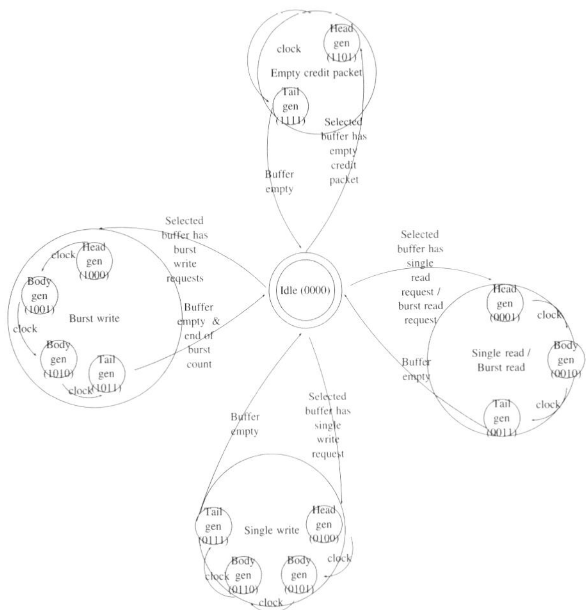

Fig. 6. State diagram of an NI with CB-EEFC (downstream of FSM)

4 Performance Analysis

4.1 Simulation Model

The performance of the network was simulated in a 3×3 mesh network with random traffic generators. Four master PEs generated exponential distributed traffic (OCP messages) with random destinations, and the five slave PEs accepted this requested traffic and generated responses to the master PEs. Moreover, the network assumed that there would be no dropping of packets using flow control between two adjacent routers. The buffer depth of the router was set to 4 flits. Basically, all kinds of end-to-end flow control methods show good performance, but only for heterogeneous networks. This means that the processing speeds of PEs are different. If the destination PE is slower than the source PE, then it degrades network performance due to the limited buffer at the destination NI. In this simulation, the speeds of the slave PEs were assumed to be 8 or 16 times lower than the master PEs.

4.2 Latency Performance

Fig. 7 and Fig. 8 show the latency performance of CB-EEFC and non-EEFC in a 3×3 mesh network. In these figures, the speeds of the slave PEs were assumed to be 1/8 and 1/16 times as fast as the speed of the master PEs, respectively. For a fair comparison, the NIs in the two simulations have the same amount of buffers with 128 flits. As shown in the two graphs, although the two methods show the same performance in the low load region, the CB-EEFC method has better performance in the high load region (a 3 cycle gap at 0.041 packet/cycle, one packet is generally composed of 4 flits). However, this improvement in terms of performance clearly appears only when slave PEs are very slow (about 1/16 the processing speed of the master PEs). Also, the CB-EEFC method does not allow the injection of inject data when the network is congested, so the network latency does not increase over 10 or 11 cycles. In the case of the non-EEFC network, the PEs generate traffic without considering network conditions, so the network latency can go upward to an infinite value.

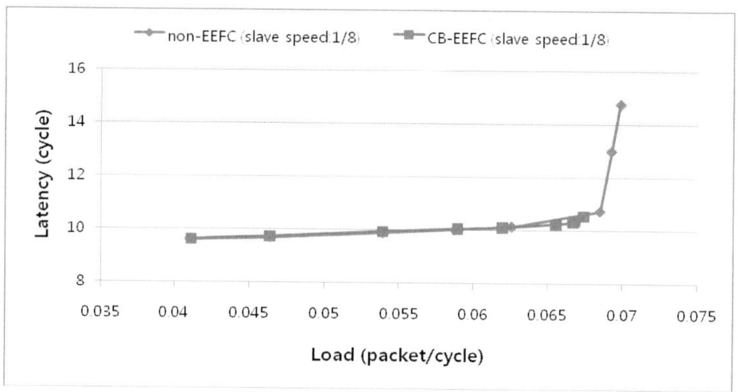

Fig. 7. Comparison of network latency between non-EEFC and CB-EEFC simulations (with slaves 8 times slower than masters)

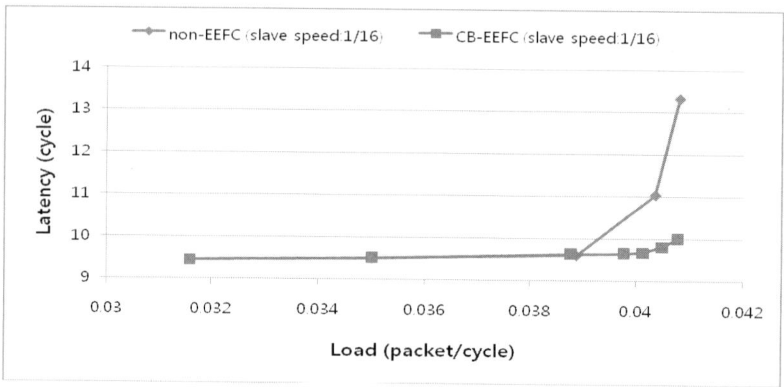

Fig. 8. Comparison of network latency between non-EEFC and CB-EEFC simulations (with slaves 16 times slower than masters)

4.3 Throughput Performance

Throughput performances for the CB-EEFC and non-EEFC methods in a 3×3 mesh networks are compared in Fig. 9 and Fig. 10. For throughput calculation, empty credit packets are excluded, hence only data packets are considered.

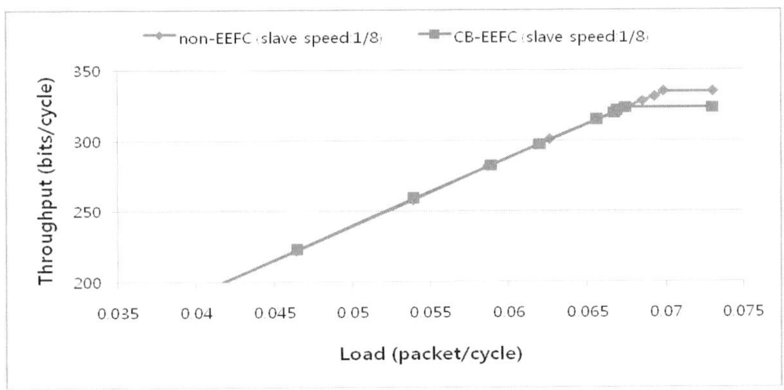

Fig. 9. Comparison of network throughput between non-EEFC and CB-EEFC simulations (with slaves 8 times slower than masters)

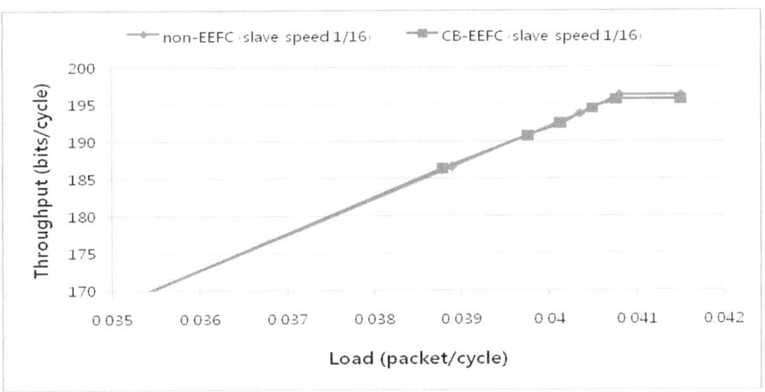

Fig. 10. Comparison of network throughput between non-EEFC and CB-EEFC simulations (with slaves 16 times slower than masters)

As shown in the figures, the two networks present the same performances at low and moderate load regions, but the CB-EEFC method has lower saturated throughput compared to the non-EEFC network. The amount of this low saturated throughput is about 0.5% up to 3%, and it is caused by the empty credit packet overhead of the CB-EEFC method.

5 Complexity Analysis

Two NIs (with CB-EEFC and without CB-EEFC) were implemented using HDL and synthesized with SMIC 0.18 um technology. The synthesis tool is the Synopsys Design Compiler. Table 1 presents the comparison of H/W complexity of the two NIs. The NI with CB-EEFC has a 31.4% increased complexity in terms of the area compared to the NI without EEFC. This increased complexity mainly comes from arbitration logic for several queues, space update logic and credit packet generation or acceptance logic in the packetizer and depacketizer.

Table 1. Complexity comparison of an NI with and an NI without CB-EEFC

Parameters	Radulescu, et. al [6]	NI without CB-EEFC	NI with CB-EEFC
Area	0.158 mm2	0.188 mm2	0.247 mm2
Max operating frequency	500 MHz	237.5 MHz	198.4 MHz
Latency	4 10 cycle	2 cycle	2 cycle
Remark	0.13um technology	0.18um technology	0.18um technology

6 Conclusion

In this paper, we implemented a router and network interface with credit-based end-to-end flow control, which can provide better performance in an NoC environment. By simulating two 3×3 mesh networks with heterogeneous processing elements, the performance and complexity of the CB-EEFC method were tested and the results analyzed. The CB-EEFC method shows latency-controlled characteristics and slightly low saturated throughput. In addition, the CB-EEFC method on a network interface has about 31.4% increased complexity as a penalty of the complex control logic. Therefore, CB-EEFC can be applied to a network which has slow PEs and needs the reduction of latency for a high network load.

References

1. Benini, L., et al.: Networks on chips: A New SoC Paradigm. Computer 35, 70–78 (2002)
2. Henkel, J., et al.: On-chip Networks: A Scalable, Communication-Centric Embedded System Design Paradigm. VLSI Design, pp. 845–851 (2004)
3. Dally, W., et al.: Route packets, not wires: On-chip interconnection networks. In: Proc. DAC (June 2001)
4. Jalabert, A., et al.: XpipesCompiler: A Tool for Instantiating Application Specific Networks on Chip. In: Proc. DATE (March 2004)
5. Zeferino, C.A., et al.: Paris: A Parameterizable Interconnect Switch for Networks-on-Chip. In: Proc. Symp. on IC and Systems Design (2004)
6. Radulescu, A., et al.: An Efficient On Chip NI Offering Guaranteed Services, shared-memory abstraction, and flexible network configuration. IEEE Trans. on CAD of ICs and Systems 24(1) (2005)

7. Iren, S., et al.: The Transport Layer: Tutorial and Survey. ACM Computing Surveys 31(4) (December 1999)
8. Arthurs, E., et al.: Theoretical Performance Analysis of Sliding Window Flow Control. IEEE Journal of Selected Areas In Communications SAC-1(5) (November 1983)
9. Micheli, G.D., et al.: Networks on Chip. Morgan Kaufmann, San Francisco (2006)
10. OCP International Partnership: Open Core Protocol Specification. 2.0 Release Candidate (2003)
11. Dally, W., et al.: Principles and Practices of Interconnection Networks. Morgan Kaufmann, San Francisco (2004)

An QoS Aware Mapping of Cores Onto NoC Architectures

Huy-Nam Nguyen[1], Vu-Duc Ngo[1], Younghwan Bae[2], Hanjin Cho[2], and Hae-Wook Choi[1]

[1] System VLSI Lab, SITI Research Center, School of Engineering
Information and Communications University (ICU)
Yusong P.O. Box 77, Taejon 305-714, Korea
[2] Basic Research Laboratory, ETRI, Daejeon, Korea
{huynam,duc75,hwchoi}@icu.ac.kr, {yhbae,hjcho}@etri.re.kr

Abstract. Network-on-chip (NoC) is being proposed as a scalable and reusable communication platform for future SoC applications. The NoC, somewhat, resembles the parallel computer network. However, the NoC design highly requires the certain satisfaction of latency, power consumption, and area constraints. The latency of the network relates much to throughput and power consumption. Moreover, the IPs and the network are heterogeneous. Hence, a certain mapping of IPs onto a certain architecture produces a certain value of network latency as well as power consumption. The change of mapping scheme leads to a significant change of the values of these constraints. The fact that if we want to maximize the system's throughput, the network latency also increases and if we minimize the network latency, the trade off is that the throughput will decrease. In this paper, we present an mapping scheme that does compromise between throughput maximization and latency minimization. This sub-optimal mapping is found using the spanning tree searching algorithm. The experiment architecture using here is Mesh based topology. We use NS2 to simulate and calculate the system throughput and system power consumption is calculated using Orion model.

1 Introduction

According to Moore's law, integration complexity doubles approximately every 1 to 2 years, so physical interconnections on chip are the bottleneck for performance because of delays on global wires [2]. As a pervasive interconnection fabric for on-chip communication, networks are gradually replacing buses and dedicated wires. Microprocessors and other computing resources connected by interconnection networks are widely deployed nowadays. The scalability and success of switch-based networks and packet-based communication in parallel computing and Internet has inspired the researchers to propose the Network-on-Chip (NoC) architecture as a viable solution to the complex on-chip communication problems [4]. Single chip multiprocessor systems are seeing network-on-chip as a scalable solution to communication [3]. Network-on-Chip designs have addressed the distinctive challenges of providing an efficient, reliable interaction among System-on-chip components. In the past, a low-latency and high-throughput network was the ultimate

I. Stojmenovic et al. (Eds.): ISPA 2007, LNCS 4742, pp. 278–288, 2007.

goal, resulting in prior network-on-chip designs being largely performance-driven. However, on-chip networks are also extremely power-constrained. The performance-driven design is no longer sufficient. How to map IPs onto the NoC architecture and route the packets around the network while optimizing some interest constraints like power or latency is critical in NoC design.

1.1 Related Works

Mapping application's IPs onto NoC architecture and routing information through the mapped network such that satisfies the bandwidth constraints and optimizes certain metrics like power consumption, latency or area are two important problems in NoC. In mapping problems, given an application described by a set of task and bounded to a list of IPs, designers have to decide how to map these selected IPs onto the network such that certain metrics of interest are optimized. In [6], Hu et. al. addressed the problem of IP mapping for regular NoCs. At that work, they proposed a branch and bound algorithm that map a given set of IPs onto a generic regular NoC architecture while minimizing the total communication energy. The performance of the system is also guaranteed to satisfy the designed bandwidth constraint. Similarly, Murali et. al. [7] propose a fast mapping algorithm for NoC architectures called NMAP that supports traffic splitting. This algorithm maps the core onto NoC architecture under bandwidth constraints, minimizing the average communication delay. This technique uses the average packet hop value as a cost function and relating it to the communication energy consumption. In [8], the authors also propose an mapping and deterministic routing algorithm called SUNMAP that is similar to the NMAP. The difference is that this system can automatically choose the NoC topology from the ones embedded inside it. However, the authors and research groups above did not address the currently hot issue of Quality of Service (QoS) such as throughput guarantee and latency guarantee. They also did not consider the drop packets inside the network which is the nature of packet based switching network. In addition, in their work, the power consumption was simulated with the homogeneous bit energy model but the fact that NoC system is heterogeneous. QoS issue, currently a hot topic in NoC design, was addressed by J.Nurmi [11] and it was also strongly mentioned by A.Ivanov and De Micheli [12] as an important design criterion of NoC in future. In this paper, we propose a QoS-aware mapping scheme that does compromise between throughput maximization and latency minimization. The experiment architecture using here is Mesh based topology. We use NS2 [10] to simulate and calculate the system throughput and system power consumption is calculated using Orion model [11]. The rest of the paper is as following: section 2 introduces some definitions and problem description; section 3 presents the QoS aware mapping and section 4 is simulation results and discussion.

2 Definitions and Problem Description

This section gives a formalism for application and architecture description.

2.1 Definitions

Definition 1:

Application Graph $G = G(V, A)$ is a directed graph, where each vertex $v_i \in V$ represents a selected core (IP), and each directed arc $a_{i,j} \in A$ represents the communication from core v_i to core v_j. Each $a_{i,j}$ can be tagged with application information and design constraints such as communication volume or communication bandwidth, latency requirements.
c($a_{i,j}$) is the communication volume (bits) of $a_{i,j}$
b($a_{i,j}$) is the bandwidth requirement for $a_{i,j}$

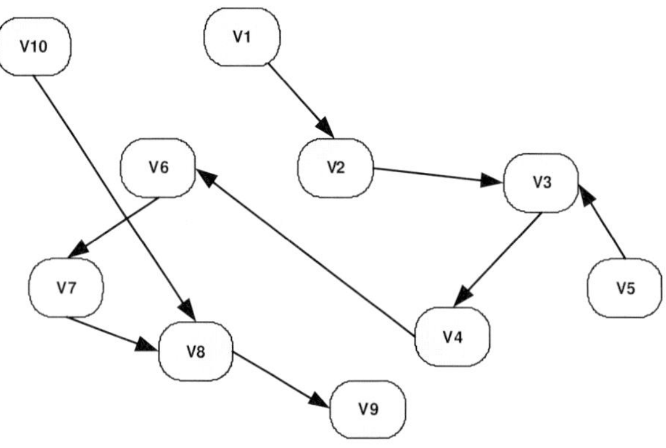

Fig. 1. Application Directed Graph G(V,A)

Definition 2:

Communication Architecture Graph $G(U, P)$ is a directed graph which describes the communication infrastructure. Each vertex $u_i \in U$ represents a node (or router)of NoC topology and each $p_(i, j) \in P$ represents the routing path from router u_i to router u_j. The routers and the paths in the network have attributes such as:
$\forall u \in U$, Ps(u) specifies the position of the router u
Ch($p_(i, j)$) is the set of channels that make up the path $p_(i, j)$
bw($p_{i,j}$) is the bandwidth available for $p_{i,j}$
$e\left(p_{u_i,u_j}\right) = E_{bit}^{u_i u_j}$ is energy consumption of sending 1 bit from router u_i to router u_j.

2.2 Mapping Problem

Mapping IPs to network topology is an important problem in NoC. Given an application described by a set of tasks, designers have to determine how to map the selected IPs onto the NoC architecture such that certain metrics are optimized. The problem can be formulated as follows:
Given an application graph $G = G(V, A)$ and a communication architecture graph $G(U, P)$, determine a mapping function:
$\mathrm{M} : G(V, A) \rightarrow G(U, P)$ such as:

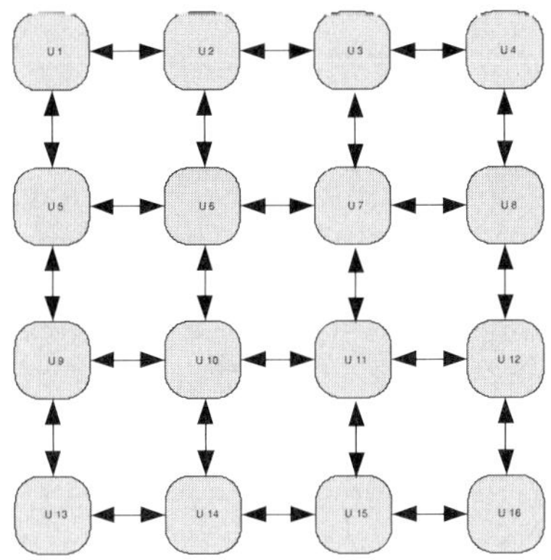

Fig. 2. Communication Architecture Directed Graph G(U,P)

- Each core $v_i \in V$ is mapped to a router $u \in U$
  $\mathrm{M}(v_i) = u_j, \forall v_i \in V, \exists u_j \in U$
  $\forall v_i \neq v_j \in V, \mathrm{M}(v_i) \neq \mathrm{M}(v_j)$
  $|V| \leq |U|$
- Optimize certain metrics:
  $\min(O(G(U,P), G(V,A)) \subseteq \{performance, energy, etc\})$
- Subject to the constraints requirement specified by:
  $Const(G(U,P), G(V,A)) \subseteq \{bandwidth, latency, area, etc\}$
  where $O(G(U,P), G(V,A))$ is a metric for performance, power or reliability of system while the constraints $Const(G(U,P), G(V,A))$ may be the amount of required constraints such as bandwidth, latency. Fig.3 is an example of mapping an application onto the 2D Mesh architecture.

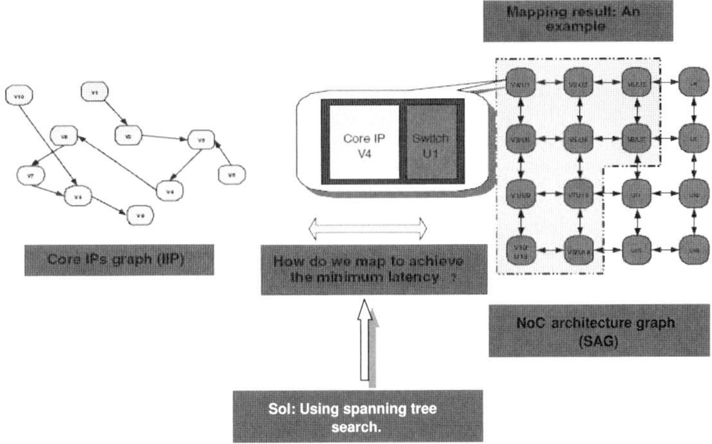

Fig. 3. Mapping example

3 QoS-Aware Mapping

In a heterogeneous system, a certain mapping of IPs onto a certain architecture produces a certain value of network latency as well as power consumption. The change of mapping scheme leads to a significant change of the values of these constraints. The fact that if we want to maximize the system's throughput, the network latency is also increase and if we minimize the network latency, the trade off is that the throughput will decrease. In this chapter we first analyze the network latency in term of queuing latency and then we use the spanning tree searching algorithm to find a sub-optimal QoS mapping scheme that does compromise between throughput maximization and latency minimization.

3.1 Latency and Throughput of NoC

The network latency is calculated by two components, queuing latency and wire latency. The queuing latency stands for the latency that occurs inside the network node (a combination of one switch and one mounted IP). While, the wire latency presents the latency occurs along the wires that connect every two neighbor switches. In this work, we just deal with the queuing latency. For the certain mapping scheme of the pre-connected IPs onto a pre-selected NoC architecture, the routing table will be determined accordingly to the used routing algorithm (with an given application, the connections between IPs are predetermined). By the known routing table, the network latency in terms of the queuing latency simply is calculated. The equation of queuing latency can be found in [13]:

$$L_{Net} = \frac{1}{m}\sum_{i=1}^{m}\left(\sum_{j}\frac{\sum_{i\in C_j}\lambda_i\frac{1}{\mu_j-\lambda_i}}{\sum_{i\in C_j}\lambda_i}\times\delta_{ij}\right) \tag{1}$$

where

$$\delta_{ij} = \begin{cases} 1, & if j^{th} node \in R_i, \\ 0, & otherwise. \end{cases} \tag{2}$$

Set C_j as the set of the incoming routes of the jth network node. m is the fixed number of routes belonging to the routing table. λ denote the arrival rate of the packet to the switch and μ is the mean of the processing rate of the network node.

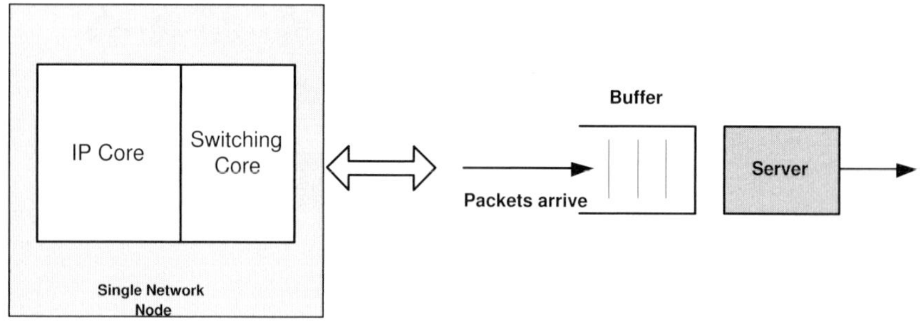

Fig. 4. Single node and Queuing model

Similarly, the network throughput equation can be drived [14]:

$$\mathcal{T_N}^{Opt} = max\left(\sum_{j=1}^{N}\left(\sum_{i=1}^{p^j}\left[\rho_i^{(k+1)}\frac{1}{p^j}\sum_{l=1}^{\varsigma_i}\lambda_{il}^j\right]\right)\right) \tag{3}$$

where ρ_i is the number of output ports of router:

$$\rho_i = \left(\frac{\sum_{l=1}^{\varsigma_i}\lambda_{il}^j}{\mu_j}\right) \tag{4}$$

The average processing time of the jth router is defined by $x_j = \frac{1}{\mu_j}$. We define the the arrival rates of the independent data flows that enter the ith input port of the jth router as $\lambda_{i1}^j, \lambda_{i2}^j, ..., \lambda_{i\varsigma_i}^j$, where ς_i denotes the number of data flows. The data flows can be generated from the certain IPs or the neighbor routers.

Straightforwardly, T_{Net} and $\mathcal{T_N}^{Opt}$ is the function of mapping IPs onto NoC architecture due to the fact that as the mapping scheme changes the given route between the two certain IPs changes accordingly. It follows that the network nodes belonging to this route are different compared to those of the other mapping schemes.

3.2 Sub-optimal Mapping Algorithm

Given an application graph $G = G(V, A)$ and a communication architecture graph $G(U, P)$ (already defined in previous section), an optimal mapping that minimize the network latency is a map:

Map : $G(V, A) \to G(U, P)$ such that:

$$L_{\min} = \min\left\{lat = \sum_{k=1}^{m}\left\{\left[\sum_j \frac{\sum_{i\neq j;i\in C_i}\lambda_i\frac{1}{\mu_j-\lambda_i}}{\sum_{i\neq j;i\in C_i}\lambda_i}\right]\delta_{kj}\right\}\right\} \tag{5}$$

The problem is that we need to find a sub-optimal mapping that compromises between throughput maximization and latency minimization. As presented

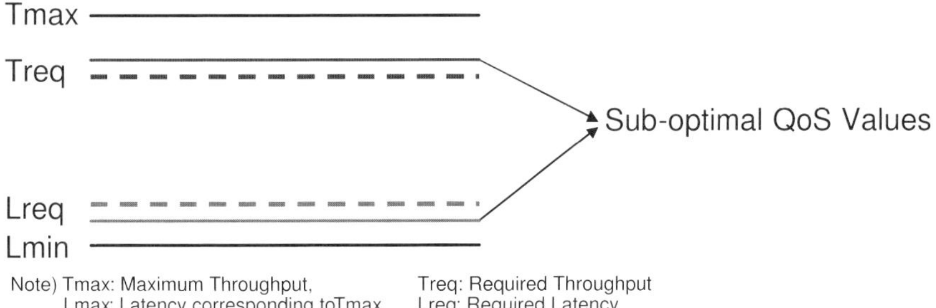

Fig. 5. Sub-Optimal QoS value

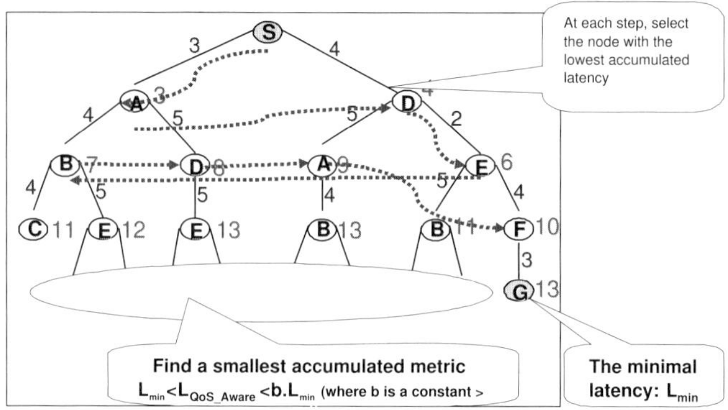

Fig. 6. Spanning Tree Algorithm

in Fig.5, our objective is to decrease the network latency to the value smaller than the required latency while trying to increase system throughput to the value greater than the required throughput. To do so we define a required latency: $L_{req} = b.L_{\min}$ (where b is a constant > 1). Then we use the spanning tree searching algorithm (Fig.6)to find out our proposed accumulated metric $L_{QoS-Aware}$ such that: $L_{\min} < L_{QoS-Aware} < b.L_{\min}$. We have to find out an QoS aware mapping that:

$\mathrm{QoS-Aware-Map}: G(V, A) \rightarrow G(U, P)$ such that:

$$L_{\min} < L_{QoS-Aware} < b.L_{\min} \tag{6}$$

4 Simulation and Discussion

In this chapter, we do the experiment with the H.264 decoder and the 4x4 Mesh NoC architecture. The switching technique is wormhole switch. Firstly, the cost function of latency:

$latency = \sum_{k=1}^{m} \left\{ \left[\sum_j \frac{\sum_{i \neq j; i \in C_i} \lambda_i \frac{1}{\mu_j - \lambda_i}}{\sum_{i \neq j; i \in C_i} \lambda_i} \right] \delta_{kj} \right\}$ is used to analytically calculate the latency and used in the spanning tree searching algorithm (written in C++) to find out the optimal latency mapping as well as minimum latency L_{min}. The inputs of this calculation are arrival rate λ_i (that is the data rates between IPs of H.264 decoder presented in Fig.7) and mean processing time μ (that is the time to transfer one flit through the router). Similarly, we find out the optimal throughput mapping and calculate the maximum throughput corresponding [14].

In case of throughput optimal mapping, the network throughput is maximum. We calculate the corresponding latency value ($L_{tmax} = 875\mu s$). In case of latency optimal mapping, the latency is $L_{\min} = 325\mu s$. Assuming that the required latency is $L_{req} = 500\mu s$ we get the constant $b = \frac{500}{325} \approx 1.54$. Then we need to find a mapping with minimal of sub-optimal latency group which satisfies: $L_{\min} < L_{QoS\_Aware} < L_{req}$.

H.264 decoder : Data transfer (단위 byte)

From/To	DB	MC	FR_MEM	ITIQ	LENT	VOM	processor	REC	MVMVD	IPRED	IS
DB	0	0	611.9596	0	0	0	0	0	0	0	0
MC	384.9207	0	29.69747	0	0	0	0	0	0	0	0
FR_MEM	227.9596	916.2545	0	0	5.401515	413.0909	0	3.410606	0	0	0
ITIQ	0	511.7301	0	0	0	0	0	55.26035	0	0	0
LENT	0	0	0	566.9904	0	0	35.05354	0	42.64444	0	0
VOM	0	0	0	0	0	0	0	0	0	0	0
processor	28.0101	27.70707	0	16.0303	20	1	0	0.59596	85.36364	5.106061	1
REC	27.6303	1.159596	2.302525	0	0	0	0	0	0	12.49773	0
MVMVD	0	0	0	0	0	0	71.23131	0	0	0	0
IPRED	0	0	0	0	0	0	0	27.6303	0	0	0
IS	0	0	5.401515	0	0	0	0	0	0	0	0

Fig. 7. Data Transaction between H.264 Decoder Blocks (Mbps)

On Chip Network model parameters	Applied NS2 constraint parameters
Switch architecture	Wormhole
Number of IPs	11
Transmission protocol	UDP
Packet size	8 bytes
Buffer size	8 packets
Queuing schemes	DropTail
Routing protocol	Deterministic
Traffic generator	Exponential

Fig. 8. NS2 Simulation environment

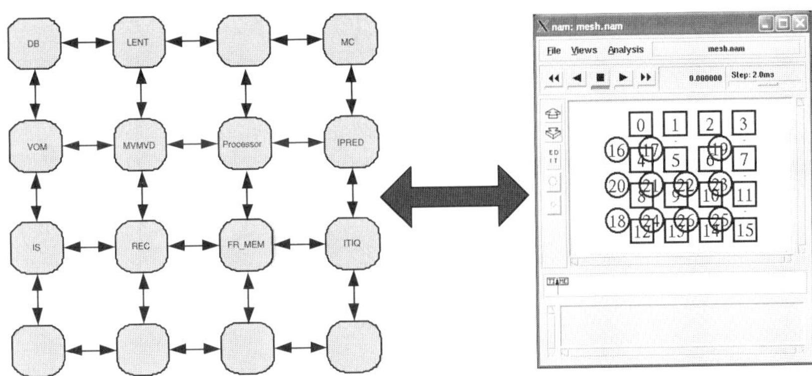

Fig. 9. Latency Optimal Mapping

Using spanning tree searching algorithm, we find out the proposed mapping that is shown in Fig.9. The corresponding latency of this QoS aware mapping is $L_{QoS\_Aware} = 416\mu s$. After having three kinds of mapping, we used NS2 to

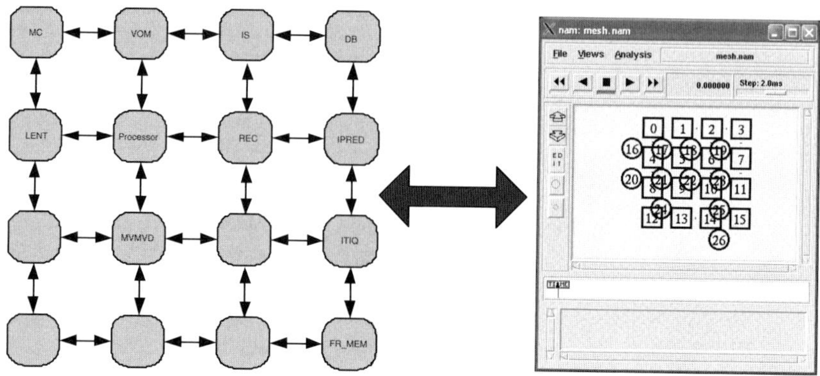

Fig. 10. Throughput Optimal Mapping

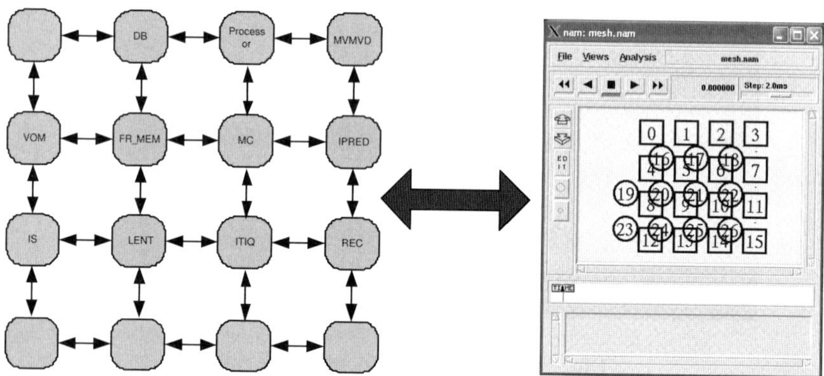

Fig. 11. QoS Aware Mapping

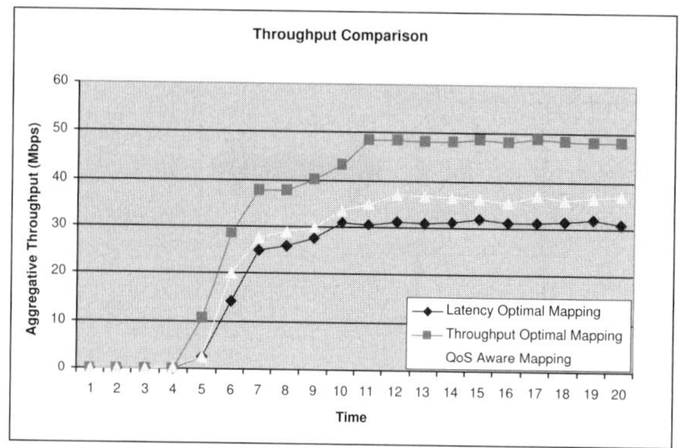

Fig. 12. Throughput Comparison of three Mapping Algorithms

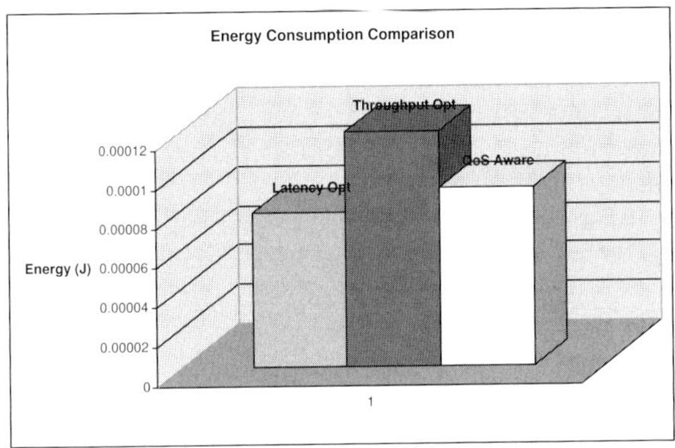

Fig. 13. Energy Comparison of three Mapping Algorithms

simulate and calculate the network throughput and total power consumption corresponding. The simulation environment is presented in Fig.8. Fig.12 depicts the throughput comparison and we can see that in our proposed mapping, the network throughput is quite greater than minimum throughput, about 19%. Fig.13 depicts the energy comparison of three mapping algorithms. These energy is calculated by counting all flits transfer through each nodes in the network including drop flits. In this work, we use Orion model [10] to calculate the heterogenous bit energy models of the different routers. The results show that our proposed mapping achieve small latency (53% compared to the maximum latency)while increase 19% throughput compared to the minimum case.

5 Conclusion

In this paper, we have been analyzed the average of heterogeneous NoC network latency in terms of the queuing latency. We also applied the Brand-and-Bound algorithm to find out the QoS aware mapping that automatically map IPs onto NoC architecture while compromising between throughput maximization and latency minimization. Our mapping algorithm decreases the network latency to the value smaller than the required latency while trying to increase system throughput. The results show that our proposed mapping achieve small latency (53% compared to the maximum latency) while increase 19% throughput compared to the minimum case.

References

1. Guerrier, P., et al.: A generic architecture for on-chip packet-switched interconnection. Design Automation and Test in Europe, 250–256 (August 2000)
2. Horowitz, M.A., et al.: The future of wires. Proceeding of IEEE 89(4), 490–504 (2001)

3. Benini, L., et al.: Networks On Chips: A new SoC paradigm. IEEE computer (January 2002)
4. Kumar, S., et al.: A network on chip architecture and design methodology. In: Proc. Symposium on VLSI, pp. 105–112 (April 2002)
5. Van der Tol, E.B., et al.: Mapping of MPEG-4 Decoding on a Flexible Architecture Platform. SPIE, 1–13 (January 2002)
6. Hu, J., et al.: Energy- and performance-aware mapping for regular NoC architectures. IEEE Trans. on CAD of Integrated Circuits and Systems 24(4) (April 2005)
7. Murali, S., et al.: Bandwidth-constrained mapping of cores onto NoC architectures. In: Proc. DATE (2004)
8. Murali, S., et al.: SUNMAP: A tool for automatic topology selection and generation for NoCs. In: Proc. DAC (2004)
9. Ns2: http://www.isi.edu/nsnam/ns/
10. Wang, H., et al.: Orion: a power-performance simulator for interconnection networks. In: Proc. Intl. Symp. on Microarchitecture, pp. 294–305 (November 2002)
11. Pande, P.P., et al.: Design, Synthesis, and Test of Network on Chips. Design and Test of Computer 22(5), 404–413 (2005)
12. Nurmi, J.: Network-on-Chip: A New Paradigm for System-on-Chip Design. SoC05, 2–6 (November 2005)
13. Ngo, V.-D., et al.: Designing On-chip Network based on Optimal latency Criteria. In: Yang, L.T., Zhou, X.-s., Zhao, W., Wu, Z., Zhu, Y., Lin, M. (eds.) ICESS 2005. LNCS, vol. 3820, pp. 287–298. Springer, Heidelberg (2005)
14. Ngo, V.-D., et al.: The Optimum Network on Chip Architectures for Video Object Plane Decoder Design. In: Guo, M., Yang, L.T., Di Martino, B., Zima, H.P., Dongarra, J., Tang, F. (eds.) ISPA 2006. LNCS, vol. 4330, pp. 75–85. Springer, Heidelberg (2006)

Latency Optimization for NoC Design of H.264 Decoder Based on Self-similar Traffic Modeling

Vu-Duc Ngo[1], June-Young Chang[2], Younghwan Bae[2], Hanjin Cho[2], and Hae-Wook Choi[1]

[1] System VLSI Lab, SITI Research Center, School of Engineering Information and Communications University (ICU) Yusong P.O. Box 77, Taejon 305-714, Korea

[2] Basic Research Laboratory, ETRI, Daejeon, Korea

{duc75,hwchoi}@icu.ac.kr, {jychang,yhbae,hjcho}@etri.re.kr

Abstract. In this article, we present analytical method to evaluate the NoC design of H.264 decoder's latency based on the self-similar traffic models of all 12 IPs. The traffic models are generated by using the superposition of four 2-state Modulated Markov Poisson Process (MMPP) and the real traced data transaction between IPs. The optimization engine is utilized to automatically allocate IPs on the desired routers to achieve the minimal latency.

1 Introduction

In [1], authors reported the optimal mapping of the general modeled processors onto NoC architecture with the latency constraint. However, this work was carried out based on Poisson traffic modelling. The reason for this traffic modelling is the simplicity and convenience in terms of implementation. However, the Poisson arrival process has a characteristic burst length that tends to be smoothed by averaging over a long enough time scale. In the other word, the Poisson process has short range dependent (SRD) characteristic. Rather, measurements of actual traffic indicate that noticeable bursts are present over a wide range of time scales. This fractal-like nature of H.264 decoder's traffic can be much better modelled using statistically self-similar processes, which have significantly different theoretical properties from the conventional Poisson process. The example of the comparison between Poisson and Self-similar process is depicted in Fig.1. Our application in this chapter is H.264 decoder. The characteristics of H.264 traffic are: Each frame includes a certain objects, all the macro blocks within a single object carries similar amount of data. Considering the data processed by each IP at the macro block level, they have almost the same number of data. Moreover, the macro blocks within an object occur next to each other in a frame. Therefore at frame level Traffic from each IP is generally similar. Consequently, self-similarity traffic is the appropriate model for modelling the real traffic. The self-similarity also is recognized by the autocorrelation of traffic (as function of time), it has the feature of long range dependent (LRD). The rest of the paper is as following: section 2 introduces some related works; section 3

I. Stojmenovic et al. (Eds.): ISPA 2007, LNCS 4742, pp. 289–302, 2007.

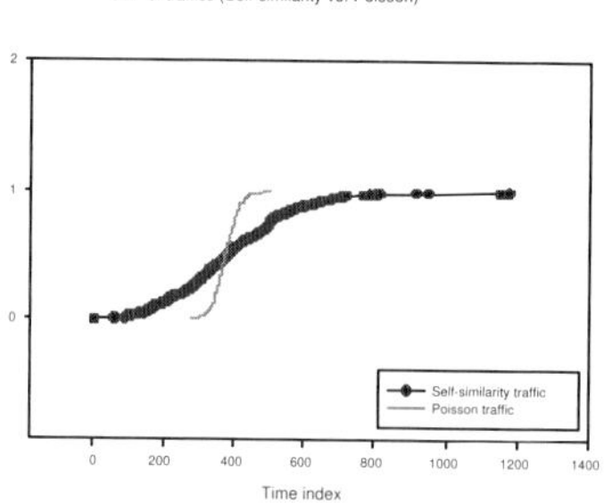

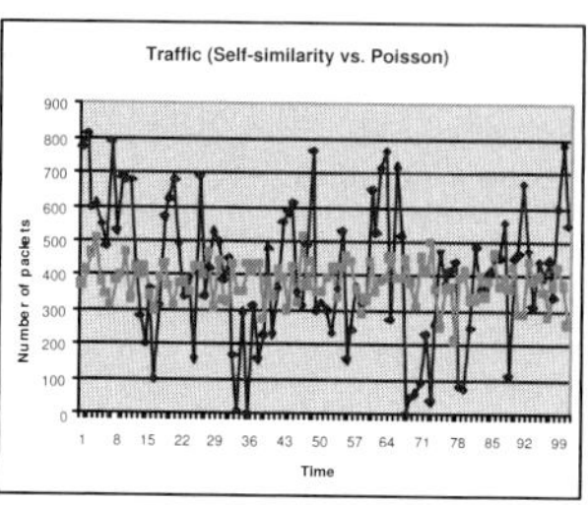

Fig. 1. Poisson process vs. Self-similar process

presents self-similarity traffic modelling for H.264 decoder; section 4 addresses the optimal latency mapping for H.264 decoder design; section 5 are simulation results and discussion and section 6 concludes our work.

2 Related Works

The authors in [2, 3] proposed the algorithms to automatically map IPs onto the target NoC architecture so as to optimize the power consumption. To do that, the authors used the same homogeneous bit energy model for their calculation of power consumption of whole network. The traffic model for their video application was model by Poisson process. Therefore, the behavior of network was not precise in terms of throughput and latency. These lead to the calculation of power consumption based on the amount of transacted data was also not precise. Recently, the authors in [4] reported their research of designing MPEG2 on NoC. They used the FGN process for representing the LRD characteristic of MPEG2 traffic. However, the FGN is shown to be not long dependent enough to present the video traffic even it is not difficult to implement. In [5, 6, 7], the superposition of MMPP (Modulated Markov Poisson Process) is proposed to present the self-similarity of data traffic in the domain of LAN network. It is also proven to be better than FGN to model the traffic of multimedia applications. G. Min et al.[11] reported the interesting result on performance evaluation of the self-similarity traffic on interconnection network. However, the architecture that they used was homogenous and therefore they did not solve the optimization for throughput and latency, consequently.

Hence in this chapter, we introduce the queuing based calculation for the network throughput and latency of NoC architecture to precisely achieve the exact amount of network traffic as well as latency. The analytical calculations are done with the MMPP traffic modelling of real trace traffic of H.264 decoder. We carry out the Self-similarity traffic modelling for H.264 traffic to best fit the real traffic. This work is done by synthesizing between trace traffic and modelled traffic. Network performance evaluation of throughput and latency are worked out by doing simulation of MMPP self-similar traffic of H.264 on 2D Mesh architecture.

Find out a mapping schemes that: maximize architectures throughput, minimize architectures latency.

2.1 Hurst Parameter

Self-similarity is measured by the Hurst-parameter H. H represents the burstiness of traffic and is a value between 0 and 1. It has been shown that the level of self-similarity in video traffic actually ranges from 0.7 to 0.98. Self-similarity can also be determined by looking at several functions. The first function is the autocorrelation function as:

$$r(k) \sim k^{-\beta} X(t) \tag{1}$$

as $k \to \infty ; 0 < \beta < 1$ and

$$\lim_{t \to \infty} \frac{X(tu)}{X(t)} = 1, \text{for} \forall u > 0. \tag{2}$$

This shows that looking at traffic at different times shows that there is a long-range dependence or correlation between the time-divisions. The second function is exactly second-order self-similar as:

$$\begin{cases} \operatorname{var}\{X(m)\} = \sigma^2 m^{-\beta}, \forall m = 1, 2, ... \\ r^m(k) = r(k), \forall k > 0. \end{cases} \tag{3}$$

The symbol m in above equation denotes the time block. This show that as all the time blocks m are added up, they equal the original time series. The third function is asymptotically second-order self-similar as: $r^m(k) = r(k)$ as $m \to \infty$. Finally, the value of H is calculated by

$$H = 1 - \beta/2. \tag{4}$$

The results of Leland's and Wilson's research [8] served to show the self-similar nature of network traffic. These results are irrespective of where or when the data is collected. They showed that the degree of self-similarity is measured in terms of the Hurst parameter H, which is typically a function of the overall utilization of the network. The discrepancy of a random process X_k is called discrepancy. To measure it, the R/S static value is used.

$$\begin{aligned} &E[R(n)/S(n)] = cn^H \\ &where: \\ &R(n) = \max(0, W_0, ..., W_n) - \min(0, W_0, ..., W) \\ &S^2(n): \text{is the sample variance} \\ &W_k = \sum_{i=1}^{n} X_i - k\overline{X}_n, \text{for } k = \overline{1..n} \\ &n: \text{block size} \end{aligned} \tag{5}$$

3 Self-similarity Traffic Modelling for H.264 Decoder

In this section, we analyze how MMPP traffic can be generated to best fit the traced traffic. At first, according to [9], we can model the self-similar traffic by the superposition of L two-state of MMPP. The mathematical model is presented as follows:

$$\begin{cases} \Lambda_{IP} = \Lambda_1 \oplus \Lambda_2 \oplus .... \oplus \Lambda_L \oplus \lambda_{IP} \\ R_{IP} = R_1 \oplus R_2 \oplus .... \oplus R_L \end{cases} \tag{6}$$
$$\oplus : \text{Kronecker sum}$$

Where the ith stage of MMPP is given by:

$$\Lambda_i = \begin{bmatrix} \lambda_{i1} & 0 \\ 0 & \lambda_{i2} \end{bmatrix}, R_i = \begin{bmatrix} -r_{i1} & r_{i1} \\ r_{i2} & -r_{i2} \end{bmatrix}, i = \overline{1..L} \tag{7}$$

The R_i is the infinitesimal matrix at i^{th} stage, meanwhile, λ_{i1}, and λ_{i2} are the arrival rates of first state and second state at i^{th} stage. In this chapter, we use the synthesis procedure between MMPP modeled traffic and traced H.264 decoder traffic as Fig.2.

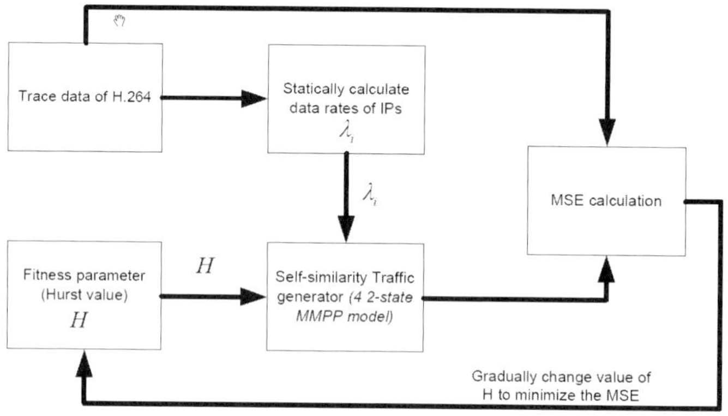

Fig. 2. Self-Similar traffic generation model

The MSE calculation of modeled traffic and traced traffic allows us to ensure the best fitness between them. The feedback in this calculation is done based on changing value of H. It follows that the values of λ_{i1}, and λ_{i2} and r_{i1}, and r_{i2} will change accordingly. The iterative process is stopped when MSE is minimum. As can be seen in Fig.2, we set value of $L = 4$. This is due to the complexity of calculation would increase 2^L when we increase L. Indeed, more big L is the more precise of modeled traffic compared to traced traffic is obtained. The modeled traffic of the IPs of H.264 decoder are generated by using algorithm in [9]. This algorithm is applied for statistically traced data. In this section, we report several experiments of generating traffic of several IPs such as DMA, IPRED, MVMVD, and MC. The traced traffic of DMA and its modeled traffic are shown in Fig.3 and Fig.4, respectively.

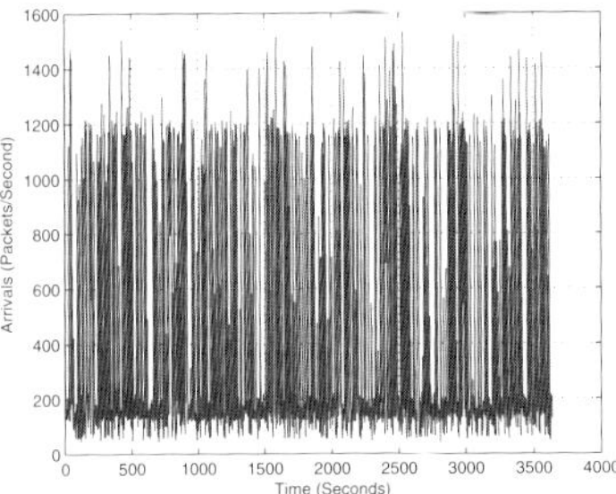

Fig. 3. Traced traffic of DMA

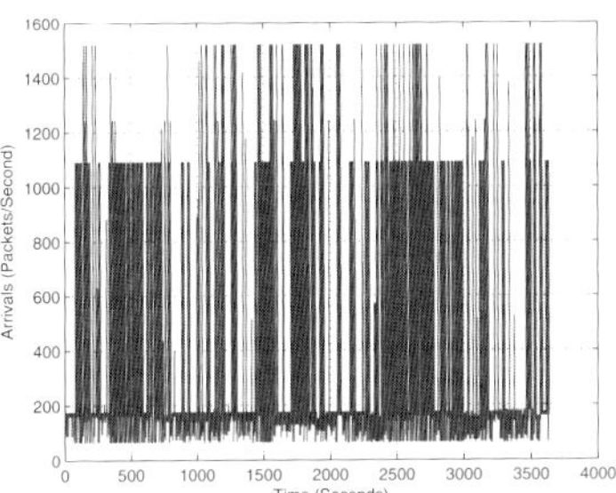

Fig. 4. Modeled traffic of DMA

Table 1. MMPP parameters of modeled DMA traffic

λ_i	r_{1i}	r_{2i}
127.91	0.01	0.79
102.87	2.3e-4	0.017
40.19	5.05e-6	3.6e-4
56.73	1.09e-7	7.9e-6

The Hurst value $H = 0.85$, $MSE = 0.001$ and the $\lambda_{IP} = 310$. The MMPP values are respectively depicted in Table 1.

We also can compare the similarity of the traced traffic and modeled traffic by the *Quantile* function. This function shows how similar of two random processes in terms of distribution. The *Quantile* of two DMA traffics is shown in Fig.5. The blue line stands for the modeled DMA traffic.

We repeat the traffic generation for the other IPs such as MC, IPRED and MVMVD. Their traced and modeled traffics are shown in Fig.6 - Fig.11 .

MC: The Hurst value $H = 0.83$, $MSE = 3.26$ and the $\lambda_{IP} = 103$. The MMPP values are respectively depicted in Table.2.

IPRED: The Hurst value $H = 0.80$, $MSE = 0.53$ and the $\lambda_{IP} = 12.9$. The MMPP values are respectively depicted in Table.3.

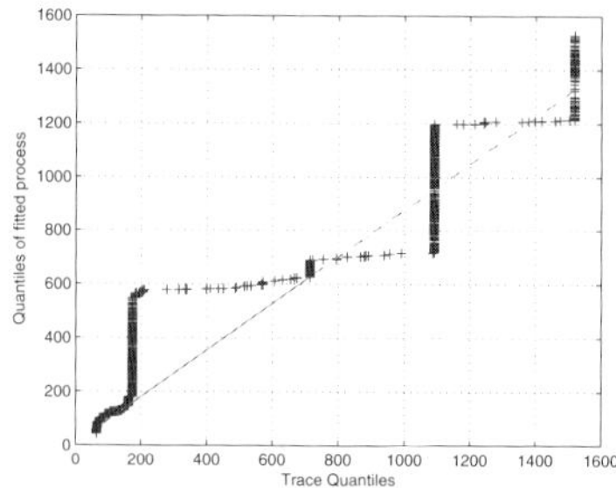

Fig. 5. Quantile function of two DMA traffics

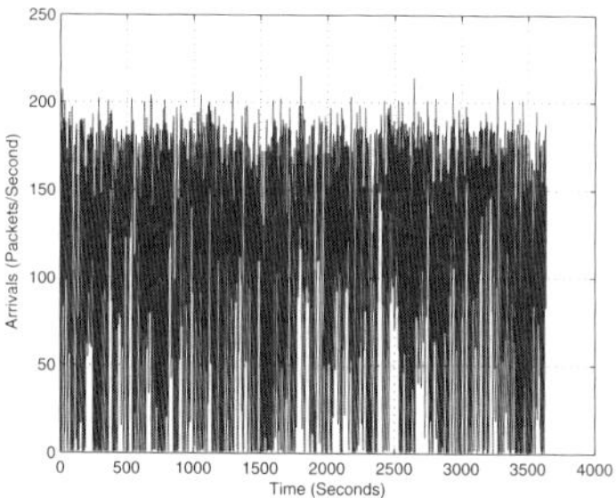

Fig. 6. Traced traffic of MC

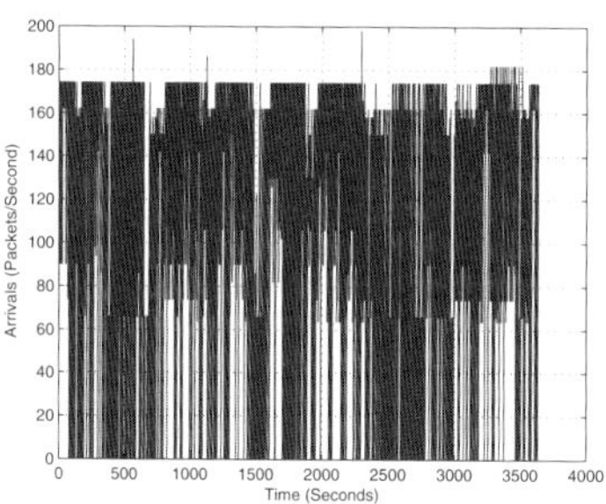

Fig. 7. Modeled traffic of MC

Table 2. MMPP parameters of modeled MC traffic

λ_i	r_{1i}	r_{2i}
56.175	0.04	0.76
28.107	8.6e-4	0.016
12.16	1.86e-5	3.5e-4
12.001	4.01e-7	7.6e-6

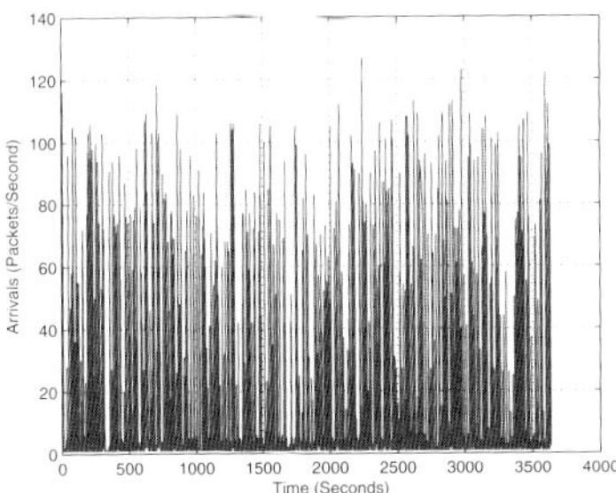

Fig. 8. Traced traffic of IPRED

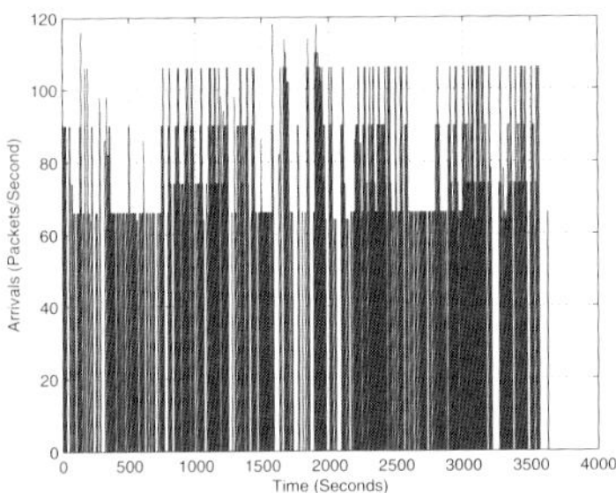

Fig. 9. Modeled traffic of IPRED

Table 3. MMPP parameters of modeled IPRED traffic

λ_i	r_{1i}	r_{2i}
10.29	0.23	0.56
4.70	5e-3	0.012
2.00	1.1e-4	2.6e-4
1.42	2.35e-6	5.6e-6

Table 4. MMPP parameters of modeled MVMVD traffic

λ_i	r_{1i}	r_{2i}
11.37	0.04	0.6
5.69	0.2	0.013
2.46	9.2e-5	2.8e-4
2.42	2e-6	6e-6

MVMVD: The Hurst value $H = 0.83$, $MSE = 0.27$ and the $\lambda_{IP} = 16.5$. The MMPP values are respectively depicted in Table 4. The other remaining IPs are similarly modeled as aforementioned 4 IPs. Finally, we can have the self-similar traffic models of all 12 IPs for the performance evaluation work which is done in the next section.

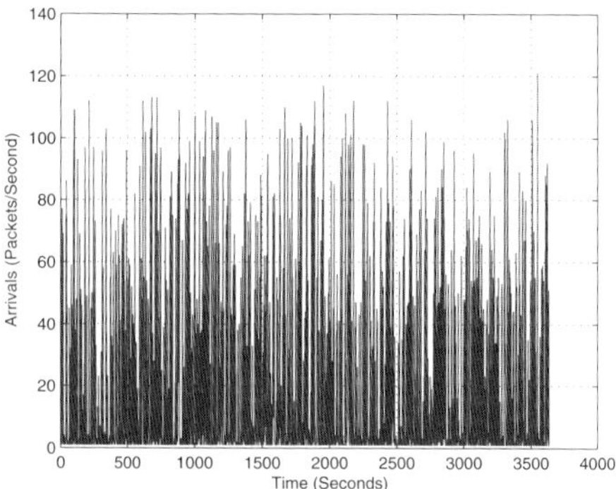

Fig. 10. Traced traffic of MVMVD

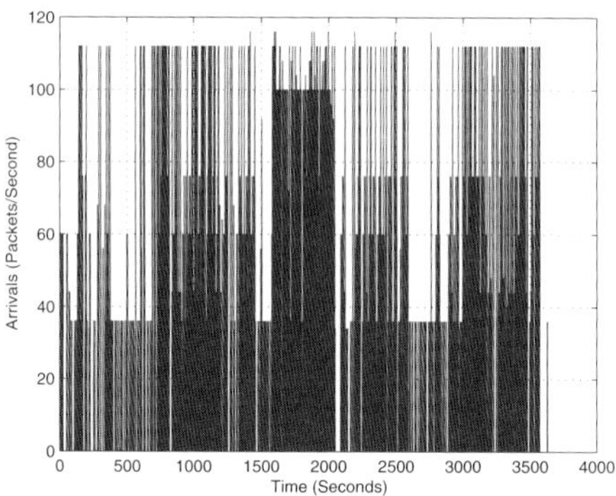

Fig. 11. Modeled traffic of MVMVD

4 Optimal Latency Mapping for H.264 Decoder Design

In this section, we analyze the network latency in terms of queuing latency. The difference from [1] is that the IP is modeled by MMPP. As mentioned previously, the characteristic of self-similar traffic affects very much on network performance, especially the network latency. Similar to previous subsection, we consider the combination of an IP and a router as a single server. From [10], the waiting time function $W(t)$ of this server can be presented by:

$$W(t) = (1-\rho)\, g - \int_0^t W(x)\, dx R_{IP} + \int_0^t W(t-u)\left[1 - H(u)\right] du \Lambda_{IP}. \quad (8)$$

Where ρ denotes the load and is given by:

$$\rho = \pi \lambda_{IP} E\left\{H(t)\right\}. \quad (9)$$

$H(t)$ is the distribution function of the waiting time of router. To calculate $W(t)$ as equation (8), the vector g must be known. We can calculate this vector through the following equation.

$$\begin{cases} gG = g \\ ge = 1. \end{cases} \tag{10}$$

The G matrix in the above equation is recursively obtain by the following steps [4].

– Initial step:

$$\begin{array}{l} G_0 = 0; F_{0,k} = I, k = 0, 1, 2, ... \\ \Theta = \max\limits_i \left(\left(\Lambda_{IP} - R_{IP} \right)_{ii} \right), \\ \gamma_n = \int_0^\infty e^{\Theta t} \frac{(\Theta x)^n}{n!} dH(t); n = 0, 1, ..., n^* \text{and} \sum\limits_{k=1}^{n^*} \gamma_k > 1 - \varepsilon_1, \\ \varepsilon_1 << 1 \end{array}$$

– Recursive:

$$\begin{array}{l} F_{n+1,k} = \left[I + \frac{1}{\Theta} \left(R_{IP} - \Lambda_{IP} + \Lambda_{IP} G_k \right) \right] F_{n,k}; n = 0, 1, ..., n^* \\ G_{k+1} = \sum\limits_{n=0}^{n^*} \gamma_n F_{n,k} \end{array}$$

– Stopping criteria

$$\|G_{k+1} - G_k\| < \varepsilon_2 << 1$$

We can realize that this stopping criteria ensures that the matrix G does converge.

We also can calculate the transform of waiting time function by taking the laplace transform of equation (8) as follows:

$$\begin{array}{l} W(s) = L\{W(t)\} \\ = \int_0^\infty W(t) e^{-st} dt \\ = \int_0^\infty \left\{ \begin{array}{l} (1-\rho) g - \\ \int_0^t W(x) dx R_{IP} + \int_0^t W(t-u) [1 - H(u)] du \Lambda_{IP} \end{array} \right\} e^{-st} dt \\ = \begin{cases} s(1-\rho) g \left[sI + R_{IP} - \Lambda_{IP} (1 - H(s)) \right]^{-1}, \text{for } s > 0, \\ \pi, \text{for } s = 0. \end{cases} \end{array} \tag{11}$$

$H(s)$ in above equation stands for the laplace transform of the distribution function $H(t)$. To figure out the latency of one given route or entire network, we need to calculate the mean value of $W(t)$. Let define it by $\bar{w} = E\{W(t)\}$. And we have:

$$\bar{w} = \frac{1}{2(1-\rho)} \left[\begin{array}{l} 2\rho + \chi E\{H^2(t)\} - \\ 2E\{H(t)\} \left((1-\rho) g + E\{H(t)\} \pi \Lambda_{IP} \right) \times \\ \left(R_{IP} + e\pi \right)^{-1} \pi^{-1} \chi. \end{array} \right] \tag{12}$$

The χ in above equation can be represented by:

$$\chi = \pi \left(\Lambda_{IP}^{1,1}, \Lambda_{IP}^{2,2}, ..., \Lambda_{IP}^{2^L, 2^L} \right)^T, \tag{13}$$

and if $\rho = \pi \lambda_{IP} E\{H(t)\} = \pi \lambda_{IP} \mu_{router}$, then finally we obtain:

$$\bar{w} = \frac{1}{2(1-\rho)} \begin{bmatrix} 2\rho + \chi\mu^{(2)}_{router} - \\ 2\mu_{router}\left((1-\rho)g + \mu_{router}\pi\Lambda_{IP}\right) \\ (R_{IP} + e\pi)^{-1}\pi^{-1}\chi \end{bmatrix} \tag{14}$$

We realize that if μ_{router} is constant value, then $\mu^{(2)}_{router} = 0$. Therefore equation (V.29) can be simplified as follow:

$$\bar{w} = \frac{1}{2(1-\rho)} \begin{bmatrix} 2\rho - \\ 2\mu_{router}\left((1-\rho)g + \mu_{router}\pi\Lambda_{IP}\right) \\ (R_{IP} + e\pi)^{-1}\pi^{-1}\chi \end{bmatrix} \tag{15}$$

The latency behavior of a single server with the IP of the modeled traffic of DMA is depicted in Fig.12.

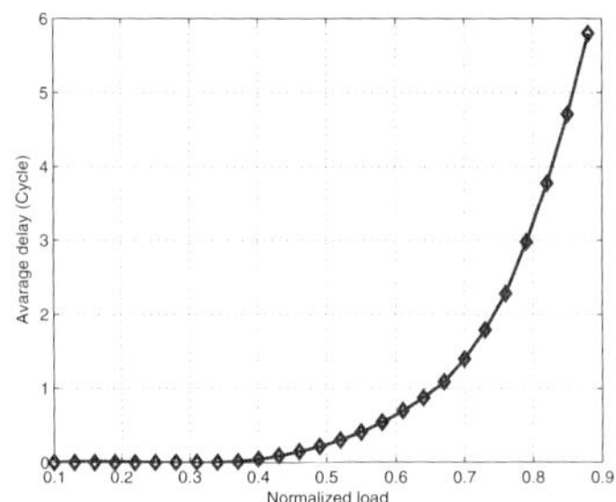

Fig. 12. Latency of a single server

For the case of complex node, in which several data streams $\lambda^{1,j}_{IP}, \lambda^{2,j}_{IP}, ..., \lambda^{C_j,j}_{IP}$ are independently associated, the mean of nodes latency is formulated by:

$$\begin{aligned} \bar{w}^{IP,complex} &= \frac{1}{2\left(1-\mu^{j}_{router}\sum_{i=1}^{C_j}\lambda^{i,j}_{IP}e\right)} \times \\ &\begin{bmatrix} 2\mu^{j}_{router}\sum_{i=1}^{C_j}\Lambda^{i,j}_{IP}e + \chi\mu^{(2),j}_{router} - 2\mu^{j}_{router} \\ \left(\left(1-\mu^{j}_{router}\sum_{i=1}^{C_j}\Lambda^{i,j}_{IP}e\right)g + \mu^{j}_{router}\pi\sum_{i=1}^{C_j}\Lambda^{i,j}_{IP}\right) \\ \left(\sum_{i=1}^{C_j}R^{i,j}_{IP} + e\pi\right)^{-1}\pi^{-1}\chi \end{bmatrix} \end{aligned} \tag{16}$$

C_j in above equation is the number of data flows enter the jth node. For a certain k^{th} route, the mean of route's latency is consequently given by:

$$\begin{aligned} \bar{w}^{k}_{route} &= \sum_{j\in route_k} \bar{w}^{IP,complex}_{j} \times \delta_{jk} \\ &= \sum_{j\in route_k} \left\{ \begin{aligned} &\frac{1}{2\left(1-\mu^{j}_{router}\sum_{i=1}^{C_j}\lambda^{i,j}_{IP}e\right)} \times \\ &\begin{bmatrix} 2\mu^{j}_{router}\sum_{i=1}^{C_j}\Lambda^{i,j}_{IP}e + \chi\mu^{(2),j}_{router} - 2\mu^{j}_{router} \\ \left(\left(1-\mu^{j}_{router}\sum_{i=1}^{C_j}\Lambda^{i,j}_{IP}e\right)g + \mu^{j}_{router}\pi\sum_{i=1}^{C_j}\Lambda^{i,j}_{IP}\right) \\ \left(\sum_{i=1}^{C_j}R^{i,j}_{IP} + e\pi\right)^{-1}\pi^{-1}\chi \end{bmatrix} \end{aligned} \right\} \times \delta_{jk} \\ &= f\left(\lambda^{i,j}_{IP}, \Lambda^{i,j}_{IP}, R^{i,j}_{IP}, \mu^{j}_{router}\right) \end{aligned} \tag{17}$$

We assume that there are totally m routes, finally the mean of the entire network latency is presented by:

$$\begin{aligned} L_{Net} &= \sum_{k=1}^{m} \bar{w}_{route}^{k} \\ &= \sum_{k=1}^{m} \left[\sum_{j \in route_k} \left\{ \begin{array}{l} \frac{1}{2\left(1-\mu_{router}^{j} \sum_{i=1}^{C_j} \lambda_{IP}^{i,j} e\right)} \times \\ \left[\begin{array}{l} 2\mu_{router}^{j} \sum_{i=1}^{C_j} \Lambda_{IP}^{i,j} e + \chi \mu_{router}^{(2),j} - 2\mu_{router}^{j} \\ \left(\left(1-\mu_{router}^{j} \sum_{i=1}^{C_j} \Lambda_{IP}^{i,j} e\right) g + \mu_{router}^{j} \pi \sum_{i=1}^{C_j} \Lambda_{IP}^{i,j}\right) \\ \left(\sum_{i=1}^{C_j} R_{IP}^{i,j} + e\pi\right)^{-1} \pi^{-1} \chi \end{array} \right] \end{array} \right\} \right] \\ &= f\left(\lambda_{IP}^{i,j}, \Lambda_{IP}^{i,j}, R_{IP}^{i,j}, \mu_{router}^{j}\right) \end{aligned} \tag{18}$$

As we can see in equation (18), network latency is the function of the combination of $\lambda_{IP}^{i,j}, \Lambda_{IP}^{i,j}, R_{IP}^{i,j}, \mu_{router}^{j}$. With the given architecture we have fixed routers or have the values of μ_{router}^{j} unchanged despite of the change of allocation scheme of the IPs onto the routers. Therefore, the value of network latency depends very much on the applied mapping scheme of the IPs onto the architecture. In other words, it turns out to be that we need to find out the optimal map to minimize the latency value.

$$L_{Opt} = \min \{L_{Net}\} = \min \left\{ \sum_{k=1}^{m} \bar{w}_{route}^{k} \right\} \tag{19}$$

The solution is once again the linear programming or BnB applied for the cost function of L_{Net} in equation (18). To do that we have several definitions in terms of graph as follows:

Definition 1. An IPs Implementation Graph (IIG) $\mathcal{G} = G(V, \lambda)$ is a directed graph where

- Each vertex v_i represents a certain IP.
- Each directed arc as the combination of $(\Lambda_{IP}^{ij}, R_{IP}^{ij})$ represents the arrival rate of the data packets generated from the ith IP toward j^{th} IP.

Definition 2. An Switching Architecture Graph (SAG) $\mathcal{G}' = G(U, R)$ is a directed graph where

- Each vertex u_i presents a certain switch core, the corresponding $1/\mu_j$ denotes its switch's mean of processing time.
- Each directed arc r_{ij} represents the route from u_i to u_j in the routing table.

Now we can state our mapping problem as follows:
Given an IIG and a SAG graphs that satisfy

$$Size(IIG) \leq Size(SAG). \tag{20}$$

The $Size()$ function presents the number of vertexes on the graph.The shortest path routing is applied in this context and the cost function of found path is the accumulated throughput after every hop.

Find a mapping scheme *map()* from IIG onto SAG which:

$$L_{Opt} = \min \left\{ \sum_{k=1}^{m} \left[\sum_{j \in route_k} \left\{ \begin{array}{l} \frac{1}{2\left(1-\mu^j_{router}\sum_{i=1}^{C_j} \Lambda^{i,j}_{IP} e\right)} \times \\ \left[\begin{array}{l} 2\mu^j_{router} \sum_{i=1}^{C_j} \Lambda^{i,j}_{IP} e + \\ \chi \mu^{(2),j}_{router} - 2\mu^j_{router} \\ \left(\left(1 - \mu^j_{router} \sum_{i=1}^{C_j} \Lambda^{i,j}_{IP} e\right) g + \right. \\ \left. \mu^j_{router} \pi \sum_{i=1}^{C_j} \Lambda^{i,j}_{IP} \right) \\ \left(\sum_{i=1}^{C_j} R^{i,j}_{IP} + e\pi \right)^{-1} \pi^{-1} \chi \end{array} \right] \end{array} \right\} \right] \right\} \quad (21)$$

such that:

$$\begin{cases} map(v_i) = u_j, \\ \forall v_i \in V, \exists u_j \in U, \\ \forall v_i \neq v_j, map(v_i) \neq map(v_j). \end{cases} \quad (22)$$

As we know the order of complexity of Min-Max algorithm returns the NP-hard search. Therefore, as mentioned above, we apply Branch and Bound technique not only to obtain the optimal mapping but also reduce significantly the complexity of the searching issue.

5 Simulation Results and Discussion

In this section, we once again simulate two cases of mapping the H.264 decoder's IPs onto the 2-D Mesh architecture including two mapping schemes for 2-D Mesh topology, i.e. random mapping and optimal latency mapping. The random mapping scheme is carried out by randomly allocating the IPs onto the routers. The optimal latency mappings of the H.264 decoder is worked out by applying the BnB algorithm for the cost function presented by equation (18). Our simulations are done based on the data transaction between IPs modeled by MMPP models which are synthesized with the traced data of H.264 decoder which are the results of section. 5.2. This procedure is used to guarantee the similarity between the generated data and the real data. The transmission protocol is defined as UDP. The routing strategy is shortest path. We set the packet size of 64 bytes or

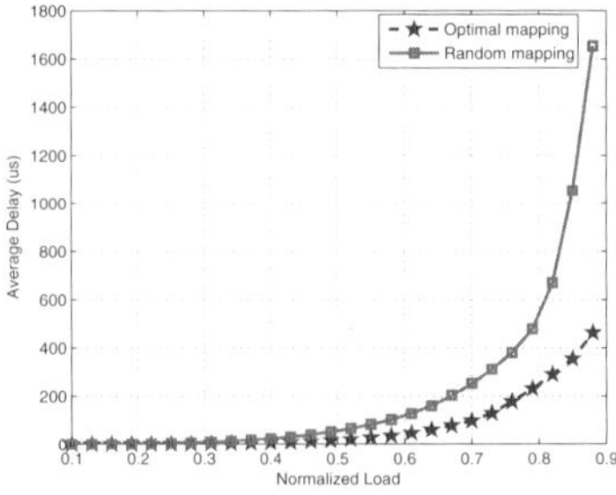

Fig. 13. Latency comparison: Random map vs. Optimal map

four flits of 128 bits. The buffer scheme of DropTail is utilized. Since the H.264 decoder is composed by 12 IPs, therefore the 4×4 Mesh is used as the target architectures.

As the simulation result shown in Fig.13, the experiments are done with the reference of load. In the area of light load, the difference between two mapping schemes is not significant. However, when the load value is greater than 0.5, the optimal mapping yields very better performance. Fig.18 shows that the latency of the random mapping goes to infinity very fast when the load value approaches to one.

6 Conclusion

In this paper, the heterogeneous NoC architecture are considered for designing based on the optimal latency criteria. Self-similarity traffic modeling for H.264 decoder trace data is carried out: based on MMPP model. The throughput and latency of heterogeneous NoC architecture with the modeled self-similarity data sources are derived. Linear programming is adopted to automatically map the IPs onto the NoC architectures with optimal latency and throughput metrics. The experiments 2D Mesh for the application of H.264 are carried out. Result are the latency of optimal mapping are significantly reduced.

References

1. Ngo, V.-D., et al.: Designing On-chip Network based on Optimal latency Criteria. In: Yang, L.T., Zhou, X.-s., Zhao, W., Wu, Z., Zhu, Y., Lin, M. (eds.) ICESS 2005. LNCS, vol. 3820, pp. 287–298. Springer, Heidelberg (2005)
2. Hu, J., et al.: Exploiting the Routing Flexibility for Energy Performance Aware Mapping of Regular NoC Architectures. In: Proc. Design, Automation and Test in Europe Conf. (March 2003)
3. Hu, J., et al.: Energy-Aware Communication and Task Scheduling for Network-on-Chip Architectures under Real-Time Constraints. In: Proc. Design, Automation and Test in Europe Conf. (February 2004)
4. Murali, S., et al.: Bandwidth-Constrained Mapping of Cores onto NoC Architectures. In: DATE, International Conference on Design and Test Europe, pp. 896–901 (2004)
5. Park, K.: Future directions and open problems in performance evaluation and control of self-similar network traffic. In: Self-Similar Network Traffic and Performance Evaluation, ch. 21, Wiley-Interscience, Chichester (2000)
6. Park, K., et al.: Performance evaluation of multiple time scale TCP under self-similar traffic conditions. ACM Transactions on Modeling and Computer Simulation (2000)
7. Heffes, H., et al.: A Markov modulated characterization of packetized voice and data traffic and related statistical multiplexer performance. IEEE J. on selected areas in Comms. 4(6), 856–868 (1986)
8. Leland, W.E., et al.: On the Self-Similar Nature of Ethernet Traffic (Extended Version). IEEE/ACM Transactions on Networking 2(1), 1–15

9. Andersen, A.T., Nielsen, B.F.: A Markovian Approach for Modeling Packet Traffic with Long-Range Dependence. IEEE JSAC 16(5) (1998)
10. Marcel, F.N.: Generalizations of the Pollaczek-Khinchin Integral Equation in the Theory of Queues. Advances in Applied Probability 18(4), 952–990 (1986)
11. Min, G., et al.: A Performance Model for Wormhole-Switched Interconnection Networks under Self-Similar Traffic. IEEE Transactions on Computers 53(5), 601–613 (2004)
12. Ramaswami, V.: The N/G/1 Queue and Its Detailed Analysis. Advances in Applied Probability 12(1), 222–261 (1980)

Hardware Implementation of Common Protocol Interface for a Network-Based Multiprocessor

Arata Shinozaki[1], Mitsunori Kubo[1], Takayuki Nakatomi[1], Baoliu Ye[2], and Minyi Guo[2]

[1] Future Creation Lab., Olympus Corp., Shinjuku-ku, Tokyo, 163-0914 Japan
{arata_shinozaki,mi_kubo,t_nakatomi}@ot.olympus.co.jp
[2] School of Computer Science and Eng., Aizu Univ., Aizu-Wakamatsu, Fukushima-ken 965-8580 Japan
{yebl,minyi}@u-aizu.ac.jp

Abstract. Our research project "UMP-PJ" has suggested the UMP Network Architecture for the next-generation computing infrastructure, in which each network node is coordinated each other. We have conducted the research on the basic architecture of the UMP Network, and shown its usefulness in the last papers. We defined a Processing Element (PE) comprised of PE Wrapper and PE Core. PE Wrapper is a common network interface of network node for UMP Network, and PE Core is an appreciation-specific function module. This paper evaluates the hardware implementation of PE. Especially, PE Wrapper is the key to satisfy the scalability and flexibility of UMP Network Architecture. The experimental model processed JPEG encoding application successfully with a PE implemented with an FPGA board on PC in conjunction with other software PEs. Experimental results demonstrate that no system bottleneck and redundant processing are caused by PE Wrapper implemented with hardware. This implies UMP Network Architecture is suitable for hardware implementation.

1 Introduction

Network-based computing environment becomes common among general people, which interconnects various network nodes including PDAs, mobile PCs, and cell phones through various kinds of network including home network, office network, adhoc network. However, these network nodes are poorly coordinated. Our research aims to realize ubiquitous computing environment for large-scale processing with highly coordinated network nodes as one of the next generation computing infrastructures. Concretely, our research is conducted on network-based multiprocessor network with interconnected nodes including application-specific miniature processors and sensors. We propose this processor network architecture as UMP (Ubiquitous MultiProcessor) Network Architecture.

A ubiquitous computing environment will be realized by embedding UMP in many home appliances, PCs, and mobile gadgets, which surround current living spaces. On this environment, living space will become intelligent providing context-aware service for scenes and events of users' life.

I. Stojmenovic et al. (Eds.): ISPA 2007, LNCS 4742, pp.303–313,2007.

Our project constructed a high-performance simulation environment for heterogeneous multiprocessor system [8], verified a basic framework for inter-processor communication, optimized communication algorithm to cope with processing speed using double-buffered model [9]. In the next step, UMP-PerComp [5] was proposed with basic communication protocol, which is pipeline processing architecture to provide services independent from users' execution environment. A software model implemented based on UMP-PerComp executed JPEG encoding application, and demonstrated the validity of the protocol.

This paper will examine the possibility to implement a node of the UMP Network with hardware, and validate system bottlenecks caused by the hardware-implemented node.

2 UMP Network

Fig.1 shows a schematic diagram of a multiprocessor system. In the part (a), each CPU can be defined as a Processing Element (PE). Also, the system bus connecting these CPUs can be defined as a PE Network. From this point of view, a part of multiprocessor system can be simplified as PEs connected with a PE Network.

PE can be also defined as a processor, which contains a general purpose processor, a DSP, and a processor specific for special function, with application-specific instruction sets and functions. Furthermore, PE contains peripherals including a monitor, a keyboard, or an HDD. Similarly, PE Network can be defined as a peripheral bus, a system bus, the Internet, or other networks. Expanding the definition, we express a multiprocessor system only with PEs and PE Network. In this paper, we define a multiprocessor system organized with PE and PE Network as UMP Network.

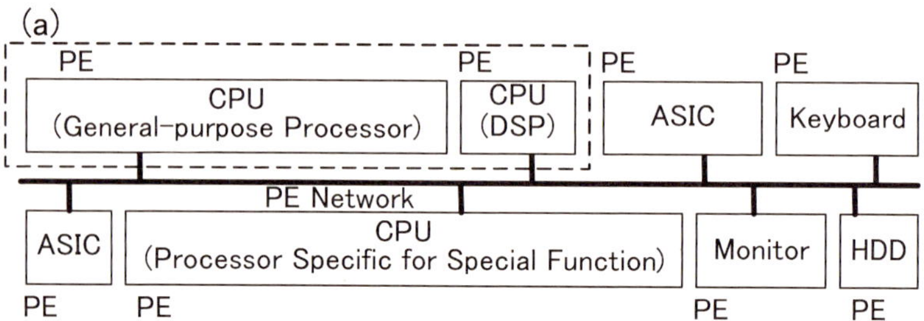

Fig. 1. Schematic Diagram of Multiprocessor System

3 Related Works

In recent years, a number of research projects have been exploring how to build pervasive applications in a global computing infrastructure. The one.world [3] framework presents a component-oriented approach for pervasive application development. It concentrates on the separation of data and functionality and exposes change to promote application level handling. Aura project [2] is characterized as "distraction-free ubiquitous computing" which focuses on user mobility within ubiquitous environments. By monitoring their environment, the Aura framework captures information about the user's task, preferences, and intentions, using this information to "shield the user from the heterogeneity of computing environments as well as from the variability of the resources". Endeavour project (http://endeavour.cs.berkeley.edu/) focuses on the specification, design, and prototype implementation of a planet-scale, self-organizing, and adaptive "information utility". Oxygen project (http:// www.oxygen.lcs.mit.edu/) envisions a future in which computation will be freely available everywhere like oxygen in the air, resting on an infrastructure of mobile and stationary devices connected by a self-configuring network. The goal of Oxygen is to supply abundant computation and communication for users via harnessing existing system, perceptual, and software technologies. EasyMeeting [1] presents middleware agent architecture, named the Context Broker Architecture (Cobra), to support context-aware agents in a smart space. Cobra's intelligent broker agent maintains a shared context model for all computing entities in the space and enforces user-defined privacy policies.

Various programming models have also been proposed for pervasive computing. Song and his colleagues [10] create a user-oriented framework that allows a user to specify a behavior as a set of tasks that need to be completed using service descriptions. It, however, does not have a utility model for choosing the best way of performing tasks. Julien et al. [4] present a novel programming architecture for managing the resulting context-aware interactions to provide transparent, lightweight decision support for a variety of domain specific application. It takes the current notion of sensor networks from a unified collecting apparatus to a fluid and information rich environment that is directly accessed by mobile users moving in an information-rich environment, and takes advantage of the differences among devices to appropriately distribute application functionality throughout the network. [11] presents a two-tiered approach where the lower tier employs peer-to-peer interactions for managing the network infrastructure and the upper tier provides a mobile agent-based programming framework for developing ubiquitous applications and services. ICrafter [6] provides a service framework for interactive pervasive workspace, with the purpose of letting users flexibly interact with services within their environment using a variety of modalities and input devices. Olympus [7] is a high-level programming model that allows developers to specify active space entities (including services, applications, devices, physical objects, locations and users) at an abstract, high level and refer to these entities as virtual entities in their programs. The inner framework associated with Olympus model takes care of resolving these virtual entities into actual active space entities based on constraints specified by developers as well as other context information. Thus, it relieves users from the task of discovering appropriate entities for performing a task.

Different from previous work, we propose P2P processing network with highly coordinated nodes, and construct a system over these nodes implemented with hardware and software. We present the system using our proprietary communication protocol and common network interface.

4 UMP-PerComp

4.1 Architecture Requirement

Although applications based on pervasive computing technology are expected to achieve high performance, the development of these kinds of applications has many challengeable problems to solve. First, ubiquitous devices span a wide range of platforms, computing power, storage capacity, form factors, and user interfaces. Hence, applications must deal with the interoperability among heterogeneous devices. Second, these devices are dispersed over the physical environment, operating autonomously and independently without any centralized control. Thus, interactions typically involve several autonomous administrative domains. Third, although novel wireless networking technologies such as Bluetooth, 802.11, infrared provide local connectivity for mobile nodes, they lead to the growth of infrastructure-less pervasive environment where the previous stable network backbone is weakening. As a result, network connectivity in ubiquitous environment is often limited, intermittent, and, at least, fluctuating.

To solve three problems above, there are three architecture requirements for our processing architecture for UMP Network.

1. Considering locations where the application is executed and execution context will constantly change, the new architecture must support contextual changes flexibly and execute a user's request without degrading the QoS.
2. For infrastructure-less pervasive environments, the new architecture must support dynamic service composition and migration, while making no assumption about underlying network environments.
3. Since resources are totally distributed over the physical space without any centralized control, the new architecture must support resource sharing among applications, devices, and users appropriately.

To meet the above requirements, we present a pipeline processing architecture over UMP Network for pervasive computing. We call this new architecture UMP-PerComp.

4.2 Architecture

Fig. 2 shows the high-level architecture design of the UMP-PerComp. The UMP-PerComp is a three-tire architecture comprising of three distinct parts, named UMP Network, Ubiquitous Service Broker (USB) and User Space, respectively.

An application requested by a user is received in User Space as a user task. USB decomposes the task into several subtasks, schedules them, and assigns them to UMP Network that can collaboratively perform them.

UMP Network dynamically reconfigures the PE Network with heterogeneous PEs and highly coordinates them for application processing. PEs' functions are abstracted as one or more services with a set of service interfaces. When a PE joins the UMP Network, it registers service to the service management component in service layer. Meanwhile, it registers its context information regarding system, network, and resource to the context management component. A PE will unsubscribe its services as well as other registered information from the system before leaving.

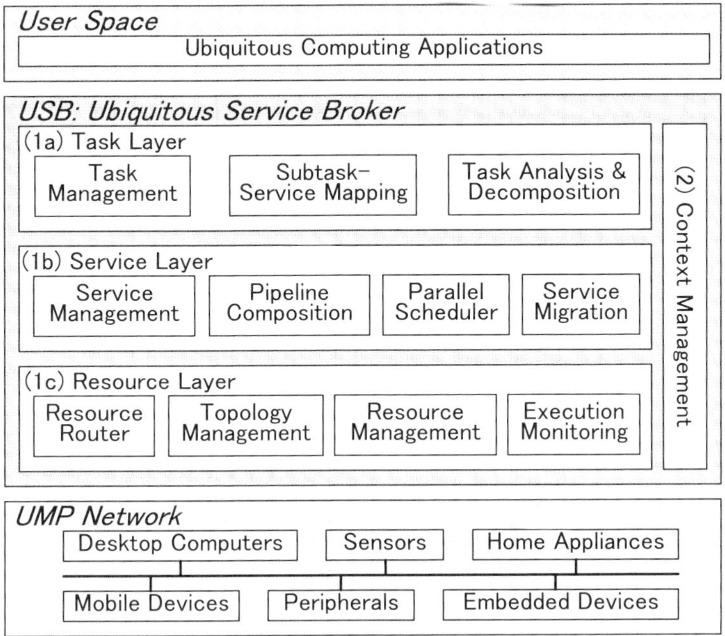

Fig. 2. The UMP-PerComp Architecture

USB: Ubiquitous Service Broker consists of the following three layers (1a)-(1c), and the Context Management Part (2).

(1a) Task layer serves as the service portal for pervasive users, accepts user tasks, decomposes them into subtasks, and maps them into a set of services.
(1b) Service layer is in charge of managing registered PE services, organizing the selected services into a pipeline structure, dispatching it to a group of PEs for parallel processing, and migrating services according to resource status on-the-fly.
(1c) Resource layer monitors the real-time resource information of the UMP Network, observes the execution status of a service, and manages the network topology.
(2) Context Management maintains the contextual information acquired from PEs, services, and users.

User Space is an interface which provides application processing for users on the UMP Network.

5 System Overview

We implemented one of PEs with hardware and connected it to the other software PEs based on the UMP-PerComp architecture. This research aims to confirm seamless connection among these PEs using common network protocol (UMP Protocol), independency of UMP Protocol from the implementation of PEs, and no system bottleneck caused by the hardware PE.

A common network interface, which is named PE Wrapper, is the key factor to realize seamless connection among every computing resource as a PE regardless of its implementation. The PE Wrapper analyzes UMP Protocol. The execution unit of PE is defined as PE Core, which provides application-specific function for users' task.

Considering the feedback and improvement in architecture of PE, a pair of PE Wrapper and PE Core was implemented on an FPGA. A commercially-available FPGA board with PCI interface was selected to keep a focus on the logic of PE and shorten the development period. Table 1 shows its basic specification and Fig. 3 illustrates its basic schematic diagram.

Table 1. Basic Specification of FPGA Board

FPGA	Xilinx Spartan-3 XC3S1000
FPGA Freq.	50MHz
PCI-I/F	33MHz (PCI 2.1-compliant)
Memory	SRAM 4MByte x 4

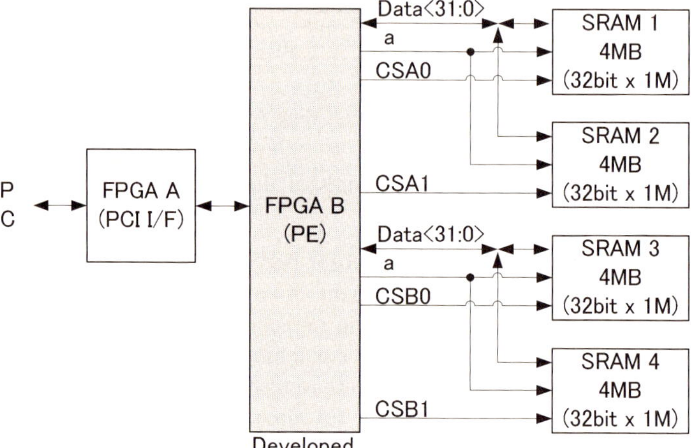

Fig. 3. Basic Schematic Diagram of FPGA Board

Concurrently, support programs were developed to interface with software PE for conversion of UMP Protocol, calling API for PCI, processing of interrupt, and communication over Ethernet. The relation of connection among these modules is shown in Fig. 4 in a layer model. The shaded area is developed for this research.

Implementing the PE Core with minimum necessary function enables to examine the feasibility of implementing the entire UMP Network with hardware. Accordingly, the function of the PE Core was limited to rotation of a bitmap image at 90 degrees. The PE Wrapper was implemented with principal part of UMP Protocol under the limitation of the number of logic cells in the FPGA. The implemented UMP Protocol has data structure including the following information:

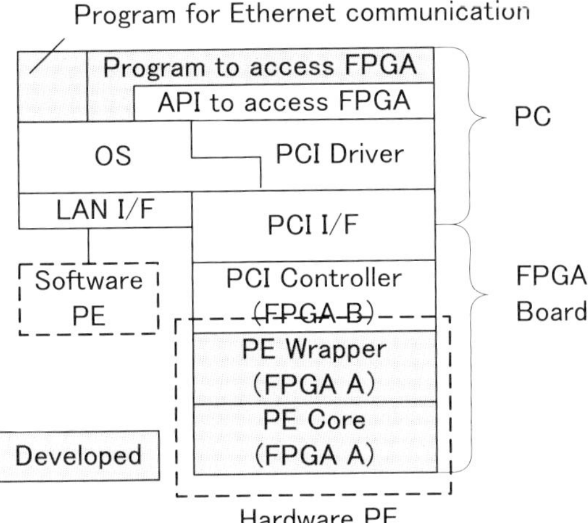

Fig. 4. Layer Model of Connection to Hardware PE

1 Memory Address to store data before/after processing
2 Control code (ex. 01: Writing data, FF: Processing Status Initialization)
3 Parameters necessary for processing (such as image size)
4 Image data

After the PE Wrapper analyzes the UMP Protocol, it requests task processing to PE Core. The above mentioned support programs send rotated image data through PCI and Ethernet after receiving interrupt issued by PE Wrapper when finished processing.

The fundamental point of this research is that the architecture of PE Wrapper must be non-redundant without interrupting processing of PEs to avoid bottleneck. Furthermore, the architecture must work without support software everywhere through various communication interfaces including on-chip bus, HyperTransport, PCI, USB, and Ethernet using the same UMP Protocol.

6 Experiment

6.1 Experimental Model

Shown in Fig.5, our experimental model executed JPEG encoding and image rotation at 90 degrees with 7 sub-functions. Each function was implemented as a PE. A PE for image rotation was implemented in two types with hardware and software respectively. The performance of each PE was measured on the two systems integrated with the two kinds of PE (rotate). We describe the former system as HW and the latter as SW. These systems need a client, which requests application processing, and a Resource Router (RR), which maintains computing resources. Each PE model, the Client, and the Resource Router were assigned to one PC whose specification is listed in Table 2 respectively. An input image was 24-bit-depth bitmap format with the size of landscape VGA (640x480), and an output image was JPEG format with the size of portrait VGA (480x640), the sampling factor of 4:2:2, and the quality of 75.

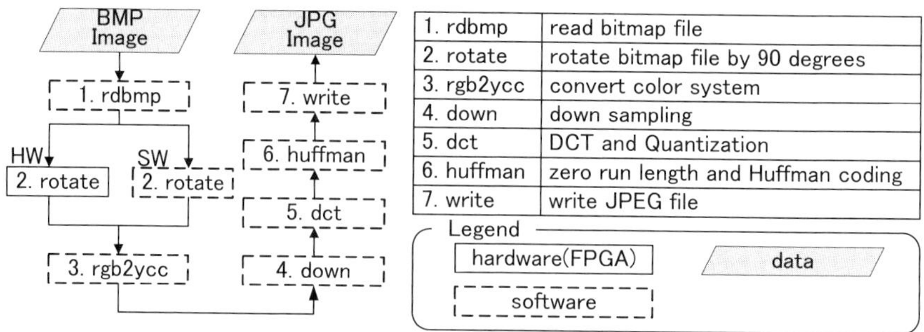

Fig. 5. Structure of Experimental Model

Table 2. Specification of PCs for PEs

	Function	Host Name	Processor: Model	Processor: Clk. Freq.	OS	Memory: Spec.	Memory: Size
	Client	PC1	PentiumM 753	1.2GHz	Win XP Pro SP2	PC2-3200	512MB
	RR	PC2	Core2 Duo E6600	2.4GHz	Win XP Pro SP2	PC2-5300	2GB
1	**rdbmp**	PC3	Pentium4 631	3.0GHz	Fedora Core 5	PC2-4300	1GB
2	**rotate**	PC4	Pentium4 550	3.4GHz	Win XP Pro SP2	PC2-4300	1GB
3	**rgb2ycc**	PC5	Pentium4 631	3.0GHz	Fedora Core 5	PC2-4300	1GB
4	**down**	PC6	Pentium4 631	3.0GHz	Fedora Core 5	PC2-4300	1GB
5	**dct**	PC7	Pentium4 631	3.0GHz	Fedora Core 5	PC2-5300	2GB
6	**huffman**	PC8	Pentium4 631	3.0GHz	Fedora Core 5	PC2-5300	2GB
7	**write**	PC9	Pentium4 631	3.0GHz	Fedora Core 5	PC2-5300	2GB

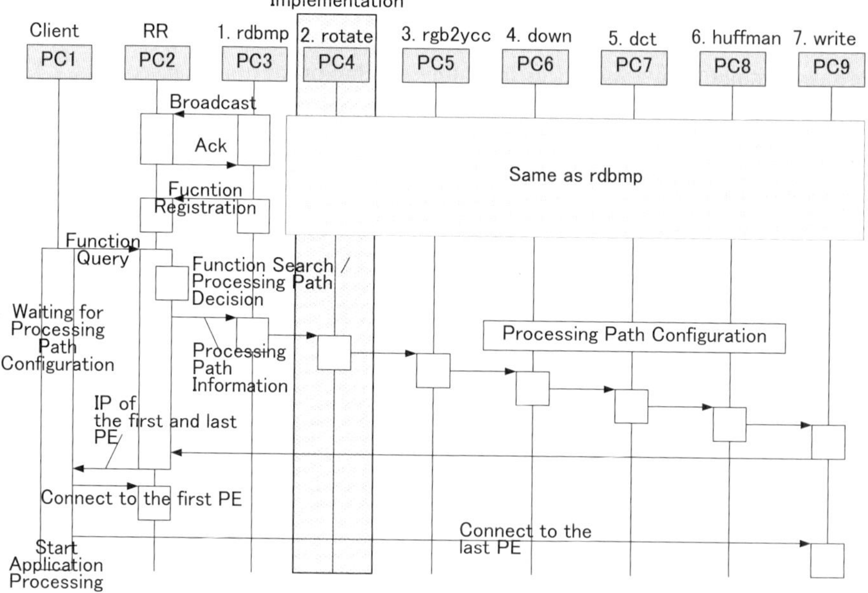

Fig. 6. Communication Sequence Diagram in Experimental Model

Each PE communicates through Ethernet according to a sequence diagram shown in Fig. 6 to process an image.

6.2 Experimental Result

The experimental model generated a correct JPEG image using the hardware PE in conjunction with software PEs. Table 3 shows the experimental result. PE Processing Time T_{proc} [s] is the time to compute for each function of PE Core. Since the result of PE (rdbmp) had large fluctuation, the best value was selected. The result of PE (write) was not measured.

Table 3. Experimental Result where *HW* indicates that only PE (rotate) was implemented with hardware, and *SW* represents that all PEs were implemented with software

		rdbmp	rotate	rgb2ycc	down	dct	huffman
T_{op} [ms]	HW	25.0	252.0	48.6	54.4	75.2	82.4
	SW	21.0	68.5	48.0	53.0	75.0	81.0
T_{proc} [ms]	HW	2.0	114.6	3.0	0.6	10.0	4.2
	SW	5.0	2.0	7.0	1.0	14.0	5.0
T_{OH} [ms]	HW	23.00	147.86	45.60	53.80	65.20	78.20
	SW	16.00	66.50	41.00	52.00	61.00	76.00
$D_{in}+D_{out}$[MB]		1.84	1.84	1.84	1.38	1.84	0.94
P_w [MB/s]	HW	80.14	12.47	40.42	25.70	28.27	12.07
	SW	115.20	27.72	44.96	26.58	30.22	12.42

The ratio of clock frequency of CPU and FPGA was 68, where the ratio of T_{proc} of hardware implementation and software one for PE(rotate) was 58. Furthermore, the hardware PE was developed under the following restriction because of the number of available logic cell on FPGA.

- Our logic in the FPGA deals with 4 bytes as 1pixel to handle memory addresses for image rotation, but 1 pixel is 3 bytes actually. Therefore, dummy data are required for image rotation
- The logic should follow the timing characteristics for asynchronous SRAM
- The logic has no issue buffer of instruction for controlling SRAM

Our logic may fail to start reading SRAM after sending previous data without inserting a waiting phase because of the above restrictions. This is the reason the result of simulation demonstrated the degradation on SRAM accesses efficiency. Since these are caused by the restriction of design, and the performance improvement will be easy.

T_{op} in Table 3 involves the time for communication over Ethernet. Although T_{proc} for the hardware PE directs the time for both PE Core and PE Wrapper, for software PEs, it shows the time to process the function itself. Considering these difference to compare the hardware implementation and the software one, Overhead Time T_{OH} and PE Wrapper Performance P_w were defined as follows.

$$\text{Overhead Time } T_{OH} = \begin{cases} T_{op} - T_{proc}, \text{if PE is software} \\ T_{op} - T_{proc} + T_{init}, \text{if PE is hardware} \end{cases} \tag{1}$$

Where:

T_{op} [s] is PE operating time from right before sending the last processed image data unit to right after receiving the first processing image data unit on each PE.

T_{proc}[s] is the time to process image data.
T_{init}[s] is the time for initialization and setup of hardware PE

$$\text{Performance of PE Wrapper } P_w = \frac{D_{in} + D_{out}}{T_{OH}} \tag{2}$$

Where:

D_{in}[B] is the size of input data.
D_{out}[B] is the size of output data.

Fig. 7 shows the comparison of PE Wrapper Performance P_w between HW system and SW system. The PE Wrapper Performance P_w of every PEs after PE (rotate) is independent from the implementation of PE (rotate). We deducted partial implementation of the UMP Protocol and the overhead time to communicate through PCI cause the degradation of PE Wrapper Performance P_w of PE (rotate). Full implementation of the UMP Protocol with hardware will enable direct communication and improve P_w. The PE Wrapper Performance P_w of hardware PE (rotate) is higher than that of PE (huffman). These conclude that no system bottleneck and redundant processing are caused by hardware PE (rotate).

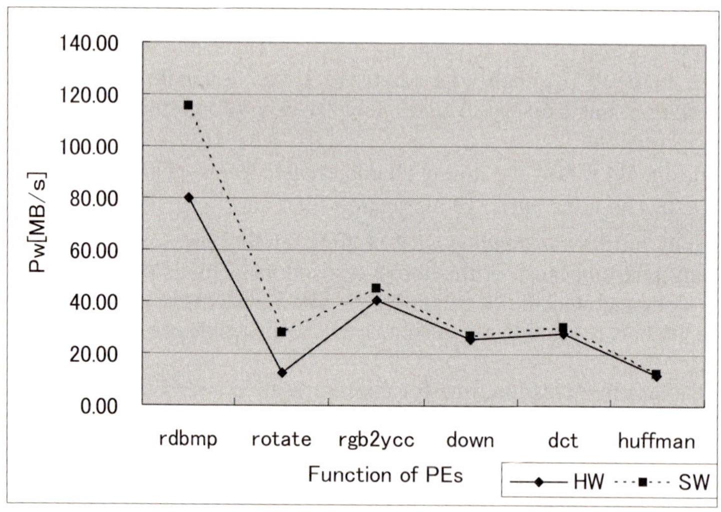

Fig. 7. Comparison of PE Wrapper Performance: P_w

7 Conclusion

We defined PE Wrapper as common network interface for UMP Network, and PE Core as appreciation-specific function module. PE Wrapper and PE Core could be implemented with FPGA successfully. The hardware PE worked without problem in conjunction with other software PEs, and generated correct JPEG image using the UMP Protocol. No system bottleneck and redundant processing were caused by PE Wrapper. This demonstrates the feasibility and usefulness of UMP Network implemented with only hardware PEs. We will develop fully-implemented hardware PE and UMP Network with two or more PEs using switch fabric to confirm the usefulness of the UMP Protocol.

References

1. Chen, H., Finin, T., Joshi, A., Perich, F., Chakraborty, D.: Intelligent agents meet the semantic web in smart spaces. IEEE Internet Computing 8(6), 69–79 (2004)
2. Garlan, D., Siewiorek, D., Smailagic, A., SteenKiste, P.: Project aura: Towards distraction-free pervasive computing. IEEE Pervasive Computing 21(2), 22–31 (2002)
3. Grimm, R.: One world: Experiences with a pervasive computing architecture. IEEE Pervasive Computing 3(3), 22–30 (2004)
4. Julien, C., Hammer, J., O'Brien, W.J.: A dynamic programming framework for pervasive computing environments. In: Proceedings of The Workshop on Building Software for Pervasive Computing in conjunction with OOPSLA 2005, San Diego, CA, USA (2005)
5. Kubo, M., Ye, B., Shinozaki, A., Nakatomi, T., Guo, M.: UMP-PerComp: A Ubiquitous Multiprocessor Network-Based Pipeline Processing Framework for Pervasive Computing Environments. In: Proceedings of the IEEE 21st International Conference on Advanced Information Networking and Applications, Niagara Falls, Canada, pp. 611–618. IEEE Computer Society Press, Los Alamitos (2007)
6. Ponnekanti, S.R., Lee, B., Fox, A., Hanrahan, P., Winograd, T.: Icrafter: A service framework for ubiquitous computing environments. In: Proceedings of Ubicomp 2001, Atlanta, Georgia, pp. 56–75 (2001)
7. Ranganathan, A., Chetan, S., Al-Muhtadi, J., Campbell, R.H., Mickunas, M.D.: Olympus: A high-level programming model for pervasive computing environments. In: Proceedings of PerCom 2005, Kauai Island, Hawaii, USA, pp. 7–16 (2005)
8. Shinozaki, A., Shima, M., Guo, M., Kubo, M.: A High Performance Simulator System for a Multiprocessor System Based on a Multi-way Cluster. In: Jesshope, C., Egan, C. (eds.) ACSAC 2006. LNCS, vol. 4186, pp. 231–243. Springer, Heidelberg (2006)
9. Shinozaki, A., Shima, M., Guo, M., Kubo, M.: Multiprocessor Simulator System Based on Multi-way Cluster Using Double-buffered Model. In: Proceedings of the IEEE 21st International Conference on Advanced Information Networking and Applications, Niagara Falls, Canada, pp. 893–900. IEEE Computer Society Press, Los Alamitos (2007)
10. Song, Z., Labrou, Y., Masuoka, R.: Dynamic service discovery and management in task computing. In: Proceedings of 1st Ann. Int'l Conf. Mobile and Ubiquitous Systems, Boston, Massachusetts, USA, pp. 310–318 (2004)
11. Stevenson, G., Nixon, P., Ferguson, R.I.: A general purpose programming framework for ubiquitous computing environments. In: Dey, A.K., Schmidt, A., McCarthy, J.F. (eds.) UbiComp 2003. LNCS, vol. 2864, Springer, Heidelberg (2003)

A Distributed Hebb Neural Network for Network Anomaly Detection

Daxin Tian[1,2], Yanheng Liu[1,2], and Bin Li[3]

[1] College of Computer Science and Technology
[2] Key Laboratory of Symbolic Computation and Knowledge Engineering of Ministry of Education
[3] Mathematics College,
Jilin University, 130012, China
daxin222@email.jlu.edu.cn, lyh_lb_lk@yahoo.com.cn

Abstract. One of the most challenging problems in anomaly detection is to develop scalable algorithms which are capable of dealing with large audit data, network traffic data, or alter data. In this paper a distributed neural network based on Hebb rule is presented to improve the speed and scalability of inductive learning. The speed is improved by randomly splitting a large data set into disjoint subsets and each subset data is presented to an independent neural network, these networks can be trained in distributed and each one in parallel. The analysis of completeness and risk bounds of competitive Hebb learning proof that the distributed Hebb neural network can avoid the accuracy being degraded as compared to running a single algorithm with the entire data. The experiments are performed on the KDD'99 Data set, which is a standard intrusion detection benchmark. Comparisons with other approaches on the same benchmark demonstrate the effectiveness and applicability of the proposed method.

Keywords: Intrusion detection system, Scaling up, Distributed learning, Neural network.

1 Introduction

With the widespread use of networked computers for critical systems, computer security is attracting increasing attention and intrusions have become a significant threat in recent years. As a second line of defense for computer and network systems, intrusion detection system (IDS) has been deployed more and more widely along with network security techniques such as firewall. Intrusion detection techniques can be classified into two categories: misuse detection and anomaly detection. Misuse detection looks for signatures of known attacks, and any matched activity is considered an attack; anomaly detection models a user's behaviors, and any significant deviation from the normal behaviors is considered the result of an attack. Many anomaly detection techniques have been applied to intrusion detection. The vast majority of the research has concentrated on mining various types of system audit data, or raw network traffic in order to build more accurate IDS devices[1-3]; and classifying alarms into attack and benign categories[4-6].

I. Stojmenovic et al. (Eds.): ISPA 2007, LNCS 4742, pp. 314–325, 2007.

The main shortcoming of IDS is false alarm which is caused by misinterpreting normal packets as an attack or misclassifying an intrusion as normal behavior. This problem is more severe under large-scale heterogeneous networks generate large amounts of temporal event data in diverse formats[7,8]. To overcome this problem some scalable anomaly detection algorithms have been proposed to dealing with large audit data, network traffic data, or alter data. For example, Khan L. et al [9] present a new approach of combination of SVM and DGSOT for enhancing the training time of SVM specifically when dealing with large data sets. The main idea of this approach is starting with an initial training set and expanding it gradually using the clustering structure produced by the DGSOT algorithm; Li X.Y. et al [10] introduce a supervised clustering and classification algorithm (CCAS) and its application in learning patterns of normal and intrusive activities and detecting suspicious activity records from a large set of computer audit data. This algorithm utilizes a heuristic in grid-based clustering. Several post-processing techniques including data redistribution, supervised grouping of clusters, and removal of outliers, are used to enhance the scalability and robustness; Li X.B. [11] propose a new decision tree algorithm SURPASS in which the information required to build a decision tree is summarized into a set of sufficient statistics, which can be gathered incrementally from the data, by reading a subset of the data from storage space to main memory one at a time. As a result, the data size that can be handled by this algorithm is independent of memory size.

The knowledge discovery and data mining community has also challenged itself to develop inductive learning algorithm that scales up to large data sets. For scaling up learning algorithms, the crucial issue is seldom "how fast" you can run on a certain problem, but instead "how large" a problem can you deal with. In traditional applications of knowledge discovery and data mining method, sample size tends to be the dominant limitation. Thus overfitting avoidance was the main concern. In contrast, in many present-day data mining applications, enough data to model very complex phenomena is available, but inappropriately simple models are produced because it is impossible with current KDD systems to make use of all of the data within the available time and memory, Thus the development of highly efficient algorithms to avoid underfitting becomes the main concern. Now many diverse techniques have been proposed for scaling up inductive algorithms, the three main approaches are design a fast algorithm[12-14], use a relational representation[15,16], and partition the data[17-19]. In partition data approach, the scaling up method almost is based on the decision tree algorithms, the reason is that with partition data techniques, accuracy may be degraded as compared to running a single inductive algorithm with the entire data, and decision tree learner can cooperates to obtain a global view of the problem by combined the local trees[20,21]. Although neural networks have inherent massively parallel features, their distributed aspects have been proved difficult to be captured, since the learning algorithm requires all the training data to be submitted to the network one by one until the network is stable after one or more epochs. Thus a group of neural networks can't run in distributed to cope with one problem corporately.

In this paper we present a distributed Hebb neural network which uses independent neural networks process part of the training data. These independent neural networks can run in distributed and each one processes in parallel, thus it can not only take advantage of the neural network's parallel character but also overcome the drawback of concentrated training. The rest of this paper is organized as follows. Section 2 describes the main idea of distributed Hebb neural network and details the basic learning algorithm. The experimental results on dataset KDDCUP99 are given in Section 3, and conclusions are made in Section 4.

2 Distributed Hebb Neural Network

2.1 The Learning Process

The main process of the distributed neural network involves two phases learning: in the first phase (distributed learning), large data are splitted randomly and sent to independent neuron networks, all the independent neuron networks learn the knowledge of each slice in distributed and every one in parallel; in the second phase (concentrated learning), the training data is built from the training results of the distributed neural networks. Since the new data is much less than the original training data, it can be learned by one neural network in finite time and memory. The process is shown in Fig.1.

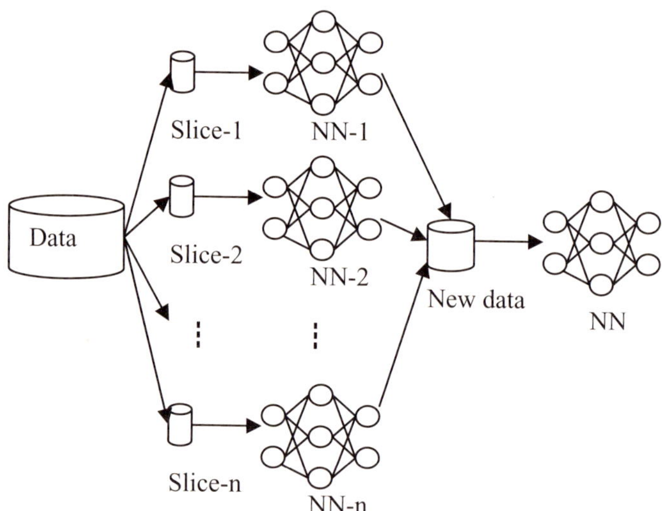

Fig. 1. Learning process of distributed neural network

A stable neural network maintains the knowledge learned from the sample data in the weight matrix $\mathbf{W}_{(m\times n)}$, m is the number of neurons, n is the dimension of each neuron. In Hebb rule, the dimension value of each neuron is equal to the sample vector $\mathbf{x}_{(1\times n)}$'s dimension. After the distributed neural network is stable, each row of $\mathbf{W}$ can be regarded as one clustering center of the slice data. During the process the whole original data set $\mathbf{X}$ has $p\times q$ samples, $\mathbf{X}$ is splitted into p slices and each slice ${}^{(i)}\mathbf{X}$ ($i = 1,\cdots,p$) has q samples; after the neural network trained by the slice data ${}^{(i)}\mathbf{X}$ is stable, its weight ${}^{(i)}\mathbf{W}$ is composed of ${}^{(i)}r$ rows (${}^{(i)}r << q$). since ${}^{(i)}r$ is much less than q, the whole new data set $\tilde{\mathbf{X}}$ is much less than the whole original data set $\mathbf{X}$.

2.2 Hebb Rule Risk Bounds

The main reason of Hebb rule can be used to achieve distributed learning is that it is a local learning algorithm. In the learning process, neural network first measures the similarity between sample $\mathbf{x}$ and neuron $\mathbf{W}_j$ through competitive leaning algorithm and then adjusts $\mathbf{W}_j$ according to Hebb rule. The risk functional is defined as

$$RC(f_{\mathrm{W}}(\mathbf{x}),\lambda) = \int C(\mathbf{x},\mathbf{W},\lambda)L(y,f_{\mathrm{W}}(\mathbf{x}))\mathrm{d}p(\mathbf{x},y) \tag{1}$$

where $L(y,f_{\mathrm{W}}(\mathbf{x}))$ is the loss function measuring the error when predicting y by $f_{\mathrm{W}}(\mathbf{x})$; $C(\mathbf{x},\mathbf{W},\lambda)$ is the competitive function,

$$C(\mathbf{x},\mathbf{W},\lambda) = \begin{cases} 1, \text{ if } d(\mathbf{x},\mathbf{W}_j) \le \lambda \\ 0, \text{ else} \end{cases} \tag{2}$$

and the empirical risk functional is

$$RC_{emp}(f_{\mathrm{W}}(\mathbf{x}),\lambda) = \frac{1}{n}\sum_{i=1}^{n} C(\mathbf{x}_i,\mathbf{W},\lambda)L(y,f_{\mathrm{W}}(\mathbf{x}_i)) \tag{3}$$

To analyze the generalization ability of the principle of empirical risk minimization and the rate of convergence of the learning process, based on the statistical learning theory, we look for the bounds that estimate the value of achieved risk for the function minimizing the empirical risk and the difference between the value of achieved risk and the value of minimal possible risk for a given set of functions.

Theorem 1: For all r indicator functions in the set $\{C(\mathbf{x},\mathbf{W},\lambda)L(y,f_{\mathrm{W}}(\mathbf{x}))\}$ and n randomly drawn samples, if $(f_{\mathrm{W}}{}^{\alpha}(\mathbf{x}),\lambda^{\alpha})$ minimizes $RC_{emp}(f_{\mathrm{W}}(\mathbf{x}),\lambda)$, then with probability $1-\mu$, the inequality

$$RC(f_{\mathrm{W}}{}^{\alpha}(\mathbf{x}),\lambda^{\alpha}) \le RC_{emp}(f_{\mathrm{W}}{}^{\alpha}(\mathbf{x}),\lambda^{\alpha}) + \sqrt{\frac{\ln 2r - \ln \mu}{2n}} \tag{4}$$

holds true.

Proof: Glivenko-Cantelli theorem proves that for any given probability measure P and positive β

$$P\{\sup|P(A)-v_n(A)|>\beta\}\underset{n\to\infty}{\to}0 \tag{5}$$

where $v_n(A)$ is the frequency of occurrence an event A in a series of independent, random trials. And the Chernoff inequalities

$$P\{\sup(P(A)-v_n(A))>\beta\}\leq 2\exp\{-2\beta^2 n\} \tag{6}$$

$$P\{\sup(v_n(A)-P(A))>\beta\}\leq 2\exp\{-2\beta^2 n\} \tag{7}$$

describes the rate of convergence. For indicator functions the risk functional $RC(f_{\mathbf{W}}(\mathbf{x}),\lambda)$ defines probabilities and the empirical risk functional $RC_{emp}(f_{\mathbf{W}}(\mathbf{x}),\lambda)$ defines frequency, thus from (6) we can obtain

$$\begin{aligned} &P\left\{\sup_{1\leq j\leq r}\left(RC\left(f_{\mathbf{W}}{}^{j}(\mathbf{x}),\lambda^{j}\right)-RC_{emp}\left(f_{\mathbf{W}}{}^{j}(\mathbf{x}),\lambda^{j}\right)\right)>\beta\right\} \\ &\leq\sum_{j=1}^{r}P\left\{\left(RC\left(f_{\mathbf{W}}{}^{j}(\mathbf{x}),\lambda^{j}\right)-RC_{emp}\left(f_{\mathbf{W}}{}^{j}(\mathbf{x}),\lambda^{j}\right)\right)>\beta\right\} \\ &\leq 2r\exp\{-2\beta^2 n\} \end{aligned} \tag{8}$$

if define

$$\mu=2r\exp\{-2\beta^2 n\} \tag{9}$$

then

$$\beta=\sqrt{\frac{\ln 2r-\ln\mu}{2n}} \tag{10}$$

From inequality (8) we can find that for all r indicator functions in the set $\{C(\mathbf{x},\mathbf{W},\lambda)L(y,f_{\mathbf{W}}(\mathbf{x}))\}$, with probability $1-\mu$, the inequality

$$RC\left(f_{\mathbf{W}}{}^{j}(\mathbf{x}),\lambda^{j}\right)-RC_{emp}\left(f_{\mathbf{W}}{}^{j}(\mathbf{x}),\lambda^{j}\right)\leq\beta \tag{11}$$

holds true. Thus for function $\left(f_{\mathbf{W}}{}^{\alpha}(\mathbf{x}),\lambda^{\alpha}\right)$ which minimizes $RC_{emp}(f_{\mathbf{W}}(\mathbf{x}),\lambda)$, inequality (11) also holds true. Substituting (10) into (11) we can obtain with probability $1-\mu$, the inequality (4) holds true. End

For the function $\left(f_{\mathbf{W}}{}^{\varepsilon}(\mathbf{x}), \lambda^{\varepsilon}\right)$ which minimizes $RC\left(f_{\mathbf{W}}(\mathbf{x}), \lambda\right)$, from inequality (7) we can obtain

$$P\left\{\left(RC_{emp}\left(f_{\mathbf{W}}{}^{\varepsilon}(\mathbf{x}), \lambda^{\varepsilon}\right) - RC\left(f_{\mathbf{W}}{}^{\varepsilon}(\mathbf{x}), \lambda^{\varepsilon}\right)\right) > \beta_1\right\} \leq 2\exp\left\{-2\beta_1{}^2 n\right\} \tag{12}$$

if define $2\exp\left\{-2\beta_1{}^2 n\right\} = \mu$ then

$$\beta_1 = \sqrt{\frac{\ln 2 - \ln \mu}{2n}} \tag{13}$$

From inequality (12) we can obtain with probability $1-\mu$ inequality

$$RC\left(f_{\mathbf{W}}{}^{\varepsilon}(\mathbf{x}), \lambda^{\varepsilon}\right) \geq RC_{emp}\left(f_{\mathbf{W}}{}^{\varepsilon}(\mathbf{x}), \lambda^{\varepsilon}\right) - \sqrt{\frac{\ln 2 - \ln \mu}{2n}} \tag{14}$$

holds true. Since $\left(f_{\mathbf{W}}{}^{\alpha}(\mathbf{x}), \lambda^{\alpha}\right)$ minimizes $RC_{emp}\left(f_{\mathbf{W}}(\mathbf{x}), \lambda\right)$, the inequality

$$RC_{emp}\left(f_{\mathbf{W}}{}^{\varepsilon}(\mathbf{x}), \lambda^{\varepsilon}\right) \geq RC_{emp}\left(f_{\mathbf{W}}{}^{\alpha}(\mathbf{x}), \lambda^{\alpha}\right) \tag{15}$$

is valid. From theorem 1 and inequality (14), (15) we can derive with probability $1-2\mu$,the inequality

$$RC\left(f_{\mathbf{W}}{}^{\alpha}(\mathbf{x}), \lambda^{\alpha}\right) - RC\left(f_{\mathbf{W}}{}^{\varepsilon}(\mathbf{x}), \lambda^{\varepsilon}\right) \leq \sqrt{\frac{\ln 2r - \ln \mu}{2n}} + \sqrt{\frac{\ln 2 - \ln \mu}{2n}} \tag{16}$$

holds true.

2.3 Completeness Analysis

The key issue to scaling up inductive learning is whether the partition data learning result is equal to the learning on the whole data by one method. The main difficulty in finding $f(\mathbf{x}, \mathbf{w})$ from samples stems from the fact that this is an ill-posed problem. For solving this problem Tikhonov presents regularization method

$$R(\mathbf{w}) = R_s(\mathbf{w}) + \lambda R_c(\mathbf{w}) \tag{17}$$

where $R_s(\mathbf{w})$ is the true risk and $R_c(\mathbf{w})$ is the regularization item and λ is the Tikhonov factor. We will proof that distributed Hebb neural network is equal to regularization method.

After training each row of the ith neural network's weight matrix ${}^{(i)}\mathbf{W}$ represents some samples of ${}^{(i)}\mathbf{X}$, that is the distance between these samples and the corresponding row is lower than one threshold value. So we can get

$$^{(i)}\mathbf{W}_j = {}^{(i)}\mathbf{X}_k + \mathbf{A}_k \tag{18}$$

in the new data set $^{(i)}\tilde{\mathbf{X}}$

$$^{(i)}\tilde{\mathbf{X}}_l = {}^{(i)}\mathbf{W}_j + \mathbf{B}_m \tag{19}$$

where $\left|\mathbf{A}_{ki}\right| \le \beta$, $\left|\mathbf{B}_{mi}\right| \le \beta$, combine (17) and (18)

$$^{(i)}\tilde{\mathbf{X}}_l = {}^{(i)}\mathbf{X}_k + \mathbf{A}_k + \mathbf{B}_m \tag{20}$$

In new data set the loss function is $L(y, f_{\mathrm{w}}(\mathbf{x}+\mathbf{a}+\mathbf{b}))$, and expanding $f_{\mathrm{w}}(\mathbf{x}+\mathbf{a}+\mathbf{b})$ into Taylor series:

$$\begin{aligned} f_{\mathrm{w}}(\mathbf{x}+\mathbf{a}+\mathbf{b}) &= f_{\mathrm{w}}(\mathbf{x}) + \nabla f_{\mathrm{w}}(\mathbf{x}+\mathbf{a}+\mathbf{b})^T(\mathbf{a}+\mathbf{b}) \\ &\quad + \frac{1}{2}(\mathbf{a}+\mathbf{b})^T \nabla^2 f_{\mathrm{w}}(\mathbf{x}+\mathbf{a}+\mathbf{b})(\mathbf{a}+\mathbf{b}) + \cdots \\ &= f_{\mathrm{w}}(\mathbf{x}) + \Delta g(\mathbf{x}) \end{aligned} \tag{21}$$

where $\left|\mathbf{a}_i + \mathbf{b}_i\right| \le 2\beta$ $\nabla f(\mathbf{z})$ is gradient $\nabla^2 f(\mathbf{z})$ is Hessian matrix. The expected value of $L(y, f_{\mathrm{w}}(\mathbf{x}+\mathbf{a}+\mathbf{b}))$ is

$$\begin{aligned} R(\mathbf{w}) &= \int (y - f_{\mathrm{w}}(\mathbf{x}+\mathbf{a}+\mathbf{b}))^2 \mathrm{d}p(\mathbf{x}, y) \\ &= \int (y - f_{\mathrm{w}}(\mathbf{x}))^2 \mathrm{d}p(\mathbf{x}, y) + \int \left((y - f_{\mathrm{w}}(\mathbf{x}))\Delta g(\mathbf{x}) + \Delta g(\mathbf{x})^2\right) \mathrm{d}p(\mathbf{x}, y) \end{aligned} \tag{22}$$

From (22) we can find that distributed Hebb neural network is adding a penalty term $\int \left((y - f_{\mathrm{w}}(\mathbf{x}))\Delta g(\mathbf{x}) + \Delta g(\mathbf{x})^2\right) \mathrm{d}p(\mathbf{x}, y)$ to the error function $\int (y - f_{\mathrm{w}}(\mathbf{x}))^2 \mathrm{d}p(\mathbf{x}, y)$, thus it is equivalent to the technique of regularization which adds a penalty term to the error function for controlling the bias and variance of a neural network[22,23].

3 Experiments

KDDCUP 99 data set contains of 22 kinds of intrusion behaviors and 494,019 records among which 97,276 are normal connection records. The test set is another data set which contains 37 kinds of intrusion behaviors and 311,029 records among which 60,593 are normal records.

3.1 Performance Measures

The recording format of test results is shown in Table 1. False alarm is partitioned into False Positive (FP, normal is detected as intrusion) and False Negative (FN, intrusion is not detected). True detect is also partitioned into True False (TF, intrusion is detected rightly) and True Negative (TN, normal is detected rightly).

Table 1. Recording format of test result

		Detection Results				
		Normal	**Intrusion-1**	**Intrusion-2**	---	**Intrusion-n**
Actual Behaviors	**Normal**	TN00	FP01	FP02	---	FP0n
	Intrusion-1	FN10	TP11	FP12	---	FP1n
	Intrusion-2	FN20	FP21	TP22	---	FP2n
	⋮	⋮	⋮	⋮	⋮	⋮
	Intrusion-n	FNn0	FPn1	FPn2	---	TPnn

Definition 1. The right detection rate of ith behavior $TR = T_{ii} \Big/ \sum_{j=1}^{n} R_{ij}$, where T_{ii} is the value lies in table1's ith row and ith column.

Definition 2. The right prediction rate of ith behavior $PR = T_{ii} \Big/ \sum_{j=1}^{n} R_{ji}$, where T_{ii} is the value lies in table1's ith row and ith column; R_{ji} is the value lies in table1's jth row and ith column.

Definition 3. Detection rate (DR) is computed as the ratio between the number of correctly detected intrusions and the total number of intrusions. If regard table's record as an $(n+1)\times(n+1)$ metric $\mathbf{R}$, then $DR = \sum_{i=1}^{n}\sum_{j=1}^{n} R_{ij} \Big/ \sum_{i=0}^{n}\sum_{j=0}^{n} R_{ij}$.

Definition 4. False positive rate (FPR) is computed as the ratio between the number of normal behaviors that are incorrectly classifies as intrusions and the total number of normal connections, according to the Table's record $FPR = \sum_{i=1}^{n} FP0i \Big/ \sum_{i=1}^{n} FP0i + TN00$.

3.2 Experiment Results

3.2.1 Training Results

To test the performance of distributed algorithm, we first divided the 494,019 records into 50 slices, each slice contains 10,000 records except the last contains 4,019 records. the learning results are shown in Fig. 2 and 3. In Fig. 2 X-axis represents each slice and Y-axis records the corresponding number of neurons after the neural networks are stable. In Fig. 3 Y-axis records the corresponding number of behaviors included in each slice. From the results we can find that the distribution of neurons and behaviors are similar which indicates the sensors have learned the knowledge. Since the behaviors recorded in 18th-36th slices and 43th-46th are all "smurf" intrusion, the number of behavior is 1 and the number of neurons are 1-5. After the training on the distributed learning result, the knowledge is represented by 368 neurons.

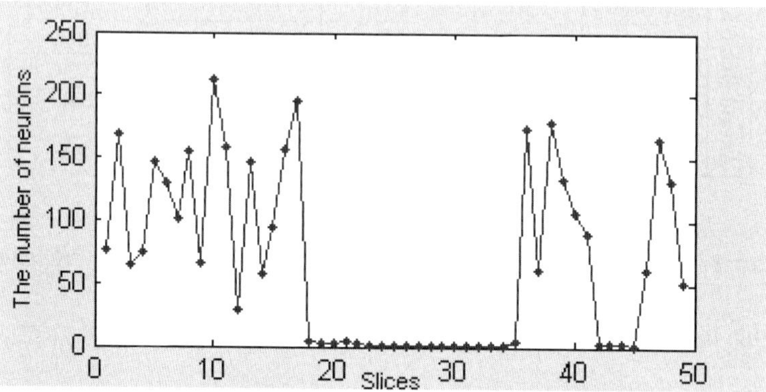

Fig. 2. The number of neurons of each corresponding slices

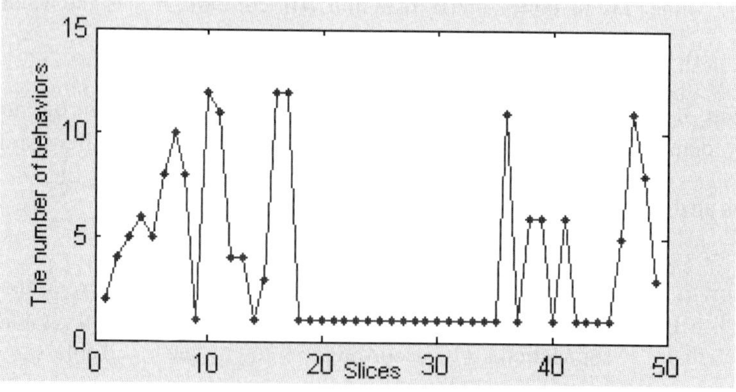

Fig. 3. The number of behaviors of each corresponding slices

3.2.2 Detection Results

There are 37 kinds of intrusion behaviors in the test set. We first separate them into four kinds of attacks:

Probe: {portsweep, mscan, saint, satan, ipsweep, nmap}

DOS: {udpstorm, smurf, pod, land, processtable, warezmaster, apache2, mailbomb, Neptune, back, teardrop}

U2R: { httptunnel, ftp_write, sqlattack, xterm, multihop, buffer_overflow, perl, loadmodule, rootkit, ps}

R2L: { guess_passwd, phf, snmpguess, named, imap, snmpgetattack, xlock, sendmail, xsnoop, worm}

The test results are summarized in Table 2.

Table 2. Testing Results

		Detection Results					
		Normal	**Probe**	**DOS**	**U2R**	**R2L**	**TR**
Actual Behaviors	**Normal**	58120	927	649	64	833	96.0%
	Probe	357	3546	174	21	118	85.1%
	DOS	256	5092	223518	52	435	97.2%
	U2R	143	39	0	23	23	10.1%
	R2L	14443	14	1	271	1460	9%
	PR	79.3%	36.9%	99.6%	5.3%	50.9%	

Comparing the result with the first winner of KDD CUP 99 we can find the TR is almost equal to the first winner. There are two reasons lead to the low TR of U2R and R2L: first, the size of attack instance that pertained to U2R and R2L is much smaller than that of other types of attack; second, U2R and R2L are host-based attacks which exploit vulnerabilities of the operating systems, not of the network protocol. Therefore, these are very similar to the "normal" data. Table 3 shows the DR and FPR of the first and second winner of the KDD CUP 99 competition, other approaches[24] and distributed Hebb neural network.

Table 3. Comparison with other approaches

Performances / Algorithms	Detection Rate (DR)	False Positive Rate (FPR)
Winning Entry	91.9%	0.5%
Second Place	91.5%	0.6%
Best Linear GP - FP Rate	89.4%	0.7%
Best GEdIDS - FP Rate	91%	0.4%
Distributed Hebb NN	93.9%	0.4%

4 Conclusions

In the fields of anomaly intrusion detection the amount of data available for building classifiers or regression models is growing very fast. Therefore, there is a great need for scaling up inductive learning algorithms that are capable of handling very-large datasets and, simultaneously, being computationally efficient and scalable. In this paper a distributed neural network based on Hebb rule is presented to improve the speed and scalability of inductive learning. The speed is improved by doing the algorithm on disjoint subsets instead of the entire dataset. The analysis of completeness and risk bounds of competitive Hebb learning proof that the distributed Hebb neural network can avoid the accuracy being degraded as compared to running a single algorithm with the entire data. In the experiments, the KDD cup 99 data set is used which is the common data set used in IDS research papers and the results demonstrate the performance potential of this approach.

Acknowledgement

This research is supported by both the National Natural Science Foundation of China under Grant No.60573128 and the National Research Foundation for the Doctoral Program of Higher Education of China No.20060183043.

References

1. Ingham, K.L., Somayaji, A., Burge, J., Forrest, S.: Learning DFA Representations of HTTP For Protecting Web Applications. Computer Networks 51(5), 1239–1255 (2007)
2. Özyer, T., Alhajj, R., Barker, K.: Intrusion Detection By Integrating Boosting Genetic Fuzzy Classifier and Data Mining Criteria for Rule Pre-screening. Journal of Network and Computer Applications 30(1), 99–113 (2007)
3. Wang, W., Guan, X.H., Zhang, X.L., Yang, L.W.: Profiling Program Behavior for Anomaly Intrusion Detection Based on The Transition and Frequency Property of Computer Audit Data. Computers & Security 25(7), 539–550 (2006)
4. Julisch, K.: Clustering Intrusion Detection Alarms to Support Root Cause Analysis. ACM Transactions on Information and System Security 6(4), 443–471 (2003)
5. Lee, W., Stolfo, S., Kui, M.: A Data Mining Framework for Building Intrusion Detection Models. In: IEEE Symposium on Security and Privacy, Oakland, pp. 120–132 (1999)
6. Shin, M.S., Jeong, K.J: An Alert Data Mining Framework for Network-based Intrusion Detection System. In: Song, J., Kwon, T., Yung, M. (eds.) WISA 2005. LNCS, vol. 3786, pp. 38–53. Springer, Heidelberg (2006)
7. Huang, M.Y., Jasper, R.J., Wicks, T.M.: A Large Scale Distributed Intrusion Detection Framework Based on Attack Strategy Analysis. Computer Networks 31, 2465–2475 (1999)
8. Julisch, K.: Clustering Intrusion Detection Alarms to Support Root Cause Analysis. ACM Transactions on Information and System Security 6(4), 443–471 (2003)
9. Khan, L., Awad, M., Thuraisingham, B.: A New Intrusion Detection System Using Support Vector Machines and Hierarchical Clustering. The International Journal on Very Large Data Bases, online first, 1–15 (2006)

10. Li, X.Y., Ye, N.: Mining Normal and Intrusive Activity Patterns for Computer Intrusion Detection. In: Chen, H., Moore, R., Zeng, D.D., Leavitt, J. (eds.) ISI 2004. LNCS, vol. 3073, pp. 226–238. Springer, Heidelberg (2004)
11. Li, X.B.: A Scalable Decision Tree System and Its Application in Pattern Recognition and Intrusion Detection. Decision Support Systems 41(1), 112–130 (2005)
12. Wei, C.P., Lee, Y.H., Hsu, C.M.: Empirical Comparison of Fast Partitioning-based Clustering Algorithms for Large Data Sets. Expert Systems with Applications 24, 351–363 (2003)
13. Peter, W., Chiochetti, J., Giardina, C.: New Unsupervised Clustering Algorithm for Large Datasets. In: Proceedings of the Ninth ACM SIGKDD International Conference on Knowledge Discovery and Data Mining, Washington, D.C, pp. 643–648. ACM Press, New York (2003)
14. Gursoy, A.: Data Decomposition for Parallel K-means Clustering. In: Wyrzykowski, R., Dongarra, J.J., Paprzycki, M., Waśniewski, J. (eds.) PPAM 2004. LNCS, vol. 3019, pp. 241–248. Springer, Heidelberg (2004)
15. Ceglar, A., Roddick, J.F.: Association Mining. ACM Computing Surveys 38(2), 1–42 (2006)
16. Parthasarathy, S., Zaki, M.J., Ogihara, M., Li, W.: Parallel Data Mining for Association Rules on Shared-memory Systems. Knowledge and Information Systems 3, 1–29 (2001)
17. Jia, C.Y., Gao, X.P.: Multi-scaling Sampling: an Adaptive Sampling Method for Discovering Approximate Association Rules. Journal of Computer Science and Technology 20(3), 309–318 (2005)
18. Tuv, E., Borisov, A., Torkkola, K.: Best Subset Feature Selection for Massive Mixed-type Problems. In: Proceedings of the 7th International Conference on Intelligent Data Engineering and Automated Learning, Burgos, Spain, pp. 1048–1056 (2006)
19. Tang, W.Y., Mao, K.Z.: Feature Selection Algorithm for Data with Both Nominal and Continuous Features. In: Ho, T.-B., Cheung, D., Liu, H. (eds.) PAKDD 2005. LNCS (LNAI), vol. 3518, pp. 683–688. Springer, Heidelberg (2005)
20. Amado, N., Gama, J., Silva, F.: Parallel Implementation of Decision Tree Learning Algorithms. In: Proceedings of the 10th Portuguese Conference on Artificial Intelligence, Porto, Portugal, pp. 6–13 (2001)
21. Todorovski, L., Dzeroski, S.: Combining Classifiers With Meta Decision Trees. Machine Learning 50(3), 223–249 (2003)
22. Bishop, C.M.: Training With Noise is Equivalent to Tikhonov Regularization. Neural computation 7(11), 108–116 (1995)
23. Geman, S., Bienenstock, E., Doursat, R.: Neural Networks and The Bias/variance Dilemma. Neural Computation 4, 1–58 (1992)
24. Folino, G., Pizzuti, C., Spezzano, G.: GP Ensemble for Distributed Intrusion Detection Systems. In: Proceedings of the 3rd International Conference on Advanced in Pattern Recognition, Bath, UK, pp. 54–62 (2005)

Processing Global XQuery Queries Based on Static Query Decomposition

Jong-Hyun Park and Ji-Hoon Kang*

Dept. of Computer Science, Chungnam National University
Gung-Dong, Yuseong-Gu, Daejeon, 305-764, South Korea
{jonghyunpark,jhkang}@cnu.ac.kr

Abstract. The concept of XML views is proposed to integrate heterogeneous data sources in XML, and a global XML view can represent the distributed heterogeneous data sources as single XML document. XQuery is one of the standard query languages for searching XML data. How to process efficiently of global XQuery queries, which are written under a global XML view, emerges as a new research topic. Popular techniques of distributed query processing are based on decomposition, and static decomposition is one of the processing techniques for the traditional query language. However, XQuery has a complex syntax such as FOR clauses that are not supported by other query languages, and its structural complexity causes some considerations for the decomposition of global XQuery queries. In this paper, we propose a method to decompose a global XQuery query into local XQuery queries and to construct the result of the global XQuery query from the results of the local XQuery queries.

Keywords: XQuery Decomposition, Processing Global XQuery.

1 Introduction

XML has emerged as the leading language for representing and exchanging data on the Internet. In recent years, there have been a number of researches focusing on the integration of XML data and heterogeneous data like relational data or Web information source described by URI [1, 2]. One of the integrating methods is using the global XML view [2]. The global XML view integrates local XML views in which users can see and search distributed heterogeneous data as a single XML document via global XML view. At this time, the query language used for searching and interoperability is XQuery language because it is a standard language for searching data written by XML.

XQuery is a standard query language proposed by W3C, and its expressive power is very rich [3]. However, the syntax of XQuery is quite complex because it borrows features from several other languages, including XPath, XQL, XML-QL, SQL, and OQL. Therefore, the efficient processing of XQuery query is not easy, and the processing of global XQuery query over a distributed environment is especially difficult.

* Corresponding author.

I. Stojmenovic et al. (Eds.): ISPA 2007, LNCS 4742, pp. 326–336, 2007.

In order to execute a traditional query on a distributed environment, one has to decompose a global query into local queries which are to be run by a number of participating servers. Unfortunately, it is difficult to decompose XQuery queries due to the irregular and non-orthogonal syntax of XQuery language [4]. One of the popular techniques of traditional distributed query processing like SQL, OQL is based on approach which decomposes a global query into several subqueries to be sent to local systems simultaneously [4, 5]. Local systems work in parallel. The global query processor collects the local results and constructs a global result by using local results. This method does not require any information for the processing of global query and can be extended to a dynamic or hybrid decomposition method regarding application. Therefore, determining a static decomposition method for the processing of global XQuery query is one of the research topics of the current paper. However, since XQuery is proposed for searching semi-structured data, its characteristic is different from SQL, and its syntactical complexity is high [6]. For example, an iteration generated by FOR clause in XQuery query is one of the considerations for global XQuery query processing, but is not in other query languages like SQL. Therefore, we have to consider some characteristics of XQuery query to apply the static decomposition technique to global XQuery query processing.

In order to search and integrate heterogeneous data with XML data over a distributed environment, this paper proposes a method to extract local XQuery queries from global XQuery query based on the static query decomposition technique and to generate the fusion XQuery query for constructing the result of global XQuery query from the local results. Although the XQuery query is written under global XML view, the real destination of global XQuery query is distributed local systems. Therefore, the efficient processing of global query depends on the data size extracted from the local system. To this end, we propose the decomposition method to obtain the minimized local results.

The rest of the paper is organized as follows. In Section 2, we present related works on processing global query. In Section 3, we introduce some considerations in XQuery query decomposition and show how we can decompose the global XQuery query into local XQuery queries and the fusion XQuery query for these considerations. In Section 4, we introduce the global XQuery query processor in which our decomposer runs. Finally, we summarize the contributions of this paper and indicate some directions for future research work in Section 5.

2 Related Work

An increasing number of business users and software applications need to process information that is accessible via multiple diverse information systems, such as data systems, file systems, legacy applications, or Web services. There are some studies on the integration of distributed relational data [7, 9], integration of relational data with semi-structured data [10, 11, 12], and efficient XQuery processing in a single system [13, 14]. However, these approaches are not direct methods for the integration of heterogeneous data with XML data. There are some proposed methods for global query processing in a distributed environment, and query decomposition is one of the popular and basic methods [4, 5, 6]. XQuery is the natural choice for data integration using XML view. However, it involves some problems in the application of previous decomposition methods into the global XQuery query because of its structural characteristics [6].

[15, 16] introduce the XQuery-based data integration systems that provide a queryable integrated view of such information. Their system architecture and function are very similar to those of our global XQuery query processor. Moreover, they also describe some considerations for global XQuery query processing. However, their focus is just the architecture and requirement of the integration system for efficient processing. They do not describe any specific algorithm which considers the structural characteristics of XQuery.

[17] proposes an extension to XQuery query by an additional expression that allows users to express queries over multiple, heterogeneous data sources. The goal of their extension is to generate local queries for the local system and to make a plan for local queries. This paper also introduces the usefulness of the local XQuery query for global XQuery query processing. However, their extended XQuery is quite complex to users, although they also propose a tool for generating XQuery query. Their processing method for global XQuery query involves the extension of XQuery, but XQuery in our method is purely XQuery proposed by W3C.

The system proposed in [8] is designed to enable users to pose the XML query over the Internet, and their goal is the same as our global XQuery query system. However, their query language is XML-QL and they do not use the global view for integration. [19, 20, 21] propose some methods for the efficient processing of distributed streaming XML data. However, their approaches define and use the interface for interaction between the mediator for global query processing and the wrappers for local systems. In other words, their systems use a dynamic query execution plan based on the special interface which is predefined for streaming XML data processing with wrappers for local systems. However, this paper assumes that we cannot obtain any information from local systems, and we know that all wrappers support XQuery query. This assumption supports the flexibility and extensibility of our system; thus, our system can be applied to any XQuery processor on a distributed environment that focuses on the global XQuery query processing based on the XML view. In addition, our method can be extended to make a dynamic XQuery execution plan which is considered as a feature of the application.

3 Decomposition of Global XQuery Queries

3.1 Some Considerations for XQuery Query Decomposition

The real destination of global XQuery queries is distributed local systems. Therefore, one consideration for the efficient processing of the global XQuery queries is how the global XQuery queries can be decomposed into local XQuery queries for the distributed local systems. In case of the SQL queries, the decomposition of the global SQL queries is not difficult because the SQL queries are written on relational data with flat structure. However, in case of XQuery queries, its data source is semi-structured data, and its expression contains some special expressions dependent on the data structure such as the FOR clauses. The FOR clauses are used to describe the repetition of nodes in an XML document, but it is one of the obstacles of XQuery query decomposition because of the scope of loops generated by the FOR clauses [6]. In other words, the FOR clauses in single XQuery query influence the reminder expressions of this query which are described below these FOR clauses. Moreover, all FOR clauses in a query always influence the RETURN clause because the latter is declared at the bottom of the query. For example, Table 1 shows the sample global XQuery query (GQ) and two XML documents which are "a.xml" and "x.xml." The destinations of sample XQuery query are the "A" local system and the "X" local system which store "a.xml" documents and "x.xml" documents, respectively. The left XML document is an "a.xml," and the right one is an "x.xml." The sample global query has some FOR clauses and a RETURN clause which has three variables defined in the FOR clause. The iterations generated by each FOR clause influences the RETURN clause. Consequently, the node structure of the result document returned by global query depends on the FOR clauses in the query. Therefore, we have to consider the FOR clauses to decompose global XQuery queries into local XQuery queries and to construct the result of global XQuery query from the local results.

Table 1. The global XQuery query and sample XML documents stored in a local system

Global XQuery query (GQ)	Local XML documents	
<Results>{ for $a in doc("a.xml")/root/a *for $x in doc("x.xml")/root/x* for $b in $a/b *for $y in $x/y* let $d := $b/d for $c in $a/c *for $z in $x/z* for $g in $a//g where $g = *$z* and $d > 2 return <result>{$c/h, *$y*, $b}</result> }</Results>	<root> <a> <b><d>1</d></b> <c><h>h1</h></c> <g>gz1</g> </a> <a> <b><d>3</d></b> <c><h>h2</h></c> <c><h>h3</h></c> <g>gz2</g> </a> <a> <b><d>5</d></b> <c><h>h3</h></c> <g>gz3</g> </a> </root>	<root> <x> <y>y1</y> <z>gz2</z> </x> <x> <y>y2</y> <z>gz3</z> </x> </root>

One of the simplest and basic methods for extracting local XQuery query from global XQuery queries is clustering the expressions with the same destination and then generating the local XQuery queries consisting of clustered expressions. This decomposition method can be applied for query languages with a flat structure such as relational data. However, the decomposition of XQuery is different from that of SQL because XML is semi-structured data. Although we can obtain the result set of local XQuery queries by this decomposition method, we have to know the order of nodes to reconstruct the result document of global XQuery queries. For example, we can decompose the GQ in Table 1 into two local XQuery queries. Table 2 shows two local XQuery queries (LQ1 for "A" local system and LQ2 for "X" local system) decomposed by clustering expressions. By these local queries, we can obtain the results which are described in Table 3. Also Table 3 shows the result of the GQ

Table 2. The global XQuery query and the local XQuery queries generated by expression clustering

Local XQuery queries (LQ1 and LQ2)	
<Results>{ for $a in doc("a.xml")/root/a for $b in $a/b let $d := $b/d for $c in $a/c for $g in $a//g where $d > 2 return <SubResult1>{$c/h, $b, $g}</SubResult1> }</Results>	<Results>{ for $x in doc("x.xml")/root/x for $y in $x/y for $z in $x/z return<SubResult2> {$y, $z}</SubResult2> }</Results>

Consequently, we have to reconstruct the result of the GQ by the results of LQ1 and LQ2 in Table 2. However, this reconstruction is not easy because we do not know the order information for node combination. Therefore, in order to adapt decomposition method for SQL, we have to consider the reconstruction of result of global query when decomposing global XQuery queries. Furthermore, we need an algorithm to reconstruct. This paper proposes the fusion XQuery queries which are used to reconstruct the global query results.

Table 3. The result of GQ in Table 1 and the results of LQ1 and LQ2 in Table 2

The result of GQ in Table 1	The results of LQ1 and LQ2 in Table 2	
<Results> <result> <h>h2</h> <y>y1</y> <b> <d>3</d> </b> </result> <result> <h>h3</h> <y>y1</y> <b> <d>3</d> </b> </result> <result> <h>h3</h> <y>y2</y> <b> <d>5</d> </b> </result> </Results>	<Results> <SubResult1> <h>h2</h> <b> <d>3</d> </b> <g>gz2</g> </SubResult1> <SubResult1> <h>h3</h> <b> <d>3</d> </b> <g>gz2</g> </SubResult1> <SubResult1> <h>h3</h> <b> <d>5</d> </b> <g>gz3</g> </SubResult1> </Results>	<Results> <SubResult2> <y>y1</y> <z>gz2</z> </SubResult2> <SubResult2> <y>y2</y> <z>gz3</z> </SubResult2> </Results>

Another consideration is reducing the size of the result document received from the local system because of the distributed environment. The FOR clauses in XQuery queries generate iterations, and these iterations cause the repeated construction of a node declared in the RETURN clause. Of course these repetitions are necessary in order to construct the correct structure of the result document. However, these repetitions can be executed in the global XQuery query processor. Consequently, in order to efficiently process a global XQuery query on a distributed environment, our global

XQuery query processor has to obtain the minimized result set from the local system and reconstruct the result of the global XQuery query by obtained results.

3.2 Generating the Local XQuery Queries and the Fusion XQuery Queries

The first step to generate the local XQuery queries is to define the information needed for processing global XQuery queries from the local system. The global XQuery query processor can see the data of the local system via XML view; thus, we can define the structure and content of the node needed for the processing of global XQuery query by XML tree structure. Figure 1 shows the information trees for processing the GQ as described in Table 1, and these trees contain the relationship of the nodes for extraction from two local systems.

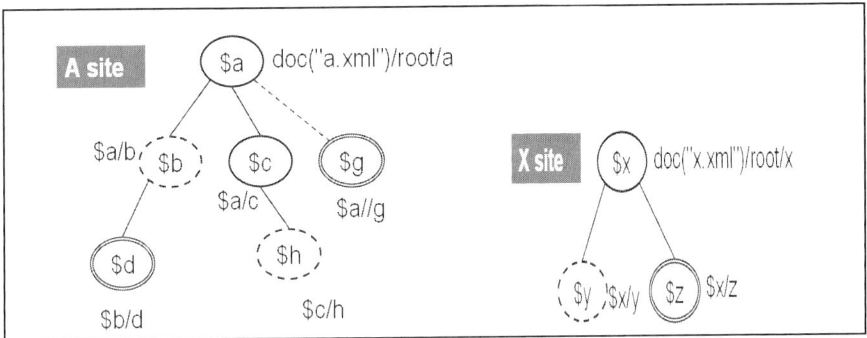

Fig. 1. The trees which express the structure of data needed for processing GQ in Table 1

The left and right trees in Figure 1 express the structure of nodes for extracting from the "A" local system and the "X" local system, respectively. Nodes circled by a double line in the tree express the nodes for processing conditions which are declared in GQ, while those nodes circled by a dotted line express the return nodes declared in the RETURN clause of the GQ. Single line edges express the parent-child relationship, while dotted line edges express the ancestor-descendant relationship. In case of the tree for the "A" local system, nodes required for processing the GQ are bound to variable $b, $h, and $g. Nodes bound to $b and $h include the result nodes of the GQ because these variables are declared in the RETURN clause of the GQ. Nodes bound to variable $g are used as an operand for the binary operation declared in the WHERE clause of the GQ, as the other operand node is other local systems. Therefore, the local XQuery query has to extract the nodes bound to $g to process the condition using $g in the GQ. In case of nodes bound to $d, although these nodes are used as an operand for the condition in the WHERE clause, the result of local XQuery query does not contain these nodes because this condition can be processed in single local system without referencing other system.

Table 4 shows the basic algorithm which generates the local XQuery queries from a global XQuery query. The result of local XQuery query generated by our algorithm is the subset of the XML document stored in a local system such as Figure 1. Table 5 shows the local XQuery queries which are generated by our algorithm to the GQ in Table 1.

Table 4. The algorithm for generating local XQuery queries from global XQuery query

```
■ LXQ : A Set of Local XQuery obtained by expression clustering
■ lxq : Local XQuery query
■ LETClauses : A Set of LET Clause
■ FORClauses : A Set of FOR Clause

TempLXQ = seperateGlobalXQuery(GXQuery);
            //Generate a local XQuery query by clustering expressions with the same destination
While(TempLXQ!= null){
   tlxq = TempLXQ.getLocalQuery(); // Get a temporal Local XQuery query
   LETClauses=getLETClauses(tlxq); //Extract all LET clause in Local XQuery query
   FORClauses=getFORClauses(tlxq);//Extract all FOR clause except first FOR clause in Local XQuery
        query
   for(each LETClause in LETClauses){
        FORclauses.add(translateLETtoFOR(LETClause));
        //translate LET clause to FOR clause and then insert translated FOR clause into FORClauses }
   LocalXQueryquery = Wrapper(first FOR clause in tlxq); //FOR clause declared doc() function
   LocalXQueryQueries.add(LocalXQueryquery);
   TempLXQ.remove(tlxq); //remove a temporal Local XQuery query }

Function Wrapper(FORclause, FORclauses){
   BoundVariable = FORclause.getBoundVariable();
   While(the BoundVariable is used in XPath Expression of other FORClause){
      WrappedFORClause = Wrapping(FORclause, other FORClause);
      //Create outer LET clause nesting other FORclause as its inner query and then Append the LET
      clause to FORClause
      Wrapper(other FORClause, FORclauses); }
   createWHEREandRETURNclause(WrappedFORClauses);
   //Create WHERE and RETURN Clause concerning WrappedFORClauses }
```

The first step of our algorithm is clustering the expressions which have the same destination and then generating the initial local XQuery queries. The second step is translating all LET clauses in the initial local XQuery queries into the FOR clause. The LET and FOR clauses are different. The LET clause generates one tuple that contains all the nodes bound to a variable, while the FOR clause generates a multiple tuple for each node binding. In case of the variable $d that is introduced in LQ1 in Table 2, this variable is declared in the LET clause and is also used as an operand of comparison operation in the WHERE clause. Consequently, the result set of this local XQuery query contains all nodes bound to variable $d, if at least one node value in the result set is greater than 2. However, the node needed for global XQuery query processing is just the node with a value greater than 2. Therefore, we can detect the creation of redundant nodes in local query result by translating the LET clause into FOR clause. The third step of the algorithm is creating a new outer LET clause for every FOR clause, including the translated FOR clauses and excluding the FOR clause described for root node. The inner query in the new LET clause consists of a single FOR clause and RETURN clause which returns the variable described in the FOR clause. In order to generate the local XQuery query from the left tree in Figure 1, the FOR clauses for addressing each node except the root node are generated, and then the LET clauses, including each FOR clause as their inner query, are generated. This step is used to obtain the local query result in order to keep the structure of the original XML document stored in the local system because some FOR clauses generate an XML document with a new structure.

The exists() functions are used to check the existence of the node bound to a variable which is an argument of this function. In case of Figure 1, if a node bound to variable $h in the XML document does not exist, this XML document is not useful for global XQuery query processing. If a node addressed by the FOR clause is just used to link two nodes such as variable $c in Figure 1, the node constructor for the construction of this node in the local XQuery query is declared such as line 15 of left query in Table 5. This node constructor is used to keep the structure of the left tree in Figure 1.

Table 5. The local XQuery queries generated from GQ and their result

Queries	<SubResult1>{ 1. for $a in doc("a.xml")/root/a 2. let $Wrapper0 := 3. for $b in $a/b 4. let $Wrapper1 := 5. for $d in $b/d 6. where $d > 2 7. return $d 8. where exists($Wrapper1) 9. return $b 10. let $Wrapper2 := 11. for $c in $a/c 12. let $Wrapper3 := 13. for $h in $c/h 14. return $h 15. return <c> {$Wrapper3} </c> 16. let $Wrapper4 := 17. for $g in $a//g 18. return $g 19. where exists($Wrapper0) and exists($Wrapper2) and exists($Wrapper4) 20. return <a>{$Wrapper0, $Wrapper2, $Wrapper4}</a> }</SubResult1>	<SubResult2>{ for $x in doc("x.xml")/root/x let $Wrapper0 := for $y in $x/y return $y let $Wrapper1 := for $z in $x/z return $z where exists($Wrapper0) and exists($Wrapper1) return <x>{$Wrapper0, $Wrapper1} </x> }</SubResult2>
Results	<SubResult1> <a> <b> <d>3</d> </b> <c> <h>h2</h> </c> <c> <h>h3</h> </c> <g>gz2</g> </a> <a> <b> <d>5</d> </b> <c> <h>h3</h> </c> <g>gz3</g> </a> </SubResult1>	<SubResult2> <x> <y>y1</y> <z>gz2</z> </x> <x> <y>y2</y> <z>gz3</z> </x> </SubResult2>

The fusion XQuery query is used to construct the result of global XQuery queries from the results obtained by local XQuery queries. Table 6 shows the fusion XQuery query for the GQ in Table 1. The doc() function in Table 6 addresses the result document obtained by local XQuery queries and returns their document node. The method to generate fusion XQuery queries is to translate global XQuery queries.

The FOR, LET, and RETURN clauses in a fusion XQuery query are the same with each clause in a global XQuery query, except FOR clauses including the doc() function. The fusion XQuery query includes JOIN operations of the global query which join between two local systems. The result of the fusion query in Table 6 is the same as the result of GQ in Table 3.

Table 6. The fusion XQuery query for constructing the result of GQ from the results obtained by local XQuery queries in Table 5

```
<Results> {
    for $a in doc("a'.xml")/SubResult1/a
    for $x in doc("x'.xml")/SubResult2/x
    let $b := $a/b
    for $y in $x/y
    for $d in $b/d
    for $c in $a/c
    for $z in $x/z
    for $g in $a//g
    where $g = $z
    return <result> {$c/h, $y, $b} </result>
}</Results>
```

4 Global XQuery Query Processor

Figure 2 shows an architecture of Global XQuery query processor which has been developed by the Electronics and Telecommunications Research Institute. The Global XQuery query processor uses our XQuery decomposer.

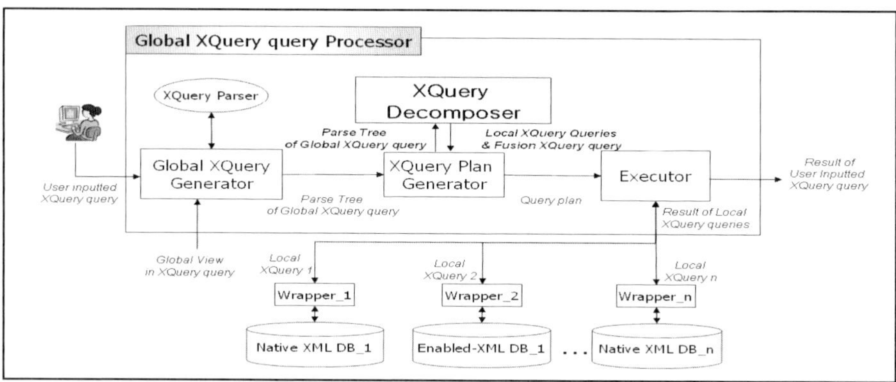

Fig. 2. An architecture of Global XQuery query processor

The Global XQuery generator produces the global XQuery query from the user-inputted XQuery query and global XML view. The XQuery Plan Generator interacts with our Decomposer and generates the query execution plan. As previously mentioned, the current XQuery plan generator statically generates the execution query plan based on decomposed local XQuery queries and the fusion XQuery query. However, our plan generator can be extended to make a dynamic execution query plan which considers a variety of factors such as joint strategies, selectivity, and indexing. The executor executes decomposed local XQuery queries and gets all the results from the local systems. Then executor runs the fusion XQuery query and obtains the final result.

5 Conclusion

In this paper, we have proposed a processing method of global XQuery query based on decomposition. For this method, we have addressed some considerations for XQuery query decomposition and correspondingly proposed a decomposition algorithm. Our result can obviously be applied to any XQuery processor that focuses on the integration and search of distributed data, since our decomposition approach is a general method and does not refer any information.

Currently, our decomposition method is statically executed to generate local XQuery queries. In the future, we will propose a dynamic or hybrid decomposition considering the characteristics of application.

Acknowledgement. This research is supported by the ubiquitous Computing and Network (UCN) Project, the Ministry of Information and Communication (MIC) 21st Century Frontier R&D Program in Korea.

References

1. Manolescu, I., Florescu, D., Kossmann, D.: Answering XML Queries over Heterogeneous Data Sources. In: Proc. VLDB, Roma, Italy (September 2001)
2. Shanmugasundaram, J., Kiernan, J., Shekita, E., Fan, C., Funderburk, J.: Querying XML Views of Relational Data. In: Proc. 27th VLDB, Roma, Italy (September 2001)
3. XQuery 1.0: An XML Query Language (April 2005), http://www.w3.org/TR/2005/WD-xquery-20050404/
4. Kozankiewicz, H., Stencel, K., Subieta, K.: Distributed Query Optimization in the Stack-Based Approach. In: Proc. HPCC 2005, Sorrento, Italy (September 2005)
5. Josifovski, V., Risch, T.: Query Decomposition for a Distributed Object-Oriented Mediator System. Distributed and Parallel Databases 11(3), 307–336 (2002)
6. Suciu, D.: Query Decomposition and View Maintenance for Query Languages for Unstructured Data. In: Proc. VLDB 1996, Mumbai (Bombay), India (September 1996)
7. Kossmann, D.: The state of the art in distributed query processing. ACM Computing Surveys 32(4), 422–469 (2000)
8. Smiljanic, M., Feng, L., Jonker, W.: Web-Based Distributed XML Query Processing. In: Proc. Intelligent Search on XML Data 2003 (September 2003)
9. Suciu, D.: Distributed query evaluation on semistructured data. ACM Transaction Database System 27(1), 1–62 (2002)
10. Zhang, X., Pielech, B., Rundensteiner, E.A.: Honey, I shrunk the XQuery!: an XML algebra optimization approach. In: Proc. WIDM 2002, McLean, Virginia, USA (November 2002)
11. Su, H., Rundensteiner, E.A., Mani, M.: Semantic Query Optimization in an Automata-Algebra Combined XQuery Engine over XML Streams. In: Proc. VLDB 2004, Toronto, Canada (September 2004)
12. Zhang, X., Rundensteiner, E.A.: XAT: XML Algebra for the Rainbow System. Technical Report WPI-CS-TR-02-24, Worcester Polytechnic Institute (July 2002)
13. Koch, C., Scherzinger, S., Schweikardt, N., Stegmaier, B.: FluXQuery: An Optimizing XQuery Processor for Streaming XML Data. In: Proc. VLDB 2004, Toronto, Canada (September 2004)

14. Yang, L.H., Lee, M.L., Hsu, W.: Finding hot query patterns over an XQuery stream. VLDB Journal 13(4), 318–332 (2004)
15. Papakonstantinou, Y., Vassalos, V.: Architecture and Implementation of an XQuery-based Information Integration Platform. IEEE Data Engineering Bulletin 25(1), 18–26 (2002)
16. Gardarin, G., Mensch, A., Dang-Ngoc, T., Smit, L.: Integrating Heterogeneous Data Sources with XML and XQuery. In: Proc. DEXA Workshops 2002, Aix-en-Provence, France (September 2002)
17. Re, C., Brinkley, J.F., Hinshaw, K.P., Suciu, D.: Distributed XQuery. In: Proc. IIWeb, Toronto (May 2004)
18. Naughton, J., DeWitt, D., Maier, D., Chen, J., Galanis, L., Tufte, K., Kang, J., Luo, Q., Prakash, N., Tian, F., et al.: The Niagara Internet Query System. IEEE Data Engineering Bulletin 24(2), 27–33 (2001)
19. Ives, Z.G., Florescu, D., Friedman, M., Levy, A.Y., Weld, D.S.: An Adaptive Query Execution System for Data Integration. In: Proc. SIGMOD Conference, Philadelphia, Pennsylvania, USA (June 1999)
20. Ives, Z.G., Levy, A.Y., Weld, D.S.: Adaptive Query Processing for Internet Applications. IEEE Data Engineering Bulletin 23(2), 19–26 (2000)
21. Ives, Z.G., Halevy, A., Weld, D.S.: An XML Query Engine for Network-Bound Data. VLDB Journal 11(4), 380–402 (2002)

Formal Verification and Performance Evaluation of User Query Pattern-Based Relational Schema-to-XML Schema Translation Algorithm*

Jinhyung Kim[1], Dongwon Jeong[2], and Doo-Kwon Baik[1]

[1] Dept. of Computer Science and Engineering, Korea Univerisity
136-713, 5 ga, Anam dong, Sungbuk gu, Seoul, Republic of Korea
{koolmania, baikdk}@korea.ac.kr

[2] Dept. of Informatics and Statistics, Kunsan National University
573-701, San 68, Myryong dong, Kunsan, Jollabuk do, Republic of Korea
djeong@kunsan.ac.kr

Abstract. This paper describes formal verification and quantitative performance evaluation for validating of query pattern-based relational schema-to-XML Schema translation (QP-T) algorithm. Many translation algorithms such as FT, NeT, CoT, ConvRel, and VP-T have been introduced on structural and/or semantic aspect for exact and effective translation. However, conventional algorithms consider only explicit referential integrity specified by relational schema or limitations regarding on reflection of implicit referential integrity information. It causes several problems such as incorrect translation, abnormal relational model transition, and so on. The QP-T algorithm analyzes query pattern and extract implicit referential integrities by interrelationship of equi-join in user queries. The QP-T algorithm can make up for weak points of the VP-T algorithm and create more exact XML Schema as a result by using with VP-T algorithm together.

1 Introduction

With XML emerging as the data format of the Internet era, there is a considerable increase in the amount of data encoded in XML [1, 2]. However, the majority of data is still stored and maintained in relational database [3]. Therefore, we need to translate such relational data into XML document.

Many translation algorithms have been developed on structural aspects and/or semantic aspects; User-specific translation algorithms, structural translation algorithm, and semantic translation algorithm. FT, NeT, CoT, ConvRel, and VP-T algorithm are representative algorithms for relational schema-to-XML DTD/Schema translation [8, 14, 15, 20, 22]. However, conventional algorithms just consider syntax part or restricted semantic part during translation. To solve this problem, the implicit referential integrity issues by value and query pattern analysis have been considered over the conversion [22, 23].

* This paper is supported by the second Brain Korea (BK) 21 Project.

I. Stojmenovic et al. (Eds.): ISPA 2007, LNCS 4742, pp. 337–346, 2007.

Researches about syntactic/semantic structure reconstruction also have been introduced in reverse-engineering part [4, 5, 6]. The CASE tool [4] can help analysis of structure for database reconstructing. The CASE tool considers structure and constraints by many analysis such as physical structure analysis, data flow analysis, usage pattern analysis, name analysis, domain analysis, data analysis, and program analysis. However, the processing steps of analysis are so complicate and some analysis is not necessary for relational schema-to-XML Schema translation. A [5] proposes a method for extracting an entity relationship schema by using node rules, link rules, and refinement rules. This method analyzes queries and reconstruct conceptual model by rules. However, this method is not effective to relational schema-to-XML Schema translation because there are too many rules and steps for reconstruction.

Therefore, the QP-T algorithm was proposed to solve many problems of conventional methods [23]. However, the performance evaluation of the VP-T algorithm was not enough to validate predominant characteristics. In consequence, we execute formal verification about extraction results of the QP-T algorithm and performance evaluation for validation about superiority of the QP-T algorithm in this paper.

2 Formal Verification

In this section, we use set theory for formal verification about implicit referential integrity relation extraction of the QP-T algorithm with simple dataset shown in Table 1. Set theory is the mathematical theory of sets, which represent collections of abstract objects. In most modern mathematical formalisms, set theory provides the language in which mathematical objects are described. It is (along with logic and the predicate calculus) one of the axiomatic foundations for mathematics, allowing mathematical objects to be constructed formally from the undefined terms of "set."

Table 1. Simple Dataset

< Student >

SID	Sname	PID
s01	Tom	p01
s02	John	P02
s03	Cathy	p02
s04	Brown	p03
s05	Cabin	p03
s06	Tom	p04

< Professor >

PID	Pname	Office
p01	Kim	217
p02	Lee	633
p03	Park	121
p04	Jean	222

< Class >

Cname	Room	Time
Database	701	2
Automata	702	1
Simulation	703	2
Algorithm	702	3

< Taking Lecture >

Seq_ID	SID	Cname
1	s01	Database
2	s01	Automata
3	s02	Simulation
4	s02	Algorithm
5	s02	Automata
6	s03	Database
7	s04	Simulation
8	s04	Algorithm

< Project >

Projname	PID	SID
Data Integration in Sensor Network	p01	s01
Wireless SN Design	p02	s02
Ontology Systme for DI	p03	s03
Integration System based on XML	p04	s05

First, for formal verification about extraction process of the QP-T algorithm, we need to formulate database model. The database model consists of four elements: database schema, initial referential integrity relation, extracted referential integrity relation, database language.

Definition 1. A Database model M_D is a set of database schemas $S = \{R_1, R_2, \cdots, R_n\}$. The database schema is a set of rules describing the structural format of the database. The database model M_D is also a set of referential integrity relation information defined in initially as $RI_{ini} = \{A_{22} \xrightarrow{RI_{ini}} A_{11}, A_{34} \xrightarrow{RI_{ini}} A_{21}\}$. The referential integrity relation information extracted by the VP-T and QP-T algorithm can be added to the data model as $RI_{VP} = \{A_{35} \xrightarrow{RI_{VP}} A_{21}, A_{44} \xrightarrow{RI_{QP}} A_{31}\}$.

Definition 2. A database schema R_i consists of relation name and a list of attributes $R_1 = \{A_{11}, A_{12}, \ldots, A_{1n}\}$, $R_2 = \{A_{21}, A_{22}, \ldots, A_{2m}\}$. Each attribute Ai includes many instances as $A_i = \cup Ins(A_{in})$. Each attribute A_i is also associated its domain $Dom(A_i)$. $Dom(M_D)$ can be defined as $Dom(M_D) = Dom(A_{11}) \times Dom\ (A_{12}) \times \cdots \times Dom(A_{nm})$.

Definition 3. The domain includes data type and semantic description information. The domain has the following property. Iff $A_{11} \neq A_{12}$ then $Dom(A_{11}) \neq Dom(A_{12})$, $\therefore$ Iff $Dom(A_{11}) \cap Dom(A_{12}) = \Phi$ then $A_{11} \neq A_{12}$.

Example 1. Data model definition about simple dataset shown in Table 1 by definition 1,2, and 3 is as follow.

- $M_D = \{S, RI_{ini}, RI_{VP}, L_S\}$
- S = {Student, Professor, Class, Taking Lecture, Project}
- Student = {SID, Sname, PID}, Professor = {PID, Pname, Office}, Class = {Cname, Room, Time}, Taking Lecture = {Seq_ID, SID, Cname}, Project = {Projname, PID, SID}
- INS(SID) = {s01, s02, s03, s04, s05, s06}, INS(Sname) = {Tom, John, Cathy, Brown, Cabin. Tom}, INS(PID) = {p01, p02, p02, p03, p03, p04}
- INS(PID) = {p01, p02, p03, p04}, INS(Pname) = {Kim, Lee, Park, Jean}, INS(Office) = {217, 633,121,222}
- INS(Cname) = {Database, Automata, Simulation, Algorithm}, INS(Room) = {701, 702, 703, 702}, INS(Time) = {2, 1, 2, 3}
- INS(Seq_ID) = {1, 2, 3, 4, 5, 6, 7, 8}, INS(SID) = {s01, s01, s02, s02, s02, s03, s04, s04}, INS(Cname) = {Database, Automata, Simulation, Algorithm, Automata, Database, Simulation, Algorithm}
- INS(Projname) = {Data Integration in Sensor Network, Wireless SN Design, Ontology System for DI, Integration System based on XML }, INS (PID) = {p01, p02, p03, p04}, INS(SID) = {s01, s02, s03, s05}
- $RI_{ini} = \{ A_{13} \xrightarrow{RI_{ini}} A_{21}, A_{43} \xrightarrow{RI_{ini}} A_{31} \}$
- $RI_{VP} = \{ A_{42} \xrightarrow{RI_{VP}} A_{11} \}$, $RI_{QP} = \{ A_{52} \xrightarrow{RI_{QP}} A_{21}, A_{53} \xrightarrow{RI_{QP}} A_{11} \}$

{PID column of Student table and PID column of Professor table} and {Cname column of TakingLecture table and Cname column of Class table} are explicit referential integrity relation information. {SID column of TakingLecture table and SID column of Student table} can be extracted by the VP-T algorithm because two columns have 1:N relation. However, {PID column of Project table and PID column of Professor table} and {SID column of Project table and SID column of Student table} can be extracted by not the VP-T algorithm but QP-T algorithm because two columns have 1:1 relation not 1:N relation.

Example 2. Domain information of each attribute includes data type information of instances (Dom_{DT}) and semantic description (Dom_{SD}). The semantic description is related column list by analysis of user query.

- Dom_{DT}(SID) = {String}, Dom_{SD}(SID) = {TakingLecture.SID, Project.SID}, Dom_{DT}(Sname) = {String}, Dom_{SD}(Sname) = {Null}, Dom_{DT}(PID) = {String}, Dom_{SD}(PID) = {Professor.PID, Project.PID}
- Dom_{DT}(PID) = {String}, Dom_{SD}(PID) = {Student.PID, Project.PID}, Dom_{DT}(Pname) = {String}, Dom_{SD}(Pname) = {Null}, Dom_{DT}(Office) = {Integer}, Dom_{SD}(Office) = {Null}
- Dom_{DT}(Cname) = {String}, Dom_{SD}(Cname) = {TakingLecture.Cname}, Dom_{DT}(Room) = {Integer}, Dom_{SD}(Room) = {Null}, Dom_{DT}(Time) = {Integer}, Dom_{SD}(Time) = {Null}
- Dom_{DT}(Seq_ID) = {Integer}, Dom_{SD}(Seq_ID) = {Null}, Dom_{DT}(SID) = {String}, Dom_{SD}(SID) = {Student.SID, Project.SID}, Dom_{DT}(Cname) = {String}, Dom_{SD}(Cname) = {Class.Cname}
- Dom_{DT}(Projname) = {String}, Dom_{SD}(Projname) = {Null}, Dom_{DT}(PID) = {String}, Dom_{SD}(PID) = {Student.PID, Professor.PID}, Dom_{DT}(SID) = {String}, Dom_{SD}(SID) = {TakingLecture.SID, Student.SID}

Definition 4. The Primary Key is a subset of $\{A_{i1}, A_{i2}, \cdots, A_{in}\}$ and can be represented as $R_i[PK] = \{A_{i1}\}$. The Foreign Key is also a subset of $\{A_{j1}, A_{j2}, \cdots, A_{jn}\}$ and can be represented as $R_i[FK] = \{A_{j2}\}$.

Example 3. The representation of PK and FK information about simple dataset shown in Table 1 is as follow.

- Student[PK] = {SID}, Professor[PK] = {PID}, Class[PK] = {Cname}, Taking Lecture[PK] = {Seq_ID}, Project[PK] = {Projname}
- Student[FK] = {PID}, Taking Lecture[FK] = {SID, Cname}, Project[FK] = {PID, SID}

We defined data model and detail information such as the domain information, the primary key information, and the foreign key information. With these information defined by definition 1,2,3, and 4, we execute formal verification about implicit referential integrity relation information extraction of the QP-T algorithm. Through the formal verification, we can validate that extracted implicit referential integrity relation information by the QP-T algorithm is exact. Before validation, we define referential integrity relation.

Definition 5. If column A_{22} is the foreign key, A_{11} is the primary key, and there is referential integrity between column A_{22} and A_{11}, the referential integrity relation can be represented as $A_{22} \xrightarrow{RI} A_{11} \Leftrightarrow (\forall_x)(x \subseteq R_2 \Rightarrow (\exists_y)(y \subseteq R_1 \wedge x.A_{22} = y.A_{11}))$.

To validate extracted implicit referential integrity relation information by the QP-T algorithm we check four points. First, if there is the referential integrity relation between column A_{22} and A_{11}, the data type in domain information of column A_{22} and A_{11} are same. Second, if $A_{22} \xrightarrow{RI_{QP}} A_{11}$, the semantic description in domain information of column A_{22} includes column name of A_{11}. Third, if $A_{22} \xrightarrow{RI_{QP}} A_{11}$, some instance in the foreign key column of relation 2 are the same as instance in the primary key column of relation 1. Fourth, if column A_{22} refers to A_{11} as the referential integrity relation, union of instances in column A_{22} is a subset of union of instances in column A_{11}.

Definition 6. If there is the referential integrity relation between column A_{11}(Primary Key) and A_{22} (Foreign Key), there exist following relations.

- Iff $A_{22} \xrightarrow{RI_{QP}} A_{11}$ then $Dom_{DT}(A_{22}) = Dom_{DT}(A_{11})$
- Iff $A_{22} \xrightarrow{RI_{QP}} A_{11}$ then $(\exists_i)(Dom_{SDi}(A_{22})) = A_{11}$
- Iff $A_{22} \xrightarrow{RI_{QP}} A_{11}$ then $(\exists_i)(INS_i(R_2[FK])) = (\exists_j)(INS_j(R_1[PK]))$
- Iff $A_{22} \xrightarrow{RI_{QP}} A_{11}$ then $\cup INS_i(R_2[FK]) \subset \cup INS_i(R_1[PK])$

Example 4. Through the QP-T algorithm, two implicit referential integrity relations are extracted as $RI_{QP1} = \{A_{52} \xrightarrow{RI_{QP}} A_{21}\}$, $RI_{QP2} = \{A_{53} \xrightarrow{RI_{QP}} A_{11}\}$ is extracted.

- A_{52} = {Project.PID}, A_{21} = {Professor.PID}, A_{53} = {Project.SID}, A_{11} = {Student.SID}
- $Dom_{DT}(A_{52})$ = {String}, $Dom_{DT}(A_{21})$ = {String}, $Dom_{DT}(A_{53})$ = {String}, $Dom_{DT}(A_{11})$ = {String}
- $Dom(A_{52}) = Dom(A_{21})$ = {String}, $Dom(A_{53}) = Dom(A_{11})$ = {String}
- $\therefore$ ***iff*** $A_{52} \xrightarrow{RI_{QP}} A_{21}$ ***then*** $Dom_{DT}(A_{52}) = Dom_{DT}(A_{21})$ ***[True]***
- $\therefore$ ***iff*** $A_{53} \xrightarrow{RI_{QP}} A_{11}$ ***then*** $Dom_{DT}(A_{53}) = Dom_{DT}(A_{11})$ ***[True]***

- $Dom_{SD}(A_{52})$ = {Student.PID, Professor.PID}, (A_{21}) = {Professor.PID}, $Dom_{SD}(A_{53})$ = {TakingLecture.SID, Student.SID}, (A_{11}) = {Student.SID}
- $Dom_{SD}(A_{52}) = A_{21}$, $Dom_{SD}(A_{53}) = A_{11}$
- $\therefore$ ***iff*** $A_{52} \xrightarrow{RI_{QP}} A_{21}$ ***then*** $Dom_{SD}(A_{52}) = A_{21}$ ***[True]***
- $\therefore$ ***iff*** $A_{53} \xrightarrow{RI_{QP}} A_{11}$ ***then*** $Dom_{SD}(A_{53}) = A_{11}$ ***[True]***
- $INS_1(A_{52})$ = {p01}, $INS_2(A_{52})$ = {p02}, $INS_3(A_{52})$ = {p03}, $INS_4(A_{52})$ = {p04}, $INS_5(A_{52})$ = {p03}, $INS_1(A_{21})$ = {p01}, $INS_2(A_{21})$ = {p02}, $INS_3(A_{21})$ = {p03}, $INS_4(A_{21})$ = {p04}, $INS_1(A_{53})$ = {s01}, $INS_2(A_{53})$ = {s02}, $INS_3(A_{53})$ = {s03}, $INS_4(A_{21})$ = {s04}, $INS_5(A_{53})$ = {s03}, $INS_2(A_{11})$ = {s01}, $INS_2(A_{11})$ = {s02}, $INS_3(A_{11})$ = {s03}, $INS_4(A_{11})$ = {s04}, $INS_5(A_{11})$ = {s05}, $INS_6(A_{11})$ = {s06}

- $INS_1(A_{52}) = INS_1(A_{21}) = \{p01\}$, $INS_2(A_{52}) = INS_2(A_{21}) = \{p02\}$, $INS_3(A_{52}) = INS_5(A_{52}) = INS_3(A_{21}) = \{p03\}$, $INS_4(A_{52}) = INS_4(A_{21}) = \{p04\}$
- $\therefore$ ***Iff*** $A_{52} \xrightarrow{RI_{QP}} A_{21}$ ***then*** $(\exists_i)(INS_i(R_5[FK])) = (\exists_j)(INS_j(R_2[PK]))$ ***[True]***
- $INS_1(A_{53}) = INS_1(A_{11}) = \{s01\}$, $INS_2(A_{53}) = INS_2(A_{11}) = \{s02\}$, $INS_3(A_{53}) = INS_5(A_{53}) = INS_3(A_{11}) = \{s03\}$, $INS_4(A_{53}) = INS_4(A_{11}) = \{s04\}$
- $\therefore$ ***Iff*** $A_{53} \xrightarrow{RI_{QP}} A_{11}$ ***then*** $(\exists_i)(INS_i(R_5[FK])) = (\exists_j)(INS_j(R_1[PK]))$ ***[True]***
- $\cup INS_i(R_5[FK]) = \{p01, p02, p03, p04\}$, $\cup INS_i(R_2[PK]) = \{p01, p02, p03, p04\}$
- $\therefore$ ***Iff*** $A_{52} \xrightarrow{RI_{QP}} A_{21}$ ***then*** $\cup INS_i(R_5[FK]) \subset \cup INS_i(R_2[PK])$ ***[True]***
- $\cup INS_i(R_5[FK]) = \{s01, s02, s03, s04\}$, $\cup INS_i(R_1[PK]) = \{s01, s02, s03, s04, s05, s06\}$
- $\therefore$ ***Iff*** $A_{53} \xrightarrow{RI_{QP}} A_{11}$ ***then*** $\cup INS_i(R_5[FK]) \subset \cup INS_i(R_1[PK])$ ***[True]***

✓ ***Because RI_{QP1} and RI_{QP2} meet all of condition 1, 2, 3, and 4 in definition 6, RI_{QP1} and RI_{QP2} are exact implicit referential integrity relation information. Implicit referential integrity relation information extracted by the QP-T algorithm is right.***

3 Performance Evaluation

3.1 Dataset for Experiments

For the performance evaluation of the QP-T algorithm, we use a MS Access Northwind Sample Database, a TPC-H sample schema v1.2.0[22], and Oracle Business Database Sample Schema. The MS Access Northwind Sample Database consists of 9 tables, 87 columns, and 7 foreign key constraints. The TPC-H sample schema v.1.2.0 consists of 8 tables, 59 columns, and 8 foreign key constraints. These 2 sample databases are simple and small databases for scholar experiment, but Oracle Business Database Sample Schema is a practical database which consists of 24 tables, 122 columns, and 37 referential integrities about goods selling, order, and human resource management. Basis information and limitation of experimental data are as in Table 2.

At present, all referential integrity relation in MS Access NorthWind Database and TPC-H Sample Schema are defined explicitly. Therefore, we modify some referential integrity relation of these experimental data by removing a part of physical relation for clear and precise experiment.

Table 2. DataSet Information

Sample Data Sets	T	C	RI_{exp}	RI_{imp}	$RI_{no\text{-}value}$	$RI_{imp\text{-}QP}$
MS Access Northwind	9	87	7	2	1	1
TPC-H Sample Schema	8	59	8	2	1	1
Oracle Business Sample Schema	24	122	37	24	4	2

RI_{exp}: Numbers of Explicit RI, RI_{imp}: Numbers of Implicit RI, $RI_{no\text{-}value}$: Numbers of Implicit RI that the VP-T cannot extract, $RI_{imp\text{-}QP}$: Numbers of Implicit RI that QP-T can extract in $RI_{no\text{-}value}$.

3.2 Translation Accuracy

The translation accuracy of the relational schema-to-XML Schema translation represents how many referential integrity relations are reflected during translation. Fig. 1 shows the translation accuracy of three sample data sets. The NeT algorithm does not consider referential integrity relation and only considers structural translation. Therefore, the NeT algorithm cannot extract and reflect referential integrity relation information during relational schema-to-XML Schema translation. The CoT and ConvRel algorithms can extract RI_{exp} of sample data sets because algorithms only consider referential integrity relation defined explicitly. Therefore, CoT and ConvRel algorithm cannot extract implicit referential integrity relation information and also cannot

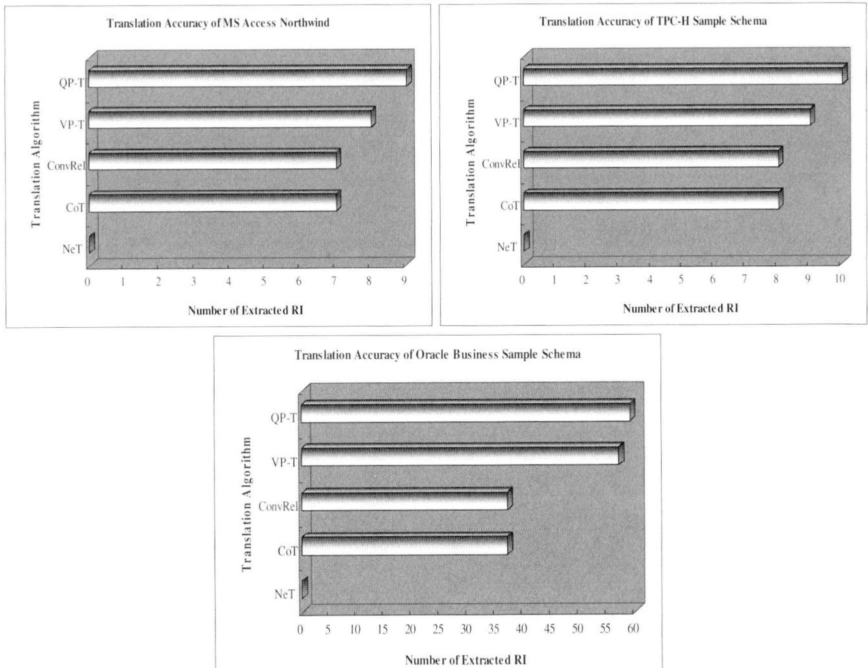

Fig. 1. Translation Accuracy of Sample Datasets

guarantee translation accuracy during relational schema-to-XML Schema translation. The VP-T algorithm can extract both explicit and implicit referential integrity relation information and present better translation accuracy than NeT or CoT algorithms. However the VP-T algorithm has a limitation that only 1:N cardinality can be extracted by the VP-T algorithm. That is, if the PK field and FK field does not have 1:N cardinality, VP-T algorithm cannot reflect that referential integrity relation during translation. Therefore, the VP-T algorithm cannot extract $RI_{no\text{-}value}$ in RI_{imp}. However, the QP-T algorithm can overcome drawback of the VP-T algorithm by query pattern analysis. The QP-T algorithm can extract $RI_{imp\text{-}QP}$ in $RI_{no\text{-}value}$ additionally compared to the VP-T algorithm.

3.3 Referential Integrity Relation Loss Ratio

The referential integrity relation information loss ratio during the relational schema-to-XML Schema translation is as in Fig. 3. The loss ratio represents rate that how much referential integrity relation information is not extracted and lost during the translation. The formula for the referential integrity relation loss ratio is shown as in Fig. 2.

$$RI_{LR} = \frac{RI_{all} - (RI_{\exp} + RI_{imp}) + RI_{no-value} - RI_{imp-QP}}{RI_{\exp} + RI_{imp}} * 100(\%)$$

Fig. 2. Formula for RI Loss Ratio

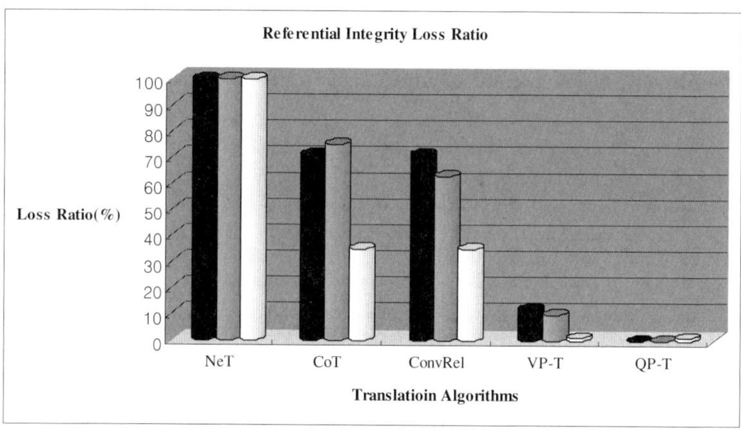

Fig. 3. RI Loss Ratio of Sample Datasets

The referential integrity relation loss ratio of the NeT algorithm is always 100% because the NeT algorithm only translates structural part such as tables and columns exactly and lost all of information about semantic part such as referential integrity and constraints during translation. The CoT algorithm can extract and reflect explicit referential integrity relation information without loss but it loses all of implicit referential integrity relation information. The referential integrity relation loss ratio of the

VP-T algorithm is lower than NeT or CoT because the VP-T algorithm can extract and reflect not only explicit referential integrity relation information but also implicit referential integrity relation information by analysis of value pattern. However, if there are not enough instances, the loss ratio of the VP-T algorithm become bigger. The QP-T algorithm can complement to the VP-T algorithm by user query analysis and presents the lowest loss ratio in translation algorithms.

4 Related Works

Various translation algorithms have been proposed. Translation algorithms are classified into 3 groups such as user specific translation methods, structural translation methods, and semantic translation methods. XML Extender from IBM, XML-DBMS [9], SilkRoute [10], XPERANTO [11], and DB2XML [12] are included in user specific translation methods. User-specific translation methods have the drawback that users have to provide rules for mapping additionally. FT [8] and NeT [8, 14] are typical methods of structural translation methods. However, demerit of structural translation methods is that these algorithms cannot reflect referential integrity relation information during relational schema-to-XML schema translation. CoT [14, 15], ConvRel [18], and VP-T [22] are classified as semantic translation methods. However, the CoT and ConvRel algorithm can only reflect explicit referential integrity relation. The VP-T algorithm can reflect implicit referential integrity relation but, it has a limitation that PK fields and FK fields must have 1:N relation. That is, the VP-T algorithm cannot extract implicit referential integrity relation which does not have 1:N cardinality.

5 Conclusion and Future Works

In this paper, we validate extraction result of the QP-T algorithm by formal verification. We also evaluate translation accuracy from relational schema-to-XML Schema and referential integrity relation information loss ratio through quantitative experiments. Consequently, extraction results of the QP-T algorithm are proved as exact and reliable results and the translation accuracy and the RI loss ratio of the QP-T algorithm shows better result compared to conventional algorithms such as NeT, CoT, ConvRel, and VP-T algorithm.

References

1. Bray, T., Paoli, J., Cavary, M. (eds.): Extensible Markup Language (XML) 1.0, 2nd edn. W3C Recommendation (October 2000)
2. ISO / IEC JTC 1 SC 34, ISO / IEC 8839:1986: Information processing – Text and office systems – Standard Generalized Markup Language (SGML) (August 2001)
3. Elmasri, R., Navathe, S. (eds.): Fundamental of Database Systems, 4th edn. Addison-Wesley, Reading (2003)
4. Hainaut, J., Henrard, J., Roland, D., Englebert, V., Hick, J. (eds.): Structure Elicitation in Database Reverse Engineering. In: Proceedings of the 3rd Working Conference on Reverse Engineering. IEEE, Los angeles (1996)

5. Anderson, M. (eds.): Extracting an Entity Relationship Schema from a Relational Database through Reverse Engineering. In: Proceedings of the 13th Int. Conf. on ERA. Springer, Manchester (1994)
6. Hainaut, J., Chandelon, M., Tonneau, C., Joris, M. (eds.): Transformational techniques for database reverse engineering. In: Proceedings of the 12th Int. Conf. on ERA. EIR Institute and Springer-Verlag (1993)
7. Fan, W., Simeon, J. (eds.): Integrity Constraints for XML. In: Proceedings of the ACM PODS, Dallas, TX (May 2000)
8. Lee, D., Mani, M., Chiu, F., Chu, W.W. (eds.): Nesting-based Relational-to-XML Schema Translation. In: Proceedings of the Int'l. Workshop on the Web and Databases, Santa Barbara, CA (May 2001)
9. Naughton, J., DeWitt, D., Maier, D.: The Niagara Internet Query System. Proceedings of the IEEE Data Engineering Bulletin 24(2), 27–33 (2001)
10. Fernandez, M., Tan, W., Suciu, D. (eds.): SilkRoute: Trading between Relations and XML. In: Proceedings of the Int'l. World Wide Web Conf. Amsterdam, Netherlands (May 2000)
11. Carey, M., Floirescu, D., Ives, Z., Lu, Y., Shanmugasundaram, J., Shekita, E., Subramanian, S. (eds.): XPERANTO: Publishing Orbject-Relational Data as XML. In: Proceedings of the Int'l. Workshop on the Web and Databases, Dallas, TX (May 2000)
12. Turau, V. (eds.): Making Legacy Data Accessible for XML Applications (1999)
13. Kurt, C., David, H. (eds.): Beginning XML, 2nd edn. John Wiley & Sons Inc., Chichester (2001)
14. Lee, D., Mani, M., Chit, F., Chu, W.W. (ed.): Effective Schema Conversions between XML and Relational Models. In: Proceedings of the European Conference on Artificial Intelligence and the Knowledge Transformation Workshop, Lyon, France (July 2002)
15. Lee, D., Mani, M., Chiu, F., Chu, W.W. (eds.): NeT&CoT: Translating Relational Schemas to XML Schemas using Semantic Constraints. In: Proceedings of the 11th ACM Int'l. Conference on Information and Knowledge Management, McLean, VA, USA (November 2002)
16. Goodson, J.: Using XML with Existing Data Access Standards. Enterprise Application Integration Knowledge Base Journal, 43–45 (2002)
17. Widom, J.: Data Management for XML: Research Directions. Proceedings of the IEEE Data Engineering Bulletin, 44–52 (1999)
18. Seligman, L., Rosenthal, A.: XML's Impact on Databases and Data Sharing. IEEE 34(6), 59–67 (2001)
19. Witkowski, A., Bellamkonda, S., Bozkaya, T., Folkert, N., Gupta, A., Haydu, J., Sheng, L., Subramanian, S.: Advanced SQL Modeling in RDBMS. Proceedings of the ACM Transactions on Database Systems 30(1), 83–121 (2005)
20. Duta, A.C., Barker, K., Alhajj, R.: ConvRel: Relationship Conversion to XML Nested Structures. In: SAC 2004. LNCS, vol. 3357, Springer, Heidelberg (2004)
21. Transaction Processing Performance Councill: Available at: http://www.tpc.org/tpch/spec/h130.pdf
22. Jinhyung, K., Dongwon, J., Dookwon, B.: An Algorithm for Automatic Inference of Referential Integrities During Translation from Relational Database to XML schema. In: Hao, Y., Liu, J., Wang, Y.-P., Cheung, Y.-m., Yin, H., Jiao, L., Ma, J., Jiao, Y.-C. (eds.) CIS 2005. LNCS (LNAI), vol. 3802, pp. 161–170. Springer, Heidelberg (2005)
23. Jinhyung, K., Dongwon, J., Yixin, J., Dookwon, B.: QP-T: Query Pattern-Based RDB-to-XML Translation. In: Meersman, R., Tari, Z., Herrero, P. (eds.) On the Move to Meaningful Internet Systems 2006: OTM 2006 Workshops. LNCS, vol. 4278, pp. 1844–1853. Springer, Heidelberg (2006)

Adaptive Processing for Continuous Query over Data Stream

Misook Bae, Buhyun Hwang[*], and Jiseung Nam

Dept. of Computer Science, Chonnam National University
300 Yongbong-Dong, Gwangju, Republic of Korea
{msbae,bhhwang,jsnam}@chonnam.ac.kr

Abstract. Stream applications such as sensor data processing, financial tickers and Internet traffic analysis require that information, naturally, occur as a stream of data values. Due to a late and out-of-order arrival of infinite, unbound and multiple input streams, processing continuous queries over them may lead to producing an incorrect answer or delaying query execution. Hence to minimize this waiting time, previous works have used timeout technique without considering the frequency of timeouts. It results in decreasing the accuracy of query execution results, since the more the frequency of timeouts, the more the loss of data. We propose an AP-STO method using StB that stores operator's state and a window time-out method based on the waiting time for the next tuple by resetting the size of a window according to the frequency of timeouts. It reduces a data lost rate and increases the tuples output-rate. We compare AP-STO method with an existing method and use output-rate and response time as criteria for performance evaluation. Our proposed method shows a substantial improvement in system performance in terms of the accuracy of query execution and the increment of tuples output-rate per a query due to the reduction in loss rate of data.

Keywords: data stream, latency, processing continuous query, timeout, inaccuracy, sliding window.

1 Introduction

A middleware which supports application service in a ubiquitous environment must, in real-time process continuous and unbounded input data, acquire and transfer the results that application users require. And queries in DSMS (Data Stream Management System) are different from those in DBS (DataBase System). Firstly, DSMS uses continuous queries while DBS does one-time queries. Secondly, most DSMSs approximately answer queries while DBSs produce correct answers for a query. So, we need an approach to process continuous data streams separately from their existing ways. Stream systems must resolve the issues to unpredictable and various characteristics such as stream type with bursty or rare input rate and continuous query over stream data. Data sources, e.g. sensors, continuously push tuples in the form of stream. The tuples may arrive late and they may be out of order,

[*] Corresponding author.

I. Stojmenovic et al. (Eds.): ISPA 2007, LNCS 4742, pp.347–358,2007.

since they are volatile and unpredictable. So, a data stream is a sequence of real-time, continuous and ordered items. Stream processing applications include senor-based environment monitoring, Internet track analysis, and financial tickers. Most of the stream processing applications depend on the windows technique that restricts an interesting scope to answer a continuous query over an unbounded stream. Windows is a mechanism to extract finite relations from infinite streams. That is, window defines the set of tuples to consider by restricting scope of unbounded tuples to produce outputs on continuous query. Currently, several window execution styles such as windows based on time, tuple counts, explicit markers and etc. are proposed. However, a time-based sliding window has been widely used in a stream data system. A time-based sliding window refers to a sliding window that includes items arrived during the last t time unit. A sliding window is used as an approximation tool for a continuous query to expire stale data from affecting with analysis and statistics in the bounded memory. When a query is processed on the sliding window, the recomputation strategy and the tuple expiration procedure affect its response time [1, 2].

This paper deals with the issues on incorrect query processing as a result of native latency of multiple sensor input streams. Hence, it presents an example scenario about the delay of query execution and the products of incorrect query execution results due to different arrival rates on the time-based sliding window. Existing methods use a timeout technique without considering the frequency of timeouts to resolve a delay of query execution. Amount of lost data is proportional to the frequency of timeouts due to the recomputation of a system. It, therefore, results in to decreasing the accuracy of query execution results. We propose AP-STO method using StB which stores operator's state and a new window time-out mechanism which resets the size of a window according to the frequency of timeouts. It decreases the data lost rate and increases the tuple output-rate. The proposed algorithm is compared with an existing method using response time and output-rate as the performance measures while varying waiting time.

The remainder of this paper is organized as follows: Section 2 is about the related work on the existing data stream processing. Section 3 presents the problem that can be experienced when processing queries over data stream. The section also proposes a system model and algorithm for effective query processing. Section 4 deals with the implementation and performance evaluation of the proposed algorithm. Section 5, finally, concludes this paper.

2 Related Work

Nowadays a variety of projects have been progressed to process data stream efficiently. Aurora project [3,4,5] among them supports a new operator set such as filter, union, aggregate, join that includes window-based operators that can be operated in bounded region over continuous input stream. It satisfies real-time requirements of users by defining QoS specification and making possible dynamic resource allocation. STREAM project [2,6,7,11] defined and used CQL similar to SQL for defining continuous query over data stream. CQL regards data stream and window as a sorted table with timestamp, and supports conversion operator to transform the result table of a query into a data stream. Telegraph CQ project supports routing over input data stream, scheduling to operator, and sharing of resource to process a query over continuous data stream. But these researches focused only operator itself. NILE project [8,9] studied optimizer-based query evaluation plan and dealt with the interaction across operators. It deals with the ordered data to induce correct execution by timestamping every stream tuple to resolve problem such as different arrival rate of infinitely incoming data stream and uses temporary memory to store operator's state and processed tuples. But this approach needs the time to sort tuples according to timestamp every time processed tuples insert and waste memory due to storing all of processed tuple set. Also [10] studied in-order execution but did not consider late arrival of data stream.

Querying over data stream includes producing a new answer when query runs a period of time and arrives new item on this continuous query in online stream processing. Because data streams do not store the whole in memory, they ordered temporally and streaming query plan do not use blocking operator that must consume the whole before a result produces. [6] indicated that these problems must be recognized and resolved. These come out conception of window. Specially, [7] is indicated that continuous query in DSMS depends on time as a base to define consistent semantics to be related to window and multiple stream updatable and the possibility of late arrival of data stream due to out of ordered and uncooperative data stream.

A sliding window query over data streams composes multiple operators. Operators are executed in form that the output from an operator is pipelined as input to next operator. This execution model is used typically in stream processing systems such as Fjord, Borealis, STREAM [1,3,4,5,6]. Proposed algorithm presents and resolves problem of the latency of tuples across operators in environment based this model.

3 AP-STO

In this section, our proposed algorithm and performance evaluation are detailed described.

3.1 Problem Statement

When a query runs, late arrival and disorder of tuples may produce incorrect result or may increase a response time in continuous query over infinite multiple input streams. An example is depicted as follows. Let's assume that there is a health care program that diagnoses disease by using data sent in a blood pressure sensor, S1, and a pulse sensor, S2. Supposed that if the frequency presented by the case that an output value of the blood pressure is larger than 160 and an output value of the pulse pressure is larger than 100 outputted repeats more than 5 times within 300 seconds, it would be possible to break out the disease to be called AA. To check a health condition, there is a continuous query Q that computes a total count of tuples which satisfies an upper condition every 300 seconds. The query Q is presented as follows.

```
Q: Select count  (S1.value, S2.value) from HealthStream S1, S2
        where  (S1.value>160 & S2.value>100)
        window on 300 seconds;
```

Each stream, among S1 and S2, is a stream as an input to select an operator and then to count the operator in a pipelined query evaluation. Fig. 1 simplifies each of the input stream data items of query Q (they are composed of only one digit of integer). Fig. 1(a) shows a pipelined query evaluation plan for example query Q. We assume that the outputs of plan are ordered. Fig. 1 (b) shows that tuple 7 in S1 is delayed by 4 time units while tuple 2 in S2 arrives without latency. This latency may occur when tuples incur different operators with different speeds.

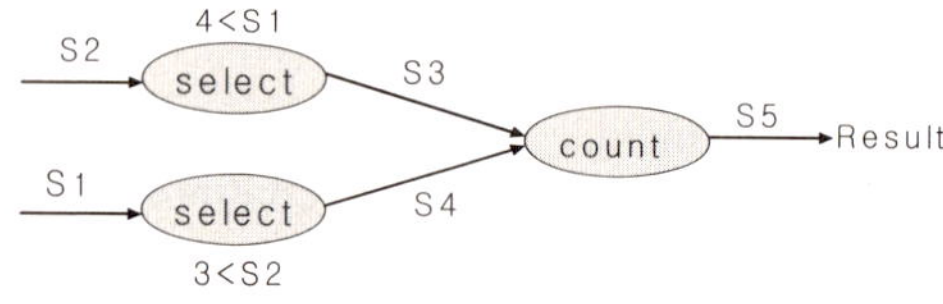

(a) Plan for Example query Q

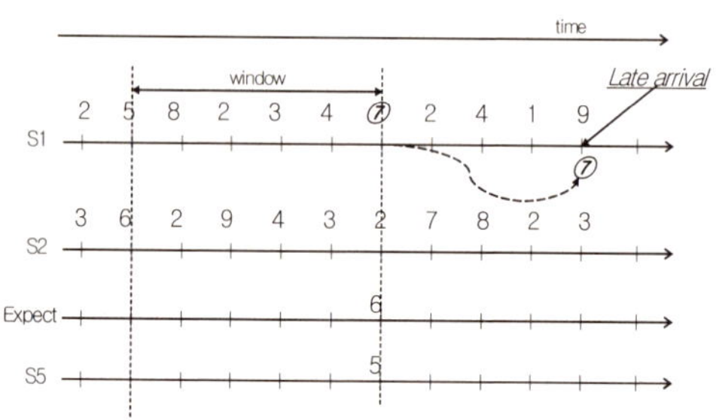

(b) Example of Latency Occurrence

Fig. 1. Motivating Example

It is issued based on how tolerable a system is in the aspects of delay time. A new tuple must be waited for until it arrives to acquire the correct query execution results, but it results in decreasing the system performance to that extent of delay. So, we need a new method to reduce response time and to increase accuracy of query execution results by restricting a waiting time so that a delay can be minimally influenced on the system performance. The existing methods have used window-timeout approach, but they have been using a fixed window size regardless of the frequency of timeouts and this has been increasing loss of data even when a recomputation happens after a timeout. We propose a method to increase the accuracy of query execution results due to decreasing the loss of data as a result of recomputation after a timeout by resetting the size of a window according to the system state monitored.

3.2 System Model and Environment

An application user raises a query and receives an answer through a DSMS. The DSMS is composed of an input manager that timestamps every incoming tuple. There is also a stream query processor which executes an optimization of a query plan and a real query, and puts the result to an output buffer. The stream query processor has three principal components: a re-optimizer, which ensures that the plans are the most efficient for the current input characteristics; an executor, which runs the query plans to produce the results; and a TOF monitor, which collects statistics about the FT (Frequency of Timeout) and the TFTO (Tolerable maximal Frequency of TimeOut). A data stream is assumed to come from a variety of data sources such as computer programs that generate values at regular/irregular intervals or from H/W sensors. A data stream is the one that we will use for the collection of data values presented by a data source. Each data source is assumed to have a unique source identifier. It is illustrated in Fig. 2.

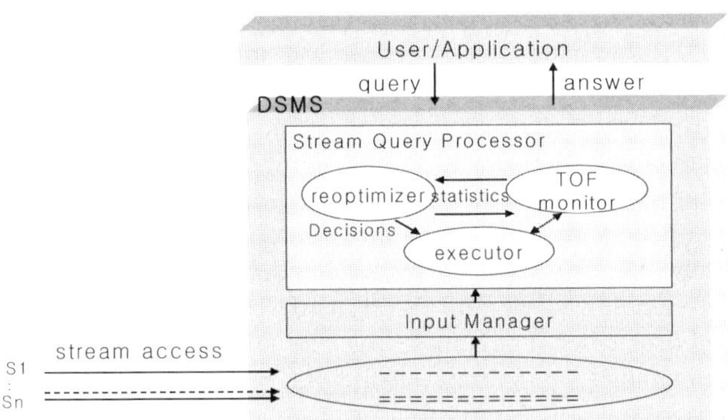

Fig. 2. Query Model

This paper focuses on sliding window query in the query evaluation system which is composed of multiple pipelined operators and considers centralized stream data system where data is collected from the sensors. The proposed method is assumed as follows.

- An input manager timestamps incoming tuples in increasing order as soon as they arrive from each source and stores it in a attribute part of the data.
- The stream items are assumed to relational tuples. They are composed of timestamps and attributes value.
- Data is eventually delivered and each data stream may have a different arrival rate.
- Time-based sliding window technique is used and the size of a window is suitable for the capacity of the main memory.

The structure for an adaptive query processing is presented as follows. It includes a user, a scheduler, operators, and the queues. A scheduler calls an operator, synchronizes rates among the operators and across the operators in a query plan, allocates the memory across the operators, and manages buffers for the incoming streams. A sliding window query includes multiple operators. An operator has an IQ (Input Queue) and an OQ (Output Queue). A data stream is inserted in an IQ and then an operator reads and writes it in an OQ. A pipelined operator is connected through a

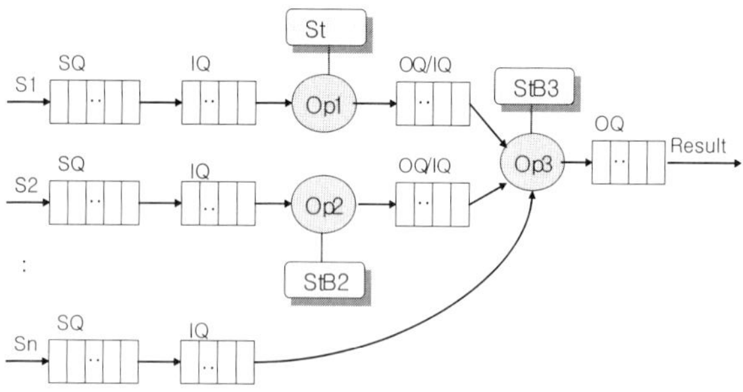

Fig. 3. Query Processing Structure

FIFO queue. Fig.3. illustrates a query processing structure to execute a query plan of an example mentioned above.

We use StB to store its state at every operator. StB keeps information about the list of tuples processed, W_timeout length that refers to the length of a window timeout, the value and the timestamp of a LPT (Lastly Processed Tuple), the value and the timestamp of a FPT (Firstly Processed Tuple), a FT, which indicates the frequency of timeout, and a TFTO, which indicates the maximal frequency of timeout that is tolerable to a system. W_timeout length field is necessary to set the maximal waiting time when a new tuple does not arrive. It, additionally, needs not to sort the incoming tuples, since they always arrive at the operator with increasing timestamps. The status of each StB for each operator of the example under discussion is illustrated in Table 1.

Table 1. Any status of each StB of Operator

StB1

Processed-tuples	{5,8}
W_timeout	5
LPT value	4
LPT_timestamp	6
FPT value	5
FPT_timestamp	2
TFTO	3
FT	1

StB2

Processed-tuples	{6,9,4}
W_timeout	6
LPT value	2
LPT_timestamp	7
FPT value	6
FPT_timestamp	2
TFTO	0
FT	0

StB3

Processed-tuples	{5,8,7,6,9,4}
W_timeout	7
LPT value	4
LPT_timestamp	5
FPT value	6
FPT_timestamp	2
TFTO	0
FT	0

A TFTO is monitored by a TOF monitor, as described in Fig.6. The TFTO can be obtained by producing the relation between the FT and the count of the tuples processed. The TFTO and the FT are stored to be used by each operator when the FT reaches the TFTO. Then, the operator controls the size of the queue.

When a continuous query is processed, the proposed method uses an eager re-evaluation strategy that re-evaluates a point of the new tuple's arrival time and an eager expiration procedure that scans the sliding window and drops the old tuple at that time to reduce the response time. We process the input tuples gradually when the new tuple arrives in a query plan. An operator processes the tuples within this window when they arrive at the window moved upon a constant time interval. That is, when a tuple arrives every t, it is expired at time t+N. We assume that N is the window size and t (tick/times) has an uniform interval of size. For example, if an expired tuple exists in s1 and joins with a new tuple when it arrives at s2 in a join operator that has two input streams, s1 and s2, we could not acquire the correct result, because the result may include and compute the expired tuple. So, the proposed method uses the timestamp of the FPT to decide whether to expire the stored tuple or not.

This paper deals a sliding window query composed of multiple operators and presents an efficient method to resolve the reduced accuracy of query excution results due to the latency of tuples accross the operators based on the pipelined query execution model.

3.3 AP-STO Algorithm

We now call our proposed algorithm for the AP-STO (Adaptive query Processing using StB and window-TimeOut).

A data source continuously pushes data streams. An AP-STO algorithm uses 3 queues, that is, the SQ (Stream Queue), the IQ and the OQ to evaluate continuous query over unbounded data stream. An SQ is used to temporally store a data stream from the data source. When a tuple arrives, it is uniquly timestamped in an increased fashion by an input manager. Tuples within a window are processed in the order of the timestamp. Tuples arrive at the queue in the order of the timestamp within a stream but does nothing to the accross streams. So, every tuple has a pair of a timestamp and a value. The SQ size that is equal to or larger than the window size refers to the scope of tuples to be processed. Each size of the IQ and the OQ is equal to the window size at the inital state of a system and the tuples within the window are only inserted into them to easily know whether a new tuple delays or not by checking the state of a queue. Each operator keeps own up-to-date state by updating the own information in the StB whenever a new tuple arrives. A window is composed of times (ticks) set with uniform interval of time.

The existing methods fix the size of a queue (window size) regardless of the frequency of timeout. On the other hand, our newly proposed algorithm changes the size of a queue according to the frequency of timeouts. That is based on the assumption that timeout may frequently occur ever since. W_timeout field in the StB means the maximal waiting time until a next tuple arrives. A window timeout occurs when a new tuple arrives late at a window waiting time. If a new tuple arrives within the window timeout length, it would be possible to acquire the correct results. However, if the timeout occurs in an operator, the operator would be initialize to recompute. That makes the values in StB and the queue of an operator to be deleted, and this results in the loss of data as much as the degree of the size of the queue. The more the loss of data occurs, the lesser the accuracy of the query execution result. Hence, we need to manage the streamed data by dynamically and adaptivly changing the size of the queue. The proposed method controls the size of the queue whenever the FT reaches the TFTO. If the FT reaches the TFTO, its size would be decreased to minimize the loss of data. If not, it would be increased (till inital size). It is possible to improve the system performance through an adaptive queue management by monitoring the relation between the FT and the count of the prccesed tuples according to the length of the timeouts.

A query execution example to comprehensively explain the proposed AP-STO algorithm is shown in Fig.4. using the latency problem as mentioned in the previous sections. As it can be clearly clarified from Fig.6, we assume that the TFTO is 3 times in magnitude because the result of this experiment shows that the case the frequency of timouts is 3 times better than the other case's results and the normal occasion is the case that the OS (Optimal States) is over 20 times. The OS implies the stability of a system performance. Fig.4. illustrates the case that the timeout occurs due to a late arrival of tuple 7 in S1. Supposed that W_timeout is assigned to 4, tuple 7 must arrive during times T1 to accquire the correct results, but it does not. So, it is waited for till times T4 (maximal waiting time is 4 since W_timeout is assigned to 4). However, timeout occurs since tuple 7 arrives at times T5. In such a case, information of TFTO is checked. Consequently, the size of the queue is decreased when the FT presents over 3 times, whereas it is taken up to its old position to steadily process the tuples when the FT presents 0 times and when it is under normal circumstances. After all, AP-STO checks the frequency of timeouts during query execution and then changes the size of the window when the FT reaches the TFTO. Ultimately, it results to the reduction of the loss rate of data.

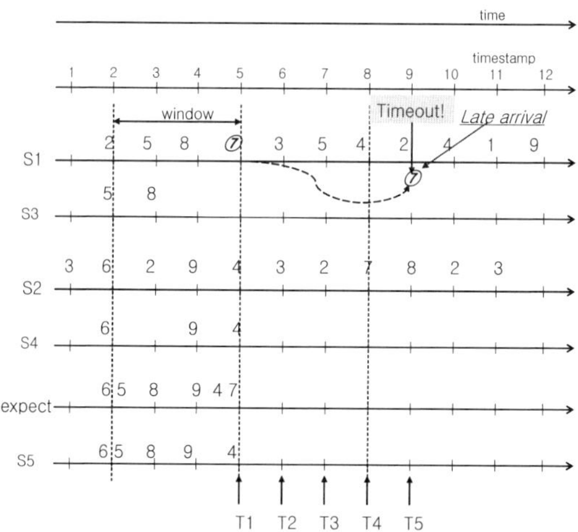

Fig. 4. Example of a Query Execution

AP-STO algorithm is briefly described by pseudo code as follows

```
//initialize each stream
Timestamp in the order of arrival of tuple in SQ;
Insert input tuple within window to IQ in operator;
ct= position of FPT //assign start position in window
while (ct <= ct+w_size) do {
  produce new output in OQ   //operate function;
  create StB and record state of operator;
  ct=ct+1;
}
```

```
//execute operators
tsLPT=ts(LPT); //assign timestamp of LPT
tsFPT=ts(FPT);//assign timestamp of LPT
v_w=w_size+w_to; //extend window size
while (input tuple) {
if (arrival of new tuple(NT)in stream(S1))
   //check arrival of NT at intervals of tick
then {
   if (tsLPT-tsFPT>w_size) //whether oldest tuple(FPT) expire or not
        then oldest_tuple_expired(FPT) ;  //delete FPT in IQ
   insert NT; //insert NT in IQ;
   produce new output in OQ  ; //re-evaluate
  update StB;   }
else {
  wait for NT until v_w;
  if w_timeout()    // occur timeout
      then  {
        recompute; //initialize all resource(IQ, OQ, StB)
        tocnt=tocnt++;  //check frequency of timeout }
      else  {
        if(Qsize != initial size of queue)
        NormaltimeFlag++;      }
}
endif
}
```

```
//control the size of queue
TimeoutFlag=0;  //check a series of timeout
NormaltimeFlag=0;   //check a series of normal processing
TimeoutFlag=tocnt;
if(TimeoutFlag == TFTO )
then {
   Qsize--;
   TimeoutFlag = 0;      } ;
if(NormaltimeFlag == OS)
then  {
   Qsize=initial size of queue
   NormaltimeFlag = 0;
 }
```

Fig. 5. Pseudo code of AP-STO algorithm

3.4 Performance Evaluation

AP-STO algorithm was implemented using Java 2 Platform Standard Ed. 5. 0. To evaluate the performance of the proposed algorithm, we have used the output-rate and the response time as the performance measures. The proposed method (AP-STO) has been compared with the known existing method (FxTO) while varying the timeout length (waiting time). The response time means the total time a query to take to be submitted by user, processed and returned by the system. The output-rate means the ratio of the number of the output tuples to the number of the input tuples per a query, and it is also a factor that affects the accuracy of the query execution results. Because the higher the output-rate the lesser the loss of data, it means that the accuracy of the query execution results increases.

This paper presents and implements an effective method to increase the output-rate by adaptivly managing the size of the queue according to the frequency of timeouts using monitoring TFTO. If the frequency of timeout reaches TFTO, the size of queue would be decreased to minimize loss of data. If not, it would be increased (till inital size) to rise the output-rate. Fig.6. shows the relation between the frequency of timeouts and the count of tuples prccessed while varying TFTO. The more the time passes the more the frequency of timeouts occurs and the more the count of tuples prccessed increases. Fig.6. shows the count of the tuples prccessed is the most while varying the TFTO when the TFTO is equal to 3 in this experiment. Due to the restricted spaces, only the case for the length of timeout equal to 4 is presented.

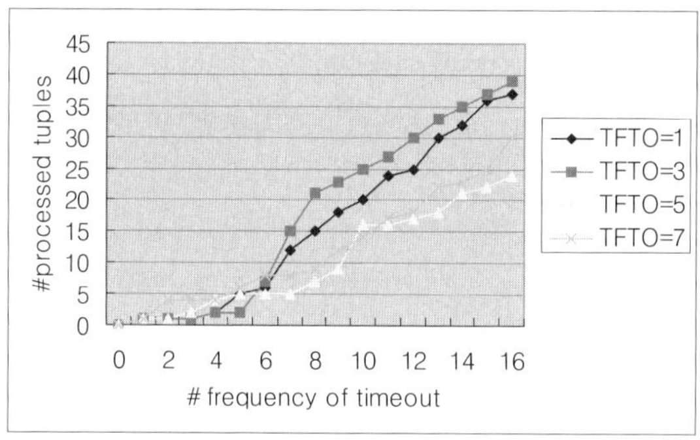

Fig. 6. Relation between FT and the count of processed tuples while varying TFTO

After all, the proposed method was evaluated by changing the size of the queue according to the frequency of timeouts during a query execution. The consequence was that the reduced loss of data resulted in to increasing the output-rate. Generally, shortening the length of timeout is proportional to increasing frequency of timeouts. The performance comparison has been done while varying the length of timeouts: 1, 3, 5 and 7 using the response time and the output-rate. Experimental results are illustrated in Fig.7 and Fig.8. Even though the proposed method (AP-STO) may require more response time than the existing method (FxTO), since it is timely necessary to control the size of the queue and to check the frequency of timeouts, Fig.7 shows that there is a little difference between the proposed AP-STO and the existing FxTO in terms of the response time, considering the average for the frequencies of timeouts in this experiment (FxTO=16, AP-STO=18). Fig.8. shows that AP-STO has better tuples output-rate than the FxTO, regardless of the length of timeout.

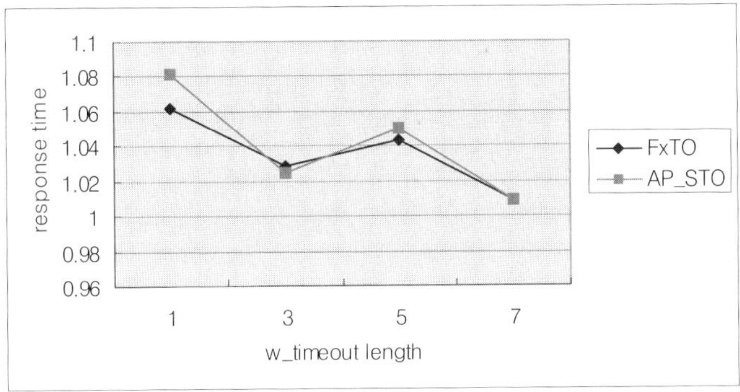

Fig. 7. Response time for timeout length

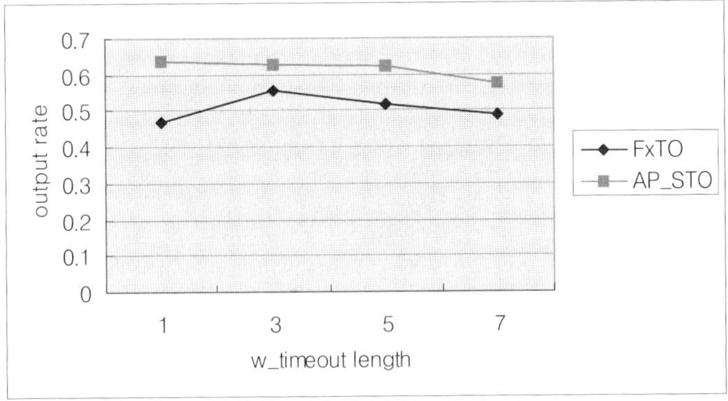

Fig. 8. Output-rate for timeout length

Consequently, the result of the experiment shows that an AP-STO has a better performance than the FxTO, since the tuples output-rate has increased.

4 Conclusion

We need an approach to process continuous data streams in the ways separate from the existing ones. Data sources push tuple streams continuously and sometimes make them arrive late and be out of order. This may result in delaying query execution and, hence, increasing loss of data due to the occurrence of timeout. Hence, we have proposed an AP-STO method using an StB which stores the operator's state and window time-out method by resetting the size of the window according to the frequency of timeouts. This mechanism decreases the data lost rate and increases the tuples output-rate. We have compared an AP-STO method with the existing method using the output-rate and the response time as the measure of performance evaluation. We have found out that there is an improvement in the system performance in terms of the accuracy of query execution results and the tuples output-rate per a query due to a decreasing of the loss of data. In a near future, we will establish a customized and event-driven system by setting the accuracy of data that users may demand.

Acknowledgments. This research was supported by the 2nd Phase Scheme of BK21 program.

References

[1] Motwani, R., Widom, J., Arasu, A., Babcock, B., Babu, S., Datar, M., Manku, G., Olston, C., Rosenstein, J., Varma, R.: Query Processing, Resource Management, and Approximation in a Data Stream Management System. In: Proc. of CIDR (2003)

[2] Babcock, B., Datar, M., Motwani, R.: Sampling from a Moving Window over Streaming Data. In: Proceedings of Thirteenth Annual ACM-SIAM Symposium on Discrete Algorithms (SODA'02), pp. 633–634 (2002)

[3] Arasu, A., Babu, S., Widom, J.: The CQL Continuous Query Language: Semantic Foundations and Query Execution. VLDB Journal ((2005)

[4] Carney, D., Cetintemel, U., Cherniack, M., Convey, C., Lee, S., Seidman, G., Stonebraker, M., Tatbul, N., Zdonik, S.: Monitoring Streams: A New Class of Data Management Applications. In: proceedings of the 28th International Conference on Very Large Data Bases (VLDB'02), Hong Kong, China (2002)

[5] Madden, S., Franklin, M.J.: Fjording the Stream: An Architecture for Queries over Streaming Sensor Data. In: ICDE Conference (2002)

[6] Babcock, B., Babu, S., Datar, M., Motwani, R., Widom, J.: Models and Issues in Data Stream Systems. In: Proc. of 21st ACM Symposium on Principles of Database Systems (PODS), Madison, Wisconsin (2002)

[7] Srivastava, U., Widom, J.: Flexible Time Management in Data Stream Systems. In: Proc. of PODS (2004)

[8] Hammad, M.A., Aref, W.G., Elmagarmid, A.K.: Optimizing In-Order Execution of Continuous Queries over Streamed Sensor Data. In: Proceedings of the International Conference on Scientific and Statistical Database Management (SSDBM), Santa Barbara, CA (2005)

[9] Hammad, M.A., Ghanem, T.M., Aref, W.G., Elmagarmid, A.K., Mokbel, M.F.: Efficient Pipelined Execution of Sliding-Window Queries Over Data Streams. Purdue University Department of Computer Sciences Technical Report CSD TR#03-035 (2004)

[10] Golab, L., Ozsu, M.T.: Processing Sliding Window Multi-Joins in Continuous Queries over Data Streams. In: Proc. of VLDB (2003)

[11] Babu, Shivnath, Widom, Jennifer: StreaMon: An Adaptive Engine for Stream Query Processing. In: Demonstration Proposal in ACM SIGMOD2004 Conference, Paris, France (2004)

Parallel Computation of Closed Itemsets and Implication Rule Bases

Jean François Djoufak Kengue[1] and Petko Valtchev,[1] and Clémentin Tayou Djamegni[2]

[1] LATECE, Université du Québec À Montréal, Canada
[2] Laboratoire d'informatique, Faculté de Sciences, Université de Dschang, Cameroun
djoufak.jean_francois@courrier.uqam.ca, valtchev.petko@uqam.ca, dtayou@yahoo.com

Abstract. Formal concept analysis has been successfully applied as a data mining framework whereby target patterns come in the form of intent families and implication bases. Since their extraction is a challenging task, especially for large datasets, parallel techniques should be helpful in reducing the computational effort and increasing the scalability of the approach. In this paper we describe a way to parallelize a recent divide-and-conquer method computing both the intents and the *Duquenne-Guiges* implication basis of dataset. Wile intents admit a straightforward computation, adding the basis — whose definition is recursive — poses harder problems, in particular, for parallel design. A first, and by no means final, solution relies on a partition of the basis that allows the crucial and inherently sequential step of redundancy removal to be nevertheless split into parallel subtasks. A prototype implementation of our method, called PARCIM, shows a nearly linear acceleration w.r.t. its sequential counter-part.

Keywords: Data mining, concept analysis, parallel algorithmic design.

1 Introduction

Data mining [1] is the process of discovering patterns and trends in large datasets in order to transform these into a knowledge which in turn supports decision making. In real-world data mining applications, datasets are continually growing larger, noisier and more decentralized [1]. As a result the size of the mining output is constantly increasing whereas the quality of the discovered patterns is harder to ensure. This makes their interpretation for decision making a laborious and error-prone activity. A way out seems to lay in the use of well formalized reduced representations of pattern families such as the closed itemset families [2] or the non-redundant sets of association rules [3].

Formal concept analysis (FCA) [4] has been exploited in the recent years as a framework for the design of reduced representations. In its original settings, FCA extracts concepts, conceptual hierarchies and implication rule bases from data represented as two-way objects $\times$ attributes tables. It presents a number of attractive features for mining: First, concept intents represent maximal patterns which usually represent a small subset of the entire pattern family. Then, the size of specific implication bases such

I. Stojmenovic et al. (Eds.): ISPA 2007, LNCS 4742, pp. 359–370, 2007.

as the *Duquenne-Guiges* (D&G) is provenly a minimal bound [5]. Finally, the concept lattices taken as classification hierarchies are easily browsable and admit intuitive visualization [6].

Despite an extensive research on data mining-oriented tasks in FCA, the basic computation problems still withhold some challenge, especially in case of very large and/or dense contexts [7]. Therefore, we believe that parallel approaches and methods could be a way to reduce computational cost and hence increase the scalability [8] of FCA-based mining techniques. The field of parallel computation of FCA constructs is relatively new as most of the existing algorithms, e.g., the classical NextClosure [9], are inherently sequential. However, recently, a new trend in FCA algorithmic design has been initiated with the publication of the first divide-and-conquer method for lattice construction [10]. A sequel of the work applying the same split/merge approach focused on intent and D&G basis computation [11].

While a parallel version of the first algorithm has been reported in [12], here we focus on the joint construction of intents and implications. The design of parallel method for the task is a challenge since beyond some obvious parallelization spots, the reference algorithm carries out sequential calculations following the recursive definition of the D&G basis skeleton, i.e., the *pseudo-closed* sets of a context. Only after a detailed examination of the pseudo-closed family and its partition into classes became it possible to split the most challenging and inherently sequential step of the computation, i.e., the reduction of a slightly larger set of implications to the D&G basis, into independent tasks to be assigned to different CPUs. The resulting parallel algorithm, called PARCIM, has been straightforwardly implemented as a prototype so that some preliminary tests could be carried out. Experimental evidence suggests that the new algorithm behaves well w.r.t. its sequential counterpart, e.g., in one test instance nearly linear acceleration was reached in the number of CPUs used.

The parallel algorithm presented here, called PARCIM, falls under lines of parallel algorithms described in [8]. Indeed, 1) it is designed from a sequential algorithm and, 2) it computes frequent closed itemsets, and association rules with 100% confidence. In the remainder of the paper, section 2 summarizes basic results from FCA on intent families and implication rules. Next, section 3 presents the reference sequential algorithm. Finally, sections 4 and 5 are dedicated to PARCIM design and implementation, and to its performance, respectively.

2 Background on Concept Lattices and Implications

FCA defines a *context* as a triple $\mathcal{K} = (O, A, I)$ made of a set O of *objects*, a set A of *attributes*, and an *incidence* relation $I \subseteq O \times A$ (oIa means object o has attribute a).

For convenience reasons, hereafter objects and attributes will be respectively denoted by numbers and lower-case letters, respectively, while set separators will be usually skipped. Our running example is presented on the left of figure 1. The pairs of the incidence relation are drawn as crosses, underlining the asymmetric nature of the FCA-reasoning, i.e., unlike in classical logic, absence of a attribute is not a property on its own (hence it does not lead to a shareable specification).

A context defines two *derivation operators*, both denoted $'$ since symmetric, mapping object sets to attribute ones and *vice versa*, respectively. For instance, the object operator

Context $\mathcal{K}$									
	a	b	c	d	e	f	g	h	i
1	×		×		×		×	×	
2		×		×	×	×			×
3	×		×		×		×	×	
4		×	×	×		×			×
5	×			×	×			×	×
6	×	×		×		×	×		
7			×	×	×	×		×	
8	×			×	×		×		×

Intents of $\mathcal{K}$			
$abcdefghi$	$cdefh$	$bdefi$	$adehi$
$adegi$	$bcdfi$	$acegh$	$abdfg$
$bdfi$	$adei$	dei	deh
def	ceh	cdf	bdf
aeh	aeg	adg	eh
di	df	ag	de
ae	ad	e	d
c	a	$\emptyset$	

Fig. 1. A context and its corresponding intent family

$i \to d$	$h \to e$	$g \to a$	$b \to df$
$f \to d$	$dfi \to b$	$dehi \to a$	$ac \to egh$
$defh \to c$	$ce \to h$	$cd \to f$	$abdefgi \to ch$
$aegh \to c$	$adi \to e$	$adf \to bg$	$bdef \to i$
$ade \to i$	$bcdf \to i$		

$i \to d$	$h \to e$	$g \to a$	$bcdf \to i$
$f \to d$	$dfi \to b$	$dehi \to a$	$aceh \to g$
$defh \to c$	$ce \to h$	$cd \to f$	$adf \to bg$
$bd \to f$	$aegh \to c$	$adi \to e$	$bdef \to i$
$ade \to i$			

Fig. 2. D&G basis for the running context (left) and its hybrid implication set (right)

is defined as $' : \wp(O) \to \wp(A)$ with $X' = \{a \in A | \forall o \in X, oIa\}$ (e.g., $45' = di$ and $di' = 2458$ within our example). Both derivation operators constitute a *Galois connection* [4]. Hence, the two compound operators $''$ are closure operators inducing two families of closed sets ($X = X''$) on $\wp(O)$ and $\wp(A)$, respectively. For instance, the attribute closures of our example are given in figure 1 (on the right).

Closed sets of objects, or *extents*, and of attributes, or *intents* (denoted $\mathcal{C}^A$ hereafter), are in one-to-one correspondence that materializes in the $'$ operators. Moreover, pairs of mutually corresponding sets (X, Y), i.e., where $X' = Y$ and $Y' = X$, are called *concepts* (e.g., (2458, di)). Concepts are partially ordered by a *sub-concept* relation $\leq$ that follows extent inclusion and the resulting structure is known to be a *complete lattice* [13] called the *concept lattice* [4]. Moreover, the precedence relation $\prec$, i.e., the transitive reduction of $\leq$, organizes the concept set into a directed acyclic graph that, whenever drawn is called the *Hasse diagram* of the lattice (not given here due to space limitations). Given a context, an *implication* is a pair of attribute sets $X \to Y$, where X and Y are respectively called *premise* and *conclusion*. Implications are close relatives to functional dependencies from relational database theory [14] where premise and conclusion respectively refers to *antecedent* and *consequent*. However, we will use FCA-based naming conventions in this paper. An implication $X \to Y$ is said to be *valid* in a context if whenever an object has all the attributes in X it also has all those in Y. The latter boils down to $Y \subseteq X''$. The set of all implications valid in context $\mathcal{K}$ is denoted by $\Sigma_{\mathcal{K}}$. $\Sigma_{\mathcal{K}}$ is typically huge and contains rules which are *redundant* since they can be derived from others by using an appropriate inference system, e.g., *Armstrong axioms* [15]. The *derivability* between implication sets is denoted $\models$ with $\Sigma_1 \models \Sigma_2$ meaning each rule in Σ_2 is valid whenever Σ_1 as a whole is. Σ_1 is called a *cover* of Σ_2.

Practical detection of redundant implications in any implication set Σ usually applies the associated closure operator $\_^{\Sigma} : \wp(A) \to \wp(A)$. It is defined as follows:

$$X^{\Sigma} = X^{\infty} : X^0 = X, X^{k+1} = X^k \cup \bigcup_{Y \to Z \in \Sigma; Y \subseteq X^k} Z.$$

Now an implication $X \to Y$ is derivable from a set Σ whenever $Y \subseteq X^{\Sigma}$. In particular, $X \to Y \in \Sigma$ is redundant whenever it is derivable from the rest, $Y \subseteq X^{\Sigma-\{X\to Y\}}$. A set Σ is *non-redundant* if no redundant rule is comprised. Correspondingly, any Σ includes at least one non-redundant subset of implications Σ_r such that $\Sigma_r \models \Sigma$. Moreover, for such Σ one is usually interested in covers $\Sigma_c \models \Sigma$ of minimal size among all covers of Σ, a.k.a. *minimal covers*. The problem of computing a minimal cover from a set Σ is known to be solvable in polynomial time w.r.t. the size of Σ [14].

Back to FCA, a known result in the field states that given a context $\mathcal{K}$, the two closure operators on $\wp(A)$ coincide, i.e., $\_'' = \_^{\Sigma_{\mathcal{K}}}$. Moreover, research on FCA has yielded a uniquely defined minimal cover for the family $\Sigma_{\mathcal{K}}$, called the *Duquenne-Guigues* (D&G) basis [5]. The basis, hereafter denoted $\mathcal{D}$ is made of all rules $X \to Y$ whose premise X is a *pseudo-closed* set [5] and the conclusion Y is the respective closure. A pseudo-closed set P for a family of closures is defined by the following two conditions: (i) P is not closed and (ii) for any other pseudo-closed Q, $Q \subset P$ forces $\bar{Q} \subset P$ ($\bar{Q}$ is the closure of P, e.g., $\_''$ or $\_^{\Sigma}$). Obviously, a pseudo-closed sets and hence a D&G basis is defined for both a context and an implication family. The left-hand side of figure 2 illustrates the D&G basis of our example (figure 1). For compactness reasons, implication conclusions are reduced to those attributes that are not in the premise. Sets i and f are pseudo-closed since they are minimal non-closed (part (ii) of the definition satisfied *a fortiori* since inapplicable), whereas dfi is pseudo-closed by both parts of the definition. Another D&G basis is given on the right-hand side of figure 2. It is the cover of an implications set called hybrid (see section 3).

The next section describes a computation method for both the intent family and the D&G basis of a context that uses partial constructs, i.e., pertaining to fragments of the context, as starting point and merges those into the global results.

3 Divide-and-Conquer Computation of Intents and D&G Basis

3.1 Overview

The work published in [11] introduces a new algorithm which can be summarized as follows. First, at an *initialization* step, the input context $\mathcal{K}$ is recursively partitioned into smaller ones by binary splits of the attributes while keeping all the objects at each step. The recursion represents a binary tree whose leaves are one-attribute contexts hence their intent families and D&G basis are readily computed. Second, subsequent merges of factor intents and implications are carried out until a single global result is yielded. At each context $\mathcal{K}_r$, the merge of the results for its two fragments, or *factors*, is a two-step process. Step one, further referred to as *assembly*, amounts to traversing the direct product of factor intents in the search of global intents and pseudo-intents called *hybrid*. Step two is a *reduction* of the set made of the hybrid D&G basis and both factor D&G bases to their common D&G basis which is exactly the one of $\mathcal{K}_r$. The left part of figure 3 illustrates different steps of the global computation process. In that figure, arrows show the sequencing of tasks. Main steps of the process are detailed in the following sections.

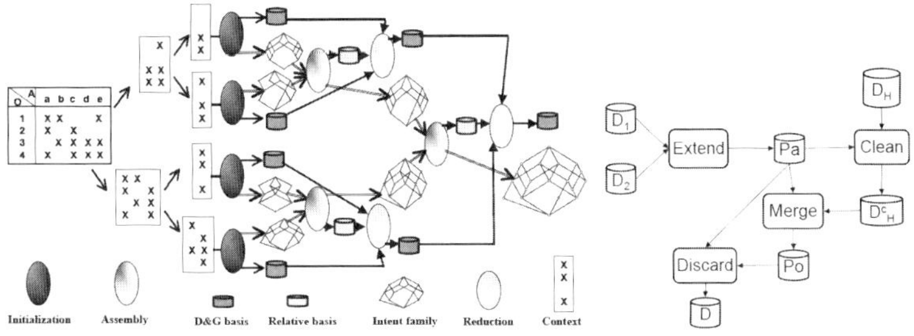

Fig. 3. Computation schemes for the D&C algorithm (left) and its reduction step (right)

3.2 Initialization Step

For a one-attribute context, there are only two possibilities for its intent family and D&G basis, depending on whether its unique attribute, say a, is shared by all objects or not. In the first case, a is the only intent and $\emptyset$ the only pseudo-closed, whereas in the second case $\emptyset$ is an intent beside a hence the pseudo-intent family is void (see [10,11]).

3.3 Assembly

Let $\mathcal{K}$ be the current context and $\mathcal{K}_1$ and $\mathcal{K}_2$ the two sibling sub-contexts of $\mathcal{K}$ with respective intent families $\mathcal{C}^{A_1}$ and $\mathcal{C}^{A_2}$. It is easily seen that intents in $\mathcal{K}$ are unions of two *factor* intents, one from $\mathcal{K}_1$ and $\mathcal{K}_2$ each. This makes the direct product of factor intent families $\mathcal{C}_{1,2} = \mathcal{C}^{A_1} \times \mathcal{C}^{A_2}$ the ideal search space for $\mathcal{C}^A$. Indeed, [10] presents a characterization of factor intent combinations $Y_1 \cup Y_2$ ($(Y_1, Y_2) \in \mathcal{C}_{1,2}$) in terms of extent intersection minimality.

Unfortunately, pseudo-closed sets of $\mathcal{K}$ have not been yet proven to split along the factor attribute sets A_1 and A_2, i.e., the direct product of factor pseudo-closed families is not a good search space for them. In contrast, another implication family, called *hybrid*, has its own pseudo-closed in $\mathcal{C}_{1,2}$ whereas the resulting hybrid D&G basis is a tight approximation of the D&G basis of $\mathcal{K}$. First, hybrid implications have the form $Y_1 \cup Y_2 \rightarrow (Y_1 \cup Y_2)''$ where $(Y_1, Y_2) \in \mathcal{C}_{1,2}$ and $Y_1 \cup Y_2$ is not closed in $\mathcal{K}$ (i.e., members of $\mathcal{C}_{1,2}$ correspond either to a global intent or to a hybrid implication premise). As shown in [11], the hybrid implication set, here denoted $\mathcal{H}$, has closed sets that equal the intents of $\mathcal{K}$. Moreover, its D&G basis $\mathcal{D}_{\mathcal{H}}$ together with the factor bases $\mathcal{D}_1$ and $\mathcal{D}_2$ constitutes a cover for the target basis $\mathcal{D}_{\mathcal{K}}$:

$$\mathcal{D}_{\mathcal{H}} \cup \mathcal{D}_1 \cup \mathcal{D}_2 \models \mathcal{D}_{\mathcal{K}}.$$

The assembly task only focuses on the computation of $\mathcal{C}^A$ and $\mathcal{D}_{\mathcal{H}}$ whereas the reduction of the three implication families to yield $\mathcal{D}_{\mathcal{K}}$ is done on the following step. The computation of intents and hybrid pseudo-closed is basically a traversal of $\mathcal{C}_{1,2}$ with an application of a common closure property. Indeed, whenever a given set $Y \subseteq A$ satisfies the property that for any hybrid pseudo-closed P, $P \subseteq Y$ forces $P'' \subseteq Y$, it is necessarily either a hybrid pseudo-closed itself or a hybrid closed, i.e global closed ($Y = Y''$).

Thus, the computation of intents and hybrid pseudo-closed is done step-wise, i.e., by starting from the smallest members of $\mathcal{C}_{1,2}$ and going towards larger ones, following a linear extension of the inclusion order. At each step, the candidates $Y = Y_1 \cup Y_2$ ($(Y_1, Y_2) \in \mathcal{C}_{1,2}$) are only tested against the currently known part of the hybrid basis $\mathcal{D}_{\mathcal{H}}$. Whenever a set Y passes all tests, its effective closure Y'' is computed to determine whether it is an intent or a hybrid pseudo-closed.

3.4 Reduction to D&G Implication Basis

The computation of $\mathcal{D}_{\mathcal{K}}$ from $\mathcal{D}_{\mathcal{H}} \cup \mathcal{D}_1 \cup \mathcal{D}_2$ is a four step process as shown in figure 3, on the right-hand side. In that figure, reduction steps are represented by rounded rectangles, implication rule sets by cans and, sequencing of steps by arrows connectors.

The aim of the first step, referred to as **Extend**, is to ensure that the implications from $\mathcal{D}_1 \cup \mathcal{D}_2$ have the form $X \rightarrow X''$. To that end, the conclusion of each rule from $\mathcal{D}_1 \cup \mathcal{D}_2$ is replaced (*Closer* task) with its closure w.r.t context $\mathcal{K}$ and the resulting rules are stored in the set $\mathcal{P}_a$. The left part of figure 4 illustrates that step. In that figure, as in figure 5, circles represent tasks while circle's incoming (resp. outgoing) arrows shows input (resp. output) implication rules or sets. Also, rounded rectangles represent merging of task outputs into implication rule sets, each represented by a can.

The second step amounts to removing redundant implications from $\mathcal{P}_a \cup \mathcal{D}_{\mathcal{H}}$. Redundancies in $\mathcal{D}_{\mathcal{H}}$ are readily spotted and need not a full-scale reduction. As indicated in [11], implication $X \rightarrow X'' \in \mathcal{D}_{\mathcal{H}}$ is redundant in $\mathcal{P}_a \cup \mathcal{D}_{\mathcal{H}}$ if there is an implication $Y \rightarrow Y'' \in \mathcal{P}_a$ such that $Y \subseteq X$ and $Y'' \nsubseteq X$ (X is not a global pseudo-closed). Finally, the non-redundant set $\mathcal{D}^c_{\mathcal{H}}$ is composed. The process behind this step, called **Clean** here, is depicted in the right part of figure 4, rules at the left-hand side of tasks being those of $\mathcal{D}_{\mathcal{H}}$. If a rule of $\mathcal{D}_{\mathcal{H}}$ is redundant the corresponding task output is empty.

The third step, referred to as **Merge**, amounts to merge sets $\mathcal{D}^c_{\mathcal{H}}$ and $\mathcal{P}_a$ into set $\mathcal{P}_o$.

In the final step, referred to as **Discard** (see figure 5), the redundancies in $\mathcal{P}_a$ are detected (*Deducer* tasks). Indeed, only factor implications in $\mathcal{P}_a$ require full-scale redundancy tests since the rules in $\mathcal{D}^c_{\mathcal{H}}$ are necessarily non-redundant. Given a rule $X \rightarrow X'' \in \mathcal{P}_a$ (rules at the left hand of *Deducer* tasks), the test amounts to computing the implication closure of X, i.e., $X^{\mathcal{P}_a - \{X \rightarrow X''\}}$ and comparing it to X''. The LINCLOSURE algorithm [14] is used to that end. Any redundant implication is immediately removed (Remove tasks) from $\mathcal{P}_o$. For non-redundant implications, the premise X is

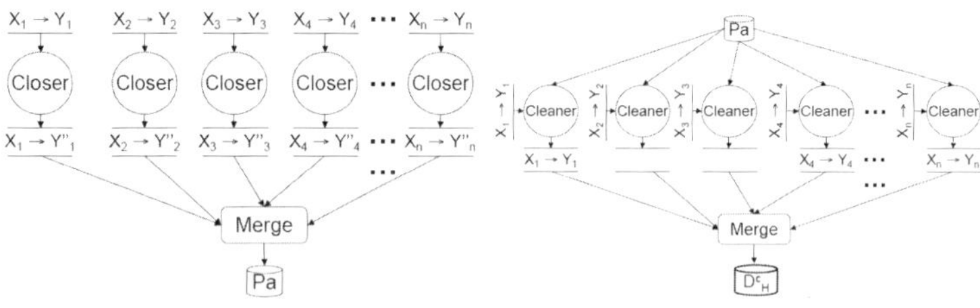

Fig. 4. First (left) and second (right) step of the reduction process, resp. rounded rectangle *Extend* and *Clean* in figure 3

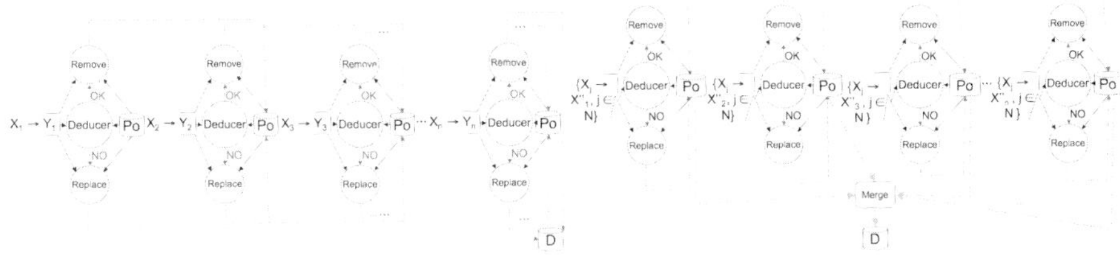

Fig. 5. Fourth step of the reduction process (left), i.e *Discard* in figure 3, and update (right)

immediately replaced (Replace tasks) by its newly computed pseudo-closed. Technically speaking, a non-reduntant $X \rightarrow X''$ becomes $X^{\mathcal{P}_a - \{X \rightarrow X''\}} \rightarrow X''$. Please notice that dashed lines on the left-hand side of figure 5 show the update of set $\mathcal{P}_o$ while revealing the strong sequentiality of the step (deducers constantly update $\mathcal{P}_o$).

3.5 Example of Assembly and Reduction

Let us consider contexts $\mathcal{K}_1$ and $\mathcal{K}_2$ to be respectively restriction of context $\mathcal{K}$ in figure 1 to the first five and the last four attributes. Intent families of $\mathcal{K}_1$ and $\mathcal{K}_2$ are respectively obtained as union of intents in the left- and right-hand part of figure 6. The lattice at the right-hand part of that figure is encapsulated in each node of the lattice at the left-hand part in order to represent the search space $\mathcal{C}_{1,2}$. Arrows are used to show the traversal order of $\mathcal{C}_{1,2}$. Inner nodes represent pairs of intents from $\mathcal{C}_{1,2}$. For example, the upper most node represents the pair of intents $(\emptyset, \emptyset)$ and the lower most $(abcde, fghi)$. In the resulting nested line diagram (see [4]), nodes representing unions that are closed, i.e., global intents, are filled in black, whereas the others are not. The unfilled nodes generate hybrid implication rules in $\mathcal{D}_{\mathcal{H}}$. The right-hand part of figure 1 depicts intents computed at the end of the assembly step while the right-hand part of figure 2 depicts $\mathcal{D}_{\mathcal{H}}$.

D&G basis corresponding to contexts $\mathcal{K}_1$ and $\mathcal{K}_2$ are respectively given by left and center part of figure 7. Going into the reduction process, set $\mathcal{P}_a$ obtained at the end of the first step is given by the right part of figure 7 while set $\mathcal{D}^c_{\mathcal{H}}$ is obtained by removing

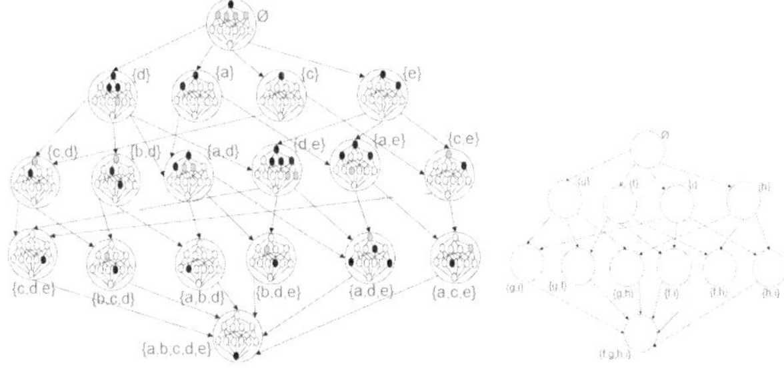

Fig. 6. Representation of intent and hybrid rule search space (left): the lattice of $\mathcal{K}_2$ (right) is encapsulated within each node of the lattice of $\mathcal{K}_1$

D&G basis of context $\mathcal{K}_1$	
$b \rightarrow d$	$bcde \rightarrow a$
$acde \rightarrow b$	$abde \rightarrow c$
$ac \rightarrow e$	

D&G basis of context $\mathcal{K}_2$	
$ghi \rightarrow f$	$fhi \rightarrow g$
$fgh \rightarrow i$	$fgi \rightarrow h$

$\mathcal{P}_a$		
$fgh \rightarrow abcdei$	$bcde \rightarrow afghi$	$b \rightarrow df$
$fhi \rightarrow abcdeg$	$acde \rightarrow bfghi$	$ac \rightarrow egh$
$abde \rightarrow cfghi$	$ghi \rightarrow abcdef$	$fgi \rightarrow abcdeh$

Fig. 7. D&G basis of neighbor contexts of our running example (left and center), together with implication rules set $\mathcal{P}_a$ (right)

implication rules $bd \rightarrow f$ and $aceh \rightarrow g$ from D&G basis at the right-hand part of figure 2. The final result, i.e., the D&G basis, corresponds to the implication set on the left-hand side of figure 2.

4 Parallel Computation of Intents and D&G Basis

We call *computation sequence* (CS) a sequence of an assembly task followed by a reduction. Here, we suppose that the number of CPUs equals the CSs at the leaf-level of the binary tree of recursive context splits.[1] In that case, an immediate way to parallelize amounts to simultaneously executing CSs corresponding to contexts at the same depth of the tree. Following the parallel design requirements we not only need algorithms for executing several CSs simultaneously but also for executing a CS on several CPUs so that a good overall charge balance is achieved. In other terms, we must design parallel algorithms for both the assembly and the reduction steps.

A generic parallel method that satisfies the above requirements is given by algorithm 1. Using function $ChooseLeafContext()$ a CPU chooses a leaf-level context from which it computes intents and D&G rules during initialization (function $Initiali-zation()$). With function $JoinComputationSequence()$ CPUs which contribute to parallel execution of a CS (function $ParallelComputationSequence()$) identify themselves. The algorithm halts when all CSs have been executed. Hereafter, we identify the appropriate computation model for parallel assembly/reduction.

Algorithm 1. PARCIM's Algorithm

In: $\mathcal{K} = (\mathcal{O}, \mathcal{A}, \mathcal{I})$ a context, CPU P
Out: $\mathcal{C}$ an intents set, $\mathcal{D}$ a D&G basis

```
ChooseLeafContext()
Initialization()
JoinComputationSequence()
while(exist(ComputationSequence()))
    ParallelComputationSequence()
    JoinComputationSequence()
```

4.1 CGM Parallel Computation Model and Algorithms

Parallel computation models aims at analyzing parallel algorithms and predicting their runtimes [16]. The CGM (Coarse Grained Multi-computer) model [16] underlies algorithms alternating computation and communication rounds. Its aim is to obtain parallel algorithms whose performances does not depends on the target architectures. To that end, communication rounds are minimized since intense communications knowingly

[1] Leaf-level contexts may have more than one attribute.

have a negative impact on performances [16]. Moreover, if two communication rounds occur in a parallel procedure, we expect involved CPUs to exchange results they have computed between the two rounds.

As it will be seen further, CGM is the model suggested by the first three steps of the reduction process. However, to embrace CGM [17], we should provide CGM algorithms for both assembly and reduction.

A CGM Assembly Algorithm: Let c_1 be any intent from intent family $\mathcal{C}^{A_1}$. Figure 6 illustrates the partitioning of search space $\mathcal{C}_{1,2}$ into coarse-grained tasks, each of which amounts to searching intents and relative basis implication rules in a partition $c_1 \times \mathcal{C}^{A_2}$. In the following, each task will be assimilated with its corresponding partition.

The dependency graph between coarse-grained tasks follows the lattice corresponding to intent family $\mathcal{C}^{A_1}$. We define *level task sets* as sets of tasks $c_1 \times \mathcal{C}^{A_2}$ such that the number of attribute in intents c_1 are the same. Considering the left part of figure 6, three successive level task sets are $\{\emptyset \times \mathcal{C}^{A_2}\}$, $\{d \times \mathcal{C}^{A_2}, a \times \mathcal{C}^{A_2}, c \times \mathcal{C}^{A_2}, e \times \mathcal{C}^{A_2}\}$, and $\{cd \times \mathcal{C}^{A_2}, bd \times \mathcal{C}^{A_2}, ad \times \mathcal{C}^{A_2}, de \times \mathcal{C}^{A_2}, ae \times \mathcal{C}^{A_2}, ce \times \mathcal{C}^{A_2}\}$.

Since tasks at each level are independent, they are executed in parallel thus constituting computation rounds. Communication rounds correspond to transfers of intents and hybrid implication rules, following dependency graph arrows, between two tasks at consecutive levels, i.e two successive computation rounds.

CGM Algorithms for First, Second and Third Reduction Steps: Closers and cleaners (see figure 4) can be evenly divided among available CPUs so as to have coarse-grained tasks whose executions can be seen as computation rounds while merging operations correspond to communication rounds.

A CGM algorithm for the Fourth Reduction Step: As it was shown in section 3.4, this step of the reduction is strongly sequential. A key concern here is that a pseudo-closed can be generated by several rules from $\mathcal{P}_a$. The strong sequentiality ensures an ordering of the rules in $\mathcal{P}_a$ so that each pseudo-closed is effectively generated by the last implication that is in a position to do this. n fact, all other rules for the same pseudo-closed are eliminated beforehand as redundant. This imposes a consistency constraint on the parallel reduction since a CPU in charge of a specific rule should not miss the elimination of a comparable rule assigned to another CPU.

A way out seems to consist in assigning all rules generating the same pseudo-closed set to the same reduction task. However, the pseudo-closed set produced by an implication is not known before-hand. HEnce we allow for larger sets of implications to undergo reduction within the same task. These groups are based on shared conclusion parts, i.e., closures, and therefore necessarily comprise the pseudo-closed-based implication classes which are strictly finer.

Thus, in order to get a CGM algorithm for the last step of the reduction process, implication rules leading to a same intent are assigned to a unique task. The right-hand side of figure 5 illustrates the corresponding algorithm. In that figure, dotted arrows shows sets that are merged to get expected D&G basis.

Since the new algorithm is similar to those of the first and the second reduction steps, i.e independent computations followed by merging of the results, the proof that CGM model applies is identical.

Number of Communication Rounds: Let n be the number of attributes of context $\mathcal{K}$ and let P be the number of CPUs in the target parallel architecture. The number of communication rounds for the parallel assembly is at most equal to the number of attributes of corresponding contexts. Since assemblies of contexts at the same tree depth execute simultaneously, the total number communication rounds executed during parallel assemblies is at most $n \times \sum_{k=0}^{\ln P} \frac{1}{2^k}$. There are 4 communication rounds during the parallel reduction, one for each merging of implication rules. Therefore, the number of communication rounds executed during parallel reductions is at most $4 \times \ln P$. Consequently, the number of communication rounds executed by PARCIM is an $\mathcal{O}(n \ln P)$.

4.2 Parallel Assembly and Parallel Reduction Algorithms

Assuming that CPUs are fed with the required datasets during communication rounds, computation rounds correspond to executions of the corresponding sequential algorithm on provided data sets. A CPU which is assigned tasks $\{c_1 \times \mathcal{C}_2, c_2 \times \mathcal{C}_2, ..., c_m \times \mathcal{C}_2\}$, $c_1, c_2, ..., c_m \in \mathcal{C}_1$, executes the sequential assembly on intent families $\{c_1, c_2, ..., c_m\}$ and $\mathcal{C}_2$. In the same way, a CPU which is assigned *Closer* tasks related to implication rules $X_1 \rightarrow Y_1$, $X_2 \rightarrow Y_2$, ..., $X_n \rightarrow Y_n$, executes first reduction step sequential algorithm on implication rules set $\mathcal{D}_1 \cup \mathcal{D}_2 = \{X_1 \rightarrow Y_1, X_2 \rightarrow Y_2, ..., X_n \rightarrow Y_n\}$. Same reasoning applies to other reduction's steps. Consequently, PARCIM's performances depend on design and execution of communication rounds.

5 Prototype and Experimental Results

Before we start working on communication rounds, we felt interesting to validate our design. To that end, we use STL[2] [18] and MPI[3] [19] standard libraries to straightforwardly implement a prototype for PARCIM. Since that prototype was implemented on a cluster of 8 CPUs networked through a star network (Myrinet switch), we allow any CPU to communicate with any other as required.

The drawback for such a choice is that some communication operations are blocked because other are executing [12].

Two contexts have been used in our experiments. The first one is made up of the thousand first objects of a sparse context called *Mushroom*. It has 32514 intents and 1987 D&G rules. The second is composed of the two hundred and fifty first objects of a dense context called *Chess*. It has 108036 intents and 921 D&G rules. PARCIM's prototype have been executed with 1, 2, 4 and 8 CPUs. Corresponding runtimes was used to divide sequential algorithm [11] runtime to get PARCIM's prototype speedup. Figure 8 summarizes obtained results and shows that in spite of weak communication scheme, PARCIM's prototype executes at least twice as quickly as its homologue sequential algorithm. Moreover, speedup increase with the number of CPUs used.

---

[2] **S**tandard **T**emplate **L**ibrary.

[3] **M**essage **P**assing **I**nterface.

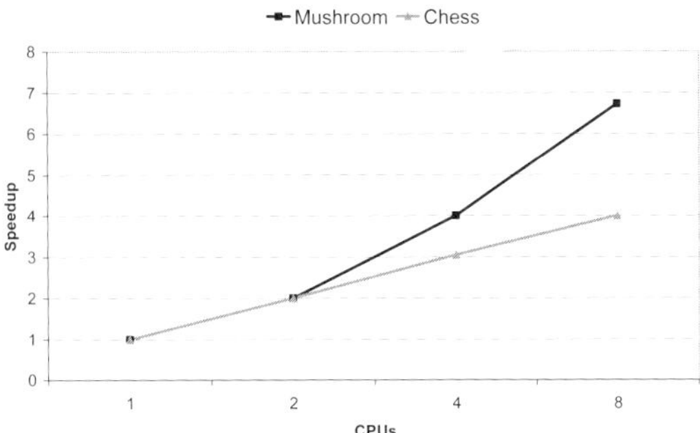

Fig. 8. Speedup of PARCIM's prototype

6 Conclusion

In this paper, we have designed and experimented the first parallel algorithm, called PARCIM, that computes both intents and D&G rules. We have shown that CGM parallel computation model is well suited for PARCIM's implementation and complexity analysis. This work also contributes to the general understanding of reduction mechanisms embroiled in the introductory sequential algorithm.

In the near future, we will work on maximizing PARCIM's speedup. To this end, we plan to improve the parallel merge algorithm [20] and the communication model [21]. Then, the algorithms will be compared to other parallel frequent closed itemset and association rule miners. In a different vein, we shall be looking at the possible increases of the degree of parallelism in the sequential algorithm. Indeed, PARCIM has a sequential spine since a parallel reduction always follows a parallel assembly. Thus, a new sequential algorithm will be studied with a dependancy graph where assemblies and reductions are simultaneous. Based on this improvement, we anticipate the design of an optimized parallel method that computes intent families, concept lattices and implication rule bases simultaneously.

Acknowledgments

This work was partly supported by Canadian Research Council (NSERC) grants and by Université du Québec À Montreal scholarships held by the first author.

References

1. Han, J., Kamber, M.: Data Mining: Concepts and Techniques, 1st edn. Morgan Kaufmann Publishers, San Francisco, California, USA (2001)
2. Wang, J., Han, J., Pei, J.: Closet+: searching for the best strategies for mining frequent closed itemsets. In: KDD '03: Proceedings of the ninth ACM SIGKDD. ACM Press, New York (2003)
3. Zaki, M.J., Hsiao, C.J.: Charm: An efficient algorithm for closed itemset mining. In: Proceedings of the Second SIAM International Conference on Data Mining, SIAM (2002)

4. Ganter, B., Wille, R.: Formal Concept Analysis: Mathematical Foundations. Springer, Heidelberg (1997)
5. Duquenne, V., Guigues, J.L.: Famille minimale d'implications informatives résultant d'un tableau de données binaires. Mathématiques et Sciences Sociales 95, 5–18 (1986)
6. Carpineto, C., Romano, G.: A lattice conceptual clustering system and its application to browsing retrieval. Mach. Learn. 24, 95–122 (1996)
7. Pasquier, N., Bastide, Y., Taouil, R., Lakhal, L.: Efficient mining of association rules using closed itemset lattices. Inf. Syst. 24, 25–46 (1999)
8. Zaki, M.J.: Parallel and distributed association mining: A survey. IEEE Concurrency 7, 14–25 (1999)
9. Ganter, B.: Two basic algorithms in concept analysis. Technical Report Preprint 831, Technische Hochschule, Darmstadt, Germany (1984)
10. Valtchev, P., Missaoui, R., Lebrun, P.: A partition-based approach towards constructing galois (concept) lattices. Discrete Math. 256, 801–829 (2002)
11. Valtchev, P., Duquenne, V.: Towards scalable divide-and-conquer methods for computing concepts and implications. Preprint accepted to Discrete Applied Mathematics (2006)
12. Djoufak, J.F.K., Valtchev, P., Djamegni, C.T.: A parallel algorithm for lattice construction. In: Ganter, B., Godin, R. (eds.) ICFCA 2005. LNCS (LNAI), vol. 3403, pp. 249–264. Springer, Heidelberg (2005)
13. Davey, B.A., Priestley, H.A.: Introduction to Lattices and Order. Cambridge University Press, Cambridge (1990)
14. Maier, D.: The Theory of Relational Databases. Computer Science Press (1983)
15. Armstrong, W.W.: Dependency structures of data base relationships. In: IFIP Congress, pp. 580–583 (1974)
16. Goetz, S.: Algorithms in cgm, bsp and bsp* model: A survey. Technical report, Carleton Unviversity, Ottawa (1997)
17. Dehne, F., Fabri, A., Rau-Chaplin, A.: Scalable parallel computational geometry for coarse grained multicomputers. Journal of Computational Geometry and Applications 6, 379–400 (1996)
18. Robson, R.: Using the STL: the C++ standard template library, 2nd edn. Springer, Heidelberg (2000)
19. Gropp, W., Lusk, E., Skjellum, A.: Using MPI: Portable Parallel Programming with the Message Passing Interface, 2nd edn. MIT Press, Cambridge, MA (1999)
20. Parka, H.K., Chi, D.H., Lee, D.K., Ryu, K.W.: An efficient parallel algorithm for merging in the postal model. ETRI Journal 21, 31–39 (1999)
21. Djamegni, C.T.: Mapping rectangular mesh algorithms onto asymptotically space-optimal arrays. J. Parallel Distrib. Comput. 64, 345–359 (2004)

An Optimal Share Transfer Problem on Secret Sharing Storage Systems*

Toshiyuki Miyamoto and Sadatoshi Kumagai

Osaka University, Osaka 565-0871, Japan
miyamoto@eei.eng.osaka-u.ac.jp

Abstract. We have been developing a secure and reliable distributed storage system, which uses a secret sharing scheme. In order to efficiently store data in the system, this paper introduces an optimal share transfer problem, and proves it to be, generally, NP-hard. It is also shown that the problem can be resolved into a Steiner tree problem. Finally, through computational experiments we perform the comparison of heuristic algorithms for the Steiner tree problem.

1 Introduction

We propose a distributed storage system[1] that uses a (k, n) threshold scheme[2] as the data encryption technique. The (k, n) threshold scheme creates n pieces of cipher data called shares, from an original datum according to encryption. Since k shares are required for data decoding, this is called the (k, n) threshold scheme. If the (k, n) threshold scheme is used, the datum cannot be decoded if unless k shares are collected. However, the datum can be decoded even if $n - k$ shares are lost. In the distributed storage system that we propose, n shares are stored on storage nodes that are distributed in an ultra fast network. Even if some storage nodes fail, since data can be recovered by collecting shares from other nodes, reliability can be increased according to the existing storage systems. In addition, secrecy can be improved, since original data cannot be recovered, even if some of shares are stolen by a cracker.

This paper addresses an optimization problem of calculation and transmission of shares. Kaneko et. al. discussed computational complexity of a File Transfer Problem (FTP)[3]. Unfortunately, it was not possible to apply the FTP to our storage system directly, and therefore a share transfer problem is introduced in this paper.

2 Secret Sharing Storage System

2.1 (k, n) Threshold Scheme

This section presents an overview of the (k, n) threshold scheme[2].

* This work was supported in part by Grant-in-Aid for Encouragement of Young Scientists No. 17700061 and 19700060 from the Ministry of Education, Culture, Sports and Technology, Japan.

I. Stojmenovic et al. (Eds.): ISPA 2007, LNCS 4742, pp. 371–382, 2007.

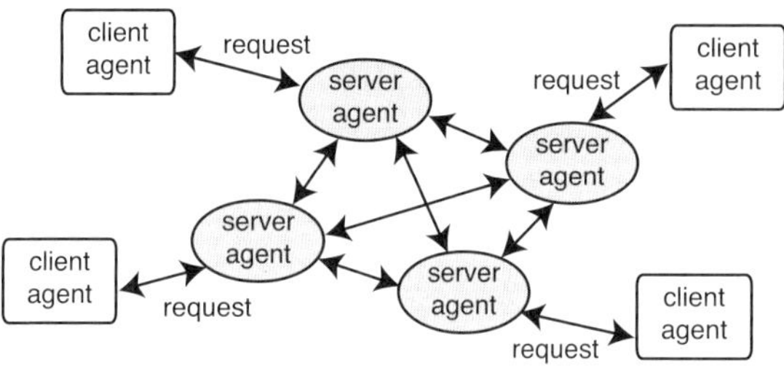

Fig. 1. Secret Sharing Storage System

First, we explain a technique for creating n shares from secret information $s \in F$, where F is an algebraic field. We use secret information s and random coefficients $r_i \in F$ $(i = 1, \cdots k-1)$ to create the following $k-1$ degree polynomial:

$$f(x) = \sum_{i=0}^{k-1} r_i x^i \tag{1}$$

where $r_0 = s$. Encryption is performed by obtaining $w_j = f(x_j)$ for n different $x_j \in F$ $(j = 1, \cdots n)$. In matrix form, the encryption can be described as follows:

$$\begin{bmatrix} w_1 \\ w_2 \\ \vdots \\ w_n \end{bmatrix} \equiv \begin{bmatrix} 1 & x_1 & x_1^2 & \cdots & x_1^{k-1} \\ 1 & x_2 & x_2^2 & \cdots & x_2^{k-1} \\ \vdots & \vdots & \vdots & \ddots & \vdots \\ 1 & x_n & x_n^2 & \cdots & x_n^{k-1} \end{bmatrix} \begin{bmatrix} r_0 \\ r_1 \\ \vdots \\ r_{k-1} \end{bmatrix} \tag{2}$$

w_j is referred to as a share, and x_j is referred to as the ID of share w_j.

Since $f(x)$ is a $k-1$ degree polynomial, it is uniquely determined by k points $(x_j, f(x_j))$. Secret information s can be obtained from $s = f(0)$.

2.2 Distributed Storage System Using a Threshold Scheme

Figure 1 shows an image of an autonomous distributed storage system: a Secret Sharing Storage System (SSSS). The SSSS is a multi-agent system consisting of server agents that reside on storage nodes scattered throughout the network and client agents that receive requests from users.

A client agent receives a user request, transfers it to a server agent, and returns its result to the user.

All server agents have functions for encrypting and decrypting data and for storing and acquiring shares. When a client agent requests a server agent to store a file on the storage, the server agent encrypts the file and sends shares to other server agents. If there is a file fetch request from a client, a server agent collects together a total of k shares to decrypt the file, performs a decryption, and returns the file to the client.

3 Share Transfer Problem

In the developd system, a file encryption is performed on one server and shares are transmitted to other servers. However, it is necessary to perform a multiplication operation kn times for the encryption of each secret information. In addition, the file must be divided into some blocks and the encryption must be performed by each block. Calculation load in this encryption is one of the problems of the SSSS. Each line of expression (2), however, could be carried out individually if the same random coefficients $r_1, \cdots, r_{k-1}$ are used. In this paper, we allow for distributed processing to encrypt secret information by plural servers and consider a minimization issue of the sum of encryption and transmitting costs.

3.1 Formulation of Share Transfer Problem

Let $\mathbb{Z}+$ be the set of positive integers, and $\mathbb{Z}_0+ = \mathbb{Z} + \cup\{0\}$.

Consider a communication network N, called a *share transmission net*, of servers in an SSSS. A share transmission net N is a 6-tuple $N = (V, E, c_v, c_e, s, D)$. (V, E) is a connected and undirected graph with the set V of vertices and the set E of edges. Each vertex is a server in the SSSS, and each edge is a communication link between servers. A vertex cost function $c_v : V \to \mathbb{Z}+$ gives cost $c_v(v)$ to calculate one share on the server v. An edge cost function $c_e : E \to \mathbb{Z}+$ gives cost $c_e(e)$ to transmit one original datum or one share through the edge e. $s \in V$ is a source, and indicates the server which has received a request from a client. $D \subseteq V$ is the set of destinations. We need to transmit a different share for each server in D. Hereafter, we assume that $|D| = n$. A share transfer problem is a problem to find routes from s to each $d \in D$, and place (server) where the datum is encrypted for each $d \in D$.

For a mapping f on E to $\mathbb{Z}_0+$, if a path P satisfies $f(e) > 0$ for all edges e on P, then we say that P is f-connected. Consider a mapping $\psi\colon D \to V$. An f-connected path from s to $d \in D$ containing $\psi(d)$ is called a *transmission route* from s to d, and denoted by $P(s, d)$. The mapping f gives the number of data types through edges, and the mapping ψ gives the server on which encryptions are performed. A prefix and postfix path of $P(s, d) = (V_d, E_d)$ for $\psi(d)$ is denoted by $P(s, \psi(d)) = (V_{\to\psi(d)}, E_{\to\psi(d)})$ and $P(\psi(d), d) = (V_{\psi(d)\to}, E_{\psi(d)\to})$, respectively. Define a function $T_d\colon E_d \to \{o, d\}$[1] that gives type of data through edges in a path $P(s, d)$ as follows:

$$T_d(e) = \begin{cases} o & \text{if } e \in E_{\to\psi(d)}, \\ d & \text{if } e \in E_{\psi(d)\to}. \end{cases}$$

Definition 1. *A pair of mappings $\psi\colon D \to V$ and $f\colon E \to \mathbb{Z}_0+$, denoted by $S = (\psi, f)$, of N is called a share transfer of N if the following conditions are satisfied:(C1) $\forall d \in D$, there exists a transmission route form s to d, and (C2) $\forall e \in E$, $|\cup_{d\in D} \{T_d(e)\}| \leq f(e)$.*

[1] The d in the region of the function T_d is different from $d \in D$, but it shows the type of the share going to the destination $d \in D$. Therefore the same symbol is used.

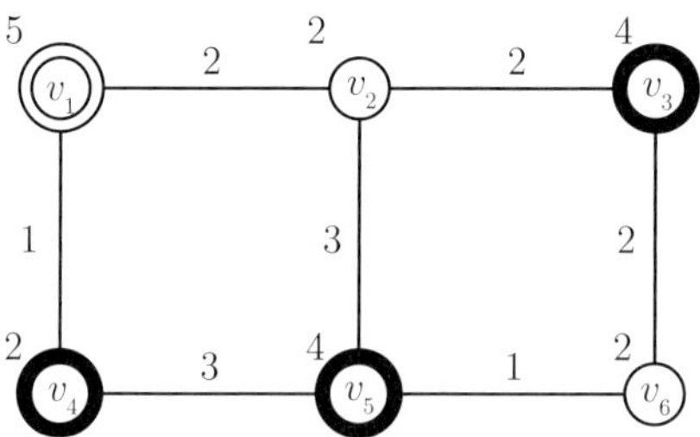

Fig. 2. Share Transmission Net N_1

Definition 2. *For a share transfer $S = (\psi, f)$, a cost $C(S)$ is defined by the following expression:*

$$C(S) = \Sigma_{d \in D} c_v(\psi(d)) + \Sigma_{e \in E} c_e(e) \cdot f(e).$$

A share transfer S is called an optimal share transfer of N if $C(S) \leq C(S')$ for every other share transfer S'.

An optimal share transfer problem is a problem to find an optimal share transfer for given N.

As an example, let us consider the share transmission net N_1 shown in Fig. 2, where $s = v_1$ and $D = \{v_3, v_4, v_5\}$. In this case, we are going to deliver a share for each server in D from v_1, and we need to find a transmission route for each $d \in D$. The number attached to each vertex indicates its share calculation cost for one share, and the number attached to each edge indicates its transmission cost for one original datum or one share. When mappings f and ψ are given as follows:

$$f(e) = \begin{cases} 1 & \text{if } e = (v_1, v_4), (v_1, v_2), (v_2, v_3), (v_2, v_5) \\ 0 & \text{otherwise,} \end{cases}$$

$$\psi(v_3) = v_2, \psi(v_4) = v_4, \psi(v_5) = v_2,$$

then the pair S of f and ψ becomes a share transfer. According to the share transfer, the original datum is transmitted to v_2 and v_4. The share to v_4 is encrypted on v_4, and shares to v_3 and v_5 are encrypted on v_2. Shares to v_3 and v_5 are transmitted though (v_2, v_3) and (v_2, v_5), respectively. The cost of this share transfer is calculated as follows:

$$\begin{aligned} C(S) &= (2 + 2 + 2) + (1 \cdot 1 + 2 \cdot 1 + 2 \cdot 1 + 3 \cdot 1) \\ &= 14 \end{aligned}$$

3.2 Complexity of Optimal Share Transfer Problem

This section discusses NP-hardness of the optimal share transfer problem. In relation to basic terminologies such as a decision problem, a non-deterministic algorithm, please refer to text books about computer science. We will show that any instance of the Steiner tree problem, which is known as an NP-complete problem, can be reduced into the share transfer problem.

Consider a graph $G = (V, E, w)$ with the set V of vertices, the set E of edges and the cost function $w \colon E \to \mathbb{Z}+$. Let $R \subseteq V$, a sub-tree of G which spans all elements in R and whose weight is minimum is called a Steiner tree for R. Then the following decision problem is NP-complete[4].

Definition 3 (Steiner Tree Problem; STP)
Given a graph $G = (V, E, w)$, $R \subseteq V$, and $K \in \mathbb{Z}+$, does G contain a Steiner tree for R whose weight is $\leq K$?

For a graph (V, E, w) and R of an instance of the STP, we define a share transmission net $N(R)$ as follows.

Definition 4. *Suppose that a graph (V, E, w) and a vertex set $R \subseteq V$ are given. Then, a share transmission net induced by R, which is denoted by $N(R)$, is defined as follows:*

$$\forall e \in E, c_e(e) = w(e),$$
$$\forall v \in V, c_v(v) = 1,$$
$$s = r \in R, \text{and}$$
$$D = R \backslash \{r\},$$

where we can choose the r arbitrarily.

In relation to a share transfer on the above share transmission net $N(R)$, we have the following lemmas.

Lemma 1. *Each share transfer (ψ, f) on $N(R)$ satisfies*

$$\Sigma_{d \in D} c_v(\psi(d)) = |R| - 1. \quad (3)$$

Proof. By Definition 4, we can prove this lemma. □

Lemma 2. *There must exist an optimal share transfer on $N(R)$ which satisfies*

$$\forall d \in D, \psi(d) = d. \quad (4)$$

Proof. Assume that for any optimal share transfer there exists $d' \in D$ such that $\psi(d') \neq d'$. Let $P(\psi(d'), d') = (V_{\psi(d')\to}, E_{\psi(d')\to})$ be a postfix path on a transmission route from s to d', then we can say that $E_{\psi(d')\to}$ is not empty.

Consider a case where the path $P(\psi(d'), d')$ shares an edge $e \in E_{\psi(d')\to}$ with another transmission route to $d'' \in D$. Note that without loss of generality, we can assume that $\psi(d'') = d''$ and d'' is only one. From the condition (C2) of Def. 1 and optimality of the share transfer, we can say that $f(e) = |\{o, d'\}| = 2$. In this case, we can find better share transfer such that $\psi(d') = d'$, since this share transfer has the same calculation cost (from Lemma 1) and less transmission cost(from $f(e) = 1$). This contradicts the optimality of (ψ, f).

Next, consider a case where the path does not share any edge with another transmission route to $d'' \in D$. In this case a share transfer such that $\psi(d') = d'$ is also an optimal share transfer.

As a result, there must exist an optimal share transfer such that $\psi(d) = d$ for any $d \in D$. □

Lemma 3. *Suppose that $\psi(d) = d$ for all $d \in D$. An optimal share transfer (ψ, f) on $N(R)$ satisfies*
(a) $\forall e \in E$, $f(e) \in \{0, 1\}$, and
(b) $E' = \{e \in E \mid f(e) = 1\}$ is an edge set of a Steiner tree for R.

Proof. (a) Since $\psi(d) = d$, only original data o flows on the share transmission net. From condition (C2) of Def. 1 and optimality, $f(e) = 1$ for edges on transmission routes and $f(e) = 0$ for other edges.

(b) Conditions $\forall d \in D, \psi(d) = d$ and $\forall e \in E$, $f(e) \in \{0, 1\}$ show that finding an optimal share transfer for $N(R)$ is equivalent to finding a Steiner tree that spans every elements in $\{s\} \cup D (= R)$. Therefore $E' = \{e \in E \mid f(e) = 1\}$ is an edge set of Steiner tree for R.

A decision problem version of the share transfer problem is given as follows.

Definition 5 (SHare Transfer Problem; SHTP).
Given a share transmission net $N = (V, E, c_v, c_e, s, D)$ and $K' \in \mathbb{Z}+$, does N contain a share transfer (ψ, f) whose cost is $\leq K'$?

A relationship between the STP and the SHTP is as follows.

Proposition 1. *There exists a share transfer whose cost is $\leq |R| - 1 + K$ on $N(R)$ iff there exists a Steiner tree for R whose weight is $\leq K$ on G.*

Proof. ($\Rightarrow$) Suppose that there exists a share transfer whose cost is $\leq |R| - 1 + K$ on $N(R)$. From Lemma 1 and Def. 2,

$$\Sigma_{e \in E} c_e(e) \cdot f(e) \leq K.$$

From Lemma 3, $\Sigma_{e \in E} c_e(e) \cdot f(e)$ is weight of a Steiner tree for R. The existence of a Steiner tree with weight $\leq K$ has been shown.

($\Leftarrow$) Suppose that there exists a Steiner tree whose weight is $\leq K$ on G. Get $N(R)$ according to Def. 4, and assume that $S = (\psi, f)$ satisfies

$$\forall d \in D, \psi(d) = d$$

$$f(e) = \begin{cases} 1 & \text{if } e \in E', \\ 0 & \text{otherwise.} \end{cases}$$

Obviously, S satisfies the conditions of Def. 1. From Def. 2 and Lemma 1,

$$\begin{aligned} C(S) &= |R| - 1 + \Sigma_{e \in E'} c_e(e) \\ &\leq |R| - 1 + K. \end{aligned}$$

Existence of a share transfer whose cost is $\leq |R| - 1 + K$ has been shown. □

Finally, we can obtain the following theorem.

Theorem 1. *Share Transfer Problem is NP-complete.*

Proof. Prop.1 shows that any instance of the STP which is NP-complete could be reduced into an instance of the SHTP. By Def.4, such reduction can be executed in polynomial time.

We can check in polynomial time for a given share transfer whether that its cost is less than or equal to a given positive integer.

Hence we have this proposition.

Since decision problem of the SHTP is NP-complete, and its optimization problem is NP-hard.

4 Reduction into Steiner Tree Problem

We argued about computational complexity of the SHTP in the previous section. This section examines a solution of the SHTP. In addition, in the SSSS, it is desirable to solve the SHTP by a distributed algorithm to lower dependence on a special node. Therefore we suggest a method to reduce the SHTP into the STP. Then we can use existing distributed algorithms such as [6,7] for the STP.

Definition 6. *For a given share transmission net $N = (V, E, c_v, c_e, s, D)$, define a weighted graph $G(N) = (V', E', w')$ for N as follows:*

$$V' = V \cup \bigcup_{d \in D} V_d, and \tag{5}$$

$$E' = E \cup \bigcup_{d \in D} E_d \cup E_v, \tag{6}$$

where $V_d = \{v_{i,d} \mid \forall v_i \in V\}$, and $E_d = \{(v_{1,d}, v_{2,d}) \mid \forall (v_1, v_2) \in E, v_{1,d}, v_{2,d} \in V_d\}$, $E_v = \{(v_i, v_{i,d}) \mid \forall d \in D, v_i \in V, v_{i,d} \in V_d\}$. Weight w' is defined as follows:

$$w'(e) = \begin{cases} c_e(e) & \text{if } e \in E, \\ c_e(e') & \text{if } e = (v_{1,d}, v_{2,d}) \in E_d \text{ and } e' = (v_1, v_2) \in E, \\ c_v(v) + \mathbf{D}(N) & \text{if } e = (v, v_d) \in E_v, \end{cases} \tag{7}$$

where $\mathbf{D}(N)$ is a larger number than the diameter of (V, E, c_e).

Figure 3 shows an weighted graph $G(N_1)$ for the share transmission net N_1 shown in Fig. 2. In the figure, $v_{4,3}$ is v_{4,v_3} in more precisely, an edge in E_v is drawn by a broken line, and $\mathbf{D}(N) = \sum_{e \in E} c_e(e) = 14$.

$G(N)$ is composed by $|D| + 1$ layers, and the bottom layer is a layer for transmitting an original data and layer d is a layer for transmitting a share going to the destination $d \in D$. The edge in E_v indicates that the original data is encrypted to the share.

Let $T = (V'_T, E'_T)$ be a Steiner tree for $R = s \cup \{d_d \mid d \in D\}$ on $G(N)$.

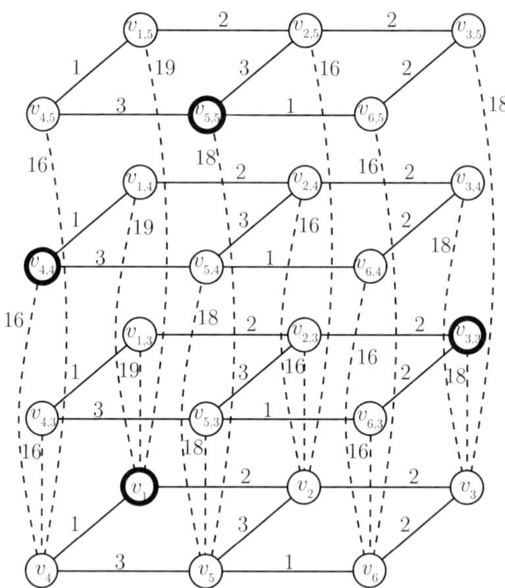

Fig. 3. An weighted graph $G(N_1)$ for the share transmission net N_1

Definition 7. *For a given T, define $S^* = (\psi^*, f^*)$ as follows:*

$$\psi^*(d) = v \ s.t.\ (v, v_d) \in E'_T, \text{and} \tag{8}$$

$$f^*(e) = |\{e' \in E'_T \mid e' = e \vee \exists d \in D, e' = e_d\}|, \tag{9}$$

where e_d is an instance of e in the layer d.

In relation to S^*, the following theorem holds.

Theorem 2. *S^* is an optimal share transfer.*

Proof. From Def. 7 we cannot obtain unique $\psi^*(d)$ when multiple edges in E_v are included in a path $P(s, d_d)$ from s to d_d on T. First, we show that we can obtain unique ψ^* from any Steiner tree T.

Assume that there exist multiple edges in E_v on the path $P(s, d_d)$ on T, see Fig. 4. Let $\pi = s \cdots v_i v_{i,d'} \cdots v_{j,d'} v_j \cdots v_k v_{k,d} \cdots d_d$ be a sequence of nodes on the path such that it moves up to a layer d' at v_i, moves down to the bottom layer at v_j, and moves up to the layer d at v_k. In this case, $(v_i, v_{i,d'}), (v_{j,d'}, v_j), (v_k, v_{k,d}) \in E_v$.

Let us consider a case such that π does not share any part of sub-sequence from v_i to $v_j (\pi_{i,j} = v_i v_{i,d'} \cdots v_{j,d'} v_j)$ with another path $P(s, d'_{d'})$ from s to $d'_{d'}$. In this case, we can obtain a path $P(s, d_d)'$, whose weight is smaller than the weight of $P(s, d_d)$, by projecting sub-path which contains $\pi_{i,j}$ from the layer d' to the bottom layer, since the calculation cost c_v is positive and the transmission cost c_e is same between the bottom layer and the layer d'. This contradicts that T is a Steiner tree.

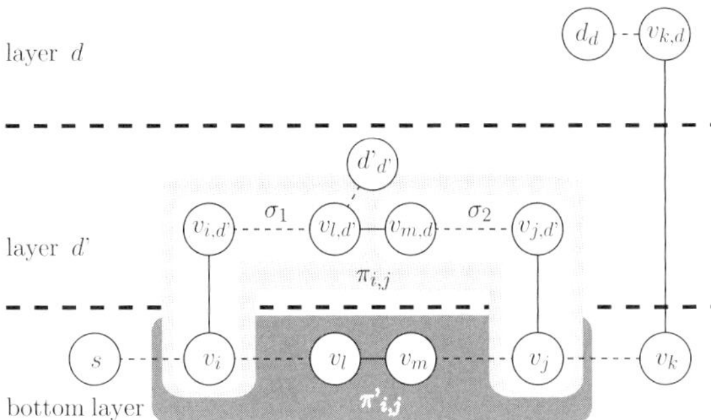

Fig. 4. Multiple edges in E_v are included in a path from s to d_d on T

Next, let us consider a case such that only $P(s, d_d)$ shares a part ($\sigma_1 = v_i v_{i,d'} \cdots v_{l,d'}$) with $P(s, d'_{d'})$ Let $\sigma_2 = v_{m,d'} \cdots v_j$, and $\pi_{i,j} = \sigma_1 \sigma_2$. When we choose the same path $P(s, d_d)'$ of the previous case, total weight will increase $\Delta = w'(\pi'_{i,j}) - (w'(v_{l,d'}, v_{m,d'}) + w'(\sigma_2))$. From eq. (7), $w'(\sigma_2)) > \mathbf{D}(N) \geq w'(\pi'_{i,j})$, and therefore Δ is negative. This contradicts that T is a Steiner tree.

Finally, let us consider a case such that also $P(s, d''_{d''})$ shares a part or the whole of $\pi_{i,j}$ with $P(s, d'_{d'})$. When $P(s, d''_{d''})$ shares the whole of $\pi_{i,j}$, by projecting sub-path which contains $\pi_{i,j}$ from the layer d' to the bottom layer for both of $P(s, d_d)$ and $P(s, d''_{d''})$, we can reduce total weight by Δ. When $P(s, d''_{d''})$ shares a part of $\pi_{i,j}$, $P(s, d''_{d''})$ goes down from the layer d' to the bottom layer at a different point from v_j. Then we can remove one more edge with weight $\mathbf{D}(N)$ by projecting from layer d' to the bottom layer. This means that by projecting both of $P(s, d_d)$ and $P(s, d''_{d''})$, we can reduce total weight. This contradicts that T is a Steiner tree.

We have shown that $\psi^*(d)$ is unique. Next we show that (ψ^*, f^*) is a share transfer.

From the definition of R, for all $d \in D$ there exists a path from s to d_d. Let us project the path to the bottom layer, and $P(s, d)$ be the image. From the definition of $f^*(e)$ at Def. 7, $P(s, d)$ is f-connected, and from the definition of $\psi^*(d)$, $\psi^*(d)$ is included in $P(s, d)$. Therefore $P(s, d)$ is a transmission route. (Def. 1, (C1))

The condition (C2) at Def. 1 requires that $f(e)$ is larger than the number of data types through e. In $G(N)$, each layer shows that a data type, and $f^*(e)$ at Def. 7 returns the number of layers including e. Therefore the condition (C2) is satisfied.

Finally, we show that S^* is optimal. Assume that there exists a share transfer (ψ', f') such that $C(\psi', f') < C(\psi^*, f^*)$. Consider transmission routes which is expressed by (ψ', f') on $G(N)$. Obviously, it is a sub-tree which spans R on $G(N)$. This contradicts that T is optimal. In addition, let S be an optimal share transfer on N, then $C(S) = C(S^*) - |D| \times \mathbf{D}(N)$. This means that by adding $\mathbf{D}(N)$ to c_v the optimal share transfer does not change. Therefore S^* is optimal. □

5 Evaluation of Heuristic Algorithms for the STP

It is known that the problem of computing an optimal Steiner tree is NP-hard, and many heuristic algorithms have been proposed as a practical alternative. However Th. 2 uses optimality of a Steiner tree, and thus we cannot assure that solutions are feasible[2] if we used heuristic algorithms. This section applies heuristic algorithms for the STP to the SHTP, and evaluates by computational experiments from solution quality and feasibility points of view.

5.1 Methods for the STP

Exact. This is an exact algorithm for the STP[8], and constructs a Steiner tree with complexity $O(|V|^3 + 2^{|S|}|R|^2)$, where $S = V \backslash R$.

Pruned-MST. This method constructs a minimal spanning tree first and then prunes unnecessary sub-graphs. Prim and Kruskal are well-known polynomial and exact algorithm for a minimal spanning tree problem. There exists a distributed algorithm GHS of Kruskal[9]. Competitiveness of Pruned-MST is $|V| - |R| + 1$.

Shortest-Paths. This method finds a shortest path from s to d for each $d \in D$, and merges them. Dijkstra and Floyd-Warshall are well-known polynomial and exact algorithm for a shortest paths problem. Many research exists on distributed algorithms for the shortest paths problem. For example, Haldar showed a distributed algorithm that uses $2 \cdot |V|^2$ messages in the worst case[5]. An advantage of this method is that this method can find a *feasible* solution in any cases, because any shortest path form s to d must be a transmission route.

WWW. Kou et. al. proposed a houristic algorithm based on Distance Network Heuristics in [10]. Wu et. al. extended Kou's algorithm in [11]. In this paper this algorithm is expressed by WWW. Chen et. al. proposed a distributed algorithm of WWW in [6], and Kamei et. al. proposed a self-stabilising distributed algorithm of Chen's algorithm in [7]. Competitiveness of WWW is $2(1 - 1/l)$, where l is the number of leafs in the Steiner tree($l \leq |R|$).

5.2 Experiments Conditions

We implemented the above four methods in Java language. For graph implementation, we used a Java package, called OpenJGraph[3], and used APIs provided by OpenJGraph to derive minimal spanning trees and shortest paths. The OpenJGraph uses Kruskal algorithm to obtain minimal spanning trees and Dijkstra algorithm to obtain shortest paths.

[2] 'Feasible' means that the mapping method defined in Def. 7 is able to obtain a share transfer, namely $\psi(d)$ can be found uniquely, from a given tree.

[3] http://openjgraph.sourceforge.net

Table 1. Results for the complete graph C_5

	Pruned-MST	Shortest-Paths	WWW
Best	1	1	1
Mean	1.40	1.04	1.04
Worst	3.73	1.37	1.37
Fail	0	0	0

Table 2. Results for the middle network N_m

	Pruned-MST	Shortest-Paths	WWW
Best	0.88	1	–
Mean	1.95	1	–
Worst	4.55	1	–
Fail	8	0	0

We compared the above methods on the two types of networks as follows:

Complete graph C_5. C_5 is a complete graph with five vertices. We prepared one hundred instances of C_5 by changing the edge cost c_e and the vertex cost c_v. Cost values were selected randomly from one to ten, and $|D| = 2$.

Middle network N_m. N_m is shown at Fig. 1 in [7], and the number of nodes is sixteen. The number of instances for N_m is one hundred. Cost values were selected randomly from one to ten, and $|D| = 4$. We did not apply the algorithm Exact for this network due to the computational complexity.

5.3 Results and Consideration

Experimental results are shown in Tables 1 and 2. Best, Mean, and Worst are best, mean, and worst value of resulting costs, respectively. For network C_5, each value is the ratio of the cost to the cost by the algorithm Exact. For the network N_m, each value is the ratio to the cost by the algorithm WWW. A value in the row Fail is the number of instances which the algorithm found as infeasible share transfer.

In relation to quality of solutions, generally Shortest-Paths and WWW succeeded to find good solutions, which were in error by less than small percentage, but in the worst case error was more than 30 %. There might be still room for improvement. Moreover solutions by Shortest-Paths and WWW were the same. As described above, although behaviors of these algorithms are quite different, by adding $\mathbf{D}(N)$ on the calculation of w' these algorithms tend to behave in the same way.

For N_m Pruned-MST outputs infeasible solutions for eight instances among one hundred instances. This shows that we have to apply heuristic algorithms carefully to the SHTP. As described before Shortest-Paths algorithm can find a feasible solution for any instances, and WWW outputs the same solutions with Shortest-Paths. Although detail analysis about relations between WWW and

Shortest-Paths is left for our future works, these algorithms can be considered as one of efficient methods for the SHTP.

6 Conclusions

This paper discussed an optimal share transmission method for a distributed storage system which uses a secret sharing scheme. We introduced a Share Transfer Problem, and proved NP-hardness of the problem. Moreover, we proposed a reduction method for the Share Transfer Problem into a Steiner Tree Problem. Finally, we applied several heuristic algorithms for the Steiner Tree Problem to the Share Transfer Problem, and evaluated by computational experiments. According to results, Shortest-Paths and WWW algorithms work well, but there may be still room for improvement.

References

1. Miyamoto, T., Doi, S., Nogawa, H., Kumagai, S.: Autonomous Distributed Secret Sharing Storage System. Syst. & Comp. in Jpn. 37(6), 55–63 (2006)
2. Shamir, A.: How to Share a Secret. communication of the ACM 22(11), 612–613 (1979)
3. Kaneko, Y., Shinoda, S.: The Complexity of an Optimal File Transfer Problem. IEICE Trans. Fund. E82-A(2) (1999)
4. Karp, R.M.: Reducibility among combinatorial problems. Plenum Press, New York (1972)
5. Haldar, S.: An All Pairs Shortest Paths Distributed Algorithm Using $2n^2$ Messages. J. of Algorithms 24, 20–36 (1997)
6. Chen, G.-H., Houle, M.-E., Kuo, M.-T.: The Steiner problem in distributed computing systems. Inf. Sci. 74, 73–96 (1993)
7. Kamei, S., Kakugawa, H.: A Self-Stabilizing Distributed Algorithm for the Steiner Tree Problem. IEICE Trans. Fund. E87-D(2), 299–307 (2004)
8. Jungnickel, D.: Graphs, Networks and Algorithms, 2nd edn. Springer, Heidelberg (2004)
9. Tel, G.: Introduction to Distributed Algorithms. Cambridge University Press, Cambridge (2004)
10. Kou, L., Markowsky, G., Berman, L.: A fast algorithm for steiner trees. Acta Informatica 15, 141–145 (1981)
11. Wu, Y.F., Widmayer, P., Wong, C.K.: A faster approximation algorithm for the Steiner problem in graphs. Acta Informatica 23, 223–229 (1986)

Deadline and Throughput-Aware Control for Request Processing Systems

Pedro Furtado and Ricardo Antunes

Universidade de Coimbra
Portugal
pnf@dei.uc.pt, rantunes@dei.uc.pt

Abstract. Congestion Control is a necessary tool in Transaction Processing Systems (TPS), to avoid excessive degradation of response times. But it should have an autonomic behavior, adapting automatically to request characteristics to deliver the best possible service. Given that every request has either explicit or implicit deadlines (maximum acceptable response times), we analyze strategies that target request deadlines and throughput. These include maximum throughput seeker strategies, strategies using feedback control on miss rate and an additional proposal for preventive control of miss rates and throughput. Another goal of our proposal is for the control to be external and it should not rely on analytic models for control (because the predictions may be erroneous due to physical system issues). We analyze and compare alternative designs for the control including our own proposals and related ones. Our experiments consider both varied request inter-arrival and duration distributions and a real transaction processing benchmark.

1 Introduction

Transaction Processing Systems (TPS) need some form of Admission Control to avoid excessive request service degradation under congested conditions. For this reason, systems do have control over admission at least by using static configuration parameters (e.g. maximum number of transactions in a DBMS), but these are coarse-grain. With that basic admission control there are no guarantees that requests will be fulfilled in due time and the control parameter may be set too high (with degraded response times while under congestion) or too low (under-utilizing resources). In order to improve this, we propose that the coarse-grain controls be supplemented by adaptive fine-grained Admission Control. A TPS should be able to decide whether requests should be accepted for execution or not, delivering service with quality and predictability. It tries to enforce two possible outcomes: request fulfillment in due time (as expressed by deadlines) or rejection for client notification or for further admission testing in a multiple servers scenario. Approaches that do not offer these alternatives result in requests being stuck in the system for too long during congested periods and therefore result in annoying latencies. The approach should be applied as-is to any system, platform, application or context. Given that we target deadlines, we review some works related to this subject in the real-time systems domain, but the assumptions and objectives there are different. In real-time systems, execution time is

I. Stojmenovic et al. (Eds.): ISPA 2007, LNCS 4742, pp.383–394,2007.

assumed known with great precision and only processing requirements are significant, while I/O and other resource requirements are assumed completely negligible and tasks are assumed totally independent. Physical issues such as I/O, DBMS cache hits/misses and data-dependent transaction execution issues make our context much less predictable than the typical real-time systems scenario. Nevertheless, runtime prediction is still a necessary condition to handle deadlines in our approach, but it has a statistic nature – we show how we characterize the durations of transactions in an application, with the TPCC transactional benchmark [21] used as an example. Another characteristic of real time systems is that scheduling assumes execution of one task at a time and preemption. Our external congestion control does not control preemption and instead decides on admission of further requests while multiple requests are already admitted and in execution within the system.

We characterize strategies as seeking the maximum throughput, using feedback control on miss rate or doing some form of preventive control of miss rates and throughput. After proposing a runtime prediction approach, we propose a throughput seeker strategy and a preventive control one. Then we compare experimentally these approaches and include existing strategies in the comparison. We also test our proposals against the TPCC benchmark [21] and conclude on the relative merits of the strategies. Our major contributions are the strategy for response times prediction, the maximum throughput and preventive control approaches, the characterization of admission control alternatives into groups according to their characteristics, the experimental comparison of alternatives and conclusions.

The paper is structured as follows: section 2 reviews related work. Section 3 discusses assumptions, variables and a model for the adaptable Admission Control work. Section 4 shows how the necessary statistics are collected and section 5 presents the adaptable strategies. Section 6 compares the strategies against varied workload distributions and the TPCC benchmark. Section 7 concludes the paper.

2 Related Work

This work is related to real-time systems and real-time databases, load balancing and quality-of-service concerning information systems. Most typical assumptions in real-time systems theory and task assignment do not hold in our context. Classical uniprocessor scheduling algorithms assume at least the following points: tasks are preemptable, only processing requirements are significant, while I/O and other resource requirements are completely negligible, all tasks are independent and execution time is precisely known. Well known scheduling algorithms include Rate Monotonic (RM), which assumes periodic tasks and favors those with smallest period, and Earliest-Deadline-First (EDF), which favors tasks with earliest deadlines. Another important aspect of these schedulers when comparing with our context is that their schedule puts a single task to execution at each time, while our external control decides on submitting multiple tasks based on an execution cardinality and does not control preemption. Real-time databases raise other relevant predictability issues, due to factors such as database cache hits/misses, data-dependent transaction variations (e.g. the number of lines of an order affect order-related transactions in transaction processing systems), transaction locks among others. Most real-time databases have soft real-time constraints, meaning that those constraints are desired targets, as opposed to hard real-time databases where deadlines must be guaranteed at any cost. Typically, in soft real-time databases transactions that miss their deadline still execute to the end (soft deadline), but hard deadlines may also be used in specific applications. The problem of scheduling transactions in real-time databases is reviewed in [13]. It has been shown to be a NP-hard problem for which some kind of heuristic can be used. One alternative is to use the EDF algorithm to schedule among transactions that did not miss their deadline and transactions that missed the deadlines are put into a low priority bag and executed when the system would otherwise be idle. Congestion control is necessary in a heavy loaded system to ensure that transactions do not have too long response times. The Adaptive Earliest Deadline (AED) algorithm [11] combines congestion with EDF. It basically has a MISS and a HIT group and the algorithms adjusts a threshold defining the number of transactions in the HIT group using a miss rate target. Transactions within the HIT group are scheduled using EDF, the MISS group transactions execute in order, only when processing would be idle otherwise. Our time-constraint approach can run with any scheduling policy, but both EDF and AEF have a serious limitation that they discriminate against long transactions, which end up with large deadline miss rates. AEVD [17] attempts at decreasing the magnitude of this problem.

The works in [8, 9, 10] focus QoS for request processing in real-time databases, specially aimed at applications with strict time-requirements such as military ones [1, 9]. They propose strategies to meet deadlines for individual requests, but the authors consider an all-in-memory context, as this renders the system more predictable and controllable. In [14, 20] the authors propose feedback control to adapt the admission procedure to guarantee deadlines in real time systems, using control theory strategies such as a PID controller. Admission Control was also studied for Web Servers. In [6] the authors propose session-based Admission Control (SBAC), noting that longer sessions may result in purchases and therefore should not be discriminated in overloaded conditions. They propose self-tunable admission control based on hybrid or predictive strategies. [5] uses a rather complex analytical model to perform admission control. There are also approaches proposing some kind of service differentiation: [3] proposes architecture for Web servers with differentiated services; [4] defines two priority classes for requests, with corresponding queues and admission control over those queues. [18] proposes an approach for Web Servers to adapt automatically to changing workload characteristics and [12] proposes a strategy that improves the service to requests using statistical characterization of requests and services. [2, 15] propose and evaluate QoS control in computer systems (e.g. web servers) using an analytic model. The model uses a combination of Markov Chains and Queuing Model, requiring knowledge of resource capacities and service demand by requests. [19] and [7] consider a maximum throughput [19] or capacity [7] as we do, but [19] does not explore adaptability further and [7] does not consider deadlines, QoS targets or response time vs EC.

3 Basic Transaction Processing Model

Admission or Congestion Control is based on a feedback controller over the Transaction Processing System (TPS). Figure 1 shows the components of our Admission Control system.

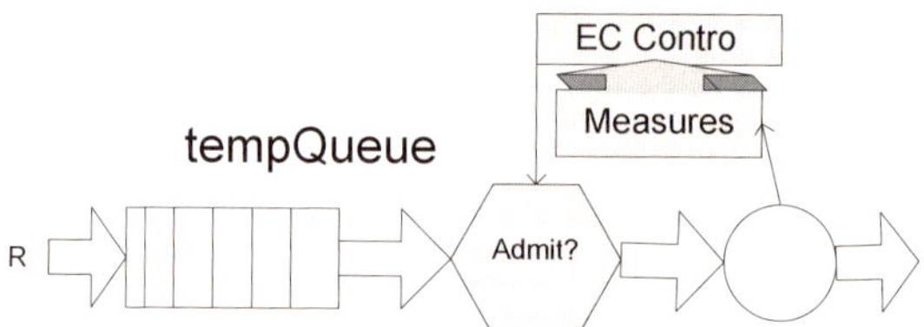

Fig. 1. System Model with Controller

Requests (R_i) enter a queue (tempQueue) and are evaluated for admission as soon as there is a free execution slot. Measures are taken during execution and fed to an "Execution Cardinality" component (EC Control), which decides the number of simultaneous executions at each control moment.

Queuing and Admission Control: waiting in a queue is not productive. It serves to hold requests temporarily during request arrival bursts, but the maximum amount of time waiting should be constrained. The queue may implement any policy, including EDF, LIFO or FIFO (FIFO is often the policy of choice). There needs to be an additional control on the size of the queue to reject requests based on the waiting time. In our proposal this is implemented by means of an Admittance Decision Time limit (ADT) that is contracted for all requests, for an individual application or for a specific request. For instance, ADT<=1 sec or ADT<=max{1 sec,20%RT}, where RT is the expected runtime of the request. Given this parameter, the system may simply put the request in the queue and, if ADT is reached, reject the request. The total number of requests in the system is the number of requests running plus the number of requests in the queue. The admission control piece of the system tests requests for admission whenever admission is possible according to execution cardinality constraints given by the admission control algorithm.

The algorithms themselves control the maximum value for the number of simultaneous executions or execution cardinality, which we denote as ECmax. Figure 2 shows the possible states for requests in the system.

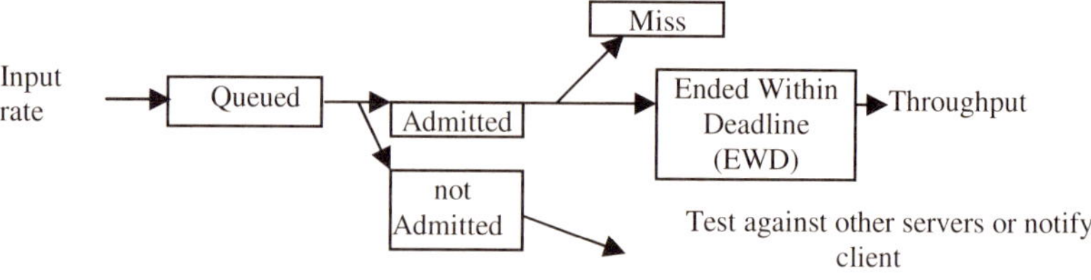

Fig. 2. Possible Request States

Considering a deadline, there are two options: requests miss their deadline but continue running until the end (soft deadlines) or they are removed from execution when they miss their deadline (hard deadlines). We introduce a metric "End within the Deadline" (EWD), which considers only requests that ended without missing the deadline. Instead of maximizing the number of requests that ended, it makes sense to maximize the number of EWD requests. The rationale is that the servicing rate should not be wasted serving requests that miss their deadlines. Likewise, when we talk about throughput (T), we can consider the Throughput with all admitted requests or the EWD throughput (T_{EWD}). Unless stated explicitly, we consider the second alternative. The objective of the control is to maximize T_{EWD} and to minimize the miss rate. We introduce now a model to reason about execution time and therefore to control deadlines.

Multi-Transaction Execution Model: the model intends to reason about an approximate expectation on the time transactions would take to execute in a multi-transaction scenario, outside factors not considered. We consider a standalone duration d_{ij} being the measure of the time transaction T_i would take to execute a run r_j if it were alone in the system. For simplicity we denote d_{ij} as d from now on. The execution in a multi-transaction environment is modeled as follows: transaction T_i ends run r_j as soon as it consumes the duration d. This duration is consumed at a rate that is dependent on the number of transactions executing simultaneously. simultaneously in the time interval Δt, T_i consumes $f(\Delta t, n)$ of d. For simplicity, we use a "linear" model in this description and in the next section we show how we were able to apply a much more precise model by collecting actual runtimes. In the "linear" model $f(\Delta t, n) = \Delta t / n$. If we apply this model (the linear version, for simplicity) to a transaction running alone, $n=1$ and d is consumed precisely in time d, as expected. For the linear model the duration is proportional to the number of simultaneous transactions (e.g. it predicts a duration $n \times d$ when n transactions with the same duration d are executed simultaneously). Given a contract specifying that transactions should not take more than D to execute (limit threshold or deadline), under a *best-effort* approach a transaction with standalone duration d will miss the deadline if there are in (time-weighted) average at least D/d transactions in the system (e.g. if the standalone duration is 1 second and the transaction should not take more than 10 seconds, 10 transactions would cause a deadline break using the linear model). More generically, if $n \rightarrow \infty$, the elementary consumption $\Delta t / n$ of d tends to 0, which means that in the limit the *best-effort* alternative becomes stuck and transactions do not progress.

Because the *best-effort* approach does not limit the number of simultaneous transactions, deadlines are missed whenever there is congestion, with bad results to the user or application that has to wait a long time to get an answer or a system busy timeout. In the next section we describe how we obtained statistics for $f(\Delta t, n)$ in our Multi-transaction execution model.

4 TPM and Response-Time Statistics

In this section we describe the information collected by our approach to support the statistical Admission Control procedure. The objective is to characterize the throughput and expected request response times by running tests offline. The system is given a workload – request types with frequency of occurrence of each type in the workload and runs automatic tests varying the number of simultaneous requests. The tests start with EC=1 and run the workload for a time $t_T(1)$, choosing the next transaction to run randomly using the workload transaction frequencies. EC is then successively incremented by ec_{INC} (we used ec_{INC}=2) until an upper value is reached (the figure shows EC=50) and each test is ran for a configurable time $t_T(EC)$.

Figure 3 shows our throughput results for a test ran using TPC-C with 100 warehouses on a Pentium 4 with 5 disks, 1GB of memory and PostgreSQL version 8.1. In the Figure the maximum throughput EC (EC_{TPM}) was achieved with 21 simultaneous executions. The value for EC_{TPM} is dominated by a few key factors, including the workload type (CPU-bound or I/O bound) and the number of resources available [19].

Figure 4 shows response time results obtained by the tests. The figure depicts the statistic <average+stdev>.

The controller uses statistic the results from the test runs to predict response times and throughput during normal system operation.

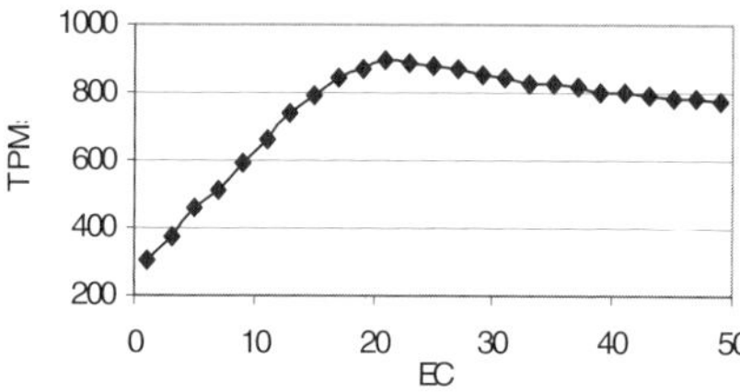

Fig. 3. Results for Test run 1

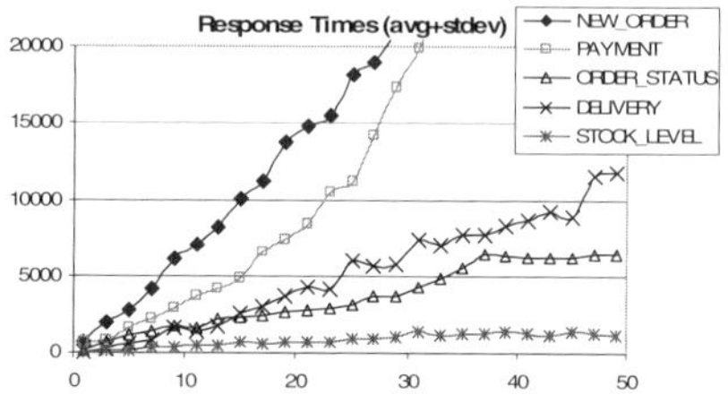

Fig. 4. Average Response Time Results

5 The Control Proposals

In this section we propose the strategies that control the maximum value for EC (EC_{max}) autonomically. One simple alternative is to use the EC that maximizes throughput, as obtained through the test runs above (EC_{MT}).

Maximum Throughput (EC_{MT})**:** this strategy considers simply $EC_{max} = EC_{TPM}$ that was obtained using the test runs described in the previous section. This EC is the one that had the best throughput according to the test runs, so the objective is to try to achieve the best throughput. However, deadlines are not taken into account in this strategy, so that if we want requests to meet deadlines and use the throughput of those that met the deadlines, this strategy will typically do worse than deadline-conscious ones.

The remaining strategies adjust the maximum execution cardinality EC_{max} within a configuration interval [EC_{low}, EC_{high}] to account for deadlines. Deadline compliance requirements may push EC_{max} down towards EC_{low} (we used a default value of 8) and if there are no deadlines $EC_{max} = EC_{high}$. We used a default value EC_{high}=50.

Exhaustive Search EC(ES): this strategy predicts the appropriate EC_{max} for the set of currently executing requests plus recently ran requests within a window frame, using exhaustive what-if prediction tests. Although they are exhaustive, the tests are not very expensive computationally, because they require only in-memory retrieval of statistics. Given an interval [EC_{low}, EC_{high}], EC_i iterates from EC_{low} to EC_{high} and, for each request, the corresponding response time is predicted by retrieving the corresponding statistical response time. The frequency of occurrence of each request is used together with the predicted response time and extrapolated to compute a utility function. In the following example of Figure 5 we maximize the number of requests that are admitted and do not miss their deadlines. The EWD (%) column records the fraction of requests that end within the deadline considering a specific $EC_{proposal}$. The "miss?" columns indicate if the corresponding request ends well (1) or misses the deadline (0) and the two last columns show the EWD($EC_{proposal}$). The highlighted cells mark the ECproposal above which each request misses the deadline. The maximum EWD value, with corresponding $EC_{decision}$ = 11 is also highlighted.

		request 1 times		request 2 times		request 3 times				
	ECproposal	5000 (deadline)	miss?	1000 (deadline)	miss?	5000 (deadline)	miss?	EWD (%)	EWD(Ecproposal)	Ecmax Choice
history	3	2000.00	1	50	1	900	1			
	4	2666.67	1	200	1	1800	1	3.0	1.0	4
	5	3333.33	1	250	1	2250	1	3.0	1.0	5
	6	4000.00	1	300	1	2700	1	3.0	1.0	6
	7	4666.67	1	350	1	3150	1	3.0	1.0	7
	8	5333.33	0	400	1	3600	1	2.0	0.7	5
	9	6000.00	0	450	1	4050	1	2.0	0.7	6
	10	6666.67	0	500	1	4500	1	2.0	0.7	7
	11	7333.33	0	550	1	4950	1	2.0	**0.7**	7
	12	8000.00	0	600	1	5400	0	1.0	0.3	4
	...	...	...	...	...	...	...	...	...	...

Fig. 5. Example of EC determination for EC_{ES}

Deadline-based EC(d): this strategy determines the miss rate for a recent window w of already ended requests, and if the miss rate is above a value m_{max} EC is reduced; if it is below m_{min}, EC is increased.

These approaches represent three different perspectives when looking at the control algorithm. The EC(MT) alternative seeks to maximize the throughput, but does not look at deadlines; the EC(d) approach is a typical feedback controller that looks at the miss rate for already ended requests and adjusts EC_{max} in monitorization iterations either up or down according to the miss rate. EC(ES) is the most reactive approach because it predicts response times at request entry times to determine if there is the risk for missing deadlines and acts accordingly.

Besides the strategies proposed above, w also want to compare them to related strategies proposed by other authors. The approach in [7] uses offline tests to compute a server capacity [7] and request requirements in terms of capacity. We name it the Cap strategy in the experimental section. The capacity is the maximum load level that produces highest throughput for the server and is expressed in msecs (e.g. a server capacity may be 20.000 msecs, meaning that it can run requests that total up to 20.000 msecs at once); requests get to execute if their recent average running time plus those of executing requests do not reach the capacity. This approach is related to our EC(MT) proposal, but instead of the number of requests executing simultaneously it uses sums of response times. The other strategy that we compare to ours is the one in [15], which controls the queue size and EC simultaneously to achieve certain Quality-of-service (QoS) objectives. It is a typical feedback control loop – we denote it as QoS strategy - and we also show that the results of this approach are comparable with the results of EC(d) above. Feedback control approaches such as EC(d) and QoS need to specify a relatively large interval between monitorization instants, because they monitor variables such as the miss rate. If the monitor interval is too small, a control action will not have enough time to bring changes into the observed variables and therefore it will act erroneously. This is the major limitation of the feedback control approaches.

6 Experimental Results

Our experimental objective was to compare the throughput using each of the strategies we defined in the previous sections and also compare to approaches proposed by other authors. We report the throughput considering only requests that ended within the deadline (T_{EWD}), as our objective is to maximize these and minimize the miss rate. We compare EC(d), EC(ES) with EC(TPM), *Best Effort* (accepting every request into the system) and also the two related strategies we reviewed before: [7], which we called Cap (because it is based on resource capacities and request requirements) and the approach in [15], which we called QoS, because it is based on a QoS objective function. The Cap strategy does not consider deadlines. For the QoS strategy, the user can specify targets for deadline, rejection probability (the approach adapts the size of the queue and the number of simultaneous executions) and the throughput. The user also gives weights to each target. However, not only we do not want to specify a throughput target, because the objective is the maximum throughput, as mixed targets are difficult to establish in this approach because the three variables (deadline, rejection probability and throughput) are not independent. For this reason, we configured a miss rate target of 5% and did not use the remaining parameters, and configured the minimum control rate for this strategy and for EC(d) to 60 seconds, because these strategies act on request miss rate statistics, so they must wait enough time to have meaningful statistics (we tested 15 seconds, 30 seconds and 120 seconds as well, but the results were worse with any of these alternatives). For the reactive EC(ES) approach, on the contrary, we configured the control interval to 50 msecs, which was chosen for presenting an acceptably low overhead (we show more on the overhead later on). We did two types of experiments: a simulation experiment to compare all the alternatives, for which we have built an event-driven simulator to model the effects of multiple simultaneous executions. We also ran experiments with the TPCC benchmark to compare EC(MT) to EC(ES) in a real setting.

For the simulation experiments we have set request deadlines to 10 seconds and used statistical distributions for both arrivals and durations (Exponential, Uniform, Gaussian, Poisson). For these distributions the expected standalone durations were (100 ms to 1.5 seconds) and expected inter-arrival time was 100ms. Each simulation run submitted 10000 transactions according to the arrival rate distribution and statistics. The results were consistent over the above distributions. The requests were configured to stay at most 5 seconds in the queue.

Figure 6 compares the throughput (T_{EWD}) of the strategies, considering Exponential durations and Uniform arrival distributions. Figure 6b details the congested fraction of the result in Figure 6a. In these experiments we are considering "soft deadlines", that is, requests that miss the deadline still execute to the end. EC_{max} is fixed at 21, the maximum throughput point obtained from the offline test runs. The arrival rate is 600 TPMs and the throughput is practically equal to the arrival rate if request durations (expected value) are small. However, as the request duration increases, the throughput (T_{EWD}) decreases significantly, because the system becomes unable to meet deadlines (EC(MT) and Cap) or restricts admission to guarantee deadlines (EC(d), EC(ES), QoS). The *Best Effort* alternative shows that the miss rate sky-rockets and the T_{EWD} throughput plunges to zero in congested states if no control is introduced over the number of simultaneous executions. The results also show that EC(ES) achieves the best throughput under congestion and the smallest miss rate as well, and this is because it is able to prevent misses. The QoS and EC(d) strategies achieve a smaller throughput and higher miss rate than EC(ES) because while EC(ES) acts preventively on request misses by looking at executing and recent requests and choosing the EC value that maximizes T_{EWD}, these other strategies react much later (they have to, because they use miss rate statistics) and bounce between decreasing EC below the desired miss rate objective and increasing it because it is too low. EC(MT) and Cap exhibit worse throughput than the other alternatives (except *Best Effort*) and behave very similarly. They both strive for the best Throughput EC value, but do not consider deadlines to determine that value. As a result, they miss too many deadlines when compared to deadline-conscious alternatives. Still, their behavior is much better than Best Effort.

Figure 7 summarizes the comparison between EC(ES) and EC(MT) under congestion for varied arrival and duration distributions (Exponential=EXP, Gaussian=GAU, Poisson=POI, Uniform=UNIF, expected duration =1.3 secs). There are differences depending on the distribution, but the adaptable strategy was always able to have a much larger throughput (the throughput of EC(MT) was even 0 for the Gaussian durations because every request would miss the 10 seconds deadline).

For runs with the TPCC benchmark (100 warehouses) we used a Pentium 4 machine with 1 GB of memory and a Postgres DBMS. The run used transaction distributions (new-order 15%, payment 20%, order-status 25%, delivery 15%, stock-level 25%). The results are shown in Figure 8 and compare the throughput of transactions that ended within the deadline using EC(ES) (Tewd in the Figure) with EC(MT) (Tewd (no control) in the Figure, corresponding to a fixed EC_{max}=21). The results show that, by controlling the execution cardinality, this transactional benchmark improved

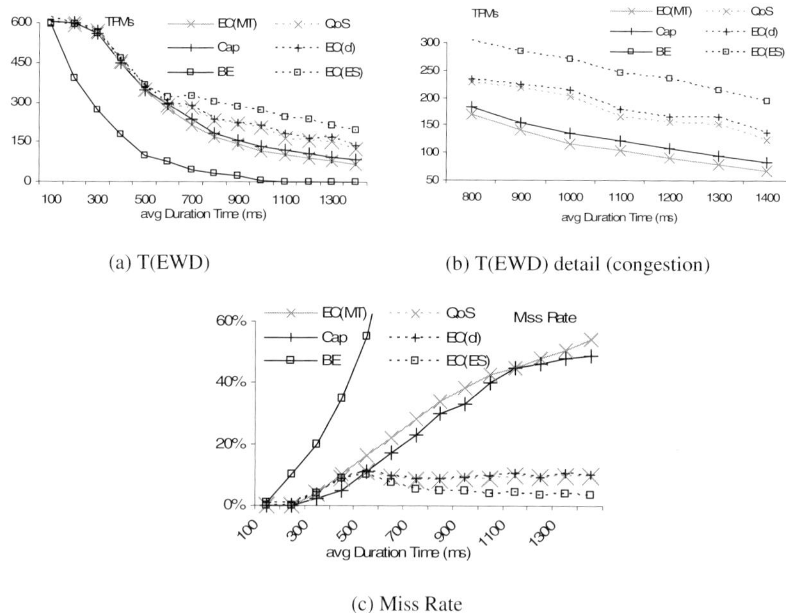

(a) T(EWD)

(b) T(EWD) detail (congestion)

(c) Miss Rate

Fig. 6. Comparison of Strategies (T_{EWD}, Miss Rate)

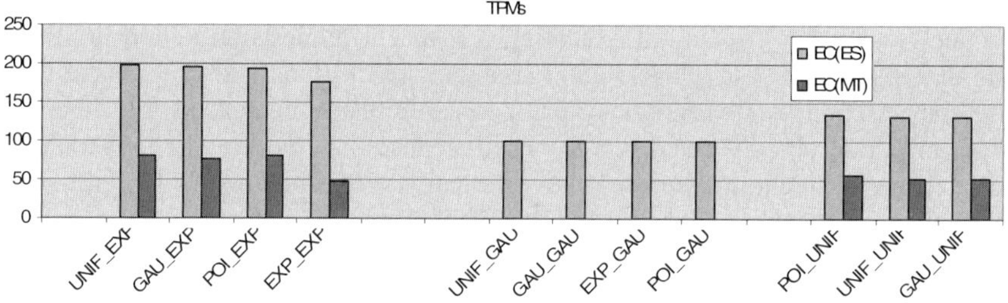

Fig. 7. Summary of T_{EWD} for Varied Distributions

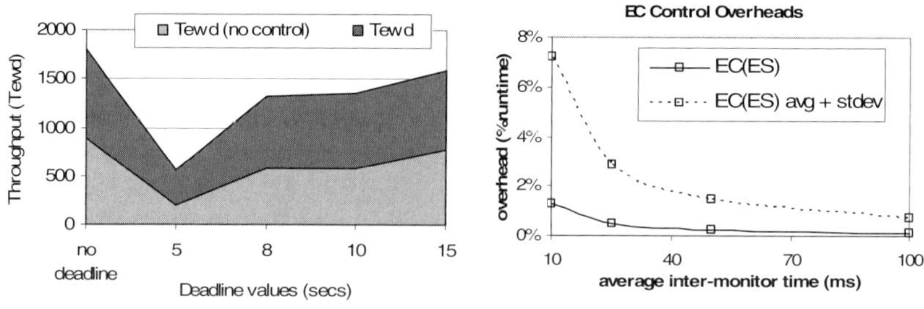

Fig. 8. Throughput T_{ewd} for TPCC

Fig. 9. Overhead of EC Control

the throughput significantly when compared with a fixed execution cardinality, even though that fixed cardinality corresponded to the maximum throughput point from offline throughput tests, not considering deadlines.

Figure 9 shows the overhead we have observed for the EC control functionality, by timing the runs of the control part. The values in the Figure are expressed in percentage of the total runtime. Only EC(ES) is depicted because the remaining strategies that were compared have no significant overhead (they either do not control or have a very small control rate). These results show that the overhead varies significantly (large standard deviation), but with 50 msecs control period it is smaller than 2% and smaller than 1% if a 100 msecs control rate is chosen.

Conclusions from the experiments: as we described before, the strategies tested can be divided into four groups – *best effort*, maximum throughput without considering deadlines, feedback control on the miss rate and preventive control, which is one of the proposed strategies in this paper. The tests show that *best effort* is useless under congestion; maximum throughput alternatives result in acceptable throughput but fail to consider deadlines; feedback control strategies are slow to react and bounce; we found out that the preventive approach yields the best results, as it adapts to each incoming request requirements for processing. This preventive approach can be applied together with maximum throughput by restraining the EC_{high} limit.

7 Conclusions and Future Work

In this paper we proposed, analyzed and compared external adaptable Admission Control, an approach that can be readily deployed in any context. The strategies controlling execution cardinality include fixing it at the best throughput value, controlling it by periodically looking at miss rates and a preventive alternative that uses statistics on runtimes to adjust the execution cardinality without missing deadlines. We have compared the approaches and shown that the preventive alternative is able to provide better results in what concerns miss rate minimization and throughput maximization simultaneously. This approach can be used in a multiple servers scenario for load-balancing decisions, which is our current focus.

References

1. Abbott, R., Garcia-Molina, H.: Scheduling Real-Time Requests: A Performance Evaluation. ACM Trans. Database System 17, 513–560 (1992)
2. Bennani: Autonomic Computing Through Analytic Performance Models. Ph.D in CS dissertation, George Mason University (2006)
3. Bhatti, N., Friedrich, R.: Web server support for tiered services. IEEE Network 13(5), 64–71 (1999)
4. Bhoj, Rmanathan, Singhal.: Web2K: Bringing QoS to Web servers. Tech. Rep. HPL-2000-61, HP Labs (2000)
5. Chen, X., Mohapatra, P., Chen, H.: An admission control scheme for predictable server response time forWeb accesses. In: Proceedings of the 10th World Wide Web Conference, Hong Kong (2001)

6. Cherkasova, Phaal: Session-based admission control: A mechanism for peak load management of commercial Web sites. IEEE Req. on Computers 51(6) (2002)
7. Elnikety, S., Nahum, E., Tracey, J., Zwaenepoel, W.: A Method for Transparent Admission Control and Request Scheduling in E-Commerce Web Sites. In: WWW2004. The Thirteenth International World Wide Web Conference, New York City, NY, USA (2004)
8. Kang, K.D., Son, S.H., Stankovic, J.A.: Managing Deadline Miss Ratio and Sensor Data Freshness in Real-Time Databases. IEEE Trans. on Knowledge and Data Engineering 16(10), 1200–1216 (2004)
9. Kang, K.D.: QoS-Aware Real-Time Data Management. PhD thesis, U. of Virginia (2003)
10. Kang, K.D., Son, S.H., Stankovic, J.A., Abdelzaher, T.F.: A QoSSensitive Approach for Timeliness and Freshness Guarantees in Real-Time Databases. In: Proc. 14th Euromicro Conf. Real-Time Systems (2002)
11. Haritsa, J., Livny, Carey, M.: Earliest Deadline Scheduling for Real-Time Database Systems. In: Proc. IEEE Real-Time Syst. Symp., pp. 232–242. IEEE, Los Alamitos, CA (1991)
12. Kanodia, V., Knightly, E.W.: Ensuring latency targets in multiclass Web servers. IEEE Requests on Parallel and Distributed Systems 13(10) (2002)
13. Krishna, C., Shin, Kang: Real-Time Systems. McGraw-Hill, New York (1997)
14. Lu, C., Stankovic, J., Tao, G., Son, S.: Feedback Control Real-Time Scheduling: Framework, Modeling and Algorithms, special issue of Real-Time Systems. Journal on Control-Theoretic Approaches to Real-Time Computing 23, 85–126 (2002)
15. Menasce, Bennani: On the Use of Performance Models to Design Self-Managing Computer Systems. In: Proc. 2003 Comp. Measur. Group Conf. Dallas, TX (December 7-12, 2003)
16. Mogul, J.C., Ramakrishnan, K.K.: Eliminating receive livelock in an interrupt-driven kernel. ACM Requests on Computer Systems 15(3), 217–252 (1997)
17. Pang, H., Livny, M., Carey, M.: Transaction Scheduling in Multiclass Real-Time Database Systems. In: Proc. IEEE Real-Time Systems Symposium, pp. 22–34. IEEE, Los Alamitos, CA (1992)
18. Pradhan, P., Tewari, R., Sahu, S., Chandra, A., Shenoy, P.: An observation-based approach towards self managing Web servers. In: International Workshop on Quality of Service, Miami Beach, FL (2002)
19. Schroeder, Mor Harchol-Balter, Iyengar, Nahum, Wierman: How to determine a good multi-programming level for external scheduling. In: 22nd International Conference on Data Engineering (2006)
20. Stankovic, J., Lu, C., Son, S., Tao, G.: The Case for Feedback Control Real-Time Scheduling. In: EuroMicro Conference on Real-Time Systems (1999)
21. TPCC: http://www.tpc.org

Cluster Recovery for Fault Tolerance of Spatial Database Cluster in Sensor Networks*

Byeong-Seob You[1], Gyung-Bae Kim[2], and Hae-Young Bae[1]

[1] Department of Computer Science and Information Engineering, Inha University
Younghyun-dong, Nam-ku, Incheon, 402-751, Korea
subi@dblab.inha.ac.kr, hybae@inha.ac.kr
[2] Department of Computer Education, Seowon University
231 Mochung-dong Heungduk-gu Cheongju-si Chungbuk, 361-742, Korea
gbkim@seowon.ac.kr

Abstract. In sensor networks, a huge amount of data is collected by millions of sensors and small mobile devices need to be processed fast. And database which stores those data always should be able to response for any requirement. Spatial database cluster provides high performance and high availability. That suits sensor networks because spatial database cluster can efficiently manage and process much amount of data. The previous system, however, should write external logs every transaction for high availability in all nodes. So, all of update transactions are slowly processed because of writing external logs. Also, recovery time of the failed node is increased because external logs for all of database are written in only single storage. In this paper, we propose the cluster recovery of spatial database cluster. The proposed method has cluster logs in each table unit for consistency among nodes. Also, the cluster log is written just in case any node is failed. Therefore the proposed method is processed more fast because all update transactions don't write cluster logs. And the proposed method provides fast recovery because each table can be recovered concurrently.

1 Introduction

Sensor technology has been developing for the last several years. As a result of it, the size of sensor is more and more small and sensor is used many fields such as perception of temperature, door locks, position of cellular phone or vehicle and so on [3, 6, 12]. Because millions of sensors including small-scale mobile devices collect a huge amount of data, it is important to study the efficient system for management and processing.

Spatial database cluster is a system composed with set of nodes which can process a query independently. That has high performance and high availability because each node has one of fragmented data for parallel processing and all of data is replicated into other nodes [11]. Therefore spatial database cluster is suitable for the environment of

* This research was supported by the MIC(Ministry of Information and Communication), Korea, under the ITRC(Information Technology Research Center) support program supervised by the IITA(Institute of Information Technology Assessment). And this research was supported by the Brain Korea 21 Project in 2007.

I. Stojmenovic et al. (Eds.): ISPA 2007, LNCS 4742, pp.395–406,2007.

processing much amount of data in sensor networks. For high performance and high availability, fast recovery of failed node is important [2].

Usually, the recovery work of shared nothing spatial database cluster is consisted of two stages. The first stage is node recovery (NR). To recover the failed node is by restarting from main-memory or disks as stand-alone database systems do. It is accomplished by recording internal logs (IL) to each node. And the second stage is cluster recovery (CR). It is the recovery for preserving data consistency to each node. After NR has been completed, the failed node should be joined in cluster system. So each node records external logs (EL) for preserving data consistency. Especially, CR considerably affects the system performance since this is on-line work [1, 17].

In previous recovery methods of cluster system, those approaches have two problems. First, EL should be recorded in all nodes even if the failed node does not exist. So update transactions are slowly processed. Secondly, recovery time of the failed node increases since a single storage for all databases is used to record EL in each node [7, 8].

In this paper, we propose the novel recovery method for shared-nothing spatial database cluster. The proposed method has been operating on GMS/Cluster [18]. Each node manages two kinds of logs (one is IL for NR and another log is EL for CR). IL is equal to log of traditional database system. In case of EL, we use logical log like a SQL since spatial data have various size of data. If we use physical log for EL, it must be transferred very large physical spatial data to its replicated node. Also we will record EL only when there is a failed node in the system. And EL is independently recorded each master table (not all tables or databases) in a node.

Therefore, the proposed method has the following advantages. First, maintenance cost of EL decreases since it is independently recorded for each master table in a node. Secondly, update transactions record EL only when there is a failed node. So we can increase the performance of query processing when there is no failed node. Thirdly, a cost of CR decreases since the failed node receives EL from each active node. Finally, we can process transactions even if entire CL doesn't finish yet. So we can provide a stable service.

This paper is organized as follows. Section 2 introduces related works. The proposed recovery method is described in Section 3. Section 4 evaluates the performance of our method. Section 5 concludes the paper.

2 Related Works

In this chapter, we will discuss ClustRa's recovery technique and Replication Server's recovery technique for CR.

2.1 Recovery Technique of ClustRa

The ClustRa is a cluster system that supports none-stop service for non-spatial data using main-memory based database system [4]. Its' nodes are linked into high speed network, such as a gigabit network. And a node can independently processes transactions. Also a group is consisted of two nodes. Each node has a mirror node that contains identical data. If one node in the group is crashed, its mirror node would take over its role instantly to ensure continuous database operations [7].

There are two types of logs in ClustRa: A node-internal log (NI-log) and a distributed tuple log (TL-log). The NI-log stores IL for transactions that are associated with the physical structures inside a node. The TL-log stores EL records relating to all fragment replicas on a node. EL has to be stored certainly to the stable storage. These logs are produced for replica propagation in general query processing and the replication controls simultaneity by this log's sequence. Therefore the response time for update transactions increases since it must record EL for propagation queries [7, 16].

When the failed node processes CR, a node that EL has been recorded sends EL to the failed node sequentially. The recovery node (node that is being recovered) receives EL and processes CR. The recovery node takes back responsibility for the data from its mirror node. And then it can continue a service normally [7, 16]. But ClustRa's CR has some problems. First, the performance of general transactions is fallen since it records EL for all update transactions. Secondly, the recovery time is limited by how long all logs are transferred since each node sends EL node by node. Therefore the recovery nodes are recovered sequentially.

2.2 Recovery Technique in Replication Server

Replication Server allows nodes to process transactions independently [5]. Replication Server provides a replication method but does not provide a partition method. It improves concurrent executions to read transactions since it provides fully replication technique by replicating more than two nodes. So service is available even if more than two nodes crash [10]. All nodes are classified into master and backup table. If a node owns master table, the other nodes owns backup table. In the case of read transactions, they can be processed at any nodes independently. However update transactions should be processed at the node owning master table, and it must propagate to backup tables.

When a node failed, service can be continued at any nodes except the failed node. After the failed node finishes NR, Replication Manager does CR for synchronizing with replicas. At this time, the recovery node informs message to all nodes with last *Log Subsequence Number* (LSN) of Replication Manager. And nodes received this LSN decide a *helper node* to help the recovery node. If a helper node is decided, logs greater than the received LSN are transmitted to the recovery node. The recovery node is recovered using the received logs. If it has been finished, client's queries can be processed normally. At this time, for recovering in parallel, it uses the methods that maintain several databases in node and records logs to several storages for each database.

Replication Server has some problems as follow. First, the cost of logging increases since the same logs must be recorded in the nodes that owned the backup tables as well as the master table. So the performance of update transactions falls down. Secondly, transactions can be processed normally after the recovery of a database is finished.

3 The Parallel Cluster Recovery Method

In this chapter, we propose the parallel recovery method in shared-nothing spatial database cluster system. First, we discuss GMS/Cluster. And then we describe a logging scheme to recover the failed node and a parallel recovery method using these logs.

3.1 GMS/Cluster

GMS/Cluster has architecture of shared-nothing. And each node in GMS/Cluster has a processor, memory and disk independently [18]. A group is consisted of nodes more than two. The number of node in a group is unlimited, and a node can be joined to a group at any time. All nodes in a group are fully replicated. So read transactions are processed in parallel using replicas.

GMS/Cluster provides high availability since replicated node continues service even if any node was crashed. Also it provides partition methods for concurrent execution of update transactions [13]. Partition distributes a load of update transactions to each group.

Spare node is a node that is waiting to join into the system. This node doesn't process any transactions and will join the system when the system is scaling due to overload [15].

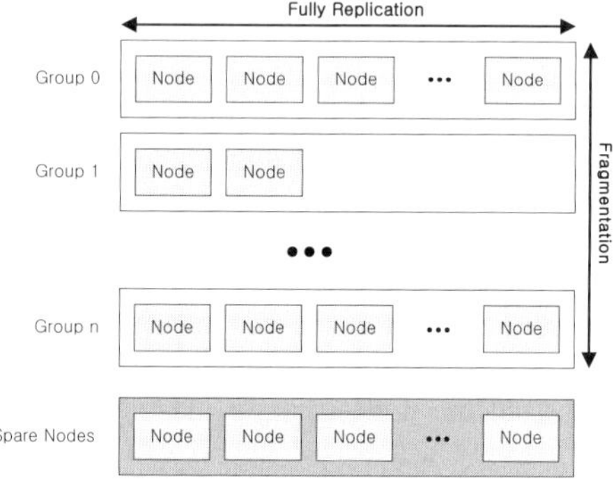

Fig. 1. Architecture of GMS/Cluster

In GMS/Cluster, the replication protocol is very important since all node of a group is fully replicated and the number of a group is unlimited. There have been considerable works in replication protocol. The lazy replication reduces response times since transactions can be executed and committed locally and only the updates are propagated to the other sites [14]. However, atomicity cannot be guaranteed at all. If a node fails before it propagates the updates of a committed transaction to the other sites, then consistency between replicas is lost. Therefore, many lazy schemes have been used a master copy approach, that is, update transactions must be submitted at the site with the corresponding primary copies and transactions whose primary copies reside at different sites are not allowed. The eager replication can achieve 1-copy-serializability and atomicity [9]. Replica's control is combined with the concurrency control mechanism to guarantee serializability. For example, there are 2-phase-locking (2PL) or timestamp based algorithms. Furthermore, an atomic commitment protocol like 2-phase-commit (2PC) is run at the end of the transaction to provide atomicity. However, despite this advantage of eager replication, we implement lazy solutions due to the simplicity and high performance of lazy replication.

3.2 Logging

There are two types of logs in GMS/Cluster: IL and EL. IL is the logs associated with the physical structures inside a node. IL contains information about physical operations regarding to the maintenance of access methods. IL is used for NR, and the system restarts based on this. EL is not directed to physical position in disk but a logical query. EL is just used for replication. A Log record in the EL is identified by queries such as a SQL.

When a failed node is detected, all nodes in a group must record EL for CR. Each node records EL for owned master tables. The system decides a node to takes over the master table the failed node has been owned, and the selected node records EL instead of the failed node.

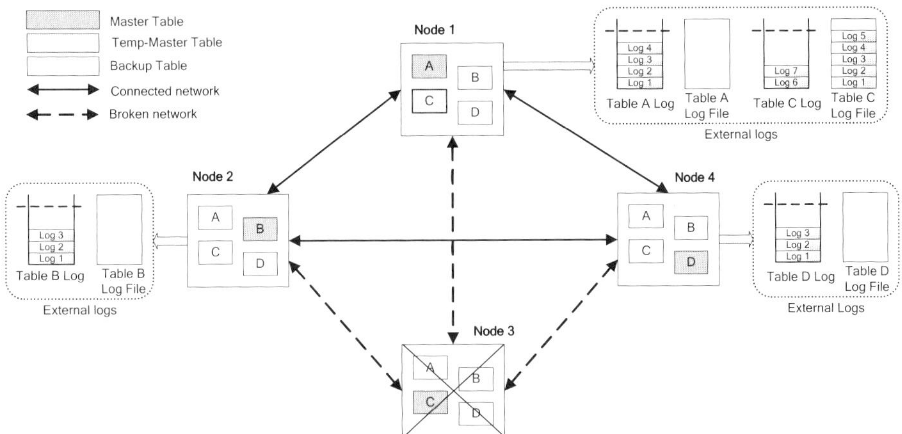

Fig. 2. The process recovering the failed node

In Fig. 2, we assume that node 3 is crashed. Node 1 takes over a role of master table C in node 3. Node 1 records EL for master table A, C. Node 2 and 3 also record EL for table B and D. The recorded EL will be used for CR of node 3. After Node 3 has been recovered, node 3 takes back a role of master table C, a role of table C in node 1 will be changed as backup.

3.3 A Changing Role of Tables and Node

If a node fails, that node cannot provide a service. However we can provide a service continually since there are backup tables for master tables of the failed node in the same group. In such a case, a role of tables in the failed node must be changed. The roles of tables are classified into two cases, i.e., master table and backup table.

Usually, if a node fails, a backup table in other nodes must take a role of master table instead of the failed node. In GMS/Cluster, the role of a backup table in the group belonging to the failed node will be changed into temporary master table. It is called as *temp-master table*. In such a situation, we must decide which node takes a role of a master table. First, we check the number of master tables in each node. A backup table of a node which owns the smallest master table becomes temp-master table. If there are nodes more than two, a backup table of a node which owns the smallest node identifier becomes temp-master table.

In the case of a backup table, we classify a role of a backup table into two cases, i.e., normal backup table and consistent backup table. Normal backup table is called as just backup table. Changing a role of backup table is may not consider. Consistent backup table is called *consist-backup table*. A node which has consist-backup table is called *consistent node*. Consist-backup table is also the same to normal backup table except following aspects. When clients send update transactions to a node owned master table, transactions are executed in local system first, and then it is forwarded to only the consistent node (not all nodes owned backup table). If the forwarding process has been finished, clients receive a message "transaction is committed" even if the transaction is not completed actually. A consistent node forwards this transaction to nodes owned backup table by Lazy protocol. If there is no consistent node, it cannot preserve a consistency. For example, after a node replies the commit message to client without forwarding transaction to consistent nodes, if a node fails, transactions cannot be forwarded to backup tables. In the case of a consist-backup table, the next node of the failed node takes a role of consist-backup table.

3.4 The Parallel Recovery Method

The parallel cluster recovery method is related to helper nodes and recovery node. Helper nodes help the failed node. It has to send external logs to the failed node. Recovery node is a node that trying to recovery for join to cluster system. It has to receive external logs from helper nodes.

First, recovery node tries to node recovery. And then it request external logs to helper nodes. After sending the request message to helper nodes, the recovery node has preparation that receives external logs from helper nodes. The recovery node will receive external logs from each helper nodes in parallel. Secondly, in such a parallel transmission, all external logs are processed in parallel for recovering. Thirdly, if a table has been reflected by external logs, it tries to synchronize temp-master and backup table since clients may send update queries to temp-master table of helper node since a table is processing cluster recovery. Fourthly, the role of nodes returns back as role before the failed node crashed. Finally, the role of node is taken back as role before failure. This is a sequence of parallel cluster recovery method.

In following steps, we describe the parallel recovery method in detail.

STEP 1: Parallel transmits external logs

For a fast recovery of the failed node, it is important that other nodes transmit EL to the failed node as soon as possible. Most previous work has saved logs to a single storage, it enforces the serializable transmission of EL to the failed node. But we enable parallel transmission that all nodes transmit to the failed node, since EL is managed for every table.

First, recovery node request EL to helper nodes. After sending request messages to helper nodes, the recovery node has preparation that receives external logs from

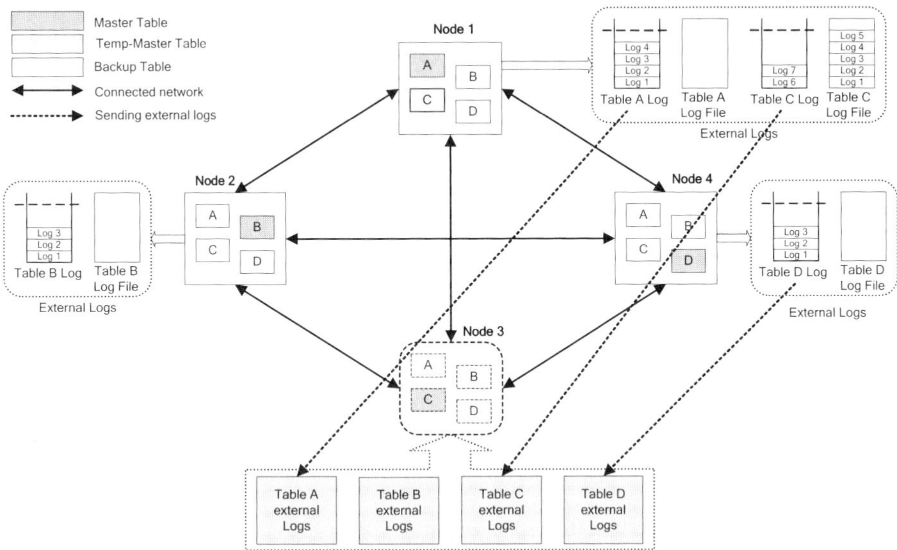

Fig. 3. The parallel transmission of external logs

helper nodes. Recovery node will receive EL from each helper nodes in parallel. Helper nodes search ELs in saved logs. If there is no EL concerned with recovery node, this helper node doesn't join recovery process. Otherwise helper node searches the first log should be sending. It is maybe 1, because we begin a record of EL when a node fails. EL is sent to recovery node sequentially. If recovery node has received all EL for a table, it will recover a table. Tables finished recovery can process the forwarding queries from other nodes even if all cluster recovery finish not yet. Furthermore we can save a cost of logging since helper node that has been finished the transmission of logs doesn't logging EL.

In figure 3, Node 3 requests EL to Node 1, 2, 4. In case of node 1, there is EL for two tables. Node 1 will try to establish connection to node 3 twice. One is connection for table A, and another is connection for table B. And node 1 transmits EL to node 3 in parallel. In case of node 2 and 4, there are EL for only one table. Node 2 and 4 will try establishes connection to node 3 once. Node 2 will be connected for transmitting logs of table B. and node 4 will be connected for transmitting table D. Therefore node 3 receives EL for four tables in parallel, such as table A, B, C and D. So we are enable fast failover of the failed node.

STEP 2: Recovers each table

The recovery node receiving EL does CR using logs. First, when the recovery node requests EL, the recovery node establishes connection as number of tables. Through this connection, the recovery node receives EL of tables from helper nodes and does CR for each table at the same time. When all external logs for a table have been received, CR for a table has been also finished. If the table has been finished CR, it does synchronization with other active nodes, and then executes queries that was requested during CR.

Fig. 4 describes a process of CR for tables in recovery node. As shown Fig. 4, four tables (A ~ D) exist in recovery node. The recovery node receives parallel EL that are kept in different nodes. The right side of recovery node shows transfer of packets relevant to each table. Packets in same vertical line mean that they arrive at the same time and they are to be handled at the same time.

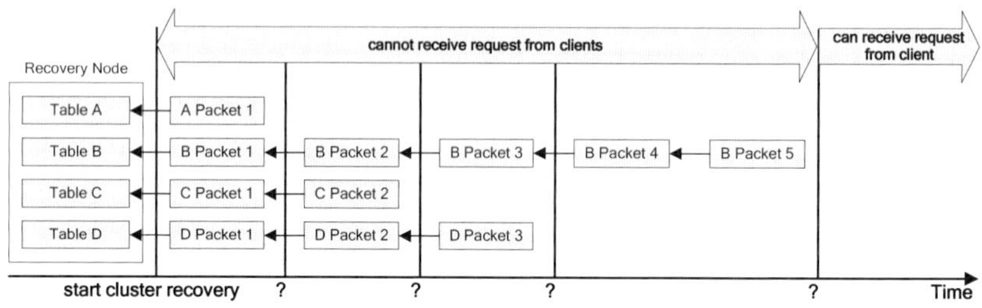

Fig. 4. A cluster recovery for tables

In the following subsections, we will describe each process of Fig. 4.

① It is the case receiving each packets for A ~ D tables. This packets are reflected in relevant each table at the same time. At this time, queries for replica propagation can be executed in <Table A> since <Table A> has been finished CR. So queries for <Table A> can be forwarded normally via synchronization process.

② It is the case received the second EL packets for B ~ D tables. EL is reflected on each table at the same time. Queries for replica propagation can be executed in <Table C>

③ It is the case received each the third EL packet for B, D tables. After EL is reflected, Queries for replica propagation can be executed in <Table D>.

④ It is the case received the fourth and fifth external log packet for B table. After EL is reflected, Queries for replica propagation can be executed in <Table D>.

After ④'s process, recovery node can play as an active node and can receive client's requests. Therefore, parallel transmission of EL and parallel CR of table unit will eliminate transfer time and recovery time. Also, a load of cluster system can be reduced progressively.

STEP 3: Synchronizes master table and backup table

The proposed recovery method processes a recovery by unit of table. After all EL have been reflected in the tables, it tries to synchronize the master and the backup table. When a table processes CR, clients may send update queries to master table of helper node. Forwarding queries can be processed in the table. The synchronization of master table and backup table has been finished even if CR of failed node has not been finished yet. Therefore we can eliminate loads of cluster system progressively.

In GMS/Cluster, nodes that own replicas maintain a queue for saving forwarding queries. If clients send update transactions to the master table, these transactions are to be executed in local node which owns the master table, and then it is to be forwarded to nodes owned replicas of master table. Nodes having received the forwarding transactions save in the queue sequentially.

If clients send update transactions to temp-master table in helper nodes during sending EL to recovery node, first the helper node executes update transactions in local system, and then this node sends update transactions to recovery node. The recovery node records the received transactions in queue. After all ELs have been reflected, it tries to synchronize the master and the backup table using transactions recorded in queue. Transactions are to be recorded sequentially to recovery node, and are to be executed sequentially. Therefore we can preserve serializability.

STEP 4: Takes back *a role of table*

After synchronizing a table, recovery node has to return back role of tables before the failed node crashes. That is, tables that had being master before the node failure should be master tables. GMS/Cluster uses a master copy approach, that is, update transactions must be sent at the node owned master tables. Therefore the node owning many master tables is overloaded by update transactions. For distributing load of a node, it has to takes back a role of table before the failed node crashes.

According to the role of a table before crashes, it is classified into two cases, i.e., master table and backup table. In the case of backup table, it is no need to change its role. Especially in the case of master table, it is necessary to change the role since other nodes in the group have taken roles of recovery node. Update transactions don't allow for this table during returning the role of master table. After prohibit of execution of update transactions, the cluster system changes the current master table into backup table, and propagates the changed information to all nodes in the cluster system.

STEP 5: Takes back *a role of node*

If clients send update transactions to a node owning master table, firstly these transactions are executed in local system, and then these are forwarded to only consistent node (not all nodes owning backup table). After the forwarding process has been finished, it replies message, "transaction has been committed", to client. Consistent node forwards transactions to nodes owning backup tables by Lazy protocol. After these transactions have been forwarded to backup node, if a node crashes, it can preserve a consistency using transactions saved in consistent node. So if recovery node was a consistent node for any node, it must return to a consistent node.

The role of consistent node can be returned after CR of all tables has been finished since consistent node has only one for each node. Like STEP 4, STEP 5 also update transactions are not allowed, and the recovery node propagates the changed information to all nodes. And it takes back a role of consistent node.

4 Experiments

In this chapter, we present performance evaluation between previous methods and the proposed method. We applied each technique to GMS/Cluster and achieved comparison with each technique. We applied each technique in the GMS/Cluster.

ClustRa has configuration that has one master node and one backup node. So, in case of ClustRa, one group has two nodes and each node have 5 master tables. In case of Replication Server, we configure that one group has four nodes (one master node and three backup nodes) and each node have 2~3 master tables. In case of proposal technique, we configure such as a Replication Server.

In the following sections, we examined CR time and average query processing time during CR by number of master tables.

4.1 Cluster Recovery Time by Number of Master Tables

We examine CR time as increasing number of master tables. Amount of logs for each master table is the same, and amount of logs for whole nodes increases proportionally as many as the number of master tables increase. During the recovery time we send fixed amount of queries.

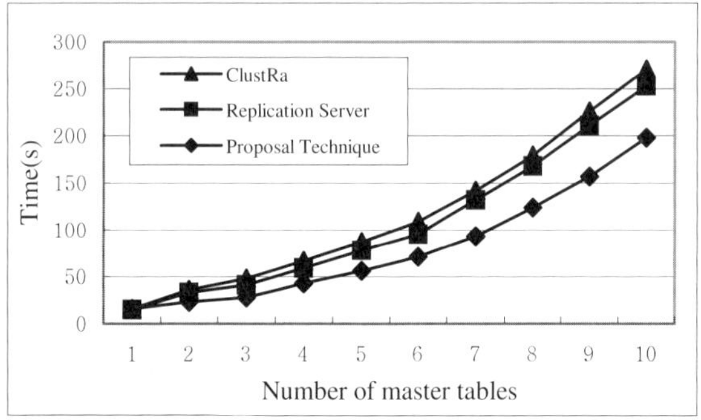

Fig. 5. Recovery time comparison by number of master tables

As we can see in Fig. 5, with the number of master tables increases, all of the techniques' recovery time increases. As quantity of log increases, recovery time takes a long time. As a result, synchronization costs and recovery time increases as non-linear. In the case of our proposed method, recovery time decreases compared with the previous methods.

4.2 Average Query Processing Time During Cluster Recovery

We examine query processing during CR about 10 master tables for each methods.

As you can see in Figure 6, ClustRa's query processing time does not decrease during recovery since it records only one log. However it increases for replicas synchronizing during CR. Also, query processing time decreases slowly after the failed node has been recovered. In the case of Replication Server, query processing time decreases much faster than that of ClustRa since it does CR in each database. However recovery time is slower than the proposed method since the recovery unit of Replication Server is large. In the case of proposed method, at first, load of query processing increases for transferring EL, but it can executes queries to tables that CR has been finished. As a result, query processing time decreases much more than previous methods.

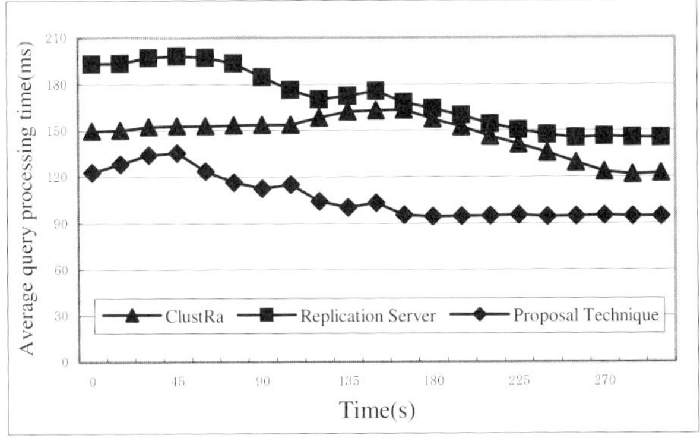

Fig. 6. Average query processing time comparison during cluster recovery

5 Conclusions

This paper has presented the parallel cluster recovery method that offers a fast recovery and eliminates load of cluster system progressively. First, we analyze other recovery methods, and discuss their problems. Based on this analysis, we propose the parallel cluster recovery method.

Most previous work save logs to a unique single storage, and sends sequentially logs to recovery node. So the failed node must be recovered sequentially. Although NR has been finished, recovery node cannot process transactions since the database of recovery node is not in a consistent state. In the proposed method, recovery node processes EL in parallel.

The proposed method has the following advantages. First, the maintenance cost of EL decreases since it is independently recorded for each master table in a node. Secondly, update transactions record EL only when there is a failed node. So we can increase the performance of query processing when there is no failed node. Thirdly, a cost of CR decreases since the failed node receives EL from each active node. Finally, we can process transactions even if the whole of CL haven't finished yet.

In our experimental, it can be seen that recovery time decreases greatly than previous methods. And load of query processing time decreases much more than previous methods during CR.

References

1. Bamford, R., Ahad, R., Pruscino, A.: A Scalable and Highly Available Networked Database Architecture. In: Proceedings of the 25th VLDB Conference, Edinburgh, Scotland (1999)
2. Bernstein, P.A., Goodman, A.: The Failure and Recovery Problem for Replicated Databases. In: Second ACM Symposium on the Principles of Distributed Computing (1983)
3. Bonnet, P., Gehrke, J., Mayr, T., Seshadri, P.: Query Processing in a Device Database System. Technical Report: TR99-1775, Cornell University, Ithaca, NY, USA (1999)
4. Bratsberg, S.E., Hvasshovd, S.O., Torbjornsen, O.: Parallel Solutions in ClustRa. IEEE Computer Society Technical Committe on Data Engineering (1997)

5. Clifford, C.B.: SYBASE: Replication Server Primer. Computing McGraw-Hill (1995)
6. Considine, J., Li, F., Kollios, G., Byers, J.: Approximate Aggregation Techniques for Sensor Databases. ICDE (2004)
7. Hvasshovd, S.O., Torbjornsen, O., Bratsberg, S.E.: The ClustRa Telecom Database: High Availability, High Throughput, and Real-Time Response. In: Proceedings of the 21st VLDB Conference (1995)
8. Jimenez-Peris, R., Martinez, M.P., Alonso, G.: An Algorithm for Non-Intrusive, Parallel Recovery of Replicated Data and its Correctness. In: IEEE Symp. on Reliable Distributed Systems (2002)
9. Kemme, B., Alonso, G.: A New Approach to Developing and Implementing Eager Database Replication Protocols. ACM Transactions on Database Systems 25 (2000)
10. Kemme, B.: Database Replication for Clusters of Workstations. PhD thesis, Department of Computer Science, ETH Zürich, Switzerland (2000)
11. Koudas, N., Faloutsos, C., Kamel, I.: Declustering spatial databases on a multi-computer architecture (1996)
12. Lazaridis, I., Mehrotra, S.: Progressive approximate aggregate queries with a multi-resolution tree structure. In: ACM SIGMOD (2001)
13. Mehta, M., DeWitt, D.J.: Data Placement in Shared-nothing parallel database systems. The VLDB Journal 6 (1997)
14. Pacitti, E., Minet, P., Simon, E.: Fast algorithms for maintaining replica consistency in lazy master replicated databases. In: Int. Conf. on VLDB, Edinburgh (1999)
15. Pirahesh, H., Mohan, C., Cheng, J., Liu, T.S., Selinger, P.: Parallelism in Relational Data Base Systems: Architectural Issues and Design Approaches. In: Proceedings Int'l Symp. on Databases in Parallel and Distributed Systems (1990)
16. Torbjornsen, O., Hvasshovd, S.O., Kim, Y.K.: Towards Real-Time Performance in a Scalable, Continuously Available Telecom DBMS. ClustRa (2001)
17. Wiesmann, M., Pedone, F., Schiper, A., Kemme, B., Alonso, G.: Understanding Replication in Databases and Distributed Systems. In: Proceedings of the 20th International Conference on Distributed Computing Systems (2000)
18. You, B.S., Kim, M.G., Kim, J.H., Bae, H.Y.: Design and Implementation of GMS/Cluster. In: Proceedings of the Korea Open GIS Association (2003)

A Secure Energy-Efficient Routing Protocol for WSN*

Al-Sakib Khan Pathan and Choong Seon Hong

Department of Computer Engineering, Kyung Hee University
1 Seocheon, Giheung, Yongin, Gyeonggi, 449-701, South Korea
spathan@networking.khu.ac.kr, cshong@khu.ac.kr

Abstract. The intent of this paper is to propose an energy-efficient routing protocol with data transmission security for wireless sensor networks. We create an energy and distance aware sink-rooted tree in the network which is used for secure data transmissions from the source sensors to the base station. We mainly focus on ensuring authenticity and confidentiality of the sensor reports by adopting one-way hash chain and pre-loaded shared secret keys. To achieve data freshness, there is an optional key refreshment mechanism in our protocol. Along with the detailed description of our protocol, we present an analysis and performance evaluation of our proposal.

1 Introduction

Wireless sensor networks (WSNs) could be very useful for providing support for some specific purposes like target tracking, surveillance, environmental monitoring etc [1], [2]. Today's sensors can monitor temperature, pressure, humidity, soil makeup, vehicular movement, noise levels, lighting conditions, the presence or absence of certain kinds of objects or substances, mechanical stress levels on attached objects, and other properties. As such types of networks are composed of resource-constrained tiny sensors, many research works have tried to focus on efficient use of the available resources of sensors. Energy is in fact, one of the most critical factors that play a great role to define the duration of an active WSN. So, any protocol should ensure a good structure of the network based on the energy levels of the participating nodes or a competent way of utilizing the energies of the sensors in the network. Energy-efficiency is also very necessary to maximize the lifetime of the network. Security on the other hand, is another critical issue especially for ensuring the legitimacy of transmitted reports from the sensors to the base station (BS) [3], [4]. The task of securing a WSN is however, complicated by the fact that the sensors are mass-produced anonymous devices with a severely limited energy budget and initially with no knowledge of their locations in the deployment environment (in general cases).

In this paper, we deal with the challenge of energy-efficiency and secure routing in WSN in a highly dense deployment scenario. We propose a protocol which aims at minimizing the wasteful energy consumption by energy-efficient structuring of the network and then secure the data transmissions from the sensors to the base station

* This work was supported by the MIC and ITRC. Dr. C.S. Hong is the corresponding author.

I. Stojmenovic et al. (Eds.): ISPA 2007, LNCS 4742, pp.407–418,2007.

using one-way hash chain and shared secret keys. The rest of the paper is organized as follows: Section 2 states the related works, section 3 presents our assumptions and preliminaries, Section 4 describes our protocol in detail, performance evaluation and analysis are presented in section 5, and section 6 concludes the paper.

2 Related Works

[5] proposed an energy-efficient security protocol for wireless sensor network by using symmetric key cryptography and NOVSF code-hopping technique. The basic idea is to implement two algorithms in the sensor nodes and in the base station which the sensor nodes and the base station would follow at the time of transmitting data within the network. To ensure better security they introduced NOVSF technique which basically scrambles the data blocks using a multiplexer in the system while transmitting data from the sensor nodes. [5] is claimed to be secure and energy efficient considering the fact that, it increases the level of security during data transmission using the NOVSF technique without utilizing any additional power. However, this scrambling technique increases the complexity of tasks for the base station. To address the issue of energy efficient data aggregation with secure data transmission, ESPDA protocol [6] is proposed. Ye et al. [7] proposed a statistical en-route filtering (SEF) scheme to detect and drop false reports during the forwarding process. In their scheme, a report is forwarded only if it contains the message authentication codes (MACs) generated by multiple nodes, by using keys from different partitions in a global key pool. Zhu et at. [8] proposed the interleaved hop-by-hop authentication scheme that detects false reports through interleaved authentication. Their scheme guarantees that the base station can detect a false report when no more than t nodes are compromised, where t is a security threshold. Motivated by [8], Lee and Cho [9] proposed an enhanced interleaved authentication scheme called the key inheritance-based filtering. In their scheme, the keys of each node used in the message authentication consist of its own key and the keys inherited from its upstream nodes. Every authenticated report contains the combination of the message authentication codes generated by using the keys of the consecutive nodes in a path from the base station to a terminal node. Other than these, [10], [11], [12], [22] focused only on energy efficiency and [3], [4], [13] dealt with the security measures for routing in WSN.

3 Network Assumptions and Preliminaries

We consider a WSN with dense deployment of sensors, where initially all nodes and the BS have same transmission ranges and all of their clocks are synchronized. The BS has unlimited resources. The sensors have the resources like the MICA2 motes [14]. Once they are deployed, they remain relatively static in their respective positions. Each node transmits within its transmission range isotropically (in all directions) so that each message sent is a local broadcast. The link between any pair of nodes in the network is bidirectional, that is, if a node n_i gets a node n_j within its transmission range (i.e. one hop), n_j also gets n_i as its one-hop neighbor.

The BS cannot be compromised in any way and no node could be compromised by any adversary while creating the tree structure in the network (i.e., section 4.1). Each sensor has a shared secret key with the BS which is pre-loaded into its memory.

An accurate model for energy consumption per bit at physical layer is given by $E = E_{elec}^{trans} + \beta d^{\alpha} + E_{elec}^{recv}$, where, E_{elec}^{trans} is the distance-independent amount of energy consumed by the transmitter electronics and digital processing, E_{elec}^{recv} is the energy utilized by receiver electronics, while βd^{α} accounts for the radiated power necessary to transmit over a distance d between source and destination.

Like [15], [16] we assume that $E_{elec}^{trans} = E_{elec}^{recv} = E_{elec}$. So, overall energy consumption between source and destination within 1-hop is calculated by $E = 2.E_{elec} + \beta d^{\alpha}$. Broadly speaking, hierarchical routing protocols use control packets for topology construction phase. For a particular node i, control packet transmission cost is,

$$C_i^{ctrl}(r) = \left[L_{ctrl} \times \beta r^{\alpha} + (nbr_i(r)+1) \times L_{ctrl} \times E_{elec}\right]\frac{1}{T}$$

where, α : the path loss exponent ($2 < \alpha < 5$), β: a constant [joule/bit.m^2], r : transmission range, L_{ctrl} : length of control packet (bits), nbr_i : number of neighbors of i for range r, L_{elec} : energy needed by the transceiver circuitry to transmit/receive a packet and T : the time period between two consecutive restructuring of network.

For a particular path p, data communication cost from source i to the BS is,

$$C_i^{data}(p) = \left[\sum_{i=1,j=2}^{N}(nfrd_p(d_i)+1) \times L_{data} \times \beta d_{i,j}^{\alpha} + (nbr_p(d_i)+1) \times L_{data}\right] \times E_{elec}$$

Here, N : total number of nodes in the network, $i, j \in 0,1,2,....,N$: node index, p: the path associated for data transmission from i to sink, d_i : transmission range set by i, $d_{i,j}$: distance between the i and j, $nfrd_p(d_i)$: number of forwarding nodes for a path p and range d, $nbr_p(d_i)$: the number of neighboring nodes for a path p and range d, L_{data} : length of data packets (bits), and finally, α and β are same as previous equation. Total communication cost for sending a data packet from source i is:

$$C_i^{total}(p) = \sum_{i=1}^{N}\left[C_i^{ctrl}(r)\right] + C_i^{data}(p)$$

The observations from the above equation are, (a) Wasteful (due to idle listening, overhearing etc.) energy consumption (WEC) increases as the number of redundant forwarder increases, (b) WEC increases as the number of idle nodes increases, (c) Energy consumption increases exponentially as the distance increases, and (d) Frequency of control packet transmission is proportional to the energy consumption. To reduce energy consumption following things could be done, (a) Reducing the number of forwarding nodes (keeping the level of connectivity and reliability of network intact), (b) Putting certain portion of the nodes in sleep mode, (c) Employing adaptive transmission range according to the distance from the forwarder to save energy, and, (d) Fixing network restructuring frequency to ensure balanced energy consumption.

We consider three states of the nodes in our protocol during its operation: (a) *Non-forwarding* - the nodes keep their radio transceivers 'Off' but the sensing circuitry 'On', (b) *Forwarding* - both the transceiver and sensing circuits remain 'On' in this state, (c) *Active* – during the tree construction and OHC initialization phase (section 4.1), all nodes remain in the active state. In active state, both the sensing and radio circuitries of the sensors remain 'On'. Basically, there is no major difference between these two states. We use two terms to differentiate two phases in our protocol.

Determining Active State Time. Let, v be a node and $N_1(v)$ be the number of one-hop neighbors of v for a particular transmission range r (r is same for all nodes). Let, T_{rtt} be the round trip time for data propagation between the longest distant pair within one hop neighbors. Then, the active state time for v is given by the equation, $T_{active} = T_{rtt} \times N_1(v)$. In our protocol, within the time T_{active}, a node could be able to determine whether it should participate in the tree as a forwarding node or not.

To ensure security for data transmissions from sensors to BS, we use pre-stored shared secret keys and one-way hash chain. A one-way hash chain [17] is a sequence of numbers generated by one-way function F that has the property that for a given x, it is easy to compute y = F(x). However, given F and y, it is computationally infeasible to determine x, such that x = F^{-1}(y). An one-way hash chain (OHC) is a sequence of numbers K_n, K_{n-1}, ..., K_0, such that, $\forall i : 0 \leq i < n$, $K_i = F(K_{i+1})$. To generate an OHC, first a random number K_r is selected as the seed, and then F is applied successively on K_r to generate other numbers in the sequence.

4 Our Proposed Protocol

4.1 Tree Construction and OHC Initialization Phase

We create a sink rooted tree (SRT) in the network. During the tree construction, all nodes keep their radio transceivers 'On' to verify whether it should remain active as a forwarder or not. A timer parameter is defined to ensure each node's active participation in this process for a specific period of time. Each node is prioritized for transmission according to its residual energy and distance from the sink.

According to our assumption, all the sensors and the BS have pre-loaded shared secret keys which could be used to provide confidentiality of the reports. However, to provide authenticity of the transmitted data, all the intermediate nodes between any source node and the base station must be initialized with the basic one-way hash chain number. Let us suppose the initial OHC number is $I_{OHC} = HS_0$.

To initiate the network structuring and OHC number initialization phase, the base station B generates a control packet containing HS_0, a MAC (Message Authentication Code) for the control packet using the key K_i, where K_i is the number in the key chain number corresponding to time slot t_i and some other parameters. The format of the control packet is: *bcm*: $B|sid|ren|dist|fid|HS_0|MAC_{K_i}(B|sid|ren|dist|fid|HS_0)$, where, *sid* indicates the sender's id, *ren* is the remaining energy of the sender, *dist* is the calculated cumulative distance to reach the BS using forwarder(s), and *fid* is the id of the upstream node (i.e. immediate parent or immediate forwarding node) selected by the current node for forwarding data towards the sink. The sink node initiates *bcm* with sender id *B*, and the values of *sid*, *ren*, *dist* and *fid* as -1, as according to our assumption, the base station has unlimited energy compared to the energies of the sensors in the network, and in this case, no forwarding node is needed to reach itself.

When the BS transmits *bcm*, at first its one-hop neighbors get the message. Receiving the message, each node in the one-hop neighborhood of the BS first calculates its distance from the base station based on the received signal strength, stores the value of HS_0 and sets *B* as its forwarder node (the ultimate destination is the BS). Now, each of these nodes transmits the message again within its own one-hop neighborhood (i.e., local broadcast). In this case, the *sid* is set to its own id, *ren* is its own residual energy and the MAC part is kept the same as the message, *bcm*.

To ensure prioritization of the transmission of control messages, each node waits for a threshold time before each further transmission. Waiting time of a node before further transmission is defined by the following equation, $T_{wait} = \{D_s/E_r\} \times R$, where, D_s is the cumulative distance between the sink and the node, E_r is the residual energy of the node, and R is a constant that is needed to normalize the value of T_{wait} . As with the course of time, the sensors lose their energy levels and the value of the ratio of distance and residual energy increases; we need to normalize this value. In our case, R is the ratio of node's initial energy and transmission range.

Each node receiving the control messages from one or more upstream neighboring nodes, first calculates the distance of each sender based on the received signal strength, then calculates the cumulative distances up to the BS via different possible forwarders, stores the id and residual energy information of each sender and stores HS_0 from the message sent by the first sender. To choose its forwarder node, it compares the values of the distance and energy ratios (D_s/E_r) of the neighboring upstream nodes and chooses the node with the least value of the ratio as its forwarder node.

It then senses the channel and if the channel is idle, it waits for T_{wait} time and then re-transmits the message containing its own status information and with its chosen forwarder id as its *fid*. As the selected upstream node could also get the message (because of bidirectional link), it sets itself as a forwarding node for this transmitting node. This process continues and eventually a tree-structure is created in the network where, each node has a forwarder node on the way to reach to the base station and possibly one or more downstream nodes that can send data to it destined to the base station. Here, the value of T_{wait} depends mainly on the values of E_r and D_s.

To authenticate HS_0, *B* releases the key K_i in time slot t_{i+d}. On receiving this key, a node can verify the integrity and source authentication of HS_0. Thus, along each path the initial OHC number is initialized. It is to be noted that, *bcm* won't bring any attack against the network even if the nodes on the other side of the network don't receive K_i at t_{i+d}. Since, the messages that are MACed by K_i are supposed to be sent out at time slot t, an adversary cannot launch any attacks with K_i when it gets K_i at t_{i+d}. Within the time T_{active}, a node which does not get any message from any of its neighbors that, it should be a forwarding node, sets itself as a non-forwarding node.

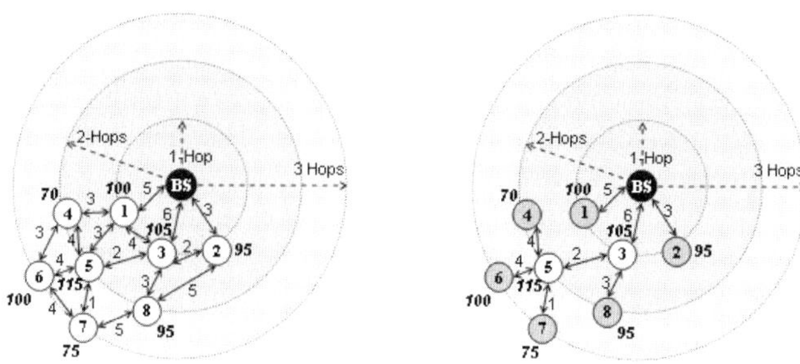

Fig. 1. (left) Before execution of the first phase (right) After execution of the first phase. The gray nodes are in non-forwarding status while the other two nodes are in forwarding status. In these figures, we have shown the N-hop (N = 1, 2, 3 ...) neighbors of the BS on the circumference of the same circle regardless of their actual calculated distances from the BS.

Let us illustrate the first phase of our protocol with an example. Figure 1 shows a portion of a network where there are 8 nodes. The black filled circle is the base station and the white circles are the sensors. The bold italic numbers beside each node indicate the residual energies of the nodes and the number in between any pair of nodes indicates the distance between those two nodes. For simplicity here we assume that *R* is 1. The base station initiates the first phase. The 1-hop neighbors of the base station in Figure 1, nodes 1, 2 and 3 get the message first. All of these nodes calculate their T_{wait} and T_{active} values. Here, the T_{wait} values for the nodes 1, 2, and 3 are 0.05, 0.057 and 0.03 respectively. In this dense deployment scenario, let us suppose that the node 2 and 3 are within the transmission ranges of each other, but as node 2 has lower T_{wait} value, it transmits the message before node 3 does. Here, when node 2 transmits the message, node 3 and 8 get the message (as its one hop neighbors), store the id, E_r and D_s of 2 for future computations. In case of node 1 and node 3, node 1 transmits before node 3 can do the transmission. The local broadcast of node 1 is heard by node 3, 4 and 5. Eventually, these nodes store the required information from this message. It should be noted here that, as node 1, 2 and 3 get the control message directly from the base station, they set the base station as their *fids*.

After node 1 and node 2 have done the transmissions, let us take a sample case. Say, node 3 and 5 are neighbors of each other. Now, node 3 has T_{wait} value 0.057 and node 5 has T_{wait} value 0.069. So, node 3 gets the chance of further transmission before node 5. Now node 8 is a neighbor of node 3. So, node 3's transmission is heard by node 5 and 8. As a 1-hop neighbor of the base station, node 3 does not need to select a forwarder, rather base station is its forwarder. When node 4's turn comes, it chooses node 5 as a forwarder node for itself. Node 5 knows this as it is a 1-hop neighbor of node 4. This process continues, and the whole network is structured as a sink rooted tree where there are several paths from the base station to the leaf nodes. Along the path, the initial OHC number is also initialized. Figure 1(right) shows the resultant structure of the network after the first phase is executed.

4.2 Network Operation and Secure Data Transmission Phase

After the tree is constructed within the network, all nodes are either in forwarding or non-forwarding states. All nodes try to sense any change of parameters within their vicinities and upon detecting any event, the non-forwarding nodes turn their radios on and transmit data towards the base station via their selected forwarding nodes.

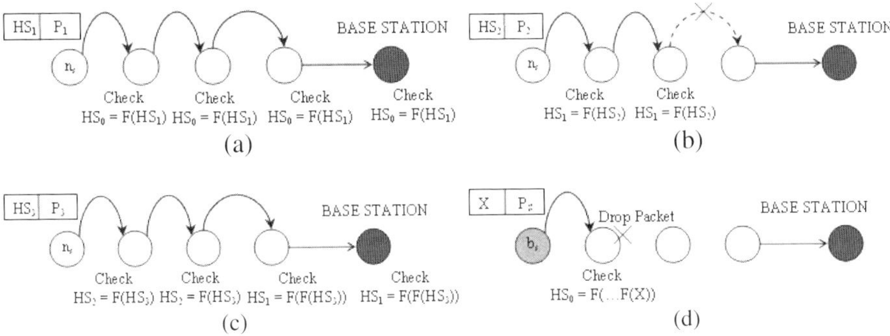

Fig. 2. (a) Authenticated packet delivery to the BS (b) Packet could not reach the BS (c) But it cannot affect the OHC verification technique (d) A bogus packet is dropped

To send the data securely to BS, each source node n_s maintains a unique one-way hash chain, HS: $<HS_n, HS_{n-1}, \ldots, HS_1, HS_0>$. When a source n_s sends a report to the sink using the path created in the sink-rooted tree (for example, $n_s \rightarrow \ldots \rightarrow n_{m-1} \rightarrow n_m \rightarrow B$), it encrypts the packet with its shared secret key with the BS, includes its own id and an OHC sequence number from HS in the packet. It attaches HS_1 for the first packet, HS_2 for the second packet, and so on. To validate an OHC number, each intermediate node $n_1,\ldots,n_m$ maintains a verifier I_{n_s} for each n_s. Initially, I_{n_s} for a particular source is set to HS_0. When n_s sends the *i*th packet, it includes HS_i with the packet.

When any intermediate node n_k receives this packet, it verifies, whether $I_{n_s} = F(HS_i)$ or not. If so, n_k validates the packet, it forwards it to the next intermediate node, and sets I_{n_s} to HS_i. In general, n_k can choose to apply the verification test iteratively up to a fixed number *w* times, checking at each step whether, $I_{n_s} = F(F\ldots(F(HS_i)))$. If the packet is not validated after the verification process has been performed *w* times, n_k simply drops the packet. By performing the verification process *w* times, up to a sequence of *w* packet losses can be tolerated, where the value of *w* depends on the average packet loss rate of the network. Here an intermediate node needs not to decrypt the packet rather it can check the authenticity of the packet before forwarding to its immediate forwarder. Figure 2 illustrates the procedure. In Figure 2(d) an adversary tries to send a bogus packet with a false HS number and it is detected in the next upstream node. Eventually such bogus packet fails to pass the authentication check and is dropped in the very next hop. This feature saves energy as the bogus packets cannot travel through the network for more than one hop.

After the tree construction, at the time of data transmission, each node could dynamically set its transmission range according to the distance of the immediate forwarder. If the distance of the forwarding node is less than the initially used transmission range for tree construction, the node decreases the range by decreasing the transmission energy. This feature gives the flexibility in our protocol to dynamically set the transmission ranges and thus helps for conserving network-wide energy. The first phase is executed every T time, where T is an application dependent parameter, which depends on the event generation rate as well as on the load of the network.

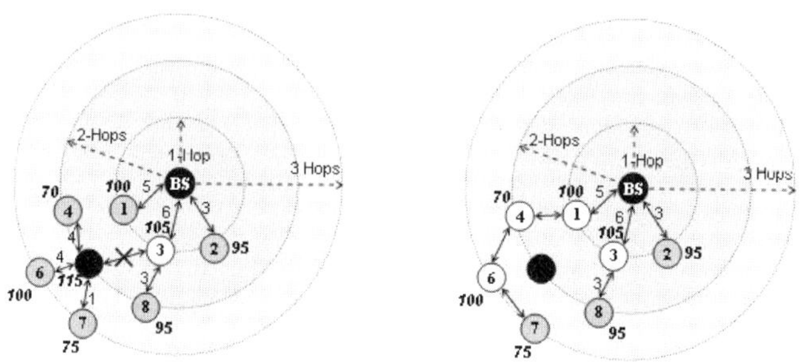

Fig. 3. (left) Node 5 failed (right) Repairing a broken path

4.3 Optional Key Refreshment

To provide data freshness and to increase the level of security, our scheme has an optional key refreshment mechanism. In this case, the base station periodically broadcasts a new session key to the sensors in the network. The format for this message is: $B|K_s|$ $MAC_{K_j}(B|K_s)$), where, K_j is the number in the key chain number corresponding to time slot t_j. To authenticate K_s, like the OHC initialization phase, B releases the key K_j in time slot t_{j+d}. On receiving this key, the nodes can verify the integrity and source authentication of K_s. Then each node gets the new key by performing an X-OR (exclusive OR) operation with its old shared key. This method could also be utilized for refreshing the keys of a specific number of nodes. In that case, the base station could simply send the K_s to the specific node by encrypting it with its previous shared secret key. Upon receiving the new key, the node can perform the X-OR operation and could use the newly derived key for subsequent data transmissions. Changing encryption keys time-to-time has an advantage as it guarantees data freshness in the network. Moreover, it helps to maintain confidentiality of the transmitted data by preventing the use of the same secret key at all the times.

4.4 Repairing a Broken Path and OHC Re-Initialization

If in any case, any node between the source node and the BS fails, it could make one or more paths useless. Eventually, in such a case all the downstream nodes along that particular path get disconnected from the base station. To repair such a broken path, we use the stored upstream knowledge of the sensors. We know that, in the first phase each downstream node stores the ids of the one-hop upstream senders of the control message. So, this knowledge could be used for repairing the path quickly. Figure 3 shows a failed node (black) and the new path after broken path recovery.

As we are considering a highly dense deployment scenario, we believe that, in most of the cases, a node might initially get two or more upstream senders who would try to be its forwarder. This procedure works fine as long as no more than w packets are lost on the way, from any source node (after a path is broken due to a node failure). If within the time of repairing the path, more than w packets are lost from a particular source, the OHC chain along that path breaks down. In fact, this is the worst case where all the downstream nodes along the path become invalid to the base station and their sent data are discarded on the way to reach the base station. To overcome this problem, the entire OHC initialization phase could be made periodic (after certain interval). Determining the best possible time interval for re-initialization of the first phase is kept as our future work.

5 Analysis and Performance Evaluation

To understand the performance of our proposed protocol, we simulated the network using NS-2 [18] with 50 to 300 nodes uniformly distributed in a 100m×100m square sensor field. The transmission range of each sensor node was set to 25 meters. Each node was provided with 2 Joule of initial energy. Transmitter and receiver electronics were set to dissipate 50nJ/bit.m^2. The data packet length was set to 2 KB. Sink or base station was located at (150, 150) co-ordinates. We varied the number of sources from 1 to 7 and data generation interval was randomly chosen. Initially Tree construction time was set to 10 seconds. As our protocol creates a hierarchical structure in the network, we compared our protocol with two other hierarchical energy-aware routing protocols LEACH [10] and EAD [11].

Figure 4(left) shows the percentage of forwarding nodes among the total number of nodes in LEACH, EAD and our protocol. Figure 4(right) shows the energy dissipation given a number of source nodes. Less energy dissipation eventually helps for increasing the lifetime of the network. The relative gain of our proposed scheme compared to LEACH and EAD increases with the increase of number of sources. Figure 5(left) presents the number of alive nodes versus simulation time with 100 nodes. Our proposed scheme generates less number of forwarders compared to EAD. As a result, the energy dissipation is much less than that of EAD as there are less nodes participating actively in the network operation phase. Our experimental results show that, our algorithm achieves better lifetime compared to LEACH and EAD.

The method of generating and storing a long OHC in a sensor node is a little difficult. But, recently, some efficient OHC generation algorithms for resource-constrained platforms have been proposed [19], [20], [21]. Among these algorithms, the fractal graph traversal algorithm [19] could perform well on the traditional sensor nodes. This algorithm stores only some of the intermediate numbers, called pebbles, of an OHC, and uses them to compute other numbers. If the size of an OHC is n (there are total n numbers in this OHC), the algorithm performs approximately $(1/2)\log_2 n$ one-way function operations to compute the next OHC number, and requires a little more than $\log_2 n$ units of memory to save pebbles.

The length of an OHC that is needed for a source node is also an important factor. The typical length is between 2^{11} to 2^{22}. If the length of an OHC is 2^{22} and a node uses one OHC number per second, it will take more than a month to exhaust all numbers from this chain. Figure 5(right) shows the storage requirements for storing pebbles for different lengths of an OHC. This includes a skipjack based one-way function and OHC generation based on [19]. We see that a node needs about 930 bytes to maintain an OHC of length 2^{22}. This includes 256 bytes lookup table for skipjack, which can be shared with other applications. Other than this, each node has to store only a few ids and neighbor information of its one-hop neighbors. Overall, the memory requirement for our scheme could be well afforded with today's sensor nodes.

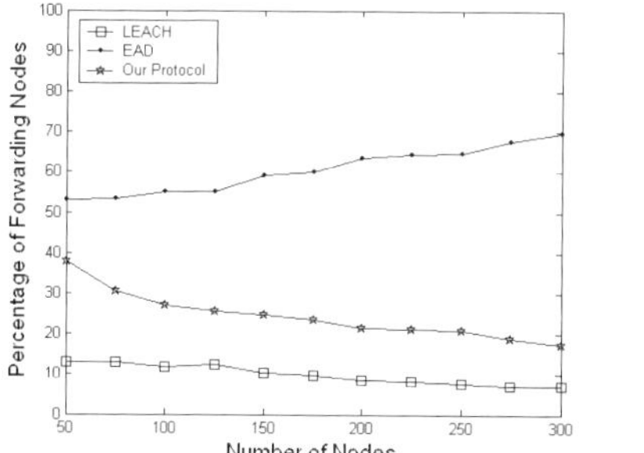

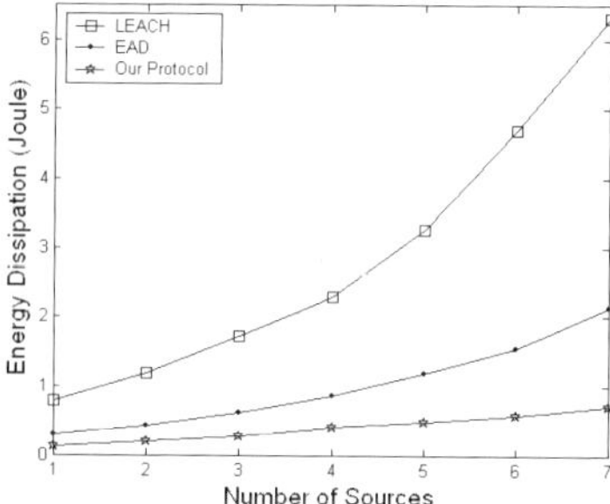

Fig. 4. (left) Percentage of forwarding nodes in total number of nodes in the network (right) Energy dissipation for different number of sources in LEACH, EAD and our protocol

We analyze the security of our scheme with respect to two design goals; the ability of BS to detect a false report, and en-route detection and filtering of false reports.

Base Station Detection. In our scheme whenever the BS receives a report from any sensor, it first checks the id of the sensor, checks the authenticity of the report by verifying the one-way hash chain number for that particular source, looks for the corresponding shared secret key and decrypts the packet. The base station could not be compromised in any way. So, it is in fact the final entity that could confirm the authenticity, confidentiality and integrity of the transmitted reports. Our security scheme is designed in a way that, any bogus report cannot reach the base station, rather would be detected and dropped by the intermediate nodes. However, if somehow a bogus packet is sent directly to the base station, it would certainly be discarded by it, for the failure of authentication check. If in any application, the optional key refreshment mechanism is employed, once the time slot of releasing the new session key is over, the base station first tries to decrypt the incoming packets from any particular source with the X-ORed new key for that node. In case, if it produces garbage result, the base station tries with the previous shared secret key with that node (the previous key could easily be obtained again by X-ORing the most recent session key with the newly computed key for that node). This case might happen when somehow some node cannot get the new session key released by the base station.

Detection by the Intermediate Nodes. (a) *Outsider Attack.* In this case, as shown in figure 2(d) that, if an outsider node generates a packet with fake OHC number, the authentication must be failed in the very next node in the path and as a result this packet would never be forwarded even to the node which is only two hops away from it. Simple verification of the OHC number prohibits the forwarding of such bogus packets. (b) *Insider Attack.* If a legitimate node along any path is compromised, the attacker could grab the OHC sequence and the shared secret key with the base station. However, it should be noticed that, to use the OHC numbers successfully, the adversary should also know the last OHC number used by that particular node to send packet to the base station. If it gets the last used OHC number, then it could use this for sending false packets successfully. Otherwise, any arbitrary use of the OHC number from that source might not be forwarded by the next intermediate node because of authentication failure. Now, in case if a node is fully compromised, that is if the adversary obtains all the required information, it actually gets the status of a legitimate node in the network. This fully compromised node could be used to generate false reports with valid authentication numbers. To prevent such type of malicious adversary, there are several factors come into play to detect the abnormal behavior of the node. In our scheme, the BS considers a report legitimate if it is reported by at least δ number of source nodes in the network, where δ is an application dependent parameter. So, the different or modified reports from a single source cannot convince the base station about any event.

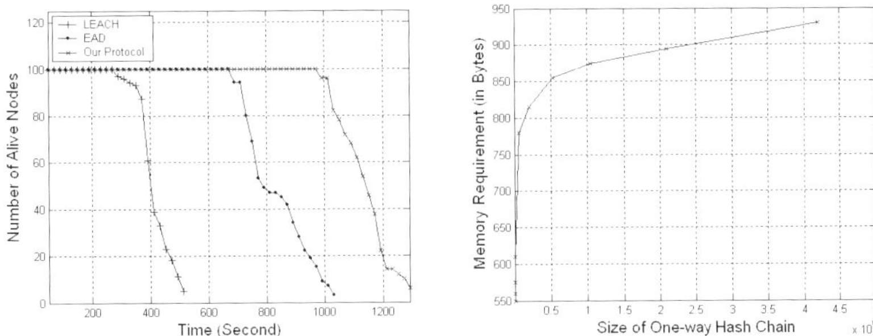

Fig. 5. (left) No. of alive nodes vs time (right) Memory requirement for OHC generation

The worst case scenario occurs if more than δ nodes in a particular region in the network are somehow compromised. This sort of collaborative and large scale attack is handled by the periodic restructuring of the whole network.

6 Conclusions

In our protocol, we mainly structured the network in a way that it could ensure the delivery of authenticated and confidential data to the BS from any source node, which is also aware of the limited energy budget of the network. According to our simulation results and analysis, our protocol demonstrates a good performance regarding energy-efficiency and security in data transmission. In future, we would like perform a detailed analysis to find out an optimal value of the interval of restructuring the network.

Acknowledgments

We would like to give special thanks to Md. Mamun-Or-Rashid for his generous help for this work.

References

1. Akyildiz, I.F., Su, W., Sankarasubramaniam, Y., Cayirci, E.: Wireless Sensor Net-works: A Survey. Computer Networks 38, 393–422 (2002)
2. Dai, S., Jing, X., Li, L.: Research and analysis on routing protocols for wireless sensor networks. In: Proc. of Int. Conf. on Comm. Circuits and Systems, vol. 1, pp. 407–411 (2005)

3. Karlof, C., Wagner, D.: Secure routing in wireless sensor networks: Attacks and countermeasures. Elsevier's Ad Hoc Network Journal, 293–315 (September 2003)
4. Pathan, A.-S.K., Lee, H.-W., Hong, C.S.: Security in Wireless Sensor Networks: Issues and Challenges. In: Proc. of the 8th IEEE ICACT 2006, Korea, vol. II, pp. 1043–1048 (2006)
5. Çam, H., Özdemir, S., Muthuavinashiappan, D., Nair, P.: Energy Efficient Security Protocol for Wireless Sensor Networks. Proc. of IEEE VTC 5, 2981–2984 (2003)
6. Çam, H., Özdemir, S., Nair, P., Muthuavinashiappan, D., Sanli, H.O.: Energy-efficient secure pattern based data aggregation for wireless sensor networks. Computer Communications 29(4), 446–455 (2006)
7. Ye, F., Luo, H., Lu, S., Zhang, L.: Statistical En-Route Filtering of Injected False Data in Sensor Networks. IEEE Jrnl. on Selected Areas in Communications 23(4), 839–850 (2005)
8. Zhu, S., Setia, S., Jajodia, S., Ning, P.: An Interleaved Hop-by-Hop Authentication Scheme for Filtering of Injected False Data in Sensor Networks. In: Proceedings of S&P, pp. 259–271 (2004)
9. Lee, H.Y., Cho, T.H.: Key Inheritance-Based False Data Filtering Scheme in Wireless Sensor Networks. In: Madria, S.K., Claypool, K.T., Kannan, R., Uppuluri, P., Gore, M.M. (eds.) ICDCIT 2006. LNCS, vol. 4317, pp. 116–127. Springer, Heidelberg (2006)
10. Heinzelman, W.R., Chandrakasan, A., Balakrishnan, H.: Energy-Efficient Communication Protocol for Wireless Microsensor Networks. In: Proc. of HICSS, pp. 3005–3014 (2000)
11. Azzedine, B., Xiuzhen, C., Joseph, L.: Energy-aware data-centric routing in microsensor networks. In: Proceedings of the 8th MSWiM 03, San Diego, pp. 42–49 (2003)
12. Hyunh, T.T., Hong, C.S.: An Energy*Delay Efficient Multi-Hop Routing Scheme for Wireless Sensor Networks. IEICE Trans. on Info. & Sys. E89-D(5), 1654–1661 (2006)
13. Yin, C., Huang, S., Su, P., Gao, C.: Secure routing for large-scale wireless sensor networks. In: Proceedings of IEEE ICCT 2003, 9-11 April 2003, vol. 2, pp. 1282–1286. IEEE Computer Society Press, Los Alamitos (2003)
14. Xbow Sensor Networks: Available at: http://www.xbow.com/
15. Hass, Z.J.: Design methodologies for adaptive and multimedia networks. IEEE Communications Magazine 39(11), 106–107 (2001)
16. Heinzelman, W.B., Chandrakasan, A.P., Balakrishnan, H.: An application-specific protocol architecture for wireless microsensor networks. IEEE Transactions in Wireless Communications 1(4), 660–670 (2002)
17. Lamport, L.: Constructing digital signatures from one-way function. Technical report SRI-CSL-98, SRI International (October 1979)
18. The Network Simulator - ns-2: http://www.isi.edu/nsnam/ns/
19. Coppersmith, D., Jakobsson, M.: Almost Optimal Hash Sequence Traversal. In: 6th International Financial Cryptography 2002, Bermuda (March2002)
20. Jakobsson, M.: Fractal hash sequence representation and traversal. In: 2002 IEEE International Symposium on Information Theory, Switzerland. IEEE Computer Society Press, Los Alamitos (2002)
21. Sella, Y.: On the computation-storage trade-offs of hash chain traversal. In: The 7th International Financial Cryptography Conference, Guadeloupe (January 2003)
22. Mamun-Or-Rashid, Md., Alam, M.M., Hong, C.S.: Energy Efficient Routing for Highly Dense Sensor Networks Based on Residual Energy and Distance. In: Proc. of IEEE ICNEWS, Dhaka, Bangladesh, pp. 52–56 (2006)

Designing Scalable Self-healing Key Distribution Schemes with Revocation Capability

Ratna Dutta[1] and Sourav Mukhopadhyay[2]

[1] Computing Division
Systems and Security Department
Institute for Infocomm Research
21, Heng Mui Keng Terrace, Singapore 119613
dratna@i2r.a-star.edu.sg

[2] School of Computing
National University of Singapore
3 Science Drive 2, Singapore 117543
sourav@comp.nus.edu.sg

Abstract. Self-healing key distribution is a potential candidate to establish session keys for secure communication to large and dynamic groups in highly mobile, volatile and hostile wireless network, where frequent membership changes may be necessary and ability to revoke users during certain exchanges is desirable. The main property of self-healing key distribution scheme is that even if during a certain session some broadcast messages are lost due to network faults, the users are capable of recovering lost session keys on their own, without requesting additional transmission from the group manager. In this paper, we propose a scalable self-healing key distribution with t revocation capability. Our proposed scheme has improvement in storage overhead over the previous approaches with the same communication cost required by the most optimal previous scheme. The scheme is supported by a proper security analysis in an appropriate security model. We prove that it is unconditionally secure and achieve both forward secrecy and backward secrecy. Our proposed self-healing key distribution is not restricted to m sessions in *Setup* phase. Besides, we develop a construction for self-healing key distribution that enables key recovery from a single broadcast message.

Keywords: session key distribution, rekeying, self-healing, revocation.

1 Introduction

The ever growing Internet features many new applications requiring multicast services. A non-exhaustive list of such applications include military operations, rescue missions, scientific explorations, pay-TV applications, distance education, collaborative work, teleconferencing, distributed interactive games, secret distribution of copyright-protected materials, audio and video streaming *etc.* The critical issue of multicast technology deals with the following problem of broadcast

I. Stojmenovic et al. (Eds.): ISPA 2007, LNCS 4742, pp. 419–430, 2007.

encryption: how the content provider can securely communicate with a dynamically changing group of users over the insecure broadcast channel, so that the content can be viewed only by the legitimate users, while minimizing the key management overhead.

Secure group communication model is at the heart of securing multicast communication. In this model, authorized members of the group share a symmetric group key that is used to encrypt/decrypt the content. The shared group key, called the *session key* is refreshed on each membership change and securely distributed to the existing members of the group. This is referred to as group rekeying. For large groups with dynamic membership changes, the cost of rekeying the group can be quite substantial. Scalable rekeying is therefore an important and challenging problem to support secure group communication for dynamic wireless network, where typical systems are large: tens of millions of users.

Key distribution and key management are on the other side of the coin. Security of multicast communication for large dynamic wireless networks, especially mobile wireless ad hoc networks hinges on efficient key distribution and key management mechanisms. Sensor nodes in mobile wireless networks are typically powered by batteries and may move in and out of range frequently. As a result, the traditional approaches for key distribution and group re-keying, used for reliable network, are not suitable for large and dynamic wireless networks.

Self-healing Key Distribution: The work presented in this paper focuses on key distribution schemes with *self-healing* property and revocation capability for large and dynamic groups over an unreliable and lossy wireless ad hoc network in a manner that is resilient to collusion attacks and packet lost. The main property of self-healing ensures that the qualified users can recover the lost session keys on their own from the broadcast packets and some private information, without any additional communication with the group manager, thus decreasing the load on the group manager. The only requirement for a user to recover the lost session keys, is its membership in the group both before and after the sessions in which the broadcast packets containing the keys are sent. Self-healing approach of key distribution is stateless in the sense that a user who has been off-line for some period is able to recover the lost session keys immediately after coming back on-line. The group membership is dynamic. The group manager can periodically add/revoke members to/from the group to start multiple sessions in a manner that is collusion resistant. The scheme has t-revocation capability if the key distribution mechanism cannot be broken by any coalition of up to t users.

The self-healing key distribution with revocation reduces network traffic and work load on the group manager. There are useful military-oriented applications of self-healing key distribution schemes with revocation capability, where the session keys need to be used for a short time-period or need to be updated frequently. For instance, consider the scenario where sensor nodes are user mobile devices powered by batteries, communicate over an unreliable wireless network. Once a battery is off, or a node is caught by the enemy, it must be removed from the group. It can rejoin the group once the power in on again or the node has been recovered. Such settings can benefit from self-healing key distribution schemes. Another application of self-healing key distribution with revocation is the broadcast communication over low-cost pay TV channel: the live-event transmissions (*e.g.* concerts, formal ceremonies *etc.*) can be viewed by the users who have paid for the service. There are several other applications that can take advantage from self-healing key distribution scheme with revocation capability, where frequent session key changes may be necessary and the ability to revoke users during certain exchanges is desirable.

Our Contributions: In this paper, we focus on designing unconditionally secure and efficient group key distribution scheme with self-healing property and revocation capability for large and dynamic groups over unreliable wireless networks. We propose two new constructions for key distribution with revocation capability adopting two different self-healing approaches. The main attraction of our schemes is that they have significant improvements in terms of both storage and communication overhead compared to the previous works [1], [5], [8]. Both our proposed schemes require the storage overhead of personal key for each user $O((t+1)\log q)$ and communication bandwidth $O((tj+j-t-1)\log q)$, where j is the current session number, t is the maximum number of compromised group members that may collude and q is a large prime number. Although, our schemes have the same communication complexity as the most recent schemes presented in [4], the storage overhead in our schemes is minimal.

The storage overhead and their communication complexity for our schemes depend on the number t of compromised group members that may collude, not on the size of the group. This reduces power consumption and increases lifetime of wireless devices. Thus our key distribution schemes are scalable to very large groups in highly mobile, volatile and hostile wireless network. Besides, our second scheme enables a user to recover all lost session keys (for sessions in which it was a group member) by using only the current broadcast message. On a more positive note, our schemes overcome the session limitation in previous works [1], [4], [5], [8], where self-healing key distribution is restricted to m sessions in *Setup* phase. We obtain all these results without sacrificing the unconditional security of key distribution. Our security analysis is in an appropriate security model and we have also shown that our schemes achieve both forward secrecy and backward secrecy.

2 Applications and Previous Work

Applications: The self-healing key distribution with revocation reduces network traffic and work load on the group manager. The spectrum of applicability of self-healing key distribution is quite large. Self-healing key distribution is a potential candidate to establish session keys for secure communication to large and dynamic groups in highly mobile, volatile and hostile wireless network, where frequent membership changes may be necessary and ability to revoke users during certain exchanges is desirable. In such situations the session keys need to be used for a short time-period or need to be updated frequently. This apealing approach of key distribution is quite suitable where frequent session key changes may be necessary and the ability to revoke users during certain exchanges is desirable. There are useful military-oriented applications of self-healing key distribution schemes with revocation capability, where the session keys need to be used for a short time-period or need to be updated frequently. For instance, consider the scenario where sensor nodes are user mobile devices powered by batteries, communicate over an unreliable wireless network. Once a battery is off, or a node is caught by the enemy, it must be removed from the group. It can rejoin the group once the power in on again or the node has been recovered. Such settings can benefit from self-healing key distribution schemes. Another application of self-healing key distribution with revocation is the broadcast communication over low-cost pay TV channel: the live-event transmissions (*e.g.* concerts, formal ceremonies *etc.*) can be viewed by the users who have paid for the service. Mobile wireless ad hoc networks have wide applications in military operations, rescue missions and scientific explorations, where there are usually no network infrastructure support and the adversary may intercept, modify, and/or partially interrupt the communication. In such applications, security becomes a critical concern. The traditional approaches for key distribution and group re-keying used for reliable network, are not suitable for large and dynamic wireless networks because of the lossy nature of wireless medium. Therefore, self-healing is a good property for key distribution in wireless mobile and ad hoc networks, where the nodes/devices are powered by batteries and have the unique feature of moving in and out of range frequently. Hence expensive computations like the ones required by public key cryptography are not suitable for such networks. There are several other applications that can take advantage from self-healing key distribution scheme with revocation capability.

Previous works: Self-healing key distribution with revocation was first introduced by Staddon *et al.* in [8]. They provide formal definitions and security notions that were later generalized by Liu *et al.* [5] and Blundo *et al.* [1]. The constructions given in [8] suffers from high storage and communication overhead. Liu *et al.* [5] introduced a novel personal key distribution scheme and combining it with the self-healing technique in [8], they proposed a new construction that improves the storage and communication overhead greatly. Blundo *et al.* [1] showed an attack to the first construction in [8] and developed a new self-healing technique different from [8] under a slightly modified framework. More recently, Hong *et al.* [4] proposed self-healing key distribution constructions having less storage and communication complexity.

3 Preliminaries

In this section, we briefly review the security model for self-healing key distribution. For more details, we refer [5]. Notations used throughout this paper are summarized below:

$\mathcal{U}$: the set of all users in the networks
U_i : the i-th user

GM : the group manager
n : the total number of users in the network
m : the total number of sessions
F_q : a field of order q
S_i : the personal secret of user U_i
K_j : the session key generated by the GM in session j
$\mathcal{B}_j$: the broadcast message by the GM during session j
H : the entropy function of information theory
$Z_{i,j}$: the information learned by U_i through $\mathcal{B}_j$ and S_i
L_j : the set of all revoked users in session j
t : the maximum number of compromised user

3.1 Our Security Model

Using entropy function, we state the following definitions that are aimed to unconditional security adopting the security model of [8], [5].

Definition 3.1 *(Session Key Distribution with b-bit privacy [5]) Let $t, i \in \{1, \ldots, n\}$ and $j \in \{1, \ldots, m\}$.*

1. *$\mathcal{D}$ is a session key distribution scheme with b-bit privacy if*
   (a) for any user U_i, the session key K_j is determined by $Z_{i,j}$, which in turn is determined by $\mathcal{B}_j$ and S_i. i.e.
   $$H(K_j|Z_{i,j}) = 0,$$
   $$H(Z_{i,j}|\mathcal{B}_j, S_i) = 0.$$
   (b) for any $L \subseteq \mathcal{U}$, $|L| \leq t$, and $U_i \notin L$, the uncertainty of users in L to determine S_i is at least b bits. i.e.
   $$H(S_i|\{S_l\}_{U_l \in L}, \mathcal{B}_1, \ldots, \mathcal{B}_m) \geq b.$$
   (c) what users $U_1, \ldots, U_n$ learn from $\mathcal{B}_j$ cannot be determined from the broadcasts or personal keys alone. i.e.
   $$H(Z_{i,j}|\mathcal{B}_1, \ldots, \mathcal{B}_m) = H(Z_{i,j}) = H(Z_{i,j}|S_1, \ldots, S_n).$$
2. *$\mathcal{D}$ has t-revocation capability if given any $L \subseteq \mathcal{U}$, where $|L| \leq t$, the group manager GM can generate a broadcast $\mathcal{B}_j$, such that for all $U_i \notin L$, U_i can recover K_j, but the revoked users cannot.* i.e.
   $$H(K_j|\mathcal{B}_j, S_i) = 0,$$
   $$H(K_j|\mathcal{B}_j, \{S_l\}_{U_l \in L}) = H(K_j).$$
3. *$\mathcal{D}$ is self-healing if the following is true for any j, $1 \leq j_1 < j < j_2 \leq m$: For any user U_i who is a member in sessions j_1 and j_2, the key K_j is determined by the set $\{Z_{i,j_1}, Z_{i,j_2}\}$.* i.e.
   $$H(K_j|Z_{i,j_1}, Z_{i,j_2}) = 0.$$

Definition 3.2 *(t-wise forward and backward secrecy [5]) Let $t, i \in \{1, \ldots, n\}$ and $j \in \{1, \ldots, m\}$.*

1. *A key distribution scheme $\mathcal{D}$ guarantees t-wise forward secrecy if for any set $L \subseteq \mathcal{U}$, where $|L| \leq t$, and all $U_l \in L$ are revoked before session j, the members in L together cannot get any information about K_j, even with the knowledge of group keys before session j.* i.e.,

$$H(K_j | \mathcal{B}_1, \ldots, \mathcal{B}_m, \{S_l\}_{U_l \in L}, K_1, \ldots, K_{j-1}) = H(K_j).$$

2. *A session key distribution $\mathcal{D}$ guarantees t-wise backward secrecy if for any set $J \subseteq \mathcal{U}$, where $|J| \leq t$, and all $U_l \in J$ join after session j, the members in J together cannot get any information about K_j, even with the knowledge of group keys after session j.* i.e.

$$H(K_j | \mathcal{B}_1, \ldots, \mathcal{B}_m, \{S_l\}_{U_l \in J}, K_{j+1}, \ldots, K_m) = H(K_j).$$

Remark 3.3 *t-wise forward secrecy and t-wise backward secrecy of a key distribution scheme ensure that the scheme is forward and backward secure and has the property of key independence and group key secrecy. Also t-wise forward secrecy implies t-revocation capability.*

4 Our Protocol

4.1 Protocol Requirements

In our setting, there is a group manager (GM) and n (fixed) users $\mathcal{U} = \{U_1, \ldots, U_n\}$. We never allow a revoked user to rejoin the group in a later session. All operations are done over a finite field, F_q, where q is a large prime number ($q > n$). Let f be a random one way permutation over F_q such that $f^i(u) \neq f^j(u)$ for all positive integers i, j and $u \in F_q$. By f^i, we mean that the permutation f is applied i-times to $u \in F_q$.

4.2 Self-healing Session Key Distribution

A high-level description of our self-healing key distribution scheme with revocation is presented below.

Setup : Let t be a positive integer. The group manager GM chooses at random a polynomial $\Psi(x, y) = a_{0,0} + a_{1,0}x + a_{0,1}y + \cdots + a_{t,t}x^t y^t$ from $F_q[x, y]$ and a random initial session identifier $\mathsf{sid}_0 \in F_q$. Each user U_i, for $1 \leq i \leq n$, receives sid_0 and the t-degree polynomial $\Psi(i, y)$ as its personal secret from the GM via the secure communication channel between them.

Broadcast : In the j-th session key distribution, $j \geq 1$, the GM first computes its j-th session identifier $\mathsf{sid}_j = f(\mathsf{sid}_{j-1})$. For $j = 1$, it stores sid_1 and for $j > 1$, it replaces the previous session identifier sid_{j-1} by the current value sid_j. It selects a random prime key $K_j \in F_q$. Let $L_j = \{U_{l_1}, \ldots, U_{l_{w_j}}\}$, $|L_j| = w_j \leq t$, be the set of all revoked users for sessions in and before

j. The GM computes the polynomial $\Phi_j(x) = \Lambda_j(x)K_j + \Psi(x, \mathsf{sid}_j)$, where $\Lambda_j(x) = (x - l_1)(x - l_2) \cdots (x - l_{w_j})$. Here the polynomial $\Lambda_j(x)$ is called revocation polynomial and $\Psi(x, \mathsf{sid}_j)$ performs the role of masking polynomial. Note that each user $U_i \in \mathcal{U}$ knows a single point, namely $\Psi(i, \mathsf{sid}_j)$ on the polynomial $\Psi(x, \mathsf{sid}_j)$. The GM broadcasts the following message:

$$\begin{aligned}\mathcal{B}_j &= \{L_1, L_2, \ldots, L_j\} \\ &\cup \{\Phi_1(x) + \Phi_2(x), \ldots, \Phi_{j-2}(x) + \Phi_{j-1}(x), \Phi_j(x)\}\end{aligned} \qquad (1)$$

Session Key Recovery: When a non-revoked user U_i receives the j-th session key distribution message $\mathcal{B}_j$, it first computes the j-th session identifier $\mathsf{sid}_j = f(\mathsf{sid}_{j-1})$ and replaces the previous session identifier sid_{j-1} by the current value sid_j for $j > 1$ (in case $j = 1$, sid_1 is stored). Then U_i evaluates $\Psi(i, \mathsf{sid}_j)$, $\Phi_j(i)$ and $\Lambda_j(i)$. Finally, U_i computes the current session key

$$K_j = \frac{\Phi_j(i) - \Psi(i, \mathsf{sid}_j)}{\Lambda_j(i)}.$$

Note that from the set $\{L_j\}$ in the broadcast message $\mathcal{B}_j$, all users U_i can compute the polynomial $\Lambda_j(x)$ and consequently, can evaluate the value $\Lambda_j(i)$. In particular, for $U_i \in L_j$, $\Lambda_j(i) = 0$. Hence the revoked users can not recover the current session key K_j from the broadcast message $\mathcal{B}_j$.

Add Group Members : When the GM wants to add a new user U_v starting from session j, where $v \neq 1, \ldots, n$, it gives to this new member U_v a t-degree polynomial $\Psi(v, y)$ as its personal secret and sid_j through the secure communication channel between them.

We now explain our self-healing mechanism: Let U_i be a group member that receives session key distribution messages $\mathcal{B}_{j_1}$ and $\mathcal{B}_{j_2}$ in sessions j_1 and j_2 respectively, where $1 \leq j_1 < j_2$, but lost the session key distribution message $\mathcal{B}_j$ for session j, where $j_1 < j < j_2$. User U_i can still recover all the lost session keys K_j for $j_1 < j < j_2$ as follows:

(a) U_i receives $\Phi_{j_1}(x)$ from the broadcast message $\mathcal{B}_{j_1}$ in session j_1 and $\Phi_{j_1}(x) + \Phi_{j_1+1}(x), \ldots, \Phi_{j_2-2}(x) + \Phi_{j_2-1}(x), \Phi_{j_2}(x)$ from the broadcast message $\mathcal{B}_{j_2}$ in session $j_2 (> j_1)$. Subsequently, U_i recovers the polynomials $\Phi_{j_1+1}(x), \ldots, \Phi_{j_2-1}(x)$ and computes $\Phi_j(i)$ for $j_1 < j < j_2$.
(b) U_i computes $\mathsf{sid}_j = f^j(\mathsf{sid}_0)$ for $j_1 < j < j_2$.
(c) U_i then computes K_j for all j, $j_1 < j < j_2$ as: $K_j = \frac{\Phi_j(i) - \Psi(i, \mathsf{sid}_j)}{\Lambda_j(i)}$.

The above scheme requires that the sets of revoked users must change monotonically. That is, $L_{j_1} \subseteq L_{j_2}$ for $1 \leq j_1 \leq j_2$. Otherwise, a group member that is revoked in session j and rejoins the group in a later session can recover the key for session j, due to the self-healing capability of the protocol. We will show later that our scheme achieves t-revocation capability which means that a coalition of t-revoked users will not be able to learn any information about the current session key.

5 Security Analysis

We now show that our protocol realizes a secure self-healing key distribution with revocation capability in the model as described in Section 3.1. More precisely, we have the following Theorems and proofs.

Theorem 5.1 *The protocol $\mathcal{P}$ presented in Section 4 is an unconditionally secure, self-healing session key distribution scheme with* $\log q$*-bit privacy and* t*-revocation capability.*

Proof: We will show our protocol $\mathcal{P}$ satisfies all the conditions required by Definition 3.1.

1. (a) Session key recovered by a user U_i is described in the third step of our protocol $\mathcal{P}$. Therefore, it follows that

$$H(K_j|\mathcal{B}_j, S_i) = H(K_j|Z_{i,j}) = 0.$$

   (b) For any set $L \subseteq \mathcal{U}$, $|L| \leq t$, and any non-revoked user $U_i \notin L$, we show that the coalition of L knows nothing about the personal secret S_i of U_i. For any session j, U_i's personal secret $S_i = \Psi(i, \mathsf{sid}_j)$ is a point over a t-degree polynomial $\Psi(x, \mathsf{sid}_j)$. Since the coalition L gets at most t points over the t-degree polynomial $\Psi(x, \mathsf{sid}_j)$, it is impossible for coalition L to learn $\Psi(i, \mathsf{sid}_j)$. Since U_i's personal secret $\Psi(i, \mathsf{sid}_j)$ is an element of F_q, we have $H(\Psi(i, \mathsf{sid}_j)) = \log q$. Hence we have

$$\begin{aligned} H(S_i|\{S_l\}_{U_l \in L}, \mathcal{B}_1, \ldots, \mathcal{B}_m) &= H(\Psi(i, \mathsf{sid}_j)|\{\Psi(l, \mathsf{sid}_j)\}_{U_l \in L}, \mathcal{B}_1, \ldots, \mathcal{B}_m) \\ &= H(\Psi(i, \mathsf{sid}_j)) \\ &= \log q \end{aligned}$$

   (c) The j-th session key K_j is chosen according to the uniform distribution and so is independent of the personal secret $S_i = \Psi(i, \mathsf{sid}_j)$ for $i = 1, \ldots, n$. This, in turn, implies that the personal secret keys alone do not give any information about any session key. We now show that the broadcast messages $\mathcal{B}_1, \ldots, \mathcal{B}_m$ alone give no information about the session keys. Given the broadcast messages $\mathcal{B}_1, \ldots \mathcal{B}_m$, one may compute the polynomials $\Phi_1(x), \ldots, \Phi_m(x)$. But the polynomial $\Psi(x, \mathsf{sid}_j)$ cannot be determined unless one gets at least $t+1$ points on this polynomial. Hence the session keys $K_1, \ldots, K_m$ cannot be determined only by broadcast messages. Thus $Z_{i,j} = \{K_j\}$ cannot be determined by only personal key S_i or broadcast message $\mathcal{B}_j$. It follows that

$$H(Z_{i,j}|\mathcal{B}_1, \ldots, \mathcal{B}_m) = H(Z_{i,j}) = H(Z_{i,j}|S_1, \ldots, S_n).$$

2. (t-revocation property) Let L be a collection of t-revoked users collude in session j. It is impossible for coalition L to learn the j-th session key K_j because knowledge of K_j implies the knowledge of the personal secret $\Psi(i, \mathsf{sid}_j)$ of user $U_i \in L$. This coalition L has no information on $\Psi(i, \mathsf{sid}_j)$ for $U_i \notin L$.

L knows the points $\{\Psi(i, \mathsf{sid}_j) : U_i \in L\}$. The size of the coalition L is at most t. Consequently, the colluding users only have at most t-points on the polynomial $\Psi(x, \mathsf{sid}_j)$. But degree of the polynomial $\Psi(x, \mathsf{sid}_j)$ is t. Hence the coalition L cannot recover $\Psi(x, \mathsf{sid}_j)$, which in turn makes K_j appears to be randomly distributed to L. Therefore, K_j is completely safe. Hence,

$$H(K_j|\mathcal{B}_j, S_i) = 0,$$

$$H(K_j|\mathcal{B}_1, \ldots, \mathcal{B}_j, \{S_l\}_{U_l \in L}) = H(K_j).$$

3. (Self-healing property) From the third step of our protocol $\mathcal{P}$, any user U_i that is a member in sessions j_1 and j_2 ($1 \leq j_1 < j_2$), can recover $\{\Phi_{j_1}(x), \Phi_{j_1+1}(x), \ldots, \Phi_{j_2-1}(x), \Phi_{j_2}(x)\}$ and compute the values $\{\Phi_{j_1}(x), \Phi_{j_1+1}(x), \ldots, \Phi_{j_2-1}(x), \Phi_{j_2}(x)\}$. Also U_i has the personal key $\Psi(i, y)$. U_i can compute the j_1-th session identifier $\mathsf{sid}_{j_1} = f^{j_1 - j_3}(\mathsf{sid}_{j_3})$, where j_3 is the number of the session at which user U_i joins the group. So U_i can compute $\mathsf{sid}_{j_1+1}, \ldots, \mathsf{sid}_{j_2}$. Subsequently, U_i can recover the whole sequence of session keys K_j for $j = j_1, \ldots, j_2$ as: $K_j = \frac{\Phi_j(i) - \Psi(i, \mathsf{sid}_j)}{\Lambda_j(i)}$. Hence

$$H(K_j|Z_{i,j_1}, Z_{i,j_2}) = 0$$ □

Theorem 5.2 *The protocol $\mathcal{P}$ presented in Section 4 achieves t-wise forward secrecy and t-wise backward secrecy.*

Proof: We will show our protocol $\mathcal{P}$ satisfies all the conditions required by Definition 3.2.

1. (t-wise forward secrecy) Let $L \subseteq \mathcal{U}$, where $|L| \leq t$ and all user $U_l \in L$ are revoked before the current session j. The coalition L can not get any information about the current session key K_j even with the knowledge of group keys before session j. This is because of the fact that in order to know K_j, $U_l \in L$ needs to know at least $t + 1$ points on the polynomial $\Psi(x, \mathsf{sid}_j)$. But the coalition L has at most t personal secrets $\Psi(i, \mathsf{sid}_j)$, *i.e.* gets t points on the polynomial $\Psi(x, \mathsf{sid}_j)$. Consequently, our protocol is t-wise forward secure and we have

$$H(K_j|\mathcal{B}_1, \ldots, \mathcal{B}_m, \{S_l\}_{U_l \in L}, K_1, \ldots, K_{j-1}) = H(K_j).$$

2. (t-wise backward secrecy) Let $J \subseteq \mathcal{U}$, where $|J| \leq t$ and all user $U_l \in J$ join after the current session j. The coalition J can not get any information about any previous session key K_{j_1} for $j_1 \leq j$ even with the knowledge of group keys after session j. This is because of the fact that in order to know K_{j_1}, $U_l \in J$ requires the knowledge of the session identifier sid_{j_1} and also the knowledge of at least $t + 1$ points on the polynomial $\Psi(x, \mathsf{sid}_{j_1})$. Now when a new member U_v joins the group starting from session $j + 1$, the GM gives the new member a t-degree polynomial $\Psi(v, y)$ as its personal secret and the $j + 1$-th session identifier sid_{j+1}. Note that $\mathsf{sid}_{j+1} = f(\mathsf{sid}_j)$, where f is a random one-way permutation. Hence the newly joint member can not

trace back for previous session identifiers sid_{j_1} for $j_1 \le j$ because of the one-way property of the function f unless it guesses sid_j. Also the coalition J knows only t points on the polynomial $\Psi(x, \mathsf{sid}_j)$ and thus can not compute $\Psi(x, \mathsf{sid}_j)$. Consequently, our protocol is t-wise backward secure and we have

$$H(K_j|\mathcal{B}_1, \ldots, \mathcal{B}_m, \{S_l\}_{U_l \in J}, K_{j+1}, \ldots, K_m) = H(K_j) \qquad \square$$

Remark 5.3 *The backward secrecy of our scheme is achieved in the computational sense under the assumption that one cannot invert the one-way function f.*

6 Efficiency

We now compare our protocol with the other similar schemes. Table 1 compares storage overhead and communication complexity of our proposed scheme with the previous approaches. At the j-th session, the broadcast message $\mathcal{B}_j$ consists of set of revoked users $\{L_1, L_2, \ldots, L_j\}$ and $j-1$ polynomials $\Phi_1(x) + \Phi_2(x), \ldots, \Phi_{j-2}(x) + \Phi_{j-1}(x), \Phi_j(x)$, each of degree t. One can ignore the communication overhead for the broadcast of the set $\{L_1, L_2, \ldots, L_j\}$, because the member IDs can be selected from a small finite field [4]. Then the size of the broadcast message at the j-th session is $(t+1)(j-1)\log q$ which is same as that required for the most optimized scheme [4].

The storage requirement in our scheme comes from *Setup* phase and after receiving the session key distribution message. In the *Setup* phase, each user stores the initial session identifier sid_0 and a t-degree polynomial as its personal secret key (*e.g.* $\Psi(i, y)$ for user U_i). After receiving the broadcast message, each user stores the j-th session identifier sid_j. Each of these elements belongs to F_q. Hence, the total memory required for each user in $(t+1)\log q$, which is constant. This is the most important result of our scheme. Moreover, the personal key is reused to next m sessions without any alteration and the maximum session number (m) is no longer needed to be determined in *Setup* phase. Consequently, our scheme eliminates the limitations of m sessions in previous works [1], [4], [5], [8].

Table 1. Comparison among different self-healing key distribution schemes in the j-th session.

Schemes	Storage Overhead	Communication Overhead
C3 of [8]	$(m-j+1)^2 \log q$	$(mt^2 + 2mt + m + t)\log q$
Scheme 3 of [5]	$2(m-j+1)\log q$	$[(m+j+1)t + (m+1)]\log q$
Scheme 2 of [1]	$(m-j+1)\log q$	$(2tj+j)\log q$
C1 of [4]	$(m-j+1)\log q$	$(tj+j-t-1)\log q$
Our scheme	$(t+1)\log q$	$(tj+j-t-1)\log q$

Remark and Future Work: Our security model excludes the following property of self-healing key distribution unlike the security model provided by [5], [8]: Let $1 \le j_1 < j < j_2 \le m$. For any disjoint subsets $L_1, L_2 \subset \mathcal{U}$, where $|L_1 \cup L_2| \le t$, no information about the session key SK_j, $j_1 < j < j_2$ can be obtained by the coalition $L_1 \cup L_2$, where the set L_1 is a coalition of users removed before session

j_1 and the set L_2 is a coalition of users joined from session j_2. Our protocol does not satisfy this property. As a future work we are interested to incorporate this property in our scheme.

7 Key Recovery from a Single Broadcast

Note that in our previous construction for self-healing key distribution, the users can recover the lost session keys only if it is present in the group both before and after the sessions in which the broadcast packets containing the key are lost. However, if the user loses the first message $\mathcal{B}_1$ and gets message $\mathcal{B}_j$ for a certain session j, then there is no means for the user to recover the lost session key in that session.

In this section, we describe a slightly modified variant of our previous schemes, enabling a user to recover all lost session keys, for sessions in which it belongs to the group, by using only the current broadcast message.

Setup : Same as the Setup in our construction described in Section 4.2.

Broadcast : Same as in our construction described in Section 4.2 except the fact that the GM broadcasts the following message:

$$\begin{aligned}\mathcal{B}_j &= \{L_j\} \cup \{\Phi_j(x)\} \cup \mathcal{B}_{j-1}(x)\\ &= \{L_1, L_2, \ldots, L_j\} \cup \{\Phi_1(x), \Phi_2(x) \ldots, \Phi_{j-1}(x), \Phi_j(x)\}\end{aligned} \quad (2)$$

Session Key Recovery : This is done exactly in the same way as in our construction in Section 4.2.

Add Group Members : Same as in our construction described in Section 4.2.

As the broadcast message transmitted by the GM is different, performing self-healing for lost session key recovery is different. We now explain our self-healing mechanism. The self-healing key recovery property required for this scheme replaces $1(a)$ and 3 in Definition 3.1 by the following:

Definition 7.1 *For any $l < j < m$, and any user U_i, which has not revoked before session j, the key K_l is determined by $\mathcal{B}_j$ and S_i. Formally, we have,*

$$H(K_l|\mathcal{B}_j, S_i) = 0.$$

For our present scheme, from any broadcast packet $\mathcal{B}_j$, user U_i, who is not revoked in session $l \leq j$, can compute session key $K_l = \frac{\Phi_l(i) - \Psi(i, \mathsf{sid}_l)}{\Lambda_l(i)}$ for all l, $l \leq j$. *i.e.* $H(K_l|\mathcal{B}_j, S_i) = 0$ for all $l \leq j$.

Following the same line of proof of Theorem 5.1, we have:

Theorem 7.2 *The above construction is unconditionally secure key distribution scheme with key recovery and t-revocation capability, having* $\log q$ *bits privacy and resilient to collusion attacks.*

The storage requirement and communication complexity of this scheme is same as that of our previous scheme described in Section 4. Table 1 compares our scheme with the previous approaches.

8 Conclusion

This paper presents an efficient unconditionally secure self-healing key distribution scheme with revocation capability, enabling a very large and dynamic group of users to establish a common key for secure communication over an unreliable wireless network. Our proposed key distribution mechanism reduces both the storage and communication overhead over the previous approaches, and is scalable to very large groups in highly mobile, volatile and hostile wireless network. In contrast to the previous constructions, the personal key of a user can be reused to next m sessions without any alteration in our proposed scheme, thus eliminating the limitations of m sessions in the *Setup* phase. The scheme is properly analyzed in an appropriate security model to prove that it is unconditionally secure and achieves both forward secrecy and backward secrecy. We also propose another self-healing key distribution scheme that enables key recovery from a single broadcast message.

References

1. Blundo, C., D'Arco, P., Santis, A., Listo, M.: Design of Self-healing Key Distribution Schemes. Design Codes and Cryptology 32, 15–44 (2004)
2. Blundo, C., D'Arco, P., Santis, A., Listo, M.: Definitions and Bounds for Self-healing Key Distribution. In: Díaz, J., Karhumäki, J., Lepistö, A., Sannella, D. (eds.) ICALP 2004. LNCS, vol. 3142, pp. 234–245. Springer, Heidelberg (2004)
3. Cover, T.M., Thomas, J.A.: Elements of Information Theory. John Wiley & Sons, Chichester (1991)
4. Hong, D., Kang, J.: An Efficient Key Distribution Scheme with Self-healing Property. IEEE Communication Letters'05. 9, 759–761 (2005)
5. Liu, D., Ning, P., Sun, K.: Efficient Self-healing Key Distribution with Revocation Capability. In: Proceedings of the 10th ACM CCS'03, pp. 27–31 (2003)
6. More, S., Malkin, M., Staddon, J.: Sliding-window Self-healing Key Distribution with Revocation. In: ACM Workshop on Survivable and Self-regenerative Systems'03, pp. 82–90 (2003)
7. Saez, G.: On Threshold Self-healing Key Distribution Schemes. In: Smart, N.P. (ed.) Cryptography and Coding'04. LNCS, vol. 3796, pp. 340–354. Springer, Heidelberg (2005)
8. Staddon, J., Miner, S., Franklin, M., Balfanz, D., Malkin, M., Dean, D.: Self-healing key distribution with Revocation. In: Proceedings of IEEE Symposium on Security and Privacy'02, pp. 224–240 (2002)

Key Predistribution Using Partially Balanced Designs in Wireless Sensor Networks

Sushmita Ruj and Bimal Roy

Applied Statistics Unit, Indian Statistical Institute,
203 B T Road, Kolkata 700 108, India
{sush_r,bimal}@isical.ac.in

Abstract. We propose two deterministic key predistribution schemes in a Wireless Sensor Network (WSN), in which sensor nodes are deployed randomly. Both the schemes are based on Partially Balanced Incomplete Block Designs (PBIBD). An important feature of our scheme is that every pair of nodes can communicate directly, making communication faster and efficient. The number of keys per node is of the order of $\sqrt{N}$, where N is the number of nodes in the network. Our second design has the added advantage that we can introduce new nodes in the network keeping the key pool fixed. We study the resiliency of the network under node compromise and show that our designs give better results than the existing ones.

Keywords: Combinatorial Design, PBIBD designs, Resiliency.

1 Introduction

Distributed Sensor Networks (DSN) consist of sensor nodes with very limited memory and power, and are scattered randomly in large numbers over a target area. The networks are used for both military and civilian purposes. Sensor nodes can communicate with each other within a particular range called the Radio Frequency (RF) range. To ensure secure communication, any two sensor nodes should communicate in an encrypted manner using a common secret key.

The keys are either predistributed in the sensor nodes or online key exchange protocols can be used. Though public key cryptosystems using RSA and ECC have been used in low end devices [6], they are not efficient where several hundred thousand nodes with very limited resources are required. Hence key predistribution is an attractive option.

Key predistribution techniques can be randomized, deterministic or hybrid. In randomized technique of key predistribution [5,2], keys are drawn randomly from a key pool and placed in each sensor node. This technique does not guarantee that any two nodes will be able to communicate directly. If direct communication is not possible, then a path needs to be established between the two nodes. This makes communication slower and power consuming.

In deterministic key predistribution, keys are placed in sensor nodes in a predetermined manner. Deterministic key predistribution using combinatorial

I. Stojmenovic et al. (Eds.): ISPA 2007, LNCS 4742, pp. 431–445, 2007.

designs have been studied in [1,8,3]. Hybrid designs combine the above two approaches and have been studied in [1,3].

Here we consider a deterministic key predistribution scheme using Partially Balanced Incomplete Block Designs (PBIBD). We will consider the dual of a $PBIBD(v, b, r, k, \lambda_1, \lambda_2)$. Let us consider a network containing v nodes containing r keys each. So any two nodes share either λ_1 or λ_2 ($\lambda_1, \lambda_2 \neq 0$) common keys. Unlike most of the previous designs, our design ensures that any two nodes can communicate directly thus making communication faster and efficient. Considering a network consisting of N many nodes, the number of keys per node is also low, equal to $O(\sqrt{N})$.

We study the resiliency of such a system in terms of two parameters. One of the parameters consider the proportion of nodes disconnected when a certain number of nodes are compromised. The other parameter considers the proportion of links broken under node compromise. We show that our design results in much better connectivity and resiliency compared to [8].

The rest of the paper is organized as follows. In Section 2 we define a few terms and concepts. We give a key predistribution scheme based on triangular $PBIBD$ in Section 3. In Section 4 we study the resiliency of the network under node capture. We define two parameters $E(s)$ and $V(s)$, where s nodes are compromised. We give an upper bound for $E(s)$ and $V(s)$. In Section 5 we discuss another design and conduct an experimental study of $E(s)$ and $V(s)$ on that design. We compare our results with [8] in Section 6 and show that our design fares better in terms of resiliency and connectivity. We conclude with some open problems in Section 7.

2 Preliminaries

2.1 BIBD and PBIBD

A *set system* or *design* [8] is a pair (X, A), where A is a set of subsets of X, called *blocks*. The elements of X are called varieties. A $BIBD(v, b, r, k, \lambda)$, is a *design* which satisfy the following conditions:

1. $|X| = v$, $|A| = b$,
2. Each subset in A contains exactly k elements,
3. Each variety in X occurs in r many blocks,
4. Each pair of varieties in X is contained in exactly λ blocks in A.

Suppose that (X, A) is a set system, where

$$X = \{x_i : 1 \leq i \leq v\}$$

and

$$A = \{A_j : 1 \leq j \leq b\}.$$

The *dual set system* of (X, A) is any set isomorphic to the set system (X', A') where

$$X' = \{x'_j : 1 \le j \le b\},$$

$$A' = \{A'_i : 1 \le i \le v\},$$

and where

$$x'_j \in A'_i \iff x_i \in A_j.$$

It follows that if we take the dual of a $BIBD(v, b, r, k, \lambda)$, we arrive at a design containing b varieties, v blocks each block containing exactly r varieties and each variety occurring in exactly k blocks. We also note that any two blocks contain λ elements in common. When $v = b$ the $BIBD$ is called a *symmetric BIBD* and denoted by $SBIBD(v, k; \lambda)$.

An *association scheme with m associate classes* [9, Section 11] on the set X is a family of m symmetric anti-reflexive binary relations on X such that:

1. any two distinct elements of X are i-th associates for exactly one value of i, where $1 \le i \le m$,
2. each element of X has n_i i-th associates, $1 \le i \le m$,
3. for each i, $1 \le i \le m$, if x and y are i-th associates, then there are p^i_{jl} elements of X which are both j-th associates of x and l-th associates of y. The numbers v, $n_i(1 \le i \le m)$ and $p^i_{jl}(1 \le i, j, l \le m)$ are called the *parameters of the association scheme.*

A *partially balanced incomplete block design with m associate classes*, denoted by $PBIBD(m)$ [9] is a design on a v-set X, with b blocks each of size k and with each element of X being repeated r times, such that if there is an association scheme with m classes defined on X where, two elements x and y are i-th $(1 \le i \le m)$ associates, then they occur together in λ_i blocks. We denote such a design by $PB[k, \lambda_1, \lambda_2, \cdots, \lambda_m; v]$.

We use PBIBD with two associate classes in our design. We use a triangular association scheme [4, Page 14] in our design.

A *triangular association scheme* is a partially balanced design with two associate classes in which the number of varieties is $v = n(n-1)/2$ and the association scheme is an array A of n rows and n columns with the following properties:

1. The positions in the principal diagonal (from top left to bottom right) are left blank.
2. The $n(n-1)/2$ positions above the principal diagonal are filled by the numbers $1, 2, \cdots, n(n-1)/2$ corresponding to the varieties.
3. The $n(n-1)/2$ elements below the diagonal are filled so that the array is symmetrical about the principal diagonal.
4. For any variety i, the first associates are those elements which lie in the same row (or same column) as i, the second associates are the rest of the elements.

The parameters of the association scheme are

$$v = n(n-1)/2, \quad n_1 = 2(n-2), \quad n_2 = (n-2)(n-3)/2$$

and

$$P_1 = \begin{pmatrix} n-2 & n-3 \\ n-3 & (n-3)(n-4)/2 \end{pmatrix}, P_2 = \begin{pmatrix} 4 & 2n-8 \\ 2n-8 & (n-4)(n-5)/2 \end{pmatrix}.$$

3 A key Predistribution Scheme Using Triangular PBIBD

We use a triangular association scheme to predistribute the keys in the sensor network. Corresponding to any variety x ($x = 1, 2, \cdots, v$) of the triangular association scheme with parameter n ($n \geq 5$) we form a block of size n_1 by taking as elements in the block the n_1 first associates of the variety x. We use the association corresponding to the array A given by:

$$A = \begin{array}{cccccc} * & 1 & 2 & \cdots & n-2 & n-1 \\ 1 & * & n & n+1 & \cdots & 2n-3 \\ 2 & n & * & 2n-2 & \cdots & 3n-6 \\ \vdots & \vdots & \vdots & * & \vdots & \vdots \\ n-1 & 2n-3 & \cdots & \cdots & n(n-1)/2 & * \end{array}$$

Thus $n(n-1)/2$ blocks are formed, where each element appears n_1 times and each block is of size n_1. We also note that the varieties that are first associates occur together in p_{11}^1 blocks. Thus

$$v = b = n(n-1)/2,\ r = k = n_1 = 2(n-2),$$
$$\lambda_1 = p_{11}^1 = (n-2),\ \lambda_2 = p_{11}^2 = 4.$$

This is a symmetric design so the number of common keys between the blocks will either be $\lambda_1 = p_{11}^1$ or $\lambda_2 = p_{11}^2$.

We present an example to demonstrate the above scheme. We consider $n = 5$. Then the array A containing the varieties will be represented by

$$A = \begin{array}{ccccc} * & 1 & 2 & 3 & 4 \\ 1 & * & 5 & 6 & 7 \\ 2 & 5 & * & 8 & 9 \\ 3 & 6 & 8 & * & 10 \\ 4 & 7 & 9 & 10 & * \end{array}$$

In the above design, $v = b = 10$, $r = k = 6$, $\lambda_1 = 3$, $\lambda_2 = 4$.

The blocks so formed are: $\{2,3,4,5,6,7\}$, $\{1,3,4,5,8,9\}$, $\{1,2,4,6,8,10\}$, $\{1,2,3,7,9,10\}$, $\{1,2,6,7,8,9\}$, $\{1,3,5,7,8,10\}$, $\{1,4,5,6,9,10\}$, $\{2,3,5,6,9,10\}$, $\{2,4,5,7,8,10\}$, $\{3,6,8,4,7,9\}$.

We now map this design to the our key predistribution scheme. We assume a DSN where there are $N = n(n-1)/2$ nodes. The total number of keys in the key pool is also $n(n-1)/2$. Each sensor node contains $2(n-2)$ keys. Since the above design is symmetric, we note that any two blocks will share either $n-2$ or 4 keys. Let P and Q be two nodes whose positions in the matrix A are given by (x_1, y_1) and (x_2, y_2). This implied that P lies in x_1th row and y_1th column and Q lies in x_2th row and y_2th column. If $x_1 = x_2$ (when nodes belong to the same row), then the keys shared between them will be the set $\{a_{x_1 j} : 0 \leq j < n, j \neq x_1, y_1, y_2\} \bigcup \{a_{y_1 y_2}\}$. $n-2$ keys are similarly shared when two nodes belong to the same column. When P and Q belong to different rows and columns, then four keys $a_{x_1 x_2}$, $a_{x_1 y_2}$, $a_{y_1 x_2}$ and $a_{y_1 y_2}$ are shared between P and Q. So every pair of node can communicate with each other directly. If we number the nodes $1, 2, \cdots, n(n-1)/2$, then any two nodes which lie in the same row (or column) of A will share $n-2$ keys. Any other pair of nodes will share four keys. We observe that if the number of sensor nodes is N, then the number of keys present in each sensor node is $O(\sqrt{N})$.

For our first design we consider a network containing $N = n(n-1)/2$ sensor nodes, each node containing $k = 2(n-2)$ keys, and any two nodes have either $\lambda_1 = n-2$ or $\lambda_2 = 4$ keys in common.

4 Study of Resiliency

Sensor nodes when deployed in an hostile environment are prone to be captured or compromised by adversaries. When nodes are compromised, the keys contained therein are exposed and so cannot be used for communication. In some cases only the links that share the exposed keys will be broken. In other cases, sensor nodes may contain all the keys that have been exposed. In such a situation, the node will be disconnected altogether. We give two measures of resiliency. First study the fraction of nodes that will be disconnected when a given number of nodes are compromised. We denote this by $V(s)$, where s is the number of nodes compromised. We give an upper bound for $V(s)$. Secondly we study the fraction of links that will be broken when s nodes are compromised. We denote this by $E(s)$. We give an upper bound for $E(s)$ and compare it with the experimental values.

4.1 Analysis of $V(s)$

$V(s)$ is defined as the proportion of nodes disconnected, when s nodes are compromised. That is,

$$V(s) = \frac{\text{Number of nodes disconnected when } s \text{ nodes are compromised}}{N-s}$$

It has already been pointed out that any two sensor nodes share either $n-2$ keys or four keys. We recollect that any two nodes which lie in the same row (or column) of A will share $n-2$ keys. We consider any two nodes P and Q. Suppose they belong to positions (x_1, y_1) and (x_2, y_2) in the array A (as defined in Section 3). Since matrix A is symmetric about the principal diagonal, position of P and Q can also be stated as (y_1, x_1) and (y_2, x_2) respectively. If P and Q belong to the same row, then $x_1 = x_2$. Then the common keys between P and Q will be $\{a_{x_1 i} : 0 \leq i < n, i \neq x_1, y_1, y_2\} \bigcup \{a_{y_1 y_2}\}$. So $n-2$ keys are shared between P and Q. If P and Q do not belong to the same row (or column), then the four common keys will be in positions $a_{x_1 x_2}$, $a_{x_1 y_2}$, $a_{y_1 x_2}$ and $a_{y_1 y_2}$. It is easy to see that if only one node is compromised, then no node is disconnected.

Proposition 1. *When two nodes in the same row (or column) are compromised, then exactly one node will be disconnected.*

Proof. Suppose two nodes C and C' at positions (x_1, y_1) and (x_1, y_2) are compromised. Due to the compromise of C, the keys, $a_{x_1 i}$ and a_{jy_1} are lost, where $0 \leq i, j < n$, $i, j \neq x_1, y_1$. Also, due to the compromise of C', the keys, $a_{x_1 l}$ and a_{my_2} are lost, where $0 \leq l, m < n$, $l, m \neq y_2, x_1$. So all keys, $a_{y_1 i}$, where $0 \leq i < n$ and $i \neq y_1$ and a_{jy_2}, where $0 \leq j < n$ and $j \neq y_2$ are lost. Thus all keys belonging to node at (y_1, y_2) are exposed. Hence the node at (y_1, y_2) is disconnected. □

Observation 1: It can be noted that any two nodes belonging to different row (or column) in array A will not disconnect any other node.
Observation 2: It follows from Proposition 1 and by Pigeon Hole Principle, that on compromising $\lceil \frac{n}{2} \rceil + 1$ nodes, at least two nodes will be in the same row or column. So at least one node will be disconnected.
Observation 3: If $\lceil \frac{n-2}{2} \rceil$ nodes are so compromised that the row and column to which they belong are all distinct, then only one node is disconnected. Suppose, nodes at position (a_0, a_1), (a_2, a_3), $\cdots$, (a_i, a_{i+1}), (a_{i+3}, a_{i+4}), $\cdots$, (a_j, a_{j+1}), (a_{j+3}, a_{j+4}), $\cdots$, (a_{n-2}, a_{n-1}) are compromised. Then the node at position (a_{i+2}, a_{j+2}) has all the keys common to the compromised nodes and so it will be compromised.

Theorem 1. *Maximum number of nodes disconnected when s nodes are compromised is $s(s-1)/2$.*

Proof. From Proposition 1 when any two nodes which belong to the same row (column) of array A are compromised, one node is disconnected. For every pair of compromised nodes in the row (column), one node is disconnected. Hence, for $\binom{s}{2}$ pairs of compromised nodes $\binom{s}{2}$ nodes are disconnected. This is the maximum number of nodes disconnected, since by Observation 1, any two node not belonging to the same row (column) will not disconnect any other node. □

We give some experimental values for $V(s)$. The results in Table 1 clearly show that very few nodes will be disconnected when nodes are compromised randomly. The values of $V(s)$ have been obtained by compromising s nodes randomly and the experiment is conducted for 100 runs for each s. The results for the upper bound show that even if nodes are compromised in a predetermined manner, very few nodes (other than the compromised nodes) will be disconnected.

4.2 Analysis of $E(s)$

Let B = Number of links broken when s nodes are compromised. $E(s)$ is the proportion of links disconnected when s nodes are compromised, that is,

$$E(s) = \frac{2B}{(N-s)(N-s-1)}.$$

Let the s nodes being compromised be $C_1, C_2, \cdots, C_s$ which belong to positions (x_1, y_1), (x_2, y_2), $\cdots$, (x_s, y_s) in array A.

Table 1. Experimental value of $V(s)$ for 100 runs and bound for $V(s)$, when number of nodes is $N = n(n-1)/2$ and keys per node is k

n	N	k	s	$V(s)(Experimental)$	Upper bound for $V(s)$
20	190	38	7	0.0765	0.1147
30	435	56	10	0.0753	0.1059
40	780	76	10	0.0351	0.0584
50	1225	96	10	0.0156	0.0370
60	1770	116	10	0.0085	0.0255
70	2415	136	10	0.0058	0.1871

Given any two nodes P and Q belonging to positions (x'_1, y'_1) and (x'_2, y'_2) in the array A, we can check whether the link PQ will be disconnected in the following way.

1. If P and Q do not belong to the same row(or column) in the matrix A, then
   (a) We note the four keys shared by P and Q. As has been discussed in Section 4.1, the keys will be $a_{x'_1,x'_2}$, $a_{x'_1,y'_2}$, $a_{y'_1,x'_2}$ and $a_{y'_1,y'_2}$.
   (b) The link PQ will not be broken if any of the five conditions is satisfied.
      i. If x'_1th and x'_2th row (column) do not contain a compromised node;
      ii. If x'_1th and y'_2th row (column) do not contain a compromised node;
      iii. If y'_1th and x'_2th and (column) do not contain a compromised node;
      iv. If y'_1th and y'_2th and (column) do not contain a compromised node;
      v. If any of the nodes (x'_1, x'_2), (x'_1, y'_2), (y'_1, x'_2) and (y'_1, y'_2) is a compromised node, and there is no other compromised node belonging to that row or column.
   (c) For all other conditions, the link PQ will be broken.

2. Suppose P and Q belong to the same row $(x'_1 = x'_2)$ (or column $(y'_1 = y'_2)$) in the array A: Suppose at least two compromised nodes (x'_1, s) and (x'_1, t) belong to the same row as P and Q. Then all the $a_{x_1 j}$ keys $(0 \leq j < n, j \neq x_1)$ are exposed. Then the link PQ will be broken if $a_{y'_1 y'_2}$ is also exposed.

We give an upper bound on the number of links broken when s nodes are compromised.

4.3 Calculation of Upper Bound for B

Let the compromised s nodes $C_1, C_2, \cdots, C_s$ belong to positions (x_1, y_1), (x_2, y_2), $\cdots$, (x_s, y_s). Let there be d distinct values among $x_1, x_2, \cdots, x_s, y_1, y_2, \cdots, y_s$. Let us denote the set of rows (or columns) containing the compromised nodes by $S_1 = \{l_1, l_2, \cdots, l_d\}$. The rest of the rows (or columns) not containing any compromised node is denoted by $S_2 = \{m_1, m_2, \cdots, m_{n-d}\}$. Clearly, $S_1 \bigcap S_2 = \phi$. Let B_d denote the number of links broken when the compromised nodes belong to d distinct rows and columns. We first note that the link between any two nodes which do not share a row (or column) as any of the compromised nodes is not broken. This is because none of the keys are exposed. To calculate the number of links broken B_d, we consider the following two cases:

1. The number of links broken, such that the nodes forming the link both do not belong to a row (or column) containing a compromised node. This number is denoted by b'_d. So,

$$b'_d = |\{\{(x'_1, y'_1), (x'_2, y'_2)\} : x'_1 \neq x'_2 \neq y'_1 \neq y'_2, \text{ at least one of } x'_1, y'_1 \in S_1 \text{ and at least one of } x'_2, y'_2 \in S_1\}|$$

2. The number of links broken, such that the nodes forming the link both belong to the same row (or column) as a compromised node. This number is denoted by b''_d. So,

$$b''_d = |\{\{(x'_1, y'_1), (x'_2, y'_2)\} : x'_1 = x'_2 \text{ or } y'_1 = y'_2 \text{ or } x'_1 = y'_2 \text{ or } x'_2 = y'_1 \text{ and at least one of } x'_1, y'_1, x'_2, y'_2 \in S_1\}|$$

So, $B_d = b'_d + b''_d$. Let p_d denote the probability that the compromised nodes belong to exactly d distinct rows (or columns). Then

$$B = \sum_{d=s}^{2s} p_d(b'_d + b''_d) \tag{1}$$

Lemma 1. *Let the compromised nodes belong to the set of columns (rows) $S_1 = \{l_1, l_2, \cdots, l_d\}$. Let $S_2 = \{m_1, m_2, \cdots, m_{n-d}\}$ be the set of the columns (rows) not containing any compromised nodes, so $S_1 \bigcap S_2 = \phi$. Then, $b'_d \leq \binom{d}{2}\binom{n-d}{2} + \frac{1}{4}\binom{d-1}{2}(d-3)d + \binom{d}{2}(d-2)(n-d)$.*

Proof. The broken links connecting the nodes not belonging to the same row (or column) share four keys. By the definition of b'_d, such a shared key a_{ij} $(i \neq j)$ will be such that either $i \in S_1$ or $j \in S_1$ or $i, j \in S_1$. We distinguish two types of keys.
Type I keys:

$$\begin{matrix} a_{m_1 l_1}, & a_{m_1 l_2}, & \cdots, & a_{m_1 l_d} \\ a_{m_2 l_1}, & a_{m_2 l_2}, & \cdots, & a_{m_2 l_d} \\ \vdots & \vdots & \vdots & \vdots \\ a_{m_{n-d} l_1}, & a_{m_{n-d} l_2}, & \cdots, & a_{m_{n-d} l_d} \end{matrix}$$

and Type II keys :

$$\begin{matrix} * & a_{l_1 l_2}, a_{l_1 l_3}, & \cdots, & a_{l_1 l_d} \\ a_{l_2 l_1}, & * \quad a_{l_2 l_3}, & \cdots, & a_{l_2 l_d} \\ \vdots & \vdots \quad\quad \vdots & \vdots & \\ a_{l_d l_1}, & a_{l_d l_2}, \cdots, & a_{l_d l_{d-1}} & * \end{matrix}$$

The four common keys belonging to any two links must belong to the Type I and Type II keys. Also we note that two among the four keys belong to the same row and the other two to a different row of the matrix A but in the same column as the first pair. To calculate all such combinations of Type I and Type II nodes, we consider the following cases:

Case (a) : all four keys are of Type I (one pair from one row),
Case (b) : all four keys are of Type II (one pair from one row),
Case (c) : the four keys are a combinations Type I keys (two from same row) and Type II keys (two others from a different row). We later show this is an overestimation.

To enumerate Case (a), we choose two keys from a row of Type I keys. This can be done in $\binom{d}{2}$ ways. It has been discussed earlier that the other two keys will also belong to the same column as the first pair. The first pair can be chosen from $n-d$ rows in $n-d$ ways. Corresponding to the $n-d$ ways, the second pair can be chosen in $n-d-1$ ways. However this involves double counting. So the two pairs (four keys)can be chosen in $\binom{d}{2}\binom{n-d}{2}$ ways.

To enumerate Case (b), we choose two keys from a row in $\binom{d-1}{2}$ ways (since there are $d-1$ Type II keys in each row as shown above). Since for each of these pairs the other pair must be chosen from the remaining $d-3$ rows (we note that a pair will not occur together in two rows as shown) in $\binom{d-1}{2}(d-3)$ ways. Since there are d rows, the four keys (all of Type II) can be chosen in $\binom{d-1}{2}(d-3)d$ ways. However this sort of counting considers each of the quadruples two times. Also because of the symmetry of Matrix A, this enumeration results in double counting. For example the key $a_{l_1 l_2}$ is the same as $a_{l_2 l_1}$. So the number of possible combinations for Case (b) is $\frac{1}{4}\binom{d-1}{2}(d-3)d$.

We next enumerate the number of possible combinations for Case (c). We can choose the first two shared keys from a rows of Type I keys in $\binom{d}{2}$. For each of ways the second pair must be chosen $d-2$ possible rows of Type II keys in $\binom{d}{2}(d-2)$ ways. Since there are $n-d$ rows of Type I keys, the possible combinations satisfying Case (c) will be $\binom{d}{2}(d-2)(n-d)$.

A few things should be observed here.

1. The calculation above gives the correct number of links affected for Case (a).
2. We over estimate the number of links affected for Case (b). We note that a key $a_{l_x l_y}$ will not be an exposed key, if only one node is compromised in the l_x-th row and l_y-th column of A. So all links which contain shared keys of this form will remain unaffected.
3. We also over estimate the number of links for Case (c). This is also because we over estimate the number of Type II keys as discussed above.

So $b'_d \leq \binom{d}{2}\binom{n-d}{2} + \frac{1}{4}\binom{d-1}{2}(d-3)d + \binom{d}{2}(d-2)(n-d)$. □

We now find an upper bound for b''_d.

Lemma 2. *Let the compromised nodes belong to the set of columns (or rows) $S_1 = \{l_1, l_2, \cdots, l_d\}$. Let $S_2 = \{m_1, m_2, \cdots, m_{n-d}\}$ be the set of the columns not* *containing any compromised nodes, so* $S_1 \bigcap S_2 = \phi$. *Then,* $b_2 \leq d(n-d)(d-1) + \binom{d-1}{2}d$

Proof. Let us consider the i-th column, where $i \in S_1$. We consider the two nodes at positions (j,i) and (k,i), where $i \in S_1$ and $j,k \in \{1,2,\cdots,n\}$, $j,k \neq i$. Two cases will arise here:

1. If $j \in S_2$ and $k \in S_1$, the link between the nodes (j,i) and (k,i) will be broken, if there are at least two compromised nodes belonging to the i-th column. To obtain an upper bound we relax this constraint. So in this case, the maximum number of links broken will be $(n-d)(d-1)$ (Since we do not consider the node at (i,i) in our calculation).
2. If $j,k \in S_1$, then the number of links broken will be $\binom{d-1}{2}$. This is also an over estimate, since the common key a_{jk} may not be an exposed key. This happens when we have a compromised node at (j,k) but no other compromised node in the j-th and k-th row (or column).

So, for d columns the number of broken links will be given by $b''_d \leq d(n-d)(d-1) + \binom{d-1}{2}d$ □

From Lemma 1 and Lemma 2 and the definition of B_d we arrive at the following theorem.

Theorem 2. *Let* p_d *denote the probability that the nodes compromised belong to* d *distinct rows (or columns). The total number of links broken, will be given by* $B \leq \sum_{d=s}^{2s} p_d(\binom{d}{2}\binom{n-d}{2} + \frac{1}{4}\binom{d-1}{2}(d-3)d + \binom{d}{2}(d-2)(n-d) + d(n-d)(d-1) + \binom{d-1}{2}d)$

Exact value of B_{2s}: We discuss a special case where all the compromised nodes belong to distinct rows (columns). So, $d = 2s$. Let the s compromised nodes belong to position $(l_1,l'_1), (l_2,l'_2), \cdots, (l_s,l'_s)$. We calculate the exact value of B_{2s} under such a circumstance.

Theorem 3. $B_{2s} = s(2s-1)(n-2s)(n-2s+1)/2 + s(s-1)(2s-3)/2 + s(s-1)(s-2)(2s-5) + 2s(s-1)(n-2s) + 4s(s-1)(s-2)(n-2s) + 2s(n-2)$.

Proof. We define b'_{2s} and b''_{2s} as in the first part of this section. Proceeding as in the proof of Lemma 1, we find the possible common keys that two nodes belonging to a broken link can share. We find the exact keys that can be shared and define then as Type I' and Type II' keys (Similar to Type I and Type II keys). Type I' keys:

$$\begin{array}{cccccccc} a_{m_1l_1}, & a_{m_1l'_1}, & a_{m_1l_2} & a_{m_1l'_2} & \cdots, & a_{m_1l_s} & a_{m_1l'_s} \\ a_{m_2l_1}, & a_{m_2l'_1}, & a_{m_2l_2} & a_{m_2l'_2}, & \cdots, & a_{m_2l_s} & a_{m_2l'_s} \\ \vdots & \vdots & \vdots & \vdots & & & \end{array}$$

$$a_{m_{n-2s}l_1}, a_{m_{n-2s}l'_1}, a_{m_{n-2s}l_2}, a_{m_{n-2s}l'_2}, \cdots, a_{m_{n-2s}l_s}, a_{m_{n-2s}l'_s}$$

and Type II' keys :

$$\begin{array}{cccccccc}
* & * & a_{l_1 l_2}, & a_{l_1 l'_2}, & a_{l_1 l_3}, & a_{l_1 l'_3}, & \cdots, & a_{l_1 l_s}, \; a_{l_1 l'_s} \\
* & * & a_{l'_1 l_2}, & a_{l'_1 l'_2}, & a_{l'_1 l_3}, & a_{l'_1 l'_3}, & \cdots, & a_{l'_1 l_s} \; a_{l'_1 l'_s} \\
\vdots & \vdots & \vdots & \vdots & \vdots & \vdots & & \\
a_{l_s l_1}, & a_{l_s l'_1}, & a_{l_s l_2}, & a_{l_s l'_2}, & a_{l_s l_3}, & a_{l_s l'_3} & \cdots \quad \cdots & * \quad * \\
a_{l'_s l_1} & a_{l'_s l'_1} & a_{l'_s l_2}, & a_{l'_s l'_2}, & a_{l'_s l_3}, & a_{l'_s l'_3} & \cdots \quad \cdots & * \quad *
\end{array}$$

Proceeding as in the proof of Lemma 1 number of combinations satisfying Case (a) is given by $\binom{2s}{2}\binom{n-2s}{2}$.

For Case (b) we first consider the number of ways in which the pair of nodes chosen from the same row will be the pair (l_x, l'_x). Two such pairs can be chosen from a row in $s-1$ ways. Corresponding to this, any other pair can be chosen from the other rows in $2(s-2)+1$ ways. Since there are $2s$ rows, the number of ways of selecting the four keys will be $2s(s-1)(2s-3)$. However each quadruple is counted twice, and since each shared key is also counted twice the exact number of ways of selecting the four keys will be $s(s-1)(2s-3)/2$.

When the nodes chosen are not of the form (l_x, l'_x), then the number of ways of selecting a pair will be $4\binom{s-1}{2}$ ways. The second pair can be chosen from the remaining rows in $2(s-3)+1$ ways. Since there are $2s$ rows the number of four tuples will be $2s(4\binom{s-1}{2})(2s-5)$. However as before each quadruple is calculated four times. So the number of ways of selection is $s(s-1)(s-2)(2s-5)$. Hence the number of cases which satisfy Case (b) will be given by $s(s-1)(2s-3)/2 + s(s-1)(s-2)(2s-5)$.

By a similar argument we can show that the number of cases which satisfy Case (c) will be given by $2s(s-1)(n-2s) + 4s(s-1)(s-2)(n-2s)$. Hence $b'_{2s} = s(2s-1)(n-2s)(n-2s-1)/2 + s(s-1)(2s-3)/2 + s(s-1)(s-2)(2s-5) + 2s(s-1)(n-2s) + 4s(s-1)(s-2)(n-2s)$.

b''_{2s} can be calculated in the following way. We know that no two compromised nodes belong to the same row (or column). Suppose there is a compromised node at location (l_x, l'_x). Suppose we consider the nodes at positions (i, l'_x) and (j, l'_x), $i, j \in \{1, 2, \cdots, n\}, i, j \neq l_x, l'_x$. The key $a_{l_x l'_x}$ is shared by the nodes but not exposed. So all such links are unaffected. The only links affected within the column l'_x will be between the nodes (i, l_x) and (l_x, l'_x), where $i \in \{1, 2, \cdots, n\}, i \neq l'_x, l_x$. For each of the $2s$ columns there are $n-2$ such links. Hence $b''_{2s} = 2s(n-2)$. Hence the theorem. □

A tighter bound for B: From Theorem 1 we find an upper bound for B. We can show that B_d is an increasing function of d. The number of ways we can choose s nodes from the whole network consisting of $N = n(n-1)/2$ nodes, is $\binom{N}{s}$. To find the number of ways of choosing s nodes such that all the rows and columns are distinct we choose $2s$ rows (or columns) to which these nodes belong in $\binom{n}{2s}$ ways. Now we form s pairs from among these $2s$ rows (or columns) in $\frac{1}{s!}\binom{2s}{2}\binom{2s-2}{2}\binom{2s-4}{2}\cdots\binom{2}{2} = \frac{(2s)!}{2^s s!}$. So the number of ways of choosing s nodes such that all the rows and columns are distinct is $\frac{n!}{(n-2s)!2^s s!}$. So $p_{2s} = \frac{n!(N-s)!}{N!(n-2s)!2^s}$. We know the exact value of B_{2s} from Theorem 3. Hence we arrive at the theorem:

Theorem 4. $B \leq \frac{n!(N-s)!}{N!(n-2s)!2^s} B_{2s} + (1 - \frac{n!(N-s)!}{N!(n-2s)!2^s}) B_{2s-1}$

The Table 2 represent the experimental values of $E(s)$. The values of $E(s)$ have been obtained by compromising s nodes randomly and the experiment is conducted for 100 runs for each s. The theoretical upper bound are also given.

Table 2. Experimental value of $E(s)$ for 100 runs and bound for $E(s)$, when number of nodes is $N = n(n-1)/2$ and keys per node is k

n	N	k	s	$E(s)(Experimental)$	$E(s)$(Theoretical Upper Bound)
30	435	56	10	0.3500	0.63
40	780	76	10	0.2510	0.3900
50	1225	96	10	0.1800	0.2417
60	1770	116	10	0.1314	0.1740
70	2415	136	10	0.07241	0.1382

5 A Second Design : Introducing New Sensor Nodes

In the previous design we saw that the size of the key pool is the same as the size of the network. Suppose we want to increase the size of the network, without adding new keys in the key pool. The design presented in this section augments the size of the network, keeping the same number of keys in each node. The keys in the key pool also remain the same. We show that network size can be increased in steps, keeping the same number of keys per node. However to ensure that any pair of nodes can communicate directly, we cannot go on adding nodes. We calculate the values of $E(s)$ and $V(s)$ when we double the size of the network. This design also uses triangular $PBIBD$. The main idea is to add new blocks to the existing $PBIBD$, thus increasing the number of sensor nodes.

5.1 Construction of the Network

We use triangular $PBIBD$ designs in the key predistribution scheme. We consider two triangular $PBIBD$ schemes [4, Page 18] with parameters

$$v', r', k', b', n_i', \lambda_i', (p_{jk}^i)'$$

and

$$v'', r'', k'', b'', n_i'', \lambda_i'', (p_{jk}^i)'' \ (i, j, k = 1, 2)$$

and having two identical association schemes. Then we can construct another triangular $PBIBD$ having the parameters

$$v = v' = v'', r = r' + r'', k = k' = k'', \ b = b' + b'',$$
$$\lambda_1 = \lambda_1' + \lambda_1'', \lambda_2 = \lambda_2' + \lambda_2'', \ n \geq 5.$$

We consider two $PBIBD$ schemes both having the same parameters:

$$v' = n(n-1)/2, b = n(n-1)/2, r' = 2(n-2), k' = 2(n-2),$$
$$\lambda_1' = n-2, \lambda_2' = 4.$$

The first association scheme results from the array A as given in Section 3, whereas the second $PBIBD$ has the association scheme resulting from the array

$$A' = \begin{array}{cccccc} * & 1 & n & \cdots & n(n-1)/2-2 & n(n-1)/2 \\ 1 & * & 2 & \cdots & \cdots & n(n-1)/2-1 \\ n & 2 & * & 3 & \cdots & n(n-1)/2-3 \\ \vdots & \vdots & \vdots & * & \vdots & \vdots \\ n(n-1)/2 & n(n-3)/2-1 & \cdots & \cdots & n-1 & * \end{array}$$

We can then construct a $PBIBD$ having $n(n-1)$ blocks each containing $2(n-2)$ elements. When we map this to a sensor network we arrive at a network having $n(n-1)$ sensor nodes. As an example we consider a network having 20 nodes. Apart from the ten blocks (here sensor nodes) constructed in Section 3, we add the following ten nodes having the following keys: $\{2,5,6,9,8,10\}$, $\{1,3,5,6,7,9\}$, $\{2,4,5,6,7,8\}$, $\{3,6,7,8,9,10\}$, $\{1,2,3,7,8,10\}$, $\{1,2,3,4,8,9\}$, $\{2,3,4,5,9,10\}$, $\{1,3,4,5,6,10\}$, $\{1,2,4,6,7,10\}$, $\{1,4,5,7,8,9\}$. Each of the nodes contains $2(n-2)$ keys.

Table 3. Experimental value of $V(s)$ for 100, when number of nodes is $N = n(n-1)$ and keys per node is k

n	N	k	s	$V(s)(Experimental)$
20	380	36	7	0.0400
30	870	56	10	0.0313
40	1560	76	10	0.0116
50	2450	96	10	0.0066
60	3540	116	10	0.0031
70	4830	136	10	0.0019

Table 4. Experimental value of $E(s)$ for 100 runs, when number of nodes is $N = n(n-1)$ and keys per node is k

n	N	k	s	$E(s)(Experimental)$
30	870	56	8	0.2043
40	1560	76	10	0.1855
50	2450	96	10	0.1174
60	3540	116	10	0.08942
70	4830	136	10	0.06742

We study the effect of node compromise on such a network. We give the experimental results for $V(s)$ and $E(s)$ for this network in Table 3 and Table 4 respectively. We observe that for networks of comparable sizes, the design given in Section 3 gives better results in terms of $E(s)$, however at the cost of more number of keys per node. This design also results in a network in which every pair of nodes share at least one common key. Thus all pairs of nodes can communicate directly, making communication faster. We can also add more nodes in the network in a recursive manner.

6 Comparison of Our Design with Existing Schemes

Our design fares better than the scheme discussed in [8] in terms of resiliency and connectivity. Our design ensures that every pair of nodes can communicate directly. In [8] communication between all nodes are not possible. We consider the example in [8]. For a network of containing 2401 nodes, any two nodes can communicate with each other with a probability of 0.6. However even for a network of larger size (containing 2415 nodes) our scheme results in cent percent connectivity of the network. Thus using our design communication will be faster and efficient, since decreasing the average path length for communication reduces time delays and minimizes errors. Secondly, we calculate the resiliency of our network based on two parameters $V(s)$ and $E(s)$ which have been discussed in Section 4. When we calculate the values of $E(s)$, we find that our design gives much better connectivity under node capture. This is because in our design initially every pair of nodes share more than one keys. So when nodes are compromised, the connectivity of the network is still very high. The Table compares the values of $E(s)$ for our approach and that given in [8] for networks of comparable sizes. We compare the values of $E(s)$ in Table 5 for different values of s for the following design schemes:

1. Our scheme I having a network consisting of 2415 nodes, each node containing 136 keys.
2. Our scheme II having a network consisting of 2450 nodes, each node containing 96 keys.
3. The scheme in [8] having a network consisting of 2209 nodes, each node containing 30 keys.

The improved connectivity and resiliency of our design comes at the cost of more number of keys per node. However, the number of keys is of the order of the size of the network as in [8].

Table 5. Comparison of the values of $E(s)$ of our schemes with those given in [8] for varying s

Scheme	$s = 2$	$s = 4$	$s = 6$	$s = 8$	$s = 10$
Our scheme I	0.0020	0.01316	0.0300	0.0536	0.0724
Our scheme II	0.0023	0.0190	0.0398	0.0718	0.1174
Scheme in [8]	0.4000	0.4469	0.4469	0.4687	0.4901

7 Conclusion

In this paper we discuss two key predistribution schemes. Both predistribution schemes are deterministic and are based on combinatorial objects called *PBIBD*. The most important feature of our design is that any pair of nodes can communicate with each other directly. This reduces the cost of communication and makes it faster and efficient. We also study the resiliency of the network under node compromise. Our results give better resilience that the prevailing designs. Also the number of keys per node is small, of the order of $\sqrt{N}$, where N

is the size of the network. Our second design is an extension of the first one. According to this design we can increase the size of the network, keeping the number of keys per node fixed. We can also use this design repeatedly. However, as one goes on increasing the number of nodes in the network, the probability that two nodes will still be able to communicate directly will decrease. In such cases, the resiliency will be adversely affected. One open problem will be to find the optimal size of the network (increased recursively) such that direct communication is possible between all pair of nodes. The network must be resilient at the same time. Though our design has keys per node equal to $O(\sqrt{N})$, this is quite large for small networks. It will be interesting to develop schemes which has fewer number of keys per node, not compromising the resiliency too much.

References

1. Camtepe, S.A., Yener, B.: Combinatorial design of key distribution mechanisms for wireless sensor networks. In: Samarati, P., Ryan, P.Y A, Gollmann, D., Molva, R. (eds.) ESORICS 2004. LNCS, vol. 3193, pp. 293–308. Springer, Heidelberg (2004)
2. Chan, H., Perrig, A., Song, D.: Random key predistribution schemes for sensor networks. In: IEEE Symposium on Security and Privacy, California (2003)
3. Chakrabarti, D., Maitra, S., Roy, B.K.: A key pre-distribution scheme for wireless sensor networks: merging blocks in combinatorial design. International Journal of Information Security 5(2), 105–114 (2006)
4. Clatworthy, W.H.: Tables of Two-Associate-Class Partially Balanced Designs. NBS Applied Mathematics Series, vol. 63 (1973)
5. Eschenauer, L., Gligor, V.D.: A key-management scheme for distributed sensor network. In: Proc. of the 9th ACM Conference on Computer and Communication Security, Washington D.C, pp. 41–47. ACM Press, New York (2002)
6. Gura, N., Patel, A., Wander, A., Eberle, H., Shantz, S.C.: Comparing elliptic curve cryptography and RSA on 8-bit CPUs. In: Joye, M., Quisquater, J.-J. (eds.) CHES 2004. LNCS, vol. 3156, pp. 119–132. Springer, Heidelberg (2004)
7. Liu, D., Ning, P.: Establishing pairwise keys in distributed sensor networks. In: Proc. of ACMCCS, pp. 52–61. ACM Press, New York, USA (2003)
8. Lee, J., Stinson, D.: A combinatorial approach to key predistribution for distributed sensor networks. In: IEEE Wireless Communications and Networking Conference (WCNC 2005), New Orleans, LA, USA (2005)
9. Street, A.P., Street, D.J.: Combinatorics of Experimental Design. Clarendon Press, Oxford (1987)

An Efficient ID-Based Authenticated Key Agreement Protocol with Pairings

Jai-Boo Oh, Eun-Jun Yoon, and Kee-Young Yoo[1,*]

Department of Computer Engineering, Kyungpook National University,
Daegu 702-701, South Korea
Tel.: 82-53-950-5553, Fax: 82-53-957-4846
Jboh0515@hotmail.com, ejyoon@infosec.knu.ac.kr, yook@knu.ac.kr

Abstract. In 2003, Shim proposed an efficient ID-based authenticated key agreement protocol based on Weil pairings [1]. Sun et al. raised the potential of a man-in-the-middle attack in [2]. In 2004, Ryu et al. proposed an efficient ID-based authenticated key agreement protocol from pairings [3]. In 2005, however, Boyd et al. noted security problems of Ryu et al.'s protocol in [4]. In 2005, Yuan et al. also pointed out the same weakness [5] in Ryu et al.'s protocol. Then, they proposed a new protocol that combines Ryu et al.'s protocol with Shim's protocol. In this paper, we demonstrate that Shim's protocol does not provide KGC forward secrecy, then we propose a more efficient and secure protocol which does provide such security. As a result, our protocol does not need an additional ECC point-addition unlike Yuan et al.'s protocol and our's can generate two secure session key to perform the secure message transmission.

Keywords: ID-based encryption, Key Agreement protocol, Bilinear Pairing.

1 Introduction

The key agreement is one of the fundamental cryptographic primitives which allow two or more entities to establish a shared secret key and agree upon a common session key for use in securing subsequent communication over an insecure channel. Thus, secure key agreement protocols are the basis for constructing secure and more complex protocols.

The pioneering work on key agreements was the Diffie-Hellman protocol. In their seminal paper [6], W. Diffie and M. Hellman proposed the public key cryptography and revolutionized the field of modern cryptography. Since their protocol, however, does not authenticate two parties, it was vulnerable to a man-in-middle attack by active adversaries who have control over the channel.

Recently, an identity-based (ID-based) approach has been the subject of much interest. One of the first feasible solutions for ID-based encryption was Boneh et al.'s scheme [7], which was based on the pairings on elliptic curves. Other ID-based key agreements based on this pairing technique have been suggested; in particular, Smart [8] proposed an ID-based authenticated key agreement protocol which combined

[*] Corresponding author.

I. Stojmenovic et al. (Eds.): ISPA 2007, LNCS 4742, pp.446–456,2007.

ideas from [9] and [10]. Shim, however, pointed out that this protocol does not provide full-forward-secrecy and her protocol was proposed in [1]. Sun et al., however, pointed out that Shim's protocol was susceptible to a man-in-the-middle attack in [2]. Since then, many protocols have been proposed [3], [11] and [12]. Recently Ryu et al. have put forth a new ID-based protocol in [3]. It is more efficient, and it requires only one pairing computation and two point-multiplication processes. Boyd et al. and Yuan et al.'s, however, have independently pointed out that Ryu et al.'s protocol can be the subject of a key compromise impersonation attack, which was described in [4] and key reveal attack have been identified in [13]. In this paper, we demonstrate that Shim's protocol does not provide KGC (Key Generation Center) forward secrecy. Then we propose a more efficient protocol. As a result, our protocol does not need an additional ECC point-addition unlike Yuan et al.'s protocol and it can generate two secure session keys to secure message transmission.

The rest of this paper is organized as follows: In Section 2, we describe definitions and parameters, and the security properties of the ID-based protocol. In Section 3, we briefly review previously proposed protocols. In Section 4, we outlined demonstrate the security of Shim's protocol. In Section 5, we propose a more efficient and secure protocol. In Section 6, we analyze our protocol. Finally, concluding remarks are presented in section 7.

2 Preliminaries

In this section, we refer to the basic definitions of the bilinear map, the Bilinear Diffie-Hellman Generator, and related computational problems which are used throughout this paper. Most of the results in this section come from [14, 15].

2.1 Bilinear Map

Let G_1 be an additive group of a large prime q and P be a generator of G_1. Let G_2 be a multiplicative group with the same order q. A pairing is map $\hat{e}$: $G_1 \times G_1 \rightarrow G_2$ which has the following properties:

(1) The map $\hat{e}$ is bilinearity: Given $Q, W, Z \in G_1$, we have

$$\hat{e}(Q, W + Z) = \hat{e}(Q, W)\, \hat{e}(Q, Z) \text{ and } \hat{e}(Q + W, Z) = \hat{e}(Q, Z)\, \hat{e}(W, Z)$$

Consequently, for any $a, b \in Z_q$:

$$\hat{e}(aQ, bW) = \hat{e}(Q, W)^{ab} = \hat{e}(abQ, W) = \hat{e}(Q, abW) = \hat{e}(bQ, W)^{a} = \hat{e}(bQ, aW).$$

(2) The map $\hat{e}$ is non-degenerate: If P is a generator of G_1, then $\hat{e}(P, P)$ is a generator of G_2. In other words, $\hat{e}(P, P) \neq 1$.

(3) The map $\hat{e}$ is efficiently computable. This map $\hat{e}$ is called an admissible pairing and it is symmetric because $\hat{e}$ has a bilinear property.

2.2 Related Hard Problems

Many pairing-based cryptographic protocols are based on the hardness of the BDHP for their security [7]. Other computational problems related to the elliptic curve discrete logarithm (ECDL) are as follows:

(1) **Discrete Logarithm Problem** (DLP)**:** Given two elements P, $Q \in G_1$, find an integer $a \in Z_q^*$, such that $Q = aP$, whenever such an integer exists.
(2) **Computational Diffie-Hellman Problem** (CDHP)**:** Given (P, aP, bP) for any a, $b \in Z_q^*$, compute abP.
(3) **Decisional Diffie-Hellman Problem** (DDHP)**:** Given (P, aP, bP, cP) for any a, b, $c \in_R Z_q^*$, decide whether $c = ab \bmod q$.

2.3 Security Attributes

A number of desirable security attributes have been identified. We refer to these attributes which were defined in [14]. In the following, we assume that A and B are two honest entities.

Known-key security. If one session key is compromised, this suould not affect the secrecy of other session keys, such as parallel sessions, previous sessions, and future sessions. Then, we can say the protocol provides a known-key security.

Forward secrecy. If the disclosure of the long-term private keys of one or more entities does affect the secrecy of previously established session keys, we can say that a protocol has partial forward secrecy. Perfect forward secrecy refers to the scenario when the long term private keys all of the participating entities are compromised.

Key compromise impersonation resilience. If a compromise of the long-term key of an entity A does not allow the Adv to masquerade as a different entity, protocol provides resistance to a key compromise impersonation.

Unknown key share resilience. An entity, A, should not be coerced into sharing a key with another entity, C, if A thinks it is actually sharing the key with B. In this situation, whenever entity A receives a message from C, it believes the message actually came from B.

3 Review of Previous Protocols

In this section, we briefly review recently-published literature regarding ID-based authenticated key agreement protocols. An ID-based key agreement protocol adopts the following ID-based encryption scheme concepts [7] which is specified by three randomized algorithms: Setup, key extract, and key agreement.

Setup: Let k be a security parameter. Let E be a super-singular curve defined by $y^2 = x^3 + 1$ over F_p. The algorithm works as follows:

(1) KGC runs randomized algorithm $\mathcal{G}$, which is a Bilinear Diffiee-Hellman (BDH) parameter generator on input k, which is a large k-bit prime such that $p = 2(\bmod 3)$ and $p = 6q - 1$ for some k-bit prime q, to generate output groups G_1 and G_2 with

a prime order q, a generator P of G_1, a bilinear map $\hat{e}$: $G_1 \times G_1 \rightarrow G_2$ and a master key $s \in Z_q^*$. KGC chooses an arbitrary point $P \in E/F_q$, with a prime order q. Then, it computes its public key $P_{PUB} = sP$.

(2) KGC chooses $H_1 : \{0, 1\}^* \rightarrow G_1$ that maps a message of arbitrary length into a non-zero point of G_1, as described in [8], and a key derivation function H which is typically a secure hash function.

(3) KGC publishes the system parameters *parms* = (p , q, G_1, G_2, E, P, P_{PUB}, H_1 H, $\hat{e}$) and secures the master-key s.

Extract: Taken as input system parameters, a master-key and an arbitrary $ID \in (0, 1)^*$ and a private key S_{ID} is returned for a given A's identity ID_A. The algorithm builds a private key S_A as follows:

(1) Use $MapToPoint_H$ to map ID_A to a point $Q_A \in E/F_P$ of order q.
(2) Set the private key S_A to be $S_A = sQ_A$, where s is the master-key.
(3) KGC sends S_A to A over a secure channel. Then, A accepts S_A as its private key.

Key agreement: Entities should be identified by the KGC and requests can be made to the KGC to issue a private key.

3.1 Shim's Protocol

Shim [1] proposed an ID-based, two-pass authenticated key agreement protocol based on the pairings as follows:

(1) A chooses $a \in Z_q^*$ at random, computes $T_A = aP$, and sends T_A to B.
(2) B chooses $b \in Z_q^*$ at random, computes $T_B = bP$, and sends T_B to A.
(3) A computes the shared security

$$K_{AB} = \hat{e}(aP_{pub} + S_A,\ T_B + Q_B).$$

(4) Similarly, B computes the shared security

$$K_{BA} = \hat{e}(T_A + Q_A,\ bP_{pub} + S_B).$$

(5) If both A and B follow the protocol, they can compute the same shared secret:

$$K_{AB} = K_{BA} = \hat{e}(P, P)^{abs}\ \hat{e}\ (P, Q_B)^{as}\ \hat{e}(Q_A, P)^{bs}\ \hat{e}(Q_A, Q_B)^s,$$

the session key is $H(A, B, K_{AB})$.

A		B
$a \in_R Z_q^*$	T_A →	
$T_A = aP$	← T_B	$b \in_R Z_q^*$
		$T_B = bP$
$K_{AB} = \hat{e}(aP_{pub} + S_A,\ T_B + Q_B)$		$K_{BA} = \hat{e}(T_A + Q_A,\ bP_{pub} + S_B)$

Fig. 1. Shim's Protocol

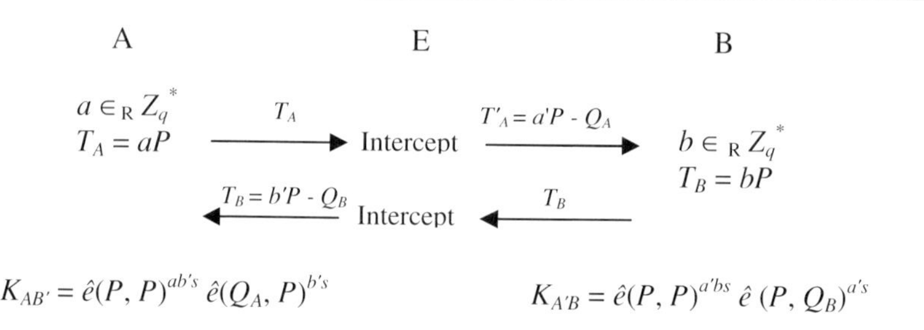

Fig. 2. Man in the middle Attack on Shim's Protocol

On this protocol, Sun et al. [12] pointed out the weakness of the man-in-the middle attack. The Adv intercepts T_A from A and T_B from B, and it sends $T'_A = a'P - Q_A$ to B and $T_B = b'P - Q_B$ to A, where a' and b' are selected value. Then, the Adv shares the secret

$$K_{AB'} = \hat{e}(P, P)^{ab's} \hat{e}(Q_A, P)^{b's} \text{ and } K_{A'B} = \hat{e}(P, P)^{a'bs} \hat{e}(P, Q_B)^{a's}.$$

3.2 Ryu et al.'s Protocol

Ryu et al.'s key agreement protocol [3], which followed the typical structure of an ID-based key agreement is as follows:

(1) A chooses $a \in Z_q^*$ at random, computes $T_A = aP$, and sends T_A to B.
(2) B chooses $b \in Z_q^*$ at random, computes $T_B = bP$, and sends T_B to A.
(3) A computes the session key

$$K_{AB} = H(A, B, a\,T_B, \hat{e}(S_A, Q_B))$$

and B computes

$$K_{BA} = H(A, B, bT_A, \hat{e}(Q_A, S_B)).$$

(4) If both A and B follow the protocol, they will compute the same session key

$$K_{AB} = K_{BA} = H(A, B, abP, \hat{e}(Q_A, Q_B)^s).$$

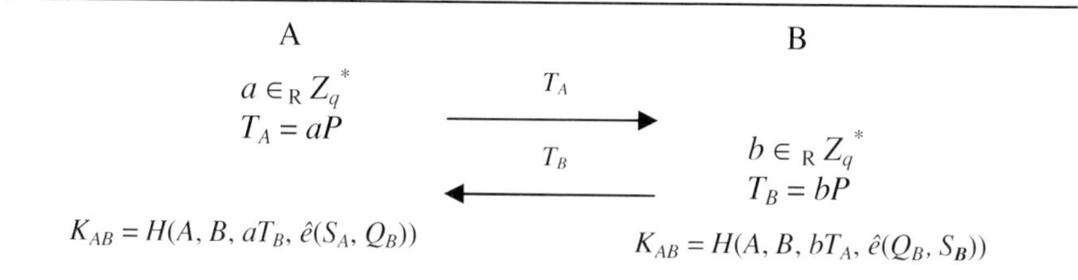

Fig. 3. Ryu et al.'s Protocol

For this protocol, Boyd et al. [4] pointed out a weakness against a key compromise impersonation attack [16] and a key reveal attack [13]. They did not propose a new scheme. That is, E knows A's long-term private key S_A and it impersonates B to A.

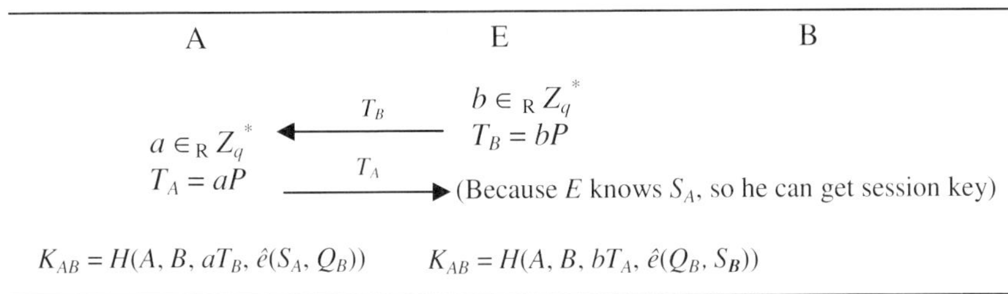

Fig. 4. Key Compromise Impersonation Attack on Ryu et al.'s Protocol

4 The KGC Forward Secrecy Problem of Shim's Protocol

In addition to Sun et al.'s attacks, Shim's protocol does not provide the KGC forward secrecy. The master key of the KGC is another secret that could become compromised. When this happens, it is clear that the long-term keys of all users will be compromised, but it is possible that a protocol can provide forward secrecy generally, but still give away old session keys if the master key becomes known. We will say that a protocol that retains confidentiality of session keys, even when the master key is known, provides the *KGC forward secrecy* [17].

Shim's protocol, however, did not provide the KGC forward secrecy. In Shim's protocol, the shared session key is

$$K_{AB} = K_{BA} = \hat{e}(P, P)^{abs}\, \hat{e}\,(P, Q_B)^{as}\, \hat{e}(Q_A, P)^{bs}\, \hat{e}(Q_A, Q_B)$$
$$= \hat{e}(saP, bP)\, \hat{e}(aP, sQ_B)\, \hat{e}(sQ_A, bP)\, \hat{e}(Q_A, Q_B)$$

In order to provide KGC forward secrecy, Shim's protocol must retain confidentiality even though the master key s is compromised. Suppose that the master key s is compromised. In Shim's protocol, Q_A and Q_B are public values and aP and bP are exchanged over an insecure channel. Therefore, the Adv can easily obtain these values from an open network. Finally, by using a master key s and (Q_A, Q_B, T_A, T_B), the Adv can obtain the shared session key between A and B by computing $\hat{e}(saP, bP)$,) $\hat{e}(aP, sQ_B)$, $\hat{e}(sQ_A, bP)$, $\hat{e}(Q_A, Q_B)$. Therefore, Shim's protocol does not provide KGC forward secrecy.

5 Proposed Protocol

In this section, we propose an ID-based key agreement protocol which is a more efficient and secure than Shim's, Ryu et al.'s and Yuan et al.'s. Our protocol can provide the level of secrecy which was suggested by Blake-Wilson et al. in [16].

The Setup and Extract process are same as the previous protocol. The Key Agreement protocol as follows.

(1) A chooses $a \in Z_q^*$ at random, computes $T_A = aP$, and sends T_A to B.
(2) B chooses $b \in Z_q^*$ at random, computes $T_B = bP$, and sends T_B to A.

(3) A computes the shared secret

$$K_{AB} = \hat{e}(aQ_B, P_{pub}) = \hat{e}(Q_B, P)^{as} \text{ or } K'_{AB} = \hat{e}(S_A, T_B) = \hat{e}(Q_A, P)^{bs}.$$

(4) B computes the shared secret

$$K_{BA} = \hat{e}(S_B, T_A) = \hat{e}(Q_B, P)^{as} \text{ or } K'_{BA} = \hat{e}(bQ_A, P_{pub}) = \hat{e}(Q_A, P)^{bs}.$$

(5) A and B compute two shared session keys

$$K = kdf\,(A, B, h, K_{AB}) = kdf\,(A, B, abP, K_{BA})$$

and

$$K' = kdf\,(A, B, h, K'_{AB}) = kdf\,(A, B, abP, K'_{BA}),$$

where kdf is a key derivation function.

The following procedure illustrates our improved scheme.

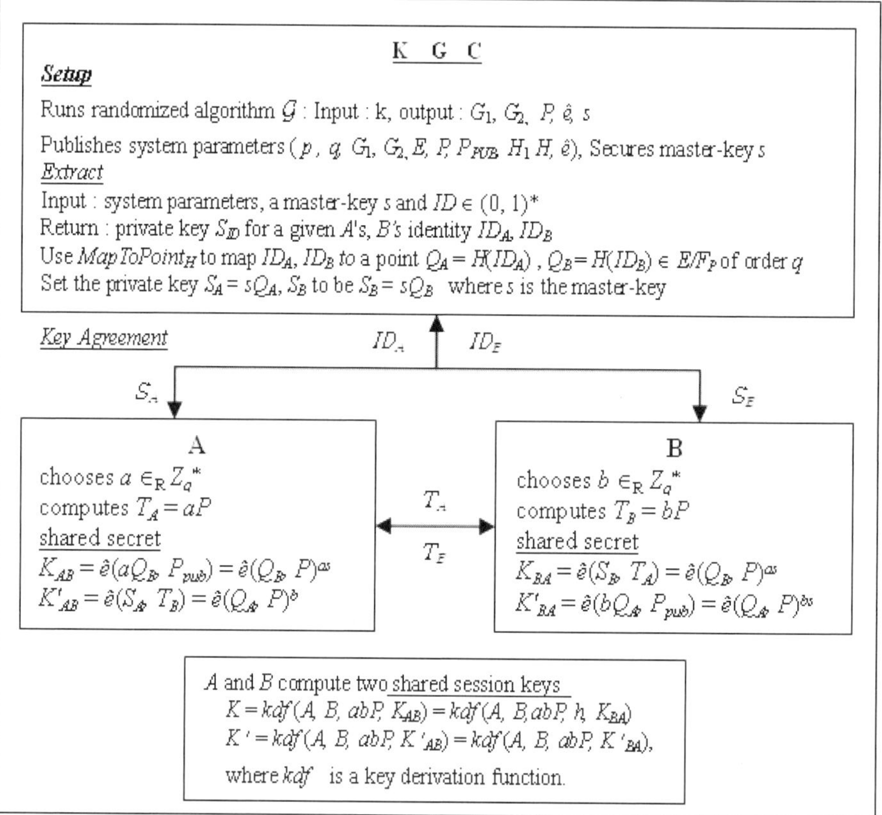

Fig. 5. Proposed ID-based authenticated key agreement protocol

6 An Analysis of the Efficiency and Security of the Proposed Protocol

In this section, we analyze the efficiency and security of the proposed protocol in accordance with the performance and security attributes defined in [16].

6.1 Efficiency

As summarized in Section 2, our protocol is role symmetric in that both communication entities execute the same operations. As shown in Table 1, we compare the efficiency of our protocol with each protocol regarding the number of parings, point-addition, point-multiplication and blocks. The process of these calculations is computationally an expensive one. Regarding the number of pairings, our protocol is more efficient than that of Smart's, Choie-Jeong-Lee's [11] and McCullagh-Barreto's [12]. Regarding blocks, our protocol needs only one large data block exchange in comparison with Chen-Kudla's protocol [17]. Although our protocol is not as efficient as Shim's and Ryu et al.'s in terms of the number of point-multiplications, we use only one more point-multiplication to make up for these flaws. Finally, concerning point-addition, our protocol is more efficient than Yuan et al.'s protocol, because our protocol does not need the extra point-addition that Yuan et al. does.

Table 1. A comparison of protocol efficiency

Protocol	Weakness	P	A	M	B
Smart [8]	Forward secrecy	2	1	2	1
Shim [1]	Man-in-the-middle attack, KGC Forward secrecy	1	2	2	1
Chen-Kudla [17]	-	1	1	4	2
Choie-Jeong-Lee 1 [11]	-	2	0	3	2
Choie-Jeong-Lee 2 [11]	-	2	0	4	1
Ryu-Yoon-Yoo [3]	Key compromise impersonate, Key reveal attack	1	0	2	1
McCullagh-Barreto [12]	Key compromise impersonate, Key reveal attack	1	1	2	1
Yuan-Li [5]	-	1	2	3	1
Our Proptocol	-	1	0	3	1

* P = Pairing, A = Point-Addition, M = Point-Multiplication, B = Blocks.

6.2 Security

We can verify that the proposed protocol provides secrecy described in Section 2.3 security attributes and sugessted in recently literatures.

Passive attack: If an Adv is able to compute the keyed point $abP \in G_1$ using only information obtained over a public channel, the other two points $T_A = aP$ and $T_B = bP \in G_1$, then Adv can also solve the CDHP in G_1. This is exactly an instance of the

CDH problem in G_1. Therefore, we can claim that our protocol is secure against a passive attack, because the CDH problem in G_1 is hard.

Man-in-the-middle attack: If the Adv wants to implement a man-in-the-middle attack, Adv replaces $T_A = aP$ with $a'P$ and substitutes $T_B = bP$ with $b'P$, Then $K_{AB'} = \hat{e}(aQ_B, P_{pub}) = \hat{e}(Q_B, P)^{as} = \hat{e}(sQ_B, aP)$. If the Adv computes the value of $K_{AB'}$, it must know b', aP , and S_B or asP. But the Adv only knows b' and aP, so it can't computes $\hat{e}(sQ_B, aP)$. If the Adv can compute S_B or asP from aP, bP , it must be broken the CDH problem.

Key reveal attack: Proposed protocol does not contain asymmetry in the formation of the session key. Therefore, we can avoid key reveal attack because K_{AB} has some asymmetry between a and b.

Known key security: Each run of the protocol computes a unique session key that depends on the ephemeral private keys a and b. If the Adv knows other session keys, it also needs to computer abP, this is the CDH problem. There does not appear to be any easier way for it to carry out an expensive brute-force attack. This means it can't gain any more information from other session keys.

Forward secrecy: If the long-term private key S_A or S_B is compromised, previous established session key $K = kdf(A, B, h, K_{BA})$ is not affected. This is because the Adv also needs to compute abP from aP and bP, which is the CDH problem. Even though two private keys S_A and S_B are compromised, the Adv also needs to compute abP from aP and bP. Our protocol, therefore, provides full-forward-secrecy.

KGC forward secrecy: If the KGC's secret s is compromised at any stage, this should not compromise the previously established session keys. In this case, the Adv must derive $h = abP$ from (s, T_A, T_B, Q_A, Q_B) to compute a session key. From the given Parameters, to derive h is CDH problem. Then, the proposed protocol provides KGC forward secrecy.

Key compromise impersonation: We assume that the Adv knows A's private key S_A. If the Adv wishes to impersonate B and sends messages to A, it chooses $b \in Z_q^*$, and sends bP to A. The Adv receives $T_A = aP$ from A. Then the Adv knows S_A, aP and bP. From this the Adv can compute the first secret $\hat{e}(Q_B, P)^{as} = \hat{e}(sQ_B, aP) = \hat{e}(S_B, aP)$, but it can't compute the second secret $\hat{e}(Q_A, P)^{bs}$. On the other hand, if the Adv knows B's private key S_B, it can compute the second secret, but it can't compute the first secret. Regardless though the Adv computes a secret values, it can't compute $h = aT_B = abP$, which is the CDH problem.

Unknown key share: We use A's public key Q_A, or B's public key Q_B to compute a session keys. So, we are able to know who shares the session key with us.

Imperfect key control: None of the entities can decide the key separately. Thus, we must note that one entity will receive the key component of another party. One party receives peer's key component material earlier than another [18]. The entity who receives these materials later has an unfair advantage in terms of controlling the value of the shared session key. Therefore, each protocol examined in this paper does not possess full key control, as mentioned in [17].

7 Conclusions

In this paper, we demonstrated that Shim's protocol does not provide KGC forward secrecy. Then, we proposed a more efficient and secure ID-based key agreement protocol which does provide KGC forward secrecy. As a result, our protocol does not need an additional ECC point-addition unlike Yuan et al.'s protocol and it is able to generate two secure session keys in order to secure message transmission.

Acknowledgement

This work was supported by Grant No. R01-2006-000-10614-0 from the Basic Research Program of the Korea Science & Engineering Foundation.

References

1. Shim, K.: Effient ID-based authenticated key agreement protocol based on the Weil pairing. Electron. Lett. 39(8), 653–654 (2003)
2. Sun, H., Hsieh, B.: Security Analysis of Shim's Authenticated Key agreement Protocols from Pairings. Cryptology ePrint Archive, Report 2003/113 (2003), http://eprint.iacr.org/2003/113
3. Ryu, E., Yoon, E., Yoo, K.: An Efficient ID-Based Authenticated Key Agreement Protocol. In: Mitrou, N.M., Kontovasilis, K., Rouskas, G.N., Iliadis, I., Merakos, L. (eds.) NETWORKING 2004. LNCS, vol. 3042. Springer, Heidelberg (2004)
4. Boyd, C., Choo, K.: Security of Two-Party Identity-Based Key Agreement. In: Dawson, E., Vaudenay, S. (eds.) Mycrypt 2005. LNCS, vol. 3715, pp. 229–243. Springer, Heidelberg (2005)
5. Yuan, Q., Li, S.: A New Efficient ID-based Authenticated Key Agreement Protocol. Cryptology ePrint Archive, Report 2005/309 (2005), http://eprint.iacr.org/2005/309
6. Diffie, W., Hellman, M.: New Directions in Cryptography. IEEE Transaction on Information Theory IT-22(6), 644–654 (1976)
7. Boneh, D., Franklin, M.: Identity-based encryption from the Weil pairing. In: Kilian, J. (ed.) CRYPTO 2001. LNCS, vol. 2139, pp. 213–229. Springer, Heidelberg (2001)
8. Smart, N.P.: An identity based authenticated key agreement protocol based on the Weil pairing. Electronics Letters 38, 630–632 (2002)
9. Joux, A.: A one-round protocol for tripartite Diffie-Hellman. In: Bosma, W. (ed.) Algorithmic Number Theory. LNCS, vol. 1838, pp. 385–394. Springer, Heidelberg (2000)
10. Menezes, A., Qu, M., Solinas, J., Vanstone, S.: Some new key agreement protocols providing mutual implicit authentication. In: proceedings of the second workshop on Selected Area in Cryptography, pp. 22–32 (1995)
11. Choie, Y., Jeong, E., Lee, E.: Efficient identity-based authenticated key agreement protocol from pairings. Applied Mathematics and Computation 162, 179C188 (2005)
12. McCullagh, N., Barreto, P.S.L.M.: A New Two-Party Identity-Based Authenticated Key Agreement. Cryptology ePrint Archive, Report 2004/122 (2004). In: Proceeding of CT-RSA 2005, http://eprint.iacr.org/2004/122
13. Bellare, M., Rogaway, P.: Entity Authentication and Key Distribution. In: Stinson, D.R. (ed.) CRYPTO 1993. LNCS, vol. 773, pp. 110C125. Springer, Heidelberg (1994)

14. Blake, I., Seroussi, G., Smart, N.: Elliptic curve in cryptography. Cambridge University Press, Cambridge (1999)
15. Al-Riyami, S.S.: Cryptographic Schemes based on Elliptic Curve Pairings. Ph.D Thesis, University of London (2004)
16. Blake-Wilson, S., Johnson, D., Menezes, A.d.: Key Agreement Protocols and their Security Analysis. In: Darnell, M. (ed.) Cryptography and Coding. LNCS, vol. 1355, pp. 30C45. Springer, Heidelberg (1997)
17. Chen, L., Kudla, C.: Identity based authenticated key agreement protocols from pairings. Cryptology ePrint Archive, Report 2002/184 (2002), available at http://eprint.iacr.org/2002/184/
18. Mitchell, C., Ward, M., Wilson, P.: Key control in key agreement protocols. Electronics Letters 34(10), 980–981 (1998)

Leveraging Many Simple Statistical Models to Adaptively Monitor Software Systems*

Mohammad Ahmad Munawar and Paul A.S. Ward

Shoshin Distributed Systems Group
Department of Electrical and Computer Engineering
University of Waterloo, Waterloo, Ontario N2L 3G1, Canada
{mamunawa,pasward}@shoshin.uwaterloo.ca

Abstract. Self-managing systems require continuous monitoring to ensure correct operation. Detailed monitoring is often too costly to use in production. An alternative is adaptive monitoring, whereby monitoring is kept to a minimal level while the system behaves as expected, and the monitoring level is increased if a problem is suspected. To enable such an approach, we must model the system, both at a minimal level to ensure correct operation, and at a detailed level, to diagnose faulty components. To avoid the complexity of developing an explicit model based on the system structure, we employ simple statistical techniques to identify relationships in the monitored data. These relationships are used to characterize normal operation and identify problematic areas.

We develop and evaluate a prototype for the adaptive monitoring of J2EE applications. We experiment with 29 different fault scenarios of three general types, and show that we are able to detect the presence of faults in 80% of cases, where all but one instance of non-detection is attributable to a single fault type. We are able to shortlist the faulty component in 65% of cases where anomalies are observed.

Keywords: Self-managing systems, adaptive monitoring, root-cause analysis.

1 Introduction

Enterprise software systems are mission critical. They are required to operate without failure, around the clock, with an acceptable level of service. Failure is expensive, leading to loss of sales, customer dissatisfaction, penalties for failing to meet service-level agreements, *etc*. However, as software is not perfect and fault-protection mechanisms are not always present, system failures occur. The major manifestations of failure are unavailable systems, exceptions and access violations, incorrect answers, data loss and corruption, and poor performance [1].

Businesses address this problem by having administrators/operators actively monitor this critical infrastructure, identifying system failures, diagnosing the faulty component(s), and restoring the system to a correctly functioning state.[1] Software systems

* Supported in part by an IBM Centre of Advanced Studies (CAS), Toronto PhD fellowship.

[1] As of 2004 there were approximately 900,000 such administrators in America, with that number expected to grow 30% by 2014 [2], making this a $100 billion solution.

I. Stojmenovic et al. (Eds.): ISPA 2007, LNCS 4742, pp. 457–470, 2007.

increasingly offer a large amount and variety of monitoring data to aid in this task, including log records, management extensions, performance metrics, *etc.* Despite the availability of this information, or perhaps because of it, effectively managing these systems is still very challenging, with 40% of system failures attributable to operator mistakes [3] and a further 40% to software [1,3]. While in principle the availability of logs and monitoring data can help in identifying failures and finding their causes, in practice faults are often hard to diagnose quickly in a sea of data. A solution to this problem is to have the system continuously self-monitor, analyze the collected data, and only report when some aspect of the system's operation fails or is going to fail. In this work we mainly deal partial system failures whereby one of more parts (components) fails while the rest of the system continues to function in line with the expectation.

The level of monitoring used in production systems is often insufficient to effectively detect and diagnose faulty components, and increasing it is deemed too costly to collect [4,5] and analyze [6]. An alternative solution is to mimic expert administrator behaviour, and monitor a small set of important information, collecting additional information only when it is deemed necessary [7]. By reducing monitoring, we not only reduce the adverse effect of measurement on system performance, but also diminish the overhead associated with storing, transmitting, analyzing, and reporting information. In this paper we present our approach for such adaptive monitoring of J2EE applications. We model the system both at a minimal level, to ensure correct operation, and at a detailed level, to diagnose faulty components. We demonstrate the effectiveness of our approach through a prototype and fault-injection experiments.

The remainder of this paper is organized as follows: In Section 2 we provide some background on enterprise software systems, especially on J2EE and describe related prior work. In Section 3 we present our method in detail and evaluate it experimentally.

2 Background and Related Work

Large enterprise applications are often developed using standardized component frameworks such as .Net [8] and J2EE [9]. These frameworks provide common services such as transactions, remote communication, data persistence, *etc.* and offer features to make applications scale. A typical application consists of many components that leverage facilities offered by the underlying framework. For example, a typical J2EE business application would comprise Servlets and Java Server Pages (JSPs) to handle the presentation logic, session Enterprise Java Beans (EJBs) to deal with the business logic, entity EJBs to manage data persistence, *etc.* In this paper we focus on the J2EE platform, though we believe our approach can work in other component-based software systems.

Most J2EE servers can be monitored using the standardized Java Management eXtensions (JMX) interface [10]. Typically, very detailed information is available. Each component may expose data related to its activity, failures, and performance. Collecting this data, however, is not free. The cost varies with the amount of data and the rate at which it is collected. In WebSphere Application Server version 6, which we use in our experiments, the overhead caused by continuously collecting all the JMX data can reach 25% of total execution time [5]. This is unacceptable on a permanent basis in a production environment, which is which is why we recently proposed adaptive monitoring of enterprise software systems [7].

Adaptive monitoring requires three key mechanisms: the ability to control collection of data, a basis for deciding what to collect when, and algorithms for detecting presence of faults and diagnosis. Recently, much work has taken place on mechanisms for adaptive monitoring (*e.g.*, [10,11,12]). Our work simply uses one such mechanism (*viz.* JMX) and focuses instead on the remaining two problems. In a separate work [13] we have looked at integrating data from different sources for problem determination.

Current solutions to fault detection and diagnosis in enterprise software systems use some form of statistics and/or machine learning, differing according to their specific objectives and the degree of system knowledge and instrumentation required. For example, some focus on performance issues and violations of service-level objectives [14,15], rather than the more-general problem determination. Kiciman and Fox [16] address the diagnosis problem, but do so by capturing execution paths of normal transactions and detecting deviations from the typical patterns. In general we have found that most prior approaches assume that detailed monitoring is always enabled, which is not, as we have noted, feasible in a production environment.

Our work makes use of statistical correlation among metrics of the system. These correlations may either reflect cause-and-effect dependencies between components or arise because of shared causes. Brown *et al.* [17] use correlations to infer dependencies between components under perturbance. Hauswirth *et al.* [18] leverage correlation information directly to investigate causes of problems. Recently, Agarwal *et al.* [19] described how correlation among change points in different metrics can allow the creation of problem signatures. These works are based on the idea that faults induce correlations. Analyzing these correlations to localize faulty components requires that all metrics of interest be always monitored. When faults occur, unexpected correlations could help diagnose faulty components. Our approach takes the complementary view that such correlations exist in a well-behaved system. These correlations may be disturbed when faults occur. With this approach all metrics need not be monitored all the time; the relevant ones can be collected when needed to ensure that their correlations still hold.

The existence of many linear relationships between pairs of metrics in transaction-oriented software systems was reported in our previous work [7] as well as by Jiang *et al.* [20]. Both these works proposed the use of these relationships for fault detection and diagnosis. Our work differs from that of Jiang *et al.* in our focus on adaptive monitoring and our study of diagnosis in this context. We consider monitoring overhead while still allowing for effective problem determination. Jiang *et al.* emphasize fault detection and assume the continuous availability of arbitrary monitoring data. Our use of simple linear regression allows for models that are easily interpreted. Jiang *et al.* employ Auto-Regressive models with eXogenous inputs (ARX), which, though more general, may not be intuitive (*e.g.*, negative parameters) and may be less efficient (*e.g.*, determining best order). In our experiments we use more fine-grained monitoring data which includes several hundred metrics from the Application Server alone. This data contains response-time metrics, which are ignored by Jiang *et al.* Finally, Jiang *et al.* proposed a technique for diagnosis without evaluating its accuracy. We present an experimental assessment of the effectiveness of our diagnosis approach.

3 Our Approach

Our approach to adaptive monitoring consists of three phases: model building (MB), minimal monitoring (MM), and problem determination (PD). In the MB phase, a model of normal system behaviour is learned. During the MM phase, the target system is overseen at a high level. Finally, in the PD phase, the scope of monitoring is changed to permit diagnosis of faulty components. Algorithm 1 presents a high-level description of our approach.

```
begin ModelBuilding
    Collect data
    Find correlated pairs of metrics
    For each pair, estimate parameters of LR models
    Collect data
    Test models and retain the robust ones
end
begin Monitoring
    mode := MINIMAL_MONITORING
    while true do
        switch mode do
            case MINIMAL_MONITORING
                Monitor a small set of low-overhead metrics
                if anomaly detected then
                    Increase monitoring
                    mode := PROBLEM_DETERMINATION
            case PROBLEM_DETERMINATION
                Use LR models to find outliers
                if models reported outliers then
                    foreach metric in models reporting outliers do
                        Compute anomaly score
                Rank metrics and components
                Report diagnosis
                if monitoring level = maximum or diagnosis remains unchanged then
                    Stop using LR models to find outliers
                    Decrease monitoring
                    mode := MINIMAL_MONITORING
end
```

Algorithm 1. High-level pseudo-code of our approach

The target system consists of many components. Each components is associated with one or more metrics. The continuous collection of these metrics at runtime generates time series data. Model building entails learning models of normal behaviour using these series. We consider departures from the behaviour predicted by the models to be anomalies. Two types of models are considered in this work: single-metric models and multiple-metrics models. Our single-metric models consist of static and dynamic thresholds which are meant to detect significant departures from the behaviour seen in the recent past. These models act as triggers to enable the more-detailed multiple-metrics models. Modeling metrics individually is difficult because they often are non-linear. Our multiple-metrics models are based on the idea that there exist simple relationships among metrics of the system which are easier to characterize. For example, the number of requests received at an Internet server may be highly correlated with the number of worker-threads activated. A simple linear regression (LR) model would easily model this relationship. When two such metrics are affected by a shared disturbance (*e.g.*, a cron job), the model may factor out the latter's effect. This obviates the need for the model to represent the potentially non-linear factor. Our detailed monitoring leverages many such simple LR models, which can automatically be derived from the monitoring data.

During the MM phase, only a small set of metrics is overseen. Our choice of metrics in this set is motivated by four factors: first, metrics in this set are affected by a large class of internal components so as to detect a broad range of problems; second, these metrics are directly relevant to users' perception of service; third, these metrics are not expensive to measure and collect; fourth, we presume that problems that do not affect them are not pressing enough to warrant further investigation. For example, in our experiments we choose to monitor the time taken to deliver pages to users and the number of failures encountered in doing so. When an anomaly is detected during the MM phase, monitoring is increased to help diagnose faulty components. The logic for augmenting monitoring is based on the learned LR models, *i.e.*, we enable collection of all or a subset of metrics associated with these models. Newly collected data allows us to determine which LR models report outliers. Metrics pertaining to such models constitute valuable information for diagnosis purposes.

In this work we consider two approaches to the adaptation of monitoring: (1) stepwise increase, and (2) immediate increase to all metrics associated with any LR model. The stepwise approach consists of considering metrics that are associated with models reporting outliers in the previous step and increasing monitoring such that metrics correlated with them are collected. This cycle continues until either the maximum level of monitoring is reached or the diagnosis stops changing. In the immediate-increase approach, this condition is immediately met when monitoring is increased. In general, stepwise increase is required when the cost of monitoring all metrics is high. Conversely, immediate increase is preferred when the cost of monitoring all metrics is acceptable, provided it is infrequent.

3.1 Diagnosing Faulty Components

Every metric pertains to some component of the target system. The outcome of model building is to associate each metric with zero or more other metrics via the LR models. To narrow down on faulty components we compute an anomaly score α_m for each metric m thus:

$$\alpha_m = \frac{|O(m)|}{|M(m)|} \tag{1}$$

where $M(m)$ is the set of LR models in which metric m is a variable and $O(m) \subseteq M(m)$ is the subset of $M(m)$ models which report outliers. We rank the metrics by their anomaly score, allowing us to shortlist components that are most-believed to be at fault. A component that fails will cause many of its related metrics to misbehave, which makes it rank high. One important advantage of this approach is that information from different metrics is corroborated to reduce the likelihood of a wrong diagnosis.

3.2 Detecting Outliers with Linear-Regression Models

For each LR model, we compute the regression model parameters during the MB phase. When anomalies are detected in the MM phase, we enter the PD phase whereby the LR models are used to assess the observed behaviour. For each new sample, we compute the DFFITS [21] diagnostic to detect outliers. $DFFITS$ estimates the level of change in prediction with or without incorporating a new sample.

$$DFFITS = \frac{\hat{y}_i - \hat{y}_{(i)}}{s_{(i)}\sqrt{h_{(i)}}} \quad (2)$$

where $\hat{y}_i$ is the predicted value with the ith observation, $\hat{y}_{(i)}$ is the predicted value without the ith observation, $s_{(i)}$ is the standard deviation of the residual without the ith observation, and $h_{(i)}$ is the leverage of point i. The *leverage* of a point is a measure of the latter's influence, and it indicates distance of the point to the mean of the predictor variable. If $DFFITS > MAX\_DFFITS$, the observation is considered to be influential and an outlier is reported. We have found $DFFITS$ to be more robust than prediction with confidence intervals and the Student's t-test.

3.3 Identifying Robust Linear-Regression Models

Our approach presumes that faults do not occur during the MB phase, otherwise their effects become part of the learned behaviour. Model building includes two activities: identifying correlated metrics and models testing. Part of the data collected during the MB phase is used for the first activity while the rest is applied to the second. During models testing, all models of pairs of correlated metrics are checked to see if they report outliers when the system operates without faults. All models which report outliers are discarded. The two important parameters here are: the minimum required statistical correlation coefficient (MIN_R) and the minimum percentage of observations for which a model should not report outliers during the testing period (MIN_VALID). The lower these values are, the more correlated pairs we retain. However, many of these correlations may be spurious and thus may limit the accuracy of the diagnosis. Conversely, too high values will lead to fewer models, and thus limit our ability to pin down faulty components.

4 Experimental Evaluation

We have developed a prototype that implements the proposed approach. Our experimental setup (shown in Figure 1) consists of a DB2 UDB 8.2 database server, a WebSphere 6 Application Server (WAS), a workload generator, and the monitoring engine. We use the Trade application benchmark [22], which implements an online stock-brokerage system, running on WAS and with a DB2 backend as our system to be monitored. Trade is a J2EE application comprising standard components such as Servlets, JSPs and EJBs.

4.1 Monitoring Engine

The monitoring engine uses JMX to collect data from WAS. The JMX interface enables individual metric collection. Prior to the MB phase, the engine collects all available metrics for a short period. With this data, it filters out metrics whose values do not change (*e.g.*, a metric reflecting a static configuration parameter) and metrics which can

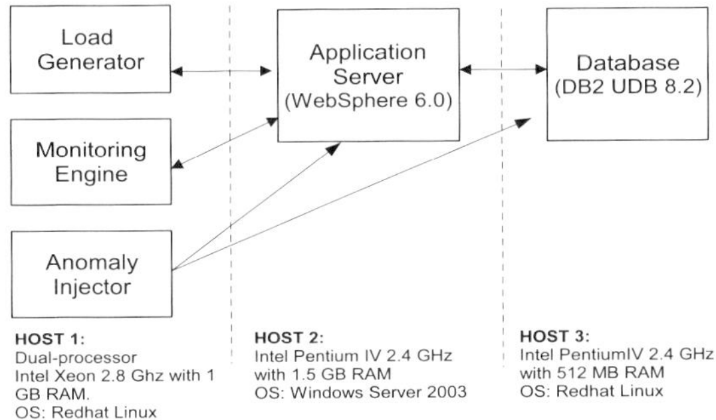

Fig. 1. Experimental Setup

be determined to be redundant using naming conventions (*e.g.*, a metric that is simply the sum of two other metrics). In our experiments up to 1900 metrics are available before filtering, which reduces it to an average of 380. The ensuing MB phase further reduces this number to roughly 280. These metrics cover an average of 30 different components. During MM phase, an average of 45 metrics are collected.

4.2 Models Calibration

4.2.1 Thresholds for Minimal Monitoring

In the Trade application web pages are the only interface through which users interact with the system. During the MM phase, the monitoring engine oversees two types of metrics relating to these web pages: failure and response time statistics. We use different thresholding schemes for each type. Setting thresholds is difficult. If the threshold is set to too low, it may be easily violated even without a fault. This will cause an unnecessary increase in the monitoring level, slowing down the target system. Conversely, if the threshold is too high, then we may not detect that a failure has occurred. We have taken an empirical approach to setting these thresholds, *i.e.*, we determine these by experimenting with different values and opting for ones that give a good trade-off between the ability to detect presence of faults and false alarms. In practice, values for these thresholds will depend on the requirements for the particular system being monitored and preferences of those administering it.

We use a static threshold for the rate of failures in web pages, which represents the maximum ratio of failed requests to the total number of requests serviced during a sampling interval. This threshold was set to 0.01 for all pages. For response time statistics we use dynamic thresholds because response time metrics vary with the load in the system. These thresholds try to detect any abrupt changes in response time when compared to recent observations which were considered normal. We compare the mean and the variance of a newly observed sample with a window of past mean and variance values representing normal behaviour. Such a window allows us to accommodate slowly drifting values, which may be the result of shifting load. Each comparison with a sample statistics in a window slot provides a vote as to whether the just observed sample has a different distribution. The latter is determined by computing the effect size (Cohen's d [23]):

$$d = \frac{\mu_w - \mu_n}{s_w} \quad (3)$$

where μ_w and s_w are the mean and standard deviation of a sample in a window slot respectively, and μ_n is the mean of the newly observed sample. We set a maximum threshold on d at 0.8, which is considered to be a large effect [23]. If $d \geq 0.8$, an anomaly is likely and we record this information; after three consecutive such occurrences, an anomaly is reported. On the other hand, if $d < 0.8$ for the majority of the window slots, it is added to the window of normal entries, dropping the oldest observation if the window is full. We have found a window size of 5 to work well in our experiments. In practice, the right value for this parameter will depend on the load pattern typically experienced for the target system.

To further increase robustness, violation of the above thresholds (failure and response time) are reported only if they repeat in three consecutive samples.

4.2.2 Linear-Regression Models for Detailed Monitoring

For model building, we fixed MIN_R to 0.8, which is generally considered to indicate a strong association between two variables. We experimentally determined adequate levels for MAX_DFFITS and MIN_VALID. To mark an observation as outlier for any LR model, we set MAX_DFFITS to 3, which is slightly less conservative than the generally suggested cut-off of 2 [24]. As for MIN_VALID, with a high value, we tend to identify very strong correlations, mostly involving metrics representing activity levels such as number of requests executed in dependent components, while ignoring response time metrics. However, correlation between response time-based metrics do exist, though they are noisier. For example, often a method of a component contributes to the bulk of the response time of a transaction; this combined with the fact that reported response time metrics are often cumulative result in many correlations. In order to keep the strong correlations between activity metrics and at the same time leverage the noisier response time metrics, we opted for two separate thresholds for MIN_VALID. We accept LR models of response time metrics if $MIN\_VALID_t \geq 90\%$ and LR models of other types of metrics if $MIN\_VALID_o \geq 95\%$ during models testing. Among the combinations we tried, this produced the best tradeoff between false positives and diagnosis accuracy.

4.3 Fault Injection

We devised a number of fine-grained probabilistic faults. Examples of faults we developed include emitting exceptions inside components, executing busy loops to delay requests, emulating thread unavailability via sleep, locking database tables, leaking connections to the database, *etc*. In this paper we only report experiments with three types of faults, namely: exceptions thrown on purpose within JSPs and EJBs, deliberate execution of busy loops inside the same components, and locking of database tables to which *entity beans* of the Trade application are mapped.

The logic for the exception and loop-based faults is embedded inside the benchmarking application. In order to inject faults, we specify the component name, the maximum number of occurrences, a probability of occurrence, and magnitude information (*e.g.*,

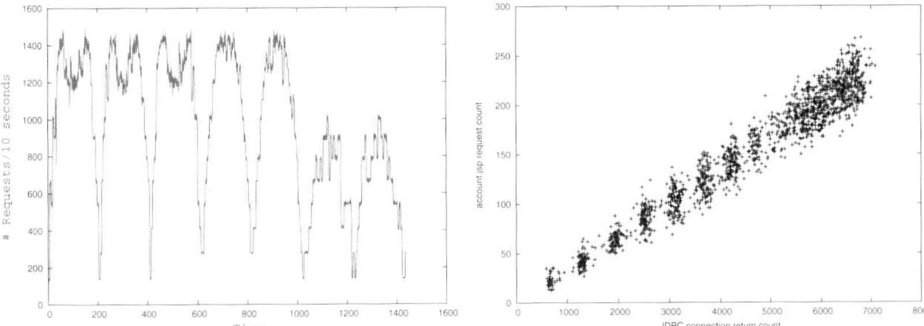

Fig. 2. (a) Example of workload pattern (b) Example of correlation between requests to a page and database connections returned

duration of a loop execution). The table-locking module is a stand-alone application that directly connects to the database. It requires a table name and a periodic trigger interval. The table-locking module itself is enabled for a specified lapse of time during which it alternates between periods in which it locks and unlocks a table.

4.4 Experiments

All our experiments use a workload that mimics day-of-the-week cycles as well as some level of random variations (See Figure 2(a)). Such a pattern reflects a typical load on business-oriented Internet services (See, *e.g.*, [25]). We have implemented a custom closed-loop load generator to emulate the described pattern. Figure 2(b) shows one example of a correlated pair of metrics found in the monitoring data collected while applying such a load. In this example the number of requests completed for the page `account.jsp` are plotted against the number of JDBC connections returned to the connection pool.

4.4.1 Adaptive Monitoring and Overhead

In our experiments the stepwise increase approach to adaptive monitoring was less effective than the immediate increase one. The main reason was the absence of metrics in the minimal monitoring metrics set that could provide the linkage for increasing monitoring for a wide range of fault scenarios. For example, all requests to the application are executed by invoking a single Servlet. These requests differ according to the parameters passed with them. Unfortunately, the available JMX data does not contain sufficiently fine-grained statistics to distinguish between requests according to their parameter names. In the future we plan to add instrumentation to collect this information. For this paper we present results using the immediate increase approach.

Our prototype operates in either the minimal-monitoring or the detailed-monitoring mode (*i.e.*, enabling all metrics associated with LR models). We ran several experiments to assess the overhead involved in operating in these mode. Each experiment runs for 35 minutes during which the target system is subject to a simulated load. In order to remove any transient effects, we discard the first 12 minutes of the gathered data and only

Table 1. Effect of Monitoring on CPU Utilization and Throughput

	CPU Utilization (%)		Throughput (requests/second)	
Monitoring Level	*Mean*	*Std. Dev.*	*Mean*	*Std. Dev.*
None	42.83	8.45	28.06	4.44
Minimal	44.45	7.57	28.29	2.51
Detailed	54.72	7.26	26.97	3.80

consider 15 minutes of the data thereafter. Since we use a closed-loop workload generator, we report both the impact on CPU utilization of the application server machine and throughput of the application. Table 1 shows the average periodic CPU utilization and throughput sampled at 10-seconds intervals. We observe that minimal monitoring causes little overhead and is thus likely acceptable for continuous operation in production. By contrast, detailed monitoring significantly affects CPU utilization and reduces throughput. As such, detailed monitoring would adversely impact performance, and thus, requires limited use. These results are consistent with data reported in the literature [5].

4.4.2 Anomaly Experiments

We now evaluate our approach by injecting faults in a running system and assessing the ability to detect presence of faults and accuracy of diagnosis. In each experiment, we inject a single type of fault in one component. Throughout all our experiments, the target system is subjected to a simulated load and the monitoring data it provides is collected for analysis. Unless stated otherwise, each experiment described below consists of a warm-up period of 5 minutes, a models learning period of 15 minutes, a models testing period of 7.5 minutes, a waiting period of approximately 7 minutes, a maximum fault activation period of 3 minutes and a 10-minute fault-free period. After models testing, the system enters the MM phase. When an anomaly is detected, the system shifts to the PD phase and diagnoses are reported to the administrator.

Results of our experiments are summarized in Table 2 and 3. Each table shows how the various components in which we inject faults appear in the ranking produced by the diagnosis engine. In each table we show two columns: one for the first diagnosis after having collected data for three consecutive sampling intervals and one for the second diagnosis after three additional sampling intervals. In these tables, cells containing 'X' represent cases where the faulty component did not rank among the top ten components suspected as being faulty. Similarly, cells with '-' represent cases where the presence of a fault was not detected and where no diagnosis could be performed.

Table 2 presents the results of diagnosing faulty components when locking database tables used by the Trade application. We observe that for three cases the diagnoses are effective as the EJBs to which the tables map rank high. In the case of the ORDEREJB table, the anomaly could not be detected. This is because this table is mostly used during buy and sell operations which are infrequent in our workload mix. In the case of ACCOUNTEJB, while we can detect a response time anomaly, the diagnosis is not precise. This is because many components depending on the ACCOUNTEJB table end up ranking higher than the `AccountEJB` component. In this particular case the top anomalous metric listed by the diagnosis was the response time of the method`getAccountData` of the `TradeEJB` component, which directly depends on the `AccountEJB` component.

Table 2. Ranking of faulty components in the diagnosis for table-locking faults

Database Table	*Diagnosis I*	*Diagnosis II*
QUOTEEJB	3	4
HOLDINGEJB	2	2
ACCOUNTEJB	X	X
ACCOUNTPROFILEEJB	2	2
ORDEREJB	-	-

Table 3. Ranking of faulty components in the diagnosis for exception and loop-based faults

	Exceptions		Loops	
Component	*Diagnosis I*	*Diagnosis II*	*Diagnosis I*	*Diagnosis II*
AccountEJB	2	3	X	2
AccountProfileEJB	6	8	-	-
QuoteEJB	7	7	X	5
OrderEJB	8	7	1	1
HoldingEJB	2	2	6	7
tradehome.jsp	X	X	2	6
portfolio.jsp	X	X	-	-
quote.jsp	X	X	9	3
order.jsp	X	X	-	-
account.jsp	X	X	-	-
marketsummary.jsp	X	X	4	4
register.jsp	X	X	-	-

Diagnosis results for both the exception and the loop-based faults are presented in Table 3. With exception-based faults, we observe that our approach is relatively effective in ranking the anomalous components in the EJB cases. Anomalies in EJB components cause more disturbance, as they are used more frequently and because they are found deeper in the underlying structure of the target system, therefore they have far greater impact. However, the ranking of the EJB components is affected the most by dependent or related components. For example, in the three cases related to `AccountProfileEJB`, `QuoteEJB`, and `OrderEJB`, the `TradeEJB` component ranks higher. The `TradeEJB` component is a facade that mediates most calls to other EJBs, making the latter dependent.

Diagnosis for anomalies in the JSPs is not accurate. JSPs in the Trade application are only used to display results of various operations. When exceptions are thrown in these pages, the data these pages require are still computed and fetched. This prevents many LR models from detecting outliers. In some cases Table 3 shows that diagnosis was carried out but the faulty pages did not rank high. Very few models reported outliers in these cases and the metrics' anomaly score were very low. With such little data, it was not surprising to see inaccurate diagnoses.

The right half of Table 3 shows the results for loop-based faults. These faults mostly affect response time metrics because many such metrics tend to be related, mostly because of their cumulative nature. For the affected metrics, loop-based faults change the relative proportion of the related metrics. Loop-based faults affect metrics reflecting activity levels much less, as they cause dependent components to be called less often, thus saving LR models from reporting outliers. We can see that in all cases where the existence of the fault is detected, we were able shortlist the faulty component in the diagnosis. Cases where the the fault's presence was not detected involve components that are not frequently used. As for the anomalies in the JSP pages that were not detected, diagnosing them would have been difficult even if the anomaly was detected. These components do not have response time metrics that are correlated with metrics of other components. For example, the component `register.jsp` has no metric correlated with any other. In the case of faulty components that are shortlisted correctly, some dependent components tend to rank higher. For example, when injecting the loop anomaly in `marketsummary.jsp`, which is embedded inside `tradehome.jsp`, `tradehome.jsp` is reported as being more likely faulty.

Our experiments suggest that the nature of faults and characteristics of the components in which these faults are injected play an important role in determining the accuracy of the diagnosis. In order to assess the contribution of the modeling technique, in a separate study [26] we have explored the use of different regression techniques for modeling relationships between pairs of metrics. In that study we found that very basic data pre-processing can improve results obtained with simple linear regression.

4.4.3 Models Robustness

To evaluate the robustness of monitoring in the MM phase, we ran an experiment without injecting any fault and using the same configuration as above except for the fact that monitoring engine continues to execute for 12 hours after the MB phase. In this experiment we detected one anomaly approximately 10 hours after the start of the experiment. The collected data shows that some requests could not be processed for a brief lapse of time. The resulting diagnosis pointed to some components directly depending on the database. While we are suspecting a problem on the database machine, we could not correlate this anomaly with any event in the database log files. It is possible that the anomaly arose as a result of an event on the database machine, but not initiated by the database itself.

In order to evaluate the robustness of the LR models learned, we ran a 12-hour experiment in which we first identify robust models. The duration of the learning and testing phases are the same in the anomaly experiments and no faults were injected during this experiment. After every 15-minutes interval, we collect data for all metrics associated with LR models for for 5 minutes and test the models for outliers. We apply the same acceptance conditions as identified in Section 4.2.2 and count the number of models which report outliers, without discarding them. Fig. 3 illustrates how the number of LR models reporting outliers changes with respect to an increasing lag between learning and testing. We observe that the number of models indicating outliers rises continually in the beginning but then stabilizes close to 260. This represents a small fraction, less than 5%, of the 7200 models learned. Some of the these models represent spurious correlations, which the monitoring engine could not eliminate. For others, the parameters learned drift over time. In these cases, it is likely that the window over which the regression was carried out was not representative enough of the typical behaviour. It should

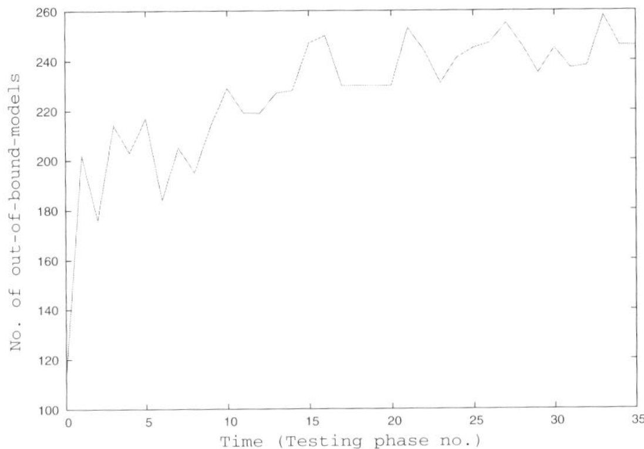

Fig. 3. Number of failing models after an increasing lapse of time

be noted that in case the target system is expected to change with time, LR models can efficiently be updated in an incremental fashion.

5 Conclusions

In this paper we have described our approach for adaptive monitoring of component-based software systems. We have shown that it is possible to create a system model based on linear relationships between monitoring metrics. The proposed approach creates models that are simple, general, robust, and require little cost to create. We have studied the effectiveness of our approach by injecting different faults in the target system. We were able to shortlist the faulty component in 65% of cases where anomalies were detected.

References

1. Pertet, S., Narasimhan, P.: Causes of failure in web applications. Technical Report CMU-PDL-05-109, Carnegie Mellon University Parallel Data Lab (December 2005)
2. Hecker, D.E.: Occupational employment projections to 2014. Monthly Labor Review, pp. 70–101 (November 2005)
3. Topal, B., Ogle, D., Pierson, D., Thoensen, J., Sweitzer, J., Chow, M., Hoffmann, M.A., Durham, P., Telford, R., Sheth, S., Studwell, T.: Autonomic problem determination: A first step toward self-healing computing systems. Technical report, IBM (2003)
4. Fox, A., Patterson, D.: Self-repairing computers. Scientific American (June 2003)
5. IBM Corp.: IBM WebSphere Application Server V6 Performance Tools, http://publib.boulder.ibm.com/infocenter/ieduasst/v1r1m0/topic/com.ibm.iea.was_v6/was/6.0/Performance/WASv6_PerformanceTools.pdf
6. Kephart, J.O., Chess, D.M.: The vision of autonomic computing. IEEE Computer 36(1), 41–50 (2003)
7. Munawar, M.A., Ward, P.A.: Adaptive monitoring in enterprise software systems. In: Tackling Computer Systems Problems with Machine Learning Techniques (SysML) (June 2006)
8. Microsoft Corp.: .NET Platform http://www.microsoft.com/net/

9. Sun Microsystems, Inc.: Java 2 platform enterprise edition, v 1.4 API specification, `http://java.sun.com/j2ee/1.4/docs/api/`
10. Sun Microsystems Inc.: JMX — Java Management Extensions, `http://java.sun.com/-products/JavaManagement/`
11. Dmitriev, M.: Profiling java applications using code hotswapping and dynamic call graph revelation. In: International Workshop on Software and Performance, pp. 139–150 (2004)
12. Mirgorodskiy, A.V., Miller, B.P.: Autonomous analysis of interactive systems with self-propelled instrumentation. In: Multimedia Computing and Networking (2005)
13. Munawar, M.A., Quan, K., Ward, P.A.: Interaction analysis of heterogeneous monitoring data for autonomic problem determination. In: The IEEE International Symposium on Ubisafe Computing. IEEE Computer Society Press, Los Alamitos (2007)
14. Appleby, K., Faik, J., Kar, G., Saile, A., Agarwal, M., Neogi, A.: Threshold management for problem determination in transaction based e-commerce systems. In: Integrated Network Management, pp. 733–746 (May 2005)
15. Cohen, I., Goldszmidt, M., Kelly, T., Symons, J., Chase, J.: Correlating instrumentation data to system states: A building block for automated diagnosis and control. In: Symposium on Operating Systems Design and Implementation (OSDI), pp. 231–244 (December 2004)
16. Kiciman, E., Armando, F.: Detecting application-level failures in component-based internet services. IEEE Transactions on Neural Networks 16(5), 1027–1041 (2005)
17. Brown, A., Kar, G., Keller, A.: An active approach to characterizing dynamic dependencies for problem determination in a distributed environment. In: Integrated Network Management, pp. 377–390 (May 2001)
18. Hauswirth, M., Sweeney, P.F., Diwan, A., Hind, M.: Vertical profiling: Understanding the behavior of object-oriented applications. In: Object-Oriented Programming, Systems, Languages, and Applications (2004)
19. Agarwal, M., Anerousis, N., Gupta, M., Mann, V., Mummert, L., Sachindran, N.: Problem determination in enterprise middleware systems using change point correlation of time series data. In: Network Operations and Management Symposium (April 2006)
20. Jiang, G., Chen, H., Yoshihira, K.: Modeling and tracking of transaction flow dynamics for fault detection in complex systems. IEEE Transactions Dependable and Secure Computing 3(4), 312–326 (2006)
21. Belsley, D.A., Kuh, E., Welsch, R.E.: Regression Diagnostics: Identifying Influential Data and Source of Collinearity. John Wiley and Sons, New York (1980)
22. IBM Corp.: Trade 6 Performance Benchmark Sample for WebSphere Application Server, `http://www-306.ibm.com/software/webservers/appserv/was/performance.html`
23. Cohen, J.: Statistical Power Analysis for the Behavioral Sciences. Lawrence Erlbaum Associates, Mahwah (1988)
24. SAS Institute Inc.: SAS OnlineDoc Version8. `http://v8doc.sas.com/`
25. Hellerstein, J.L., Zhang, F., Shahabuddin, P.: Characterizing normal operation of a web server: Application to workload forecasting and problem detection. In: Proceedings of Computer Measurement Group (December 1998)
26. Munawar, M.A., Ward, P.A.: A comparative study of pairwise regression techniques for problem determination. Technical Report 2007-15, ECE, University of Waterloo (2007)

Binomial Graph: A Scalable and Fault-Tolerant Logical Network Topology

Thara Angskun, George Bosilca, and Jack Dongarra

Dept. of Computer Science, The University of Tennessee, Knoxville, USA
{angskun,bosilca,dongarra}@cs.utk.edu

Abstract. The number of processors embedded in high performance computing platforms is growing daily to solve larger and more complex problems. The logical network topologies must also support the high degree of scalability in dynamic environments. This paper presents a scalable and fault tolerant topology called binomial graph (BMG). BMG provides desirable topological properties in terms of both scalability and fault-tolerance for high performance computing such as reasonable degree, regular graph, low diameter, symmetric graph, low cost factor, low message traffic density, optimal connectivity, low fault-diameter and strongly resilient. Several fault-tolerant routing algorithms are provided on BMG for various message types. More importantly, BMG is able to deliver broadcast messages from any node within $log_2(n)$ steps.

1 Introduction

Recently, several high performance computing platforms have been installed with more than 10,000 CPUs, such as Blue-Gene/L at LLNL, BGW at IBM and Columbia at NASA [1]. However, as the number of components increases, so does the probability of failure. To satisfy the requirements of such a dynamic environment (where the available number of resources is fluctuating), a scalable and fault-tolerant communication framework is needed. The communication framework is important for both runtime environments of MPI libraries and the MPI libraries themselves. The communication frameworks are based on a logical topology. The design of logical topologies should meet the following important criteria: (a) Low degree - the degree of a node is the number of links incident to the node. The degree number should be kept to a minimum to reduce the state management load on each node. (b) Regular graph - every node has the same degree. (c) Low diameter - the diameter of a graph is the longest shortest path between any two nodes. This number represents the worst case performance (a maximum number of hops) of the topology. (d) Symmetric graph - the average inter-nodal distance should be the same from any source node. (e) No numbers of node restriction - unlike the physical network topology, the logical network topology should be able to handle any number of nodes to support large scale parallel applications. In addition to the mentioned criteria, the routing protocol of the topology should be able to deliver the control messages in both normal and failure circumstances.

I. Stojmenovic et al. (Eds.): ISPA 2007, LNCS 4742, pp. 471–482, 2007.

There are several existing logical network topologies that can be used in high performance computing (HPC). The fully connected topology is good in terms of fault-tolerance, but it is not scalable because of high degree. The bidirectional ring topology is more scalable, but it is not fault-tolerant. Hypercube [2] and its variants FPCN [3], de Bruijn [4] and its variants , Kautz [5] and ShuffleNet [6] have a number of node restrictions. They are either not scalable or not fault-tolerant. The Manhattan Street Network (2D Torus) [7] is more flexible (no restriction in numbers of node) than Hypercube-like topologies. However, it has a much higher average hop-distance. Variants of k-ary tree, such as Hierarchical Clique (HiC) [8] and k-ary sibling tree (Hypertree [9]) used in SFTP [10, 11], are scalable and fault-tolerant. They are good for both unicast and broadcast messages. However, all nodes in their topologies are not equal (the resulting graph is not regular). Topologies, used in structured peer-to-peer networking based on distributed hash tables such as CAN [12], Chord [13], Pastry [14] and Tapestry [15], are also scalable and fault-tolerant. They were designed for resource discovery in dynamic environment. Hence, they may not be efficiently used in HPC owing to the overhead for managing highly dynamic applications.

This paper presents a new scalable and fault tolerant logical network topology called binomial graph (BMG). BMG provides desirable topological properties in terms of both scalability and fault-tolerance for high performance computing. The structure of this paper is as follows. Section 2 describes the structure and initialization scheme of BMG. Some topological properties of BMG are discussed in section 3 and section 4. Section 5 presents the fault-tolerant routing algorithm, followed by conclusions and future work in the section 6.

2 Structure of BMG

BMG is an undirected graph G:=(V,E) where V is a set of nodes (vertices); $|v|$ = n and E is a set of links (edges). Each node i, where $i \in V$ and i=1,2,...,n, has links to a set of nodes U, where $U=\{i\pm1, i\pm2, ..., \pm 2^k | 2^k \leq n\}$ in circular space, i.e., node i has links to a set of clockwise (CW) nodes $\{(i+1) \bmod n, (i+2) \bmod n, ..., (i+2^k) \bmod n | 2^k \leq n\}$ and a set of counterclockwise (CCW) nodes $\{(n\text{-}i+1) \bmod n, (n\text{-}i+2) \bmod n, ..., (n\text{-}i+2^k) \bmod n \mid 2^k \leq n\}$. The structure of BMG can also be classified in the circulant graph family.[1] A circulant graph with n nodes and jumps $j_1, j_2, ..., j_m$ is a graph in which each node i, $0 \leq i \leq n-1$, is adjacent to all the vertices $i \pm j_k$ mod n, where $1 \leq k \leq m$. BMG is a circulant graph where j_k is the power of 2 that is less than or equal n.

Fig. 1(a) illustrates an example of 12-node binomial graph. All the lines represent all connections in the network. The other way to look at the binomial graph is that it is a topology, which is constructed from merging all necessary links being able to create binomial trees from each node in the graph. Fig. 1(b) shows an example of a binomial tree when node 1 is the root node. The arrows point in the direction of the leaf nodes. For each link in a binomial graph, a

[1] Although BMG can be categorized into a class of a well-known graph, this particular configuration have never been analyzed.

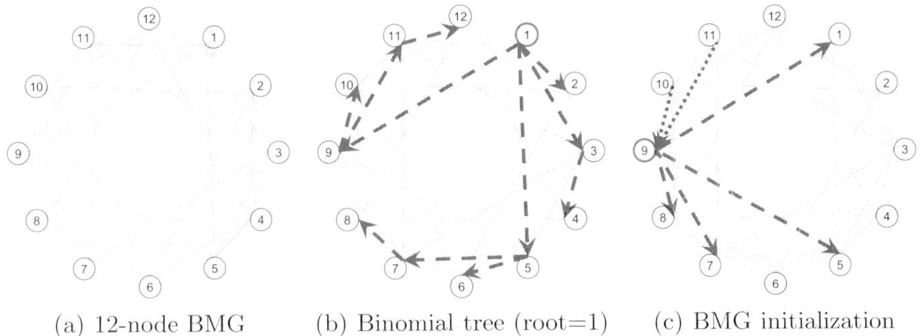

(a) 12-node BMG (b) Binomial tree (root=1) (c) BMG initialization

Fig. 1. Binomial graph structure

node which has a higher ID will initiate the connection to the node that has the lower ID. Assume that the nodes are started in order, i.e., node 1 is started before node 2, node 2 is started before node 3 and so on. When node i starts up, it will try to establish a connection to each $u \in U$, where $u < i$. The dashed lines of Fig. 1(c) represent all the connections that are linked to node 9 in the 12-node binomial graph. The arrows point from the initiators (connectors) to the acceptors. Node 9 initiates connections to node 1, 5, 7 and 8, while it accepts connections from node 10 and 11. Their structured initialization procedure is capable of handling any number of nodes in a scalable manner, i.e, there is no number of node restriction for BMG.

3 Properties of BMG

This section presents several basic properties in graph theory of BMG such as degree, diameter, average distance, message traffic density and cost factor. Several evaluations comparing BMG with other related topologies are presented. Properties of related topologies were obtained from respective theorems given in the reference papers.

3.1 Degree

If a node in a graph has δ connections that are linked to it, the node has degree δ. The minimum degree δ_{min} of a graph is the smallest node degree, while the maximum degree δ_{max} of a graph is the largest node degree. If every node has the same degree ($\delta_{min} = \delta_{max}$), the graph is *regular*. A *regular* graph also means that all the nodes are equivalent and can use the same routing and fault-handling algorithms. Those algorithms are also simpler compared to non-regular topologies, such as tree-based topologies, because they don't need to handle special cases. BMG is a regular graph. Fig. 1(a) is an example of a 12-node BMG, where each node has degree 6. For a BMG of size n (having n nodes), each node has a degree δ

as shown in Equation (1).

$$\delta = \begin{cases} (2 \times \lceil \log_2 n \rceil) - 1 & \text{For } n = 2^k, \text{where } k \in \mathbb{N} \\ (2 \times \lceil \log_2 n \rceil) - 2 & \text{For } n = 2^k + 2^j, \text{where } k, j \in \mathbb{N} \wedge k \neq j \\ 2 \times \lceil \log_2 n \rceil & \text{Otherwise} \end{cases} \quad (1)$$

Although BMG has higher degree than other related topologies, it has lower distance than the related properties. The trade-off between degree and distance for a fair comparison between topologies is discussed later in section 3.5.

3.2 Diameter

The distance $d(i,j)$ between a node i and a node j in a graph is defined as the length of the shortest path from i to j in the graph. The diameter D of a graph is given by $\max(d(i,j))$ over all possible pairs (i,j) of nodes in the graph. The diameter D is the longest shortest path between any two nodes in the graph. The BMG diameter, along with the diameter of related networks such as 2D Torus, binary Hypercube, Chord, $HiC_{(4,h)}$ and 4-ary Hypertree, is shown in Fig. 2(a). BMG has the lowest diameter among them.

3.3 Average Distance

The average distance $\bar{d}_i$ of node i is obtained from Equation (2).

$$\bar{d}_i = \frac{\sum_{j=1}^{n} d(i,j)}{n-1}, \text{ where } i \neq j \quad (2)$$

A graph is symmetric (in the sense of average distance) if all the nodes have the same average inter-nodal distance ($\bar{d}_i$, where $i \in \mathbb{N}$), which is also the same as average distance of the graph $\bar{d}$. The average distance $\bar{d}$ of a graph is given by Equation (3).

$$\bar{d} = \frac{\sum_{i=1}^{n} \sum_{j=1}^{n} d(i,j)}{n \times (n-1)}, \text{where } i \neq j \quad (3)$$

Fig. 2(b) illustrates that BMG has the lowest average distance (of a graph) when comparing with 2D Torus, binary Hypercube, Chord, $HiC_{(4,h)}$ and 4-ary

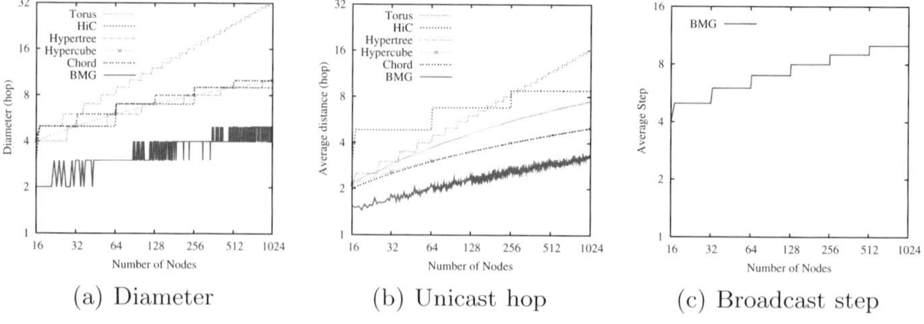

(a) Diameter (b) Unicast hop (c) Broadcast step

Fig. 2. BMG distance related properties

Hypertree topologies. The average distance also reflects the unicast performance (in terms of hop).

If node i uses S_i steps to send broadcast messages, the average number of broadcast steps of a graph is computed by $\frac{\sum_{i=1}^{n} S_i}{n}$. Fig. 2(c) illustrates the average number of broadcast steps of BMG. The number of broadcast steps from any node in BMG is $log_2(n)$ because a binomial tree can always be created from any node of BMG.

BMG is also a symmetric graph in terms of performance. Both the average inter-nodal distance (unicast) and the number of steps required for broadcast are the same for all nodes.

3.4 Message Traffic Density

Assuming each node is sending one message to a node at average distance $\bar{d}$, the message traffic in the network can be estimated by the message traffic density (ρ). This factor is given by $\rho = \frac{\bar{d} \times n}{L}$, where L is the total number of links. BMG has the number of links $L = \frac{\delta \times n}{2}$. Fig. 3(a) shows that BMG has the lowest message traffic density when comparing with 2D Torus, binary Hypercube, Chord, $HiC_{(4,h)}$ and 4-ary Hypertree topologies. Nevertheless, ρ of BMG does not exceed 0.5 even for large systems.

3.5 Cost Factor

A network with large diameter usually has a small degree, but it may suffer from high latency, e.g., the ring topology has $\delta = 2$ and $D = \lfloor \frac{n}{2} \rfloor$. On the other hand, a small-diameter network may have a higher degree, e.g., the fully connected topology (complete graph) has $D = 1$ and $\delta = n - 1$. It is desirable to have a logical topology with both small diameter (low latency) and small degree (low state management). Thus, for a symmetric network, a cost factor [16] (ξ) is defined as the product of diameter (D) and degree (δ). In general, the cost of a particular topology [17] can also be defined as the product of the diameter (D) and the number of links (L) in the network.

Fig. 3(b) and Fig. 3(c) present a cost factor comparison. Although 4-ary Hypertree has lower cost factor than BMG, it has significantly higher message traffic

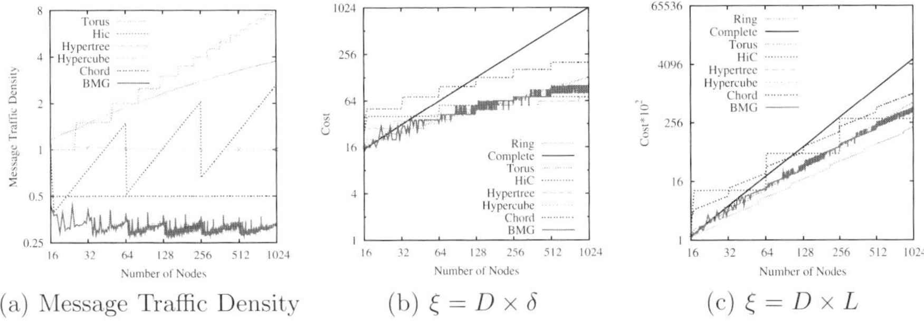

(a) Message Traffic Density (b) $\xi = D \times \delta$ (c) $\xi = D \times L$

Fig. 3. ρ and ξ properties of BMG

density and average distance. The results show that BMG has comparable cost factor to binary Hypercube and Torus. It also has significantly lower cost factor than $HiC_{(4,h)}$, Chord, ring and fully connected topologies.

All of the properties presented in this section illustrate the scalable capability of BMG. It has a reasonable degree, a low diameter, a low average (unicast and broadcast) distance, a low message traffic density and a low cost factor. The capabilities of BMG in terms of fault-tolerance are presented in the next section.

4 Fault Tolerant Capabilities of BMG

This section presents several properties in terms of fault-tolerance to illustrate the fault-tolerant capability of BMG such as connectivity and fault-diameter.

4.1 Connectivity

The node-connectivity (κ) of BMG is defined as the minimum number of nodes of which removal can result in disconnecting the network, i.e., the smallest number of node-distinct paths between any two nodes. The link-connectivity (λ) of BMG is defined as the minimum number of link of which removal can result in disconnecting the network, i.e., the smallest number of link-distinct paths between any two nodes. Fig. 4(a) illustrates that node-connectivity and link-connectivity of BMG are equal to the degree, i.e., the BMG is $\delta - 1$ node fault-tolerant and $\delta - 1$ link fault-tolerant. However, some cases, where δ nodes fail, will result in disconnecting the network. In fact, the percentage for n-node BMG being disconnected by a δ-node fault set is minimal (less than one percent) as shown in Fig. 4(b). Fig. 4(c) compares the node-connectivity and link-connectivity of $HiC_{(4,h)}$ and BMG at the same degree. BMG is twice as robust as $HiC_{(4,h)}$.

For any graph, $\kappa \leq \lambda \leq \delta_{min}$. However if $\kappa = \lambda = \delta_{min}$, the graph is *optimally connected* [18] because the node and link connectivities are as high as possible, i.e., the network is as robust as it could be, and that is the case for BMG. The optimal connectivity is also important in reducing the impact of node destruction on link load [19]. In general, traffic can be distributed over at least λ link-disjoint paths

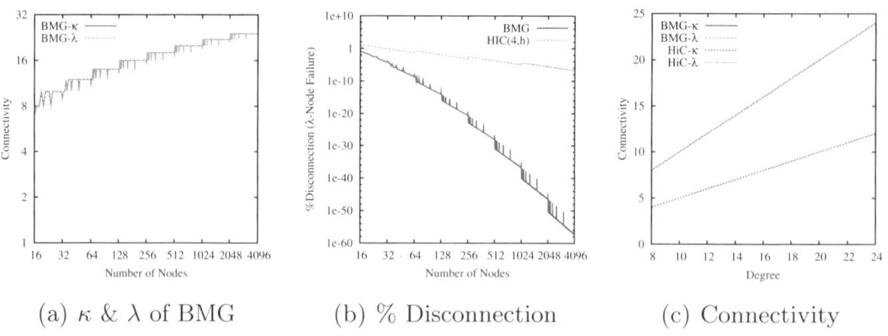

(a) κ & λ of BMG (b) % Disconnection (c) Connectivity

Fig. 4. Connectivity

between two nodes. If $\kappa < \lambda$, the number of link-disjoint paths may drastically drop after the loss of a critical node. However, if $\kappa = \lambda$ (optimal connectivity), the node failure can destroy, at most, one of the λ link-disjoint paths.

4.2 Fault Diameter

The fault diameter F is the largest diameter of the network when there are $\lambda - 1$ node failures (a maximum number of failure nodes before the network becomes bipartite). Fig. 5(a) depicts that the fault diameter of BMG is lower than other topologies. There are two classes of graph G distinguished by the relationship between the fault diameter (F) and the diameter (D) of the graph [20], called *strongly resilient* and *weakly resilient*. A graph is considered *strongly resilient* if there exists a constant ϕ such that $F(G) \leq D(G) + \phi$ for all graph sizes n, where $n \in \mathbb{N}$. On the other hand, a graph is considered *weakly resilient* if there exists a constant ϕ such that $F(G) \leq D(G) \times \phi$ for all graph sizes n, where $n \in \mathbb{N}$. BMG is considered *strongly resilient* as shown in Fig. 5(b), where $\phi = 2$, i.e., $F(BMG) \leq D(BMG) + 2$. This indicates that, even under faulty conditions, the performance of BMG will not be severely degraded.

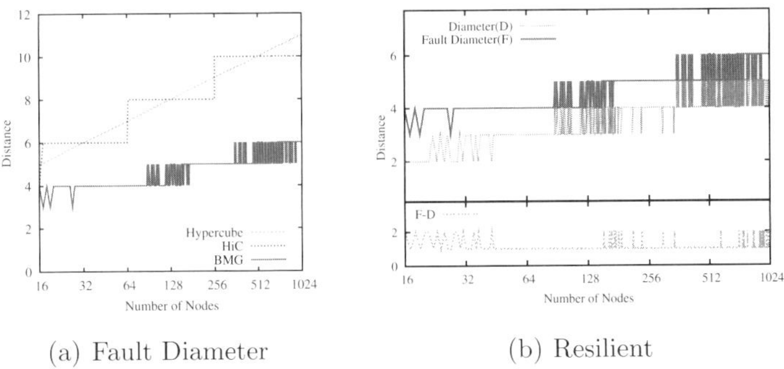

(a) Fault Diameter (b) Resilient

Fig. 5. Fault diameter

5 Fault-Tolerant Routing

This section presents several routing algorithms that can handle different message types (unicast, multicast and broadcast) under both normal and failure circumstances. Due to the fact that all nodes in BMG are equal (both regular and symmetric), each node in the graph can run the same routing algorithm. In BMG, each node only needs to maintain the contact information, node ID and status of its δ direct neighbors. This information will be used for searching the shortest path from a source to a destination in both normal and failure modes.

5.1 Unicast Routing Algorithm

Under normal circumstances (no failures), the unicast message routing could be optimally done by searching for the shortest path between the source and destination. However, the complexity of the algorithm is more than sub-optimal, which could estimate the shortest path with rule-based techniques.

Optimal Algorithm. The optimal routing algorithm can use the breadth-first search technique with a modified graph coloring algorithm. Although this algorithm gives the optimal result, the complexity of the algorithm is $O(|V| + |E|)$. A routing table could be used to keep the result of the neighbors sorted by the shortest path from the node itself to all other nodes in BMG. The lower priority neighbor node will be used as an alternative for the next hop when the highest priority neighbor dies. In practice, the routing table can be implemented with a data structure that has the search complexity $O(log_2 n)$ such as a red-black tree.

Sub-Optimal Algorithm. A basic algorithm to estimate the shortest path between nodes is to use a rule-based method that sends the unicast messages to the neighbor that has the closest ID to the destination ID as shown in Algorithm 1. The complexity of the basic unicast routing algorithm is $O(\delta)$.

Algorithm 1. Find neighborID which has the shortest distance to destID

Require: $1 \leq myID \leq n \wedge 1 \leq destID \leq n, n \in \mathbb{N}$

Min $\Leftarrow \infty$
Get neighborID of myID
for $i = 0$ to $(Numbersofneighbor) - 1$ **do**
    Distance $\Leftarrow |destID - neighborID[i]|$
    if Distance < Min **then**
        Min $\Leftarrow$ Distance
        nextHopID=neighborID[i]
    end if
end for
Return nextHopID

The basic routing algorithm becomes sub-optimal when the destination is one of the neighbors (or a neighbor of neighbors) of a node (including a source node) of which ID is not the closest ID compared to the destination, e.g., if the node 1 is the source and the node 12 is the destination of unicast messages in a 23-node configuration The basic routing algorithm will route messages from node 1 to node 12 using node 9 and node 11 as the intermediate nodes, while the shortest path would use node 5 as the intermediate node to route unicast messages from node 1 to node 12.

To overcome this shortcoming, a unicast message routing algorithm (called variant) has been introduced. It is the variant of the basic algorithm, which allows messages forward to a neighbor which its ID is not the closest ID to the destination ID if the destination is directly connected to the neighbor, e.g., in case of sending unicast messages from node 1 to node 12 on 23-node BMG. Node 1 will forward messages to neighbor node 5 (even node 9 has a closer ID to node 12), because node 12 is directly connected to node 5. Fig. 6(a) illustrates the average ($\bar{d}$) and maximum (d_{max}) distance of the variant routing algorithm compared with the basic and optimal routing algorithm. Fig. 6(b) and Fig. 6(c) depict that the variant algorithm is marginally better than the basic algorithm in terms of d_{max} and $\bar{d}$.

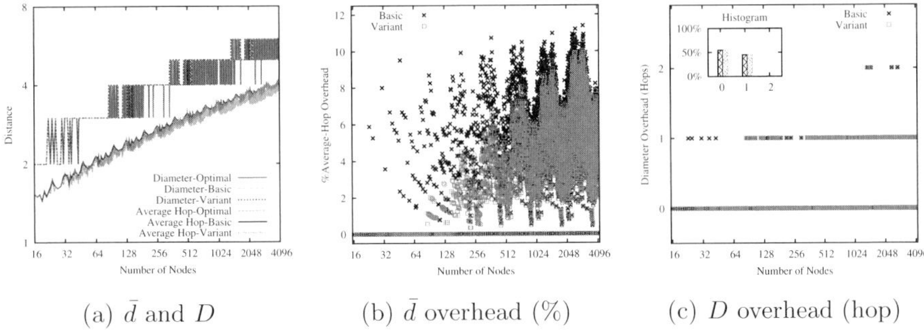

(a) $\bar{d}$ and D (b) $\bar{d}$ overhead (%) (c) D overhead (hop)

Fig. 6. Variant routing performance

The average d_{max} overhead of a configuration between 16 and 4096 nodes is reduced from 0.454 to 0.449 hops, while the average $\bar{d}$ overhead is also decreased from 5.55% to 4.69%. The complexity of the variant unicast routing algorithm is $O(\delta^2)$. This algorithm could be extended by recursively finding if the destination is directly connected to the neighbor of a neighbor and so on. The complexity of the extended version is $O(\delta^{r+1})$, where r is the recursive level.

In normal circumstances, each of the unicast routing algorithms is loop avoidance, i.e., it prevents problems of duplicate packet, broadcast storm and deadlock. The messages will always get closer to the destination at every hop. However, this is not the case under failure circumstances. The messages can be looped. Thus, additional loop prevention is needed. The loop can be prevented by techniques such as adding transit list fields in the packet header. The transit list fields may contain 3-tuple consisting of incoming neighbor, transit node and outgoing neighbor. These fields do not only prevent a node from sending a packet to the same neighbor twice, but also help in backtracking to the originator of the packet and finding an alternative route. The transit list may be added to the header only when a node detects that its neighbor, which is in the outgoing direction of the packet, died or when the packet has already had the transit list.

5.2 Multicast Routing Algorithm

The multicast from any nodes in BMG is the capability to send messages to several destinations (1 to m, where $m < n$). Unlike the IP multicast, multicast group management (group creation and termination) is not required. The multicast group members are embedded in the message header. The multicast routing algorithms are all based on unicast algorithms. All capabilities in both normal and failure circumstances are the same, except that the multicast messages can also be split at an intermediate node. The messages will be split, if the shortest paths to those destination nodes are not in the same direction from the intermediate node point of view. However, if there is more than one shortest path to a destination, the intermediate node will choose the next hop which can go along with other destinations. When a node receives a multicast message, it will first determine the header and choose the next hop for each multicast destination according to the shortest path to them. The node will recreate the header corresponding to the direction of each next hop. Messages that contain the largest number of hops will be forwarded first to increase network throughput by utilizing multiple links simultaneously.

5.3 Broadcast Routing Algorithm

Broadcast messages from any node in BMG are handled by creating a binomial spanning tree from the source. Under normal circumstances, only the links of the binomial spanning tree of BMG are used to prevent loop (broadcast storm problems). There are two steps involving the next hop calculation. The first step is to create a binomial spanning tree using the source node as the root node of the tree. The second step is to calculate the next hop. The next hop is chosen from the children of each node according to the spanning tree that has the highest cost among its children. The cost is computed from the number of steps used to send a message to all nodes in the subtrees of children.

There are two algorithms for creating a binomial spanning tree and finding a parent and children of a node, according to the binomial spanning tree from the source. The first algorithm creates the tree by choosing the closest ID first as shown in Fig. 7(a), while the second algorithm chooses the closest ID last as shown in Fig. 7(b)

Both of the algorithms only use the existing links in BMG to create the binomial tree from any node in BMG. This means that broadcast messages from any node in BMG can always be delivered within $O(log_2 n)$ steps.

In case of failure, a broadcast message is encapsulated into a multicast message, and then the message is sent from a parent of the failed node to its children in the binomial spanning tree. The children will de-capsulate the multicast message and continue to forward the initial broadcast message. If the children of the failed node also die, the message will be rerouted to its grandchildren automatically.

Under normal circumstances, all of the broadcast routing algorithms in BMG are loop avoidance because they always send broadcast messages using links that exist in the binomial spanning tree. Under failure circumstances, the rerouting mechanism is based on multicast messages, so the loop avoidance procedures are inherited from the multicast algorithms.

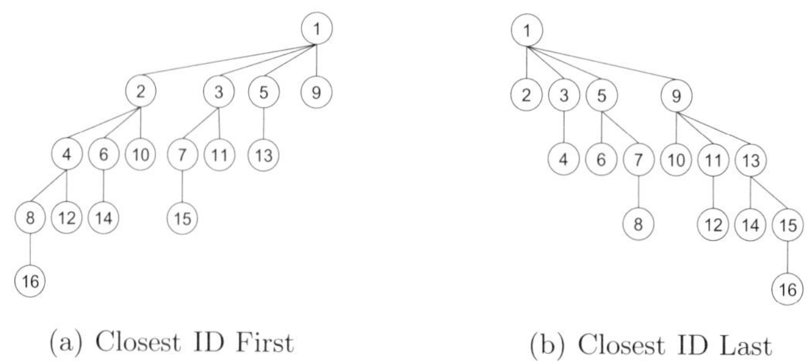

(a) Closest ID First

(b) Closest ID Last

Fig. 7. Binomial Broadcast Tree

6 Conclusions and Future Work

This paper presents a scalable and fault tolerant topology called binomial graph (BMG). The capabilities in terms of both scalability and fault tolerance have been analyzed. The results show that BMG provides desirable topological properties for high performance computing. It has scalable capability properties such as reasonable degree, regular graph (every node has the same degree), low diameter, low average distance (both unicast and broadcast), symmetric graph (in the sense that average inter-nodal distance is the same from any source node), no numbers of node restriction, low cost factor and low message traffic density. The BMG also has good fault-tolerant properties such as optimal connectivity, low fault-diameter, strongly resilient and good optimal probability in failure cases. The paper also discusses several routing algorithms that can deliver the shortest path, while it maintains low complexity. These routing algorithms are suitable under both normal and failure circumstances.

There are several improvements that we plan for the near future. Making the routing algorithm aware of the underlying network topology (in both the LAN and WAN environments) will greatly improve the overall performance for both the unicast and broadcast message transmissions. This is equivalent to adding a function cost on each possible path and integrating this function cost to the computation of the shortest path. In the longer term, we hope that BMG will become the basic logical topology of the runtime environments within the FT-MPI and Open MPI libraries.

References

1. Dongarra, J.J., Meuer, H., Strohmaier, E.: TOP500 supercomputer sites. Supercomputer 13, 89–120 (1997)
2. Saad, Y., Schultz, M.H.: Topological properties of hypercubes. IEEE Transactions on Computers 37, 867–872 (1988)
3. Ohring, S., Das, S.K.: Folded petersen cube networks: New competitors for the hypercubes. IEEE Transactions on Parallel and Distributed Systems 7, 151–168 (1996)
4. Sivarajan, K.N., Ramaswami, R.: Lightwave networks based on de bruijn graphs. IEEE/ACM Trans. Netw. 2, 70–79 (1994)
5. Panchapakesan, G., Sengupta, A.: On a lightwave network topology using kautz digraphs. IEEE Transactions on Computers 48, 1131–1138 (1999)
6. Karol, M.J.: Optical interconnection using shufflenet multihop networks in multi-connected ring topologies. In: SIGCOMM '88. Symposium proceedings on Communications architectures and protocols, pp. 25–34. ACM Press, New York (1988)
7. Maxemchuck, N.F.: Regular mesh topologies in local and metropolitan area networks. AT&T Technical Journal 64, 1659–1685 (1985)
8. Campbell, S., Kumar, M., Olariu, S.: The hierarchical cliques interconnection network. Journal of Parallel and Distributed Computing 64, 16–28 (2004)
9. Goodman, J.R., Sequin, C.H.: Hypertree: A multiprocessor interconnection topology. IEEE Transactions on Computers 30, 923–933 (1981)

10. Angskun, T., Fagg, G.E., Bosilca, G., Pješivac–Grbović, J., Dongarra, J.: Scalable fault tolerant protocol for parallel runtime environments. In: Mohr, B., Träff, J.L., Worringen, J., Dongarra, J. (eds.) Recent Advances in Parallel Virtual Machine and Message Passing Interface. LNCS, vol. 4192, pp. 141–149. Springer, Heidelberg (2006)
11. Angskun, T., Fagg, G.E., Bosilca, G., Pješivac–Grbović, J., Dongarra, J.: Self-healing network for scalable fault tolerant runtime environments. In: Proceedings of 6th Austrian-Hungarian workshop on distributed and parallel systems, Innsbruck, Austria. Springer, Heidelberg (2006)
12. Ratnasamy, S., Francis, P., Handley, M., Karp, R., Shenker, S.: A scalable content addressable network. Technical Report TR-00-010, Berkeley, CA (2000)
13. Stoica, I., Morris, R., Karger, D., Kaashoek, F., Balakrishnan, H.: Chord: A scalable Peer-To-Peer lookup service for internet applications. In: Proceedings of the 2001 ACM SIGCOMM Conference, pp. 149–160 (2001)
14. Rowstron, A., Druschel, P.: Pastry: Scalable, decentralized object location, and routing for large-scale peer-to-peer systems. In: Guerraoui, R. (ed.) Middleware 2001. LNCS, vol. 2218, pp. 329–350. Springer, Heidelberg (2001)
15. Zhao, B.Y., Kubiatowicz, J.D., Joseph, A.D.: Tapestry: An infrastructure for fault-tolerant wide-area location and routing. Technical Report UCB/CSD-01-1141, UC Berkeley (2001)
16. El-Amawy, A., Latifi, S.: Properties and performance of folded hypercubes. IEEE Transactions on Parallel and Distributed Systems 2, 31–42 (1991)
17. Louri, A., Neocleous, C.: A spanning bus connected hypercube: A new scalable optical interconnection network for multiprocessors and massively parallel systems. Journal of Lightwave Technology 15, 1241–1252 (1997)
18. Gibbons, A.: Algorithmic graph theory. Cambridge University Press, Cambridge (1985)
19. Dekker, A.H., Colbert, B.D.: Network robustness and graph topology. In: ACSC '04: Proceedings of the 27th Australasian conference on Computer science, pp. 359–368. Australian Computer Society, Inc., Darlinghurst, Australia (2004)
20. Krishnamoorthy, M.S., Krishnamurthy, B.: Fault diameter of interconnection networks. Computers and Mathematics with Applications 13, 577–582 (1987)

Eventually Perfect Failure Detectors Using ADD Channels

Srikanth Sastry and Scott M. Pike*

Texas A&M University
Department of Computer Science
College Station, TX 77843-3112, USA
{sastry,pike}@cs.tamu.edu

Abstract. We present a novel implementation of the *eventually perfect failure detector* ($\diamond\mathcal{P}$) from the original hierarchy of Chandra-Toueg oracles. Previous implementations of $\diamond\mathcal{P}$ have assumed models of partial synchrony where point-to-point message delay is bounded and/or communication is reliable. We show how to implement this important oracle under even weaker assumptions using Average Delayed/Dropped (ADD) channels. Briefly, all messages sent on an ADD channel are *privileged* or *non-privileged*. All non-privileged messages can be arbitrarily delayed or even dropped. For each run, however, there exists an unknown window size w, and two *unknown* upper-bounds d and r, where d bounds the average delay of the last w privileged messages, and r bounds the ratio of non-privileged messages to privileged messages per window.

Keywords: Failure Detectors, Partial Synchrony, Communication Models.

1 Introduction

A *failure detector* can be viewed as a distributed oracle that can be queried for (potentially unreliable) information about process crashes. Unreliable oracles can make mistakes by wrongfully suspecting correct processes, and/or not suspecting crashed processes. Despite such mistakes, many oracles are sufficiently powerful to solve important problems that are *not* solvable in crash-prone asynchronous systems. For example, the hierarchy of Chandra-Toueg oracles [1] was originally introduced to circumvent impossibility results for fault-tolerant consensus [2].

Oracle-based algorithms achieve an essential separation of concerns between detection properties and detection mechanisms. To be implemented in practice, most failure detector classes require some degree of partial or even full synchrony. The timing assumptions for fault detection, however, are encapsulated by the oracle abstraction. Since oracle-based algorithms depend only on the assertional *properties* of fault detection, they are effectively decoupled from the underlying implementation mechanisms and network timing parameters.

* This work was supported by the Advanced Research Program of the Texas Higher Education Coordinating Board under Project Number 000512-0007-2006.

I. Stojmenovic et al. (Eds.): ISPA 2007, LNCS 4742, pp. 483–496, 2007.

This separation of concerns has spawned two basic lines of research. One examines the weakest detection properties sufficient for solving fundamental problems using oracles. The other examines increasingly weaker models of computation for implementing oracles in real systems. These two trajectories are complementary. The former extends our knowledge of relative solvability, while the latter addresses the practical implications of implementing such oracles, typically for providing fault-detection capabilities as a system service.

We contribute to the second line of research by defining a novel implementation of the *eventually perfect failure detector* $\diamond\mathcal{P}$ from the original Chandra-Toueg hierarchy [1]. Informally, $\diamond\mathcal{P}$ can give arbitrarily unreliable information about process crashes for a finite computation prefix of unknown length. Eventually, however, it provides perfect information about crash faults. Unfortunately, the time to convergence is not known, so it is not generally decidable whether the output of $\diamond\mathcal{P}$ during a given segment of computation is reliable or not. More precisely, $\diamond\mathcal{P}$ satisfies the following two properties [1]:

- **Strong Completeness:** Every crashed process is eventually and permanently suspected by every correct process.
- **Eventual Strong Accuracy:** For each run, there exists an unknown time after which no correct process is suspected by any correct process.

The oracle $\diamond\mathcal{P}$ is of interest for two primary reasons: it is relatively powerful, and yet realistically implementable. First, $\diamond\mathcal{P}$ is sufficiently powerful to solve many fundamental problems which are otherwise unsolvable without some recourse to fault detection. $\diamond\mathcal{P}$ is more than sufficient to solve fault-tolerant consensus [1], but its computational power is better illustrated by its sufficiency for harder problems like stable leader election [3], quiescent reliable communication [4], wait-free non-blocking contention management [5], wait-free eventual weak exclusion [6], crash-locality-1 dining philosophers [7], and wait-free eventually k-bounded schedulers under eventual weak exclusion [8].

Beyond its theoretical significance, $\diamond\mathcal{P}$ is also realistically implementable. Among other relatively powerful oracles — such as the Perfect ($\mathcal{P}$) [1], Strong ($\mathcal{S}$) [1], and Marabout [9] detectors — $\diamond\mathcal{P}$ is the only oracle implementable in partially synchronous systems. This result is from [10], where Larrea, *et al.*, prove that failure detectors with perpetual accuracy (including $\mathcal{P}$, $\mathcal{S}$, and Marabout) cannot be implemented in classical models of partial synchrony [1,11]. As such, $\diamond\mathcal{P}$ has both theoretical as well as practical importance, insofar as it can solve important fault-tolerant problems, while being implementable in systems subject to timing uncertainties characterized by partial synchrony.

Ideally, we would like to know the weakest system model for implementing $\diamond\mathcal{P}$. This challenge has dual significance, because it underpins the fundamental solvability and portability of $\diamond\mathcal{P}$-based algorithms. Accordingly, the contributions of this paper are twofold: (1) we articulate a new, weaker model of partially synchronous communication called Average Delayed/Dropped (ADD) Channels, and (2) we implement $\diamond\mathcal{P}$ in the ADD model, which permits unbounded message loss and unbounded point-to-point message delay. Our results characterize one of the weakest models to date for implementing $\diamond\mathcal{P}$.

2 Motivation

Classical models of partial synchrony ([1, 12, 13, 14, 15, 3, 16, 17]) for implementing $\diamond\mathcal{P}$ make certain assumptions about the reliability and timeliness of the underlying communication channels. The models cited above assume that the communication channels are either always reliable[1], or eventually reliable (i.e., can lose at most finitely-many messages over some prefix, followed by an infinite reliable suffix). Additionally, these models assume the existence of upper-bounds (known or unknown) on point-to-point message delay, or average message delay.

In many systems, however, message loss and/or delays occur intermittently throughout the computation. For instance, consider a communication system with (1) an unknown upper-bound on channel delay, (2) bounded buffers at each in-bound channel interface, and (3) a load-shedding policy (such as *milk* or *wine*) for congestion control. Suppose process p persistently sends messages to q at a rate faster than q can process them. In finite time, the in-bound buffer at q becomes full and activates the load-shedding policy: for milk, buffered messages are dropped in favor of (fresh) arriving messages; for wine, arriving messages are dropped in favor of (aged) buffered messages. For every message that arrives when the buffer at q is full, some message is lost. However, q processes messages infinitely often, so infinitely many messages are also delivered reliably. Upper-bounds on channel delay and buffer delay translate into an upper-bound on ene-to-end message delay. Therefore, an infinite subset of messages are delivered within some bounded delay, but an infinite subset of them are also dropped.

Existing implementations of $\diamond\mathcal{P}$ can be trivially adapted to withstand certain subsets of messages being arbitrarily delayed or dropped. For instance, consider a system E where only the odd-numbered messages may be delayed or dropped, but all the even-numbered messages are delivered reliably within some unknown bound on delay. Implementing $\diamond\mathcal{P}$ in such a system is trivial, because the infinite pattern of potentially delayed and dropped messages in known, and hence can be used to advantage. Such applications can simply send dummy information in the odd-numbered messages and use the even-numbered messages to communicate. Effectively, the applications have access to a reliable sub-channel consisting of the even-numbered messages. However, consider a system T where, during every prefix of computation, at most 50% of the messages sent may be delayed or dropped, but all other messages are delivered within some (unknown) bound on delay. Implementing $\diamond\mathcal{P}$ in such a system becomes non-trivial.

In this paper, we consider systems in which an infinite subset of messages can be *non-privileged*, insofar as they may be arbitrarily delayed or even dropped. We assume that non-privileged messages follow some distribution, about which we have only limited knowledge. All we assume is that each sufficiently long window of communication contains at least one message that is neither dropped, nor arbitrarily delayed. Our system model and implementation of $\diamond\mathcal{P}$ follow next.

---

[1] A communication channel is said to be reliable if every message sent to any correct process is delivered in finite time, and is neither lost, duplicated, nor corrupted.

3 System Model

We introduce a new model of partial synchrony based on unreliable communication links called *Average Delayed or Dropped* (ADD) Channels, and show how to implement $\diamond\mathcal{P}$. To our knowledge, the ADD system model is weaker than peer models of partial synchrony for implementing $\diamond\mathcal{P}$ using only bounded space.

3.1 Communication Model – ADD Channels

Every *Average Delayed or Dropped* (ADD) channel is a unidirectional communication link connecting two process. All messages sent on an ADD channel can be logically partitioned into two disjoint sets: *privileged* and *non-privileged*. This distinction is merely a modeling device which is known neither to the channel, nor to the application processes using such channels. Non-privileged messages have no timing or reliability guarantees. As such, infinitely many messages may be arbitrarily delayed or even dropped. By contrast, ADD channels provide the following guarantees for privileged messages:

1. If a process p sends infinitely-many messages to a correct process q on an ADD channel, then some infinite subset of those messages will be privileged. All such privileged messages will be delivered reliably to q.
2. For every execution of an ADD channel, there exists an unknown window size $w \in \mathbb{N}^+$, an unknown message delay $d \in \mathbb{N}^+$, and an unknown message ratio $r \in \mathbb{N}^+$, such that for every sending interval containing a subsequence S of exactly w privileged messages:
   (a) The average delay of all privileged messages in S is at most d.
   (b) The average number of non-privileged messages sent between any consecutive pair of privileged messages in S is at most r.

Intuitively, privileged messages are delivered reliably, and, on average, are neither too late nor too sparse. Privileged and non-privileged messages can be interleaved, but any interval containing w privileged messages is subject to the bounds d and r, which restrict the average delay of privileged messages, and the average ratio to non-privileged messages, respectively. Although the bounds w, d, and r exist for each ADD channel, they are unknown and may vary per run.

3.2 Simplified Reduction of ADD Channel Properties

Consider any run of an ADD channel with window size w and average privileged delay d. For contradiction, suppose that some privileged message m is delayed for more than $w \times d$ time units in this run. Consider any sequence S containing w privileged messages including m. The average delay of privileged messages in S must exceed d. Thus, the unknown window size w and the unknown bound d on *average* privileged delay actually induce an unknown bound on the *absolute* delay of privileged messages; specifically, no privileged message can be delayed more than $w \times d = D$ time units.

Similarly, let r bound the average number of non-privileged messages between any consecutive pair of privileged messages in windows of size w. Again, suppose for contradiction that more than $w \times r$ non-privileged messages are sent between some consecutive pair of privileged messages, say, m_i and m_j. Consider any sequence S containing w privileged messages including m_i and m_j. The average ratio of non-privileged to privileged messages in S must exceed r. Thus, the unknown window size w and the unknown bound r on *average* message ratio actually induce an unknown bound on the maximum number of non-privileged messages which can be sent between any consecutive pair of privileged messages; specifically, at most $w \times r = R$ non-privileged messages can be sent between any consecutive pair of privileged messages.

The foregoing analysis yields a simplified specification of the timeliness and reliability properties of ADD channels. This equivalent characterization will be used throughout the remainder of the paper in our analysis and proofs.

1. If a process p sends infinitely-many messages to a correct process q on an ADD channel, then some infinite subset of those messages will be privileged. All such privileged messages will be delivered reliably to q.
2. For every execution of an ADD channel, there exist two unknown bounds $D \in \mathbb{N}^+$ and $R \in \mathbb{N}^+$ such that:
   (a) The absolute delay of all privileged messages is at most D.
   (b) The maximum number of non-privileged messages sent between any consecutive pair of privileged messages is at most R.

3.3 ADD System Model

An ADD system consists of a finite set of processes Π where:

1. Processes can fail only by *crashing*, which occurs when a process ceases execution without warning and never recovers. Any process that is not crashed is considered to be *live*.
2. Each pair of processes is connected via two reciprocal ADD channels, and message passing is the only means of interprocess communication.
3. There exists an unknown *lower-bound* on the absolute speed of live processes. No bounds on relative process speeds are assumed.
4. Each process has access to a local clock which generates ticks at a constant rate. Different clocks can tick at different rates and be unsynchronized. In physical systems, this is typically realized by a crystal oscillator which generates clock ticks at a constant frequency.

4 Implementation

In this section, we describe a heartbeat-based implementation of $\Diamond\mathcal{P}$ in the ADD model for a system S with n processes. Our implementation has two types of modules: *heartbeat generators* and *heartbeat witnesses*. Each process p has a single heartbeat generator, and n heartbeat witnesses (one for each process in S). Note that p has a heartbeat witness for itself as well. Thus, there are n generators and n^2 witnesses globally in the system.

Each heartbeat generator periodically sends n heartbeats, one to each process in S. The heartbeat frequency at each process is not necessarily known; moreover, it may vary from process to process due to local differences in hardware, server loads, and operating system scheduling policies. Nonetheless, we will show that each generator satisfies a *lower-bound* on heartbeat frequency. In conjunction with ADD channels, such heartbeat generators will yield an *upper bound* on the heartbeat inter-arrival times at each recipient. Although such bounds are not necessarily known, they can be adaptively estimated by the witness modules to provide an eventually reliable time-out mechanism.

Each heartbeat witness monitors the heartbeat traffic received on a given ADD channel. The role of each witness is to maintain a time-out variable that eventually converges to the de facto upper-bound on heartbeat inter-arrival time. Each witness starts with an initial estimate of the inter-arrival bound. If no heartbeat is received within the estimated bound, then the process sending heartbeats on this channel is suspected. False-positive suspicions may result if the estimated bound is too low, but such mistakes will be detected whenever a subsequent heartbeat is received. If so, the witness exonerates the previously suspected process, and increases its estimate of the inter-arrival bound.

The adaptive time-out mechanism just described is a common approach to implementing $\diamond\mathcal{P}$. The informal basis for correctness is as follows. Consider two processes p and q. If q crashes, then p receives at most finitely many messages from q. After the final such message, p will eventually time-out and permanently suspect q thereafter. This satisfies the strong completeness requirement of $\diamond\mathcal{P}$. By contrast, if p and q are both correct, then p can falsely suspect q at most finitely many times. Since q sends infinitely many heartbeats, each false suspicion of q will be detected by p, thereby causing p to increase its estimated bound on inter-arrival time. This estimate can only increase finitely many times before eventually exceeding the actual bound on inter-arrival time. Thereafter, p never suspects q again. This satisfies the eventual strong accuracy requirement of $\diamond\mathcal{P}$.

The foregoing argument for correctness depends on the critical assumption that there exists an upper bound on heartbeat inter-arrival times. The primary contribution of our work is to demonstrate that inter-arrival times can be bounded in the ADD system model, despite the fact that (1) there is no upper bound on relative process speeds, (2) there is no upper bound on message delay, and (3) infinitely many messages can be dropped. Nevertheless, we will prove that the ADD system model is sufficient to implement heartbeat generators with a lower bound on heartbeat frequency, and that ADD channels are sufficiently timely and reliable to convert lower bounds on heartbeat frequency into upper bounds on heartbeat inter-arrival times.

The remainder of this section describes the heartbeat generator and heartbeat witness modules, and defines a scheduler for fairly interleaving the actions of each module as threads within a single process.

4.1 Communication Patterns

Sending pattern and receiving pattern. In an execution, we refer to the set of messages sent by one process to another as a *sending pattern*. Some messages in the sending pattern may be dropped. Therefore, only a subset of the sending pattern is delivered. We refer to the set of messages (sent by some process) that is delivered to a process as a *receiving pattern*.

Bounded persistent sending pattern. Consider a sending pattern s consisting of an infinite number of messages. If there exists an upper-bound on the duration between every pair of consecutive messages, then s is referred to as a *bounded persistent* sending pattern.

4.2 Timer

In order to send heartbeats at regular intervals, and to implement an adaptive timeout mechanism, we need a mechanism to measure time. We accomplish this through a countdown timer. A class called *timer* implements such a countdown timer using the local clock available at each process. The pseudo-code for the class is show in Fig. 1.

The class *timer* uses the local clock primitive *clock_tick*() to measure time. The primitive *clock_tick*() is the output of the local clock provided by the system that generates ticks at a constant rate. *clock_tick*() generates an event (tick) that is used by *timer* to count down.

The class *timer* has two methods associated with it: *start*, and *stop*. The method *timer.start* accepts a countdown value, and starts counting down from the given value to zero. The counter is decremented for each clock tick. When the counter reaches zero, and a notification is sent to the process that called that timer. The method *timer.stop* simply sets the counter value to zero, and no notification is sent.

```
class timer()
    method timer.start(integer countervalue)
        counter := countervalue
        while (counter > 0)
            upon event clock_tick() decrement counter
        send notification
    end method
    method timer.stop()
        counter := 0
    end method
```

Fig. 1. Implementation of a timer using the local clock

4.3 Heartbeat Generator

The pseudo-code in Figure 2 implements the heartbeat generator. The parameter p is the local client process of the heartbeat generator. The variable *hb_tmr* is

```
function generator(process p)
1 :   param:
2 :       p ∈ Π /* p is the client process */
3 :   var:
4 :       const inter_hb_time /* timer for sending heartbeats periodically */
5 :   primitive:
6 :       timer hb_tmr /* timer is the class from Fig. 1.1 */
7 :   begin
8 :       loop forever
9 :               hb_tmr.start(inter_hb_time)
10 :                  wait until notification from hb_tmr
11 :                  foreach q ∈ Π
12 :                      send a heartbeat to q
13 : end
```

Fig. 2. Pseudo-code *generator* implements the heartbeat generator at process p, periodically sending heartbeats to all process

an instance of the *timer* class in Fig. 1. The variable *inter_hb_time* determines the interval between two heartbeats sent to a process. This variable is constant, and is determined before the execution begins.

Heartbeat generator sends heartbeats at regular intervals. The regularity of the interval is maintained by the *loop forever* construct in lines 8–12 in Fig. 2. The timer *hb_tmr* starts (line 9) in the beginning of each iteration of the loop for a duration of *inter_hb_time* time units. In line 10, the heartbeat generator waits for the timer to expire. Upon timer expiry, the heartbeat generator receives a notification. After receiving the notification, the heartbeat generator sends one heartbeat each to all the processes in the system. When *generator* reenters the loop, it restarts the timer for *inter_hb_time* time units. In other words, *generator* sends heartbeats after every *inter_hb_time* time units.

4.4 Heartbeat Witness

The pseudo-code in Fig. 3 implements the heartbeat witness. The function *receiver* (in Fig. 3), monitors heartbeats from a single process q. To monitor heartbeats from all processes in the system, a process p runs *receiver* for all processes $q \in \Pi$, concurrently.

The parameter p is the process that is receiving the heartbeats, the parameter q is the process whose heartbeats are being monitored by p. The integer variable *max_inter_arrival* stores the current estimate on the heartbeat inter-arrival time, and initialized to some positive value. The timer *tmr* counts down from *max_inter_arrival* to zero. The boolean variable *suspect* stores the current suspicion status of process q. If *suspect* is *true*, then p currently suspects q.

In Fig. 3, the timer *tmr* starts with some initial estimate of the upper-bound on inter-arrival time of heartbeats from q (line 8). The function *receiver* goes into an infinite loop (lines 11–18) waiting for either a heartbeat from q (line 12), or expiry of *tmr*. If a heartbeat is received from q (line 12), then *receiver* checks

```
function receiver(process p, process q)
1 :  param:
2 :      p ∈ Π /* p is the client process */
3 :      q ∈ Π /* q is the monitored process */
4 :  var:
5 :      integer max_inter_arrival := initial estimate
6 :      boolean suspect := false
7 :  primitive:
8 :      timer tmr /* timer is the class from Fig. 1.1 */
9 :  begin
10 :   tmr.start(max_inter_arrival)
11 :     loop forever
12 :         if (receive heartbeat from q)
13 :             if (suspect = true)                       /* wrongful suspicion */
14 :                 suspect := false
15 :                 increment max_inter_arrival          /* increase timeout */
16 :             tmr.start(max_inter_arrival)
17 :         if (receive notification from tmr)
18 :             suspect := true
19 : end
```

Fig. 3. Pseudo-code *receiver* implements the heartbeat witness monitoring process q, at process p

to see if q is already in the suspect list (line 13). If q is in the suspect list, then its a wrongful suspicion. Therefore, q is removed from the suspect list (line 14). A wrongful suspicion implies that the current estimate on the upper-bound on the inter-arrival time was less than the de-facto upper-bound. Hence, *receiver* increases the estimate on the the upper-bound (line 15). In line 16, the timer *tmr* is restarted. If the timer *tmr* expires (line 17), then q is added to the suspect list.

4.5 Scheduler

The threads *generator* (in Fig. 2) and *receiver* (in Fig. 3) are scheduled by a round-robin pre-emptive scheduler $\Diamond\mathcal{P}$-exec as shown in Figure 4. The set of processes Π is finite and static. Therefore, the number of threads executed by $\Diamond\mathcal{P}$-exec are finite and constant. The round-robin scheduling ensures that there is an upper-bound on how long the threads *generator*, and *receiver* have to wait in the queue before being scheduled for execution.

The lower-bound on absolute process speed translates to an upper-bound on the physical time it takes for $\Diamond\mathcal{P}$-exec (in Figure 4) to execute each instruction in its code. Round-robin scheduling of threads bounds the physical time that each *generator*, and *receiver* thread waits to be executed. The composition of the two bounds translates to an upper-bound on the physical time it takes for each thread to be scheduled and run on the processor.

Note that an upper-bound on physical time translates to an upper-bound on local time measured as the number of local clock ticks. This follows from the assumption that ADD system model provides a local clock that measures time at a uniform rate.

```
◇P−exec (process p)
    cobegin
        foreach q ∈ Π
            task receiver(p, q)
        end foreach
        task generator(p)
    coend
```

Fig. 4. Eventually Perfect Failure Detector ($\diamond\mathcal{P}$) in the ADD model

5 Proof of Correctness

5.1 Proof Outline

To prove correctness, we need to show that the implementation in Sec. 4 satisfies $\diamond\mathcal{P}$ specifications *viz.*, *strong completeness* and *eventual strong accuracy.*

The proof of correctness is divided into three parts:

- In the first part, we prove that *generator* (in Fig. 2) described in Sec. 4.3 always generates a bounded persistent sending pattern.
- In the second part, we show that when a bounded persistent sending pattern is transmitted on an ADD channel, the channel yields a receiving pattern with an upper-bound on inter-arrival time.
- In the third part, we show that if *receiver* (in Fig. 3) described in Sec. 4.4 witnesses a receiving pattern with an upper-bound on inter-arrival time, *receiver* satisfies *strong completeness* and *eventual strong accuracy.*

The composition of the above three parts demonstrates that the implementation described in Sec. 4 satisfies $\diamond\mathcal{P}$ specification.

5.2 Generating Bounded Persistent Sending Patterns

Lemma 1. *The heartbeat generator in Fig. 2 always generates a bounded persistent sending pattern.*

Proof. The following three arguments hold:

1. All the lines in the code take bounded local time to execute.
2. The scheduler (Sec. 4.5) guarantees that every time the *generator* thread enters the queue, waiting to be executed on the processor, there is an upper-bound on the duration (measured in local time) that the *generator* thread waits before executing on the processor.
3. Visual inspection of the pseudo-code in Fig. 2 reveals that notification for the expiry of timer *hb_tmr* is sent every constant number of clock ticks.

From the above three arguments it follows that there is an upper-bound on time between two consecutive executions of lines 10–12 in Fig. 2. In other words, there is an upper-bound on the time between every pair of consecutive heartbeats to each process. Given that the timer *hb_tmr* is started infinitely often, heartbeats are sent infinitely often. In other words, the sending pattern generated by these heartbeats is a *bounded persistent* sending pattern. □

5.3 Upper-Bound on Heartbeat Inter-arrival Time

Let a bounded persistent sending pattern, transmitted on an ADD channel, yield a receiving pattern V. We show that there exists an upper bound on the inter-arrival time of the privileged messages in V. We use this result to prove that there exists an upper bound on on the inter-arrival time of all messages in V.

Lemma 2. *If a bounded persistent sending pattern of heartbeats is sent on an ADD channel, then there exists an upper-bound on the inter-arrival time of privileged heartbeats in the receiving pattern.*

Proof. ADD channel properties (Sec. 3.1) guarantee an unknown upper-bound R on the number of non-privileged messages between every pair of consecutive privileged messages. In other words, in every sequence of $2(R+1)$ consecutive heartbeats in an ADD channel, at least two of them are privileged.

The sending pattern is bounded persistent; by definition, there exists some upper-bound on the duration between the send times of every pair of consecutive heartbeats. Let us denote this bound as B time units. This implies that the upper-bound on time taken to send $2(R+1)$ heartbeats in the sending pattern is given by $2B(R+1)$ time units. In other words, the upper-bound between send times of every pair of consecutive privileged heartbeats is $2B(R+2)$ time units.

ADD channels also guarantee an unknown upper-bound D on the message delay of privileged messages. Thus, the upper-bound on the difference between message delays of two consecutive privileged messages is D time units. Therefore, the upper-bound on time elapsed between the arrivals of two consecutive privileged heartbeats is given by $A_p = 2B(R+1) + D$ time units, which is an upper-bound on the inter-arrival times of privileged heartbeats. □

Lemma 3. *A bounded persistent sending pattern of heartbeats, when sent on an ADD channel, yields a receiving pattern V with upper-bound on inter-arrival time.*

Proof. Let m be the earliest arriving privileged heartbeat in V. Let the arrival time of m be t_m. Let $V_m \subset V$ be the set of all heartbeats in V that arrived before, or at time t_m. Let $V_{m+} \subset V$ be the set of all heartbeats in V that arrived after, or at time t_m. Note the following: (1) $V_m \cup V_{m+} = V$, (2) all privileged heartbeats are in the set V_{m+}, and (3) heartbeat m is an element of both V_m and V_{m+}.

The set V_{m+} has all the privileged heartbeats. From Lemma 2, we know that there exists some unknown upper bound A_p on inter-arrival time of privileged heartbeats. Therefore, for every heartbeat $g \in V_{m+}$ there exists some privileged heartbeat $h \in V_{m+}$ that arrives within A_p time units after the arrival of g. Therefore, the upper-bound on inter-arrival time of heartbeats in V_{m+} is A_p.

If $|V_m| > 1$, then the inter-arrival time of heartbeats in V_m is at most t_m. This follows from the fact that $m \in V_m$ and m arrived at time t_m.

From the above argument it follows that the upper-bound on inter-arrival time for all the heartbeats that arrived before time t_m is t_m, and the upper-bound on the inter-arrival time for all the heartbeats that arrived at or after time t_m is A_p. Therefore, the upper-bound on the inter-arrival time for all heartbeats in V is given by $A = max(A_p, t_m)$. □

5.4 Strong Completeness and Eventual Strong Accuracy

If there exists an upper-bound on the heartbeat inter-arrival time, then *receiver* in Figure 3 satisfies Strong Completeness and Eventual Strong Accuracy.

Strong completeness. The strong completeness property states that every correct process eventually, and permanently suspects all crashed processes.

Lemma 4. *The heartbeat witness in Fig. 3 satisfies* ***strong completeness****.*

Proof. A faulty process crashes after some finite time, and therefore, sends only a finite number of heartbeats. Consider a run where process q crashes at time t_c. Let t_f be the time of the last receipt of heartbeats sent by q to a correct process p. After time t_f, process p does not receive any heartbeat from q, therefore the *if* condition in line 12 of *receiver* (Fig. 3) at p will evaluate to $false$ in the infinite suffix. In other words, if q is suspected by p after time t_f, then p will suspect q permanently thereafter.

At time t_f, process p has some finite value of timer *tmr*. Since *tmr* eventually expires, let it expire at time $t_s > t_f$. This implies that the *if* condition in line 17 of Fig. 3 evaluates to true at time t_s. Therefore the correct process p adds q to its suspect list at t_s.

From the above arguments it follows that all correct processes eventually and permanently suspect q, and hence, all crashed processes. □

Eventual strong accuracy. Eventual strong accuracy states that for each run, there exists a time after which no correct process is suspected by any correct process.

Lemma 5. *If there exists an upper-bound on the heartbeat inter-arrival time, receiver in Fig. 3 satisfies* ***eventual strong accuracy****.*

Proof. For a given run, for each pair of correct processes p and q, let the upper-bound on inter-arrival time of heartbeats from q to p be A time units.

The thread *receiver* at process p maintains an estimate on the upper-bound on the inter-arrival time of heartbeats (variable $max\_inter\_arrival$ in Fig. 3) from q. If the current estimate on the upper-bound on inter-arrival time, at some time t, is equal to, or greater than A, then in the infinite suffix process p will receive a heartbeat from q before timer *tmr* expires at p. Therefore, process q is never suspected by p after time t.

However, if the current estimate on the upper-bound on inter-arrival time is less than A, then timer *tmr* at process p may expire before p receives a heartbeat from q, resulting in a false suspicion. However, within A time units after such a false suspicion, p will receive a heartbeat from q. Consequently, p will take q off the suspect list and increment the estimate on the upper-bound on inter-arrival time. The estimate on the upper-bound on inter-arrival time can be incremented only finitely many times before it exceeds A. Therefore, p can suspect q only finitely many times before the estimate on the upper-bound on inter-arrival time exceeds A. Therefore, in the infinite suffix following the last instance of p suspecting q, process p never suspects process q.

Since p and q are any two correct processes, the above argument applies to every pair of correct processes. In other words, there exists a time after which no correct process is suspected by any correct process. □

Theorem 6. *The algorithm described in Sec. 4 implements an eventually perfect ($\diamond\mathcal{P}$) failure detector in the ADD model.*

Proof. From Lemmas 1 and 3, it follows that the heartbeat generator module *generator* produces a bounded persistent sending pattern, which when transmitted on an ADD channel, yields a receiving pattern with an unknown upper-bound on the inter-arrival time.

From Lemmas 4 and 5 we conclude that if there exists an upper-bound on the inter-arrival time in the receiving pattern, the heartbeat witness module *receiver* satisfies strong completeness and eventual strong accuracy.

Thus, it follows that the algorithm described in Sec. 4 implements $\diamond\mathcal{P}$ in the ADD model. □

6 Conclusion

We have shown that one can implement eventually perfect failure detector ($\diamond\mathcal{P}$) in the weak, unreliable, partially synchronous ADD model with unbounded message loss as well as unbounded message delay for the majority of messages. Our work demonstrates a proximate but essential understanding of unreliable, partially synchronous communication via ADD Channels, and their sufficiency for implementing $\diamond\mathcal{P}$. This work is a fundamental step toward the ultimate goal of understanding the minimal assumptions on reliability and partial synchrony necessary to implement this oracle.

References

1. Chandra, T.D., Toueg, S.: Unreliable failure detectors for reliable distributed systems. Journal of the ACM 43, 225–267 (1996)
2. Fischer, M.J., Lynch, N.A., Paterson, M.S.: Impossibility of distributed consensus with one faulty process. Journal of the ACM 32, 374–382 (1985)
3. Aguilera, M.K., Delporte-Gallet, C., Fauconnier, H., Toueg, S.: Stable leader election. In: Proceedings of the 15th International Symposium on Distributed Computing, pp. 108–122. Springer, Heidelberg (2001)
4. Aguilera, M.K., Chen, W., Toueg, S.: On quiescent reliable communication. SIAM Journal on Computing 29, 2040–2073 (2000)
5. Guerraoui, R., Kapałka, M., Kouznetsov, P.: The weakest failure detectors to boost obstruction-freedom. In: Proceedings of the 20th International Symposium on Distributed Computing, pp. 399–412. Springer, Heidelberg (2006)

6. Pike, S.M., Song, Y., Ghoshal, K.: Wait-free dining under eventual weak exclusion. Technical Report TAMU-CS-TR-2006-5-1, Texas A&M University (2006)
7. Pike, S.M., Sivilotti, P.A.G.: Dining philosophers with crash locality 1. In: Proceedings of the 24th International Conference on Distributed Computing Systems, pp. 22–29. IEEE Computer Society Press, Los Alamitos (2004)
8. Song, Y., Pike, S.M.: Eventually k-bounded wait-free distributed daemons. Technical Report TAMU-CS-TR-2007-2-1, Texas A&M University (2007)
9. Guerraoui, R.: On the hardness of failure-sensitive agreement problems. Information Processing Letters 79, 99–104 (2001)
10. Larrea, M., Fernández, A., Arévalo, S.: On the implementation of unreliable failure detectors in partially synchronous systems. IEEE Transactions on Computers 53, 815–828 (2004)
11. Dwork, C., Lynch, N., Stockmeyer, L.: Consensus in the presence of partial synchrony. Journal of the ACM 35, 288–323 (1988)
12. Mostéfaoui, A., Mourgaya, E., Raynal, M.: Asynchronous implementation of failure detectors. In: Proceedings of the 33rd International Conference on Dependable Systems and Networks. IEEE Computer Society Press, Los Alamitos (2003)
13. Bertier, M., Marin, O., Sens, P.: Implementation and performance evaluation of an adaptable failure detector. In: Proceedings of the 32nd International Conference on Dependable Systems and Networks, pp. 354–363. IEEE Computer Society Press, Los Alamitos (2002)
14. Larrea, M., Arévalo, S., Fernández, A.: Efficient algorithms to implement unreliable failure detectors in partially synchronous systems. In: Proceedings of the 13th International Symposium on Distributed Computing, pp. 34–48. Springer, Heidelberg (1999)
15. Fetzer, C., Raynal, M., Tronel, F.: An adaptive failure detection protocol. In: Proceedings of the 7th Pacific Rim International Symposium on Dependable Computing, pp. 146–153. IEEE Computer Society Press, Los Alamitos (2001)
16. Fetzer, C., Schmid, U., Süsskraut, M.: On the possibility of consensus in asynchronous systems with finite average response times. In: Proceedings of the 25th International Conference on Distributed Computing Systems, pp. 271–280. IEEE Computer Society Press, Los Alamitos (2005)
17. Larrea, M., Lafuente, A.: Communication-efficient implementation of failure detector classes $\diamond\mathcal{P}$ and $\diamond\mathcal{Q}$. In: Proceedings of the 19th International Symposium on Distributed Computing, pp. 495–496. Springer, Heidelberg (2005)

Stochastic Communication Delay Analysis of Adaptive Wormhole-Switched Routings in Tori with Faults

Farshad Safaei[1,2], Mahmood Fathy[1], Ahmad Khonsari[3,2], Mohamed Ould-Khaoua[4,5]

[1] Dept. of Computer Eng., Iran Univ. of Science and Technology, Tehran, Iran
[2] IPM School of Computer Science, Tehran, Iran
[3] Dept. of ECE, Univ. of Tehran, Tehran, Iran
[4] Dept. of Electrical and Computer Eng., Sultan Qaboos Univ., Al-Khodh, Oman
[5] Dept. of Computing Science, Univ. of Glasgow, UK
{f_safaei,mahfathy}@iust.ac.ir, {safaei,ak}@ipm.ir, mohamed@dcs.gla.ac.uk

Abstract. This paper proposes a novel analytical modeling approach to investigate the performance of five prominent adaptive routings in wormhole-switched 2-D tori fortified with an effective scheme suggested by Chalasani and Boppana [1], as an instance of a fault-tolerant method. This scheme has been widely used in the literature to achieve high adaptivity and support inter-processor communications in parallel computers due to its ability to preserve both communication performance and fault-tolerant demands in such networks. Analytical results of the model are confirmed by comparing with those obtained through simulation experiments.

1 Introduction

Flow control in interconnection networks deals with the allocation of channel and buffer resources to packets as they proceed through the network. The wormhole switching has been dominant for its low latency communication, and it has been adopted by most of the contemporary massively parallel machines. In wormhole switching, a message is divided into flow control digits (or *flits*). The flits are routed through the network one after another in a pipeline fashion. A flit of the message is designated as the *header flit*, which leads the message through the network. When the header flit is blocked due to lack of output channels, all of the flits wait at their current nodes for available channels.

Routing is the process of transmitting data from one node to another in a given system. Most past multicomputers have adopted deterministic routing where messages with the same source and destination addresses always take the same network path. This form of routing has been popular because it requires a simple deadlock-avoidance algorithm, resulting in a simple router implementation [2]. However, if any channel along the message path is heavily loaded, the message experiences large delays and if any node/channel along the path is faulty, the message cannot be delivered at all. Alternatively, adaptive routing improves both the performance and fault-tolerance of an interconnection network and, more importantly, it has the ability to provide performance, which is less sensitive to the communication

I. Stojmenovic et al. (Eds.): ISPA 2007, LNCS 4742, pp.497–508,2007.

pattern [2]. Fault-tolerance is the ability of a routing algorithm to bypass faulty nodes/links in the network.

This paper proposes a novel analytical model to assess the performance behavior of a number of prominent adaptive routing algorithms in wormhole-switched 2-D tori [3] fortified with an efficient scheme suggested by Chalasani and Boppana [1], as an instance of routing methodology widely used in the literature to achieve high adaptivity and fault-tolerance capability in communication networks.

The remainder of the paper is structured as follows. Section 2 reviews some definitions and background that will be useful for the subsequent sections. Section 3 describes the analytical model while Section 4 validates the model through simulation experiments. Finally, in Section 5, we summarize the results presented in the paper.

2 Preliminaries

2.1 Torus Network Topology

A (k, 2)-torus is a direct network with $N=k^2$ nodes; k is called the radix. Links (channels) in the torus can be either uni- or bi-directional. In this paper, we will focus on 2-D torus with bi-directional links as they have been more popular in parallel systems. Each node can be identified by a 2-digit radix k address (x_1, x_2). Nodes, with address (x_1, x_2), (y_1, y_2) are connected iff $x_1=(x_2+1) \bmod k$ or $y_1=(y_2+1) \bmod k$. We denote the link between nodes x and y by $<x, y>$.

2.2 The Chalasani-Boppana's Routing Scheme

Several fault-tolerant fully adaptive routings on the tori have been characterized in [3] out of which the one using negative hop-based deadlock-free routing, augmented with a new idea called *bonus cards*, has shown to have the best performance. Chalasani and Boppana [1] have proposed an efficient framework to enhance wormhole switching for deadlock-free fault-tolerant routings in the torus networks. They considered arbitrary-located faulty blocks and assumed only local knowledge of faults. The key concept used in their method is that, for each connected fault region of the network, it is feasible to connect the fault-free components around the fault to form a ring. This is the fault ring, f-ring, for that fault and consists of the fault-free nodes and channels that are adjacent (row-wise, column-wise, or diagonally) to one or more components of the fault region.

3 The Analytic Model

This section describes first the assumptions and then the derivation of the analytical model. Our analysis focuses on the PHop, Pbc, Nbc, Duato-Pbc, and Duato-Nbc routing algorithms introduced in [3].

3.1 Assumptions

The model makes assumptions, which are commonly used in the literature [5-10], and are listed below.

- Nodes generate traffic independently of each other, following a Poisson process with an average rate of λ_{node} messages per cycle.
- Messages destinations are uniformly distributed across the network nodes.
- The message length is M flits, each of which requires one cycle transmission time between two adjacent routers.
- Each node is failed with probability θ_p. The probabilities of node failure in the network are equally likely and independent of each other. Furthermore, faults are static [1-3, 10] and do not disconnect the network.
- Nodes (processors) are more complex than links and thus have higher failure rates [1, 2]. So, we assume only node failures.
- The local queue at the injection channel in the source node has infinite capacity. Messages at the destination node are transferred to the local PE one at a time through the ejection channel.
- V virtual channels per physical channel are used. These virtual channels are used according to the routing scheme. This number of virtual channels yields the optimal performance compared to the other schemes proposed in [3], but, of course, at the expense of high implementation cost.

3.2 Outline of the Model

The mean message latency consists of the mean network latency, $E(L)$, that is the mean time to cross the network and the mean waiting time seen by messages at the source node, $E_s(W)$. However, to model the effect of virtual channel multiplexing, the mean message latency has to be scaled by a factor, say $E(V)$, representing the average degree of virtual channel multiplexing, that takes place at a given physical channel. Therefore, the mean message latency can be approximated as [7]

$$\textit{Mean Message Latency} = [E\,(L) + E_s\,(W)].\ E\,(V) \tag{1}$$

Under the uniform traffic pattern the average number of channels that a message makes along a given dimension and across the fault-free network, $E(k)$, $E(d)$, respectively, are given by Agarwal [8]

$$E\,(k\,) = \begin{cases} k\;/\,4 & k \text{ is even} \\ 1/\,4(k\;-1/\,k\,) & k \text{ is odd} \end{cases} \quad , E(d) = 2\ E(k) \tag{2}$$

In view of the above equations, it is also easy to check that they are true if there are no faults in the network. Hence, it is needed to recalculate these expressions due to the existence of faulty regions in the network. In this section, to make the representation easier, we focus on representing a technique to compute the average number of hops across each dimension, $E_f\,(k)$, with a rectangular fault region. In order to calculate the $E_f\,(k)$, two cases should be considered:

(i) A message may face the f-ring with probability P_{hit}. In this case, $E_f(k)$ can be computed by multiplying the average number of hops, $E(\omega)$, by P_{hit}.

(ii) A message may not face the f-ring (with probability $P_{miss} = 1-P_{hit}$). Therefore, the $E_f\,(k)$ can be obtained by multiplying the average number of hops in the normal case, $E(k)$, by P_{miss}.

Taking into account two different cases mentioned above, $E_f\,(k)$ is calculated by weighting average of the average number of hops taken in each case. Thus, $E_f\,(k)$ can be computed by

$$E_f(k) = P_{hit}E(\omega) + P_{miss}E(k) \tag{3}$$

where $P_{miss} = 1 - P_{hit}$.

It is noteworthy that a fault-free node is in the f-ring only if it is at most two hops away from a faulty node. Thus, the distance of route between two nodes may be greater than or equal to 2 and is at most h. We get the average number of hops as

$$\begin{aligned} E(\omega) &= 2\left[\sum_{i=0}^{h/2} 2(h/2-i) + w + \sum_{j=0}^{w/2} 2(w/2-j) + h\right] \Big/ (h+w) \\ &= \left[2(h/2+1)(w+3h/4) + 2(w/2+1)(h+3w/4)\right] \Big/ (h+w) \end{aligned} \tag{4}$$

Calculating the probability of facing the fault ring (P_{hit})

Consider a torus with k vertices along in each dimension and a block fault region containing some faulty nodes embedded in the network. The probability that the path from an arbitrary source node $s \in S$ to any arbitrary destination node $d \in D$ being along the shortest path and blocked by the f-ring is defined as

$$P_{hit} \triangleq \frac{\text{The number of paths that cross the block fault region}}{\text{The total number of minimal paths that pass through the network}} \tag{5}$$

Let us first calculate the total number of paths that pass through the torus. In general, if there are n dimensions numbered 0 to $n - 1$ and there are Δ_t hops from a source node, s, to a destination node, d, in the t-th dimension, then the total number of minimal routes from s to d can be calculated as

$$\|\Im\|_{(s,d)}^{n} = \prod_{t=0}^{n-1} \binom{\sum_{j=t}^{n-1} \Delta_j}{\Delta_t} = \left(\sum_{t=0}^{n-1} \Delta_t\right)! \Big/ \prod_{t=0}^{n-1} \Delta_t\,! \tag{6}$$

To calculate the message blocking probability in the vicinity of fault regions, there is a need to find the probability of facing fault rings. We denote the probability of occurring such event by P_{hit}. When the faults are randomly distributed through the network, this parameter is equal to an independent node failure probability (i.e., θ_p). But, in the vicinity of fault rings, the P_{hit} will be calculated in a different approach. The details of calculation of P_{hit} using adaptive routing scheme have been reported elsewhere [10]. Now, let us calculate the average message arrival rate on a given channel $<a, b>$ where a and b are two adjacent nodes. Because a link survives if and only if both nodes at its ends survive, it is followed that

$$\Pr\{A\ link\ survives\} = (1 - \theta_p)^2 \tag{7}$$

For every source-destination pair of surviving nodes, s and d, for which channel $<a, b>$ may be used, the probability that channel $<a, b>$ is traversed is calculated as

$$P_{(s,d),<a,b>} = \|\Im\|_{<s,a>}^{2} \cdot \|\Im\|_{<b,d>}^{2} \cdot (1-\theta_p)^2 \Big/ \|\Im\|_{(s,d)}^{2} \tag{8}$$

The rate of messages produced at a specific node and destined to another surviving node is equal to the ratio of the message generation rate, λ_{node}, to the number of surviving nodes in the network except itself. Therefore, the rate of messages generated at a specific node, *s*, and destined to another surviving node, *d*, that traverse a surviving channel <*a*, *b*> on its path is measured as

$$\lambda_{(s,d),<a,b>} = \lambda_{node} \cdot P_{(s,d),<a,b>} / (N(1-\theta_p)-1) \tag{9}$$

The rate of messages traversing a specific channel can be calculated as the aggregate of Eq. (9) over all source-destination pairs that have at least one path between each other that traverses surviving channel <*a*, *b*>. Thus

$$\lambda_{<a,b>} = \sum_{(s,d)\in G_{<a,b>}} \lambda_{(s,d),<a,b>} \tag{10}$$

where $G_{<a,\,b>}$ is the set of all pairs of source and destination nodes that have at least one path between each other that traverses channel <*a*, *b*>.

3.2.1 Calculation of the Message Blocking Probability

We assume that the total *V* virtual channels associated to each physical channel are grouped into some different classes. According to the PHop routing scheme [4], if a message has already completed *i* hops, it can use only a virtual channel of class *i*. In other words, if the virtual channels of class *i* are occupied, the message is blocked even if virtual channels in other classes are free. In what follows, we calculate the message blocking probability in each routing algorithms introduced in [3].

Message blocking probability in PHop scheme

We denote the probability of blocking for a message after passing *i* hops by PHop (*i*). Throughout the paper we will assume that the number of virtual channels in different classes, say *k*', are equal. Using the following theorem, we see that PHop (*i*) is constant for each $0 \le i \le r$.

Theorem 1. *If the virtual channels selection rule is PHop and there are k' and V virtual channels in each class and physical channel, respectively, the message blocking probability is given by*

$$\text{PHop}\ (i) = \sum_{j=k'}^{V} P_j \cdot \binom{V-k'}{j-k'} \Big/ \binom{V}{j} \tag{11}$$

where P_j is the probability that j virtual channels at a specific physical channel are busy. The probability P_j is obtained later from Eq. (37) *using a Markovian model.*

Proof: According to the behavior of the PHop routing scheme, when the message is blocked at the *i*-th hop channel, all the virtual channels that are elements of the class *i* are occupied. Thus, there are $j \ge k'$ busy virtual channels such that *k*' of which are all in class *i*. It is clear that the probability of occurrence of such event is equal to $\binom{V-k'}{j-k'} \Big/ \binom{V}{j}$. Since *j* could take all the values between *k*' and *V*, the result follows. ♦

Message blocking probability in Pbc scheme

Suppose that *C* is the number of virtual channel classes and each class contains *k*' virtual channels. Using virtual channel selection rule by Pbc, the number of usable virtual channels of class *i*, when (*r* – *i*) hops are going to be taken to reach the destination, can be given as

$$j = C - r + I \tag{12}$$

We denote the probability of message blocking at the i-th hop channel, using the Pbc routing scheme by $P^b_{\text{Pbc}}(i,r)$, where r is the distance (in hops) that a message makes from source to destination.

Theorem 2. *If the virtual channels selection rule is Pbc and there are k' and V virtual channels in each class and physical channel, respectively, the message blocking probability for an r-hop message is given by* $P^b_{\text{Pbc}}(i,r) = \left[\sum_{l=k'}^{V} P_l \cdot \binom{V-k'}{l-k'} \Big/ \binom{V}{l}\right]^{j-i}$

***Proof*:** After crossing the i-th hop channel, the usable classes are between $i+1$ and j. Therefore, the message is blocked at the i-th hop channel if all the virtual channel classes between $i+1$ and j are busy. We then deduce that $P^b_{\text{Pbc}}(i,r) = \prod_{l=i+1}^{j} PHop(l) = \left[\sum_{l=k'}^{V} P_l \cdot \binom{V-k'}{l-k'} \Big/ \binom{V}{l}\right]^{j-i}$ which completes the proof. ♦

Message blocking probability in Nbc scheme

For the negative-hop with bonus cards, Nbc, the number of bonus cards is equal to the number of virtual classes minus the number of required negative hops to reach the destination. Using the same approach for Pbc scheme, we can show that the probability of blocking for an r-hop message in Nbc routing algorithm is equal to

$$P^b_{\text{Nbc}}(i,r) = P^b_{\text{Pbc}}\left(\lfloor i/2 \rfloor, \lfloor r/2 \rfloor\right) \qquad 0 \le i \le r \tag{13}$$

Note that, the number of virtual channel classes (i.e., C) is different in Pbc and Nbc schemes.

Message blocking probability in Duato- Pbc scheme

Now, assume that the virtual channel selection rule is Duato-Pbc where V_1 and V_2 virtual channels are used in fully adaptive and deadlock-free classes, respectively. In what follows, we determine the blocking probability of an r-hop message in Duato-Pbc scheme. By defining the notation $P^b_{\text{Pbc}}(i)$ as the probability of blocking for the i-hop channel in Pbc routing, the $P^b_{\text{Pbc}}(i)$ condition on selecting a class such that all its virtual channels in each hop be busy, is computed as follows. Let $\Phi(i)$ be the probability of class utilization at the i-th hop channel, which is defined by

$$\begin{aligned}\Phi(i) &\triangleq \frac{\text{The number of usable classes in Category II at } i\text{-th hop channel}}{\text{The total number of usable classes at } i\text{-th hop channel}} \\ &= (V_2 - i + 1)/(V_1 + V_2 - i + 1)\end{aligned} \tag{14}$$

For a message visiting the i-hops, $0 \le i \le E(d)$, the probability of selecting a class that can be done in the i trials is given by

$$(\Phi(\text{i}))^i \tag{15}$$

Thus, the probability that all virtual channels of Category II are busy, is given by

$$P^b_{\text{Category II}}(r) = \sum_{i=0}^{r} P^b_{\text{Pbc}}(i,r) \cdot (\Phi(i))^i \tag{16}$$

We can therefore obtain the probability of blocking for an r-hop message in Duato-Pbc scheme as

$$P^b_{\text{Duato-Pbc}}(r) = \sum_{j=V_1}^{V} P_j \cdot \left[\binom{V-V_1}{j-V_1} \Big/ \binom{V}{j} \right] \cdot P^b_{\text{Category II}}(r) = \text{PHop}(V_1) \cdot P^b_{\text{Category II}}(r) \tag{17}$$

Message blocking probability in Duato-Nbc scheme

Finally, by means of the similar approach developed in the previous sections, we can easily establish the probability of message blocking in Duato-Nbc routing algorithm as

$$P^b_{\text{Duato-Nbc}}(r) = \text{PHop}(V_1) \cdot \sum_{i=0}^{r} P^b_{\text{Pbc}}(i) \cdot (\Phi(\lfloor i/2 \rfloor))^i \tag{18}$$

3.2.2 Calculation of the Mean Network Latency

Let the channels traversed by the message be numbered from 1 to $E(d)$, with the lower-numbered channels being crossed first (the destination node is at the fictive channel $E(d)+1$). We derive a recurrent relation in which latency is determined first at the destination (i.e., at channel $E(d)+1$) and then is propagated backward to the source (i.e., at channel 1). Suppose that message flits are serviced as soon as they arrive at their destinations, the latency seen at the fictive channel is given by

$$L_{E(d)+1} = M \tag{19}$$

where M is the message length in terms of flits. Let us now determine the latency L_i, $(1 \le i \le E(d))$, seen by a message when it is crossing channel i towards its destination. In the event of blocking, a message may wait up indefinitely, for one of the required virtual channels to become free. If it successes to acquire a virtual channel, it advances in one cycle to the next node. If the message faces the fault ring (with probability P_{hit}), it is delivered to the Chalasani-Boppana's scheme to be routed through the network. Let $P^b_{\Re}(i)$ be the probability that a message experiences blocking situation when the routing scheme $\Re$ is used at the i-th hop channel. The routing scheme $\Re$ can be identified as

$$\Re = \{[R] \subset \text{Fully adaptive routings} : R \in \Gamma\} \tag{20}$$

where $[x]$ signifies the class of x and Γ is the set of routing algorithms that are developed in [3]. That is

$$\Gamma = \{\text{PHop, Pbc, Nbc, Duato-Pbc, Duato-Nbc}\} \tag{21}$$

Taking into account all the cases that a message may experience when crossing an intermediate channel, the latency L_i, $(1 \le i \le E(d))$, seen by the message when crossing channel i can be written as

$$L_i = \left[1 - \left(P^b_{\Re}(i) + P_{hit}\right)\right] \cdot \left[L_{i+1} + 1 + P^b_{\Re}(i) \cdot E_{<a,b>}(W)\right] + P_{hit} \cdot \left[\Lambda + M + E(d) \cdot \left[\sum_{j=1}^{i-1} \left(1 + P^b_{\Re}(j) \cdot E_{<a,b>}(W)\right)\right]\right] \tag{22}$$

In the equation above, the first term accounts for the cases when the message neither experiences a blocking nor faces the fault ring at the i-th hop channel. The message may wait $E_{<a,\, b>}(W)$ with probability $P_{\Re}^{b}(i)$ to access one of the required virtual channels to advance to the next channel (i+1), where it sees the latency L_{i+1} to complete its journey. The second term, on the other hand, accounts for the case when the message has faced the fault ring. In this case, the message is transferred to the Chalasani-Boppana's routing scheme after M cycles to account for the message transmission time. It also encounters a delay overhead of Λ cycles due to routing decision time using the Chalasani-Boppana's scheme. Finally, the mean network latency, $E(L)$, seen by a message visiting $E_f\,(d)$ channels to cross from source to destination is given by

$$E(L) = L_1 \tag{23}$$

3.2.3 Calculation of the Mean Waiting Time

We now want to provide the mean message waiting time, $E_{<a,\, b>}(W)$, to acquire a virtual channel that may be treated as an M/G/1 queue [6]. Since the minimum service time at a given channel is equal to the message length, M, following a suggestion proposed by Draper and Ghosh [9], the variance of the service time distribution can be approximated by $(E_{<a,\, b>}(S) - M)^2$; where $E_{<a,b>}(S)$ is the average service time of channel $<a, b>$. Hence, the mean waiting time becomes

$$E_{<a,b>}(W) = \lambda_{<a,b>} \cdot \left(E_{<a,b>}(s)\right)^2 \left(1 + \left(E_{<a,b>}(s) - M\right)^2 \Big/ \left(E_{<a,b>}(s)\right)^2\right) \Big/ \left(2\left(1 - \lambda_{<a,b>} \cdot E_{<a,b>}(s)\right)^2\right) \tag{24}$$

In order to calculate the $E_{<a,\, b>}(S)$ we must consider that a message may successfully reach its destination, or in the case of facing, the message is delivered to the Chalasani-Boppana's scheme and visits $E_f\,(d)$ channels, on average, between the source and destination nodes. Let us refer to these cases as "normal" and "affected" messages, respectively. Taking into account all the above cases, we can write the mean service time seen by the message when crossing the network as

$$E_{<a,b>}(S) = P_n \cdot E_n(S) + \sum_{i=1}^{E_f(d)} P_f(i) \cdot E_i(L) \tag{25}$$

where P_n is the probability of successful normal transmission, i.e., a message has successfully arrived at its destination without facing the fault ring. Because a normal message visits, on average, $E(d)$, channels to reach its destination, P_n is calculated by

$$P_n = \prod_{i=1}^{E(d)} \left[1 - \left(P_{\Re}^{b}(i) + P_{hit}\right)\right] \tag{26}$$

The second term of Eq. (26) denotes the state when a message is affected due to facing the fault ring. Moreover, a normal message reaches the i-th hop channel if it has not met the fault ring at the previous (i −1) hop channels. Therefore, the probability $P_f\,(i)$ that a message faces the fault ring at the i-th hop channel can be described as

$P_f(i)$ =Pr{*the message faces the f-ring at the i-th hop channel* | *the message neither experiences blocking nor faces the f-ring at the previous (i*−1*) hop channels*} $= P_{hit} \cdot \prod_{j=1}^{i-1} \left[1 - \left(P_{\Re}^{b}(j) + P_{hit}\right)\right]$ (27)

Consider a normal message that has not met the fault ring at any of the intermediate channels, and therefore was transmitted successfully in the network. The mean network latency of a normal transmission consists of two parts: one delay is due to the actual message transmission time and the other is due to waiting times at network channels during transit from source to destination. Given that a message crosses, on average, $E(d)$ channels; the mean network latency, $E_n(S)$, in the case of a normal transmission can be written as

$$E_n(s) = \sum_{i=1}^{E(d)} \left[1 + P_{\Re}^{b}(i) \cdot E_{<a,b>}(W)\right] \tag{28}$$

where M signifies the message length, and $E_{<a,b>}(W)$ is the mean waiting time seen by a message at channel $<a, b>$. Now, consider again a message that faces the fault ring at the i-th hop channel ($1 \leq i \leq E_f(d)$). The message that has already passed (i–1) channels along the normal channels is routed in the f-ring for the rest of its journey until it is delivered to its destination. The mean network latency seen by a message in the case of an affected transmission due to the fault situation at the i-th hop can be written as

$$E_i(L) = \sum_{j=1}^{i-1} \left[1 + P_{\Re}^{b}(j) \cdot E_{<a,b>}(W)\right] + E_{f-ring}(L) \tag{29}$$

where the first term denotes the latency in the normal channels and the second term, $E_{f\text{-}ring}(L)$, signifies the approximated latency seen by an affected message from the i-th hop channel in the f-ring until it reaches its destination. $E_{f\text{-}ring}(L)$ is obtained by

$$E_{f-ring}(L) = M + E_{f-ring}(\omega) \cdot \left[1 + E_{f-ring}(b) \cdot E_{f-ring}(W)\right] \tag{30}$$

where $E_{f\text{-}ring}(\omega)$ is the average number of hops that an affected message makes along the f-ring, and $E_{f\text{-}ring}(b)$, $E_{f\text{-}ring}(W)$ are the mean blocking and waiting times at a channel along the f-ring, respectively. In what follows we calculate the quantities $E_{f\text{-}ring}(\omega)$, $E_{f\text{-}ring}(b)$, and $E_{f\text{-}ring}(W)$.

In order to estimate the average number of hops that a message can make along the f-ring, we consider a rectangular fault region embedded in a torus parameterized by h and w which are concerning the height and width of the region, respectively. Then, it turns out that

$$\begin{aligned} E_{f-ring}(\omega) &= \frac{4}{h^2+2hw}\left(\sum_{i=0}^{h}\sum_{j=0}^{w} i+j\right) + \frac{2}{h^2+2hw}\left(\sum_{i=0}^{h}\sum_{j=0}^{i-1} j+h-i+w\right) \\ &+ \frac{2}{h^2+2hw}(h/2+1)(w+3h/4)\frac{2}{h^2+2hw}\left(\sum_{i=0}^{w}\sum_{j=0}^{i-1} j+w-i+h\right) + \frac{2}{h^2+2hw}(w/2+1)(h+3w/4) \end{aligned} \tag{31}$$

The traffic on a channel in the f-ring is composed of messages that are affected by the faults and are also blocked at each node in the network. If P_{hit} and $P_{\Re}^{b}(i)$ are the probability of facing the fault ring and probability of blocking at a given channel, respectively; a normal message can become an affected message at the i-th hop channel ($1 \leq i \leq E_f(d)$) with probability (P_{hit}+ $P_{\Re}^{b}(i)$). Considering that, on average, there are $E_{f\text{-}ring}(\omega)$ channels in the f-ring and only nodes in the path which is crossing the f-ring may be contributed with blocked messages; therefore we need to estimate the mean arrival rate in the f-ring. To do so, we ought to obtain the set of pair nodes such that there exists one or more points from that set of points reside on the f-ring along the given path. Thus, we define the set A as

$$\mathcal{A}=\{(a,b)\in v(T_{k\times k})\times v(T_{k\times k}): y_a, y_b < h+3, |x_b - x_a| > \lfloor k/2 \rfloor \text{or } x_a, x_b < w+3, |y_b - y_a| > \lfloor k/2 \rfloor\} \quad (32)$$

where $T_{k\times k}$ and $v(T_{k\times k})$ are the $k\times k$ torus network and the set of its vertices, respectively. So, the approximate mean arrival rate in the f-ring, $\lambda_{f\text{-}ring}$, can be provided as

$$\lambda_{f-ring} = \|A\| \cdot \sum_{i=1}^{E(d)} \left(P_{hit} + P_{\Re}^{b}(i)\right) \cdot \lambda_{<a,b>} \Big/ E_{f-ring}(\omega) \quad (33)$$

where the symbol || || indicates the cardinality of set A.

Knowing that the traffic on network channels is uniform when adaptive routing is used, the mean service time seen by a given message is the same across all channels, regardless of their position, and is equal to the mean of the network latency, $E_{f\text{-}ring}(L)$. We can obviously conclude

$$E_{f\text{-}ring}(b) = \lambda_{f\text{-}ring} E_{f\text{-}ring}(L) \quad (34)$$

A message that is affected by faults at its i-th hop channel will traverse, on average, $E_{f\text{-}ring}(\omega)$ channels along the f-ring to reach its destination, requiring one cycle at each hop in the absence of blocking. To simplify the model derivation, the channels in the f-ring are assumed to have the same statistical behavior. Let us now calculate the mean waiting time at a channel in the f-ring. Modeling the channel as an M/G/1 queue [6] with a mean arrival rate, $\lambda_{f\text{-}ring}$ and approximated mean service time $E_{f\text{-}ring}(L)$ and an approximated variance $(E_{f\text{-}ring}(L) - M)^2$, as suggested by [9], yields the mean waiting time in the f-ring as

$$E_{f-ring}(W) = \lambda_{f-ring} \cdot \left(E_{f-ring}(L)\right)^2 \left[1 + \left(E_{f-ring}(L) - M\right)^2 \Big/ \left(E_{f-ring}(L)\right)^2\right] \Big/ \left(2\left(1 - \lambda_{f-ring} \cdot E_{f-ring}(L)\right)^2\right) \quad (35)$$

3.2.4 Calculation of the Mean Waiting Time at the Source Node

In this section, we compute the average waiting time at the source node, $E_s(W)$. Since a message in the source node can enter the network through any of the V virtual channels, the average arrival rate to the queue is λ_{node}/V and service time $E_{<a,b>}(s)$ with an approximated variance $(E_{<a,b>}(s) - M)^2$. Applying the Pollaczek-Khinchine (P-K) mean value formula [6] yields the average waiting time experienced by a message at the source node as

$$E_s(W) = \left(\lambda_{node}/V\right)\left(E_{<a,b>}(s)\right)^2 \left[1 + \left(E_{<a,b>}(s) - M\right)^2 \Big/ \left(E_{<a,b>}(s)\right)^2\right] \Big/ \left(2\left(1 - \lambda_{node} \cdot E_{<a,b>}(s)/V\right)^2\right) \quad (36)$$

3.2.5 Calculation of Average Degree of Virtual Channels Multiplexing

The probability, P_j $(0 \le j \le V)$, that j virtual channels at a given physical channel are busy can be determined using a Markovian model (details of the model can be found in [5, 7, 10]). In the steady state, the model yields the following probabilities [5]

$$P_j = \begin{cases} Q_0 = 1 & P_0 = \left(\sum_{j=0}^{V} Q_j\right)^{-1} \\ Q_j = Q_{j-1}\lambda_{<a,b>}E_{<a,b>}(S) \quad (0<j<V) & P_j = P_{j-1}\lambda_{<a,b>}E_{<a,b>}(S) \quad (0<j<V) \\ Q_j = \dfrac{Q_{j-1}\lambda_{<a,b>}}{1/E_{<a,b>}(S)-\lambda_{<a,b>}} \quad (j=V) & P_j = \dfrac{P_{j-1}\lambda_{<a,b>}}{1/E_{<a,b>}(S)-\lambda_{<a,b>}} \quad (j=V) \end{cases} \tag{37}$$

When multiple virtual channels are used per physical channel, they share the bandwidth in a time multiplexed manner. The average degree of virtual channel multiplexing, that takes place at a given physical channel, can be estimated by [5]

$$E(V) = \sum_{i=1}^{V} i^2 \cdot P_i \Big/ \sum_{i=1}^{V} i \cdot P_i \tag{38}$$

The above equations reveal that there are several inter-dependencies between the different variables of the model. Given that closed-form solutions for such models are very difficult to determine, the equations of the proposed model here are solved using an iterative technique [6].

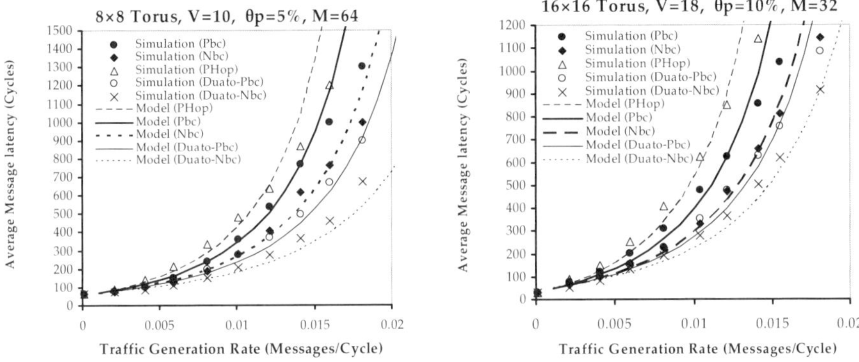

Fig. 1. Average message latency calculated by the model vs. simulation in the 8×8 and 16×16 torus networks for V=10, 18 virtual channels per physical channel, message lengths M=32 and 64 flits and failure rate θ_p= 5%, 10%

4 Simulation Experiments

To further understand and evaluate the performance issues of the routing algorithms, we have developed an event-driven simulator at flit-level. The simulator mimics the behavior of Chalasani-Boppana's scheme in (k, 2)-tori with and without faults. We ran each simulation for 300,000 flit times and sufficient warm-up times (by discarding the information obtained during the first 10,000 flit times) provided to allow the network reach the steady state. We have simulated the 8×8 and 16×16 torus networks with 5% and 10% of total network nodes faulty. The values obtained from different fault sets are averaged and shown in Fig. 1. The x-axis in this figure represents the traffic rate injected by a given node in a cycle (λ_{node}) while the y-axis shows the average message latency (in flit cycles). Each graph illustrates the simulation results and the analytical model prediction for two message length M = 32, 64 flits and

V =10, 18 virtual channels per physical channel. The figure indicates that the simulation results and the values predicted by the proposed model are in good agreement under steady state regions, i.e. under light and moderate traffic and near the saturation point. Since the independence assumptions are essential in ensuring a tractable model, and given that most evaluation studies concentrate on network performance in the steady state regions, it can be concluded that the present analytical model constitutes a cost-effective evaluation tool for assessing the performance behavior of fully adaptive routing algorithms in torus networks.

5 Conclusions

In this paper, we have presented a novel analytical modeling approach to capture the mean message latency for five adaptive routing algorithms, namely PHop, Pbc, Nbc, Duato-Pbc, and Duato-Nbc using an efficient scheme suggested by Chalasani and Boppana in 2-D tori with faults. We showed that the proposed analytical model manages to achieve a good degree of accuracy while maintaining simplicity, making it a practical evaluation tool that can be used by the researchers in the field to gain insight into the performance behavior of fully adaptive routings in wormhole-switched torus networks. As future direction a number of interesting topics can be studied by tuning the model parameters in order to extend the proposed model to higher order dimensional network and consider the performance evaluation of interconnection networks with an arbitrary topology.

References

1. Chalasani, S., Boppana, R.V.: Adaptive wormhole routing in tori with faults. IEE Proc.-Comput. Digit. Tech. 42(6), 386–394 (1995)
2. Dally, W.J., Towles, B.: Principles and practices of interconnection networks. Morgan Kaufman Publishers, San Francisco (2004)
3. Safaei, F., et al.: Performance Comparison of Routing Algorithms in Wormhole-Switched Fault-Tolerant Interconnect Networks. In: International Conference on Network and Parallel Computing (2006)
4. Boppana, R.V., Chalasani, S.: A Framework for Designing Deadlock-Free Wormhole Routing Algorithms. IEEE Transactions on Parallel and Distributed Systems 7(2), 169–183 (1996)
5. Dally, W.J.: Virtual channel flow control. IEEE Transactions on Parallel and Distributed Systems 3(2), 194–205 (1992)
6. Kleinrock, L.: Queueing Systems, vol. 1. John Wiley, New York (1975)
7. Ould-Khaoua, M.: A Performance model for Duato's adaptive routing algorithm in k-ary n-cubes. IEEE Trans. Computers 48(12), 1–8 (1999)
8. Agarwal, A.: Limits on interconnection network performance. IEEE Transactions on Parallel and Distributed Systems 2(4), 398–412 (1991)
9. Draper, J., Ghosh, J.: A comprehensive analytical model for wormhole routing in multicomputers systems. Journal of Parallel and Distributed Computing 32, 202–214 (1994)
10. Safaei, F., et al.: Performance Analysis of Fault-Tolerant Routing Algorithm in Wormhole-Switched Interconnections. Journal of Supercomputing (2007)

An Efficient Fault-Tolerant Routing Methodology for Fat-Tree Interconnection Networks*

Crispín Gómez, María E. Gómez, Pedro López, and José Duato

Dept. of Computer Engineering,
Universidad Politécnica de Valencia,
Camino de Vera, s/n, 46071–Valencia, Spain
crigore@gap.upv.es, {megomez,plopez,jduato}@disca.upv.es

Abstract. In large cluster-based machines, fault-tolerance in the interconnection network is an issue of growing importance, since their increasing size rises the probability of failure. The topology used in these machines is usually a fat-tree. This paper proposes a new distributed fault-tolerant routing methodology for fat-trees. It does not require additional network hardware. It is scalable, since the required memory, switch hardware and routing delay do not depend on the network size. The methodology is based on enhancing the Interval Routing scheme with exclusion intervals. Exclusion intervals are associated to each switch output port, and represent the set of nodes that are unreachable from this port after a failure appears. We propose a mechanism to identify the exclusion intervals that must be updated after detecting a failure, and the values to write on them. Our methodology is able to support a relatively high number of network failures with a low degradation in network performance.

1 Introduction

Nowadays, large parallel computers with thousands of nodes have been or are being built [1,3,8]. In such systems, fault-tolerance in the interconnection network is an issue of growing importance since the high number of components significantly increases the probability of failure. In order to deal with permanent faults in a system, two different fault models can be used. In a static fault model, once a failure is detected, the system activity is stopped, appropriate actions to handle the failure are taken and then, the system activity is resumed. It needs to be combined with checkpointing techniques to be effective. In a dynamic fault model, once a new failure is found, actions are taken in order to appropriately handle the faulty component in parallel with the system activity.

There exist several approaches to tolerate permanent faults in the interconnection network. Replicating components incurs in a high extra cost. Another powerful technique is based on dynamically reconfiguring the routing tables. This technique is extremely flexible but it may kill performance, since it uses a generic routing algorithm that does not take advantage of the topology [20]. However, most of the solutions proposed in the literature are based on designing fault-tolerant routing algorithms that find an alternative path when packets may encounter a fault [7].

* This work was supported by the Spanish MEC under Grant TIN2006-15516-C04-01, by CONSOLIDER-INGENIO 2010 under Grant CSD2006-00046 and by the European Commission in the context of the SCALA integrated project #27648 (FP6).

I. Stojmenovic et al. (Eds.): ISPA 2007, LNCS 4742, pp. 509–522, 2007.

Many of the large parallel computing systems are cluster-based machines. In clusters, routing is usually distributed and based on forwarding tables. There is a table at each switch that stores, for each destination node, the output port that must be used. This scheme can be extended to support adaptive routing by storing several outputs in each table entry [16]. The main advantage of table-based routing is that any topology and any routing algorithm can be used. However, routing based on forwarding tables suffers from a lack of scalability, as table size and access time to it grow linearly with the network size. Therefore, a routing strategy for cluster machines that is scalable, flexible to support the most commonly-used routing algorithms in widely-used topologies and fault-tolerant would be desirable. In this paper, we take on such a challenge.

In large cluster-based machines, the chosen topology is based on either direct (tori and meshes) [3] or indirect multistage networks (MINs) [24]. In particular, fat-trees have risen in popularity in the past few years [15].

A scalable distributed routing scheme is Interval Routing (IR) [19]. IR groups those destinations that are physically reachable from the same output port into an interval. Each packet is forwarded through the output port whose interval contains the destination of the packet. To implement IR, it is sufficient to store the bounds of each interval and perform a parallel comparison. Hypercube and n-dimensional meshes with deterministic routing and multistage networks support IR [2]. Some generations of the Quadrics network [18] have used IR. Moreover, in [9], IR was extended with the proposal of Flexible Interval Routing (FIR), a routing strategy for switch-based networks that allows to implement the most commonly-used deterministic and adaptive routing algorithms in meshes and tori, requiring a very small amount of memory.

The goal of this paper is to propose a distributed fault-tolerant methodology for fat-trees that is scalable, since the required amount of memory and routing time do not depend on network size. Moreover, the hardware required at the switches is very simple. Unlike other previous proposals for fat-trees [21, 10, 6], it does not require extra links or switches, since it exploits the inherent path diversity of the fat-tree topology, and does not disconnect any physically-connected node. The proposed methodology is based on IR, enhancing that scheme with exclusion intervals. Exclusion intervals are associated to each output port and represent the set of nodes that become unreachable from that output port after a fault appears. Moreover, it only nullifies the strictly necessary paths due to failures, allowing adaptive routing through all the healthy paths. Furthermore, our proposal is fully compatible with FIR, which would allow to obtain a extremely flexible and fault-tolerant routing strategy with very low memory requirements for the most commonly-used topologies in cluster-based machines.

The rest of the paper is organized as follows. Section 2 describes the fat-tree topology. Section 3 describes the proposed fault-tolerant routing methodology. Section 4 evaluates the proposal. Section 5 briefly summarizes previous work devoted to fault-tolerance in MINs. Finally, some conclusions are presented.

2 Fat-Tree Topology

A multistage interconnection network (MIN) is a regular topology in which switches are identical and organized as a set of stages. Each stage is only connected to the previous and the next stage using a regular connection pattern. Processing nodes are attached only to the switches of the first stage. In particular, we focus on the fat-tree topology [14], since it is the most-commonly used MIN in commercial machines. A fat-tree topology is a complete tree that gets thicker near the root. The number of ports of the switches increases as we go nearer to the root, which makes the physical implementation unfeasible. For this reason, some alternative implementations keep a fixed switch degree. We focus on k-ary n-trees, where bandwidth is increased as we go near the root by replicating switches. Figure 1 shows a k-ary n-tree with 8 processing nodes.

k-ary n-trees are a parametric family of regular topologies that can be built by varying two parameters, k (the arity or the number of links of a switch that connects to the previous or next stage; i.e. the switch degree is $2k$) and n (the number of stages). A k-ary n-tree is able to interconnect $N = k^n$ processing nodes using nk^{n-1} switches. Each processing node is represented as a n-tuple $\{0, 1, ..., k-1\}^n$, and each switch is defined as a pair $\langle s, o \rangle$, where s is the stage at where the switch is located, $s \in \{0..n\text{-}1\}$, and o is a $(n-1)$-tuple $\{0, 1, ..., k-1\}^{n-1}$ which identifies the switch inside its stage. Figure 1 shows a 2-ary 3-tree, with 8 processing nodes and 12 switches.

Two switches, $\langle s, o_{n-2}, ..., o_1, o_0 \rangle$ and $\langle s', o'_{n-2}, ..., o'_1, o'_0 \rangle$, are connected if $s' = s + 1$ and $o_i = o'_i$ for all $i \neq s$. There is a link between the switch $\langle 0, o_{n-2}, ..., o_1, o_0 \rangle$ and the processing node $p_{n-1}, ..., p_1, p_0$ if $o_i = p_{i+1}$ for all $i \in \{n-2, ..., 1, 0\}$. We will use this link numbering in the switches of a k-ary n-tree: descending links are labeled from 0 to $k-1$, and ascending links from k to $2k-1$.

In a k-ary n-tree, minimal routing can be accomplished by sending packets forward to one of the nearest common ancestors of both, source and destination, and then, from there, backwards to the destination [7]. When crossing stages in the forward direction, several paths are possible, so adaptive routing is provided. In fact, each switch can select any of its upward output ports. Once a nearest common ancestor has been reached, the packet is turned around and sent backwards to its destination. Once the turnaround is crossed, a single path is available to the destination node. That is, the upwards phase is fully adaptive while the backwards phase is deterministic.

Adaptive routing in fat-trees can be easily implemented by using Interval Routing. By properly configuring the interval associated to every switch port, packets can be correctly routed to their destinations. Notice that cyclic intervals are required, as shown in Fig. 1. A packet generated at node 0 destined to node 2 may choose two routing options at switch $\langle 0, 00 \rangle$, since node 2 belongs to both up link intervals of the switch, reaching either switch $\langle 1, 00 \rangle$ or $\langle 1, 01 \rangle$. From these switches, only port number 1 forwards the packet to switch $\langle 0, 01 \rangle$ (node 2 is only inside the interval associated to link 1) which delivers the packet to node 2 through port number 0.

3 Fault-Tolerant Routing Methodology with Exclusion Intervals

The proposed methodology provides fault-tolerant adaptive routing for fat-tree networks. We will only consider permanent faults. It can work with both link and switch faults. However, a switch fault can be modeled by the fault of all the links connected to it. Therefore, we focus only on link faults.

A static fault model is assumed. Therefore, once a new fault is detected, the system activity is stopped, then the new routing information is computed and distributed, and finally the system activity is resumed from the last performed checkpoint. The

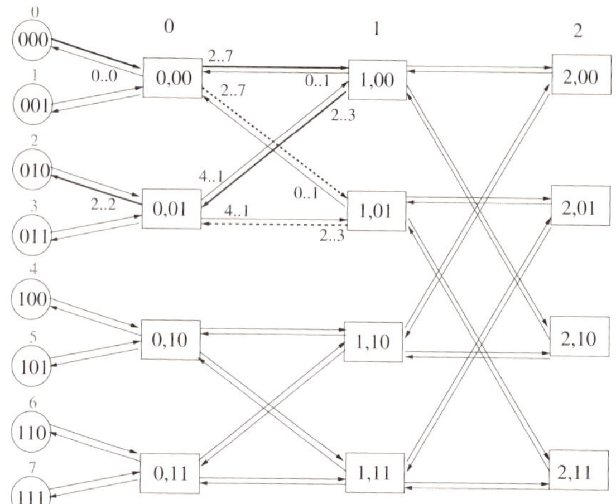

Fig. 1. A 8-node 2-ary 3-tree

proposed methodology will be focused only in the computation of the fault-tolerant routing information. Fault detection and checkpointing are out of the scope of this paper.

Our proposal uses Interval Routing (IR) for adaptively routing packets in k-ary n-tree networks. As we showed in Fig. 1, IR allows a simple and intuitive implementation of the commonly-used routing algorithm in fat-trees. We extend IR with *exclusion intervals* for the purpose of providing fault-tolerance. The original IR uses an interval per output port to indicate the reachable destinations through that output port. We associate an additional interval to each output port, the exclusion interval, that indicates the destinations that become unreachable through that output port after a fault. The exclusion interval contains nodes that belong to the inclusion interval, but due to a fault, they must be excluded. Therefore, the nodes that are now reachable through that output port are the ones that are in the inclusion interval but are not in the exclusion interval. In this way, we can avoid paths that use faulty links. For instance, assume that the interval associated to a given output port is $[0..11]$. After excluding the interval $[4..7]$, the set of reachable nodes is reduced to $[0..3, 8..11]$. In Sect. 3.1 we will show an example of computing the exclusion intervals for a faulty network. The proposal will be referred as FT^2EI (Fat-Tree Fault-Tolerant routing with Exclusion Intervals).

This implementation of fault-tolerant routing in fat-trees is very simple. Only two sets of registers that store the inclusion and exclusion intervals plus some logic to check whether the destination address is inside these bounds are required per output port[1]. These operations are done in parallel in all the output ports, introducing a very low delay, much smaller than the one incurred by forwarding tables. As adaptive routing is supported, a given destination address may be inside several intervals. The selection function will select the final output port from this set.

[1] In fact, exclusion intervals are only required at ascending output ports (see Sect. 3.1).

3.1 Computing the Exclusion Intervals

Every link in the network connects two switches, through an output port of a switch to an input port of the other switch. When a link fails, we will call faulty switch to the switch that is connected to the faulty link through its output port, since in our methodology this is the switch that has to take actions to tolerate the fault.

In a k-ary n-tree, we can consider two different types of link faults from the point of view of the faulty switch: ascending (up) link faults and descending (down) link faults, which correspond to links that forward packets to upper or lower stages respectively. The management of both faults is different. The up link fault management is extremely easy. As all nodes reachable through an up link at a switch can be also reached by any of its ascending links, the method just nullifies the faulty link. This is done by associating to the faulty link an exclusion interval that includes all the nodes in the network. As the upwards phase is fully-adaptive, all the network traffic that was sent through the faulty link will be sent through any of the other up links of the switch.

On the other hand, a fault in a down link of a switch requires the updating of several exclusion intervals, even exclusion intervals of other switches. Remember that, in a k-ary n-tree, the down routing phase is deterministic. Once a packet has arrived to one of the common ancestors between source and destination nodes, it has only one possible down path. So, our methodology must avoid that packets arrive to any common ancestor whose down path to destination goes through the faulty link, which requires updating the exclusion intervals of previous switches. In the next sections we explain how to update the exclusion intervals to do that.

An Example of Exclusion Interval Computing. We will explain the methodology with the example shown in Fig. 2. Figure 2 assumes that link 1 of switch 18 has failed and, as a consequence, nodes 4 to 7 are not longer reachable from it. Therefore, packets with destination 4, 5, 6 or 7 should not arrive at switch 18 in the descending phase. Hence, switches 26 and 30 should not receive packets destined to nodes 4, 5, 6 or 7, since their unique path to arrive to these nodes is through switch 18. To make this possible, switches that connect to switches 26 and 30 through up links, should exclude nodes from 4 to 7 in their associated output ports. Therefore, switches[2] 18 and 22 should update the exclusion interval of their up output ports to exclude nodes 4, 5, 6 and 7. Again, switches of the previous stage should avoid forwarding packets destined to nodes 4 to 7 to switches 18 and 22, because now these switches cannot forward packets to those destinations through any of its output ports. These switches are 8, 12 and 14, which should exclude nodes 4 to 7 in the exclusion interval associated to output port 3. They will now route packets to these destinations through output port 2. Notice, though, that as long as the exclusion intervals of switches 8, 12 and 14 have been set, it is not longer necessary to update the exclusion intervals of switches located at stage 2 (i.e. switches 18 and 22) since packets destined to nodes 4, 5, 6 and 7 will never reach them, because switches 8, 12 and 14 already exclude those nodes in output port 3. Figure 2 shows the exclusion intervals that should be updated in the network.

Computing Exclusion Intervals in the General Case. Let $\langle e, v_{n-2}, ..., v_1, v_0 \rangle$ and l be the faulty switch and link, respectively. As it can be seen this switch belongs to

[2] Notice that switch 18 will not actually send any packet to nodes 4-7 through its up links.

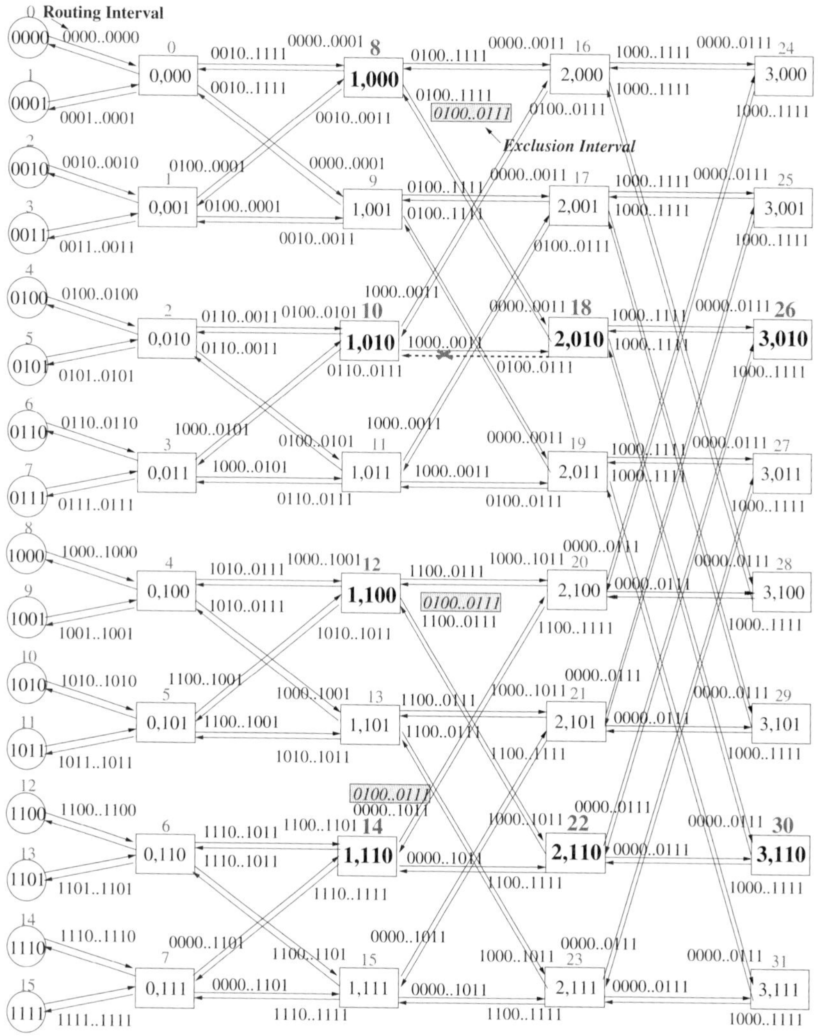

Fig. 2. A 2-ary 4-tree with a faulty link at switch 18

stage e . As shown in the previous example, only some switches at stage $e - 1$ should be updated. These switches can be classified according to their connection to the faulty switch, as they may be directly or indirectly connected to it.

First, we will identify the switches that are directly connected to the faulty switch. In Fig. 2, these switches are 8 and 10 (but switch 10 routes packets to the affected destinations through its down links, so it is not really necessary to update it). According to Sect. 2, the switches that are directly connected to the faulty switch may differ only by the $e-1$ digit of the second component of the switch identifier with the faulty switch. Hence, these switches are given by $\langle e-1, v_{n-2}..v_e, X, v_{e-2}, .., v_1, v_0\rangle$, being X any value between 0 and $k-1$. The port to update in them is the up one that is connected to the faulty switch and is given by the v_{e-1} digit (the e less significant digit) of the second component of the faulty switch. According to our link numbering (where up links start from k), the link to be updated is the $k + v_{e-1}$ one. As it was stated above, there is a switch (switch 10 in the example) in the previous stage that does not need to be updated, despite the fact of accomplishing the previous equation. This switch does not need to be updated because it will never forward through its up links packets whose destination is included in the exclusion interval. This switch is the one directly connected to the faulty switch through the link in the opposite direction of the faulty link, and is given by $\langle e - 1, v_{n-2}..v_e, l, v_{e-2}, .., v_1, v_0 \rangle$.

The rest of the switches of the $e - 1$ stage to be updated are the ones that may forward packets to the faulty switch following any of the possible paths provided by the routing algorithm. These switches are given by $\langle e - 1, X, .., X, v_{e-2}..., v_1, v_0 \rangle$. This expression also includes the switches directly connected to the faulty switch. The link to update in those switches is also given by $k + v_{e-1}$. Finally, the nodes to include in the exclusion interval should be computed. The exclusion interval may contain the nodes included in the inclusion interval associated to the faulty link. This interval is given by $[v_{n-2}, ..., v_{n-e}, l, 0, ..., 0 \,..\, v_{n-2}, ..., v_{n-e}\, , l, (k-1), ..., (k-1)]$. The computation cost of this algorithm is $O(k^{n-1})$, that is, the number of switches in a stage of the fat-tree.

Let us apply these equations to the example shown in Fig. 2 in order to prove that we get the same result shown in Sect. 3.1. The link 1 of switch 18 $\langle 2, 010 \rangle$ has failed. The switches to be updated are $\langle 1, XX0 \rangle$, that is, switches 8 $\langle 1, 000 \rangle$, 10 $\langle 1, 010 \rangle$, 12 $\langle 1, 100 \rangle$ and 14 $\langle 1, 110 \rangle$. The link to be updated in these switches is $k + v_{e-1}$, that is, $k + v_1 = k + 1 =$ link 3. The values to fill in the exclusion intervals are given by [0100..0111], which is the interval that includes nodes 4, 5, 6 and 7. Finally, the switch 10 $\langle 1, 010 \rangle$ may not be updated. So, the same result is obtained.

Notice that in both up and down link faults, it is only required to associate exclusion intervals to up links, since what we do is to eliminate the ascending paths that cross the faulty link. Notice that, only the paths that make use of the faulty link are eliminated, allowing adaptive routing through all the healthy paths. By using one exclusion interval per output link, the network is able to tolerate at least 1 fault.

3.2 Extension to More Than One Fault

In this section, we analyze how our methodology deals with more than one fault in the network. When considering multiple faults, we have analyzed two alternative approaches. First, we will consider the existence of only one exclusion interval per output port, as assumed up to this point. Second, we will consider the possibility of associating multiple exclusion intervals to each ascending output port.

One Exclusion Interval Per Output Port. The methodology could be directly applied to tolerate multiple link faults, provided that these faults affect exclusion intervals associated to different output ports. The problem arises when two different faults need to update the exclusion interval associated to the same output port.

In order to tolerate multiple faults regardless of the exclusion intervals to be updated, we have designed a methodology to merge two exclusion intervals, the one previously stored that avoids the previous faults, and the one required to tolerate a new fault. The resulting merged exclusion interval should contain all the nodes contained in both exclusion intervals, but it may also contain some nodes that do not belong to any of the initial intervals. We will refer to these nodes as victim nodes. Victim nodes are nodes that should be reachable through this output port, but are included in the exclusion interval in order to obtain a single interval[3]. This is necessary if a single exclusion interval is associated to each output port and the old and new intervals do not intersect. As the inclusion of victim nodes in the exclusion interval reduces the number of paths to these nodes, care must be taken to minimize the number of victim nodes in the exclusion interval. As an example, consider the network status shown in Fig. 2, with a faulty link in switch 18. If, at this point, a new fault is found in link number 1 of switch 22, the interval [12..15] should be excluded in link number 3 of switches 8, 10 and 12. These links already have their exclusion interval registers set to [4..7]. The only possible way of avoiding the use of the faulty links for both set of destinations is to merge both exclusion intervals to obtain a new one [4..15], which will include victim nodes 8 to 11.

Due to the use of cyclic intervals, obtaining a single exclusion interval is not simple, as several cases must be considered. Moreover, the processing is different depending on whether the initial intervals overlap or not. If they overlap, the resulting interval will be the union of the two intervals. Otherwise, either a cyclic or non-cyclic interval can be chosen. The option that reduces the number of victim nodes will be finally selected.

Furthermore, after updating each exclusion interval, it must be checked if there is a set of nodes that are now unreachable from the updated switch. These nodes were reachable through its up links, but due to multiple link faults they may have been excluded in all the up links of the switch. If this is the case, the switches of the previous stage that connect to this switch should also exclude that set of nodes in the links that connect to it. Once these switches are updated, they must perform the same checking, and so on. For instance, using the scenario shown in Fig. 2, if a new fault is detected at link 1 of switch 16, link 2 of switches 8, 12 and 14 should exclude the interval [4..7]. Now, these switches will have the interval [4..7] excluded in all their up links, hence switches of the previous stage directly connected to them should not forward packets with destination between 4 and 7 to them. So, this interval should be excluded at link number 2 of switches 0, 1, 4, 5, 6 and 7. No more iterations are needed, because these switches have other ports that can forward packets to nodes [4..7]. Anyway, once the lowest stage is reached, no more iterations are possible.

Multiple Exclusion Intervals Per Output Port. The task of minimizing the number of victim nodes in a network with several faults can be improved if there are more than one exclusion interval per output port. In this way, if merging two intervals include some victim nodes, we could instead store them into two different exclusion intervals associated to the same output port, thus, not excluding any victim node. The routing function will now exclude those nodes that are included in any of the exclusion intervals associated to the output port. So, no healthy path is sacrificed and therefore we should get better performance. However, if we consider the possibility of having a higher number of faults than the number of exclusion intervals associated to each output port, victim nodes could be again included in the exclusion intervals associated to output ports, but

[3] Notice that these nodes are still reachable through other paths, but not using this output port. So, these nodes are not eliminated from the system.

it is expected that the number of victim nodes will be smaller than the one obtained with just one exclusion interval per output port. In order to fill exclusion intervals in the output ports, the methodology follows the next steps every time a new fault is treated. First, it checks if the exclusion interval associated to the new fault intersects with any of the exclusion intervals already stored at the output port. If so, a new exclusion interval is obtained by merging both of them. In this case, it is not necessary to use another physical exclusion interval, as there are no victim nodes. If the new exclusion interval does not intersect with any of the intervals already stored in the output port, and there are physical exclusion intervals available, then a new one is used to store the exclusion interval associated to the new fault. Finally, if there are not physical exclusion intervals available to assign to the new non-overlapping one, it is merged with the exclusion interval that leads to the minimum number of victim nodes.

As stated in the previous section, once a physical exclusion interval has been updated at a switch, it must be checked if there are nodes that have become unreachable from that switch, accordingly updating the exclusion intervals in the previous stage. This process should be repeated as many times as required.

Notice that the exclusion intervals do not induce new dependencies in the channel dependency graph (CDG) associated to the routing function [7]. On the contrary, every time a exclusion interval is updated, the number of channel dependencies is reduced as the number of possible paths is reduced. Therefore, the resulting fault-tolerant routing algorithm is deadlock free, since the routing algorithm on which it is based is deadlock-free and our proposal removes some channel dependencies.

4 Evaluation

Now, we evaluate FT^2EI, analyzing both its fault–tolerance and performance. We have not considered faults in the injection links, as these faults physically disconnect the processing node. Only network link faults have been modeled.

We will say that the proposal is $n-$fault tolerant, if it is able to tolerate any combination of n faults. Indeed, we say that one given combination of n faults is tolerated if the methodology is able to provide at least one path to communicate every source-destination pair in the network, thus avoiding the faults. A fault combination is not tolerated, if there is at least a source-destination pair for which the methodology can not provide a path. When possible, we have analyzed all the possible combinations for a given number of faults (2-ary 2-trees and 2-ary 3-trees). For networks with a larger number of links, we have analyzed up to 10,000 randomly selected fault combinations. The error caused due to not analyzing all the cases is obtained by a statistical method that considers the total number of fault combinations and the number of analyzed ones, and represents the maximum probability that a fault combination is not tolerated. This probability is quite low (i.e. fault combinations are likely to be tolerated). As an example, in the 4-ary 3-tree, this probability is 0.0081 for 2 faults and 0.0098 for 15 faults.

For the performance evaluation, a detailed event-driven simulator has been developed. It models a k-ary n-tree cut-through network with point-to-point bidirectional serial links. Routers has a non-multiplexed crossbar with queues only at the input ports. The queues can store five packets. Packets are adaptively routed using the mechanism

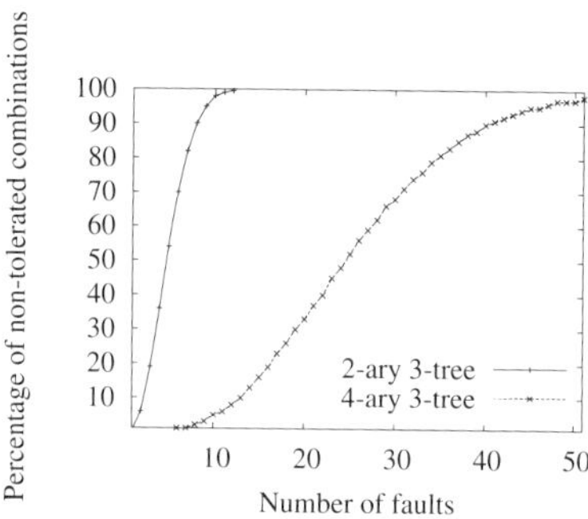

Fig. 3. Pct. of non-tolerated combinations vs. nr. of faults

proposed in this paper. Routing, switching and link time is assumed to be 1 clock cycle. We assume an uniform traffic pattern where the packet generation rate is constant and the same for all the nodes. The packet length is set to 16 bytes.

4.1 One Exclusion Interval Per Output Port

The number of tolerated faults is $k-1$, 1 fault can be tolerated when $k=2$, 2 faults when $k=3$, and so on. The non-tolerated combinations for more than $k-1$ faults in our methodology correspond to the combinations where there is at least a switch in the first stage, stage 0, where all the up links exclude a common subset of processing nodes. In this way, processing nodes connected to that switch have no available path to the excluded set of nodes. When this happens in upper stages, it can be solved by excluding the interval in the previous stage, but this is not possible for stage 0.

Figure 3 shows the number of non-tolerated fault combinations for two network sizes (2-ary 3-tree and 4-ary 3-tree) when varying the number of faults. As it can be seen, in a 2-ary 3-tree, all the combinations of 1 faults are tolerated, and for 2 faults there is a 6% of non-tolerated combinations. In a 4-ary 3-tree, all the combinations of 3 faults are tolerated, and for 4 faults, there is only a 0.23% of non-tolerated combinations. Notice that, for more than $k-1$ faults, the percentage of non-tolerated combinations decreases as we increase the network size.

Now, we analyze how network performance is degraded when some faults are produced and solved with only one exclusion interval. Figure 4 shows the throughput degradation for several k-ary n-trees[4] when varying the number of faulty links from 0 to 5. Each point represents the mean of 500 simulations, each one of them corresponding to a different randomly selected fault combination tolerated by our methodology (if there is a small number of tolerated fault combinations, all them are simulated). The error bars are always smaller than 0.05, so, for the sake of clarity, they are not shown. For one fault, the performance degradation varies from 6% to 14%; for five faults the performance goes down between 8% and 25%. Again, the larger the network, the lower performance degradation due to the higher number of alternative paths.

[4] For a 2-ary 2-tree and 5 faults, there are not tolerated combinations.

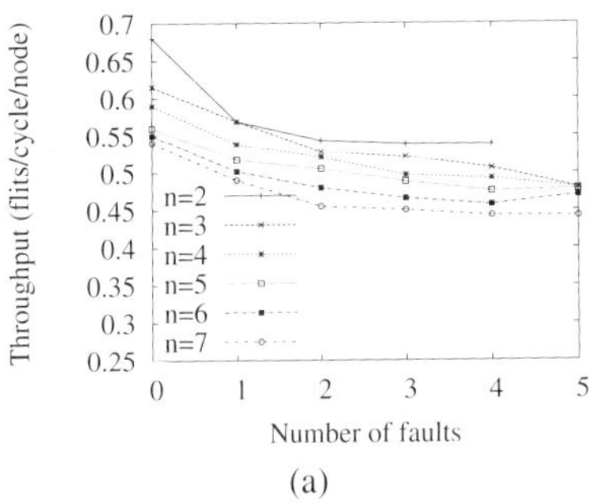

(a)

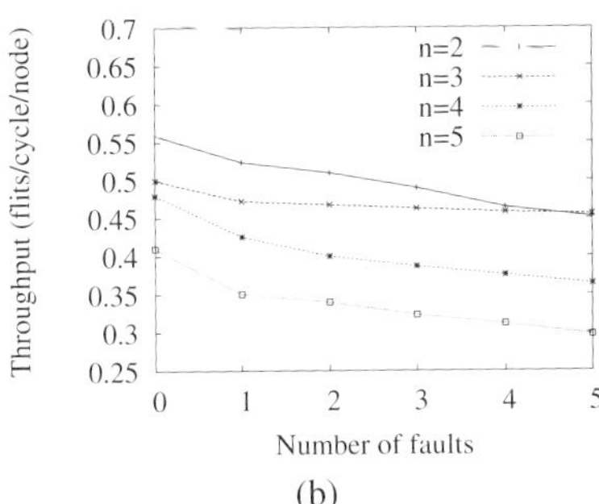

(b)

Fig. 4. Network throughput degradation for one exclusion interval: (a) For several 2-ary n-trees (b) For several 4-ary n-trees

4.2 Multiple Exclusion Intervals Per Output Port

Concerning fault-tolerance, having multiple exclusion intervals does not increase the number of tolerated faults. That is, the methodology remains $k-1$ fault-tolerant. Multiple exclusion intervals help to reduce the number of victim nodes, but with k faults the worst-case scenarios are those in which the exclusion intervals associated to all the faults share a set of destinations and affect the same switch at stage 0. In this situation, no physical path is available for these nodes. So, multiple exclusion intervals do not help in tolerating more faults. Nevertheless, multiple exclusion intervals help to reduce the number of non-tolerated combinations for k and more faults. That is, the percentage of non-tolerated combinations gets smaller as the number of intervals increases. Therefore, fault combinations that do not disconnect any node are easier to be tolerated, since there is a lower number of victim nodes. Figure 5.(a), as an example, shows the percentage of non-tolerated fault-combinations for a 4-ary 3-tree for different number of exclusion intervals per output port. As it can be seen, adding a second exclusion interval has a large influence, specially when more than 15 faults are present in the network. The third exclusion interval also gets improvements but adding more exclusion intervals has a lower impact. For smaller networks (2-ary 3-tree) and a limited number of faults, as it can be seen in Fig. 5.(b), it is not interesting having more than two exclusion intervals. Nevertheless, for larger networks (4-ary 3-tree) and considering a very high number of faults (see Fig. 5.(b)), it can be worth to have more exclusion intervals (up to 5 in this case). Hence, we can say that two exclusion intervals are enough, except for large systems when a high number of faults can appear in the network.

Figure 6, show, as an example, the performance degradation for 4 faults[5] when considering several exclusion intervals. As it can be seen, from 1 to 2 exclusion intervals, the performance degradation is reduced, but for more intervals, no additional improvements are obtained. Nevertheless, again, when considering a large network with a lot of faults (see Fig. 7), additional improvements are obtained when increasing the number of exclusion intervals to tolerate faults, since less healthy paths are eliminated.

[5] The error bars are again smaller than 0.05.

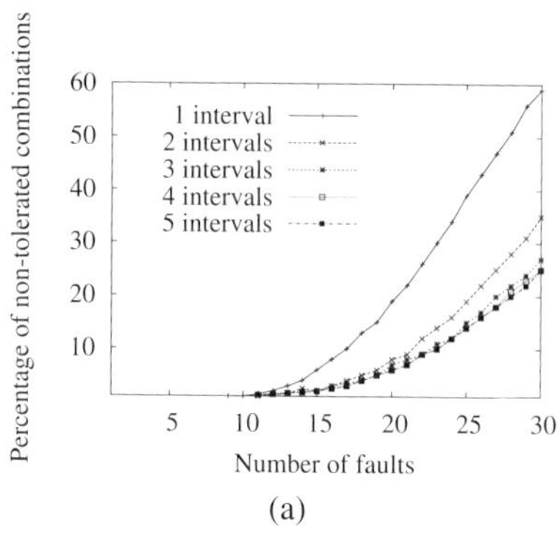

(a)

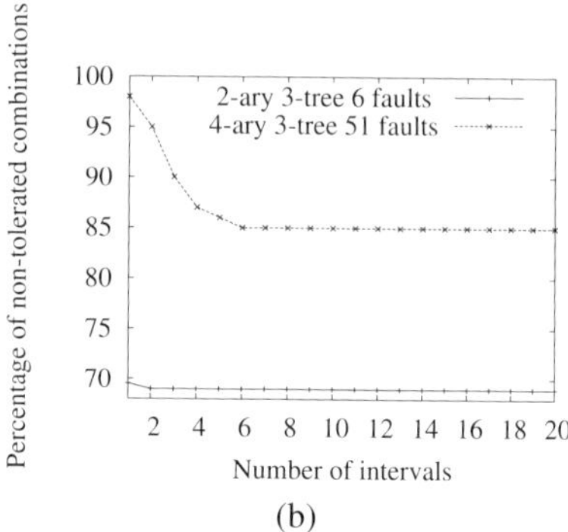

(b)

Fig. 5. Pct. of non-tolerated fault combinations: (a) versus number of faults for different nr. of exclusion intervals in a a 4-ary 3-tree (b) versus number of exclusion intervals in a 2-ary 3-tree with 6 faults and in a 4-ary 3-tree with 51 faults

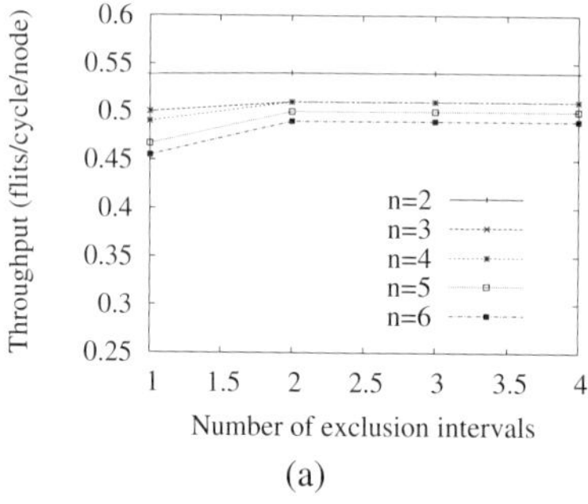

(a)

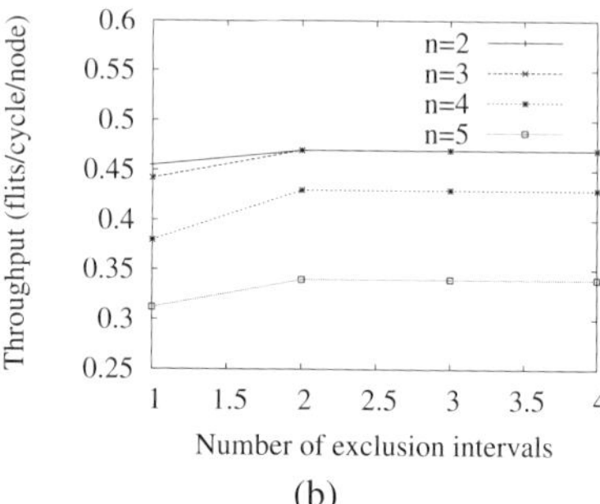

(b)

Fig. 6. Network throughput degradation for multiple exclusion intervals: (a) For several 2-ary n-trees with 4 faults (b) For several 4-ary n-trees with 4 faults

5 Related Work: Fault-Tolerance in MINs

A large amount of work to provide fault-tolerance in MINs is based on using additional hardware to increase the number of alternative paths: adding links between switches in the same stage, more links between stages, or extra stages [10, 11, 25]. Another approach is to misroute packets by routing in multiple passes [26, 12, 5], providing therefore longer paths and increasing latency. In [23], the author proposes a hybrid approach combining multiple paths and multiple passes to forward packets in a faulty network. The authors in [17] presents a comparative study of four fault-tolerant MINs. The study reveals that columnwise redundancy (extra stages) is much more effective than the rowwise approach (extra rows of switches along with extra links between switches). In [22] the authors use several parallel MINs to create redundancy without any interconnecting links between them, increasing the hardware cost of the network. In [21], a new topology that consists of two parallel fat-trees with crossover links between the switches in the same position in both networks is proposed. It is able to tolerate only one faulty link with a very high extra hardware cost. The work in [4] describes a method of creating

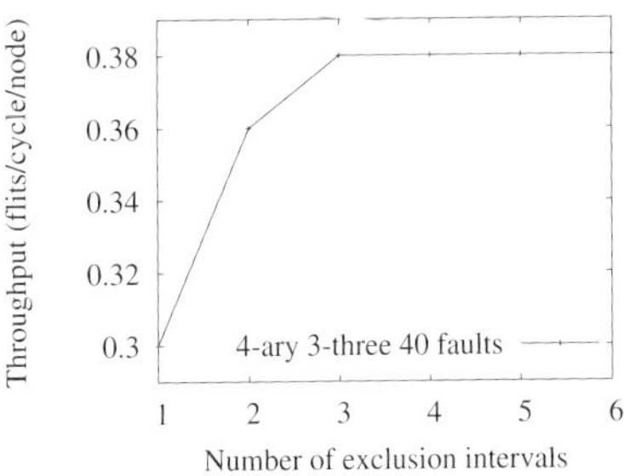

Fig. 7. Network throughput degradation, multiple exclusion intervals, 4-ary 3-tree, 40 faults

routing tables for irregular faulty networks. In [6], different choices in the construction of multiple paths in MINs are analyzed, and the authors describe methods for fault identification and network reconfiguration in MINs. They found that to achieve a good computational performance it is necessary to eliminate nodes with poor network connectivity in order to maintain high network throughput.

6 Conclusions

We have proposed an efficient fault-tolerant distributed adaptive routing strategy ($FT^2 EI$) for k-ary n-tree interconnection networks that it is scalable in memory requirements and router delay. The FT^2EI methodology does neither need complex hardware nor replicating any network component. It is based on enhancing the well-known Interval Routing scheme with exclusion intervals. Each output port is provided with an exclusion interval, that represents the set of nodes that become unreachable after a fault. We have also proposed a simple algorithm to calculate the exclusion intervals of the affected switches, avoiding penalizing those nodes that are not affected by the fault and allowing adaptive routing in all the healthy paths. The results show that the FT^2EI methodology is able to completely tolerate all the fault combinations of $k-1$ links. Moreover, for medium and large networks, FT^2EI is able to tolerate a large number of fault combinations with a high probability (98.05% of probability for 8 faults in a 4-ary 3-tree network). The price paid is some performance degradation, which depends on the number of faults. Although associating several exclusion intervals per output port does not help in increasing the number of tolerated faults for a given topology, the percentage of non-tolerated combinations of faults is strongly reduced, and also the performance degradation of the network. We have obtained that two exclusion intervals per output port is enough for small and medium networks. More than two exclusion intervals make only sense for large networks and a high number of faults.

References

1. ASCI Red Web Site, `http://www.sandia.gov/ASCI/Red/`
2. Bakker, E., et al.: Linear Interval Routing. Algorithms review 2, 45–61 (1991)
3. IBM BG/L Team: An Overview of BlueGene/L Supercomputer. ACM Supercomputing Conference (2002)

4. Broder, A., Fischer, M., Dolev, R., Simons, B.: Efficient fault-tolerant routings in networks. In: Proc. of the 16th annual ACM Symp. on Theory of Computing, ACM Press, New York (1984)
5. Chalsani, S., Raghavendra, C., Varma, A.: Fault-tolerant routing in MIN based supercomputers. In: Proc. of the 4th Int. Conf. on Supercomputing (1990)
6. Chong, F.T., et al.: Design and performance of multipath MIN architectures. In: Proc. of the 4th annual ACM Symp. on Parallel Algorithms and Architectures, ACM Press, New York (1992)
7. Duato, J., Yalamanchili, S., Ni, L.: Interconnection Networks. An Engineering Approach. Morgan Kaufmann, San Francisco (2004)
8. Earth Simulator Center: `http://www.es.jamstec.go.jp/esc/eng/index.html`
9. Gómez, M.E., López, P., Duato, J.: A Memory-Effective Routing Strategy for regular Interconnection Networks. In: Proc. Int. Parallel and Distributed Processing Symp. (2005)
10. Kamiura, N., Kodera, T., Matsui, N.: Design of a fault-tolerant multistage interconnection network with parallel duplicated switches. In: Proc. of the 15th IEEE Int. Symp. on Defect and Fault-Tolerance in VLSI Systems, IEEE Computer Society Press, Los Alamitos (2000)
11. Konstantinidou, S.: The selective extra stage butterfly. Transactions on Very Large-Scale Integration Systems (1993)
12. Lee, T.H., Chou, J.J.: Some directed graph theorems for testing the dynamic full access property of multistage interconnection networks. In: IEEE TENCON, IEEE Computer Society Press, Los Alamitos (1993)
13. Leighton, T., Maggs, B., Sitaraman, R.: On the fault-tolerant of some popular bounded-degree networks. SIAM J. Comput. 27(5) (1998)
14. Leiserson, C.E.: Fat-trees: Universal networks hardware-efficient supercomputing. IEEE Transactions on Computers 34(10) (1985)
15. Liu, J.: Microbenchmark Performance Comparision of High-Speed Cluster Interconnetcs. IEEE Micro (2004)
16. Martinez, J.C., Flich, J., Robles, A., Lopez, P., Duato, J.: Supporting Adaptive Routing in IBA Switches. Journal of Systems Architecture 49, 441–449 (2004)
17. Mun, Y., Youn, H.Y.: On performance evaluation of fault-tolerant multistage interconnection networks. In: Proc. of the 1992 ACM/SIGAPP Symp. on Applied Computing, ACM Press, New York (1992)
18. Quadrics Home Page, `http://www.quadrics.com`
19. Santoro, N., Khatib, R.: Labelling and Implicit Routing in Networks. Computer Journal 28(1), 5–8 (1985)
20. Scott, S.L., Thorson, G.M.: The Cray T3E Network: Adaptive Routing in a High Performance 3D Torus. In: Symposium on High Performance Interconnects (1996)
21. Sem-Jacobsen, F.O., et al.: Siamese-Twin: A Dynamically Fault-tolerant Fat-tree. In: Proc. Int. Parallel and Distributed Processing Symp (2005)
22. Sengupta, J., Bansal, P.: Fault-tolerant routing in irregular MINs. IEEE Region 10 Int. Conf. on Global connectivity in Energy, Computer, Communication and Control 2 (1998)
23. Sharma, N.: Fault-tolerance of a MIN using hybrid redundancy. In: Proc. of the 27th Annual Simulation Symp. (1994)
24. Tera-10 at Commissariat a l'Energie Atomique, `http://www.cea.fr`
25. Valerio, M., et al.: Fault-tolerant orthogonal fat-trees as interconnection networks. In: Proc. 1st Int. Conf. on Algorithms and Architectures for Parallel Processing (1995)
26. Varma, A., Raghavendra, C.: Fault-tolerant routing in multistage interconnection networks. IEEE Trans. on Comput. 38(3), 385–393 (1989)

On the Optimality of Rollback-Recovery Protocol Preserving Session Guarantees*

Jerzy Brzeziński, Anna Kobusińska, and Jacek Kobusiński

Institute of Computing Science
Poznań University of Technology,
ul. Piotrowo 2, 61-965 Poznań, Poland
{Jerzy.Brzezinski,Anna.Kobusinska,Jacek.Kobusinski}@cs.put.poznan.pl

Abstract. The rVsAll rollback-recovery protocol assures that consistency models, called session guarantees, are provided for mobile clients and unreliable servers. The protocol is optimized according to the required consistency model by taking into account properties of session guarantees and integrating their consistency management with known rollback-recovery techniques: message-logging and checkpointing. We have proved the correctness of rVsAll protocol in terms of safety and liveness properties. These properties assert that clients access object replicas maintained by servers according to the required session guarantee regardless of server's failures, and state that each access operation issued by clients will eventually be performed (in a finite time), even in the presence of server's failures.
In this paper, we show that the proposed protocol is also optimal, in the sense that, the consistent global checkpoint taken in rVsAll protocol contains the minimal number of operations indispensable to fulfill the required session guarantees after server's failure and its recovery. The paper presents the proof of the optimality property of the proposed protocol.

Keywords: fault tolerance, rollback-recovery, mobile systems, session guarantees, optimality.

1 Introduction

Recent advances in wireless technologies and portable information appliances, have engendered a new paradigm of computing, in which users carrying portable devices have an access to data and information services, regardless of their physical location or movement behavior. Such users expect to see the consistent system state, despite their switching among different servers. Intuitively: the user wants to continue processing after a switch to another server so that new operations will remain consistent with previously issued operations during the execution of a client application. Therefore, in [11] a new class of consistency models, called

* This work was supported in part by the State Committee for Scientific Research (KBN), Poland, under grant KBN 3 T11C 073 28.

I. Stojmenovic et al. (Eds.): ISPA 2007, LNCS 4742, pp. 523–533, 2007.

session guarantees (or *client-centric consistency models*) and recommended for mobile environment, has been proposed to define the required properties of the system observed from client's point of view. There are four session guarantees proposed [11]: *Read Your Writes (RYW)*, *Monotonic Writes (MW)*, *Monotonic Reads (MR)*, and *Writes Follow Reads (WFR)*. RYW expresses the user expectation not to miss his own modifications performed in the past, MW ensures that the order of writes issued by a single client is preserved, MR ensures that the client's observations of the data storage are monotonic and finally, WFR keeps the track of causal dependencies resulting from operations issued by a client.

There are some consistency protocols of session guarantees provided for mobile systems [11,3,10]. Unfortunately, as far as we know, all these protocols do not ensure that required session guarantees are obeyed in the face of server's crashes. In practice, failures do happen. Therefore, the existing consistency protocols should be provided with the fault–tolerant techniques, which allow servers to provide required session guarantees despite their failures. This reveals an open research area concerning a problem of integrating the consistency management of session guarantees with recovery mechanisms. Such a problem was undertaken, and in [1] we proposed rVsSG rollback-recovery protocol guarantying session guarantees for mobile clients and unreliable servers. The proposed protocol takes advantage of the known rollback-recovery techniques, like logging and checkpointing. While applying these techniques, the semantics of operations is taken into account. Consequently, in rVsSG protocol, only the operations essential to provide session guarantees are logged. To further optimize rVsSG, we proposed rVsAll rollback-recovery protocol in which the moments of taking checkpoints are chosen with respect to session guarantees requirements [2]. We proved that the rVsAll protocol is correct, i.e. clients performing this protocol access object replicas maintained by servers according to the required session guarantee, regardless server's failures. Moreover, each access operation issued by such clients will eventually be performed (in a finite time) by servers according to required session guarantee, even in the presence of failures [2].

On the other hand, in general, checkpointing and rollback-recovery protocols should minimize the loss of computation in an environment subject to failures. Therefore, besides the above mentioned optimization according to session guarantees demands, in rVsAll protocol also the overall expected time of completing the computation in case of failures should be attenuated and thus, the computational efficiency of the protocol increased and the reliability of the system enhanced. To reduce the overall expected time of computation, the obsolete operations should not be saved in the stable storage. The excessive access to stable storage, made by logging or checkpointing operations irrelevant to providing session guarantees, would result in performance degradation by slowing down the processing. Additionally, it leads to the unnecessary limitation of stable storage space. On the other hand, the deficient number of the saved operations might incur an expensive recovery overhead.

In this paper, we prove that the proposed rVsAll protocol is optimal in the sense that its consistent global checkpoint contains the minimum number of operations issued by clients and indispensable to fulfill the required session guarantees in the case of the server's failure and its recovery.

2 Related Work

Session guarantees have been introduced in the context of Bayou replicated storage system [11] to allow mobile clients to implicitly define sets of writes that must be performed by servers. Since in Bayou each server's state is maintained in the database, adding a persistent and crash resisting log is enough to provide fault-tolerance in case of server's failure. CASCADE — a caching service for distributed CORBA objects [4], is another system using consistency conditions based on session guarantees. In CASCADE it is assumed that processes do not crash during the execution and all communication links are eventually operational. The Globe system [7] follows the approach similar to CASCADE, by providing a flexible framework for associating various replication coherence models with distributed objects. Among the coherence models supported by Globe are also client-based models, although they are combined with object-based consistency models in a single framework. Finally, Pastis — a highly scable, multi-user, peer-to-peer file system [8] implements a consistency model based on RYW session guarantee. In Pastis it is assumed that at least one replica is not faulty and all users allowed to write to a given file trust one another regarding the update of that file.

3 System Model, Basic Definitions and Notations

Throughout this paper, a replicated distributed storage system is considered. The system consists of a number of unreliable *servers* holding a full copy of *shared objects* and *clients* running applications that access these objects. Clients are mobile, i.e. they can switch from one server to another during application execution. To access the shared object, clients select a single server and send a direct request to this server. Operations are issued by clients sequentially, i.e. a new operation may be issued after the results of the previous one have been obtained. The storage replicated by servers does not imply any particular data model or organization.

Operations are issued by clients synchronously, and are basically divided into *reads*, *writes*, or *irrelevant*, and denoted respectively by r, w and o, depending on an operation type. The operation o performed by server S_j will be denoted by $o|_{S_j}$, the operation performed on object x will be denoted by $o|_x$.

The server, which first obtains the write from a client, is responsible for assigning it a globally unique identifier. Clients can concurrently submit conflicting writes at different servers, e.g. writes that modify the overlapping parts of data storage. Operations on shared objects issued by client C_i are ordered by a relation $\overset{C_i}{\rightarrow}$ called *client issue order*. A server S_j performs operations in an order represented by a relation $\overset{S_j}{\rightarrowtail}$. Relevant writes $RW(r)$ of a read operation r is a set of writes that has influenced the current state of objects observed by the read r. In the paper, it is assumed that clients perceive the data from the replicated storage according to session guarantees. Below, we present their formal definitions, brought in [10] and give the examples of their applications:

Definition 1. *Read Your Writes session guarantee is defined as follows:*

$$\forall C_i \, \forall S_j \left[w \overset{C_i}{\rightharpoonup} r|_{S_j} \implies w \overset{S_j}{\rightarrowtail} r \right]$$

To illustrate RYW session guarantee, let us consider a user writing a TODO list to a file. After traveling to another location, the user wants to recall the most urgent tasks, and reads TODO list. Without RYW the read may return any previous (possibly empty) version of the document.

Definition 2. *Monotonic Writes session guarantee is defined as follows:*

$$\forall C_i \, \forall S_j \left[w_1 \overset{C_i}{\rightharpoonup} w_2|_{S_j} \implies w_1 \overset{S_j}{\rightarrowtail} w_2 \right]$$

Let us consider a counter object with two methods: `increment()`, and `set()`, which increment value of the counter, and set its new value, respectively. A user issues the `set()` function, and then updates the counter by calling `increment()` function. Without MW the final result would be unpredictable.

Definition 3. *Monotonic Reads session guarantee is defined as follows:*

$$\forall C_i \, \forall S_j \left[r_1 \overset{C_i}{\rightharpoonup} r_2|_{S_j} \implies \forall w_k \in RW(r_1) : w_k \overset{S_j}{\rightarrowtail} r_2 \right]$$

In case of MR, a mailbox of a traveling user is considered. The user opens the mailbox at one location, reads emails, and afterwords opens the same mailbox at different location. With MR, the user sees at least all the messages he has read previously.

Definition 4. *Writes Follow Reads session guarantee is defined as follows:*

$$\forall C_i \, \forall S_j \left[r \overset{C_i}{\rightharpoonup} w|_{S_j} \implies \forall w_k \in RW(r) : w_k \overset{S_j}{\rightarrowtail} w \right]$$

Let us consider a user that reads a file, and prepares some notes he wants to add to this file. After switching to another server in the meantime, the user should be able to append his note, as the new server was properly updated due to WFR.

In the paper, it is assumed, that data consistency is managed by the formerly proposed *consistency protocol, called* VsSG [3] that uses a concept of server-based version vectors having the following form: $V_{S_j} = \left[v_1 \; v_2 \; ... \; v_{N_S} \right]$, where N_S is a total number of servers in the system and single position v_i is the number of writes performed by server S_j. Vector V_{S_j} is incremented in position j, when server S_j performs write w received directly from client C_i. Such a write is labeled with a *vector timestamp*, denoted by $T(w)$ $(T : \mathcal{O} \mapsto V)$ and set to the current value of the vector clock V_{S_j}. The timestamped operations are recorded in history H_{S_j}. $\mathcal{O}_{S_j}$ is a set of all writes performed by the server in the past — the ones received by S_j from clients or those incorporated from other servers during the synchronization procedure. The VsSG protocol eventually propagates all writes to all servers. At the client's side, vector R_{C_i} representing writes relevant to reads issued by the client C_i is maintained. The linearly ordered set $\left(\mathcal{O}_{S_j}, \overset{S_j}{\rightarrowtail}\right)$ of past writes is denoted by H_{S_j} and called *history* [3]. During synchronization of servers, their histories are *concatenated*. The concatenation of histories H_{S_j} and H_{S_k}, denoted by $H_{S_j} \oplus H_{S_k}$, consists in adding new operations from H_{S_k} at the end of H_{S_j}, preserving at the same time the appropriate relations [3].

4 Checkpoint and Log Definitions

In this paper we assume the *crash-recovery* failure model, i.e. servers may crash and recover after crashing a finite number of times [6]. Servers can fail at arbitrary moments and we require any such failure to be eventually detected, for example by failure detectors [9]. Below, we propose formal definitions of fault-tolerance mechanisms used by rVsAll protocol:

Definition 5. *Log Log_{S_j} is a set of triples:*

$$\{\langle i_1, o_1, T(o_1)\rangle \langle i_2, o_2, T(o_2)\rangle \ldots \langle i_n, o_n, T(o_n)\rangle\},$$

where i_n represents the identifier of the client issuing a write operation $o_n \in \mathcal{O}_{S_j}$ and $T(o_n)$ is timestamp of o_n.

During a rollback-recovery procedure, operations from the log are executed according to their timestamps, from the earliest to the latest one.

Definition 6. *A checkpoint $Ckpt_{S_j}$ is a pair $\langle V_{S_j}, H_{S_j}\rangle$, of a version vector V_{S_j} and a history H_{S_j} maintained by server S_j at the time t, where t is a moment of taking a checkpoint.*

A global checkpoint is a set of local checkpoints, one per each process from a system. Formally it is defined in the following way:

Definition 7. *Global checkpoint Ckpt is a tuple $\langle Ckpt_{S_1}, Ckpt_{S_2}, .., Ckpt_{S_n}\rangle$, of local checkpoints, one for each server in the system.*

Although a consistency issues of global checkpoints in distributed systems have received a considerable attraction [5], a throughout investigation of this subject shows that proposed solutions can not be readily applied to distributed systems where clients are mobile and require given session guarantees to be fulfilled. Therefore, in this section the definition of consistent global checkpoint taken from the client C_i's viewpoint is proposed. We will say that a global checkpoint

$Ckpt$ is *consistent* with respect to appropriate session guarantee, if there exists server S_j, whose checkpoint $Ckpt_{S_j}$ belongs to $Ckpt$, and the following conditions are fulfilled: if C_i requires RYW — for every write operation w issued by C_i before a read operation r, checkpoint $Ckpt_{S_j}$ includes the operation w; if C_i requires MW — for every write operation w_1 issued by C_i before write operation w_2, checkpoint $Ckpt_{S_j}$ includes the operation w_1; if C_i requires MR — for every write operation w relevant to read operation r_1 issued by C_i before read operation r_2, checkpoint $Ckpt_{S_j}$ includes the operation w; if C_i requires WFR — for every write operation w_k relevant to read r issued by C_i before write w, checkpoint $Ckpt_{S_j}$ includes the operation w_k. Below the formal definition of a global checkpoint consistent according to appropriate session guarantees is given:

Definition 8. *Global checkpoint $Ckpt$ is consistent with respect to given session guarantee from client C_i point of view, if for:*

- *RYW:* $\forall w \in \mathcal{O}_{C_i} :: w \stackrel{C_i}{\rightarrow} r :: \left[\exists S_j :: \left(w \in Ckpt_{S_j} \wedge Ckpt_{S_j} \subset Ckpt\right)\right]$
- *MW:* $\forall w_1 \in \mathcal{O}_{C_i} :: w_1 \stackrel{C_i}{\rightarrow} w_2 :: \left[\exists S_j :: \left(w_1 \in Ckpt_{S_j} \wedge Ckpt_{S_j} \subset Ckpt\right)\right]$
- *MR:* $\forall w_1 \in \mathcal{O}_{C_i} :: w_1 \stackrel{C_i}{\rightarrow} w_2 :: \left[\exists S_j :: \left(w_1 \in Ckpt_{S_j} \wedge Ckpt_{S_j} \subset Ckpt\right)\right]$
- *WFR:* $\forall w_k \in RW(r) : r \stackrel{C_i}{\rightarrow} w|_{S_k} \wedge w_k \stackrel{S_k}{\rightarrowtail} w ::$
$\left[\exists S_j :: \left(w \in Ckpt_{S_j} \wedge Ckpt_{S_j} \subset Ckpt\right)\right]$

In this paper we assume, that the log and the checkpoint are saved by the server in the stable storage, able to survive all failures [5]. Additionally, we assume that the newly taken checkpoint replaces the previous one, so just one checkpoint for each server is kept in the stable storage.

Checkpoints taken in the proposed protocol contain only such operations, which are indispensable for recovering the failed server state with respect to session guarantees issued by clients before the failure. In other words, only the operations essential to preserve required session guarantees are saved in the stable storage. Thus, the minimal stable storage space is occupied. Because checkpoints contain only the minimal, required number of operations, the time of taking a checkpoint is reduced and the excessive access to stable storage is avoided.

The definition of optimality property reflects the above facts and says that any operation can not be removed from the checkpoint. Otherwise the saved operations are insufficient to recover the server's state according to the required earlier session guarantees. The definition of optimality property is defined as follows:

Definition 9. *The protocol is said to be optimal, if there is no write operation w belonging to the consistent global checkpoint $Ckpt$, such that after the removal of w from the checkpoint $Ckpt$, $Ckpt$ is still consistent with respect to the required session guarantee.*

5 The rVsAll Rollback-Recovery Protocol

To preserve the required session guarantee, the rollback-recovery protocol must ensure that writes issued by a client and essential to preserve this guarantee are

```
Upon sending a request ⟨o⟩ to server S_j at client C_i

W ← 0
if (iswrite(o) and MW ∈ SG) or (not iswrite(o) and RYW ∈ SG) then
    W ← max(W, W_{C_i})
end if
if (iswrite(o) and WFR ∈ SG) or (not iswrite(o) and MR ∈ SG) then
    W ← max(W, R_{C_i})
end if
send ⟨o, W, i⟩ to S_j

Upon receiving a request ⟨o, W, i⟩ from client C_i at server S_j

while (V_{S_j} ≱ W) do
    wait()
end while
if iswrite(o) then
    V_{S_j}[j] ← V_{S_j}[j] + 1
    timestamp o with V_{S_j}
    Log_{S_j} ← Log_{S_j} ∪ ⟨o, T(o)⟩
    perform o and store results in res
    H_{S_j} ← H_{S_j} ⊕ {o}
    if (MW ∈ SG and i ∈ CW_{S_j}) or (WFR ∈ SG and RW_{S_j}[i] > 0) then
        Ckpt_{S_j} ← ⟨V_{S_j}, H_{S_j}⟩
        Log_{S_j} ← ∅
        CR_{S_j} ← ∅
        CW_{S_j} ← ∅
        nWrites ← 0
        RW_{S_j} ← 0
    else
        CW_{S_j} ← CW_{S_j} ∪ i
        nWrites ← nWrites + 1
    end if
end if
if (not iswrite(o)) then
    if (RYW ∈ SG and i ∈ CW_{S_j}) or (MR ∈ SG and RW_{S_j}[i] > 0) then
        Ckpt_{S_j} ← ⟨V_{S_j}, H_{S_j}⟩
        Log_{S_j} ← ∅
        CR_{S_j} ← ∅
        CW_{S_j} ← ∅
        nWrites ← 0
        RW_{S_j} ← 0
    else
        RW_{S_j}[i] ← nWrites
    end if
    perform o and store results in res
end if
send ⟨o, res, V_{S_j}⟩ to C_i

Upon receiving a reply ⟨o, res, W⟩ from server S_j at client C_i

if iswrite(o) then
    W_{C_i} ← max(W_{C_i}, W)
else
    R_{C_i} ← max(R_{C_i}, W)
end if
deliver ⟨res⟩

Every Δt at server S_j
foreach S_k ≠ S_j do
    send ⟨S_j, H_{S_j}⟩ to S_k
end for

Upon receiving an update ⟨S_k, H⟩ at server S_j

foreach w_i ∈ H do
    if V_{S_j} ≱ T(w_i) then
        perform w_i
        V_{S_j} ← max(V_{S_j}, T(w_i))
        H_{S_j} ← H_{S_j} ⊕ {w_i}
    end if
end for
signal()

On rollback-recovery
⟨V_{S_j}, H_{S_j}⟩ ← Ckpt_{S_j}
Log'_{S_j} ← Log_{S_j}
CR_{S_j} ← ∅
CW_{S_j} ← ∅
RW_{S_j} ← 0
nWrites ← 0
foreach o'_j ∈ Log'_{S_j} do
    choose ⟨o'_i, T(o'_i)⟩ with minimal T(o'_j) from Log'_{S_j} where T(o'_j) > V_{S_j}
    V_{S_j}[j] ← V_{S_j}[j] + 1
    perform o'_j
    H_{S_j} ← H_{S_j} ⊕ {o'_j}
    CW_{S_j} ← CW_{S_j} ∪ i'
    nWrites ← nWrites + 1
end for
```

Fig. 1. Checkpointing and rollback-recovery rVsAll protocol

not lost after the server's failure and its recovery. In rVsAll protocol, servers save only some of obtained operations, namely those received directly from clients. Operations obtained during synchronization procedure, even if required by session guarantee, are just performed by the server, because they have already been saved in the stable storage (in the log or in the checkpoint) of other servers. Hence, even if writes obtained in the result of synchronization procedure are lost, the required session guarantee is not violated. This stems from the fact, that such writes will be obtained again during consecutive synchronizations.

The server, which obtains the write request directly from client C_i, checks whether the request can be performed accordingly to required session guarantees (line 9). If the state of server S_j is not sufficiently up to date, the obtained request is postponed (line 10), otherwise server's S_j data structures are updated: the value of version vector V_{S_j} is increased and operation o is timestamped, to give o a unique identifier (lines 13-14). Afterward, o is logged to stable storage (line 15). After the operation is performed (line 16), it is added to the history H_{S_j} of performed writes (line 17). With every logged operation the size of the log is increased, and thus a recovery takes more time. Therefore, in order to bound a recovery time after the server failure, the server state is checkpointed. The moment of taking a checkpoint is optimized by considering the properties of session guarantees, for example in the case of RYW session guarantee, when write operations are not followed by a read request, the consistency protocol does not need to take them into account when preserving RYW. Thus, in rVsAll protocol checkpoints are taken in the following moments: for RYW session guarantee it is a moment of obtaining read request (line 32). For MR session guarantee it is a moment of obtaining read request that follows in the server execution order another read issued by the same client (line 32) . In the case of MW session guarantee it is moment of obtaining write request following in the server execution order all writes issued by the same client (line 19). Finally, for WFR session guarantee, it is a moment of obtaining write request, following in the server execution order the read request issued by the same client (line 19). After the checkpoint is taken, log Log_{S_j} is cleared (line 20 respectively for MW and WFR; 33 for RYW and MR).

The update message received from other servers changes the state of server S_j, only if the history H contains writes that has not been performed by S_j yet (line 54). Such update operations are performed (line 55) and processed by S_j(lines 56-57). After the failure occurrence, the failed server restarts from the latest checkpoint (line 61) and replays operations from the log (lines 67-74) according to their timestamps, from the earliest to the latest one.

The safety property of such a rVsAll protocol is formally proved [2].

6 Protocol Optimality

The optimality of checkpointing and rollback-recovery protocol in terms of checkpointing is formally defined in Definition 9. Below we prove that rVsAll protocol preserves the optimality property with respect to RYW session guarantee.

Theorem 1. *Rollback-recovery protocol rVsAll is optimal with respect to RYW i.e.:*

$$\nexists w' \in Ckpt :: w' \stackrel{C_i}{\rightarrow} r ::$$

$$[Ckpt' = Ckpt \setminus \{w'\} \wedge Ckpt' \text{ is consistent global checkpoint}]$$

where w' and r are write and read operations issued by client C_i and Ckpt is a consistent global checkpoint.

Proof. Let us assume for the sake of contradiction, that there exists operation w' issued by client C_i that belongs to consistent global checkpoint $Ckpt$, and after the removal of w' from $Ckpt$, it is still consistent with respect to RYW session guarantee from client's C_i viewpoint. Further, without the lost of generality, let us consider the system state only at moments of obtaining by servers read operations issued by clients.

According to the definition, global checkpoint $Ckpt$ is consistent according to RYW, if:

$$\forall w \in \mathcal{O}_{C_i} :: w \stackrel{C_i}{\rightarrow} r :: \left[\exists S_j :: \left(w \in Ckpt_{S_j} \wedge Ckpt_{S_j} \subset Ckpt\right)\right] \tag{1}$$

Because from the assumption also $Ckpt \setminus \{w'\}$ is consistent, then

$$\forall w \in \mathcal{O}_{C_i} :: w \stackrel{C_i}{\rightarrow} r :: \left[\exists S_j :: \left(w \in Ckpt_{S_j} \wedge Ckpt_{S_j} \subset Ckpt \setminus w'\right)\right] \tag{2}$$

Since, from the definition, global checkpoint $Ckpt$ is composed from local checkpoints $Ckpt_{S_j}$, one for each server S_j, then if $Ckpt$ does not include the operation w', then none of local checkpoints $Ckpt_{S_j}$ includes it. In other words:

$$\forall S_j : w \notin Ckpt_{S_j} \tag{3}$$

This implies, that:

$$\forall S_j : \mathcal{O}_{C_i} \cap \mathcal{O}_{S_j} = \emptyset, \tag{4}$$

However, rVsAll rollback-recovery protocol ensures that there is at least one server (the one, which has obtained the write request directly from the client) that eventually performs write requested by the client and in the case of the failure this server does not lost the results of performed write. The checkpoint $Ckpt_{S_j}$ of server S_j consists of version vector V_{S_j} and history H_{S_j} maintained by server S_j at the time t (as it was assumed earlier in the paper, without loosing the generality, we consider a moment t of performing by S_j the read request issued by client C_i). The history is a linearly ordered set $\left(\mathcal{O}_{S_j}, \stackrel{S_j}{\rightarrowtail}\right)$ of all writes performed by server S_j. Thus there exists at least one server S_j, for which the following condition holds:

$$\exists S_j : \mathcal{O}_{C_i} \cap \mathcal{O}_{S_j} \neq \emptyset \tag{5}$$

If (5) is fulfilled, then (4) can not be truth, thus rollback-recovery protocol rVsAll is optimal with respect to RYW.

The proofs of optimality of rVsAll protocol with respect to MW, MR and WFR session guarantees are carried out analogically, however, because of the lack of space we do not run them in this paper. Full versions of the theorems and proofs can be found in [2].

7 Conclusions

This paper has dealt with the problem of integrating the consistency management of distributed systems with mobile clients with the recovery mechanisms. To solve such a problem, the rollback-recovery protocol rVsAll, preserving session guarantee has been proposed.

The novel optimization of rVsAll protocol comes from the fact that every server S_j saves only some of performed operations (these obtained directly from clients). However, although only some of operations performed by the server are saved, the protocol is safe, i.e. MW session guarantee is fulfilled in the case of server's failure. Moreover, the optimality of the proposed protocol, in the sense, that the consistent global checkpoint taken in rVsAll contains the minimum number of operations issued by clients and indispensable to fulfill the required session guarantee after the server's failure and its recovery, has been formally proved.

Our future work encompasses the evaluation of the overhead of rVsAll protocol quantitatively, by carrying out appropriate simulation experiments.

References

1. Brzezinski, J., Kobusinska, A., Kobusinski, J.: Bounding recovery time in rollback-recovery protocol for mobile systems preserving session guarantees. In: Eliassen, F., Montresor, A. (eds.) DAIS 2006. LNCS, vol. 4025, pp. 187–198. Springer, Heidelberg (2006)
2. Brzezinski, J., Kobusinska, A., Kobusinski, J., Szychowiak, M.: Optimised mechanism of rollback-recovery in mobile systems with session guarantees. In: Technical Report RA-028/06, Institute of Computing Science. Poznan University of Technology (2006)
3. Brzezinski, J., Sobaniec, C., Wawrzyniak, D.: Safety of a server-based version vector protocol implementing session guarantees. In: Sunderam, V.S., van Albada, G.D., Sloot, P.M.A., Dongarra, J.J. (eds.) ICCS 2005. LNCS, vol. 3516, pp. 423–430. Springer, Heidelberg (2005)
4. Chockler, G., Dolev, D., Friedman, R., Vitenberg, R.: Implementing a caching service for distributed CORBA objects. In: Proceedings of Middleware 2000: IFIP/ACM Int. Conf. on Distributed Systems Platforms, pp. 1–23. ACM Press, New York (April 2000)
5. Elmootazbellah, N., Elnozahy, Lorenzo, A., Wang, Y-M., Jonson, D.B.: A survay of rollback-recovery protocols in message-passing systems. ACM Computing Surveys 34(3), 375–408 (2002)
6. Guerraoui, R., Rodrigues, L.: Introduction to distributed algorithms. Springer, Heidelberg (2004)

7. Kermarrec, A-M., Kuz, I., van Steen, M., Tanenbaum, A.S.: Aframework for consistent, replicated Web objects. In: Proceedings of the 18th Int. Conf. on Distributed Computing Systems (ICDCS) (May 1998)
8. Picconi, F., Busca, J-M., Sens, P.: Pastis: a highly-scable multi-user peer-to-peer file system. EuroPar, 1173–1182 (2005)
9. Sergent, N., Defago, X., Schiper, A.: Failure detectors: Implementation issues and impact on concsensus performance. Technical Report SSC/1999/019. Ecole Poytechnique Federale de Lausanne, Switzerland (May 1999)
10. Sobaniec, C.: Consistency Protocols of Session Guarantees in Distributed Mobile Systems. PhD thesis, Institute of Computing Science, Poznan University of Technology (September 2005)
11. Terry, D.B., Demers, A.J., Petersen, K., Spreitzer, M., Theimer, M., Welch, B.W.: Session quarantees for weakly consistent replicated data. In: PDIS 94. Proceedings of the Third Int. Conf. on Parallel and Distributed Information Systems, Austin, USA, September 1994, pp. 140–149. IEEE Computer Society, Los Alamitos (1994)

A Replication Software Architecture(RSA) for Supporting Irregular Applications on Wide-Area Distributed Computing Environments*

Jaechun No[1], Chang Won Park[2], and Sung Soon Park[3]

[1] Dept. of Computer Software
College of Electronics and Information Engineering
Sejong University, Seoul, Korea
jano@sejong.ac.kr

[2] Intelligent IT System Research Center
Korea Electronics Technology Institute
Bundang-gu, Seongnam-si, Korea
cwpark@keti.re.kr

[3] Dept. of Computer Science & Engineering
College of Science and Engineering
Anyang University, Anyang, Korea
sspark@aycc.anyang.ac.kr

Abstract. In the distributed computing environment, many large-scale scientific applications are irregular applications which perform their computation and I/O on an irregularly discretized mesh. However, most of the previous work in the area of irregular applications focuses mainly on the local environments. In distributed computing environments, since many remotely located scientists should share the data to produce useful results, providing a consistent data replication mechanism to minimize the remote data access time is a critical issue in achieving high-performance bandwidth. We have developed a replication software architecture(RSA) that enables the geographically distributed scientists to easily replicate irregular computations with minimum overheads, while safely sharing large-scale data sets to produce useful results. Since RSA uses database support to store the data-related and computational-related metadata, it can easily be ported to any computing environments. In this paper, we describe the design and implementation of RSA for irregular applications and present performance results on Linux clusters.

1 Introduction

In distributed computing environments, many large-scale scientific applications are I/O intensive and generate large amount of data(on the order of several hundred gigabytes to terabytes) [1,2]. Many of these applications perform their computation and I/O on an irregularly discretized mesh. The data accesses in those applications make extensive use of arrays, called indirection array [3] or

* This work was supported in part by a Seoul R&BD program.

I. Stojmenovic et al. (Eds.): ISPA 2007, LNCS 4742, pp. 534–544, 2007.

map array [4], in which each value of the array denotes the corresponding data position in memory or in the file.

The data distribution in irregular applications can be done either by using compiler directives with the support of runtime preprocessing [5] or by using a runtime library [3]. Most of the previous work in the area of irregular applications focuses mainly on computations on the local environments.

In distributed computing environments, since many remotely located scientists should share the data to produce useful results, providing a consistent data replication mechanism to minimize the remote data access time is a critical issue in achieving high-performance bandwidth.

The usual way of managing consistent data replicas between distributed sites is to periodically update the remotely located data replicas, as implemented in Globus toolkit [8,9]. This method is implemented under the assumption that the data being replicated is read-only so that once it has been generated would not it be modified in any remote site. This assumption is no longer true in such a case that a remote site may modify or update the data replicated in its local storage. If another remote site tries to use the same data before the data is updated with the new one, the data consistency between distributed sites would then fail and the scientist would get wrong results.

We have developed a replication software architecture(RSA) that enables the geographically distributed scientists to easily replicate irregular computations with minimum overheads, while safely sharing large-scale data sets to produce useful scientific results. First, in order to replicate a fast irregular computation on remote sites, RSA uses the concept of history file to optimize the cost of the index distribution, using the metadata stored in database. Secondly, in order to support a fast and consistent data replication, RSA provides two kinds of data replication methods, called owner-initiated data replication and client-initiated data replication, that are combined with data compression.

The rest of this paper is organized as follows. In Section 2, we discuss an overview of irregular problems and the way of locally solving the irregular computations in RSA. In Section 3, we present the design and implementation of compression and replication methods of RSA. Performance results on the Linux cluster located at Sejong University are presented in Section 4. We conclude in Section 5.

2 An Overview of RSA for Solving Irregular Applications

Figure 1 shows a typical irregular application that sweeps over the edges of an irregular mesh. In this problem, `edge1` and `edge2` are two arrays representing nodes connected by an edge, and array `x` and `y` are the actual data associated with each edge and node, respectively. After the computation is completed, the results `p` and `q` are written to a file in the order of global node numbers.

Figure 2 shows the steps involved in solving the problem described in Figure 1. The partitioning vector is the one generated from a partitioning tool, such as MeTis [12]. Each value of the vector denotes a processor order where the node should be assigned.

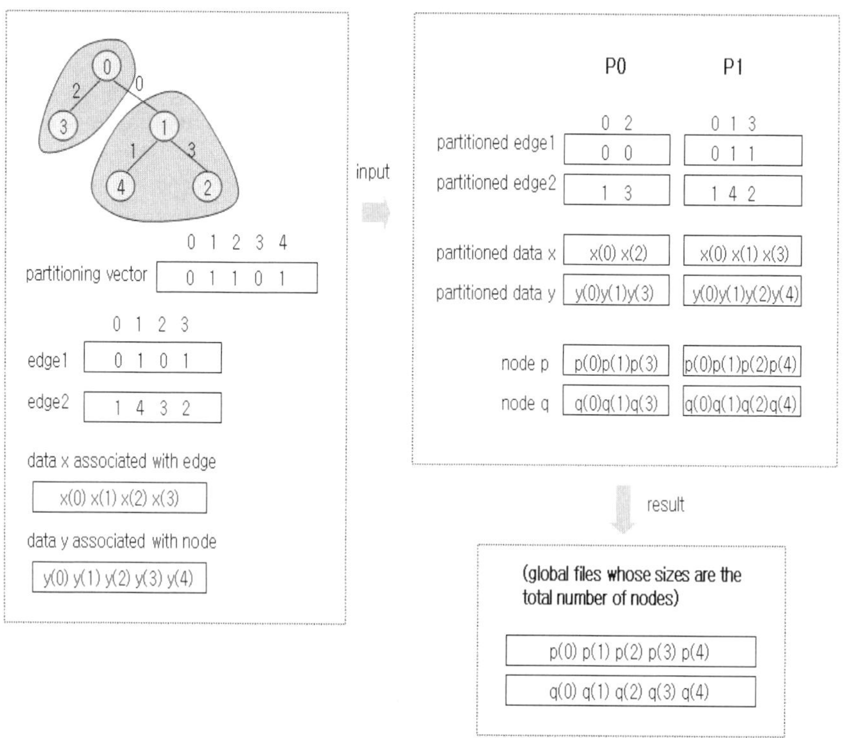

Fig. 1. An example of irregular problems

In the initial stage, the metadata associated with the application and data attributes are stored in the application_registry_table, run_registry_table, and data_registry_table. By using the partitioning vector imported to RSA, the index values, `edge1` and `edge2`, are partitioned among processes. The partitioned index values are asynchronously written to a history file to be retrieved in subsequent runs requiring the same edge distribution. Also, the associated metadata are stored to index_table and index_history_table.

The use of the history file significantly affects the performance. With the history file, an application just reads the already partitioned `edge1` and `edge2` from the history file and converts them to the localized edges by the partitioning vector. This avoids the communication costs to exchange each process's edges and the computation costs to choose the edges to be assigned. The disadvantage of the history file is that it cannot be used if the program runs on a different number of processes than when the file was created.

One efficient use of the history file is to create it in advance for the various numbers of processes of interest. As long as the user runs the application with any of those numbers of processes, an appropriate history can be chosen to reduce communication and computation costs.

With the aim of reducing the I/O and communication overheads, RSA combines MPI-IO [10,11] with data compression using lzrw3 algorithm. After merging the I/O data domain in MPI-IO, if the data compression is applied, the compression library is then linked to RSA. Otherwise, the native file system I/O call is used.

3 Data Replication in RSA

3.1 Client Grouping and Communication

RSA supports the client grouping to eliminate unnecessary communication overheads. By making the client groups, RSA can easily detect the other clients who share the same data replicas and can let them take the new copy of the modified data, without affecting other clients.

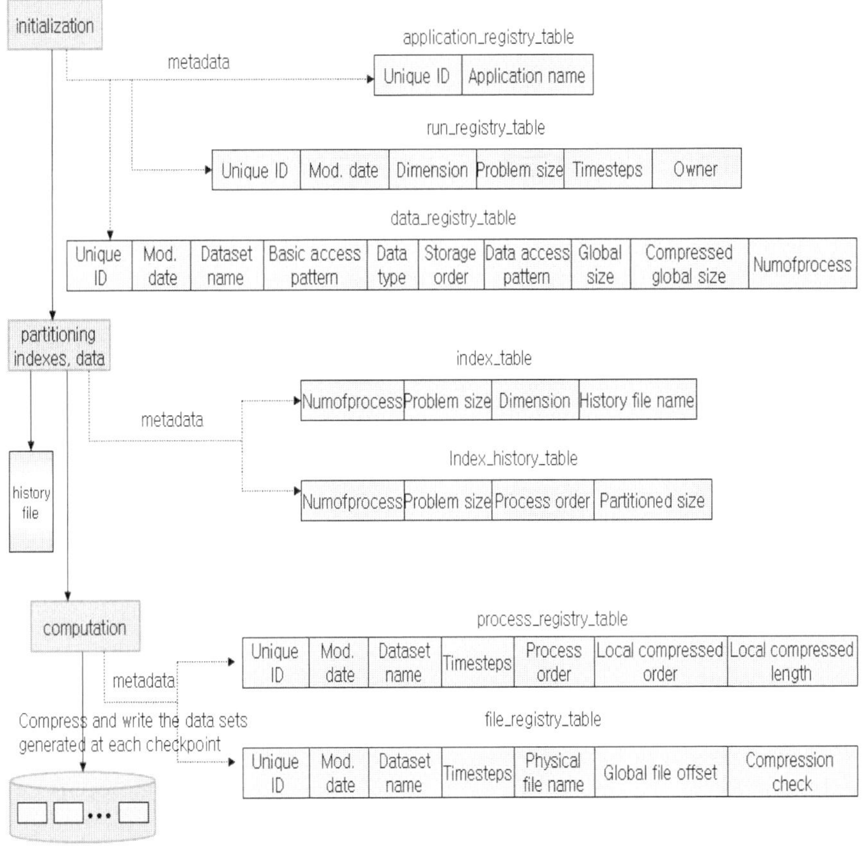

Fig. 2. RSA steps to solve an irregular problem

If there is a group who has already registered to share the same data sets, the new client will then be a member of the existing group. Otherwise, a new group where the new client belongs to is created by taking the new group ID in the client_registry_table. Also, the replication_registry_table is appended to reflect the new client registration.

The communications for the metadata, real data, and history data are separately performed through the different communication ports. The I/O forwarder is responsible for the real data communication and invokes MPI-IO processes to perform I/O. If a remote client wants to receive a history file to replicate irregular computations, the history forwarder is responsible for transferring the desired history file. The metadata requester is responsible for transferring the metadata accessed from the metadata database table located at the data owner.

Suppose that a remote client requests data sets from the data owner. If the data sets being requested have already been compressed, the data sets are then retrieved from the file using the compression-related metadata selected from the metadata database table.

The compressed real data sets and the associated metadata are transferred to the requesting client, by the I/O forwarder and metadata requester. If a history file is requested by a client, the desired file is also transferred by the history forwarder.

3.2 Data Replication Methods

RSA supports two kinds of data replication methods to maintain the consistent data replicas over the geographically distributed sites. In the owner-initiated data replication, when user generates data sets at the data owner, RSA replicates them to the remote clients to share the data sets with the data owner. Also, when a remote client changes the data replicas stored in its local storage, it broadcasts the modifications to the members in the same group and to the data owner for replica consistency. Figure 3 shows the steps taken in the owner-initiated replication.

At time t_i, since the client A and client B want to receive the same data sets, a and b, from the data owner, they are grouped into the same client group. When an application generates the data sets at time t_j, a and b are replicated to the client A and client B.

Suppose that the client A modifies the data replicas at time t_k. The client A requests for the IP address of other members in the same group, sends the modified data sets to them, and waits for the acknowledgements.

When the data owner receives the modified data, it updates them to the local storage and sets the status field of the replication_registry_table to "holding" to prevent another client from accessing the data sets while being updated. When the data owner receives the notification signal from the client who initiated the data modification, it sets the status field to "done", allowing another client to use the data replica.

The owner-initiated data replication approach allows remote clients to share the data replicas safely, provided that they find out the corresponding status

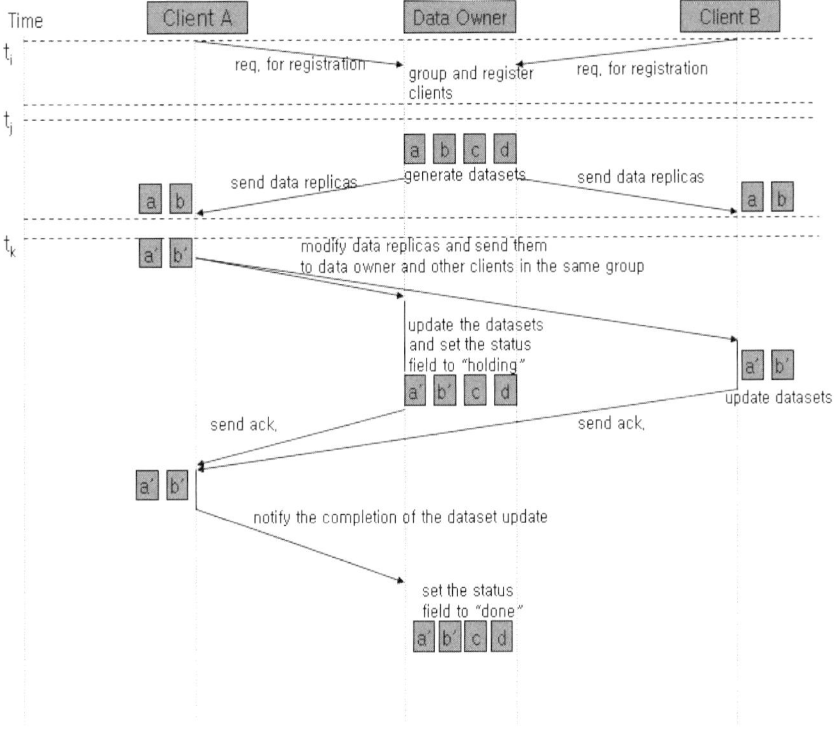

Fig. 3. Owner-initiated replication

field is set to "done". Moreover, even though a remote client crashes, it doesn't affect the data consistency since as soon as the data replicas are modified the change is immediately reflected to the data owner and to the other clients in the same group. However, if the data modification to the data replicas frequently happens, the heavy communication bottleneck then causes even if no one else would use the data sets modified.

Figure 4 shows the client-initiated data replication where only when the modified data replicas are needed by users are those data replicas sent to the requesting client and to the data owner. Unlike in the owner-initiated data replication, there is no data communication when users on the data owner produce the application data sets. If a client needs to access the remote data sets stored in the data owner, he will then get the data replica while registering to our architecture.

In Figure 4, after the application generates the data sets at time t_i, the client A and client B request for the data sets, a and b, from the data owner at time t_j. Because they want to receive the same data sets, they become the member of the same client group.

Suppose that client A modifies the data replica at time t_k. He just sends a signal to the data owner to update the corresponding status field of the data set with the IP address of client A.

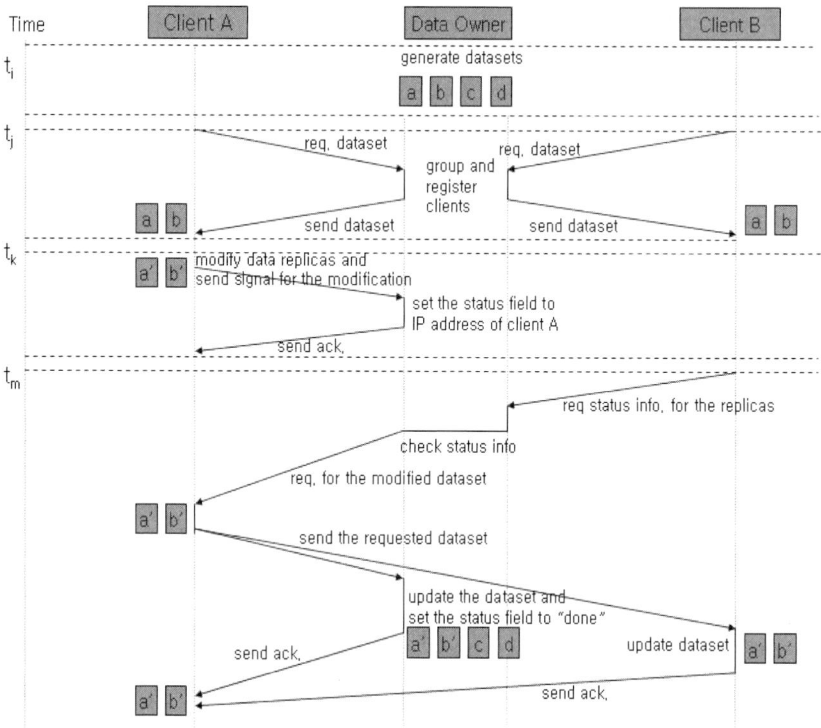

Fig. 4. Client-initiated replication

At time t_m, suppose that the client B accesses the data replica stored in its local storage but not having been updated by client A. In order to check the replica consistency, client B first requests the status information of the data replica from the data owner. The data owner finds out that the data set has been modified by client A and that requests the data from client A. Client A sends the modified data to the data owner and to the client B, and then waits for the acknowledgements from both. After the data owner updates the modified data set and sets the status field to "done", it sends back an acknowledgement to the client A.

In the client-initiated data replication approach, the data replicas are sent to the remote clients only when the data sets are actually needed by them. Therefore, unlike in the owner-initiated data replication approach, the client-initiated data replication does not cause unnecessary data communication. However, if a client who keeps the modification of the data replica crashes before the data modification is updated to the data owner and to the other members of the same group, a significant data loss will then happen.

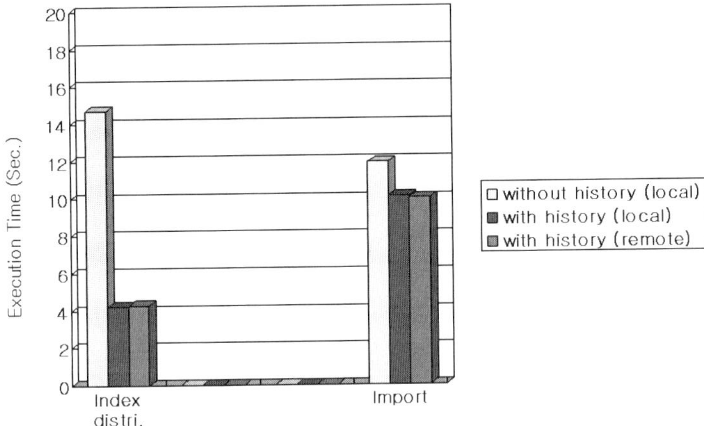

Fig. 5. Execution time for partitioning indices and data at the data owner(local) and at the remote client(remote)

4 Performance Evaluation

In order to measure the performance of RSA, we used two Linux clusters, located at Sejong university. The performance results were obtained using the template implemented based on a tetrahedral vertex-centered unstructured grid code. The mesh we used had about 9 million edges and 1 million nodes. At the initial stage, the application imports edges, four data arrays associated with edges, and another four data arrays associated with nodes. The total imported data size was about 402MB. As a result of computations, the application wrote about 4MB of four data sets each and 12MB of a single data set at the data owner. These data sets are replicated among clients.

In order to evaluate two replication approaches, a randomly chosen remote client modified 28MB of replicas at time steps 5, 10, and 15, respectively, and spread those replicas to the data owner and to the clients, according to the owner-initiated data replication and to the client-initiated data replication. At each time step, a maximum execution time measured among the remote clients was selected as a performance result. This time includes the cost for metadata accesses to the data owner, real data communication, and I/O operations.

Figure 5 shows the cost for partitioning indirection arrays among 4 processes. Without using the history file, after importing the edges, each process determines the amount of memory to store the partitioned edges while distributing the index values, according to the partitioning vector.

When partitioning the edges with a history file, the cost of `index distri.` is nothing but reading the history file of the edges in a contiguous way, including the database cost to access the metadata. Figure 5 also shows that the cost for importing indices and data, `import`, is decreased with a history file. Therefore, we can see that with the history file replicated, any client can easily repeat the irregular problems with the small index distribution cost.

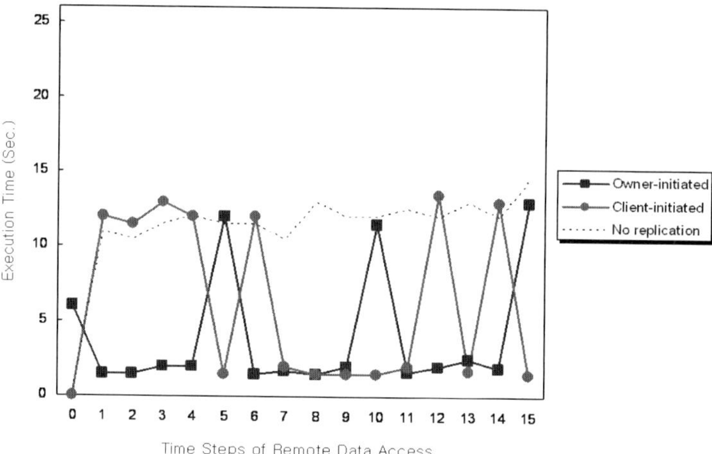

Fig. 6. Execution time for replicating 28MB data on the remote clients as a function of time steps for accessing remote data sets. Two client groups were made, each group consisting of two nodes.

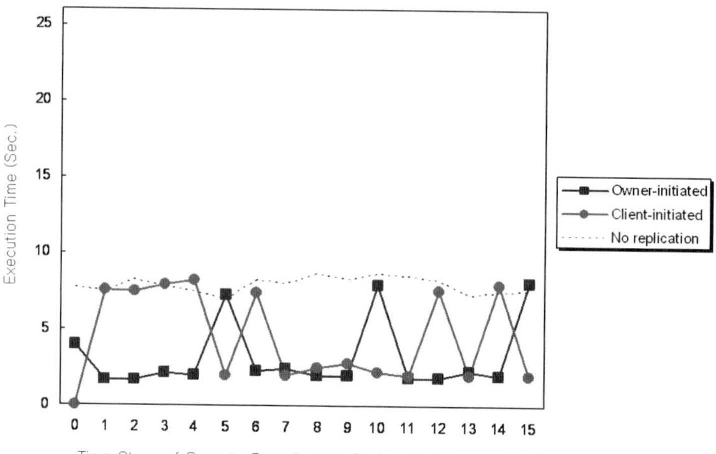

Fig. 7. Execution time for replicating compressed data on the remote clients as a function of time steps for accessing remote data sets. Two client groups were made, each group consisting of two nodes.

In Figure 6, we created two client groups, each group consisting of two nodes. At each time step, a client accesses either 28MB of replicas stored in the local storage, or 28MB of remote data sets stored on the data owner in such a case that the data sets required are not replicated to the local storage.

When the replicas stored in the local storage are used, the execution time for accessing data sets drops to almost 3 seconds needed for communicating the corresponding data properties. If the modification to the replicas happens at time steps 5, 10, and 15, respectively, the modified replicas are then broadcast to the data owner and to the clients in the sample group, thereby increasing the execution time for accessing remote data sets.

In Figure 7, we replicated the compressed data sets on the two client groups, each group consisting of two nodes. The total data size being transferred was about 20MB, which shows about 30% of reduction in the data size. Due to the data compression, the I/O times for retrieving the compressed data sets on the data owner and for writing them to the remote clients are significantly reduced.

The communication time for transferring the compressed data sets to the remote client is also decreased. However, because we use a single I/O forwarder to merge the compressed data sets from multiple MPI-IO processes, the reduction in the communication time is not as large as we expected.

5 Conclusion

We have developed a data replication software architecture(RSA) that enables the geographically distributed scientists to easily repeat the irregular computations, while safely sharing large-scale data sets to produce useful scientific results. First, in order to remotely replicate the irregular computations, the partitioned index values stored in the index history file are sent to the remote client so that he can repeat the irregular computations without performing the index distribution. Secondly, in order to reduce the I/O and communication costs in replicating the data sets on the remote clients, we used MPI-IO and data compression, and then they showed the clear benefits in the execution time. Thirdly, in order to maintain the consistency in case of replica modifications or updates, we developed two kinds of data replication methods. In the owner-initiated data replication, the replication occurs when applications generate the data sets in the data owner location. In the client-initiated data replication, only when the data sets are needed by a remote client are the necessary data sets replicated to the requesting client. In the future, we plan to use our replication techniques with more applications and evaluate both the usability and performance.

References

1. Rosario, J.M., Choudhary, A.: High performance I/O for parallel computers: Problems and prospects. IEEE Computer 27, 59–68 (1994)
2. Allcock, B., Foster, I., Nefedova, V., Chervenak, A., Deelman, E., Kesselman, C., Leigh, J., Sim, A., Shoshani, A., Drach, B., Williams, D.: High-Performance Remote Access to Climate Simulation Data: A Challenge Problem for Data Grid Technologies. In: Reich, S., Tzagarakis, M.M., De Bra, P.M.E. (eds.) SC 2001. LNCS, vol. 2266. Springer, Heidelberg (2002)
3. Das, R., Uysal, M., Saltz, J., Hwang, Y.-S.: Communication optimizations for irregular scientific computations on distributed memory architectures. Journal Parallel and Distributed Computing 22, 462–479 (1994)

4. Gropp, W., Lusk, E., Thakur, R.: Using MPI-2: Advanced Features of the Message-Passing Interface. MPI Press (1999)
5. Hanxleden, R.V., Kennedy, K., Saltz, J.: Value-Based Distributions and Alignments in Fortran D. Journal of Programming Languages - Special Issue on Compiling and Run-Time Issues for Distributed Address Space Machines (1994)
6. Moore, R., Rajasekar, A.: Data and Metadata Collections for Scientific Applications. High Performance Computing and Networking (2001)
7. Chervenak, A., Deelman, E., Kesselman, C., Pearlman, L., Singh, G.: A Metadata Catalog Service for Data Intensive Applications. GriPhyN technical report (2002)
8. Chervenak, A., Schuler, R., Kesselman, C., Koranda, S., Moe, B.: Wide Area Data Replication for Scientific Collaborations. In: Proceedings of 6th IEEE/ACM International Workshop on Grid Computing (2005)
9. Cai, M., Chervenak, A., Frank, M.: A Peer-to-Peer Replica Location Service Based on A Distributed Hash Table. In: Proceedings of the SC2004 Conference (2004)
10. Thakur, R., Gropp, W.: Improving the Performance of Collective Operations in MPICH. In: Proceedings of the 10th European PVM/MPI Users' Group Conference (2003)
11. No, J., Thakur, R., Choudhary, A.: High-performance scientific data management system. Journal Parallel and Distributed Computing 63, 434–447 (2003)
12. Karypis, G., Kumar, V.: A Fast and High Quality Multilevel Scheme for Partitioning Irregular Graphs. Journal on Scientific Computing (1997)

Cooperative Grid Jobs Scheduling with Multi-objective Genetic Algorithm

Bin Zeng, Jun Wei, Wei Wang, and Pu Wang

Department of management, Naval University of Engineering, Wuhan, China
zbtrueice@163.com

Abstract. Job scheduling on computational grids is a key problem in large scale grid-based applications for solving complex problems. The aim is to obtain an efficient scheduler able to allocate dependable jobs originated from large scale applications on hierarchy based grid computing platforms with heterogeneous resources. In contrast to satisfying multi objectives of different levels, which is NP-hard in most formulations, a set of cooperative multi-objective genetic algorithm (MOGA) is presented. Using this scheme, the application level generates multiple local schedules based on local nodes and objectives to a schedule pool, from which the system level can assemble a set of global schedules according to global objectives. The MOGA scheduling scheme is shown to perform well on the experimental scenario, which shows its flexibility and possible application to more complex job scheduling scenarios with multiple and diverse tasks and nodes.

Keywords: job scheduling; grid computing; Multi-objective genetic algorithm; optimal scheduling scheme.

1 Introduction

Grids are responsible for integrating heterogeneous network resource and coordinating resource sharing in the dynamic and multi-scheme virtual organizations in order to solve the large scale challenging problems. As a cooperative environment of solving problem, it is necessary for the grids to develop efficient job scheduling schemes and resource management policies in regard to their objectives, scope, and structure. However, there exists different and somewhat conflicting QoS objectives for management and security policies among the hierarchy based grid entities such as grid users (applications), grid resource administrative and virtual organization administrative. Therefore, it has become one of hotspots of grid researches for its resource management and job scheduler to coordinate different levels of grid entities [1].

This scheduling task in grid is much more complex than its version in traditional computing environments. Indeed, the fact that objective function of different QoS constraints are independent and somewhat conflicting making thus the job scheduling a complex large scale optimization problem [2][3]. This problem

I. Stojmenovic et al. (Eds.): ISPA 2007, LNCS 4742, pp. 545–555, 2007.

is multiobjective in its general definition, as several optimization criteria such as makespan, flowtime and node utilization are to be matched [4].

Due to its theoretical and practical relevance, the evolutionary computing research community has started to examine this problem [5][6]. Braun compared the performance of different job schedulers such as Min-min, GA and GENITOR-style GA based on the QoS model for tasks with dependencies, priorities, deadlines, and multiple versions and made the conclusion that GENITOR-style GA can achieve the best performance and Min-min algorithm is also a good scheduler for its minimum time cost [7]. Dogan defined the job scheduling problem based on different QoS levels of both users and systems,designed the QSMTS_IP algorithm to schedule the grid jobs according, and maximize objective functions of multi QoS dimensions[8]. In [9], a QoS model is presented and the performance of QSMTS_IP, Min_min, GA, Least Slack First and Sufferage[10] is compared based on the model. However, the existing approaches in the literature show several limitations: in their works just the uniobjective case is considered by deducing multiobjective functions into an uniobjective function and usually either monolithic grid environments or the static version of the problem are considered [11].

In this paper, we propose a MOGA based scheduling scheme for optimizing the execution of jobs in a Grid. The scheme is designed for a service Grid focusing on distributed cooperative services such as strategic distributed system that often involve a lot of heterogeneous resources and dependable real-time tasks (Observe, Orient, Decide and Act) requiring enough resources to minimize its execution time. The lower level Grid admin domain generate multiple local schedules based on local resources, constraints, and interests (objectives). An adaptive application-level scheduling algorithm is developed to maximize the service for resources requirement of local jobs and at the same time minimize the execution cost. These local schedules correspond to a schedule pool, from which the system level Grid admin can assemble a set of ranked K-Neighboring global schedules according to global objectives. An adaptive system-level job scheduling algorithm is used to find a set of ranked schedules.Global feasibility is ensured at the upper level Gird domain, while local autonomies are maintained among lower application level domains due to the characteristics of the proposed organizational control architecture. The experimental scenario results have shown that the scheduling system can ensure the global feasibility and local autonomy at the same time.

2 Job Scheduling Framework

With the development of network computing and cooperative distributed resource management, Researchers have taken more and more importance on the building of large scale grid to integrate all the computational resource of many organizations into a networked environment. Logically, the architecture of such Grid is divided into three levels: the system level, the admin domain (AD) level and the node level. The node can be a computer, a sensor monitor or a resource controller which providing some types of services. The admin domain level consists of machine groups, in which all nodes belong to one organization or team. An AD can locally control the resources of its nodes but cannot operate the resources of nodes in other ADs directly. A Grid system has many ADs connected together through data link and has good collaboration and trust relationship between the ADs of a virtual organization. The design of scheduling scheme for such a Grid need to consider the following issues:

1. Limitation of resources: In general, a Grid is provided with limited resources with which to accomplish their objectives.
2. Autonomy of Grid ADs: Each AD is independent. An AD itself determines whether or not to run a new job, how to schedule and how to optimize node utilization.
3. Multiplication of Tasks Objectives: In an AD, the tasks of a job are dependable and have multi objectives.
4. Adaptation of Grid:Various tasks consume different nodes, including computing power and storages.

The multi objective model includes tasks, nodes, task precedence constraints, and scheduling parameters.

A task, derived from job decomposition, is characterized as T_i ($i = 1, \cdots, N$, where N is the number of tasks) by specifying the following basic attributes:

(1) Task start time $t_{s,i}$; (2) Task processing time $t_{p,i}$; (3) Task finish time $t_{f,i}$; (4) Task resource requirement vector $R_i = [r_{i,1}, \cdots, r_{i,k}, \cdots, r_{i,K}]$, where $r_{i,k}$ is the number of resource $k (k = 1, \cdots, K)$, where K is the number of resource types, in this paper a resource can represent a software service provided by a node required for successful execution of task T_i.

For each node $S_i (i = 1, \cdots, M)$, where M is the number of nodes, we define the basic attributes as follows: (1) Node resource capability vector $C_i = (c_{i,1}, \cdots, c_{i,k}, \cdots, c_{i,K})$, where $c_{i,k}$ is the number of service k processed by node S_i; (2) $E_{i,j}$ as the energy consumption of node S_j finishing T_i.

We define the set of successor tasks of task T_i as T_i^s. Then, the task precedence constraints are given by:

$$t_{s,i'} \geq t_{f,i} + t^{to}, \text{with} \quad T_{i'} \in T_i^s \tag{1}$$

where t^{to} is the required 'timeout' between task T_i and its successor tasks. The scheduler parameters include the following attributes: (1) Task to AD assignment, which is given by:

$$p_{i,m} = \begin{cases} 1, & \text{if task } T_i \text{ is assigned to } AD_m \\ 0, & \text{otherwise} \end{cases} \tag{2}$$

(2) Node to AD allocation, which is given by:

$$q_{i,m} = \begin{cases} 1, & \text{if resource } S_i \text{ is allocated to } AD_m \\ 0, & \text{otherwise} \end{cases} \tag{3}$$

(3) We define the near optimal node to task scheduling variable as follows:

$$v_{i,j}(T_1,T_2) = \begin{cases} 1, & \text{if resource } S_j \text{ is allocated to } T_i \text{ durning interval } [T_1,T_2] \\ 0, & \text{otherwise} \end{cases} \tag{4}$$

3 Job Scheduling Models and Algorithms

3.1 Application Level Scheduling

At the application level, each admin domain seeks to fulfill the tasks assigned to it. The multiple objectives are:

(1) Maximize task resources availability (TRA)

When all resources required by a real-time task T_i are available,it means the QoS of task completion equals 100%. However, in realistic applications of a mobile grid, where the resources are scarce, the AD may wish to reduce the task resources availability in order to achieve lower cost. In order to accommodate cost-availability trade-off, the resource availability for a task T_i executed by AD_m is defined as

$$A_{i,m} = \sum_{k=1}^{K} a_{i,k} \times p_{i,m} \tag{5}$$

Where $a_{i,k}$ is the resource availability for T_i in terms of each resource type k, which identifies the percentage of satisfied resources for the corresponding resource type and is evaluated via $a_{i,k} = \frac{\tilde{r}_{i,k}}{r_{i,k}}$, where $\tilde{r}_{i,k}$ is the number of resources of type k actually used to process task T_i:

$$\tilde{r}_{i,k} = min\{r_{i,k}, \sum_{S_j \in S'_m} v_{i,j}(t_1,t_2) \times r_{i,j}\} \tag{6}$$

Where S'_m is the node set allocated to AD_m. Then, the TRA maximization problem is formulated as follows:

$$\max_{v_{i,j}(t_1,t_2)} \frac{1}{N_m} \sum_{i=1}^{N_m} A_{i,m}, \quad \text{subject to (1)} \tag{7}$$

Where N_m is the number of tasks assigned to AD_m.

(2) Minimize Task Execution Cost

If a certain TRA requirement is satisfied, AD would prefer to allocate minimum resources in order to low down the power consumption (energy is a limited resource in a mobile grid) and preserve enough resources for other concurrent tasks. The optimization problem can be formalized as:

$$\min_{v_{i,j}(t_1,t_2)} \sum_{i=1}^{N_m} E_{i,j} \times v_{i,j}, S_j \in S'_m, \quad \text{subject to (1)} \tag{8}$$

In our model, the two objectives are somewhat conflicting.If task execution cost is reduced, it may result in a decrease in task resources availability. On the other hand, higher task resources availability may increase the task execution cost. The multiple objective optimization problem is to find a set of trade-offs (Pareto front) between these two objectives. To solve the scheduling problem, we improve the NSGA [12] algorithm by adding a fast sorting scheme and a Pareto-based scale-independent fitness function.

The key problem is to find an appropriate assignment of nodes to tasks within each AD during a certain time interval, $v_{i,j}(t_1, t_2)$. We encode the chromosome with the number of $N_m \cdot L_m$ genes, where N_m and L_m are the number of nodes and tasks controlled by AD_m respectively. For example, for a three-task and three-node problem, a chromosome taking the form [(1 0 0), (1 0 1), (0 1 0)] indicates that S_1 is allocated to T_1; T_2 will be processed by S_1 and S_3; and S_2 will execute T_3.

For a solution s_k, The generalized Pareto-based scale-independent fitness function is given by:

$$FITNESS(s_k) = p_k + q_k + c_k \tag{9}$$

p_k denotes the number of solutions that can be dominated by s_k, q_k denotes the number of solutions that can dominate s_k, c_k denotes the number of total solutions. We apply a pre-sorting scheme, which is tailored for the bi-objective problem, to accelerate the sorting process of NSGA. The population of size K is sorted in ascending order with respect to one of the values of the two objectives, i.e., $O_{1,k}$, Within this pre-sorted set, the Pareto front is found by sweeping the individual solution one by one with respect to the second objective values, i.e., $O_{2,k}$. It guarantees that if an individual solution s'_k is swept after s_k, then s_k dominates s'_k. The pseudo code of this algorithm is shown as follows:

Step 1: Sort the solutions in ascending order by one objective $O_{1,k}$, where $k = 1, K$, denote the sorted set as Ω;

Step 2: For an individual solution $s_k \in \Omega$, set
$p_k = |\{s_i | s_i(o_2) < s_k(o_2), s_i \in \Omega, i = 1, \cdots, k-1\}|$,
$q_k = |\{s_j | s_j(o_2) > s_k(o_2), sj \in \Omega, j = k+1, \cdots, K\}|$

Step 3: Repeat Step 2 until $k == K$.

3.2 Cooperative Node Re-allocation

If an AD cannot complete a task assigned to it using local resources with certain task resources availability (TRA), it may find other candidate ADs with the necessary resources to coordinate on the task. The cooperation is typically achieved via finding a set of nodes that satisfy the timing constraints of the task. The objective is to maximize the mean task completion accuracy given by (12).The procedures for this mechanism are (i) identifying the tasks whose TRA have not reached certain criterion; (ii) selecting the candidate nodes that can execute the task. The set of tasks assigned to AD_m that have not satisfied their TRA requirements after AD scheduling are given by:

$$\breve{T}_m = \{T_i | A_{i,m} < \alpha\} \tag{10}$$

Where α is a constant denoting the TRA threshold. The AD_m requires coordination with other ADs for processing the tasks in $\breve{T}_m$. The candidate AD are those ADs that (a) possess the required resources; and (b) own resources that satisfy the timing restrictions on the coordinated tasks. For a task $T_i \in \breve{T}_m$, the candidate set of nodes that can satisfy the requirement (a) is given by:

$$\breve{S} = \{S_j | c_{j,l} \times r_{j,l}, l = 1, \cdots, K\} \tag{11}$$

The requirement (b) is introduced in (13) as a constraint. The objective for negotiation is given by:

$$\max_{v_{i,j}(t_1,t_2)} \frac{1}{|\breve{T}_m|} \sum_{i=1}^{\breve{T}_m} A'_{i,m}, T_i \in \breve{T}_m, S_j \in \breve{S} \tag{12}$$

Subject to

$$\begin{array}{c} v_{i,j}(t_1, t_2) = 0, T_i \in \breve{T}_m \\ S_j \in \breve{S}, t_1 = t_{s,i}, t_2 = t_{f,i} \end{array} \tag{13}$$

Where $A'_{i,m}$ is the TRA of T_i requiring more than one AD. Since some tasks require more than one AD to process, we redefine the task resources availability for task T_i as:

$$A_i = \begin{cases} A_{i,m}, & \text{if } \mathrm{T_i} \notin \mathrm{\breve{T}_m} \\ A'_{i,m}, & \text{if } \mathrm{T_i} \in \mathrm{\breve{T}_m} \end{cases} \tag{14}$$

This is a single-objective optimization problem, and we employ a GA to find the best task-to-node assignment. A binary chromosome contains $|\breve{T}_m| \cdot |\breve{S}|$ genes, where $|\breve{T}_m|$ and $|\breve{S}|$ are the number of the unfinished tasks and the number of candidate nodes, respectively. The mean task resources availability is used as the fitness function, which is given by (12). The GA uses Arithmetic and Multipoint crossover operators and Multi-nonuniform mutations. For the selection operator, the new population is comprised of the following three parts: (a) 50% of the new population is from the best 50% of the previous population; (b) 20% of the new population is from crossover; and (c) 30% new population comes from mutations. By doing this, we can keep both elitism and the diversity of the population. The size of initial population is set at $N = 100$, which is sufficient to cover the problem of any size. The number of iterations is set to 50 based on our experimental observation that the GA usually converges within 50 iterations.

4 System Level Scheduling

The system level need to integrate multiple distributed schedules (denoted as S) from each AD to achieve the following two objectives: (a) complete the job (consisting of a set of dependable tasks) as rapidly as possible; (b) complete the job with maximum degree of accomplishment.

The overall task resources availability at the system level is the mean value of the task resources availability. The resulting TRA optimization problem is given by:

$$\max_S = \max_S \frac{1}{N} \sum_{i=1}^{N} A_i, \qquad \text{Subject to (1)} \tag{15}$$

We assume that the job start time (t_{Start}) is 0 and job end time is t_{End}. Minimization of the makespan is equivalent to minimizing the t_{End}. Since tasks are parallel and are distributed among ADs, the makespan is calculated by assembling the schedule from each AD. The problem is thus given by:

$$\min_S t_{end}, \qquad \text{Subject to (1)} \tag{16}$$

The MOGA proposed for solving the global schedule building problem, except for the encoding, is similar to the one we used in application level scheduling. The index of one of the local schedules in each AD is encoded in the corresponding gene in a chromosome with M genes, where M is the number of ADs. For example, a chromosome [1 3 2 5] indicates that the first schedule of AD1, the third schedule of AD2, the second schedule of AD3, and the fifth schedule of AD4 are selected to assemble a global schedule. The MOGA will enumerate the of these indices until a set of K- Neighboring schedules are found.

Two issues are involved in building a global schedule: (a) to maintain the feasibility of the global schedule; and (b) to converge to a stable schedule state in terms of start time of each task. We use shifting algorithm to build the global schedule and maintain its feasibility, that is, local AD schedules are reassembled according to the task graph. The start times of tasks that have precedence constraints will be shifted to a time when all its preceding tasks have been accomplished. We employ the following iterative scheme to achieve the stability of the schedule: once the shifting algorithm is complete, a set of new start times is obtained. We start the entire process with the set of new start times. This iteration is repeated till the task start times do not change. At this stage, the global schedule reaches its stable state. This process is depicted in Fig. 1.

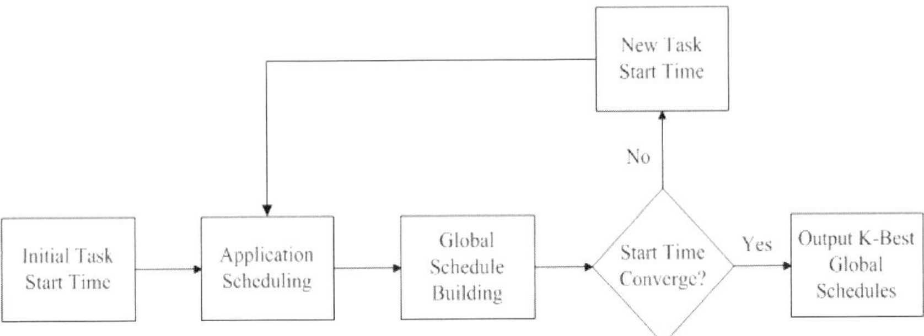

Fig. 1. The system level scheduling procedure

5 Experimental Results and Analysis

The Experiment was conducted in a small 20-node Grid which belong to 4 admin domain. The parameter of tasks and resources including task resource requirement vector and node resource capability vector can be adjusted according to the real operational equipments and mission.

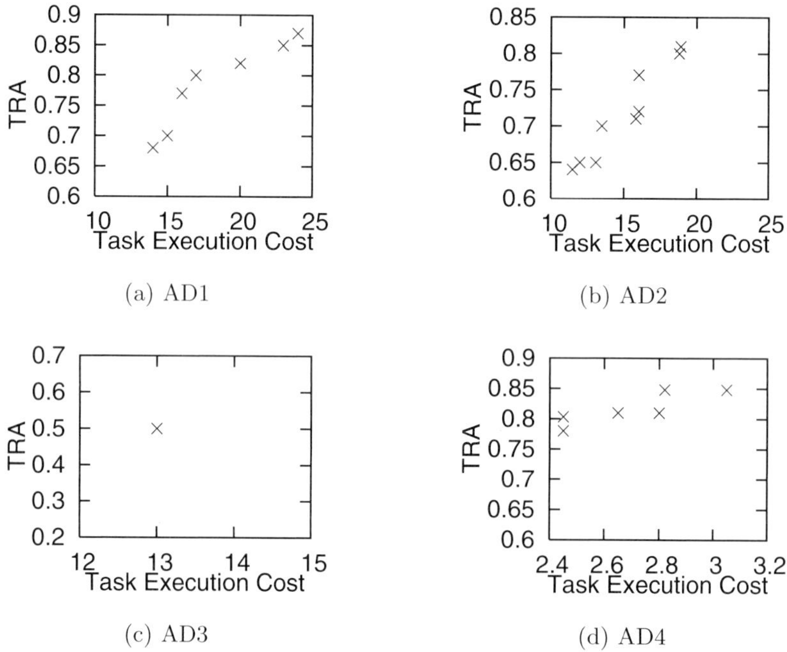

Fig. 2. The Pareto Front found for each AD

After it is finished, each AD produces $N_{i,m}(m = 1, \cdots, 4)$ Pareto optima. $N_{i,m}$is different for each AD. The Pareto front for each AD is shown in Fig. 2. We note that the $N_{i,m}$for each AD is 7, 9, 1, 7, respectively. Each local Pareto optimum corresponds to a task resource allocation matrix, therefore, a local Pareto optimal schedule.

The system level schedule building process is responsible for assembling local schedules to form ranked K-Neighboring global schedules. The objective function values, i.e., the overall TRA, and makespan for the 14 Pareto optima are listed in Table 1. We notice that the range of the TRA is from 88.27% to 90.81%, and the makespan ranges from 120 to 122. This information tells us that even if the job shifts from the best schedule to the lowest ranked schedule, the performance of the job will not deteriorate much.

In the second experiment, the number of delayed tasks was chosen to compare the performance of our MOGA algorithm with that of Min_min and Sufferage. The delayed tasks will be rescheduled later since their resource requirements can't be satisfied. The less the number of delayed tasks, the more user satisfied

Table 1. The Objective Functions Values for Pareto Optima

Rank	TRA	Makespan	Fitness Value
1	90.81%	120	106
2	90.32%	121	86
3	90.25%	121	86
4	89.61%	120	83
5	88.86%	120	81
6	88.51%	120	80
7	88.27%	120	78
8	86.37%	120	66
9	88.79%	121	63
10	88.30%	121	61
11	90.03%	122	61
12	89.95%	122	61
13	89.60%	122	60
14	89.50%	122	60

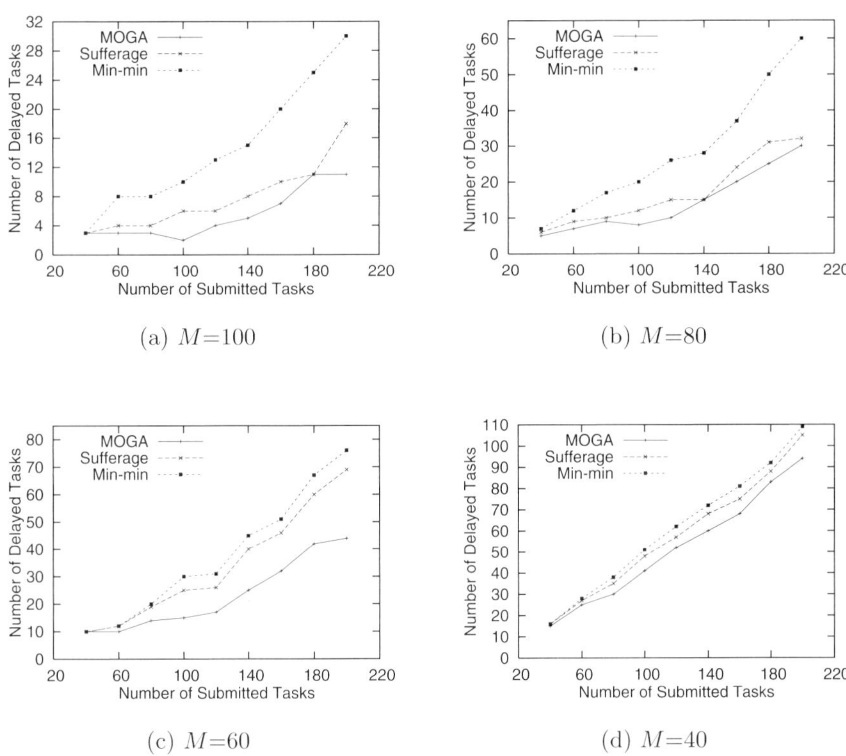

(a) M=100 (b) M=80

(c) M=60 (d) M=40

Fig. 3. Comparsion of delayed task numbers using MOGA, Min_min and Sufferage

and the less resource consumption for rescheduling.It can be seen from Fig. 3 that the number of delayed tasks increase with the increase of submitted tasks when the number of nodes, M,changes. We also see that MOGA algorithm delayed the less tasks than the other two algorithms, since it has the ability of obtaining resources from other Grid admin domains. Sufferage can also decrease the number of delayed tasks by preserving the urgent tasks and scheduling them with a higher priority.

6 Conclusion

In this paper, an efficient flexible Grid job scheduling scheme applying Multi-Objective Genetic Algorithms is proposed. Each admin domain provides multiple Pareto optimal local schedules that satisfy local objectives, while the system level assembles these local schedules, generate a set of ranked K-Neighboring global schedules. When facing environmental disturbances (some nodes may break down due to incidents), the upper level resource manager can either shift to different stages of alternative schedules or adjust current schedule by learning from the history of the current or alternative schedules. The advantage of this scheduling scheme is that it generates multiple neighboring candidate schedules in one run, which avoids the costly rescheduling process and also minimizes the adaptation cost.

References

1. Kurowski, K., Nabrzyski, J., Pukacki, J.: User preference driven multiobjective resource management in grid environments. In: Proceedings First IEEE/ACM International Symposium on Cluster Computing and the Grid, pp. 114–121 (2001)
2. Anstreicher, K., Brixius, N., Goux, J.P., Linderoth, J.: Solving large quadratic assignment problems on computational grids. Mathematical Programming 91, 563–588 (2002)
3. Paniagua, C., Xhafa, F., Caballé, S., Daradoumis, A.: A parallel grid-based implementation for real time processing of event log data in collaborative applications. In: PDPTA, pp. 1177–1186 (2005)
4. Beynon, M., Sussman, A., Catalyurek, U., Kurc, T., Saltz, J.: Performance optimization for data intensive grid applications. In: Proceedings Third Annual International Workshop on Active Middleware Services, pp. 97–105 (2002)
5. Di Martino, V.: Sub optimal scheduling in a grid using genetic algorithms. In: Proceedings International Parallel and Distributed Processing Symposium, pp. 553–565 (2003)
6. Braun, T.D., Siegel, H.J., Beck, N., Boloni, L.L., Maheswaran, M., Reuther, A.I., Robertson, J.P., Theys, M.D., Yao, B., Hensgen, D., Freund, R.F.: A comparison of eleven static heuristics for mapping a class of independent tasks onto heterogeneous distributed computing systems. Journal of Parallel and Distributed Computing 61, 810–837 (2001)
7. Braun, T., Siegel, H., Maciejewski, A.: Static mapping heuristics for tasks with dependencies, priorities, deadlines, and multiple versions in heterogeneous environments. In: Proceedings 16th International Parallel and Distributed Processing Symposium, pp. 78–85 (2002)

8. Dogan, A., Ozguner, F.: On qos-based scheduling of a meta-task with multiple qos demands in heterogeneous computing. In: Proceedings 16th International Parallel and Distributed Processing Symposium, pp. 477–482 (2002)
9. Golconda, K., Ozguner, F., Dogan, A.: A comparison of static qos-based scheduling heuristics for a meta-task with multiple qos dimensions in heterogeneous computing. In: Proceedings 18th International Parallel and Distributed Processing Symposium, pp. 106–115 (2004)
10. Weng, C., Lu, X.: Heuristic scheduling for bag-of-tasks applications in combination with qos in the computational grid. Future Generation Computer Systems 21, 271–280 (2005)
11. Page, A.J., Naughton, T.J.: Dynamic task scheduling using genetic algorithms for heterogeneous distributed computing. In: Proceedings 19th IEEE International Parallel and Distributed Processing Symposium, pp. 189–197. IEEE Computer Society Press, Los Alamitos (2005)
12. Deb, K., Pratap, A., Agarwal, S., Meyarivan, T.: A fast and elitist multiobjective genetic algorithm: Nsga-ii. IEEE Transactions on Evolutionary Computation 6, 182–197 (2002)

A Pro-middleware for Grids Computing

Raihan Ur Rasool and Qingping Guo

Wuhan University of Technology, Mail Box 114, Yujiatou, Wuhan, 430063, P.R. China
{raihan,pguo}@whut.edu.cn

Abstract. Several works on grid computing have been proposed during the last few years. However, most of them including available software, can not deal properly with some issues related to abstraction and friendliness of grid. A much wider variety of applications and large community of users can get benefit once grid computing technologies become easier to use and more sophisticated. This work concentrates on presenting 'Users-Grid' (pro-middleware), which sits between the grid middleware and user applications. It introduces a high-level abstraction layer and hides the intricacies of the grid middleware. It attempts to make the grid-related aspects transparent to the end users. Its main features are automatic DAG inference and seamless job submission. It facilitates end-users to directly run their applications on grid by themselves without depending on the expertise of support teams.

1 Introduction

The computational grids offer applications the collective computational power of distributed but typically shared heterogeneous resources. But the current grid computing software is rather low-level, immature, difficult to set up and use, and requires substantial technical expertise. Due to the labor and expertise required, small scale research groups and individual researchers cannot access the Grid's computational power.

Grid standards change at a rapid pace. For example during the last few years, the Globus Toolkit has moved from a non-SOA version (Globus Toolkit 2.0) to a WS-RF compatible version (GT4) [1]. The unstable Grid standards can also be held responsible for the hesitancy of many academic or industrial organizations to adopt Grid technologies [2]. A much wider variety of applications and large community of users can get benefit once grid computing technologies become easier to use and more sophisticated. In order to expand access to the latest advances in computer science, it is necessary to develop tools that simplify their use for non-specialists [3, 4].

The Globus Grid Toolkit is a set of low-level tools, protocols and services that has become a de facto standard for basic grid computing infrastructure. However, even after the advent of Grid services, the use of Grid requires a group of knowledgeable, dedicated specialists [3]. Developing Grid services with the WS-RF [5] standard is a complex process, which consists of several steps to develop a single service and requires proficiency in Grid technologies [4]. The problems with the current Grid applications development model can be avoided by introducing a high-level

I. Stojmenovic et al. (Eds.): ISPA 2007, LNCS 4742, pp.556 – 562,2007.

abstraction layer [1]. We still need to develop tools to facilitate end-users to directly run their applications on grid by themselves without depending on expertise of support teams [6]. We are still in need of tools to effectively utilize such resources. The two most popular grid-aware systems are Condor [7] and Globus [8]. Developing Grid applications using the core Globus Toolkit, the de facto standard Grid middleware, is still far from straightforward [9]. Many users are often hesitant to port their programs to make them Grid-enabled due to complexities in this approach. There are a large number of existent non-Grid applications that could potentially be moved to a Grid environment [10]. However, a complete reengineering of the application is not realistic. Tools like the Java Community Grid Toolkit (Java CoG Kit) [11] have helped facilitate the user; but even with the many facilities that Java CoG Kit provides, a good understanding of the grid is still required [12].

The challenge is to efficiently execute applications in grid environments, without placing the burden on users. Few systems (for example EasyGrid [13]) help the programmer (not the end users) to enable applications to execute in grid environments. On the contrary, Users-Grid pro-middleware attempts to make the aspects related to the grid, transparent to the end users. It enables applications to draw computational power transparently from the grid. This paper aims to present a tool [14, 15] which sits between the grid middleware (Globus) and user applications, hence named 'pro-middleware'. It provides a high-level abstraction layer to grid applications and hides the intricacies of the grid middleware. Several works on grid computing have been proposed in the last years. However, most work presented in the literature can not deal properly with some issues related to abstraction and friendliness of the grid.

Our work differs from those in the literature. We designed an architectural model to be implemented at a pro-middleware level. We handle three problems: automatic DAG inference, automatic application partitioning and automatic job submission. To the best of our knowledge, no other work in the literature considers this approach to solve the problem of grid friendliness. It's to emphasize that we do not propose a full grid solution (as the Globus project does, for example): we assume that issues like authorization and certification are provided to grant access to the grid nodes, as well as we assume each grid node has its own local resource manager. The remaining of this text is organized as follows. Section 2 presents our pro-middleware approach. Section 3 discuses experimental results and finally, section 4 concludes this text.

2 A Pro-middleware Approach

Grids for "big science" or specific applications tend to be deployed for long term needs, with significant investment of project specific resources. There is a strong need for a utility grid that is differentiated from such application specific grids [16]. Users-Grid provides computing power transparently and turns grid into a utility. Its defining feature is automatic or seamless job submission. It enables existing software or applications to run on the grid. With Users-Grid, user only runs the heavy applications on his own machine without knowing the details and complexities of Grid, and Users-Grid seamlessly makes the job(s) request and automatically submits it after analyzing and partitioning.

In Users-Grid architecture, we model tasks and resources as graphs. This approach has been borrowed from [17]. Each node at resource side is considered as a grid site, and therefore has information about individual resources in the site, including access restrictions, computational power, costs etc. The edges of the resources graph correspond to the connections available between the grid nodes. At the application side, each node corresponds to an application task, and each edge represents a task dependence that indicates a precedence order. This architectural model relies on already available software components to solve issues such as allocation of tasks within a grid node, or authorization control. The conception of our work is based on the following assumptions. Each grid node has its Resource Management System (RMS) and it allows dynamic resource discovery and allocation. Tasks can have dependencies on other tasks only through file sharing. And tasks do not communicate by message passing in our applications. Moreover, we consider that the application graph is a directed acyclic graph (DAG). This is a common assumption as presented in Condor's DAGMan [7] and Globus Chimera [18]. Users-Grid pro-middleware has three main parts: a monitor, worker and Personal Automatic Job Submission Agent (PAJA). A general idea of Users-Grid and its internal working have been demonstrated in fig 1.

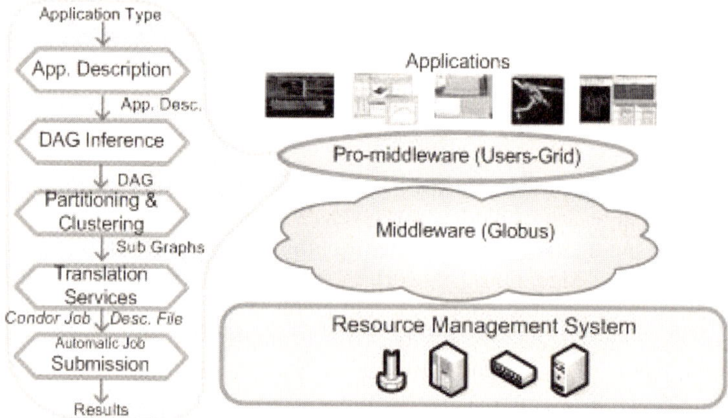

Fig. 1. General Idea of Users-Grid pro-middleware

2.1 Users-Grid Monitor

As stated above, the main task of monitor is to analyze and know the type of applications currently running. The 'Application Enabler Daemon' of Users-Grid monitor can already be active or can be started by Users-Grid control panel. Users can make policies and set their choices in this control panel. When the user runs the application the daemon collects the information about the running applications. It helps to decide the type of application (independent, loosely coupled, or tightly coupled tasks). Knowing the application type can further help to decide the suitability of that application to run on the Grid. The monitor generates the application description in XML format and passes it to Users-Grid worker. It is also responsible to show the status and monitoring information about the application in a user friendly way.

2.2 Users-Grid Worker

It gets the application descriptions as an input from the monitor and automatically infers the DAG. It is also responsible to partition the application into sub-graph. The basic description file is parsed, and the application graph is built in memory. A clustering algorithm (fig 2) is executed, and the sub-DAGs of the application graph are obtained [17]. Knowing the kind of application improves performance when trying to infer the DAG.

```
Data: graph of tasks
Result: set of clusters
begin
        initialize set of clusters as empty;
        initialize current cluster as empty;
        while not at end of the graph do
            get next task;
            if current cluster reached granularity limit then
                add current cluster to set of clusters;
                initialize a new current cluster as empty;
            end
            add next task to current cluster;
        end
        add current cluster to set of clusters;
        return set of clusters
end
```

Fig. 2. Clustering Algorithm

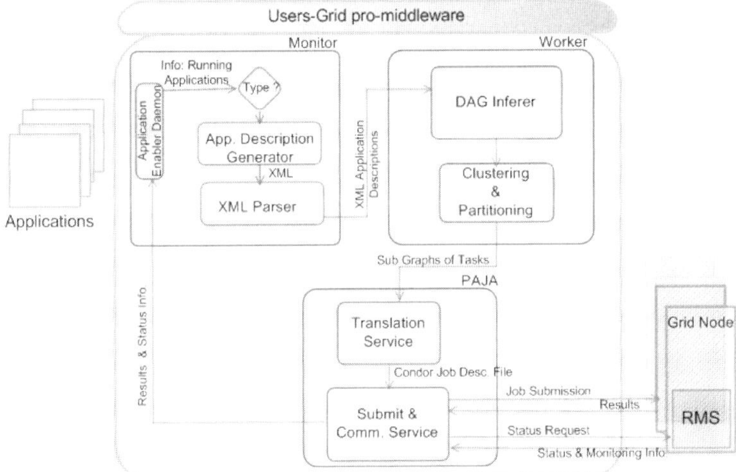

Fig. 3. Users-Grid components working detail

2.3 Personal Automatic Job Submission Agent (PAJA)

It is responsible for translating the internal sub-graph description to the appropriate format for an automatic tasks submission to Condor. PAJA translates GXML description to a condor-job submission format and is capable of submitting tasks to RMS (Condor). It has a job submission and communication service; which is responsible for automatic job submission, status and monitoring information, and collection of results. Fig 3 explains the architectural details and internal working of Users-Grid pro-middleware system.

Currently, the jobType field in the standard GRAM RSL supports only two special types of job, MPI and Condor. The Condor glidein mechanism effectively bypasses the GRAM and its limitations [17]. Condor is a special case that has built-in support in the GRAM to handle jobType=condor, as well as an alternate job manager, jobmanager-condor. Extending RSL seems to be a solution but it's not easy. So currently Users-Grid only supports Condor as a RMS at the grid nodes.

3 Results and Discussion

Users-Grid introduces a high-level abstraction layer to facilitate end-users to directly run their applications on grid by themselves without depending on the expertise of support teams. The first promising outcome of this research has been achieved in the form of a prototype development of a part of this project. So it is still work-in-progress and here we want to show few results from our early findings. We intend to compare the Users-Grid (with Condor) and Condor-only approaches. Our experimental setup includes seven Intel Core 2 Duo processors; with 2.0 GHz CPU clock speed. Each computer has 1 GB DDR with 667 MHz FSB (Front Side Bus). And all of them have been connected with 10/100 Mbps LAN. We ran a program that performs mathematical calculation in a local area network. Following fig 4 clearly shows that Users-Grid completes an application in a little longer time as compared to Condor-only. Tasks actually take longer to be dispatched and to start running in Users-Grid, which delays the whole application progress. It's because of the overhead of job preparation time.

We had to compromise on efficiency to provide real virtualization, automatic job submission and ease of use to users. We prove our statement by considering an example of Matlab. It provides an easy-to-use programming language, sophisticated graphics features, statistics and optimization tools. We can easily observe that all the convenience of Matlab came at the cost of performance [19]. The graphical user interface, parser, interpreter and lack of type inference take away processor cycles which could be used for computation. Also, the interpreted scripts could not match the performance of compiled C or FORTRAN code. Still Matlab is a huge success. We can see that what the users really want is ease of use, not only the peak performance. Users prefer a system that is easy to use and has good performance over a system with peak performance but is hard to use and clumsy [19].

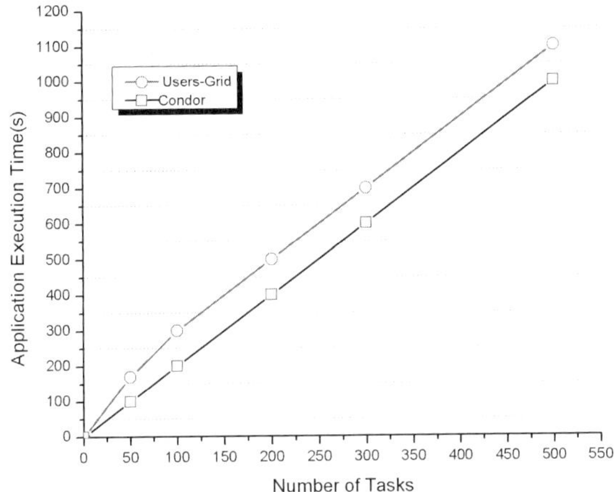

Fig. 4. Application execution time for Users-Grid and Condor

4 Conclusions and Future Work

Current grid computing software is low-level and difficult to set up which requires substantial technical expertise. Due to its complexity, many researchers have not adopted this new way of working yet. Small scale research groups and individual researchers are still 'waiting' for this technology. A much wider variety of applications and large community of users can get benefit once grid computing technologies become easier to use and more sophisticated. We argue that the problems can be avoided by introducing a high-level abstraction layer between the existing middleware (Globus) and software applications. Our work focuses on providing a tool that can seamlessly enable (existing) applications to run on Grid. So, users will remain blissfully unaware that they are using any computer but the one on their desktop. Experimental results show that application execution time taken by Users-Grid is not equal to Condor-only approach. But considering Matlab as an example, clarifies that users prefer a system that is easy to use and has good performance over a system with peak performance but is hard to use and clumsy.

Acknowledgments

We are thankful to Shadi Hamza, Oyang Lin, Sun Qiang, Feng Miao and Ahmad for their support in ideas, programming, user interface designing and valuable suggestions. We are also indebted to Francisco and Patrícia for providing us supportive material and help which became a base of this work. This work borrows much from their ideas and technical work.

References

1. Hernández, F., Bangalore, P.: A Graphical Modeling Environment for the Generation of Workflows for the Globus Toolkit. In: Kielmann, V.G.a.T. (ed.) Workshop on Component Models and Systems for Grid Applications, Saint Malo, France, pp. 79–96 (2004)
2. Cline, K., Cohen, J.: Toward Converging Web Service Standards for Resources, Events, and Management. Verision 1.0. Hewlett Packard Corporation, IBM Corporation, Intel Corporation and Microsoft Corporation (2006)
3. Parashar, M., Lee, C.: Special Issue on Grid Computing. In: IEEE Conference on Computer Science, vol. 93(93), pp. 479–484. IEEE, Los Alamitos (2005)
4. Hernández, F., Bangalore, P.: End-User Tools for Grid Computing. In: International Conference on Software Engineering, pp.1–5 (2005)
5. Foster, I.: A Globus Toolkit Primer (2006), http://www.globus.org/toolkit/docs/4.0/key/GT4_Primer_0.6.pdf
6. Smarr, Catlett, E.C.: Metacomputing. Communications of the ACM 35 (1992)
7. Thain, D., Tannenbaum, T., Livny, M.: Condor and the Grid. John Wiley, Chichester (2003)
8. Foster, I., Kesselman, C., Nick, J., Tuecke, S.: Grid services for distributed system integration. IEEE Computer 35(36) (2002)
9. Chua, C., Tang, F., Issac, P., Krishnan, A.: GEL: Grid Execution Language. Journal of Parallel and Distributed Computing (2004)
10. Goyeneche, P.K., Delaitre, A., Kiss, T., Farkas, T., Boczkó, Z., Highlevel, T.: Grid Application Environment to Use Legacy Codes as OGSA Grid Services. In: 5th IEEE/ACM International Workshop on Grid Computing, Pittsburgh, PA, vol. 3004 (2005)
11. Laszeweski, V., Foster, I., Gawor, J., Lane, P.: A Java Commodity Grid Kit, Concurrency and Computation: Practice and Experience. Concurrency and Computation: Practice and Experience 13(8-9), 643–662 (2001)
12. Hernández: Domain-Specific Models and the Globus Toolkit. Department of Computer and Information Sciences, University of Alabama at Birmingham, UABCIS-TR-2004-0504-1, Birmingham, AL (2004)
13. Boeres, C., Rebello, V.E.F.: EasyGrid: Towards a framework for the automatic grid enabling of legacy MPI applications. Concurrency and Computation: Practice and Experience 16(5), 425–432 (2004)
14. Rasool, R.U., Guo, Q.P.: Users-Grid Matlab Plug-in: Enabling Matlab for the Grid. In: IEEE International conference on e-business Engineering, Shanghai, pp. 472–479 (2006)
15. Rasool, R.U., Guo, Q.P.: A proposal of next generation Grid-operating system. In: International Conference on Grid Computing and Applications, Las Vegas, USA, pp. 90–96 (2005)
16. Vandenberg, A.: Grid computing for all. In: 43rd annual southeast regional conference, Kennesaw, Georgia, p. 3 (2005)
17. Mangan, P.K.V.: GRAND: UM MODELO DE GERENCIAMENTO HIERÁRQUICO DE APLICAÇÕES EM AMBIENTE DE COMPUTAÇÃO EM GRADE. vol. Dorctor of Philosophy. RIO DE JANEIRO, RJ - BRASIL (2006)
18. Foster, I., Voeckler, J., Wilde, M., Zhao, Y.: Chimera: A virtual data system for representing, querying and automating data derivation. In: 14th Conference on Scientific and Statistical Database Management, Edinburgh, Scotland (2002)
19. Choy, A.E.: Parallel MATLAB: doing it right. IEEE Journal 93, 331–341 (2005)

On Formal MOM Modeling

Hanmei Cui and Jessica Chen

School of Computer Science, University of Windsor
Windsor, Ont. Canada N9B 3P4
{duan1,xjchen}@uwindsor.ca

Abstract. Distributed applications are usually concurrent and nondeterministic. For this reason, formal verification on their design specifications is an essential technique for us to gain more confidence in the correctness of the behavioral aspects of our design before putting them into coding stage. Message-Oriented Middleware (MOM) is widely used to simplify the task of interprocess communications in distributed applications. To model the MOM-based applications for verification purpose, the services provided by MOM must also be integrated into the models. However, MOM modeling is non-trivial. While providing high-level program interfaces which shield programmers from the complexity of the underlying operating systems and networks, MOM may also conceals under such interfaces the concurrency and nondeterminism present in the underlying networks. This increases the possibility of misinterpreting the behavior of the applications, which in turn causes design errors. An over-abstracted MOM model based on Application Programming Interface may bury such design errors while an over-detailed model may consume too much resource and render the verification infeasible. As a guideline for MOM modeling, we present several formal models of various behavioral aspects of MOM in terms of Promela, the specification language used in SPIN model checker. Based on our empirical study, we also discuss the impact of incorporating these formal models in different settings into the MOM-based application models, in terms of increased state space for model checking.

Keywords: distributed applications, message-oriented middleware, nondeterminism, model checking.

1 Introduction

A middleware encapsulates the heterogeneity of the distributed computing environment and provides a consistent logic communication media for distributed applications. This greatly reduces the design and coding effort. On the other hand, the introduction of middleware technology has raised several important issues on our state-of-the-art methodologies for software quality control in terms of software testing/monitoring and formal verification.

There are two major middleware families: *Distributed Object System (DOS) middleware* and *message-oriented middleware(MOM)*. In this paper, we consider

I. Stojmenovic et al. (Eds.): ISPA 2007, LNCS 4742, pp. 563–576, 2007.

the issues arising from applying model checking technique to verify the correctness of design specifications of distributed applications that rely on MOM as media for interprocess communication [1].

MOM exposes only high-level Application Programming Interface (API) to the users: Many communication management tasks such as load balance, identification, authorization, authentication, encryption/decryption and wiring protocols are handled by the MOM at the back-end.

From the user's view point, with MOM, the processes in an application communicate with each other by exchanging messages through universally identifiable MOM *message queue* components. A process may create and register message sender and message receiver components to the message queues or share an existing sender or receiver component created by another process. The message senders and message receivers are MOM components acting as the *gates* of a message queue. Senders inject messages into the message queue while receivers extract messages from it. MOM may unicast a message to be received by a single registered receiver or multicast it to a group of registered receivers.

While simplifying the task of interprocess communication, the inherent nature of MOM services originated from the difficulties in network communication also complicates our task to reason about the correctness of MOM-based distributed applications.

- Message loss and message reordering are both possible. Although techniques are available to prevent such phenomena, they are not always implemented due to the efficiency concern.
- Application level multicasting is usually implemented by a group of unicasts with a dedicated central dispatcher. The dispatcher can be a resource bottleneck and cause livelock or deadlock problem.
- MOM may conceal the concurrency and nondeterminism in the underlying networks.

If these features in the underlying MOM services are not taken into account, our verdict on the correctness of the distributed application may be serious flawed. Such errors are hard to identify, hard to catch, and very often overlooked. This is because (i) the middleware APIs distances the programmers from the reality of the network communications; and (ii) the errors only appear occasionally.

Thus, in order to check the correctness of a MOM-based application, the design specification should include the modeling of not only the distributed application itself, but also the important aspects of the MOM system: the services provided by MOM which affect the business logics of the application must also be integrated into the model.

Model checking is a well-known technique (see e.g. [2,3,4]) for systematically reasoning about the correctness of a design specification against the requirement specifications. An essential issue in applying model checking technique is that the verification model constructed must be highly abstract, so that the size of the model is manageable by the chosen model checker. On the other hand, the abstract model should also be property-preserving in the sense that the truth-value of the desired property is preserved during the abstraction. As a consequence, the task of constructing succinct design models is time-consuming and heavily depends on the designer's expertise on formal modeling. Modeling MOM services faces the same challenge: An over-abstracted MOM model may bury the design errors or introduce false errors while an over-detailed model may consume too much system resource to carry out the verification.

To serve as a guideline for MOM modeling, we present in this paper several formal models on various behavioral aspects of MOM, extracted from open MOM specifications such as CORBA Messaging and Java Messaging Services. These models combine to form a single MOM model appropriate for a given application. They are capable of representing popular COTS (Commercial-Off-The-Shelf) MOM products such as SUN ONE, MQSeries and Message Queue Server.

Our formal MOM models are expressed in terms of Promela [5,3], the formal specification language used in SPIN model checker. We have chosen Promela/SPIN in our research because of (i) SPIN's popularity and its ability to handle large state space; and (ii) Promela's power on modeling interprocess communication. Although the formal models are presented in terms of a particular language, most of our discussions are also valid for the modeling in other similar languages as long as they support the FIFO (First-In-First-Out) message queues.

Based on our empirical study using SPIN, we also discuss the impact of incorporating these formal models in different settings into the distributed application models built on top of the MOM, in terms of the increased state space for model checking.

Our MOM models are designed in such a way that it can be directly plugged into an application model through UML interface. Unified Modeling Language (UML) has been widely recognized as an industrial standard for designing object-oriented software applications. Various automated tools are available to generate formal specifications, including Promela specifications, from system models described in UML (see e.g. [6]). For a MOM-based application modeled in UML, we have defined a set of messaging primitives in terms of UML classes for expressing the MOM interprocess communication in UML application models. The designers simply use these primitive classes as the messaging interface according to the MOM chosen, and we developed a tool which generates the Promela model with integrated MOM features. Due to the lack of the space, we have omitted the presentation of this part of our work.

In the next section, we compare related work. Then in Section 3, we give a motivating example and discuss the important aspects in MOM to be modeled. In Section 4 we discuss the details of the MOM modeling in Promela. The experimental results are provided in Section 5. Conclusion and final remarks are given at the end.

2 Related Work

Middleware has raised several important issues for software quality control in terms of software testing/monitoring and formal verification.

For software testing and monitoring, many middleware implementations provide us with a proper interface to intercept the executions of the distributed applications [7]. On the other hand, the internal middleware implementation may also interfere with the testing procedure on the distributed applications supported by the middleware. It has been shown that, for example, when we apply reproducible testing to distributed systems where *remote method invocations* are used as communication facilities, new deadlocks may be introduced when we incorporate the test control mechanism to the execution of the *program under test*. A static analysis technique has been thus explored to solve this problem [8].

For formal verification, the emergence of middleware technology raised two major issues: one is the verification of the correctness of the middleware itself, and the other is the verification of the correctness of the middleware-based applications.

Along the first line of research, various pieces of research work have been conducted to verify the correctness of communication protocols on different layers. For example, the specifications of CORBA ORB (Object Request Broker) properties are discussed in [9]. The descriptions of CORBA GIOP (General Inter-ORB Protocol) in Promela can be found in [10].

Our work belongs to the second line of research [11,12,13,14,15,16], which involves the formalism of the middleware as well as its use in the design specifications of the applications.

As we mentioned before, there are two major families of middleware: the DOS middleware and the MOM middleware. For the DOS middleware, we have discussed in [12] how to automatically generate a Promela model of a CORBA-based application from its adapted UML diagram. Earlier work on DOS middleware also includes [16]. The present work is dedicated to the discussion on MOM middleware.

For MOM, in [14], the authors described a generic *publish-subscribe* framework in model checking tool SMV (Symbolic Model Verifier). The framework is more general and not tailored for distributed applications. In principle, the *dispatching service* presented in [14] is similar to our *Static Universal Pace* model with *triggering service* but implemented differently. In our work, we have included more features such as *message priority*, *browsing vs. retrieval*, *message selection*, etc. In addition, we have discussed various implementations of the same service aspect when possible and provided guidelines for the selection. The framework in [14] needs to be generated separately and integrated into formal application models manually. Our model, on the other hand, can be customized and integrated into the application model automatically through a UML → Promela translator we developed.

Of course, it is also possible to embed various models of middleware features into the model checker itself. [11] gives a short proposal on embedding the middleware asynchronous communication mechanisms of *publish-subscribe* infrastructures into model checking tool Borgor. In doing so, we can take advantage of the features of a particular model checking tool to consider state space reduction. However, such an approach will be tied to a particular model checking tool. Our discussion on the other hand is quite general: as we mentioned in the Introduction, although the formal models we presented are in terms of Promela, most of our discussions are also valid for the modeling in other similar languages as long as they support the FIFO message queues.

3 MOM and its Modeling

3.1 Motivating Example

First, let us consider an example where an improper model of the MOM leads to incorrect fault detection.

A company owns several beach condos that are available to its employees for vacations. A reservation request from an employee needs to be approved by two parties: the manager and the secretary. The manager will see if the employee can go on vacation on the requested days while the secretary will see whether there is any condo available. A reservation request is made as a multicast message to both the manager and the secretary. Each party will give approval to the employees' requests based on the first-come-first-serve policy.

Consider the scenario when there is only one condo still available. Two employees, Bob, who is working in Chicago and Richard, who is working in New York, would like to request for vacation for the same day and each of them needs a condo.

Suppose that they made their requests at roughly the same time. On application level, Bob sent the message before Richard, yet on MOM layer, the messages to the two parties interleaved: The MOM used by the company implements multicast with multiple unicast sessions between Bob and the manager, Bob and the secretary, Richard and the manager, Richard and the secretary. There is no guarantee that one request will arrive before the other at both parties. As a result, it is possible that the request from Bob arrived first at the manager's while the request from Richard arrived first at the secretary's. The manager decided that Bob and Richard cannot go on vacation during the same period. Since the request from Bob arrived first, he approved the Bob's request and denied the Richard's. At the same time, the secretary found out there was only one condo left. Since the request from Richard arrived first, she approved Richard's request and denied Bob's. As the two parties gave split consent, neither Bob nor Richard succeeded in obtaining a condo even though one of them was still available.

Now, if we use a MOM model which, in order to reduce the size of its model, forces the multicast to be completed in one atomic step, which in reality is not possible on different machines, the above fault will be buried and not present in the application model. On the other hand, a MOM model which uses unicast to model multicast may put too much burden on the model checker and result in an application model that is too large to verify.

As we can see, a balance must be found between the completeness and the verification cost while modeling MOM.

3.2 Aspects of MOM for Modeling

Not all aspects of MOM need to be considered in its model. For verification purpose, we are only interested in those that may affect the logic of the application. For example, the encryption/decryption algorithm in MOM are transparent to the applications and do not have to be included into the model. In fact, while constructing a MOM model, only those aspects that affect the interprocess communication logic of the application should be considered. In this section, we look into these aspects.

As we mentioned before, with MOM, the processes in an application communicate with each other by exchanging messages through universally identifiable MOM message queue components. MOM may provide both unicast and multicast services. In unicast service, messages are injected into a *unicast queue* by *sender* components registered to the queue. Messages in such queues can be retrieved by only one of the *receiver* components registered to the queue. However, multiple registered receivers may browse (i.e. read without removing) the message before it is retrieved.

In multicast service, messages are injected into a *multicast queue* by sender components registered to the queue. Such components are also called *publishers*. MOM will duplicate each message in such queues and send a copy of the message to each registered receiver who is interested in it. The receiver components in this case are also called *subscribers*.

A number of issues need to be considered while modeling MOM unicast and multicast services:

- *triggering service*. A MOM may provide *triggering service* to notify the registered receivers when a message it required becomes available. This eliminates busy-waiting phenomenon of the process on the receiver side when no message is available to it.
- *message selection*. A MOM may allow a receiver to select only the messages it is interested in: The receivers retrieve the oldest message that matches a desired pattern.
- *message browsing*. A MOM may allow a message in the message queue to be read without being removed from the queue.
- *message loss*. Since preventing message loss may be too costly for those applications with high bandwidth requirement, a MOM may provide at-most-once (transient) delivery besides the guaranteed once-and-only-once (persistent) delivery. The former is much faster.
- *message priority*. A MOM may allow messages to be assigned with various priorities and provide expeditious delivery for messages with higher priority.
- *resource contention*. When multiple processes share senders or receivers, they must compete for the access to the MOM message queue. This may raise the deadlock or livelock problems.
- *delivery mode*. In MOM, messages are typically delivered asynchronously. The process that produces the message will continue its execution without

waiting for any feedbacks. Synchronous delivery mode is also implemented by some MOM implementations such as JMS, in which the process who produced a message will be blocked until another process acknowledges the consumption of the message.
– *message reordering*. To reduce bandwidth penalty, a MOM may prevent two messages from reordering only if they are from the same sender to the same receiver.

An application may not need all these aspects in its model, depending on the MOM chosen and the properties that we are interested in. For example, if message receivers are all activated before any message is sent, then there is no need to model a *dynamic receiver pool* in multicast service model.

In the following section, we present several formal models dealing with these MOM aspects.

4 MOM Modeling in Promela

SPIN is an on-the-fly LTL (Linear-time Temporal Logic) model checker that exploits efficient partial order reduction techniques and BDD-like storage techniques to optimize verification runs. Our MOM models are written in Promela [5], the formal language used in SPIN.

A Promela program consists of a set of processes running concurrently. For interprocess communication, it provides complex FIFO queues called *channels*, which enables both rendezvous and buffered message passing. A *rendezvous channel* cannot hold any message: it acts as hand-shaking gate for *synchronous* message passing. Messages in a Promela channel can be retrieved in FIFO order or by matched-retrieval, in which case only the matched message will be retrieved. A message may also be browsed instead of being retrieved, in which case the receiver reads the message but leaves it in the queue. If no suitable message is available in the queue, the receiver who tries to browse or retrieve the message will be blocked until one is available.

Using Promela channels as the base for MOM message queues, *triggering service*, *message selection* and *message retrieval/browsing* can be modeled directly:

– *triggering service*. An attempt to retrieve message from an empty Promela channel will automatically block the process until a message is available. This is identical to the *triggering service* provided by MOM.
– *message selection*. Promela allows *matched retrieval* and *matched browsing* by comparing message fields with constants. This can be used to model *message selection* in an abstracted form.
– *message browsing*. Promela allows a process to read messages in a channel without removing it. This is similar to, though more restrictive than, the *message browsing* in MOM.

There are various ways to model *message loss* and *message priority*:

- *message loss.* Message loss can be modeled in three possible ways. (i) let the *sender* randomly select a message to discard; (ii) let the *receiver* randomly select a message to discard; (iii) introduce an additional process to randomly *steal* messages from the queue.
- *message priority.* Message priority can be modeled as *split queue* or *priority augmentation.*
  - *split queue.* The unicast queue is implemented as multiple channels and messages of different priorities are injected to separate channels. The receivers process the messages according to the channels.
  - *priority augmentation.* A priority field is added to each message to identify the priority. The receivers process the messages according to the priority field using *matched retrieval* or *matched browsing.*

Regarding the *delivery policies* for prioritized messages, both Higher-Priority-First (HPF) and Higher-Priority-More-Frequently (HPM) policy may be implemented.

- *HPF.* Along the *split queue* approach, a receiver processes messages in lower priority channels only when the higher priority channels are empty. Along the *priority augmentation* approach, a receiver processes messages with lower priority value only when no message matching a higher priority value exists in the channel.
- *HPM.* A receiver processes the higher priority channels or retrieves higher priority messages more often.

Regarding *resource contention*, we create sender and receiver processes to simulate the sender and receiver components in MOM.

For *delivery mode*, an asynchronous message passing in MOM can be directly modeled by using buffered Promela channels. Synchronous message passing can be modeled by the rendezvous Promela channels, with the following restrictions:

- The queue for synchronous message passing only supports one receiver;
- The queue does not support asynchronous message passing, message selection or message priority.

A more complete model, which represents a MOM message queue that supports both delivery modes and multiple receivers, can also be achieved: Messages are augmented with a *delivery mode flag* and an *acknowledgement channel.* A process that may produce synchronous messages is associated with a rendezvous Promela channel, serving as the acknowledgement channel. The process sends any asynchronous messages to the message channel and continues. On the other hand, after sending an asynchronous message, the process will block on the acknowledgement channel. The process that consumed a message first examines message *delivery mode.* If the message is synchronous, the process will extract the information about the acknowledgement channel from the message and send an acknowledgement message to that channel to re-activate the producer process. Naturally, the verification cost for such a model is much higher.

Message reordering can be realized by creating a *sender process* and a *receiver process*, each representing a sender or a receiver component. A rendezvous *gate* channel is associated with each sender or receiver process and the application processes must send or receive messages through these gate channels instead of communicating with the queue channel directly. The sender and receiver processes store-and-forward messages between application processes and proper queue channels. Message reordering is then achieved through the interleavings among the sender and the receiver processes.

Another complex feature to model is the *multicast service*. There are several criteria to consider, the critical ones being:

- will message loss be tolerable?
- will the subscribers be able to retrieve messages with different paces? In other words, will a slower subscriber block other subscribers?
- will subscribers be *static* or *dynamic*? That is, will the number of the active subscribers grow and shrink during the execution?

According to these criteria, we present six different multicast models:

- *Static Universal Pace* (SUP): This is the basic model. The number of receivers is static and the receivers are forced to retrieve messages with the same pace: If any receiver has not retrieved the oldest message, those who did are blocked and cannot retrieve the next message. The senders are blocked when there is no room to hold the new one.
- *Dynamic Universal Pace* (DUP): Similar to the SUP model except that the number of receivers can grow or shrink.
- *Static Differentiated Pace with message Loss* (SDPL): Receivers retrieve messages with their own paces but message loss may occur: If a message arrives but a receiver cannot accept it, the message is dropped for that receiver to avoid blocking others.
- *Dynamic Differentiated Pace with message Loss* (DDPL): Similar to the SDPL model except that the number of receivers can grow or shrink.
- *Static Differentiated Pace with message Blocking* (SDPB): Receivers retrieve messages with their own paces unless the channel is full and there is a receiver who is not ready to retrieve the oldest message. To avoid message loss, both message senders and the other receivers are blocked to prevent message loss.
- *Dynamic Differentiated Pace with message Blocking* (DDPB): Similar to the SDPB model except that the number of receivers can grow or shrink.

Message selection, *message loss*, *message priority* and *message reordering* can be integrated into these multicast models.

In the next section, we study the impact on the increased size of the verification models by adding specific MOM features to an application model. We present our empirical study on *message priority* and *message reordering* in unicast models, followed by those of the basic multicast models.

5 Empirical Study

In this section, we use variants of the producer/consumer example to study the impact of adding specific MOM features to the application model on the increased size of the model. The model size is measured by the number of *stored states* consumed by SPIN during the model checking procedure. We examine such impact when different number of producers, consumers and channel sizes are used.

5.1 Message Priority in Unicast

We implemented three MOM models: the HPF and HPM *split queue* models and the HPM *priority augmentation* model. All of them provide two levels of message priority.

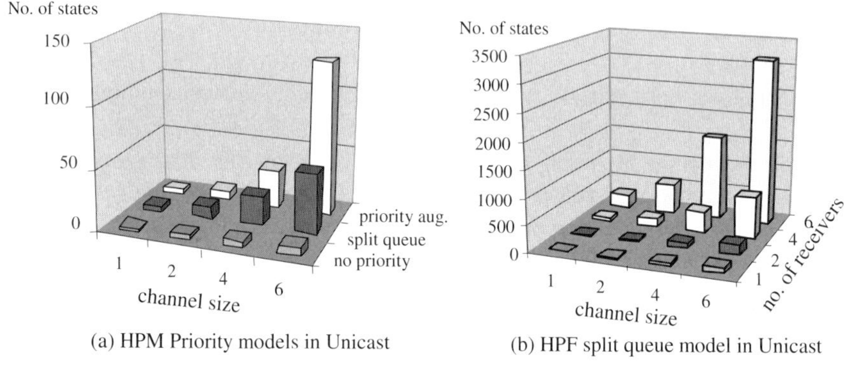

(a) HPM Priority models in Unicast (b) HPF split queue model in Unicast

Fig. 1. Comparison of the model sizes with different unicast priority MOM models

Figure 1(a) compares the state-space used in the HPM approach when: (i) No priority is implemented; (ii) Split queue model is implemented; and (iii) Priority augmentation model is implemented. From the figure we can draw the conclusion that the *split queue* approach performs better with larger channel sizes while with small channel sizes, the *priority augmentation* approach is less expensive. Since the channel size chosen in an application model is usually very small, the figure argues for the *priority augmentation* approach. When the number of data fields in a message increases, the impact of the added priority field will decrease even further.

Figure 1(b) shows the result of the *split queue* model with the HPF approach under different numbers of consumers and different channel sizes. Compared with the previous HPM result and the state-space shown here, the conclusion is that the HPM model is superior.

Similar result is obtained for the HPF in the *priority augmentation* approach, which we have omitted here due to the lack of space. Since HPM is also a more accurate model for messages sent across the networks, there is a strong argument for choosing HPM instead of HPF.

As we can see, choosing the *priority augmentation* model with small channel sizes, which is feasible in most cases, can introduce the MOM priority feature into the application with acceptable increase in the verification cost.

5.2 Message Reordering and Resource Competition in Unicast

Now we study the impact of including sender or receiver processes in MOM unicast models for simulating message reordering and resource competition phenomena. We implemented three MOM models:

- Sender process is not used. Each producer process communicates with the queue channel directly.
- A single sender process is shared by all producers.
- Two sender processes are shared by producers.

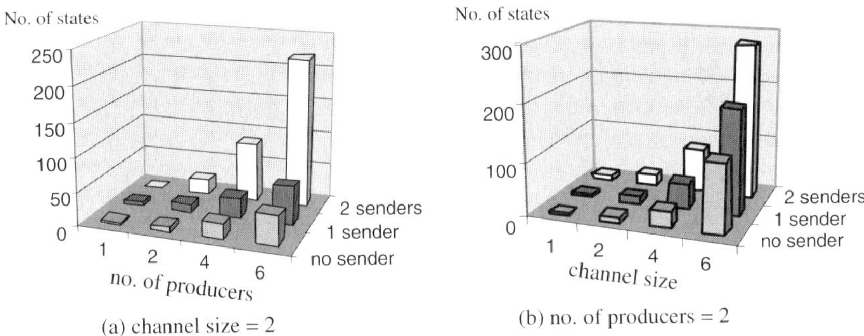

Fig. 2. Comparison of model sizes with message reordering unicast models (one consumer)

Figure 2 compares the state-space used in these three models with different number of producers and different channel sizes. In Figure 2(a), the channel size is fixed and the number of producers varies; In Figure 2(b), the number of producers is fixed and the channel size varies. From the figures we can see that the impact of including senders in the model decreases with the channel size and increases exponentially with the number of senders in the model. The latter is expected due to the state explosion problem in model checking.

Thus, the application model should use as few senders as possible, to reduce the burden on the model checker.

The result on the receiver processes is similar and is omitted here.

5.3 MOM Multicast Models

Now we compare SUP, DUP, SDPL and SDPB multicast models introduced in the previous section. Due to the lack of space, we have omitted DDPL and

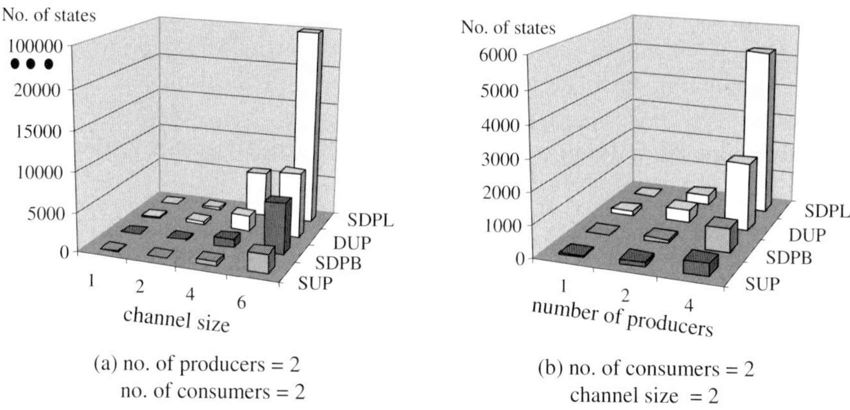

Fig. 3. Comparison of the model sizes with multicast models

DDPB models: we use only SUP and DUP models to demonstrate the cost of adding the dynamic feature.

We use a variant of the producer/consumer application, in which each message produced is multicasted to all the consumers. Figure 3 compares the state-space used in these three models with different numbers of producers, consumers and different channel sizes.

Figure 3(a) shows the change of number of states in different models according to the channel size while the number of producers and consumers is fixed; Figure 3(b) shows the change of number of states in different models according to the number of producers while the channel size is fixed and the number of consumers (receivers) is fixed.

Apparently, the SUP model is the least stressful. Then again, such a model is often too restrictive since it can easily introduce false deadlock errors into the model. From DUP model we can see that implementing a *dynamic subscriber pool*, even when it is used on top of the simplest *Universal Pace* model, is too expensive to be feasible in most cases: the designers should try to abstract the application model to avoid such a situation. The SDPL model stays closer to the real MOM *multicast service* than SUP model does, since it allows subscribers to retrieve messages with their own paces and can be used to substitute DUP model when the producer number and the channel size are small. In some cases, it is even more expensive than the DUP model. Comparably, the SDPB model may be the best choice. The pace of subscribers is less restrictive and it actually outperforms the SUP model with small queue sizes and large subscriber numbers.

6 Conclusion and Final Remarks

In this paper, we have discussed various aspects of MOM, formally modeled these aspects and studied their impact on the increased cost to model checking the models of the applications with the MOM features included.

Since there is a trade-off between the accuracy of the model and the cost to verify its correctness, and some models outperform others under certain circumstances, choosing a suitable model plays an important role in successfully carrying out the model checking. Our work may serve as a guideline for choosing an appropriate MOM model while modeling a MOM-based application: Our study shows that (i) the *triggering service*, *message loss* and *message priority* can be included in the model with acceptable expenses; (ii) The message interleaving in unicast services should be considered carefully; (iii) Though the *multicast service* is in general expensive to model no matter which approach we use, some are more acceptable than others; (iv) The SUP model is in general the least expensive, yet the SDPB model is more accurate and it outperforms SUP in certain cases.

Acknowledgements

This work is supported by the Natural Sciences and Engineering Research Council of Canada under grant number RGPIN 209774.

References

1. Linthicum, D.S.: Next Generation Application Integration: From Simple Information to Web Services, 1st edn. Addison-Wesley, Reading (2003)
2. Cleaveland, R., Sims, S.: The NCSU concurrency workbench. In: Alur, R., Henzinger, T.A. (eds.) CAV 1996. LNCS, vol. 1102, pp. 394–397. Springer, Heidelberg (1996)
3. Holzmann, G.: The model checker SPIN. IEEE Transactions on Software Engineering 23 (1997)
4. McMillan, K.L.: Symbolic Model Checking. Kluwer Academic Publishers, Dordrecht (1993)
5. Holzmann, G.: The Design and Validation of Computer Protocols. Prentice-Hall, Englewood Cliffs (1991)
6. Latella, D., Majzik, I., Massink, M.: Automatic Verification of a Behavioural Subset of UML Statechart Diagrams Using the SPIN Model-checker. Formal Aspect of Computing 11, 637–664 (1999)
7. Chen, J., Cui, H.: DOS middleware instrumentation for ensuring reproducibility of testing procedures. IEEE Transactions on Instrumentation and Measurement 56, 56–62 (2007)
8. Chen, J.: Building test constraints for testing distributed systems with middleware. In: van der Hoek, A., Coen-Porisini, A. (eds.) SEM 2002. LNCS, vol. 2596, pp. 216–232. Springer, Heidelberg (2003)
9. Duval, G.: Specification and verification of an object request broker. In: Proc. of the 20th International Conference on Software Engineering, pp. 43–52 (1998)
10. Kamel, M., Leue, S.: Validation of remote object invocation and object migration in CORBA GIOP using Promela/Spin. In: Proceedings of SPIN Workshop'98, Paris, France (1998)

11. Baresi, L., Ghezzi, C., Mottola, L.: Towards fine-grained automated verification of publish-subscribe architectures. In: Najm, E., Pradat-Peyre, J.F., Donzeau-Gouge, V.V. (eds.) FORTE 2006. LNCS, vol. 4229, pp. 131–135. Springer, Heidelberg (2006)
12. Chen, J., Cui, H.: Translation from adapted UML to promela for CORBA-based applications. In: Graf, S., Mounier, L. (eds.) Model Checking Software. LNCS, vol. 2989, pp. 234–251. Springer, Heidelberg (2004)
13. Deng, X., Dwyer, M., Hatcliff, J., Jung, G., Robby, Singh, G.: Model-checking middleware-based event-driven real-time embedded software. In: de Boer, F.S., Bonsangue, M.M., Graf, S., de Roever, W.-P. (eds.) FMCO 2002. LNCS, vol. 2852, pp. 154–181. Springer, Heidelberg (2003)
14. Garlan, D., Khersonsky, S., Kim, J.: Model checking publish-subscribe systems. In: Ball, T., Rajamani, S.K. (eds.) Model Checking Software. LNCS, vol. 2648, pp. 166–180. Springer, Heidelberg (2003)
15. Hatcliff, J., Deng, X., Dwyer, M., Jung, G., Ranganath, V.P.: An integrated development, analysis, and verification environment for component-based systems. In: Proc. of the 25th International Conference on Software Engineering, pp. 160–173. IEEE Computer Society Press, Los Alamitos (2003)
16. Kaveh, N., Emmerich, W.: Deadlock detection in distributed object systems. In: Proc. of the Joint 8th European Software Engineering Conference (ESEC) and 9th ACM SIGSOFT Symposium on the Foundations of Software Engineering (FSE-9), pp. 44–51. ACM Press, New York (2001)

Performability Analysis of Grid Architecture Via Queueing Networks

Haijun Yang[1], Minqiang Li[2], and Qinghua Zheng[3]

[1] Beijing University of Aeronautics & Astronautics, Beijing 100083, P.R. China
navy@buaa.edu.cn

[2] Institute of Systems Engineering, Tianjin University, Tianjin 300072, P.R. China
mqli@tju.edu.cn

[3] Guangxi University of Technology, Liuzhou 545006, P.R. China
qinghuazheng@ncic.ac.cn

Abstract. One of the major challenges for grid technologies is to create the scientific and technological base for share, collaboration, large-scale distributed systems. Theories and models of grid architectures are important to this endeavor as well as to providing the foundations for constructing grid systems able to work effectively. It is important to model and analyze the grid architecture so that it can evolve guided by scientific principles. On the basis of a coarse-grain classification of grid applications, we present a novel grid architecture taxonomy, interaction-intensive and computation-intensive architecture. In this paper, we will give some new grid performance metrics and model grid architectures mathematically via queueing networks. In addition, we obtain some scientific principles guiding the grid architecture design.

1 Introduction

The past several years have seen a remarkable progress of grid technologies. The grid assembles a set of geographically distributed, heterogeneous resources via the underlying networks to provide much more easier resource sharing and more efficient collaboration to users, which can be considered as a distributed system augmented with special grid features[1]. One of the major challenges for grid technologies in the next decade is to create the scientific and technological base for share, collaboration, large-scale distributed systems. Theories and models of grid architectures are important to this endeavor as well as to providing the foundations for constructing grid systems able to work effectively. The motivation for modeling grid architectures is to find the advantages of different grid architectures and point out their different application scenarios. It is important to model and analyze the grid architecture so that it can evolve guided by scientific principles. Grid architectures have evolved greatly in recent years. From the initial layered architecture to the famous Open Grid Services Architecture(OGSA) which is being exemplified in the Open Grid Services Infrastructure(OGSI)[1-4], more recently, Web Services Resource Framework(WSRF) is introduced as a new architecture to deeply support Web Services [5,6]. WSRF defined conventions for managing state of Web services, and WS-Notification defined mechanisms[7].Using WSRF and WS-Notification, Grid technology can be employed by Web Services specifications. This is a recognized classification of grid architectures,

I. Stojmenovic et al. (Eds.): ISPA 2007, LNCS 4742, pp. 577–588, 2007.

which is based on the different grid technologies and functions. However, this approach is not the only way to categorize the grid architectures. We believe that different grid applications need different grid architectures to improve the gird performance. Therefore, a novel grid architecture classification is helpful to understand and promote grid applications.

The main contributions of the work are as follows:

- We present a novel grid architecture taxonomy, interaction-intensive architecture and computation-intensive architecture.
- Our work differs significantly from previous work in that using queueing networks modeling grid architectures, and pointing out some scientific principles to guide the design of grid architectures.
- We define a novel conception-performability, and depict the grid availability and grid efficiency by ergodic results.

The remainder of this paper is organized as follows. In section 2, we define grid performability mathematically. We give the classification of grid applications in section 3. In section 4, we model the computation-intensive and interaction-intensive architecture with queueing networks, and compare the two architectures. Section 5 summarizes this paper and gives some open issues.

2 Performance Metrics

Grid technology promises much for high performance service-oriented computing but can also suffer from overheads introduced by cross domain connectivity, extensive middleware and unreliable infrastructure. Consequently, the grid performance study is becoming an ongoing critical problem. However, it is difficult to determine appropriate performance metrics. Especially, quantifying the performance metrics of grid system and its applications is a crucial issue. In this paper, we focus on the performance metrics-performability, i.e., the joint consideration of performance and dependability. For performability, we are interested in properties such as responsiveness, throughput, availability and efficiency. How to formulize grid availability and efficiency? Which mathematical tool should be employed to depict the concepts?

In this section, we will first prove that the model is a birth-death process. The availability and efficiency of a grid system can be described by ergodic theory.

Lemma 1. If a grid application can be depicted as a stochastic sequence $\{Q_n,\ n=1,2,...\}$, then, Q_n is a time-homogeneous birth-death process.

Proof: We first prove that $\{Q_n,\ n=1,2,...\}$ is a birth-death process. The transition probability of Q_n can be depicted as following:

$$Q_n(x,y)=\begin{cases} p_n(x) & \text{if } y=x+1, \\ q_n(x) & \text{if } y=x-1, \\ 0 & \text{otherwise} \end{cases} \quad (1)$$

Where $p_n(x)+q_n(x)=1$ .So, according the birth-death process definition, it is clear that $\{Q_n,\ n=1,2,...\}$ is a birth-death process.

Then, we prove that the time n and $p_{i,j}(n,n+1)$ are independent.

When $|i-j| \geq 2$, $p_{i,j}(n,n+1)=0$, i.e. the transition probability $p_{i,j}(n,n+1)$ is independence with the time n.

When $i-j=1$, $p_{i,j}(n,n+1)=q_n(i)$, $q_n(i)$ is just related with the node i, if the node i is availability.

Similarly, we can prove that $p_{i,j}(n,n+1)$ is independence with the time n when $j-i=1$ .This completes the proof.

Assuming the condition of lemma 1 being satisfied, we get two definitions as follows.

Definition 1. In a grid system, the availability from node i to node j can be described as following:

$$A_{i,j} = \sum_{n=1}^{\infty} A_{i,j}^{(n)} \tag{2}$$

$$A_{i,j}^{(n)} = P(x_{m+n} = j, x_{m+k} \neq j, k = 1,2,\ldots n-1 | x_m = i) \cdot \prod_{k=0}^{n} s_{m+k}(t) \cdot s_{m+k}(t+1),$$

Where $s_{m+k}(t) = \begin{cases} 1 & \text{node (m + k) is available at time } t \\ 0 & \text{otherwise} \end{cases}$.

Definition 2. In a grid system, the efficiency from node i to node j can be described as following:

$$E_{i,j} = \sum_{n=1}^{\infty} n \cdot A_{i,j}^{(n)} \tag{3}$$

$$A_{i,j}^{(n)} = P(x_{m+n} = j, x_{m+k} \neq j, k = 1,2,\ldots n-1 | x_m = i) \cdot \prod_{k=0}^{n} s_{m+k}(t) \cdot s_{m+k}(t+1),$$

Where $s_{m+k}(t) = \begin{cases} 1 & \text{node (m + k) is available at time } t \\ 0 & \text{otherwise} \end{cases}$.

3 Grid Architecture Taxonomy

Without user's supports, the grid technology is going to be a failure. It is important to stimulate the use of the grid technologies by the research of grid architectures and applications. There is a tight relation between grid architectures and its applications. Furthermore, grid architectures are determined by its applications, i.e., different type of grid applications need different type of grid architectures. To pursue optimal system performance, we think that there is no omnipotent grid architecture for various grid applications. Academia and industry have been accepting this standpoint[1,8]. We believe that classification of grid applications is the foundation of grid architectures. So, in order to study grid architectures, we must first distinguish the applications from interaction-intensive and computation-intensive.

In this section, on the basis of prior work[9,10], we will present a coarse-grain taxonomy of grid applications. And then, a novel Oriented-Application grid architecture taxonomy will be given on the basis of the taxonomy of grid applications.

3.1 Classification of Grid Applications

According of the scenarios of grid applications, we present two classes grid applications from the view of computation-intensive and interaction-intensive.

(1)Computation-intensive. Grid technology promises to share computing and information resources at different geographical location. Computational scientist, experimental scientist and engineers employed grid technologies to visualize their applications and obtain enough computational power. These users need so huge computational power that now none of a supercomputer can offer enough computational power to perform their applications. That is to say, computational power is their first goal. For example, the TeraGrid project, is an open scientific grid combining eight supercomputing centers to provide global, persistent computational resources. This project was launched by the National Science Foundation, and has been completed in September 2004, bringing over forty teraflops of computing power and nearly two petabytes of rotating storage, and specialized data analysis and visualization resources into production, interconnected via a dedicated national network. Another example is FusionGrid, which was found by National Fusion Collaboratory Project. FusionGrid created and deployed collaborative software tools throughout the magnetic fusion research community. There are many analogous grid applications which pursue much more computational power, such as Comb-e-chem, one of the e-Science Projects, AVO(Astrophysical Virtual Observatory) Project, and so on. Representative grid applications of above mentioned share some common characteristics. All of them chase huge computational power to perform their applications better for special users. This class application needs great computational power provided by connecting some supercomputers being located in different geographical positions via grid technologies. They are sensitive to computational power than other demands. So, this class application is called computation-intensive.

(2)Interaction-intensive. Supporting collaboration is another important goal of the grid technology, which makes it easier to perform some grid applications for facilitating grid users. There are frequent interactions between the grid users(clients) and the grid services in this class application. Furthermore, in the grid environment, the interaction is a critical method to complete the collaboration between the clients and the grid services. Applications in this class are the major demands in modern society. So far, lots of grid projects have been founded to meet the demands. For instance, the famous grid organization, Globus Alliance, has released GT3.2 and GT4.0, which emphasize the Service-Oriented application being increasing demands in grid environment [11]. The interaction not only completes the services, but also can improve the quality of grid services. Moreover, we believe that interaction is the inherent essence of the Service-Oriented applications. We can find other famous examples to support our viewpoint. The DAME(Distributed Aircraft Maintenance Environment) is an e-Science pilot project to implement a distributed decision support system for deployment in maintenance applications and environments through the grid technology[12]. The VEGA grid system is a system platform being compliant with current computing technologies and providing service-oriented applications [13].

Web service is the main type of service-oriented application. It is becoming a trend for grid technologies to support Web Service. The major grid projects announce to support the Web Services, such as Globus Alliance, e-Science, and so on.

3.2 Application-Oriented Grid Architecture Taxonomy

In this subsection, we will present a novel grid architecture taxonomy, which is based on the above taxonomy of grid applications. This classification of grid architecture is focused on the characteristics of grid applications. It is helpful to analyze and predict the behaviors of different gird systems.

(1)Interaction-intensive Architecture. In this class architecture, all components of grid system are called grid components. In order to complete interaction-intensive services, the grid components must exchange messages with each other via interactions. From the view of usage time, there are no dominative interactions in this architecture. The web service architecture is a paradigm. Furthermore, we employ the web service to explain our viewpoint in the below. As the literatures have shown[11,14], the architecture, implemented via WSRF/WSN, can be described by the grid components. In order to make it clear, we depict this architecture by a detailed process. A grid user(Client) interacts the service's security component firstly. The security component authenticates the grid user's information, and sends an authorization or not. Then, the satisfied interaction information is dispatched to a target WS-Resource through a correct URL address. Otherwise, the security component rejects the client's request, and the process is over. If the service implementation component receives the correct information, it will complete the service request. The service implementation component is not just a single service provider. Note that the component can possibly be a service composition, which integrates some services to obtain new functionality. However, from the grid user's view, there is no difference between them and all of them can be considered as the former one. This grid component is responsible for receiving, processing information, and providing functional responses to a client by interactions. The grid component sends the result to the client through the security component. This architecture can be illustrated as following figure1.

(2)Computation-intensive Architecture. In this class architecture, grid resources were mapped as services, after user authentication, grid users can directly connect grid resources. For computation-intensive applications, the time of user authentication is far less than that of computation, and thus can be neglected from the viewpoint of occupation time. So, this class architecture can be abstracted as a simple Client/Server architecture. The client is thin, after authentication, all most computing works will be completed by the servers. That is to say, in this class architecture, except the computing tasks, other processes between grid users and grid resources occupy little usage time. Thus, we can abstract this class architecture via some simple queueing system models.

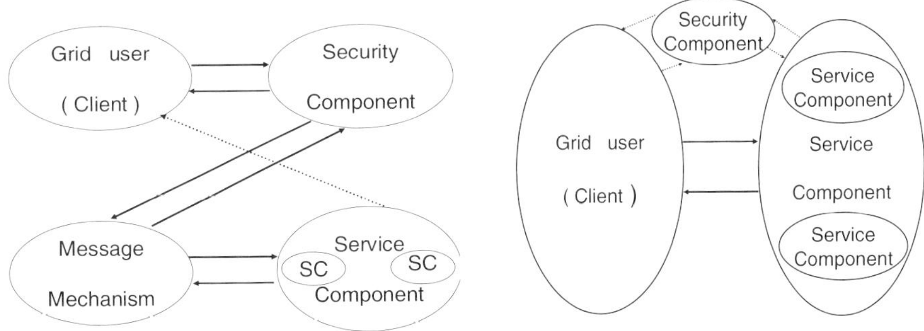

Fig. 1. Interaction-intensive Architecture **Fig. 2.** Computation-intensive Architecture

4 Modeling and Analysis

In this section, we model the two grid architectures, the computation-intensive architecture and interaction-intensive architecture, with queueing networks models. We put emphasis on the comparison of the two different architectures. And, queueing networks is just an appropriate tool to depict and compare these models. This comparison can help us to understand the difference between both grid architectures in performance. Furthermore, the analysis result is useful to design and optimize grid architectures for different grid applications. According of various service types, some models will be presented and analyzed in detail.

4.1 Results of Interaction-Intensive Architecture

The interaction-intensive architecture is illustrated as above Fig.1, which can be depicted via queueing network models as Fig.3. In Fig.3, client, security component, message mechanism and service component are abstracted as nodes of a queueing networks model. In this paper, we assume that the principle is first come, first served(FCFS) policy.

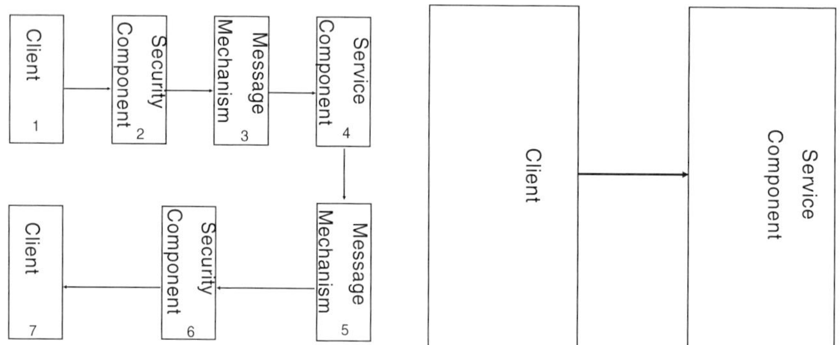

Fig. 3. Interaction-intensive Model

Fig. 4. Computation-intensive Model

Why can it be modeled as a tandem network instead of a cyclic queue? This is because the different processes in one grid component are independent, and they have different service time in it. For example, the message mechanism sending and receiving messages are independent. Moreover, they spend respective service time. In this queueing networks model, requests enter and leave the system only at the client node. To complete an application, it must interact with the grid components in turn. The application using interaction-intensive architecture must proceed through a series of grid components, each component performing a given task. In addition, Fig.3. shows that the output of previous node is the input of next node. In such a situation, we first consider the tandem model with no restriction on the waiting room's capacity between the grid components (i.e., we assume that each component has the ability to accept no limit requests). Then, we assume that client requests arrive according to a Poisson process with mean λ , and the service time of each grid component is exponential with mean $1/\mu_i$,$(i=1,2,\ldots,7)$. Meanwhile, we define $\rho_i=\lambda_i/\mu_i$ for $i=1,2,\ldots,7$. Furthermore, the seven nodes are independent, and each one can be considered as a $M/M/1$ model[15]. The steady-state is an important state, in which every node of the system has the same flow of requests.

We first analyze every node via $M/M/1$ model respectively. Let $N_i(t)$, $i=1,2,\ldots,7$ denote the number of requests in the ith node at time t after the last departure. $p_{i,n_i}=(N_i(t)=n_i)$, $i=1,2,\ldots,7$ denotes the distribution of $N_i(t)$ in steady-state state. The $p_{i,n}$ can be written as following:

$$p_{i,n_i}=(1-\rho_i)\cdot\rho_i^{ni} \tag{4}$$

Where $\rho_i=\lambda_i/\mu_i$, $i=1,2,\ldots,7$.

Let $p_n=(N_1(t)=n_1,N_2(t)=n_2,\ldots,N_7(t)=n_7)$ denote the distribution of the tandem model in steady-state state. Because these nodes are independent, the joint probability distribution can be derived straightly.

$$p_n=\prod_{i=1}^{7}(1-\rho_i)\cdot\rho_i^{ni} \tag{5}$$

Where $\rho_i=\lambda_i/\mu_i$, $i=1,2,\ldots,7$.

Using the above results, we can calculate the mean queue length, waiting time and sojourn time of this model in steady-state state, which can be denoted as L , W , and W_s respectively.

$$L=\sum_{i=1}^{7}\rho_i/(1-\rho_i)=\sum_{i=1}^{7}\frac{\lambda_i}{\mu_i-\lambda_i}=\sum_{i=1}^{7}\frac{\lambda}{\mu_i-\lambda} \tag{6}$$

On the basis of formula (6), using Little's theorem, we can obtain the whole waiting time of the system in steady-state state.

$$W=\sum_{i=1}^{7}(\rho_i/(1-\rho_i))/\lambda_i=\sum_{i=1}^{7}\frac{1}{\mu_i-\lambda_i}=\sum_{i=1}^{7}\frac{1}{\mu_i-\lambda} \tag{7}$$

From formula (7), we get the sojourn time of the model in steady-state state.

$$W_s=\sum_{i=1}^{7}\left(\frac{1}{\mu_i-\lambda_i}+\frac{1}{\mu_i}\right)=\sum_{i=1}^{7}\frac{2\mu_i-\lambda_i}{\mu_i(\mu_i-\lambda_i)}=\sum_{i=1}^{7}\frac{2\mu_i-\lambda}{\mu_i(\mu_i-\lambda)} \tag{8}$$

Formula (6) depicts the mean queueing length of interaction-intensive architecture with no limit capacity, which is positive related with the latency with throughput being λ . Formula (7) and (8) describe the mean waiting time and total spending time on this situation.

Secondly, we consider this tandem model with restriction on the waiting room's capacity between the grid components. There is a limit K_i, $i=1,2,\ldots,7$ places on the number allowed in every node in this model (i.e., K_i is the maximum request number that the ith component can accept). Then, these seven nodes are independent also, and each one can be considered as a $M/M/1/K$ model[15]. Using literature results and methodology similar to that of above where $M/M/1$ model is derived, the results of $M/M/1/K$ model in steady-state state are presented as follows.

$$\rho_{i,n_i} = \begin{cases} \dfrac{(1-\rho_i)\cdot \rho_i^{n_i}}{1-\rho_i^{K_i+1}} & (\rho_i < 1) \\ \dfrac{1}{K_i+1} & (\rho_i = 1) \end{cases} \tag{9}$$

$$L_i = \begin{cases} \dfrac{1}{1-\rho_i} - \dfrac{1+K_i\cdot \rho_i^{K_i+1}}{1-\rho_i^{K_i+1}} & (\rho_i < 1) \\ \dfrac{K_i}{2} & (\rho_i = 1) \end{cases} \tag{10}$$

$$L^K = \sum_{i=1}^{7} L_i = \begin{cases} \sum_{i=1}^{7}\left(\dfrac{1}{1-\rho_i} - \dfrac{1+K_i\cdot \rho_i^{K_i+1}}{1-\rho_i^{K_i+1}}\right) & (\rho_i < 1) \\ \sum_{i=1}^{7}\dfrac{K_i}{2} & (\rho_i = 1) \end{cases} \tag{11}$$

$$W^K = \sum_{i=1}^{7} L_i / \lambda = \begin{cases} \sum_{i=1}^{7}\left(\dfrac{\mu_i}{\lambda\cdot\mu_i - \lambda^2} - \dfrac{\mu_i^{K_i+1} + K_i\cdot\lambda^{K_i+1}}{\lambda\cdot\mu^{K_i+1} - \lambda^{K_i+2}}\right) & (\rho_i < 1) \\ \sum_{i=1}^{7}\dfrac{K_i}{2\cdot\lambda} & (\rho_i = 1) \end{cases} \tag{12}$$

$$W_S^K = \begin{cases} \sum_{i=1}^{7}\left(\dfrac{\mu_i}{\lambda\cdot\mu_i - \lambda^2} - \dfrac{\mu_i^{K_i+1} + K_i\cdot\lambda^{K_i+1}}{\lambda\cdot\mu_i^{K_i+1} - \lambda^{K_i+2}} + \dfrac{1}{\mu_i}\right) & (\rho_i < 1) \\ \sum_{i=1}^{7}\left(\dfrac{K_i}{2\cdot\lambda} + \dfrac{1}{\mu_i}\right) & (\rho_i = 1) \end{cases}$$

$$= \begin{cases} \sum_{i=1}^{7}\left(\dfrac{\mu_i^2 + \lambda\mu_i - \lambda^2}{\lambda\cdot\mu_i^2 - \mu_i\lambda^2} - \dfrac{\mu_i^{K_i+1} + K_i\cdot\lambda^{K_i+1}}{\lambda\cdot\mu_i^{K_i+1} - \lambda^{K_i+2}}\right) & (\rho_i < 1) \\ \sum_{i=1}^{7}\left(\dfrac{K_i}{2\cdot\lambda} + \dfrac{1}{\mu_i}\right) & (\rho_i = 1) \end{cases} \tag{13}$$

Formula (11) depicts the mean queueing length of interaction-intensive architecture with restricted capacity, which is positive related with the latency with throughput being λ. Formula (12) and (13) describe the mean waiting time and total spending time on this situation.

4.2 Results of Computation-Intensive Architecture

On the other hand, the computation-intensive architecture is illustrated as above Fig.2, which can be depicted via queueing models also as following figure. In Fig.4, the client and the service component are abstracted as nodes of a queueing model. Comparing with Fig.2 and Fig.4, we can find that the security component has been omitted. Why can the security component be neglected from the model? Because the security component is responsible for the client authentication, and this process only consumes very little time. In grid system, the client authentication just consumes very little time (e.g. 0.1 second), while the computation task might occupy much time (e.g. several hours or even several days), which is million times than the former. Hence, Fig.4 can exactly abstract the computation-intensive architecture.

In this subsection, we model the computation-intensive architecture as Fig.4. Methodology similar to the above, we consider two service conditions, one with no restriction on the waiting room's capacity(i.e., we assume that the service component has the ability to accept no limit requests), another with restriction on the waiting room's capacity(i.e., we assume that the service component has the ability to accept only K requests). On the basis of the previous works, we can obtain the results of $M/M/1$ and $M/M/1/K$ straightly.

4.3 Analysis of the Interaction-Intensive and Computation-Intensive Architecture

In subsection 4.1 and 4.2, we have obtained some performance results(the mean queue length, waiting time and sojourn time) about the two architectures. On the basis of them, some comparative results will be given in this subsection.

Assuming that an application can be used in the two architectures, and it spends the same service time on the different situations(i.e., $\sum_{i=1}^{7} 1/\mu_i = 1/\mu$). In addition, we assume that the two systems share the same arrival rate λ. There are two conditions: one with no restriction on the waiting room's capacity, another with restriction K on the waiting room's capacity. We only compare the architectures under the situation that $\rho_i < 1, (i = 1,2\ldots,7)$ and $\rho < 1$ being satisfied.

1) No restriction

We compare with the mean queue length, waiting time and sojourn time respectively.

$$L_1/L_2 = (\sum_{i=1}^{7}\frac{\lambda}{\mu_i - \lambda})/(\frac{\lambda}{\mu - \lambda}) = \sum_{i=1}^{7}\frac{\mu - \lambda}{\mu_i - \lambda} \tag{14}$$

$$\sum_{i=1}^{7} 1/\mu_i = 1/\mu \Rightarrow \sum_{i=1}^{7} \lambda/\mu_i = \lambda/\mu \Rightarrow \sum_{i=1}^{7} \rho_i = \rho \tag{15}$$

Utilizing (14) in equation (15), we obtain

$$L_1/L_2 = \sum_{i=1}^{7}\frac{\mu - \lambda}{\mu_i - \lambda} = \sum_{i=1}^{7}\frac{\rho_i}{1-\rho_i}\cdot\frac{1-\rho}{\rho}$$

$$\begin{aligned}\prod_{i=1}^{7}(1-\rho_i) &= \prod_{i=1}^{3}(1-\rho_i)\cdot\prod_{i=4}^{7}(1-\rho_i)\\ &> (1-\rho_1-\rho_2-\rho_3)\cdot(1-\rho_4-\rho_5-\rho_6-\rho_7)\\ &> 1-\sum_{i=1}^{7}\rho_i = 1-\rho\end{aligned}$$

$$\sum_{i=1}^{7}\frac{\rho_i}{1-\rho_i}\cdot\frac{1-\rho}{\rho} = \frac{1-\rho}{\rho}\cdot\sum_{i=1}^{7}\frac{\rho_i}{1-\rho_i} = \frac{1-\rho}{\rho}\cdot\frac{\sum_{i=1}^{7}\rho_i\prod_{j=1,j\neq i}^{7}(1-\rho_j)}{\prod_{i=1}^{7}(1-\rho_i)} < \frac{1-\rho}{\rho}\cdot\frac{\sum_{i=1}^{7}\rho_i\prod_{j=1,j\neq i}^{7}(1-\rho_j)}{1-\rho}$$

$$= \frac{\sum_{i=1}^{7}\rho_i\prod_{j=1,j\neq i}^{7}(1-\rho_j)}{\rho} < \frac{\sum_{i=1}^{7}\rho_i}{\rho} = 1 \tag{16}$$

So that, we get $L_1/L_2<1 \Rightarrow L_1<L_2$, which presents that the mean queue length of the interaction-intensive architecture is less than that of the computation-intensive architecture, if they share the same service time.

In a manner similar to that used in compare of the mean length and the fact that $\lambda_1=\lambda_2=\lambda$, we obtain the following results.

$$W_1/W_2=\sum_{i=1}^{7}\frac{1}{\mu_i-\lambda}\Big/\frac{1}{\mu-\lambda}<1 \quad W_{S,1}-W_{S,2}=\sum_{i=1}^{7}\frac{2\mu_i-\lambda}{\mu_i(\mu_i-\lambda)}-\frac{2\mu-\lambda}{\mu^2-\lambda\cdot\mu}=W_1-W_2$$

$$\because\ W_1/W_2<1,\ \text{and}\ W_i>0,\quad i=1,2 \qquad \therefore\ W_1-W_2<0\Rightarrow W_{S.1}<W_{S.2}$$

These results show that $W_1<W_2$ and $W_{S.1}<W_{S.2}$, i.e., the waiting time and sojourn time of the interaction-intensive architecture are less than those of the computation-intensive architecture. Thus, we obtain the proposition 1.

Proposition 1. Consider two models with no limit capacities. If $\sum_{i=1}^{7}1/\mu_i=1/\mu$ and $\lambda_1=\lambda_2=\lambda$, then $L_1/L_2<1$, $W_1<W_2$ and $W_{S.1}<W_{S.2}$.

Proposition1 states that for arbitrary applications employed on these two architectures, if they have same arrival rate and spend the same service time, the mean queue length, waiting time and sojourn time of the interaction-intensive architecture are less than those of computation-intensive architecture. From the above results, we can find that the more nodes in interaction-intensive architecture do not delay the waiting time and sojourn time.

2) Restriction with K and K_i, $i=1,2,\ldots,7$

We compare the mean queue length, waiting time and sojourn time respectively in restriction with K and K_i, $i=1,2,\ldots,7$. We first consider the condition, $\rho_i<1$, (for $i=1,2,\ldots,7$) and $\rho<1$.

$$L_1^K/L_2^K=\sum_{i=1}^{7}\left(\frac{1}{1-\rho_i}-\frac{1+K_i\cdot\rho_i^{K_i+1}}{1-\rho_i^{K_i+1}}\right)\Big/\left(\frac{1}{1-\rho}-\frac{1+K\cdot\rho^{K+1}}{1-\rho^{K+1}}\right)=\sum_{i=1}^{7}\left[\frac{\sum_{j=1}^{K_i}(\rho_i^j-\rho_i^{K_i+1})}{(1-\rho_i^{K_i+1})}\frac{(1-\rho^{K+1})}{\sum_{j=1}^{K}(\rho^j-\rho^{K+1})}\right]$$

$$\because\ (1-\rho_i^{K_i+1})<1 \quad \therefore\ (1-\rho_i^{K_i+1})\cdot\sum_{j=1}^{K}(\rho^j-\rho^{K+1})<\sum_{j=1}^{K}(\rho^j-\rho^{K+1})$$

$$\therefore\ L_1^K/L_2^K<\frac{\sum_{i=1}^{7}(\sum_{j=1}^{K_i}(\rho_i^j-\rho_i^{K_i+1}))\cdot(1-\rho^{K+1})}{\sum_{j=1}^{K}(\rho^j-\rho^{K+1})}$$

If $\sum_{i=1}^{7}\sum_{j=1}^{K_i}(\rho_i^j-\rho_i^{K_i+1})\le\frac{\sum_{j=1}^{K}\rho^j-K\rho^{K+1}}{(1-\rho^{K+1})}$ holds, so that $L_1/L_2<1$.

Then, we consider the waiting time and sojourn time of the two architectures in restriction with K. When $\lambda_1=\lambda_2=\lambda$, $W_1/W_2=\frac{L_1/\lambda_1}{L_2/\lambda_2}=L_1/L_2$, on the basis of above results, we obtain the proposition 2.

Proposition 2. Consider two models with restrict capacities, K and K_i, $i=1,2,\ldots,7$. If $\lambda_1=\lambda_2=\lambda$ and $\sum_{i=1}^{7}\sum_{j=1}^{K_i}(\rho_i^j-\rho_i^{K_i+1})\ge\frac{\rho}{(1-\rho^2)}$, then $L_1^K<L_2^K$, and $W_1^K<W_2^K$.

Furthermore, we calculate the difference of the sojourn time.

$$W_{1,S}^K-W_{2,S}^K=W_{1,S}-W_{2,S}+(\sum_{i=1}^{7}1/\mu_i-1/\mu) \tag{17}$$

If $\sum_{i=1}^{7}1/\mu_i>1/\mu$ (i.e., $\sum_{i=1}^{7}\rho_i>\rho$) is satisfied, then equation(23) is positive. Hence, we get the following proposition.

Proposition 3. Consider two models with restrict capacities, K and K_i, $i=1,2,\ldots,7$. If the conditions $\lambda_1=\lambda_2=\lambda$, $\sum_{i=1}^{7}\sum_{j=1}^{K_i}(\rho_i^j-\rho_i^{K_i+1})\ge\frac{\rho}{(1-\rho^2)}$ and $\sum_{i=1}^{7}\rho_i\ge\rho$ hold, then $W_{1,S}^K<W_{2,S}^K$ are satisfied.

Proposition2 and 3 address the condition on which the performance of interaction-intensive architecture is prior to that of computation-intensive architecture.

On the other hand, we can present some contrast results about the mean queue length, waiting time and sojourn time.

Proposition 4. Consider two models with restrict capacities, K and K_i, $i=1,2,\ldots,7$. If $1>\rho_i>\rho$, $(i=1,2,\ldots,7)$, $\lambda_1=\lambda_2=\lambda$ and $\sum_{i=1}^{7}\sum_{j=1}^{K_i}(\rho_i^j-\rho_i^{K_i+1})\ge\frac{\rho}{(1-\rho^2)}$, then $L_1^K>L_2^K$, and $W_1^K>W_2^K$.

Furthermore, we calculate the difference of the sojourn time.

$$W_{1,S}^K-W_{2,S}^K=W_{1,S}-W_{2,S}+(\sum_{i=1}^{7}1/\mu_i-1/\mu) \tag{18}$$

If $\sum_{i=1}^{7}1/\mu_i>1/\mu$ (i.e., $\sum_{i=1}^{7}\rho_i>\rho$) is satisfied, then equation(24) is positive. Hence, we get the following proposition.

Proposition 5. Consider two models with restrict capacities, K and K_i, $i=1,2,\ldots,7$. If the conditions $1>\rho_i>\rho$, $(i=1,2,\ldots,7)$, $\lambda_1=\lambda_2=\lambda$, $\sum_{i=1}^{7}\sum_{j=1}^{K_i}(\rho_i^j-\rho_i^{K_i+1})\ge\frac{\rho}{(1-\rho^2)}$ and $\sum_{i=1}^{7}\rho_i>\rho$ are satisfied, then $W_{1,S}^K>W_{2,S}^K$ is satisfied.

On the contrary, proposition4 and 5 state the condition on which the performance of computation-intensive architecture is prior to that of interaction-intensive architecture.

5 Conclusion and Future Work

We have categorized grid applications into two classes, the computation-intensive and the interaction-intensive applications. On the basis of the classification, we presented a novel grid architecture taxonomy, the computation-intensive and interaction-intensive grid architecture. Then, we modeled the two grid architectures with queueing networks models. One of our key insights is the comparison of the two grid architectures. Furthermore, some propositions were obtained, which can guide the grid architecture in the future. Another insight is that we give grid performance metrics, performability. Moreover, we described grid availability and efficiency mathematically.

In this paper, we assume that the service time of grid component is an exponential distribution. It is an important problem to study when the service time of grid component is arbitrary distribution. Furthermore， modeling and analyzing the grid architecture deeply is our next focused work.

Acknowledgments

Supported in part by National Science Fund China(No. 70571057).

References

[1] Foster, I., Kesselman, C.: The Grid: Blueprint for a New Computing Infrastructure, 2nd edn. Morgan Kaufmann, Amsterdam (2004)

[2] Foster, I., Kesselman, C., Tuecke, S.: The Anatomy of the Grid: Enabling Scalable Virtual Organizations. Int. J. of Supercomputer Applications 15(3), 200–222 (2001)

[3] Foster, I., Kesselman, C., Nick, J.M., Tuecke, S.: Grid Services for Distributed System Integration. Computer 35(6), 37–46 (2002)

[4] Talia, D.: The Open Grid Services Architecture: where the grid meets the Web. IEEE Internet Computing 6(6), 67–71 (2002)

[5] Baker, M., Foster, I.: On recent changes in the grid community. Distributed Systems Online, IEEE 5(2), 4/1–4/10 (2004)

[6] Open Grid Services Architecture: available on-line at http:// www.globus.org /ogsa/

[7] Foster, I., et al.: Modeling and managing State in distributed systems: the role of OGSI and WSRF. Proceedings of the IEEE 93, 604–612 (2005)

[8] Foster, I.: Service-Oriented Science. Science 308(5723), 814–817 (2005)

[9] Raicu, I., et al.: The Design, Performance, and Use of DiPerF: An automated Distributed Performance evaluation Framework. J. Grid Comput. 4(3), 287–309 (2006)

[10] Wolski, R., Nurmi, D., et al.: Models and Modeling Infrastructures for Global Computational Platforms. In: IPDPS'05 - Workshop 10, Denver Colorado, p. 224a (2005)

[11] Humphrey, M., et al.: State and Events for Web Services: A Comparison of Five WS-Resource Framework and WS-Notification Implementations. In: Feldman, S., Uretsky, M., Najork, M., Wills, C. (eds.) HPDC-14, pp. 24–27 (2005)

[12] http://www.cs.york.ac.uk/dame/summary.htm

[13] Yang, H., Xu, Z., Sun, Y., Zheng, Q.: Modeling and Performance Analysis of the VEGA Grid System. In: Pan, Y., Chen, D., Guo, M., Cao, Dongarra, J. (eds.) e-Science and grid computing, Melbourne, pp. 296–303 (2005)

[14] Zheng, Q., Yang, H., Sun, Y.: How to Avoid Herd: A Novel Stochastic Algorithm in Grid Scheduling? In: Grimshaw, A., Parashar, M., Schwan, K. (eds.) HPDC-15, Paris, France, pp. 267–278 (2006)

[15] Donald, G., Carl, H.H.: Fundamentals of Queueing Theory, 3rd edn. John Wiley & Sons, Inc., New York (1998)

An Effective Approach Based on Rough Set and Topic Cluster to Build Peer Communities*

Quanqing Xu, Zhihuan Qiu, Yafei Dai, and Xiaoming Li

Department of Computer Science and Technology,
Peking University, 100871 Beijing, China
{xqq, qzh, dyf, lxm}@net.pku.edu.cn

Abstract. A peer community is composed of a number of peers who share files about the same topic in the file sharing P2P applications. Building peer communities can benefit content location and retrieval in P2P systems. We propose an effective approach based on rough set and topic cluster to build peer communities. Firstly, we compute one of the best reduced sets of all the same type files, such as the video files, with files' attributes in a peer. Secondly, topic clusters of a peer are calculated, which represent the interests of it. Finally, we build peer communities using the super peer technique. Experiments performed on the real data sets prove that our approach is effective. Experimental results verify that our approach works much better compared with that of previous approaches.

Keywords: P2P, Rough Set, Topic Cluster, Peer Community, Entropy.

1 Introduction

As we know, file sharing has become an important P2P application. The emergence of file sharing applications such as Napster, Maze (maze.pku.edu.cn), Gnutella, and Freenet [1] has been the catalyst in drawing a great deal of attention to P2P systems. Most of the current shared files are audio or video files [2]. P2P systems are a special type of distributed systems, in which peers collectively share and/or consume services and resources. Information retrieval in P2P systems (P2P IR) is a complex problem because of the properties of P2P systems, such as the large amount of involved peers, the dynamic attribute of peers and so on.

If we were to design the search mechanism based on grouping the files of the same topic together, the retrieval performance in P2P systems will be substantially improved. Files of the same category, for example, being on the same topic, are called similar files and file collections about the same topic are called similar collections. Therefore, the peers which own similar collections are called similar peers. For example, if the file collections in peer p_1 and peer p_2 are both *action video files*, we call p_1 and p_2 similar peers. A peer community is composed of similar peers.

* This research has been supported by the National Natural Science foundation of China under Grant No.90412008, National Grand Fundamental Research 973 program of China under Grant No.2004CB318204.

I. Stojmenovic et al. (Eds.): ISPA 2007, LNCS 4742, pp. 589–600, 2007.

Recently, building communities in P2P systems has been a popular research topic, which helps discover resources and prune the searching space. We can see that the idea has been adopted by [3][4][5][6]. Therefore, it is important for us to build peer communities in P2P systems, which will benefit P2P search and retrieval.

One of the new data mining theories is the rough set theory [17] which can be used for reduction of data sets. This can help us compute one of the best reduced sets *RS* and reduce the size of sets of all the same type files of a peer. From the *RS*, we can extract several topic clusters. In this paper, we suggest an effective approach to build communities based on rough set and topic cluster (RSTC). The similarity between two peers is determined by the similarity between their topic clusters. We organize our paper as follows: In Section 2, we describe user's interest model in P2P system. We propose a method of building peer communities and give performance analysis in Section 3. The experiments and experimental results are discussed in Section 4. Related works are briefly introduced in Section 5. We conclude the paper in Section 6.

2 User's Interest Model in the P2P System

All the files of the same type of a peer *p* are viewed as a set *S*, so we can extract some interests of *p* from *S*. There are two key programs: (1) One of the best reduced sets should be calculated in order to reduce the size of *S* and decrease the computational cost of extracting topic cluster(s); (2) The interests of *p* are expressed by topic cluster(s), which should be computed.

To facilitate our discussion, we will first make an introduction about the theory of rough set, and then calculate one of the best reduced sets *RS*, which can be computed with files' attributes, for example, name, size, md5, and etc. We will then extract topic clusters from *RS*.

2.1 Background

Maze is a P2P file-sharing system that is developed and deployed by our research team. It is currently deployed across a large number of hosts inside China's internal network and has become an excellent platform to observe many important activities inside the P2P network. More details of the Maze architecture are available in [7].

Each peer in P2P system adds plenty of descriptive information to the titles of sharing files in order to easily be found. We counted respectively the number of occurrence of the length of filename of *Perhaps Love* and *The Transporter* video file, which were first downloaded(6860 and 3627 times) on 05-12-10 and 05-12-12 in the Maze system. We conclude that sharing directories and files of a peer include a large quantity of information, which show the interests of him/her.

2.2 Calculate One of the Best Reduced Sets

A peer often uploads the same series of files in P2P systems, such as soap opera *Friends*. So, we can view the same video files as an equivalence class.

Definition 1(Quotient Set). Given a set **S** and an equivalence relation R on **S**, R is defined by

$$\mathrm{IND}(\mathbf{S})=\{(x, y)\in \mathbf{S}\times\mathbf{S}:\ f(x, a)=f(y, a),\ \forall a\in \mathbf{S}\} \tag{1}$$

The set of all equivalence classes in **S** given an equivalence relation R is usually denoted as **S** / R and called the quotient set of **S** by R. We adopt the theory of concept lattice to compute equivalence relation IND(**S**). Because the structure of concept lattice is unique, it is simple to compute equivalent relation based on it. The IND(**S**) is the union of the least upper bound set of the entire node (**X, X'**)$\in L$.

$$\mathrm{IND}(\mathbf{S})=\cup\{\mathbf{S}\subseteq\mathbf{X'},(\mathbf{X},\mathbf{X'})\in L\} \tag{2}$$

Based on a concept lattice L, an algorithm computes a quotient set with hasse diagrams which come from structures of lattice. Hasse diagrams [8] represent a structure of concept hierarchy. It reads as follows:

```
Algorithm 1. Computing of quotient set of F
 Input: the set of all the vectors of filenames F
 Output: the set of result R
 ComputeIND(F){
 1)Initialization: let R=Φ, we initialize each node's flag
 with zero, which comes from the concept lattice's Hasse
 graph;
 2)For each H=(X, X')∈L, X≠Φ, according to ||X'||'s sort
 ascending:
  If Flag(H)!=1 and I⊆Attrib(X'), then process the Hasse
 graph's each node N: Flag[N]=1, add X into R;
 3) Return R; }
```

Definition 2(Important degree). While attribute *ele* is added into R, the degree of important of it in the U/IND(F) is defined by

$$SGF(ele,R)=\gamma_R(F)-\gamma_{R-\{ele\}}(F) \tag{3}$$

Where $\gamma_R(F)$ is referred to [17] for details. When SGF(*ele*, R)>0, attribute *ele* is necessary in R, the aggregation of all the necessary attributes constitutes the core of R.

Theorem 1. All of the necessary relations of **F** compose a set, which is called the core of **F,** CORE(**F**). We use REDU(**F**), which represents all of the reductions of **F**. CORE(**F**)=$\cap$ REDU(**F**). (The proof details are skipped).

There are two purposes about the core concept. Firstly, it may be accepted as the foundation of computing all reduced sets. Secondly, it is a set, which can not be removed from an original set. We used the set to compute one of the best reduced sets.

```
Algorithm 2: Computing one of the best reduced sets of F
 Input: the set of all the vectors of filenames F
 Output: a best reduced set: BestRedu
 ComputeBestRedu(F) {
 1)Initialization: according to ComputeIND(F) and theorem
  1, we compute CORE(F), and then BestRedu=CORE(F), F'=F-
  CORE(F);
```

```
2)for each attribute ele∈F', Compute SGF(ele, BestRedu)
  and sort descending according to it;
3)while( γ(BestRedu)≠γ(F) ) {
  Get SGF(a_i,BestRedu) a_i ∈ F', (i=1,2,…,m), at the same
  time, add a_i into BestRedu, F'=F-{a_i} (i=1, 2,…,m);
  Compute γ(BestRedu); }
4) for each a_i ∈ BestRedu {
  if a_i ∉ CORE , then BestRedu=BestRedu-{a_i}, and then
compute γ(BestRedu);
  if γ(BestRedu)≠γ(F) , then BestRedu = BestRedu + {a_i}; }
5) return BestRedu; }
```

Table 1. The golf dataset

ID	outlook	temperature	humidity	windy	play
1	sunny	hot	high	false	no
2	sunny	hot	high	true	no
3	overcast	hot	high	false	yes
4	rain	mild	high	false	yes
5	rain	cool	normal	false	yes
6	rain	cool	normal	true	no
7	overcast	cool	normal	true	yes
8	sunny	mild	high	false	no
9	sunny	cool	normal	false	yes
10	rain	mild	normal	false	yes
11	sunny	mild	normal	true	yes
12	overcast	mild	high	true	yes
13	overcast	hot	normal	false	yes
14	rain	mild	high	true	no

Example 1

We adopt the dataset *golf* of UCI [9] (Table 1). Firstly, we make use of the algorithm ComputeIND(*golf*) and theorem 1 compute CORE(*golf*), initialization: BestRedu=CORE, G'=G-CORE; Secondly, we compute one of the best reduced set according to ComputeBestRedu(F). One of the best reduced set is as follows (Table 2). Subsequently, we process the follow ten datasets from UCI: Breast, Breast-cancer, Iris-disc, Monk1, Monk3, Parity5+5, Tic-tac-toe, Vote, Vote-Irvine and Zoo. Only the number of the Tic-tac-toe dataset is equal to the number of one of the best reduced set of it. The number of the best reduced set is less than one of the original dataset in the other nine datasets. The number of the original Parity5+5 dataset is 1024, while the number of the best reduced set is only 32.

Table 2. One of the best reduced sets of the golf dataset

ID	outlook	temperature	windy	play
1	sunny	hot	false	no
2	sunny	hot	true	no
3, 13	overcast	hot	false	yes
4, 10	rain	mild	false	yes
5	rain	cool	false	yes
6	rain	cool	true	no
7	overcast	cool	true	yes
8	sunny	mild	false	no
9	sunny	cool	false	yes
11	sunny	mild	true	yes
12	overcast	mild	true	yes
14	rain	mild	true	no

2.3 Compute Topic Clusters of a Peer

Definition 3(Topic Cluster). Topic cluster T = $\{f_i \mid f_i$ is a file which describes the same topic with the other files in the same set, $f_i \in F$, i=0... m-1$\}$. The interest set of a peer is composed of one or more topic clusters.

Definition 4(the Nearest Topic Cluster). Among the interest sets of a peer, the nearest topic cluster of T_i is defined by

$$T_i.\text{nearest} = \{T_j \mid \max(\text{Simi}(T_i, T_j)),\ j=0 \ldots n-1 \text{ and } j \neq i\} \quad (4)$$

Where Simi(T_i, T_j) is calculated by using Vector Space Model (VSM).

Based on CURE[10], the following two algorithms are presented for extracting topic cluster(s) from a peer, which are respectively the description of merging two topic clusters into a topic cluster and extracting topic cluster(s) from a peer.

```
Algorithm 3. Merging two topic clusters into a topic
 cluster
 Input: Tx, Ty
 Output: Tz
 MergeTopicCluster(Tx, Ty){
 1) Compute the centroid vector v⃗ of Tz = Tx∪Ty;
 2) Select representative filename vectors of Tz
   a) Select the most similar filename vector to v⃗ as the 1st
 representative vector;
   b) Let R is a set of representative vectors of Tz;
      R̄ = Tz - R;
      While(R̄≠Φ) {
        MaxSimiSet = Φ;
        for each f⃗∈R̄ {
          Max={f⃗ |max{Simi(f⃗, g⃗), g⃗ ∈R} };
          MaxSimiSet += Max; }
        Remove the vector of maximum similarity in the
        MaxSimiSet from R̄, place it in R }
 3) for each filename vector f⃗∈R, f⃗=(1-α)f⃗+αv⃗ (α [10] is a
   shrink factor)
 4) return the topic cluster Tz }
```

```
Algorithm 4. Extracting topic cluster(s) from a peer
Input: all the filenames S of the same type of p, the
number of topic clusters t, if threshold is set b
Output: the list L of the topic clusters
ExtractTopicCluster(S, t, b){
1)Initialization: for each f ∈ S, segment word(Chinese,
Japanese, Korean(CJK) and etc) and compute the idf value
of each word, extract vectors(tfidf) for each filename,
and then are normalized, obtain all the vectors(F) of S;
2)BestRedu=ComputeBestRedu(F), L=Φ;
  for each record ∈ BestRedu, Compute the nearest topic
cluster of record; Insert record into the List L;
```

```
3)While(L.size>t){
   Tx = max_element(L);/* according to sort by the
similarity of a topic cluster T and the nearest topic
cluster of T */
   Tz = MergeTopicCluster(Tx, Ty);/* Ty is the nearest topic
cluster of Tx */
   for each T∈L, compute maxSimi=max{Simi(T, Tz);
   if( b && maxSimi < threshold ) break;
   if (T.nearest==Tx or Ty) {
      if (Simi(T, Tz) > Simi(T, Tx or Ty))
         T.nearest = Tz;
      else // record is belonged to the remainder of L
          T.nearest = {record | max{Simi(T, record)}}; }
   else if Simi(T, Tz)>Simi(T, T.nearest)
      T.nearest=Tz; }
4)for each T∈L, sort terms by TFIDF and compute the top-n
topic terms of T
5) return the list L of topic clusters }
```

Example 2

After extracting *t* topic clusters from the *golf* dataset, the results are as follows.

Table 3. Extracting *t* (*t*=2, 3, 4) topic clusters from the *golf* dataset

t (the number of topic clusters)	The topic clusters
2	{1, 2, 4, 5, 6, 8, 9, 10, 11, 14} {3, 7, 12, 13}
3	{1, 2, 4, 5, 6, 8, 9, 10, 11} {3, 7, 12, 13} {14}
4	{1, 2, 4, 10, 8, 11} {3, 7, 12, 13} {5, 6, 9} {14}

We took continuous change of uploading files in P2P systems into account. When some files are added to the sharing directory by a peer, they are also added to the most similar topic cluster respectively. When some files are removed from the sharing directory, they are also removed from the topic cluster which they resided in. If there are some changes in a topic cluster, its top-n topic terms are computed and are compared with its top-n topic terms before changing. If the change number of its top-n topic terms exceed a threshold, its topic clusters are extracted again.

3 Building Peer Communities

It is important for us to automatically build peer communities in P2P systems. A peer community is composed of peers sharing the same topic. The interests of a peer are reflected by the topics of sharing files in the file sharing application. Algorithm 5 outlines the main procedures of building peer communities.

```
Algorithm 5. Building Peer Communities
 1)Initialization: The functions of becoming a super peer
 and extracting topic cluster(s) are placed in each peer
 in the P2P system. By design, peers with high system
 resources and bandwidth can volunteer to become a super
 peer, whereas peers with low system resources and
```

bandwidth can remain regular peers.

2) In the start stage,

If a peer *p* is an old peer, it saves an IP list of super peers.

If *p* is a newcomer, it may find its neighbors or build a friend list, and then get an IP list of super peers from its neighbors or friends. Subsequently, it tries to connect those IP addresses until it can find an active super peer. It gets a list of all the active super peers and updates its list of active super peers.

3) *p* sends its centroid (term, frequency) of its topic clusters to a super peer *sp* (The centroid is represented by split bloom filter [11] in order to support membership lookup), which there are some communities' record in *sp*

Algorithm 3 is adopted to add *p* to the most similar community to *p*.

If the very worst thing happens, there are no communities in all the super peers. *p* is viewed as a community.

If there are enough friends, *p* sends the information of building a community to its friends to construct a new one.

4) If the change number of its top-n topic terms of a topic cluster of *p* exceeds a given threshold, its topic clusters are extracted again, go to 3).

5) Super peers communicate with each other to find some communities of bad performance, and then make use of algorithm 3 and algorithm 4 to adjust them.

Definition 5(the Same Topic in a Community). Let A and B be topic clusters in a community C, if the similarity of $A.\vec{v}$ and $B.\vec{v}$ is greater than *threshold*, A and B are viewed as two elements of a Same Topic *ST*. *ST* is composed of all the similar elements, such as A, B, in the community C.

We present a simple performance analysis for building peer communities that serves as a feasibility check with regard to scalability. We focus on message costs, as storage and local-processing costs are relatively uncritical in our setting. We assume that we have P = 1, 000, 000 peers, each with N = 30, 000 files. We further assume that each peer has C = 3 topic clusters, and that each topic cluster is assumed to contain 10, 000 files. Each centroid of topic clusters is assumed to contain 3,000 dimensions (the concrete numbers are for illustration of the magnitudes that we would expect in a real system), which are represented by split bloom filter (k=6, m=40, 000, s=2 and $P_{err}=1.3\times10^{-4}$). Each dimension is represented by a pair (term, frequency), which will be parsed (term, TFIDF) by a super peer.

When a peer joins peer communities, each centroid of topic clusters and its maximal frequency of term (2 bytes) is sent to a super peer, which results in a message size of (2+40, 000*2/8) * 3= 30, 006 bytes. We further assume that half of all the peers join peer communities within 5 hours. This results in (P/2) * 30, 006/(5*3600) = 833, 300 bytes or approximately 0.795 Mbytes per second, far behind 10-100Mbytes/s for the entire P2P system. When the change number of its top-n topic terms of a topic cluster of p exceeds a threshold, its topic clusters are extracted, and then are sent to a super peer with changed terms. Its cost can be much blow the previous cost. The bottom line of this coarse analysis is that the approach does not present any critical performance challenges and seems very feasible also from a scalability viewpoint.

There are many topic clusters in a community. Algorithm 3 and 4 are adopted to compute a same topic, which is constituted by one or more topic clusters. Our rule of building peer communities is an automatic and autonomous mechanism, so we use *entropy* [12] to evaluate the quality of the built communities. The autonomy determines that several built communities could be about the same topic.

Definition 6(Entropy of a Community). The entropy of a community C is defined by

$$\text{Entropy}(C) = \sum_{i=1}^{t} -\frac{P_i}{P}\log(\frac{P_i}{P}) \tag{5}$$

Where P is the number of peers belonging to C; t is the number of topics in C; and P_i is the number of peers having topic T_i. If all the peers in C are about the same topic T, entropy(C) = 0.

4 Experimental Results

4.1 Datasets

We performed our experiments on the upload file data of all the live users in the Maze system from 2005-12-10 to 2005-12-16. The information from this data as follows.

Table 4. Comparing the *N*umber of *P*eer with *V*ideo *F*ile (NPVF) with the *T*otal *N*umber of *P*eer (TNP)

Date	NPVF	TNP	Weight
05-12-10	5832	7656	76.18%
05-12-11	9385	11881	78.99%
05-12-12	16210	19779	81.96%
05-12-13	29172	35661	81.80%
05-12-14	28576	34887	81.91%
05-12-15	14899	18579	80.19%
05-12-16	19407	23649	82.06%

Table 5. Comparing the *N*umber of *D*ownloaded *V*ideo *F*iles (NDVF) with the *T*otal *N*umber of *D*ownloaded *F*iles (TNDF)

Date	NDVF	TNDF	Weight
05-12-10	407536	962956	42.32%
05-12-11	441437	1108058	39.84%
05-12-12	333382	841076	39.64%
05-12-13	322027	822135	39.17%
05-12-14	323613	811639	39.87%
05-12-15	329459	843887	39.04%
05-12-16	290709	787293	36.93%

As can be seen the Table 4, over 80% of peers upload video files in the Maze system. From the Table 5, an approximate 40% of files downloaded are video files. In our opinions, it is very interesting for us to find interest similar peers about video files.

In our experiment, we used the following parameter and settings (Table 6). There are 109, 762 words in our dictionary (Dict.dat: 647, 386 bytes/ 637K); There are 98, 467 words with IDF value (IDF.dat: 1, 778, 278 bytes/ 1.7M), which can be calculated from 34, 202, 752 video file names in the Maze share resource lists. The two files are released in the P2P systems.

Table 6. Parameter and settings

Parameter name	Default value	Description
k	6	The number of hash function
n	3, 000	The maximal dimension of a topic cluster
m	40, 000	The bit number of bloom filter
s	2	Multiple
thrs	0.45	The threshold of merging two topic clusters
File attributes include: name, type, size, date, path, md5, and etc;		

4.2 Experimental Results

In this experiment, all the video files (VF) of a peer are considered as a set in the first. Second, we compute one of the best reduced sets (BRS) in it, which aims to reduce the original dataset without losing accuracy. Finally, we get the statistical information which is shown in the Table 7. From the Table 7, we can see that the number of experiment datasets decrease over 10% and below 15%, which is beneficial to compute topic clusters. When peers remove some video files, it is possible to get similar datasets reduction, while still maintaining the right communities in this experiment.

Table 7. Comparing experiment datasets with the best reduced set of them

Date	VF	BRS	Weight
2005-12-10	665145	587988	88.40%
2005-12-11	1173842	1028286	87.60%
2005-12-12	2444048	2153206	88.09%
2005-12-13	4272000	3836256	89.80%
2005-12-14	4182993	3626655	86.70%
2005-12-15	2051477	1786836	87.10%
2005-12-16	2854226	2523136	88.40%

We made use of the following approaches to build peer communities: RSTC, topic model(*tm*) [6][14], shortcut [4] and extend community [3]. Fig. 1 depicts the number of peer communities when using these algorithms for constructing communities. The vertical axis is the number of peer communities and the horizontal axis is the date on which the observation was made.

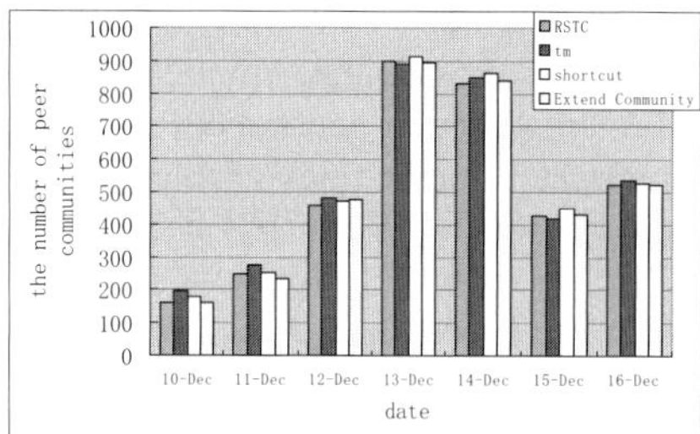

Fig. 1. The number of peer communities using the four algorithms

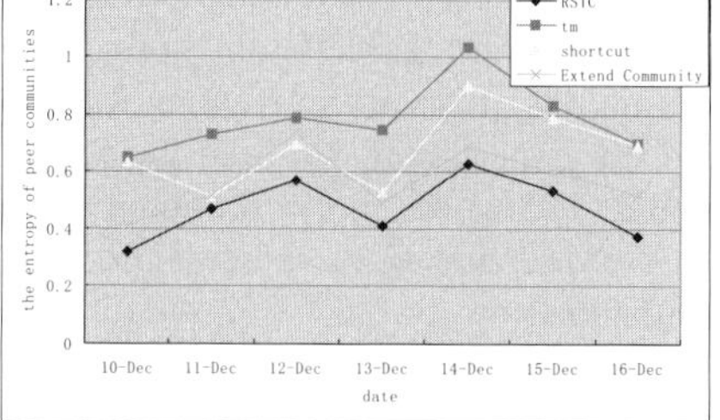

Fig. 2. The entropy of peer communities using the four algorithms

The entropies in Fig. 2 are the averaged entropies of all built communities. From the figure, we can see that RSTC approach works better than the other approaches. The topic model(*tm*) is least effective the four approaches. The reason is that *tm* only deals with a topic. It is difficult for it to extract a topic from a large number of documents[1]. In our opinions, it is an approach of ideal conditions. The approach using shortcuts [4], is based on the following hypothesis: if a peer was able to successfully respond to a query sent by another peer, it is likely that he/she will also be able to successfully respond to future queries sent by the same peer. Our experiments show that there are some deviations from a real P2P system about the hypothesis. Fig. 2 shows that the experiment result of the extend community approach is close to that of RSTC. The extended community approach periodically adds *n* nodes to a peer's community list which currently share the largest number of files with that peer and varies the maximum community size. So, its performance is worse than that of RSTC.

5 Related Works

In [3], interest-based communities were built by analyzing the content of the documents of various peers, which was based on the following principle: two peers are more similar only if they shared more same files. Content comparison is required in the approach so that network bandwidth cost and computing cost are potentially highly expensive if peers own large document collections.

[6] required that there is only one topic of all the files in a peer. In fact, there are multiple topics in a peer. The files should be clustered according to their topics to find similar peers in P2P systems. In [13] and [15], authors used the *tf* approach to find similar peers in a "centralized" manner, but the approach does not apply to a purely P2P system. The topic model(*tm*) approach is used in [6] and [14]. When the finding task is performed in a pure P2P environment, each peer just knows the resource descriptions of its neighbors. [14] used *Kullback-Leibler divergence* to define the similarity between two peers, while [6] employed the fuzzy correlation coefficient of *fuzzy set* theory to define the similarity between two peers. In fact, the *cosine* formula is the most effective and efficient method to define the similarity between two peers.

[1] A document is represented by its file name in this paper.

[4] proposed to find similar peers by analyzing the query history and proposed the interest-based algorithm using shortcuts. [16] proposed to find similar peers according to users' interests which were denoted by attributes, which could be explicitly provided by the peers or implicitly discovered from the history queries. Taking the privacy and security problem into account is the main advantage of attribute mechanism.

6 Conclusions and Future Work

In this paper, we propose an effective mechanism based on rough set and topic cluster to build peer communities in P2P systems. We solved the problems with calculating one of the best reduced sets of all the same type (video) files of a peer and topic cluster(s) of it, and then built peer communities with the super peer technique in P2P systems. One contribution of our work is that we've manage to solve a best reduced set to decrease the size of the destination object without losing accuracy. The other contribution is that we've extracted topic(s) from a peer and build peer communities with the super peer technique. Our experiments proved that our approach greatly advances efficiency without losing accuracy compared with that of previous methods and will be feasible for the real large-scale P2P systems.

We believe that possible directions to future work include some research topics such as extending our performance evaluation to accommodate other built communities algorithms, evaluating the algorithms under dynamic conditions (i.e., peers joining and leaving the system at unpredictable time) and etc. Search and retrieval based on peer communities is a hot research topic in P2P system, which is worth of further theoretical research, especially in dynamic distributed environment.

Acknowledgments. We are grateful to Jing Tian, Mao Yang, Mingzhong Xiao and Yu Peng for their suggestion and help.

References

1. Clarke, I., Sandberg, O., Wiley, B., Hong, T.W.: Freenet: A distributed anonymous information storage and retrieval system. In: Workshop on Design Issues in Anonymity and Unobservability, Berkeley, CA, USA, pp. 311–320 (July 2000)
2. Miller, J.: Characterization of data on the gnutella peer-to-peer network. In: Proceedings of 1st IEEE Consumer Communications and Networking Conference, pp. 489–494 (2004)
3. Barbosa, M.W., Costa, M.M., Almeida, J.M., Almeida, V.A.F.: Using locality of reference to improve performance of peer-to-peer applications. In: Proceedings of the 4th International Workshop on Software and Performance, pp. 216–227, Shores, California, USA (2004)
4. Sripanidkulchai, K., Maggs, B.M., Zhang, H.: Efficient content location using interestbased locality in peer-to-peer systems. In: IEEE INFOCOM 2003, San Francisco, CA, USA (2003)
5. Bawa, M., Manku, G.S., Raghavan, P.: Sets: Search enhanced by topic segmentation. In: Proceedings of the 26th Annual International ACM SIGIR Conference on Research and Development in Information Retrieval, pp. 306–313, Toronto, Canada (2003)

6. Zhu, X., Han, D., Zhu, W., Yu, Y.: An Effective Resource Description Based Approach to Find Similar Peers. In: Proc. of the Fifth IEEE International Conference on Peer-to-Peer Computing, pp. 191–198, Konstanz, Germany (2005)
7. Yang, M., Zhang, Z., Li, X., Dai, Y.: An Empirical Study of Free-Riding Behavior in the Maze P2P File-Sharing System. In: Proceedings of IPTPS, Ithaca, NY (February 2005)
8. Wille, R.: Restructuring lattice theory: An approach based on hierarchies of concepts. Ordered Sets, pp. 445–470. Reidel, Dordrecht Boston (1982)
9. Merz, C., Murphy, J.: UCI repository of machine learning database [EB/OL], http://www.cs.uci.edu/ mlearn/MLRepository.html 2000-10-25/2002-02-27
10. Guha, S., Rastogi, R., Shim, K.: CURE: an efficient clustering algorithm for large databases. In: Haas, L.M., Tiwary, A. (eds.) Proceedings of the ACM SIGMOD International Conference on Management of Data, pp. 73–84. ACM Press, Seattle (1998)
11. Xiao, M., Dai, Y., Li, X.: Split bloom filters. Chinese Journal of Electronic 32, 241–245 (2004)
12. Steinbach, M., Karypis, G., Kumar, V.: A comparison of document clustering techniques. Technical Report #00-034, Department of Computer Science and Engineering, University of Minnesota (2000)
13. Bawa, M., Manku, G.S., Raghavan, P.: Sets: Search enhanced by topic segmentation. In: Proceedings of the 26th Annual International ACM SIGIR Conference on Research and Development in Information Retrieval, pp. 306–313, Toronto, Canada (2003)
14. Xu, J., Croft, W.B.: Cluster-based language models for distributed retrieval. In: Proceedings of the 22th Annual International ACM SIGIR Conference on Research and Development in Information Retrieval, pp. 254–261, Berkley, CA, USA (August 1999)
15. Klampanos, I.A., Jose, J.M.: An architecture for information retrieval over semi-collaborating peer-to-peer networks. In: Proceedings of the 19th ACM Symposium on Applied Computing, pp. 1078–1083, Nicosia, Cyprus (2004)
16. Khambatti, M., Ryu, K., Dasgupta, P.: Efficient discovery of implicitly formed peer-topeer communities. International Journal of Parallel and Distributed Systems and Networks 5(4) (2002)
17. Pawlak, Z.: Rough Sets. International Journal of Computer and Information Sciences 11, 341–356 (1982)

Evaluation on the UbiMDR Framework*

Jeong-Dong Kim[1], Dongwon Jeong[2], Jinhyung Kim[1], and Doo-Kwon Baik[1]

[1] Dept. of Computer Science and Engineering, Korea University, 1, 5-ga, Anam-dong, Sungbuk-gu, Seoul, 136-701 Republic of Korea
{kjd,koolmania,baik}@software.korea.ac.kr
[2] Dept. of Informatics and Statistics, Kunsan National University, San 68, Miryong-dong, Kunsan, Jollabuk-do, 573-701 Republic of Korea
djeong@kunsan.ac.kr

Abstract. This paper describes the performance evaluation to validate the superiority of UbiMDR framework. In ubiquitous application, the semantic operability is one of the most important issues to maximize the usability of sensors in sensor fields. However, existing frameworks are not suitable for the ubiquitous computing environment because of data heterogeneity between data elements. The MDR-based framework in ubiquitous computing provides the semantic interoperability among ubiquitous applications or sensor fields. In addition, the UbiMDR framework represents low costs for mapping or addition of new elements or operation compared to conventional framework.

1 Introduction

Ubiquitous computing (Ubicomp) encompasses a wide range of research topics, including distributed computing, mobile computing, sensor networks, human-computer interaction, and artificial intelligence. Ubicomp has also a variety of terms in use to describe Pervasive Computing and Ambient Intelligence.

Ubicomp can be defined as the anytime/anywhere/any device [1]. Under ubiquitous environment, applications can gather and utilize various sensing information. It allows the applications to provide high quality services with context, sensing information from sensors. Although current applications use sensing information, they are dependent on and restricted in a correspondent sensor field. That is, existing frameworks are not suitable for the Ubicomp environment allowing applications to use the context at anytime, anywhere, and with any devices.

To solve this problem, we already proposed the MDR (Metadata Registry)-based framework to provide sensor field with independent semantic interoperability in Ubicomp environment [11]. UbiMDR is a MDR-based framework to achieve the semantic consistency (interoperability) between ubiquitous applications.

In addition, MDR is a framework for interoperability of databases and is the international standard developed by ISO/IEC JTC 1/SC 32. The MDR has been used to

* This research is supported by BK(Brain Korea)21.

I. Stojmenovic et al. (Eds.): ISPA 2007, LNCS 4742, pp. 601–611, 2007.

implement applications in various domains [3, 4, 5, 6, 7, 8, 9] and facilitates sharing and exchanging of data in such as e-Commerce [10]. Most applications in Ubicomp environment require real-time data processing and precise semantic interpretation of gathered information from many sensors. Therefore, UbiMDR framework with UMDR concept is appropriate to prevent semantics from mapping incorrectly or abnormally. Consequently, UbiMDR allows applications to gather, interpret, and utilize information from sensor fields in real-time without semantic inconsistency. However, the performance evaluation of the UbiMDR framework is not enough to validate outstanding characteristics in [11]. In addition, we perform formal comparison model definition and performance evaluation for certification about predominance of the UbiMDR framework.

2 Overview of UbiMDR

This section describes the conceptual model, system architecture and UMDR structure of UbiMDR.

2.1 Conceptual Model

Fig. 1 shows the conceptual model for the UbiMDR.

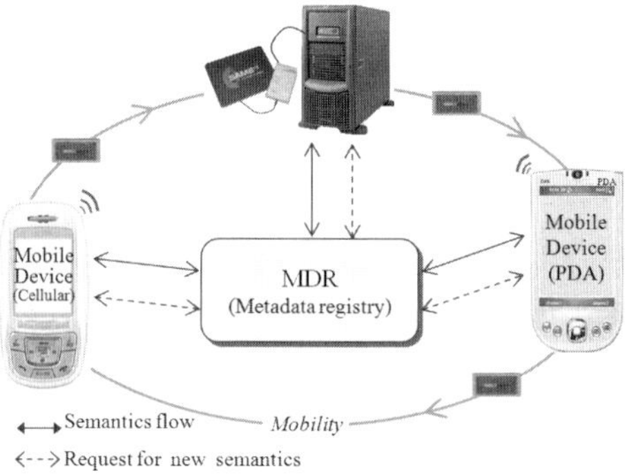

Fig. 1. Conceptual model of UbiMDR

In Fig. 1, the MDR is used for the semantic interoperability between devices and tags. In other words, information of tags as well devices is formed according to the MDR. The MDR has been developed to maximize the semantic interoperability between databases. We employ the advantages of the MDR to achieve the semantic consistency of data in ubiquitous environment.

2.2 System Architecture

The UbiMDR should support these processes and the architecture is illustrated in Fig. 2. Two types of users (sensor designer and application designer) are in the UbiMDR

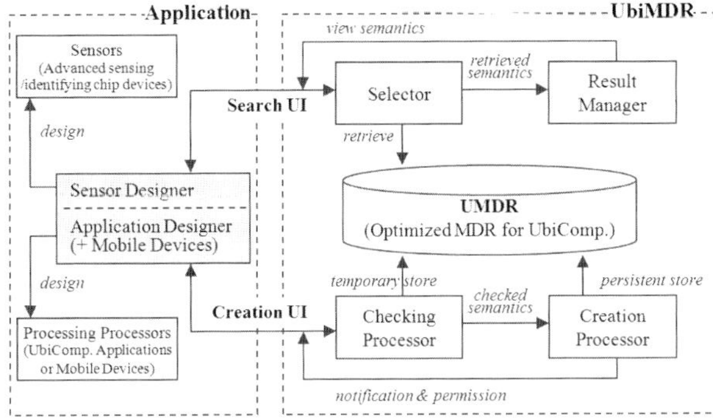

Fig. 2. The UbiMDR architecture

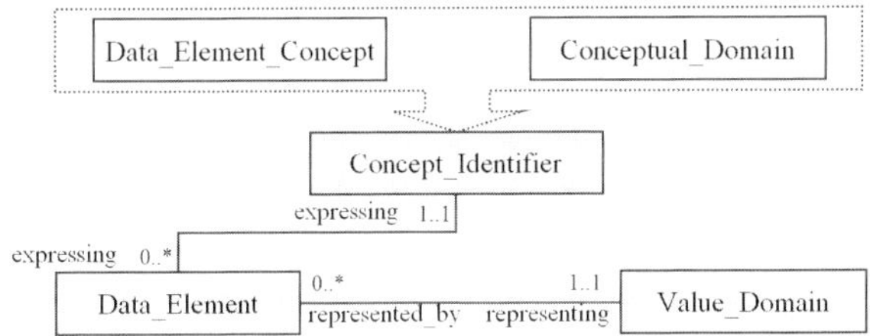

Fig. 3. Conceptual model of UMDR

architecture. The role of sensor designer is to define semantics for sensor data (tag information) and push value to the sensors/tags. To define semantics the sensor designer select proper semantic candidates through a component "Selector". Its result delivered by "Result Manager". Application designers also define necessary semantics for their application following the same process. "Checking Process" and "Creation Processor" are used for users (designers) to suggest and create new semantics which are not predefined in the UMDR.

2.3 UMDR Structure

The original MDR is more complicated for the ubiquitous applications, thus the definition of an optimized MDR is need to be suitable for the ubiquitous environment.

One of the core components of the architecture is UMDR (Ubiquitous Metadata Registry). In the ubiquitous environment, data set is smaller than database (application) level. It means the original MDR structure should be optimized for the ubiquitous environment. This property is one of the reasons why we must optimize and simplify the original MDR developed by ISO/IEC JTC 1/SC 32 [2].

Fig. 3 shows the UMDR metamodel for the UbiMDR. Compared with the original MDR, a novelty of the UMDR is the integration of the Data_Element_Concept and Conceptual_Domain, which result in a Concept_Identifier. The benefit brought by this integration enable the management of data element concept with a less storage cost. In the UMDR, the conceptual domain and data element concept are no longer been manipulated separately but are two attributes of the Concept_Identifier.

3 Performance Evaluation

This section describes preliminary constraints, notations, and symbols models. In addition, we describe comparison evaluation between conventional Ubicomp framework and UbiMDR framework with data interoperability. Comparison evaluation includes the evaluation model, mapping cost, adding cost for new sensor fields, adding cost for new data elements to sensor fields and operating cost for interoperability.

3.1 Notations and Symbols

Notations and symbols are used to describe evaluation models. Table 1 shows notations and symbols and their description.

Table 1. Summary of Notations and Symbols

Notations & Symbols	Description
SenFN	# of SF (the number of SF)
SemN	# of semantic per SF (the number of semantics (meanings) in a specific SF.)
SF	A set of sensor fields; SF={SF_1, SF_2, …, SF_n}
s_i	A set of semantics
S_{ij}	A semantic s_j in SF_i
SF_u	The UMDR including standardized semantics; the UMDR
$AnaT_{ij}$	Time for interpreting the meaning of a semantic, s_j in SF_i
InterpretSem()	Interpreting time of semantic in Sensor Fields
MapN	# of mapping number or mapping table number
LSenFN	# of existing sensor fields (the number of existing(local) SF)
NSenFN	# of new SF (the number of new SF)
AddT	Time for saving a new data element to a SFor the UMDR
X	The number of data elements that a reader get from a tag
χ	The number of data elements to be added in SF

3.2 Assumptions

For comparison evaluation, we need assumptions. Assumptions are listed to support the evaluation models about mapping cost, adding cost for new sensor fields, adding cost for new data elements to sensor fields and operating cost.

- ✓ The semantic analysis time of sensor field (or UMDR) is generated by random number generator. $x \in (a,b]$; (0.0sec<semantic analysis time≤1.0sec)
- ✓ AddT is analysis time of saving for adding new data elements. This is generated by random number generator; $x \in (a,b]$; (0.0sec<AddT≤ 10.0sec)
- ✓ The number of sensor fields is bigger than 1; sensor field >1.

3.3 Cost Evaluation for Integrating Initial Built-in Semantics

Fig. 4 describes the model for comparing cost evaluation for integrating initial built-in semantics.

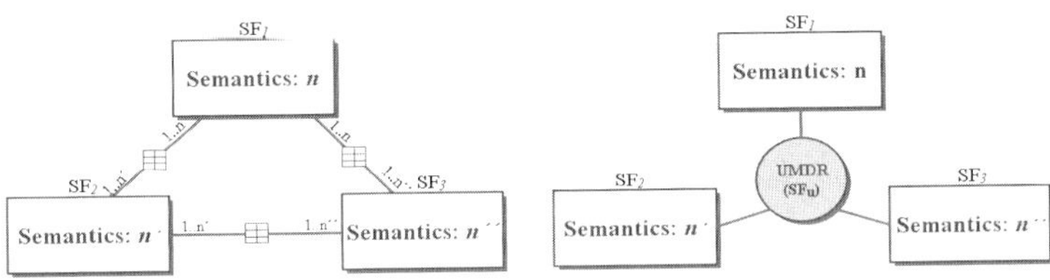

Fig. 4. Evaluation for comparing mapping cost in the previous approach (*Left*) and the UbiMDR approach (*Right*)

The formula for estimating the mapping cost of the previous approach is as follows:

Formula 1: *Previous framework*

$$Cost(MSF_{PREV})$$
$$= \sum_{i=1}^{SenFN-1}\left[\sum_{j=i+1}^{SenFN}\left\{\sum_{k=1}^{SemN_{SF_i}} InterpretSem(SF_i.s_k) + \sum_{l=1}^{SemN_{SF_j}} InterpretSem(SF_j.s_l)\right\}\right]$$
$$= \sum_{i=1}^{SenFN-1}\left[\sum_{j=i+1}^{SenFN}\left\{\sum_{k=1}^{SemN_{SF_i}} InterpretSem(S_{ik}) + \sum_{l=1}^{SemN_{SF_j}} InterpretSem(S_{jl})\right\}\right]$$
$$= \sum_{i=1}^{SenFN-1}\left\{\sum_{j=i+1}^{SenFN}\left(\sum_{k=1}^{SemN_{SF_i}} AnaT_{ik} + \sum_{l=1}^{SemN_{SF_j}} AnaT_{jl}\right)\right\}$$

InterpretSem(SF$_i$*.s*$_k$*)* is the time for analyzing and describing a $SF_i.s_k$ and its semantic data set, *InterpretSem(S*$_{ik}$*)* is a random number which represents Interpretation time of semantic data between sensor fields (0<Interpretation time$\leq$1), *AnaT* is semantic analysis time that value is randomly generated (0<Analysis time$\leq$1).

The UbiMDR framework only uses one mapping table (UMDR) to gather semantic data from the sensor fields. The UMDR of UbiMDR contains predefined semantic data element used in the sensor fields. Therefore, the mapping cost of UbiMDR approach is independent of the number of sensor fields. Formula of mapping cost of the UbiMDR framework is as follows:

Formula 2: *UbiMDR framework*

$$Cost(UbiMDR_{UMDR})$$
$$= \sum_{i=1}^{SenFN}\left[\sum_{j=1}^{SemN_{SF_i}}\left\{InterpretSem(SF_i.s_j) + \sum_{k=1}^{SemN_{SF_u}} InterpretSem(SF_u.s_k)\right\}\right]$$
$$= \sum_{i=1}^{SenFN}\left[\sum_{j=1}^{SemN_{SF_i}}\left\{InterpretSem(S_{ij}) + \sum_{k=1}^{SemN_{SF_u}} InterpretSem(S_{uk})\right\}\right]$$
$$= \sum_{i=1}^{SenFN}\left\{\sum_{j=1}^{SemN_{SF_i}}\left(AnaT_{il} + \sum_{k=1}^{SemN_{SF_u}} AnaT_{uk}\right)\right\}$$

InterpretSem(SF$_u$*.s*$_k$*)* is the time for analyzing and describing a SF_u and it's the UMDR including standardized semantics.

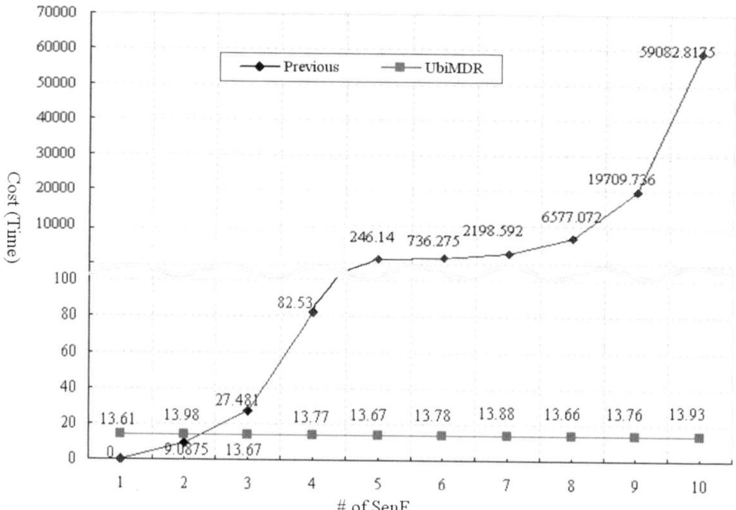

Fig. 5. Integration cost of initial built-in semantics

Fig. 5 shows mapping cost between previous framework and UbiMDR framework. As shown in Fig. 5, the UbiMDR framework is more efficient than the previous approach. When the number of sensor fields is 10, UbiMDR : Previous = 13.93 : 59082.81 (that is, about 1: 4241).

3.4 Cost Evaluation for Adding New Sensor Fields

The model for calculate the number of required mapping tables by adding new sensor fields, *MapN* is defined as Fomular 3. Fig. 6 illustrates the relationship between the number of mapping tables and the number of sensor fields for integrating new sensor fields.

Formula 3:

$$MapN = \frac{SenFN \cdot (SenFN - 1)}{2} = \frac{(SenFN^2 - SenFN)}{2}$$

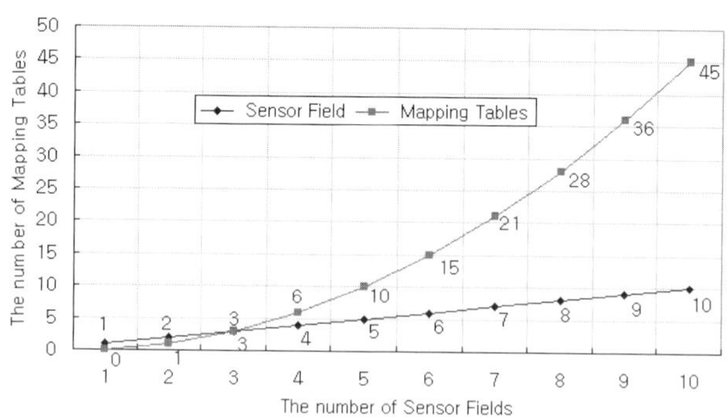

Fig. 6. Relation between sensor fields and mapping tables

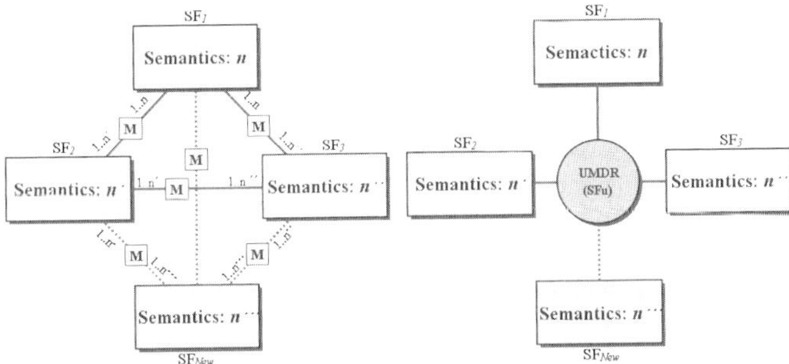

Fig. 7. Evaluation for comparing cost of adding a new sensor field in the previous approach (*Left*) and the UbiMDR approach (*Right*)

Fig. 7 illustrates the evaluation models for adding new sensor fields to the existing sensor fields.

As the previous approach shown in Fig. 7 (Left), a new sensor field should creates and shares adapters as the number of sensor fields. The existing sensor fields also need to create an additional mapping to share their semantic data with the new sensor field. The cost calculation model of the previous approach is as follows and *LSenFN* is the number of local (existing) sensor fields.

Formula 4:

$$Cost(NewADD_{PREV})$$
$$= C_{PREV} \cdot \left\{ \frac{(NSenFN + LSenFN) \cdot (NSenFN + LSenFN - 1)}{2} - \frac{LSenFN(LSenFN - 1)}{2} \right\}$$
$$= C_{PREV} \cdot \left\{ \frac{(NSenFN + LSenFN) \cdot (NSenFN + LSenFN - 1) - (LSenFN^2 - LSenFN)}{2} \right\}$$

In case of the UbiMDR approach in Fig. 7 (Right), only new sensor field requires one adapter, and thus the calculation formula of the UbiMDR approach is defined as Formular 5.

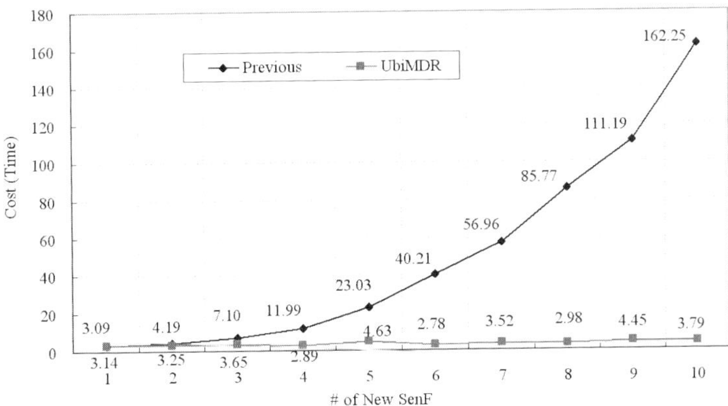

Fig. 8. Cost of adding new sensor field

Formula 5:

$$Cost(NewADD_{UbiMDR}) = C_{UMDR} \cdot NSenFN$$

Fig. 8 shows the evaluation result for adding new sensor fields. As shown in the result, the UbiMDR approach is more efficient than the previous approach. When the numbers of sensor fields and new sensor field are 5 and 1 respectively, UbiMDR: Previous = 2.22 : 40.21 (that is, about 1: 18).

3.5 Costs for Adding New Data Element(s)

In previous framework, if a new data element is added in one sensor field, data element is mapped into Null or a correspondent data element in another sensor field. The formula for adding cost of new data element in the previous approach is as follows:

Formula 6: *Previous framework*

$$\begin{aligned} & Cost(NewAddDE_{PREV}) \\ & = \sum_{i=1}^{\chi Num} \left\{ \sum_{j=1}^{SenFN} InterpretSem(SF_j \cdot \chi) \right\} \\ & = \sum_{i=1}^{\chi Num} \left\{ \sum_{j=1}^{SenFN} AddT_j \chi \right\} \end{aligned}$$

χNum is the number new data elements to be added in the sensor fields, $SenFN$ is the number of sensor fields where new data element are added, $InterpretSem(SF_j, \chi)$ means that SF_j is a target the matching sensor fields about χ (if exist matching data in other sensor fields (mapping table), should be matched to data element but, do not exist matching data element, should be matched to NULL).

In UbiMDR framework, if a new data element is added in one sensor field, data element is just added to UMDR. The formula for adding cost of new data element in the previous approach is as follows:

Formula 7: *UbiMDR framework*

$$\begin{aligned} & Cost(NewAddDE_{UbiMDR}) \\ & = \sum_{i=1}^{\chi Num} InterpretSem(SF_u) \\ & = \sum_{i=1}^{\chi Num} AddT\chi \end{aligned}$$

Fig. 9 illustrates adding cost of new data element with simple example.

In previous framework, new data elements should be added in adapters as many as the sensor fields.

Previous approach and UbiMDR approach have different rules definition and methods for adding a new semantic data element. Previous approach solves heterogeneity between different sensor fields by mapping tables. However, UbiMDR approach has already defined semantic data element lists in UMDR.

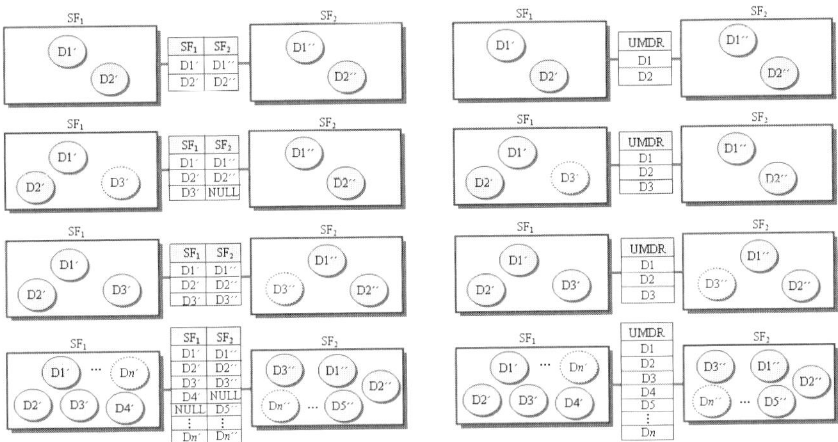

Fig. 9. Data Elements Adding Cost Evaluation models of Previous (left) and UbiMDR Framework (right)

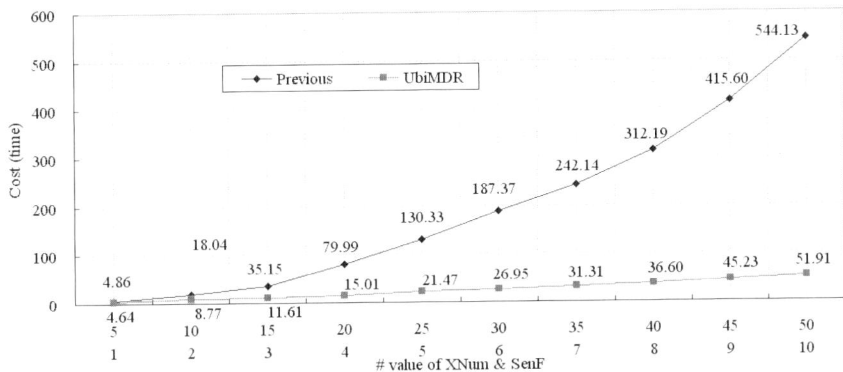

Fig. 10. Adding Cost of New Data Elements

Fig. 10 shows the evaluation result of the cost of adding new data element(s). As shown in the result, the UbiMDR approach has lower cost than the previous approach.

3.6 Operating Cost

This section compares previous approach with UbiMDR approach in operating aspect. Previous approach requires all of semantics in sensor fields, but UbiMDR approach requires only SF_u because semantic data element is already defined in UMDR. Previous approach has to compare semantic data element with each mapping table. Therefore, as data elements increase, the operating cost increase. The formula for the previous and UbiMDR framework is as follows:

Formula 8: *Previous framework*

$$Cost(Spend_{PREV}) = \sum_{i=1}^{X}\left[\sum_{j=1}^{SenFN-1}\left\{\sum_{k=j+1}^{SemN_{SF_k}} InterpretSem(SF_k.s_k)\right\}\right] = \sum_{i=1}^{X}\left[\sum_{j=1}^{SenFN-1}\left\{\sum_{k=j+1}^{SemN_{SF_k}} InterpretSem(S_{kk})\right\}\right] = \sum_{i=1}^{X}\left\{\sum_{i=1}^{SenFN-1}\left(\sum_{k=j+1}^{SemN_{SF_k}} AnaT_{kk}\right)\right\}$$

Formula 9: *UbiMDR framework*

$$Cost(Spend_{UbiMDR}) = \sum_{i=1}^{X}\left[\sum_{j=1}^{SemN_{SF_u}} InterpretSem(SF_u.s_i)\right] = \sum_{i=1}^{X}\left[\sum_{j=1}^{SemN_{SF_u}} InterpretSem(S_{ui})\right] = \sum_{i=1}^{X}\left(\sum_{j=1}^{SemN_{SF_u}} AnaT_{ui}\right)$$

Fig. 11 illustrates operating procedure of previous and UbiMDR framework. Diagram is as follows:

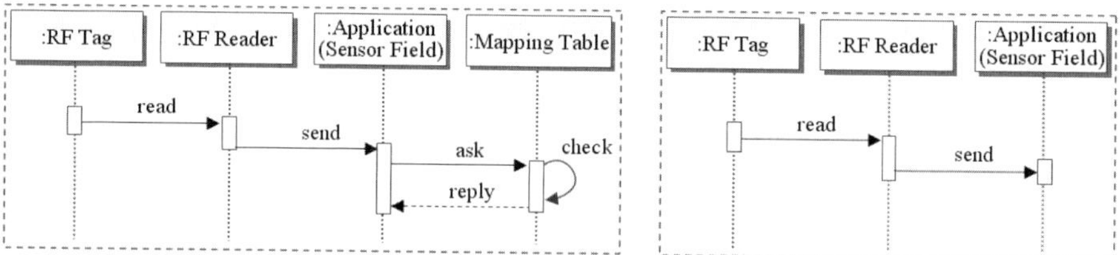

Fig. 11. Operating Procedure of Previous (left) and UbiMDR Framework (right)

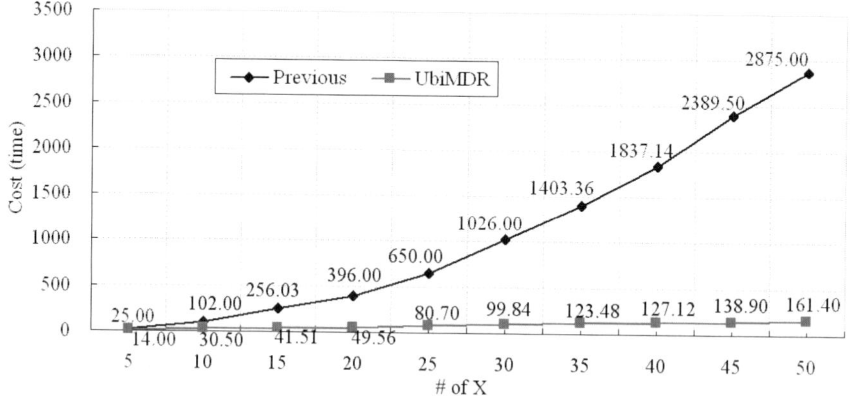

Fig. 12. Operating Cost

Fig. 12 shows the evaluation result of the operating cost. As shown in the result, the UbiMDR approach is more efficient compared to the previous approach. For example, when the number of X is 50, the difference between the two approaches is more then 26. In other words, the previous approach creates an additional 26 costs.

4 Conclusion and Future Works

In this paper, we describe the performance evaluation to validate the superiority of UbiMDR framework. This framework can provide the semantic interoperability among ubiquitous applications or various sensor fields. The UMDR is an optimized MDR for exchanging heterogeneous RFID data values under the same semantic meaning. Also, we described comparison evaluation model between conventional Ubicomp framework and UbiMDR framework with data accuracy of interoperability, mapping cost, adding cost of new sensor field(s), adding cost of new data element(s), and operating cost. The UbiMDR framework represents low costs in mapping, adding new elements, and operating compared to conventional framework.

In future study, we will focus on the deployment of the UbiMDR to encourage its flexible utilization in a larger scale. The UbiMDR will be extended to support the situation awareness concept [12]. This work can provide higher quality services with context information. Finally, security issue will be studied and added to the UbiMDR.

References

1. Weiser, M.: http://www.ubiq.com/hypertext/weiser/Ubi- Home.html
2. ISO/IEC JTC 1/SC 32, ISO/IEC 11179: Information Technology - Metadata Registries (MDR) - Part 1 Part 6 (2004)
3. Jeong, D., In, P., Jarnjak, F., Kim, Y., Baik, D.-K.: A Message Conversion System, XML-based Metadata Semantics Description Language, and Metadata Repository. Journal of Information Science (JIS) 31(5), 394–406 (2005)
4. Environmental Protection Agency (EPA): Environmental Data Registry (EDR) (2004), http://www.epa.gov/edr/
5. Australian Institute of Health and Welfare: Australian National Health Information Knowledgebase (2004), http://www.aihw.gov.au/
6. U.S. Department of Transportation, U.S. Intelligent Transportation System (ITS) (2004), http://www.dot.gov/
7. Environmental Protection Agency: Data Standards Publications and Guidances (2003), http://oaspub.epa.gov/edr/ stddoc$document_type_vw.acti onquery
8. Australian National Health Data Committee: National Health Data Dictionary (2003), http://www.aihw.gov.au/
9. ITS Architecture Development Team, ITS Logical Architecture: Vol. I, Vol. II: Process Specifications. Vol. III: Data Dictionary (2003), http://www.itsa.org/
10. OASIS: ebXML Registry Information Model (April 2002), http://www.oasis-open.org/specs/index.php
11. Kim, J.-D., Jeong, D., Jing, H., Baik, D.-K.: UbiMDR: Supporting Application-Independent Semantic Interoperability for Ubiquitous Applications. In: International Conference on Computational Intelligence and Security (CIS 2006), China Guangzhou, pp. 1155–1158 (November 2006)
12. Jeong, D., Kim, Y., In, H.: New RFID System Architectures Supporting Situation Awareness under Ubiquitous Environments. Journal of Computer Science 1(2), 114–120 (2005)

Distributing Fixed Time Slices in Heterogeneous Networks of Workstations (NOWs)

Yassir Nawaz and Guang Gong

Department of Electrical and Computer Engineering
University of Waterloo
Waterloo, ON, N2L 3G1, Canada
ynawaz@engmail.uwaterloo.ca, G.Gong@ece.uwaterloo.ca

Abstract. Heterogeneous Networks of Workstations (NOWs) offer a cost-effective solution for parallel processing. The completion time of a parallel task over NOWs depends on how the task is divided and distributed among the heterogeneous workstations. In this paper we present a distribution scheme which attempts to minimize the task's completion time over a heterogeneous NOWs. The scheme is based on the idea of distributing fixed time slices of work as opposed to fixed work slices. Our simulations show that the proposed scheme outperforms both fixed and variable work distribution schemes commonly in use. The scheme is very simple and requires no active monitoring of the network. Furthermore it is adaptive and copes very well with the changes in background loads on workstations and network interference.

Keywords: Networks of workstations, parallel processing, fixed work slices, fixed time slices.

1 Introduction

Heterogeneous parallel computing environments are becoming increasingly popular. Advances in commodity technology and increase in network bandwidth have made networks of workstations (NOWs) a viable alternative to parallel computers with large aggregate power and memory [1]. Many parallel machines are now infact, based on workstation chips. Despite the available power and memory, running parallel tasks over NOWs pose distinct challenges. These challenges mainly arise due to the workstation heterogeneity, background load on the workstations, dynamic variation of this background load and interference on the network.

In this paper we address the problem of load distribution in heterogeneous NOWs based parallel systems. Our goal is to minimize the execution time of parallel applications in a master/slave configuration. A number of solutions to this problem have been presented [2, 3, and 4]. The most popular solutions either distribute equal slices of work among the workstations or they distribute variable slices of work according to a predetermined fashion. Another approach is the adaptive distribution where the work slices are adapted according to the slave's behavior. We present an adaptive work distribution solution based on the

I. Stojmenovic et al. (Eds.): ISPA 2007, LNCS 4742, pp. 612–621, 2007.

idea of distributing equal time slices and compare it with previously proposed load distribution schemes. The proposed solution is faster than equal work slice distribution and has less communication overhead than most of the variable work slice distribution techniques. These differences are further highlighted in the applications that require frequent synchronizations. Furthermore the proposed solution is simple and requires no active monitoring on the part of the master.

The rest of the paper is organized as follows. The next section gives a brief description of some of the popular workload distribution strategies. Section 3 describes the equal time slice distribution strategy and its implementation. The experimental results are discussed in section 4. Conclusions and possible future directions are provided in section 5.

2 Background

In this section we present several algorithms for load distribution in NOWs. The work is assumed to be divisible i.e. it can be partitioned into arbitrary chunks or slices such as matrix multiplication and Jacobi iteration. All the algorithms presented here are based on master/slave paradigm in which master is responsible for work distribution among the slaves and also for collecting the partial results from the slaves and integrating them into the final result. The amount

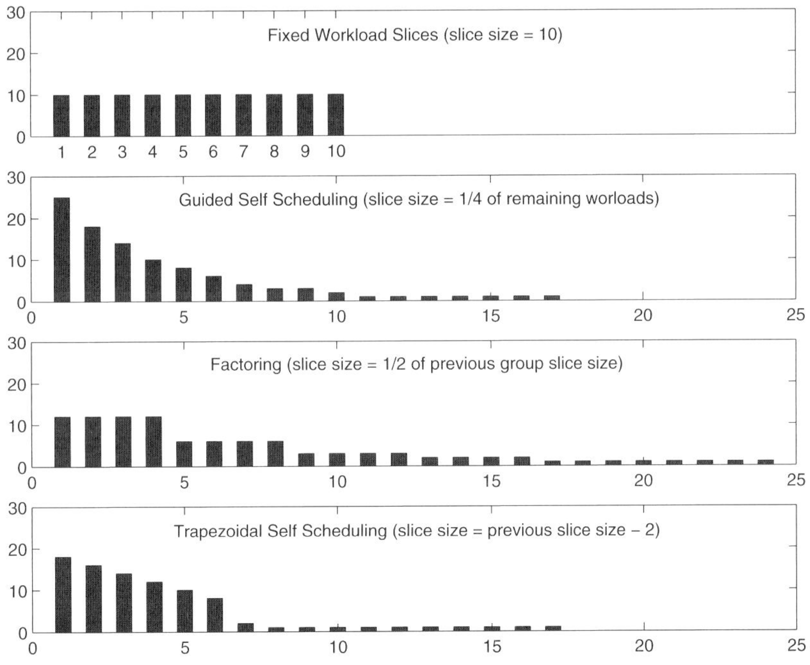

Fig. 1. Load distribution in fixed and variable workload schemes

of work assigned to each slave is determined by the master according to one of the load distribution algorithm described below.

2.1 Fixed Work Slice

In this algorithm workload is divided into equal slices. In case of matrix multiplication or Jacobi iteration each slice consists of a fixed number of rows or columns. Each slave is assigned a slice of the work. The slave processes its slice and returns the results to the master. The master collects the results and assigns a new slice to the slave. The process continues until all the work slices have been assigned. Figure 1 shows the distribution of a task consisting of 100 subtasks. Each workload slice is of size 10 i.e. it contains 10 subtasks.

The algorithm is straightforward and works under the assumption that in a heterogeneous environment faster slaves will finish their slice quickly and will return for new work more often than the slower slaves. This means that work done by the slaves will be in proportion to their speed, reducing their idle times and minimizing the overall execution time. However if the last work slice is assigned to a slower slave it will delay the completion of the task as faster slaves will be sitting idle. This uncertainty is further increased if the task involves frequent synchronizations of all slaves i.e. in Jacobi iteration. One possible solution is to reduce the slice of the workload to minimize the uncertainty however it results in increased communication overhead.

2.2 Variable Work Slice

These algorithms try to strike a balance between uncertainty and communication overhead by starting with large slices of workload but decreasing the size of the slice with time.

Guided Self Scheduling: In Guided Self Scheduling the size of a work slice is determined by the size of the remaining workload [3]. Typically the size is set to $1/G$ of the remaining workload. For example if there are 100 rows remaining to be distributed and G is 4 then the size of the next work slice will be 25 rows. A complete example which consists of 100 subtasks is shown in Figure 1. This results in diminished load sharing and reduces the uncertainty towards the end.

Factoring: Factoring creates smaller and more uniform work slices than guided self-scheduling [2]. The slices are divided into groups and slices in each group are of same size. The size of the group is usually equal to the number of slaves. The size of work slices in a group is a constant factor of the size of the work slices in the previous group. The factors can be calculated based on a-priori knowledge of task computation times. If that is not possible an arbitrary factor can be chosen. Figure 1 shows an example where the initial slice size is 12 and the reduction factor is 2.

Trapezoidal Self Scheduling: In this scheme the size of the work slice decrease linearly as opposed to exponentially as was the case in guided self-scheduling and factoring [4]. Figure 1 shows an example of Trapezoidal self scheduling where the initial size of the work load slice is 18 and each new slice is calculated by subtracting 2 from the previous slice.

2.3 Adaptive Load Distribution

In adaptive load distribution strategies the distribution decisions are based on slave's previous performance. The objective in these strategies is to prevent the last workload slice being assigned to a slow slave. One such scheme that uses fixed size workload slices is proposed in [5]. This scheme keeps track of the amount of work done by each slave and is used to estimate the speed of each client. Before assigning a workload slice to a slave an estimate of the time remaining in finishing the entire workload is made. If this time is less than the estimated time required by the slave to finish the workload slice, the slave is dropped from the computation and no more work is assigned to it. Therefore towards the end slower slaves are dropped preventing them from delaying the completion of the task. However the drawback of this scheme is that the exclusion of slower slaves reduces the available computation power and may also result in a deadlock if all the slaves are dropped. In this case a new round must be started and the remaining workload slices be distributed among all the slaves to finish the workload. If the workload slice is small it also suffers from communication overhead.

3 Distributing Fixed Time Slices

Most of the load distribution schemes presented in the last section have their advantages and disadvantages. These schemes attempt to minimize the total execution time by striking a balance between two conflicting requirements: minimizing the uncertainty in task completion and, the communication overhead. The uncertainty in task completion depends on the size of the last workload slice assigned to the slaves and the communication overhead depends on the total number of messages exchanged between the master and slaves. Variable workload slices reduce the uncertainty, however if the communication overhead is significant they perform poorly [6]. The reason is that towards the completion message size gets smaller and the amount of messages increase rapidly destroying the gains achieved due to larger slices distributed in the initial phase of the computation. This is evident from Figure 1. The adaptive scheme described in section 2.3 minimizes uncertainty by eliminating the slower slaves towards the completion of the task.

A better and more efficient approach is to minimize the uncertainty without eliminating the slower slaves or significantly increasing the number of message exchanges. This can be achieved by distributing fixed time slices as opposed to fixed work slices. The objective is to pick a suitable time slice and adjust the work slice of each slave such that the time taken by that slave to finish the work slice is equal to the chosen time slice.

3.1 Uncertainty Comparison

In order to see how distributing time slices significantly reduces uncertainty let us consider an example: The computing environment consists of master and 3 heterogeneous slaves, $S1$, $S2$ and $S3$, with different speeds. Given a workload slice of size n, $S1$ takes n seconds to compute the workload, $S2$ takes $2n$ seconds and $S3$ takes $4n$ seconds. Now let's estimate the uncertainty for $n = 20$ in distributing fixed work slices and fixed time slices.

Fixed Work Slice: In worst case scenario the master has one work slice left to distribute, all the three slaves, $S1$, $S2$ and $S3$, request for work at the same time, and the work slice is assigned to the slowest slave $S3$. This is the worst case because it maximizes the idle times of the two faster slaves $S1$ and $S2$. The time required to finish the task is $4 \times 20 = 80s$, whereas if this task was assigned to $S1$ the completion time would have been $1 \times 20s$. So there is an uncertainty of $60s$. This uncertainty can be generalized as:

$$Uncertainty = (R - 1)T, \tag{1}$$

where R is the ratio of the speed of fastest slave to the slowest slave and T is the time required to finish the work slice on the fastest machine.

Fixed Time Slice: Consider that a fixed time slice of $20s$ is being distributed to all the slaves' i.e.,

- $S1$ gets a workload slice of size $20(20/1)$
- $S2$ gets a workload slice of size $10(20/2)$,
- $S3$ gets a workload slice of size $5(20/4)$.

If $S1$, $S2$ and $S3$, request for work at the same time there are several possibilities depending on the order in which they are served:

- $S1$ gets 20: completion time 20s.
- $S2$ gets 10 and $S1$ gets 10: completion time $20s$.
- $S2$ gets 10, $S3$ gets 5, and $S1$ gets 5: completion time $20s$.
- $S3$ gets 5, $S1$ gets 10, and $S2$ gets 5: completion time $20s$.

Therefore no matter which slave is assigned the last workload the time required to complete the entire task is constant.

Now let's consider a case where the last workload is of size 5, all slaves request for work at the same time and $S3$ gets selected. This represents the worst case scenario in fixed time slice scheme. Since $S1$ could have finished this work slice in 5 seconds worst case uncertainty in this case is $15s$, which is significantly less than $60s$. It can be generalized as:

$$Uncertainty = \frac{1}{R} \times (R - 1)T \tag{2}$$

where R is the ratio of the speed of fastest slave to the slowest slave and T is the size of the time slice. If the time slice in fixed time slice scheme is set equal to the time taken by the fastest slave to finish a work slice in fixed workload scheme, uncertainty can be improved by a factor of R.

3.2 Communication Comparison

Let us assume that we are willing to permit uncertainty of 60s in our above example and calculate the number of messages exchanged in fixed work slice and fixed time slice schemes. Assume that the task is divisible in 200 subtasks.

Fixed Work Slice: Since work slice consists of 20 subtasks the total number of messages exchanged between the master and slaves S1, S2 and S3 are 10(200/20).

Fixed Time Slice: The permissible uncertainty is 60s so we calculate the corresponding time slice from Equation 2 as:

$$\begin{aligned} 60 &= \frac{1}{4} \times (4-1)T \\ 80 &= T \end{aligned} \tag{3}$$

The maximum time slice is $80s$ which implies that the work slices of $S1$, $S2$ and $S3$ are 80, 40 and 20 respectively. The minimum number of message exchanges required to finish the task is 4 ($S1 : 80, S2 : 40, S3 : 20, S1 : 60$) and the maximum is 5 ($S1 : 80, S2 : 40, S3 : 20, S3 : 20, S2 : 40$). Even in the worst case messages exchanged are half of those exchanged in fixed work slice scheme.

3.3 Choosing Optimum Time Slice

The choice of the time slice can affect the overall completion time of the computation. If the communication overhead is significant a small time slice is a poor choice. On the other hand a very large time slice can result in increased uncertainty as is evident from Equation 2. The time slice should also be small enough to allow all the slaves to take part in the computation. We will study the affect of time slice size on the performance of computation in section 4.

3.4 Calculating Workload for Fixed Time Slice

One of the major challenges in implementing fixed time slice scheme is to calculate the size of the work slice, for each slave, to match the chosen time slice. If the speeds of all the slaves are known, the size of work slice for each slave can be calculated before hand. However if the speed or the number of slaves are not known or can change dynamically due to slaves dropping out or variation in background loads, an adaptive approach is required. We describe one such approach: A time slice T is chosen along with a small variation d. As the computation starts each requesting slave is assigned a fixed work slice W by the master. For each slave, master records the size of the work slice and the time of allocation. When the slave returns to submit results, master calculates the time, t_{last}, taken by the slave to compute the last work slice and adjusts the next work slice by a factor f according to Algorithm 1. The functionality of the procedures and functions in the algorithm are evident from their name. When the time taken by the slave equals the chosen time slice T, the size of the corresponding work slice is associated with that slave. When all the slaves are assigned work slices that match

Algorithm 1. Fixed time slice distribution algorithm

```
while not_end_of_task do
    accept_request(slave);
    if(not_first_request(slave))
        store_results(slave);
        t_last=calculate_t_last(slave);
        W=get_last_workload(slave);
        if(t_last > T + d): W ← W − f;
        elseif(t_last < T − d): W ← W + f;
    update(slave);
    assign_load(slave, W);
```

the fixed time slice, no further adaptation is necessary. Figure 2a demonstrates the load distribution in a heterogeneous NOW at the start of the computation and Figure 2b shows the distribution after the adaptation.

3.5 Variations in Background Load and Network Traffic

The proposed scheme has the added advantage that it can cope very well with the variations in the background loads on slaves. This is a realistic assumption as many heterogeneous NOWs are based on the concept of 'stealing cycles' i.e. the slaves machines are not dedicated and only free computing cycles are made available to the distributed application. Therefore if the slave machine gets heavily loaded during the computation, the completion time of the workload slice on it will increase. In such an environment Algorithm 1 can be used to adjust the workloads on the slaves dynamically. The master in such a case will progressively decrease the work slice of the loaded slave machine until it matches the chosen time slice. Since the slaves may be geographically distributed, increased network interference on a certain connection may result in the larger communication overheads. If the work slices are fixed the uncertainty in the completion time will increases from master's perspective. However if Algorithm 1 is being used the work slice of the slaves on this connection will be decreased accordingly thus reducing the uncertainty. The reason for this decrease is that the completion time t_{last} computed by the master includes the transmission delays.

4 Results

This section presents the results of the simulations conducted to evaluate the performance of three load distribution strategies: Fixed work slices, Variable work slices (Guided Self-Scheduling) and fixed time slices.

4.1 Simulation Setup

The simulated heterogeneous NOWs consists of a master M and 3 slaves: $S1$, $S2$, and $S3$. $S1$ is the fastest slave with $S2$ being twice as slow as $S1$ and $S3$

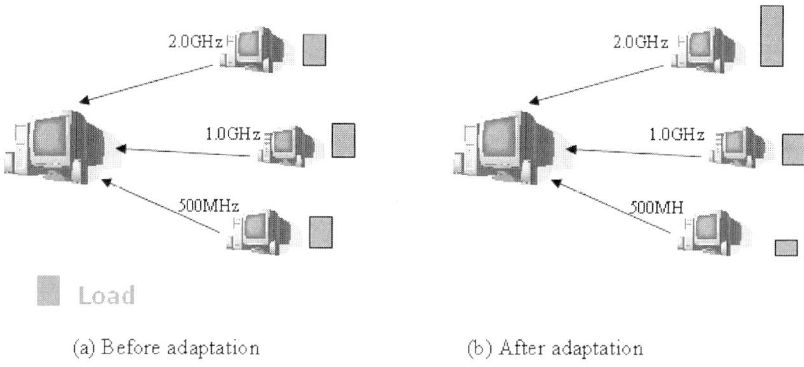

Fig. 2. Adaptation in a HNOW (fixed time slice distribution)

four times as slow as $S1$ i.e. a work slice finished by $S1$ in time t will be finished by $S2$ in time $2t$ and by $S3$ in time $4t$. This is achieved by using three identical SUN UltraSPARC workstations and making the first workstation perform the computation once, the second workstation perform the computation twice and the third workstation perform the computation four times. Apart from the transmission delay which is proportional to the message size, there is an overhead of $0.5s$ associated with each message transmission. This simulates the cost associated with communicating between geographically distributed workstations (delay experienced at the routers etc). The NOWs is used to solve a problem that involves ten matrix multiplications. Each matrix has dimension of 1000×1000. The results of each multiplication are used in the next multiplication therefore all the slaves must work on the same multiplication and synchronize before the next multiplication can begin. There are several scientific applications which require similar synchronizations such as Jacobi iteration. The size of the workload slice is equal to the number of rows in that workload. The height of vertical bars in the Figures 3 and 4 represents the time taken to finish the entire task. These reported times have been averaged over 50 simulated tasks.

4.2 Fixed Work Slice

Figure 3a shows the performance of this scheme for various work slices. When the work slice is very small communication overhead dominates the benefits achieved due to reduced uncertainty which explains the poor performance for a work slice of size 8. As the size increases communication overhead decrease and the performance increase. However when the work slice increases beyond a certain limit, performance begins to suffer again. This is due to the increased uncertainty introduced by larger work slice.

4.3 Guided Self Scheduling

Recall from section 2.2 that as we increase G the granularity of the workload slice increases. If G is too small a large workload slice assigned to a slower slave

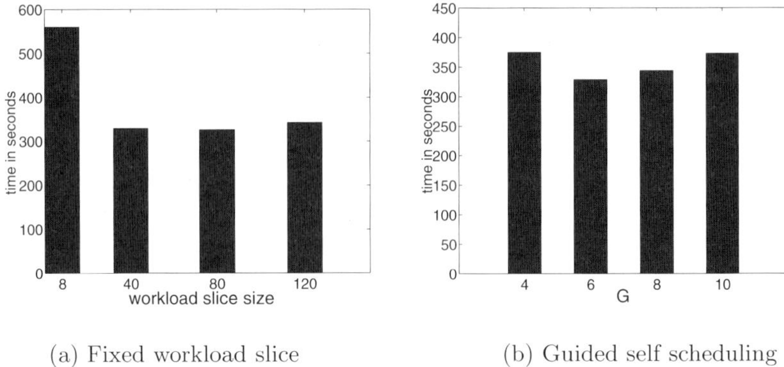

(a) Fixed workload slice

(b) Guided self scheduling

Fig. 3. Performance of fixed workload slice distribution and guided self scheduling

initially, may delay the synchronization of all slaves. On the other hand if G is too large performance suffers due to increased communication overhead. The optimum G for this example as shown in the Figure 3b is 6.

4.4 Fixed Time Slice

The performance of fixed time slice scheme is shown in Figure 4a. If time slice is very small the overall performance suffers due to high communication overhead however as the time slice increases performance improves. This improvement is due to reduced communication overhead which dominates a slight increase in uncertainty. However for a very large time slice the uncertainty in completion becomes significant (see equation 2).

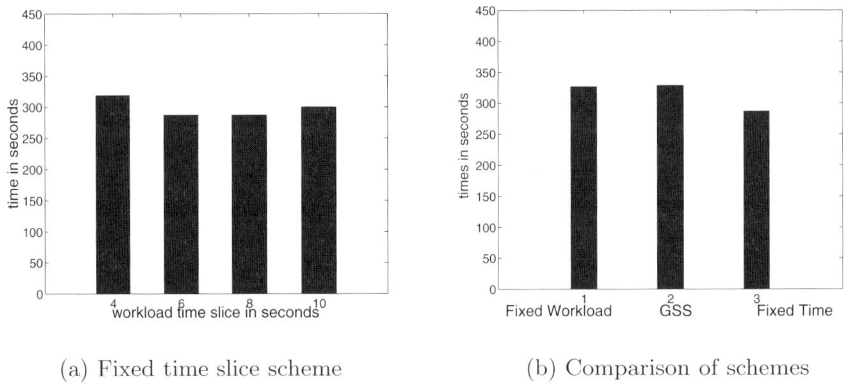

(a) Fixed time slice scheme

(b) Comparison of schemes

Fig. 4. Performance of fixed time slice scheme and its comparison to other schemes

4.5 Comparison

The results in the previous subsections show that fixed and variable workload schemes have comparable performances for the described problem. The fixed time slice scheme proposed in section 3 however outperforms both fixed and variable workload schemes. To do a more precise evaluation we select the best performance of each scheme from Figures 3a, 3b, and 4a, and compare them in Figure 4b. The time taken by fixed time slice is 287s where as time taken by fixed work slice and guided self scheduling is 327s and 329s respectively, thus making fixed time slice approximately 12 percent faster. The fixed time slice load distribution scheme wins because it not only minimizes the uncertainty of the fixed work slice scheme but does so without an increase in the communication overhead exhibited in variable work slice schemes. These gains are further enhanced with an increase in the number of synchronizations and heterogeneity of the network.

5 Conclusions

In this paper we have presented a load distribution scheme for heterogeneous NOWs, based on distributing fixed time slices of work. The proposed scheme has been compared with fixed and variable workload distribution schemes. The results indicate that fixed time slice scheme outperforms both fixed and variable workload distribution schemes as it incorporates the advantages of both i.e. low communication overhead and low uncertainty. Furthermore it is self optimizing and automatically takes into account the latency of distant connections to remote slaves. These properties are highly desirable in the presence of dynamic background load on slave workstations and network interference. Another advantage of the scheme is its non intrusive behavior towards the slaves and its tendency to get out of the way thus facilitating efficient use of the fixed computational resource in a multi-user environment.

In future we intend to conduct experiments to verify the performance of the proposed scheme in the presence of variable background load on slave workstations. Another consideration is to deal with the possibility of a slave going offline indefinitely thus requiring reallocation of its work.

References

1. Anderson, T., Culler, D., Patterson, D.: NOW team: A Case for NOW (Networks of Workstations). IEEE Micro 15(2), 54–64 (1995)
2. Hummel, S.F., Schonberg, E., Flynn, L.E.: Factoring: A Method for Scheduling Parallel Loops. Comm. ACM 35(8), 90–101 (1992)
3. Polychronopoulos, C., Kuck, D.: Guided Self Scheduling: A Practical Scheduling Scheme for Parallel Computers. IEEE Trans. Computers C-36(12), 1425–1439 (1987)
4. Tzen, T.H., Ni, L.M.: Dynamic Loop Scheduling for Shared-Memory Multiprocessors. IEEE Trans. Parallel Dist. Syst. 4(1), 87–98 (1993)
5. Hargrove, W., Hoffman, F.: Optimizing Master/Slave Dynamic Load-Balancing in Heterogeneous Parallel Environments, `http://research.esd.ornl.gov/hnw/sc99/`
6. Piotrowski, A., Dandamudi, S.P.: Performance Sensitivity of Variable Granularity Load Sharing on Networks of Workstation. In: Intl. Conference on Massively Parallel Computer Systems, Colorado Springs, pp. 6.12–6.19 (April 1998)

A Grid Resources Valuation Model Using Fuzzy Real Option*

David Allenotor** and Ruppa K. Thulasiram

Department of Computer Science,
University of Manitoba
Winnipeg, MB R3T 2N2.
Canada
{dallen,tulsi}@cs.umanitoba.ca

Abstract. In this study, we model pricing of grid/distributed computing resources as a problem of real option pricing. Grid resources are non-storable compute commodities (eg., CPU cycles, memory, etc). The non-storable characteristic feature of the grid resources hinders it from fitting into a risk-adjusted spot price model for pricing financial options. Grid resources users pay upfront to acquire and use grid compute cycles in the future, for example, six months. The user expects a high and acceptable degree of satisfaction expressed as the Quality of Service (QoS) assurance. This requirement further imposes service constraints on the grid because it must provide a user-acceptable QoS guarantee to compensate for the upfront value. This study integrates three threads of our research; pricing the grid compute cycles as a problem of real option pricing, modeling grid resources spot price using a discrete time approach, and addressing uncertainty constraints in the provision of QoS using fuzzy logic. We have proved the feasibility of this model through experiments and we have presented some of our pricing results and discussed them.

1 Introduction

A financial option is defined (see e.g., [5]) as the right to buy or to sell an underlying asset that is granted in exchange for an agreed-upon sum. The right expires if it is not exercised on or before a specific period and the option buyer forfeits the premium paid at the beginning of the contract. The exercise price *(strike price)* specified in an option contract is the stated price at which the asset can be bought or sold at a future date. A *call option* grants the holder the right to purchase (sell the underlying asset in a *put option*) the underlying asset at the specified strike price. The price of their underlying asset at any future time may not be predicted with certainty hence the option holder has no assurance

* The last author acknowledges partial financial support from the Natural Sciences and Engineering Research Council (NSERC) Canada through Discovery Grants and to the University Research Grants Program (URGP) of the University of Manitoba.
** Correspondence author.

I. Stojmenovic et al. (Eds.): ISPA 2007, LNCS 4742, pp. 622–632, 2007.

that the option will be *in the money* (i.e., yields a non-negative reward), before expiry. In contrast to financial options, real options deal with the possibility of a choice from two decisions – the choice for or against an investment decision without necessarily binding oneself upfront. Grid resources are non-storable compute commodities (CPU cycles, memory, network bandwidths, throughput, computing power, disks, processor, and various measurements and instrumentation tools). Their non-storable characteristics hinder them from fitting into a risk-adjusted spot price model for pricing financial options. We assume the following in a hypothetical computing grid systems: (1) The price of the underlying grid resources at time $t_1, t_2, \cdots, t_n$ is associated with some level of uncertainty and varies based on new technology, improved solution methodology (that may require either more or less of the available compute commodities), and the prices of acquiring new hardware and software. (2) Our pricing model depends on the future prices rather than the spot prices since the request for grid compute cycles follows a stochastic process.

Based on assumption (1), we introduce a Price Variant Multiplier (PVM) α_f. The PVM is a fuzzy number defined as a membership function $0 \leq \alpha_f \leq 1$. The price of the underlying resources at $t_1, t_2, \cdots, t_n$ depends on the value of α_f, e.g., at t_1, with more computing facilities and same technology, α_f takes a lower value (e.g., 0.1) and with new technology, α_f takes a higher value closer to 1. Therefore, our model adjusts by a value of $(\alpha_f)^{-1}$. Assumption (2) facilitates the application of risk neutral approach in our model.

Our model starts with a continuous-time stochastic process (Geometric Brownian Motion (GBM)). It provides a mathematical description of the change in asset[1] prices with time. It assumes proportional changes in the asset price S to have a constant instantaneous drift μ, and volatility σ. The stochastic differential equation is;

$$dS = \mu S dt + \sigma S dz \tag{1}$$

where dS denotes increments in the asset price process during an infinitesimally small time interval dt, and dz is the underlying uncertainty that drives the model and indicates some incremental value in dt in a Wiener process.

The rest of this paper is organized as follows. Section 2 reviews related work. Section 3 explores real option concepts as a grid pricing tool. Section 4 presents the results of our model and Section 5 conclude our study.

2 Related Work

Some notable methodologies for pricing financial options include closed-form equations such as the Black-Scholes [4] model and its modifications, Monte Carlo path-dependent simulation methods (see e.g., [8]), lattices (binomial and trinomial (e.g., [6], [9])), and other numerical techniques (e.g., [10], [11], [14]). In real options analysis, the mainstream approaches include the closed-form solutions

[1] Asset here means any of the non-storable compute resources such as compute cycles, memory etc (listed in section 3) with respect to distributed/grid computing.

and the binomial lattice. The closed-form solutions such as the Black-Scholes formula solves the partial differential equation for the option price evolution under certain unrealistic assumptions. These schemes are exact and easy to implement, however they lack modeling flexibility for valuing non-capacity options. In [13], d'Halluin et al. apply modern financial option pricing methods to network investment decision problem. Their framework applies estimation techniques to manage the resultant network bandwidth capacity uncertainties. In contrast to [13], we capture uncertainty in our model parameters using fuzzy logic methods. In [2], Gray et al. provide a real option framework for valuing a space mission design project. Their valuation accuracy is based on the value of Net Present Value (NPV) using the binomial method. In real options, the value of NPV [5] must be high enough (i.e., $NPV > 0$). The results obtained in [2] did not take into cognizance the value of the project cost and inherent uncertainty associated with the stochastic variables of their framework. Carlsson and Fullér in [3] apply a hybrid approach (real option, fuzzy logic, and probability theory) to value future options. The results given in [2] and [3] have no formal reference to the QoS that characterize a decision system. Carlsson and Fullér [3] apply fuzzy methods to measure the level of decision uncertainties, however, there is a lack of indication on how accurate the decisions could be. Other literatures [7], [9] evaluated real options and applied it to spot pricing. These research did not show capabilities for pricing non-storable components of a grid resource. In a grid system, resources are non-storable and a user who predicts that he/she might need more computing power in the future must pay upfront today to hold the right to exercise the option when he/she needs the computing resources in the stated future date. In this study, we integrate real options for pricing compute cycles and apply the trinomial approach to capture our data for analysis.

3 Grid Resources Pricing

Grid resources are capacity-type non storable resources [12]. Their availability is governed by a high degree of uncertainty in the prices of future compute commodities. Any previously unutilized capacity may not have value in the current time. Consequently, it is hard to develop an inventory to equalize price fluctuations and jumps in spot prices of the grid resources. Similarly, it is hard to determine the amount of reservations (compute resource requirements) necessary to satisfy computational demands. It is therefore hard to guarantee a grid resource availability without overcommitting the resources and compromising the QoS guarantees.

We model grid resources based on the transient availability[2] of the grid compute cycles, the availability of compute cycles, and the value of volatility of prices associated with the compute cycles. Given maturity date t, expectation of the risk-neutral value ($\hat{E}$); the future price of a contract on grid resources could be expressed as;

$$F(t) = \hat{E}[S(t)] = S(0)e^{\int_0^t \mu(\tau)d\tau} \tag{2}$$

[2] A reserved quantity at a certain time (t_{n-1}) may be unavailable at t_n.

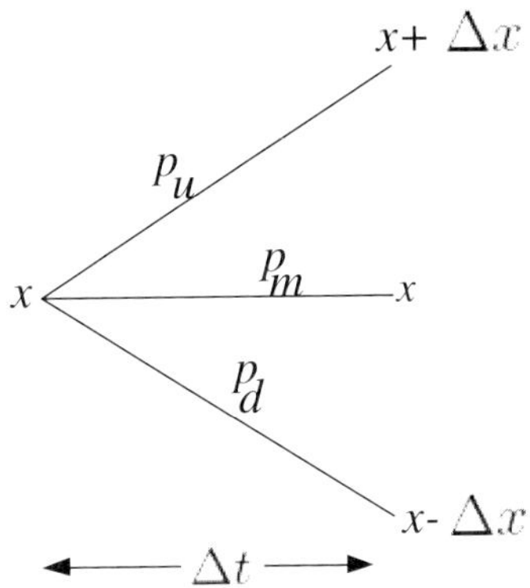

Fig. 1. One-Step Trinomial Lattice

To solve the partial differential equation of the option price by the explicit finite difference method [16] is equivalent to performing discounted expectations in a trinomial-tree. Consider a trinomial model (see e.g., [5], [15]) of asset price in a small time interval Δt, the asset price increases by Δx, remain the same or decreases by Δx, with probabilities; probability of up movement p_u, probability of steady move (staying at the middle) p_m, and probability of a downward movement p_d. Figure 1 shows a one-step trinomial lattice expressed in terms of Δx and Δt. The drift and volatility parameters of the asset price can be captured in the simplified discrete process using $\Delta x, p_u, p_m$, and p_d. The space step can be computed (with a choice) using $\Delta x = \sigma\sqrt{3\Delta t}$. The transitional probabilities can be derived as

$$p_u = 0.5 * ((\sigma^2 \Delta t + v^2 \Delta t^2)/(\Delta x^2) + (v\Delta t)/\Delta x)) \tag{3}$$

$$p_m = 1 - ((\sigma^2 \Delta t + v^2 \Delta t^2)/\Delta x^2) \tag{4}$$

$$p_d = 0.5 * ((\sigma^2 \Delta t + v^2 \Delta t^2)/(\Delta x^2) - (v\Delta t)/\Delta x)) \tag{5}$$

Consider the grid as a resources system with multiple resources $cc_i = \{cc_1, cc_2, \cdots, cc_n\}$ where n is a finite number (the number of available grid resources). To price the multi-resources system (such as the grid resources), we suppose a real option depends on some other variables such as the expected growth rate cc_μ and the volatility respectively cc_σ. Then if we let

$$dcc_i/cc_i = cc_\mu dt + cc_\sigma dz_i \tag{6}$$

for any number of derivatives of cc such as $(cc_1, cc_2, \cdots, cc_n)$ with prices p $(p_1, p_2, \cdots, p_n)$ respectively, we have

$$d\ln S = dp_i/p_i = \mu_i dt + \sigma_i dz \tag{7}$$

where the variables $cc_i = \{the\ set\ of\ resources\}$ i.e., if cc_1 = CPU cycles, cc_2 =bandwidths, cc_3 = memory, cc_4 = throughput, cc_5 = disks,cc_6 = processor

cc_7 = network, cc_8 = computing power, cc_9 = instrumentation tools, and cc_{10} = visualization tools, from Equation (7), we apply the mean reverting process[3] for pricing options [5]:

$$d \ln S = [cc(t) - a \ln S]dt + [stochastic\ term] \tag{8}$$

where σdz is called the stochastic term and a is the mean reverting factor. The strength of the mean reverting process is determined by the value of a (high for $a > 0$). For a multi-asset problem, we have:

$$d \ln S_i = [cc_i(t) - a \ln S_i]dt + \sigma_i dz_i|_{i=1,2,\cdots,n} \tag{9}$$

The value of $cc(t)$ is determined such that $F(t) = \hat{E}[S(t)]$ i.e., the expected value of S is equal to the future price. A scenario similar to what we may get is a user who suspects that he might need more compute cycles (bandwidth) in 3, 6, and 9 months from today and therefore decides to pay some amount, $\$s$ upfront to hold a position for the expected increase. We illustrate this process using a 3–step trinomial process. If the spot price for bandwidth is $\$s_T$ bit per second (bps) and the projected 3, 6, and 9 months future prices are $\$s_1$, $\$s_2$, and $\$s_3$ respectively. In this scenario, the two uncertainties are the amount of bandwidth that will be available and the price per bit. However, we can obtain an estimate for the stochastic process for bandwidth prices by substituting reasonably some assumed values of a and σ (e.g., $a = 10\%$, $\sigma = 20\%$) in Equation (8) and obtain the value of S from Equation (9). Suppose $V_{l,j}$ represents the option values at l for $l = 0, 1, \cdots, n-1$ level and j node for $j = 1, 2, 3$ (for a trinomial lattice only); i.e., $V_{1,1}$ represents the option value at level 1 and at p_u. Therefore, the displacement for the node is $V_{l,j} + \alpha_j$. If there are displacements $\alpha_{p_u}, \alpha_{p_m}$, and α_{p_d} for p_u, p_m, and p_d respectively, the expected future price for bandwidth is given as:

$$\hat{E}[S(t)] = p_u e^{V_{l,j}} + p_m e^{V_{l,n}} + p_d e^{V_{l,n}} \tag{10}$$

where $l = 0, 1, \cdots, n-1$ and $j = 1, 2, 3$

3.1 Fuzzification of Model Parameters

We specify the model parameters (S, t, α_f in Equation (10)) using fuzzy logic [1] to capture the inherent uncertainty of the stochastic behavior of option prices. Using the predefined fuzzification parameters, the LHS of Equation(10) can be shown as

$$\hat{E}(S(t)) \equiv \hat{E}(\tilde{S}(\tilde{t})) \equiv E[\alpha_s, a_s, b_s, \beta_s](p_u, p_m, p_d) \tag{11}$$

and the RHS is equivalent to:

$$\alpha_{p_u} e^{V_{i,j}} + \alpha_{p_m} e^{V_{i,j}} + \alpha_{p_d} e^{V_{i,j}}|_{i=0,1,2,\cdots,n-1}\ ;\ j = 1, 2, 3. \tag{12}$$

$$\tilde{\alpha}_{p_u} e^{V_{i,j}} + \tilde{\alpha}_{p_m} e^{V_{i,j}} + \tilde{\alpha}_{p_d} e^{V_{i,j}}|_{i=0,1,2,\cdots,n-1}\ ;\ j = 1, 2, 3. \tag{13}$$

[3] Mean reverting factor damps price variation effect on the model.

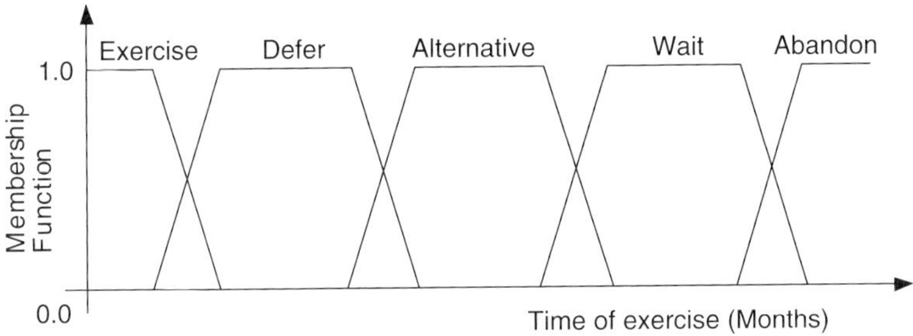

Fig. 2. Trapezoidal Membership Function For Flexibility Opportunity

where (a_s, b_s) is called the core of the fuzzy membership function of $\mu_S(x)$; and (α_s, β_s) are the end values. The model is given as:

$$E[\alpha_s, a_s, b_s, \beta_s](p_u, p_m, p_d) = \tilde{\alpha}_{p_u} e^{V_{i,j}} + \tilde{\alpha}_{p_m} e^{V_{i,j}} + \tilde{\alpha}_{p_d} e^{V_{i,j}} \quad (14)$$

where $i = 0, 1, 2, \cdots, n-1$ and $j = 1, 2, 3$. We associate the model with an equivalent trapezoidal fuzzy membership function such as the opportunity to defer (within a specified time frame), opportunity to abandon, opportunity to exercise, opportunity with other alternatives, and the opportunity to wait (without any given time frame). Figure 2 depicts the classes of our defined options. Defers defines a choice for a postponed right to exercise in a future known date, abandon defines an option that will never be exercised. Exercise refers to the choice of exercising the options, alternative defines the choice of abandonment with alternatives, and the choice to wait refers to future an option exercised without any specific date.

4 Experimental Results

4.1 Fuzzy Logic Approach to Pricing Grid Resources

Our resources pricing framework combines the perspectives of fuzzy logic and option pricing. We use two inputs variables; QoS which takes the form of High, Mid, Low, X-Low, Unacceptable and fuzzy real options given as: Exercise, Defer, Alternative, Wait, and Abandon respectively. Table 1 shows the relationship between the QoS values, fuzzified real option values, and price. From table 1 the fuzzy value (membership function for the flexibility to exercise the option) is high i.e., "Exercise" with a corresponding "High" QoS and Price respectively. The following provides the resulting inference rule:

$$If\ Input\ is\ \{QoS\}\ and\ \{Fuzzy\ Options\}\ Output\ is\ \{Class\ of\ Options\} \quad (15)$$

Equation (15) defines the fuzzy inference engine for evaluating the class of real options. Figure 3 shows the corresponding inference rule of our model. The QoS obtained from our model depends on the value of the class of options obtained

Table 1. QoS, Option Values, and Flexibility Opportunities to Exercise Option

Flexibility Opportunity	Exercise	Defer	Alternative	Wait	Abandon
QoS	High	Mid	Low	-	-
Price	High	Mid	Low	-	-

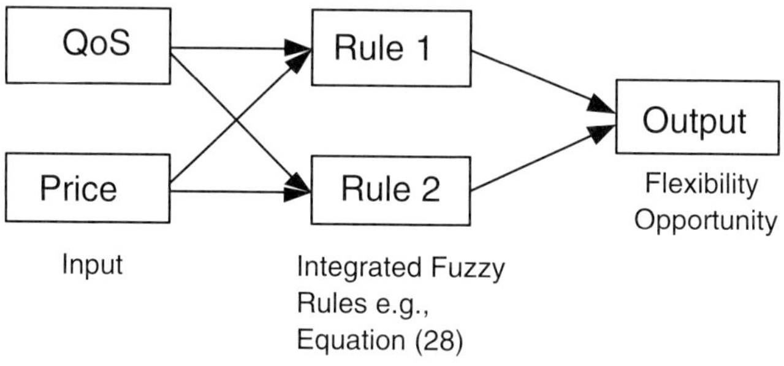

Fig. 3. Inference Rule Engine For Table 1

from the fuzzy inference rules. Figure 5 shows the relationship between QoS, exercise price, and flexibility opportunity for pricing grid resources. For example, a resource user would prefer a high level of flexibility opportunity and ready to exercise the option with a corresponding high value for QoS. Figure 5 $(a) - (f)$ shows the effects of the time of exercising a real option (ie., the time of actual use of the infrastructure in the future). In Figure 5 $(a) - (f)$, the price increases with the time. This indicates that for a non-storable compute grid cycles, earlier exercise enjoys more profitability from the holder's (consumer) point of view because as the time of exercise draws near, the service provider will want to keep the grid busier for the next near future period by reducing the price for a higher QoS. By doing this, the service provider can also try to optimize the return on his/her investment. For an assumed volatility of the availability of future compute commodities, we can predict the value of such resources.

The flexibility of choosing low QoS at lower price should not exist in the market place. This could be inferred from the implementation of the fuzzy rule for the current study depicted in Figure 4. At the same time, higher QoS at a lower price is a possibility where the demand on the infrastructure is small or when the time of consumption is very near in the future. From our experiment, it is hard to provide a high quality of flexible service at low cost, given the constraints on the resources cost. This is a consequence of the non-storability behavior of the grid compute commodities. For example, grid compute cycles must be produced at virtually the same instant that they are utilized coupled with high resources price volatility. As a result, the grid resources do not follow a familiar and notable option pricing process for exercising options over an elongated period e.g., American option for oil, gas, or gold. Therefore, pricing grid compute commodities must be done at shorter time interval (few months, say at the most 6 months) to deal with fluctuations in resources demand on

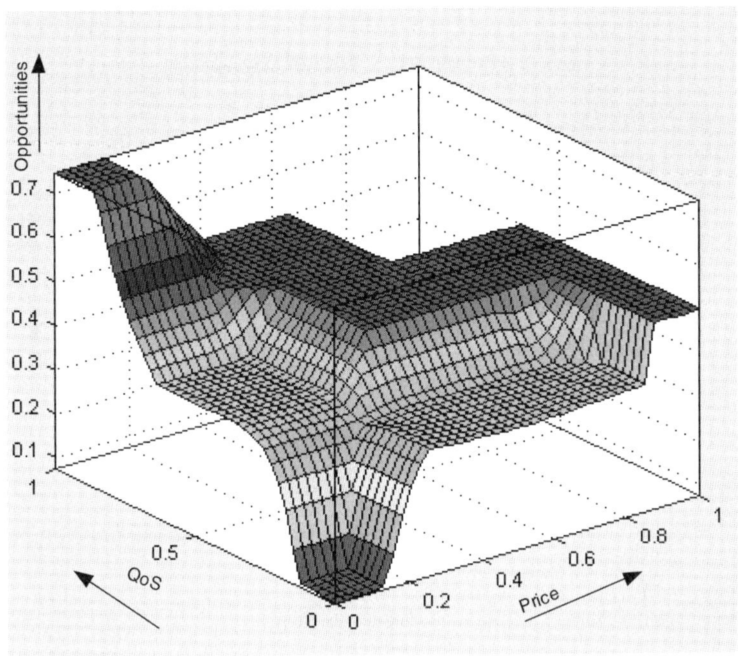

Fig. 4. Relationship Between QoS, Exercise Price, and The Flexibility Opportunity

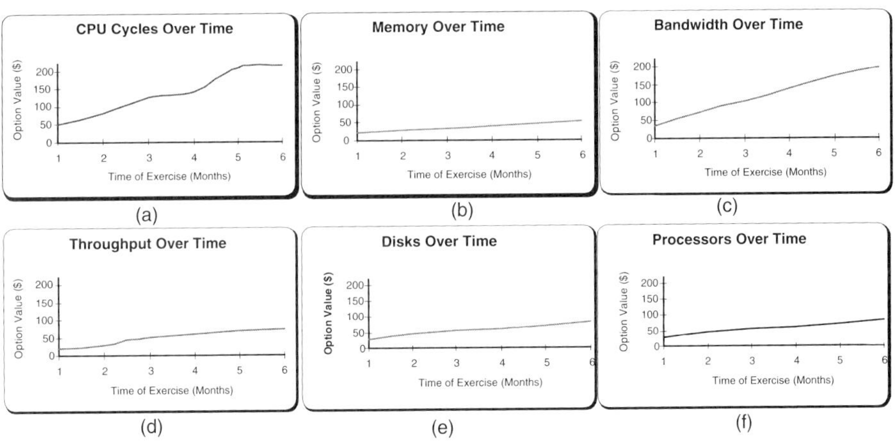

Fig. 5. Effects of Time of Exercise on Option Price (a): CPU Cycles, (b): Memory, (c): Bandwidth, (d): Throughput, (e): Disks, (f): Processors

the grid. Figure $7(i - vi)$ shows users' resources usage (option values/month). For example, during the third month, the user receives grid resources of cc_1 for \$124.00, cc_2 for \$102.00, cc_3 for \$33.21, cc_4 for \$52.55, cc_5 for \$58.13, and cc_6 for \$36.76 whereas in the fourth month, s/he would have to pay for corresponding

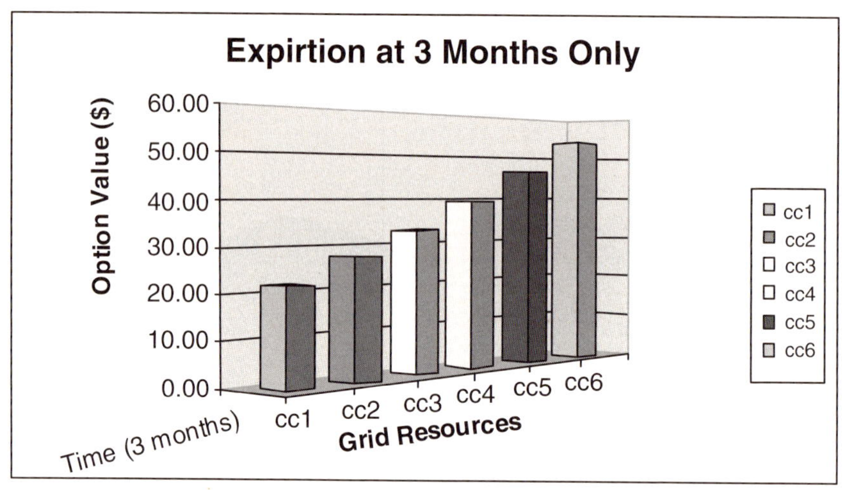

Fig. 6. Compute Cycles Obtained for Three Months Expiration

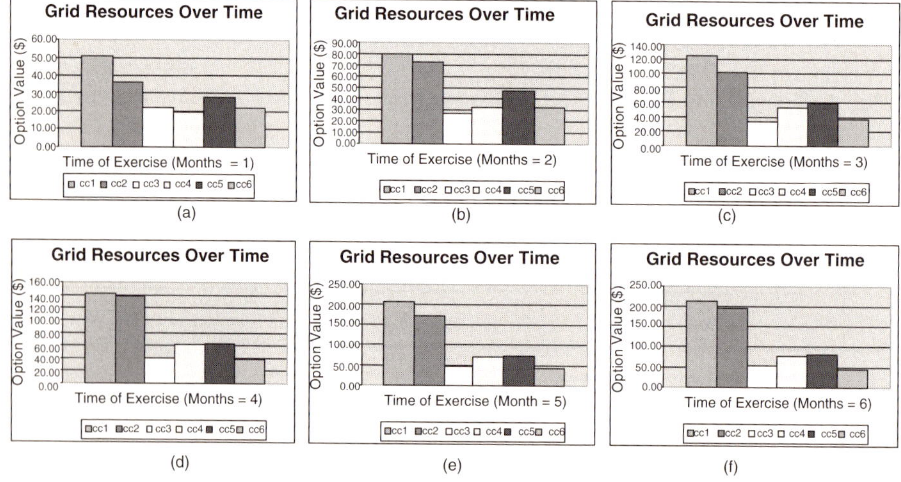

Fig. 7. Grid Resources Usage in Months 1 – 6

grid resources at cc_1 for \$142.00, cc_2 for \$138.00, cc_3 for \$39.79, cc_4 for \$62.00, cc_5 for \$63.22, and cc_6 for \$38.73. Figure 6 shows a snapshot of the costs for the resource $(cc_1, cc_2, \cdots, cc_6)$ utilization at the end of third month. Options value at $t_1 < t_2$ for the same grid resources because a guaranteed availability of grid resources in terms of QoS is hard to ascertain – assumption (1). The result obtained also shows a dependence on the future price rather than the spot price.

5 Conclusions

This study focused on an emerging research area of computational finance application to grid economics. Our specific contribution from this study is on the development of a model for pricing grid resources as real options. For an assumed volatility of the availability of future compute commodities, we can determine the value of such resources using the proposed model. We presented some preliminary results on the option values with QoS. The QoS was ascertained by introducing some fuzzy rules. We obtained and analyzed various scenarios of option pricing using a trinomial lattice method. What we showed in this paper is that the price of a grid resource is determined by the effects of time and volatility (one of the most subjective and perhaps the most difficult factor to quantify) and therefore must be priced as real options. This study opens up many challenging issues for further study in the computing market for providing QoS in grid/distributed computing. Together with technical services, the proposed model will help achieve high dependability in complex distributed systems.

References

1. Zadeh, L.A.: Fuzzy Sets. Information and Control 4, 338–353 (1965)
2. Gray, A.A., Arabshahi, P., Lamassoure, E., Okino, C., Andringa, J.: A Real Option Framework for Space Mission Design, NASA – Jet Propulsion labouratory (2003)
3. Carlson, C., Fuller, R.: A Fuzzy Approach to Real Option Valuation. Fuzzy Sets and Systems 139, 297–312 (2003)
4. Black, F., Scholes, M.: The Pricing of Options and Corporate Liabilities. Journal of Political Economy 3, 637–659 (1973)
5. Hull, J.C.: Options, Futures, and Other Derivatives, 6th edn. Prentice-Hall, Englewood Cliffs (2006)
6. Thulasiram, R.K., Litov, L., Nojumi, H., Downing, C.T., Gao, G.R.: Multithreaded Algorithms for Pricing a Class of Complex Options. In: Proceedings (CD-ROM) of the International Parallel and Distributed Processing Symposium (IPDPS), San Francisco, CA (2001)
7. Gupta, A., Zhang, L., Kalyanaraman, S.: Simulation for Risk Management: A Two-component Spot Pricing Framework For Loss-rate Guaranteed Internet Service Contracts. In: Winter Simulation Conference'03: Proceedings of the 35th Conference on Winter Simulation, pp. 372–380 (2003)
8. Rahmail, S., Shiller, I., Thulasiram, R.K.: Different Estimators of The Underlying Asset's Volatility and Option Pricing Errors: Parallel Monte-Carlo Simulation. In: Proceedings of the International Conference on Computational Finance and its Applications (ICCFA), Bologna, Italy, pp. 121–131 (April 21-23, 2004)
9. Amico, M., Pasek, Z.J., Asl, F., Perrone, G.: Simulation Methodology For Collateralized Debt and Real Options: A New Methodology to Evaluate The Real Options of Investment Using Binomial Trees and Monte Carlo Simulation. In: Winter Simulation Conference '03: Proceedings of the 35th Conference on Winter Simulation, pp. 351–359 (2003)
10. Barua, S., Thulasiram, R.K., Thulasiraman, P.: High Performance Computing for a Financial Application using Fast Fourier Transform. In: Cunha, J.C., Medeiros, P.D. (eds.) Euro-Par 2005. LNCS, vol. 3648, pp. 1246–1253. Springer, Heidelberg (2005)

11. Thulasiram, R.K., Zhen, C., Chhabra, A., Thulasiraman, P., Gumel, A.: A Second Order L_0 Stable Algorithm for Evaluating European Options. Int'l Journal of HPC and Networking (IJHPCN) (2006)
12. Kenyon, C., Cheliotis, G.: Grid Resource Commercialization: Economic Engineering and Delivery Scenarios. In: Nabrzyski, et al. (ed.) [17] 1st edn., ch. 26, vol. 64 (November 2003)
13. d'Halluin, Y., Forsyth, P.A., Vetzal, K.R.: Managing Capacity For Telecommunications Networks Under Uncertainty. IEEE/ACM Transaction on Networking 10 (2002)
14. Thulasiram, R.K., Thulasiraman, P.: Performance Evaluation of a Multithreaded Fast Fourier Transform Algorithm for Derivative Pricing. The Journal of Supercomputing 26(1), 43–58 (2003)
15. Cox, J.C., Ross, S.A., Rubinstein, M.: Option Pricing: A Simplified Approach. Journal of Financial Economics 7, 229–263 (1979)
16. Tavalla, D., Randall, C.: Pricing Financial Instruments: The Finite Difference Method. John Wiley and Sons, New York (2000)
17. Nabrzyski, J., Schopf, J., Weglarz, J. (eds.): Grid Resource Management: State of the Art and Future Trends. Int'l Series in Operations Research & Management Science, 1st edn. vol. 64. Kluwer Academic Publishers, Springer (November 2003)

Enhancing Data Replication with Greedy Pipeline-Based Aggressive Copy Protocol in Data Grids

Reen-Cheng Wang, Su-Ling Wu, and Ruay-Shiung Chang

Department of Computer Science and Information Engineering
National Dong Hwa University
{rcwang,rschang}@mail.ndhu.edu.tw

Abstract. To gain high performance computing or store large amount of data using inexpensive devices, grid system is one of the well-known solutions. In most cases, the grid can be categorized into two types: computational grid and data grid. Data grid is used for data intensive applications. In data grids, replication is used to reduce access latency and bandwidth consumption. Furthermore, it can also improve data availability, load balancing and fault tolerance. If there are many replicas, they may have coherence problems while being updated. In this paper, based on the aggressive-copy method, we propose a novel Greedy Pipeline-based Aggressive Copy (GPAC) protocol. The performance of pipelining dataset blocks and greedy sequencing in the GPAC can accelerate data replication speed in compared with previous works. Both analytical and experimental results show promising performance enhancements.

1 Introduction

The computers become more and more powerful as predicted by Moore's Law since 1965. Using a high performance computer, lots of complicated problems can be solved easily today. However, a single high performance computer, such as a supercomputer, is very expensive and unaffordable. To solve this problem, scientists interconnect many inexpensive systems to expand storage spaces and enhance computing power. The whole system can perform as well as a supercomputer does. The grid [1] system is one of these technologies. In a grid system, heterogeneous devices are connected together via networks to become a large-scale computing infrastructure. From users' perspective, the grid is liked a single powerful computer. No matter where the resources or storages are, every task will be assigned to the suitable sites for processing or storing.

A data-intensive computing consists of applications that produce, manipulate, or analyses data in the range of hundreds of Megabytes to Petabytes and beyond [2]. How to manage these data effectively becomes a great challenge. The Data Grid [3][4][5], therefore, is proposed to provide a platform for users to execute their data-intensive applications on aggregated computational, storage and networking resources. The real examples are such as the experiments at the Large Hadron Collider [6] at Conseil Européen pour la Recherche Nucléaire (CERN). The huge amounts of data will be generated and replicated to hundreds of institutions worldwide. Thousands of physicists will be involved to analyze terabytes of data

I. Stojmenovic et al. (Eds.): ISPA 2007, LNCS 4742, pp. 633–644, 2007.

daily. Undoubtedly, replication is one of the important functions inside. It is used to reduce access latency, provide load balancing, and also improve data availability. For example, if a data is very popular in the system and only exists in a single site, the access load of this site will become very heavy. With replication mechanism, many sites can have the data simultaneously. Users can access the data from a suitable place.

However, if there are many replicas, they will have coherence problems when data is updated. Some of the sites may have the newest data while others still hold old ones. This may cause unpredictable errors in the system. To overcome this problem, many mechanisms are proposed. In this paper, we propose a novel Greedy Pipeline-based Aggressive Copy (GPAC) method based on the aggressive-copy mechanism and the greedy method to reduce the effect. It can accelerate the update speed and decrease users' waiting time.

The rest of this paper is organized as follows. Section 2 presents an overview of the previous works about coherence problem. Section 3 introduces our method. Experimental results are shown in Section 4. And finally, the conclusions and future works are presented in Section 5.

2 Related Works

The major coherence problem happens when a user is updating a file and another user wants to access the same data. It will cause the dirty read problem. Dullmann D. et al [7] addressed a basic consistency scheme called Possibly Inconsistent Copy, with several well known ways to tackle this problem: standard locking, optimistic locking and snapshot. Standard locking obtains a file write lock before performing the file access and release the lock after processing. Optimistic locking is used in case of a very low probability of lock contention on the file. One could alternatively access without getting a lock and test the modification date of the file after the process. In case the file was updated, one really gets a lock and retries. Snapshots keep an old version of the file until the access process is finished, but allow writers to update simultaneously.

Home-based Lazy consistency (HLRC) [8] provides another kind of lock protocol. Every data has its designated home to which all update are propagated. To make home up-to-date, differences of each modified data are sent to its home at the end of an interval. At the time of data acquisition, acquiring process receives write notices from releasing process and invalidates pages indicated by them. When an actual access happens on an invalidated file, faulting process update its stale copy by fetching the fresh copy from the home location.

Yun H. et al. improved the lock performance of HLRC in [9]. The new lock protocol for HLRC updates data that is expected to be accessed inside a critical section. The operations have three phases: lock request, lock grant, and data fault handling. The advantage of their proposed protocol reduces page fault handling time and lock-waiting time.

Domenici A. et al [10] presented an architecture of the replica consistency service. Their method is based on the middleware which is mainly developed by the European

Data Grid Project. The architecture includes three functions: client interface for the consistency service, file update mechanism, and update propagation protocol. They lay out a high-level architectural design for a Replica Consistency Service.

Two coherence protocols, which are named lazy-copy and aggressive-copy, were introduced in [11]. In the lazy-copy based protocol, replicas are only updated as needed if someone accesses it. It can save network overhead without transferring up-to-date replicas every time when some modifications are made. However, lazy-copy protocol has to pay the penalties for access delay when inter-site updating is required. For the aggressive-copy protocol, replicas are always updated immediately when the original file is modified. With linear and star topologies, we reference the aggressive-copy protocol as "1 to 1" and "1 to All" method in our experiments.

In [12] the model of multi-master copies was used to adapt replica consistency service for data grids. Improved from [13], replicas are separated into two categories: a master replica and secondary replicas. A master copy can only be modified by end users. In opposition to the master replica, a secondary replica is read-only. A secondary replica is forced to renew according to the last contents of the master replica as a master replica is altered. The replica catalogue should be in conformity with the master replicas in order to keep track of the up-to-date file information.

Izmailov R. et al. [14] proposed Fast Parallel File Replication (FPFR) for point-to-multipoint transfer. It starts from creating multiple distribution trees and replicates data to multiple sites simultaneously by pipelining point-to-point transfer. It can reduce the total time of replication procedure. One of the problems of FPFR is the pipelining method is file basis. It is good for multiple small files replication. But if the replication dataset is a huge single file, the performance will not enhance so much. The FPFR is named as "N to N" model and compared in our experiments.

In passive coherence problem solving methods, such as HLRC, lazy-copy, or lock mechanism, only partial consistency is achieved. On the other hand, in active methods, such as aggressive-copy or FPFR, full consistency for replica is guaranteed. Compared with each other, access delay time can be reduced by active mechanisms without suffering from long update time during each replica access. In the following section, based on the aggressive copy mechanism, we propose a novel pipeline-based method to enhance the update speed in data grid.

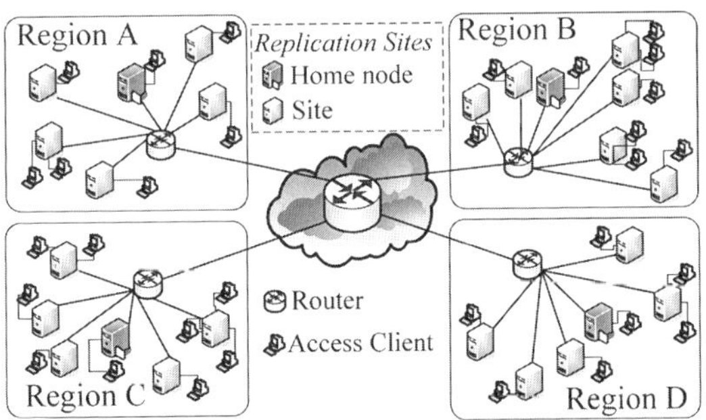

Fig. 1. The network architecture

3 The Greedy Pipeline-Based Aggressive Copy

3.1 Network Architecture

Fig. 1 is an example of network architecture. Several regions are connected together to form the data grid. Each region contains many replication sites. In each region, there is a home node which is used to manage the information of replicas.

3.2 Pipeline Transfer Method

The first part of our method adopts the pipeline concept to improve the update speed. It is inherited from our previous work in [15]. But we are more focusing on optimization in heterogonous environments in this paper. Extend from [15], assume a file with size M has to be transfer to N nodes with/without P-level pipeline transfer method. Here the P-level pipeline means that we cut the update dataset into P blocks to perform a pipeline transfer for each block. If the grid is constructed in a heterogonous environment with different network speed and process overhead at each site. Assume each site i is attached to a speed S_i network and its processing overhead is δ_i. Without pipeline transfer method, the total time T^*_{np} (the lower index "np" means with No-Pipeline process) to finish the process will be:

$$T^*_{np} = \left(\frac{M}{S_1} + \delta_1\right) + \left(\frac{M}{S_2} + \delta_2\right) + \cdots + \left(\frac{M}{S_N} + \delta_N\right) = \sum_{i=1}^{N}\left(\frac{M}{S_i} + \delta_i\right) \tag{1}$$

And for those with P-level pipeline transfer method, we must find out the bottleneck site which causes the longest propagation delay in the environment first. The bottleneck site b can be found using equation (2).

$$\exists site(b) \quad which\ makes \left(\frac{M}{S_b * P} + \delta_b\right) = \left(\max\left(\frac{M}{S_i * P} + \delta_i\right)\middle| \forall i \in N\right) \tag{2}$$

With (2), we can have the total time T^*_p (the lower index "p" means with Pipeline process) to finish the process of P-level pipeline transfer as (3).

$$\begin{aligned} T^*_p &= \left(\frac{M}{S_1 * P} + \delta_1\right) + \left(\frac{M}{S_2 * P} + \delta_2\right) + \cdots + \left(\frac{M}{S_N * P} + \delta_N\right) + \left(\frac{M}{S_b * P} + \delta_b\right) * (P-1) \\ &= \sum_{i=1}^{N}\left(\frac{M}{S_i * P} + \delta_i\right) + \left(\frac{M}{S_b * P} + \delta_b\right) * (P-1) \end{aligned} \tag{3}$$

For proving the pipeline transfer method can have shorter delay in a heterogonous environment, with minus (1) from (3), we can get the equation (4).

$$T^*_p - T^*_{np} = \sum_{i=1}^{N\ except b}\left(\frac{M}{S_i} * \left(\frac{1}{P} - 1\right)\right) + \delta_b * (P-1) \tag{4}$$

Because the applications are data-intensive, the data block transmit time $M/(P*S_i)$ on each hop will always extremely larger then overhead δ_b at the bottleneck. That is

$$M/(P*S_i) >> \delta_b \tag{5}$$

If a proper P, which is an integer greater than 1, can be chosen, and we put (5) into (4), we will get an inequality (6).

$$T_p^* - T_{np}^* = \sum_{i=1}^{N\,except\,b}\left(\frac{M}{S_i}*\left(\frac{1}{P}-1\right)\right) + \delta_b*(P-1) \cong \sum_{i=1}^{N\,except\,b}\left(\frac{M}{S_i}*\left(\frac{1}{P}-1\right)\right) < 0 \tag{6}$$

It proves the pipeline-based aggressive copy can take more advantages then non-pipelined method with proper P.

3.3 The Ordering Problem

In our study, we notice that there is an ordering problem in pipelined-based aggressive copy which will affect the results in data replication. Take a simple network as Fig. 2 for example. If there is a 15Mbytes (120Mbits) file updated in Site 1 and it has to be replicated to Site 2 and Site 3, there are two sequence orders: Site 1 -> Site 2 -> Site 3 and Site 1 -> Site 3 -> Site 2. Assume it is an ideal network and the propagation delays between each site are the same and equal to 1 sec. We ignore the packet process time in each site because it is quite small. A 3-level pipeline transfer is applied to the file. The different sequences will cause different finish time as illustrated in Fig. 3. In Fig. 3 (a), for transferring each block, it takes 2 sec from Site 1 to Site 2, and 4 sec from Site 2 to Site 3. Besides, in Fig. 3 (b), it takes 4 sec for each block transferring from Site 1 to Site 3, and 4 sec from Site 3 to Site 2. Finally, the sequence Site 1 -> Site 2 -> Site 3 finishes at 21 sec and the other sequence Site 1 -> Site 3 -> Site 2 finishes at 23 sec.

In real environments, aggressive copy coherence protocol usually updates a large number of sites. This will make the ordering problem more serious because of the delay accumulation. In order to optimize the sequence of update, we propose a method using the greedy algorithm.

While a region is initiated, all sites will measure the transfer speed with each other. The measure will be performed periodically for updating the current available bandwidth. The transmission time, which is the inverse of measured speed, will transfer to home node to construct the peering transmission time matrix, such as Table 1. Because the connected network may be asymmetric like ADSL, or there may have huge download stream while measuring, the matrix can be non-symmetric. According

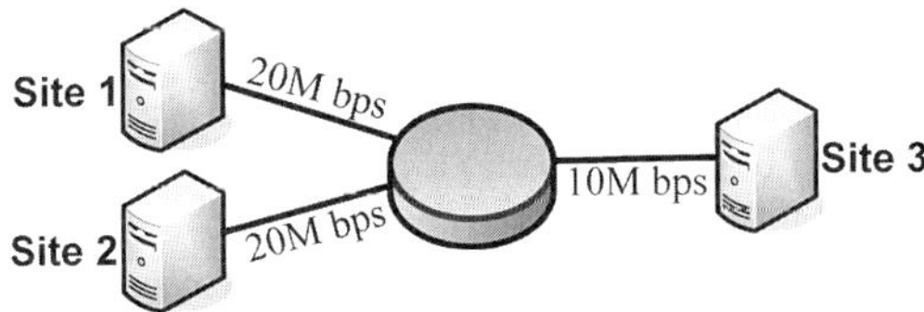

Fig. 2. Simple network

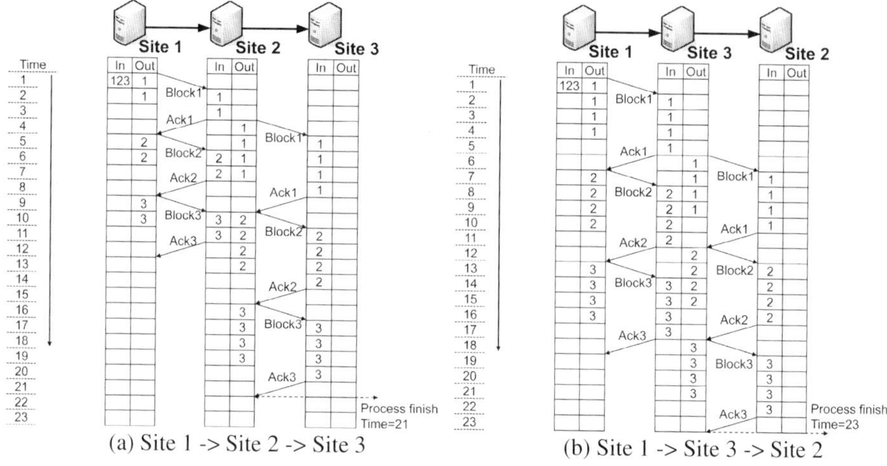

Fig. 3. The effect of different sequences

to this matrix, a home node will calculate an optimized updating path for each node. The sequences will send to each site for their usage.

Take the Table 1 for example. Starting from the Home node (labeled as "*H*" in Table 1 and following), the greedy algorithm will select the shortest transmission time which is the 2 at column "*e*" first. It constructs the *H* -> *e* sequence. Then both row "*H*" and column "*e*" will be pruned and continue the greedy algorithm from row "*e*" with downsized matrix. After a few iterations, the sequence *H* -> *e* -> *a* -> *c* -> *f* -> *d* -> *b* will be setup. If site *c* is the updated server, it will replicate to *H* first than following the *H* -> *e* -> *a* -> *f* -> *d* -> *b* order which discard the original site *c* in the sequence.

Table 1. Peering transmission time matrix

	H	a	b	c	d	e	f
H	X	3	4	5	4	2	2
a	2	X	3	1	4	3	2
b	4	5	X	6	5	5	2
c	2	5	4	X	4	3	3
d	2	3	3	4	X	4	5
e	4	1	3	5	2	X	4
f	4	5	3	4	1	3	X

3.4 The Greedy Pipeline-Based Aggressive Copy

With integrating pipeline method with greedy algorithm, we improve the [15] to a new Greedy Pipeline-based Aggressive Copy (GPAC in brief) protocol. Assume the home node of each region has the information of other regions and sites in its region. The pipeline method is used to construct a new four step fast file transfer structure. As shown in Fig. 4. First, we measure the peering transmission time matrix of cross region home nodes and sites in each region. Second, while a dataset is updated, it will

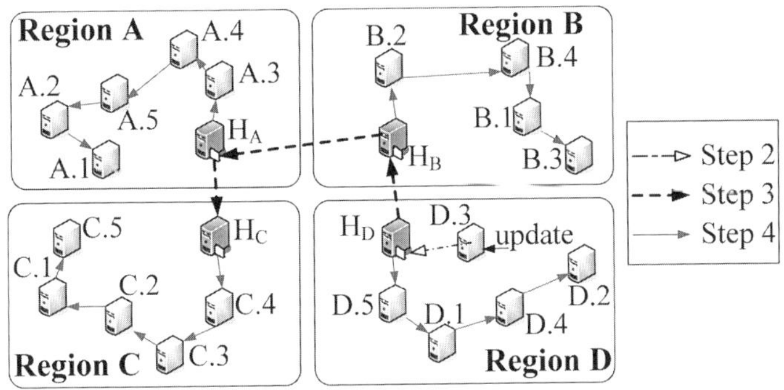

Fig. 4. The transmission in the entire network

cut the dataset into blocks and update its corresponding home node. Third, we update all home nodes one by one with the pipeline update method. Fourth, when a home node is updated, it starts to update other sites in its region respectively. The pipeline method is used in step 4, too. In this way, the replicas in the entire network can be updated quickly.

```
Algorithm GPAC:

Step 1: <initialization>
  1. Probe and define number of blocks to be cut for each
     file
  2. Measure the peering transmission time matrix of
     cross region home nodes and define the home node
     update sequence with the greedy method
  3. Measure the peering transmission time matrix of
     sites in each region and define the update sequences
     of local sites with the greedy method
Step 2: <update site>
  1. Inform corresponding home node
  2. Cut the file into pre-defined pieces
  3. Starts to transfer block by block
  4. When corresponding home node received first block,
     it goes to Step 2.
Step 3: <home nodes replication>
  1. Corresponding home node inform the next home node
     based on the sequence defined by Step 1.2
  2. After each block received, pipeline it to next home
     node
  3. If there is no block to be transferred, go to Step 3
Step 4: <local sites replication>
  1. If it is the corresponding home node of updated
     site, delete the updated site from pipeline sequence
  2. Home node begins to transmit blocks to next site in
     local site sequence generated by Step 1.3
  3. After each block received, pipeline it to next local
     site
  4. Until all processes finish
```

Take Fig. 4 for example. Site *D.3* updates a file. Assume in Step 1.1, the number of blocks is set to 3. In Step 1.2, after measuring and computing the Table 1 liked peering matrix, the home node update sequence is defined as H_D->H_B->H_A->H_C for Home node D. The Step 1.3 will construct the local site sequence H_A->*A.3*->*A.4*->*A.5*->*A.2*->*A.1* in Region A, H_B->*B.2*->*B.4*->*B.1*->*B.3* in Region B, H_C->*C.4*->*C.3*->*C.2*->*C.1*->*C.5* in Region C, and H_D->*D.5*->*D.1*->*D.3*->*D.4*->*D.2* in Region D.

In Step 2.1, H_D will be informed the dataset is being modified. In Step 2.2, *D.3* will split the file into 3 blocks: block1, block2, and block3. In Step 2.3, *D.3* starts to transfer block1 followed by block2 and block3 to H_D. In Step 2.4, when H_D received block1, it goes to Step2.

In Step 3.1, GPAC is performed in H_D->H_B->H_A->H_C. When H_D finished replication process with H_B, it goes to Step 4. So for the other home nodes except the last H_C. Because there is no next home node for H_C, it will goes to Step 4 immediately after it received block1.

In Step 4.1, H_D will delete site *D.3* from the local site sequence in its region. Thus, the local site sequence in region D becomes H_D->*D.5*->*D.1*->*D.4*->*D.2*. This sequence is used in Step 4.2 and Step 4.3 to do local GPAC. H_B, H_A, and H_C will do their local GPAC based on their local site sequence, too. The whole process will be finished in Step 4.4.

4 Experimental Results and Analysis

We implement our GPAC method with greedy algorithm using Globus Toolkit version 4.0 [16][17] and run it on Taiwan Unigrid [18] with two regions. In region 1, there are five servers which are named from uniblade01 to uniblade05. The sites are located in National Tsing Hua University, Taiwan. The region 2 contains six servers which are named from grid1 to grid6. They are placed in National Dong Hwa University, Taiwan. The uniblade01 and grid1 were assigned to be the home node in each region. Two regions are connected via Internet.

4.1 Probing the Network

The Step 1 in the algorithm is used to probe the network status at the beginning.

The Proper Number of Blocks. In Step 1.1, we probe the grid with different updated file size to observe the proper *P* value. The probing result is shown in Fig. 5, we can find that the total transmission time decreases when the number of blocks increased. After the trend curve analysis using quadratic polynomial regression model, we define the pipeline level *P*=8 for our following tests.

Node Sequences. Because our experiment environment has only two home nodes, we can skip Step 1.2. In Step 1.3, both transmission time matrix in region 1 and 2 are measured. For more accurate results, we test the update time of each file for 50 times and average the values. Results are shown in Table 2 and 3. Based on the greedy algorithm, our GPAC method will transfer in the sequence of uniblade01-> uniblade04-> uniblade02-> uniblade05-> uniblade03 in region 1 and grid1 -> grid2 -> grid3 -> grid4 -> grid5 -> grid6 in region 2.

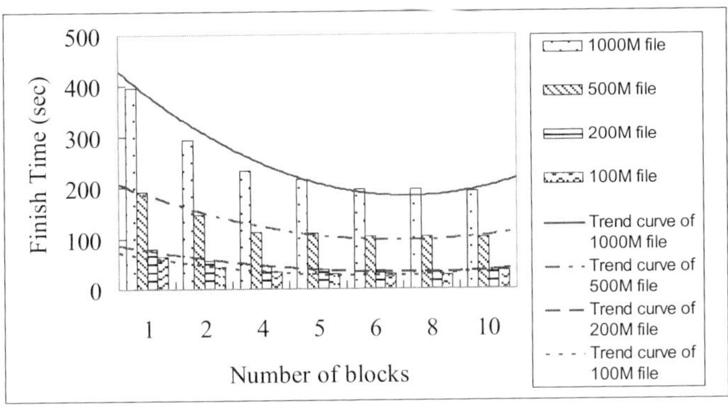

Fig. 5. The blocks-time relation

Table 2. Transmission time matrix in region 1

	uniblade01	uniblade02	uniblade03	uniblade04	uniblade05
uniblade01	X	0.24	0.26	0.22	0.23
uniblade02	0.24	X	0.29	0.20	0.22
uniblade03	0.38	0.41	X	0.37	0.38
uniblade04	0.21	0.20	0.27	X	0.20
uniblade05	0.24	0.28	0.31	0.23	X

Table 3. Transmission time matrix in region 2

	grid1	grid2	grid3	grid4	grid5	grid6
grid1	X	1.16	1.24	1.24	1.25	1.80
grid2	1.09	X	0.93	0.93	0.94	1.65
grid3	1.00	0.95	X	0.96	0.96	1.61
grid4	1.03	0.97	0.97	X	0.98	1.06
grid5	1.04	0.97	0.97	0.9	X	1.65
grid6	1.40	1.35	1.35	1.37	1.35	X

4.2 Comparing the Transmission Speed

In this section, we compare our GPAC method with three different methods described in section 2: 1 to 1, 1 to All, and N to N. 1 to 1 means the file is transferred one site after another sequentially until all relevant sites are updated. It is also the traditional aggressive-copy protocol with linear topology. 1 to All means all sites request the file from one site. It performs traditional aggressive-copy protocol with star topology. N to N means sites will construct a hierarchical structure, and transfer in FPFR manner. Two tests are performed. In the first experiment, we test a smaller scale with only six machines. And in the other, we enable all the servers in our environment. The initial updated server is randomly selected. Different size of dataset 100M, 200M, 500M, and 1000M were tested. Each condition is run 50 times and the results are averaged for more accurate.

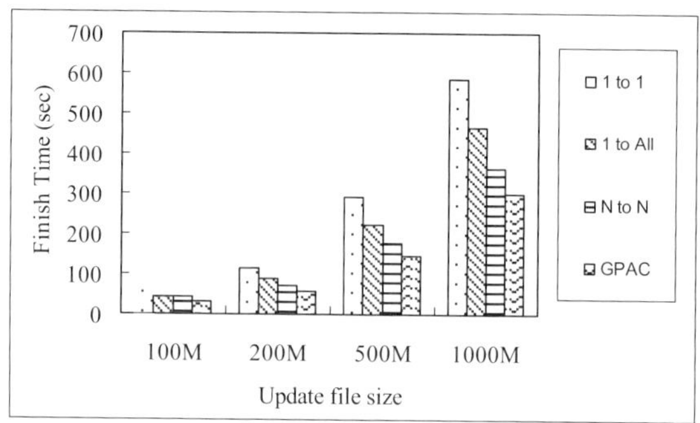

Fig. 6. The update time in local grid

Table 4. The finish time reducing of our GPAC in compare with others in local grid test

Update File Size \ Compared With	1 to 1	1 to All	N to N
100M	50.77%	25.58%	25.58%
200M	49.57%	35.56%	19.44%
500M	49.48%	34.08%	16.48%
1000M	48.72%	35.48%	17.13%

Fig. 6 shows the average results of our first experiment. The 1 to 1 method is the worst and followed by the 1 to All method. The N to N method improves a lot but our GPAC method does better. The finish time reducing of our GPAC in compare with others in this experiment is calculated and summarized in Table 4.

Fig. 7 shows the average results of our second experiment. Because the number of the sites is increased, the update time increases a lot. In the test, because the 1 to all method will transmit file to lot of cross region sites (based on the randomly picked up first updated server), it performs worth than 1 to 1 method which only has one cross region file transfer here. The finish time reducing of our GPAC in compare with others in this experiment is calculated and summarized in Table 5. Our GPAC method is still faster than others.

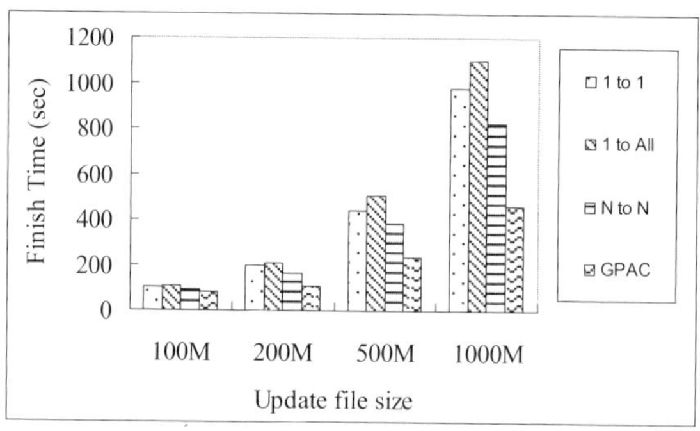

Fig. 7. The update time in cross region grid

Table 5. The finish time reducing of our GPAC in compare with others in cross region grid test

Update File Size \ Compared Method	1 to 1	1 to All	N to N
100M	19.19%	23.81%	13.98%
200M	46.97%	50.00%	34.38%
500M	46.35%	53.56%	38.64%
1000M	49.80%	55.39%	40.44%

5 Conclusions and Future Works

Data replication is necessary in many kinds of grid applications. For data consistency, aggressive copy coherence protocol is a good choice but it costs a lot of time to update all replicas. In this paper, we propose a faster transmission method to update all the files, called Greedy Pipeline-based Aggressive Copy (GPAC).

The GPAC is event driven. When a dataset has to be cohered, the process will pipeline each subset of data one by one. The datasets those have only a read pattern of access will remain unchanged after their first synchronization. Their corresponding home node will take care of their status. The dataset pipelining with block basis and greedy sequencing are the mainly improved in this protocol. While the file cut in GPAC will add additional overhead, the benefits outweigh the overhead. In compared with other three “1 to 1”, “1 to All”, and “N to N” methods, the experimental results show the GPAC can reduce 13.95% - 50.77% finish time in real experiment. This definitely proves that GPAC is a better solution for aggressive copy coherence protocol for data intensive applications.

The other problems which are unsolved in this paper include fault tolerance issue and dynamic peering transmission time matrix measuring. In this version of GPAC, a fail transmit of a dataset block in pipelining may mess up the whole process in replication. Some fault tolerance processes should be added to reduce this effect for practical use. Also, the peering transmission time matrix measuring at the first step can be improved if it can be calculated in coherence process. This can take great benefit not only faster the initiate process but also approach the best solution dynamically if the network condition varies frequently. These are our future works.

Acknowledgements

This research is supported in part by ROC NSC under contract numbers NSC95-2422-H-259-001 and NSC94-2213-E-259-005.

References

1. Foster, I., Kessekman, C.: The Grid: Blueprint for a New Computing Infrastructure. Morgan-Kaufmann, San Francisco, USA (1999)
2. Moore, R., Prince, T.A., Ellisman, M.: Data-intensive Computing and Digital Libraries. Communications of the ACM 41(11), 56–62 (1998)

3. Chervenak, A., Foster, I., Kesselman, C., Salisbury, C., Tuecke, S.: The Data Grid: Towards an Architecture for the Distributed Management and Analysis of Large Scientific Datasets. J. of Network and Computer Applications 23(3), 187–200 (2000)
4. Hoschek, W., Jaen-Martinez, J., Samar, A., Stockinger, H., Stockinger, K.: Data Management in an International Data Grid Project. In: IEEE/ACM Int. Workshop on Grid Computing, London, UK (2000)
5. The EU Data Grid Project: http://www.eu-datagrid.org/
6. LHC: The Large Hardon Collider, http://lhc.web.cern.ch/lhc/
7. Dullmann, D., Hoschek, W., Jaen-Martinez, J., Segal, B.: Models for replica Synchronisation and Consistency in a Data Grid. In: Proc. 10th IEEE Int. High Performance Distributed Computing Symposium, pp. 67–75 (2001)
8. Zhou, Y., Iftode, L., Li, K.: Performance Evaluation of Two Home-Based Lazy Release Consistency Protocols for Shared Virtual Memory Systems. In: Proc. USENIX OSDI (1996)
9. Yun, H., Lee, S., Lee, J., Maeng, S.: An Efficient Lock Protocol for Home-based Lazy Release Consistency. In: Proc. IEEE/ACM Int. Cluster Computing and the Grid Symposium, pp. 527–532 (2001)
10. Domenici, A., Donno, F., Pucciani, G., Stockinger, H., Stockinger, K.: Replica consistency in a Data Grid. Nucl. Instrum. Methods Phys. Res. 534, 24–28 (2004)
11. Sun, Y., Xu, Z.: Grid Replication Coherence Protocol. In: Proc. 18th Int. Parallel and Distributed Processing Symposium, p. 232 (2004)
12. Chang, R.S., Chang, J.S.: Adaptable Replica Consistency Service in Data Grid. In: Proc. 3rd Int. Conf. on Info. Tech.: New Generations, pp. 646–651 (2006)
13. Guy, L., Kunszt, P., Laure, E., Stockinger, H., Stockinger, K.: Replica Management in Data Grids. Technical report, GGF5 Working Draft, Edinburgh, Scotland (2002)
14. Izmailov, R., Ganguly, S., Tu, N.: Fast Parallel File Replication in Data Grid. Future of Grid Data Environments Workshop, GGF - 10, Berlin (2004)
15. Wang, R.C., Wu, S.L., Chang, R.S.: A Novel Data Grid Coference Protocol Using PAC Method. In: Cerin, C., Li., K.C. (eds.) Advances in Grid and Pervasive Computing. LNCS, vol. 4459, pp. 484–495. Springer, New York (2007)
16. The Globus Toolkit version 4, http://www-unix.globus.org/toolkit/docs/4.0/
17. Foster, I.: Globus Toolkit Version 4: Software for Service-Oriented Systems. In: Proc. IFIP Int. Conf. on Network and Parallel Computing, pp. 2–13 (2005)
18. Taiwan UniGrid Project Portal Site: http://www.unigrid.org.tw/

A Performance Comparison of the Contiguous Allocation Strategies in 3D Mesh Connected Multicomputers

Saad Bani-Mohammad[1], Mohamed Ould-Khaoua[1], Ismail Ababneh[2], and Lewis Mackenzie[1]

[1] Department of Computing Science
University of Glasgow, Glasgow G12 8QQ, UK
{saad,mohamed,lewis}@dcs.gla.ac.uk
[2] Department of Computing Science
Al al-Bayt University, Mafraq, Jordan
ismail@aabu.edu.jo

Abstract. The performance of contiguous allocation strategies can be significantly affected by the distribution of job execution times. In this paper, the performance of the existing contiguous allocation strategies for 3D mesh multicomputers is re-visited in the context of heavy-tailed distributions (e.g., a Bounded Pareto distribution). The strategies are evaluated and compared using simulation experiments for both First-Come-First-Served (FCFS) and Shortest-Service-Demand (SSD) scheduling strategies under a variety of system loads and system sizes. The results show that the performance of the allocation strategies degrades considerably when job execution times follow a heavy-tailed distribution. Moreover, SSD copes much better than FCFS scheduling strategy in the presence of heavy-tailed job execution times. The results also show that the strategies that depend on a list of allocated sub-meshes for both allocation and deallocation have lower allocation overhead and deliver good system performance in terms of average turnaround time and mean system utilization.

1 Introduction

The mesh has been one of the most common networks for recent multicomputers due to its simplicity, scalability, structural regularity, and ease of implementation [1, 6, 12]. Meshes are suited to a variety of applications including matrix computation, image processing and problems whose task graphs can be embedded naturally into the topology [25].

Efficient processor allocation and job scheduling are critical to harnessing the full computing power of a multicomputer [1, 4, 5, 28]. The goal of job scheduling is to select the next job to be executed while the goal of processor allocation is to select the set of processors on which parallel jobs are executed [1].

In distributed memory multicomputers, jobs are allocated distinct contiguous processor sub-meshes for the duration of their execution [1, 4, 5, 6, 7, 12, 28, 29]. Most existing research studies [1, 4, 6, 11, 12, 29] on contiguous allocation have been carried out mostly in the context of the 2D mesh network. There has been relatively

I. Stojmenovic et al. (Eds.): ISPA 2007, LNCS 4742, pp. 645–656, 2007.

very little work on the 3D version of the mesh. Although the 2D mesh has been used in a number of parallel machines, such as iWARP [2] and Delta Touchstone [8], most practical multicomputers, like the Cray XT3 [3], Cray T3D [19], and the IBM BlueGene/L [14], have used the 3D mesh and torus as the underlying network topology due to its lower diameter and average communication distance [27].

Most existing contiguous allocation strategies for the 3D mesh, mainly the early ones, have time complexities that grow linearly with the size of the mesh [5, 7, 28]. The recent contiguous allocation strategies have time complexities that can be less sensitive to the size of the mesh [20, 23]. They build lists of the busy sub-meshes with the goal of achieving time complexities that depend on the number of allocated sub-meshes instead of the mesh size [20, 23]. Time complexities in $O(m^2)$, where m is the number of allocated sub-meshes in the busy list, were achieved [20, 23]. An advantage of the busy-list approach is that the list of busy sub-meshes is often small even when the mesh size becomes large, which decreases the allocation overhead.

The efficacy of most contiguous allocation strategies has been assessed under the assumption of exponentially distributed execution times [4, 5, 6, 7, 11, 12, 20, 23, 28, 29], which may not reflect all possible practical scenarios. For instance, a number of measurement studies [9, 15, 16, 17, 26] have convincingly shown that the execution times of many computational jobs are characterised by heavy-tailed execution times; that is, there are typically many short jobs, and fewer long jobs. Heavy-tailed distributions capture this variability and behave quite differently from the distributions more commonly used to evaluate the performance of allocation strategies (e.g., the exponential distribution). In particular, when sampling random variables that follow heavy-tailed distributions, the probability of large observations occurring is non-negligible.

In this paper, the performance of the existing contiguous allocation strategies for 3D mesh-connected multicomputers is revisited in the context of heavy-tailed job execution times. Existing strategies were typically evaluated with the assumption of First-Come-First-Served (FCFS) job scheduling. In this paper, a Shortest-Service-Demand (SSD) scheduling strategy is also used because it is expected to reduce performance loss due to blocking. This strategy was found to improve performance significantly [10, 21, 22]. Also in this paper, the performance of allocation strategies is measured in terms of usual performance parameters [4, 5, 6, 7, 20, 21, 22, 23, 24, 28, 29] such as the average turnaround time and mean system utilization. Algorithmic efficiency is measured in terms of the mean measured allocation overhead that allocation and deallocation operations take per job. The results show that the performance of the allocation strategies degrades when the distribution of job execution times is heavy-tailed. As a consequence, an appropriate scheduling strategy should be adopted to deal with heavy-tailed execution times. Our analysis reveals that the SSD scheduling strategy exhibits superior performance than the FCFS scheduling strategy in terms of average turnaround time and mean system utilization.

The rest of the paper is organised as follows. The following section contains relevant preliminaries. Section 3 contains a brief overview of the allocation strategies compared in this study. Section 4 contains a brief overview of the scheduling strategies considered. Simulation results are presented in Section 5, and Section 6 concludes this paper.

2 Preliminaries

The target system is a $W \times D \times H$ 3D mesh, where W is the width of the cubic mesh, D its depth and H its height. Each processor is denoted by a coordinate triple (x, y, z), where $0 \le x < W$, $0 \le y < D$ and $0 \le z < H$ [24]. A processor is connected by bidirectional communication links to its neighbour processors. The following definitions have been adopted from [4, 24].

Definition 1. *A sub-mesh $S(w,d,h)$ of width w, depth d, and height h, where $0 < w \le W$, $0 < d \le D$ and $0 < h \le H$ is specified by the coordinates (x, y, z) and (x', y', z'), where (x, y, z) are the coordinates of the base of the sub-mesh and (x', y', z') are the coordinates of its end, as shown in Fig. 1.*

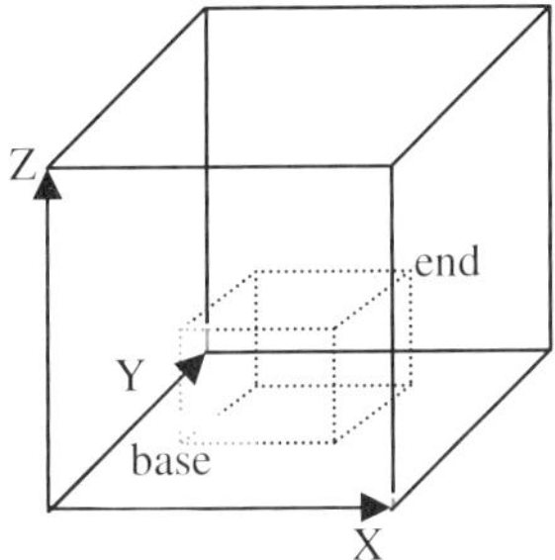

Fig. 1. A sub-mesh inside the 3D mesh

Definition 2. *The size of $S(w,d,h)$ is $w \times d \times h$.*

Definition 3. *An allocated sub-mesh is one whose processors are all allocated to a parallel job.*

Definition 4. *A free sub-mesh is one whose processors are all unallocated.*

Definition 5. *The list of all sub-meshes that are currently allocated to jobs and are not available for allocation to other jobs is called the busy list.*

Definition 6. *A prohibited region is a region consisting of nodes that can not be used as base nodes for the requested sub-mesh.*

Definition 7. *The Right Border Plane (RBP) of a sub-mesh $S(x_1, y_1, z_1, x_2, y_2, z_2)$ with respect to a job $J(\alpha \times \beta \times \gamma)$ is defined as the collection of nodes with address $(x_2 + 1, y', z')$ where $\max(y_1 - \beta + 1, 0) \le y' \le y_2$ and $\max(z_1 - \gamma + 1, 0) \le z' \le z_2$. A RBP of sub-mesh S is a plane located just off the right boundary of S.*

3 Processors Allocation Strategies

Contiguous allocation has been investigated for 2D and 3D mesh-connected multicomputers [1, 4, 5, 6, 7, 11, 12, 28, 29]. The main shortcoming of the very few existing contiguous allocation strategies for the 3D mesh is that they achieve complete sub-mesh recognition capability with high allocation overhead. Below we describe some of the strategies that have been proposed for the 3D mesh.

First Fit (FF) and Best Fit (BF): In these two strategies [7], the free sub-meshes are scanned and FF allocates the first sub-mesh that is large enough to hold the job, whereas BF allocates the smallest suitable sub-mesh. Simulation results have shown that these two strategies have comparable performance in terms of average turnaround time and mean scheduling effectiveness; the performance of FF is close to that of BF, therefore we only consider the FF strategy for comparison in this paper. The strategies FF and BF are not recognition-complete. An allocation request is allocatable only if there is a large enough sub-mesh with the same orientation as the allocation request. Bit arrays are used for the scanning of available processors.

Turning First Fit (TFF) and Turning Best Fit (TBF): The problem of missing an existing possible allocation explained above is solved using TFF and TBF allocation strategies [7]. In these two strategies, turning the allocation request is used to improve the performance of contiguous FF and BF allocation in 3D mesh. The TFF and TBF allocation algorithms support the rotation of the job request. Let (a,b,c) be the width, depth and height of a sub-mesh allocation request. The six permutations (a,b,c), (a,c,b), (b,a,c), (b,c,a), (c,a,b) and (c,b,a) are, in turn, considered for allocation using the allocation strategy. If allocation succeeds for any of these permutations the process stops. For example, assume a free mesh (3, 3, 2) and the job requests (2, 3, 2) and (3, 2, 1) arrive in this order. The second job request cannot be allocated until it is rotated to (1, 3, 2). Simulation results have shown that the TFF strategy can greatly improve performance in terms of average turnaround time and mean scheduling effectiveness. Changing the orientation of allocation requests can alleviate external fragmentation. Moreover, the performance of TFF is almost identical to that of TBF; therefore the TFF strategy is considered for comparison in this paper. In [7], different scheduling strategies, such as First-Come-First-Served (FCFS) and Out-of-Order (OO) have been studied to avoid potential performance loss due to blocking.

The allocation and deallocation times of the algorithms proposed in [7] depend on the number of processors in the mesh system, n. The time complexity of the allocation algorithm is in $O(n^2)$, and the deallocation algorithm has time complexity in $O(n)$.

Busy List (BL) and Turning Busy List (TBL): In these strategies [20, 23], allocation is based on maintaining a busy list of allocated sub-meshes. The list is scanned to determine all prohibited regions. The prohibited region of job $J(\alpha\times\beta\times\gamma)$ with respect to an allocated sub-mesh $S(x_1, y_1, z_1, x_2, y_2, z_2)$ is defined as the sub-mesh represented by the address $(x', y', z', x_2, y_2, z_2)$, where $x' = \max(x_1-\alpha+1, 0)$, $y' = \max(y_1-\beta+1, 0)$ and $z' = \max(z_1-\gamma+1, 0)$. The sub-meshes $(W-\alpha+1, 0, 0, W-1, D-1, H-1)$, $(0, D-\beta+1, 0, W-1, D-1, H-1)$, and $(0, 0, H-\gamma+1, W-1, D-1, H-1)$ are automatically not available for accommodating the base node of a free $\alpha \times \beta \times \gamma$ sub-mesh for $J(\alpha \times \beta \times \gamma)$, whether the nodes in these sub-meshes are free or not; otherwise, the sub-mesh would grow out of the corresponding mesh boundary plane (rightmost, deepest and highest planes) of $M(W, D, H)$. These three sub-meshes are called automatic prohibited regions of $J(\alpha \times \beta \times \gamma)$ and must always be excluded during the sub-mesh allocation process. A job $J(\alpha \times \beta \times \gamma)$ is allocatable if there exists at least one node that does not belong to any of the prohibited regions and the three automatic prohibited regions of $J(\alpha \times \beta \times \gamma)$.

All prohibited regions that result from the allocated sub-meshes are subtracted from each RBP of the allocated sub-meshes to determine the nodes that can be used as base nodes for the required sub-mesh size. Simulation results have shown that the performance of the allocation strategy in [20, 23] is at least as good as that of the existing allocation strategies. Moreover, the mean measured allocation time of these strategies is much lower than that of the existing strategies. The results have also revealed that the rotation of the job request improves the performance of the contiguous allocation strategies.

The allocation and deallocation times of the algorithms proposed in [20, 23] depend on the number of elements in the busy list, m. The time complexity of the allocation algorithms is in $O(m^2)$, and the deallocation algorithm has time complexity in $O(m)$. These allocation strategies maintain a busy list of m allocated sub-meshes. Thus, the space complexity of the allocation algorithms is in $O(m)$. This space requirement is small compared to the improvement in performance in terms of allocation overhead, as we will see in the simulation results. Also, this space requirement is small compared to the space requirement of FF, BF, TFF and TBF, which is in $O(n)$. An array is used for storing the allocation states of processors.

The time and space complexities of the allocation and deallocation algorithms considered in this paper are summarized in Table 1. Notice that the strategies that depend on a list of allocated sub-meshes for both allocation and de-allocation can entail smaller time complexity because m does not always depend on the size of the mesh for both allocation and deallocation. For job size distributions typically assumed in simulation studies (e.g., the uniform distribution used in [18]), the number of allocated sub-meshes remains small as the size of the mesh increases.

Table 1. Time and Space Complexity for Allocation and Deallocation Algorithms

Algorithm	Allocation Complexity	Deallocation Complexity	Space Complexity
TBL/BL	$O(m^2)$	$O(m)$	$O(m)$
TFF/FF	$O(n^2)$	$O(n)$	$O(n)$

m : Number of allocated sub-meshes in the busy list.
n : Total number of processors in the mesh.

4 Job Scheduling Strategies

The order in which jobs are scheduled first can have a considerable effect on the performance. In FCFS scheduling strategy, the allocation request that arrived first is considered for allocation first. Allocation attempts stop when they fail for the current FIFO queue head, while in SSD scheduling strategy, the job with the shortest service demand is scheduled first [10, 21, 22]. Any of them can start execution if its allocation request can be satisfied. Job scheduling has substantial effect on the performance of the allocation strategies. In [21, 22], the authors showed that the effect of the SSD scheduling strategy on the performance of the allocation strategies is substantially better than that of the FCFS scheduling strategy.

The performance of contiguous allocation strategies compared can be significantly affected by both a distribution adopted for job execution times and the scheduling strategy. To illustrate this, the performance of allocation strategies in this paper is evaluated in the context of heavy-tailed job execution time under both FCFS and SSD scheduling strategies. SSD scheduling strategy should be adopted to deal with heavy-tailed job execution times and to avoid potential performance loss due to blocking.

5 Simulation Results

Extensive simulation experiments have been carried out to compare the performance of the allocation strategies considered in this paper, with and without change of request orientation. Switching request orientation has been used in [5, 7, 20, 23, 28].

We have implemented the allocation and deallocation algorithms, including the busy list routines, in the C language, and integrated the software into the ProcSimity simulation tool for processor allocation in highly parallel systems [10, 18].

The target mesh is cube with width W, depth D and height H. Jobs are assumed to have exponential inter-arrival times. They are scheduled using First-Come-First-Served (FCFS) and Shortest-Service-Demand (SSD) scheduling strategies. The FCFS scheduling strategy is chosen because it is fair and it is widely used in other similar studies [6, 11, 12, 20, 21, 22, 23, 24], while the SSD scheduling strategy is used to avoid potential performance loss due to blocking [21, 22]. The execution times are modeled by a Bounded Pareto [13] (exhibiting a heavy-tailed property) as follows:

$$f(x) = \frac{\alpha k^{\alpha}}{1-(k/q)^{\alpha}} x^{-\alpha-1} (k \le x \le q)$$

where k and q are the lower and upper limit of job execution time, and α is a parameter that reflects the variability of job execution time. In the experiments, these parameters are set to: $k = 15.0$, $q = 4241.0$, and $\alpha = 1.0$ as suggested in [13].

Uniform distribution is used to generate the width, depth and height of job requests. The uniform distribution is used over the range from 1 to the mesh side length, where the width, depth and height of the job requests are generated independently. This distribution has often been used in the literature [1, 4, 6, 7, 11, 12, 20, 21, 22, 23, 24, 28, 29]. Each simulation run consists of one thousand completed jobs. Simulation results are averaged over enough independent runs so that the confidence level is 95% that relative errors are below 5% of the means. The main performance parameters observed are the average turnaround time of jobs, mean system utilization and average allocation overhead. The turnaround time is the time that a parallel job spends in the mesh from arrival to departure. The utilization is the percentage of processors that are utilized over time. The allocation overhead is the time that the allocation algorithm takes for allocation and deallocation operations per job. The independent variable in the simulation is the system load. The system load is defined as the inverse of the mean inter-arrival time of jobs.

The notation <allocation strategy>(<scheduling strategy>) is used to represent the strategies in the performance figures. For example, TBL(SSD) refers to the Turning Busy List allocation strategy under the scheduling strategy Shortest-Service-Demand.

Figure 2 depicts the average turnaround time of the allocation strategies (TBL, TFF, BL, and FF) for the heavy-tailed and exponential job execution times under FCFS scheduling strategy. The simulation results in this figure are presented for a heavy system load. It can be seen in this figure that the performance of the allocation strategies degrades when the distribution of job execution times is heavy-tailed. For example, the average turnaround time of TBL(FCFS) under exponential job execution time is 49% of the average turnaround time of TBL(FCFS) under heavy-tailed job execution time, therefore, the SSD strategy should be adopted to deal with heavy-tailed job execution times as it avoids performance loss due FCFS blocking.

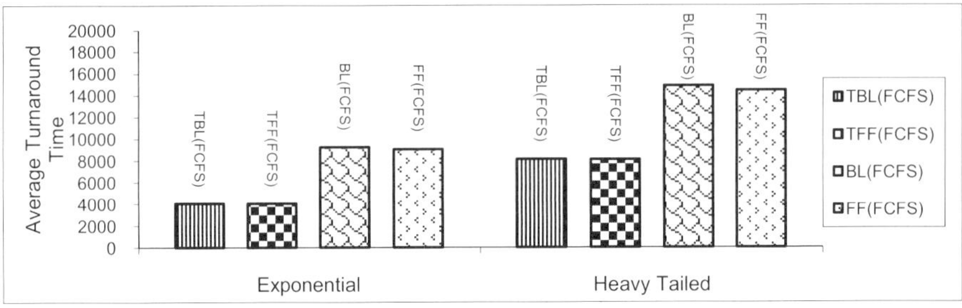

Fig. 2. Average turnaround time in BL, FF, TBL, and TFF under the exponential and heavy-tailed job execution times with FCFS scheduling strategy in an $8 \times 8 \times 8$ mesh

In Figure 3, the average turnaround time of jobs is plotted against the system load for both scheduling strategies considered in this paper. It can be seen in the figure that the strategies with rotation under SSD strategy (TBL(SSD) and TFF(SSD)) have almost identical performance, and that they are superior to all other strategies. They are followed, in order, by the strategies BL(SSD), FF(SSD), TBL(FCFS), TFF(FCFS), BL(FCFS), and FF(FCFS). When compared to TBL(SSD) and TFF(SSD), BL(SSD) increases the average turnaround times by about 31% and 57% for the loads 0.025 and 0.105 jobs/time unit, respectively. It can also be seen in the figure that the average turnaround times of the strategies that depend on the busy list is very close to that of the strategies that depend on the number of processors in the mesh system. For example, the average turnaround time of TBL(SSD) is very close to that of TFF(SSD). However, the time complexity of the strategies that depend on the busy list (TBL and BL) is in $O(m^2)$ [20, 23], whereas it is in $O(n^2)$ for the other strategies (TFF and FF) [7]. The time complexity of TBL and BL does not grow with the size of the mesh as in TFF and FF. It can also be seen in the figure that the average turnaround time of the strategies with rotation is substantially superior to the strategies without rotation because it is highly likely that a suitable contiguous sub-mesh is available for allocation to a job when request rotation is allowed. It can also be noticed in the figure that the SSD strategy is much better than the FCFS strategy. This finding demonstrates that the scheduling and allocation strategies both have substantial effect on the performance of allocation strategies in the 3D mesh.

In Figure 4, the mean system utilization of the allocation strategies is plotted against the system loads for the two scheduling strategies considered in this paper. In this figure, TBL(SSD) and TFF(SSD) again have almost identical performance, and they are slightly superior to the other strategies. Also, these results show that switching request orientation improves performance substantially. This is indicated by the largely superior mean system utilization of the strategies that can switch the orientation of allocation requests (TBL(SSD), TBL(FCFS), TFF(SSD), and TFF(FCFS)) when they are compared to the strategies without rotation (BL(SSD), BL(FCFS), FF(SSD), FF(FCFS)). Moreover, the contiguous allocation strategies with rotation under SSD scheduling strategy achieve system utilization of 52%, but the contiguous allocation strategies without rotation can not exceed 42%. Also, higher system utilization is achievable under heavy loads because the waiting queue is filled very early, allowing each allocation strategy to reach its upper limits of utilization.

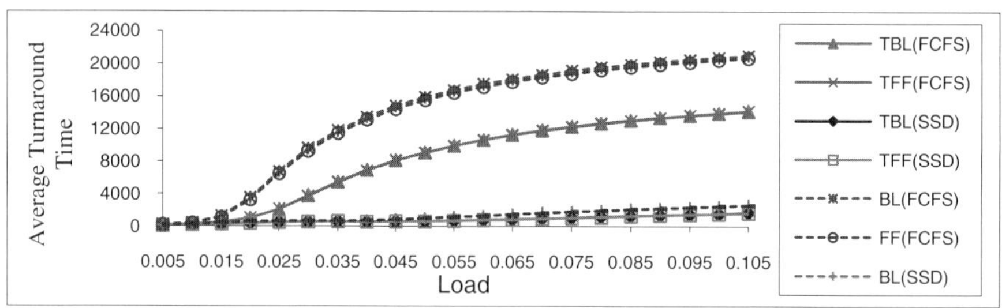

Fig. 3. Average turnaround time vs. system load in BL, FF, TBL, and TFF under the FCFS and SSD scheduling strategies in an $8 \times 8 \times 8$ mesh

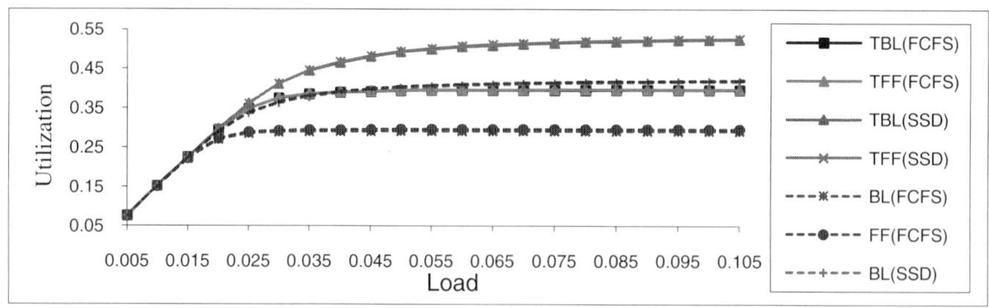

Fig. 4. Mean System utilization in BL, FF, TBL, and TFF under the FCFS and SSD scheduling strategies in an $8 \times 8 \times 8$ mesh

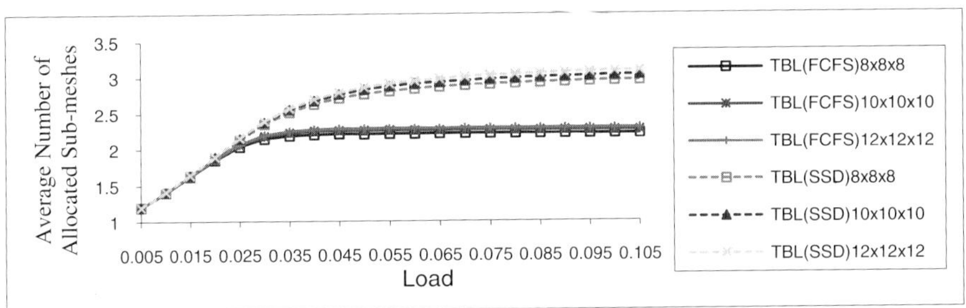

Fig. 5. Average number of allocated sub-meshes (m) in TBL under the FCFS and SSD scheduling strategies in $8 \times 8 \times 8$ mesh, $10 \times 10 \times 10$, and $12 \times 12 \times 12$ mesh

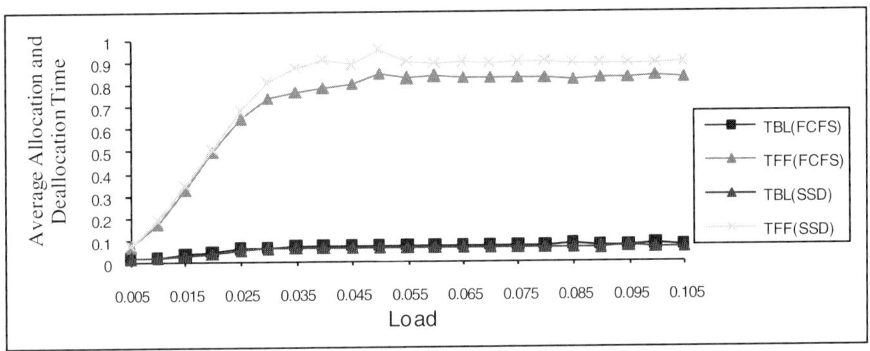

Fig. 6. Average allocation and deallocation times in TBL and TFF under the FCFS and SSD scheduling strategies in an $8 \times 8 \times 8$ mesh

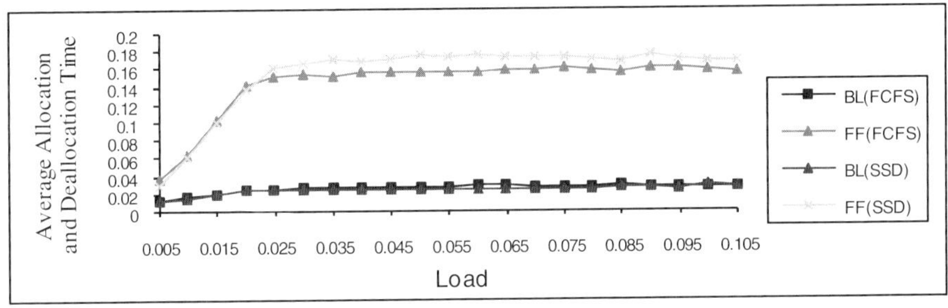

Fig. 7. Average allocation and deallocation times in BL and FF under the FCFS and SSD scheduling strategies in an $8 \times 8 \times 8$ mesh

In Figure 5, the average number of allocated sub-meshes (m) in TBL is plotted against the system load for different mesh sizes under both FCFS and SSD scheduling strategies. It can be seen in the figure that the average number of allocated sub-meshes (m) is much lower than the number of processors in the mesh system (n). It can also be seen in the figure that for larger mesh sizes, the results show that m does not grow with n. It can also be noticed in the figure that the average number of allocated sub-meshes under SSD is higher than that under FCFS. In SSD, the job with the shortest service demand is scheduled first, meaning that allocation and deallocation operations are more numerous resulting in more allocated sub-meshes in the busy list.

Figures 6 and 7 show the average allocation and deallocation time (allocation overhead) for the allocation strategies against the job arrival rate in an $8 \times 8 \times 8$ mesh under the two scheduling strategies FCFS and SSD. We observe that the strategies that depend on the busy list (TBL, BL) take much smaller allocation overhead than the strategies that depend on the number of processors in the mesh system (TFF, FF) under both FCFS and SSD scheduling strategies. In Figure 6, for example, the time needed to carry out the allocation and deallocation operations of TBL(FCFS) strategy is 9% of the time taken by these operations in TFF(FCFS) strategy under the arrival rate 0.075 jobs/time unit. It can also be seen in the figures that the time needed for both allocation and deallocation for the strategies with rotation is higher than that of the strategies without rotation because in the worst case, the allocation process for the strategies with rotation, is repeated for all possible permutations (six permutations) of the job request while this process is repeated only one time for the other strategies. Moreover, it can be seen in the figures that the difference in allocation time gets much more significant as the system load increases. Thus, the strategies which depend on the busy list for both allocation and deallocation can be said to be more effective than the strategies that depend on the number of processors in the mesh system.

6 Conclusion and Future Directions

We have compared the performance of contiguous processor allocation strategies proposed for 3D mesh connected multicomputer for a wide range of system load and system sizes when the distribution of job execution times is heavy-tailed (e.g. Bounded Pareto distribution). These allocation strategies cover a wide range of choices, including traditional First Fit (FF), Turning First Fit (TFF), Busy List (BL) approach that maintains a list of allocated sub-meshes to determine the regions consisting of nodes that cannot be used as base nodes for the requested sub-meshes, and Turning Bust List strategy (TBL), that attempts to maintain a good performance in terms of utilization, turnaround time, and allocation overhead.

In this study, the allocation overhead (i.e., allocation and deallocation time) is taken into account. A new scheduling strategies (SSD) has been used to deal with heavy-tailed job execution times to avoid performance loss due to blocking that results from largest jobs.

Simulation results have shown that the TBL(SSD) strategy is superior overall to all other strategies. It is as effective as the best competitor TFF(SSD) strategy, yet it is substantially more efficient. Moreover, the results have shown that the performance of the allocation strategies that depend on the number of allocated sub-meshes in the busy list (TBL and BL) is at least as good as that of the allocation strategies that depend on the number of processors in the mesh system in terms of average turnaround time and mean system utilization. The results have also shown that, the average allocation and deallocation time of the strategies that depend on the bust list (TBL and BL) is much lower than that of the other strategies that depend on, for both allocation and deallocation, the number of processors in the mesh system (TFF and

FF). The results have also revealed that the rotation of the job request can greatly improve the performance of the contiguous allocation strategies. Moreover, the simulation results have shown that the effects of the SSD scheduling strategy on the performance of the allocation strategies is substantially better than that of the FCFS scheduling strategy in terms of performance parameters used in this study.

The busy list strategies (TBL and BL) can be efficient because it is implemented using a busy list approach. This approach can be expected to be efficient in practice because job sizes typically grow with the size of the mesh. The length of the busy list can be expected to be small, even when the size of the mesh scales up.

As a continuation of this research in the future, it would be interesting to implement the allocation strategies based on real workload traces from different parallel machines and compare it with our results obtained by means of simulations.

References

[1] Yoo, B.-S., Das, C.-R.: A Fast and Efficient Processor Allocation Scheme for Mesh-Connected Multicomputers. IEEE Transactions on Parallel & Distributed Systems 51(1), 46–60 (2002)

[2] Peterson, C., Sutton, J., Wiley, P.: iWARP: a 100-MPOS, LIW microprocessor for multicomputers. IEEE Micro 11(3), 26–29, 81-87 (1991)

[3] Cray: Cray XT3 Datasheet (2004)

[4] Chiu, G.-M., Chen, S.-K.: An efficient submesh allocation scheme for two-dimensional meshes with little overhead. IEEE Transactions on Parallel & Distributed Systems 10(5), 471–486 (1999)

[5] Choo, H., Yoo, S., Youn, H.-Y.: Processor scheduling and allocation for 3D torus multicomputer systems. IEEE Transactions on Parallel & Distributed Systems 11(5), 475–484 (2000)

[6] Ababneh, I.: An Efficient Free-list Submesh Allocation Scheme for two-dimensional mesh-connected multicomputers. Journal of Systems and Software 79(8), 1168–1179 (2006)

[7] Ababneh, I.: Job scheduling and contiguous processor allocation for three-dimensional mesh multicomputers. AMSE Advances in Modelling & Analysis 6(4), 43–58 (2001)

[8] Intel Corporation: A Touchstone DELTA system description (1991)

[9] Wei, J., Zhou, X., Xu, C-Z.: Robust Processing Rate Allocation for Proportional Slowdown Differentiation on Internet Servers. IEEE Transactions on Computers 54(8), 964–977 (2005)

[10] Windisch, K., Miller, J.V., Lo, V.: ProcSimity: an experimental tool for processor allocation and scheduling in highly parallel systems. In: Proceedings of the Fifth Symposium on the Frontiers of Massively Parallel Computation (Frontiers'95), Washington, DC, USA, pp. 414–421. IEEE Computer Society Press, Los Alamitos (1995)

[11] Seo, K.-H.: Fragmentation-Efficient Node Allocation Algorithm in 2D Mesh-Connected Systems. In: Proceedings of the 8th International Symposium on Parallel Architecture, Algorithms and Networks (ISPAN'05), pp. 318–323. IEEE Computer Society Press, Los Alamitos (2005)

[12] Seo, K.-H., Kim, S.-C.: Improving system performance in contiguous processor allocation for mesh-connected parallel systems. The Journal of Systems and Software 67(1), 45–54 (2003)

[13] He, L., Jarvis, S., Spooner, D., Jiang, H., Dillenberger, D., Nudd, G.: Allocating Non-Real-Time and Soft Real-Time Jobs in Multiclusters. IEEE Transactions on Parallel and Distributed Systems 17(2), 99–112 (2006)

[14] Blumrich, M., Chen, D., Coteus, P., Gara, A., Giampapa, M., Heidelberger, P., Singh, S., Steinmacher-Burow, B., Takken, T., Vranas, P.: Design and Analysis of the BlueGene/L Torus Interconnection Network, IBM Research Report RC23025, IBM Research Division, Thomas J. Watson Research Center (December 3, 2003)

[15] Harchol-Balter, M.: The Effect of Heavy-Tailed Job Size Distributions on Computer System Design. In: Proceedings of ASA-IMS Conference on Applications of Heavy Tailed Distributions in Economics, Engineering and Statistics, Washington, DC (June 1999)

[16] Crovella, M.E., Lipsky, L.: Long-Lasting Transient Conditions in Simulations with Heavy-Tailed Workloads. In: Proceedings of the 1997 Winter Simulation Conference, December 7-10, pp. 1005–1012 (1997)

[17] Harchol-Balter, M., Crovella, M.E., Murta, C.D.: On Choosing a Task Assignment Policy for a Distributed Server System. Journal of Parallel and Distributed Computing 59(2), 204–228 (1999)

[18] ProcSimity V4.3 User's Manual: University of Oregon (1997)

[19] Kessler, R.E., Swarszmeier, J.L.: Cray T3D: a new dimension for Cray research. In: Proc. CompCon., pp. 176–182 (1993)

[20] Bani-Mohammad, S., Ould-Khaoua, M., Ababneh, I., Mackhenzie, L.M.: An Efficient Turning Busy List Sub-mesh Allocation Strategy for 3D Mesh Connected Multicomputers. In: Proceedings of the 7th Annual PostGraduate Symposium on the Convergence of Telecommunications, Networking & Broadcasting (PGNET, Liverpool John Moores University, UK, June 26-27, 2006, pp. 37–43 (2006)

[21] Bani-Mohammad, S., Ould-Khaoua, M., Ababneh, I., Mackhenzie, L.M.: An Efficient Processor Allocation Strategy that Maintains a High Degree of Contiguity among Processors in 2D Mesh Connected Multicomputers, 2007. In: ACS/IEEE International Conference on Computer Systems and Applications (AICCSA 2007), Amman, Jordan, 13-16 May. IEEE Computer Society Press, Los Alamitos (2007)

[22] Bani-Mohammad, S., Ould-Khaoua, M., Ababneh, I., Machenzie, L.: A Fast and Efficient Processor Allocation Strategy which Combines a Contiguous and Non-contiguous Processor Allocation Algorithms. Technical Report; TR-2007-229, DCS Technical Report Series, University of Glasgow (January 2007)

[23] Bani-Mohammad, S., Ould-Khaoua, M., Ababneh, I., Machenzie, L.: A Fast and Efficient Strategy for Sub-mesh Allocation with Minimal Allocation Overhead in 3D Mesh Connected Multicomputers. Ubiquitous Computing and Communication Journal 1 (2006) ISSN 1992-8424

[24] Bani-Mohammad, S., Ould-Khaoua, M., Ababneh, I., Machenzie, L.: Non-contiguous Processor Allocation Strategy for 2D Mesh Connected Multicomputers Based on Sub-meshes Available for Allocation. In: Proceedings of the 12th International Conference on Parallel and Distributed Systems (ICPADS'06), Minneapolis, Minnesota, USA, vol. 2, pp. 41–48. IEEE Computer Society Press, Los Alamitos (2006)

[25] Varavithya, V.: Multicasting in wormhole routed multicomputers, Ph.D. Thesis, Department of Electrical and Computer Engineering, Iowa State University (1998)

[26] Tabatabaee, V., Tiwari, A., Hollingsworth, J.K.: Parallel Parameter Tuning for Applications with Performance Variability. In: SC 2005 (2005)

[27] Athas, W., Seitz, C.: Multicomputers: message-passing concurrent computers. IEEE Computer 21(8), 9–24 (1988)

[28] Qiao, W., Ni, L.: Efficient processor allocation for 3D tori, Technical Report, Michigan State University, East Lansing, MI, 48824-1027 (1994)

[29] Zhu, Y.: Efficient processor allocation strategies for mesh-connected parallel computers. Journal of Parallel and Distributed Computing 16(4), 328–337 (1992)

An Enhanced Approach for PDA and Cellular Clients to Submit and Monitor Applications in the Mobile Grid

Vinicius C.M. Borges, Anubis G.M. Rossetto, Frank J. Knaesel, and Mario A.R. Dantas

Federal University of Santa Catarina (UFSC),
Department of Informatics and Statistics (INE),
Laboratory of Research in Distributed Systems (LaPeSD),
88040-900 Florianopolis - SC, Brazil
{vcunha,anubis,fknaesel,mario}@inf.ufsc.br

Abstract. Some challenges in the mobile grid environments are not handled by some related works, for example, adapting to heterogeneous interfaces of different mobile devices (PDAs and cellular) for submission and monitoring of applications in grid environments. This article presents an approach that employs the workflow concept for providing automated and adapted features for executing applications in grid mobile configurations. The approach, coined as SuMMIT, enabled to consume less battery energy of PDAs and more agility for submitting and monitoring applications in comparison with some related works. In addition, the SuMMIT environment provides an execution flow adjustment, in case of disconnection, matching requirements of submitted application and options defined by the user. The SuMMIT also has adapted and optimized characteristics according to some limitations and problems found in different devices.

1 Introduction

Limitations usually found in mobile devices impose great difficulties to provide to users an option for solve complex problems when using these devices. The infrastructure of mobile grid [1, 2, 3] integrates mobile devices with the grid environment. It is important to point out that the use of mobile devices in grid environments may have two interaction aspects [1, 2]: devices are considered as users of grid resources (interfaces) or as grid resources. The computing power of mobile devices has presenting a growing rate of improvements in the last years. However, the actual processing capacity and storage still does not enable the resolution of complex problems inside these devices. Therefore, in our research work, devices are considered as users of resources.

The majority of researches [2, 3, 4, 5] only allow submission and monitoring features of a task per time from a specific device. Therefore, users can submit tasks in an inappropriate order for solving a problem. It is also possible to occur delays between tasks submission due to retransmissions caused by the high error

I. Stojmenovic et al. (Eds.): ISPA 2007, LNCS 4742, pp. 657–668, 2007.

rate of wireless networks. It would be interesting to have an approach which mobile devices inside their context could show an automated and coordinated facility related to executions flow of tasks in grid configurations to execute an application.

In addition, these devices are more susceptible to disconnections, due their limited resources and mobile nature. For example, disconnections can be caused by the battery lifetime reduced or interferences in the wireless network. The occurrence of a voluntary (or involuntary) disconnection of the mobile device is a fault. This fault can provoke an error, and this error can generate a failure. For instance, a fault is the connection interruption with the device, the error is the impossibility to receive information of the mobile user (when it is necessary), and this error can generate a failure state, i.e., a incorrect result of the execution flow. Therefore, it becomes necessary detected the disconnection and adjust the execution flow, preventing a failure state.

The main objective of this paper is to present a research work that allows different mobile devices submission and monitoring applications to grid environments, taking into consideration also problems mentioned. In this context, an approach, called as *SuMMIT* (***Su**bmission, **M**onitoring and **M**anagement of **I**nteractions of **T**asks*) was conceived to perform for applications submission and monitoring in an automatic, coordinate and organize form, based on the workflow concept. As differential contribution, the approach presents adaptived and optimized characteristics for providing a more appropriated form for adjusting to the set of problems and limitations found in different mobile devices.

The article is organized as follows. In section 2, it is presented some characteristics considered in related research works. Aspects concerned to the *SuMMIT* approach and the design and implementation of the prototype are shown in the section 3. In the section 4, it is presented a comparison between this approach and approach proposed in the majority of related works. Finally, in the section 5 some conclusions and future research directions are pointed out.

2 Related Works

Research works were implemented in [3, 4, 5] and they are examples from the literature that do not consider the challenge of submission and monitoring of applications tasks in grid resources to solve a single problem in a automated manner. These approaches allow to submit and to monitor a task for time in the interface of the device and their order of submission controlled for the mobile user.

The approach presented in [6], suggests that PDA client can submit several tasks that work together for solving a problem employing workflow concept. However, this approach shows clearly that PDA clients implement a small set of workflow functionalities. The contribution also does not show functionalities that are implemented. Others aspects that can be observed from the research work present in [6] is: it does not mention any functionalities adaptation of the application submission and monitoring for the context of the mobile devices, with intention of better adjusting this approach to the set of limitations found in the environment of mobile devices. Lastly, this approach is developed specifically in PDAs, not taking into consideration the cellular devices as access terminals to the grid.

In [2], authors particularly focus on a disconnected operation problem that is frequent due to their confined communication range and device mobility. However in [2], mobile devices work as grid resources for applications executions. Therefore, this approach do not handle the disconnection from viewpoint that the mobile device works as an interface of interaction with grid for solving complex problems (i.e., adapting execution flow on disconnection cases).

The main focus of [6] is the security implementation in the PDA clients, tasks submission in UNICORE middleware requires mandatorily a safe communication between clients and the grid middleware. Moreover, none related works shown in [2, 3, 4, 5, 6] argue or show solutions for limitations (or serious problems) of mobile devices, for example: small and different size of screens, maximize the battery lifetime and the adaptation of the execution flow in cases of disconnection of devices. These problems are considered in the proposed approach and they are tackled in a differential way as special features of our proposal.

3 SuMMIT Approach

In this section, it is described the approach of the SuMMIT environment and their characteristics of design and development. The approach is shown in the Figure 1. It was conceived with main components: **Mobile GUI**, **Agent** and **Workflow Manager**.

Components of the approach from top to bottom are as follows:

- **Mobile GUI** presents mobile-adapted interfaces of unique access to the grid;
- **Workflow Manager** processes and manages requests (e.g. submission, monitoring and download of application results) coming from mobile devices to execute in a grid environment. This component enables the execution of applications in which can coordinate distributed resources in multiple virtual

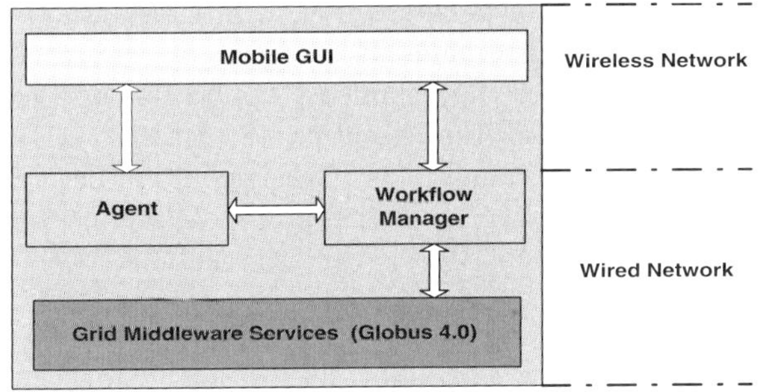

Fig. 1. SuMMIT Approach

organizations, it obtains specific capacities of processing through the integration of multiple teams involved in different parts of the workflow and thus, promoting inter-organizational collaborations;
- **Agent** adapts the execution flow to guarantee the consistency of the application in a eventual disconnection;

3.1 Workflow Manager

Due to the advent of grid computing, providing several services, resources and the capacity to solve complex problems, it is becoming each time more common the execution of application with several tasks for the resolution of a unique problem. In general, this aggregate of tasks has interactions and dependences, requiring the use of some computational tools (e.g., software and/or database) that are shared by virtual organizations of the grid.

These tasks represent a work flow which data are send/receive among tasks obeying certain rules. Therefore, it becomes necessary the utilization of a mechanism for control, organize and have some automatization of tasks execution flow. For this purpose, the workflow concept is employed in our approach, similar to some research projects of grids [7, 8, 9]. The proposal presents a thin and generic solution for definition of grid resources used in each stage of application execution in a automated and coordinated way. The classic concept of workflow is presented in [10].

Beyond this component processes and manages requests coming from mobile devices to execute in a grid environment, it also collects related information to tasks execution, realizing all these functionalities of transparent way to a mobile user. Lastly, it provides automatization for mobile user, dispatching all tasks to the grid scheduler without necessity of user interaction. Therefore, it allows more agility in the tasks execution that work together to solve a problem. Three modules comprise this component: **Controller**, **Engine** and **Collector**.

Each submitted application by mobile users has its proper **Engine** instance, proper **Collector** instance and an unique Identifier. The Java CoG Kit package [11] was used for interacting this component and Globus 4.0 [12]. The **Controller** module is responsible for receiving requests that arrive from mobile devices and order these requests, commanding and controlling their order through the Identifier. When this module receives a submission request, it creates an instance of the **Engine** module and it directs the request to this instance.

The **Engine** is the main module of this component. This module interprets the workflow definition file of the submitted application for knowing how it must be to submit and control the execution of all tasks, i.e., data and flow control and invoking computational tools. These definition files are described in the ***Karajan*** workflow language [9] of the Java CoG Kit package. These files are stored in the metadata repository. After, the submission is done through GRAM grid service [12]. The Condor scheduler [13] is responsible for scheduling tasks in grid resources, status of submitted tasks are informed through events generated during the execution. Therefore, the **Engine** creates an instance called **Collector** for capturing this information and store them in checkpoint files (i.e., XML files) that reports the updated status of each task.

3.2 Agent

Our approach adapt the execution flow to guarantee the consistency of the application in a personalized way for the user when there is a disconnection. For this purpose, the **Agent** component verifies the environment and it adapts the execution flow of submitted application from devices. Therefore, it was possible to detect the disconnection and it also adjusts the flow, preventing a failure. Interactions among components of the SuMMIT are shown in the Figure 2.

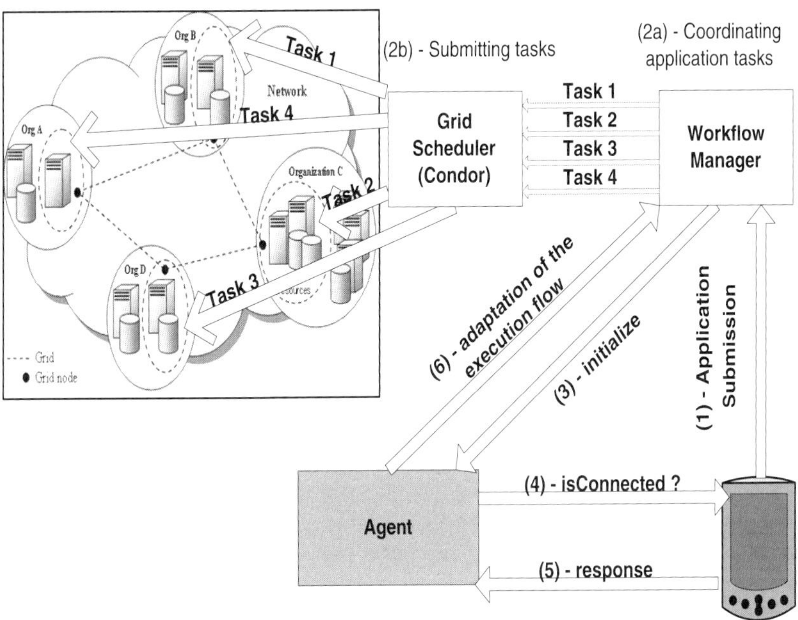

Fig. 2. SuMMIT Components Interactions

Firstly, the user submits the application to the **Workflow Manager** (step (1)) that coordinates and orchestrates application tasks (e.g., an application with 4 tasks), i.e., controlling the execution flow according to workflow definition file (step (2a)). Next, it dispatches tasks for the Condor, used as scheduler of the Globus middleware (step (2b)). Afterwards, the **Manager** creates an instance of the **Agent** (step (3)) that it will verify in an determined time interval (it was defined an time interval of 20s) if the device that sent the submission request is connected (steps (4) e (5)). The **Agent** continues verifying until the moment that submitted application complemented its execution. If the **Agent** does not receive a response from the device in this time interval, it is characterized a disconnection and it is adapted the execution flow (step (6)). The **Agent** module has three basic operations: **Observe**, **Analyze** and **Adapt**.

The **Observe** operation has the function to verify the connection status with the device. The detection of the disconnection that submitted the application was the first step to develop the **Agent** component. In this situation, determining how it will be the execution flow of tasks. There are cases which an application may have dependences in relation to the mobile device or user, for example, user can need to provide input parameters in a specific task according to obtained results in previous tasks, or still to reference data stored in the device.

The **Observe** is performed by means of one thread that was created for each device connected in this component. A thread waits successive communication from the device. When the thread does not receive a return in an time interval, it is considered that the device is disconnected and then, the **Analyze** operation is activated. For instance, if some application task needs from data of the mobile user, the **Workflow Manager** stops the application execution and it waits for this data during the defined time interval, if the data does not arrive during this interval, an exception is generated and **Analyze** operation is activated.

The **Analyze** operation examines application requirements (i.e., dependences) and it decides how it must process in this situation. Another interesting aspect of the proposal refers to the fact that the user can define options, when a disconnection occurs during an application execution in situations where an application does not have any dependence from a mobile user. Therefore, an user can decide to stop the application until the connection returns. If the application has dependence, it must mandatorily stops (or aborts) in the specific task that has the dependence. This feature provides facility to the approach for treating the disconnection and if necessary, it adapts the execution flow considering the nature of the application. In other words, this characteristic providess a personal profile to the user, allowing a personalized application execution.

After the definition of the **Analyze**, the **Adapt** is responsible for modifications, when it is necessary. It has three possible situations of intervention in the execution flow: aborting, stopping for later restart or allowing that the application continues executing. In these cases, the **Adapt** communicates with the **Engine** module to proceed adaptations. If the **Analyze** identified that application may continue the execution, results are stored to deliver to the user after.

When the **Adapt** operation defines that the application must be stopped to restart later, the **Workflow Manager** will store states of the execution in the checkpoint file. Thus, when a device reconnects to the **Manager**, it will be verified if some task did not complete yet. If it was not completed, it will notify to the user that there is a submitted application which it has not completed the execution yet. If the user confirms the restart of this application, tasks states will be recovered and it will restart the execution in the point that it had stopped.

3.3 Mobile GUI

This component was designed and developed for providing interfaces of unique access to the grid specially for cellular phones and PDAs. Thus, we use tools and communication protocols that allow to provide portability for the different devices. Therefore, this component was implemented using J2ME (*Java 2 Micro Edition*) *Wireless Toolkit* [14] and HTTP communication protocol, for providing portability and support a great number of devices. Examples of interfaces are:

application submission; visualization of final and partial results of the application in a optimized way, only parts of resultant files that are considered relevant for user are loaded in the interface of mobile devices and lastly, to monitor application execution, following the progress of the execution through status of each task.

The SuMMIT approach provides an interface with same functionalities for PDAs and cellular telephones. Therefore, it allows that user has flexibility for choosing which device to use, depending of different necessities of each user. In other words, users can utilize of advantages offered for both PDAs (for example, less resource limitation than cellular and it does not possess financial cost for data transmission) or/and cellular (for example, lower acquisition cost and a bigger covering ray). It is important to point out, some of these interfaces are adapted in agreement with the restrictions of different devices. Adaptations challenges are argued in this section.

The application monitoring can be an interesting functionality for mobile users of the grid and clusters, as it observed in the [15], because these devices allows the presentation wherever and whenever how it is advancing the execution in the grid resources. Once these devices allow better portability than desktops computers, due they were weightless and small. Moreover, some application executions can take hours (or even days) to conclude [7]. Therefore, it becomes necessary to provide alternatives to users to have knowledge of the progress of its execution from different localities.

Our approach provide a monitoring interface according to screen restrictions of each device. Thus, the monitoring is initiated without necessity of any interaction (or intervention) from the user with the interface of the **Mobile GUI**. The monitoring was developed to provide an enhanced capability to follow the execution of each application task. This aspect can be possible using updated information of status and adapted interfaces for PDAs and cellular. The Figure 3 illustrates the monitoring interface.

We implemented a PDA interface that represents the workflow of the application graphically in a single structure and providing a organized way of tasks status in the interface. Moreover, allowing to follow simultaneously the execution of the several application tasks. Among options shown in the [8], the non-DAG

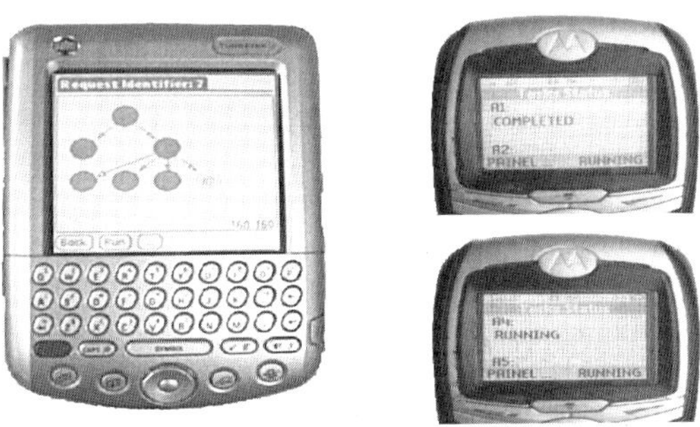

Fig. 3. Application Monitoring Interface

formalism of workflow representation was the most ideal for our approach, because it is flexible, allowing to represent all definition structures (such as, sequential, loops and parallelism) also contained in other formalism options. Therefore, our interface can represent workflows with complex structures and relationships. In addition, it also presents a graphic representation that allows saving spaces in the screen of devices. In other words, utilizing the minimum of graphic elements where circles (or nodes) indicate tasks and arches indicate transitions or dependences among these tasks. In addition, the PDA monitoring interface also has a standard of colors in each circle that indicates the updated status of each task. Thus, when the monitoring interface receives information from status, it translates this information in colors that are filled in the corresponding circles that represent tasks.

The cellular GUI has the same functionalities contained in PDA GUI. However, the monitoring interface is presented of different way in the cellular phone. In other words, due the KVM (Kilobyte Virtual Machine) of some cellular phones have not provided support to some classes and methods used to draw the structure of application workflow in the interface of the PDA (including cellular used in our approach). Therefore, it was necessary to present the status of the tasks in another way. At the cellular, the monitoring interface of the workflow presents tasks statuses in a form with text fields for each task. As shown in the right side of the Figure 3.

Although, the cellular monitoring interface of the workflow makes possible the characteristic to present a adapted and unique structure in its context to monitor application tasks simultaneously, it does not has colors standard to indicate the status. Instead of a colors standard, notifications of messages in the screen and emission of sounds was used to report the tasks status in the cellular.

In addition, the problem of DNA sequencing of a bacterium implemented in [16] produces texts files with size varying from few bytes to 10 Kilobytes. However, we noticed that the transfer time of files in the cellular telephone took an amount of time considerably larger than the time verified in PDA, due the transmission rate of these devices are less than PDAs, i.e., in the cellular have a rate of 32 - 48 kbps and a PDA can have a rate of 11Mbps or more. Moreover, the cellular utilizes GPRS (General Packet Radio Service) technology to transmit data in the network which there is a financial cost for volume of transmitted data. Therefore, we decided to employ a compression method of text files called GZIP [17] to reduce the financial cost and the transference time of the transmitted data to the cellular, the files size are: Major (6 KB to 10KB), Medium (3 KB to 6KB) e Minor (512 bytes to 3KB) . Therefore, we choose files of 512 bytes, 5KB e 10KB for representing respectively the 3 size types.

The total time of transfer and the cost of the files received on the cellular in a total of 10 experiments (as shown at graphs of the Figure 4) presented in average a minor value when using the compression, i.e., 45% (Major), 31% (Medium) and 20% (Minor) in transfer time and 65% (Major), 77% (Medium) and 34% (Minor) in costs. Important to point out that total mean time of transfers of the compacted files shown in the graph of left side in the Figure 4 make accounts

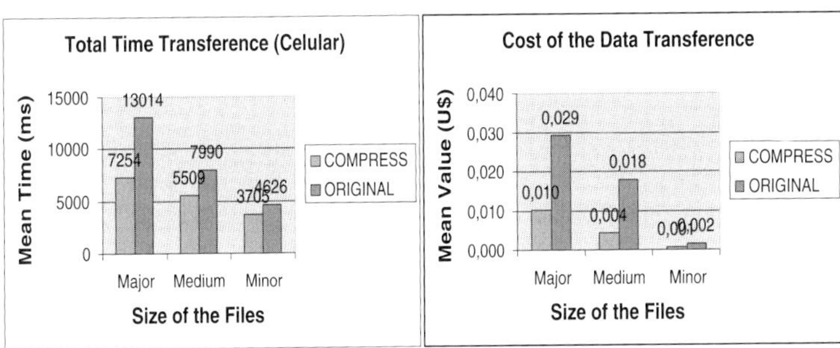

Fig. 4. Data Compression in the Cellular

the time to compress, to transfer in the wireless and wired networks and to decompress on the cellular.

4 Experimental Results

The configuration chosen for the experimental tests was a real scenario in a WLAN (Wireless LAN) and communications towers of cellular operators. This environment is projected to reach one real evaluation of the application execution and related cases. Characteristics of the PDA are: Palm Tungsten C executing the operating system Palm 5.2.1 with processor 400MHz, 64 MB RAM, Built-in Wi-Fi (802.11b).

The **SuMMIT** approach allows the submission and monitoring of applications through a single submission request. In other words, *Workflow Manager* controls the execution flow and it invokes the necessary computational tools without requesting interaction of users for performing all steps. This is differential aspect when compared to the **Other** approach presented in [3, 5, 4], which each application task is submitted of each time through the user interface. Therefore, in these others research works, the user controls the submission order of each task that work together cooperatively to solve the same problem.

We realized 10 executions to compare the execution time between two approaches, as it can be shown at the right side of Figure 5. In the case of the **Other** approach, the calculated total time in each execution is the execution time summed up of each task. Already in the **SuMMIT** approach, the calculated total time is about the total execution time of the application. In the two approaches, the total time of execution does not contain the consumed time to interact with GUI, it is checked the time from the moment that the user sends submission request of each one of the 9 tasks (in the case of the **Other** approach) or when it sends submission request of the application (in the case of the **SuMMIT** approach) and it is going until the end of the application execution. The total execution times of all the submission requests showed minor in the **SuMMIT** approach. This result is justified by the fact of the **SuMMIT** approach to be an automated procedure, saving the consumed time to process the

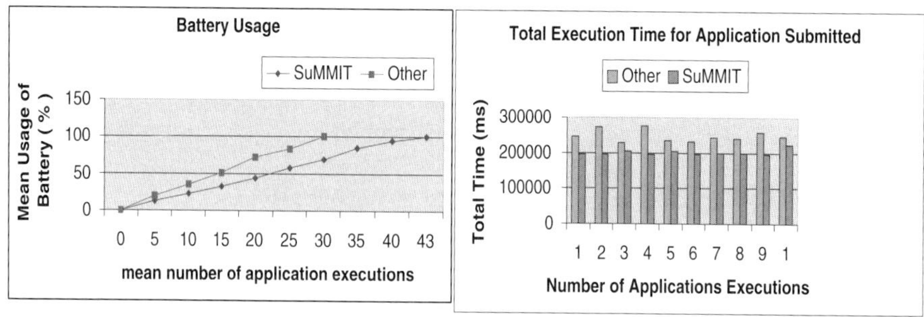

Fig. 5. Battery Usage

request of sending and receiving of each task and also occurring less access the wireless network, differently of the **Other** approach.

In other hand, it is well known that a reduction in the access to wireless network can provide a smaller dissipation of battery energy of these devices, i.e., increasing its lifetime. Extending the battery lifetime is one of the more critical and challenger problems in theses devices [18, 19]. Therefore, one approach that provides more automatization for applications submission, as it happens in our approach; it sends fewer submission requests and consequently, it may reduce the dissipation of battery energy of these devices.

At the left side of the Figure 5 is presented a comparison of the mean battery consumption in the PDA for submitting and monitoring tasks for resolution of a problem. The comparison considers the use of the **SuMMIT** in contrast to the **Other** approach implemented in [2, 3, 5, 4]. The application considered is a DNA sequencing that requires the execution of 9 tasks that must be executed in an organized and controlled way to reach its resolution. The implementation was obtained from in [16]. The result shows that **SuMMIT** reached an average saving of 28% when compare to the **Other** approach. The **SuMMIT** allows a larger number of executions, i.e., on average more 12 application executions than **Other**, as it can be seen in the graph.

It was performed 24 experiments in each approach, each experiment represents the percentage of the battery consumption of 5 application executions of the sequencing problem. In each application execution, it was summed up the consumption percentage for submitting and monitoring each task in the **Other** approach and it was checked consumption percentage for submitting and monitoring the application execution in the **SuMMIT** approach. Besides, in each experiment, grid resources were exclusively dedicated for tests and the time interval of sending of notifications were equals in both approaches. Therefore, these variables do not influence the result.

The average and confidence interval of battery consumption for each experiment was respectively 11% and *(+/-)* 1,6603% in **SuMMIT**, while in the **Other** approach was 16,17% and *(+/-)* 1,6323%. A ***2-Sample T*** Test [20] was used to compare if there is a significant difference between **SuMMIT** and the **Other** approach. In a significance level of 95%, the ***2-Sample T*** test evidenced a significant difference between the two samples, due the resultant ***P-value*** = 0,0002, as [20] observes, when ***P-value*** < 0,05, it indicates a significant difference between two samples. In other words, **SuMMIT** saves significantly more battery energy than the **Other** approach for submitting and monitoring an application.

5 Conclusions and Future Works

In this article, we presented an approach, called as SuMMIT, for tasks submission and monitoring to grid environments from PDAs and cellular clients. The proposal was designed and implemented considering three components, **Workflow Manager**, **Agent** and **Mobile GUI**. These components enable the resolution of complex problems using the concept of workflow. The environment provides to a mobile user a more coordinated, organized and automated form for executing applications in the grid.

The developed prototype provided a transparent facility with adaptive feature according to disconnection problem that exits in mobile devices. In other words, it provides an adjustment for the execution of the tasks flow, matching requirements of submitted application and options defined by a user. Therefore, this functionality guarantees the consistency of the flow in a personalized manner for the mobile user. The SuMMIT also provides GUI with adapted and optimized characteristics according to some limitations and problems found in different devices. In addition, the experimental result indicated that the proposed approach enabled to consume less battery energy of PDAs for submitting and monitoring applications and it also reduces the total time for executing applications.

As step forward of the present research, it will be also elaborated an algorithm that provides an time interval for verification of the disconnection state and for monitoring workflow in a more dynamic fashion. This mechanism will consider input parameters, e.g., battery lifetime and/or traffic volume in the wireless network.

References

1. Bruneo, D., Scarpa, M., Zaia, A., Puliafito, A.: Communication paradigms for mobile grid users. In: 3rd (CCGrid'03), pp. 669–676 (2003)
2. Park, S.M., Ko, Y.-B., Kim, J.H.: Disconnected operation service in mobile grid computing. In: Orlowska, M.E., Weerawarana, S., Papazoglou, M.M.P., Yang, J. (eds.) ICSOC 2003. LNCS, vol. 2910, pp. 499–513. Springer, Heidelberg (2003)
3. Shi, W., Li, S., Lin, X.: Towards merging pervasive computing into grid - light weight portal, dynamic collaborating and semantic supporting. IMSCCS 1, 560–563 (2006)
4. Sajjad, A., Jameel, H., Kalim, U., Han, S.M., Lee, Y.K., Lee, S.: Automagi - an autonomic middleware for enabling mobile access to grid infrastructure. ICAS-ICNS, 73 (2005)

[5] Grabowski, P., Kurowski, K., Nabrzyski, J., Russell, M.: Context sensitive mobile access to grid environments and vo workspaces. MDM, 87 (2006)

[6] Brooke, J., Parkin, M.: A pda client for the computational grid. In: WETICE '05, Washington, DC, USA, pp. 325–330. IEEE Computer Society Press, Los Alamitos (2005)

[7] Schneider, J., Linnert, B., Burchard, L.O.: Distributed workflow management for large-scale grid environments. SAINT, 229–235 (2006)

[8] Yu, J., Buyya, R.: A taxonomy of workflow management systems for grid computing. SIGMOD'05 34, 44–49 (2005)

[9] Laszewski, G., Hategan, M.: Workflow concepts of the java cog kit. Journal of Grid Computing 3, 239–259 (2005)

[10] Hollingsworth, D.: Workflow management coalition. reference model and api specification. WfMC-TC00-1003 (1996)

[11] Laszewski, G.V., Foster, I., Gawor, J., Lane, P.: A java commodity grid kit. Concurrency and Computation: Practice and Experience 13, 643–662 (2001)

[12] Foster, I.: Globus toolkit version 4: Software for service-oriented systems. In: Jin, H., Reed, D., Jiang, W. (eds.) NPC 2005. LNCS, vol. 3779, pp. 2–13. Springer, Heidelberg (2005)

[13] Thain, D., Tannenbaum, T., Livny, M.: Condor and the Grid. John Wiley and Sons, NJ, USA (2003)

[14] Sun Java Wireless Toolkit. Java 2 Platform, Micro Edition (J2ME) Wireless Toolkit. Web Page (2007), [Online]. Disponivel em: `http://java.sun.com/products/sjwtoolkit/`

[15] Dantas, M.A.R., Rista, C.: A wireless monitoring approach for a ha-oscar cluster environment, 302–306 (2005)

[16] Lemos, M.: Workflow para Bioinformática. PhD thesis, Pontificia Universidade Católica do Rio de Janeiro - Brazil (PUC-Rio) (2004)

[17] Deutsch, P.: Rfc 1952 - gzip file format specification version 4.3 (1996)

[18] Rong, P., Pedram, M.: Extending the lifetime of a network of battery-powered mobile devices by remote processing: a markovian decision-based approach. In: proceedings of DAC '03, pp. 906–911. ACM Press, New York (2003)

[19] Mohapatra, S., Cornea, R., Oh, H., Lee, K., Kim, M., Dutt, N.D., Gupta, R., Nicolau, A., Shukla, S.K., Venkatasubramanian, N.: A cross-layer approach for power-performance optimization in distributed mobile systems. In: IPDPS (2005)

[20] Montgomery, D.: Design and Analysis of Experiments. John Wiley and Sons Ltd., Chichester (2005)

[21] Foster, I., Kesselman, C.: The Grid 2: Blueprint for a new Computing Infrastructure. John Wiley and Sons Ltd., Chichester (2003)

GiPS: A Grid Portal for Executing Java Applications on Globus-Based Grids

Yudith Cardinale and Carlos Figueira

Universidad Simón Bolívar, Departamento de Computacióny T. I.,
Apartado 89000, Caracas 1080-A, Venezuela
{yudith,figueira}@usb.ve

Abstract. Grids are becoming the platform of choice for high performance computing. Although grids present a unified view of resources, they need evolved user interfaces in order to fully take advantage of their potential for real applications. Grid portals can deliver complex grid solutions to users; they do so without the need to download or install specialized software, or worrying about setting up networks, firewalls, and port policies. Due to the powerful, general-purpose nature of grid technology, and the nature of the grid resources they expose, the security of portals or points of access to such resources must be carefully considered. In this paper we present `GiPS`, the SUMA/G Grid Portal, a user-specific portal which allows Java applications to access grid resources for execution. We describe how the portal exploits standard, off-the-shelf commodity software together with existing grid infrastructures in order to facilitate security and data access. The main technologies used by `GiPS` are GSI, MyProxy, Java CoG Kit, GridSphere, and SUMA/G middleware. In SUMA/G, Java classes and files are loaded on demand from the user's machines. We describe how the SUMA/G Grid Portal supports this execution model and how it allows users to access controlled external data servers (users' *local* file systems and file systems accessible from their local workstations), under a secure platform.

Keywords: Grid Portals, Grid Computing, Grid Security, Portal Development Kit, Java Execution Model.

1 Introduction

Distributed platforms for compute-intensive processing and resource sharing, known as *grids* [1], provide basic technologies for integrating multi-institutional sets of computational resources to better utilize them to solve a particular problem or set of problems. However, grid infrastructure only provides a common set of services and capabilities that are deployed across resources: it is the responsibility of the applications, scientists, or final users to devise methods and approaches for accessing grid services. For this reason, higher-level tools, often in the form of problem solving environments (PSE) [2], are designed for specific application areas to more effectively take advantage of grid infrastructure. Traditionally, specialized PSE's were developed in the form of higher-level client

I. Stojmenovic et al. (Eds.): ISPA 2007, LNCS 4742, pp. 669–682, 2007.

side tools, with the foremost difficulty in the deployment and configuration of specialized software. This leads to require scientists and researchers to download and install specialized software libraries and packages.

Grid portals [3] can deliver complex grid solutions to users wherever they have access to a web browser running on the Internet without the need to download, install specialized software or worry about setting up networks, firewalls, and port policies. Grid portals are a class of *WWW* application servers that provide secure online environments for gathering information about grid services and resources, as well as offering tools to harness these grid services and resources in order to perform useful tasks. Grid portals have been proven to be effective mechanisms for exposing computing resources and distributed systems to general user communities without forcing them to deal with the complexities of the underlying systems. Grid portals can be subdivided in two categories: *application-specific* and *user-specific* portals. An application specific portal provides scientists with a customized view of software and hardware resources specific to their particular problem domain. User portals generally offer site specific services for a particular community or research center. In both cases, Grid portals are a single point of access to grid resources which applications and users have already been authorized to use.

Due to the powerful, general-purpose character of grid technology, and to the nature of the grid resources they expose, the security of any portal or entry point to such resources cannot be taken lightly. Many grids link together powerful clusters of computational power and large scale data stores containing confidential, classified or proprietary information, or simply resources with specific local usage policies. Security in terms of privacy, integrity, and general protection services on grid-based communication has to be assured, such as to prevent, for instance, network sniffing and man-in-the-middle attacks. Authentication is necessary for verifying the identity of a user, as well as for single sign-on and delegation capabilities. Authorization is used to determine the allowed actions of an authenticated user.

The *de facto* standard for grid security is the Grid Security Infrastructure (GSI) [4]. GSI is a public key based X.509 conforming system that relies on trusted third parties for signing user and host certificates. Typical usage models require that each user be assigned a user credential consisting of a public/private pair of keys. Users generate delegated proxy certificates with short life spans that pass from one component to another, making up the basis of authentication, access control, and logging. Users can typically manage the credentials (and proxy) manually or use a number of command line-based utilities to manage their credentials. In case of grid portals, it is necessary to integrate this security model with easy-to-use interfaces such that the portal manage the credentials automatically. Furthermore, an on-line proxy certificate repository (i.e., MyProxy [5]) could be highly beneficial. The grid portal can take care of transferring the user's credential from the PKI certificate to a *proxy certificate* issued by an online server, thus enabling a web user to be easily authenticated through a web client to any grid service.

In this paper we introduce GiPS (Grid Portal for SUMA/G), a user-specific portal for execution of Java applications on grid resources. We describe how GiPS uses standard, off-the-shelf commodity software together with existing grid infrastructures in order to facilitate security and data access. The main technologies used by our Portal are GSI, MyProxy, Java CoG Kit [6], GridSphere [7], and SUMA/G middleware [8].

SUMA/G[1] (Scientific Ubiquitous Metacomputing Architecture/Globus), the underlying grid infrastructure of GiPS, is a grid middleware specifically targeted at executing Java bytecode on top of Globus grids. The Portal integrate the SUMA/G middleware execution services, by using SUMA/G's command-line tools: when a user interacts with the browser, an appropriate tool with the right parameters is invoked. GiPS supports the suite of SUMA/G command-line tools to execute Java applications. Particularly, it supports launching of, and monitoring executions of Java applications. Services such as security and data transfer are transparently supported. We also show how the security approach of SUMA/G is extended with GiPS. In SUMA/G Java classes and files are loaded on demand from the user's machines, which means that it is not necessary either previous installation of the user's Java code on the execution node nor packing all classes for submission. Instead, only the reference to the main class is submitted; all Java class files, as well as data files, are loaded on demand, with prefetching and buffering support in order to reduce communication overheads [9]. We describe how GiPS supports this execution model and how it allows for user controlled external data servers access, namely users' *local* file systems and file systems accessible from their local workstations, under a secure platform.

2 Related Work

Due to the increasing importance of developing grid portals, there have been proposed many frameworks relying on reusable portlets and add-on technology. Together these technologies comprise a component architecture that allows the scientific grid portal developers to build a portal from well-tested and highly configurable pieces, which in turn enable easy and secure access to grid resources through the portal. With these frameworks, it is possible to rapidly plug new functionality into a portal server, making it easily available for its users.

Nowadays, the most popular frameworks for developing grid portals are the Grid Portal Development Kit (GPDK) [2], the Clarens web-based framework [10], the GridSphere portal framework [7], the GridPort Toolkit [11], and the Open Grid Computing Environment (OGCE) [12].

GPDK, GridSphere, GridPort, and OGCE mainly rest on several major foundational elements: standardized portlet containers based on the Java Specification Request 168 (JSR 168); grid standards for security, file transfer and remote execution based on the Globus toolkit that are accessed through the Commodity Grid (CoG) programming interfaces; and the emerging web-service architecture, including Java Server Pages and servlets. This combination of elements allow

[1] http://gryds.labf.usb.ve

grid resources and scientific applications hosted on remote resources to be easily and securely accessed through the portal.

In contrast to portlet-based frameworks, which mostly focus on implementations on the server side, Clarens enables development of both client and server-side in a generic way (portlet clients are assumed to be web browsers). Services in Clarens are usually XML-RPC or SOAP-speaking web services; clients thus just need to understand these web services standards. It was originally developed for Apache/mod-phyton, but there is also now a Java implementation available [13].

The utility of grid portal technologies for computational science has been established by the number of portals being developed for: i) application specific purposes customized for a particular domain, and ii) general purpose functionality such as launching jobs for remote execution or retrieving remotely-stored data. The former are called application-specific portals, while the latter are called user-specific portal.

Application-specific portals now exist for a broad range of scientific collaborations, including efforts in chemistry (such as GridChem [14], a Java-base grid portal), astronomy (such as the Astrophysics Simulation Collaboratory Portal [15]), physics (e.g. PPDG [16]), medical/biology (BIRN [17], a GridSphere-based portal for biomedical scientists), nanotechnology (nanoHUB Portal [18]), geophysics (NASA QuakeSim Portal [19]), climate and weather (LEAD [20]), and oil industry [21].

Examples of user-specific portals for basic operations such as job submission, file transfer and querying of information services are: the NPACI (National Partnership for Advanced Computational Infrastructure) Portal [22] (based on GridPort), the GENIUS Portal [23] to access the EGEE grid infrastructure [24], and the Legion Portal [25]. All of them allow investigators to seamlessly exploit grid services via a browser-based view of a well defined set of grid resources.

Regarding grid portal architecture, most of grid portals follow the standard three layers [26]: user access, grid services, and resources layers. The top layer is composed by user and portal interfaces. At this layer, the end-user interacts with the system through a web browser. It is responsible for portal content displaying. The second layer consists of the actual portal (portlet container) along with grid services such as security, user profiles, file transfer, job submission and information services. The third layer consists of the underlying system in terms of grid infrastructure as well as legacy systems. It provides information about storage and computational resources regarding to number, status, and relational information of processing capability to portal and applications. The architecture proposed in [27] introduce a *Mobile Agent Layer* to monitor and obtain information about grid resources. The agents are responsible for achieving the status of different dynamic resources and grid nodes.

Security gains prominence in grid portals largely because of the nature of the grid resources they expose. In this sense, one of the most important issue considered in grid portals is related to authentication, authorization, session management, and auditing (logging) [28]. Many grid portals base their security infrastructure on GSI, which is a public key-based X.509 conforming system that relies on trusted third parties for signing user and host certificates; it also combines with an on-line proxy certificate repository (i.e., MyProxy), which keeps the user certificates and manages the creation of proxy certificates. Recent works describe this basic security architecture [29,30].

GiPS is a portlet-based user-specific portal, which offers services for executing Java applications on grid resources. Particularly, it supports launching of, and monitoring executions of Java applications. Services such as security and data transfer are transparently supported. Like most grid portals, GiPS integrates well known technologies: GSI, MyProxy, Java CoG Kit, and GridSphere. The main innovative features of GiPS compared to other grid portals are:

- support for both sequential and parallel Java applications;
- support for the Java execution model: Java classes are loaded on demand from the user's machines without the need of previous installation of the users Javacode on the execution node nor packing all classes for submission;
- access to user controlled external data servers, namely users' *local* file systems and file systems accessible from their local workstations, which are not part of the grid;
- no need for client software install on the user's workstation apart from the web browser with its usual plug-ins

3 SUMA/G: The Underlying Middleware

SUMA/G is a grid middleware that transparently executes Java bytecode on remote machines. In SUMA/G, Java classes and files are loaded on demand from the user's machines, which means that it is not necessary either previous installation of the user's Java code on the execution node nor packing all classes for submission. Instead, only the reference to the main class is submitted; all Java class files, as well as data files, are loaded on demand with prefetching and buffering support in order to reduce communication overheads [9]. Bytecode and data files servers may be located on machines belonging to the grid, or in user controlled external servers.

SUMA/G was originally built on top of commodity software and communication technologies, including Java and CORBA [31]. While it has been gradually incorporating Globus general services by using the Java CoG Kit, CORBA is still needed to allow for transparent remote I/O handling, mainly for interactive job execution. The SUMA/G architecture is depicted in Figure 1. SUMA/G security and resource management are based on Globus components [32]. Details of SUMA/G components could be found in [31]. In this section we concentrate in the description of the Security and Job Submission SUMA/G models, which are the main issues regarding to GiPS, the SUMA/G Grid Portal, functionalities.

3.1 SUMA/G Security Model

SUMA/G uses the GSI through the Java CoG Kit, for user authentication and authorization, as well as a mechanism for including all SUMA/G components into

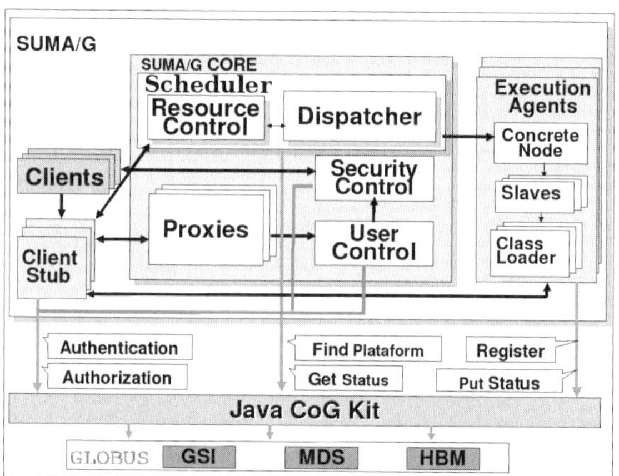

Fig. 1. SUMA/G architecture

the grid security space. All SUMA/G components exchange messages through encrypted channels using SSL. The main SUMA/G components involved in the security model are the `User Control` and the `Security Control`.

The `User Control` is in charge of user registration and authentication. SUMA/G users must have a valid certificate installed on their machines. Certificates must be signed by a SUMA/G Certification Authority. Users must register before the `User Control`, providing the Virtual Organization (VO) they belong to. VOs are specially important for users authorization. One or more VOs for SUMA/G users should be registered at the `User Control`. The `User Control` authentication relies on the `Security Control` certificates verification.

The `Security Control` serves all GSI certificates generation and verification requests. This module's design follows a General Responsibility Assignment Software Patterns (GRASP). It is composed by the following main classes: **SecurityMessage**, an object containing a message signed with the user's private key, and a certificate or certificate chain; **KeyStoreHandler**, which handles certificates loading from the keystore; and **ManageCertificate**, which initializes and verifies SecurityMessages for users authentication.

The `Security Control` offers a number of services for certificates handling in SUMA/G:

- **Certificates keystore:** Users may store/retrieve certificates from a keystore, controlled by a password.
- **Serialization**: Certificates are serialized/deserialized for transmission/ reception through CORBA.
- **Message encryption, signing and verification:** Both public and private keys handling is necessary to accomplish these tasks.

– **Certificates verification:** Includes usual certificates checking, such as dates, CA signature, revocation, integrity and certification chain coherence.

Figure 2 shows the authentication and authorization processes to gain access to resources. The `Client` uses the `Security Control` API to get the SecurityMessage signed with the user's private key (SecurityMessage), which contains at least an X.509 credential with a VO attribute assertion (step 1). The SecurityMessage is sent through CORBA to the `User Control` (step 2). The `User Control` verifies the SecurityMessage with the `Security Control` API and matches the X.509 credential to a VO group to authorize access to a subset of grid resources (step 3).

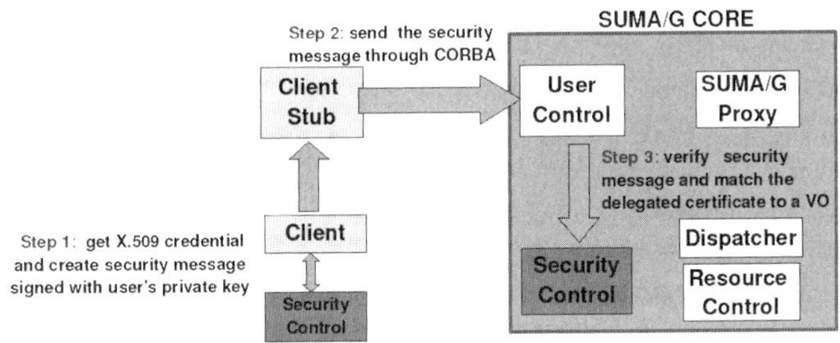

Fig. 2. SUMA/G security model

3.2 SUMA/G Job Submission

The basics of executing Java programs in SUMA/G are simple. Users start the execution of programs through a shell running on the client machine. They can invoke either the `Execute` service, corresponding to the on-line execution mode, or the `Submit` service, which allows for off-line execution (batch jobs). At this time a proxy credential is generated (by using GSI) that allows processes created on behalf of the user to acquire resources, without additional user intervention. Once the SUMA/G `CORE` receives the request from the client machine, it authenticates the user (through GSI), transparently finds a platform for execution (by querying the MDS), and sends a request message to that platform. An `Execution Agent` at the designated platform receives an object representing the application and starts, in an independent JVM, an `Execution Agent Slave`, which actually executes the application. The SUMA/G Class Loader is started in that new JVM, whose function is to load classes and data during execution. Supported classes and input files sources, as well as output destinations, include: a) the machine (client) where the application execution command is run and, b) a remote file server on which the user has an account. A pluggable interface allows for implementing several protocols in order to manage remote files access. Currently, schemes for CORBA and sftp are available; support for gridFTP and others will also be provided. In order to execute an application, either on-line or off-line, the user has only to specify the main class name. In the case of `Execute` service, the rest of the classes and data files are loaded at run-time, on demand, without user intervention. For the `Submit` service, SUMA/G `Client` transparently packs all classes together with input files and delivers them to SUMA/G `CORE`; the output is kept in SUMA/G until the user requests it.

4 GiPS: SUMA/G Grid Portal

This section describes the `GiPS` architecture and its main functionalities regarding to job submission, data access, and security.

4.1 GiPS Architecture

The architecture of the `GiPS` follows a standard three-tier model: i) the highest layer represented by the user's workstation running a web browser to display the portal interfaces; ii) the middle layer consisting of the set of portlets that implement the execution services along with state information; and iii) the lowest layer consisting of the actual grid: SUMA/G components, and the resources registered on it.

An important benefit of `GiPS` is that it does not require downloading any of the SUMA/G software on a user's machine. Since the Portal operates entirely on the web server, the client machine requires merely a browser installed on it.

`GiPS` is built on the GridSphere framework, which provides a portlet API implementation fully JSR 168 compliant. We employed GridSphere and the associated GridPortlets package to develop our own customized portlets, and Hibernate as the database interface. Our Portal integrates customized grid-enabled portlet components to ensure job submission, data management, user credential management, and resource management. Following sections explain some details.

4.2 Execution Services

The `GiPS` execution services consist on transparent job management on the grid. Through the Portal, users can submit a job to SUMA/G `CORE`, monitor its current status, inspect the output "on the fly" and save it on the local workstation. To support these functionalities we developed two important portlets:

SubmitPortlet: It is mainly in charge of executing the SUMA/G SUBMIT command with the appropriate parameters. Figure 3(a) shows the graphic interface for job submission. Additionally it takes care of user authentication, proxy certificate management, and user *log* file handling, with historical information for auditing. When a user submits a job, a JOB-ID is returned, which will be used later to ask for the status and results of that job.

JobResultPortlet: It has the responsibility of executing SUMA/G commands in order to get status (*Running, Ready, Waiting, Completed*) of submitted jobs and restore results once they have been finished. All JOB-IDs returned by the SUBMIT service are kept on a per user file. `GiPS` lists the status of all pending jobs, and the user can select a JOB-ID(s) to obtain the corresponding results (see Figure 3(b)).

SUBMIT JOBS

Welcome To SUMA/G

Login:
Password:
Address:
Main-Class:

Option:
Parameters
Object File
Files
Prot
Buffer Size
Types
Number of Hosts
Keep Submiting
Submit

a) Submit a Job

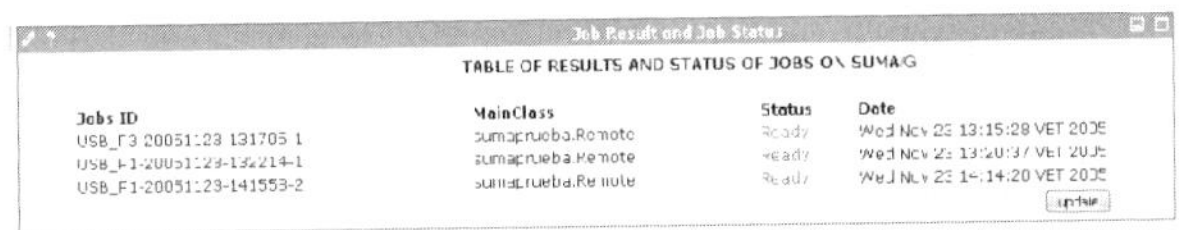

b) Get Status and Results

Fig. 3. (a) Submit a job, (b)Get status and results

4.3 Java Execution Model Support: Loading Classes and Data on Demand from User's File Systems

SUMA/G implements a number of mechanisms to handle remote access to data and classes. All data files and classes requests issued by applications are redirected to the client, which in turn connects to local file systems (i.e., at the client machine) or to remote file systems specified by the user (e.g., at machines in which the user has an account) to serve the requests. Figure 4 shows current SUMA/G I/O subsystem.

The remote data and classes access mechanisms are:

1. Dynamic class loading. Each application instantiates its own SUMA/G `Class Loader`, which handles the dynamic class loading from the client up to the `Execution Agent` at run time.
2. Standard input, output and error redirection. For interactive applications, the execution environment is modified such that the standard input, output and error are connected to the client issuing the execution request, thus behaving as if it were a local execution.
3. `java.io` redirection. A new package, `suma.io` redefines the basic classes in `java.io`. Using *callbacks* to the client, the data files can be accessed by applications. If the required data is not present at the user machine, the `Client Stub` locates and accesses the remote file system who keeps the data. Data is transferred from the remote file system to the user machine, through a secure channel (by using https or sftp), and then to the `Execution Agent`, in a GSI realm. Note that files are not transferred as a whole but in blocks;

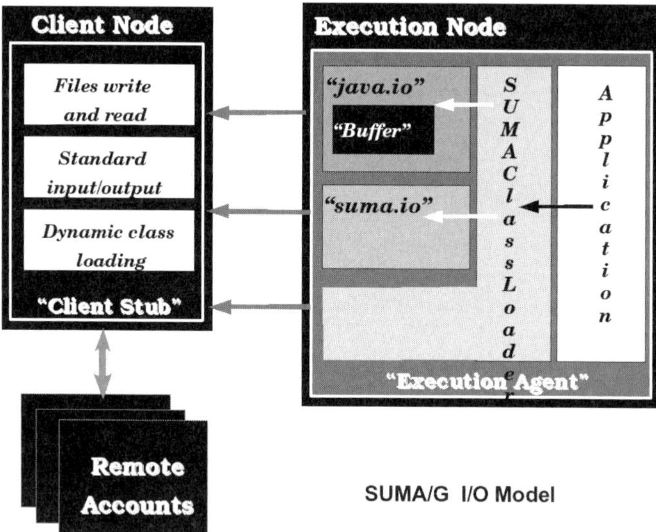

Fig. 4. SUMA/G I/O subsystem

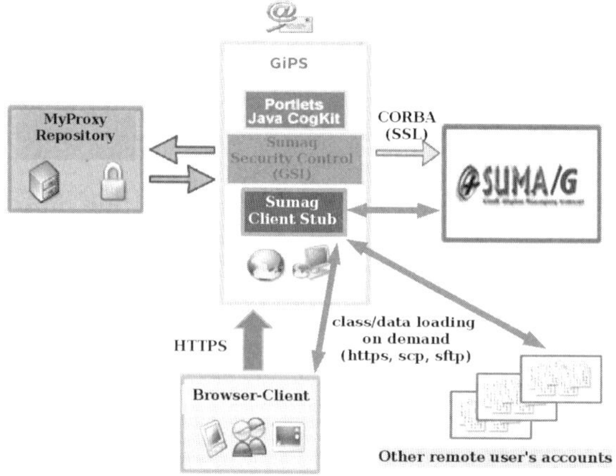

Fig. 5. GiPS access scheme

hence, there is never a file's complete copy in local storage, thus reducing the risk of obtaining a copy of the file.

4. Buffering. Remote file accesses use buffering to improve performance, by reading or writing blocks, hence reducing the number of *callbacks* to data sources. At execution time a block size is specified and the data transfer is performed on demand, when the application executes a read on the file. The data block transferred from the remote file system starts at the first byte accessed by the application. If the application tries to access a byte not

contained in the transferred data block, another data block is transferred, overwriting the previous block.

GiPS supports the SUMA/G remote class and file access mechanisms. The main benefit of the Portal is that a single grid username provides access not only to the resources allowed for the VO the user belongs to, but also to the file systems accessible from the local workstation. In this case the local workstation does not run a SUMA/G client, but a standard web browser. A modified SUMA/G Client Stub runs at the web server side. The access to the local file systems is made by this SUMA/G Client Stub, through a file server, such as *sshd* or *apache*, which must be locally installed. Not only the local file systems can be accessed from the grid side, but also other file systems available in different machines that are not part of the grid. Users grant access to their accounts, after the connection from the web browser to the web Portal is conceded. Figure 5 depicts the access scheme provided by the GiPS. File access is done through the Portal on demand, relieving the user of uploading data and classes into the grid.

4.4 Job Control

A directory structure was designed such that GiPS could keep per user jobs handling and control information, as well as the job's results. In this structure, each user is assigned a unique directory where all results and a log file are stored (see Figure 6). The log file keeps track of date, name, JOB-ID and status for each submitted job by that user. A new feature was added to SUMA/G JobResult service in order to pack the results and download them from GiPS to a directory on a local or remote user account.

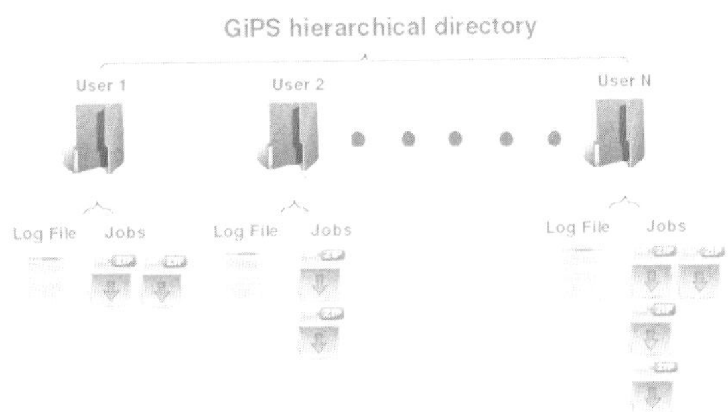

Fig. 6. GiPS directory

4.5 Security

Security is provided at two levels: Portal and Grid, as shown on Figure 7. At the Portal level, the user authenticates herself using login and password; thus, a number of services, not necessarily directly related to grid job executions (e.g., forums, Wiki) could be accessed by authenticated users (step 1 on Figure 7).

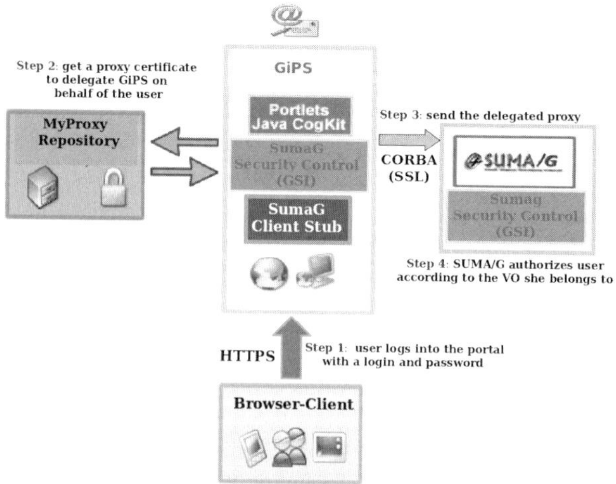

Fig. 7. GiPS authentication and authorization

Once authenticated at the Portal level, GiPS takes care of user authentication before the grid, by requesting a delegated proxy for the user from a MyProxy server (step 2 on Figure 7). Interaction with the MyProxy server through a secure channel is transparently handled by GiPS, by using *GridPortlets*, which are portlets built on top of Java CoG Kit. By taking advantage of the MyProxy package, users can use GiPS to gain access to remote resources from anywhere without requiring their certificate and private key be located on the same machine/device running a web browser. The MyProxy server is responsible for maintaining user's delegated proxy, that can be securely retrieved by a portal for later use. Next, the user request is sent to the grid along with the delegated proxy, which is used by SUMA/G `User Control` and `Security Control` to authorize grid resources access (steps 3 and 4 on Figure 7), as explained on Section 3.1. Logs for every GiPS access are kept on files stored on the directory structure described on Section 4.4 for auditing purposes.

5 Conclusions

Exploiting the whelm of resources offered by grids needs execution environments that relieve users from the burden imposed by current systems. Portals emerged as a panacea, by easing access through a well-known web interface. GiPS come as a choice for easily executing Java applications on grids under a secure platform.

With GiPS, users can securely access the grid, submit sequential and parallel Java applications to the distributed computing resources and take back their outputs. It supports the Java execution model, where Java classes are loaded on demand from the user's machines without the need of previous installation of the users Javacode on the execution node nor packing all classes for submission. Additionally, through GiPS, it is possible to access to user controlled external data servers, namely users' *local* file systems and file systems accessible from their local workstations, which are not part of the grid.

Future work in GiPS involves developing special portals, providing greater support for grid administrators, exploring interoperability between grid infrastructures, providing a programming interface to grids, and offering increasing support to grid users in the form of *superschedulers*, information services, interfaces for special services, etc.

References

1. Foster, I., Kesselman, C.: Computational Grids. In: The Grid: Blueprint for a New Computing Infrastructure, pp. 15–51. Morgan Kaufmann Publishers, Inc., San Francisco (1999)
2. Novotny, J.: The grid portal development kit. Concurrency and Computation: Practice and Experience 14, 1129–1144 (2002)
3. Fox, G., Gannon, D., Thomas, M.: Editorial: A Summary of Grid Computing Environments. Concur. and Computat.: Practice and Experience 14 (2002)
4. Foster, I.T., Kesselman, C., Tsudik, G., Tuecke, S.: A security architecture for computational grids. In: ACM Conf. on Computer and Communic. Security, ACM Press, New York (1998)
5. Novotny, J., Tuecke, S., V.W.: An online credential repository for the grid: Myproxy. In: Proc. of the 10th IEEE Internat. Symp. on High Perf. Distrib. Comp., IEEE Computer Society Press, Los Alamitos (2001)
6. von Laszewski, G., Foster, I., Gawor, J., Smith, W., Tuecke, S.: CoG Kits: A Bridge between Commodity Distributed Computing and High-Performance Grids. In: ACM Java Grande 2000 Conference, pp. 97–106. ACM Press, New York (2000)
7. Novotny, J., Russell, M., Wehrens, O.: GridSphere: a portal framework for building collaborations. Concurrency - Practice and Experience 16(5), 503–513 (2004)
8. Cardinale, Y., Hernández, E.: Parallel Checkpointing on a Grid-enabled Java Platform. In: Sloot, P.M.A., Hoekstra, A.G., Priol, T., Reinefeld, A., Bubak, M. (eds.) EGC 2005. LNCS, vol. 3470, pp. 741–750. Springer, Heidelberg (2005)
9. Cardinale, Y., De Oliveira, J., Figueira, C.: Remote class prefetching: Improving performance of java applications on grid platforms. In: Guo, M., Yang, L.T., Di Martino, B., Zima, H.P., Dongarra, J., Tang, F. (eds.) ISPA 2006. LNCS, vol. 4330, pp. 594–606. Springer, Heidelberg (2006)
10. Steenberg, C., Bunn, J., Legrand, I., Newman, H., Thomas, M., van Lingen, F., Anjum, A., Azim, T.: The Clarens Grid-Enabled Web Services Framework: Services and Implementation. In: CHEP 2004. Proceedings of The Conference for Computing in High Energy and Nuclear Physics (2004)
11. Thomas, M., Boisseau, J., Mock, S., Dahan, M., Mueller, K., Sutton, D.: The GridPort Toolkit Architecture for Building Grid Portals. In: Proc. of the 10th IEEE Internat. Symp. on High Performance Distributed Compumputing, IEEE Computer Society Press, Los Alamitos (2001)
12. Amin, K., Hategan, M., von Laszewski, G., Zulezec, N.: Abstracting the grid. In: Proc. of The 12 Euromicro Conf. on Parallel, Distributed and Network-Based Processing (2004)
13. Ali, A., Anjum, A., Haider, R., Azim, T., ur Rehman, W., Bunn, J., Newman, H., Thomas, M., Steenberg, C.: JClarens: A Java Based Interactive Physics Analysis Environment for Data Intensive Applications. In: Proc. of the Internat. Conf. of Web Services (2004)

14. The GridChem Project: GridChem Portal (2007), https://www.gridchem.org/index.php
15. Bondarescu, R., Allen, G., Daues, G., Kelley, I., Russell, M., Seidel, E., Shalf, J.: The astrophysics simulation collaboratory portal: a framework for effective distributed research. Future Generation Computer Systems 21, 259–270 (2005)
16. The Particle Physics Data Grid Collaboratory: PPDG Portal (2007), http://www.ppdg.net/
17. Biomedical Informatics Research Network Project: BIRN Portal (2001), http://www.nbirn.net/cyberinfrastructure/portal.shtm
18. nanoHUB Project: nanoHUB Portal (2006), http://www.nanohub.org/
19. NASA Jet Propulsion Laboratory: QuakeSim Portal (2007), http://complexity.ucs.indiana.edu:8282/
20. Gannon, D., Plale, B., Christie, M., Marru, S., Kandaswamy, G., Fang, L., Huang, Y., Lee-Palickara, S., Jenson, S., Liu, N., Shirasuna, S., Simmhan, Y., Slominski, A., Ramachandran, R., Clark, R.D., Lawrence, K., Kim, I.H.: The LEAD Science Portal Problem Solving Environment. In: Proceedings of AMS Conference (2007)
21. Lewis, J., Allen, G., Chakraborty, P., Huang, D., Li, Z.L.X., White, C., Zhang, C.: Developing a grid portal for large-scale reservoir studie. In: Annual Argonne Undergraduate Symposium (2006)
22. Thomas, M., Mock, S., Boisseau, J.: Development of Web toolkits for computational science portals: The NPACI HotPage. In: Proc. of The 9th IEEE Internat. Symp. on High Performance Distributed Computing, IEEE Computer Society Press, Los Alamitos (2000)
23. Barbera, R., Falzone, A., Rodolico, A.: The genius grid portal. In: Proc. of The Conference for Computing in High Energy and Nuclear Physics (2003)
24. EGEE Team: Enabling Grids for E-SciencE (2006), http://public.eu-egee.org/
25. Natrajan, A., Nguyen-Tuong, A., Humphrey, M., Grimshaw, A.: The legion grid portal. Concurrency and Computation: Practice and Experience 14 (2002)
26. Thomas, M.P., Burruss, J., Cinquini, L., Fox, G., Gannon, D., Gilbert, L., von Laszewski, G., Jackson, K., Middleton, D., Moore, R., Pierce, M., Plale, B., Rajasekar, A., Regno, R., Roberts, E., Schissel, D., Seth, A., Schroeder, W.: Grid Portal Architectures for Scientific Applications. Journal of Physics: Conference Series 16, 596–600 (2005)
27. Fang, J.: Multi-layer grid portal architecture based on mobile agent. In: Proc. of the Second Internat. Conf. on Semantics, Knowledge, and Grid, pp. 98–99 (2006)
28. Vecchio, D.D., Hazlewood, V., Humphre, M.: Evaluating grid portal security. In: Proceedings of Supercomputing 2006, Tampa, FL (2006)
29. Jiang, J., Chen, D., Chen, T., Shen, X.: A security grid portal using pki and online proxy certificate repository. In: IMSCCS'06. Proc. of The First Internat. Multi-Symposiums on Computer and Computational Sciences, vol. 2 (2006)
30. Wu, X., Yang, G., Shen, J., Zhou, Q.: A novel security model based on virtual organization for grid. In: Proc. of the Sixth Internat. Conf. on Parallel and Distributed Computing Applications and Technologies, pp. 106–109 (2005)
31. Cardinale, Y., Curiel, M., Figueira, C., García, P., Hernández, E.: Implementation of a CORBA-based metacomputing system. In: Hertzberger, B., Hoekstra, A.G., Williams, R. (eds.) High-Performance Computing and Networking. LNCS, vol. 2110, Springer, Heidelberg (2001)
32. The Globus Alliance: The Globus Toolkit (2006), http://www.globus.org/

Advanced Grid DataBase Management with the GRelC Data Access Service

Sandro Fiore, Alessandro Negro, Salvatore Vadacca, Massimo Cafaro, Maria Mirto, and Giovanni Aloisio

SPACI Consortium & University of Salento, Italy
Euro Mediterranean Centre for Climate Change, Italy
{sandro.fiore,alessandro.negro,salvatore.vadacca,massimo.cafaro, maria.mirto,giovanni.aloisio}@unile.it

Abstract. Many data grid applications manage and process huge datasets distributed across multiple grid nodes and stored into heterogeneous databases; e-Science projects need to access widespread databases within a computational grid environment, through a set of secure, interoperable and efficient data grid services. In the data grid management area several projects aims at addressing these issues providing different solutions and proposing a set of data access and integration/federation services.

In this paper we present the GRelC Data Access, a WS-I based data grid access service developed by SPACI Consortium and the University of Salento. Its architectural design is discussed and experimental results related to an European testbed are also reported.

1 Introduction

Several grid projects [1] have generally focused on contexts where data is stored on files. However, many e-Science applications have an urgent need to access and interconnect legacy and independently operating large databases [2] (e.g., protein data banks in the bioinformatics field), that is, working at a finer grain level. Such applications could improve their performance and quality of results by using efficient, cross-DBMS and specialized data access services in a grid environment supplying high-performance storage and retrieval mechanisms.

DataBase Management Systems (DBMSs) represent a reliable, accepted and powerful instrument to store persistent data. An efficient and secure data grid middleware able to interact with relational databases and based on standard and interoperable protocols represents a key service/building block for advanced and complex data grid management services.

Even though in the last few years many efforts have been concentrated in this direction, basically providing services for data access and integration [3], [4], [5], performance has not been fully addressed. This paper presents the GRelC Data Access, a WS-I based grid data access service (it represents the evolution of the GRelC Server [6], [7]), discussing its architectural design and reporting experimental results related to an European testbed. Extreme performance, interoperability and security represent the main requirements addressed by this service.

I. Stojmenovic et al. (Eds.): ISPA 2007, LNCS 4742, pp. 683–694, 2007.

The outline of the paper is as follows: in Section 2 we recall related work, whereas in Section 3 we address the main requirements of the system. In Section 4 we describe the GRelC Data Access architecture presenting its main subcomponents and highlighting user and query management as well as technological and security issues. In Section 5 we report on the experimental results within an European grid context (the SEPAC Production Grid [8]) and finally, in Section 6, we draw our conclusions and highlight future work.

2 Related Work

The Spitfire Project [9] is part of the Work Package 2 in the European Data Grid Project and provides a means to access relational databases from the grid. It is a very thin layer on top of an RDBMS (by default MySQL) that provides a JDBC driver. Web Service technology (Jakarta Tomcat) is used to provide SOAP-based RPC (through Apache Axis) to a few user-definable database operations. Spitfire provides just a basic set of functionalities w.r.t the GRelC DAS (for instance it does not implement advanced delivery mechanisms, as described in Section 4.1.2).

The Open Grid Services Architecture Data Access and Integration (OGSA-DAI) [10] is another project concerning the development of middleware to assist with access and integration of data from separate data sources via the grid. The project was conceived by the UK Database Task Force and it is working closely with the Open Grid Forum DAIS-WG [11] and the Globus Alliance [12]. This project is strongly related to data access and integration services. OGSA-DAI provides a Distributed Query Processor (DQP) [13] middleware for data integration whereas the GRelC project provides the GRelC Gather [14], a grid enabled P2P (peer-to-peer) approach to carry out data federation. Technological differences are related to the programming language (Java against C for services and Java Swing against Qt for graphical interfaces) that can widely affect performance. Moreover, we provide a WS-I approach owing to the fact that WSRF (Web Services Resource Framework) specifications and middleware support for the C programming language (the Globus Toolkit 4.0.3 C-WS-Core container is not yet production-level, since it misses a proper authorization framework) are not mature enough.

The GRelC Server was the precursor of the GRelC DAS [7],[14]. It was based on a client/server approach, proprietary protocols and provided support for several kinds of queries. As reported in [15], the GRelC Server efficiently performed query management. An inherent drawback was related to interoperability, which was not addressed owing to the Grid/Web Service technologies and related grid standards and specifications in constant flux.

3 DAS Requirements

As described in [15], the main challenges of a DAS service are: transparency (the ability to manage different DBMSs, concealing data sources heterogeneity), robustness and efficiency (performance issues), uniformity (the ability to provide uniform access, standardized error management and exception handling) and security (ability to perform authorization and authentication as well as data encryption, data integrity etc.).

Moreover, since Grid standards and related middleware continually evolve, a new requirement becomes important: interoperability.

Within the proposed DAS service, we addressed transparency and uniformity by means of the Standard Database Access Interface (Section 4.1.3), security by means of the Globus Toolkit Grid Security Infrastructure, (Section 4.1.4) and performance through appropriate design and technological choices (Sections 4.1.2). Finally, we achieved interoperability by means of a modular architecture based on W3C and OASIS standard protocols such as XML, SOAP and WSDL.

4 GRelC Data Access Service Architecture

As can be seen in Fig. 1, the GRelC Data Access Service architecture (in the large) involves several components such as (i) DAS, (ii) data sources and (iii) client applications. Moreover, in grid environments the DAS supports third-party queries concerning (iv) grid storage components to store database dumps, query resultsets, etc.

In the following subsections we will detail the key component of the GRelC DAS architecture, presenting its main subcomponents, query and user management, technological choices, heterogeneous database access and security issues. Finally, we will briefly mention command-line and graphical client applications.

4.1 GRelC DAS

Within the proposed data grid architecture, the GRelC DAS (Fig. 2) represents the key component. It is a service providing an uniform access interface to relational and non-relational (i.e., textual databases) data sources. It offers a unique front-end to store, manage and retrieve data hiding all of the physical details such as database location, name, user login, etc.

The aim of this data grid service is to efficiently, securely and transparently manage databases on the grid, across virtual organizations, with regard to modern grid standards and specifications (OGSA [16] and WSRF [17]).

4.1.1 DAS Subcomponents

The DAS includes the following subcomponents: server front-end, data access component, user, grid-DB and enterprise grid management, metadata catalogue and GRelC Standard Database Access Interface (SDAI).

The Server Front-end listens for incoming client requests dispatching them to the proper request handler. It relies on the GSI (Grid Security Infrastructure [18]) protocol and provides security by means of mutual authentication and authorization, using X509v3 certificates and Access Control Lists (ACL). It also creates the user's environment and sets up the user's data access policies.

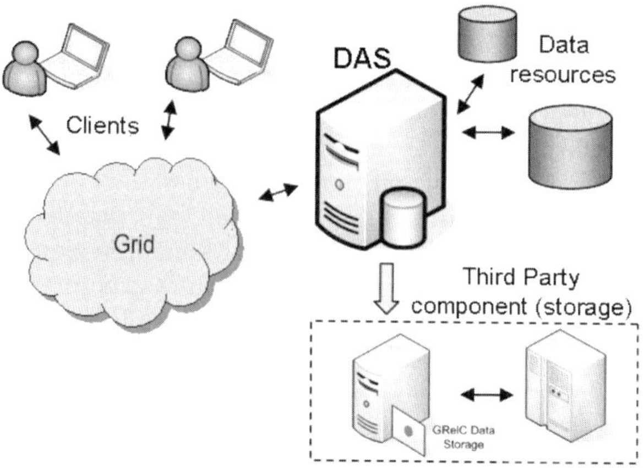

Fig. 1. DAS architecture in the large

The Data Access component provides functionalities related to database (i) bind, (ii) query and (iii) unbind. Moreover, interaction with third-party storage (which is out of the scope of this paper) is also provided by this component. Query Management is a multifaceted issue; additional details are provided in Section 4.1.2.

The User Management component provides several functionalities. Among the others it allows (i) adding and (ii) deleting users to/from grid-DB, (iii) changing privileges (both for administrators and end users), (iv) managing profiles, etc. Additional details about this fundamental issue are provided in Section 4.1.3. The Grid-DB component provides several functionalities related to

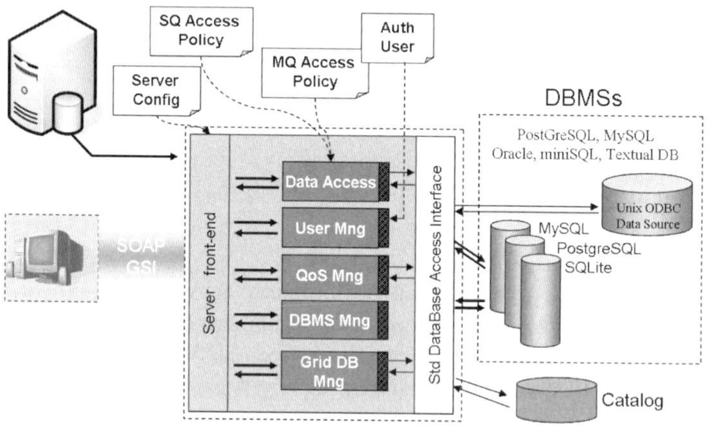

Fig. 2. DAS Internal Architecture

grid-DB management. It allows (i) creating, (ii) registering, (iii) dropping, and (iv) managing a grid-DB. By registration we mean the possibility to map a legacy database onto a grid-DB instance, automatically importing all of the database related metadata (tables, attributes, types, domains, etc.).

The Enterprise Grid management component supplies a set of methods to mainly (i) add, (ii) delete and (iii) manage the Enterprise Grid (EG) of the user. Each user can define a set of hosts, the available DBMSs, the connection strings, etc. in order to provide the system with basic information for grid-DB management.

The Metadata Catalog, is a system (relational) database containing information about users, VOs, access control policies, grid-databases (DBMS type, port, login, etc.), and so on. It currently runs on PostgreSQL, MySQL, SQLite, Unix ODBC and Oracle DBMSs by means of the GRelC SDAI library, which provides transparent and uniform access to a relational database through a plug-in based architecture leveraging dynamic libraries. An SQLite implementation has a twofold benefit: it provides extreme performance (due to the embedded database management) and it increases service robustness and reliability owing to the fact that it does not depend on external DBMS servers.

The Server Management component provides support for (i) logging, to keep track of information related to all of the operations carried out at the server-side by the users, and (ii) monitoring, to check the availability of hosts and DBMSs belonging to the EG (periodic reports and event-triggered alerts can be sent to the administrator in case of problems).

Logging can be set by the grid-DB administrator at different levels. The following can be logged as needed: user's connections, read and/or write operations on data sources, read and/or write operations on metadata. The GRelC DAS also provides some methods to perform remote logging control.

4.1.2 Query Management

The GRelC DAS supplies the user with the capability to carry out several kinds of queries. The most important one is the SingleQuery. In the following subsection we detail the SingleQuery mechanism, whereas in Section 5 we propose a related performance benchmark within an European production grid context.

4.1.2.1 Single Query. The Single Query (SQ) represents the basic query provided by the DAS. By means of the SQ the user can perform SELECT, INSERT, UPDATE and DELETE operations. However, SQ SELECT queries could be very critical within a grid environment owing to the amount of data that could be asked for and then retrieved by the client. For this reason we provide the users with four types of SQ SELECT queries in grid, exploiting different data delivery mechanisms: SQ-On-line (SQOL), SQ-Memory (SQM), SQ-File (SQF) and SQ-FileZip (SQFZip). These approaches, in grid, represent an alternative solutions to non grid-enable Direct DataBase Connection ones (DDBC) implemented by means of native DBMS client APIs (in this case, clients directly contact the

DBMS). Let us better detail the grid-enabled SQ Select Queries provided by the GRelC DAS.

In the first case, SQOL, the client retrieves one row at a time. The GRelC DAS provides the client with a set of methods to retrieve the current tuple, attributes schema, number of rows, to move cursor forward and backward within the resultset and so on. The number of interactions between the client and the GRelC DAS can be high if the client is interested to the entire resultset. Indeed, this query is suitable to retrieve just a few tuples of for DML statements. To deal with high volume queries in grid environments we provide other query mechanisms.

In the SQM case the entire resultset is transferred from the server to the client as a method output parameter within a data structure. The rationale behind this kind of query is that grouping data can result in higher efficiency owing to a reduced number of interactions between client and server. The user can also specify the chunk size (number of tuples) of this data structure, in order to split the resultset into several blocks. The number of interactions between the DAS and the client, depends on the following ratio: resultsetsize/chunksize. Data chunking allows (i) performing in parallel computation of chunk 'n' at the client side and data delivery of chunk 'n+1' and (ii) beginning data computation at the client side before receiving all of the chunks. In this scenario, tuning of the chunk size can affect the performance.

In the SQF case the resultset is transferred from the server to the client within a file using the HTTPG (HTTP over GSI) data transfer protocol (GridFTP [19] support will be soon available). As in SQM, the user can specify a chunk size (number of tuples) to split the query response into several pieces.

In the last case, SQFZip, the resultset is stored within a file and then compressed (using Lempel-Ziv77 and Huffman coding) to further enhance performance w.r.t the delivery phase. As in SQM and SQF the user can specify a chunk size.

SQM, SQF and SQFZip implement enhanced delivery mechanisms to speedup performance. There are client side APIs to manage the retrieved resultset. The GRelC-Recordset client library contains among the others, the following functions: grelc-open-recordset(), grelc-movefirst(), grelc-eof(), grelc-get-value(), grelc-get-attribute-name(), grelc-get-attribute-type(), etc.

4.1.3 User Management

The proposed GRelC DAS provides fine grained support for data access policies based on three main classes of users, as described below. This choice comes from the need to provide users with different capabilities and authorization levels both as end users and as administrators.

Within the DAS service, three types of users can be defined:

- Super-User: she is the DAS administrator and can: (i) create grid-DB, (ii) define grid-DB admins, (iii) add/delete/modify properties of DAS users, (iv) manage the EG (hosts and DBMSs related metadata). She can also read log files related to all of the registered grid-DBs.

- Grid-DB Admin: she is the grid-DB administrator and can (i) assign/remove users to/from the grid-DB and (ii) grant/revoke their privileges. She manages grid-DB users and can read the grid-DB specific log file.

- End-User or grid-DB user: principals able to access a grid-DB; can be characterized by several authorization data access policies such as: create and drop (users can create and drop tables within a grid-DB) and select, insert, delete, update (users can read/add/modify/delete rows within a table). For each grid-DB, suitable policies must be assigned to every user by the relevant grid-DB administrator.

4.1.4 Technological Issues

From a technological point of view the GRelC DAS is a web service developed exploiting the gSOAP Toolkit [20]. To address security we implemented GSI support, available as a gSOAP plug-in [21]. To address efficiency we chose programming languages and technologies with the aim to ensure extreme performance; despite the fact that most grid services are extensively based on Java, the proposed data access service is entirely based on the C programming language.

To provide support for C++ developers, the DAS SDK contains a C++ proxy class wrapping all of the C methods implemented within the DAS web service (currently about 80 C++ methods are available). The proxy class allows easier development of C++ client applications (Section 4.2 describes the XGRelC GUI), concealing all of the details related to the SOAP connection, gSOAP-GSI and GRelC-Access plug-in, low-level internal DAS client data structures and so on.

4.1.5 Heterogeneous Database Access

To address the transparency and uniformity requirements, we conceived the Standard Database Access Interface, a C library leveraging a plug-in based approach. The library virtualizes data access operations; it provides high-level data access interfaces connected with database connection, query execution, data and metadata manipulation, concurrency control, transaction management, etc.

Owing to its modular design, new drivers related to other data sources can be easily plugged into the proposed library and made available to the DAS.

It is worth noting here that the GRelC DAS manages through the SDAI both system-level databases (such as for instance the Metadata Catalogue) and application-level data sources (user's databases), a feature known as DAS reflectivity property.

4.1.6 Security

Security is a crucial and complex requirement for the proposed DAS. While managing a database in a grid environment by means of a DAS, it is fundamental to address: (i) robust mutual authentication (in our case, based on public-key mechanisms) among the actors involved within the system (clients applications, DAS and third-party components such as storage services); (ii) communication protection of the data exchanged through the network, by means of data cryptography; (iii) access control policies based on Access Control Lists and role management mechanisms, to easy control and manage both principals (who can access the grid-DB) and privileges (under what conditions).

For the proposed grid service, we decided to adopt GSI, which is widely accepted and used in several grid contexts. GSI also allows performing single sign-on and delegation mechanisms, which are strongly required within a grid environment.

Moreover, we already provide Virtual Organization Membership System (VOMS) [22] support to perform scalable and flexible grid-based role management.

4.2 Client Applications

Client applications are built on top of the methods provided by the GRelC DAS. Two kinds of clients are currently available: command-line and graphical.

In the former case, C clients allow the user to submit SingleQueries, to check DAS logs, to manage DAS users, grid-DBs, etc.

In the latter case, the XGRelC graphical Management Console allows the user to create/delete grid-DBs, to submit queries, to retrieve resultsets, to manage users, etc using an intuitive graphical user interface.

The Management Console is built on top of the GRelC DAS proxy class described in Section 4.1.4 and Qt libraries. It implements all of the services provided by the GRelC DAS.

5 Experimental Results on the SEPAC Grid

In this Section, we present experimental results related to a performance comparison among the four kinds of SingleQuery illustrated before. In the first subsection we present the environment of our tests, that is the SEPAC grid, whereas in the second one we show experimental results about SingleQuery tests.

5.1 Environment and Test Database

Our tests have been conducted within the European SEPAC production grid. We deployed a GRelC DAS in Lecce (IT) and several client applications in Zurich (CH). The GRelC DAS ran on a Linux machine on which we installed the DBMS and the test database. We used the PostgreSQL RDBMS, but it is worth noting here that, as we already stated in Section 4, this is not a constraint in our implementation.

The client application ran on a Linux machine and it was developed using the C programming language. Table 1 shows the client and server specifications. On both the client and the server machines there were no other concurrent processes running.

In our experiment, we considered the 'molecule' table of our own integrated relational database related to the bioinformatics databanks UniProt [23] and UTRdb [24], retrieving the following fields: sequence identifier, molecule type, authors, creation date, description, last sequence update, last annotation update, reference field, sequence field, sequence check, notes and other minor information.

Table 1. Client and server specifications

	Server	Client
SO	OpenSuse 10.2	Fedora Core release 2 (Tettnang)
Kernel	2.6.18.2-34smp	2.6.5-1.358smp
CPU	Intel Pentium 4	Intel Pentium 4
Speed	3.00 GHz	3.00 GHz
Ram	1026112 KB	1026112 KB
Swap	2104472 KB	2040244 KB
Postgres	8.1.3	-
Network	WAN (Lecce,ITALY)	WAN (Zurich,SWISS)

5.2 Single Queries Benchmark

In this subsection, we present experimental results related to a performance comparison among the SingleQueries (SQOL, SQM, SQF and SQFZip) and the DDBC. These tests are related to client applications submitting several kinds of SingleQueries to the GRelC DAS retrieving a number of tuples ranging from one to one hundred thousand. Results provide us with some insight about the efficiency of the proposed queries. The response times for SQOL are reported in Table 2. Obviously, as described in Section 4.1.2, SQOL (which can be seen as a traditional approach to query submission leveraging grid middleware), does not provide any kind of efficient delivery mechanism and it cannot be considered a credible alternative to DDBC. On the contrary SQM, SQF and SQFZip address efficiency requirement (as pointed out by our tests) reducing (i) the number of interactions between the client and the DAS and (ii) the total connection time, by grouping and/or compressing data in memory or file.
In the following we report on our SQs comparison among DDBC, SQM, SQF, and SQFZip without chunking the resultset (chunking will be addressed in a future work providing additional tests) and then, we discuss the speedup introduced by the SQM, SQF and SQFZip w.r.t. the DDBC approach.

In our experiment, we ran several tests considering N, (the number of retrieved records) in two classes:

- SMALL: N ranging from one to one thousand;
- LARGE: N ranging from ten thousand to one hundred thousand.

Table 2. Resultset Size and SQOL Average Response time

Tuples N	Resultset Size	Avg SQOL
1	1.9 KB	0.49 sec
10	6.9 KB	0.97 sec
100	59.8 KB	6.41 sec
1000	716.3 KB	52.7 sec
10000	7.59 MB	7 min 59 sec
100000	73.7 MB	72 min 42 sec

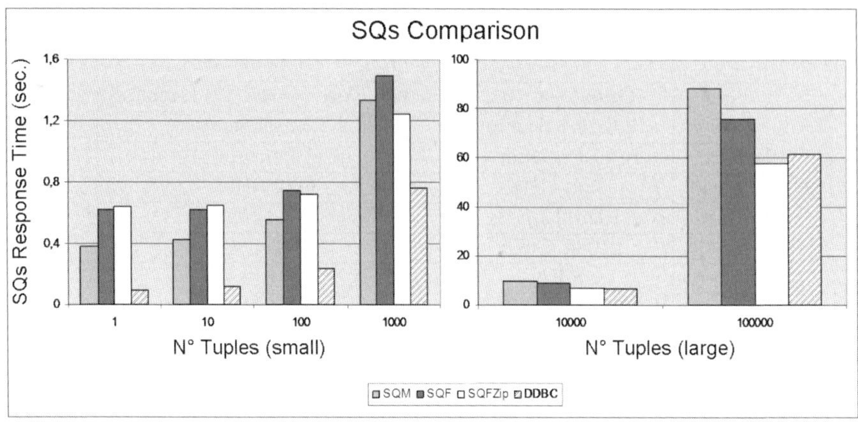

Fig. 3. Single Queries Comparison. T=SQ(N)

Regarding the SMALL case, as reported in Fig. 3, different behaviours are related to DDBC, SQM, SQF and SQFZip. DDBC is always better than the GRelC DAS queries. However considering that SQM, SQF, SQFZip carry out an additional GSI mutual authentication step (about 0.3 secs), the GRelC DAS queries can be considered comparable with the non grid enabled DDBC. Comparing the GRelC DAS queries we can state that: SQF is less efficient than SQM and SQFZip for N equal/greater to one hundred tuples whereas SQFZip is less efficient for N equal/less than ten tuples. As we expected, the bigger is N the better is the result of SQFZip w.r.t. SQM and viceversa. For N equal to one thousand tuples SQFZip is the best GRelC DAS query solution (the compression effect impacts on the performances, so SQFZip gets 7% of improvement w.r.t SQM and 20% w.r.t SQF), whereas for N equal/less than one hundred SQM is better. However, we need to take into account that in the SMALL case, the query tests related to DDBC, SQM, SQF and SQFZip took no more than 1.5 seconds in our testebed environment.

Regarding the LARGE case we can seen that: DDBC is better than SQM and SQF both for N equal to ten and one hundred thousand (29% and 24% respectively of improvement), whereas concerning SQFZip, DDBC is comparable with it for N equal to ten thousand and worse than it for N equal to one hundred thousand. So, considering N equal to one hundred thousand SQFZip is the best query solution w.r.t. DDBC, SQM and SQF (6%, 34% and 24% respectively of improvement). The results demonstrate that the new GRelC DAS queries perform well w.r.t the classic DDBC.

Finally, we remark that an important difference between GRelC DAS queries and DDBC, is that the first ones represent an efficient and robust grid solution for database management w.r.t. the non grid-enabled DDBC.

6 Conclusions

We described the GRelC DAS, a (WS-I based) grid data access service developed within the GRelC Project [25]. The aim of this service is to efficiently, securely and transparently manage databases on the grid promoting flexible, secure and coordinated resource sharing and publication across virtual organizations, taking into account modern grid standards and specifications. We also highlighted main requirements, architecture, user and query management, security issues, client SDK and applications, etc. We reported a benchmark related to SingleQueries comparison, within the European SEPAC production grid, proving how efficient data delivery mechanisms (i.e. data compression) can enhance performance connected with database query submission within a computational grid environment compared with traditional (non grid-enabled) database access approaches.

Future work is related to (i) a WSRF-based GRelC DAS, (ii) a performance comparison with existing middleware such as OGSA-DAI, (iii) a relational implementation based on the emerging Open Grid Forum specifications (WS-DAI, WS-DAIR). Jointly with the Grid Resource Broker [26] team, the main functionalities of the GRelC DAS will be integrated within a data management grid portal to provide ubiquitous and seamless access to grid databases.

References

1. Foster, I., Kesselman, C.: The Grid: Blueprint for a New Computing Infrastructure. Morgan Kaufmann, San Francisco (1998)
2. Ozsu, M.T., Valduriez, P.: Principles of Distributed Database Systems, 2nd edn. Prentice Hall, Upper Saddle River, NJ, USA (1999)
3. Antonioletti, M., Krause, A., Paton, N.W., Eisenberg, A., Laws, S., Malaika, S., Melton, J., Pearson, D.: The WS-DAI Family of Specifications for Web Service Data Access and Integration. ACM SIGMOD Record 35(1), 48–55 (2006)
4. Antonioletti, M., Atkinson, M.P., Baxter, R., Borley, A., Chue Hong, N.P., Collins, B., Hardman, N., Hume, A., Knox, A., Jackson, M., Krause, A., Laws, S., Magowan, J., Paton, N.W., Pearson, D., Sugden, T., Watson, P., Westhead, M.: The Design and Implementation of Grid Database Services in OGSA-DAI. Concurrency and Computation: Practice and Experience 17(2-4), 357–376 (2005)
5. Karasavvas, K., Antonioletti, M., Atkinson, M.P., Chue Hong, N.P., Sugden, T., Hume, A.C., Jackson, M., Krause, A., Palansuriya, C.: Introduction to OGSA-DAI Services. In: Herrero, P., Pérez, M.S., Robles, V. (eds.) SAG 2004. LNCS, vol. 3458, pp. 1–12. Springer, Heidelberg (2005)
6. Aloisio, G., Cafaro, M., Fiore, S., Mirto, M.: The GRelC Project: Towards GRID-DBMS. In: Proceedings of Parallel and Distributed Computing and Networks (PDCN) IASTED, Innsbruck, Austria, February 17-19, 2004, pp. 1–6 (2004)
7. Aloisio, G., Cafaro, M., Fiore, S., Mirto, M.: The GRelC Library: A Basic Pillar in the Grid Relational Catalog Architecture. In: Proceedings of ITCC, Las Vegas, Nevada, April 5-7, 2004, vol. I, pp. 372–376 (2004)
8. The SEPAC-Grid Project, `http://www.sepac-grid.org`
9. The Spitfire Project, `http://edg-wp2.web.cern.ch/edg-wp2/spitfire`
10. Open Grid Services Architecture Data Access and Integration, `http://www.ogsadai.org.uk`

11. Database Access and Integration Services WG, https://forge.gridforum.org/projects/dais-wg
12. The Globus Project, http://www.globus.org
13. Alpdemir, M.N., Mukherjee, A., Gounaris, A., Paton, N.W., Watson, P., Fernandes, A.A.A., Fitzgerald, D.J.: OGSA-DQP: A Service for Distributed Querying on the Grid. In: Bertino, E., Christodoulakis, S., Plexousakis, D., Christophides, V., Koubarakis, M., Boehm, K., Ferrari, E. (eds.) EDBT 2004. LNCS, vol. 2992, pp. 858–861. Springer, Heidelberg (2004)
14. Aloisio, G., Cafaro, M., Fiore, S., Mirto, M., Vadacca, S.: GRelC Data Gather Service: a Step Towards P2P Production Grids. In: Proceedings of 22nd ACM SAC, Seoul, Korea, March 11-15, 2007, vol. I, pp. 561–565. ACM Press, New York (2007)
15. Aloisio, G., Cafaro, M., Fiore, S., Mirto, M.: Advanced Delivery Mechanisms in the GRelC Project. In: MGC 2004. ACM Proceedings of 2nd Int'nl Workshop on Middleware for Grid Computing, Toronto, Ontario, Canada, October 18, 2004, pp. 69–74. ACM Press, New York (2004)
16. Foster, I., Kesselman, C., Nick, J., Tuecke, S.: The Physiology of the Grid: An Open Grid Services Architecture for Distributed System Integration. Technical Report for the Globus Project, http://www.globus.org/research/papers/ogsa.pdf
17. The WS-Resource Framework, www.globus.org/wsrf
18. Tuecke, S.: Grid Security Infrastructure (GSI) Roadmap. Internet Draft (2001)
19. GridFTP Protocol, http://www-fp.mcs.anl.gov/dsl/GridFTP-Protocol-RFC-Draft.pdf
20. van Engelen, R.A., Gallivan, K.A.: The gSOAP Toolkit for Web Services and Peer-To-Peer Computing Networks. In: Proceedings of IEEE CCGrid Conference, Berlin, Germany, May 2002, pp. 128–135. IEEE Computer Society Press, Los Alamitos (2002)
21. Aloisio, G., Cafaro, M., Epicoco, I., Lezzi, D., Van Engelen, R.: The GSI plug-in for gSOAP: Enhanced Security, Performance, and Reliability. In: Proceedings of ITCC 2005, vol. I, pp. 304–309. IEEE Press, Los Alamitos (2005)
22. Alfieri, R., Cecchini, R., Ciaschini, V., dell'Agnello, L., Frohner, A., Gianoli, A., Lorentey, K., Spataro, F.: VOMS, an Authorization System for Virtual Organizations. In: Fernández Rivera, F., Bubak, M., Gómez Tato, A., Doallo, R. (eds.) Grid Computing. LNCS, vol. 2970, pp. 33–40. Springer, Heidelberg (2004)
23. Bairoch, A., Apweiler, R., Wu, C.H., Barker, W.C., Boeckmann, B., Ferro, S., et al.: The Universal Protein Resource. Nucleic Acids Res. 33, 154–159 (2005)
24. Pesole, G., Liuni, S., et al.: UTRdb: a specialized database of 5 and 3 untranslated regions of eukaryotic mRNAs. Nucleic Acids Res. 27, 188–191 (1999)
25. Aloisio, G., Cafaro, M., Fiore, S., Mirto, M.: The Grid Relational Catalog Project. In: Grandinetti, L. (ed.) Advances in Parallel Computing, Grid Computing: The New Frontiers of High Performance Computing, pp. 129–155. Elsevier, Amsterdam (2005)
26. Aloisio, G., Cafaro, M., Carteni, G., Epicoco, I., Fiore, S., Lezzi, D., Mirto, M., Mocavero, S.: The Grid Resource Broker Portal. Concurrency and Computation: Practice and Experience. Special Issue on Grid Computing Environments (to appear)

A Generic Distributed Monitor Construct for Programming Process Synchronization in Distributed Systems

Jiannong Cao, Miaomiao Wang, Weigang Wu, Xianbing Wang, and Stephen C.F. Chan

Internet and Mobile Computing Lab, Department of Computing, Hong Kong Polytechnic University, Hung Hom, Kowloon, Hong Kong
{csjcao,csmmwang,cswgwu}@comp.polyu.edu.hk

Abstract. The monitor construct has been implemented in several concurrent and/or parallel programming languages for shared-memory system environments, Extensions of the monitor to support process synchronization in distributed systems have also been proposed. But, most existing work only provides the architecture design of the distributed monitor. There is no discussion about the algorithmic and implementation issues. Also, none of them consider how to implement conditional variables. In this paper, we present the design and implementation of a distributed monitor construct, named DisMoniC, for programming process synchronization in distributed systems. DisMoniC is generic in the sense that it can be used with any distributed mutual exclusion (DME) algorithm to implement exclusive access to the monitor operations. Time-efficient algorithms are proposed to implement conditional process synchronization in the distributed monitor. We also present performance evaluation of the proposed construct.

Keywords: Distributed monitor construct, Process synchronization, Distributed systems, Distributed mutual exclusion.

1 Introduction

Process synchronization is crucial for preserving the integrity of resources shared among a group of processes. It involves mutually exclusive access to and synchronized use of the shared resource. Being a structured and high-level programming mechanism, the monitor construct has been widely used to control and coordinate concurrent access to shared resources in multiprogramming and concurrent environments [1, 2]. It can be used for implicitly ensuring mutual exclusion and explicitly achieving conditional synchronization.

The monitor construct has been implemented in several concurrent and/or parallel programming languages for shared-memory system environments [3, 4, 5]. Extensions of synchronization constructs, including the monitor, to support process synchronization in distributed systems have also been proposed [6, 7, 8, 9, 10]. Distributed applications that require sharing of resources, such as replicated distributed databases, computer-supported collaborative works, airline reservation, and on-line network games, can be developed using distributed monitors [11, 12].

I. Stojmenovic et al. (Eds.): ISPA 2007, LNCS 4742, pp. 695–706, 2007.

However, processes in a distributed system normally communicate by passing messages, which makes the design and implementation of the monitor construct difficult. In a distributed monitor construct, the mechanisms for achieving mutual exclusion and dealing with condition variables are different from those in a classical centralized monitor construct. First, in a centralized monitor construct, when a process exits the monitor, the process on the head of the waiting queue can enter the monitor immediately. A distributed monitor, however, must first locate the next privilege node using a distributed mutual exclusion (DME) algorithm and then let the corresponding process enter the distributed monitor. Second, in a centralized monitor, when a process invokes the wait primitive on a condition variable, it is added to the waiting queue of the condition variable and then just waits for the signal primitive to wake it up. In contrast, in a distributed monitor construct, when a process invokes the wait primitive on a condition variable, the process should be appended to the waiting queue at the node of the process and other nodes should be informed of the invocation of the wait primitive.

Most existing work did not consider the algorithm and implementation issues but only provided the architecture design of the distributed monitor. Also, none of them considered how to implement conditional variables. In this paper, we present the design and implementation of DisMoniC, a generic distributed monitor construct for programming process synchronization in distributed systems communicating by passing messages. DisMoniC is generic, because it can work with any DME algorithm to realize exclusive access to the Critical Section (CS). In contrast, exiting distributed monitor structures are tightly coupled with specific DMEs. Furthermore, besides mutual exclusion, DisMoniC also addresses the conditional process synchronization problem. To achieve conditional synchronization, the condition variables are handled by using our proposed time-efficient algorithm.

DisMoniC mainly consists of the local monitor module, the distributed monitor module, the condition variables, and the distributed mutual exclusion (DME) interface. DisMoniC introduces almost no additional overhead besides the overhead of the DME algorithm itself. We have proved the correctness of the proposed construct in term of the correctness properties, *Mutual Exclusion, Deadlock Free* (liveness) *and Starvation Free* (fairness), but due to the limit in space, we omit the proof in this paper. We have implemented a prototype of DisMoniC. Performance evaluation results will be presented.

The rest of this paper is organized as follows. In Section 2, we briefly review existing works on DME and distributed monitors. Section 3 describes the design of DisMoniC. We present the algorithm implementation for DisMoniC in Section 4. The performance evaluation of DisMoniC is reported in Section 5. Finally, Section 6 concludes the paper with the discussion of our future work.

2 Related Works

The monitor construct is an encapsulation of local administrative data and procedures. The data represents the status of the shared resource controlled by the monitor, while the local procedures operate on these local data variables to change the status of the shared resources. At any time, one and only one process is allowed to execute inside a monitor. This ensures mutually exclusive access to the shared resource. Processes requesting to access a monitor that is already in use are forced to wait in an entry queue until the monitor is released.

Apart from guaranteeing mutual exclusion, a monitor can contain condition variables for the purpose of process synchronization. Condition variables can be associated with shared resources. A process which has just possessed a shared resource but subsequently requires access to another shared resource that is in use can, without leaving the monitor, wait on the condition variable that represents the availability of that shared resource. Processes waiting in condition queues are actually outside the monitor since only one process is allowed to be inside a monitor at any time. However, these processes are different from those requesting to enter the monitor in that they do not have to make a request to re-enter the monitor. This feature improves the performance of the monitor because the overhead caused by requesting, entering and exiting the monitor is reduced.

In implementing the monitor construct, four primitives are required: the *enter* and *exit* mutual exclusion primitives and the *wait* and *signal* synchronization primitives. The *enter* primitive ensures mutually exclusive access to the requested monitor while the *exit* primitive releases the mutual exclusion of the monitor being accessed to other requesting processes. The *wait* primitive blocks the execution of the calling process and releases the mutual exclusion of the monitor that is on hold to other requesting processes. The *signal* primitive activates one of the processes waiting in either the entry queue or the condition queues of the specified monitor and releases the control of the signaling process to the awaken one.

A DME algorithm is necessary for the distributed monitor construct. DME is a well studied problem and many algorithms have been proposed. Comprehensive surveys can be found in [13, 14, 15]. DME algorithms can be classified into two categories: centralized algorithm and distributed algorithm. In a centralized algorithm [16], one node in the network is designated as the control node that controls the access to the shared resource. Centralized algorithms are simple and easy to implement, but the control node may become the performance bottleneck. It can also be the single point of failure. In a distributed algorithm, all nodes have an equal amount of information and bear equal responsibility for deciding which process should access the shared resource. Distributed mutual exclusion algorithms can be further classified into two major types: quorum-based algorithm [17, 18, 19, 20, 21] and token-based algorithm [22, 23, 24, 25, 26]. Both quorum-based and token-based algorithms address the problem of centralized algorithms at the expense of increased message traffic in the system. In quorum-based algorithms, a process must request and receive the privilege from at least a quorum of processes. In token-based algorithms, processes contact more than one process to search the token or must maintain some specific logical topology of the network [23].

The importance of providing high-level support for programming process synchronization has been well recognized [6, 7, 8, 9, 10]. Extending the traditional monitor construct to distributed one has been studied. Based on Suzuki and Kasami's token-based DME algorithm [26], Mansfield proposed a distributed monitor construct for resource sharing in distributed systems [27]. However, despite being simple in concept, the mechanisms for implementation has not been described. Yuan and Hsu described the design and implementation of a distributed monitor based on the client-sever model [9]. The implementation makes use of Sun's RPC mechanism. However, since a centralized server is used, it is more like a centralized monitor construct. The server may become a performance bottleneck in a large-scale distributed system.

DisMoniC provides a generic and complete solution to the design and implementation of distributed monitor. It works with any DME algorithm to ensure mutually exclusive access to shared resource. Furthermore, besides mutual exclusion, DisMoniC also realizes conditional process synchronization which has not been considered yet in previous work.

3 Design of DisMoniC

In this section, we describe the design of DisMoniC. First, we introduce its system architecture by discussing the design principles, describing the programming primitives, and explaining the functions of major components. Then, we describe the runtime mechanisms of DisMoniC.

3.1 System Architecture

In our system model, the network consists of N nodes communicating by messages. Each pair of nodes is logically connected. As mentioned before, the distributed monitor construct is different form the centralized monitor in the ways they achieve mutual exclusion and handle conditional variables. We design the distributed monitor construct DisMoniC by addressing the above two issues.

To guarantee mutual exclusion, we divide the operations of achieving mutual exclusion into two levels. The first level is the *process level*, where the local monitor mechanism is used to serialize the access to the critical section within a node. The second level is the *node level*, where the distributed monitor construct controls the sequence of accesses to the system-wide shared resource, by using a DME algorithm. Figure 1 illustrates the two-level model. In this paper, the DME algorithm is abstracted to a distributed mutual exclusion service with specific operations for requesting and releasing the CS. The design of the DisMoniC is independent of underlying DME algorithm used.

To achieve conditional synchronization, information about the processes waiting on condition variables must be synchronized among the nodes. We provide a time-efficient mechanism to propagate the process waiting information. To propagate the waiting information, piggybacking technique is used in the underlying message passing. The queue that contains all the processes waiting on the condition variable is piggybacked on messages exchanged among the nodes for other purposes, e.g. for achieving mutual exclusion. Then, when a signal primitive is invoked, the corresponding waiting process can be informed immediately.

The system architecture of DisMoniC is shown in Figure 2. DisMoniC consists of four major parts: the local monitor module, the distributed monitor module, the condition variables, and the DME algorithm interface.

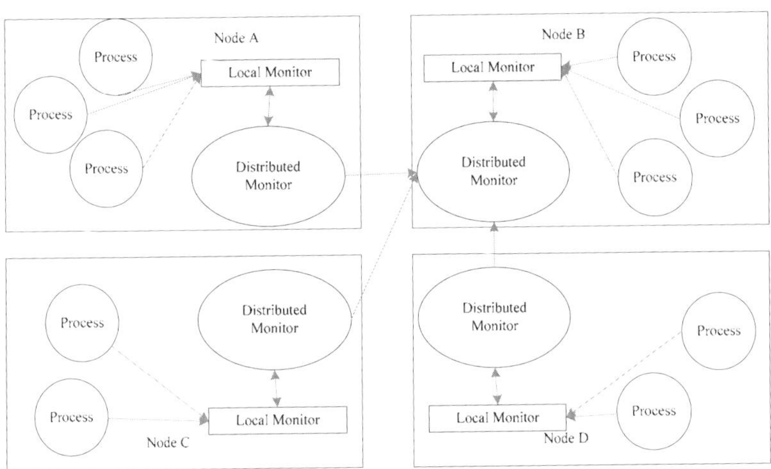

Fig. 1. Two level mutual exclusion (Node B is the privileged node)

- *Local monitor module*: All processes use the local monitor to compete for entering the distributed monitor, at the node level which is a shared resource to all the processes at the process level.
- *Distributed monitor module*: It controls the access to the DME algorithm and handles condition variables in the distributed environment.
- *Condition Variable*: We extend the functional model of condition variables to achieve system-wide synchronization of waiting process information.
- *DME algorithm interface*: Any proper DME algorithm, which implements such interface, can be plugged into our distributed monitor construct at runtime.

DisMoniC provides five APIs for application developer to use. They are *initialize*, *enter, exit, wait* and *signal.* The first method is used for specifying and combining the *user specified monitor* based on DisMoniC. User specified monitor consists of a specific DME algorithm, application specific condition variables, and monitor operations. The latter four methods are mapped to the invocations of the system primitives.

DisMoniC provides four system primitives, namely *enter()* and *exit()* (distributed mutual exclusion operations), and *wait()* and *signal()* (conditional synchronization operations) to ensure mutual exclusion and achieve conditional synchronization.

- *enter ()*: if a process wants to execute operations in CS for distributed process synchronization, it first enters the distributed monitor by obtaining permission through the DME algorithm.
- *exit ()*: after a process finishes the operation in the CS, it exits the distributed monitor, so that some other process waiting for the monitor can access the monitor.
- *wait ()*: a process invokes this primitive to wait for a signal message to achieve synchronization of using the resource.
- *signal()*: a process finishing the use of the resource signals the corresponding waiting process to continue and then it exits immediately.

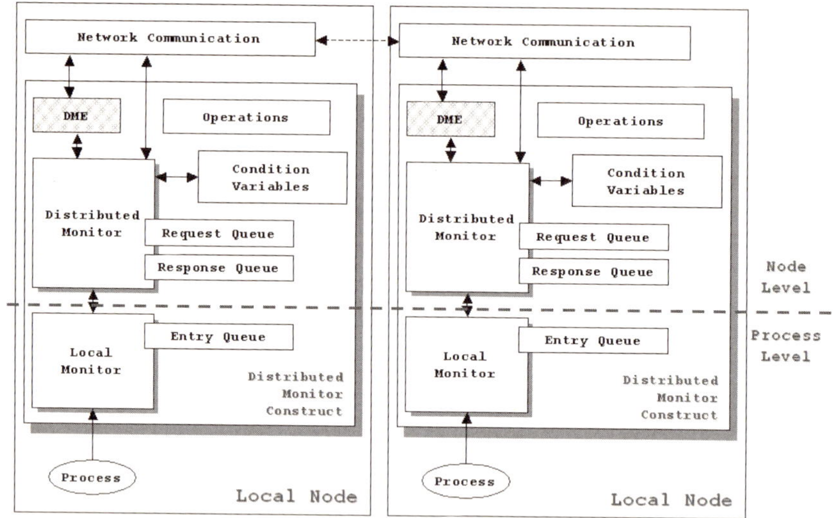

Fig. 2. System architecture of DisMoniC

These primitives will invoke the operations of the DME to request or release the privilege of entering the CS. DisMoniC defines two methods for the DME interface: *makeRequest()* and *releasePrivilege()*.

- *makeRequest()*: This method is mapped to the specific DME's privilege request method. It will be invoked by the enter() system primitive. This method is an asynchronous method and does not block the calling process.
- *releasePrivilege()*: This method is mapped to the specific DME's privilege release method. It is invoked by the exit() system primitive. An important mechanism added to this method is piggybacking the process waiting information of condition variables when the DME algorithm sends messages to pass the privilege of entering CS.

3.2 Runtime Mechanism

To explain the runtime mechanism clearly, first of all, we classify the communications between the nodes into two kinds. One is for achieving distributed mutual exclusion among the nodes using a DME algorithm. Another is for programming distributed process synchronization using the distributed monitor. Based on these two kinds of communications, we classify the executions of the distributed monitor into two modes: *DME mode* and *Signal mode*.

In the DME mode, processes compete for mutually exclusive access to the critical section in the distributed system or wait for signal primitive on some condition variables. Process waiting information will be piggybacked by the messages exchanged among the nodes via the DME algorithm.

When a process invokes a signal primitive, the execution mode is changed to the Signal mode. In the Signal mode, the execution of the DME algorithm will be blocked, and the signal information will be transmitted directly among the distributed monitor modules on the different nodes. The process waiting information will be piggybacked also. When the node that first initiates the signal mode receives a response message, the execution mode will be changed back to the DME mode.

Based on the description of the communication between nodes, we will explain the interaction between various parts of DisMoniC as shown in Figure 3. First of all, note that every process accesses the shared resource by synchronizing with other processes through the *user specified monitor*. For a process that has not entered the *user specified monitor,* to access the shared resource, the *enter* primitives of the local and distributed monitor will be invoked.

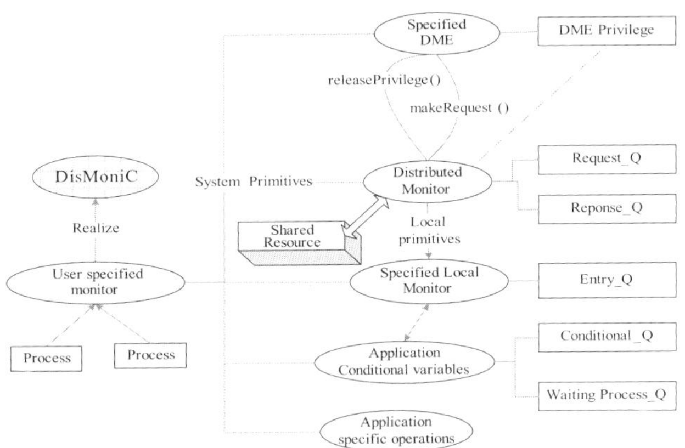

Fig. 3. Runtime mechanism of DisMoniC

When a process goes to local monitor (the process level), it will check the *InUse* attributes to find whether any other process already requests to enter the distributed monitor at the node level. If it is the case, the current requesting process needs to wait in *Entry_Q*. This mechanism ensures that, at any time, at most one process from the same node can enter the distributed monitor to apply for CS.

When a process goes through the local monitor and requests to enter the distributed monitor (the node level), it uses the method *makeRequest()* of the DME algorithm to obtain the privilege for executing operations in the *user specified monitor*. If the process does not obtain the permission, it will wait in the *Request_Q*. Upon receipt of a Privilege message, the process will be de-queued from the *Request_Q* and then can access the globally shared resource.

For a process that has entered the *user specified monitor*, to access the shared resource, it may need to wait for a signal primitive on some condition variables. The node ID of the process will be appended to the condition variables' *Condition_Q*. The ID of the process waiting on the condition variable will be appended to the condition variables' *WaitingProcess_Q*. The process waiting for a signal response message will wait in *Response_Q*. Upon receipt of a Signal response message, the node ID of the process will be dequeued from the condition variable's *Condition_Q*, and the process ID will be dequeued from *WaitingProcess_Q*. The process will be waked up and de-queued from the *Response_Q*, and then can access the shared resource associated with the condition variable.

For a process releasing the shared resource, the *exit* and *signal* primitive of the distributed and local monitor will be invoked. The process firstly checks whether the *Condition_Q* is empty. If the *Condition_Q* is empty, the *exit* primitive of distributed monitor is called, which will identify the execution mode. If the execution is in DME mode, the *releasePrivilege()* method of the DME algorithm will be invoked to allow other processes at other nodes to compete for the critical section, and then the *exit()* primitive of Local Monitor is invoked to allow other process on the same node to make requests in the node level. If the execution mode is the Signal Mode, it sends the Response message to the node which initiates the Signal Mode, piggybacking the newest waiting process information.

If the *Condition_Q* is not empty, the *signal* primitive is called. If the monitor executes in the DME mode, the process will wait for the Response message. After receiving the message, it will invoke *exit()* primitive. Otherwise, it sends a Signal message to the process at the head of the *Condition_Q* for the condition variable, piggybacking the newest process waiting information.

4 Implementation Considerations for DisMoniC

In this section, we describe the distributed implementation of the DisMoniC algorithms. For algorithm implementation, the following data structures are used:

- *Con_Vars* is a list to maintain condition variables. Because the distributed monitor construct has no real condition variable, condition variables in a *user specified monitor* will be created first and then used to initialize the distributed monitor.
- DME_Algorithm is the interface for calling the methods of the DME algorithm.
- *Signal_Flag* indicates whether a signal primitive has been invoked. In our proposed mechanism, when a signal primitive is invoked, the DME algorithm is blocked from circulating the privilege of entering the critical section until the signal primitive has been fulfilled. In this case, the Signal_Flag is set to *true*, which indicates that the execution mode is changed to the Signal mode, and the process being signaled obtains the permission to enter the critical section. Nesting signal primitives are allowed in the distributed monitor, and a nesting signal primitive means a signal primitive invoked by a process waked up by a signal primitive.
- *Signal_Source* maintains the ID of the node that first initiates the Signal mode. When the Signal_Source node receives a Response message, the Signal mode terminates.
- *Condition_Q* is a FIFO queue that stores the node ID of all the processes waiting on the condition variable.
- *WaitingProcess_Q* is a FIFO queue stores the ID of the processes waiting on the condition variable on the current node.
- *Smallest_TimeStamp* indicates the oldest process that wais on the condition variable and will be signaled next time.
- *Biggest_TimeStamp* indicates the latest process waiting on the condition variable.

A method, named *initialize(DME, Con_Vars),* is designed to initialize the distributed monitor with the user specified monitor. It sets the current node to the node identifier to be used in the DME algorithm, Signal_Source to the current node, and Signal_Flag to *false*.

As mentioned before, the distributed monitor provides four primitives: *enter()*, *exist()*, *wait()*, and signal (). Their functions have been described in Section 3.1. Due to the limited space, here we only focus on the implementation of the piggyback mechanism for handling condition variables.

The information about processes waiting on condition variables will be piggybacked when any message is passed in the DME algorithm. This is realized by the Piggyback_WaitingInfo (WaitInformation) method.WaitingInformation is a list whose elements consist of four parts, *Condition_Variable*, *Smallest_TimeStamp*, *Biggest_TimeStamp*, and *Condition_Q*. If a token-based DME algorithm is used in the distributed monitor, Smallest_TimeStamp and Biggest_TimeStamp can be ignored. Because WaitingInformation is piggybacked on only the token, every process will take this piggybacked message as the most recent process waiting information. However, for quorum-based algorithm, a process will receive permissions from more than one process, so more than one WaitingInformation will be piggybacked. In this case, Smallest_TimeStamp and Biggest_TimeStamp are used to determine the most recent process waiting information. When Smallest_TimeStamp > Biggest_TimeStamp holds, Condition_Q is empty.

When a distributed monitor receives the piggybacked message, it refreshes the process waiting information for all condition variables using the *On_Receive_PiggybackInfo()* method. Information about each condition variable will be extracted and passed to the *update()* method of the corresponding local condition variable.

Each condition variable is associated with four methods: *wait()*, *On_Recv_Signal()*, *update()* and *record()*, which are invoked by the corresponding methods in the distributed monitor. When the wait () method is invoked, the calling process is appended to *WaitingProcess_Q*, and then waits for a signal message of the condition variable. When the *On_Recv_Signal()* method is invoked, it increases *Smallest_TimeStamp* by one, dequeues the condition variable's *Condition_Q*, and dequeues a process from *WaitingProcess_Q*, and then wakes up the process.

In addition, the *record()* method of condition variable is used to update the waiting process information at the node level before the final wait() method is called. When the record() method is invoked, it increases Biggest_TimeStamp by one, and appends the node ID to the condition variable's Condition_Q. When the update() method is invoked, it synchronizes the waiting information about the current condition variable by using the piggybacked waiting information.

5 Performance Evaluation

To evaluate the performance of DisMoniC, we have implemented a prototype with our proposed algorithms and a DME algorithm. A distributed producer-consumer program is developed to run as the application of DisMoniC.

The correctness properties of the monitor construct, including safety, liveness and fairness, are validated using the results obtained from the simulations. The validation is done by monitoring the run-time behaviors of the application program.

Recall that DisMoniC is independent of the DME algorithms to be used. In our evaluation, we simply simulated a permission-based algorithm similar to

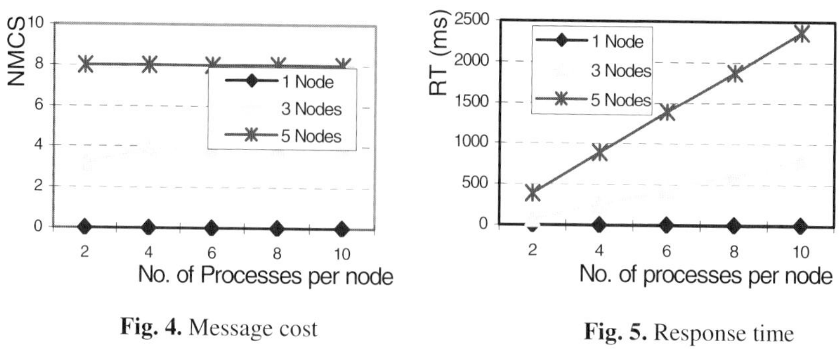

Fig. 4. Message cost

Fig. 5. Response time

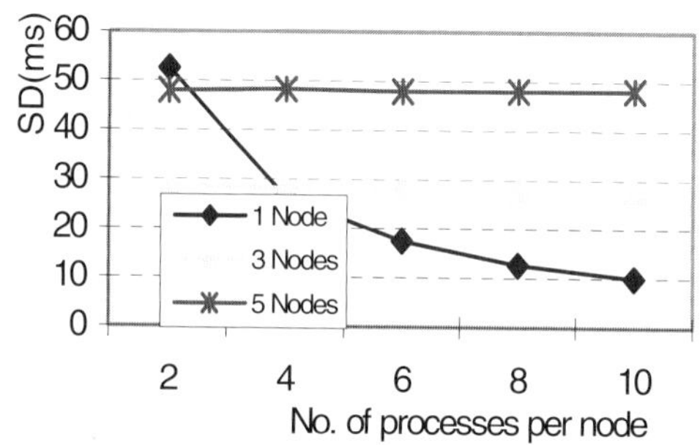

Fig. 6. Synchronization delay

Ricart-Agrawala algorithm[20]. We assume the message transmission delay is 10ms. The DisMoniC has been simulated in a system with one, three and five nodes, respectively.

Three metrics are used in the performance evaluation.

Number of Messages Per CS Entry (NMCS): the average number of messages exchanged among the nodes for each execution of the CS.

Synchronization Delay (SD): the number of sequential messages exchanged after a node leaves the CS and before the next node enters the CS.

Response Time (RT): the time interval that a node waits to enter the CS after its request for CS is issued.

The simulation results are shown in Figures 4-6. From Figure 4, it can be observed that the NMCS is about 2 * (N – 1), where *N* is the total number of nodes in the system. Theoretically, the NMCS of the DME algorithm is 2 * (N – 1). This indicates that, our DisMoniC does not introduce additional message overhead. Figure 5 shows the response time of DisMoniC, which increases linearly with the total number of processes at all the nodes.

The SD, as shown in Figure 6, is nearly equal to the transmission delay of one message, which is the minimum delay that can be achieved.

In summary, the performance of our proposed distributed monitor depends on the underlying DME algorithm. Besides the cost of DME algorithm, very little additional overhead is introduced by DisMoniC.

6 Conclusions

In this paper, we have described DisMoniC, a generic distributed monitor construct for programming distributed systems, which extends the centralized monitor by incorporating a DME algorithm to ensure distributed mutual exclusion and introducing time efficient algorithm for handling condition variables to achieve process synchronization in a distributed environment. Even with the implementation of condition variables, DisMoniC can still guarantee the correctness properties, i.e. safety, and liveness, fairness. Simulations have been conducted to evaluate the performance of DisMoniC. The simulation results show that, besides the cost of the underlying DME algorithm, almost no additional overhead is introduced by our proposed algorithms in DisMoniC.

In our future work, we are planning to optimize the piggybacked messages and the related operations of handling condition variables. Furthermore, in order to realize a robust distributed monitor construct, we will also improve DisMoniC by handling various kinds of failures, including link failures and node failures.

Acknowledgement

This work is partially supported by the University Grant Council of Hong Kong under the CERG Grant PolyU 5183/04E and the China National 973 Program Grant 2002CB3/2002.

References

1. Hoare, C.A.R.: Monitors: An Operating System Structuring Concept. Communications of the ACM 17(10), 549–557 (1974)
2. Hansen, P.B.: Operating System Principles. Prentice Hall, Englewood Cliffs, NJ (1973)
3. Lampson, B.W., Redell, D.D.: Experiences with Processes and Monitors in Mesa. Communications of the ACM 23(2), 105–117 (1980)
4. Doeppner Jr., T.W., Gebele, A.J.: C++ on a Parallel Machine. Department of Computer Science, Brown University, Technical Report, CS-87-26 (November 1987)
5. Beck, B.: Shared-Memory Parallel Programming in C++. IEEE Software 7(4), 38–48 (1990)
6. Schneider, F.B.: Ensuring Consistency in a Distributed Database System by Use of Distributed Semaphores. In: Delobel, C., et al. (eds.) Distributed Data Bases, pp. 183–189. North-Holland, Amsterdam (1980)
7. Raymond, K.: A Consensus Algorithm for Distributed Semaphores. In: Proc. 12th Australian Computer Science Conf., pp. 88–97 (February 1989)
8. Maddi, A., Raynal, M.: Implementing Semaphore on a Distributed memory Parallel Machine. In: Evans, D.J., et al. (eds.) Parallel Computing '91, pp. 407–412. Elsevier Science, Amsterdam (1992)
9. Yuan, S., Hsu, Y.: Design and Implementation of A Distributed Monitor Facility. Computer Systems – Science & Engineering 12(1), 43–51 (1997)

10. Chiao, H.-T., Wu, C.-H., Yuan, S.-M.: A More Expressive Monitor for Concurrent Java Programming. In: Bode, A., Ludwig, T., Karl, W.C., Wismüller, R. (eds.) Euro-Par 2000. LNCS, vol. 1900, Springer, Heidelberg (2000)
11. Greco, C.F.: A Simple Shared Data Space for Web-based Distributed Collaborative Applications. Department of Computer Science, Duke University, A Thesis submitted for the degree of Master of Science (1997)
12. Malkhi, D., Reiter, M.K.: Secure and Scalable Replication in Phalanx. In: Proceedings of the 17th IEEE Symposium on Reliable Distributed Systems, pp. 51–58. IEEE Computer Society Press, Los Alamitos (October 1998)
13. Sighal, M.: A Taxonomy of Distributed Mutual Exclusion. Journal of Parallel and Distributed Computing 18, 94–101 (1993)
14. Velazquez, M.G.: A Survey of Distributed Mutual Exclusion Algorithm. Department of Computer Science, Colorado State University, Technical Report, CS-93-116 (September 1993)
15. Benchaïba, M., Bouabdallah, A., Badache, N., Ahmed-Nacer, M.: Distributed Mutual Exclusion Algorithms in Mobile Ad Hoc Networks: an Overview. ACM SIGOPS Operating Systems Review 38(1) (2004)
16. Felten, E.W., Rabinovich, M.: A centralized token-based algorithm for distributed mutual exclusion. Univ. of Washington technical report TR-92-02-02 (2002)
17. Agrawal, D., El Abbadi, A.: An Efficient and Fault-tolerant Solution for Distributed Mutual Exclusion. ACM Transactions on Computer Systems 9(1), 1–20 (1991)
18. Lamport, L.: Time, clocks, and the order of events in a distributed system. Communications of the ACM 21(7), 558–565 (1978)
19. Maekawa, M.: A Sqrt(N) Algorithm for Mutual Exclusion in Decentralized Systems. ACM Transactions on Computer Systems 3(2), 145–159 (1985)
20. Ricart, G., Agrawala, A.: An Optimal Algorithm for Mutual Exclusion in Computer Networks. Communications of the ACM 24(1), 9–17 (1981)
21. Sanders, B.: The Information Structure of Distributed Mutual Exclusion Algorithms. ACM Transactions on Computer Systems 5(3), 284–299 (1987)
22. Mizuno, M., Neilsen, M.L., Rao, R.: A Token based distributed mutual exclusion algorithm based on Quorum Agreements. In: 11th Intl. Conference on Distributed Computing Systems, pp. 361–368 (May 1991)
23. Naimi, M., Trehel, M., Arnold, A.: A log(n) distributed mutual exclusion algorithm based on path reversal. Journal of Parallel and Distributed Computing 34, 1–13 (1996)
24. Singhal, M.: A Heuristically-aided Algorithm for Mutual Exclusion in Distributed Systems. IEEE Transactions on Computers 38(5), 622–651 (1989)
25. Singhal, M.: A Dynamic Information-Structure Mutual Exclusion Algorithm for Distributed Systems. IEEE Transactions on Parallel and Distributed Systems 3(1), 121–125 (1992)
26. Suzuki, I., Kasami, T.: A Distributed Mutual Exclusion Algorithm. ACM Transactions on Computer Systems 3(4), 344–349 (1985)
27. Mansfield, T.: A Decentralized Implementation of Monitors. Australian Computer Science Communications 12(1), 266–274 (1990)

Low Latency Vertical Handover Using MIH L2-Trigger Algorithm in Mobile IP Networks

Jin-Man Kim and Jong-Wook Jang

Dept. of Computer Engineering, Dong-Eui University,
995 Eomgwangno, Busanjin-gu, Busan, Korea
iricejm@nate.com, jwjang@deu.ac.kr

Abstract. Recently, information communication market is reorganized focused on the digital convergence service used for integrating the communication, broadcasting and internet media by connecting the communication equipment, broadcasting equipment and computer via a network. The mobility support protocol enabling the effective handover between heterogeneous networks is emerged as the hot issue in relation with these next generation communication networks. In this paper, we are to suggest the MIH Vertical handover procedure required for the implementation of MIH over MIPv4 Low-Latency vertical handover by analyzing the handover performance in the overlap area between wireless networks using the vertical handover function of MIPv4 Mobile IP Technology of IETF and considering the expected problems. Also, we are to suggest the MIH L2-Trigger generation algorithm required for deciding the optimal handoff. We evaluate the vertical handover performance of MIPv4 low-latency in the overlap area between wireless networks by using the NS-2 and applying the IEEE 802.21 MIH (Media Independent Handover) based on the suggested technique and algorithm.

1 Introduction

Mobile communication network is considerably developed and new wireless communication technology is introduced, so the diverse networks are provided and operated with overlapped. The mobile communication networks such as 3GPP and 3GPP2[1], WLAN[2] Service commonly provided in the hot spot area and recently commercialized Wibro[3] service are widely provided to the users as the representative services after being installed according to characteristics. The users want to access to the internet at any times and any places and require the continual service free from disconnection in this communication environment. Communication network interlocking technology and mobility support technology are essentially required for meeting these users' requirements. In this paper, we materialize the vertical handover function applicable to the heterogeneous networks by consolidating the IEEE 802.21 MIH (Media Independent Handover)[4] Technology, used for the interlocking between heterogeneous wireless access networks, and Mobile IP Technology, used for providing the mobility, and using the ns-2 (network simulator-2)[5] and then analyze and evaluate the materialized performances.

I. Stojmenovic et al. (Eds.): ISPA 2007, LNCS 4742, pp. 707–718, 2007.

In the chapter 2 of this paper, we are to review the MIH Technology as a pat of relevant research program. In chapter 3, we are to consider the problems shown in the vertical handover of MIPv4 and suggest the MIH Vertical handover procedures required for the implementation of MIH over MIPv4 low-latency vertical handover. Also, we are to suggest the MIH L2-Trigger generation algorithm required for deciding the optimal handoff. In the chapter 4, we compare the difference among MIPv4[6], MIPv4 Low-Latency[7] and MIH over MIPv4 Low-Latency vertical handover function through the NS-2 simulation. In the chapter 5, we make a conclusion as the final process.

2 Relevant Researches

2.1 IEEE 802.21 MIH Technology

The IEEE 802.21 MIH is designed by assuming that the handset is set as the multi-mode. In other words, many interfaces, where the handover occurs, are available. It is designed to be used for the handover among cable networks such as IEEE 802.3, wireless networks such as IEEE 802.11, 15, 16, 20 and other networks such as 3GPP and 3GPP2, and also, we must consider whether the areas covered by each network base station are overlapped or not for the classification. The Fig. 1 shows the concept of handover between general IEEE 802 networks.

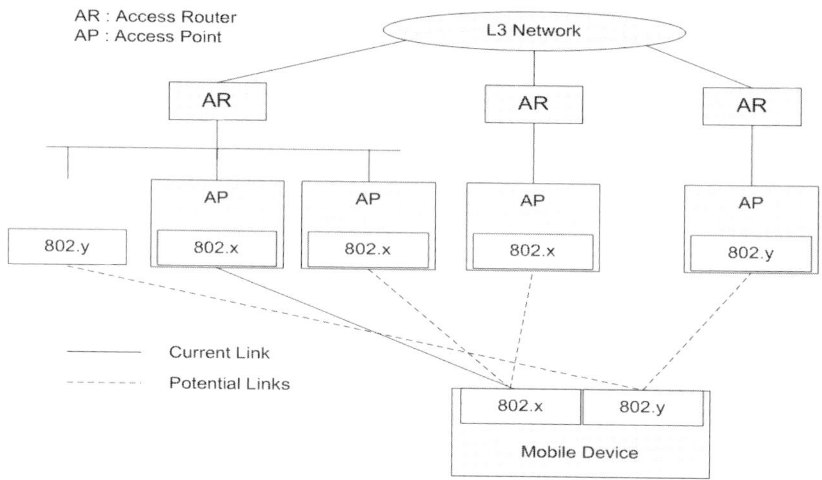

Fig. 1. The concept of handover between IEEE 802 series networks

As shown in the Fig. 1, MIH is designed in consideration of diverse networks, so the diverse handover scenarios are available. We must consider whether the user quality is guaranteed in the handover between heterogeneous networks. If the channels of layer 2 and layer 3 are reset by the handover, layer 3 is delayed for longer than layer 2, so the real time service quality is not guaranteed. The IEEE 802.21 MIH is designed focused on minimizing the delay resulted from the handover by relaying the information of layer 2 to the layer 3 by means of introducing the concept of L2 Trigger in order to solve this problem. For the current IEEE, only the layer 2 is standardized and IETF (Internet Engineering Task Force) handles the standardization of layer 3, so there is no way of solving this problem. In this regard, IETF and IEEE 802.21 are expected to take the actions required for solving this problem.

3 The Proposed MIH over MIPv4 Low-Latency Vertical Handover Procedures and MIH L2-Trigger Algorithm

3.1 Consideration of Vertical Handover Problems Shown in the Existing MIPv4

MIPv4 is the protocol designed to provide the IP Mobility using the IPv4. The MIPv4 includes the CoA (Care of Address) indicating the current location of mobile node other than home address used in its home network.

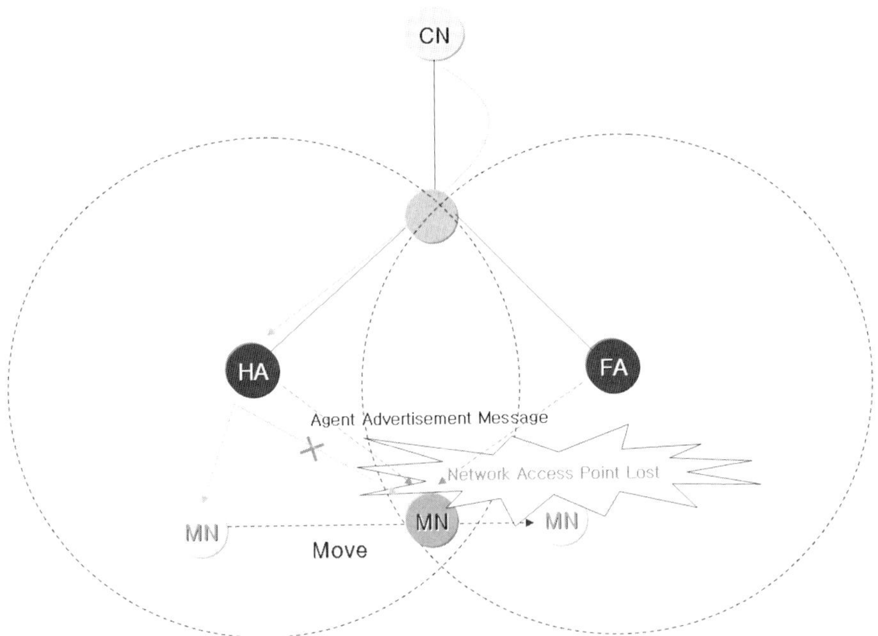

Fig. 2. The mobile node looses the attach point in the network overlap area duding the handoff process of Mobile IP

We may see whether the mobile node is positioned in the home network or moved to other networks through this CoA. For the Mobile IP, HA or FA frequently informs of its current position using the agent advertise message and mobile node requests the registration of agent using the solicitation message.The solicitation message of mobile node may request the advertise message of agent, so the mobile node may see whether it is currently located in the HA Area or FA Area. Thus, mobile node acquires its location information through the advertise message of agent and relays its location information to the HA through the registration procedures. When the mobile node is moved to new FA, HA may see new CoA of mobile node by registering the agent of mobile node and continually relay the data by setting the tunneling through this new CoA. Mobile IP provides the mobility to the mobile node through this mechanism. However, this mechanism of mobile IP may cause the problem according to applied environment.

In this paper, we are to consider the problems of mobile IP focused on two viewpoints and then solve the considered problems. First, handoff of MIPv4 is delayed in the overlap area. If the HA and FA share the overlap area and handoff occurs when the mobile node moves via a overlap area, mobile node may loose its attach point when passing through this overlap area. This phenomenon is resulted from the basic motion mechanism of Mobile IP. As shown in the Fig. 2, mobile node receives the overlapped agent advertise message of HA and FA when entering the overlap area, so the mobile node confuses its current attach point and then looses the network attach point accordingly. Second, handoff problem may be caused between heterogeneous networks. The Mobile IP is designed to provide the independent mobility to its sub-technology by providing the mobility in the layer 3. However, the mobile IP Handoff between heterogeneous networks must select and activate the L2, sub-technology, and physical layer under the actual wireless network environment. Because the Mobile IP does not include the function required for selecting and changing the interface, the handoff between heterogeneous networks is not provided under the actual environment. In this regard, we are to prove that the unnecessary handoff delay is reduced by enabling the mobile node to select the most suitable link when entering the overlap area in this paper.

3.2 MIH over MIPv4 Low-Latency Vertical Handover Procedures

In the future, next generation communication network is expected to accept the diverse access networks based on the IP Based core network. Also, the IP Technology based access networks will play the core roles. The mobile IP Technology is essentially required for providing the effective mobility under this next generation communication network environment. The Mobile IPv4/IPv6 is known as the representative IP Mobility protocol. The IPv6 is the technology intended to solve the deficient IP of IPv4. However, all IPv4s are not replaced with the IPv6 and long time is required for replacing all, so the IPv4 based access network, most widely used in the market, is expected to be positioned as the top IP Based access network in the future. In this regard, the mobility support technology of MIPv4 must be continually studied.

In this paper, MIPv4 is selected under the intention of studying the IP Mobility, and also, we use the MIPv4 Low-Latency Handover technology, Mobile IP Fast handover method, used to provide the real time service to the mobile handset as the IP Mobility support technology intended to solve the slow mobility support in the wide area, known as one of mobile IP Problems. The mobility support between IP Based access networks is essentially required in consideration of increased demand. However, IP Mobility includes the problems to solve as described in the clause 3.1. In this clause, we are to suggest the MIH over MIPv4 low-latency vertical handover

plan as an alternative to solve the vertical handover problems of mobile Ipv4 and handoff delay problems shown in the network overlap area.
MIH, IEEE 802.21, is the mobility support technology, handoff support technology between heterogeneous networks, applicable regardless of media characteristics of IP Layer.

In this paper, we intend to provide the mobility between heterogeneous networks to the MIPv4 and minimize the handoff delay in the overlap area. To accomplish these goals, we are to suggest the vertical handover procedures required for providing the mobility between MIPv4 heterogeneous networks of MIH and minimizing the handoff delay in the overlap area and compare and analyze the MIH over MIPv4 Low-Latency vertical handover performances using the NS-2.

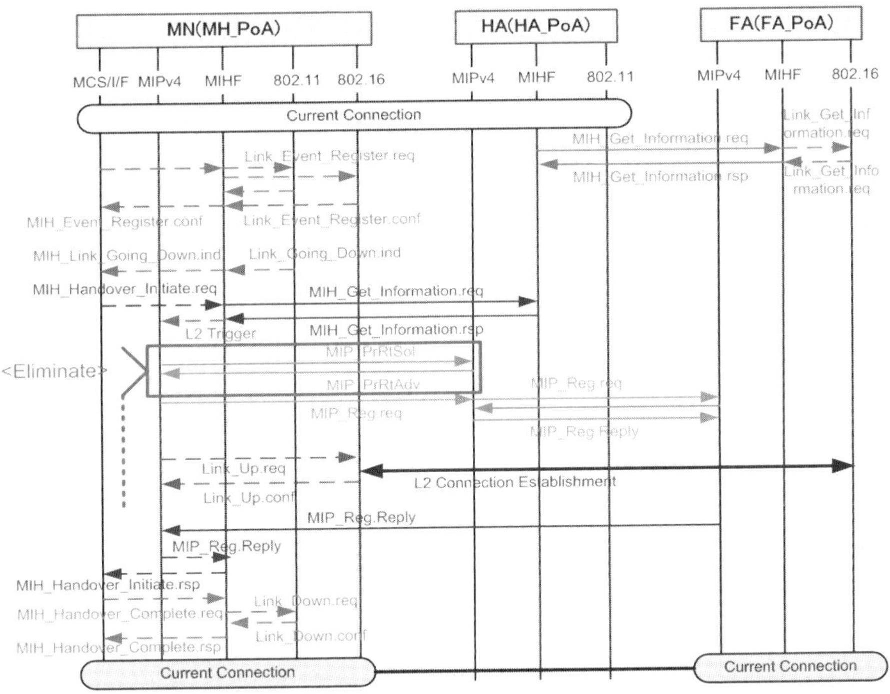

Fig. 3. MIH over MIPv4 Vertical Handover procedures using the Pre-Registration and L2-MT Methods

Fig. 3 shows the handover procedures between 802.11 WLAN and 802.16 WiBro as the vertical handover procedures suggested in this paper. As shown in the Fig. 3, PoA, HA, acquires the information of surrounding FA PoA through the MIH_Get_Information.req and mobile node performs the handover through the Handover.Initiate when moving from 802.11 network to 802.16 network. At this time, mobile node acquires the Phy_Type, MAC_Type, Channel, New CoA Address of network to move through the MIH_Get_Information.req. We simplify the whole process by reducing the MIP_PrRt_Sol, MIP_PrRt_Adv procedures, registration procedures of MIPv4. The handover delay of MIPv4 is resulted from the repeated handovers in the L2 and L3 when mobile node moves from HA, current network attach point, to FA. We may minimize the loss by activating the channel secured for the handover in the L3. However, HA Registration procedures should not be performed without completely securing the handover. In other words, the HA Registration procedures must be performed only after the mobility of mobile node is completely guaranteed. Otherwise, supply of service may be stopped. We may minimize the handoff delay time by performing the HA Registration procedures of MIP only after carefully checking the exact time when the handover event of mobile node occurs. In this paper, we allow the mobile node to acquire the PHY_Type, MAC_Type, Channel of new FA and PoA_Address information by generating the MIH_Link_Going_Down.ind if the RxPr, packet receiving power of received packet stamp, is smaller than RxThreshold value during the measuring process intended to generate the stable L2-Trigger using the MIH and perform the stable handoff by completing the L3 Registration before the L2 handoff process is completely done. Also, we allow the mobile node to keep its current attach point until the handoff is generated when the node moves from the overlap area by enabling the MIH to control the network interface of mobile node and link selection for the purpose of preventing the mobile node from confusing and loosing the network attach point when the mobile node enters the overlap area. We may reduce the MIPv4 Low-Latency Handoff delay in the overlap area between heterogeneous networks by enabling the mobile node to perform the L3 registration and L2 Handoff within the designated time. Nothing is important than detecting the accurate handover time and selecting the optimal link condition to minimize the handoff delay between heterogeneous networks. This paper shows that the handoff delay may be minimized by adjusting the registration procedures performed according to handover procedures of MIPv4 using the MIH when the vertical handover procedures are performed between heterogeneous networks of MIPv4.

3.3 MIH L2 Trigger Generation Algorithm Required for Deciding the Exact Handoff Performance Time

Nothing is more important than deciding when to start the handoff performance in deciding the handoff. Basically, Mobile IP completes the handoff procedures through the HA Registration of new FA after the L2 handoff. This hard handoff extends the time delay required for the L3 handoff, registration procedure after the L2 handoff, so it is difficult to guarantee the real time communication and continuity of service. The MIPv4-LLH-PreReg technique is suggested as an alternative to solve this problem. This technique is designed to reduce the handoff delay of existing mobile IP by completing the L3 registration using the L2 Trigger before the mobile node completes the L2 handoff. However, if this method is applied or used, handoff performance depends on the size of overlap area. The following Fig. 4 shows the handoff problem, resulted from the different size of overlap area, expected when using the MIPv4-LLH-PreReg technique:

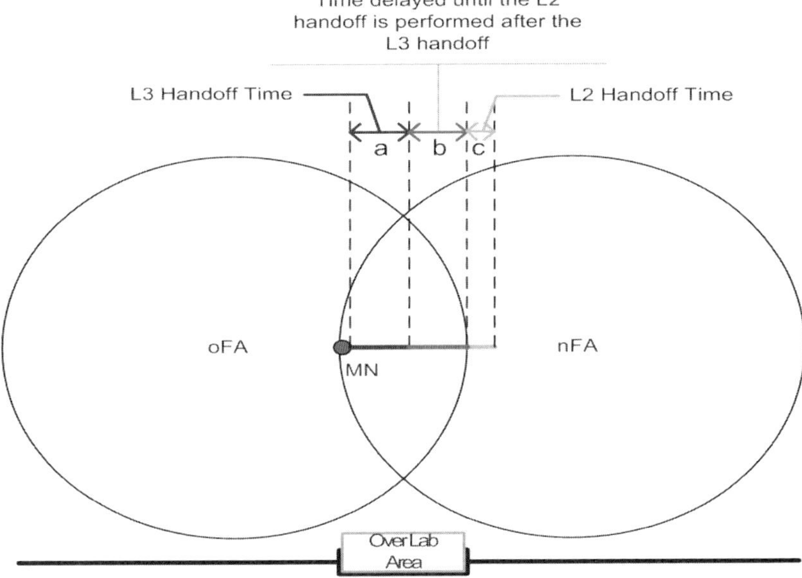

Fig. 4. Handoff problem, resulted from the different size of overlap area, expected when using the MIPv4-LLH-PreReg technique

The handoff procedure is performed when the mobile node passes through the overlap area between oFA and nFA. The problem occurs when this overlap area is too big or too small. If the overlap area is too big, time delay corresponding to b occurs as shown in the Fig. 4. On the contrary, if the overlap area is too small, it is difficult to secure the sufficient time delay, a (necessary and sufficient L3 handoff time), so the handoff delay or continuity of service is not guaranteed. When the time delay, b, is removed and sufficient L3 handoff time is guaranteed as the most ideal case, optimal handoff is performed. Thus, time to decide the handoff must be dynamically adjusted according to location of mobile node and format of network for the optimal handoff performance. The MIPv4-LLH-PreReg performs the L3 registration when passing through the boundary of nFA or receiving the L2 signal of new FA. In other words, handoff is always performed at the same time, so the problem occurs as previously explained. In this paper, we are to suggest the MIH L2-Trigger generation algorithm enabling you to decide the time to perform the handoff under the optimal condition regardless of overlap area size of network using the MIH for the purpose of solving the problem.

For the suggested algorithm, RSSI (Receive Signal Strength Indicator) is used as the source value of L2-Trigger generation. RSSI, a method used to measure the RF Signal strength, is the mechanism used to measure the RF Energy including the Wireless NIC Circuit device or element. This device or element is defined in the IEEE802.11 standard.

The mobile node periodically measures the RSSI of oFA or nFA, and if the momentarily measured oFA_RSSI Value is less than the specific threshold value, handoff will be performed. However, the momentarily measured electric wave signal is suddenly changed by the communication errors under the wireless environments.

Therefore, the handoff must be decided based on the average electric wave signal in order to perform the handoff under the more stable environment. In this paper, the 'Simple Moving Average' technique is used for acquiring the average value of receiving signals measured in the real time.

$$\begin{aligned} & m = 3 \\ & P_{MA}(t) = (P_{t-2} + P_{t-1} + P_t)/m \\ & \quad = \sum_{x=m-1}^{1} P_{t-x}/m \end{aligned} \tag{1}$$

Formula (1) is the 'Simple Moving Average' formula used for calculating the average electric wave signal. In this formula, $P_{MA}(t)$ and m mean the average electric wave signal and average moving period respectively. The signal of average electric wave is changed according to this average moving period. In this paper, m=3 is used as the basic value.

Also, RSSI_Max and RxTh, RSSI Threshold value, are considered as 100 and 16 (-96dBm) respectively for the purpose of measuring the RSSI Signal. In fact, each vendor designates the different value for the RSSI_Max, and RxTh value is different accordingly. In this regard, it is difficult to define whether the received signal strength is strong or weak. The signal strength of wireless communication equipment supplied by different vendors needs to be measured by the unified references. However, this issue on unifying the signal strength measuring methods is not included in the scope of this paper.

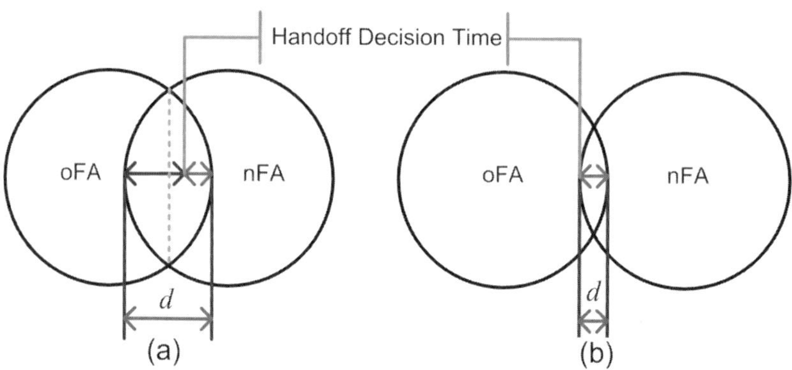

Fig. 5. Time to Decide the Handoff according to Size of Overlap Area

The mobile node must decide the handoff time when entering the overlap area between oFA and nFA after moving to these two areas. At this time, handoff time must be decided and size of overlap area must be forecasted for dynamically adjusting the handoff time. The Fig. 5 shows when to decide the handoff according to size of overlap area. If the overlap area is big as shown in the Fig. 5 (a), postpone the time to decide the handoff until the signal of nFA is bigger than the one of oFA in the overlap area, and if the overlap area is small as shown in the Fig. 5 (b), it is recommended to decide the handoff when the mobile node enters the overlap area for the optimal handoff performance.

Thus, we suggest the algorithm, which is applicable to two cases, used to decide the time to perform the optimal handoff at any circumstances. It is recommended to decide the handoff based on two different states using the difference of signal strength between nFA_RSSI(t) and oFA_RSSI_P_{MA}(t) when entering the overlap area. We set the conditions to check these two states as follows:

Conditions:

$$nFA\_RSSI(t) \geq nFA\_RSSI\_RxTh,$$
$$L3\_HO\_Interval = \Delta RSSI\_Level(Require\_L3\_HO\_Time),$$
$$if \quad \left(\frac{oFA\_RSSI\_P_{MA}(t) + oFA\_RSSI\_RxTh}{2}\right) -$$
$$oFA\_RSSI\_RxTh \geq L3\_HO\_Interval \quad then$$
$$\text{"High"} \quad else \quad \text{"Low"}$$

Under above conditions, the mobile node forecasts the RSSI Value in the area where the signals of oFA and nFA cross when receiving the RSSI Signal of nFA and another signal exceeding the threshold. The size of overlap area is forecasted through this process. The handoff time is decided by comparing the forecasted value with the RSSI Change of time required for the L3 handoff. The formula (2) is the condition used when deciding the handoff in case of "Low." This formula is used when the overlap area is relatively small and handoff is decided according to conditions stated in the formula (2) when entering the overlap area.

$$nFA\_RSSI\_P_{MA}(t) \rhd nFA\_RSSI\_RxTh \tag{2}$$

Formula (3) is used to acquire the handoff decision condition in case of "High." This formula is used when the overlap area is relatively big and handoff is decided according to conditions stated in the formula (3) when entering the overlap area. In this case, mobile node performs the handoff when the signal of nFA is bigger than the one of oFA after being crossed.

$$\begin{aligned} &nFA\_RSSI\_P_{MA}(t) \rhd nFA\_RSSI\_RxTh \quad \& \\ &oFA\_RSSI\_P_{MA}(t) \lhd nFA\_RSSI\_P_{MA}(t) \quad \& \\ &oFA\_RSSI\_P_{MA}(t) \rhd 0 \end{aligned} \tag{3}$$

4 Evaluation of Performance

Simulation is conducted to evaluate the performance using the NS-2. The Ad-hoc model developed by the Monarch Research Group, CMU (Carnegie Mellon University)[8], is used for the simulation. Set the media used in the Ad-hoc network as the wireless channel and wireless physical and use the two-ray ground reflection model for the propagation model. Use the drop-tail queue based priority queue for the queuing model and set the number of packets to queue to 50. Set the MAC Protocol to 802.11. In this paper, we perform the vertical handover test by forming the multi-interface environment by means of applying the dual channel of 802.11 for the purpose of materializing the vertical handover between 802.11 WLAN and IEEE 802.16 WiBro.

4.1 Simulation Model

Set the size of network area to 600m x 600m and refer to the Fig. 6 for the details of simulation scenario.

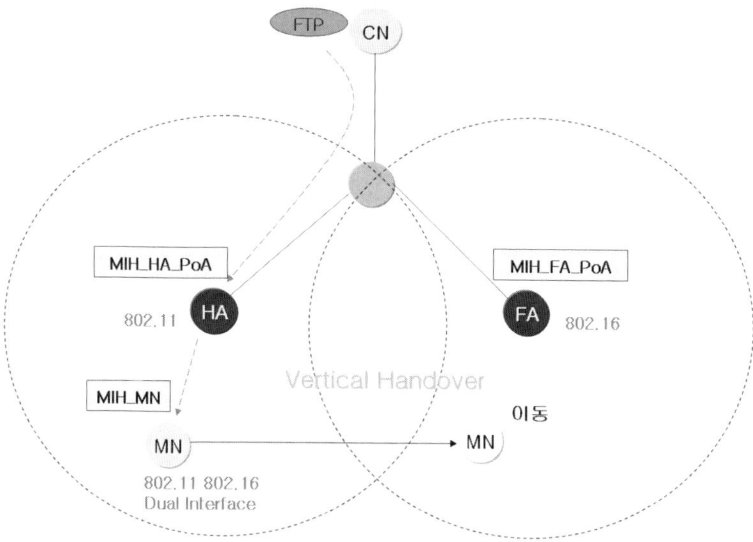

Fig. 6. Scenario for the MIH over MIPv4 Low-Latency Vertical Handover

MN includes both the 802.11 and 802.16, dual interface, when assuming that the HA is 802.11 network and FA is 802.16 network. MN is connected to the HA, initial network approach point, and adjust the TCP Protocol based FTP traffic to be generated from CN to MN. We perform the simulation for 25 seconds and set the maximum moving speed, measured when the MN moves from HA Area to FA Area, to 30m/s. We measure the handoff delay time between vertical handover in the overlap area of MIPv4 and MIPv4 Low-Latency and vertical handover of MIH over MIPv4 Low-Latency for the evaluation of performance. We measure the packet yield at every 0.5 second to check the handoff delay time. Fig. 7 shows the compared handoff delay times between vertical handover of existing MIPv4 and MIPv4 Low-Latency and vertical handover of MIH over MIPv4 Low-Latency. Fig. 7 shows that the handoff of MIPv4 is delayed for about 11 seconds. Also, the handoff delay of MIPv4 Low-Latency is considerably reduced as compared with MIPv4 through the pre-registration process using the L2 trigger. However, it looses the network attach point in the network overlap area. Anyhow, MIH over MIPv4 Low-Latency shows the less handoff delay as compared with the existing MIPv4 or MIPv4 Low latency during the vertical handover process from 802.11 to 802.16.

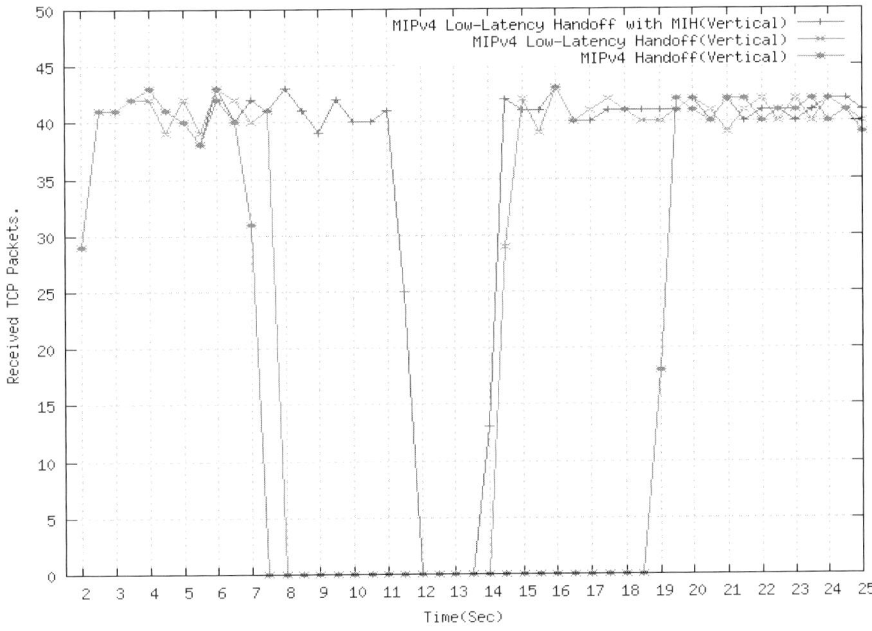

Fig. 7. MIPv4 and MIH over MIPv4 Low-Latency Vertical Handover performance analysis

5 Conclusion

In this paper, we intend to solve the vertical handover problem shown in the network overlap area of existing Mobile IPv4 as a part of program intended to solve the mobility support problem between heterogeneous networks in consideration of increased demand for the IP Based wireless access network. We suggest the handover procedures between 802.11 and 802.16 by applying the IEEE 802.21 MIH Technology as an alternative to solve this problem. We analyze the MIH over MIPv4 Low-Latency Vertical Handover performance using this handover procedure. Analyzed results show that the MIPv4 may not independently prevent the handoff delay in the overlap area between heterogeneous networks. However, we may considerably reduce the handoff delay time in the overlap area between heterogeneous networks during the vertical handover process using the MIH, layer 2.5. This result shows that the MIH may be selected as an alternative of mobility support protocol guaranteeing the continual service free from disconnection by allowing the mobile node to select the optimal network attach point when moving in the next generation network environment where the diverse IP Access networks coexist. Also, we may see that the optimal handoff is performed through the MIH L2-Trigger generation algorithm enabling you to decide the time to dynamically perform the handoff according to size of overlap area. As the future research project, we need to study the effective handover procedures and algorithm to generate the precise L2 trigger enabling the seamless handover using the MIH.

References

1. 3GPP2 P.S0001-A-1: Wireless IP Network Standard (2000)
2. ANS/IEEE Std 802.11: Wireless LAN Medium Access Control (MAC) and Physical Layer(PHY) Specifications (1999)
3. IEEE P802.16e/D6: Air Interface for Fixed and Mobile Broadband Wireless Access Systems Amendment for Physical and Medium Access Control Layers for Combined Fixed and Mobile Operation in Licensed Bands (2005)
4. IEEE P802.21/D00.01: Draft IEEE Standard for Local and Metropolitan Area Networks: Media Independent Handover Services (2005)
5. ISI: The Network Simulator: ns-2, University of Southern California, http://www.isi.edu/nanam/ns/
6. Perkins, C.: IP Mobility Support for IPv4 revised. ID draft-ietf-mip4-rfc3344bis-01.txt (2004)
7. El MalKi, K.: Mobile IP Low-Latency Handoff. Low Latency Handoffs in Mobile IPv4, ID draft-ietf-mobileip-lowlatency-handoffs-v4-09.txt (2004)
8. The CMU Monarch Project: The CMU Monarch Project's Wireless and Mobility Extensions to ns, Carnegie Mellon University (1999)

SPACC: A Simple Positioning and Coverage Control Solution for Wireless Sensor Networks

Mohsen Sharifi and Ehsan Farzad

Computer Engineering Department, Iran University of Science and Technology, University Road, Hengam Street, Resalat Square, Narmak, Tehran, Iran
{msharifi,farzad)@iust.ac.ir

Abstract. A category of wireless sensor networks consists of lots of autonomous sensor nodes with limited power and few base stations with theoretically unlimited power. A number of redundant nodes are usually deployed densely in these types of networks in order to provide redundancy for sensing and communications. There is a challenge though of which nodes must be active and which ones must be asleep, without compromising the coverage and network connectivity. To get round this challenge, each node should somehow know the position of its immediate neighbors. Previous researches have impractically assumed the existence of a GPS module in each node, which is in direct contradiction with the main constraints of low cost and size of sensor nodes. This paper proposes an energy saving solution without requiring the nodes to possess any physical GPS. The goal is to minimize the number of active sensors with respect to coverage and connectivity. Each node decides locally by itself whether to be active or not. There is no need for any global synchronization between nodes. Simulation results show that the higher density of nodes in our proposed solution leads to better coverage, higher energy saving and longer network lifetime.

1 Introduction

Recent advances in micro-electronics, digital electronics and wireless communications, prepared the area to develop tiny multi-functional sensor nodes with low cost and low energy. These sensors are able to collect and process environment data and communicate with others (sensors or sinks). A Wireless Sensor Network (WSN) consists of several sensor nodes; each of them equipped with a battery and embedded circuits for sensing and wireless communications. Sensor nodes are often deployed on hostile or remote environments for monitoring and gathering data, hence recharging or replenishment is not practical and energy is the most significant resource for them. The lifetime of a WSN is the time range that there exists enough nodes to cover the monitored area and the nodes are connected. An area is covered if it is covered by at least one active node, and this node is connected to sink, i.e. it can report events to the sink [1].

There are many differences between WSNs and other ad-hoc networks. One of the most significant issues of WSNs is redundancy. Since nodes are usually deployed

I. Stojmenovic et al. (Eds.): ISPA 2007, LNCS 4742, pp. 719–727, 2007.

densely, underlying network has more redundancy for sensing and communications. This redundancy causes collisions and collisions in turn increase retransmissions that result in waste of energy. Node redundancy leads to data redundancy since nodes have similar data to report.

One way to decrease redundancy is node scheduling. In node scheduling, nodes sleep several times through the network lifetime. But how can nodes decide to be active or not? One approach is based on centralized decisions which all nodes send their data to cluster head or a referee node and all processes are performed on that node. This increases the number of communications and results in energy waste and undesirable network traffic. Since energy consumption in communications is much more than in computations, it is better to make all decisions locally [2]. In our proposed solution, nodes decide about their own status in a fully localized manner and only by transmission of few messages between immediate neighbors.

The remaining of the paper is organized as follows. Section 2 presents relevant existing approaches in the literature. Our solution, nicknamed SPACC (Simple Positioning And Coverage Control), is presented in Section 3. Experimental results are reported in Section 4, and Section 5 concludes the paper.

2 Related Works

In this section, we present a brief description of existing solutions to the area coverage problem in WSNs. Since we are only concerned with localized or distributed solutions in this paper, we exclude centralized approaches and deterministic deployment methods [3, 4, 5] from our presentation here. Cardei et al. [6] has a rather complete presentation of existing solutions on the subject.

Tian et al. [7] present a scheduling scheme, which allows nodes to sleep or to remain active without affecting the network-monitoring task. The authors have presented a special kind of areas called "blind points". These points are created when two neighboring nodes simultaneously decide to turn off trusting each other for coverage. They introduce a timeout before making a decision. Therefore, neighboring nodes cannot decide at the same time anymore. When timeout ends, a node decides to be active if it is not fully covered. Otherwise, it emits a "withdrawal" message and goes to sleep. The authors have only addressed the coverage problem and ignored the connectivity problem. Moreover, they have used timeouts to solve the problem, while negotiations between nodes could have solved the problem more easily as is done in our approach.

Ye et al. [8] propose a distributed probing-based density control algorithm, named PEAS, that uses a simple rule for nodes to decide for activity. At first, a subset of nodes operates in the active mode to maintain coverage while others are put into sleep. Active nodes keep working until running out of energy. Any sleeping node wakes up occasionally to check if there exist working nodes in its vicinity. If no working nodes are within its adjustable probing range, it starts to operate in active mode; otherwise, it sleeps again. In this approach, no node location is needed but it does not ensure that the coverage area of a sleeping node is completely covered by working nodes, i.e., it does not guarantee complete coverage.

Zhang et al. [9] propose an Optimal Geographical Density Control algorithm (OGDC) which runs in rounds and begins with the selection of working nodes among a set of starting nodes. A power-on message is broadcasted by a starting node containing its geographical location and a random direction along which a working host should be located. This ensures that different nodes will be working at each round. Therefore, the power consumption will be distributed over the whole set of nodes. Furthermore, a back off time is needed for sending the message and permits to make the packet collision probability lower. Although random direction for power-on messages causes starting nodes not to be the same, selection of active nodes on the bases of remaining energy needs extra message passing, because nodes should be aware of energy level of their neighbors. There is also a need for time synchronization between nodes. This solution assumes that radio range is at least twice the sensing range.

Wang et al. [10] have extended the OGDC approach and proposed a Coverage and Configuration Protocol (CCP). They also observe that coverage infers connectivity if the radio range is at least twice the sensing range. In CCP, each node collects neighboring information and then uses this as an eligibility rule to decide if a node can sleep.

Carle et al. [11] present a two-step algorithm, called SCR-CADS (Surface Coverage Relay Connected Dominating Set) that uses the MPR (Multi Point Relay) approach proposed in [12]. In the first step, each node collects the locations of its neighbors and then broadcasts an SCR set to all its neighbors; this set is the minimal set of nodes that cover the area that is under coverage of each node. In the second step, each node decides locally to be either asleep or active based on a random priority. In this approach, it is assumed that radio radii are exactly equal to sensing radii.

All aforementioned solutions assume that each node knows its own location. In our SPACC solution, we remove this assumption. All is needed in 2-dimensional space is the location of 3 nodes that are not on a single line (or, 4 nodes in 3-dimensional space that are not on a single plane); one of these nodes is the sink and others are immediate neighbors of the sink. To support connectivity, we assume that radio radii are at least twice the sensing radii, as in [9].

3 SPACC Solution

Many proposed solutions on node scheduling mandate that redundant nodes should be off in order to conserve power but without compromising coverage and connectivity. In SPACC we assume that nodes are immobile and homogeneous, node density is high, and network is not sparse; the reasons for these assumptions are argued in later sections.

SPACC solution works in two phases: (1) Local Positioning, and (2) Coverage Detection.

3.1 Local Positioning

For better understanding, let's consider a graph $G(V,E)$ where $V=(v_1,v_2,\dots,v_n)$ is a set of nodes and $(v_1,v_2)\in E$ if and only if v_1 and v_2 are immediate neighbors of each other. We can then define the set of neighbors of v_1 as follows:

$$NBR(v_1) = \{v' : (v', v_1) \in E\}$$

Initially, each v_i broadcasts a *location request* message to $NBR(v_i)$. Each receiver of the location request message responds to the location message if it knows its own location. Otherwise, it waits until it receives enough location messages (at least 3 in 2-dimensional and 4 in 3-dimensional space) from other nodes so that it can calculate its own location. Having received these messages within an appropriate period and calculated its location, it can then respond to all nodes that had sent it location requests. Therefore, the location of unknown nodes is calculated using the locations of neighbors and distances to each neighbor (determined by signal power loss analysis).

In 2-dimensional space, if we have the distance between a node and 3 other nodes, the location of node can be calculated using mathematical rules. However, the exact distance between nodes is not calculable. So the approximate location of nodes is estimated through numerical analysis methods. Albowicz et al. in [13] propose a method to estimate location of a node in 3-dimensional space using location of neighbors. In this method, each node is responsible for computing its own location. Initially, each node selects some referee nodes among its neighbors and estimates its location using non-linear regression and partial distances. After location estimation, each node sends its location via location messages to requesting nodes in *NBR* set.

3.2 Coverage Detection

In the second phase of SPACC, the activity status of each node is determined. At first, each node determines its own *volunteer status* itself; the volunteer status of a node is *True* if the area under its coverage is also covered by other nodes. To find this status, each node uses a heuristic algorithm that takes the location of neighbors as input, and returns a flag representing activity status and a *rely set* containing neighbors that must be active to assure coverage if this node sleeps. A rely set is defined as follows:

$$R(v_1) = \{v'' : v'' \in NBR(v_1),\ v_1 \ relies\ on\ v''\}$$

This heuristic algorithm is a *divide and conquers* algorithm that is implemented recursively; it could have also been implemented by dynamic programming. Initially, the set *R* is empty and grows as the execution of the algorithm progresses. Depth of recursion depends on our policy that pre-defines our precision level. Higher precision levels lead to more accuracy. Each node can find a *surrounding square* encompassing its circular coverage area. The algorithm begins with a surrounding square with a side length equal to twice the sensing radius of the node. At each recursion, the square is divided into 4 equal sub-squares. Since coverage area is circular, and not rectangular, a square may be found which is out of coverage area of main circle. The algorithm ignores these out of bound sub-squares. In fact, the coverage area is divided into smaller sub-squares and depending on the number of levels, these sub-squares simulate the circular coverage area.

Each node follows 3 steps in each recursion in the heuristic algorithm:

1) If the number of recursions is more than the pre-defined precision level, this step returns *False*, else it continues to the next step.

2) If the square (initially the surrounding square) is out of bounds of coverage area of the node, this step returns *True*, otherwise it continues to the next step.
3) If there is a neighbor in *NBR* that fully covers the square, the result is *True*, otherwise the square is divided into four equal sub-squares and the algorithm runs for each sub-square in turn and the result is the logical *AND* of sub-results.

Fig. 1 shows two volunteer nodes after running the SPACC coverage detection heuristic algorithm, where $R(N_1)=\{N_2,N_3,N_4,N_5\}$, $R(N_2)=\{N_1,N_6,N_7,N_8\}$ and N_1 and N_2 (shown in grey color) are the two volunteer nodes wishing to go to sleep.

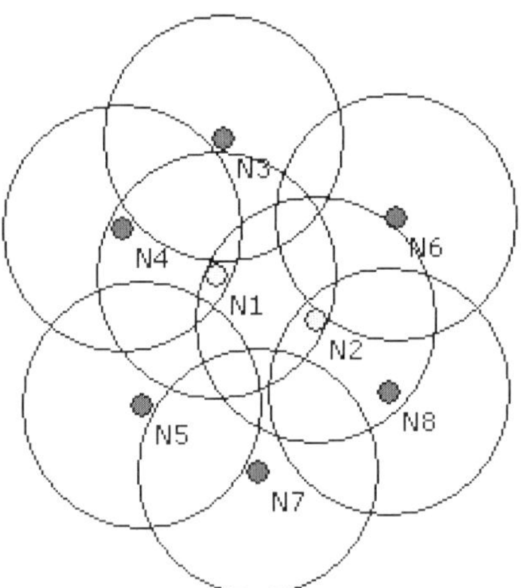

Fig. 1. N_1 and N_2 are two volunteer nodes wishing to go to sleep

After determining volunteer status, each volunteer node sends *volunteer* messages to all nodes within its own R set. Each volunteer message contains the volunteer status of the node and the number of members of R (i.e. $|R|$). Nodes that receive volunteer messages from their neighbors act differently according to their sleep priorities. Sleep priority is equal to $|R|$ and a lower number implies higher priority. This type of prioritization can also resolve the conflict between associated nodes, say v_1 and v_2 where $v_1 \in R(v_2), v_2 \in R(v_1)$, that grant sleep to their counterpart associated nodes.

Different responses of a node to volunteer messages according to sleep priorities are thus:

- When the priority of the node is higher than its neighbors, it returns *False* and goes to sleep.
- When the priority of the node is higher than the priority of some nodes, and lower than the priority of some others, it waits until it receives response messages from higher priority nodes and then sends its result to lower priority nodes.

- When the priority of the node is lowest, it waits for responses all higher priority nodes and then decides what to do.
- When a node receives a *False* message from a higher priority neighbor, it re-computes its volunteer status by considering only the remaining nodes (i.e. excluding this neighbor). It must remain active if it is not volunteer this time; otherwise, it neglects the response and waits for other responses.

It is worth to mention that the priority of associated nodes is transitive, i.e. if v_1 has higher priority than v_2 and v_2 has higher priority than v_3, then v_1 has higher priority than v_3 too. Hence, the probability of cycle in priorities is zero.

A question may arise on why a node does not immediately respond to lower priority nodes when it finds itself prior to some nodes. To find out the answer, assume v_1 with a higher priority than v_2 that cannot sleep due to v_3 – a higher priority associated node. If v_1 responds immediately to v_2, finally v_1 and v_2 will be active but v_2 can sleep because activity of v_1 is enough to ensure coverage. Therefore, a node does not send any responses until all of its higher priority neighbors respond. Fig. 2 shows a sample associated nodes and the final result of prioritization. Nodes N_1 and N_2 are volunteers to sleep but node N_1 should remain active in order to preserve the coverage.

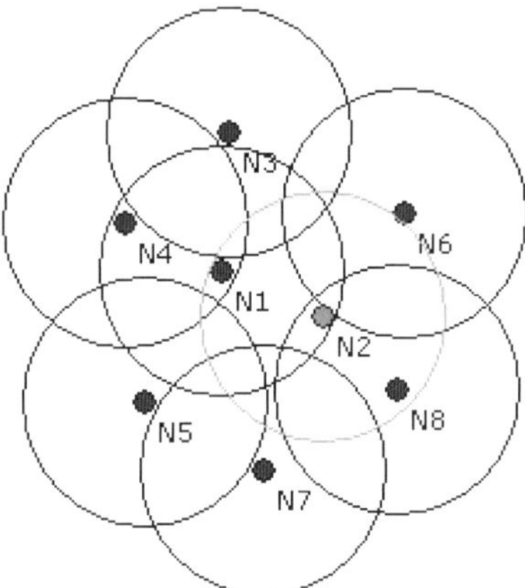

Fig. 2. Given two associated nodes N_1 and N_2, N_2 sleeps and N_1 remains active

Upon determination of activity status of nodes, they continue working until they run out of power. In case of energy shortage, the node that is running out of energy broadcasts a *low energy* message to nodes in its own *NBR* set. Each message receiver removes the sender from its NBR set and if the sender *id* exists in its R set, it turns on and starts volunteer selection phase again regarding remaining neighbors. Hence, there is no need to run the algorithm round and round and synchronize nodes at each round. Also, since only volunteer status and an integer representing the number of members of *R* are needed to be exchanged between nodes, the network traffic due to negotiation is very low.

4 Evaluation

We gathered our experimental results by simulating SPACC in a 50 meters by 50 meters field containing different numbers of nodes. Nodes had a sensing range of 10 meters, their radio range was twice their sensing range, and their initial power level was 10 units. Fig. 3 illustrates the number of active sensors along the time axis using 40, 70 and 100 sensors in total out of which nearly 20 or so nodes are selected by the algorithm to suffice to be active. Active nodes decrease their power by one unit at each time unit. Simulation ends as soon as all nodes run out of energy. For each of the above three numbers of nodes (i.e. 40, 70 and 100), simulation was run 150 times and each result shown was calculated by averaging the results of all runs; so neither of the results shown is optimal.

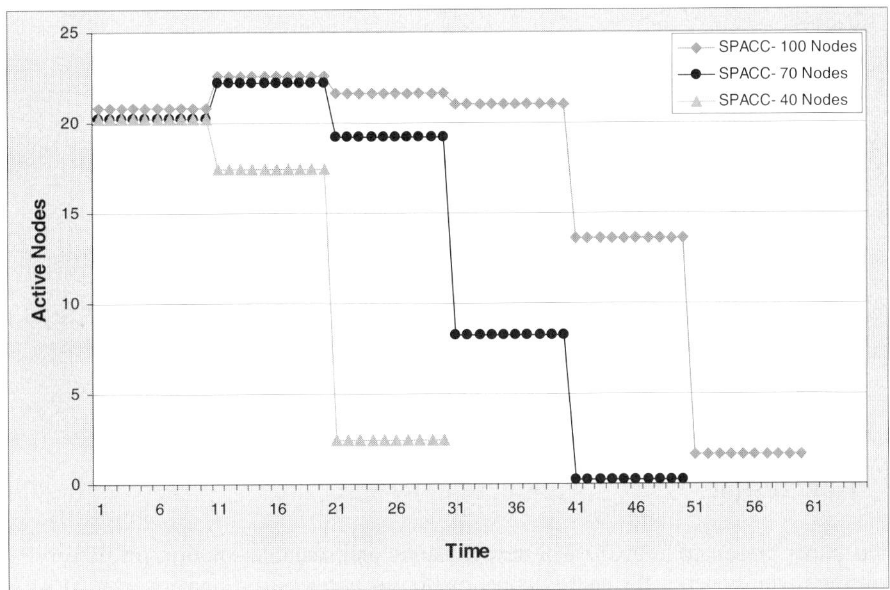

Fig. 3. The number of active nodes along time

The number of active nodes in Fig. 3 increases after time 11 when 70 and 100 nodes are used in total. No such increase happens after time 11 when 40 nodes are used in total. This is because remaining nodes are not sufficient to cover the area and almost half of them run out of energy at time 11.

Fig. 4 displays the area coverage percentage along time axis. Deployment of nodes is random and nodes initially cover the whole area.

Simulation results demonstrated that higher density of nodes increases the network lifetime. As mentioned before, simulation results are average and not optimal. With deterministic deployment, the functionality of SPACC increases. Nodes that run out of energy, inform their neighbors and therefore unlike prior solutions, there is no need for global synchronization between nodes. This removes the requirement for redundant communications and saves the power even more. Previous solutions have assumed the existence of a GPS module in each node, while SPACC removes this impractical assumption. Also in SPACC, communication traffic for local decisions is lower than previous solutions since only |*R*| and volunteer status need to be exchanged.

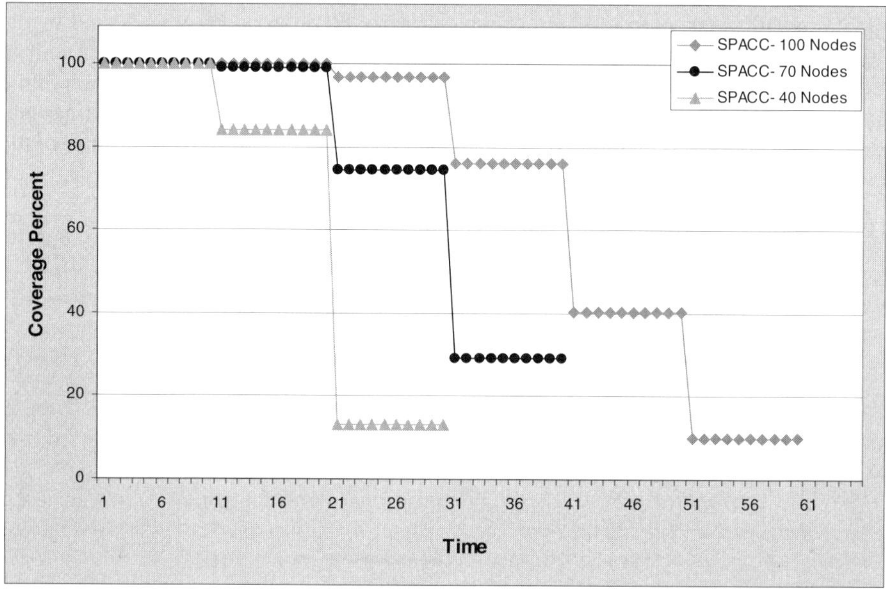

Fig. 4. The area coverage percentage through time

5 Conclusion

This paper presented SPACC as a new dynamic and scalable solution for preserving coverage with concern for energy conservation in wireless sensor networks. SPACC dismissed the requirement for GPS module in sensors for location awareness, and used a simple heuristic algorithm instead of the set-based rather complicated algorithms used by previous researches. Experimental results showed considerable improvements in network lifetime and coverage depending on node density; higher density leads to better improvements. Given these strengths, SPACC can be really considered as a near optimal solution for coverage in wireless sensor networks.

References

1. Akyildiz, I., Su, W., Sankarasubramaniam, Y., Cayirci, E.: Wireless sensor networks: a survey. Computer Networks 38, 393–422 (2002)
2. Estrin, D., Govindan, R., Heidemann, J.S., Kumar, S.: Next century challenges: scalable coordination in sensor networks. In: Proceedings of the 5th Annual ACM/IEEE International Conference (MobiCom'99), Washington, pp. 263–270 (1999)

3. Adlakha, S., Srivastava, M.: Critical density thresholds for coverage in wireless sensor networks. IEEE Wireless Communications and Networking 3, 1615–1620 (2003)
4. Kar, K., Banerjee, S.: Node placement for connected coverage in sensor networks. In: Proceedings of WiOpt 2003, Modeling and Optimization in Mobile, Ad Hoc and Wireless Networks, Sophia-Antipolis, France, pp. 50–52 (2003)
5. Liu, B., Towsley, D.: On the coverage and detectability of wireless sensor networks. In: WiOpt'03, Modeling and Optimization in Mobile, Ad Hoc and Wireless Networks, Sophia-Antipolis, France (2003)
6. Cardei, M., Wu, J.: Coverage in wireless sensor networks. In: Handbook of Sensor Networks, CRC Press, Boca Raton, USA (2004)
7. Tian, D., Georganas, N.D.: A coverage-preserving node-scheduling scheme for large wireless sensor networks. In: Proceedings of ACM Wireless Sensor Network and Application Workshop 2002, Atlanta, Georgia, USA, pp. 32–41. ACM Press, New York (2002)
8. Ye, F., Zhong, G., Cheng, J., Lu, S., Zhang, L.: PEAS: a robust energy conserving protocol for long-lived sensor networks. In: IEEE International Conference on Distributed Computing Systems (ICDCS 2003), RI, USA, IEEE Computer Society Press, Los Alamitos (2003)
9. Zhang, H., Hou, J.C.: Maintaining sensing coverage and connectivity in large sensor networks. Technical Report, UIUCDCS-R-2003-2351 (2003)
10. Wang, X., Xing, G., Zhang, Y., Lu, C., Pless, R., Gill, C.: Integrated coverage and connectivity configuration in wireless sensor networks. In: Proceedings of SenSys '03, Los Angeles, CA, USA, pp. 28–39 (2003)
11. Carle, J., Gallais, A., Simplot, D.: Preserving area coverage in wireless sensor networks by using surface coverage relay dominating sets. In: 10th IEEE Symposium on Computers and Communications (ISCC 2005), Spain, IEEE Computer Society Press, Los Alamitos (2005)
12. Adjih, C., Jacquet, P., Viennot, L.: Computing connected dominated sets with multipoint relays. In: INRIA, Technical Report 4597 (2002)
13. Albowicz, J., Chen, A., Zhang, L.: Recursive position estimation in sensor networks. In: Proceedings of 9th International Conference on ICNP 2001, Riverside, CA, pp. 35–41 (2001)

Research of Routing Algorithm in Hierarchy-Adaptive P2P Systems

Xiao-Ming Zhang[1], Yi-Jie Wang[1], and ZhouJun Li[2]

[1] National Key Laboratory for Parallel and Distributed Processing, Institute of Computer, National University of Defense Technology, Changsha, 410073, China
yolixs@163.com, wwyyjj1971@vip.sina.com

[2] School of Computer Science and Engineering, Beihang University, Beijing, 100083, China
zhoujun.li@263.net

Abstract. Recently superpeers are introduced to improve the performance of P2P systems. A superpeer is a node in a P2P system that operates as a server for a set of clients. By exploiting heterogeneity, the superpeer paradigm allows P2P systems to run more efficiently. This paper proposes a hierarchy-adaptive P2P topology DAHP2P and a hierarchical routing algorithm Hroute. Peers are grouped into clusters according to proximity and super peers form the upper-level overlay, the number of hierarchy is self-adaptively changed according to the number of nodes in the system, a hierarchical routing algorithm is designed to reduce the routing hops. Simulation results show that Hroute can significantly reduce the expected number of hops and latency of message routing, and loads of peers at different layers are relatively balanceable.

1 Introduction

P2P systems are gaining increased popularity. Recent developments of structured and unstructured overlay networks point to a new direction for overlay research to address these major challenges such as scalability, efficiency and flexibility.

Nodes in unstructured overlay network have the flexibility to choose the number and destinations of their connections, and adapt them to network heterogeneity for improved network performance. However, unstructured overlay networks often require flooding or gossip to route messages, which limits their efficiency and put more overhead on the underlying physical networks. Obviously, this approach supports arbitrarily complex queries but not scale to large size systems.

To solve the scalability problem of unstructured overlay, several approaches have been simultaneously but independently proposed, all of which support a distributed hash table (DHT) functionality; among them are Chord[1], CAN[2], Pastry [3] and Tapestry[4]. These systems are able to locate any item after querying no more than O(logN) individual peers. But they also have some limitations. First, their homogeneous design can result in inefficient group communication on heterogeneous networks. It has been observed in [5] that peers are highly diverse in terms of their network resources and their participation times. Second, they are all flat DHT designs without

I. Stojmenovic et al. (Eds.): ISPA 2007, LNCS 4742, pp. 728–739, 2007.

hierarchical routing. This approach is strikingly different from routing in the Internet, which uses hierarchical routing. Hierarchical routing offers several benefits over non-hierarchical routing, including scalability and administrative autonomy.

In this paper we explore a hierarchy-adaptive P2P topology DAHP2P and a hierarchical routing algorithm Hroute. Peers are grouped into clusters according to proximity and super peer is selected. Super peers form the upper-level overlay, and the number of layers is self-adaptively changed according to the number of nodes in the system. Inspired by hierarchical routing in the Internet, a hierarchical routing algorithm is designed to reduce the routing hops and improve routing efficiency. Super peer at different layers are assigned different responsibility. This design and routing algorithm can reduce the average number of hops in a lookup and enhance the performance of system.

2 Related Work

As for unstructured P2P systems, there are some effort to improve topology of the overlay network using nodes' heterogeneity[6,7], such as Kazaa[8] and Gnutella[9-11] and so on .They classifies nodes into two classes, namely, strong (high capability) nodes and weak (low capability) nodes and enforces capability-based restrictions on overlay network. A super peer is a specially designated node that has higher bandwidth connectivity and it maintains an index of pointers to the data stored at each of its associated low capability nodes. All queries are routed via the super peers.

As for structured P2P systems, there are also some efforts to exploit nodes' heterogeneity. Brocade[12] proposes to organize the peers in a two-layer overlay. All peers form a single overlay O_L . Geographically close peers are then grouped together and get assigned a representative called super peer. Super peers are typically well connected and situated near network access points. The super peers form another overlay O_H . Brocade is not truly hierarchical since all peers are part of O_L , which prevents it from reaping the benefits of hierarchically organized overlays.

However, the number of layers in these systems is fixed, and they also adapt flooding routing or routing based on flat DHT, in which nodes' heterogeneity isn't exploited well. These systems are also constructed with no consideration to the location information of nodes. In DAHP2P, peers are grouped into clusters according to proximity, and the number of layer can be changed accord to the number of node in system, and super peers at different layer are assigned different responsibility.

3 Hierarchical Topology

The core design of DAHP2P is showed as following. Peers are grouped into clusters according to proximity, and super peers are selected to form the upper-layer overlay. At each layer, the entire ID space is dynamically partitioned among all the super peers and the zone hold by a super peer is divided by those super peers that are clients of it at successor layer. The size of the smallest zone and the number of peers at each layer is determined by the number of dimension of ID space and layer number.

3.1 Hierarchical Arrangement of Peers

All the peers fall into two categories, super peers and client peers. At bottom layers, the client peers that don't provide any service to other peers are called pure client peers. The super peer of a cluster is called the parent of the client peers in the cluster, and the client peers are called the children of the super peer. Ancestors of a peer are the peers whose zone contains the zone of that peer, and grandchild peers of a peer are the peers whose zone was contained by the zone of that peer. The layers of system are numbered sequentially with the top layer being layer 0. In a system with a d-dimensional ID space and k to control the size of cluster that is constituted of super peers, the hierarchical architect satisfies the following restrictions:

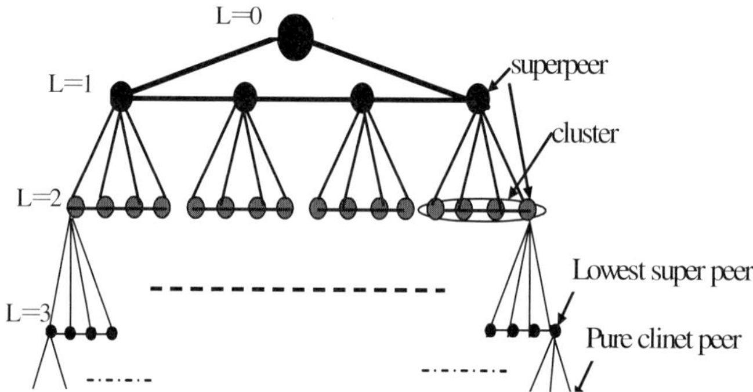

Fig. 1. Example of four-layer topology

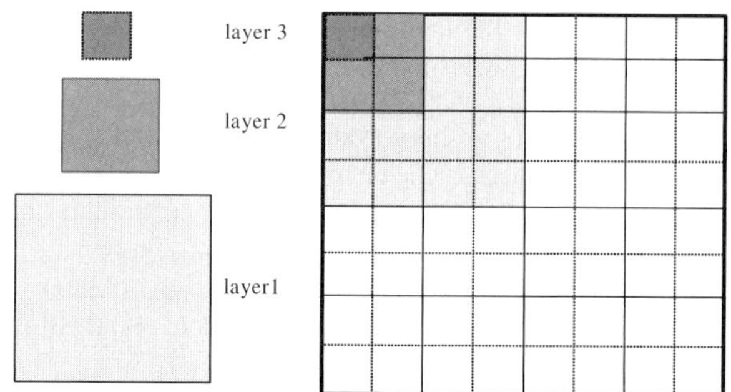

Fig.2. Example of 2-d space with four-layer partition

1. Peer in each layer can only be connected to exactly one super peer in its immediate upper-layer. Super peers in each layer are connected with their neighbor peers. Two zones are neighbors if their coordinate spans overlap along d-1 dimensions and abut along one dimension, and two super peers are neighbors if their zones are neighbor and they are in the same layer.

2. In each layer, the size of cluster that composed of super peers must be smaller than k^d, and the size of bottom cluster must be smaller than the size that the super peer of the cluster can server.
3. The hierarchical topology is constructed by a up-down approach, in which super peers of layer i+1 can't be selected when the number of super peers at layer i is smaller than k^{d*i}. The absolute value of subtraction between any two lowest super peers must be smaller than 1.
4. At layer i, the volume of zone that is k^{-i} times of the total volume of ID space is named the threshold zone. The volume of zone at each layer must be n ($1 \leq n < k*k$, n is an integer number) times of volume of the threshold zone. For $1 \leq i \leq L$, each layer-(i-1) threshold zone is divided into 2^{d*k} layer-i threshold zones, obtained by cutting the layer-i threshold zone into k parts along each of the d dimensions.

Fig.1 shows a hierarchical overlay network with 5 layer, of which 4 layer is composed of super peers and the bottom layer is composed of purely client peers. Fig.2 show the partition of a 2-dimentional ID space corresponding to the hierarchical overlay network showed in Fig.1.

4 Construction of Hierarchical Overlay Network

The construction algorithm Chpp is as following. When a new peer wants to join, it finds the closest peer, and then finds a nearby cluster that can hold new peer through the closest peer. Chpp can be used to construct hierarchical CAN, Chord and Pastry and so on. We predict distance of underlying network in term of network delay with coordinate-based approaches, and coordinate of each peer is by GNP[13].

x.ZL	Length of zone x's widest edge.
x.zone	Zone hold by peer x.
x.parent	Parent of peer x.
x.childs	Child peers connect with x.
x.L	The number of layer x is in.
x.minZL	width of the widest edge of zones hold by lowest super peers of x's grandchildren
R	List of ancestors

Fig. 3. Signification of parameters

4.1 Joining of New Peers

New peer join the system with a down-up approach, in which the new peer first find the closest and also the lowest cluster that can hold new peer. This joining approach can reduce the overhead of super peers at up-layers. For example, when a new peer A

```
A finds nearby peer B using broadcast;
A computers its own coordinate;
if (B is pure client peer)    B=B.parent;
if (B is not a lowest super peer)
   for (; B != lowest super peer; B= the closest peer in B.chinlds to A);
if (B can't hold new peer && (B.zone.ZL = = ID.ZL/k^{B.L})) {
   Z.L = B.zone.ZL*k;
   for (C = B.parent; C != null; C = C.parent)
        if (minZL of a lowest super peer of C's grandchildren ≥ ZL) break;
   if (C!=null)
   for (B = C; B != lowest super peer;
         B = the closest peer whose grandchild's minZL ≥ ZL in B.childs to A );
   else {   C, D =the two strongest peers in B.childs ∪ {A};
            C.zone = ⌊k / 2⌋ / 2 times of B.zone;
            D.zone = B.zone – C.zone,    C.L= B.L = B.L+1;
            C become a lowest super peer and C.childs = half of B.childs∪ {A};
            D become a lowest super peer and D.childs = the other half of B.childs ∪ {A};
          C.R = D.R = B.R ∪ B;
          C and D set neighbor relations with neighbor in the same layer;
          B become a super peer of C and D;
          B.childs = {C, D};   } }
else {   if (B can hold new peer)    A join the cluster B is in;
      else   if ( B.zone.ZL > ID.ZL / k^{B.L}) {
            C = the strongest peer of B.childs ∪ {A};
            C become a lowest super peer;
            C.zone = ⌊ B.zone.ZL / (ID.ZL * k^{-B.L} * 2) ⌋ * ID.ZL * k^{-B.L} times of B.zone;
            B.zone=b.zone – C.zone;
            C.L = B.L, C.R=B.R;
            C.childs = half of B.childs ∪ {A};
            C set relation with B.parent and neighbors in the same layer; }}
```

Fig. 4. Process of peer joining

wants to join, it first find a close peer E that is already in the system, and computer its own coordinate using the reference peers received from E. then it find the closest super peer that can hold new peers. It may become a super peer after competition. The signification of parameters used in this paper is showed in Fig.3, and the node-joining procedure is shown in pseudo code form in Fig.4.

4.2 Peer Departure and DAHP2P Maintenance

Each cluster selects a candidate super peer that is the second strongest peer. The candidate super peer maintains a copy of the information stored in super peer, and super peer sends periodic update messages to the candidate. Each peer in DAHP2P sends periodic messages to the peers that connect with it. These periodic messages include following types.

The periodic messages sent by a peer to its parent peers include the information about its address and capabilities. If the peer is also a super peer of an under-layer cluster, the messages also includes the biggest layer number of its grandchild peers or the length of the widest edge of the zones hold by lowest super peers that are grandchildren of it, and also include the address of the candidate super of its cluster. At any time, if there has a child peer that is stronger than its super peer, then the child peer becomes the super peer and that super peer becomes a candidate super peer.

The periodic messages sent by a parent peer to its child peers include information about its address, address of candidate super peer and a list of ancestors. A super peer send periodic message to its neighbor peers giving information about its zone, address, candidate super peer and its neighbors. When the super peer is failure, its neighbors can determine whether to takeover its cluster or to connect with its candidate.

The prolonged absence of a periodic message from a peer signals its failure. To deal with the failure or leaving of a super peer, these aspects must be considered.

(1) If the cluster whose super peer A is failure can merge with another neighbor cluster whose super peer is B, then these two cluster merge. The merger must satisfy following aspects. First, all client peers can be hold by the strongest peer of the two clusters. Second, the two zones hold by A and B can be coalesced. In a d-dimensional coordinate space, two zones can be coalesced if they have the same coordinate along d-1 dimensions and abut along one dimension. A new super peer that is the strongest peer of these two clusters is selected to hold the coalescent zone.

(2) If the cluster whose super peer is failure can't merge with any neighbor cluster, the candidate super peer becomes the super peer of that cluster. If this candidate is a super peer of an under-layer cluster, he broadcast its departure.

(3) If the cluster whose super peer is failure has no active peers, then the zone hold by the super peer is takeover by a neighbor super peer. Once a super peer has decided that all the peers of the neighbor cluster are failure, it initiates the takeover mechanism and starts a takeover timer running. Each neighbor super peer of the failed cluster will do this independently, with the timer initialized in proportion to the volume of the super peer's own zone. When the timer expires, a super peer sends a TAKEOVER message conveying its own zone volume to all of the failed super peer's neighbors. On receipt of a TAKEOVER message, a super peer cancels its own timer if the zone volume in the message is smaller then its own zone volume, or it replies with its own TAKEOVER message. In this way, a neighbor super peer is efficiently chosen which is still alive, and which has a small zone volume.

5 Hierarchical Routing

In most hierarchical P2P systems, flooding or DHT-based routing is still used in super peer layer. However, as to hierarchical P2P systems, these routing methods are not efficient, because they are all flat designed and without exploiting nodes heterogeneity, in which nodes with poor capacities and heavy loads become the bottleneck of the whole system. These routing technologies are also different from routing in the Internet, which uses hierarchical routing. Hierarchical routing offers several benefits over non-hierarchical routing, including less routing hops and scalability. In DAHP2P, a novel hierarchical routing Hroute is proposed. The core design of Hroute is that: stronger peers have more responsibility.

5.1 Routing Based on Ancestor Tables

In DAHP2P, the destination node of publish message is the lowest super peer whose zone covers the Hash(key) of published data, and if the nodes along the routing path have storage space that is free or gained by releasing other outdated data, they can cache the information of that data.

Each peer maintains three tables. One is the ancestor table $R<P_0, P_1, \ldots, P_{n-1}>$ (n is the layer number of the owner). In the ancestor table, P_i $(1<i<n)$ is a child of P_{i-1}, and P_i is a super peer at layer i. The second one is a neighbor table, and the neighbor table maintains a list of neighbor peer at the same layer. The third one is the child peers table that maintains a list of its entire child peers.

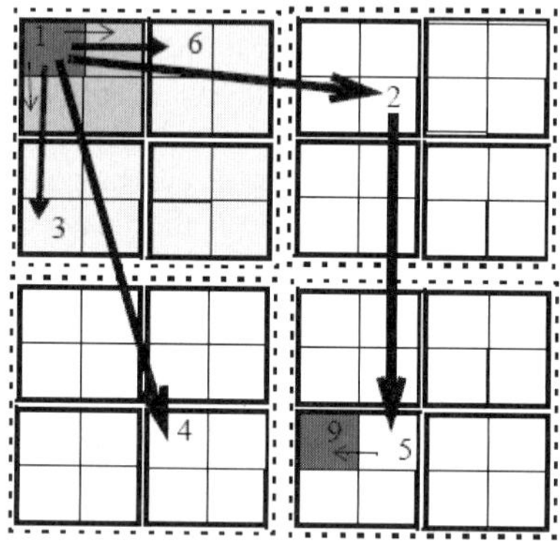

Fig. 5. Routing based on shortcuts

This routing algorithm is very simple. If the hashing value of request data is within the peer's current zone, it already reaches the destination. Otherwise, it route to the ancestor peer whose zone is the smallest one that cover that hashing value in the current ancestor table, and then iterates through the child peers whose zone cover that hashing value, until it finds a peer who maintains a information about the request data. If the entire ancestor peers whose zone cover the hashing value of destination data are failure or busy, the neighbor table is used to route messages, in which the messages are just routed to the neighbor peer with zone coordinate closest to the hashing value of request data.

5.2 Routing Based on Shortcuts

In the routing algorithm based on ancestor table, there has one critical issue. Assuming a uniform distribution of traffic, it can be shown that super peer at layer i needs to handle at most d^k times the traffic on average than super peer at layer i-1. So we must reduce the diversity of load among the super peers at different layers, since the default routing algorithm has less number of super peers to handle traffic at high layer.

The evolving routing algorithm introduces shortcuts to reduce the load of super peers at high layers. Considering the tree architecture of DAHP2P, the evolving routing algorithm make sure that some peers that are grandchild peers of x can share in the load of x, and this routing is named routing based on shortcuts.

For using shortcuts to balance load, each super peer maintains a shortcut table Ch<S_1, S_2, ..., S_{n-1}>(n is the layer number of this super peer). In the shortcut table, Si (0<i<n-1) is also a table that contains at most 2*d items and each of these items is a grandchild of a peer that is a neighbor of its ancestor peer at layer i.

```
if ( node contain index of key)
    return index;
else{
    for (i = node.L-1; i ≥ 0; i--)
      if (node.R.P_i.zone covers key) {
        L=i;
        break; }
      if (Ch.S_L+1 != null && node.zone doesn't cover key)
        d = distance between node.R.P_L+1.zone and key;
        for (i =0; i<Ch.S_i+1.size(); i++) {
          C = the i^th peer of Ch.S_L+1;
          if ( the distance between key and C.zone or C.R.P_L+1 < d) {
              B = C;
              d = the smaller value of distance between key and C.zone or
               C.R.P_L+1; }}
        node send message to B; }
    if (Ch.S_L+1 = null || node.zone covers key || B is unavailable) {
       if (node.zone covers key)
           node sends message to peer whose zone covers key in
 node.childs;
       else if ( node send message to node.R.PL unsuccessfully)
           node sends message to the closest neighbor to key;   }
```

Fig. 6. Pseudo-code for routing based on shortcuts

The routing algorithm based on shortcuts is as following. First it make outs the layer number i of the lowest ancestor peer whose zone covers the hashing value of destination data, and then check the closest peer to destination in S_{i+1}, if that peer is available, the message is sent to that peer. Fig.5 illustrates the routing path peer 1 to peer 9 based on shortcuts with an example. In this example the DAHP2P with 4 layers has a 2-dimensional ID space. The shortcuts table of peer 1 is <{2,4}, {6,3}>, and peer 1 finds that the zone of ancestor peer at layer 0 covers destination hashing valuc, it then check the {2, 4} in its shortcut table. Because peer 2 and peer 4 are all close to destination, so it can send message to either of them Fig.6 shows the pseudo-code for the basic algorithm.

The shortcuts table was maintained by a variance FIFO strategy. Information of each peer in S_i contains the time t1 when this peer joins. When a peer A responsible for a data correspond to a item that is empty in S_i, or that peer has the same ancestor P_{i-1} with the peer B of the correspond item in S_i, if the value gained by t1 subtracting from t2 in the correspond item is bigger than a given value T, peer B is replaced by A; Otherwise, if peer A is closer to the owner of the table than peer B, peer B is also replaced by A. This replacing strategy makes sure that shortcuts are composed by closer peers gradually.

6 Performance Evaluation

We test performance of DAHP2P and Hroute both on simulated topologies. The topologies we use in the simulation is produced by BRITE. BRITE [14] is a more realistic topology generator, which generates truly representative Internet topologies. Here we use a two-level hierarchical topology generated by BRITE. The hierarchical topology was generated by the bottom-up approach. The router-level topology used Waxman models, and router nodes were assigned to autonomous systems in the way of heavy-tailed.

In these simulations, we compare the average routing hops between DAHP2P and other P2P systems, and test the loading of super peers at different layers. We use two metrics to evaluate DAHP2P and Hroute. One metric is the average routing hops in different p2p overlay networks, one metric is the stretch of routing latency in DAHP2P and eCAN[15], and the last one is the loading of super peers at different layers. In all the following simulations, k=2, d=3, m=4.

1. Comparison of average routing hops

If the number of peer is N, then the number of layers is $f(N) = \lceil \log_{k^d} \frac{N(k^d-1)+1}{k^d(m+1)-m} \rceil + 1$. We assume that all the data is stored in the lowest super peers, which means that each data location must locates the lowest super peer that store the information of the destination data. Fig.7 shows the comparison of average routing hops between DAHP2P, eCAN and f(N). It can be concluded that the average routing hops of DAHP2P is only 60% of that of eCAN, and is almost the same with f(N).

Fig.8 shows the comparison of average routing hops between DAHP2P, CAN with different dimensions and Chord. It can be concluded that the average routing hops of DAHP2P with 3-dimensional ID space is smaller then that of CAN with 5-dimensional ID space, and the difference is become greater when the number of peers is become greater. This is because the average routing hops of CAN is $O((d/4)*N^{1/d})$, and the average routing hops of Chord is $O(\log_2 N)$, and all these are greater then that of DAHP2P. The space cost of super peers is $O(\log_{k^d} N/(m+1))+O(d)$ (d is the number of dimensions of ID space in DAHP2P), which is greater then CAN or Chord a little. But the average routing hops is smaller then CAN of Chord a lot.

2. Comparison of routing latency stretch

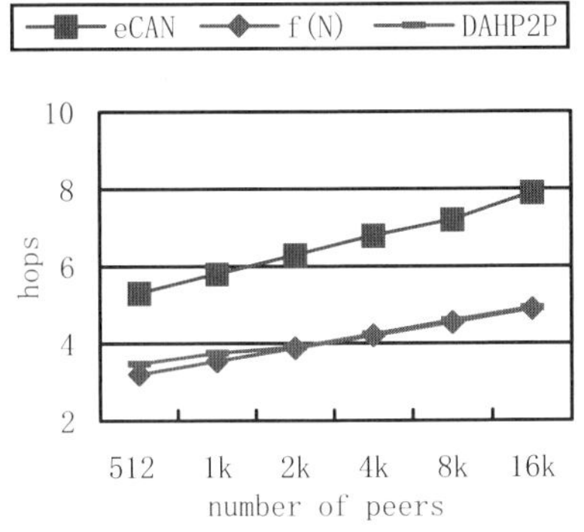

Fig. 7. Average routing hops compared with f(N)

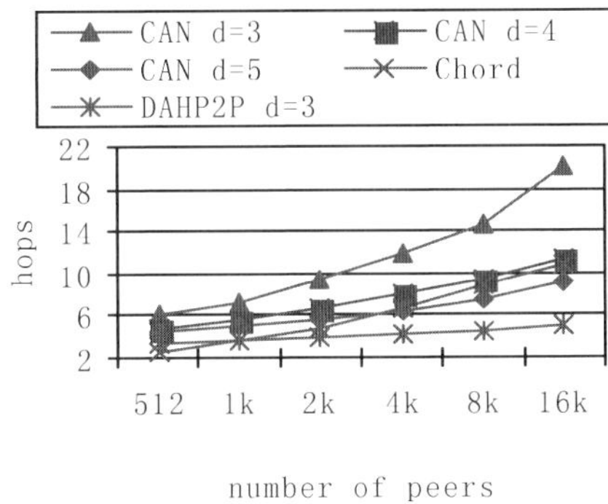

Fig. 8. Comparability of average routing hops in different P2P topology

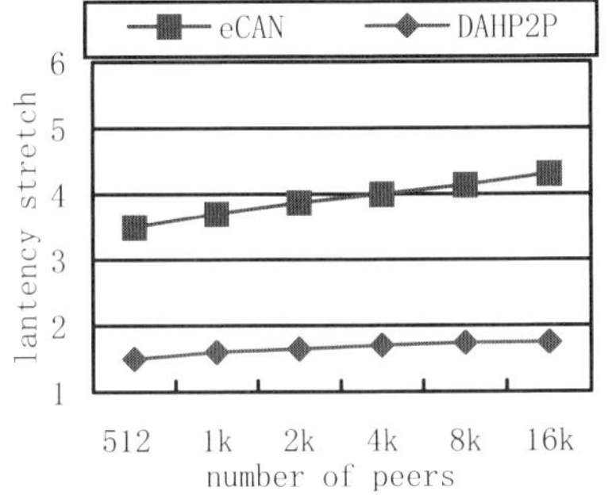

Fig. 9. Comparability of latency stretch between DAHP2P and eCAN

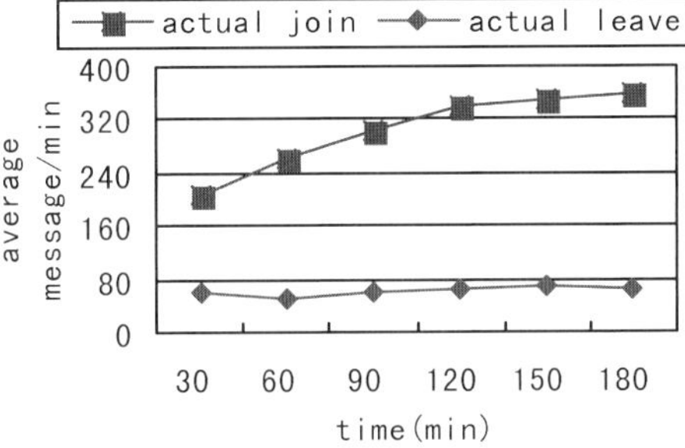

Fig. 10. Average message/min of peer joining and leaving

In this simulation we compare the routing latency stretch of DAHP2P and eCAN, and the routing latency stretch is the ratio of the routing latency in overlay network to the latency of shortest path form source to destination in underlying network. Low values of stretch are thus desired. Fig.9 shows the comparison of routing latency stretch between DAHP2P and eCAN. It can be concluded that the routing latency stretch of eCAN is above 3.5, and that of DAHP2P is no more than 2.0. This is because that clusters in DAHP2P are grouped by peers according to proximity, and Hroute is used to reduce routing hops.

3. Comparison of load between super peers at different layers

As peers join the system, the peer must find a super peer that can hold new peers, and the number of messages that is O(l) is relative to the number of layers. The maintenance traffic is the keepalive messages used to detect failures among super peers. The number of messages per peer is only relative to the number of ID dimension. When a super peer leaves the system, the total number of messages is relative to the number of super peers connected to the failure super peer, and the number of peer connected to a peer is relative to the number of ID dimension .

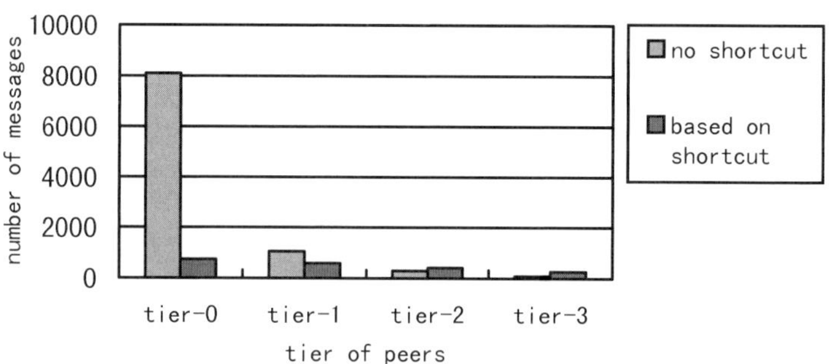

Fig. 11. Effect of shortcuts on loads of super peers at different layers

In this simulation, we aim to evaluate the maintenance traffic and the effect on the load of super peers taken by shortcuts, and the target environment is around 8000 peers. The id space is 4-dimesional and k is 2, and m is 8. The failure probability of each super peer is 0.05 over an hour. The keep-alive period for super peers is 45 seconds. The join and leave rate are 1 peer/sec, and in the first 133 minutes the leave rate is 0. The lookup rate for each peer is 0.01 lookup/sec. In a period of 10 minutes, we record loads of super peers at different layers, and the load is the number of request each super peer receives.

Fig.10 shows the average messages/min of peer joining and leaving. In the first 130 minutes the number of layers is increase with the peer joining, and so is the average messages/min. But the average message per new peer is no more then 2*O(l) (l is the number of layers). The average messages per leaving peer is about $O(2^4)$.

Fig.11 shows the effect on loads of super peers at different layers taken by shortcuts. It can be conclude that the load of a super peer is greater as the layer number is smaller without shortcuts, and the greatest ratio of load of a super peer to load of a successor-layer super peer is about 8. When shortcuts are introduced the difference of loads between super peer at different layers is reduced greatly, and the greatest ratio of load of a super peer to load of a successor-layer super peer is about 2. By using shortcuts, a node routes to x has the option of replacing x with any grandchild peer of its. Because the number of peers to replace x is proportional to the size of zone it holds, this implies that the number of peers handling its routing task corresponding to x's layer number, and the upper the layer is the more number of grandchild peers are. As a result, the loads of super peers at different layers are relatively balanceable.

7 Conclusion

In this paper, a hierarchy-adaptive P2P overlay network DAHP2P and hierarchical routing Hroute are proposed. Peers are grouped into clusters according to proximity, and super peer that is the strongest peer in each cluster is selected to provide serves for client peers. Super peers in the same layer form the up-layer overlay network, and the number of system layers is changed self-adaptively according to the number of nodes in the system. A hierarchical routing algorithm is designed to reduce the routing hops and latency. Simulation results show that Hroute can locate data with in O(l) hops(l is the number of system layers) , and loads of superpeers in different layer are relatively balanceable.

References

1. Stoica, I., Morris, R., Karger, D., Kaashoek, M., Balakrishnan, H.: Chord: A scalable peer-to-peer lookup service for internet applications. In: Proceedings of SIGCOMM (2001)
2. Ratnasamy, S., Handley, M., Karp, R., Shenker, S.: A scalable content-addressable network. In: Proceedings of SIGCOMM (2001)
3. Rowstron, Druschel, P.: Pastry: Scalable, distributed object location and routing for large-scale peer-to-peer systems. In: IFIP/ACM International Conference on Distributed Systems Platforms (Middleware) (Heidelberg, Germany), pp. 329–350 (November 2001)
4. Zhao, B.Y., Kubiatowicz, J., Joseph, A.D.: Tapestry: An infrastructure for fault-tolerant wide-area location and routing. Tech. Rep. UCB/CSD-01-1141, Computer Science Division, University of California, Berkeley (2001)
5. Ripeanu, M., Ian Foster, T.: Mapping the gnutella network: Macroscopic properties of large-scale peer-to-peer systems. In: Revised Papers from the First International Workshop on Peer-to-Peer Systems, pp. 85–93. Springer, Heidelberg (2002)
6. Yang, B., Garcia-Molina, H.: Designing a super-peer network. In: Proceedings of the 19th International conference on Data Engineering (2003)
7. Montresor, A.: A robust protocol for building superpeer overlay topologies. In: Proceedings of the 4 International Conference on P2P Computing, Zurich, Switzerland, pp. 202–209. IEEE Computer Society, Los Alamitos (2004)
8. Kazaa: Kazaa home page (2003), http://www.kazaa.com/
9. Gnutella: http://www.gnutella.com
10. Kaashoek, F., David, K., Koorde, R.: A simple degree-optimal hash table. A simple degree optimal distributed hash table. In: Proceedings of the 2nd International Workshop on P2P Systems(IPIPS'03), Berkeley, CA, pp. 98–107 (2003)
11. Singla, A., Rohrs, C.: Ultrapeers: Another step towards gnutella scalability. Whitepaper (2002)
12. Zhao, B.Y., Duan, Y., Huang, L., Joseph, A.D., Kubiatowicz, J.D.: Brocade: Landmark routing on overlay networks. In: Proceedings of IPTPS'02, Cambridge, MA (2002)
13. Ng, T.S.E., Zhang, H.: Predicting Internet network distance with coordinates-based approaches. In: Proceedings of IEEE Infocom, pp. 170–179. IEEE Computer Society Press, Los Alamitos (2002)
14. Medina, A., Lakhina, A., Matta, I., And Byers, J.: BRITE: An Approach to Universal Topology Generation. In: Proceedings of MASCOTS 2001, Cincinnati. OH (2001)
15. Xu, Z., Zhang, Z.: Building Low-maintenance Expressways for P2P Systems. Hewlett-Packard Labs, Palo Alto, CA, Tech. Rep. HPL-2002- 41 (2002)

Bandwidth Degradation Policy for Adaptive Multimedia Services in Mobile Cellular Networks*

Yide Zhang, Lemin Li, and Gang Feng

School of Communication and Information Engineering, University of Electronic Science and Technology of China, 610054, Chengdu, Sichuan, China
computium@gmail.com, {lml,fenggang}@uestc.edu.cn

Abstract. One of the key challenges in the optimal control of adaptive multimedia services transmission in mobile cellular network is to balance user satisfaction and fairness among all users, while at the same time ensuring that the scarce bandwidth be utilized efficiently. We propose a novel Bandwidth Degradation Policy (*BDP*) for Adaptive Multimedia Services which could solve the conflicting relationship between user satisfaction and fairness. The *BDP* employs specific degradation policy to accommodate more users and compensation mechanism to maintain fairness among all users, and meanwhile increasing the user satisfactions and the whole network revenue. Specifically, we introduce four new *QoS* metrics to evaluate the performances of adaptive multimedia services in mobile cellular networks. Finally we compare our *BDP* with other strategies in the literature through both of the analytical results and simulation results. The presented extensive simulation results with concerns of mobility validate our analysis.

Keywords: QoS, Degradation Policy, Adaptive Multimedia Services, Mobile Cellular Network.

1 Introduction

The scarcity and extreme fluctuation of available link bandwidth in wireless cellular networks leads to adaptive multimedia services, where the bandwidth of an ongoing multimedia call can be dynamically adjusted [2]. For most adaptive multimedia applications (e.g., voice, video telephony or video conferencing), service can be degraded in case of congestion as long as it is still within the pre-specified tolerable range. For adaptive multimedia services, the multimedia bit streams are compressed in the form of layered (scalable) coding to adapt the fluctuation in resource availability in wireless cellular networks and accommodate diverse user access devices [1], [2]. The layers could be classified into two categories: the *basic layer* and the *enhancement layers*. The *basic layer* probably means the most important part

* This work was supported by NSFC (National Science Foundation of China) and RGC (Research Grants Council of Hong Kong) grant No.60218002, and National Key Basic Research Program (2007CB307104 of 2007CB307100).

I. Stojmenovic et al. (Eds.): ISPA 2007, LNCS 4742, pp. 740–749, 2007.

which should be delivered first and given higher priority. Additionally, the data in the *enhancement layers* probably improves the perceptual quality of the adaptive multimedia services.

In order to fully utilize the system resources, degrading the *QoS* of existing multimedia traffic in a controlled manner has been shown as an effective way to improve the overall system performance [4], [5], and [7]. However, the inherent nature of the adaptive multimedia services and the using of degradation strategy will lead to a paradox. To accommodate more users, the system has to degrade some of the ongoing calls, which renders the discontent of degraded users. On the other hand, accommodating more users satisfies the new coming users and increases whole system utilization. This makes the compensation to degraded calls necessary.

Instead of focusing only on the bandwidth utilization and forced-termination probability, we adopt the Degradation period ratio (*DPR*) in the literature [5] [6], and devise other four new *QoS* metrics--Weighted Degradation period ratio (*WDPR*), Upgrade/Degrade Portion Ratio (*UPR*), Upgrade/Degrade Differentiation Ratio (*UDR*), and Satiation Ratio (*SR*). Few literatures provide analysis for service degradation of individual calls, which is crucial to *QoS* provision [8], [9].

In this paper, we fully exploit the flexibility and dynamic property of adaptive multimedia services in our proposed Bandwidth Degradation Policy (*BDP*) for Adaptive Multimedia Services. Degrading the bandwidth of a handoff call will save it out of being dropped due to insufficient bandwidth provision of target cell. Degradation also helps the system to accommodate more users thus improve the whole system utilization. Furthermore, with properly concerning about the fact that degradation will cause the inconvenience of users, we integrate compensation mechanism in our degradation policy in order to make it smarter, since the degradation and compensation will happen with concerns of the current status of the whole system. We directly name our degradation policy with integration of compensation mechanism as Bandwidth Degradation Policy (*BDP*). This policy keeps fairness among all users in the system.

The rest of the paper is organized as follows. Section 2 describes the system model. The proposed *BDP* with degradation policy and compensation mechanism is present in Section 3. Section 4 presents the analytical and simulation results with concerns of mobility. Finally, we conclude the paper in Section 5.

2 System Model

2.1 QoS Metrics

In a system with degradable service, a call may receive full or degraded service, depending on the system load at the time of its arrival (this probability is given in the previous subsection). Even if a call receives full service upon its arrival, it can be degraded when the system tries to accept more calls [8]. Thus instead of focusing only on the bandwidth utilization and forced-termination probability, we adopt the *DPR* in the literature, and devise other four new *QoS* metrics as:

1) *Weighted Degradation period ratio* (*WDPR*): *DPR* only considers the time factor, which is not enough to describe how bad the calls are degraded. For

instance, when call *A* and call *B* have the same *DPR* of 0.5, but call *A* always allocated less than 10% portion of the target bandwidth, whereas call *B* could be fulfilled more than 90% portion of the target bandwidth. Obviously we could concern that call *B* is in a situation much better than call *A*, but *DPR* lacks of the capability to reveal it. We devise *WDPR* to overcome this shortcoming. We give lower weight to the calls could receive higher bandwidth allocations when they are in their degradation period.

2) *Upgrade/Degrade Portion Ratio* (*UPR*): the ratio of the upgraded and degraded call numbers to the total call numbers.
3) *Upgrade/Degrade Differentiation Ratio* (*UDR*): We define *Upgrade Frequency* (UF) and *Degrade Frequency* (*DF*) as the frequency of switching between upgraded and degraded service by an admitted call. Then the *UDR* is defined using following equation:

$$UDR = \frac{UF - DF}{UF + DF} \times UPR \tag{1}$$

4) *Satiation Ratio* (*SR*): the ratio of the really allocated bandwidth to the target bandwidth, which describes to what extent the system could fulfill the adaptive multimedia connection requests and which also ultimately reflects the user satisfaction.

$$SR = \frac{\sum_i ALLOCATED \quad BANDWIDTH}{\sum_i REQUIRED \quad BANDWIDTH} \tag{2}$$

2.2 System Basic Considerations

We consider a wireless network with homogeneous cells. For expression simplicity, we assume the following notation and system configuration in Table 1.

Table 1. Notation explanations

Basic Layer Only services	***BLO***	**Total *BLO* call arrival rate**	λ_I
***BLO* service calls**	***Co***	**Total BEL calls arrival rate**	λ_{II}
combined Basic & Enhancement services	***BEL***	**Total data call arrival rate**	λ_d
***BEL* service calls**	***Cc***	**Total *BLO* handoff call arrival rate**	γ_I
Basic layer of the *BEL* service	***BEL-B***	**Total *BEL* handoff call arrival rate**	γ_{II}
Basic layer of the *BEL* service call	***Cb***	**Total data handoff call arrival rate**	γ_d
Enhancement layers of the *BEL* service	***BEL-E***	**average BLO call holding time**	$1/\mu_I$
Enhancement layers of the *BEL* service call	***Ce***	**average BEL call holding time**	$1/\mu_{II}$
Non real-time data service call	***Cd***	**average data call holding time**	$1/\mu_d$
Basic Bandwidth Unit	***BBU***	**Total *BBUs* in each cell**	**C**
***BBUs* of one *BEL* service call**	***m***	**Total number of BBUs**	***C*K***

In our *BDP*, in each cell there exist 3 types of adaptive multimedia services: Basic Layer Only (*BLO*) services, combined Basic Layer and Enhancement Layers (*BEL*) services, and non real-time Data services. Generally, we assume that one *BLO* service call takes up one *BBU* and several data calls could share one single *BBU*, whereas one *BEL* service call occupies *m BBUs* in that the *basic layer* of the *BEL* service call occupies one *BBU* and the *enhancement layer*s occupies the rest of (*m-1*) *BBUs*.

Moreover, we assume in each cell, the arrivals of originating *BLO* calls, handoff *BLO* calls, originating *BEL* calls, handoff *BEL* calls, originating data calls, and handoff data calls are Poisson distributed.

3 Bandwidth Degradation Policy (*BDP*)

The proposed *BDP* with compensation mechanism could solve the conflicting relationship between user satisfaction and fairness. If there is not enough bandwidth for the incoming adaptive multimedia call, degradation policies will be applied to the ongoing adaptive multimedia calls in the same cell. On the other hand, since degradation will cause the inconvenience of users, we integrate a compensation mechanism in our degradation policy. Through setting a timer to every call in the system we prevent a specific call from being degraded too many times and give a higher preference to the degraded call when it would be compensated. Consequently, the *Co* and *Cb* calls have the same highest priority, and *Ce* calls receive a lower priority, whereas the *Cd* calls have the lowest priority. Although a *BEL* service call always consists of a *Cb* call and a *Ce* call simultaneously, the *Cb* call still has priory over the *Ce* call. We presen[t our *BDP* in three aspects:

(1) Since Co and *Cb* calls are delay sensitive and delay-jitter sensitive, fixed bandwidth (e.g. 1 *BBU*) should always be maintained during the whole serving period. Thus a *Co* or *Cb* call always receives one *BBU* allocation preferentially. When an originating or incoming *Co* or *Cb* call arrives, the *BDP* will assign this idle channel to the incoming *Co* or *Cb* call. Then *BDP* seek for more bandwidth for the "counterpart" --*Ce* call, which may request several *BBUs*. On the other hand, if there is not enough bandwidth available in the cell, the *BDP* will decide which call to be degraded. They first try to randomly terminate an existing *Cd* call and preempt the occupied bandwidth. Only if there is no existing *Cd* call, the degradation policies will reclaim one *BBU* out of the several *BBU* occupied by a *Ce* call and reassign it to the incoming call. Degrading another *Ce* call and reallocating the reclaimed bandwidth to the newly coming *Co* or *Cb* call increases the system capacity.

(2) According to fact that a *Ce* call usually requests for extra several *BBUs* besides the corresponding *Cb* call, the system will try to fulfill its bandwidth requirement after allowing the corresponding *Cb* call in to the cell. Each time the *BDP* tries to preempt 1 *BBU* from an existing *Cd* call or degrading another *Ce* call which takes up too much bandwidth or lasting too long. Degrading another appropriate *Ce* call and reallocating the reclaimed bandwidth to the newly coming *Ce* call sustains fairness among every adaptive multimedia services user.

(3) Finally, the *Cd* calls receive the lowest priority. When it originates or incomes, only if there is an idle channel, the *BDP* will allocate one channel to the *Cd* call.

4 Analytical and Simulation Results

We consider the following system configuration listed in Table 2.

Table 2. Font sizes of headings. Table captions should always be positioned *above* the tables.

Number of clusters in the system	**N=7**	**Average *BLO* arrival**	**λ_I is variable**
Number of cells in each cluster	**K=7**	**Average *BEL* arrival**	**λ_{II} is variable**
Sampling time interval	**3 seconds**	**Average *BLO* handoff arrival**	**γ_I is variable**
Number of *BBUs* in each cell	**C = 50**	**Average *BEL* handoff arrival**	**γ_{II} is variable**
Cell radius	**R=1000m**	**Max BBU occupation of *BEL***	**m=4**
Number of sectors per cell	**1 sector**	**Mean holding time**	**$1/\mu=1/\mu_I=1/\mu_{II}$ =120 sec**
Distance-based propagation attenuation coefficient	**α=3.5**	**Mean speed**	**V is variable**
thermal noise	**-118 dBm**	**Velocity correlation coefficient**	**ξ is variable**
Shadow fading standard deviation	**6 dB**	**Handoff hysteresis**	**H=3 dB**
Shadow fading correlation	**0.5**	**Call dropping SIR threshold**	**d=7,13 dB**

In this section, we first present numerical results and compare our proposed BAS (Bandwidth Allocation Scheme) algorithms in *BDP* with the schemes that employ assigning requested channels as a whole to the *BEL* service calls from the very beginning. We call the latter "Constant *BAS" (CB*), which was proposed by *Dervis Z. Deniz, etc* in [3]. The system performance parameters considered here are the call blocking probability and overall Bandwidth Utilization Rates (*BUR*). Note that blocking *Ce* calls doesn't imply the termination of the corresponding *Cb* calls, instead that the high layer software would maintain the last legible video frame as an elimination of the blank screen.

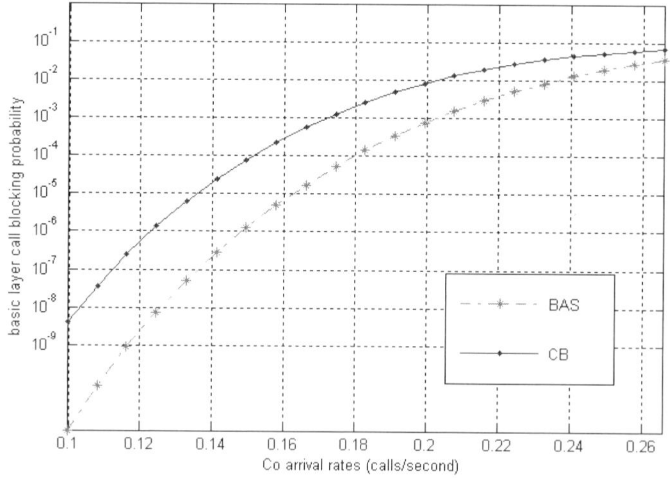

Fig. 1. Call Blocking Probability of *BAS* in *BDP* and *CB*

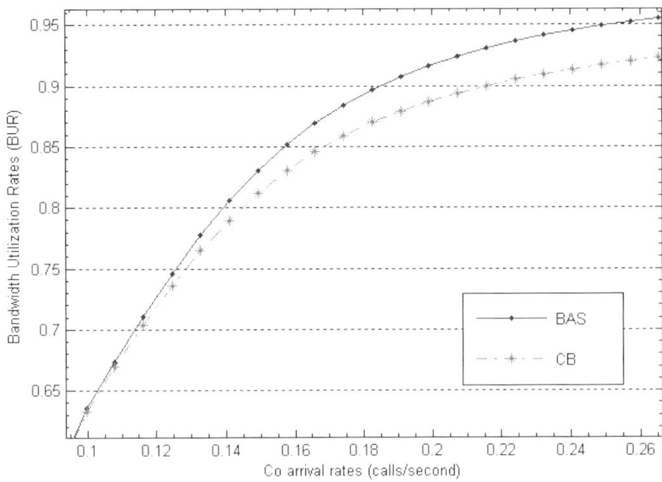

Fig. 2. *BUR* of *BAS* in *BDP* and *CB*

From the above results, in order to maintain the target system performance, we summarize our studies that our scheme *BDP* outperforms the scheme *CB* on the important system performance metric Call Blocking Probability about 47.27% and *BUR* about 0.83% on the average.

The *QoS* metrics considered in this paper are *DPR*, *WDPR*, *UPR*, *UDR* and *SR* of the adaptive multimedia services. We will investigate and compare these parameters between the *BLO* and *BEL* service call connection requests. Furthermore, we assume that the mobility varies. The average velocity spans from 0 *mps* (meter per second) to 50 *mps*, with fixed step of 10 *mps*. Value 0 stands for stationary case. We adopt 0.1 *mps* in mobility case 1 to mimic the realistic world [10].

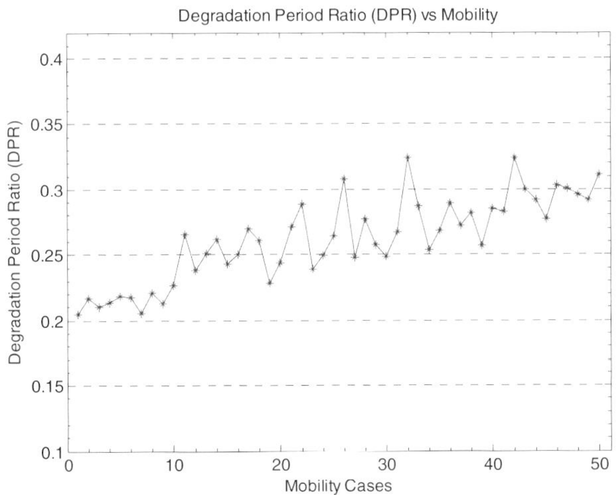

Fig. 3. Simulation result of *DPR*

The *DPR* and *WDPR* simulation results could be seen from Figs. 3 and 4. With the same *X*- and *Y*-coordinate in Figs. 3 and 4, we could see that the *WDPR* reflects the mobility influences more rationally than the *DPR*.

The *UDR* and *UPR* simulation results could be seen from Figs. 5 and 6. As the average value of *UDR* is 13.85%, we could deduce nearly 15% of the degraded *BEL* calls are upgraded or compensated after they are degraded, resulting more fairly bandwidth allocation among all users. Note that the *UDR* is virtually averaged by the corresponding *UPR*, seen in eqns. (1).

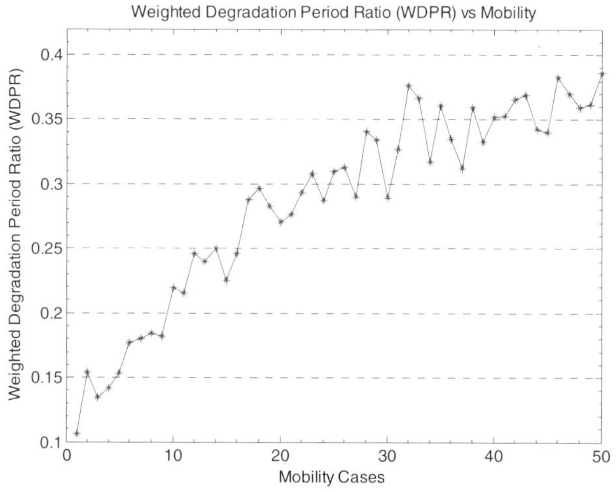

Fig. 4. Simulation result of *WDPR*

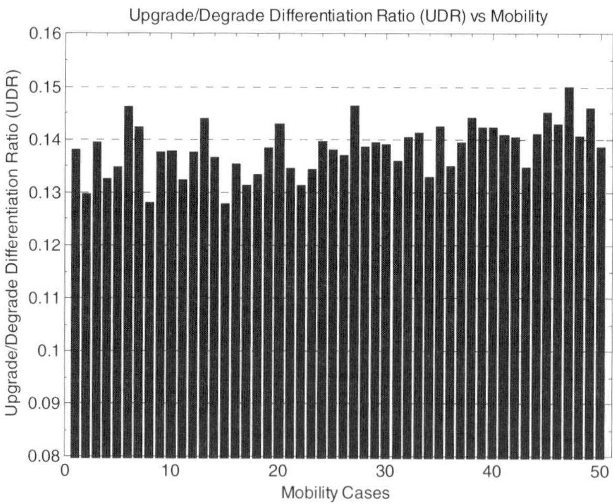

Fig. 5. Simulation result of *UDR*

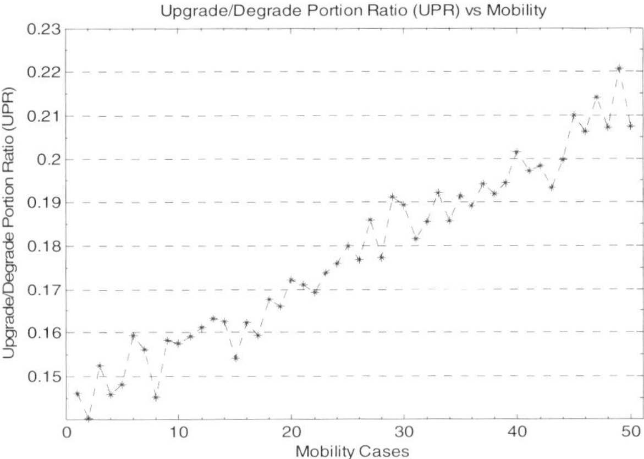

Fig. 6. Simulation result of *UPR*

As the *UPR* representing how much *BEL* call is not fulfilled and results in less satisfaction of adaptive multimedia user. The result demonstrates the *UDR* increases linearly with the mobility increasing. However, it also slightly oscillates at the small granularity. But the successive increasing of *UPR* demonstrates the great influences of the mobility following our intuition that high mobility implicates high portion of *BEL* calls are upgraded or degraded when they are moving to the neighboring cell.

The high portion of adaptive multimedia arrival achieves high *SR* of the adaptive multimedia services values with average value of 89.96%, which means almost all the bandwidth requirements of *BEL* call is fulfilled and results in much better satisfaction of adaptive multimedia user.

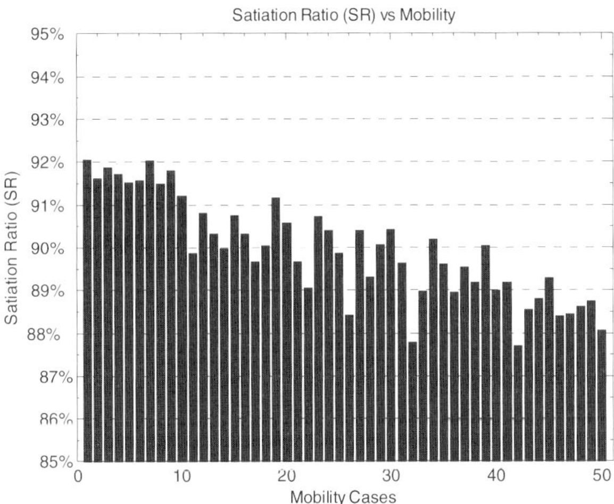

Fig. 7. Simulation result of Satiation Ratio (*SR*)

This simulation result reflects that our *BDP* with compensation mechanisms could gracefully balance user satisfaction and fairness among all users. It is necessary to mention that, when the portion of adaptive multimedia arrivals in the total arrivals is at middle-level, i.e. around 50% under any mobility conditions, our *BDP* could also retain the *QoS* metric on very high levels, which means nearly 90% of the bandwidth requirements of *BEL* calls could be satiated.

5 Conclusion

In this paper, we study and demonstrate the proposed *BDP* for adaptive multimedia services in cellular network. Specifically, we measure the *QoS* metrics such as *DPR*, *WDPR*, *UPR*, *UDR*, and *SR* of the adaptive multimedia services through extensive computer simulations. We could confirm that our study, with these simulation results, reveal the insight aspects of applying degradation policy and compensation mechanisms. Our *BDP* with compensation mechanisms could gracefully balance user satisfaction and fairness among all users, while at the same time ensuring that the scarce bandwidth be utilized efficiently. Moreover, accommodating more adaptive multimedia calls into the system without the portion limitation is detrimental to the whole system, which will either prevent more new users from entering into the system, or lower satisfaction of ongoing adaptive multimedia user, demolishing the fairness among all users.

Acknowledgment

This work was supported by NSFC (National Science Foundation of China) and RGC (Research Grants Council of Hong Kong) grant No.60218002, and National Key Basic Research Program (2007CB307104 of 2007CB307100). The authors sincerely wish to thank the anonymous reviewers for valuable reviews and suggestions.

References

1. Liu, J., Li, B., Hou, Y.T., Chlamtac, I.: On Optimal Layering and Bandwidth Allocation for Multisession Video Broadcasting. IEEE Transactions on Wireless Communications 3(2) (2004)
2. Kwon, T., Choi, Y., Das, S.K.: Bandwidth adaptation algorithms for adaptive multimedia services in mobile cellular networks. Wireless Personal Commun. 22(3), 337–357 (2002)
3. Deniz, D.Z., Mohamed, N.O.: Performance of CAC Strategies for Multimedia. IEEE J. Select Areas Commun. 21(10), 1557–1573 (2003)
4. Das, S.K., Sen, S.K., Basu, K., Lin, H.: A Framework for Bandwidth Degradation and Call Admission Control Schemes for Multiclass Traffic in Next-Generation Wireless Networks. IEEE J. Select Areas Commun. 21(10), 1790–1802 (2003)
5. Kwon, T., Choi, Y., Bisdikian, C., Naghshineh, M.: QoS provisioning in wireless/mobile multimedia networks using an adaptive framework. Wireless Networks 9, 51–59 (2003)
6. Xiao, Y., Chen, C.L.P., Wang, B.: Bandwidth degradation QoS provisioning for adaptive multimedia in wireless/mobile networks. Computer Commun. 25, 1153–1161 (2002)

7. Yu, F., Wong, V.W.S., Leung, V.C.M.: A New QoS Provisioning Method for Adaptive Multimedia in Cellular Wireless Networks. In: Proc. IEEE Infocom'04 (2004)
8. Chou, C.-T., Shin, K.G.: Analysis of Combined Adaptive Bandwidth Allocation and Admission Control in Wireless Networks. In: IEEE Infocom'02, New York (June 23-27, 2002)
9. Zhang, Y., Zhou, C., Dai, S., Li, L., Li, B.: Senior Member, IEEE, Bandwidth Allocation Scheme and Call Admission Control for Adaptive Multimedia Services in Wireless Cellular Networks–Part A:Numerical Results. In: IEEE The third International Conference on Communications, Circuits and Systems Proceedings, ICCCAS'05, Hongkong, China (May 27-30, 2005)
10. Zhang, Y., Li, L., Li., B.: Mobility Influences on the Capacity of Wireless Cellular Networks. ETRI Journal 28(6), 799–802 (2006)

On the System Performance vs. User Movement with Systematic Simulation in Mobile Cellular Networks*

Yide Zhang, Lemin Li, and Gang Feng

School of Communication and Information Engineering, University of Electronic Science and Technology of China, 610054, Chengdu, Sichuan, China,
computium@gmail.com, {lml,fenggang}@uestc.edu.cn

Abstract. We demonstrate in the paper that user movement has great influences on the system performance of mobile cellular networks. We also develop a system model to study to what extent the influences will be, with focusing on the user movement simulation. We concern the parameters that determine the system performance of mobile cellular networks. We show partially in this paper that these parameters vary while user movement changes, but the effects are interactive. Since handoff calls are given a higher priority over new calls and *GC* mechanism is employed, our analysis shows that a mature mobile cellular network should make use of user movement characteristics and dynamically adjust its reservation threshold of the handoff call requests. Extensive simulation results validate our analysis.

Keywords: User Movement, System Performance, Mobile Cellular Network.

1 Introduction

Mobile cellular networks, as exemplified by mobile phones, have provided people great freedom in mobility while enabling them to stay in touch with others and have also made information available literally at their fingertips. We have therefore recently witnessed phenomenal growth in the development and deployment of wireless services. Carriers pay much attention to the capacity of their whole mobile cellular networks, while users concern the system performance of mobile cellular networks more than before. This paper studies the mobility influences on the system performance of mobile cellular networks.

A fundamental characteristic of mobile cellular networks is the time variation of the channel strength of the underlying communication links [5, 10]. In a realistic wireless environment, system designs are confronted with interference problems, e.g. *CCI*, intrinsically limited bandwidth, and highly variable and unpredictable propagation characteristics. Specifically, the channel quality may vary widely among spatially distributed users due to distance-related attenuation. In addition, the channel conditions for a user may vary dramatically over time because of fading effects [3].

---

* This work was supported by NSFC (National Science Foundation of China) and RGC (Research Grants Council of Hong Kong) grant No.60218002, and National Key Basic Research Program (2007CB307104 of 2007CB307100).

I. Stojmenovic et al. (Eds.): ISPA 2007, LNCS 4742, pp. 750–761, 2007.

User movement is a most significant characteristic inherent to mobile cellular networks. However, as far as we know, there are few papers concerning with the user movement influences on the system performance of mobile cellular networks. This paper studies the user movement influences on the system performance of mobile cellular networks. We consider a mobile cellular network with homogeneous cells. The mobile cellular network has *N* clusters, with *K* cells in each cluster in a planar configuration. Due to the fact that dropping an ongoing call from user's perception is far more serious than blocking a new call request, we give handoff calls a higher priority over new call requests when handoff calls and new call requests originate in the same cell simultaneously. Furthermore, a portion of the total bandwidth in a cell is reserved for handoff requests from neighboring cells. Our analysis also includes the modeling of the system, with focus on the mobility model.

Our basic innovation idea comes from the following observation: in the real world a mobile user generally keeps moving in the direction it has moved before. A mobile user usually travels with a destination in mind. Thus, the variation of a mobile user velocity and direction within a short time is confined due to physical restrictions. Therefore, a mobile user's current velocity and moving direction are likely to be correlated with its past velocity and moving direction. We also devised an *Abrupt Event Influence (AEI)* factor Φ to describe the sudden diversion of the user movement variation. For example in road cross, user may change his or her direction or velocity suddenly. By adjusting some simulation parameter values, especially the devised *AEI* factor Φ, we could simulate various user movement behaviors in the real world.

This paper demonstrates that the user movement influences on the system performance of mobile cellular networks is conspicuous. The probability that an ongoing call experience more handoffs during its lifetime will increase while the call's mobility increases, with the consequence of making the system exhaust more resources to keep the same *QoS* for high mobility calls. Increasing the probability of a successful handoff results in restricting the acceptance ratio of new call requests to make more channels available for handoffs. The system performance of mobile cellular networks is highly related to the New Call Blocking Probability (P_b) and Handoff Call Dropping Probability (P_d), i.e. the probability that an unsuccessful handoff call is terminated before the connection ends [6, 7 and 10].

We perceive the relevance between our study and the phenomenal growth in the development and deployment of mobile services. The number of mobile subscribers keeps ascending rendering the cell size being systematically reduced in micro-cell and pico-cell systems in order to increase the overall network capacity. Additionally, the proliferation of cellular data services and the emerging mobile multimedia applications such as mobile video-phone and teleconference probably require the system providing more stringent *QoS* capability. Dropping a multimedia connection which may carry a bandwidth many times than that of a voice call is seemingly unacceptable following the intuition. Although our study begins in a conventional TDMA/ FDMA network, the results are likely to apply to CDMA-based networks like 3G/4G.

The rest of the paper is organized as follows. We describe the system model in section 2, as well as user movement simulation and the propagation model. We present the extensive simulation results in Section 3. We conclude the paper in Section 4 with discussions.

2 The System Model

We consider a mobile cellular network with homogeneous hexagonal cells with *N* clusters, and each cluster consists of *K* cells (the reuse pattern), with *C* Basic Bandwidth Units (*BBUs*) or channels in each cell. Moreover, the cell radius is assumed to be *R* meters. In each cell, a portion of the total *BBUs* is reserved for handoff requests from neighboring cells. We assume this portion is C_G. Since real systems can contain thousands of cells, which are extremely difficult to model, we use a wraparound technique to make all the cells appear as if they were placed in the middle of a cellular system, with capability to capture the essential characteristics to the real system.

In order to explore how user movement influences the system performance of mobile cellular networks, it is necessary to model the system. We are focusing on the user movement simulation which we are convinced has great impacts on the system performance. The propagation model is also established.

2.1 User Movement

We use a vector *(X, Y)* to represent the location of the user. The change of user's location implicates the changed values of *X* and *Y*. Then, with the perspective that the user's behaviors have some random characteristics, the disturbance of the user's movement direction is concerned. The uncorrelated normal Gaussian process is concatenated along both the *X* and *Y* coordinate, resulting in the following formulas:

$$V_x(n) = V_x(n-1) \cdot \xi + \sqrt{1-\xi^2} \cdot V_{avg} \cdot \chi \tag{1}$$

$$V_y(n) = V_y(n-1) \cdot \xi + \sqrt{1-\xi^2} \cdot V_{avg} \cdot \chi \tag{2}$$

Vx and *Vy* represent the velocity at the *X* and *Y* coordinate respectively, whereas V_{avg} means the average velocity value.χ is a uncorrelated normal Gaussian process with mean of 0 and deviation of 1. However, since the velocity of a user is correlated between two consecutive sampling times, a correlation coefficient has to be carefully modeled. First of all, the correlation coefficient ξ of the velocity of a user between two successive sampling times leads to the following formula to describe the variation of the user speed:

$$\xi = \exp(-\Delta t \cdot \beta \cdot \phi) \tag{3}$$

Δt is the time interval between two successive sampling times. βdetermines the degree of memory in the mobility pattern[9] and is an experiential coefficient. Φ is the devised "Abrupt Event Influence" factor, describing the sudden diversion of the user's movement model.

Though adjusting the value of β and the distribution of χ, especially the devised "Abrupt Event Influence" factor Φ, we could use the above equations to simulate various user movement behaviors. Here come 3 typical examples:

- User movement in business zone or downtown: This case is for micro-cell or pico-cell mobile cellular networks. User might be in Pedestrian Model or

"Bicycle Model" – which is typical in China. We design: $\xi=1$ (memoryless), $R=50$m and $V_{avg}=5$ *mps*.

- User movement in urban zone or small town: This case is for micro-cell mobile cellular networks. User might be in urban zone or small town with low density of population, while driving or taking cars, buses, taxies, etc. We design: $\xi=0.3$ (little memory), R=600m and Vavg = 15 mps = 54 km per hour. Possibility we apply will Φ -- the devised "Abrupt Event Influence" factor, describing the sudden diversion of the user's movement behavior.
- User movement in rural zone or high way: This case is for macro-cell mobile cellular networks. User might be in rural zone or high ways with very low density of population, while driving or taking wagons, cars, taxies, etc. We design: $\xi=0.1$ (deep memory), $R=1000$m and $V_{avg}=25$ *mps* = 90 *km per hour*. Possibility we apply will Φ -- the devised "Abrupt Event Influence" factor, describing the sudden diversion of the user's movement behavior. For example in road cross, user may change his or her direction or velocity suddenly.

2.2 Propagation Model

The performance of mobile communication systems depends on the mobile radio channel significantly [2]. Propagation models predict the average signal strength and its variability at a given distance from the transmitter. Different propagation models exist for outdoor and indoor propagation and for different types of environments (urban or rural) [3].

We assume that the terminal is currently located at distance d. The received power may thus be written as (in dB) [4, 5]:

$$P_r = P_t + G_p + G_s + G_r \tag{4}$$

P_r represents the received signal power of the terminal (receiver); P_t represents the transmitted signal power of the terminal (transmitter), whereas G_p, G_s and G_r represent average path loss gain, the shadow fading gain and the Rayleigh fading gain respectively.

Path-Loss Model. The average path loss is distance dependent. The dependence of the global average Gp can be modeled with a simple exponential expression:

$$G_p = C_t - 10 \cdot \alpha \cdot \lg r \tag{5}$$

This model is usually referred to as the Okumura-hata model [5].The constant C_t is used to model the effects of antenna size and other physical parameters. It can be interpreted as the path gain at a distance of on meter from the transmitter antenna. The αparameter determines how much the power decays as a function of distance from the transmitter, typically ranging from 3~5, as 4 is for the radio signal transmission in the space.

Large-Scale Fading Model. Large-scale fading is also called the shadow fading. A common model for large-scale fading is the log-normal distribution characterized by the probability density function.

$$G_s = \frac{1}{\sigma\sqrt{2\cdot\pi}}\exp(-\frac{(G_s - G_p)^2}{2\cdot\sigma^2}) \quad (6)$$

The log-standard deviation σ may be in the order of several dB, dependent on the terrain situation. In the real world the shadow fading is correlated in space. If a mobile for example is behind an obstacle it will probably still be behind that obstacle if it only moves a small distance. The autocorrelation of the log-normal shadow fading is taken into account.

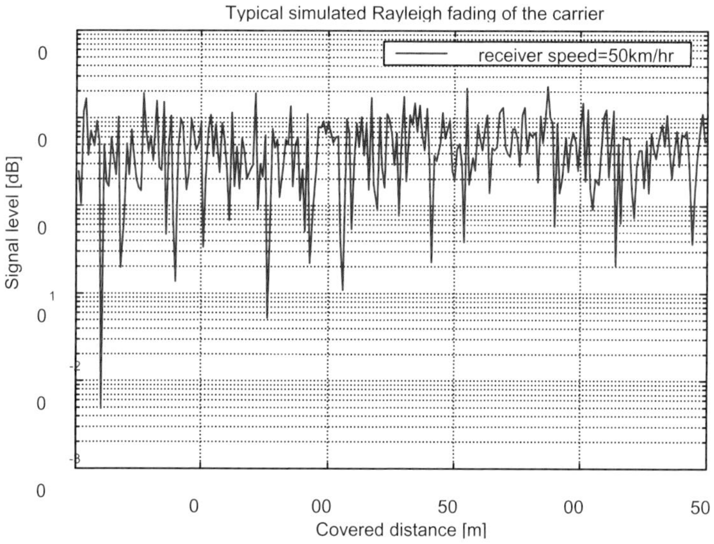

Fig. 1. The Variation of the Received Signal with the Rayleigh Fading

Small-Scale Fading Model. Small-scale fading or short term fading is usually modeled as a Rayleigh fading. It varies quickly over distance.

$$G_r = I_0(\frac{G_r\cdot\eta}{\sigma_r^2})\frac{G_r}{\sigma_r^2}\exp(-\frac{(G_r^2+\eta^2)}{2\cdot\sigma_r^2}) \quad (7)$$

$I_0()$ is the zero-order modified Bessel function and the parameter η denotes the amplitude of the dominant, constant signal.

Figure 1 depicts the typical variation of the received signal with the Rayleigh fading.

Generally speaking, the distance dependence of the global average G_p can be modeled with a simple exponential expression, the large-scale fading gain G_s could be modeled as a log-normal distribution, and the small-scale fading or short term fading is usually modeled as a Rayleigh fading.

3 Simulation Results and Discussion

In this section, we present simulation results. The parameters used in the simulation environment are listed in Table 1.

Table 1. Parameters for simulation

Number of clusters in the system	N=7
Number of cells in each cluster	K=7
Total cells	49
Number of *BBUs* in each cell	C is variable
guard channel threshold	C_G is variable
Cell radius	R=800 meters
Number of sectors per cell	1 sector
Distance-based propagation attenuation coefficient	α=3.5
thermal noise	-118 dBm
Standard deviation for shadow fading	6 dB
Shadow fading correlation	0.5
Sampling time interval	3 seconds
Average number of new call request to a cell	λ is variable
Average number of handoff call request to a cell	γ is variable
Mean holding time	$1/\mu=1/\mu_I= 1/\mu_H$ =120 sec
Mean speed	variable
Velocity correlation coefficient	β=1
Handoff hysteresis	H=3 dB
Call dropping SIR threshold	5 dB

We plot the whole system model under consideration in Figure 2. Wrap-around technique is utilized, rendering the out-going calls returning from the other size of the system.

The system performance measurement parameters considered in this paper are New Call Blocking Probability (P_b), Handoff Call Dropping Probability (P_d). Note that blocking handoff calls doesn't imply the termination of the corresponding calls. Only the finally termination of a handoff unsuccessful call due to the link quality deterioration results the dropping of a handoff call.

The arrivals of new calls are assumed to be Poisson distributed with average arrival rate λ_{avg} calls per second per cell, and generated at any place in the cell with an equal probability [1]. The average service rate is assumed to be exponentially distributed with mean holding time about 120 seconds [8]. We analyze in details the impacts of different values of C_G. We assume that C_G =0~6, other parameters are configured as in Table 1. We also plot the C_G =0 case in comparison between the systems with and without Guarded Channel (GC) mechanisms.

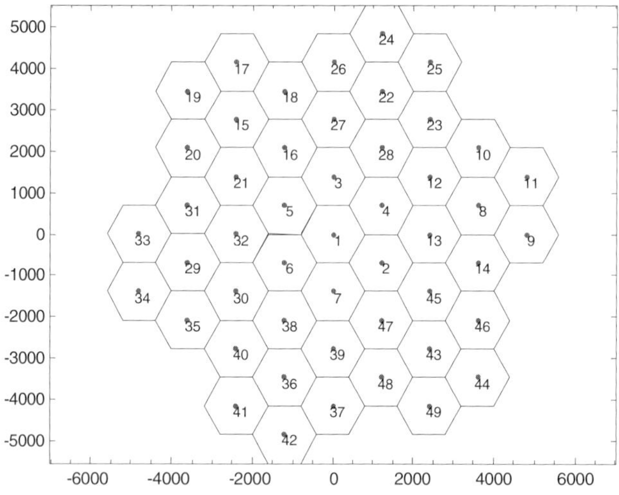

Fig. 2. System Model(Units:meter)

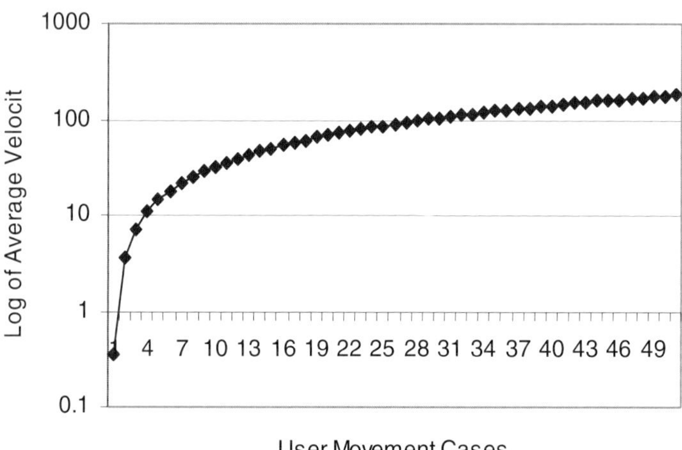

Fig. 3. Adopted User Movement Cases

Furthermore, we assume that the user movement behavior varies. The average velocity spans from 0 *mps* (meter per second) to 50 *mps*, with fixed step of 10 *mps*. Value 0 stands for stationary case. Hence the users' velocity changes from 0 *kph* (kilometer per hour) to 180 *kph*, with fixed step of 3.6 *kph*. Since in realistic world, users rarely keep absolutely "still" even when they make or answer calls with fixed phones, no mention to mobile phones, we adopt 0.5 *mps* in case 1. Figure 3 details the user movement behavior variation (the *Y* values are the log of average velocity in unit *kph*).

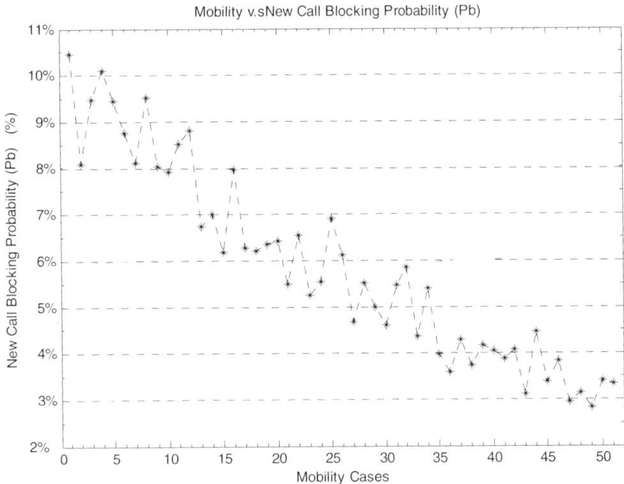

Fig. 4. New Call Dropping Probability (P_b)

Figure 4 and 5 depicts the system performance measurement parameters considered in this paper: New Call Blocking Probability (P_b) and Handoff Call Dropping Probability (P_d).

The relatively high predetermined intense simulation parameter-- the arrival rate of new calls (λ) results in slightly high New Call Blocking Probability (P_b). However, we could still see the giant influence of the user movement on the New Call Blocking Probability (P_b), seen from Figure 4. Higher user movement converts into more outgoing users leaving the current cell into another neighboring cell, rendering the chances for new call requests not being blocked by the system and therefore the lower P_b. We could obviously see that the entire trend is that the value of P_b goes decreasingly with the increment of the user movement at large granularity, whereas at the small granularity the value of P_b oscillates.

The user movement influence on the Handoff Call Dropping Probability (P_d) is more complicated and shown in Figure 5. When the average velocity of ongoing MSs is below 10 *mps*(36 *kph*) —low user movement, the impact of user movement on the P_d is so conspicuous that the value of P_d inclines linearly with the augment of user movement at the slope more than 1.732 or angle more than 60 degree. When the average velocity is between 10 *mps* (36 *kph*) and 20 *mps* (72 *kph*)--median user movement, the entire trend is rising, whereas P_d is heavily oscillating. Finally when the user movement is high enough, i.e. more than 20 *mps* (72 *kph*), P_d stays stable with very slight augment.

Moreover, we observe that the increasing of user movement significantly reduces the New Call Blocking Probability (P_b), at the expense of acceptable increment of Handoff Call Dropping Probability (P_d). However, when P_d is finely controlled below 2%, the increasing of user movement is converted into notable decreasing of P_b, which allows the system to accommodate more users. Generally speaking, the user movement is beneficial to increases the system performance of mobile cellular networks.

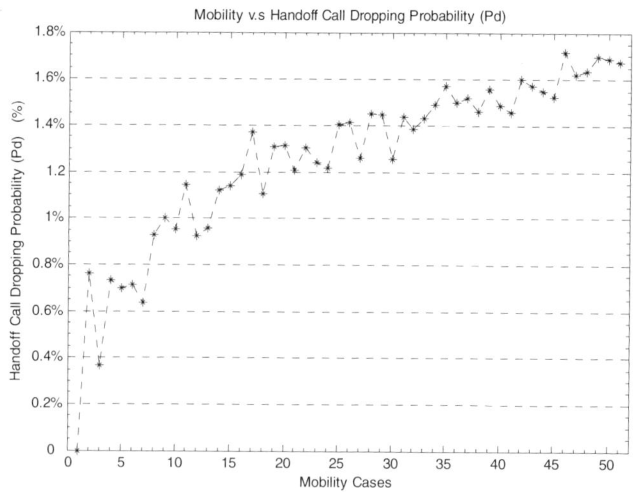

Fig. 5. Handoff Call Dropping Probability (P_d)

However whether the conclusion drawn in the last paragraph above could be held of not when we reserve guarded channels exclusively for handoff calls needs to be scrutinized. We analyze in details the impacts of different values of C_G. We assume that C_G =0~8, other parameters are configured as in Table I. We also plot the C_G =0 case in comparison between the systems with and without Guarded Channel (*GC*) mechanisms.

Figure 6 to 7 depict the system performance parameters under different C_G values and user movement cases. We let the C_G values range from 0 to 8, demonstrating the entire trends employing C_G values up to 8 and give the detail explanations of the simulation results. We employ the 3-dimensional image to exhibit the combining effects caused by both guarded channel threshold and user movement on different system parameters.

The relatively high predetermined intense simulation parameter-- the arrival rate of new calls (λ) results in slightly high New Call Blocking Probability (P_b), while the increasing C_G value worsens the situation, seen from Figure 6. Besides we could see the giant influence of the mobility on P_b, the influences of C_G value is also conspicuous. We confirm our former reasoning that higher guarded channel threshold could be applied if user movement is relatively high. The increasing user movement neutralizes the influences caused by the increment of C_G value. We also see some local extremums representing the random process in our simulation results.

The result in Figure 7 confirms the initial advantage of utilizing the Guarded Channel (*GC*) mechanisms. But we notice that the high user movement cases lessen the advantage gaining from adding more guarded channels. The explanation is that the higher user movement cases render a call experiencing more handoffs during its lifetime, however, due to the cell radius is bounded, larger user movement will loose its impacts on the Handoff Call Dropping Probability (P_d) values. Thus, the simulation results are relatively flatter in higher user movement cases than in lower ones. Also, we could say that the user movement influences on the P_d is more complicated as stated before, increasing C_G value makes the situation more complex. While the P_d value increases oscillatorily with the increment of user movement, the increasing C_G value reduces P_d at the same time. Again, the random process employed to generate the arrivals of the new and handoff calls, as well as the handoff processing, renders a few local extremums in our simulation results, which is a 3-dimensional curved surface.

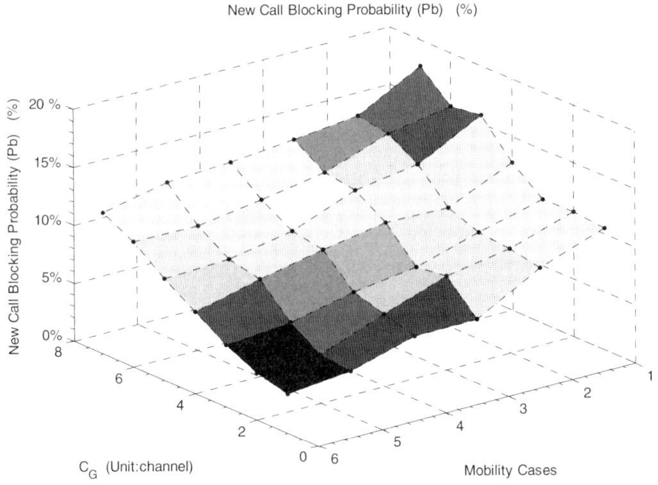

Fig. 6. Handoff Call Dropping Probability(P_d)

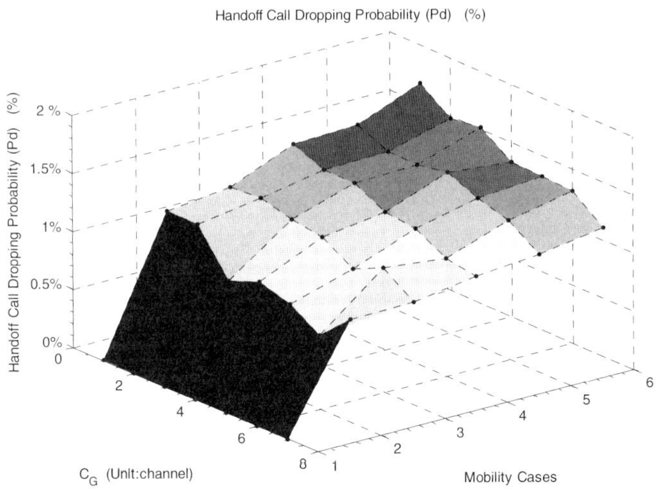

Fig. 7. New Call Dropping Probability(P_b)

Therefore, we could see from our simulation results that, when the increasing of user movement significantly reduces the New Call Blocking Probability (P_b), at the expense of acceptable increment of Handoff Call Dropping Probability (P_d), the detrimental effect on the individual system performance metric will hardly conceal the much more benefits the system could gain from the variation of the user movement. Moreover, when P_d is finely controlled below 2%, the increasing of user movement is converted into notable decreasing of P_b, which allows the system to accommodate more users. Generally speaking, the user movement is beneficial to increases the system performance of mobile cellular networks.

4 Conclusion

We demonstrate in the paper that user movement has great influences on the system performance of mobile cellular networks. We show partially that the system performance parameters vary while the user movement changes. When P_d is finely controlled below 2%, the increasing of user movement is converted into notable decreasing of P_b, which allows the system to accommodate more users. In general, the user movement is beneficial to increases the system performance of mobile cellular networks. Since handoff calls are given a higher priority over new calls and *GC* mechanism is employed, our analysis shows that a mature mobile cellular network should make use of user movement characteristics and dynamically adjust its reservation threshold of the handoff call requests. Extensive simulation results validate our analysis.

Acknowledgment

This work was supported by NSFC (National Science Foundation of China) and RGC (Research Grants Council of Hong Kong) grant No.60218002, and National Key Basic Research Program (2007CB307104 of 2007CB307100). The authors sincerely wish to thank the anonymous reviewers for valuable reviews and suggestions.

References

1. Haung, Y.-R., Lin, Y.-B., Ho, J.M.: Performance Analysis for Voice/Data Integration on a Finite Mobile Systems. Transactions on Vehicle Technology 49(2), 367–378 (2000)
2. Tripathi, N.D., Reed, J.H., VanLandingham, H.F.: Radio Resource Management in Cellular Systems. Kluwer Academic Publishers, Dordrecht (2001)
3. Rappaport, T.S.: Wireless communications: Principles and Practice, 2nd edn. Prentice-Hall Inc., Englewood Cliffs (2002)
4. Zander, J., Kim, S.-L.: Radio Resource Management for Wireless Networks. Artech House (2001)
5. Hata, M.: Empirical Formula for Propagation Loss in Land Mobile Radio Services. IEEE Transactions on Vehicle Technology VT-29(3) (1980)
6. Wu, S., Wong, K.Y.M., Li, B.: A Dynamic Call Admission Policy with Precision QoS Guarantee Using Stochastic Control for Mobile Wireless Networks. IEEE/ACM Trans. Networking 10(2) (2002)

7. Wu, H.-L., Li, L.-Z., Li, B., Yin, L., Chlamtac, I., Li, B.: On handoff performance for an voice/data integrated cellular system, part II: data buffer case. In: IEEE PIMRC'2002, Lisbon, Portugal (2002)
8. Li, L.-Z., Li, B., Li, B., Cao, X-R.: Performance analysis of bandwidth allocations for multi-services mobile wireless cellular networks. In: IEEE WCNC 2003, vol. 2, pp. 16–20, 1072–1077 (2003)
9. Liang, B., Haas, Z.J.: Predictive Distance-Based Mobility Management for Multidimensional PCS Networks. IEEE/ACM Transactions on Networking 11(5) (2003)
10. Zhang, Y., Dai, S., Zhou, C., Li, L., Li, B.: Bandwidth Allocation Scheme and Call Admission Control for Adaptive Multimedia Services in Wireless Cellular Networks–Part A: Numerical Results. In: IEEE The third International Conference on Communications, Circuits and Systems–ICCCAS'05 (2005)

Channel Assignment and Spatial Reuse Scheduling to Improve Throughput and Enhance Fairness in Wireless Mesh Networks

Nguyen H. Tran and Choong Seon Hong*

Department of Computer Engineering, Kyung Hee University
Giheung, Yongin, Gyeonggi, 449-701 Korea
nguyenth@networking.khu.ac.kr, cshong@khu.ac.kr

Abstract. In wireless mesh network, by equipped mesh router with multiple radios tuned into orthogonal channels, throughput improvement problem can be alleviated. Efficient channel assignment and link scheduling is essential for throughput improvement. Effective channel assignment schemes can greatly relieve the interference effect between nearby transmissions. However, not only the links in wireless mesh network using different channels can be activated at a time, but some links in the same channel also can be activated concurrently if the SNIR (Signal-to-Noise and Interference Ratio) at their receiver endpoints is not lower than the threshold. In this paper, we investigate the problem of how to schedule a set of feasible transmission under physical interference model by using the Spatial TDMA access scheme and channel assignment in wireless mesh networks. We also consider the fairness enhancement to prevent some border nodes of the network from starvation. By using Minimum Spanning Tree as network subgraph constructed from original network graph, we propose centralized algorithms for scheduling and channel assignment to maximize the aggregate throughput and to provide the fairness of the network. We also evaluate the throughput improvement and fairness enhancement of our algorithms through extensive simulations and the results show that our algorithm can achieve significant aggregate throughput and fairness performance.

Keywords: Wireless mesh networks, scheduling, fairness.

1 Introduction

Wireless mesh networks (WMNs) have emerged to be a new, cost-effective for the next generation wireless Internet. In such networks, mesh routers which are stationary or less mobile nodes form the infrastructure backbone for clients whereas the mesh clients are the wireless devices to which the WMN provides connectivity. Only a fraction of nodes have direct access to the Internet and serve as gateways. Based on

* This research was supported by the MIC, Korea, under the ITRC support program supervised by the IITA (IITA-2006-(C1090-0602-0002)) and Dr. C.S Hong is the corresponding author.

I. Stojmenovic et al. (Eds.): ISPA 2007, LNCS 4742, pp. 762 – 773, 2007.

the benefits of multi-radio multi-channel mesh routers, several recent works have focused on many typical problems of WMNs like channel assignment, routing, scheduling [2], [5], [7], [13], [14]. Due to the limited wireless channel capacity, the large number of clients and the emergence of real-time multimedia applications, improving network throughput has become the critical requirements in such networks.

One of the important factors to improve the network capacity is spatial reuse [9], the total number of concurrent transmissions that can be accommodated in the network. Another popular MAC protocol that attracts most of the recent work is CSMA/CA proposed in IEEE 802.11 standard. But, due to its conservative mechanism with carrier sensing and collision avoidance characteristics, when a node transmits, a number of its neighbors must be inactivated. This leads to the fact that high traffic demand can not be satisfied, especially with WMN. In mesh networks, one of the major problems caused by concurrent transmissions is the reduction of capacity due to *interference*. Mesh routers with multiple radios can greatly alleviate this problem. With multiple radios, nodes can transmit and receive simultaneously or can transmit on multiple channels simultaneously. However, due to the limited number of channels available, the interference can not be completely eliminated. So an efficient channel assignment must be done to mitigate the effect of interference. Recently, most of the interest challenges relating to WMN have been investigated under two main interference models: *protocol* and *physical* interference models, which were first proposed in [18]. Until now, the protocol interference model mostly has been used due to the fact of its simplicity. In the physical interference, the transmission between two nodes is successful if the SNIR at the receiver is not lower than a certain threshold. In this way, more than one transmission can take place as long as the condition of SNIR at the receivers satisfied. We see that the characteristic of physical model is suitable with spatial reuse. Moreover, as the majority of traffic is transferred to and from gateways, traffic flows will likely aggregate at the mesh routers close to the gateways. Therefore, without effective channel assignment and scheduling algorithm, there is probably the data starvation of the mesh clients of border mesh routers. So, besides targeting to improve the overall throughput of the system, the transmission scheduling also takes into account the fairness problem to give the communications between border nodes a higher chance for transmission.

Based on discussion above, we present two centralized heuristic algorithms. One of them is for channel assignment problem which efficiently mitigates the interference effect and the other is to address the problem of scheduling using STDMA access scheme under the physical interference model to reach the objective of throughput improvement with fairness for the system. We also present extensive simulation results to evaluate throughput improvement and fairness of our algorithms.

The remainder of our paper is organized as follows. In Section 2, we summarize related work in the literature and highlight the major differences between existing work and our work. We state our models, assumptions and definitions in Section 3. Next, we describe our algorithms for scheduling and channel assignment in Section 4 and section 5. We evaluate the performance of our algorithm in Section 6. Finally, we present our conclusions and discuss the future work in Section 7.

2 Related Work

In literature, there are many works of scheduling mechanisms proposed for STDMA access scheme defined by Nelson and Kleinrock [11] for both protocol and physical interference model. Only a few works have considered physical interference in this context [2], [3], [4], [6], [12]. In [4], Gronkvist and Hasson compare the use of physical interference in STDMA to an approach that considers interference up to a certain distance from a node. Jain et al. [6] consider throughput optimization by formulating the problem of scheduling under both protocol and physical interference model as an LP problem. However, this formulation can be computationally intensive to achieve close to optimal performance. The work of [3] also provides an exponential-time LP formulation. About channel assignment problems, in [23], Ramachandran et al. presents an interference-aware channel assignment algorithm and protocol for multi-radio wireless mesh networks. His proposed solution assigns channels to radios to minimize interference within the mesh network and between the mesh network and co-located wireless networks. In [24], Brzezinski et al. considers the interaction between channel assignment and distributed scheduling in WMNs. Heuristic approaches [14], [15] on channel assignment and load-aware routing are proposed to improve the aggregate throughput of WMNs and balance load among gateways.

About the fairness problem, in [2], Ben Salem et al. propose a scheduling that ensures per-client fairness with solution assigns transmission rights to the links in a STDMA fashion and is collision-free by constructing maximal cliques. However, due to the fact that clique enumeration problem is proven to be NP-hard, her solution just can be used for small size WMNs. In [22], Jian Tang et al. consider the bandwidth allocation problem by using a simple max-min fairness model to achieve the tradeoff between maximizing throughput and enhancing the fairness. They address the problem by considering Lexicographical Max-Min bandwidth allocation under an interference constraint in a multi-channel multi-hop wireless network to non-gateway mesh routers.

3 System Models

3.1 Network Model

We consider the backbone of WMN modeled by a *network graph* $G(V,E)$, where $V = \{1,...,|V|\}$ is the set of nodes (mesh routers) and $E = \{(i,j) : i, j \in V\}$ is the set of bi-directional links. We assume that time is slotted, denoted by t, and that the packet length is normalized in order to be transmittable in a unit time slot. We denote $Q_e(t)$ the number of packets waiting to be transmitted on link e by the end of time slot t, also known as queue length of link e. In the system, each node is equipped with one or more wireless interface cards, referred to as radios in this paper. We assume there are K orthogonal channels available in the network without any inter-channel interference. By using multiple radios and multiple channels, an interface of a node can transmit the data on one channel while another interface can receive data on a different channel.

3.2 Interference Model

Physical Interference Mode: To schedule two links at the same time slot, we must ensure that the schedule will avoid the interference. We only consider physical interference model in our work. In this model, a successful transmission from node i to node j depends on the SINR at j. Specifically, denoting RSS_j^i as the signal strength of node j received when node i transmits to node j, and ISS_j^k as interfered signal strength received by j from another node k which is also transmitting, packets along the link (i, j) are correctly received if and only if:

$$\frac{RSS_j^i}{N + \sum_{k \in V_C} ISS_j^k} \geq \alpha \tag{1}$$

where N is the white noise, V_C is the subset of nodes in V that are transmitting concurrently, and the threshold α is the constant. Based on the physical interference model, the set of communication links that interfere with each other can be represented by using *interference graph* [6]. The interference graph will be constructed based on the interference between the links using the same channel.

Interference graph: To define a interference graph $G^{'}(V^{'}, E^{'})$, we first create a set of vertices $V^{'}$ corresponding to the communication links in the network. In this interference graph, a node represents for the edge in network graph and the directed edge between two nodes $v_1^{'}$, $v_2^{'}$ (which represents two links e_1, e_2 in network graph) has a weight. The interference graph must be weighted because the more the links on the same channel are active concurrently, the more interference each link will be affected by each other until they become unacceptable for the packet reception at the receivers.

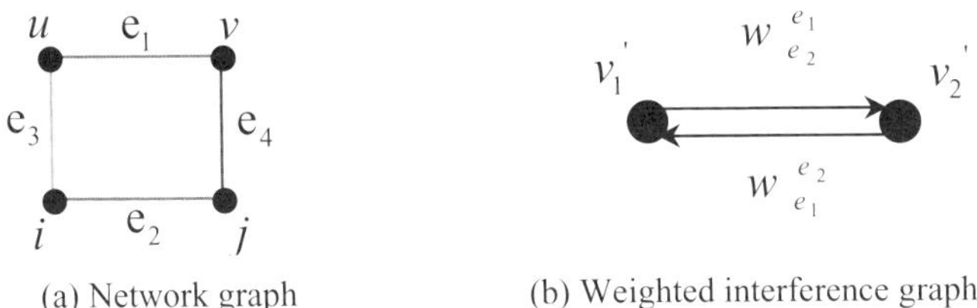

(a) Network graph (b) Weighted interference graph

Fig. 1. Network graph and weighted interference graph

Consider an example in Figure 1, the communications between node u and v, i and j are on the same channel (the same red color in the figure), for example channel 1. The communications between u and i, v and j are on channel 2 and 3 respectively. So there is interference between e_1 and e_2. Therefore, we can construct the interference graph based on the network graph as Figure 2(b). From the above definition of weighted interference graph, we can have the weight value $w_{e_2}^{e_1}$ represents for the interference contributed by e_1 to e_2 (we can calculate $w_{e_1}^{e_2}$ as this way similarly):

$$w_{e_2}^{e_1} = \frac{\max(ISS_j^{v}, ISS_j^{u})}{\frac{RSS_j^{i}}{\alpha} - N} \tag{2}$$

3.3 Conditions

We find the conditions to determine whether a certain set of concurrent transmissions on the same channel is feasible. 1) A necessary condition: The set $E_M = \{e_1, ..., e_k\} \subseteq E$ is feasible only if none of its edges is incident with each other on the same node. 2) A sufficient condition: Every receiver of all links in E_M must have $SINR \geq \alpha$. So, we can state the following corollary:

Corollary 1. *A set $G_T^{'} \in E$ of concurrent transmission on the same channel in a given network graph $G(V, E)$ is feasible under physical interference model if every vertex of the corresponding interference graph $G^{'}(V^{'}, E^{'})$ satisfies:*

$$\sum_{v_k^{'} \in V^{'} - \{v^{'}\}} w_e^{e_k} \leq 1 \tag{3}$$

Proof: We have the set of links $\{e_k = (i_k, j_k), k = 1, 2, ...\}$ transmitting concurrently with link $e = (i, j)$. Therefore, in respective interference graph, we will have of all edges incident on $v^{'}$ represents all interfering signals of all links $e_1, ..., e_k$ to link e. From Eq.(1), packets are received correctly at receiver of link e when:

$$\frac{RSS_j^{i}}{N + \sum_{(i_k, j_k) \in G_T^{'}} ISS_j^{i_k}} \geq \alpha \Rightarrow \frac{\sum_{(i_k, j_k) \in G_T^{'}} ISS_j^{i_k}}{\frac{RSS_j^{i}}{\alpha} - N} \leq 1 \Leftrightarrow \sum_{v_k^{'} \in V^{'} - \{v^{'}\}} w_e^{e_k} \leq 1. \qquad \square$$

4 Scheduling Algorithm

In this section, we present a greedy algorithm to construct a feasible schedule for a set of transmissions under physical interference model. Instead of considering for the whole network, proposed algorithm just investigates in a subgraph. The reason is to improve the fairness characteristic. If we consider the feasible schedule for whole network, the links close to management nodes have higher priority will take over the right to be scheduled first. It leads to some links at the border of system may not have a chance to transmit the data. When setting feasible schedule for a subgraph in each period, the number of high priority links has been reduced, so the border links can transmit with higher probability.

Consequently, we decide to choose Minimum Spanning Tree (MST) as the subgraph of the network graph $G(V,E)$ in our algorithm because MST has all characteristics appropriate for the purpose of our algorithm. First, MST is a spanning subgraph that contains all vertices of $G(V,E)$ so it gives an equal chance for all links incident with all nodes to be considered in each period of the schedule. Second, MST of a graph defines the cheapest subset of edges that keeps the graph in one connected component. So each link in a MST will have the higher priority than the others incident on the same node with it. It satisfies the condition that links with higher priority will be considered to be scheduled first. Finally, it can be computed quickly and easily, e.g. Kruskal's minimum spanning tree algorithm [21] can have the running time $O(|E|\log|V|)$. It's an important factor to reduce time complexity of our algorithm. Figure 2 is an example of MST (the bold lines) constructed from a WMN. There are total 7 links operating on channel 1 contend to be scheduled for whole network while in this MST, there are just 4 links. So with the priority criterion, links of border nodes will have higher chance to be in a schedule.

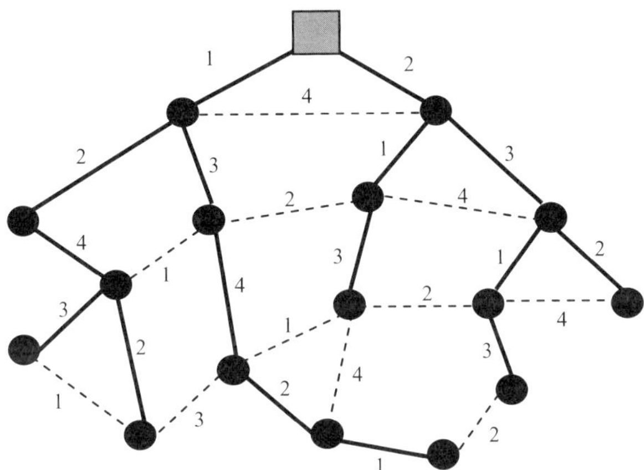

Fig. 2. A Minimum Spanning Tree of a WMN with 4 different channels

The pseudo code of scheduling algorithm is given in Figure 3. First, a MST $T(V_T, E_T)$ is constructed from the network graph. The cost of each link is computed by value $c(e) = \dfrac{1}{Q_e(t)}$ where $Q_e(t)$ is the queue size of link e by the time the algorithm starts to operate. With those edges of this MST, at least one edge of a vertex in $T(V_T, E_T)$ has the minimum cost. At first, the set of links on the same channel to be scheduled are ordered according to the decreasing order of queue lengths (step 2). After that, in step 3, Algorithm 1 finds the maximal feasible set of transmissions (E_M). Beginning with the highest queue length link, the algorithm adds next ordering links into the interference graph until there is a link making the interference graph unsatisfied with corollary 1. After having maximal feasible set of transmission, each link e in E_M will be scheduled in the first available slots beginning from slot 0 to slot $Q_e(t)$ (step 5). The period of this feasible transmission set is the maximum queue length of a link in E_M .

Algorithm 1. Scheduling Algorithm

Input: a network graph $G(V, E)$

Output: a feasible schedule with spatial reuse.

1. Creating MST $T(V_T, E_T)$ from $G(V, E)$

for $i = 1, \ldots, K$

2. initialize $G_T^{'}(i)$ with $V_T^{'}(i) = 0, E_T(i) \supseteq E_M(i) = 0$;

3. order links in $E_T(i)$ with decreasing number of queue length. Let $e_1(i), \ldots, e_m(i)$ be the resulting ordering;

4. **for** $j = 1, \ldots, m$

    $V_T^{'}(i) = V_T^{'}(i) + \{\{v^{'}(i)\} \leftrightarrow \{e^{j}(i) \in E_T(i)\}\}$;

    construct $G_T^{'}(i)$ with new vertex $v^{'}(i)$ added;

    if $G_T^{'}(i)$ satisfies corollary 1

        $E_M(i) = E_M(i) + e^{j}(i)$;

        $j = j + 1$;

    else exit;

    endif

  endfor

5. set available slots to $1, \ldots, T = \max_{e \in E_M(i)} Q_e(t)$

6. **for** $k = 1, \ldots, l = |E_M(i)|$

    schedule link $e^{k}(i) \in E_M(i)$ in the first $Q_{e^{k}(i)}(t)$ slots;

  endfor

endfor

Fig. 3. Scheduling Algorithm

5 Channel Assignment Algorithm

5.1 Overview

The channel assignment problem for mesh networks is similar to the *list coloring* problem. The list coloring problem is NP-complete [21]. Therefore, we rely on an approximate algorithm for channel assignment. Our channel assignment algorithm is also based on the MST subgraph of network graph. The rationale behind the use of MST subgraph is intuitive: we still satisfy our goal described in previous section of giving channel assignment priority to links starting from the gateway and then in decreasing levels of priority to links fanning outward towards the edge of the network. Before using the channel assignment algorithm, the gateway uses the neighbor information collected from all routers to get the link delay information. Neighbor information sent by a router can contain the identity of its neighbors delay to each neighbor. The channel assignment algorithm is summarized in Figure 4. The algorithm starts with all links emanating from the gateway which we called the first-hop level links. These links are sorted by increasing delay values (step 1). The link delay can be calculated using the Expected Transmission Time (ETT) metric [19]. ETT of a link is derived from the link's bandwidth and loss rate. A more detailed description of the metric can be found in [19]. This sort is performed in order to give higher priority to the better links emanating from the gateway. After that, it will assign the channel having better capacity to the link having higher priority that will not conflict with channel assignments of its neighbors to mitigate the effect of interference (step 2). If a non-conflicting channel is not available, a channel will be chosen randomly to be assigned (Step 3). The algorithm continues with links of second-hop level until the last-hop level, gradually fan-out from the gateway to border mesh routers.

Algorithm 2. Channel Assignment Algorithm

```
for  i = first-hop level to last-hop level from the gateway
   for all links in i -hop level
1.       sort links by increasing delay value
2.       assign higher capacity channels in K orthogonal channels to higher priority
         links that does not conflict with their neighbors
3.       if notfound channels in Step 2
            assign random channels
         endif
   endfor
endfor
```

Fig. 4. Channel Assignment Algorithm

6 Performance Evaluation

In this section, through simulation, we evaluate the performance of our scheduling algorithm by comparing with the algorithm of Alicherry, et al. [5], which uses IEEE 802.11 CSMA/CA whose behavior is similar to protocol interference model. We

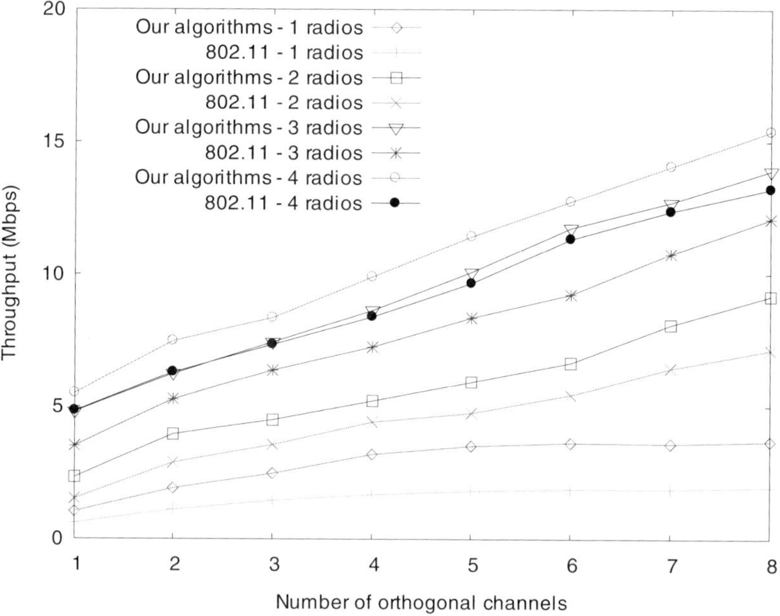

Fig. 5. Throughput Improvement Evaluation

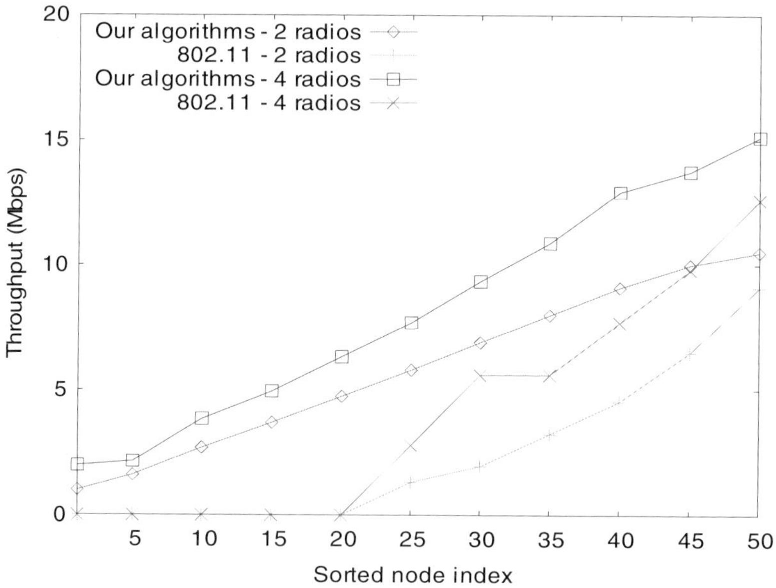

Fig. 6. Fairness Evaluation

present two sets of simulation results. The first set evaluates throughput improvement and the second set evaluates the fairness. We have implemented our algorithm in ns-2 (ver2.28). In particular, we have modified in ns-2 such that the interference perceived at a receiver is the collective aggregate interference from all the concurrent transmissions. We use two-ray propagation model. In case of 802.11, each node has the transmission range of $150\,m$, carrier sense range of $300\,m$. The simulations are carried out for a $800 \times 800\,m^2$ area in which 50 nodes are placed randomly. We use the default transmission rates 11 Mbps to reflect realistic 802.11b data rates. We also use constant bit rate (CBR) over UDP and use Adhoc On-demand Distance Vector (AODV) as the base routing protocol. We choose Kruskal's algorithm [21] to construct the MST from the network for our algorithms.

Throughput Improvements Evaluation: We compare our algorithms and Alicherry's algorithm using 802.11 based on the effect number of channels and number of radios. We vary the number of orthogonal channels available from 1 to 8 and the number of radios is from 1 to 4 respectively. From Figure 5, we see that our algorithm can exploit effectively the increasing number of channels with different number of radios. For example, as the number of channels goes from 1 to 8, the network throughput goes from 1.3 Mbps to 4.6 Mbps, from 2.9 Mbps to 11.7 Mbps, from 5.8 Mbps to 16.86 Mbps and from 6.75 Mbps to 18.9 Mbps in case of 1, 2, 3 and 4 radios respectively. Compared with 802.11, we can see the average increase of our algorithms is respectively 45%, 36%, 30% and 25%.

Fairness Evaluation: To evaluate the fairness of our algorithm and Alicherry's algorithm using 802.11, we compare the aggregate throughput of nodes starting from the border of network towards the nodes which are near the management node. Therefore, the nodes are sorted with the order of increasing queue length. We also vary number of radios (2 and 4 radios) to show their effects on fairness evaluation. We choose the fixed number of orthogonal channels in the network $K = 8$. From Figure 6, it can be observed that the border nodes throughput of our algorithm is higher than that of 802.11. The number of nodes which are starved in case of 802.11 is significant (nearly 20 nodes). With our algorithm, the fairness has been improved much when the border nodes still can transmit the data.

7 Conclusions and Future Work

In this paper, we have investigated how to assign channels and how to schedule links in WMNs by using STDMA access scheme under physical interference model. We proposed heuristic algorithms to solve this problem. Our algorithms not only improves system throughput but also guarantees the fairness for all nodes in the system, which are proven through extensive simulations.

We have identified several future research avenues. One of them is the possibility to joint our fair scheduling and channel assignment algorithm with routing to give the better performance. Another interesting problem to be addressed is developing distributed algorithms to reduce the overhead of exchanging interference measurement information between gateway and mesh routers.

References

1. Akyildiz, F., Wang, X., Wang, W.: Wireless mesh networks: a survey. Elsevier Journal of Computer Networks 47(4), 445–487 (2005)
2. Salem, N.B., Hubaux, J.P.: A Fair Scheduling for Wireless Mesh Networks. In: Proc. IEEE Workshop on Wireless Mesh Networks (WiMesh) (2005)
3. Gronkvist, J., Hansson, A.: Comparison Between Scheduling. In: Proc. MobiHoc, pp. 255–258 (2001)
4. Gronkvist, J., Nilsson, J., Yuan, D.: Throughput of Optimal Spatial Reuse TDMA for Wireless Ad-Hoc Networks. In: Proc. IEEE Vehicular Technology Conference, pp. 2156–2160 (2004)
5. Alicherry, M., Bathia, R., Li, L.: Joint Channel Assignment and Routing for Throughput Optimization in Multi-Radio Wireless Mesh Networks. In: Proc. ACM Mobicom, pp. 58–72 (2005)
6. Jain, K., Padhye, J., Padmanabhan, V., Qiu, L.: Impact of Interference on Multi-Hop Wireless Network Performance. In: Proc. ACM Mobicom, pp. 66–80 (2003)
7. Kodialam, M., Nandagopal, T.: Characterizing the Capacity Region in Multi-Radio Multi-Channel Wireless Mesh Networks. In: Proc. ACM Mobicom, pp. 73–87 (2005)
8. Kodialam, M., Nandagopal, T.: Charactering achievable rates in multi-hop wireless mesh networks with orthogonal channels. Bell Lab. Tech. Rep (2004)
9. Kyasanur, P., Yang, X., Vaidya, N.: Mesh Networking Protocols to Exploit Physical Layer Capabilities. In: Proc. IEEE Workshop on Wireless Mesh Networks (WiMesh) (2005)
10. Kyasanur, P., Vaidya, N.: Capacity of Multi-Channel Wireless Networks: Impact of Number of Channels and Interfaces. In: Proc. ACM Mobicom, pp. 43–57 (2005)
11. Nelson, R., Kleinrock, L.: Spatial-TDMA: A Collison-free Multihop Channel Access Protocol. IEEE Trans. on Communication 33, 934–944 (1985)
12. Moscibroda, T., Wattenhofer, R.: The Complexity of Connectivity in Wireless Networks. In: Proc. IEEE Infocom (2006)
13. Tang, J., Xue, G., Zhang, W.: Interference-Aware Topology Control and QoS Routing in Multi-Channel Wireless Mesh Networks. In: Proc. ACM MobiHoc, pp. 68–77 (2005)
14. Raniwala, A., Gopalan, K., Chiueh, T.: Centralized channel assignment and routing algorithms for multi-channel wireless mesh networks. ACM Mobile Computing and Communications Review (MC2R) 8(2), 50–65 (2004)
15. Raniwala, A., Chiueh, T.: Architecture and Algorithms for an IEEE 802.11-Based Multi-Channel Wireless Mesh Networks. In: Proc. IEEE Infocom. (2005)
16. Bicket, J., Aguayo, D., Biswas, S., Morris, R.: Architecture and Evaluation of an Unplanned 802.11b Mesh Networks. In: Proc. ACM Mobicom, pp. 31–42 (2005)
17. Kyasanur, P., Vaidya, N.: Routing and Interface Assignment in Multi-Channel Multi-Interface Wireless Networks. In: Proc. IEEE WCNC (2005)
18. Gupta, P., Kumar, P.R.: The capacity of wireless networks. IEEE Transactions on Information Theory 46(2), 388–404 (2000)
19. Draves, R., Padhye, J., Zill, B.: Routing in multi-radio, multi-hop wireless mesh networks. In: Proceedings of ACM MobiCom, pp. 114–128 (2004)
20. Tang, J., Xue, G., Zhang, W.: Maximum throughput and fair bandwidth allocation in multi- channel wireless mesh networks. In: Proceedings of IEEE Infocom (2006)

21. Cormen, T.H., Leiserson, C.E., Rivest, R.L., Stein, C.: Introduction to Algorithms, 2nd edn. MIT Press, Cambridge (2001)
22. Brar, G., Blough, D., Santi, P.: Computationally Efficient Scheduling with the Physical Interference Model for Throughput Improvement in Wireless Mesh Networks. In: Proc. ACM Mobicom, pp. 48–62 (2006)
23. Ramachandran, K., Buddhikot, M.: Interference-Aware Channel Assignment in Multi-Radio Wireless Mesh Networks. In: Proc. of IEEE Infocom (2006)
24. Brzezinski, A., Zussman, G., Modiano, E.: Enabling Distributed Throughput Maximization in Wireless Mesh Networks: A Partitioning Approach. In: Proc. ACM Mobicom (2006)

Effects of Mobility on Membership Estimation and Routing Services in Ad Hoc Networks*

Juan Carlos García, Mari-Carmen Bañuls, Stefan Beyer, and Pablo Galdámez

Instituto Tecnológico de Informática,
Universidad Politécnica de Valencia, 46022 Valencia (Spain)
{juagaror,banuls,stefan,pgaldam}@iti.upv.es

Abstract. The use of MANET's (or Mobile Ad hoc NETworks) is becoming very popular. Power efficiency is a key issue in this type of network, as mobile devices usually rely on limited power supplies. One essential service, the routing protocol, employed to discover routes between nodes in the network, can greatly affect power consumption.

Furthermore, many distributed applications require an additional membership service to keep track of the nodes that make up the system at any moment. In general, this information is not provided by routing services with the exception of the Optimised Link State Routing protocol (OLSR).

The two services, routing and membership estimation, form a basic support to build other higher–level distributed services on ad hoc networks. To decrease the over-all power consumption these services should be optimized for the intended use of the network. In particular the degree of mobility can have an impact on the power consumption and performance of different approaches to routing and membership estimation.

In this paper we present a study of two different approaches that combine a routing service with membership estimation. We compare the proactive OLSR with our own approach. Our approach consists of integrating a gossip-style failure detector with the reactive Dynamic Source Routing protocol (DSR).

We present an analysis of the effects of mobility on the global performance and power consumption of the two approaches. We identify scenarios for which each approach is best suited.

Keywords: ad hoc networks, distributed systems, wireless routing, energy consumption, group membership.

1 Introduction

A Mobile Ad hoc network (MANET), is a heterogeneous wireless network without a fixed infrastructure in which the nodes can move freely and connect/disconnect from the network. Applications for this kind of system and the underlying infrastructure services require an efficient implementation to minimize power consumption, bandwidth and problems derived from the mobility of the nodes.

In MANETs, a fundamental service, the routing protocol, is in charge of discovering routes and forwarding packets between nodes in the network, thus enabling network

* This work has been partially supported by the Spanish MEC grant TIN2006-14738-C02-01.

I. Stojmenovic et al. (Eds.): ISPA 2007, LNCS 4742, pp. 774–785, 2007.

communication. A great variety of network protocols for ad hoc networks exist. These are typically optimized for low power consumption or for high–availability of routes.

Furthermore, a lot of distributed applications need to know which nodes are connected or disconnected. Commonly this information is not provided by the routing service. An extra–service must be installed, a *membership estimation service*. Only the Optimized Link State Routing protocol (OLSR) can provide this information as a by product of the routing service. One strategy to maintain membership information are gossip–style algorithms [1]. This kind of algorithms periodically interchange messages amongst the nodes of the network, in order to maintain the *liveness* information of the nodes.

Membership estimation and routing constitute basic services to build reliable communication, solve certain consensus problems and stronger membership conditions protocols, or help construct replication protocols. They are the fundamental building blocks for many distributed applications. Due to the special requirements of ad hoc networks, the optimization of these services is essential in order to decrease both the bandwidth and power consumption. For this reason, the utilization of protocols that are optimized for low power consumption or packet overhead are preferred in these kinds of networks. When multiple services are employed, it is necessary to evaluate the execution environment and utilization to determine which combination of the different services can be chosen to limit the overhead and power consumption. A good election of the different services can improve or decrease the global performance of the whole system.

In this paper we analyze two different approaches to providing routing and membership services to a node. We compare the proactive OLSR protocol with our own approach. Our own approach consists of combining the reactive Dynamic Source Routing protocol (DSR) with a gossip–style membership estimation service. In particular, we focus on the effect mobility has on the overall performance and power consumption of the two approaches. The analysis leads us to provide recommendations for the use of the approaches in different mobility scenarios.

The remainder of the paper is structured as follows: In section 2 we review some related work on ad hoc routing services and gossip–style protocols. Section 3 describes the two approaches used in our study. Section 4 shows the results obtained in the experimental evaluation. Finally, in section 5 we conclude and expose future work.

2 Related Work

2.1 Wireless Routing Protocols

Routing protocols for ad hoc networks can be classified into two types: proactive and reactive protocols (also called *on–demand*). Proactive algorithms periodically interchange messages about routes and system topology amongst nodes. Their main advantage is that routes are always available. However, there is the additional cost of a certain overhead, due to the interchange of messages with system information. Examples of proactive protocols are OLSR[2,3] and DSDV[4].

In contrast, reactive protocols only run when a packet is ready to be sent and no pre-calculated route exists in the source node's route cache. This operation mode introduces a delay in the delivery of the packet, but does not introduce constant traffic of network maintenance messages. Examples of this type of protocols are DSR[5], DyMO[6], AODV[7] and TORA[8].

Many studies have been performed to analyze the performance of these different protocols. The main parameters and characteristics of ad hoc networks are described in [9]. In [10] the authors have obtained results of energetic performance of different routing protocols measuring total, transmission, reception and packet-type dependent energy consumptions, in a 500×500 m^2 scenarios. Routing overhead and path optimality of CBR traffic in 50 nodes multi-hop scenarios has been analyzed in [11] and in [12] the authors study the control message overhead and data loss in large networks using OLSR.

However, these studies do not take into account membership information, that may have to be provided by an additional service, or, as on the case of OLSR is already available as a by product of the routing protocol.

2.2 Epidemic Protocols

Gossip-style protocols [13](also called epidemic protocols) are used in large distributed systems to spread information amongst the members. They do not provide strict guarantees of delivery but offer high probability of success. In [14] an algorithm to provide membership estimation service is proposed, whereas [1] introduces a gossip-like failure detection system to monitor the changes in a wired network. Several works [15,16] have studied some approaches to gossip protocols for routing in ad hoc networks.

For the gossip–style failure detector, which we have integrated with the DSR routing protocol, we have adapted one of these approaches to implement our gossip-style failure detector described in [1]. Our adaptation was required to allow the protocol to be used in a dynamic environment, where the neighbours of a node can change and might not be known. Whereas the original protocol selects the nodes to which it propagates information from a known set of neighbours, we propagate information by means of a broadcast packet, which may or may not be sent, depending on a probaility value, which can be configured.

3 The Analysed Approaches

3.1 Overview

In this section we describe the two approaches we have chosen for our comparison. The first approach is the use of OLSR. The protocol has been chosen because it is, as far as we know, the only protocol that provides membership information as part of the routing service. The second approach is a combination of the DSR protocol and a gossip–style membership service. The additional service adds membership information to the service provided by the routing protocol, making the two approaches directly comparable. DSR and our gossip-style membership protocol, are also described below.

3.2 The OLSR Routing Protocol

OLSR (Optimised Link State Routing) [2,3] is a proactive routing protocol in which the topology and routes of the system constantly interchange amongst the network members. OLSR is optimized to reduce the power consumption using only a minimal set of nodes (called *MPRs*) to flood the information to the network members. One feature of the protocol is that it keeps the membership information in all nodes.

OLSR bases its operation on two types of packets. *Hello* messages are used to discover links between neighbouring nodes, whereas *TC* messages (Topology Control) are employed by the selected *MPR's* to spread the network topology in the system.

To establish the frequency of the packet interchange, OLSR uses four relevant parameters: the frequency of the interchange of *Hello* messages H_i, the frequency of the interchange of *TC* messages TC_i, the temporal validity of information in a *Hello* message H_t and the temporal validity of information in a *TC* message TC_t.

3.3 DSR

DSR (Dynamic Source Routing) [5] is a reactive routing protocol for MANET's. The service only runs when a packet is ready to be sent and there is no route to the target in the *route cache* of the sender node. DSR has three packet types. *Route request* packets are employed to find routes to target notes by means of successive broadcasts amongst the nodes of the path. Intermediate nodes that overhear the process add the route to their cache for future use. A *route reply* message containing the complete discovered route to the sender is sent once a Route Request message has reached the actual target of the route request. *Route error* messages serve to re–start the route discovery process, when a link in the path is found to be broken. One of the features of DSR is that is optimized for low power consumption due to his own reactive nature. If the topology of the network does not vary, the power consumption can be reduced to a minimun.

3.4 Gossip–Style Failure Detection in DSR (GDSR)

The service provided by routing protocols, such as DSR, may be not sufficient to implement many distributed services. A global knowledge of the members that compound the system may be required. Membership estimation service can provide a first view of the nodes in the system. These two services (routing and membership service) constitute a basic set to support the implantation of other higher–level distributed systems protocols on ad hoc networks. Examples of distributed services that may require this are reliable communication, strong membership or replication. OLSR, as described above, is only routing protocol we know of that provides membership information.

Our approach, GDSR, is a combination of DSR and a memberhip estimation serveice. In order to add membership information to DSR we have added a gossip–style service to the system. By doing so, we have added a certain degree of proactivity to system with a reactive routing protocol. We have previously published the details of GDSR in [17]. In this paper we focus on the effect of mobility on our approach and on OLSR, and on identifying scenarios for the use of each approach, rather than the actual architecture. However, below we provide a quick overview of the gossip protocol, in order to understand the parameters that affect our experiments.

We have adapted the gossip protocol described in [1] for wireless networks. Each node in the network manages a membership table. In the membership table we keep an integer value (called *heartbeat*) for each known node of the system. We also keep a value indicating the time the heartbeat was last updated. Each node increases its own *heartbeat* every T_g seconds. When a node increments its hearbeat, it decides whether to perform a broadcast of its own membership table with the probability P_{hb}. All nodes that receive this broadcasted membership table, merge their own table with the received one and update the *heartbeat* values for each node. If there were changes to the table, the node decides whether to forward the new table with the probability P_s. If a *hearbeat* in the membership table of a node is not updated after the timeout T_f, the state of the stale node is set to *failed* and the node will be erased from the table T_{cleanup} seconds later.

When a node wants to join the network, it waits T_{start} seconds listening to possible gossip messages generated by the members of the network. Any information received in this time is used to build its own membership table. If this time expires without receiving any message, the node enters normal mode of operation, forwarding its own membership table, which only contains its own id and *heartbeat*. The protocol has many parameters; the most important ones are the periodic value of *heartbeat* increment (T_g), the time of validity of the *heartbeat* (T_f) (generally $T_f \geq 2T_g$), the waiting value before a node joins the network (T_s) and the probabilities of performing a broadcast after a *hearbeat* increment (P_{hb}) or when the reception of a packet produces changes (P_s).

4 Measurements and Results

We have compared the OLSR protocol with our GDSR approach. To this end, we have run the set of experiments to study the effect of mobility on the two approaches. In previous studies [18,17] we have shown the *liveness* properties of the proposed GDSR approach. The study centers on the power consumption of the nodes. We have measured the averaged energy consumed by all nodes in order to quantify the energetic performance of the simulations. To simulate a high–level application we have employed a CBR (Constant Bit Rate) traffic which sends an individual message to another node by means of the routing service.

Previous studies [19,20] compare the performance of routing protocols, measuring the throughput or the power consumption. Nevertheless, to our knowledge, no work exists on how different services running on the nodes could affect these results. In our opinion, it is more sound to study of all the services of the system, in order to obtain a characteristic value for the general performance of nodes.

4.1 Experimental Setup

Simulations were run in the ns2 2.27 [21] network simulator. This version has an integrated implementation of the DSR routing protocol, but has no implementation of the OLSR. For this reason, a third party implementation from NRL Protean Group [22] was integrated. Finally, the gossip protocol was integrated into the simulator by us [17].

We have divided our experiments into two scenarios: *single–hop* that consists of a $200 \times 200\ \mathrm{m}^2$ flat grid that is used to simulate enclosed situations, such connections between attendants of a meeting, or handheld visitor guide devices in a museum, and *multi–hop* that consists of a 600×600 m^2 flat grid. This scenario is used to simulate "open-air" situations and lager distance wire-less networks.

In each experiment we employed four patterns of node mobility following a *Random WayPoint* mobility model. Nodes wait a certain *pause* time before every random change of direction and speed. The four configurations used were as follows: *static* (the nodes do not move at all during the simulation), *low–mobility* (the *pause* time was set to 50s), *mid–mobility* (the *pause* time was set to 25s) and *high–mobility* (the *pause* time was set to 10s). The nodes we set to change their direction and speed randomly. The maximum speed that could be reached was $5m/s$.

We performed a series of experiments to measure the energetic performance of the services varying the total number of nodes N in the network between 4 and 40 for both the GDSR and the OLSR approach. Every series of experiments consisted of a set of 10 simulations over which the results were later averaged. The topology of the network was constructed for each repetition by randomly locating the nodes in the grid. The simulation time was established at 300 seconds. The CBR was configured to sent a packet of 128 bytes at a rate of $1p/s$ to other nodes in the network. We established the values for the energy consumption model approximately as those of the real network interface *Lucent WaveLAN*.

In all experiments, the performance of both approaches had to be compared when the parameters and factors were comparable. In the case of GDSR the main parameters are the gossip interval (T_g), the time to determine that a node has failed (T_f) and the probabilities to broadcast the membership information when a packet is received (P_s) or forward local information (P_{hb}). On the other hand, in the OLSR protocol the main parameters are the frequency of refreshing the information for both message types (H_i and TC_i) and the temporal validity of them (H_t and TC_t). In our simulations we set $P_{hb} = P_s$ (also called P). We decided to use a T_g value of 1 and a T_f value of 2, whereas for OLSR we used the comparable values of $H_i = TC_i = T_g/P$ and $H_t = TC_t = 1.5$ (due to the implementation of OLSR, a H_t value greater than H_i is required). The value of P_g was fixed initially to 0.06 to avoid simulator overhead.

We also performed another set of experiments, varying the P parameter for Gossip service only between the values of 0.03 and 0.01. This was done to reduce the power consumption, whilst mainting better *liveness* than the OLSR protocol, which we studied in our previous works [18,17].

4.2 Results

Single–hop scenario. Figure 1 shows the total power consumption in a static single–hop scenario on a logarithmic scale. We can see that GDSR with P set to 0.06 has the worst performance of the approaches. Nevertheless, decreasing the value of P to 0.03 produces a slightly better performance than with the OLSR protocol. When we decrease the value of P to 0.01, the performance increases even more. Analyzing the individual energy consumption for the plain protocols in this scenario with P value of 0.06, we see that the Gossip service scales worse with respect to an increment in the number of nodes. This can be seen in figure 3. We observe that the DSR routing protocol seems more suited to single–hop scenarios that OLSR. Routes are valid for a long period of time and there is no necessity to discover new routes. The proactive nature of the OLSR routing protocol causes an implicit power consumption, although the routes do not change.

Nevertheless, the overload on the networks growns due to the increase of Gossip messages. If there is a large number of nodes in a single–hop partition, traffic is increased due to the large probability of sending a packet that notifies changes or updates (i.e. *heartbeat* increment or an update of the membership table). This increases power consumption. When the number of packets increases the possibilities of collisions or erroneous packets increases, which causes more retransmissions of packets. Furthermore, the broadcasts message generated by the Gossip protocol mean that all nodes must overhear all Gossip packets. Therefore more energy is consumed.

This situation is accentuated in single–hop dynamic scenarios, as we can see in figure 2, which shows the total power consumption for high mobility of the nodes. We observe that GDSR with a P value set to 0.06 saturates the network and has a notably poor performance compared to OLSR. Nevertheless, when we decrease the P value to 0.03, the results obtained are better than for OLSR as long as the number of nodes is low. When we reduce the P value to 0.01, we obtain better results than OLSR for all numbers of nodes in the experiment.

To further study the loss of performance of the Gossip protocol in this kind of scenario, we analyzed the energy spent in send and receive mode, including collisions or packets received with errors. Figure 4 shows the energy consumption for different values of P of the Gossip protocol on a logarithmic scale. We observe that an increase in the number of nodes causes higher power consumption in receive mode. This is due to the larger probability that a node sends a message, especially when the P value increases. Furthermore, there is a increment of error packets reception and collisions. Fine tuning of the Gossip parameters can avoid this situation, obtaining better power consumption.

Multi–hop scenario. We have repeated the experiments in the multi–hop scenario described above. Figure 6 shows the total power consumption of both approaches as a function of the number of nodes (N) in the multi–hop scenarios with high–mobility nodes. The results show that OLSR has a better performance than GDSR in all cases, when the value P value is set to 0.06. We can see that OLSR scales better than the GDSR approach, when the number of nodes increase and the mobility appears. When the mobility increases, there is a slight increment of total power consumption. Analyzing the power consumption of the individual protocols (DSR and Gossip separately), we observe that DSR has a higher energy cost than in single–hop scenarios. As routes to nodes change, the routing protocol needs to start the *route discovery* processes to maintain routes updated. Using OLSR the power consumption also increases slightly, due to the same reason. In OLSR, changes in network topology must be updated on all nodes. The Gossip service does not suffer significantly from increased node numbers and shows lineal behavior.

On the other hand, in the static multi–hop scenario, we see that the total energy consumption decreases, compared to the dynamic scenario (Figure 5). In this case, the routes discovered by the the routing protocols are valid during a long period of time, decreasing energy cost. Analyzing again the power consumption of two protocols combined in the GDSR approach separately, we observe in figure 7 that DSR has a lower

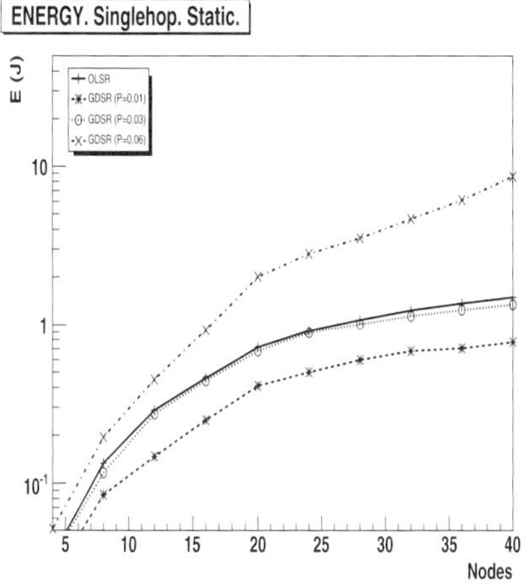

Fig. 1. Total averaged power consumption, single–hop scenarios, static nodes

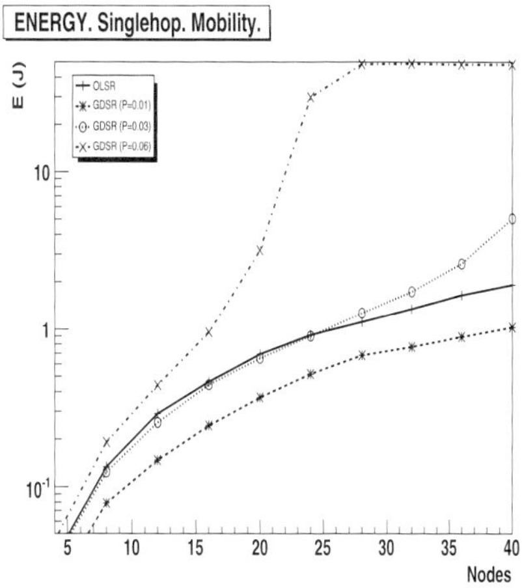

Fig. 2. Total averaged power consumption, single–hop scenarios, high mobility of nodes

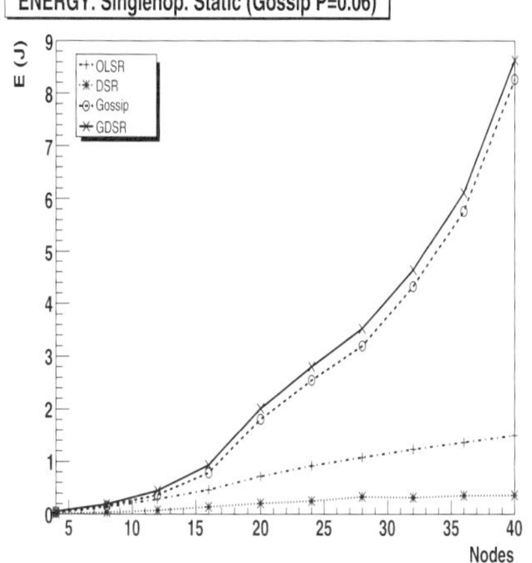

Fig. 3. Total averaged power consumption for protocols (P=0.06), single–hop scenarios, static nodes

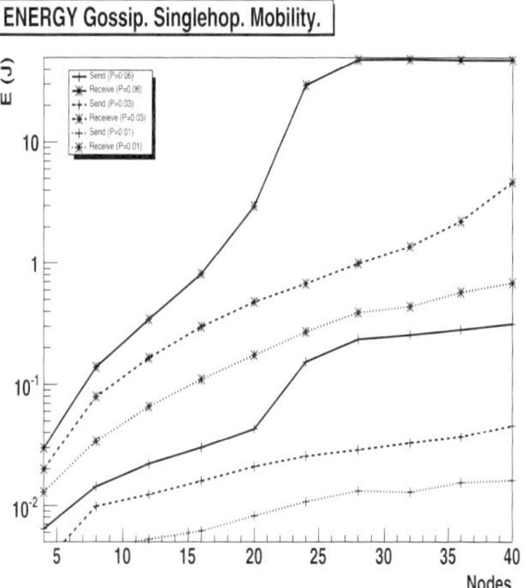

Fig. 4. Send/Receive power consumption Gossip, single–hop scenarios, high mobility of nodes

energy cost than Gossip in the static case. This is because the DSR routing protocol is optimized for this kind of scenario. The ability to learn routes by means of overheard messags and the long life–time of the routes reduces the power consumption.

When we repeated the experiments, varying the value of P in Gossip to 0.03 and 0.01 we obtained better results for GDSR than OLSR in all cases. The resulting reduction in power consumption of Gossip causes DSR to now consume the main part of the total energy in GDSR. Figure 8 shows the performance of all protocols in the multi–hop

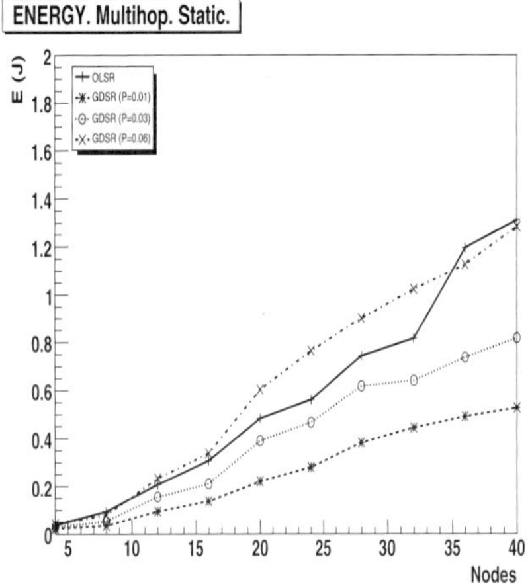

Fig. 5. Total averaged power consumption, multi–hop scenarios, static nodes

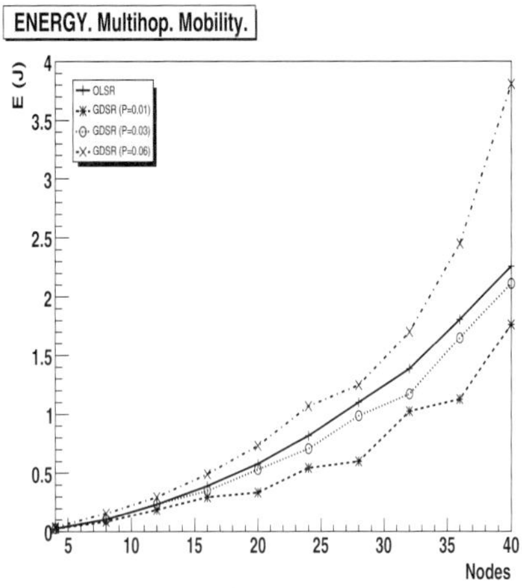

Fig. 6. Total averaged power consumption, multi–hop scenarios, high mobility nodes

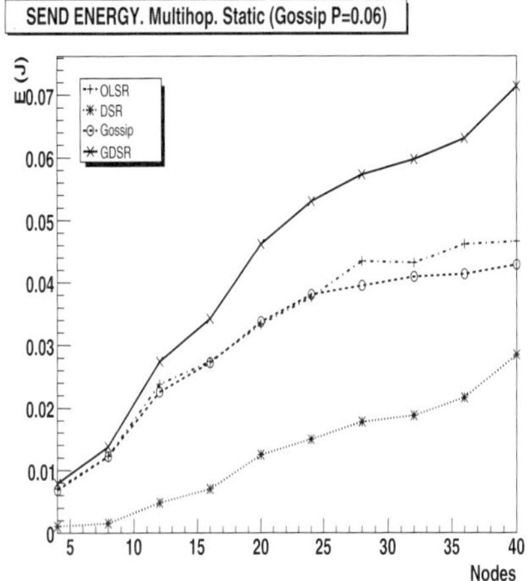

Fig. 7. Send power consumption for protocols (P=0.06), multi–hop scenarios, static nodes

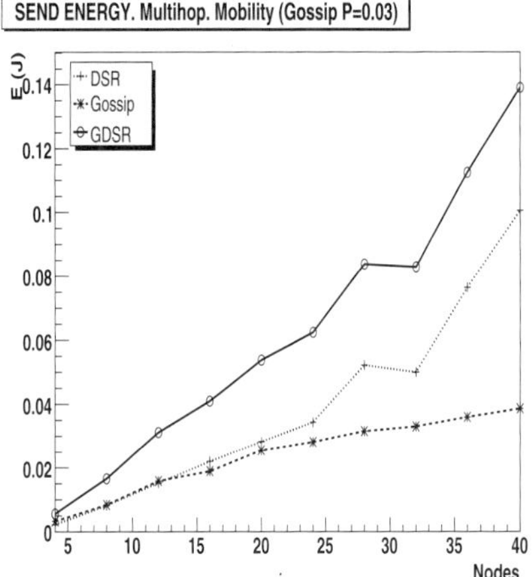

Fig. 8. Send power consumption for protocols (P=0.03), multi–hop scenarios, high mobility nodes

scenario with high–mobility. Furthermore, we observe a large increment in the power consumption of DSR when the number of nodes is around 28 nodes or higher. This may be caused by overloading of the *route cache*. The size of the route cache in the DSR protocol is set to 30 paths. When mobility appears routes have a short lifetime and need to be replaced in cache frequently. To obtain better results the cache management algorithms can be fine–tuned or the cache size increased.

Summary. We have presented the energy performance of a set of services that can be used as basis to build more complex distributed applications on ad hoc networks: routing and membership estimation services. We used two different approaches to providing these services. The first, is the use of the OLSR routing protocol that offers these two basic services in a single component. The other approach is the joint combination of a routing protocol (DSR) and membership estimation service (Gossip) that we called GDSR.

We have seen that the OLSR solution has better performance than GDSR in all cases when the P value of GDSR is set to 0.06. In the static scenario, the DSR routing service performs well reducing the power consumption of the protocol. This means, in comparison to the routing service, membership has the bigger overhead and power consumption in GDSR solution. Furthermore, in scenarios with massive mobility and a high number of nodes, the OLSR solution seems to work better because the DSR routing protocol has a higher energetic cost, due to the short period of validity of the routes stored in the route cache and the necessity to discover new routes and manage broken links. Furthermore, a high number of an incerase in power consumption of the Gossip protocol.

Nevertheless, setting the P value of the Gossip protocol to 0.03 we can obtain better results in multi–hop scenarios with better liveness that OLSR. Finally, setting the P value to 0.01 we can obtain better results in both cases, single–hop and multi–hop. We therefore see, that allowing the fine-tuning of the parameters of the membership service can improve greatly the energy performance. OLSR does not provide this option as the membership information is a by product of the routing protocol.

Mobility affects the services differently. The power consumption of Gossip (membership-service) does not depend exclusively on the mobility but on the size of the network and possible partitions that can occur. In DSR, when mobility increases, routing protocol traffic also increases, due to route changes. This produces a higher power consumption. OLSR does not distinguish between the two services and does not suffer considerably from node mobility, but the impossibility to tune the parameters of the two services independently makes it difficult optimize for certain scenarios. This highlights the convenience of having separated services. In addition of the ease of fine–tuning, poor performance of one service does not affect the other service.

5 Conclusions and Future Work

We have presented a study of a two services that are often needed to implement high–level distributed systems on ad hoc networks: routing and membership estimation. We compare two different approaches that provide these services. Firstly, a single protocol that integrates both services (OLSR) and secondly our own approach, a combination of a routing service (DSR) and a membership estimation service (Gossip) called GDSR. The two services can be the basis to build more complex distributed services, such as reliable communication, strong membership or replication.

One advantage of the proposed GDSR solution is that it offers more tuning flexibility, as it is possible to adjust the parameters of the two services independently. Moreover, the independence of the two services means that faulty operation or bad performance of one service has not collateral effects on the other service. Furthermore, we combine the advantages of proactive protocols with the advantages of reactive protocols, by adding a degree of proactivity to a reactive service. The degree of proactivity is configurable, by adjusting the parameters of the Gossip protocol.

We have studied the effects of mobility on the power consumption of the two approaches. We have performed our simulations of both approaches with comparable parameters whenever it was possible. The results obtained show that, depending on the topology and value of certain parameters, one solution or the other one is advisable. OLSR has better energy performance in a general purpose configuration. However, GDSR parameters can perform better than OLSR, if fine–tuned for the specific environment the protocol is used in.

The work in this paper focuses on the OLSR and DSR routing protocols, but we plan to extend our analysis to other proactive and reactive algorithms with similar arguments. Furthermore, we will study how the co–operation between these services can improve the global performance of the system. The information managed by one of the services may be interesting for the other service. For example, the membership estimation service may know certain routes to nodes that can be passed to the routing service.

References

1. Renesse, R.V., Minsky, Y., Hayden, M.: A gossip-style failure detection service. In: Proceedings of Middleware'98, IFIP, The Lake District, UK, pp. 55–70 (1998)
2. Jacquet, P., Mühlethaler, P., Clausen, T., Laouiti, A., Qayyum, A., Viennot, L.: Optimized link state routing protocol for ad hoc networks. In: Proceedings of the 5th IEEE Multi Topic Conference (INMIC 2001). IEEE Computer Society Press, Los Alamitos (2001)
3. J, P., et al.: Optimized link state routing protocol (olsr). Internet Draft (draft-ietfmanet -olsr-09.txt), INRIA Rocquencourt (2003)
4. Perkins, C., Bhagwat, P.: Highly dynamic destination-sequenced distance-vector routing (DSDV) for mobile computers. In: ACM SIGCOMM'94 Conference on Communications Architectures, Protocols and Applications, pp. 234–244. ACM Press, New York (1994)
5. Johnson, D.B., Maltz, D.A., Broch, J.: Dsr: the dynamic source routing protocol for multihop wireless ad hoc networks, 139–172 (2001)
6. Chakeres, I., Belding-Royer, E., Perkins, C.: Dynamic manet on-demand routing protocol (dymo). Internet Draft (2005)
7. Perkins, C.E., Royer, E.M.: Ad-hoc on-demand distance vector routing. In: WMCSA '99: Proceedings of the Second IEEE Workshop on Mobile Computer Systems and Applications, Washington, DC, USA, p. 90. IEEE Computer Society Press, Los Alamitos (1999)
8. Park, V.D., Corson, M.S.: A highly adaptive distributed routing algorithm for mobile wireless networks. In: INFOCOM '97: Proceedings of the INFOCOM '97. Sixteenth Annual Joint Conference of the IEEE Computer and Communications Societies. Driving the Information Revolution, Washington, DC, USA, pp. 1405–1413. IEEE Computer Society Press, Los Alamitos (1997)
9. Corson, S., Macker, J.: Mobile Ad hoc Networking (MANET): Routing Protocol Performance Issues and Evaluation Considerations (1999)
10. Cano, J.C., Manzoni, P.: A performance comparison of energy consumption for mobile ad hoc network routing protocols. In: MASCOTS '00: Proceedings of the 8th International Symposium on Modeling, Analysis and Simulation of Computer and Telecommunication Systems, Washington, DC, USA, pp. 57–64. IEEE Computer Society Press, Los Alamitos (2000)

11. Broch, J., Maltz, D.A., Johnson, D.B., Hu, Y.C., Jetcheva, J.: A performance comparison of multi-hop wireless ad hoc network routing protocols. Mobile Computing and Networking, 85–97 (1998)
12. Laouti, A., Mühlethaler, P., Najid, A., Plakoo, E.: Simulation results of the olsr routing protocol for wireless network. Technical Report RR-4414, INRIA (2002)
13. Eugster, P.T., Guerraoui, R., Handurukande, S.B., Kouznetsov, P., Kermarrec, A.M.: Lightweight probabilistic broadcast. ACM Trans. Comput. Syst. 21(4), 341–374 (2003)
14. Golding, R.A.: Weak-Consistency Group Communication and Membership. PhD thesis, University of California at Santa Cruz (1992)
15. Haas, Z.J., Halpern, J.Y., Li, E.L.: Gossip-based ad hoc routing. In: INFOCOM (2002)
16. Li, X.Y., Moaveninejad, K., Frieder, O.: Regional gossip routing for wireless ad hoc networks. Mob. Netw. Appl. 10(1-2), 61–77 (2005)
17. García, J.C., Bañuls, M.C., Galdámez, P., Miedes, E.: Membership estimation service for high availability support in ad hoc networks. In: Proceedings of the VI IEEE International Symposium and School on Advanced Distributed Systems. LNCS, Guadalajara, México. Springer (to appear 2006)
18. García, J.C., Bañuls, M.C., Galdámez, P.: Trading off consumption of routing and precision of membership. In: Proceedings of the 3rd International Conference Communications and Computer Networks, Marina del Rey, CA (USA), October 24–26, pp. 108–113. ACTA Press (2005)
19. Feeney, L.M., Nilsson, M.: Investigating the energy consumption of a wireless network interface in an ad hoc networking environment. In: IEEE INFOCOM. IEEE Computer Society Press, Los Alamitos (2001)
20. Feeney, L.M.: An energy consumption model for performance analysis of routing protocols for mobile ad hoc networks. Mobile Networks and Applications 6(3), 239–249 (2001)
21. project, T.V.: The NS2 manual. Technical report, ISI (2004), http://www.isi.edu/nsnam/ns/ns-documentation.html
22. Group, N.P.: (2005), http://pf.itd.nrl.navy.mil

Hamiltonicity and Pancyclicity of Binary Recursive Networks

Yun Sun[1], Zhoujun Li[2], and Deqiang Wang[3]

[1] School of Computer, National University of Defense Technology, China
cloud_sun76@126.com

[2] School of Computer Science and Engineering, Beihang University, China
lizj@buaa.edu.cn

[3] Institute of Nautical Science and Technology, Dalian Maritime University, China
dqwang@dlmu.edu.cn

Abstract. By means of analysis and generalization of the hypercube and its variations of the same topological properties and network parameters, a family of interconnection networks, referred to as binary recursive networks, is introduced in this paper. This kind of networks not only provides a powerful method to investigate the hypercube and its variations on the whole, but also puts forth an effective tool to explore new network structures. A constructive proof is presented to show that binary recursive networks are Hamiltonian based on their recursive structures, and an approach to prove 4-pancyclicity of a subfamily of binary recursive networks is outlined.

Keywords: Interconnection network, Hypercube, Binary recursive networks, Hamiltonian cycle, Pancyclicity.

1 Introduction

Network topology is a crucial factor for interconnection networks since it determines the performance of networks. Many interconnection network topologies have been proposed for the purpose of connecting thousands of processing elements. The hypercube is one of the most popular interconnection networks since it's structure is simple and it is easy to implement. But it has been shown that hypercube does not achieve the smallest possible diameter for its resources. Therefore, many variants of hypercube were proposed. The most well-known variants are the crossed cube [4,5], the Möbius cube [3], the generalized twisted cube [2], the twisted n-cube [6] and the twisted-cube connected network [14]. We find that these variations have many attractive topological properties and good parameters which are the same as hypercube: they are n-regular graphs with 2^n vertices and $n \times 2^{n-1}$ edges, their shortest cycles are 4-length (when $n \geq 2$), and their structures are strictly recursive (every n-dimensional network is constructed by two $(n-1)$-dimensional networks). The family of these networks is referred to as binary recursive networks in this paper.

An interconnection network can be represented by a undirected graph $G = (V, E)$, where $V = V(G)$ is the set of nodes and $E = E(G)$ is the set of edges of the networks. We adopt the fundamental graph terminology in [1,5,11] when using an undirected graph

I. Stojmenovic et al. (Eds.): ISPA 2007, LNCS 4742, pp. 786–796, 2007.

to model an interconnection network. A path $P(v_0, v_t) = \langle v_0, v_1, \cdots, v_t \rangle$ is a sequence of nodes where two consecutive nodes are adjacent. A cycle (denoted as C_v hereafter), which is a path with at least three vertices where the first vertex is the same as the last vertex [8,13], is widely used in interconnection networks, owing to its good properties such as low connectivity, simplicity, extensibility, as well as its feasible implementation. An l-cycle is a cycle of length l . A cycle which visits each vertex of a graph exactly once is called a Hamiltonian cycle. $G = (V, E)$ is L-pancyclicity if G contains any cycle of length $L \leq l \leq |V|$, where L is a positive integer. G is Hamiltonian if there exists a Hamiltonian cycle in it.

One way to evaluate an interconnection network (a host graph) is to see how well other existing networks (the guest graphs) can be embedded into it. The embedding problem, which maps a guest graph into a host graph, is an important topic of recent studies, since it can make us apply existing algorithms for the guest graphs to the host graph. This paper will discuss the cycle-embedding properties of the binary recursive networks. The 4-pancyclicity of the crossed cubes, the Möbius cube and the twisted-cube connected network are proven in [10,12,17] respectively. And the Hamiltonian cycles have been found in some binary recursive networks [2,3,4,5,6,14,15]. However, for different topologies, the methods of searching for Hamiltonian cycles and the approaches of proof for pancyclicity are quite different and only suit their own special structures. Since there is no unified perspective to these variants, it is difficult to extend the results from the individual topology to the whole family. Park et al. [9] tried to use the induction principle to prove the existence of Hamiltonian cycle, but he failed to find out the uniform method for searching the Hamiltonian cycle of the family. Hu et al. [16] proposed an approach to prove the 4-edge-pancyclicity of some hypercube variants, but his approach could't be taken shape in searching cycles for any length l ($L \leq l \leq |V|$) of the family. The reasons lie in the lack of an algebraical definition for the family. In this paper, however, we first redefine the family using an algebraic method and analyze the topology properties of the family. Next we use this definition to prove the fact that the whole family of binary recursive networks is Hamiltonian. The proof is constructive, which offers us a method for constructing a Hamiltonian cycle in any binary recursive network. Then we outline an approach to prove the 4-pancyclicity of a sub family of the binary recursive networks. The proof is constructive too, which help us to search cycles of any length l ($L \leq l \leq |V|$) in the subfamily.

The rest of this paper is organized as follows: In section 2 we explain the basic definitions of the binary recursive networks. The Hamiltonian property is proved in Section 3. In section 4 we propose a method to prove the pancyclicity of a sub family of the binary recursive networks. We release our conclusions and future works in Section 5.

2 Binary Recursive Networks

Let $G = (V, E)$, if $x = x_n x_{n-1} \cdots x_{i+1} x_i x_{i-1} \cdots x_1 \in V$ then denote $\mathrm{bit}_i(x) = x_i$ and $\mathrm{pre}_{n-i}(x) = x_n x_{n-1} \cdots x_{i+1}$. If $x_n x_{n-1} \cdots x_{i+1} = y_n y_{n-1} \cdots y_{i+1}$ and $x_i \neq y_i$, then $\sigma(x+y) = i$. Suppose α and β be two binary strings and $|\alpha|+|\beta| \leq n$, let $\Gamma_G(\alpha)$($\Gamma(\alpha)$ for short if there is no confusion) be an subgraph of G, where $V(\Gamma(\alpha)) = \{x|x \in V(G)$ and $\mathrm{pre}_{|\alpha|}(x) = \alpha\}$, $E(\Gamma(\alpha)) = \{(x, y)|x, y \in V(\Gamma(\alpha))$ and $(x, y) \in E(G)\}$. Denote $\Gamma^{(\alpha)}(\beta) = \Gamma(\alpha\beta)$.

2.1 Definition of Binary Recursive Networks

Definition 1. *Let $n \geq 1$ be an integer. The graph G is n-labeled, i.e. each of its vertex is labeled by an n-bit binary string. $*^{n-i}$ is a $(n-i)$-length binary string ($* \in \{0,1\}$, $1 \leq i \leq n$). If R_i is a one-to-one mapping from $\Gamma(*^{n-i}0)$ to $\Gamma(*^{n-i}1)$, we call it an i-dimensional binary recursive adjacent function (i-dimensional adjacent function for short).*

Let R_i be an i-dimensional adjacent function of the n-labeled graph G, then according to the property of one-to-one mapping, we can obtain

(1) $\forall x \in \Gamma_G(*^{n-i}0)$, $\exists y \in \Gamma_G(*^{n-i}1)$ such that $y = R_i(x)$, or

(2) $\forall y \in \Gamma_G(*^{n-i}1)$, $\exists x \in \Gamma_G(*^{n-i}0)$ such that $y = R_i(x)$, i.e. $x = R_i^{-1}(y)$.

(3) $\forall x_1, x_2$, if $x_1 \neq x_2$, then $R_i(x_1) \neq R_i(x_2)$.

We denote the relationship of vertices x and y as $y = R_i^*(x)$, if they satisfy the above statements.

Definition 2. *Let G be an n-labeled graph and R_i $(1 \leq i \leq n)$ an i-dimensional adjacent function of G. $\forall x, y \in V(G)$, if and only if $x, y \in V(G)$, there exists an integer $k(\in 1, 2, \cdots, n)$ such that $y = R_k^*(x)$, then we call G an n-dimensional binary recursive network determined by $R_1, R_2, \cdots, R_n$, denoted as RN_n. If $y = R_k^*(x)(k \in 1, 2, \cdots, n)$, we call $(x, y) \in E(G)$ a k-dimensional conjunction edge (k-conjunction edge for short), where x and y are the k-adjacent vertex of each other's.*

According to the definitions of the hypercube, the crossed cube, the Möbius cube, the generalized twisted cube, the twisted n-cube and the twisted-cube connected network, we obtain their adjacent function (see Table 1).

According to Definition 2, we know the networks above are all binary recursive networks.

Table 1. Adjacent functions of typical binary recursive networks

Type of networks	Adjacent functions of networks $(i = 1, 2, \cdots, n)$
The hypercube	$H_i(x) = x + \varepsilon_i$
The crossed cube	$C_i(x) = x + \varepsilon_i + \sum_{k=1}^{\lceil i/2-1 \rceil} \mathrm{bit}_{2k-1}(x)\varepsilon_{2k}$
The Möbius cube	$M_i(x) = \begin{cases} x + \varepsilon_i, & \mathrm{bit}_{i+1}(x) = 0 \\ x + \sum_{k=1}^{i} \varepsilon_k, & \mathrm{bit}_{i+1}(x) = 1 \end{cases}$
The generalized twisted cube	$G_i(x) = \begin{cases} x + \varepsilon_i, & \mathrm{mod}(i,3) = 1, 2 \\ x + \varepsilon_i + \mathrm{bit}_{i-1}(x)\varepsilon_{i-2}, & \mathrm{mod}(i,3) = 0 \end{cases}$
The twisted n-cube	$T_i(x) = \begin{cases} x + \varepsilon_1 + \varepsilon_2, & i = 2, x \in \Gamma(0^{n-2}) \\ x + \varepsilon_i, & i = 1, 3, \cdots, n \end{cases}$
The twisted-cube connected network	$N_i(x) = x + \varepsilon_i + \sum_{k=1}^{\lceil i/2-1 \rceil} \mathrm{bit}_{2k-1}(x)\varepsilon_{2k} + \sum_{k=3}^{i-1} \mathrm{bit}_k(x)\varepsilon_2$

2.2 Topology of Binary Recursive Networks

For a thorough understanding of the structures of the binary recursive networks, we need to study its low-dimensional topologies, and comprehending the concepts of its sub-network and super-network.

Let $R_i (i \in \{1, 2, \cdots, n\})$ be the i-dimensional adjacent function of an n-dimensional binary recursive network, so $R_i : \Gamma_G(u_n u_{n-1} \cdots u_{n-i}0) \rightarrow \Gamma_G(u_n u_{n-1} \cdots u_{n-i}1)$ is a one-to-one mapping.

(1) when $n = 1$, there is only one adjacent function (1-dimensional) $R_1(1) = 1$, so 1-dimensional binary recursive networks have only one topological structure, i.e. K_2.

(2) when $n = 2$, there are two 2-dimensional adjacent functions, $R_2(0*) = 1*$ and $R_2(0*) = 1\bar{*}$, where $* = 0, 1$. So there are two 2-dimensional binary recursive networks determined by R_1 and R_2, they are

$$\langle 00, 01, 11, 10, 00 \rangle \quad \text{and} \quad \langle 00, 01, 10, 11, 00 \rangle.$$

But from the point of view of topology isomorphs, the two 2-dimensional binary recursive networks have only one topology, i.e. a 4-length cycle.

(3) By means of the isomorph of topologies, we also know that there are only 2 different topologies in 3-dimensional binary recursive networks. One is normal 3-cube; the other is twisted 3-cube (see Fig.1).

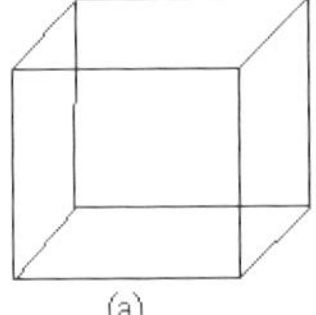

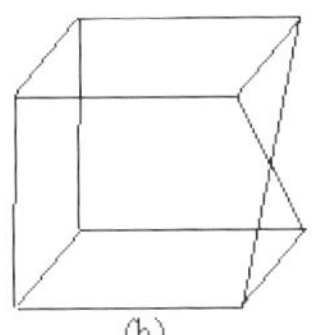

Fig. 1. Topologies of RN_3 . (a) Normal 3-cube Q_3 . (b) Twisted 3-cube TQ_3.

Definition 3. *Let H be a subgraph of RN_n, if $\exists i \in \{1, 2, \cdots, n\}$ s.t. $H \cong RN_i$, i.e. H and RN_i are isomorphic, then H is a (i-dimensional) sub-network of RN_n.*

Theorem 1. *If $u = u_i u_{i-1} \cdots u_1$ is an $i (0 \leq i \leq n)$-length binary string, then $\exists RN_{n-i}$ s.t.*

$$\Gamma_{RN_n}(u) \cong RN_{n-i}.$$

Proof. Let $\varphi : \Gamma_{RN_n}(u) \rightarrow RN_{n-i}$, $\forall u_i u_{i-1} \cdots u_1 x_{n-i} x_{n-i-1} \cdots x_1 \in \Gamma_{RN_n}(u)$ s.t.

$$\varphi(u_i \cdots u_1 x_{n-i} \cdots x_1) = x_{n-i} \cdots x_1.$$

Obviously, φ is a bijection. Let $s = \varphi(x)$, $t = \varphi(y)$, for any $x = u_i u_{i-1} \cdots u_1 x_{n-i} x_{n-i-1} \cdots x_1$ and $y = u_i u_{i-1} \cdots u_1 y_{n-i} y_{n-i-1} \cdots y_1 \in V(\Gamma_{RN_n}(u))$, there are $\text{bit}_k(s) = \text{bit}_k(x)$ and $\text{bit}_k(t) = \text{bit}_k(y)$ $(1 \leq k \leq n - i)$. If $(x, y) \in E(RN_n)$, then $\exists j = \sigma(x + y) \in \{1, 2, \cdots, n - i\}$ s.t. $x = R_j^*(y)$ and $\text{pre}_{n-j}(x) = \text{pre}_{n-j}(y)$ for $\sigma(x + y) \leq n - i$.

Defining the mapping $S_j (j \in \{1, 2, \cdots, n - i\})$ on RN_{n-i} as follows:

$$S_j^*(y_{n-i} \cdots y_1) = x_{n-i} \cdots x_1 \quad \Leftrightarrow \quad R_j^*(u_i \cdots u_1 y_{n-i} \cdots y_1) = u_i \cdots u_1 x_{n-i} \cdots x_1.$$

It is a one-to-one mapping on $V(RN_{n-i})$.Thereby $S_1, S_2, \cdots, S_{n-i}$ are adjacent functions on RN_{n-i}, moreover, $\varphi(x) = S_j^*(\varphi(y))$, so $\varphi(x)$ and $\varphi(y)$ are j-adjacent vertex in RN_{n-i}. Thus φ is an isomorphic mapping, $\Gamma_{RN_n}(u) \cong RN_{n-i}$.

Definition 4. *Let $R_1, R_2, \cdots, R_n$ be the adjacent functions of an n-dimensional binary recursive network RN_n. α, β are two different binary strings, and $|\alpha| = |\beta|$.*

(1) $\Gamma_{RN_n}(\alpha)$ and $\Gamma_{RN_n}(\beta)$ are conjunction, if $\exists x \in \Gamma_{RN_n}(\alpha)$ and $\exists y \in \Gamma_{RN_n}(\beta)$ s.t. $(x, y) \in E(RN_n)$.

(2) $\Gamma_{RN_n}(\alpha)$ and $\Gamma_{RN_n}(\beta)$ are m-dimensional adjacent (denoted as $\Gamma_{RN_n}(\alpha) = R_m^*(\Gamma_{RN_n}(\beta))$), if $\exists R_m \in \{R_1, R_2, \cdots, R_n\}$ s.t. $\forall x \in \Gamma_{RN_n}(\alpha)$ there is always $R_m^*(x) \in \Gamma_{RN_n}(\beta)$, and $\forall y \in \Gamma_{RN_n}(\beta)$ there is always $R_m^*(y) \in \Gamma_{RN_n}(\alpha)$.

Theorem 2. *Let α and β be two different binary strings and $|\alpha| = |\beta| = i (i \in \{1, 2, \cdots, n\})$, and let $R_1, R_2, \cdots, R_n$ be the adjacent functions of RN_n. If $\exists R_m \in \{R_1, R_2, \cdots, R_n\}$ s.t. $\Gamma_{RN_n}(\alpha) = R_m^*(\Gamma_{RN_n}(\beta))$, then $\exists RN_{n-i+1}$ s.t. $\Gamma_{RN_n}(\alpha, \beta) \cong RN_{n-i+1}$.*

Proof. (Skeletony) $\alpha \neq \beta$, so if $x \in \Gamma_{RN_n}(\alpha)$ and $y \in \Gamma_{RN_n}(\eta)$ then $m = \sigma(x + y) > n - i$. And by $|\alpha| = |\beta| = i$, there is $|\Gamma_{RN_n}(\alpha)| = |\Gamma_{RN_n}(\beta)|$. Based on these conditions, let $\varphi : x \in \Gamma_{RN_n}(\alpha, \beta) \rightarrow x_m x_{n-i} x_{n-i-1} \cdots x_1$ s.t. $\forall x \in \Gamma_{RN_n}(\alpha, \beta)$ there is

$$\varphi(x) = x_m x_{n-i} x_{n-i-1} \cdots x_1 .$$

So φ is a bijection. According to φ and the interconnection relationship between $\Gamma_{RN_n}(\alpha)$ and $\Gamma_{RN_n}(\beta)$, we can make out the adjacent functions S_{n-i+1}. Because $|\Gamma_{RN_n}(\alpha)| \cong RN_{n-i}^{(\alpha)}$ and $|\Gamma_{RN_n}(\beta)| \cong RN_{n-i}^{(\beta)}$, there is a RN_{n-i+1} to satisfy $\Gamma_{RN_n}(\alpha, \beta) \cong RN_{n-i+1}$.

Definition 5. *Let RN_n be an n-dimensional binary recursive network determined by R_1, $R_2, \cdots, R_n$, and*

$$\mathcal{V}_{RN_n}^{(i)} = \{\Gamma(\alpha) || \alpha| = i\},$$

$$\mathcal{E}_{RN_n}^{(i)} = \{(\Gamma(\alpha), \Gamma(\beta)) | \Gamma(\alpha), \Gamma(\beta) \in \mathcal{V}_{RN_n}^{(i)} \text{ and } \Gamma(\beta) = R_l^*(\Gamma(\alpha)), n - i \leq l \leq n\}.$$

For some integer $i (1 \leq i \leq n)$, $\forall \Gamma_{RN_n}(\alpha), \Gamma_{RN_n}(\beta) \in \mathcal{V}_{RN_n}^{(i)}$, once $\exists x \in \Gamma(\alpha)$ and $\exists y \in \Gamma(\beta)$ such that $(x, y) \in E(RN_n)$, there exists an integer $l (n - i + 1 \leq l \leq n)$ such that $\Gamma(\beta) = R_l^*(\Gamma(\alpha))$, then we call $(\mathcal{V}_{RN_n}^{(i)}, \mathcal{E}_{RN_n}^{(i)})$ a i-rank super-network of RN_n, $\mathcal{V}_{RN_n}^{(i)}$ the super-vertex set, $\mathcal{E}_{RN_n}^{(i)}$ the super-edge set.

Actually, $(\mathcal{V}_{RN_n}^{(i)}, \mathcal{E}_{RN-n}^{(i)})$ is the i-rank super-network of RN_n, if and only if there exists a RN_i such that $(\mathcal{V}_{RN_n}^{(i)}, \mathcal{E}_{RN-n}^{(i)}) \cong RN_i$.

Theorem 3. *Let $RN_n (n \geq 2)$ be a binary recursive network determined by $R_1, R_2, \cdots$, R_n. For some integer $j (1 \leq j \leq n - 1)$, $\forall u, v \in V(RN_n)$, once $\text{pre}_{n-j}(u) = \text{pre}_{n-j}(v)$, there is always $\text{pre}_{n-j}(R_l^*(u)) = \text{pre}_{n-j}(R_l^*(v))$ for any $R_i \in \{R_1, R_2, \cdots, R_n\}$, then there exists a $(n - j)$-rank super-network of this binary recursive network.*

Proof. From definition 5.

3 Hamiltonian Cycles in RN_n

Theorem 4. *$RN_n(n \geq 2)$ are Hamiltonian graphs.*

Proof. $\forall x \in \Gamma(00)$, let

$$P_x = \langle x, R_n^*(x), R_{n-1}^*(R_n^*(x)), R_n^*(R_{n-1}^*(R_n^*(x)))\rangle$$

where $R_n^*(R_{n-1}^*(R_n^*(x))) \in \Gamma(01)$. So P_x is a 3-length path ($3 = 2^2 - 1$) (see Fig. 2).

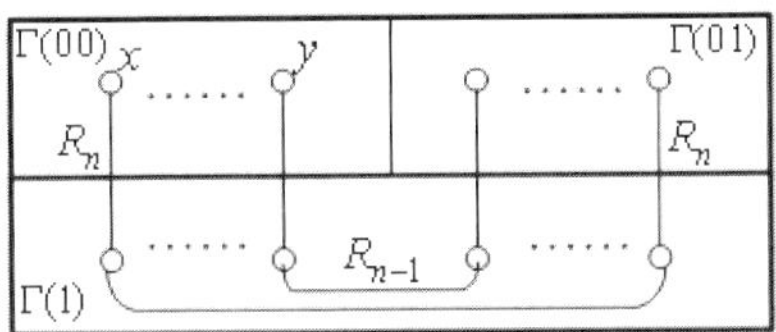

Fig. 2. (2^2 – 1)-length paths

$R_i(i = 1, 2, \cdots, n$) are one-to-one mappings, so if $x \neq y$, there are no same vertices in P_x and P_y for any $x, y \in \Gamma(00)$. Thus, we gain $|\Gamma(00)| = 2^{n-2}$ disjoint 3-length paths, their endvertices (the first vertex and the last vertex) are in $\Gamma(00)$ and $\Gamma(01)$ respectively.

From the presentation above, we know that the $2 \times 2^{n-2} = 2^{n-1}$ endvertices of the 2^{n-2} disjoint paths $\{P_x | x \in \Gamma(00)\}$ are all in $\Gamma(0)$. Whereas, each vertex in the $\Gamma(0)$ is a endvertex of some disjoint path because $|\Gamma(0)| = 2^{n-1}$. Furthermore, both $\Gamma^{(0)}(10)$ and $\Gamma^{(0)}(11)$ have 2^{n-3} vertices (other 2^{n-2} vertices in $\Gamma^{(0)}(0) = \Gamma(00)$). According to

$$R_{n-2}(\Gamma^{(0)}(10)) = \Gamma^{(0)}(11),$$

we connect the $(n-2)$-adjacent vertices between $\Gamma^{(0)}(10)$ and $\Gamma^{(0)}(11)$ (i.e. select every $(n-2)$-conjunction edge in $\Gamma^{(0)}(1)$). Then the original 2^{n-2} disjoint (2^2-1)-length paths become 2^{n-3} disjoint $(2^3 - 1)$-length paths (see Fig.3).

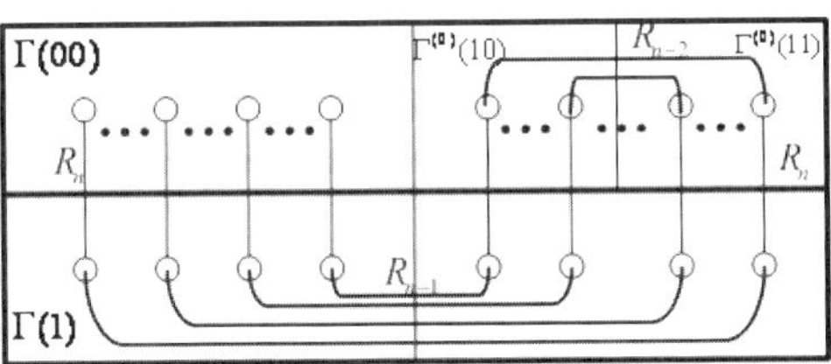

Fig. 3. (2^3 – 1)-length paths

We deal with the 2^{n-2} endvertices in $\Gamma(00)$ in the same way. There are 2^{n-4} vertices in $\Gamma^{(00)}(10)$ and $\Gamma^{(00)}(11)$ respectively, after connecting the $(n - 3)$-adjacent vertices between $\Gamma^{(00)}(10)$ and $\Gamma^{(00)}(11)$, we gain 2^{n-4} disjoint $(2^4 - 1)$-length paths (see Fig.4).

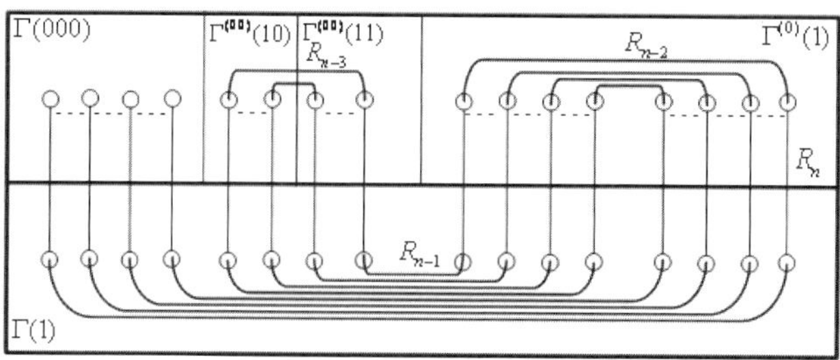

Fig. 4. $(2^4 - 1)$-length paths

Generally, there are 2^{n-k} endvertices of 2^{n-k-1} disjoint $(2^{k+1}-1)$-length paths in $\Gamma(0^k)$. Both $\Gamma^{(0^k)}(10)$ and $\Gamma^{(0^k)}(11)$ have 2^{n-k-2} endvertices. After connecting those $(n-k-1)$-adjacent vertices, we gain 2^{n-k-2} disjoint $(2^{k+2}-1)$-length paths ($k = 3, 4, \cdots, n-3$).

Finally, only $(2^2 =)4$ endvertices are left in $\Gamma(0^{n-2})$, and there are 2 endvertices in $\Gamma^{(0^{n-2})}(0)$ and $\Gamma^{(0^{n-2})}(1)$ respectively. Here $(2^0 =)1$ endvertex $u = 0^{n-2}10$ in $\Gamma^{(0^{n-2})}(10)$ and $(2^0 =)1$ endvertex $v = 0^{n-2}11$ in $\Gamma^{(0^{n-2})}(11)$. According to $u = R_1(v) = v + \varepsilon_1$, we connect them, and gain $(2^0 =)1$ disjoint $(2^n - 1)$-length path. Its endvertices are $s = 0^{n-1}0$ and $t = 0^{n-1}1$. Obviously they are 1-adjacent vertices. After connecting s and t, the path we gained becomes a cycle which is 2^n-length and its vertices are different to one another. There are exactly 2^n vertices in RN_n , so this cycle is a Hamiltonian cycle of the RN_n.

In a word, all $RN_n (n \geq 2)$ are Hamiltonian graphs.

Theorem 5. *$RN_n (n \geq 2)$ are edge Hamiltonian graphs.*

Proof. (Skeletony). $\forall (x, y) \in E(RN_n)$, let $\sigma(x + y) = j$, we would construct a Hamiltonian cycle that includes the edge (x, y) in RN_n. The following approach of the Hamiltonian cycle construction is directly derived from the proof of theorem 4.

First, if $j \neq 1$, select all j-conjunction edges in $\Gamma_{RN_n}(x_n x_{n-1} \cdots x_{j+1})$, else select all 1-conjunction edges in $\Gamma_{RN_n}(x_n x_{n-1} \cdots x_3)$;

Next, select all i-conjunction edges in $\Gamma_{RN_n}(x_n x_{n-1} \cdots x_{i+2} \bar{x}_{i+1})$ for any $i \in \{j + 1, \cdots, n-1\}$ and select all n-conjunction edges in RN_n.

Finally, if $i \geq 3$, select all $(j-l)$-conjunction edges in $\Gamma_{RN_n}(x_n x_{n-1} \cdots x_{j+1} 0^l)$ for any $l \in \{1, 2, \cdots, j-2\}$ and select all 1-conjunction edges in $\Gamma_{RN_n}(x_n x_{n-1} \cdots x_{j+1} 0^{j-3} 1)$. If $j = 2$, select all 1-conjunction edges in $\Gamma_{RN_n}(x_n x_{n-1} \cdots x_4 \bar{x}_3)$.

Thus, we obtain a Hamiltonian cycle which include the edge (x, y). So $RN_n (n \geq 2)$ are edge Hamiltonian graphs.

4 Pancyclicity of RN_n

Theorem 6. *Let RN_3 be a 3-dimensional binary recursive network determined by R_1, R_2, R_3. If $RN_3 \cong Q_3$, then for any $x \in V(Q_3)$ there are always 4, 6, and 8-length cycles that include the path $\langle R_1^*(x), x, R_1^*(x)\rangle$; If $RN_3 \cong TQ_3$, then for any $x \in V(TQ_3)$ there are always 4, 5, 6, 7 and 8-length cycles that include the path $\langle R_1^*(x), x, R_2^*(x)\rangle$.*

Proof. When $RN_3 \cong Q_3$, without losing generality we label the Q_3 as fig.5(a). Select a vertex $x_1 \in V(Q_3)$, then $\langle R_1^*(x), x, R_2^*(x)\rangle = \langle x_2, x_1, x_4\rangle$. Obviously, we can gain the 4, 6 and 8-length cycles including the path $\langle x_2, x_1, x_4\rangle$ respectively as follows:

$\langle x_2, x_1, x_4, x_3, x_2\rangle$

$\langle x_2, x_1, x_4, y_3, y_4, x_3, x_2\rangle$ and $\langle x_2, x_1, x_4, x_3, y_4, y_1, x_2\rangle$

$\langle x_2, x_1, x_4, y_3, y_2, y_1, y_4, x_3, x_2\rangle$ and $\langle x_2, x_1, x_4, x_3, y_4, y_3, y_2, y_1, x_2\rangle$

For other vertices $x \in V(Q_3)$, the 4,6 and 8-length cycles that include the path $\langle R_1^*(x), x, R_2^*(x)\rangle$ can be gained similarly.

When $RN_3 \cong TQ_3$, without losing generality we label the TQ_3 as fig.5(b). Select a vertex $x_1 \in V(TQ_3)$, then $\langle R_1^*(x), x, R_2^*(x)\rangle = \langle x_2, x_1, x_4\rangle$. Obviously, we can gain the 4,5,6,7 and 8-length cycles including the path $\langle x_2, x_1, x_4\rangle$ respectively as follows:

$\langle x_2, x_1, x_4, x_3, x_2\rangle$; $\langle x_2, x_1, x_4, y_3, y_4, x_2\rangle$; $\langle x_2, x_1, x_4, x_3, y_1, y_4, x_2\rangle$;

$\langle x_2, x_1, x_4, y_3, y_4, y_1, x_3, x_2\rangle$ and $\langle x_2, x_1, x_4, y_3, y_2, y_1, x_3, x_2\rangle$

$\langle x_2, x_1, x_4, x_3, y_1, y_2, y_3, y_4, x_2\rangle$

For other vertices $x \in V(TQ_3)$, the 4,5,6,7 and 8-length cycles that include the path $\langle R_1^*(x), x, R_2^*(x)\rangle$ can be gained similarly.

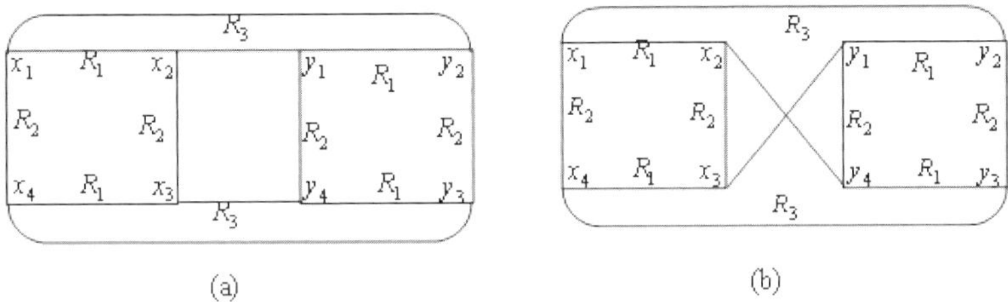

Fig. 5. Generalized RN_3. (a)$RN_3 \cong Q_3$, (b) $RN_3 \cong TQ_3$.

Theorem 7. *If RN_n ($n \geq 3$) has a $(n-2)$-rank super-network $(\mathcal{V}_{RN_n}^{(n-2)}, \mathcal{E}_{RN_n}^{(n-2)})$, and there is one $(n-2)$-rank super-edge $(\Gamma_{RN_n}(x), R_i^*(\Gamma_{RN_n}(y))) \in \mathcal{E}_{RN_n}^{(n-2)}$, $3 \leq i \leq n$, s.t.*

$$\Gamma_{RN_n}(x, y) \cong TQ_3$$

then RN_n is 4-pancyclicity.

Proof. When $n = 3$, $\mathcal{V}_{RN_3}^{(1)} = \{\Gamma_{RN_3}(0), \Gamma_{RN_3}(1)\}$ and $\mathcal{E}_{RN_3}^{(1)} = \{(\Gamma_{RN_3}(0), \Gamma_{RN_3}(1))\}$. If $\Gamma_{RN_3}(0, 1) \cong TQ_3$, Then $RN_3 \cong TQ_3$. This theorem follows theorem 6.

When $n > 3$, if RN_n has a $(n-2)$-rank super-network, then there exists a RN_{n-2} determined by $S_{n-2}, \cdots, S_2, S_1$ s.t. $(\mathcal{V}_{RN_n}^{(n-2)}, \mathcal{E}_{RN_n}^{(n-2)}) \cong RN_{n-2}$. So there is an edge $(x, y) \in E(RN_{n-2})$ s.t. $(x, y) \cong (\Gamma_{RN_n}(x), R_i(\Gamma_{RN_n}(y)))$, where $\Gamma_{RN_n}(x, y) \cong TQ_3$.

According to theorem 5, we can construct a Hamiltonian cycle including the edge (x, y) of RN_{n-2}. Because $(\mathcal{V}_{RN_n}^{(n-2)}, \mathcal{E}_{RN_n}^{(n-2)}) \cong RN_{n-2}$, there is a super Hamiltonian cycle in the super-network $(\mathcal{V}_{RN_n}^{(n-2)}, \mathcal{E}_{RN_n}^{(n-2)})$ which is isomorphic with the Hamiltonian cycle in the RN_{n-2} (see fig.6), where the super-vertices in the super Hamiltonian cycle are 2-dimentional binary recursive networks and $RN_2^1 = \Gamma_{RN_n}(x)$, $RN_2^2 = \Gamma_{RN_n}(y)$.

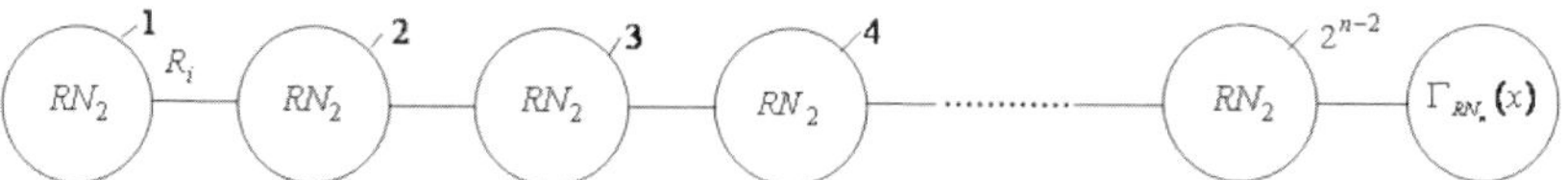

Fig. 6. The super Hamiltonian cycle in $(v^{(n-2)}_{RN_n}, \varepsilon^{(n-2)}_{RN_n})$

Actually, Because every 2-dimentional binary recursive network is a 4-length cycle in fig.6, a RN_3 is constructed by two adjacent RN_2. All topologies of super-vertices labeled 1,2 and 3 are shown in fig.7.

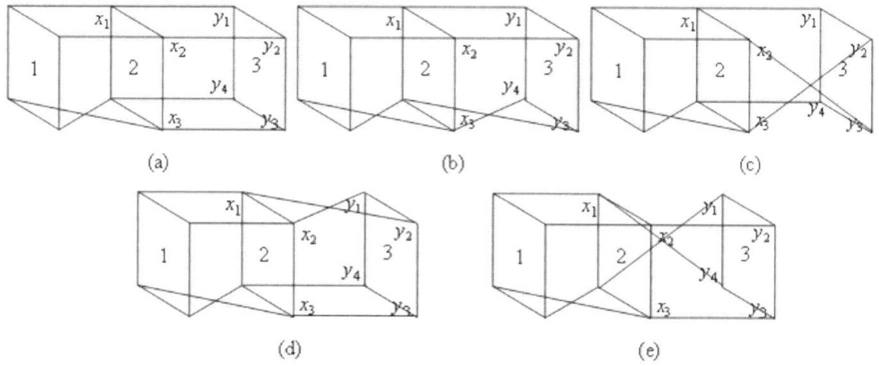

Fig. 7. All topologies of super-vertices RN_2^1 ,RN_2^2 and RN_2^3

By theorem 6, in twisted-3 cube $\Gamma_{RN_n}(x,y)$, there are always 4,5,6,7 and 8-length cycles which include a 2-length path in RN_2^2. Without losing generality, let the 2-length path be $\langle x_1, x_2, x_3\rangle$.

Because in fig.7, we have enumerated all topologies of RN_2^1, RN_2^2 and RN_2^3 in fig.6, we can conclude that there is always a 6-length cycle in the RN_3 constructed by RN_2^2 and RN_2^3. The 6-length cycle include (x_1, x_2) or (x_2, x_3), and a 3-length path in RN_2^3 whatever the RN_3 is Q_3 or TQ_3. For instance, these 6-length cycles in fig.7(a),(b),(c),(d) and (e) are $\langle x_1, y_1, y_4, y_3, y_2, x_2, x_1\rangle$ or $\langle x_2, y_2, y_1, y_4, y_3, x_3, x_2\rangle$, $\langle x_1, y_1, y_4, y_3, y_2, x_2, x_1\rangle$, $\langle x_2, y_3, y_4, y_1, y_2, x_3, x_2\rangle$, $\langle x_1, y_2, y_3, y_4, y_1, x_2, x_1\rangle$ and $\langle x_2, y_2, y_1, y_4, y_3, x_3, x_2\rangle$ respectively.

So there is always a 6-length cycle which has only one common edge with those 5,6,7 and 8-length cycles including $\langle x_1, x_2, x_3\rangle$ in $\Gamma_{RN_n}(x,y)$, and this 6-length cycle includes a 3-length path in RN_2^3. Thus, we can gain $9(=5+6-2)$, $10(=6+6-2)$, $11(=7+6-2)$ and $12(=8+6-2)$-length cycles by deleting the common edge of the 6-length cycle and these $5,6,7,8(=2\times 2^2)$-length cycles.

Similarly, we can find a 6-length cycle that includes a 3-path in RN_2^4 and a common edge with these 9, 10, 11, $12(=3\times 2^2)$-length cycles above. Thus, we can gain 13, 14, 15 and $16(4\times 2^2)$-length cycles by the same way.

Following this proceeding, and because there are 2^{n-2} different super-vertices in the super Hamiltonian cycle, we can obtain the cycles for any length $l(4 \le l \le 2^{n-2}\times 2^2 = 2^n)$ in RN_n under the precondition of this theorem.

Corollary 1. *when $n \geq 2$, the crossed cube CQ_n, the Möbius cube M_n, the generalized twisted cube GQ_n, the twisted n-cube TQ_n and the twisted-cube connected network TN_n are all 4-pancyclicity.*

Corollary 2. *when $n \geq 2$, the hypercube is 4- even pancyclicity, i.e. there are cycles for any even length $l(4 \leq l \leq 2^n)$.*

5 Conclusions

In this paper, we named a family of interconnection networks as Binary Recursive Networks. Their network structures are variations of hypercube. Then we got a general algebra expression of the binary recursive networks and analyzed its topology properties.

Using the adjacent functions, we gave a constructive proof to show that all the binary recursive networks are Hamiltonian. This proof provided a method of constructing Hamiltonian cycle in any binary recursive network. An approach to prove the 4-pancyclicity of some binary recursive networks was proposed by using the Hamiltonian and the topology properties of the binary recursive networks.

In the future, we are going on to study the searching algorithm of cycles for any length in the binary recursive networks under the direction of theorem 7.

References

1. Bondy, J.A., Murty, U.S.R.: Graph theory with applications. The Macmillan Press Ltd, NYC (1976)
2. Chedid, F.B., Chedid, R.B.: A new variation on hypercubes with smaller diameter. Infromation Processing Letters 46, 275–280 (1993)
3. Cull, P., Larson, S.M.: The Möbius cubes. IEEE Trans. Computers 44(5), 647–659 (1995)
4. Efe, K.: A Variation on the Hypercube with Lower Diameter. IEEE Trans. On Computers 40(11), 1312–1316 (1991)
5. Efe, K.: The crossed cube architecture for parallel computation. IEEE Trans. Parallel and Distributed Systems 3(5), 513–524 (1992)
6. Esfahanian, A., Ni, L.M., Sagan, B.E.: The twisted n-cube with application to multiprocessing. IEEE Trans. Computers 40(1), 88–93 (1991)
7. Gould, R.J.: Updating the hamiltonian problem – a survey. J. Graph Theory 15(2), 121–157 (1991)
8. Leighton, F.T.: Introduction to Parallel Algorithms and Architectures: Array, Tree, Hypercubes. Morgan Kaufmann, San Mateo, Calif (1992)
9. Park, C., Chwa, K.: Hamiltonian properties on the class of hypercube-like networks. Information Processing Letters 91, 11–17 (2004)
10. Rowley, R.A., Bose, B.: Fault-tolerant ring embedding in de Bruijn Networks. IEEE Trans. Comput. 42(12), 1480–1486 (1993)
11. Saad, Y., Schultz, M.: Topological properties of hypercube. IEEE Trans. Computers 37(7), 867–872 (1988)
12. Hsieh, S., Chen, G., Ho, C.: Fault-free Hamiltonian cycles in faulty arrangement graphs. IEEE Trans. Parallel and Distributed Systems 10(3), 223–237 (1999)
13. West, D.B.: Introduction to graph theory. PrenticeHall, Englewood Cliffs (1996)

14. Wang, D., Zhao, L.: The twisted-cube connected network. J. of Computer Science and Technology 14(2), 181–187 (1999)
15. Wang, D., An, T., Pan, M., et al.: Hamiltonian-like properties of k-ary n-cubes. In: The Proceeding of International Conference on Parallel and Distributed Computing, pp. 1002–1007 (2005)
16. Hu, K.S., Yeoh, S., Chen, C., Hsu, L.: Node-pancyclicity and edge-pancyclicity of hypercube variants. Information Processing Letters 102, 1–3 (2007)
17. Wang, D., Liu, Y.: Almost Pancyclic Property of the Twisted-Cube Connected Network. Chinese Journal of Northeastern University(Natural Science) 20(1), 12–14 (1999)

Strategies for Traffic Grooming over Logical Topologies

Arunita Jaekel, Ataul Bari, and Subir Bandyopadhyay

School of Computer Science, University of Windsor
401 Sunset Avenue, Windsor, ON, N9B 3P4, Canada
{arunita,bari1,subir}@uwindsor.ca

Abstract. In WDM mesh networks, low-speed data streams from individual users are combined, using the techniques of traffic grooming, for efficient utilization of the high bandwidth of a lightpath. The objective of traffic grooming is to minimize the cost of the network and/or to maximize the network throughput. Proposed solutions for this optimization problem are computationally intractable, even for networks of moderate size. In this paper, we have presented efficient Integer Linear Program (ILP) formulations for traffic grooming on mesh WDM networks, one for minimizing the congestion and the other to maximize the throughput of the network, with an assumption that the logical topology is specified. Unlike previous formulations, our formulations can be used for practical sized networks. We have simulated our formulations with networks up to 30 nodes, and with hundreds and even thousands of low-speed data streams and have shown that the formulations are able to generate optimal solutions within a reasonable amount of time.

1 Introduction

In optical networks, high throughput backbone networks using *Wavelength Division Multiplexing* (WDM) [1], [2] have become standard. A lightpath [2], in an optical network, is defined as a point-to-point communication path that optically connects an optical transmitter at a source end-node to an optical receiver at a destination end-node without any opto-electronic conversion at any intermediate node in its route from its source to its destination.

A lightpath, using current technology, can support a data rate of 2.5, 10 or even 40 giga bits per second (Gbps). Individual requests for connections are typically for a much lower data communication, of the order of mega bits per second (Mbps), compared to the data rate of a lightpath. *Traffic grooming* has been studied intensively to address this tremendous mismatch between the data rates of user requests and lightpaths. Traffic grooming may be defined as a family of techniques for combining a number of low-speed traffic streams from different users for transmission over a WDM network, to make "efficient" use of the high data rate of the lightpaths [3], [4], [5], [6], [7]. In this paper we consider static grooming with non-bifurcated model[1] for the traffic routing.

[1] A brief review of terms (e.g., static grooming, bifurcated and non-bifurcated model, logical and physical topology) relevant to this work is given in Section 2.

I. Stojmenovic et al. (Eds.): ISPA 2007, LNCS 4742, pp. 797–808, 2007.

The optimal design of WDM mesh networks with traffic grooming capabilities deals with solving the combined problem of the following subproblems:

Subproblem i) Topology Design (*TD*): find the logical topology of the network,

Subproblem ii) Route and Wavelength Assignment (*RWA*): ensure that a feasible RWA, to realize each logical edge, is possible,

Subproblem iii) Traffic Routing (*TR*): decide which logical path(s) should be used for each data stream so that the total payload of each edge in the logical topology never exceeds the capacity of a lightpath and network resources are used in an optimal way.

The Integer Linear Program (ILP) formulations, proposed in the literature [2], [8], [9] for solving the combined logical topology design and traffic grooming problem are computationally intractable, even for moderate sized networks, and the problem is solved by applying some heuristics. One widely used heuristic is to decouple the combined problem into three *independent* subproblems [8], [9] and solve them separately. In the heuristic for the TR subproblem, a common objective is to minimize the *congestion* of the network [2], defined as the total traffic on the logical edge carrying the maximum amount of traffic.

In recent years, the number of lightpaths on a single fiber has increased tremendously [2], [10] and, in most cases, WDM channels are no longer the scarce resources. It is reasonable to assume that RWA may be solved in a separate step [2], [11] or simplified considerably [12].

The traffic routing problem (TR) for the bifurcated model is relatively easier and may be solved using standard multi-commodity network flow techniques [2]. For the non-bifurcated model, traffic routing itself has been recognized as a NP-complete problem [13], and can become computationally intractable, particularly when considering hundreds, or even thousands of low-speed traffic requests.

Efficient heuristics are already available for TD as well as for RWA [2], [14]. In this paper, we have focused on the problem of non-bifurcated traffic grooming on a given logical topology. Our objective is not to solve the combined topology design and routing problem, but to determine an efficient routing scheme for a specified logical topology and set of traffic requests. We have considered two sets, $\mathcal{S}_1$ and $\mathcal{S}_2$, of ILP formulations for traffic grooming when the logical topology has been already determined by solving subproblems TD and RWA, using available heuristics. Both sets, $\mathcal{S}_1$ and $\mathcal{S}_2$, have two ILP formulations each, addressing the following popular objective functions:

Objective function 1: for a given set of traffic requests, route *all* the requests to minimize the congestion of the logical topology.

Objective function 2: for a given set of traffic requests, route *as many* requests as possible to maximize the network throughput.

The formulation *ILP1a (IL1b)* in set $\mathcal{S}_1$ consider objective function 1 (2). Both formulations in $\mathcal{S}_1$ are for optimal traffic grooming, so that each formulation takes into account *all* possible logical paths to handle the TR subproblem optimally[2].

[2] These formulations were first introduced in [15] and is included here for completeness.

It turns out that, for networks of practical size, the formulations in $\mathcal{S}_1$ often fail to find a solution within a reasonable amount of time. To make the problem tractable, when the formulations in $\mathcal{S}_1$ fail to find a solution, we have proposed formulation *ILP2a* (*ILP2b*) in set $\mathcal{S}_2$ to handle objective function 1 (2). The formulations in set $\mathcal{S}_2$ are much faster because the search spaces for these formulations are constrained. Each of these formulations restricts the search of logical paths, for each request for data communication, to k predetermined "promising" paths, for some specified k. An extreme example would be a situation where k is 1 and the predetermined path is the shortest path from the source to the destination of each request. To make the search more efficient, it may be desirable to use a higher value of k and use some heuristic to generate "promising" paths.

In summary, in this paper we have

- proposed new ILP formulations, in $\mathcal{S}_2$, for traffic grooming on a given logical topology.
- shown that, with a proper choice of the value of k, the objective value determined by each of the formulations in $\mathcal{S}_2$ is quite comparable to the optimum value obtained using the corresponding formulation in $\mathcal{S}_1$ when an optimum formulation can be determined.
- shown that, for practical networks, each of the formulations in $\mathcal{S}_2$ can find a solution quickly, even when the corresponding formulation in $\mathcal{S}_1$ fails to find a solution.

The traffic grooming problem, with a number of different objective functions has been addressed in [3], [6], [16]. To the best of our knowledge, this is the first approach for traffic grooming that finds, using an ILP, the optimal solution within the given limited search space. We also believe that this is the first study that looks at the time needed to solve the grooming problem for two different objective functions, using very similar sets of constraints.

In Section 2, we have briefly reviewed the background. In Section 3, we have presented our sets of formulations, $\mathcal{S}_1$ and $\mathcal{S}_2$. In Section 4 we have described our experiments and the results. We conclude with a summary in Section 5.

2 Review

The physical topology of a WDM network is conveniently represented by a digraph $G_P = (V_P, E_P)$, where V_P is the set of nodes in the network, and E_P is the set of edges, each directed edge $x \rightarrow y$ representing a physical link (i.e, an optical fibre) from node x to node y, $x, y \in V_P$. Each node in V_P is either an *end-node* (a potential source or destination of any communication), or a *router node* [2]. Since it is not practical to have each end-node connected to every other end-node by a lightpath, multi-hop networks [1] have been studied widely. In a multi-hop network, if there is a request for communication from a source s to a destination d and there is no lightpath from s to d, a multi-hop path involving a number of lightpaths is used for communication from s to d. In such networks, the notion of a *logical topology* (also called a *virtual topology*) [2], [8], [9] is useful for determining an efficient scheme for data communication. The logical topology may be represented by a graph $G_L = (V_L, E_L)$ where the set of nodes, V_L, is the set of all end-nodes from V_P of graph G_P and E_L is the set of *logical edges* in the network. If there is a lightpath from end-node p to end-node q, there is a logical edge $p \Rightarrow q$ from p to q in the logical topology. To communicate from s to d, a path in the logical topology G_L, often called a *logical path* (or *virtual path*) [2] has to be used. In general, there are many possible logical paths from the source to the destination of a request.

Traffic grooming maximizes the utilization of the capacity of each lightpath, and hence, minimizes the network cost, in terms of transmitters, receivers and optical switches. There are two basic approaches [5] in traffic grooming:

Approach i) for a given set of traffic requests, minimize the total network "cost"[3], with the condition that all traffic requests are satisfied.

Approach ii) for given resource limitations and traffic requests, maximize the network throughput, measured by the total amount of traffic that is successfully carried by the network.

In the literature, two models have been adopted for determining the routing strategy for traffic grooming - the *bifurcated* model and the *non-bifurcated* model. In the bifurcated model, a data stream from an individual user is allowed to be split into multiple data streams, and to be carried by different logical paths, from the source of the data stream to its destination [17]. In the non-bifurcated model, each data stream is communicated using a *single* logical path from the source of the data stream to its destination. The non-bifurcated model has a number of technological advantages [6] and has been adopted in [4], [6], [12].

Traffic grooming problem can be classified as either *static* or *dynamic*. In a *static grooming* scenario, [6] the traffic is relatively stable over longer periods of time. In *dynamic traffic grooming* scenario, requests for data communication are processed as they arrive [7].

3 ILP Formulations

In this section we present two sets of ILP formulations, $\mathcal{S}_1$ and $\mathcal{S}_2$, that address the traffic grooming problem in WDM mesh networks. Set $\mathcal{S}_1$ includes formulations *ILP1a* and *ILP1b*, and set $\mathcal{S}_2$ includes formulations *ILP2a* and *ILP2b*. Each of these formulations considers a different objective function as follows:

i) *ILP1a* (*ILP2a*) minimizes the *congestion* of the network, defined as the maximum traffic load on a logical link. This is a well-known objective that has been used for traffic routing, for the bifurcated grooming model [2], [8].
ii) *ILP1b* (*ILP2b*) maximizes the weighted sum of requests that may be handled by the network, for a specified set of network resources. Here, the *weight* of

[3] Here cost is determined by the design objective. For example, reducing the number of lightpaths directly reduces the number of transmitters and receivers in the network. Other cost functions have been proposed as well [8].

a request is the required data communication rate, in OC-n notations. This objective was also considered in [18], [19].

3.1 Notation Used in the Formulations

In the formulations *ILP1a*, *ILP1b*, *ILP2a* and *ILP2b*, we will use the following symbols to represent input data

$o(p)$: The origin of lightpath p.
$l(p)$: The destination of lightpath p.
s_q : The originating node of commodity (request for communication[4]) q.
d_q : The destination of commodity (request for communication) q.
V_L : The set of end nodes in the logical topology.
E_L : The set of logical edges in the logical topology.
$\mathcal{Q}$: The set of all request for communication, each request specified using the OC-n notation [7].
g : The capacity of a logical edge (lightpath) using the OC-n notation.
t_q : Data communication rate for the request corresponding to commodity q.
$\mathbb{R}$: The number of "promising" routes through the logical topology to be considered for routing between each ordered pair of end-nodes.
n_q : The number of elements, $|\mathcal{Q}|$, in $\mathcal{Q}$.
$\mathbb{P}$: The number of elements, $|E_L|$, in E_L.
n : The number of end-nodes, $|V_L|$, in the network.
D : A matrix of size $\mathbb{R} \times |\mathcal{Q}| \times |E_L|$ where the element $d^k_{p,q}$ of matrix D corresponds to path k, from the source s_q to the destination d_q of commodity q and lightpath p. The element $d^k_{p,q}$ is defined as follows:

$$d^k_{p,q} = \begin{cases} 1 \text{ if the } k^{th} \text{ path, from } s_q \text{ to } d_q \text{ for commodity } q \text{, uses lightpath } p, \\ 0 \text{ otherwise.} \end{cases}$$

We also define the following variables:

F : A $|E_L| \times |\mathcal{Q}|$ matrix of binary variables where the element $f_{p,q}$ defined as follows:

$$f_{p,q} = \begin{cases} 1 \text{ if commodity } q \text{ is routed over lightpath } p, \\ 0 \text{ otherwise.} \end{cases}$$

X : A $\mathbb{R} \times |\mathcal{Q}|$ matrix of binary variables where the element $x_{k,q}$ corresponds to the kth route, from the source s_q to the destination d_q of commodity q, and is defined as follows:

$$x_{k,q} = \begin{cases} 1 \text{ if commodity } q \text{ uses } k^{th} \text{ route to send data from } s_q \text{ to } d_q, \\ 0 \text{ otherwise.} \end{cases}$$

Y : A vector of $|\mathcal{Q}|$ binary variables where the element y_q corresponds to commodity q and is defined as follows:

$$y_q = \begin{cases} 1 \text{ if commodity } q \text{ is successfully routed over the logical topology,} \\ 0 \text{ otherwise.} \end{cases}$$

[4] Each request for communication constitutes a commodity, for these multi-commodity network flow formulations.

λ_{max} **:** The maximum traffic on any lightpath.

$\mathcal{H}$ **:** A $|E_L| \times |\mathcal{Q}|$ matrix of *continuous* variables where the element $\mathfrak{h}_{p,q}$ defined as follows:

$\mathfrak{h}_{p,q} = \begin{cases} 1 \text{ if commodity } q \text{ is routed over lightpath } p, \\ 0 \text{ otherwise.} \end{cases}$

This variable is similar to the binary variable F, except that it has been defined as continuous variable. Although $\mathfrak{h}_{p,q}$ is a continuous variable, the corresponding constraints are specified in such a way that $\mathfrak{h}_{p,q}$ can take integer values only. This technique helps to reduce the complexity of the formulation, by reducing the number of binary variables.

3.2 Formulation ILP1a

The objective of *ILP1a* is to minimize the *congestion* of the network. This can be achieved using the formulation given below.

$$\textbf{Minimize } \lambda_{max} \tag{1}$$

Subject to:

$$\sum_{p:o(p)=i} f_{p,q} - \sum_{p:l(p)=i} f_{p,q} = \begin{cases} 1 \text{ if } i = s_q, \\ -1 \text{ if } i = d_q, \\ 0 \text{ otherwise,} \end{cases} \quad \forall q \in \mathcal{Q}, \forall i \in V_L \tag{2}$$

$$\sum_q f_{p,q} t_q \leq \lambda_{max} \qquad \forall p \in E_L, \forall q \in \mathcal{Q} \tag{3}$$

$$\lambda_{max} \leq g \tag{4}$$

Equation (1) is the objective function that minimizes the maximum load, λ_{max}, on any given lightpath, and hence minimizes the congestion. Constraint (2) is to ensure that each request is routed from its source to its destination using a single path. The left hand side of constraint (3) computes the total traffic on each lightpath. Since the objective is to minimize λ_{max}, and the right hand side of constraint (3) is λ_{max}, the effect of this constraint is to set λ_{max} to the maximum value of the total traffic on each lightpath. Constraint (4) is used to enforce the capacity constraint on each lightpath, by ensuring that the maximum traffic λ_{max} is less than the lightpath capacity g.

3.3 Formulation ILP1b

The objective of formulation *ILP1b* is to maximize the amount of traffic that can be successfully handled by the network. This objective can be achieved using the formulation given below.

$$\textbf{Maximize } \sum_q y_q \cdot t_q \tag{5}$$

Subject to:

$$\sum_{p:o(p)=i} f_{p,q} - \sum_{p:l(p)=i} f_{p,q} = \begin{cases} y_q & \text{if } i = s_q, \\ -y_q & \text{if } i = d_q, \\ 0 & \text{otherwise.} \end{cases} \qquad \forall q \in \mathcal{Q}, \forall i \in V_L \tag{6}$$

$$f_{p,q} \leq y_q \qquad \forall p \in E_L, \forall q \in \mathcal{Q} \tag{7}$$

$$\sum_q f_{p,q} \cdot t_q \leq g \qquad \forall p \in E_L, \forall q \in \mathcal{Q} \tag{8}$$

If request q is handled by the above formulation, $y_q = 1$. Thus $y_q \cdot t_q$ gives the contribution of request q to the network throughput. The objective function (equation (5)) maximizes the weighted sum of traffic requests. Constraint (2) in *ILP1a* is replaced by constraint (6) in *ILP1b*. This enforces the flow constraints only for commodities that can be successfully routed over the network (i.e., $y_q = 1$). Constraint (7) ensures that if a request q is blocked, (i.e., $y_q = 0$), then it is not allocated any bandwidth on any lightpath ($f_{p,q} \leq y_q$, $\forall p,\ p \in E_L$). The data communication rate for commodity q is t_q and this is carried by lightpath p if $f_{p,q} = 1$. Thus $f_{p,q} \cdot t_q$ is the contribution of commodity q to the traffic on lightpath p. Constraint (8) therefore enforces the capacity constraint of the lightpaths.

3.4 Formulation ILP2a

Formulation *ILP2a* is for traffic grooming over a given logical topology to minimize the congestion using a "restricted search". We do this by pre-computing a set of $\mathbb{R}$ "promising" routes over the logical topology, for each pair of end-nodes. When searching for a logical path from the source s_q to destination d_q for a request q, we select one of the $\mathbb{R}$ routes from s_q to d_q. This can be done using the formulation given below.

$$\textbf{Minimize } \lambda_{max} \tag{9}$$

Subject to:

a) Each request must be assigned exactly one route.

$$\sum_k x_{k,q} = 1 \qquad \forall q \in \mathcal{Q} \tag{10}$$

b) Determine whether lightpath p appears in the logical path for request q.

$$\mathfrak{h}_{p,q} = \sum_k x_{k,q} \cdot d^k_{p,q} \qquad \forall p \in E_L, \forall q \in \mathcal{Q} \tag{11}$$

c) Compute the total load on a lightpath and determine the congestion.

$$\sum_q \mathfrak{h}_{p,q} \cdot t_q \leq \lambda_{max} \qquad \forall p \in E_L, \forall q \in \mathcal{Q} \tag{12}$$

d) Ensure that the capacity constraint on each lightpath is satisfied.

$$\lambda_{max} \leq g \tag{13}$$

For *ILP2a*, the objective function (equation (9)) is identical to the corresponding objective function (equation (1)) given in *ILP1a*. Constraint (10) enforces the non-bifurcation approach since this constraint forces $x_{k,q}$ to be 1 for exactly one value of k. In other words, for commodity q, $x_{k,q} = 1$ for exactly only one route k. Since $x_{k,q}$ is 1 for exactly one value of k, and, if $d^k_{p,q} = 1$, the kth route uses lightpath p. Therefore, constraint (11) sets the value of $\mathfrak{h}_{p,q}$ to 1 if and only if lightpath p is used in the logical path for commodity q. Constraints (12) and (13) serves the same purpose as constraints (3) and (4) respectively in *ILP1a*.

3.5 Formulation ILP2b

Formulation *ILP2b* given below is for traffic grooming over a given logical topology to maximize the network throughput using a "restricted search" similar to that used in *ILP2a*.

$$\textbf{Maximize} \sum_q y_q \cdot t_q \tag{14}$$

Subject to:

a) A commodity must use only one route.

$$\sum_k x_{k,q} = y_q \qquad \forall q \in Q \tag{15}$$

b) Determine whether lightpath p appears in the logical path for request q.

$$\mathfrak{h}_{p,q} = \sum_k x_{k,q} \cdot d^k_{p,q} \qquad \forall p \in E_L, \forall q \in Q \tag{16}$$

c) Ensure that the capacity constraint on each lightpath is satisfied.

$$\sum_q \mathfrak{h}_{p,q} \cdot t_q \leq g \qquad \forall p \in E_L, \forall q \in Q \tag{17}$$

For *ILP2b*, the objective function, equation (14), is identical to that in equation (5) for *ILP1b*. Constraint (15) in *ILP2b* is like constraint (10) in *ILP2a*, except that a commodity q is assigned a lightpath only if $y_q = 1$, since we need flow constraints only for commodities that can be handled by the network. The capacity constraint (17) is just like constraint (8), used in *ILP1b*.

3.6 Complexity Analysis

An integer linear program is characterized by the number of integer and continuous variables and the number of constraints. Table 1 gives the number of integer

Table 1. Number of variables and constraints in the ILP formulations

Formulation	Number of integer variables	Number of continuous variables	Number of constraints
ILP1a	$\mathbb{P} \cdot n_q$	1	$\mathbb{P} + n \cdot n_q + 1$
ILP1b	$\mathbb{P} \cdot n_q + n_q$	0	$\mathbb{P} + \mathbb{P} \cdot n_q + n \cdot n_q$
ILP2a	$\mathbb{R} \cdot n_q$	$\mathbb{P} \cdot n_q + 1$	$\mathbb{P} \cdot n_q + \mathbb{P} + n_q + 1$
ILP2b	$\mathbb{R} \cdot n_q + n_q$	$\mathbb{P} \cdot n_q$	$\mathbb{P} \cdot n_q + \mathbb{P} + n_q$

variables, continuous variables and constraints in the formulations *ILP1a*, *ILP1b*, *ILP2a* and *ILP2b*. As shown in the table, the required number of integer variables are considerably reduced in the formulation *ILP2a* (*ILP2b*) compared to *ILP1a* (*ILP1b*), at the expense of some additional continuous variables. Since the time to solve an ILP is critically dependent on the number of integer variables [20], formulations *ILP2a* and *ILP2b* can be processed by a solver much more quickly.

4 Experimental Results

For experiments, we have considered a number of networks of different sizes, ranging from 6 to 30 nodes, including the well-known NSFNET topology and the 20 node ARPANET topology [21]. The average number of traffic requests varied, from about 60, for a 6 node network, to over 1800 for a 30 node network. In each case, we have considered 3 “promising” routes through the logical topology for routing between each ordered pair of end-nodes, i.e., $\mathbb{R} = 3$. For our experiments, we have simply selected the three shortest edge-disjoint paths between each source-destination pair. If three edge-disjoint paths could not be found, we selected three shortest paths between the source-destination pair such that the number of overlapping edges is minimized. The experiments were carried out on a 900 MHz processor, using CPLEX 9.1 [22].

In order to run the formulations discussed above, it is necessary to specify a logical topology for the network. A number of heuristics are available to design logical topologies [8]. Any such heuristic may be used to design logical topologies for our formulations. For our experiments, we have used our own heuristic to design logical topologies using a minimum number of transmitters and receivers. Since the design of logical topologies is not the issue of this paper, and due to space limitations, we are not giving details of the design of logical topologies. It is important to note, however, that all the logical topologies we used were capable of carrying the traffic that we used for testing. In other words, for each situation that we have considered, there was a feasible solution to the routing problem.

When studying the performance of formulations *ILP1a* and *ILP2a* using CPLEX, we set the parameters for the absolute optimality tolerance to 5% and the time limit to 2 hours. This means that we stopped the solver either when the value of the objective function was within 5% of that of the optimal solution

Table 2. Comparison of execution times for *ILP1a*, and *ILP2a*

Number of		Execution time (Sec.)		% reduction
Nodes	Requests	*ILP1a*	*ILP2a*	of sol. time
6	63	0.45	0.1	77
8	112	9.42	0.31	96.7
10	192	1741	2.16	99.9
12	282	3252	4.4	99.9
14	385	*	14.5	
16	510	**	28.5	
20	805	**	874	
30	1842	**	2231	
* Integer feasible solution was found within two hours, but the formulation did not converge.				
** No Integer feasible solution was found within two hours.				

Table 3. Comparison of execution times for *ILP1b*, and *ILP2b*

Number of		Execution time (Sec.)		% reduction
Nodes	Requests	*ILP1b*	*ILP2b*	of sol. time
6	63	0.11	0.05	57
8	113	0.30	0.05	84
10	192	1.13	0.08	93
12	282	2.73	0.10	96
14	385	7.27	0.13	98
16	510	251	0.17	99.9
20	805	498	0.21	99.9
30	1842	**	0.52	
** No Integer feasible solution was found within two hours.				

or when the solver was unable to converge to find a solution after 2 hours of operations. Table 2 shows the time required for formulations *ILP1a* and *ILP2a* for various network sizes. As expected, formulation *ILP2a* is not only much faster than *ILP1a*, but was able to generate solutions for networks with up to 30 nodes. In contrast, formulation *ILP1a* only succeeded to converge for networks with sizes 12 or less. For networks of size 14, formulation *ILP1a* did find an initial feasible solution but failed to converge within the time limit of 2 hours. For each network with 16 or more nodes, formulation *ILP1a* failed even to find an initial feasible solution. For networks with up to 12 nodes, the values of the objective function obtained using *ILP2a* and the corresponding value obtained using ILP1a agree within the set parameters.

Table 3 shows the solution times required for *ILP1b* and *ILP2b*. For both formulations, we stopped the CPLEX solver either when the global optimum was reached or if the solver was unable to converge to find a solution after 2 hours of operations. For this set of experiments, the latter situation occurred only for formulation *ILP1b*, when processing networks with 30 nodes. As shown in the table, the formulation *ILP2b* was able to converge much faster than the formulation *ILP1b*. And as for the quality of the solution, the values of the objective function obtained using *ILP2b* and the corresponding value obtained using *ILP1b* agree in all cases, for networks with up to 20 nodes (after which, the formulation *ILP1b* failed to produce feasible solution).

5 Conclusions

In this paper we have considered two sets $\mathcal{S}_1$ and $\mathcal{S}_2$ of ILP formulations for traffic grooming in WDM mesh networks. These formulations are useful in designing traffic grooming strategies in networks where conventional strategies cannot be used due to the complexity of the problem. Formulations in the set $\mathcal{S}_1$, when they converge, give optimum solutions, for a given logical topology. We have shown that formulations in $\mathcal{S}_1$ may fail to converge in a reasonable time for large networks, particularly when the set of requests is large. The formulations in $\mathcal{S}_2$ are faster and works on large networks, with thousands of requests, because the search space for valid logical paths from the source to the destination of each request, is restricted, to a degree determined by the user, by a suitable choice of the parameter $\mathbb{R}$. It is interesting to find, from our experiments, over a large number of networks and sets of requests, that

1. when the formulation *ILP1a* does converge, the values of the objective functions obtained using *ILP2a* is within 5% of that obtained using *ILP1a*.
2. when the formulation *ILP1b* does converge, the values of the objective functions obtained using *ILP2b* is within 0.5% of that obtained using *ILP1b*.

In summary, we have shown that, for practical purpose, it is sufficient to develop a "good" logical topology using some heuristic, and then perform optimal traffic routing using an appropriate formulation from $\mathcal{S}_1$, or failing that, from $\mathcal{S}_2$.

Acknowledgment

The work of A. Jaekel and S. Bandyopadhyay have been supported by research grants from the Natural Sciences and Engineering Research Council of Canada (NSERC).

References

1. Mukherjee, B.: Optical Communication Networks. McGraw-Hill, New York (1997)
2. Ramaswami, R., Sivarajan, K.N.: Optical Networks: A Practical Perspective. Morgan Kaufmann, San Francisco (2002)
3. Dutta, R., Rouskas, G.N.: Traffic grooming in WDM networks: past and future. IEEE Network 16(6), 46–56 (2002)
4. Hu, J.Q., Modiano, E.: Optical WDM Networks: Principles and Practice. In: Traffic Grooming in WDM Networks, vol. II, Kluwer Aca. Pub., Dordrecht (2004)

5. Zang, K., Mukherjee, B.: A review of traffic grooming in WDM optical networks: Architectures and challenges. Optical Networks Magazine 4(2), 55–64 (2003)
6. Zhu, K., Mukherjee, B.: Traffic grooming in an optical WDM mesh network. IEEE Journal on Selected Areas in Communications 20(1), 122–133 (2002)
7. Zhu, K., Zhu, H., Mukherjee, B.: Traffic Grooming in Optical WDM Mesh Networks. Springer, Heidelberg (2005)
8. Dutta, R., Rouskas, G.N.: A survey of virtual topology design algorithms for wavelength routed optical networks. Optical Networks Magazine 1(1), 73–89 (2000)
9. Rouskas, G., Dutta, R.: Optical WDM Networks: Principles and Practice, chap. Design of Logical Topologies for Wavelength Routed Networks, pp. 79–102. Kluwer, Dordrecht (2000)
10. Mukherjee, B.: WDM optical communication networks: Progress and challenges. IEEE Journal on Selected Areas in Communications 18(10), 1810–1824 (2000)
11. Konda, V.R., Chow, T.Y.: Algorithm for traffic grooming in optical networks to minimize the number of transceivers. In: IEEE Workshop on High Performance Switching and Routing, pp. 218–221 (May 2001)
12. Hu, J.Q., Leida, B.: Traffic grooming, routing, and wavelength assignment in optical WDM mesh networks. In: IEEE INFOCOM, vol. 1, pp. 495–501 (2004)
13. Dutta, R., Huang, S., Rouskas, G.N.: On optimal traffic grooming in elemental network topologies. Opticomm. 13–24 (October 2003)
14. Zang, H., Jue, J.P., Mukherjee, B.: A review of routing and wavelength assignment approaches for wavelength-routed optical WDM networks. Optical Networks Magazine 18(10), 47–60 (2000)
15. Jaekel, A., Bari, A., Chen, Y., Bandyopadhyay, S.: New techniques for efficient traffic grooming in WDM mesh networks. In: IEEE ICCCN (2007)
16. Cerutti, I., Fumagalli, A.: Traffic grooming in static wavelength multiplexing networks. IEEE Communications Magazine, 101–107 (January 2005)
17. Huang, S., Dutta, R.: Research problems in dynamic traffic grooming in optical networks. IEEE Broadnets (October 2004)
18. Lee, K., Shayman, M.A.: Rollout algorithms for logical topology design and traffic grooming in multihop WDM networks. In: IEEE GLOBECOM, vol. 4, pp. 2113–2117 (2005)
19. Zhang, Y., Wu, J., Yang, O.W.W., Savoie, M.: Lagrangian-relaxation based mesh traffic grooming for network profit optimization. In: IEEE Workshop on High Performance Switching and Routing (HPSR05), pp. 406–410 (2005)
20. Nemhauser, G.L., Wolsey, L.A.: Integer and Combinatorial Optimization. John Wiley and Sons, Chichester (1988)
21. Sridharan, M., Salapaka, M.V., Somani, A.: A practical approach to operating survivable WDM networks. In: IEEE JSAC, vol. 20(1), pp. 34–46 (January 2002)
22. Ilog cplex 9.1. Documentation available at, `http://www.columbia.edu/dano/resources/cplex91man/index.html`

Implementing IPv4+4 Addressing Architecture with IPv4 LSRR Option for Seamless Peer-to-Peer (P2P) Communication

Cihan Topal and Cuneyt Akinlar

Computer Engineering Department, Anadolu University, Eskisehir, Turkey
cihant@anadolu.edu.tr, cakinlar@anadolu.edu.tr

Abstract. IPv4 architecture is well entrenched with Network Address Translation (NAT) boxes, which cause well-known problems for Peer-to-Peer (P2P) applications. IPv6 would enable end-to-end connectivity when deployed, but the industry has been slow in transitioning to IPv6. IPv4+4 has been suggested as an alternative NAT-extended addressing architecture, where the idea is to assign 64-bit end-to-end globally unique addresses for nodes on private address realms by concatenating the 32-bit globally routable IPv4 address of the realm (border) gateway with the 32-bit private IPv4 addresses of the nodes. While IPv4+4 addressing proposal is neat, existing IPv4+4 implementations require changes to all border gateways and end-hosts, which hinders its deployment. In this paper we show how the IPv4+4 addressing architecture can be implemented by using a modified version of the standard IPv4 Loose Source Record Route (LSRR) option. Our proposal requires no changes to existing IPv4 infrastructure (assuming all IPv4-compliant nodes implement LSRR as required by RFC 791), thus enabling seamless end-to-end communication for P2P applications. We demonstrate packet forwarding with the 64-bit IPv4+4 addresses, and illustrate how the widely-used P2P voice over IP protocol, the Session Initiation Protocol, can make use of our proposal for seamless end-to-end communication.

1 Introduction

While Network Address Translation (NAT) [1,2] has been proposed as a stop-gap measure to slow down IPv4 [13] address depletion, NAT boxes have been widely adapted and deployed all over the IPv4 infrastructure. Although a NAT-based Internet is suitable for the client-server type of communication, e.g., HTTP, where the server is on the public Internet and the client is on a private address realm, i.e., the client has a non-routable private IPv4 address [15], this architecture creates well-known problems for Peer-to-Peer (P2P) communication.

To enable P2P communication in the presence of NATs, hole punching techniques have been proposed exemplified by STUN [8], STUNT [9,10,11]. The general idea with these proposals is to let a node behind a NAT box talk to a server on the public Internet and learn (global IP address, port) pair assigned to its (private IP address, local port) pair for a certain session, and then disclose this information to

I. Stojmenovic et al. (Eds.): ISPA 2007, LNCS 4742, pp. 809–820, 2007.

the peer for direct communication. Although such port prediction and hole punching methods enable P2P communication in certain cases, they are not reliable and fail to work for all NAT types. Furthermore NATs exhibit different behavior for each transport layer protocol, i.e., UDP [16], TCP [17], SCTP [18], further complicating the matters for P2P communication.

IPv6, when deployed, would provide each node on the Internet with a globally routable IPv6 address, which would enable end-to-end connectivity necessary for P2P communication. But the industry has been slow in transitioning to IPv6 as it requires a complete rehaul of the network infrastructure, i.e., routers, and end-hosts. The difficulty in transition to IPv6 also stems from the fact that IPv6 addresses are not backward-compatible. Alternatively, several NAT-extended architectures have been proposed to restore end-to-end addressing and connectivity [4,5,6,7]. IPv4+4 is one such addressing architecture, which proposes assigning each node a IPv4-compatible 64-bit globally unique network address formed by concatenating the 32-bit globally routable IPv4 address of the realm (border) gateway with the 32-bit private IPv4 address of the node [4]. Although this addressing proposal is very neat, the existing IPv4+4 implementation [5] requires changes to all realm gateways and end-hosts, and is not feasible in the short term.

In this paper we dwell on the IPv4+4 addressing architecture, and show how it can be implemented with a modified version of the IPv4 Loose Source Record Route (LSRR) option [13,14]. RFC 791 states that all IPv4-compliant nodes *must* implement LSRR [13]. Thus our proposal allows immediate deployment of the IPv4+4 addressing architecture without requiring any changes to existing IPv4 infrastructure, i.e., no changes to IPv4 routers, NAT devices, and hosts, assuming they already implement LSRR. We expect the emerging P2P applications such as voice over IP, interactive gaming, file sharing etc., to benefit from our IPv4+4 implementation proposal for seamless end-to-end connectivity without the need for complex, non-deterministic port prediction techniques. We do not advocate porting the existing client-server applications to IPv4+4 as they already work through NATs.

The rest of the paper is organized as follows: In section 2, we describe the IPv4+4 addressing architecture. Then in section 3 we describe the details of the IPv4+4 implementation given in [5], which proposes a new header structure and requires changes to realm (border) gateways and all end-hosts for deployment. Then in section in section 4, we describe how IPv4+4 can be realized using a modified version of the standard IPv4 Loose Source Record Route (LSRR) option. The advantage of our proposal is that it uses the existing IPv4 infrastructure and requires no changes whatsoever to IPv4 routers, realm gateways or end-hosts. Our proposal further allows communication over all transport layer protocols, e.g., UDP [16], TCP [17] or SCTP [18], and is not specific to any of them. Finally in section 5, we show how the emerging P2P application, voice over IP using the Session Initiation Protocol (SIP) [20], can make use of the IPv4+4 addressing and LSRR-based implementation to provide seamless end-to-end communication. We conclude the paper in section 6.

2 IPv4+4 Addressing Architecture

The basic idea in IPv4+4 is provide the nodes in a private realm, i.e., nodes having private IPv4 addresses, with an end-to-end, globally unique network address. This is achieved by concatenating the public IPv4 address of the realm gateway with the private IPv4 address of the node [4].

Fig. 1. Example network with 2 private realms connected to the public Internet through realm (border) gateways A and B

Figure 1 shows an example network with 2 private realms connected to the public Internet through realms gateways with public IPv4 addresses A and B. Nodes within the private realms, e.g., X and Y, have non-unique private IPv4 addresses. In the IPv4+4 architecture, node X would have the globally unique IPv4+4 address A.X and node Y would have the globally unique IPv4+4 address B.Y [4]. Nodes in the public Internet already having a globally unique IPv4 address, e.g., node C, simply use 0.0.0.0 as their public IPv4+4 part. That is, node C's IPv4+4 address is 0.C.

3 Related Work - An IPv4+4 Implementation

In this section we talk about an IPv4+4 implementation given in [5]. We detail the proposed header structure, the packet forwarding algorithm and the deployment requirements of the proposed implementation.

3.1 Header Format

The header format for IPv4+4 is shown in Figure 2. The first 20 bytes of the header comprise the regular IPv4 header. The next 12 bytes specify the IPv4+4 extension header. Conceptually this packet structure can be viewed as an IPv4 packet encapsulated within another IPv4 packet. This is what makes IPv4+4 backward compatible. That is, legacy IPv4 routers simply look at the first 20 bytes of the header, which is exactly the same as the IPv4 header, and forward the packet properly using the destination IPv4 address. To legacy routers and hosts IPv4+4 extension header looks like a new transport layer protocol with 12 bytes of header. However IPv4+4 hosts view the full IPv4+4 header as a new network protocol with 64-bit addresses [5].

Ver.	Hlen	DS Byte		Total Length	
Identification				Flag	Fragmentation Offset
TTL		Protocol 1		Header Checksum 1	
Source Address 1					
Destination Address 1					
Source Address 2					
Destination Address 2					
Protocol 2		SPos	DPos	Header Checksum 2	

Fig. 2. IPv4+4 header structure

Protocol1 field in IPv4 header indicates IPv4+4 encapsulation, and is set to 233. *Source Address 1* and *2* fields together specify source IPv4+4 address, and *Destination Address 1* and *2* fields together specify the destination IPv4+4 address. *SPos* and *DPos* fields specify which portion of the IPv4+4 address is in the IPv4 header part, i.e., the private IPv4 portion or the public IPv4 portion. *Protocol2* field specifies the transport layer protocol, that is, UDP, TCP or SCTP among others.

3.2 Packet Forwarding

Packet forwarding between two IPv4+4 nodes is achieved as follows: Assume node X in realm A wishes to send a packet to node Y in realm B (refer to Figure 1). The source IPv4+4 address will be A.X and the destination IPv4+4 address will be B.Y[1].

Figure 3(a) shows the address fields in IPv4+4 header as the packet moves from X to Y. When the packet leaves X, IPv4 source address (SA1), contains X's private IPv4 address, and the destination IPv4 address (DA1) contains the public IPv4 address of realm B, where Y is located. IPv4+4 extended source address (SA2) contains the public IPv4 address of realm A, where X is located, and IPv4+4 extended destination address (DA2) contains the private IPv4 address of Y. IPv4 routers in realm A (if any) will look at the IPv4 header, and simply forward the packet up the realm gateway A. The realm gateway is an integral part of the IPv4+4 architecture and has the job of swapping SA1 and SA2 for outgoing packets [5]. Thus after the packet moves past realm gateway A, SA1=A and SA2=X. DA1 and DA2 are untouched. Notice that for all routers in the public Internet, which look at the IPv4 header, this is a packet coming from realm gateway A and going to realm gateway B. Using regular IPv4 forwarding the packet will be delivered to B. The realm gateway B is responsible for swapping DA1 and DA2 for incoming packets [5]. SA1 and SA2 are untouched. After the

[1] How X learns Y's IPv4+4 address is beyond the scope of this paper. In [5] authors suggest augmenting the DNS architecture for this purpose. Interested reader may refer to that paper.

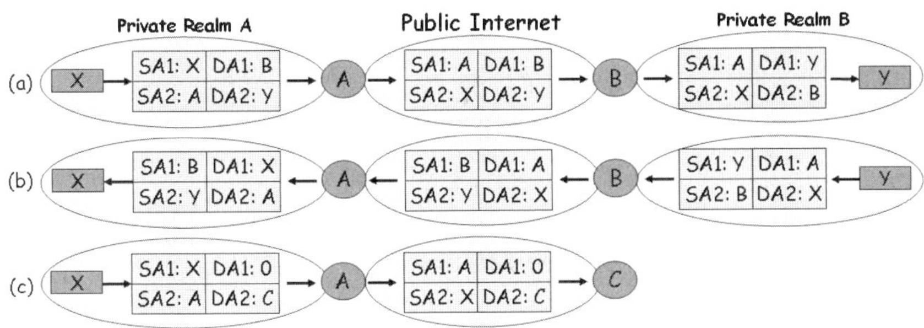

Fig. 3. Packet forwarding in the IPv4+4 architecture: (a) Packet transmission from X to Y, (b) Packet transmission from Y to X, (c) Packet transmission from X to C

packet moves past B, DA1=Y and DA2=B. Thus IPv4 routers in realm B (if any) will correctly deliver the packet to Y.

Figure 3(b) shows the packet flow in the reverse direction, from Y to X. Notice that similar translations occur as the packet moves past the realm gateways. Finally, Figure 3(c) shows a packet transmission to a host with a globally unique IPv4 address. Notice that the public IPv4+4 part of such hosts are set to 0, and the packet is delivered by regular IPv4 forwarding.

3.3 Deployment Requirements and Implementation Details

Deployment of and transition to IPv4+4 requires a stepwise upgrade of NATs and hosts. The first step in a site's transition starts with an upgrade of the NAT device to a IPv4+4 realm gateway. Recall from the previous section that a realm gateway is an integral part of the IPv4+4 architecture, and is responsible for the following tasks: (1) the swapping of addresses in IPv4+4 header, (2) the conversion of ICMPv4 message headers, (3) the participation in routing and filtering of private addresses [5]. So without an upgrade of the NAT to a realm gateway, no host inside a private realm can communicate with an external IPv4+4 host. After the NAT is upgraded with the realm gateway functionality, hosts inside the private realm can start upgrading to IPv4+4.

To program on top of IPv4+4, a new socket API with the new address space can be defined similar to IPv6 socket API. But in [5], authors report how the regular IPv4 sockets API can be used by the bump-in-the stack method [19]. That is, they use the address block 1.0.0.0/8 and assign an IPv4 address from within this range to each IPv4+4 address that the host has communication with. From the application's perspective the application is talking to an IPv4 host, but the translation layer changes between the IPv4 address and the IPv4+4 address. Regardless, using IPv4+4 at a host still requires changes to the host's protocol stack.

Although IPv4+4 header is backward compatible to IPv4, which allows legacy IPv4 routers forward IPv4+4 packets without any changes, transition to IPv4+4 still requires the upgrade of all end hosts and private realm border gateways, i.e., NAT devices. Given prevalent NAT device deployment without IPv4+4 support, it is unrealistic to expect customers to throw away their NAT devices and start buying IPv4+4-compliant border gateways. Additionally, upgrade of all end hosts to IPv4+4 is a daunting task in itself.

4 A Modified Loose Source Record Route (LSRR)-Based Implementation of the IPv4+4 Addressing Architecture

IPv4+4 addressing architecture is a very neat idea. But implementing IPv4+4 by defining a new protocol and header structure, and requiring the upgrade of realm gateways and end-hosts to the new protocol is a serious limiting factor for the transition. What we need is a way to implement IPv4+4 with minimal changes to the existing network components. In this section we show how this can be done with the IPv4 Loose Source Record Route (LSRR) option. We first detail how LSRR works, and then show how a modified version of LSRR can be used to implement IPv4+4. Finally in section 5, we put everything together with a demonstration of the proposed usage of IPv4+4 addressing in the famous voice over IP protocol, the Session Initiation Protocol.

4.1 IPv4 Loose Source Record Route (LSRR) Option

IPv4 Loose Source Record Route (LSRR) option has been defined in RFC 791 [13]. LSRR allows the sender of an IPv4 packet to specify a list of nodes (IPv4 routers) that the packet must pass through on its way to the destination, and to record the route information. Although this type of explicit source-based routing information is not necessary for the correct forwarding of the packet, the following benefits are listed in [14]: (1) To potentially specify a shorter path by the source, (2) To avoid certain networks for performance or security reasons, (3) To test and monitor certain IPv4 routers.

LSRR is implemented as an option included in the IPv4 header, and specifies a list of IPv4 addresses where the packet must make stops on its way to the destination. The destination address of the initial packet contains the IPv4 address of the first hop node. At each stop, the address pointed to by the option pointer is taken from the list and placed in the destination address field, and that element of the list is replaced by the IPv4 address of that stop [14].

Figure 4 shows an example packet flow using the LSRR option: X wishes to send a packet to Y, but wants the packet to make stops at B and C before arriving at Y. This is achieved by specifying a source route by the LSRR option as follows: When the packet leaves X, the IPv4 source address (SA) is set to X's IPv4 address and the destination IPv4 address (DA) is set to the next hop node B's IPv4 address. X also specifies the path that the packet should follow in the network after stopping at B. The LSRR option indicates that the packet needs to go to C and then to Y. LSSR option pointer (specified in parenthesis) indicates where the packet should be sent at the next hop B. At the beginning this is set

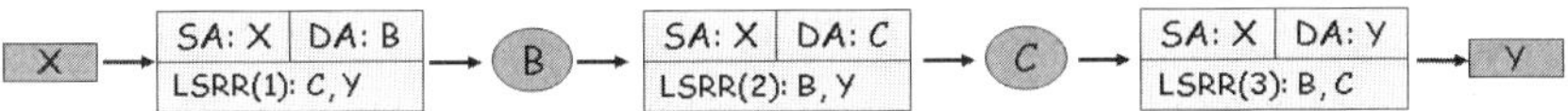

Fig. 4. Packet Transmission with IPv4 Loose Source Record Route (LSRR) option: X sends a packet to Y. The packet makes stops at B and C before arriving at Y.

to 1[2], meaning that the next hop after B is the first IPv4 address on the list, i.e., C. Since DA=B, the packet will be delivered to B. When B receives the packet, it looks at the LSRR option and realizes that the option is not exhausted yet. So it swaps DA, i.e., B, with the IPv4 address indicated by the LSSR pointer, i.e., C. B also increments the LSRR pointer to point to the next IPv4 address on the list. Notice that SA is not changed. The new packet with SA=X and DA=C will be delivered to C. C also notices that the LSRR option is not exhausted, so it performs LSRR processing similar to B: C swaps the DA with the IPv4 address pointed to by LSRR, increments the LSRR pointer, and forwards the packet onwards. The new packet has SA=X and DA=Y, and will be delivered to Y. Y realizes that LSRR processing is done and that it is the last stop on the source route. Y also learns the route back to X from the LSRR values, which contains the path in the reverse direction.

4.2 Modified LSRR to Implement IPv4+4 Addressing Architecture

In this section we show how a modified version of the IPv4 LSRR can be used to implement IPv4+4 addressing architecture. As discussed in section 2, the implementation of IPv4+4 given in [5] requires a lot of changes to the network infrastructure and is not feasible. To start using IPv4+4 addresses, a transition strategy that requires minimal or no changes to the IPv4 infrastructure is needed.

Consider the network in figure 1, and assume that X with IPv4+4 address A.X wishes to send a packet to Y with IPv4+4 address B.Y (We will demonstrate how X learns its and Y's IPv4+4 address in the context of voice over IP (VoIP) in section 5). Figure 5(a) depicts the packet flow with LSRR: X sends out a packet with IPv4 source address SA=X, and IPv4 destination address DA=A. X also specifies in LSRR that A must forward the packet to B, which must forward the packet to Y, the packet's final destination. When A receives the packet, it puts the address pointed to by LSRR pointer, the first address, into the destination address of the packet and records its own IPv4 address in the LSRR address list. So when the packet leaves A, SA=X and DA=B. When the packet is delivered to B, B performs a similar LSRR processing. Thus after the packet leaves B, SA=X and DA=Y with LSRR list containing A and B. When Y receives the packet it can realize that the packet is coming from A.X, and if a packet needs to be send back it can follow the reverse LSRR path.

[2] In a real IPv4 implementation this pointer contains the byte offset of the next IPv4 address on the list from the beginning of the LSRR option, and would initially be equal to 4. At each stop it will be incremented by 4.

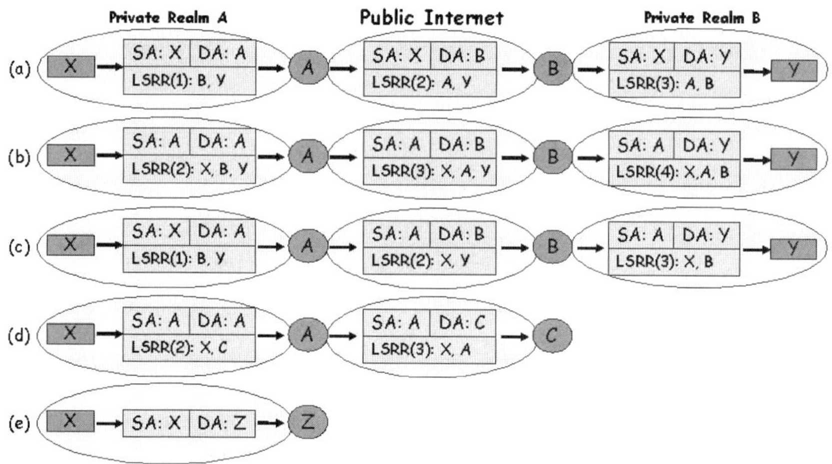

Fig. 5. Using modified LSRR to implement IPv4+4: (a) Packet transmission from X to Y with pure LSRR, (b) Packet transmission from X to Y with modified LSRR, (c) Packet transmission from X to Y where the realm gateway performs special LSRR processing, (d) Packet transmission from X to C, (e) Packet transmission between two hosts, X and Z, in the same private realm (refer to Figure 1)

The above method almost works with one flaw: Notice that due to the nature of LSRR processing, the source IPv4 address is not changed anywhere in the network. This means that when the packet leaves private realm router A and is in the public Internet its SA=X, which is a private IPv4 address. According to RFC 1918 [15], realm routers must perform packet filtering and no packet having a private source or destination address should be sent out to the public Internet. It is also well known that most ISPs perform ingress filtering for incoming packets [12]. So even if A is made to send out the packet with a private source address, the packet is most likely to be dropped by the first ISP router.

For the proposed method to work, all packets leaving private realm A must have a source IPv4 address equal to A. There are two ways to achieve this: (1) The packet leaves the sending host with SA=A, (2) The realm gateway performs special treatment to outgoing packets with the LSRR option. It changes not only the destination address but also the source address before the packet is sent out to the public Internet.

Figure 5(b) illustrates method (1): X sends out a packet with SA=A, DA=A, LSRR(2)=X, B, Y. The LSRR pointer points to the second address, B. In a sense this looks like a packet that has originated from A with SA=A, DA=X, LSRR(1)= A, B, Y, and X just performed regular LSRR processing on the packet changing the packet headers to SA=A, DA=A, LSRR(2)=X, B, Y. The packet now makes it to A, which makes DA=B and LSRR(3)=X, A, Y before sending out the packet to the public Internet. The packet will make one more stop at B, and be finally delivered to Y. With this method, no changes to realm gateways are required as long as they support LSRR processing. But the host must be able to send out packets with SA=A.

Figure 5(c) illustrates method (2): X sends out a packet with SA=X, DA=A, LSRR(1)=B, Y. When A receives this packet, it performs special treatment instead of regular LSRR processing: A moves the first address in LSRR list, B, to DA, puts the source address, X, in its place in LSRR list, and sets SA=A for the outgoing packet. So the outgoing packet will have SA=A, DA=B and LSRR(2)=X, Y. The rest of the packet delivery involves regular LSRR processing by B and Y. Although this method is ideal, it requires all existing border routers to be upgraded, and therefore it is not feasible at this time.

Figure 5(d) shows X talking to C, which has a globally routable address. As illustrated, this communication is very similar to X talking to Y. Instead less addresses need to be put into LSRR list.

Finally, figure 5(e) shows X talking to Z, which is on the same private network. Clearly the hosts can communicate over standard IPv4 without the need for source based routing.

5 Seamless P2P Communication with the Session Initiation Protocol Using IPv4+4 Addresses

The Session Initiation Protocol (SIP) [20] is the emerging Voice over IP (VoIP) signaling protocol. It is used to establish, change and terminate multimedia sessions between two or more peers on an IP network. In this section our goal is to demonstrate how P2P communication would work for voice transmission between two IPv4+4 addressed nodes. We assume that the existing realm gateways, i.e., the NAT boxes on the private realm borders, support the IPv4 LSRR option.

Consider the network shown in Figure 1. Assume that Alice logged in X and Bob logged in Y are two SIP users located behind NAT boxes. They only know about their private IPv4 address, X and Y respectively, and the public IPv4 address of the SIP server, S. Assume that they are not even aware of the public IPv4 addresses of their realm gateways. The first thing that a SIP client performs during startup is to register its current location with the SIP server. In Alice's case, she would send a registration request similar to the following (we only show the relevant fields of the SIP message. SIP message examples are taken from [22]):

```
REGISTER sip:X SIP/2.0
From: sip:alice@X
To: sip:alice@X
Contact: sip:alice@X
```

The registration packet is usually sent over UDP and would have <SA=X, DA=S>. Notice that this packet would be subject to NAT processing at the border gateway A, and have its source address changed. So the packet would have <SA=A, SA=S> on the public Internet. When S receives the registration request, it realizes that Alice is logged into a machine with private IPv4 address X (induced from Contact: sip:alice@X) located behind the NAT box A (induced from SA of the packet). With our proposal, the SIP server S would send the following reply back:

```
SIP/2.0 200 OK
From: sip: alice@X
To: sip: alice@X
Contact: sip: alice@A.X
```

Notice that Contact: header in the reply contains the full 64-bit IPv4+4 address A.X of node X. Thus Alice would learn that she is behind a NAT box with global IPv4 address A. Bob would go through a similar registration procedure and learn that he is behind a NAT box with global IPv4 address B. That is, Bob's IPv4+4 address is B.Y. The SIP server S also learns both Alice and Bob's IPv4+4 contact addresses as A.X and B.Y.

When Alice wishes to establish a VoIP session with Bob, she would send an Invite request via S. With our proposal, Alice would specify her IPv4+4 address for media exchange instead of her private IPv4 address. A sample Invite message with IPv4+4 address is shown below:

```
INVITE sip:bob SIP/2.0.
From: sip:alice
To: sip:bob
Content-Type: application/sdp

v=0
o=alice 2890844526 2890844526 IN IP4+4 A.X
s=-
c=IN IP4+4 A.X
t=0 0
m=audio 49172 RTP/AVP 0
a=rtpmap:0 PCMU/8000
```

Notice that Alice puts her IPv4+4 address A.X within the media session description by SDP [21]. Specifically, Alice indicates that she expects the media in PCM format sent to IPv4+4 address A.X:49172.

When Bob receives the invitation request, he would reply with a message similar to the following, where Bob specifies his IPv4+4 address B.Y:3456 for media exchange:

```
SIP/2.0 200 OK
From: sip:alice
To: sip:bob
Contact: sip:bob@A.Y
Content-Type: application/sdp
```

```
v=0
o=bob 2890844527 2890844527 IN IP4+4 B.Y
s=-
c=IN IP4+4 B.Y
t=0 0
m=audio 3456 RTP/AVP 0
a=rtpmap:0 PCMU/8000
```

Alice would finally send an ACK message, and the session would be established. The media exchange is now P2P between A.X:49172 and B.Y:3456, and can be achieved by IPv4 LSRR as described in section 4.2.

It is important to note that IPv4+4 addresses would be used only if the user is logged into a host behind a NAT box. If Alice were to login at a host with a globally routable IPv4 address, e.g., node C in figure 1, she would register the contact address sip:alice@C. The SIP server S would realize that Alice's host is not behind a NAT box, and so further communication with Alice would use IPv4 address C, and not an IPv4+4 address. Thus IPv4+4 addresses would only be needed for hosts behind NAT boxes.

6 Concluding Remarks

With the current NAT-based IPv4 Internet architecture nodes behind NAT boxes do not have globally unique end-to-end addresses. This creates problems for P2P applications, where the communication needs to be started from outside of the NAT box. To solve this global identification problem, IPv4+4 addressing architecture has been proposed, which suggests concatenating the global IPv4 address of the border gateway, i.e., the NAT box, with the private IPv4 address of an internal node to create a 64-bit globally unique network-layer address. With nodes on private realms having such 64-bit globally unique identifiers, the question arises as to how packet exchange will work in this addressing architecture. Although authors present one implementation method in [5], it requires changes to all end-hosts and border routers, and this is not feasible.

In this paper we presented a modified IPv4 loose source record route (LSRR)-based implementation of IPv4+4. Our proposal requires no changes to hosts, IPv4 routers or the border gateways, i.e., the NAT boxes, and enables seamless end-to-end P2P communication so long as all IPv4-compliant nodes implement the IPv4 LSRR option correctly, as required by RFC 791 [13].

Assuming proper LSRR support from the current NAT-boxes, we demonstrated how P2P would work in the context of VoIP with the SIP protocol. We are in the process of testing if the currently deployed NAT boxes implement the LSRR option correctly, if at all. If they do support the LSRR option, we believe that a LSRR-based IPv4+4 addressing is the way to go in the evolution to the next generation Internet.

References

1. Tsirtsis, G., Srisuresh, P.: Network address translation - protocol translation (NAT-PT). RFC 2766 (2000)
2. Srisuresh, P., Holdrege, M.: IP Network Address Translator (NAT) Terminology and Considerations. RFC 2663 (1999)
3. Deering, S., Hinden, R.: Internet Protocol, Version 6 (IPv6) Specification. RFC 2460 (1996)
4. Turanyi, Z., Valko, A.: IPv4+4. In: 10th International Conference on Networking Protocols (ICNP 2002) (2002)
5. Turanyi, Z., Valko, A., Campbell, A.: Design, Implementation and Evaluation of IPv4+4. In: ACM SIGCOMM, Stanford, CA, pp. 314–329. ACM Press, New York (1988)
6. Francis, P., Gummadi, R.: IPNL: A NAT-Extended Internet Architecture. In: ACM SIGCOMM. ACM Press, New York (2001)
7. Cheriton, D., Gritter, M.: TRIAD: A Scalable Deployable NAT-based Internet Architecture. Technical Report (2000)
8. Rosenber, J., Weinberger, J., Huitema, C., Mahy, R.: STUN: - simple traversal of user datagram protocol (UDP) through network address translators (NATs). RFC 3489 (2003)
9. Guha, S., Takeday, Y., Francis, P.: Simple Traversal of UDP through NATs and TCP too (STUNT) `http://nutss.gforce.cis.cornell.edu/`
10. Guha, S., Takeda, Y., Francis, P.: NUTSS: A SIP-based Approach to UDP and TCP Network Connectivity. In: SIGCOMM Workshops, Portland, OR (2004)
11. Biggadike, A., Ferullo, D., Wilson, G., Perrig, A.: NATBLASTER: Establishing TCP connections between hosts behind NATs. In: ACM SIGCOMM Asia Workshop, Beijing, China (2005)
12. Ferguson, P., Senie, D.: Network Ingress Filtering: Defeating Denial of Service Attacks which employ IP Source Address Spoofing. RFC 2827 (2000)
13. Postel, J.: Internet Protocol Darpa Internet Program Protocol Specification. RFC 791 (1981)
14. Postel, J., Reynolds, J.: Comments on the IP Source Route Option, `http://www.mirrorservice.org/sites/ftp.isi.edu/in-notes/museum/ip-source-route-comments.txt`
15. Rekhter, Y., Moskowitz, B., Karrenberg, D., de Groot, G., Lear, E.: Address Allocation for Private Internets. RFC 1918 (1996)
16. User Datagram Protocol: RFC 768 (1980)
17. Transmission Control Protocol: RFC 793 (1981)
18. Stream Control Transmission Protocol: RFC 2960 (2000)
19. Tsuchiya, K., Higuchi, H., Atarashi, Y.: Dual Stack Hosts using the Bump-in-the-Stack Technique (BIS). RFC 2767 (2000)
20. Rosenberg, J., Schulzrinne, H., Camarillo, G., Johnston, A., Peterson, J., Sparks, R., Handley, M., Schooler, E.: SIP: Session Initiation Protocol. RFC 3261 (2002)
21. Handley, M., Jacobson, V.: SDP: Session Description Protocol. RFC 2327 (2004)
22. Johnston, A., Donovan, S., Sparks, R., Cunningham, C., Summers, K.: Session Initiation Protocol (SIP) Basic Call Flow Examples. RFC 3665 (2003)

Dynamic Handover Mechanism Using Mobile SCTP in Contention Based Wireless Network

Lin-Huang Chang [1,2], Huan-Jie Lin [2], and Ing-chau Chang [3]

[1] Department of Computer and Information Science
National Taichung Univ., Taichung, Taiwan, R.O.C.
albertchang04@gmail.com

[2] Graduate Institute of Networking and Communication Engineering
Chaoyang Univ. of Technology, Taichung, Taiwan, R.O.C.
{lchang,s9330613}@cyut.edu.tw

[3] Department of Computer Science and Information Eng.
National Chunghua Univ. of Education, Chunghua, Taiwan, R.O.C.
icchang@cc.ncue.edu.tw

Abstract. Mobile SCTP (mSCTP) has been proposed to support transport layer mobility management. In this paper, we proposed a dynamic handover mechanism named Contention-based mSCTP (C-mSCTP) in the contention based wireless network. The handover strategy in C-mSCTP takes wireless bandwidth and the contention probability into account to set the primary path before transmitting data. The simulation results show that the C-mSCTP achieves much better performance in terms of transmission delay and throughput than mSCTP does.

1 Introduction

A number of mobility management schemes have been proposed in the literature using different networking layers. Mobile IP (MIP) [8], a proposed standard of the Internet Engineering Task Force (IETF), is a network layer solution to support mobility based on IP. Mobility management at the network layer requires the support of network agents/routers for tunneling between routers which makes the mobility enabled network layer "circuit switched". This involves overhead and inefficiency due to triangle routing and/or tunneling as well as security related complexities.

The Scream Control Transmission Protocol (SCTP), proposed by IETF Signaling Transport (SIGTRAN) working group in October 2000 [1] to accomplish signaling transport over IP networks, may overcome the problem of session interruption. SCTP is a new reliable transport protocol which joins Transmission Control Protocol (TCP) and User Datagram Protocol (UDP) as a general propose end-to-end protocol above the IP layer. One of the prominent features of SCTP is multi-homing which allows two end-points to set up an association with multiple IP addresses or via multiple network interface cards for each endpoint. That means it supports the switchovers of different IP addresses at one endpoint without interrupting any ongoing data transfer. So, the session continuity issue could be solved. The multi-homing feature of SCTP, therefore, is believed to be a suitable candidate for transport layer mobility management.

I. Stojmenovic et al. (Eds.): ISPA 2007, LNCS 4742, pp. 821–831, 2007.

On top of SCTP multi-homing feature, an extension called mobile SCTP (mSCTP) has been proposed to provide seamless handover for Mobile Nodes (MNs) roaming into different IP network domain during the active session [5-6]. The mSCTP utilizes ADD_IP, DELETE_IP and Set-PRIMARY extensions [7] to dynamically add or delete IP addresses to and from end points, and to replace the primary path from the exsiting association. Differently from the MIP or SIP based handover schemes, the mSCTP provides the handover management at the transport layer without help of routers.

The mSCTP therefore can be employed to the seamless handover of sessions that are triggered by MNs by selecting the primary path. However, the handover strategies in mSCTP are mostly based on the signal strength of Base Stations (BSs). It results in aggregation of MNs on one BS with strongest signal in the same signal overlapped area. In this case, the transmission probability will decrease in the contention based wireless network.

In this paper, we proposed a dynamic handover mechanism using mSCTP in contention based wireless network, named C-mSCTP. The handover strategy in C-mSCTP takes wireless bandwidth and the probability of acquiring the contention into account to set the primary path before transmit data. The detailed design and advantages of using C-mSCTP instead of mSCTP will be described in this paper.

The rest of this paper is organized as follows. Section 2 describes the related works regarding mSCTP. The proposed scheme, dynamic handover mechanism using C-mSCTP, is illustrated in detail in Section 3. Section 4 provides the performance analyses of C-mSCTP based on the simulation results. We summarize this paper and show some future works in Section 5.

2 Related Works

Mobility management issues have been discussed a lot due to the popularity of the wireless access networks and devices. In this paper, we focus on the transport layer mobility management. We will review mSCTP mechanism first and then address some related researches using mSCTP for transport layer mobility management.

The configuration of a specific strategy for switching the primary path actually is a challenge to the mSCTP. The decision to handover to the new primary path should be made carefully to maintain best transmission characteristics. One of the more preferred rules to trigger the primary path change, discussed in [5], is detection and comparison of signal strength from underlying layer.

S. J. Koh and etc. [19] [20] proposed a scheme using mSCTP for supporting soft handover in the transport layer. They conducted experiments on triggering rules for ADD_IP and PRIMARY_CHANGE during handover and found that the aggressive ADD_IP and conservative PRIMARY_CHANGE rules provided better throughput. In this case, different setting of thresholds was required in different wireless networks. And, the signal strength was the only consideration to make decision in handovers.

In order to determine when to add or delete end-point IP addresses of MN and how to change primary path when handover happens, M. J. Chang and etc. [21] proposed Address Management Module (AMM), which was based on mSCTP and utilized the link layer radio signal strength information, to improve handover latency. They also proposed error and congestion control enhancement to cope with handover efficiently. However, this scheme was still based on signal strength only.

In mSCTP mechanism, if the signal strength of the primary path is too low to transmit data, it will switch to a new path in the Association IP list. From the past related literatures, most research groups focused on the best signal strength and/or found better signal thresholds for path switching. Some researchers considered the path switch with transmission delay time. However, their designs were under static network and the possible long delay, responded from CN, in wireless network will lead the mobility issues unsatisfactory.

On the other hand, the contention condition, which affects the probability for an MN to acquire resources from BS, did not receive much attention before. Therefore, in this paper, we take into account the transmission bandwidth via the detection of the signal strength and the contention probability for an MN requesting for a BS in the contention based wireless network. Furthermore, by using heartbeat messages to detect all paths for the knowledge of the switching criteria periodically, the handover decision will be made to the best selection dynamically. The details of the design and calculation of the evaluation value for path switching will be illustrated in the next section.

3 Proposed Scheme

The MN requests BSs to contend resources in the contention based wireless network before transmit data. Based on the wireless resources and the probability of acquiring the contention, we proposed a dynamic handover mechanism using estimation values. We calculated the estimation values of different wireless transmission paths. When the highest estimation value is over a defined range the handover is triggered. The handover is deferred for a buffer range to avoid the oscillation behavior or ping-pong effect due to frequent handovers. The details of our design are described in the following.

The MN can register to different BSs to get IP addresses and manage them using mSCTP in the signal overlapped wireless network. In our design, the mSCTP IP management will lead the MN to handover to a new transmission path which provides the best throughput. Fig. 1 illustrates the scenario of dynamic handover mechanism using mSCTP in our design. When MN1 is at location (a) in Fig. 1, it will register to BS1 upon receiving the beacon sent by BS1. The MN1 will set the primary transmission path to BS1 after acquiring the IP address from it with successful registration. At this moment, MN1 can communicate with CN through BS1. In the design of mSCTP, the heartbeat messages are sent to transmission backup paths periodically to keep them alive. The heartbeat messages are not delivered to the primary path because its condition is detected during ordinary data transmission. However in dynamic handover mechanism of our design the heartbeat messages are sent to all paths periodically to calculate the estimation values for all paths.

When MN1 moves to location (b) in Fig. 1, it registers to BS2 upon receiving its beacon. While acquiring the new IP address from BS2, MN1 will add it to the association IP list. The MN1 can handover to another BS to get better transmission performance when it is located within signal overlapped area, such as location (b), (c) and (d) in Fig. 1. In most mSCTP handover strategies, the MN sets its primary transmission path according to the strongest signal strength of BSs. In our proposed scheme with dynamic handover strategy, the handover decision is made by the estimation values which are based on the wireless bandwidth via detection of the signal strength and probability of acquiring the contention. The detailed calculation of the estimation value is described in next sub-section. When MN1 moves to location (e) in Fig. 1 which is outside the signal coverage of BS1, it deletes IP address assigned by BS1 and stops sending heartbeat message to BS1 according to the mSCTP handover strategy. The dynamic handover strategy in this paper, however, keeps this IP address on the list for another heartbeat message sending interval. The MN will delete the IP address after detecting no heartbeat message response for two heartbeat sending intervals. This design can avoid additional registration and deletion overhead due to the oscillation behavior around the signal coverage border.

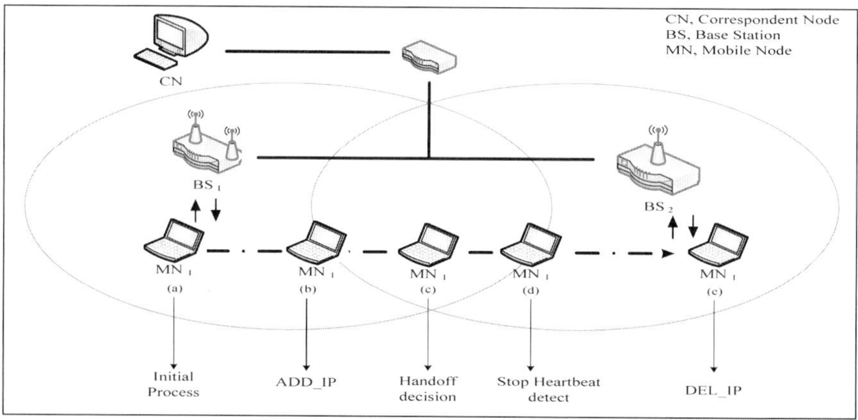

Fig. 1. The Scenario of Dynamic Handover Mechanism using mSCTP

For wireless network using contention mode, such as Institute of Electrical and Electronics Engineers (IEEE) 802.11b [23] transmission technology, all MNs wait a Distributed Coordination Function Inter-frame Space (DIFS) period and send requests to BS to contend for bandwidth resource before transmit data messages. In the contention window, if the request message of an MN collides with the other one, it starts the backoff process. If a BS provides service to many MNs, all MNs will contend and share for the bandwidth resource of the BS. In average, an MN acquires more shared resource of a BS in the condition of sparse users than dense users. For the signal strength based handover strategy, an MN handovers to a BS with strongest strength. This may lead to heavy contention for the bandwidth resource of BS with strongest strength. On the other hand, if the handover mechanism is based on the number of registered MNs in BS list, some registered MNs with no intention to send data will lead to the wrong decision in handover.

In this paper we take into account the transmission contention probability as well as wireless access bandwidth to trigger the handover. The wireless access bandwidth is decided from the detection of the signal strength of the underlying layer. The evaluation of contention probability is calculated by sending out the heartbeat message from the MN to BSs periodically to accomplish contention-based dynamic handover using mSCTP. The transmission probability proposed in our dynamic handover mechanism is calculated according to the successful rate of probing heartbeat messages in steady state under contention service. It increases the process and resource overhead and the estimation is not consistent and periodic if the detention is carried out from every transmitted data. The probability calculation in steady state, which will be discussed in more detail shortly, provides stable estimation within an interval.

The transmission probability is the successful contention rate for an MN intending to send a heartbeat message to a BS. The contention result can be success (S) or failure (F). It can be expressed in a space vector V={S, F}. When it is failed, mostly due to the collision with other transmitted messages, the backoff process is initiated. Each failed contention will hold the MN a random period of time, called backoff window. For an MN requesting for contention after backoff process, the request can be expressed in a random experiment set {1, 2, 3,.....}. The successful or failed probability can be obtained from random frequency and state space vector in each round. The stable transmission probability is calculated according to Transition Probability Process in the Markov Chain [24].

The research from Zorzi's group [25] employed one-step Markov process whose transition probabilities are a function of the channel characteristics to represent binary channel transition characteristics on a Gilbert Channel [31]. Gilbert Channel is commonly used to model symbol-error bursts. They presented the throughput performance of the Go-Back-N and selective-repeat automatic repeat request (ARQ) protocols with timer control, using the Markov process model for both forward and feedback channels. The transition model of Gilbert Channel is shown in Fig. 2. As shown in Fig. 2, the S state is the successful transmission state and the F state is the failed transmission state in the channel. The state transition probability from state F to next state S is defined as P_s. The state transition probability to stay in state F will be 1-P_s. Similarly, the state transition probability from state S to state F and keeping in the same S state will be P_f and 1-P_f, respectively.

From Fig. 2, the transition model of Gilbert Channel can be described by transition probability matrix, P_{trans}, as shown in the following equation,

$$P_{trans} = \begin{bmatrix} P_s & 1-P_f \\ 1-P_s & P_f \end{bmatrix} \tag{1}$$

In steady state, the sum of successful transmission probability, P_s, and failed transmission probability, P_f, equals to one. Therefore, 1-P_s is the transition probability from state S to state F and 1-P_f is the transition probability from state F to state S.

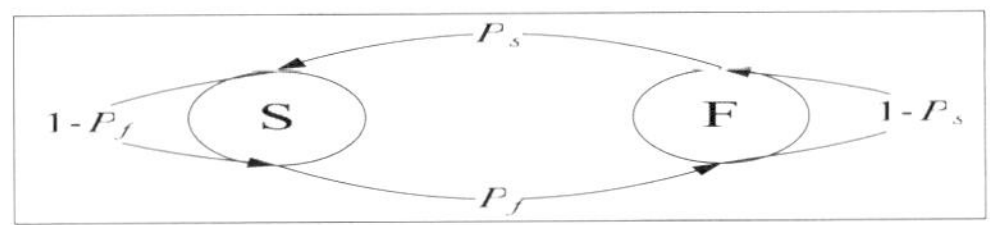

Fig. 2. Transition Model of Gilbert Channel

In this research, the collision or failure of contention message will move the state into state F in the state diagram. The success of contention message on the other hand will move the state into state S. The binary channel characteristics of Gilbert Channel can denote the contention states of the requested messages. The heartbeat message with periodic detection function in dynamic handover mechanism is applied to the calculation of transition probability factors. Therefore, the transition probabilities for successful and failed contention are denoted as P_{cs} and P_{cf}, respectively.

According to Stochastic Processes in Markov Chain [27], and the characteristic of Mean Square Convergence, the probability transition model can be described in matrix from equation (1).The dynamic handover mechanism is designed to calculate the contention probability in steady state within the heartbeat interval. This will avoid the sampling overhead and frequent calculation. Therefore, we calculate the limit state and probability matrix using iteration to obtain the transition probability in steady state. The Mean Square Convergence, called Contention-based Iteration Gilbert Convergence (CIGC) in this research, in steady state can be expressed as following equation,

$$[S', F']_{CIGC} = [a, \quad b] \cdot \begin{bmatrix} P_{cs}, & 1-P_{cf} \\ 1-P_{cs}, & P_{cf} \end{bmatrix} \tag{2}$$

where S' is the transition probability of successful contention and F' is the transition probability of failed contention in steady state. The $[a, b]$ is the limit value for a given random positive number. Since the sum of total probability is 1, the result of iteration calculation will be the same by using either [0, 1] or [1, 0] factor. That means we can choose any one of factors, [0, 1] or [1, 0], to simplify our calculation. The calculation result of $[S',F']_{CIGC}$ is a measure of contention cost for an MN to choose a BS.

For an MN to choose a BS as the primary path, the measure of contention cost should not be the only consideration. Combining the available transmission bandwidth with the contention cost, therefore, will provide an optimized estimation for an MN to select a best transmission path in the contention based wireless network. We defined the estimation value of the optimized path as contention-based estimate value (CEV), as shown in the following equation,

$$CEV = S' \times \frac{R}{Max(R)} \tag{3}$$

where R is the transmission rate of the MN corresponding to the selected BS and $Max(R)$ is the maximum transmission rate the MN can achieve. Again, S' is the successful contention probability from the calculation of $[S',F']_{CIGC}$ in steady state. From the iteration and calculation result, the BS with highest CEV value is believed to provide the optimized path selection for an MN to achieve best transmission performance in terms of transmission delay and throughput.

In summary of our proposed dynamic handover mechanism, the success or failure for an MN to contend for the wireless resource can be expressed using Gilbert Channel. Therefore, the successful and failed contention probability can be calculated from the Markov Chain state transition model. By using two-dimension Mean Square Convergence, the contention cost for an MN to choose a BS in steady state is obtained after iteration. Further, combining the transmission rate with the successful probability, the estimation value for an MN choosing a BS as the primary path is defined and expected to optimize the transmission performance.

The design of the dynamic handover mechanism is based on the contention probability and available transmission bandwidth. It does not need to change any communication protocol or scheme which makes it easy to be deployed on a large scale.

4 Performance Analyses

The experiments were conducted using Network Simulation Version 2 (NS-2)-2.28 [29] in Linux Fedora core 2 operating system. We modified NS-2 SCTP 3.5 module [30] to conform to our proposed dynamic handover scheme. The network topology of the simulation is shown in Fig. 3 which covers an 800 * 800 meter range. In Fig. 3, there are three BSs (BS1, BS2 and BS3) which comprising a basic service set (BSS). The MNs are randomly distributed in the BSS with all kinds of movement models randomly. The network traffics are generated using constant bit rate (CBR) to calculate the throughput between MN1 and CN. The simulation time is 210 seconds. The simulation will be carried out for both original mSCTP and our proposed C-mSCTP.

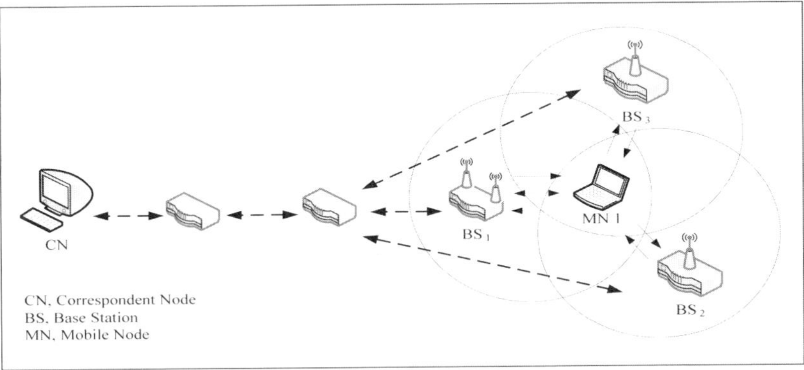

Fig. 3. Network simulation topology

To observe the throughput performance for C-mSCTP and mSCTP handover schemes, the MN1 sent out the SCTP DATA chunks in 1468 Bytes size with 30 seconds heartbeat interval for two different protocols. We applied Random Loss Error Module in the simulation environment. The throughput performance, shown in Fig. 4, is calculated based on the transmission sequence number (TSN) that CN received. In Fig. 4, the X axis stands for the simulation time in second and the Y axis represents TSN. The original mSCTP handover strategy is based on signal strength in the Distributed Coordination Function (DCF) mode. It does not consider the contention situation in the network domain. From the simulation result shown in Fig. 4, the CN received TSN about 51000 bytes with the mSCTP scheme. On the other hand, the proposed C-mSCTP scheme based on the contention probability and transmission bandwidth in the network domain will handover to a BS which provides better performance in throughput. The simulation result in Fig. 4 conforms to the deduction with TSN about 85000 bytes. More than 60% improvement in throughput was achieved by using C-mSCTP instead of mSCTP.

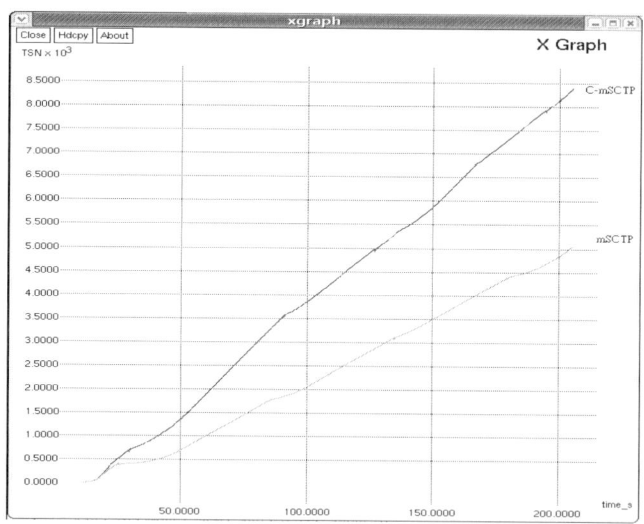

Fig. 4. Comparison of throughput between C-mSCTP and mSCTP

The total number of MNs in a BS will affect the individual and overall network traffics of the MN and BS in the domain, respectively. The more the MNs handover to the same BS, the more service overheads the BS need to provide and the less resource one MN will acquire in average. In this simulation scenario, we set different numbers of MNs in each round and observed the throughput (bytes) that CN received from MN1 with 210 seconds simulation duration. The MNs' mobility is set to be Random Mode in each round of experiments. However, the MN1 was set to be static since this experiment did not concern the handover issue of MN1 while roaming but rather measured the influence of path selection in the number of MNs in one BS. The simulation result is shown in Fig. 5.

The number of MNs in this experiment, varied from 11 to 20, comprises the X axis in Fig. 5. From the simulation result, the overall throughput decreases for both C-mSCTP and mSCTP when the number of MNs increases. It is due to the raise of processing overhead for the BS and the sharing of the network bandwidth with increase of MNs. In the same network domain, the number of MNs will affect the contention probability of MN1 to acquire access. However, the BS signal strength does not change with the number of MNs, therefore, it will not reflect the bandwidth request situation in the domain. The C-mSCTP mechanism taking into account the contention probability, which correlates with the number of MNs in the same domain, therefore provides better handover decision as compared with mSCTP scheme, shown in Fig. 5.

Furthermore, we conducted the experiments for the MN1 transmitting different sizes of files, varied from 10 MB to 50 MB, to CN using file transfer protocol (FTP). The transmission delay time for C-mSCTP and mSCTP schemes were obtained and compared in Fig. 6.

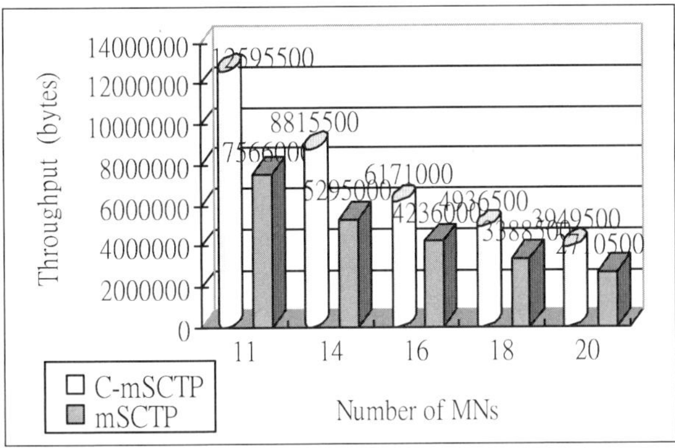

Fig. 5. Throughput of C-mSCTP and mSCTP with different numbers of MNs

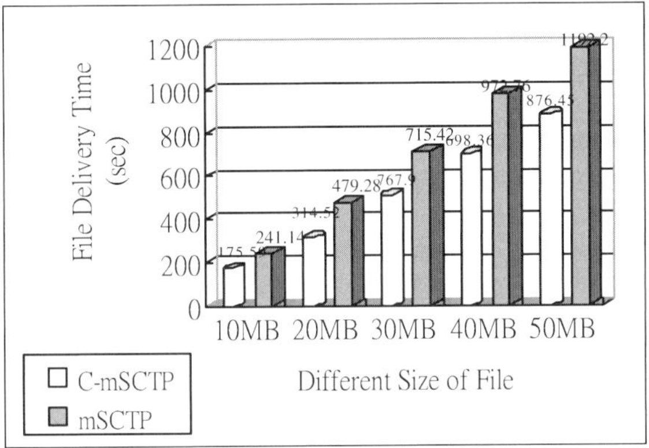

Fig. 6. File delivery time of C-mSCTP and mSCTP with different file sizes

In Fig. 6, the X axis stands for different file sizes, varied from 10, 20, 30, 40 to 50 MB and the Y axis represents the file delivery time in second. The simulation results showed that the C-mSCTP mechanism completed the file transmission with less delivery time than mSCTP scheme for each corresponding file size. Based on the highest estimation value in C-mSCTP, the MN1 selects a best transmission path dynamically for FTP session while maintaining the same session due to the characteristics of multi-homing. This avoids the unnecessary delay possibly due to the contention backoff. Therefore, the file delivery time in C-mSCTP mechanism is less than that in mSCTP scheme.

5 Conclusions

In this paper, we have proposed a dynamic handover mechanism called C-mSCTP to solve the unbalancing contention problem in mSCTP. By using Markov Chain state transition model and two-dimension Mean Square Convergence, the contention cost for an MN to choose a BS in steady state was obtained after iteration. Further, by combining the transmission rate with the successful contention probability, the contention-based estimate value (CEV) for an MN choosing a BS as the best path was defined.

From the simulation result, the BS with highest CEV value in C-mSCTP, compared with mSCTP based on signal strength handover strategy, provided the optimized path selection for an MN to achieve much better transmission performance in terms of transmission delay and throughput. More than 60% improvement in throughput was achieved by using C-mSCTP instead of mSCTP.

In the future, we will improve the dynamic handover mechanism in C-mSCTP by optimizing the heartbeat interval and providing the confidence interval to avoid ping-pong effect due to frequent handovers. Besides, we will extend the dynamic handover mechanism from contention-based to allocation-based wireless network. Also, since C-mSCTP does not change any communication protocol or scheme, it can be extended on a large scale.

Acknowledgements

This research is partially supported by the National Science Council of Republic of China, Taiwan under contracts, NSC 95-2221-E- 324-020 and NSC 95-2622-E-324-013-CC3.

References

1. Stewart, R.: Stream Control Transmission Protocol. IETF RFC 2960 (October 2000)
2. Stewart, R., Metz, C.: SCTP: New Transport Protocol for TCP/IP. IEEE Internet Computing 5, 64–69 (2001)
3. Fu, S., Atiquzzaman, M.: SCTP: State of The Art in Research, Products, and Technical Challenges. IEEE Communications Magazine 42, 64–76 (2004)
4. Postel, J.: Transmission Control Protocol. IETF RFC 793 (January 1980)
5. Koh, S.J., Xie, Q., Park, S.D.: Mobile SCTP (mSCTP) for IP Handover Support. IETF Draft, draft-sjkoh-msctp-01 (October 2005)
6. Riegel, M., Tuexen, M.: Mobile SCTP. IETF Draft, draft-riegel-tuexen-mobile-sctp-07 (October 2006)
7. Stewart, R., Xie, Q., Tuexen, M., Maruyama, S., Kozuka, M.: Stream Control Transmission Protocol (SCTP) Dynamic Address Reconfiguration. IETF Draft, draft-ietf-tsvwg-addip-sctp-17 (November 2006)
8. Perkins, C.: IP Mobility Support for IPv4. IETF RFC 3344 (August 2002)
9. Johnson, D., Perkins, C., Arkko, J.: Mobility Support in IPv6. IETF RFC 3775, (June 2004)
10. Koodli, R., Perkins, C.: Mobile IPv4 Fast Handovers. IETF Draft, draft-ietf-mip4-fmipv4-02 (October 2006)
11. Koodli, R.: Fast Handovers for Mobile IPv6 IETF RFC 4068 (July 2005)
12. Eastlake, D., Brunner-Williams, E., Manning, B.: Domain Name System (DNS) IANA Considerations. IETF RFC 2929 (September 2000)

13. Rosenberg, J., Schulzrinne, H.: Session Initiation Protocol (SIP): Locating SIP Servers. IETF RFC 3263 (June 2002)
14. Rosenberg, J.: Session Initiation Protocol (SIP). IETF RFC 3261 (June 2002)
15. Chiasserini, C.F., Meo, M.: A Reconfigurable Protocol Setting to Improve TCP over Wireless. IEEE Transactions on Vehicular Technology 51, 1608–1620 (2002)
16. Funato, D., Yasuda, K., Tokuda, H.: TCP-R: TCP Mobility Support for Continuous Operation. In: International Conference on Network Protocols, pp. 229–236 (October 1997)
17. Aydin, I., Chien-Chung, S.: Evaluating Cellular SCTP over One-Hope Wireless networks. In: IEEE Vehicular Technology Conference, vol. 2, pp. 826–830 (September 2005)
18. Ma, L., Yu, F., Leung, V.C.M., Randhawa, T.: A New Method to Support UMTS/WLAN Vertical Handover Using SCTP. IEEE Wireless Communications 11, 44–51 (2004)
19. Koh, S.J., Jung, H.Y., Min, J.H.: Transport Layer Internet Mobility Based on mSCTP. In: IEEE International Conference on Advanced Communication Technology, vol. 1, pp. 329–333 (2004)
20. Koh, S.J., Chang, M.J., Lee, M.: mSCTP for Soft Handover in Transport Layer. IEEE Communications Letters 8, 189–191 (2004)
21. Chang, M.J., Lee, M., Koh, S.J.: Transport Layer Mobility Support Utilizing Link Signal Strength Information. IEICE Transaction on Communication E87-B, 2548–2556 (2004)
22. Funasaka, J., Lshida, K., Obata, H., Jutori, Y.: A Study on Primary Path Switching Strategy of SCTP. In: International symposium on autonomous decentralized systems (April 2005)
23. IEEE 802.11 WG.: Wireless LAN Medium Access Control (MAC) and Physical Layer (PHY) Specifications. IEEE Standard, 1-445 (1997)
24. Harrison, P.G., Patel, N.M.: Performance Modeling of Communication Networks and Computer Architectures. Addison-Wesley, Reading (1993)
25. Zorzi, M., Rao, R.R., Milstein, L.B.: ARQ Error Control for Fading Mobile Radio Channels. IEEE Transactions on Vehicular Technology 46, 445–455 (1997)
26. Daigle, J.: Queueing Theory for Telecommunications. Addison-Wesley, Reading (1992)
27. Bolch, G., Greiner, S., Meer, H.D., Trivedi, S.: Queueing Networks and Markov Chains - Modeling and Performance Evaluation with Computer Science Applications. Wiley-Interscience, Chichester (1998)
28. Mason, R.D., Lind, D.A., Marchal, W.G.: Statistics. Saunders College (1994)
29. The Network Simulator version -2 (ns-2): http://www.isi.edu/nsnam/ns/
30. ns-2 SCTP module Version 3.5, http://www.armandocaro.net/
31. Gilbert, E.N.: Capacity of a burst-noise channel. Bell Syst. Tech. J. 39, 1253–1266 (1960)

A Clustering-Based Channel Assignment Algorithm and Routing Metric for Multi-channel Wireless Mesh Networks

Chao Liu[1], Zhongyi Liu[1], Yongqiang Liu[2], Huizhou Zhao[1], Tong Zhao[1], and Wei Yan[1]

[1] School of Electronics Engineering and Computer Science, Peking University, China
{liuchao,lzy,zhaohuizhou,zt,weiyan}@net.pku.edu.cn
[2] NEC Laboratory China
liuyongqiang@research.nec.com.cn

Abstract. Multiple non-overlapped channels are available in IEEE 802.11 but are rarely used today in wireless multi-hop networks. Wireless mesh network is a special type of multi-hop ad hoc network and is envisioned to provide high capacity and large coverage. In this paper, we propose a 2-hop clustering based multi-interface, multi-channel network architecture and design a novel channel assignment algorithm and routing metric. Channel assignment is composed of Inter-cluster Static Assignment and Intra-cluster Dynamic Assignment. Since traditional routing metrics, such as hop-count, may not perform well in multi-channel wireless networks, we propose the CDM routing metric, which combines hop-count, channel diversity and channel switching capability together. Simulation results show that our algorithms achieve up to 3.3 times higher end-to-end throughput.[1]

Keywords: wireless multi-hop networks, wireless mesh networks, multi-channel, multi-interface, channel assignment, routing metric.

1 Introduction

Despite significant improvement has been made in physical layer technologies, the bandwidth problem is still severe for multi-hop ad hoc networks due to interference from adjacent hops on the same path as well as from neighboring paths [1]. The IEEE 802.11b/g and 802.11a standard provide 3 and 12 non-overlapped channels respectively, which could be used simultaneously within a neighborhood. However, such bandwidth aggregation is rarely applied to 802.11-based multi-hop ad hoc networks. Most ad hoc network implementations use only a single frequency channel, wasting the rest of the spectrum.

Wireless mesh networks (WMN) is a promising technology emerged recently. The WMN backbone operates just like a network of fixed routers, except that they are connected only by wireless links. In such networks, most of the nodes are stationary

[1] This research has been supported by NSCF of china under Grant 60673181. Partially supported by NSCF Grant 60573166 and Network Key Lab Grant of Guang Dong Province.

I. Stojmenovic et al. (Eds.): ISPA 2007, LNCS 4742, pp. 832–843, 2007.

and do not rely on batteries. Hence, the focus of WMN design is on improving the network capacity, instead of coping with mobility or minimizing power usage. Providing each node with multiple wireless interfaces offers a promising approach for improving the capacity of WMNs.

A multi-interface-per-node wireless mesh network architecture raises two research questions: channel assignment and routing. Channel assignment deals with assigning a physical channel to a given interface when the number of interfaces per node is lower than the number of available channels. Channel assignment must meet the following two requirements: (1) Maintain the connectivity of the network; and (2) solve the *channel dependency problem* [12]. The second requirement is illustrated in Fig.1. Imagine that there are two interfaces per node and the initial result of channel assignment is labeled on the links. At some moment, the channel of link DE is changed from channel 3 to channel 7. This means that the channel of link EF must also do the same change, so as link DH and HI. This example shows that a change in local channel assignment could lead to a series of channel re-assignments across the network. The channel dependency problem makes it difficult to develop distributed dynamic channel assignment algorithms as local change may have global effects.

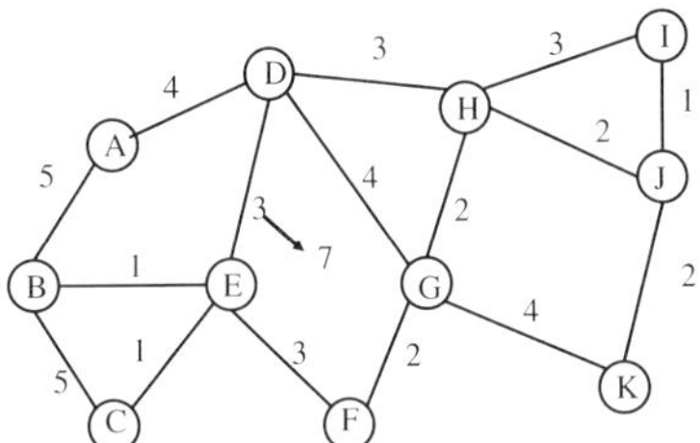

Fig. 1. The Channel Dependency

When nodes have multiple radios, the minimum-hop routing does not perform well [2]. New routing metrics must incorporate the channel diversity in the physical layer of the route. Hence, cross layer design is a key technology for the design of new routing algorithms.

In this paper we make the following research contributions:

- We propose a 2-hop clustering-based multi-interface, multi-channel wireless mesh network architecture. 2-hop clustering largely ensures that non-neighbor clusters could not interfere with each other. The connectivity problem is break up into two aspects: inter-cluster connectivity and intra-cluster connectivity. The channel dependency problem is constricted to a local cluster as channel change of a link in one cluster will not lead to changes in other clusters.
- We develop a novel channel assignment algorithm based on 2-hop clustering. Channel assignment is composed of inter-cluster static assignment and intra-cluster dynamic assignment. In this way, the connectivity of the network is maintained and channels are distributed evenly among the network.

- We propose a new routing metric- Channel Distribution Metric (CDM), which combines hop-count, channel diversity and channel switching capability together. We also modify AODV routing protocol to support CDM based routing.
- The evaluation results show that our Clustering-based Channel Assignment algorithm combining with new CDM metric improve the end-to-end throughput up to 3.3 times.

The rest of the paper is organized as follows. Section 2 reviews past works related to this research. Section 3 describes the channel assignment and routing metric. Section 4 presents the results and analysis of the proposed algorithms. Section 5 concludes the paper with a summary of research contributions and future work.

2 Related Work

Multi-channel / Multi-radio research. Several researchers have proposed MAC protocols based on IEEE 802.11 for utilizing multiple channels [3, 4]. A couple of channel assignment algorithms are also proposed. In [5], authors use multiple 802.11 NICs per node in an ad hoc network by assuming an *identical channel assignment* to all nodes. NIC-1 is assigned channel-1, NIC-2 to channel-2, and so on. This approach can only yield a maximum of factor 2 of improvement using 2 NICs. Raniwala et al. [6] proposed a load-aware channel assignment algorithm. One important assumption of Raniwala's protocol is that traffic load between all nodes are known, which is usually not held in practice.

D-Clustering. For *d-clustering algorithms* such as those presented in [7, 8], each node is either a cluster-Head or is at most *d* hops away from a cluster-Head. The value of *d* is a design parameter of the algorithm. The algorithm proposed in [7] partitions the nodes according to their IDs. The algorithm presented in [8] constructs a multi-layer hierarchy of cluster-Heads (i.e., the cluster-Heads of layer 1 are the cluster members of layer 2). Upper bounds on communication overhead for d-clustering algorithms are investigated in [9].

Routing Metrics. Draves et al. [2] proposed WCETT, a new metric for routing in multi-channel networks. The metric is used with LQSR, a source routing protocol, and ensures "high-quality" routes are selected. WCETT is defined as follows:

$$WCETT = (1-\beta) * \sum_{i=1}^{n} ETT_i + \beta * \max_{1<=j<=k} X_j \ . \quad (1)$$

where ETT_i is the expected transmission time of link *i*, *k* is the number of channels, X_j is given as:

$$X_j = \sum_{\text{Hop i is on channel j}} ETT_i \, , 1 <= j <= k \ . \quad (2)$$

As we can see, X_j is the sum of all the expected transmission time of links working on channel *j* along the route. However, if the path is so long that different links on the same channel do not interfere with each other, X_j will over estimate the cost of the route. In this paper, we propose the CDM metric, somewhat avoiding the drawback of WCETT. The description of CDM will be given in section 3.5.

3 Channel Assignment Algorithm and Routing Metric

3.1 Overview

Fig.2 is an example to explain our channel assignment algorithm. The network is partitioned into different clusters, each of which has a cluster *Head* and a *FIXED* channel, i.e. the common channel within this cluster. For example, the FIXED channel of cluster1 is channel1, and the FIXED channel of cluster2 is channel2. Different clusters are linked by *Gateway* nodes, which are the nodes on the periphery of clusters. Note that one gateway only belongs to one cluster, and there may be multiple Gateways between two clusters. All the links between Gateways are working on the same channel, named *DEFAULT* channel. Those nodes other than Gateways and Heads are called *Ordinary* nodes. After the initial assignment, the nodes may still have more idle interfaces. They set these idle interfaces to *DYNAMIC* status and switch channel according to the local traffic load. It is important to notice that we use clustering-based architecture only for channel assignment and clusters are transparent for routing algorithms and upper layer protocols.
Our algorithms are based on the following three assumptions:

- Every node has at least two network interfaces; but we don't require every node has the same number of interface.
- The network topologies seen by different network interfaces of one node are identical.
- The number of interfaces per node is lower than the number of available channels.

The execution cycle of the algorithms consists of three phases: *Clustering* phase, *Inter-cluster Static Channel Assignment* phase, and *Intra-cluster Dynamic Channel Assignment* phase.

In the Clustering phase, the network is partitioned into clusters. Each cluster has a maximum radius of 2 hops, i.e. every node is at most 2 hops away from its cluster Head.

During the Inter-cluster Static Channel Assignment phase, each cluster is assigned a FIXED channel. The principle of the inter-cluster channel assignment is that neighboring clusters are assigned with different FIXED channels as long as there are enough available channels. After the inter-cluster channel assignment, channels are well distributed in the network and connectivity of the network is maintained.

The last phase is Intra-cluster Dynamic Channel Assignment phase. The cluster Head node continually measures the available bandwidth on each channel, and periodically notifies every member with *Top_Free_Channel* message, i.e. the list of freest channels in its area. Other member nodes switch the channels of their DYNAMIC interfaces based on local traffic load to get more bandwidth. Data packets are transmitted on FIXED, DEFAULT and DYNAMIC interfaces, while all the broadcast and control/management messages, including those flood messages from upper layer, are transmitted on the FIXED and DEFAULT interfaces to guarantee every node get the messages.

To explore the potential of our multi-channel network as much as possible, we propose a new routing metric named CDM and modify the AODV routing protocol to support CDM-based routing.

One distinct characteristic of our entire algorithm is that we assign the channels based on clustering. The motivation behind that includes:

- It makes channel dependence problem restricted within the cluster since different clusters use different FIXED channel and are only connected by DEFAULT channel.
- The neighboring clusters can use non-overlap FIXED channels to decrease the interference and improve the throughput.
- Since the nodes within one cluster are connected with FIXED channel and every cluster are connected with DEFAULT channel, so the entire network maintains exactly equivalent connectivity as the single channel network.
- Since all members within a cluster share one common FIXED channel, the broadcast and flooding, which is considered to be a complicated problem in multi-channel network, can be done efficiently in our network.

3.2 Clustering Algorithm

An amount of clustering algorithms are already proposed by researchers. In this paper, we adopt the Max-Min D-cluster algorithm proposed by [7]. Max-Min D-cluster is a distributed algorithm. It partition nodes into *d*-clusters based on their IDs, where *d* is an input parameter. After the algorithm converges, every node is either a cluster Head or at most *d* hops away from its cluster Head.

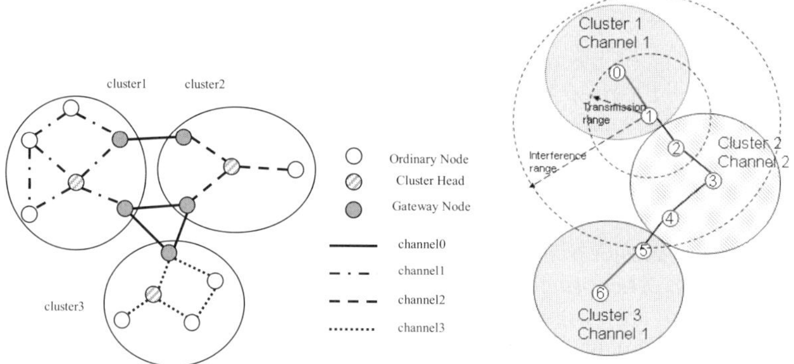

Fig. 2. Example for Channel Assignment

Fig. 3. Non-neighbor Cluster Interference in 1-cluser

One critical decision of our algorithm is how to choose the radius of clusters (i.e. the parameter *d*). We prefer 2-hop clustering due to the following reasons:

If the radius of clusters is set to 1, then two non-neighbor clusters may still interfere with each other. For example, In Fig. 3, cluster 1 and cluster 3 are non-neighbors and both choose channel 1 to be FIXED channel. Node's transmission range is 250, and interference range is 550. Node 1 and node 5 are within each other's interference range. In contrast, if the radius of the clusters is 2, then non-neighbor cluster interference can only occur when the intermediate cluster is small enough, which reduces the possibility of non-neighbor cluster interference to a very small extent.

If the radius of clusters is larger than 2, the efficiency of clustering algorithm will be reduced sharply. And the intra-cluster interference will get severe, despite the Intra-cluster Dynamic Channel Assignment.

3.3 Inter-cluster Static Channel Assignment

At first, every node set one of its interfaces to work on the DEFAULT channel (this interface is called DEFAULT interface), e.g. channel 1. Then the network performs Max-Min D-cluster on the DEFAULT channel and nodes are partitioned into clusters. After that, the inter-cluster channel assignment phase begins. It includes three steps:

1. In the first step, every cluster Head performs a conflict-avoiding algorithm to find the FIXED channel of this cluster.
2. Next, Head nodes flood this FIXED channel to its cluster members.
3. At the last step, Ordinary nodes change their DEFAULT interface to FIXED channel, and Gateway nodes set one idle interface to the FIXED channel.

After all the steps are completed, the connectivity within cluster is maintained by the FIXED channel, and neighboring clusters are linked with Gateways using the DEFAULT channel. Hence the connectivity of our network is maintained, and equivalent to the single-radio single-channel network.

The conflict-avoiding algorithm is the key design issue of the inter-cluster channel assignment. This problem can be considered as a classical graph k-coloring problem: each cluster is a vertex in the graph; two clusters are neighbors means that there is one edge connecting these two vertices in the graph; then color all vertices with k colors (k is the number of the available channels), so that neighboring vertices have different colors, or the number of conflicts is as small as possible.

To solve this problem, we design a distributed greedy algorithm. Every node runs following steps for one time:

1. Wait all the neighboring Heads that have higher IDs than its own to tell it about their FIXED channels, and store their FIXED channels in a *Neighbor_Channel* list.
2. Choose a free channel which is not included in *Neighbor_Channel*, or choose a channel which causes least conflicts if there is no free one
3. Notify all the neighboring Heads that have lower IDs than its own about the FIXED channel it chose.

To determine the minimum number of colors needed to color a given graph is NP-complete [11]. Our algorithm does not intend to color the graph with minimum colors, but gets a suboptimal solution and causes few color conflicts with a greedy method. In worst case, where all clusters are connected as a complete graph, the time complexity of the algorithm is $O(n^2)$ (n is the number of clusters). In most case, the time complexity is $O(mn)$, where n is the number of clusters, m is the maximum degree of vertices in the graph.

3.4 Intra-cluster Dynamic Channel Assignment

After all clusters get FIXED channels, the nodes may still have some idle interfaces (also called DYNAMIC interfaces), especially on those non-Gateway nodes which only use one interface on the FIXED channels. This section is about how to utilize these DYNAMIC interfaces.

It is well recognized that channel assignment and routing can be efficiently executed only if the traffic patterns are taken into account [10]. Considering that the global traffic load information is sometimes impossible to get, we will use some local information in our dynamic channel switching.

In the intra-cluster channel assignment phase, each Head node selects a particular node, called *Measurer*. If this Head is not a Gateway, it selects itself to be Measurer, else it selects the one that is non-Gateway and has largest ID. The selected Measurer sets one idle interface to hop on the available channels (i.e. all channels except those already used by this cluster). On each time slot, the Measurer node listens on that channel and gets an estimation of free time percentage. The estimation can be simply done by subtracting the channel busy time from the entire time slot. Thus the Measurer node will always get an updated list about which channels are the freest in its local area. This list is called *Top_Free_Channels*, and is periodically flooded to the cluster members.

Then cluster members can use the ranking in the *Top_Free_Channels* to adaptively switch their DYNAMIC interfaces. There are two different strategies of this dynamic switching, and we call it *Greedy Switching* and *On-demand Switching*.

The Greedy Switching is straightforward: if a node has n idle interfaces, it sets these interfaces on the first n channels in the Top_Free_Channels list. Every node use hello message to discover neighboring nodes on each interfaces and use ETT [2] metric to choose the interface to transmit data packets when there are more than one common channels between itself and another neighboring node.

Beside the Greedy Switching, another strategy of dynamic channel assignment is On-demand Switching. Normally, all nodes use FIXED channel for data packets transmitting, and Gateway nodes also use DEFAULT channel to transmit inter-cluster traffic. At the same time, nodes continually measure the free time percentage on the FIXED channel using method of promiscuous listening. If the free time percentage drops to a threshold (30% in our implementation), this node will select a channel from Top_Free_Channles list, enable an unused DYNAMIC interface to the selected channel, and then broadcast a message on the FIXED interface to notify all its neighbor nodes about the DYNAMIC channel it just enabled. The broadcasted message is called *Dynamic_Change*, and includes the ID of the node and the ID of the selected channel. If the neighbor node has one DYNAMIC interface that is not used yet, it enables the interface to the selected channel, and replies a *Dynamic_Change_ACK* message to the original node. If no reply is received, the original node gives up this channel switch. After a while, if the congestion is relieved and free time percentage of FIXED channel rises to another threshold (75% in our implementation), the original node recalls this channel switch.

When a node chooses the suitable channel from the Top_Free_Channles list, it excludes those channels already selected by its own and its neighbor nodes from the list, and chooses the first channel that remains in the list.

The Greedy Switching and On-demand Switching are different in their ways of utilizing Free Channels. In Greedy Switching, every node makes use of the available channels as much as possible to achieve higher throughput. But they probably cause more interference. In On-demand Switching, nodes use the channels in a modest way, and they enable the DYNAMIC interface only when necessary. So when congestion happens in an area of the network, the free channel can be quickly enabled to relieve the heavy traffic load.

There is an assumption behind our algorithm: the measurement on the Measurer node can also reflect the channel usage situation on the positions of other member nodes. This is not always held in the wireless network. But considering that the overhearing range is much larger than the transmitting range, the Measurer node can mostly overhear the transmission of other cluster members. Besides, we only need a rough rank of the free channels, and the measurement on Measurer node is good enough. There is no need to make every node do the measurement itself, because per-channel hopping of the measurement would dedicate an interface and seems needless.

3.5 CDM Routing Metric

In this section, we propose a new routing metric – *Channel Distribution Metric* (*CDM*) and adapt AODV routing protocol to support CDM.

There are three goals for the CDM designing. First, it should take the channel diversity of a path into account, because the interference along the path is a main factor that decreases the throughput.

Second, the metric should be increasing while adding new route into the path. Because a longer path will obviously consume more resource in the network, a node should try to choose shorter path in the consideration of global optimal. A longer path would also cause longer roundtrip time and hence decrease the end-to-end TCP throughput. Last but not least, many routing protocols (e.g. DSR, AODV, DSDV and etc.) demand the metric to have non-decreasing property.

Third, the dynamic channel switching capability of nodes along the path should be explicitly considered. Intra-cluster dynamic channel assignment is a distinct characteristic of our multi-channel network. It can reduce the interference within the cluster and thus improve the throughput. The metric should make good use of this characteristic.

Our CDM metric is defined as follows:

$$\text{CDM} = \alpha \times \text{MLC} + \beta \times \text{HopCount} - \gamma \times \text{VCM} . \tag{3}$$

where α, β, γ are parameters subject to $0 < \alpha < 1$, $0 < \beta < 1$, $0 < \gamma < 1$, and $\gamma <= \beta$. A smaller CDM value indicates the route is better.

MLC donates the Maximum interfered-Link Count and is defined as

$$\text{MLC} = \max_{i=1,2\ldots n-1} \left\{ \sum_{j=i+1}^{\min(i+InterferenceLen,n)} \text{I}(\text{C}(i) == \text{C}(j)) \right\} . \tag{4}$$

where n is the hop count of the route and $I(C(i) = C(j))$ is an indicator function that is equal to one when channels being used by link i and link j are the same, otherwise set to zero. The *InterferenceLen* is the interference range measured in hop count; it can be a constant value (equal to 3 in our system). So MLC accounts for the interference along the path, and furthermore reflects the path's channel diversity.

HopCount, the second part of equation (3), is derived from the traditional minimum-hop routing. It reflects the end-to-end delay of the path and the overall transmission time it consumes.

VCM is the abbreviation of *Variable Channel Metric*, and is given as follows.

$$VCM = \sum_{i=1}^{n} HasUnusedInterface(i) \ . \tag{5}$$

Where n is hop count, *HasUnusedInterface(i)* is an indicator function which is equal to one when node i has one or more unused DYNAMIC interface, otherwise equal to zero. Thus VCM reflects the channel switching capability of a route. The reason why the *HasUnusedInterface(i)* function is not equal to the number of the idle interfaces is because the CDM metric would lose the non-decreasing property if we allow the value of *HasUnusedInterface(i)* to be more than one. Consider adding one node that has a big number of idle interfaces into the route, and this node would probably lower the entire CDM metric, which is not the situation we want. The last constraint of the parameters, $\gamma <= \beta$, is also for the assurance of the non-decreasing property, because VCM should get lower weight than HopCount.

3.6 Discussion

Our channel assignment algorithm can eliminate most interference between neighboring clusters. But the intra-cluster interference still exists, especially on the FIXED channel. The Intra-cluster Dynamic Channel Assignment is designed to mitigate the interference within cluster. But due to the limited number of non-overlapping channels (3 orthogonal channels in 802.11b/g and 12 in 802.11a), the interference is inevitable.

Max-Min D-cluster is a simple clustering algorithm, whose result depends mainly on the distribution of IDs in the network. Max-Min D-cluster may lead to some small clusters (i.e. clusters with radius equal to one or clusters with small number of members). Small cluster may cause non-neighboring interference. Fortunately, the algorithm of clustering is substitutable, and one of our future works is designing a topology-based clustering algorithm and replacing Max-Min D-cluster.

Once Clustering and Inter-channel Static Channel Assignment are done, the clustering result and FIXED channels are fixed for a long period of time, such as hours or days. When a new node appears in the network, it just scans on every channel, looks for a neighboring cluster, joins in it, and set one interface on the FIXED channel of that cluster. Then depending on whether or not this new node has other neighboring clusters, it would become a Gateway node and set another interface on DEFAULT channel. When a node in the network fails, if this node is a cluster member, nothing needs to do. If the failing node is a cluster Head, other members in this cluster will sense this event through a continual absence of Top_Free_Channel message, and elect a new cluster Head that with the largest ID.

4 Evaluation

In the evaluation, we will compare our algorithm with one algorithm proposed by [6]. [6] designed two centralized channel assignment algorithms, *neighbor partitioning scheme* and *load-aware scheme*. The load-aware scheme outperforms the other one in their evaluation, but requires global traffic profile and needs to compute routes for all flows in the beginning of the experiment, which is not always feasible in real network. So we choose the neighbor partitioning scheme for comparing.

We modify NS2 to support multiple wireless interfaces per mesh node. The data rate is fixed to 1M bits/s, and transmission range and interference range are set to 250m and 550m respectively. The number of orthogonal channels is 12, which is the situation of IEEE 802.11a. Two types of network topologies are evaluated: grid topology and random topology. Specifically, we use an 8 * 8 grid topology, and the IDs are randomly distributed and different in each run. The random topology is 50 nodes distributed randomly in a 1500m * 1500m area.CBR UDP traffic with 512 byte packet size and 0.006s interval is used. *Throughput* is defined as the correct byte received by the destination node of each CBR flow. The *aggregated throughput* is the sum of throughput of all flows in the whole network.

In the implementation of our algorithm, we use On-demand Switching scheme to do the Intra-cluster Dynamic Channel Assignment. Currently, we have not implemented the Greedy Switching scheme yet. After we complete the Greedy Switching part, comparison of these two schemes will be given. For the CDM metric, in equation (3) and (4), the parameters are set as: $\alpha = \beta = \gamma = 1/3$, $InterferenceRange = 3$.

In below sections, we will compare the aggregated throughput of three kinds of networks:

- I-NET- Every node has only one interface and the network has only one channel.
- II-NET- Every node has two interfaces. The neighbor partitioning channel assignment proposed by [6] is used. The routing protocol is unmodified AODV.
- III-NET- Every node has two interfaces and our clustering-based channel assignment algorithm is used. The routing protocol is CDM-based AODV.

3 Long flows (i.e. longer than 4 hops) and 5 short flows (i.e. equal or shorter than 4 hops) exist simultaneously in each scene. The simulation time is 400s. Every scene is run for 50 times, and the final results are the average of the 50 runs. In each run, the source and destination nodes of each CBR UDP flow are randomly generated.

We present the aggregated throughput of short flows and long flows respectively in Table 1, group by the topologies and the type of flows.

Table 1. The average aggregated throughput (in Mbps) of three networks, group by topology and flow type

	Grid topology			Random topology		
	I-NET	II-NET	III-NET	I-NET	II-NET	III-NET
Short flows	1.4	1.8	2.5	0.7	1.1	1.4
Long flows	0.3	0.6	1.0	0.1	0.1	0.3

Fig. 4 and Fig. 5 are the aggregated throughput for 5 short flows. In Grids topology, the average throughput of I-NET is about 1.4Mbps, while II-NET is 1.8Mbps (28.6% higher than I-NET) and III-NET is 2.5Mbps (78.6% higher than I-NET). In random topology, the average throughputs are 0.7Mbps, 1.1Mbps and 1.4Mbps. II-NET and III-NET improve 57.1% and 100% upon I-NET respectively. The reason why III-NET outperforms II-NET is that: in III-NET, channels are distributed more reasonably and CDM-base AODV can utilize the multi-channel better than the traditional AODV.

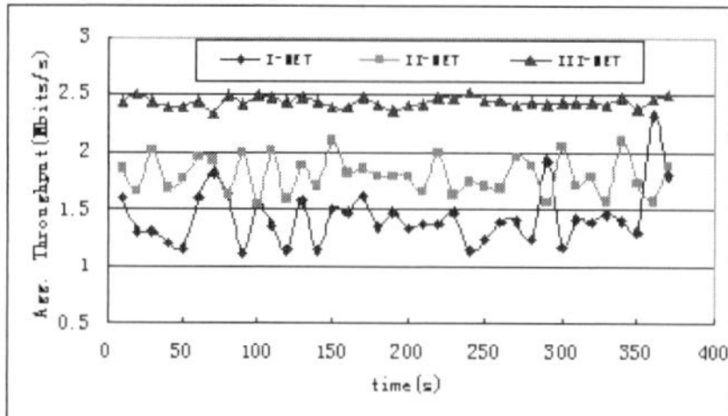

Fig. 4. Aggregated Throughput of Short Flows (Grid Topology)

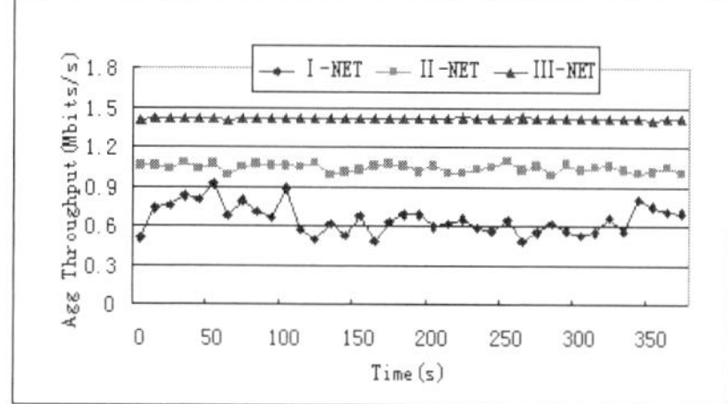

Fig. 5. Aggregated Throughput of Short Flows (Random Topology)

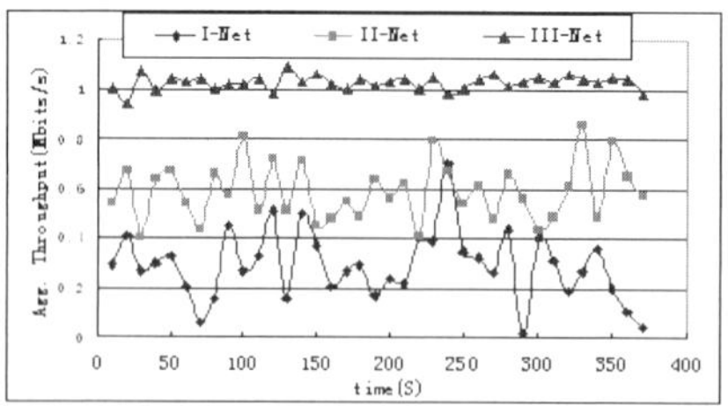

Fig. 6. Aggregated Throughput of Long Flows (Grid Topology)

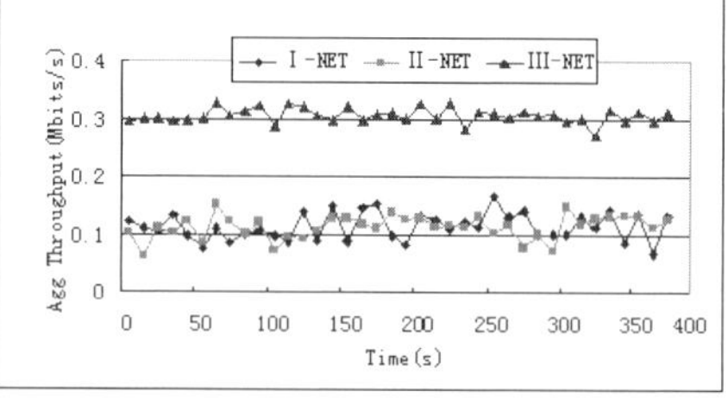

Fig. 7. Aggregated Throughput of Long Flows (Random Topology)

Fig. 6 and Fig. 7 are results for 3 long flows. As the figures indicate, in grid topology the aggregated throughput of III-NET is 3.3 times higher than I-NET while the aggregated throughput of II-NET is 2 times higher than that of I-NET. In the random topology, the results are similar for III-NET. But one notable phenomenon is that the aggregated throughput of II-NET is only slightly higher than I-NET. This is probably because the Neighbor Partitioning algorithm only considers the interference between adjacent links. Actually, the interference range is much larger than one hop, and links may interfere with each other even though they are not directly adjacent. This kind of interference gains more importance along the longer routes, and thus degrades the improvement caused by multi-channel in II-NET.

When comparing III-NET with I-NET, the improvement on long flows is much higher than that of short flows. We believe that this is caused by the following reason: the interference along the hops of one long route, which is also called *intra-route interference*, is the main factor affecting the end-to-end throughput. In III-NET, channel diversity between neighboring clusters along the route can greatly mitigate the intra-route interference, thus sharply increase the throughput. This meets our goal of enhancing the throughput of long flows to a higher extent than short flows.

5 Conclusions and Future Work

To utilize the non-overlapping channels available in IEEE 802.11a/b/g, and enhance the network capacity, we propose a channel assignment and routing algorithm based on 2-hop clustering. The channel assignment algorithm is a hybrid of static assignment and dynamic assignment: we use static channel assignment for inter-cluster assignment and dynamic switching for intra-cluster channel assignment. A new routing metric, named CDM, is proposed to enable the routing algorithm to select routes that can achieve higher end-to-end throughput. We also modify the AODV routing protocol to implement CDM based routing. Simulation results show that our algorithms can improve the end-to-end throughput up to 3.3 times.

At present, we use a simple but efficient clustering algorithm Max-Min D-cluster. However, the clustering result of Max-Min D-cluster depends on the distribution of node IDs on the plane. In the future, we may replace Max-Min D-cluster with other clustering schemes, e.g. connectivity based clustering. Our CDM metric combines hop-count, channel diversity and channel switching capability together, but the impact of weights on these three parts (i.e. the parameters in equation (3)) has not been explored. Hence the routing metric still needs to be improved. We have already developed a prototype of multi-channel wireless mesh network (called MeshNet) with 7 nodes; extensive experimental test will also be the future work.

References

1. Jain, K., Padhye, J., Padmanabhan, V.N., Qiu, L.: Impact of interference on multi-hop wireless network performance. In: Proc. IEEE/ACM MOBICOM (2003)
2. Draves, R., Padhye, J., Zill, B.: Routing in multi-radio, multi-hop Wireless Mesh Networks. In: Proc. ACM MOBICOM (2004)
3. Nasipuri, A., Zhuang, J., Das, S.R.: A multichannel CSMA MAC protocol for multihop wireless networks. In: Proc. IEEE WCNC (1999)
4. Jain, N., Das, S., Nasipuri, A.: A Multichannel CSMA MAC protocol with receiver-based channel selection for multihop wireless networks. In: Proc. IEEE International Conference on Computer Communications and Networks (IC3N). IEEE Computer Society Press, Los Alamitos (2001)
5. Kyasanur, P., Vaidya, N.H.: Routing and interface assignment in multi-channel multi-interface Wireless Networks. In: Proc. IEEE WCNC. IEEE Computer Society Press, Los Alamitos (2005)
6. Raniwala, A., Gopalan, K., Chiueh, T.: Centralized channel assignment and touting algorithms for multi-channel Wireless Mesh Networks. In: ACM SIGMOBILE Mobile Computing and Communications Review, vol. 8(2), pp. 50–65 (April 2004)
7. Amis, A., Prakash, R., Vuong, T., Huynh, D.: Max-Min D-Cluster formation in wireless ad hoc networks. In: Proc. IEEE INFOCOM. IEEE Computer Society Press, Los Alamitos (2000)
8. Banerjee, S., Khuller, S.: A clustering scheme for hierarchical control in multi-hop wireless networks. In: Proc. IEEE INFOCOM, pp. 1028–1037. IEEE Computer Society Press, Los Alamitos (2001)
9. Sucec, J., Marsic, I.: Clustering overhead for hierarchical routing in mobile ad hoc networks. In: Proc. IEEE INFOCOM, vol. 3, pp. 1698–1706 (2002)
10. Alicherry, M., Bhatia, R., Li, L.E.: Joint channel assignment and routing for throughput optimization in multi radio Wireless Mesh Networks. In: Proc. ACM/IEEE MOBICOM (2005)
11. Cheeseman, P., Kenefsky, B., Taylor, W.: Where the really hard problems are. In: Proc. 12th International Joint Conference on AI (IJCAI-91), vol. 1, pp. 331–337 (1991)
12. Raniwala, A., Chiueh, T.: Architecture and algorithms for an IEEE 802.11-based multi-channel Wireless Mesh Network. In: Proc. IEEE INFOCOM. IEEE Computer Society Press, Los Alamitos (2005)

A Hierarchical Care-of Prefix with BUT Scheme for Nested Mobile Networks

Ing-Chau Chang[1], Chia-Hao Chou[1], and Lin-Huang Chang[2]

[1] Department of Computer Science and Information Engineering, National Changhua University of Education, Changhua, Taiwan, R.O.C.
icchang@cc.ncue.edu.tw, chahau@gmail.com
[2] Graduate Institute of Networking and Communication Engineering, ChaoYang University of Technology, Wufeng County, Taichung, Taiwan, R.O.C.
lchang@cyut.edu.tw

Abstract. In this paper, we apply the hierarchical concept to the Care-of Prefix (CoP) scheme as HCoP and enhance HCoP with a novel Binding Update Tree (BUT) structure as HCoP-B for NEtwork MObility (NEMO) management of the nested mobile network. As compared to schemes such as Reverse Routing Header (RRH), Route Optimization using Tree Information Option (ROTIO) and HCoP with numerical performance evaluations, HCoP-B achieves the shortest handoff latency and significantly reduces the consumed network bandwidth of global binding update messages for route optimizations (RO) of all correspondent nodes (CN) after the nested mobile network hands over to a new AR. Consequently, HCoP-B resolves the RO storm problem.

1 Introduction

The IETF NEtwork MObility (NEMO) working group extends MIPv6 [1] as the NEMO Basic Support (NBS) protocol [2] to manage network mobility for mobile nodes (MN) in a single-layer mobile network. NBS achieves performance improvements over MIPv6 for network mobility in terms of reduced transmission powers, the number of handoffs, complexities, bandwidth consumptions and location update delays [3]. NBS creates a bi-directional tunnel between the mobile router (MR) and its home agent (MR-HA) to avoid ingress filtering. However, NBS suffers the pinball routing problem and non-optimal transmission paths [4] in the nested NEMO, which further introducing significant delays and packet overheads.

For completing route optimization (RO) with researches which inherit the concept from MIPv6, each MN must send a binding update (BU) message to notify every connecting correspondent node (CN) to divert the transmission path to the NEMO directly. Consider ten MNs in the NEMO are connecting with a CN, these MNs must immediately send ten duplicate BUs to the same CN for RO after the NEMO's handoff, which significantly wastes wireless and Internet bandwidths. We call it the *RO storm problem.* In this paper, we focus on resolving pinball routing and RO storm problems for the nested NEMO by proposing a novel *hierarchical care-of prefix*

I. Stojmenovic et al. (Eds.): ISPA 2007, LNCS 4742, pp.844–855,2007.

(CoP) with the binding update tree (BUT) scheme, which is called HCoP-B in this paper. This paper is organized as follows. Section II summarizes related works on mobility of the nested NEMO. Section III describes the HCoP-B scheme and associated algorithms. Section IV presents numerical evaluation results for performances of all schemes. Section V concludes this paper.

2 Related Works

Reverse Routing Header (RRH) [4] uses a type 4 routing header from the MN to record the home address (HoA) of each intermediate MR in the nested NEMO. As the packet arrives at the HA of the MN's serving MR, i.e., the closest MR, these routing information is stored in its binding cache for determining the optimal route of packets back to the MN in a type 2 routing header. In this way, RRH only needs to build a bi-directional tunnel between the MN's serving MR and the MR-HA, which resolves the pinball routing problem. However, RRH introduces extra packet length and processing overhead for the routing header of each packet. The CN and MR-HA need spaces to record routing information for each MN.

Based on NBS, ROTIO [5] proposes a routing optimization scheme with the extended tree information option (xTIO) [6]. Each MR in the nested NEMO sends a normal BU, which contains the home address of the top-level mobile router (TLMR), to its home agent and a local BU, which contains routing information between the issuing MR and the TLMR, to the TLMR. ROTIO suffers only two levels of nested tunnels, i.e., one between the closest MR of the MN and the MR's HA and the other between the TLMR and the TLMR's HA, to send a packet from a CN to an MN in the nested NEMO. However, ROTIO suffers the non-optimal transmission path, increased packet overhead and TLMR/MR binding cache sizes.

The Care-of Prefix (CoP) [7] proposes a routing mechanism using hierarchical mobile network prefix assignment and hierarchical re-routing to optimize the routing and to reduce handoff signal overheads. The CoP flow consists of three stages: 1) the prefix delegation; 2) the binding update; 3) packet re-transmission. CoP resolves the pinball routing problem without suffering significant packet overheads of RRH. As the NEMO is allocated a new CoP, only one BU is sent by the TLMR to the aggregate router (AGR) to modify its binding cache instead of multiple BUs sent by all MNs in the NEMO, which reduces handoff signal overheads. However, CoP introduces problems. First, CoP spends more time to delegate CoPs for MRs of each level, which in turn raises total handoff latency. Second, the AGR cannot be placed at an optimal location for all CNs, which increases transmission delay and consumed bandwidth.

None of RRH, ROTIO and CoP mentions how to cope with the RO storm problem, which seriously degrades network performances resulting from the huge amount of BU messages simultaneously sent by MNs in the NEMO to all connecting CNs for RO after the NEMO handoff. We will describe our HCoP-B in section III.

3 The HCoP-B Scheme and the BUT Handling Algorithms

We propose the hierarchical CoP (HCoP) scheme in this paper by integrating the concept of the mobility anchor point (MAP) from HMIPv6 [8] into the CoP approach. The TLMR of the nested NEMO, i.e., the MAP, manages care-of prefix allocation, maintains the binding cache for all MNs and achieves optimal routing from the CN to the MN in the nested NEMO via it. However, HCoP suffers from the RO storm problem as RRH and CoP do. Hence, we propose the HCoP with a novel binding update tree (BUT) scheme, i.e., HCoP-B, to build a BUT on the MAP to record the NEMO topology and information about all connecting CNs of MNs, MR-HAs and VMN-HAs for the nested NEMO. HCoP-B achieves the following advantages: 1) reduce the handoff latency as the level of the nested NEMO grows, by overlapping the duration to perform the prefix delegation and the local binding update (LBU) to the MAP, and the global binding update (GBU) from the MAP to HAs and CNs for RO; 2) reduce bandwidth of GBU messages for RO from MNs to all connecting CNs with our BUT handling algorithms; 3) resolve the RO storm problem existed in RRH, ROTIO and HCoP; 4) support VMN in the nested NEMO. HCoP-B Operations are described as follows.

A HCoP-B Prefix Delegation

As soon as MR1, i.e., the MAP in Fig. 1, receives new wireless beacon signals from an access router (AR), it sends a router solicitation (RS) message to the AR for requesting the AR to advertise the HMRA [9] message into the nested NEMO. With the allocated care-of prefix (A::) in the HMRA message and the MAC address (MR1_ID) of the egress network interface, MR1 can configure its new CoA as A::MR1_ID. This prefix delegation process is repeated at each MR of every level, which introduces latency in the nested NEMO. With HCoP-B, each MR records the home prefix of its upper level MR from the received HMRA message for building network topology of the NEMO at BUT at the binding update stage.

B HCoP-B Binding Update

(1) Building binding caches and NEMO topology in BUT

After the MR has configured its CoA, it sends only one LBU, which maintains the many-to-many mapping between the home prefix and the care-of prefix of this MR, to the MAP to update the binding cache for all local fixed nodes (LFN) and local mobile nodes (LMN) of the MR. This part of binding cache is called the local binding cache (LBC) in HCoP-B. For example, after MR4 configures its CoA (Aaα::MR4_ID) with the allocated CoP (Aaα::), it will send an LBU, which maintains the mapping between Prefix_MR4 and MR4_CoP (Aaα) of MR4, for both MN1 and MN2 to MR1. Oppositely, the VMN has to send its own LBU to the MAP to build the visitor binding cache (VBC), which maintains an one-to-one mapping between the HoA and CoA (Aaα::VMN_ID) of the VMN. HCoP-B gives the VBC with a higher precedence over the LBC for searching the correct CoA of the VMN when it leaves its home network. The VBC and LBC will also be built at MR-HAs, VMN-HAs and all CNs after RO by the GBU messages. For the MAP to build the LBC/VBC and nested NEMO topology in BUT, we modify the format of mobility option in the original BU message. We define a new type 16 and three new flags, V, U and R, for this modified message. If the V flag is set, the VMN sends its VMN-HoA and VMN-CoA in LBU to the MAP to create an entry in VBC; otherwise, the MR sends its home prefix (MR-HP) and corresponding CoP (MR-CoP) for updating its binding in LBC. Moreover, if the U flag is set, the MR sends the home prefix of its upper MR (Upper MR-HP) to the MAP for building correct NEMO topology.

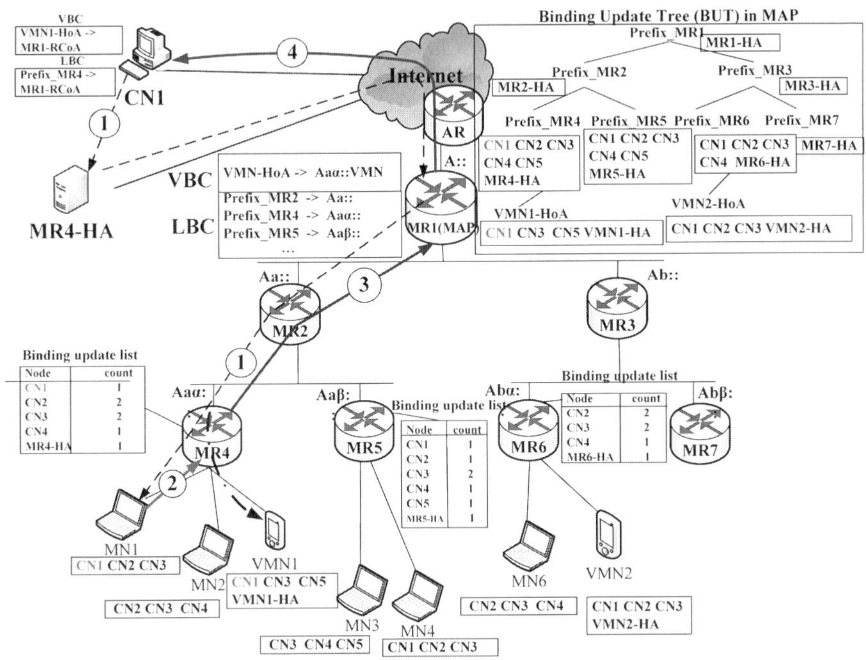

Fig. 1. The BUT building and route optimization flows in HCoP-B

(2) Processing the BUT information:

a. When a new CN sends the first packet to an MN or VMN:

Fig. 1 is illustrated as an example to exhibit how HCoP-B processes BUT information. When MN1 or VMN1 receives the first packet sent from CN1 (step 1), it will record the address of CN1 in its binding update list (BUL) [1]. With our proposed HCoP-B, MN1 will transmit this address on the modified mobility option of the LBU with the R flag set to its serving MR4 for adding CN1 with the counter value of 1 into the BUL of MR4 (step 2). This counter is used to record the total number of active connections from CN1 to MNs of MR4. Whenever the MR adds a new CN into its BUL, it will send this CN address to the MAP (MR1) on the modified mobility option of the LBU with the R flag set. Oppositely, if the counter value of a CN is greater than 1, which means this CN has ongoing connections with other MNs of the MR, the MR will not send an LBU to the MAP for reducing wireless bandwidth consumption between them. However, VMN1 itself issues an LBU to the MAP (step 3). After the MAP receives the LBU from MR4 or VMN1, it will record the address of CN1 at BUT entries of MR4 or VMN1 in the NEMO topology. Finally, the MAP will issue a GBU for MN1 or VMN1 to CN1 to create an entry in the LBC or VBC of CN1 (step 4). With cache information in the LBC and VBC, CN1 can first send packets through a single tunnel to the MAP and then the MAP forwards packets to MN1 or VMN1 without suffering the pinball routing problem. Consequently, HCoP-B achieves route optimization of CN for the nested NEMO.

b. When a mobile subnet of the NEMO hands over:

With HCoP-B, there are two handoff types for a NEMO subnet:

- *Intra-MAP Handoff*:

Whenever a mobile subnet in the nested NEMO receives more than one HMRA messages from different MRs of the same MAP, it is executing an intra-MAP handoff. The leading MR of the subnet will issue an LBU, which contains the home prefix of the new upper MR, to the MAP to modify the network topology of the NEMO. After completing the prefix delegation in the subnet, all underlying MRs or VMNs will issue LBUs to the MAP to update contents of the LBC or VBC with the newly allocated CoPs or CoAs respectively.

- *Inter-MAP Handoff*:

On the other hand, if a mobile subnet in the nested NEMO receives another HMRA message from an MR of a new NEMO, it is leaving the old MAP and executing an inter-MAP handoff to the new MAP. HCoP-B handles BUTs of the old and new MAPs in the detachment and re-attachment phases:

1) The detachment phase at the old MAP:

As shown at step 1 in Fig. 2, the leading MR (MR2) of the mobile subnet will first issue an LBU with a new flag *G* set in the BU header to notify the old MAP of its leaving. The old MAP then replies an LBA which contains BUT information for the leaving mobile subnet to the MR2 in a new mobility option (type=24), which is shown at step 2 in Fig. 2. Four new flags t, π, m and i are proposed in the LBA message. This information, which is illustrated inside the red box of Fig. 2, includes the hierarchical network topology of the leaving mobile subnet as well as HAs and connecting CNs of all MRs and VMNs.

For retrieving the hierarchical tree topology of the mobile subnet from the BUT of the old MAP, HCoP-B modifies the O-Tree algorithm [10] into the *GET_BUT()* and *PUT_BUT()* procedures in this paper. The GET_BUT() procedure uses the leading MR of the subnet as the tree root and two arrays (T, $\prod$) for the MAP to traverse the tree topology of the mobile subnet. The GET_BUT() writes "1" into array T to indicate that the visited node has child nodes or "0" otherwise, which means the tree traversal process should backtrack to the parent node. At the same time, the home prefix for the visited MR or the HoA for the visited VMN is recorded in array $\prod$. The RDN() procedure is for each visited node to remove duplicate connecting CNs, MR-HAs and VMN-HAs in the whole mobile subnet. Array I maintains the list of non-duplicate CNs, MR-HAs and VMN-HAs. Two-dimensional array M records corresponding indexes in arrray I for all connecting CNs, the MR-HA or the VMN-HA of each visited node. Table 1 lists results of GET_BUT() when the mobile subnet with its leading MR2 in Fig. 2 leaving the old MAP.

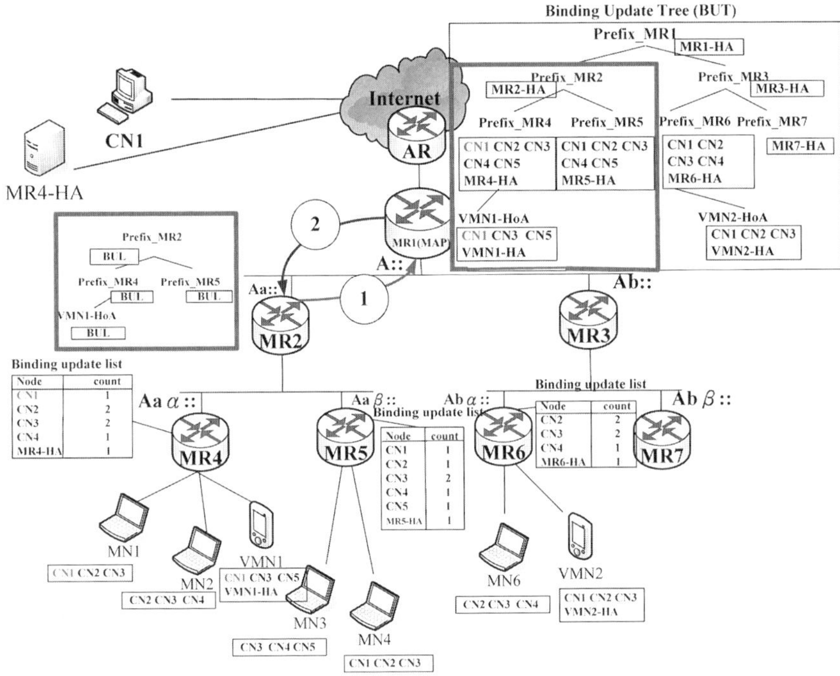

Fig. 2. The detachment phase of HCoP-B Inter-MAP handoff with MR2 as its leading MR

Table 1. Results of GET_BUT(MR2) for Fig. 2

T	1 1 0 0 1 0
Π	Prefix_MR2 Prefix_MR4 VMN1-HoA Prefix_MR5
M[Prefix_MR2]	1 0 0 0 0 0 0 0 0
M[Prefix_MR4]	0 1 1 1 1 1 1 0 0
M[VMN1-HoA]	0 1 0 1 0 1 0 1 0
M[Prefix_MR5]	0 1 1 1 1 1 0 0 1
I	MR2-HA CN1 CN2 CN3 CN4 CN5 MR4-HA VMN1-HA MR5-HA

2) The re-attachment phase at the new MAP:

As shown in Fig. 3, when the mobile subnet with MR2 as its leading MR re-attaches into the new NEMO with MRa as its new MAP and receives a new CoP, HCoP-B overlaps the following two steps to resolve the RO-storm problem with HCoP-B.

Step 1.1: MR2 sends BUT information of its mobile subnet, which is copied from the LBA message replied by the old MAP as described above, in the LBU with the mobility option (type=24) to the new MAP MRa. As soon as MRa receives this information, it copies data into arrays T, Π, M and I and then performs the PUT_BUT(MR2) procedure to restore BUT information of the MR2 mobile subnet to the BUT of the new NEMO. Operations are repeated until all elements in array T have been examined to completely rebuild the tree of the subnet in the BUT of the new MAP. Results of PUT_BUT(MR2) are shown in Table 2.

Step 1.2: At the end of PUT_BUT(), the new MAP collects non-duplicate binding update information in the mobile subnet for all MR-HAs and active CNs. Then, the new MAP can issue only one GBU, which contains all Prefix_MRs and VMN-HoAs of this node from array H. Hence, each CN, MR-HA or VMN-HA can simultaneously update all entries of these Prefix_MRs in its LBC and VMN-HoAs in its VBC with the mapping of Prefix_MR/VMN-HoA to the new MAP's RCoA or to the VMN-HA.

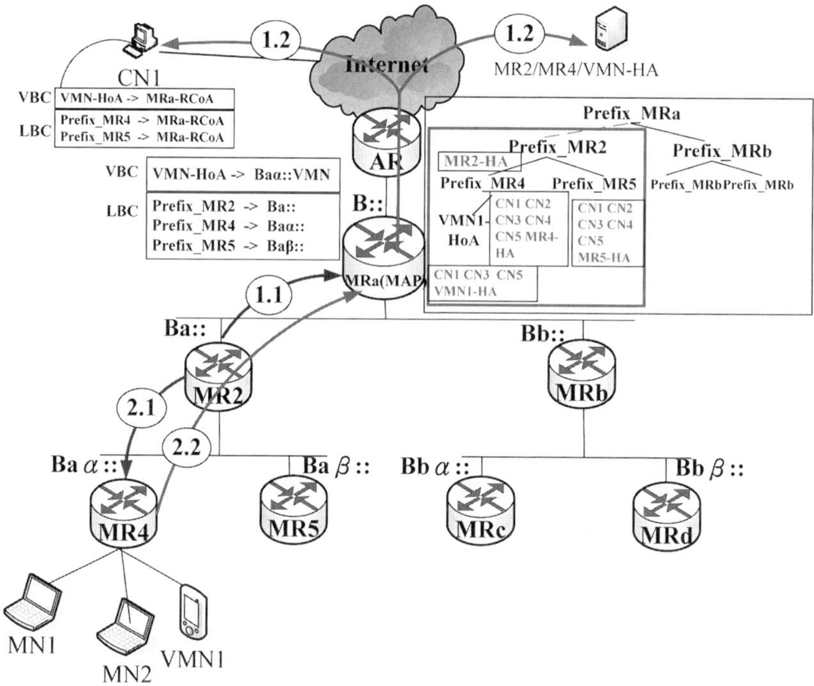

Fig. 3. The re-attachment phase of HCoP-B Inter-MAP handoff with MR2 as its leading MR

Step 2.1: MR2 continues advertising the HMRA message to delegate the CoP into the mobile subnet such that all underlying MRs and MNs can allocate new CoA addresses from the CoP in the HMRA message for later communication.

Step 2.2: After each MR/VMN acquires a new CoA, it issues an LBU to the new MAP to update its LBC/VBC with the mapping of the Prefix_MR/VMN-HoA to the new MR-CoP/VMN-CoA.]

(3) Media re-transmission after route optimization with HCoP-B

As soon as the CN has updated its VBC and LBC for RO as above, HCoP-B only needs to build a tunnel to the MAP on the path from the CN to the MN, which solves the pinball routing problem.

Table 2. Results of PUT_BUT(MR2) for Fig. 3

I	H
MR2-HA	Prefix_MR2
CN1	Prefix_MR4, VMN1-HoA, Prefix_MR5
CN2	Prefix_MR4, Prefix_MR5
CN3	Prefix_MR4, VMN1-HoA, Prefix_MR5
CN4	Prefix_MR4, Prefix_MR5
CN5	Prefix_MR4, VMN1-HoA, Prefix_MR5
MR4-HA	Prefix_MR4
VMN1-HA	VMN1-HoA
MR5-HA	Prefix_MR5
BUL[Prefix_MR2]	MR2-HA
BUL[Prefix_MR4]	CN1, CN2, CN3, CN4, CN5, MR4-HA
BUL[VMN1-HoA]	CN1, CN3, CN5, VMN1-HA
BUL[Prefix_MR5]	CN1, CN2, CN3, CN4, CN5, MR5-HA

4 Performance Evaluations

In the following, we will compare numerical results of handoff delays and consumed network bandwidth of GBUs with ROTIO, RRH, HCoP and HCoP-B schemes. The handoff latency of each scheme is defined as the time to complete its handoff flow and resume packet transmissions to the deepest MN in the nested NEMO. Notations and their values used are listed in table 3. We assume the topology of the nested NEMO is an L-level complete binary tree, as shown in Fig. 4. Hop counts from the serving AR of the nested NEMO to the HA, HA_i^l, and to the active CN of the *i*th MR, MR_i^l, at the *l*th layer are denoted as $H_{HA_i^l}$ and $H_{CN_i^l}$ respectively. Their values are assumed to be uniformly distributed among 1 to 30 Internet hops. Connecting CNs of MNs under any MR in the nested NEMO is uniformly selected from a set of ten CNs.

When the nested NEMO with ROTIO executes its handoff, the TLMR, i.e., MR_1^0, first performs prefix delegation to acquire its new MR-CoA with the time listed in Equation 1. In ROTIO, the total time for each MR to delegate CoP downward and issue the LBU to MR_1^0, i.e., Equation 3, then for each MR to send the GBU to update binding caches of HA_1^0 and active CNs, i.e., Equation 4-1, and finally for the MN to receive resumed packets, i.e., Equation 4-2, is overlapped with the time listed in Equation 2 for MR_1^0 to update HA_1^0 with the GBU. Consequently, the maximal handoff latency of ROTIO for the MN to receive resumed packets through the new AR is formulated as (1)+Max{(2),(3)+(4-1)+(4-2)}.

When the nested NEMO with RRH executes its handoff, the TLMR, i.e., MR_1^0, first performs prefix delegation to acquire its new MR-CoA with the time listed in Equation 1. After that, the TLMR issues the RA-TIO message into the nested NEMO level by level such that every underlying MR can configure its new MR-CoA and execute global binding update through the new AR to its HA. If route optimization is required for RRH, each MR must sends a GBU, containing a type 4 routing header, to each active CN for optimizing the packet route from the CN to the MN. The total time, which is shown in Equation 5 where $D \in \{\text{all } HA_i^l \text{ and } CN_j\}$, is the sum of the time spent for prefix delegation in the nested NEMO and the maximal time among

Table 3. Notations and Their Descriptions

Notations	Descriptions
L	The number of levels of the nested NEMO
MR_i^l	The *i*th MR at the *l*th layer of the nested NEMO
CN_i^l	The set of connecting CNs under the *i*th MR at the *l*th layer of the nested NEMO
N_j	The number of MRs and VMNs which have active connections with CN_j
H_D^S	Distance in hop count from the source node *S* to the destination one *D* in the nested NEMO
t_{bc}	The processing time, which value is *1ms*, for the node to update the LBC/VBC when receiving the BU.
t_{cc}	The processing time, which value is *1ms*, for the MR to configure its new CoA when receiving the CoP from the MAP.
t_{in}	The propagation delay, which value is *2ms/hop*, between any two adjacent nodes in the nested NEMO.
t_{out}	The propagation delay, which value is *10ms/hop*, between any two adjacent nodes in Internet.
t_{RS}, t_{RA}, t_{HMRA}, t_{RA-TIO}	The propagation delay, which value is *2ms/hop*, to transmit the RS, RA, HMRA or RA-TIO message between two adjacent MRs in the nested NEMO.

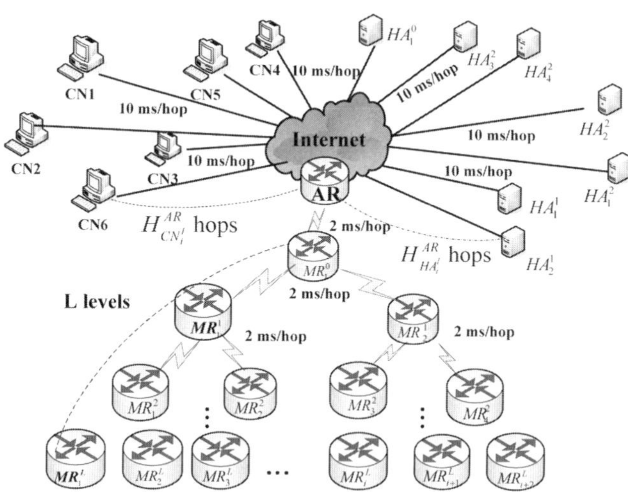

Fig. 4. The nested NEMO topology used for simulation

those for all MRs to send GBUs to their HAs and all connecting CNs. t_{in} is added to transmit packets one more hop inside the nested NEMO from the MN's serving MR

$t_{RS}+t_{RA}+t_{cc}$	**(1)**	$(t_{in}+t_{out}\times H_{HA_1^0}^{AR})\times 2+t_{bc}$	**(2)**
$t_{RA-xTIO}\times l+(t_{in}\times l\times 2+t_{bc})$	**(3)**	$t_{in}\times(l+1)+t_{out}\times(H_{HA_1^0}^{AR}+H_{CN}^{HA_1^0})+t_{bc}$	**(4-1)**
$t_{out}\times(H_{HA_1^0}^{CN}+H_{AR}^{HA_1^0})+t_{in}\times(l+1)+t_{in}$	**(4-2)**	$t_{RA-TIO}\times l+[t_{in}\times(l+1)+t_{out}\times Max(H_D^{AR})]\times 2+t_{bc}$	**(5)**
$t_{RS}+t_{HMRA}+t_{cc}$	**(6)**	$(t_{HMRA}+t_{cc})\times(l+1)$	(7)
$(t_{HMRA}+t_{cc})\times l+(t_{in}\times l\times 2)+t_{bc}$	**(8)**	$(t_{in}\times(l+2)+t_{out}\times H_{CN_i^l}^{AR})\times 2+t_{bc}$	**(9)**
$(t_{in}\times(l+1)+t_{out}\times H_{HA_i^l}^{AR})\times 2+t_{bc}$	**(10)**	$(t_{in}+t_{out}\times H_{HA_i^l}^{AR})\times 2+t_{bc}$	**(11)**
$(t_{in}+t_{out}\times H_{CN_i^l}^{AR})\times 2+t_{in}\times(l+1))$	**(12)**		

to the MN. Consequently, the handoff latency of RRH for the MN to receive resumed packets through the new AR is formulated as (1)+(5)+t_{in} .

When the nested NEMO with HCoP executes its handoff, the MAP first performs prefix delegation to acquire its new MR-CoA with the time listed in Equation 6. The MAP then issues the HMRA message to every underlying MR for configuring its new MR-CoA one level by one level with the time shown in Equation 7 and the MR executes local binding update to the MAP with the time shown in Equation 8. As soon as the MR receives the LBA from the MAP, which is the earliest time for the MN to send the GBU to its connecting CN for route optimization with the time shown in Equation 9, the MR sends the GBU to its HA and waits for the corresponding GBA, with the time shown in Equation 10. The handoff latency for the nested NEMO with HCoP to complete its handoff is the sum of the time for delegating MAP's prefix, i.e., (6), the maximal time for delegating prefixes within the nested NEMO and for updating local bindings, i.e., Max[(7), (8)], and the maximal time for MRs and MNs to update global bindings in HAs and CNs, i.e., Max[(9),(10)]. It is shown as (6)+Max[(7),(8)]+Max[(9),(10)].

As shown in Fig. 5, when the nested NEMO with HCoP-B executes its handoff, HCoP-B, like HCoP, executes prefix delegation and local binding update to the MAP with the time shown in Equation 6, 7 and 8. With the information in the BUT and operations described in section III, the MAP of HCoP-B simultaneously issues GBUs to HAs of all MRs for updating binding information with the time shown in Equation 11 and to all connecting CNs of all MNs for optimizing the media route with the time shown in Equation 12. It is obvious that HCoP-B proposes to overlap these operations and thereby to significantly reduce total handoff latency for the nested NEMO, which is shown as (6)+Max[(7),(8),(11),(12)].

As shown in Fig. 6, handoff latencies of ROTIO, HCoP, RRH and HCoP-B are grown as the level L of the nested NEMO raises, according to equations above. Because ROTIO still suffers the triangle route problem between the TLMR and its

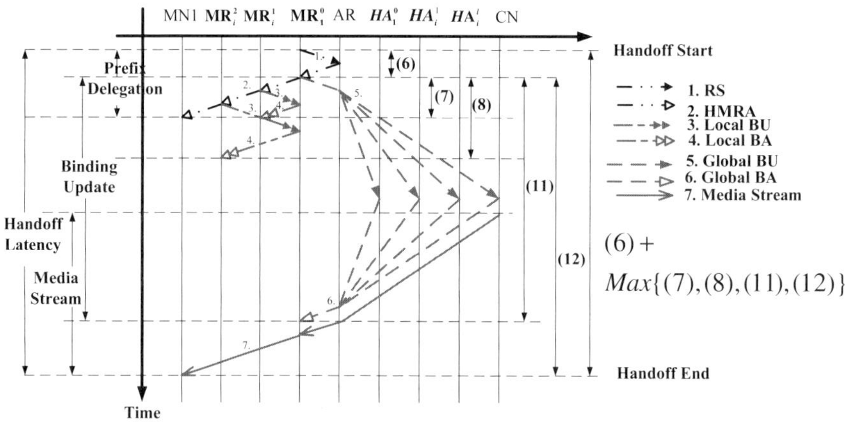

Fig. 5. Time flow of the HCoP-B handoff latency

HA, it introduces the largest handoff latencies for the MN to receive packets from the CN after the NEMO handoff. As compared to HCoP, which cannot issue the GBU message to the CN for RO until the prefix delegation and local binding update stages have been finished, RRH can immediately execute operations for RO of the CN as soon as the MR receives the RA-TIO message and thereby has smaller handoff latencies than HCoP. However, with information recorded in the BUT of the MAP, HCoP-B overlaps executions of the prefix delegation and local binding update stages inside the nested NEMO and the global binding update stage for HAs and CNs outside, which achieve the smallest handoff latencies.

Depending on the information conveyed in the GBU message, GBU messages of ROTIO, RRH, HCoP and HCoP-B for RO of CNs have different packet lengths. For RRH, the MR at level l issues the GBU message of length $(142 + 16 \times l)$ bytes, i.e., $2 \times$ IPv6 header + routing header + BU header + mobility option (TIO) = $2 \times 40 + [8 + 16 \times (l + 1)] + 6 + 32$, to record 16-byte home addresses of total $(l+1)$ MRs in the type 4 routing header. The consumed bandwidth of RRH in the nested NEMO is the sum of total GBU messages which are raised as L. GBU message lengths of ROTIO and HCoP are 144, i.e., $3 \times$ IPv6 Header + BU Header + CoA Option = $3 \times 40 + 6 + 18$, and 88, i.e., IPv6 Header + HAO + BU + CoA Option = $40 + 24 + 6 + 18$, bytes respectively such that consumed bandwidths of these two schemes are both raised as L. However, HCoP-B sends only one modified GBU message, where records address information of length $(122 + 16 \times N_j)$, i.e., IPv6 Header + HAO + BU + type 16 Mobility Option = $40 + 24 + 6 + 4 + 16 \times 3 + 16 \times N_j$, for the number of N_j MRs and VMNs which are collected in the array H of PUT_BUT(), to CN j as described in section III. As shown in Figure 7, HCoP-B consumes the least amount of bandwidth than HCoP, RATIO and RRH in the nested NEMO as the level L increases.

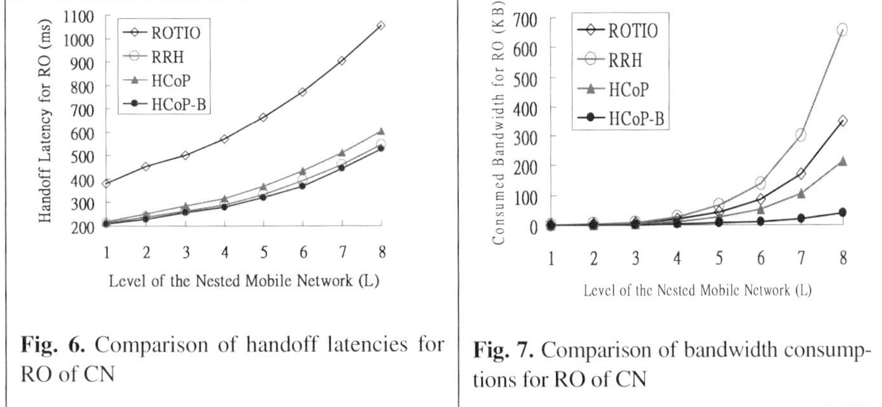

Fig. 6. Comparison of handoff latencies for RO of CN

Fig. 7. Comparison of bandwidth consumptions for RO of CN

5 Conclusions

We proposed the HCoP-B mobility management scheme for the nested NEMO with the novel BUT architecture and associated algorithms in this paper. Our HCoP-B scheme achieves the shortest handoff latency and the least amount of network bandwidth to connecting CNs for route optimization after the nested NEMO hands over to a new AR. With this mobility management scheme and the BUT architecture, the RO storm problem of the nested NEMO is solved.

References

1. Johnson, D., Perkins, C., Arkko, J.: Mobility Support in IPv6, IETF RFC 3775 (2003)
2. Devarapalli, V., Wakikawa, R.: NEMO: Basic Support Protocol, IETF RFC 3963 (2005)
3. Perera, E., et al.: Survey on Network Mobility Support. Mobile Computing and Communications Review 8(2), 7–19 (2004)
4. Thubert, P., Molteni, M.: IPv6 Reverse Routing Header and Its Application to Mobile Networks, Internet Draft: draft-thubert-nemo reverse-routing-header-05.txt (2004)
5. Cho, H., Kwon, T., Choi, Y.: Route Optimization Using Tree Information Option for Nested Mobile Networks. IEEE JSAC 24(9), 1717–1724 (2006)
6. Thubert, P., Bontoux, C., Montavont, N.: Nested Nemo Tree Discovery, Internet Draft: draft-thubert-tree- discovery-03.txt (2006)
7. Suzuki, T., et al.: Care-of Prefix Routing for Moving Networks. IEICE Trans. on Communications E88-B(7), 2756–2764 (2005)
8. Soliman, H., Castelluccia, C., MAlki, K.E., Bellier, L.: Hierarchical Mobile IPv6 Mobility Management (HMIPv6), IETF RFC 4140 (2005)
9. Cho, H., Paik, E.K.: Hierarchical Mobile Router Advertisement for Nested Mobile Networks, Internet Draft: draft-cho-nemo-hmra- oo.txt (2004)
10. Keeler, K., Westbrook, J.: Short Encoding of Planar Graphs and Maps. Discrete Applied Mathematics 58, 239–252 (1995)

Some Properties of WK-Recursive and Swapped Networks

Navid Imani[1], Hamid Sarbazi-Azad[2,1], and Albert Y. Zomaya[3]

[1] IPM School of Computer Science, Tehran, Iran
[2] Sharif University of Technology, Tehran, Iran
[3] School of Information Technologies, University of Sydney, Sydney, Australia
navid@sfu.ca, azad@sharif.edu, zomaya@it.usyd.edu.au

Abstract. The surface area which is defined as the number of vertices at a given distance from a base vertex of a graph is considered to be as one of the most useful yet abstract combinatorial properties of a graph. The applicability of surface area spans many problem spaces such as those in parallel and distributed computing. These problems normally involve combinatorial analysis of underlying graph structures (e.g., spanning tree construction, minimum broadcast algorithms, efficient VLSI layout, performance modeling). In this paper, we focus on the problem of finding the surface area of a class of popular graphs, namely the family of WK-recursive and swapped networks. These are attractive networks due to their useful recursive structures.

Keywords: Interconnection networks, WK-recursive networks, Swapped networks, Topological properties, Surface area.

1 Introduction

The surface area of a network is defined as the number of nodes at a given distance from a known base node. Apart from their mathematical elegance, the calculation of the surface area of a graph is considered as a very attractive counting problem in the field of enumerative combinatorics. Surface area can also be utilized in the context of graph theory as a strong combinatorial metric for graphs, as many of the problems that appear in graph theory involve to some extent counting the number of vertices at some distance.

Some of the most prevalent applications of the surface area property appear in the field of parallel and distributed computing. The study of surface area in the context of networking is interesting in the sense that many network properties and algorithms are directly related to an expression for the surface area of the respective graph. Surface area can be considered as a measure of the performance of broadcast and multicast in networks. It can be beneficial for generating a spanning tree of the minimum depth which useful for load balancing. It can also be used in the design of intrusion detection algorithms for a variety of network topologies. Other application arise in VLSI layout design and the analytical study of networks.

I. Stojmenovic et al. (Eds.): ISPA 2007, LNCS 4742, pp.856–867,2007.

In this paper, we study the surface area of a class of interesting recursive networks. In particular, we explore the different versions of this problem for WK-recursive networks [6], WK-pyramids [7], and Swapped Networks [15, 12, 9]. Similar studies have been conducted in relation to the calculation of the surface area of other networks. For instance, in [1], an expression for calculating the surface area of an n-dimensional hypercube is derived. The surface area for the unidirectional and bidirectional k-ary n-cube is reported in [2] while the same properties for the mesh are put forth in [3]. Similar studies have also been reported for some graphs of the Cayley family where a formula for the surface area of the rotator network was reported [5]. In [11] a closed form equation for calculation of surface area for the star graph is proposed. There might be several types of resources in a multicomputer that each processor needs to access. These resources may encompass I/O processors, memory or software packages. However, it is not often an economical nor it is a feasible or logical choice to place one resource from each type in each node of the system. In general, then, the problem of resource placement is how to disseminate some limited resources over the nodes of the network giving comparable access to all processors.

2 Preliminaries and Definitions

Definition 1 [4]. the *surface area* $A(r)$ of a graph G is defined as the number of vertices in G whose distances from a given base vertex b of G are exactly r. In other words, $A(r)$ is the surface area of a virtual sphere with radius r centered at some given vertex b.

The definition of surface area as defined above is appropriate for symmetric graphs in which any vertex of the graph can be chosen as the base vertex. However, If G is not symmetric then given u and $v \in V(G)$, the number of nodes at the distance d of v might be different from the number of nodes at the distance d of u. In order to be able to utilize the same property for any network topology, we define the *surface area of a non-symmetric network G centered at v* as the number of vertices at a known distance r from the known base vertex v (rather than from any arbitrary base vertex) of the graph. According to the latter definition, we can show that the surface area of G centered at v as $A(r,v)$ where the base node appears as the second parameter of A.

Definition 2. Given a graph G, let $A(i)$ denote the number of vertices at distance i from the base vertex in G. We define the *surface area vector* (SAV) of G as the $(k+1)$-ary ordered set $v=<A(0),\ldots,A(k)>$ containing the number of vertices at distances 0 to $Diam(G)$ of the base vertex and $k=Diam(G)$. $A(i)$ is then obtained as the $i+1^{th}$ item in v; we also call $A(i)$ as item i of v.

Definition 3. We define two operators (in addition to usual scalar multiplication and vector addition) on vector-space V containing all vectors over the infinite field of $\mathbb{N}$; Concatenation $\oplus$, and shift $\rightarrow$ operations are defined in the following way:

I) for any u and $v\in V$, $u=<u_1,u_2,\ldots,u_n>$, $v=<v_1,v_2,\ldots,v_m>$, $u\oplus v=<u_1,\ldots,u_n,v_1,\ldots,v_m>$.
II) for any $v\in V$, $v=<v_1,v_2,\ldots,v_m>$, $\vec{v}=<0,v_1,\ldots,v_m>$.

Definition 4. Given the set of vectors $v_1,\ldots,v_k$ and a vector w all defined over the same field, we denote w as a *linear concatenation* of $v_1,\ldots,v_k$ if there are scalars $c_1,\ldots,c_k\in\mathbb{N}$ such that $w=c_1v_1\oplus c_2v_2\oplus\ldots\oplus c_kv_k$.

3 Calculating the Surface Area

In this section, we derive a recursive formula for the surface area of the WK-recursive network centered at different vertices. The topology plays a crucial role in issues such as communication performance, hardware cost, better deployment of applications, and fault tolerance. The *WK-Recursive* network topology has been proposed by Vecchia and Sanges [14]. The topology has many attractive properties, such as high degree of regularity, symmetry and efficient communication. Particularly, for any specified number of degree, it can be expanded to arbitrary size level without reconfiguring the links. WK-Recursive networks have received considerable attention. Researchers have devoted themselves to various issues of WK-Recursive networks such as broadcasting algorithms, topological properties, substructure allocation and communication analysis as in [6, 8, 10]. It has been very recently shown when used as an interconnection network in systems-on-chip, the WK-recursive network can even outperform the known mesh network which has been the best known topology for network-on-chip [13].

An L-level WK-recursive network denoted by $WK_{(C,\,L)}$, consists of a set of nodes $V(WK_{(C,L)})=\{a_La_{L-1}...a_1|\,a_i\in\{0,1,..,C-1\}\ for\ 1\le i\le L\}$ where the node with address schema $A=(a_La_{L-1}...a_1)$ is connected to 1) all nodes with addresses $(a_La_{L-1}...a_2k)$ that $k\in\{0,1,..,C-1\}, k\neq a_1$, as *brother* nodes and to 2) the node $(a_La_{L-1}...a_{j+1}a_{j-1}(a_j)^j)$ if for one j, $1\le j\le L-1$, we have $a_{j-1}=a_{j-2}=...=a_1$ and $a_j\neq a_{j-1}$, as the *cousin* node. Notation $(a_j)^j$ denotes j consecutive a_j's. It is apparent that the node with address $(a_La_L..a_La_La_L)$ does not have any cousins. Such node can be called an *extern node*. So, any $WK_{(C,\,L)}$ has exactly C extern nodes. The degree of extern nodes for all $WK_{(C,\,L)}$ is C-1 and the degree of other nodes is C. As a result, the number of nodes in a $WK_{(C,\,L)}$ is calculated by $|V(WK_{(C,L)})|=C^L$ [6]. The number of edges in $WK_{(C,\,L)}$ is obtained as $|E(WC_{(C,L)})|=C^{L+1}-C$ [6].

Due to the recursive structure of $WK_{k,d}$, the extern nodes, i.e nodes labeled as J^d are isomorphic. First, we obtain an equation for the surface area of $WK_{k,d}$ centered at an extern node.

Observation 1. Let $A_d(r)$ denote the number of vertices at the distance r of the extern node in $WK_{k,d}$ labeled by J^d; then we have $A_d(r)=A_{d-i}(r)$ for any given i and d, $i<d$, such that $r<Diam(WK_{k,d-i})$.

Theorem 1. Let v_d denote the SAV of $WK_{k,d}$ centered at an extern node; then we can obtain v_d as $v_d=v_{d-1}\oplus(k-1)v_{d-1}$ and $v_0=<1>$.

Proof. If we define the $WK_{k,0}$ to be consisting of a single vertex then $Diam(WK_{k,0})=0$; hence, v_0 is a vector containing a single number, i.e. $v_0=<1>$. To prove the first argument in the theorem, we consider counting the number of vertices at different distances starting from distance zero. As a result of the recursive structure of the *WK*-recursive network, each $WK_{k,l}$ in the structure of a *WK*-recursive of higher dimension is connected to $(k-1)$ other copies of $WK_{k,l}$. Each such a copy is connected to the former $WK_{k,l}$ through a single edge branching out from its extern node. Therefore, the vertices at the distance of $Diam(WK_{k,l})+1$ are $(k-1)$ extern nodes, one in each $(k-1)$ remained copies of $WK_{k,l}$. From here counting the number of vertices at higher distances is fairly easy. Because it is similar to the process of counting nodes on $(k-1)$ independent copies of $WK_{k,l}$. Hence, we can conclude that the surface area of $WK_{k,l+1}$ at the distance $Diam(WK_{k,l})+i$, $i \leq Diam(WK_{k,l})$ would be equal to three times of the surface area of $WK_{k,l}$ at the distance i. Hence, $v_l=v_{l-1}\oplus(k-1)v_{l-1}$. As l was chosen arbitrarily, we can state the same argument for a WK subgraph of any dimension. In particular, if $l=d$, we get a recursive equation for obtaining v_d.

Theorem 2. Let $A(r)$ denote the surface area of $WK_{k,d}$ centered at a extern node, $r\leq Diam(WK_{k,d})$, then $A(r)=(k-1)^{\|r\|}$ where $\|r\|$ denotes the number of '1' bits in the binary presentation of r.

Proof. In order to obtain a non-recursive equation for the surface area we try to solve the recursive vector equation derived in theorem 1. Let us first assume that we want to calculate the surface area for some r, $0 < r < Diam(WK_{k,d})=2^d-1$. It is clear that each vector v_d is obtained from concatenating two vectors of equal lengths. If $r \leq \lfloor Diam(WK_{k,d})/2 \rfloor = Diam(WK_{k,d-1})=2^{d-1}-1$, then it is clear that $A(r)$ for a network of dimension k is exactly equal to the surface area for the sub-network of size $k-1$ at the same distance r. On the other hand, if $r > Diam(WK_{k,d-1})$, by theorem 1 we know that $A(r)$ is in the second half vector and we can calculate it as three times the surface area of $WK_{k,d-1}$ at the distance $r-Diam(WK_{k,d-1})$. In order to obtain the value of $A(r)$, we can continue this process of finding $A(r)$ in $WK_{k,d}$ by figuring out whether r is located in the first half or the second half of v_{d-1}. The value of $A(r)$, hence, depends on which half vector is chosen at each stage of locating r. With this in mind, we invoke the binary representation of r in order to facilitate the process of identifying half vectors which contain the item we are looking for. In particular, if we write the binary representation of r in d digits (for some r we may have zero digit(s) on its left) we can find out immediately whether r is in the first or second half vector in the ith step of finding r by just looking at i^{th} digit on the left. Also, in order to help with our search for r^{th} item in the vector, we imagine a tree structure namely the *vector tree* for v_d, VT_d, in the following way: each vector x_i is modeled as a vertex in VT_d while v_d is represented by a vertex located at the root of the tree. There is an edge between two vectors x and y iff x is obtained as linear concatenation of y and some other vector(s). We also label each edge to a vector v_i with the coefficient of v_i. Hence, in the case of our recursive equation, v_d has two children, namely v_{d-1} and $v'_{d-1}=v_{d-1}$. Furthermore, the edge to the left child is labeled '1' while the edge to the right child is labeled '$k-1$'. Amusingly, VT_d is a complete binary tree of height d. The vertices of VT_d at a height l correspond to vectors of length 2^l and leaves of the tree match vectors of length 1. For the given number r if we trace the item $A(r)$ in vectors starting from the base node down the vector tree, as the vector corresponding to each intermediate node is a linear concatenation of vectors corresponding to its children, no item is lost in the tree hierarchy but each item may be multiplied (divided) to scalars at each level of the hierarchy. Therefore, vertices containing $A(r)$ item are on a path from the base vertex to some leaf vertex, say x. In particular, we can obtain $A(r)$ by multiplying the edge labels on the respective path and the single value in the vector corresponding to x. If we tag each right edge in VT_d with '1' and each left edge with '0' then the concatenation of the tags on the path constructed for r corresponds to the binary representation of r. Figure 1 illustrates the structure of VT_d. Equivalently, the only leaf vertex which contains r is the rth leaf from the left of the tree. On the other hand, right edges are labeled '$k-1$' while others are labeled '1', so $A(r)$ can be obtained as $(k-1)$ to the power of the number of '1's in the binary representation of r. Figure 2 depicts the graph corresponding to the surface area function of $WK_{4,d}$ wherein the x axis is chosen to be the size of network (denoted by d).

Definition 5. Given a graph G and a subgraph H of G, we define the *Regional surface area* of G at the distance r of H denoted by $A_H(r)$ as the number of vertices v, $v \notin V(H)$, whose distance from some vertex u of H is r while v is at least at the distance r of each other vertex $u' \in V(H)$. We call H the base subgraph of G for calculating $A_H(r)$. Hence, regional surface area can be formally defined in the following way:

$$A_H(r)=card\{v\in G-H \mid (\exists u\in H \mid d(u,v)=r)\wedge(\forall u'\in H,\ u'\neq u,\ d(v,u) \geq r)\}$$

The statement above generalizes the definition of surface area as proposed in [4] such that the former definition is obtained as a specific case of regional surface area when H is chosen to be a single vertex (i.e. subgraph consisting of the base vertex only). In what follows, we obtain the regional surface area of $WK_{k,d}$ when two center nodes are chosen as the base subgraph.

Theorem 3. Let u_d denote the surface area vector of $WK_{k,d}$ calculated from the two center nodes in $WK_{k,d}$, then u_d can be calculated as $u_d=2v_{d-1}\oplus(k-2)u_{d-1}$, $u_0=<1>$.

Proof. We calculate the number of vertices at different distances assuming the two center vertices as the base subgraph (vertices at distance 0). Let us denote by S and S' the $WK_{k,d-1}$ subgraph containing either of vertices of H. Vertices at a distance $r<Diam(WK_{k,d-1})$ in $WK_{k,d}$ are vertices at distance r of either S or S'. Hence, the surface area at distances less than $Diam(WK_{k,d-1})$ is equal to twice of the surface area in the case of the extern node as the base node. On the other hand, all the vertices of S

and S' are at most at distance $Diam(WK_{k,d-1})$ of the base vertex in the respective subgraph (S and S'). Therefore, at distance $Diam(WK_{k,d-1})+1$ two vertices at each of two remained copies of $WK_{k,d-1}$ are chosen. Let us call these subgraphs R and R'. This situation for each of R and R' is similar to the one we encountered for $WK_{k,d}$ at distance 0. Hence, the regional surface area at distance $Diam(WK_{k,d-1})+i$ of $WK_{k,d}$ would be equal to twice the regional surface area of $WK_{k,d-1}$ at distance i. Therefore, we can build the regional surface area vector as $u_d=2v_{d-1}\oplus(k-2)u_{d-1}$.

In order to solve the more complex vector recursive equation derived for u_d, we would generalize the same approach which was followed in Theoreme 2 to cover theoretically any recursive equation obtained using concatenation of multiplication, addition, and shift of vectors. We would later use this main theorem as a vehicle for solving the complex recursive equations derived in the next sections.

Definition 6. Given a vector $v=<v_0,v_1,\ldots,v_n>$ and a natural number $k < n$, we define $\overset{(k)}{\vec{v}}$ as $\overset{(k)}{\vec{v}} =< \underbrace{0,\ldots,0}_{k}, v_0, v_1, \ldots, v_n >$ if $k \geq 0$, and as $\overset{(k)}{\vec{v}} =< v_{|k|+1}, \ldots, v_n >$ if $k<0$.

Theorem 4. Let $w_d = x_{d-1}^0 \oplus x_{d-1}^1 \oplus \ldots \oplus x_{d-1}^{i-1} \oplus w_{d-1} \oplus x_{d-1}^{i+1} \oplus \ldots \oplus x_{d-1}^{k-1}$ where x_{d-1}^j is defined as $x_{d-1}^j = c_j \overset{s_j}{\vec{y}}{}_{d-1}^{j}$, $0 \leq j \leq k-1$, for some vector y_{d-1}^j, natural number c_j and integer s_j; then item r of w_d, $w_d(r)$, can be obtained as:

$$w_d(r) = c_i^{\|r'\|_k^i} c_j y_{d-1}^j((r'')_{10} - s_j)$$
$$(r)_k = (r' j r'')_k$$

where $(r)_k$ is the modulo-k representation of r, r' is the left most part of $(r)_k$ containing i symbols only, $y_{d-1}^j(r)$ is the function which retrieves the item r of y_{d-1}^j vector, and $\|r'\|_k^i$ denotes the number of i symbols in modulo-k representation of r'. We also assume that all x and w vectors which are subscribed with the same number (say w_i and x_i's) are of the same length.

Proof. In order to solve the recursive equation for w_d, we generalize the tree presentation proposed in the proof of Theorem 1. Given a general recursive equation, e.g. w_d, we build the *vector tree* of w_d, $VT(w_d)$, in the following way: each vector in the recursive expansion of w_d is modeled as a vertex in $VT(w_d)$ while w_d is represented by a vertex located at the root of the tree. Hence, with some liberty in the use of notation we denote a node, v, as a node in the tree and the vector corresponding to v. There is an edge between two vectors x and y in $VT(w_d)$ iff x is obtained as a linear concatenation of y and some other vector(s). We also label each edge to a vector y_{d-1}^j with the coefficient c_j. In order to calculate $w_d(r)$, we need to track the r item down the tree hierarchy starting from the root vertex. Again, because each vertex v can be written as a linear concatenation of its children, the set of vertices which contain the r item form a path from the root to a leaf vertex. In particular, we can define a one-to-one function M to map each item $w_d(i)$ to a leaf node in $VT(w_d)$. Let us denote each such a path from root to a leaf node $M(w_d(r))$ by P_i. Thus, we can derive $w_d(r)$ by multiplying over the labels of all edges of P_i and then multiplying the result by the content of the leaf node. But as we do not know the recursive equation for y vectors, we are unable to form the tree completely and we would halt as soon as we track the rth item in some y vector; i.e. some part of P_i is unknown. Let y be the first unknown vector (y type vector) we encounter on the path from the root and let P_a be the path from w_d to y. Further, let us assume P_b is the path in $VT(y)$ containing the r item from y to $M(w_d(r))$ leaf vertex. Clearly, P_aP_b=P_r. Given a path P, we denote by $\prod P$ the multiplication of the label of all edges on P. $w_d(r)$ can then be obtained as $w_d(r) = M(w_d(r))\prod P_a \prod P_b$. It is clear that the path P_a corresponds to a sequence of vertices say $w_d, w_{d-1}, \ldots, w_{d-i}, y_j$. Obviously, all edges on this path except for the last one lead to the ith child; hence, if we rank the edges to the children of each parent vertex from left to right starting from 0, we get the following sequence for P_a : $i,i,\ldots,i,j$. On the other hand, the lengths of vectors in each level of the tree are equal and hence the numbers of leaves in the subtrees whose roots are in the same level. In particular, we can decide which subtree contains the r item using the modulo-k presentation of r. If the 1st digit from the left of $(r)_k$ is equal to i then in the 1st step of the process of finding the r item, the edge ranked i should be chosen and so on. Then, we can derive the number of edges ranked i on P_a, i.e. $|P_a|-1$, as the number of consequent i symbols which appears at the left of $(r)_k$. Therefore, we can obtain $w_d(r)$ as $c_i^{\|r\|_k^i} x_{d-1}^j((r'')_{10})$ but we know that $x_{d-1}^j = c_j \overset{s_j}{\vec{y}}{}_{d-1}^j$ and that $\overset{s_j}{\vec{y}}{}_{d-1}^j(r) = y_{d-1}^j(r - s_j)$. After a simple replacement, the final equation for $w_d(r)$ is obtain as the one proposed in the theorem. Similarly, if we know a recursive vector equation for y_{d-1}^j, based on vectors which have not been calculated previously (any vector other than w for the case of y_{d-1}^j), one can go on with the approach we followed in this proof to obtain the final closed form equation for w_d.

Theorem 5. Let $u_d(r)$ denote the number of vertices at distance r from two center vertices in $WK_{k,d}$; then $u_d(r)=2(k-2)^{\|s\|}(k-1)^{\|t\|}$ where s and t are strings of integers obtained by chopping the consequent zeros from the left side of the binary presentation of r.

Proof. We use theorem 4 in order to derive a non-recursive equation for calculating $u_d(r)$. As in each step of recursion of u_d each vector is divided into two parts, $VT(u_d)$ is a full balanced binary tree and we should choose l=2 in theorem 4. There are no shift operations present in the recursion, so we can obtain $u_d(r)=(k-1)^{\|s\|}2v_{d-1}((t)_{10})$, but we have already calculated v_d; hence, we can derive the final equation for $u_d(r)$ as $u_d(r)= 2(k-2)^{\|s\|}(k-1)^{\|t\|}$.

So far, we studied the surface area of WK-recursive network. WK-recursive is not considered as a regular network as the degree of extern nodes is $k-1$, i.e. less than the degree of other nodes in the network. If we interconnect the opposite extern nodes of

$WK_{k,d}$ together using extra wraparound edges for an even k, we obtain a regular graph which is called the torus *WK*-recursive (*TWK*). As a result of the existence of the wraparound edges at the extern nodes, calculating the surface area for *TWK* is not as straightforward as the previous cases. In what follows, we propose a formula for calculating the surface area of the torus *WK*-recursive network.

Theorem 6. Let w_d denote the surface area vector of $WK_{k,d}$ centered at a center node; we can obtain w_d recursively as:

$$w_d=(v_{d-1}\oplus(k-2)w_{d-1})+\vec{v}_{d-1}$$

Proof. In order to derive a recursive vector equation for the surface area of $WK_{k,d}$, we identify vertices at different distances starting from distance 0. Vertices at distance 1 are those which are at distance 1 from the extern node in $WK_{k,d-1}$ plus one other vertex in the second copy of $WK_{k,d-1}$. If we go on with this process, for the distance 2 we can obtain the surface area as $v_{d-1}(2)+v_{d-1}(1)$. In particular, for $r \le Diam(WK_{k,d-1})$, we can obtain the surface area at the distance r as $v_{d-1}(r)+v_{d-1}(r-1)$. At the distance $Diam(WK_{k,d-1})+1$, $(k-1)$ extern vertices are selected, one on each remained copy of $WK_{k,d-1}$. At the distance $Diam(WK_{k,d-1})+2$, the other extern of each of these copies are selected. Particularly, as a result of the fact that in the WK-recursive network extern vertices and center vertices are homogeneous (vertex transitive), this is the same situation we faced when we started counting the vertices at distance 1. Therefore, hereafter the surface area at the distance r would be equal to the surface area of $WK_{k,d-1}$ at distance $r-Diam(WK_{k,d-1})$. From the above arguments, one can easily see that w_d can be obtained as $w_d=(v_{d-1}\oplus(k-2)w_{d-1})+\vec{v}_{d-1}$.

Corollary 1. The surface area of $TWK_{k,d}$ centered at one of its center nodes is equal to the surface area of $WK_{k,d}$ centered at a extern node.

Proof. This corollary is immediately derived as a result of the vertex transitivity of the extern and center vertices in the torus *WK*-recursive network.

Theorem 7. Let $w_d(r)$ denote the surface area of $WK_{k,d}$ at the distance r from a center node; then

$$w_d(r)=\begin{cases}(k-2)^{\|s\|}\left((k-1)^{\|t\|}+(k-1)^{\|t-1\|}\right), & (\|t\|\neq 0)\vee(r=0)\\(k-2)^{\|s\|-1}\left((k-2)+(k-1)^{|t|}\right), & \text{Otherwise}\end{cases}.$$

Proof. Again, we use theorem 4 in order to derive a closed form equation for the recursive equation proposed for w_d. However, we can not solve w_d directly because its recursive equation is not in the form of the ones which theorem 4 covers. Yet, we can use the same theorem in order to obtain partial results which would later be useful in deriving the final solution. For the time being, let us assume that we want to solve the equation $w'_d=(v'_{d-1}\oplus(k-2)w_{d-1})$. Using theorem 4, we can easily derive its solution as $w'_d(r)=(k-2)^{\|s\|}v'_{d-1}((t)_{10})$. Now, if we could define $v'_d=v_d+\vec{v}_{d,1..2^d}$ where $\vec{v}_{d,1..2^d}$ is the vector containing the first 2^d items of $\vec{v}_d$, then v'_{d-1} had 2^{d-1} items and $v'_{d-1}((t)_{10})=v_{d-1}((t)_{10})+ v_{d-1}((t)_{10}-1)=(k-1)^{\|t\|}+(k-1)^{\|t-1\|}$. Therefore, we could obtain $w_d(r)$ as $w_d(r)=(k-2)^{\|s\|}[(k-1)^{\|t\|}+ (k-1)^{\|t-1\|}]$. Yet, the recursive equation we are trying to solve is $w_d=(v_{d-1}\oplus(k-2)w_{d-1})+ \vec{v}_{d-1}$ in which $\vec{v}_{d-1}$ affects not only the first half vector but also the first element of the second half vector. It is the only difference between w_d and w'_d and, hence, the elements of the two vectors are equal except for those elements which are located at the start of a half vector at some level of the recursion. In particular, as each vector is divided into two half vectors of equal size in each step of the recursion, the respective elements (which have to be treated as exceptions) are those for which t is obtained as a string of all zeros. Thus, $w_d(r)=w'_d(r)$ if $\|t\|\neq 0$. If $\|s\|\neq 0$, $\|t\|=0$ and $|t|=l>0$ then r item is the first element of w_l and, hence, $w_l(r)$ is obtained as the multiplication of the first $d-l-1$ edges on the path P_a in $VT(w_d)$ and then multiplying the result by $(k-1)^{|t|}+(k-2)(k-1)^{\|t\|}$, where $(k-1)^{|t|}$, is the last element of v_l. But $\|t\|=0$, if we can obtain $w_d(r)= (k-2)^{\|s\|-1}[(k-1)^{|t|}+(k-2)]$ for the case where $\|t\|=0$ and $\|s\|\neq 0$.

Theorem 8. Let $u_d(r)$ and $u'_d(r)$ denote the number of vertices at the distance r from the two center vertices in $WK_{k,d}$ and $TWK_{k,d}$, respectively; then $u_d(r)=u'_d(r)$.

Proof. Starting from the two center vertices in $TWK_{k,d}$, the extern nodes of two $TWK_{k,d-1}$ copies which contain initial vectors are reachable at distance $Diam(WK_{k,d-1})$. Therefore, at distance $Diam(WK_{k,d-1})+1$ we can exploit wraparound links to reach a vertex on the other $TWK_{k,d-1}$ copy but this vertex is at the distance $Diam(WK_{k,d-1})$ from one of the two center vertices and, hence, is already visited. Therefore, we can conclude that the presence of the wraparound edges makes no difference in the surface area of $TWK_{k,d}$ and $u_d(r)=u'_d(r)$.

Definition 7 [7]**.** The WK-Pyramid network, denoted as $WKP_{(C,L)}$, consists of a set of nodes $0\leq k\leq L, 0\leq a_i\leq C-1, 1\leq i\leq k$ or $k=0$ and $a_1=1\}$. A node with addressing schema $(k,(a_k a_{k-1} a_{k-2}...a_1))\in V(WKP_{(C,L)})$ is said to be a node at level k. specially, the node at level 0 is said the *apex* node. The part $(a_k a_{k-1} a_{k-2}...a_1)$ determines the address of nodes at related WK-recursive network in layer k. All the nodes in level k form a $WK_{(C,L)}$. Hence, there are totally $N=\sum_{k=0}^{L} C^k = \frac{C^{L+1}-1}{C-1}$ nodes in the $WKP_{(C,L)}$. A node with address $(k,(a_k a_{k-1} a_{k-2}...a_1))\in V(WKP_{(C,L)})$ is connected, within the mesh at level $k>0$, to node $(k,(a_k a_{k-1} a_{k-2}...a_2 j))\in V(WKP_{(C,L)})$, $1\leq j\leq C$, $j\neq a_1$, as the neighbouring *sibling* nodes, and connected to node with address schema $(k,(a_L a_{L-1}...a_{j+1} a_{j-1}(a_j)^j))$, as cousin nodes (nodes at the same level), if for one j, $1\leq j\leq L-1$, $a_{j-1}=a_{j-2}=...=a_1$ and $a_j\neq a_{j-1}$. It is also connected to nodes $(k+1,(a_k a_{k-1} a_{k-2} ... a_2 a_1 j))$, $1 \le j \le C$, in level k+1, as *child* nodes, and connected to node $(k-1,(a_k a_{k-1} a_{k-2} ... a_2))$, in level k−1, as *parent* node.

Next, we study the surface area of the WK-recursive pyramid network as a hierarchical network which benefits from WK-recursive networks of different sizes in its layers.

Theorem 9. Let $A_a(r)$ denote the number of vertices at the distance r of the apex node of a $WKP_{k,l}$, $r \le l$; $A_a(r)$ can then be obtained as $A_a(r)=(k-1)^r$.

Proof. By taking advantage of the structure of $WKP_{k,l}$, the vertices in each $WK_{k,r}$ can be reached from the apex node at the distance r by taking the vertical links. Therefore, the number of vertices at distance r of the apex node is obtained as $|V(WK_{k,r})|=(k-1)^r$.

Theorem 10 [16]. Let p_d denote the vector surface area of $WKP_{k,d}$ centered at a extern node in the base of the pyramid; then p_d is obtained as $p_d = \sum_{i=0}^{d} \vec{v}_{d-i}^{(i)}$.

Theorem 11 [16]. Let x_d denote the surface area vector of the $WKP_{k,l}$ centered at a extern node in an intermediate layer, say $WK_{k,d}$, such that $d+Diam(WK_{k,d}) \le l$ and $d \ge Diam(WK_{k,d})$. x_d is then obtained as $x_d = \sum_{i=-d}^{d} \lfloor k^i \rfloor \vec{v}_{d+i}^{\,\|i\|}$.

Theorem 12. Let $p_d(r)$ denote surface area at the distance r of a $WKP_{k,l}$ centered at a extern node in the base layer ; $p_d(r)$ can be obtained from the following equation:

$$p_d(r) = \sum_{i=0}^{r} (k-1)^{\|i\|}, \qquad r < l \cdot$$

Proof. By exploring the recursive vector equation for p_d, one can observer that for each $r<l$ only r of the vectors would have a non-zero value for their r+1th element. In particular, the value of this item for a vector such as $\vec{v}_{d-i}^{\,i}$ would be $(k-1)^{\|r-i\|}$. The final equation is easily derived by adding up the value of r+1th item for all vectors $\vec{v}_{d-i}^{\,i}$ for different values of i.

Theorem 13 [16]. Let $x_d(r)$ denote the number of vertices at the distance r of a extern node say b in an intermediate layer d of a $WKP_{k,l}$; then $x_d(r)$ can be obtained as $x_d(r) = \sum_{i=0}^{r} (k-1)^{\|i\|} + k^i (k-1)^{\|r-i\|}$.

Definition 8. *Swapped network*: the swapped network, $Sw(G)$, derived from the n-node *nucleus* or *basis* graph G, is a graph with n copies of G (clusters) numbered 0 to $n-1$, so that node j in cluster i is connected to node i of cluster j for all $i \ne j$ and $0 \le i$, $j \le n-1$ [15]. Next, we derive the surface area vector of the swapped networks assuming the surface area vector of its nucleus graph [12, 15].

Theorem 14. Given a symmetric graph G, let $w(G)$ denote the surface area vector of a swapped network with G as its nucleus. $w(G)$ can be calculated as $w(G) = v + \sum_{i=1}^{Diam(G)} \overrightarrow{(v_i v)}^{i+1}$, where $v=<v_0,v_1,\ldots, v_{Diam(G)}>$ is the surface area vector of G.

Proof. In order to count the number of vertices at different distances from the extern node, we study the structure of the swapped network. Let G' denote the swapped network with the nucleus G. Then, G' consists of $|V(G)|$ copies of G, each labeled with an integer in range of 1 to $|V(G)|$. Let us also label each vertex in G with a distinct integer in range of 1 to $|V(G)|$. Each given vertex i in some copy j of G is then by definition connected to a single group (group i) through a single edge to its j vertex, $i \neq j$. In particular, each two arbitrary x and y vertices of a group j are connected to two different copies of G, i.e. to x and y groups, respectively. Hence, each group other than j is connected to only a single vertex in group j. From this we can infer that at the distance k+1 one vertex in v_k of the groups is selected. But as G is assumed to be symmetric, the number of vertices in each of these new copies which are selected at some distance $k+\varepsilon+1$, $0 \le k \le Diam(G)$, are equal to v_k. It is as if at the distance k+1 the process of counting is initiated in v_k copies of G and, hence, a vector $\overrightarrow{(v_i v)}^{i+1}$ is added to w. The final vector equation for w is obtained by adding up these vectors for all values of i.

4 Conclusions

In this paper, we studied several combinatorial properties of some attractive network topologies. In particular, we extended the definition of the surface area to fit any network topology. We also defined the regional surface area as a generalization of the normal surface area which assumes a subgraph as the base and calculates the distances accordingly. In order to propose a solution for the surface area of the desired networks, we set forth a new vector notation, namely the surface area vector, and derived the surface area as a recursive equation based on these vectors. Next, we formulated closed-form solutions for the surface area of the WK-recursive, WK-pyramid, and swapped networks using a novel notion called recursive vector equations.

References

1. Abraham, S.: Issue in the design of direct interconnection networks schemes for the multiprocessors. PhD Thesis, University of Illinois at Urbana-Champaign (1992)
2. Sarbazi-Azad, H.: On Some Combinatorial Properties of Meshes. In: Proceedings of IEEE International Symposium on Parallel Architectures and Networks, pp. 117–122. IEEE Computer Society Press, Los Alamitos (2004)

3. Sarbazi-Azad, H., Ould-Khaoua, M., Mackenzie, L., Akl, S.G.: On the Combinatorial Properties of k-ary n-Cubes. Journal of Interconnection Networks 5, 79–91 (2004)
4. Broeg, B.: Topological properties of of k-ary n-cubes. PhD Thesis, Department of Computer Science, Oregon State Univ. (1995)
5. Cobett, P.F.: Rotator Graphs: An efficient topology for point-to-point multiprocessor networks. IEEE Transaction on Parallel and Distributed Systems 3, 622–626 (1992)
6. Duh, D.R., Chen, G.H.: Topological properties of WK-recursive networks. Journal of Parallel and Distributed Computing 23, 468–474 (1994)
7. Hoseiny Farahabady, M., Sarbazi-Azad, H.: The WK-Recursive Pyramid: An Efficient Network Topology. In: International Symposium on Parallel Architectures, Algorithms and Networks, pp. 312–317 (2005)
8. Fang, J.F., Lai, G.J., Liu, Y.C., Fang, S.T.: A novel broadcasting scheme for WK-recursive networks. Communications, Computers and Signal Processing, pp.1028–1031(2003)
9. Farahabady, M.H., Sarbazi-Azad, H.: The recursive transpose-connected cycles (RTCC) interconnection network for multiprocessors. In: Proceedings of the 2005 ACM symposium on Applied computing, pp. 734–738 (2005)
10. Fu, J.S.: Hamiltonicity of the WK-Recursive Network with and without Faulty Nodes. IEEE Transactions on Parallel and Distributed Systems 16, 853–865 (2005)
11. Imani, N., Sarbazi-Azad, H., Akl, S.G.: On Some of the Combinatorial Properties of the Star Graph. In: Proceedings of international symposium on Parallel Architectures, Algorithms and Networks, pp. 58–65 (2005)
12. Parhami, B.: Swapped interconnection networks: Topological, Performance, and robustness attributes. J. Parallel Distrib. Comput. 65, 1443–1452 (2005)
13. Rahmati, D., Kiasari, A.E., Hessabi, S., Sarbazi-Azad, H.: Performance comparison of WK-recursive and mesh networks for Networks-on-chip. In: IEEE International Conference on Computer Design, pp. 142–147. IEEE Computer Society Press, Los Alamitos (2006)
14. Vecchia, D., Sanges, C.: Recursively Scalable Networks for Message Passing Architectures. In: Proc. Conf. Parallel Processing and Applications, pp. 33–40 (1987)
15. Yeh, C.-H., Parhami, B.: Swapped networks: unifying the architectures and algorithms of a wide class of hierarchical parallel Processors. In: Proceedings of the International Conference on Parallel and Distributed Systems, pp. 230–237 (1996)
16. Imani, N., Sarbazi-Azad, H., Zomaya, A.: Some combinatorial properties of recursive networks. Technical reports, School of Computer Science, IPM, Iran (2006)

Design and Analysis of Multicast Communication in Multidimensional Mesh Networks

Ahmed Al-Dubai[1], Mohamed Ould-Khaoua[2], and Imed Romdhani[3]

[1,3] School of Computing, Napier University, 10 Colinton Road
Edinburgh, EH10 5DT, UK
{a.al-dubai,i.romdhani}@napier.ac.uk
[2] Department of Computing Science, University of Glasgow
Glasgow G12 8RZ, UK
mohamed@dcs.gla.ac.uk

Abstract. This paper addresses the issue of multicast communication in scalable interconnection networks, using path-based scheme. Most existing multicast algorithms either assume a fixed network size, low dimensional networks or only consider the latency at the network level. As a consequence, most of these algorithms implement multicast in a sequential manner and can not scale well with the network dimensions or the number of nodes involved. Furthermore, most of these algorithms handle multicast communication with low throughput. In this paper, we propose a multicast algorithm for multidimensional interconnection networks, which is built upon our Qualified Groups QG multicast scheme for ensuring efficient communication irrespective of the network sizes/dimensions or the number of the destination nodes. Unlike the existing works, this study considers the scalability and latency at both the network and node levels so as to achieve a high degree of parallelism. Our results show that the proposed algorithm considerably improves the multicast message delivery ratio, throughput and scalability.

Keywords: Mesh Networks, Path-based Multicast, Routing Algorithms.

1 Introduction

Multicast is a fundamental communication pattern for ensuring a scalable implementation of a wide variety of applications in parallel and distributed computing. In multicast communication, a source node sends the same message to an arbitrary number of destinations in the network. Multicast is widely used by many important applications. For instance, multicast is frequently used by parallel search and parallel graph algorithms [3, 14]. In more recent fields such as bioinformatics, protein sequences are clustered into families of related sequences. Multicast services are required during the creation and maintenance of theses clusters. Furthermore, multicast communication can be used as a tool that can allow efficient access and update of different types of information and finding the genes in the DNA sequences of various organisms. Moreover, multicast is also fundamental to the implementation

I. Stojmenovic et al. (Eds.): ISPA 2007, LNCS 4742, pp.868–882,2007.

of higher-level communication operations such as gossip, gather, and barrier synchronisation [1, 2, 4]. In general, the literature outlines three main schemes to deal with the multicast problem: unicast-based [1, 3], tree-based [3, 13, 17] and path-based [2, 3, 8, 14, 15]. A number of studies have shown that *path-based* algorithms exhibit superior performance characteristics over their unicast-based and tree-based counterparts, especially within *wormhole* switched networks [2, 14, 15]. In path-based multicast, when the units (called flits in wormhole switched networks) of a message reach one of the destination nodes in the multicast group, they are copied to local memory while they continue to flow through the node to reach the other destinations [2, 3, 8]. The message is removed from the network when it reaches the last destination in the multicast group.

Although many interconnection networks have been studied [3], and indeed deployed in practice, none has proved clearly superior in all roles, since the communication requirements of different applications vary widely. Nevertheless, *n*-dimensional *wormhole switched* meshes have undoubtedly been the most popular interconnection network used in practice [2, 3, 5, 6, 10, 11] due to their desirable topological properties including ease of implementation, modularity, low diameter, and ability to exploit locality exhibited by many parallel applications [3]. In wormhole switching, a message is divided into elementary units called flits, each of a few bytes for transmission and flow control. The *header* flit (containing routing information) governs the route and the remaining data flits follow it in a pipelined fashion. If a channel transmits the header of a message, it must transmit all the remaining flits of the same message before transmitting flits of another message. When the header is blocked the data flits are blocked in-situ.

Meshes are suited to a variety of applications including matrix computation, image processing and problems whose task graphs can be embedded naturally into the topology [3, 6, 10]. Wormhole switched meshes have been used in a number of real parallel machines including the Intel Paragon, MIT J-machine, Cray T3D, T3E, Caltech Mosaic, Intel Touchstone Delta, Stanford DASH [3]. Recently, among commercial multicomputers and research prototypes, Alpha 21364's multiple processors network and IBM Blue Gene uses a 3D mesh. In addition, a mesh has been recently the topology of choice for many high-performance parallel systems and local area networks such as Myrinet-based LANs. More recently, the mesh topology has been widely adopted in network-on-chip technologies, including NOSTRUM, SOCBUS, RAW (MIT) which are regular mesh architectures [11]. While our previous focused on 2D meshes, our present study investigates the multicast communication over the 3D mesh networks with the aim of generalising our previous multicast scheme [2] for higher dimensional meshes. The rest of the paper is organised as follows. Section 2 we briefly review the system. Section 3 accommodates our multicast algorithm. Section 4 conducts extensive analysis and simulation experiments and Section 5 summarises this work.

2 Preliminaries and Motivation

Definition 1: *Given a direct network composed of processors interconnected together by n-dimensional mesh topology, it can be modelled as a graph* $G = (V, E)$ *with node* *set* V *and edge set* E. *In such topology, a* $N = d_{1\max} \times d_{2\max} \times d_{3\max} \times .. d_{n\max}$ *mesh:*

$V = (d_1, d_2, d_3,..n) \in \{(d_1, d_2, d_3,..n)_1 ..... (d_1, d_2, d_3,..n)_N\}$:

$0 \le d_1 < d_{1\max}, 0 \le d_2 < d_{2\max}, 0 \le d_3 < d_{3\max} ...$

$0 \le d_n < d_{n\max}$, $E = \{(d_{1i}, d_{2i}, d_{3i,..} d_{ni}), (d_{1j}, d_{2j}, d_{3j},..d_{nj})\}$, *such that any two nodes with co-ordinates* $(d_{1i,} d_{2i}, d_{3i},..d_{ni})$ *and* $(d_{1j,} d_{2j}, d_{3j},..d_{nj})$ *are connected by a communication channel if and only if*

$$\left|d_{1i} - d_{1j}\right| + \left|d_{2i} - d_{2j}\right| + \left|d_{3i} - d_{3j}\right| + ...\left|d_{ni} + d_{nj}\right| = 1$$

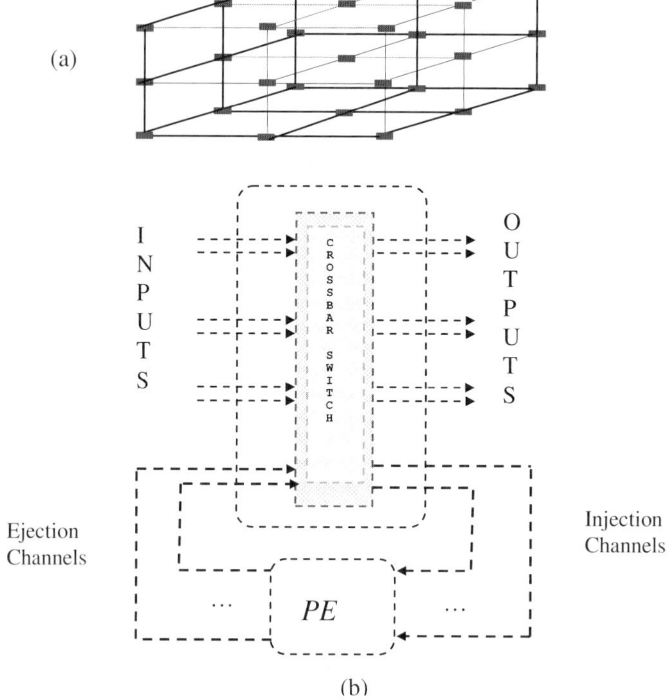

Fig. 1. (a) $3 \times 3 \times 3$ *Mesh- (b) a* node in the middle of the mesh

Fig. 1 depicts the structure of a node situated in the middle of $3 \times 3 \times 3$ mesh. The discussion can be easily extended to nodes situated at the corners and edges. A node consists of a processing element (PE) and router. The PE contains a processor and some local memory. A node uses six input and six output channels to connect to its neighbouring nodes; two in a dimension, one for each direction. There are also local channels used by the PE to inject/eject messages to/from the network, respectively.

Messages generated by the PE are injected into the network through the injection channel. Messages at the destination node are transferred to the PE through the ejection channel. The input and output channels are connected by a crossbar switch that can simultaneously connect multiple input to multiple output channels given that there is no contention over the output channels.

Definition 2: *Consider a mesh* (V, E), *with node set* V *and edge set* E, *a multicast set is a couple* $(p, Đ)$, *where* $p \in V$, $Đ = \{p_1, p_2 ..., p_k\}$ *and* $p_i \in V, i = 1,...,k$. *The node* p *is the source of the multicast message, and the* k *nodes in* $Đ$ *are the destinations. To perform a multicast operation, node* p *disseminates copies of the same message to all the destinations in* $Đ$.

Existing multicast algorithms either assume a fixed network size, low dimension networks or consider only the latency at the network level. Having surveyed the literature, existing solutions to multicast communication in interconnection networks rely on two main strategies. In view of the dominance of the start-up time in the overall multicast latency, algorithms in the first strategy try to reduce the number of start-ups required to perform multicast, but this has been shown to be inefficient under high traffic loads [8, 10, 14]. For instance, the Dual Path (DP) and Multi Path (MP) algorithms proposed in [10] use this strategy. Briefly, DP uses at most two copies of the multicast message to cover the destination nodes, which are grouped into two disjoint sub-groups. This may decrease the path length for some multicast messages. The MP algorithm attempts to reduce path lengths by using up to four copies (or $2n$ for the n-dimensional mesh) of the multicast message. As per the multi-path multicast algorithm, all the destinations of the multicast message are grouped into four disjoint subsets such that all the destinations in a subset are in one of the four quadrants when source is viewed as the origin. Copies of the message are routed using dual-path routing (see [10] for a complete description). Algorithms in the second class, on the other hand, tend to use shorter paths, but messages can then suffer from higher latencies due to the number of start-ups required [15]. Based on this strategy, for example, the Column Path (CP) algorithm presented in [15] partitions the set of destinations into at most $2k$ subsets (e.g. k is the number of columns in the mesh), such that there are at most two messages directed to each column.

Generally, most existing path-based algorithms incur high multicast latency. This is due to the use of long paths required to cover the groups serially like algorithms under the umbrella of the first multicast approach or those of the second category, in which an excessive number of start-ups is involved. In addition, a common problem associated with most existing multicast algorithms is that they can overload the selected multicast path and hence cause traffic congestion. This is mainly because most existing grouping schemes [8, 10, 15] do not consider the issue of load balancing during a multicast operation. More importantly, existing multicast algorithms have been designed with a consideration paid only to the multicast latency at the network level, resulting in an erratic variation of the message arrival times at the destination nodes. As a consequence, some parallel applications cannot be performed efficiently using these algorithms, especially those applications which are sensitive to variations in the message delivery times at the nodes involved in the multicast operation. Thus, our objective here is to propose a new multicast algorithm that can overcome the limitations of existing algorithms and thus leading to improve the performance of multicast communication in mesh networks. In our previous work [2], a new multicast scheme, the Qualified Group (QG) has been devised for meshes. Such a scheme has been studied under restricted operating conditions, such as low dimensional networks, fixed symmetric network sizes and a limited number of destination nodes [2]. In the context of the issues discussed above, this paper makes two major contributions. Firstly, the QG is generalised here with the aim of handling multicast communication in symmetric, asymmetric 3D meshes and different network sizes. Secondly, unlike many previous works, this study considers the issue of multicast latency at both the network and node levels across different traffic scenarios.

3 The Qualified Groups QG Algorithm

The QG aims at optimising the performance of message-passing communication by matching the algorithmic characteristics to the desirable properties of meshes. In other words, QG takes advantage of the partitionable structure of the mesh to divide the destination nodes into several groups of comparable sizes in order to balance the traffic load among these groups. This grouping, thus, leads to avoid the congestion problem in the network. The groups, in turn, implement multicast independently in a parallel fashion, which results in reducing the overall communication latency.

In general, the QG is composed of four phases which are described below. For the sake of the present discussion and for illustration in the diagrams, we will assume that messages are routed inside the network according to the dimension order routing. It is worth clarifying that we have adopted the dimension order routing due to the fact that this form of routing is simple and deadlock and livelock free, resulting in a faster and more compact router when the algorithm implemented in hardware, [3, 15]. However the *QG* algorithm can be used along any other underlying routing scheme, including the well-known Turn model and Duato's adaptive algorithms [3], since the grouping scheme, as explained below, in *QG* can be implemented irrespective of the underlying routing scheme (in the algorithmic level), which is not the case in most existing multicast algorithms in which destination nodes are divided based on the underlying routing used (in the routing level) [8, 10, 15]. It is worth mentioning that such a research line will be investigated further in our future works.

Phase 1: In this phase, a multicast area is defined as the smallest n-dimensional array that includes the source of the multicast message as well as the set of destinations. The purpose of defining this area is to confine a boundary of network resources that need to be employed during the multicast operation. The algorithm for computing the multicast area and division dimension is shown in Fig. 2.

Definition 3: *In the n-dimensional mesh with a multicast set* $(p, Đ)$, *a multicast area* G_{MA} *includes the source node* $p[d_1, d_2, \dots d_n]$ *and destination nodes* $Đ\ [(d_1, d_2, \dots d_n)]$ *such that* $\forall\ d_i \in \{d_1, d_2, \dots, d_n\}$, *has two corners, upper corner* $u_{d_i} = \max(Đ[d_i], p[d_i])$ *and lower corner* $l_{d_i} = \min(Đ[d_i], p[d_i])$ *such*

$$\text{that } mid_{d_i} = \begin{cases} (l_{d_i} + u_{d_i})/2 \text{ if } (l_{d_i} + u_{d_i}) \text{ is even} \\ ((l_{d_i} + u_{d_i}) - 1)/2 \text{ if } (l_{d_i} + u_{d_i}) \text{ is odd} \end{cases}$$

Procedure: the multicast area G_{MA} *and the divisor dimension* Div_{di} *in the multicast area in n-dimensional meshes.*
Input: A multicast set $(p, Ɖ)$ *destination nodes and a multicast message M*
Output: the multicast area G_{MA} *and the divisor dimension* Div_{d_i}

Begin
$\forall \; d_i \in \{d_1, d_2, ..., d_n\}$
{

$u_{d_i} = \max(Ɖ[d_i], p_{d_i})$, $l_{d_i} = \min(Ɖ[d_i], p_{d_i})$ and

$$mid_{d_i} = \begin{cases} (l_{d_i} + u_{d_i})/2 \text{ if } (l_{d_i} + u_{d_i}) \text{ is even} \\ ((l_{d_i} + u_{d_i}) - 1)/2 \text{ if } (l_{d_i} + u_{d_i}) \text{ is odd} \end{cases}$$

$$N_{d_i} = \left| Ɖ[d_i^{\Uparrow}] - Ɖ[d_i^{\Downarrow}] \right| :$$

$$Ɖ[d_i^{\Uparrow}] = \sum_{mid_{d_i}}^{u_{d_i}} Ɖ[d_i] \text{ and } Ɖ[d_i^{\Downarrow}] = \sum_{l_{d_i}}^{mid_{d_i}-1} Ɖ[d_i]$$

}
Select the divisor dimension

$Div_{d_i} = \min(N_{d_1}, N_{d_2}, ..., N_{d_n})$

Find the primary groups $= \{G_1, G_2, ... G_{g_{pr}}\}$

Fig. 2. Computing the multicast area G_{MA} and divisor dimension Div_{d_i} in *QG*

Phase 2: The multicast area G_{MA} is then divided into groups. The objective behind grouping the destination nodes is to distribute the traffic load over the multicast area in order to avoid traffic congestion, which contributes significantly to the blocking latency. Besides, grouping enables the destination nodes to receive the multicast message in comparable arrival times; i.e., this helps to keep the variance of the arrival times among the destination nodes to a minimum.

Definition 4: *In an n-dimensional mesh with a multicast set* $(p, Ɖ)$, *a divisor dimension* Div_{d_i} *for Ɖ satisfies the following condition*

$$Div_{d_i} = \min(N_{d_1}, N_{d_2}, ..., N_{d_n}), N_{d_i} = \left| Ɖ[d_i^{\Uparrow}] - Ɖ[d_i^{\Downarrow}] \right| :$$

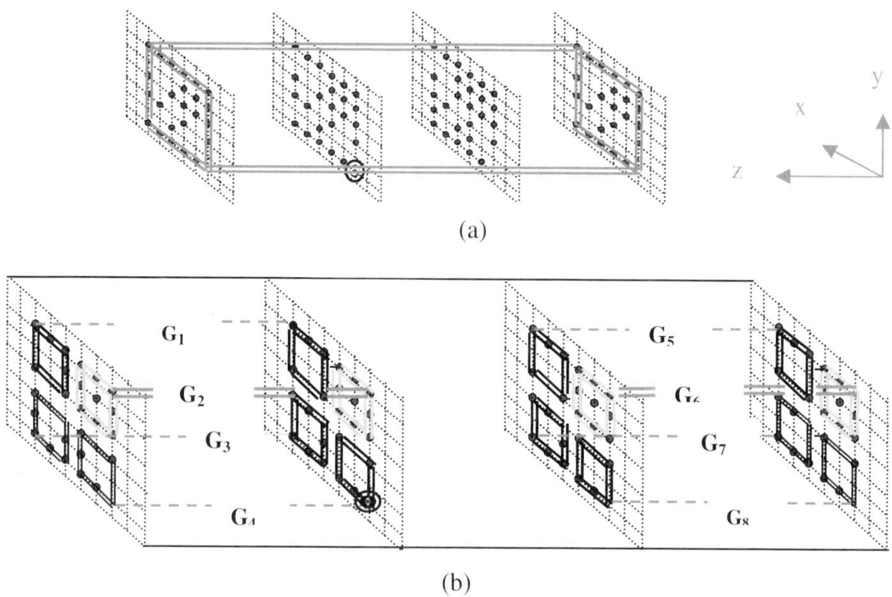

Fig. 3. (a) the multicast are in 8×10 ×4 3D mesh. (b) the grouping scheme (phase 2).
● Destination Node ◎ Source Node

$$Đ[d_i^{\Uparrow}] = \sum_{mid_{d_i}}^{u_{d_i}} Đ[d_i] \, and \; Đ[d_i^{\Downarrow}] = \sum_{l_{d_i}}^{mid_{d_i}-1} Đ[d_i]$$

Notice that if $N_{d_1} = N_{d_2}$, d_1 is given a higher priority, i.e., a higher priority is given based on the ascending order of the dimensions. For instance, if $N_x = N_y = N_z$, X dimension will be considered as a divisor dimension. The divisor dimension is used as a major axis for the grouping scheme in this phase. The multicast area G_{MA} is then divided into a number of disjoint groups as formulated in the following definition.

Definition 5: *Given an n-dimensional mesh with a multicast set* $(p, Đ)$ *and a multicast area* G_{MA}, $\forall G_i, G_j : G_i \subseteq G_{MA}$ *and* $G_j \subseteq G_{MA} \rightarrow G_i \cap G_j = \Phi$.

According to Definition 5, G_{MA} is divided into a number of primary groups as given in equation 1; where g_{pr} refers to the number of primary groups obtained after dividing the destination nodes over the division dimension, such that

$$g_{pr} = \begin{cases} p_t & \text{if } \exists G_i \subseteq G_{MA} : G_i = \Phi \\ 2^n & \text{otherwise} \end{cases} \tag{1}$$

where p_t is an integer, $1 \le p_t < 2^n$

For the sake of illustration, let the system be a $8\times10\times4$ 3D mesh, the multicast area is determined as depicted in Fig. 3.(a), the division dimension is Z and the destinations have been divided into 8 groups as illustrated in Fig. 3(b).

Phase 3: This phase is responsible for qualifying the groups already obtained in the preceding phase for a final grouping. Having obtained the primary groups, g_{pr}, we recursively find the multicast area for each group, $G_i \subseteq G_{MA}$, as defined in Definition 4, and determine the internal distance $Int(G_i)$ for each group G_i.

$$Int(G_i) = Dist(p_f(G_i), p_n(G_i)) + N_{G_i} \tag{2}$$

Where $Dist$ refers to the Manhattan distance in which the distance between tow nodes, for instance the distance between two nodes $(p1_x, p1_y)$ and $(p2_x, p2_y)$ is given by $Dist(p1, p2) = |(p1_x - p2_x)| + |(p1_y - p2_y)|$. While the first term, $Dist(p_f(G_i), p_n(G_i))$, in the above equation represents the distance between the farthest p_f and the nearest node p_n in a group G_i from/to the source node p, respectively, the second term, N_{G_i}, represents the number of destination nodes that belong to the relevant group $G_i \subseteq G_{MA}$. We then determine the external distance $Ext(G_i)$.

$$Ext(G_i) = Dist(p_n(G_i), p) \tag{3}$$

The minimum weight W_m for a group $G_i, 1 < i \leq g_{pr}$, where g_{pr} refers to the number of primary groups, is then calculated by

$$W_m(G_i) = Ext(G_i) + Int(G_i) \tag{4}$$

Definition 6: *Given a multicast area* G_{MA} *and* $G_i \subseteq G_{MA}$, *where* $1 < i \leq g_{pr}$, *the average of the minimum weights* W_{av}, *for the multicast area* G_{MA}, *is given by*

$$W_{av} = \frac{\sum_{i=1}^{g_{pr}} W_m(G_i)}{g_{pr}} \tag{5}$$

Definition 7: *Given a multicast area* G_{MA}, $G_i \subseteq G_{MA}$, *and* W_{av}, *the qualification point,* $QP(G_i)$, *for each group is calculated as follows*

$$QP(G_i) = \frac{(W_m(G_i) - W_{av})}{W_{av}} \tag{6}$$

The qualification point for each group is compared to an assumed threshold value TD, which is used to set a limit for the partitioning process.

Definition 8: *Given a multicast area* G_{MA} *and* $G_i \subseteq G_{MA}$, *we say that* G_i *is a qualified group if and only if its minimum weight* $W_m(G_i) \leq W_{av}$ *or if its qualification point* $(QP(G_i)) \leq TD$.

For example, given that the threshold value is $TD = 0.5$, each qualified group must hold at least half of the total average weight W_{av} of the groups. Once a group $G_i \subseteq G_{MA}$ does not satisfy the condition formulated in Definition 8, it is treated as an unqualified group. In this case, this unqualified group is divided into two sub-groups based on its division dimension.

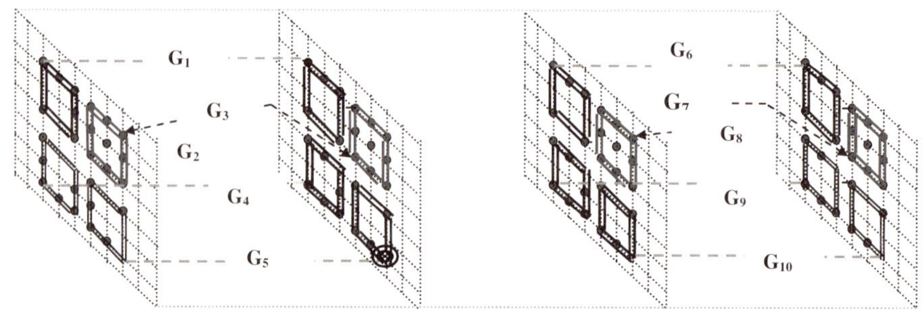

Fig. 4. The qualified groups in 8×10 ×4 3D mesh (Phase 3)

Following the example shown in Fig.3 and using a threshold value $TD = 0.5$, we find in this example that both G_2 and G_6 (as shown in Fig. 3) are not qualified (based on Definition 8). Therefore, the multicast area for each group (G_2 and G_6) is divided into two further sub-groups based on the division dimension (Z in this case) as depicted in Fig. 4. The new sub-groups are then compared to the qualified groups already obtained. After qualifying all the groups, the source node sends the message to the representative nodes in the qualified groups. If the new resulting groups are qualified the partitioning process is terminated. Otherwise, the unqualified group is divided into a number of sub-groups sb, where $2 \leq sb \leq 2^n$. For instance, for any unqualified group $G_i \subseteq G_{MA}$ in the 3D mesh, it can be divided into 8 groups at maximum, even if the new obtained groups are still larger than those which meet the qualification point. In fact, the partitioning process is terminated at this stage in order to reduce the number of comparisons during the qualifying phase. This helps to keep the algorithm simple and maintains a low preparation time.

Phase 4: For each group resulting from Phase 3, the nodes which have the lowest communication cost, in terms of distance are selected as the representative nodes of the qualified groups that can receive the multicast message from the source node. In other words, the nearest node for each qualified group is elected so that it could be sent the multicast message with a single start-up only. Concurrently, the representative nodes act as "source" nodes by delivering the message to the rest of the destination nodes in their own groups with one additional start-up time only.

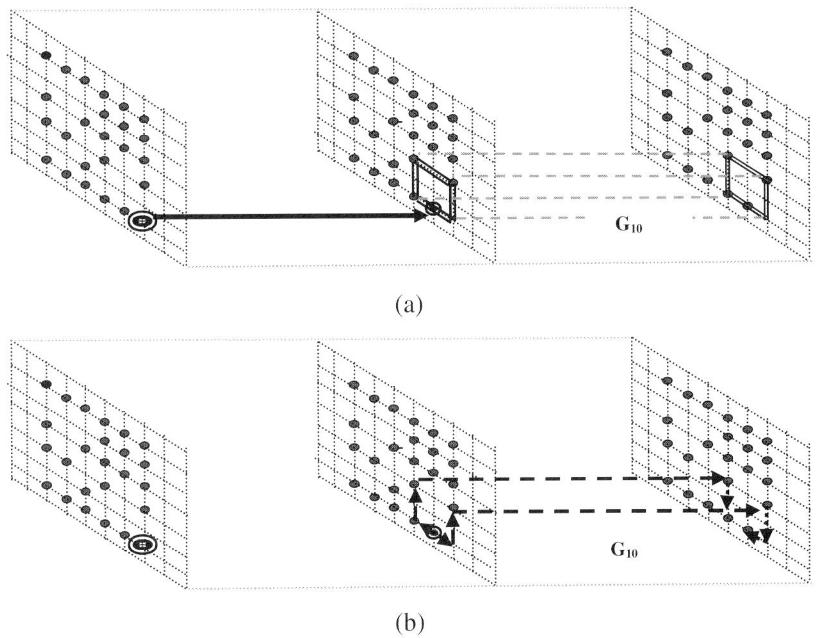

Fig. 5. (a) The first communications step (which occurs in phase 4) in the QG multicast algorithm, (b), The second communications step (which occurs in phase 4)

After qualifying all the groups, the source node sends the message to the representative nodes in the qualified groups. The source node performs this operation with a single start-up latency taking advantage of the multiple-port facility of the system by creating two disjoint paths in this step. For the sake of clarity, we have selected group G_{10} to represent this step as illustrated in Fig. 5(a), where the source node sends the message to the selected representative node. Concurrently, every representative node in each group acts as a source node and, in turn, sends the message to the rest of the destinations in its own group as the representative node does in Fig. 5(b).

4 Performance Evaluation

A number of simulation experiments have been conducted to analyse the performance of *QG* against *DP*, *MP* and *CP*. A simulation program has been developed to model the multicast operation in the mesh. The developed model has been added to a larger simulator called MultiSim [6], which has been designed to study the collective communication operations on multicomputers and has been widely used in the literature [2, 10, 12]. The simulation program was written in VC++ and built on top the event-driven CSIM-package [7]. We have used the 2D mesh with four injection channels and four ejection channels. Two unidirectional channels exist between each pair of neighbouring nodes. Each channel has a single queue of messages waiting for

Table 1. The coefficient of variation of the multicast latency in the DP, MP and CP algorithms with the improvement obtained by QG (QG_{IMPR}%) in the 10×10×10 3D mesh

	#Destinations=20		# Destinations=60		# Destinations=80	
	CV	(QG_{IMPR} %)	CV	(QG_{IMPR} %)	CV	(QG_{IMPR} %)
DP	0.4156	40.01	0.5056	62.70	0.5678	78.62
MP	0.3605	21.96	0.4710	51.77	0.4873	53.14
CP	0.4967	67.34	0.5590	79.74	0.5925	86.48
QG	CV= 0.2967		CV= 0.3107		CV = 0.3176	

transmission. In our simulations, the start-up latency has been set at 33 cycles, the channel transmission time at 1 cycle and the threshold *TD* at 0.5.

The network cycle time in the simulator is defined as the transmission time of a single flit across a channel The preparation time (which consists of dividing the destination nodes into appropriate subsets and creating multiple copies of the message as needed, depending on the underlying algorithm) of the DP, MP, CP and QG algorithms are set at 2, 2, 4 and 16 cycles, respectively. The preparation time was deliberately set higher in the QG algorithm to reflect the fact that our algorithm requires a longer time to divide the destinations into qualified groups. All simulations were executed using 95% confidence intervals (when confidence interval was smaller than 5% of the mean). The technique used to calculate confidence intervals is called batch means analysis. In batch means method, a long run is divided into a set of fixed size batches, computing a separate sample mean for each batch, and using these batches to compute the grand mean and the confidence interval. In our simulations, the grand means are obtained along with several values, including confidence interval and relative errors which are not shown in the figures. Like existing studies [1, 2, 3, 10, 15, 13], only the grand mean is shown in our figures.

4.1 Latency at the Node Level and Average Additional Traffic

This section presents the coefficient of variation of the multicast latency as a new performance metric in order to reflect the degree of parallelism achieved by the multicast algorithms. A set of simulation experiments have been conducted where the message inter-arrival times between two messages generated at a source node is set at 250 cycles. The message length is fixed at 64 flits and the number of destination nodes is varied from 20, 30, 40… to 60 nodes. The coefficient of variation (CV) is defined as SD / M_{nl}, where SD refers to the standard deviation of the multicast latency (which is also the message arrival times among the destination nodes) and M_{nl} is the mean multicast latency. The coefficient of variation of *QG* has been compared against that of *DP, MP* and *CP*. Table 1 contains performance results for the $10 \times 10 \times 10$ mesh, which have been obtained by averaging values obtained from at least 40 experiments in each case. The $QG_{IMPR}\%$ in Table 1 refers to the percentage improvement obtained by *QG* over its *DP, MP* and *CP* competitors.

As shown in Table 1, *QG* achieves a significant improvement over *DP, MP* and *CP*. This is due firstly to the efficient grouping scheme adopted by *QG* which divides the destinations into groups of comparable sizes. Secondly, and more importantly, unlike in *DP, MP* and *CP*, the destination nodes for each qualified group in *QG* (except those selected in the first message-passing step) receive the multicast message in the second message-passing step, in parallel. This has the net effect of minimising the variance of the arrival times at the node level. In contrast, *DP, MP* and *CP* perform multicast with either longer paths as in *DP* and *MP* or in an excessive number of message-passing steps, as in *CP*.

The additional traffic is computed as in [8, 10], that is, by subtracting the number of destination nodes from the number of channels involved in the multicast operation. This reflects the amount of network resources that are used to complete a multicast

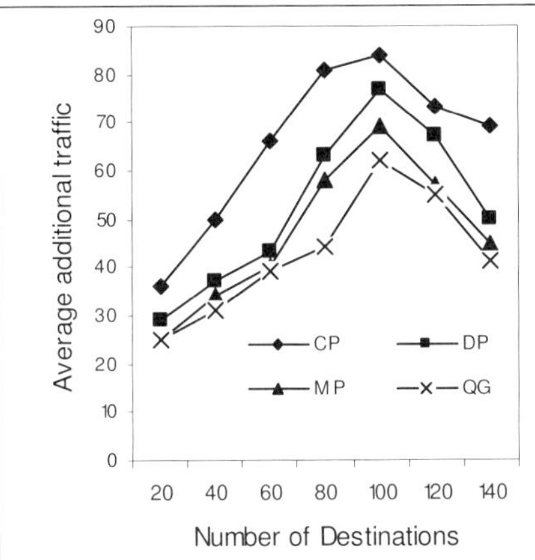

Fig. 6. Average additional traffic as a function of the number of destinations for the four algorithms, DP, MP, CP and QG in 8×8 ×8 mesh

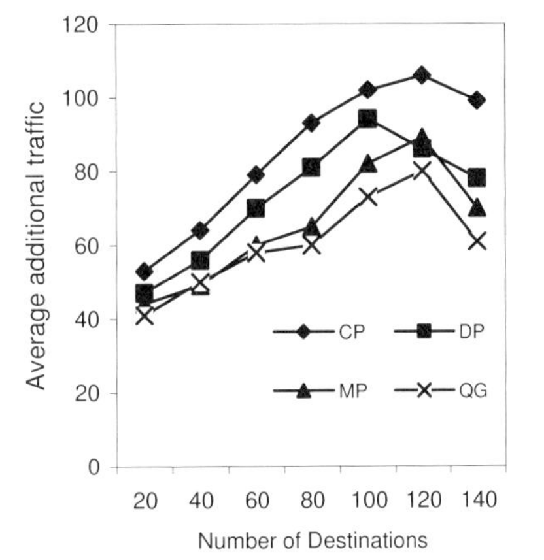

Fig. 7. Average additional traffic as a function of the number of destinations for the four algorithms, DP, MP, CP and QG in 10×10 ×10 mesh

operation. A physical channel occupied for one cycle is considered as one-traffic unit. Figs. 6 and 7 shows the resulting average additional traffic in the four algorithms for various numbers of destination nodes and two different network sizes, 8×8 ×8 and 10×10 ×10 3D meshes, respectively. To complete a multicast operation, *QG* requires fewer channels than *DP*, *MP* and *CP* since the destinations are divided into several groups which are reached in a more efficient manner.

4.2 Latency in the Presence of Multicast and Unicast Traffic

In some real parallel applications, a message may have to compete for network resources with other multicast messages or even with other unicast messages. To

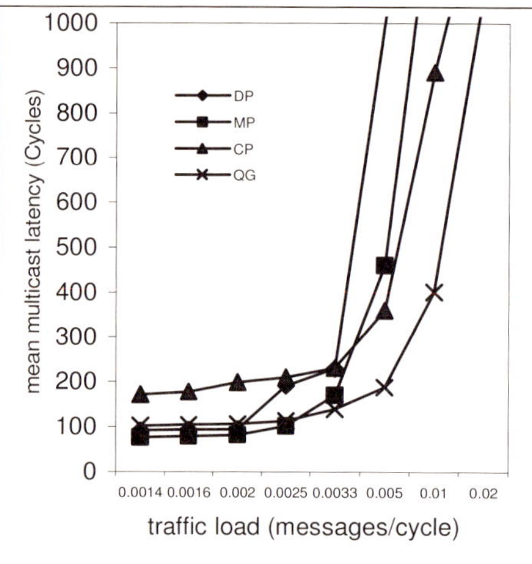

Fig. 8. Mean multicast latency in the 8×8×8 mesh. Message length is 64 flits, number of destination =10, traffic consists of multicast (10%) and unicast (90%).

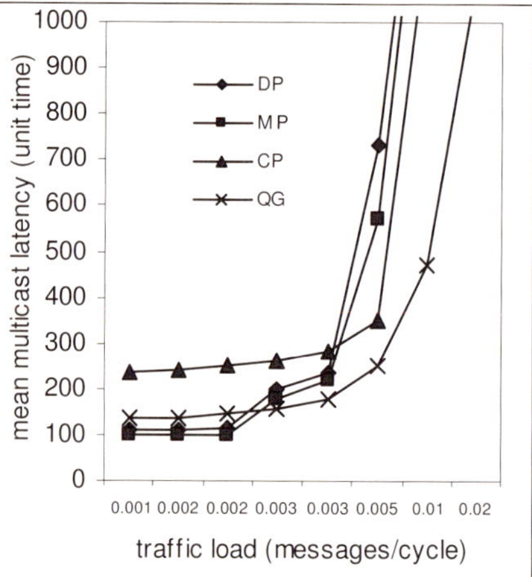

Fig. 9. Mean multicast latency in the 8×8×8 mesh. Message length is 64 flits, number of destination 20 nodes, traffic consists of multicast (10%) and unicast (90%)

examine performance in such situation, results for the mean multicast latency have been gathered in the $8\times8\times8$ mesh in the presence of both multicast (10%) and unicast (90%) traffic (similar studies are outlined in [8, 10, 15]). The message size is set at 64 flits and the number of destinations in a given multicast operation has been set to 10 and 20 nodes, respectively. The simulation results are provided in Figs. 8 and 9. Fig. 8 reports results for 10 destinations while Fig. 9 shows results for 20 destinations. Under light traffic, QG, DP and MP have comparable performance behaviour, with MP having a slightly lower latency. On the other hand, CP has a higher time. This is mainly due to the dominating effect of the start-up latency in such a situation. However, under heavy traffic, an opposite behaviour is noticed in that QG performs the best in terms of both latency and throughput, followed by CP. More importantly, we can observe from Fig. 9 that as the number of destinations increases the performance advantage of QG becomes more noticeable over that of CP. This is mainly because QG alleviates significantly the congestion problem at the source node. In contrast, the source node in CP suffers from a higher load and as more destinations are involved in the multicast operation, the more severe this limitation becomes.

5 Conclusions and Future Directions

In this study, the QG multicast algorithm has been generalised for n-dimensional meshes. In this paper, 3D meshes have been considered in our performance evaluation. Results from simulations under different conditions have revealed that the *QG* algorithm exhibits superior performance over well-known algorithms, such as dual-path, multiple-path, and column-path algorithms. Unlike existing multicast algorithms, the *QG* algorithm can maintain a lower variance of message arrival times at the node level. Consequently, most of the destination nodes receive the multicast message in comparable arrival times. Our Results show also that the QG has improved the scalability of the multicast operation in 3D meshes. It would be interesting to further investigate the interaction between the important parameters that affect the performance of the *QG* algorithm, notably the grouping scheme, network size, threshold value, multicast group size, and traffic load, with the aim of proposing an analytical model that could predict, for example, the multicast latency given a particular grouping scheme, network size, multicast group size, and traffic load. Moreover, another possible research line is to apply this multicast scheme on Network-on-Chip platforms.

References

1. Wang, N.-C., Yen, C.-P., Chu, C.-P.: Multicast communication in wormhole-routed symmetric networks with hamiltonian cycle model. Journal of Systems Architecture 51(3), 165–183 (2005)
2. Al-Dubai, A., Ould-Khaoua, M., Mackenzie, L.: An efficient path-based multicast algorithm for mesh networks. In: Proc. the 17th Int. Parallel and Distributed Processing Symposium (IEEE/ACM-IPDPS), Nice, France, April 22 -26, pp. 283–290 (2003)
3. Duato, J., Yalamanchili, C., Ni, L.: Interconnection networks: an engineering approach. Elsevier Science, Amsterdam (2003)
4. Touzene, A.: Optimal all-ports collective communication algorithms for the k-ary n-cube interconnection networks. Journal of Systems Architecture 50(4), 169–236 (2004)
5. Chen, Y.-S., Chiang, C.-Y., Chen, C.-Y.: Multi-node broadcasting in all-ported 3-D wormhole-routed torus using an aggregation-then-distribution strategy. Journal of Systems Architecture 50(9), 575–589 (2004)
6. McKinley, P.K., Trefftz, C.: MultiSim: A simulation tool for the study of large-scale multiprocessors. In: MASCOTS' 1993. Proceedings of the Int. Symp. Modeling, Analysis and Simulation of Computer and Telecommunication Systems, pp. 57–62 (1993)
7. CSIM: A C-based, process-oriented simulation language http://www.mesquite.com/
8. Fleury, E., Fraigniaud, P.: Strategies for path-based multicasting in wormhole-routed meshes. J. Parallel & Distributed Computing 60, 26–62 (1998)
9. Tseng, Y.-C., Wang, S.-Y., Ho, C.-W.: Efficient broadcasting in wormhole-routed multicomputers: A network-partitioning approach. IEEE Transactions on Parallel and Distributed Systems 10(1), 44–61 (1999)
10. Lin, X., McKinley, P., Ni, L.M.: Deadlock-free multicast wormhole routing in 2D-mesh multicomputers. IEEE Transactions on Parallel and Distributed Systems 5(8), 793–804 (1994)
11. Bjerregaard, T., Mahadevan, S.: A survey of research and practices of Network-on-Chip. ACM Computing Surveys 38, 1–51 (2006)
12. Robinson, D.F., McKinley, P.K., Cheng, C.: Path based multicast communication in wormhole routed unidirectional torus networks. Journal of Parallel Distributed Computing 45, 104–121 (1997)
13. Malumbres, M.P., Duato, J.: An efficient implementation of tree-based multicast routing for distributed shared-memory multiprocessors. J. Systems Architecture 46, 1019–1032 (2000)

14. Mohapatra, P., Varavithya, V.: A hardware multicast routing algorithm for two dimensional meshes. In: The Eighth IEEE Symposium on Parallel and Distributed Processing, News Orleans, pp. 198–205 (1996)
15. Boppana, R.V., Chalasani, S., Raghavendra, C.S: Resource deadlock and performance of wormhole multicast routing algorithms. IEEE Transactions on Parallel and Distributed Systems 9(6), 535–549 (1998)
16. Wang, S., Tseng, Y., Shiu, C., Sheu, J.: Balancing traffic load for multi-node multicast in a wormhole 2D torus/mesh. The Computer Journal 44(5), 354–367 (2001)
17. Kumar, D.R., Najjar, W.A., Srimani, P.K.: A new adaptive hardware tree-based multicast routing in k-ary n-cubes. IEEE Computer 50(7), 647–659 (2001)

Zone Based Data Aggregation Scheduling Scheme for Maximizing Network Lifetime

Sangbin Lee[1], Kyuho Han[1], Kyungsoo Lim[1], Jinwook Lee[2], and Sunshin An[1]

[1] Department of Electronics and Computer Engineering,
Korea University, Seoul, Korea
{kulsbin,garget,angus,sunshin}@dsys.korea.ac.kr
[2] Networking Technology Lab.,
Samsung Advanced Institute of Technology (SAIT), Seoul, Korea
thetruth.lee@samsung.com

Abstract. A wireless sensor network consists of many micro-sensor nodes distributed throughout an area of interest. Each node has a limited energy supply and generates information that needs to be communicated to a sink node. The basic operation in such a network is the systematic gathering and transmission of sensed data to a base station for further processing. During data gathering, sensors have the ability to perform in-network aggregation (fusion) of data packet routes to the base station. The lifetime of such a sensor system can be defined as the time during which the sensor information is gathered from all of the sensors and combined at the base station. Given the location of the sensors, the base station and the available energy at each sensor, the main interest is to find an efficient manner in which data can be collected from the sensors and transmitted to the base station, so as to maximize the system lifetime. We address the zone based data aggregation scheduling scheme for maximizing network lifetime. The experimental results demonstrate that the proposed protocol significantly outperforms other data aggregation protocols in terms of the energy saving and system lifetime.

Keywords: Data Aggregation, Maximum Network Lifetime, Spatial Correlation, TDMA Scheduing, Wireless Sensor Networks, Zone.

1 Introduction

A wireless sensor network refers to a network including tens to several thousands of sensor nodes capable of communicating with each ohter using a radio frequency (RF) to sense physical space, the network being spread over a wide area. Due to development of a sensor technique, technology for a microelctromechanical system (MEMS) can be connected via a wireless network and is embracing low power electronics engineering technology, low power RF planning technology, and the like. As a result, sensor nodes are being developed that operate at low power levels and have low costs[1],[2].

In the future, it is envisioned that sensor networks will consist of hundreds of inexpensive nodes that can be readily deployed in physical environments to

I. Stojmenovic et al. (Eds.): ISPA 2007, LNCS 4742, pp. 883–894, 2007.

collect useful information (e.g. seismic, acoustic, medical and surveillance data) in a robust and autonomous manner. However, there are several obstacles that need to be overcome before this vision becomes a reality [3]. These obstacles arise from the limited energy, computing capabilities, and communication resources available to sensors. Therefore, reducing the energy consumption of such networks is the most important design consideration.

Data aggregation has been put forward as an essential paradigm for wireless routing in sensor networks [5]. Most previous related works [6], [3] aimed to reduce the energy consumed by sensors during the process of data gathering. Directed diffusion [6] is based on a network of nodes that can coordinate their operation, in order to perform distributed sensing of an environmental phenomenon. This approach allows significant energy savings to be achieved, when intermediate nodes are employed to aggregate responses to queries. LEACH [3] analyzes the performance of the cluster-based routing mechanism with in-network data compression. In PEGASIS [4], sensors form chains so that each node transmits and receives information from a close neighbor. Gathered data moves from node to node, becomes aggregated and is eventually transmitted to the base station.

Wireless Sensor Networks (WSNs) are characterized by the dense deployment of sensor nodes that continuously observe a physical phenomenon. Due to the high density in the network topology, sensor observations are highly correlated in the space domain. These spatial correlations, along with the collaborative nature of the WSN, bring significant potential advantages for the development of efficient communication protocols well-suited for the WSN paradigm. Typical WSN applications require spatially dense sensor deployment in order to achieve satisfactory coverage [7]. As a result, multiple sensors record information about a single event in the sensor field.

Due to the high density in the network topology [7], spatially proximal sensor observations are highly correlated, with the degree of correlation increasing with decreasing inter-node separation. Therefore, it may not be necessary for every sensor node to transmit its data to the sink; instead, a smaller number of sensor measurements might be adequate to communicate the event features to the sink within a certain reliability/fidelity level. There has been some research effort to study the correlation in WSN [8],[9]. However, most of these existing studies investigated the theoretical aspects of the correlation, and they do not provide efficient networking protocols which exploit the correlation in the WSN.

In a recent effort, joint routing and source coding was introduced in [10] to reduce the amount of traffic generated in dense sensor networks with spatially correlated records. While this technique reduces the number of bits transmitted; from the network point of view, the number of transmitted packets remains unchanged, whereas it could be further minimized by regulating the network access based on the spatial correlation between the sensor nodes.

In this paper, the Zone based Data Aggregation Scheduling (ZDAS) scheme is proposed to maximize the network lifetime. ZDAS is operated in a framework that models the spatial correlations in wireless sensor networks. The proposed protocols can significantly outperform the previous protocols in terms of the energy saving and network lifetime. The remainder of this paper is organized as follows. In Section 2, we state the problem and, in Section 3, we present the ZDAS algorithm whose primary purpose is to prolong the network lifetime. In Section 4, we show the numerical results obtained using the above analytical framework. Finally, concluding remarks are discussed in Section 5.

2 System Model

In this section, we present the preliminary system model for the analysis of the network lifetime in wireless sensor network, which will be discussed in Section 3.

2.1 Network Model

We consider a multi-hop wireless network with n nodes. The nodes communicate with each other via wireless links. The nodes in the network and possible communications between the nodes are represented by a directed graph When $G = (V, E)$. Here, $V = \{ v_1, v_2, \ldots, v_n\}$ represents the set of nodes in the network and E represents the set of directed edges in the network. Given a link $e \in E, t(e)$ is used to represent the transmission end of the link e and $r(e)$ to represent the receiving end of the link e. A link e is considered to be active if there is a transmission from $t(e)$ to $r(e)$. Given a node $v \in V$, $l_{in}(v)$ denotes the set of links terminating at node. In other words, $l_{in}(v) = \{ e \in E : r(e) = v\}$. Similarly, for a given node $v \in V$, $l_{out}(v)$ denotes the set of edges emanating from $l_{out}(v) = \{ e \in E : t(e) = v\}$.

As in a previous work [3], [6], [4], we make the simplistic assumption that an intermediate sensor can aggregate multiple incoming packets into a single outgoing packet. Therefore, the value of $l_{out}(v)$ can only be one.

Note that the model includes the special case where the underlying graph is a complete graph (every pair of nodes can directly communicate with each other), in which the path loss for those nodes not in range is set to zero. We assume that each sensor generates one data packet per time unit to be transmitted to the base station. For simplicity, we refer to each time unit as a round. The information from the assigned sensors needs to be aggregated at each round and be sent to the base station. Further, each node has a battery with a finite, non-replacement energy, ε. Whenever a sensor transmits or receives a data packet, it consumes some energy from its battery. The base station has an unlimited amount of energy available to it.

2.2 Self-organization of Zone

ZDAS groups the sensor nodes into zones by using the information of sensor nodes. The prevalence of spatial correlation in environmental phenomena makes it possible to schedule the process of data aggregation of the sensor nodes. Three types of short, fixed-size signaling packets (DR, SCC, U) is used for self-organization of zone. The self-organization of zone operates in three phases as shown in Fig.1 : Data Request, SCC packet broadcast and Update.

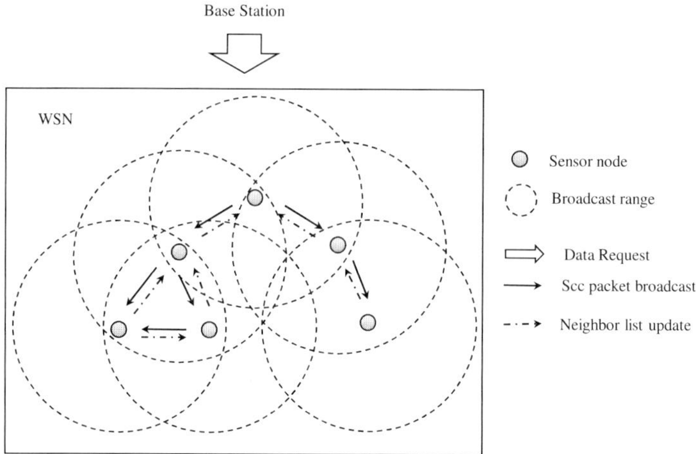

Fig. 1. Self-Organizition of Zone by Exchanging signaling packets

We assume that the base station can gather all data about sensor (sID, zID, *Location*) through exchanging the signaling packets as Fig.1. In the request phase, when user in base station wants to gather the data (e.g. temperature, light), Base station transmits the Data Request (DR) packet to the sensor network. This DR packet contains the application type (e.g. temperature, light), and the location of base station, and the user-specified error threshold, τ, interchangeable with a user-provided error-tolerance threshold. In the broadcast phase, all sensor nodes in sensor network broadcast the spatial correlation code (SCC) packets and are self-organized into zones as a TAG-like [12] forwarding tree is built using a user-specified error threshold, τ .

The SCC-packet contains the addresses (sID, zID), geographical information of the node, the user-specified error threshold, τ, and the sensing value (e.g. temperature) as shown in Fig.2.

Where sID is a identification of the sensor node and zID is a identification of the zone. A user-provided error threshold, τ, is used while building the zones.

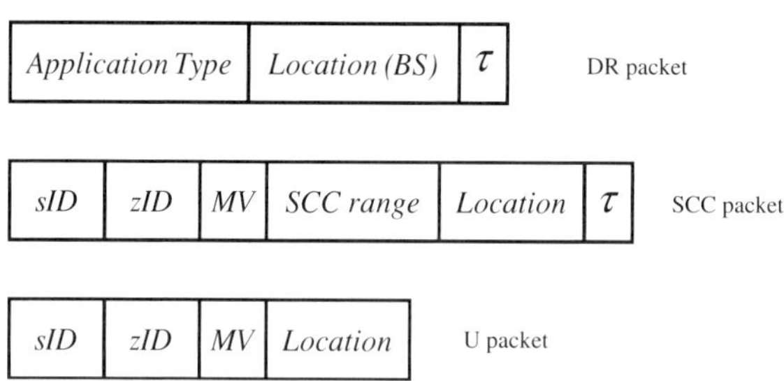

Fig. 2. Signaling Pakets

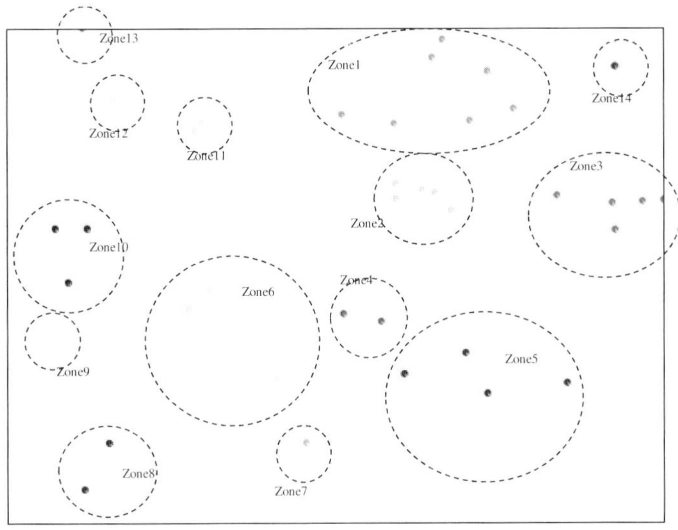

Fig. 3. Self-organized Zones

Each node decides to join a zone based on the values of Neighbor sensing Value (NV) and My local sensor Value (MV) , if $MV < NV \pm NV \times \tau$, then the sensor node registers the zID of the node that broadcasts SCC and is included in the same zone.

In the update phase, those sensor nodes that receive the SCC packet transmit the update packet, called the U-packet. This packet contains the geographical position of the node and the sensing value. As a result, Fig.3 shows zones being self-organized by exchanging signaling packets.

2.3 Energy Consumption Model

Energy consuption model determines a device lifetime by considering application specific event characteristics, and network specific data extraction model and communication method. With the notation in Table 1, a model for the energy consumption per bit at the physical layer is

$$E = E_{ctrans} + E_{crec} + E_{aggre} + \beta d_{ij}^{\alpha} \tag{1}$$

where E_{ctrans} is the energy utilized by the transmitter circuits (PLLs, bias currents, etc.) and digital processing. This energy is independent of distance; E_{crec} is the energy consumed by the receiver circuits, E_{caggre} is the energy consumed by data aggregation, and β_{ij}^{α} accounts for the radiated power necessary to transmit over a distance d_{ij} between node v_i and node v_j. As in [11], we assume that

$$E_{ctrans} = E_{crec} + E_{circuit} \tag{2}$$

Table 1. Notation

Notation	Description
α	Path loss ($2 \leq \alpha \leq 5$)
β	Constant $[Joule/(bits \cdot m^{\alpha})]$
L_{SCC}	Size of SCC packets $[bits]$
L_U	Size of location update packets $[bits]$
L_G	Size of generated packets $[bits]$
$L_{in}(i)$	The number of $l_{in}(i)$
$M(z_k)$	The number of sensor nodes grouped into $zonek$
r_i	Range of SCC_i
f	Iteration number
$\varepsilon_i^k(f)$	Residual Energy of node v_i in zone k at start of slot f
$\zeta_i(r_i)$	The set containing the indices of the nodes in range r_i of node v_i
$N_i(r_i)$	The number of neighbors of node v_i when its range is r_i

Thus, the overall expression for E in Eq.1, which we refer to as the link metric hereafter, simplifies to

$$E = 2 \cdot E_{circuit} + E_{caggre} + \beta d_{ij}^{\alpha} \tag{3}$$

According to this link metric, the *aggregation cost* for node v_i is expressed as Eq.4

$$C_i^{Aggre} = L_G\Big[(2 \cdot E_{circuit} + E_{caggre})N_{in}(i) + \sum_{l_{in}(j)=l_{out}(i)} \beta d_{ij}^{\alpha}\Big] \tag{4}$$

The *constructing zone cost* for node v_i that has range r_i can be computed from Eq.5

$$\begin{aligned} C_i^{Inf}(r_i) &= L_{SCC}\Big[\beta r_i^{\alpha} + N_i(r_i) \cdot E_{circuit}\Big] + \\ &+ L_U\Big[2N_i(r_i) \cdot E_{circuit} + \sum_{m \in \zeta_i(r_i)} \beta d_{mi}^{\alpha}\Big] \end{aligned} \tag{5}$$

Therefore, the expected residual energy for node v_i is expressed as

$$\varepsilon_i^k(f+1) = \varepsilon_i^k(f) - \frac{C_i^{Aggre}}{M(z_k)} \quad ,(\varepsilon_i^k(1) = \varepsilon_i^k(0) - C_i^{Inf}(r_i)) \tag{6}$$

The expression βr_i^{α} represents the energy needed to transmit one bit over a distance r_i ; thus $L_{SCC} \cdot \beta r_i^{\alpha} + L_{SCC} \cdot E_{circuit}$ is the energy needed for node v_i to transmit the SCC-packet in its range, whereas each of the neighbor nodes in its range expends only $L_{SCC} \cdot E_{circuit}$ to receive the SCC-packet. By adding these two components, we obtain the first line of Eq.5. Then, each of the neighbor nodes transmits an U-packet. The energy expenditure has again a constant factor,

$L_U \cdot E_{circuit}$, plus a factor, $L_U \cdot \beta d_{mi}^{\alpha}$, which depends on the distance between the transmitting node v_m and node v_i.

Moreover, v_i expends $L_U \cdot E_{circuit}$ to receive the each of the U-packets of the neighbors. By summing all of these components, which depend on the mobility rate of the nodes in the network, we obtain the final expression for P_i^{Inf}. In other words, P_i^{Inf} is the average energy which is needed to allow node v_i to obtain topology information within the range r_i.

3 Data Aggregation Scheduling Scheme

In this section, we describe the development of the data aggregation scheduling scheme based on the zone & energy model proposed in the previous section. Because sensor nodes in the same zone have high spatial correlation, there is no need for all of them to transmit their data packets. Therefore, using scheduling, we elect only one sensor node to aggregate and transmit its data packets for the sake of minimizing the network energy consumption.

3.1 TDMA Scheme

TDMA schemes have been proposed wherein the slot length is optimally assigned according to the routing requirements, while minimizing the total energy consumption across the network. In particular, during the time slot assigned by the TDMA scheme, the corresponding node works in active mode. After finishing its data transmission, it turns off all of its circuits and enters sleep mode. In this way, the energy consumption can be minimized.

In the previous section, we refer to each time slot as a round. We define the lifetime T_{net} of the network as the number of rounds until first zone is drained of its energy. A data aggregation schedule specifies, for each round, how the data packets from all of the sensors are collected and transmitted to the base station. A data aggregation schedule has one aggregation tree for each round. The lifetime of a schedule is equal to the lifetime of the network under that schedule.

The objective is to find a schedule that maximizes the network lifetime T_{net} by balancing the energy consumption of each zone.

3.2 ZDAS Algorithm

In this section, we discuss how to obtain a schedule from an admissible flow network. Recall that a schedule is a collection of directed trees, rooted at the base station, that span all of the zones, with one such tree for each round. Each such tree specifies how the data packets are aggregated and transmitted to the base station. We call these trees aggregation trees. An aggregation tree may be used for one or more rounds.

Step 1 : Constructing an Aggregation Tree - In this protocol, the sensor nodes are grouped into zones based on their spatial correlation. In Fig.4, the

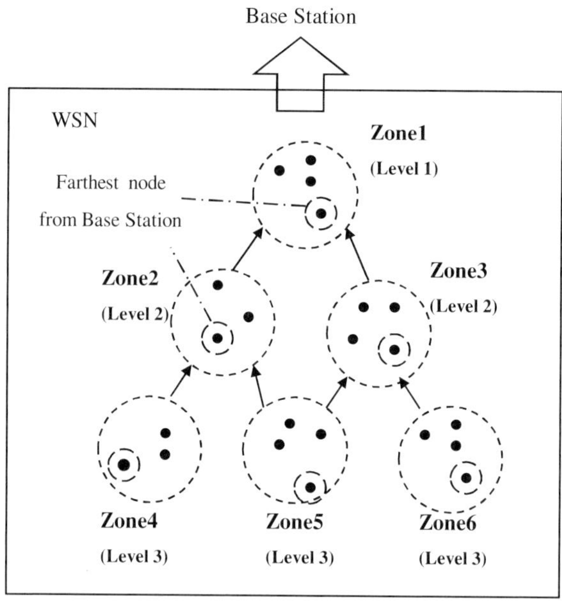

Fig. 4. Construction of Aggregation Tree

aggregation is formed among the zones at different levels of the hierarchy. The level is defined by the node which is the farthest from the base station in each zone. The hop counts of these nodes are the level of the zones. In Fig.4, the zones are used to construct the Aggregation Tree using the level of each zone. Each admissible aggregation tree is assigned to a round by the scheduling algorithm, as shown in Fig.5. After step 1 is processed, step 2 is processed at each admissible aggregation tree (Fig.5) .

Step 2 : Hierarchical election of representative node - In step 2, a schedule is constructed based on the residual energy of the sensor nodes in each zone. In order to maximize the network lifetime, the average energy consumption per zone must be minimized. Therefore, the representative node (r_{level}-node) that has the most residual energy, in the case where the data is transmitted to the next level zone, is selected among the sensor nodes in the same zone. Only the r_{level}-node aggregates and transmits the data packet to the next level zone. In this case, the most important considerations are the residual energy of the sensor node, the distance of the link, and the number of sensor nodes grouped into each zone. The greater the number of sensor nodes grouped into the zone, the lower the average energy consumption per zone.

For each zone, the algorithm first computes Eq.6 and then Eq.7. As a result, in each zone, it elects the r_{level}-node to be assigned to the TDMA slot.

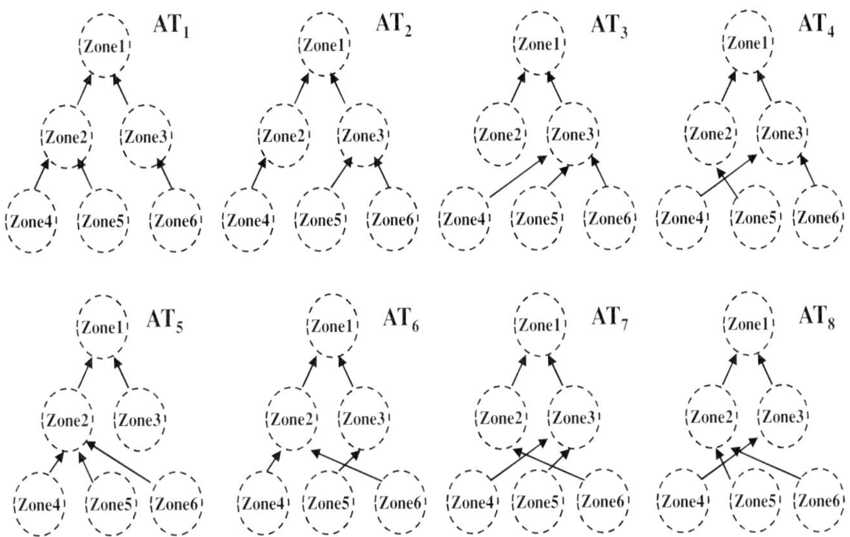

Fig. 5. Admissible Aggregation Tree

$$\varepsilon_j^k(f+1) = \max\{\varepsilon_i^k(f+1)\}, \quad \forall k \tag{7}$$

First, the algorithm elects the r_1-node by computing Eq.6 and Eq.7 among the sensor nodes in the highest level zones (1-level) that have links to the BS. Then, the algorithm elects the r_2-node by computing Eq.6 and Eq.7 among the sensor nodes in those zones of the 2-level that have links to the r_1-node.

This procedure is repeated until it elects the r_{level}-nodes for all zones. Also, step 2 is repeated for all admissible aggregation trees (Fig.5). In this case, all other nodes that are not elected switch to sleep mode. Therefore, these nodes consume only sleep power (P_{sleep}). Eq.8 shows the expected residual energy of each sleep node.

$$\varepsilon_i^k(f+1) = \varepsilon_i^k(f) - \frac{P_{sleep}}{M_k}, \quad j \neq i \tag{8}$$

Step 3 : Selection of Aggregation Tree - Based on the elected r_{level}-nodes obtained through step 2, the algorithm computes Eq.9 for all admissible aggregation trees. Eq.9 shows the residual energy of the aggregation tree after round (T) has elapsed. E_{AT} is the sum of the residual energy of all r_{level}-nodes and sleep nodes.

$$E_{AT}(f+1) = \sum_k \Big(\sum_i \varepsilon_i^k(f+1) + \sum_j \varepsilon_j^k(f+1) \Big). \tag{9}$$

Step 4 : Iterative Execution - The process of steps 2 $\sim$ 3 is iterated until the first zone is drained of its energy. $\big($ i.e. $\sum_i \varepsilon_i^k(f+1) + \sum_j \varepsilon_j^k(f+1) = 0$ $\big)$.

Through steps 2 $\sim$ 4, the appropriate aggregation tree is assigned at each round. As a result, the lifetime of the sensor network is $T_{net} = T \times f$.

4 Performance Evaluation

We evaluate the performance of the proposed algorithm via simulation in this section. The simulation settings are as follows. In our experiment, we set $\alpha = 2$, $\beta = 100pJ/bit/m^{\alpha}$, $E_{circuit} = 50pJ/bit$ and $E_{caggre} = 100pJ/bit$ for the power consumption model. The initial energy reserve ε_v on each sensor is $1J$. We set the data packet sizes, L_{SCC}= $128bits$, $L_U = 128bits$, $L_G = 1000bits$. The maximum transmission range of each sensor is $25m$ and the base station is located at (25,150). We are particularly interested in the typical scenarios encountered in sensor networks applications. The model depends on several input parameters, and on the appropriate choice of these parameters which are highly dependent on the technology and on the target applications. We vary these parameters in order to study their relevant effects on the network performance. Moreover, we believe that the realistic tuning of these parameters must be aided by the real hardware implementation of the considered protocols. We present the simulation results for the scenarios illustrated in Table 2.

In Table 2, Field is a geographical area, and n is the number of nodes, and r_i is a range of SCC_i and τ is a error threshold. We compare the performance of our protocol with that of other data aggregation protocols (PEGASIS [4], LRS, CMLDA [13]).

4.1 Experimental Results

In the case of Scenario 1, the network lifetime given by the ZDAS is longer than that given by the other protocols. In Fig.6, the ZDAS performs 1.08 to 1.73 times better than the LRS protocol and 0.98 to 1.2 times better than the CMLDA protocol. In the case of Scenario 2, the network lifetime given by the ZDAS is always significantly longer than that given by the other protocols. Fig.7, the ZDAS performs 1.81 to 2.82 times better than the LRS protocol and 1.35 to 1.83 times better than the CMLDA protocol. We observe that as the network size grows, ZDAS is able to at least double the lifetime returned by the LRS protocol. In the case of Scenario 3, Fig.8 shows the tradeoff between the energy required to construct the zone and the size of the zone. As the SCC range increases, the energy required to construct the zone increases, but the number of transmissions

Table 2. Parameters of the model used for the simulations

	Scenario 1	Scenario 2	Scenario 3	Scenario 4
Field	$50m \times 50m$	$100m \times 100m$	$50m \times 50m$	$50m \times 50m$
n	$variables$	$variables$	$variables$	$variables$
r_i	$10m$	$20m$	$variables$	$10m$
τ	5 %	5 %	5 %	$variables$

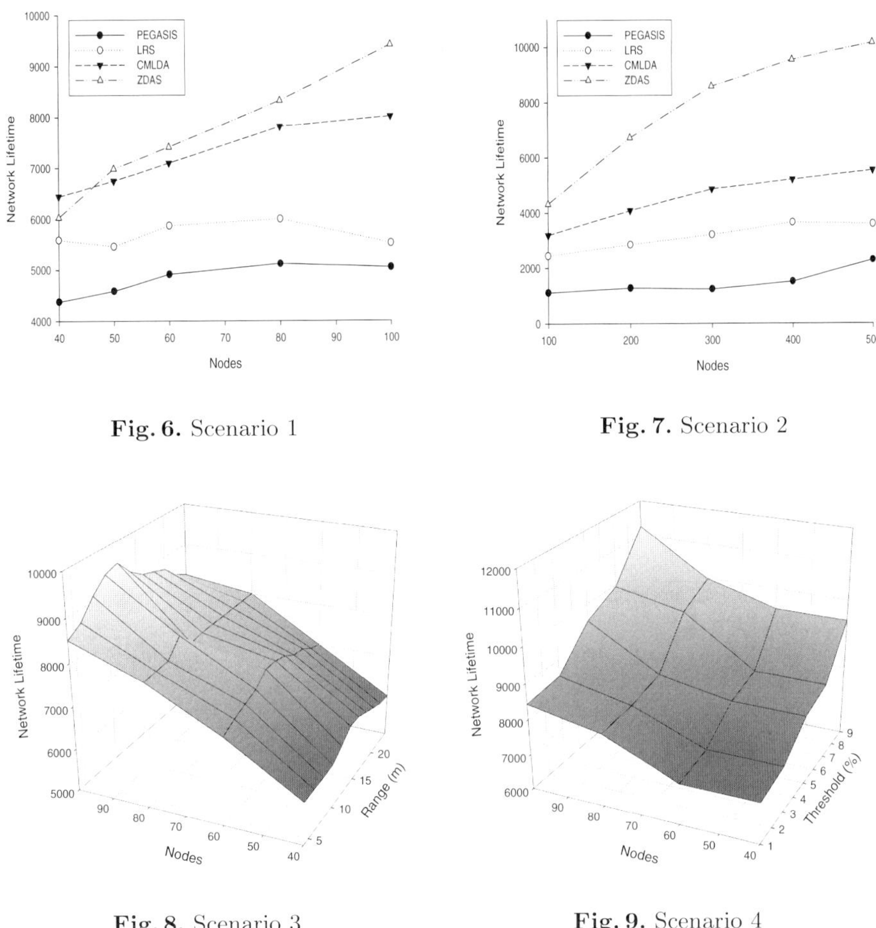

Fig. 6. Scenario 1

Fig. 7. Scenario 2

Fig. 8. Scenario 3

Fig. 9. Scenario 4

decreases. In the case of Scenario 4, we show the impact of τ on the network performance. From Fig.9, we observe that a large value of τ will slightly increase the network lifetime, because as τ increases, the size of the zone increases.

5 Conclusion

The paper investigates the zone based data aggregation scheduling scheme in wireless sensor networks. By jointly designing the routing and link layer to minimize the sum of the transmission energy and circuit processing energy, the aggregation energy and some interesting results are obtained. The benefit of spatial correlation is also studied in a sensor network, with a protocol for maximizing the network lifetime. The results show that significant energy savings can be made by taking advantage of the spatial correlation, which increase the network lifetimes compared with the other data aggregation protocols. It is also shown that the energy savings vary according to the number of nodes, range, and threshold. As a result, the network lifetimes change adaptively. In order to improve this algorithm, we will study the impact of mobile data sinks on the lifetime of sensor networks, and present our observations.

References

1. Kahn, J.M., Katz, R.H., Pister, K.S.J.: Mobile Networking for Smart Dust. In: Proceedings of 5th ACM/IEEE Mobicom Conference (1999)
2. Min, R., Bhardwaj, M., Cho, S.H., Sinha, A., Shih, E., Wang, A., Chandrakasan, A.P.: Low-Power Wireless Sensor Networks. In: Proceedings of VLSI Design (2001)
3. Heinzelman, W., Kulik, J., Balakrishnan, H.: Adaptive Protocols for Information Dissemination in Wireless Sensor Networks. In: Proceedings of 5th ACM/IEEE Mobicom Conference (1999)
4. Lindsey, S., Raghavendra, C.S., PEGASIS,: Power Efficient Gathering in Sensor Information Systems. In: Proceedings of IEEE Aerospace Conference, IEEE Computer Society Press, Los Alamitos (2002)
5. Heidemann, J., et al.: Building Efficient Wireless Sensor Networks with Low-Level Naming. In: Proceedings of 18th ACM Symposium on Operating Systems Principles, ACM Press, New York (2001)
6. Intanagonwiwat, C., Govindan, R., Estrin, D.: Directed diffusion: A scalable and robust communication paradigm for sensor networks. In: Proceedings of 6th ACM/IEEE Mobicom Conference, Boston, Massachusetts, United States (2000)
7. Vuran, M.C., Akan, O.B., Akyildiz, I.F.: Spatio-temporal correlation: theory and applications for wireless sensor networks. In: Proceedings of Computer Networks, vol. 45 (2004)
8. Clouqueur, T., Phipatanasuphorn, V., Ramanathan, P., Saluja, K.: Sensor deployment strategy for target detection. In: Proceedings of the ACM WSNA, Atlanta, USA, ACM Press, New York (2002)
9. Pradhan, S.S., Ramchandran, K.: Distributed source coding: symmetric rates and applications to sensor networks. In: Proceedings of the Data Compression Conference (2000)
10. Scaglione, A., Servetto, S.D.: On the interdependence of routing and data compression in multi-hop sensor networks. In: Proceedings of the ACM MOBICOM 2002, Atlanta, GA, USA, ACM Press, New York (2002)
11. Heinzelman, W.B., Chandrakasan, A.P., Balakrishnan, H.: An Application-Specific Protocol Architecture for Wireless Microsensor Networks. IEEE Transactions on Wireless Communications 1(4) (2002)
12. Madden, S.R., Franklin, M.J., Hellerstein, J.M., Hong, W.: TAG: Tiny AGgregation service for ad-hoc sensor networks. In: Proceedings of OSDI (2002)
13. Dasgupta, K., Kalpakis, K., Namjoshi, P.: An Efficient Clustering-based Heuristic for Data Gathering and Aggregation in Sensor Networks. In: Proceedings of WCNC (2003)
14. Heinzelman, W.B., Chandrakasan, A.P., Balakrishnan, H.: An Application-Specific Protocol Architecture for Wireless Microsensor Networks. Proceedings of IEEE Transactions on Wireless Communications 1(4) (2002)

A Robust Scalable Cluster-Based Multi-hop Routing Protocol for Wireless Sensor Networks

Sudha Mudundi and Hesham Ali

Department of Computer Science
College of Information Science and Technology
University of Nebraska at Omaha
Omaha, NE 68182
smudundi@mail.unomaha.edu, hesham@unomaha.edu

Abstract. Wireless sensor networks are widely deployed for a wide range of applications for gathering information about the environment, monitoring huge building etc. However, the limited energy of the sensor nodes requires efficient gathering of information so that the network lifetime is increased. In literature it is proved that this efficiency can be achieved by clustering the sensor nodes in the network. Previously we proposed a single hop genetic based clustering protocol (GCA) for sensor networks. However, multi-hop routing techniques are known to be a practical approach to solving the problem of routing in sensor networks. In this paper, we present a new robust clustering based multi-hop routing protocol for wireless sensor networks. The proposed genetic clustering algorithm (M-GCA) employs evolutionary techniques to form an efficient virtual backbone. This backbone is used to support routing messages to the base station. Simulation results show that the proposed multi-hop routing protocol outperforms GCA, a single-hop clustering protocol in several scenarios.

1 Introduction

Clustering is one of the conventional protocols for wireless networks. In clustering, nodes are organized into clusters, which consist of a cluster head and several other sensor nodes called cluster members or non-cluster head nodes. The cluster members send the data to their respective cluster heads and only the cluster heads communicate the data to the base station or sink, where an end user accesses it. This reduces the energy spent by the nodes that are away from the local base station/sink. Hence clustering is known to be an energy-efficient communication protocol.

In a large and distributed network consisting of thousands of nodes it might be advantageous to form a multi-hop backbone, which consists of all the cluster heads in the network. This backbone would allow us to route the data from each cluster head node to reach the base station and this will save energy by reducing the long-range transmissions by the far-away cluster heads to the base station. Further energy efficiency can be achieved if the cluster heads perform data aggregation along the route until the data is reached the base station.

The multi-hop model is known to be a practical approach to solving the problem of routing in sensor networks [15]. In the cluster-based hierarchical model the data is

I. Stojmenovic et al. (Eds.): ISPA 2007, LNCS 4742, pp. 895–907, 2007.

first aggregated in the cluster and then sent to next cluster head. As the data moves from a lower level cluster head to a higher level cluster head, large distances are covered and this reduces the latency to travel to the base station [15]. The benefits of energy efficiency, scalability and network robustness of a hierarchical multi-hop network model makes it suitable for time-critical applications [15]. Hence instead of using a single-hop routing method that is used in GCA, it would be more efficient to use a multi-hop routing amongst the clusters for routing the data to the base station.

2 Related Work

Optimal selection of cluster-heads is an NP-hard problem [9]. Thus the existing solutions in literature to this problem are based on heuristic approaches. A good clustering algorithm is the one that does not require frequent topology re-construction as this will lead to frequent information exchange among the nodes in the network. This will eventually lead to high computation overheard.

A self-organizing and adaptive clustering protocol LEACH is proposed in [2]. It aims at minimizing the energy dissipation in the sensor network. It randomly selects sensor nodes as cluster heads to evenly distribute the energy load evenly in the all the sensor nodes. A centralized version of LEACH called as LEACH-C (LEACH-Centralized) is also proposed. In this protocol a central control algorithm is used to form the clusters throughout the network.

In [3] a distributed clustering approach called HEED is proposed. In this protocol the cluster heads are periodically selected based on two parameters. They are node residual energy and cost incurred during the intra cluster communication. In [4] a distributed two-phase Bluetooth scatternet formation algorithm is proposed. The proposed scatternet formation scheme is used to form cluster-based framework for collaboration in event detection in wireless sensor networks. The Max-Min d-Cluster Algorithm in [5] generates d-hop clusters with a run-time of O (d) rounds. But this algorithm does not ensure that the energy used in communicating information to the information center is minimized.

In [6] an approach is proposed which assumes some high-energy nodes called *"Gateways"* are deployed in the network. These gateways, group sensors to form distinct clusters in the system, manage the cluster and perform data fusion to correlate sensor reports. Each sensor only belongs to one cluster and communicates with the base station only through the gateway in the cluster.

In [7] the authors propose a chain-based power efficient protocol based on LEACH. A greedy algorithm is used to construct the chain based on the global knowledge. In a chain, each node takes a turn to become the cluster head. Nodes perform fusion by fusing their own data with the received data. The TEEN [8] cluster-based routing protocol is also based on LEACH.

3 Proposed Multi-hop Genetic Algorithm

In this paper, we present M-GCA (Multi-hop Genetic Clustering Algorithm), a two-level hierarchical evolutionary cluster-based multi-hop routing protocol for wireless sensor networks. All the sensor nodes in the network are clustered using the genetic clustering algorithm (GCA) described in [17]. The protocol is explained here.

Our dynamic cluster formation protocol called the Genetic Clustering Algorithm (GCA) is based on the genetic algorithm. As mentioned earlier, forming clusters is a NP-hard problem; hence we need to use some optimization techniques to find good clusters. The genetic algorithm is one such optimization technique. We first present the concept of the proposed genetic algorithm, its sequence of steps and then illustrate how our approach uses the same sequence of steps in determining the roles for the devices in the network. Genetic algorithms are stochastic, directed search algorithms, which one finds useful in finding global optimal or at least sub-optimal solutions in both static and dynamic environments. They are used to find approximate solutions to solve hard problems through application of the principles of evolutionary techniques.

The main components of a genetic algorithm are explained in brief as follows. Each chromosome represents a legal solution to the problem and is represented using binary digits, integers or real numbers. The initial population is usually generated randomly or heuristics can used to seed the initial population for better convergence. Each chromosome is evaluated based on some fitness function. Then two parent chromosomes are selected from a population based on their fitness function depending on the application. With a crossover probability, the parents simply swap portions of the underlying chromosomes to form new offspring. With a mutation probability, offspring are randomly mutated at each position in the chromosome, which creates variation in the population.

One of the main objectives of this paper is to cluster sensor nodes efficiently using the above-mentioned evolutionary approach. This involves selecting cluster-head among cluster members. Clustering enables network scalability. It also extends the lifetime of the sensor network, as the all the sensors need not communicate to the base station. Only the cluster members communicate to their respective cluster-heads. The cluster-heads aggregates the data signal and communicates with the base station directly. In general, the increase in network lifetime is very important because of the fact that the sensors are energy limited.

We propose a three-phased clustering protocol in which the first phase consists of role determination using a genetic algorithm. The genetic algorithm finds the best role assignment and cluster formation. The second phase involves in connection establishment based on the roles determined in the first phase. It also involves creating TDMA schedules by the cluster-head nodes. The final phase is the data transmission phase. During this phase, all the nodes in the cluster send data to their cluster-head and the cluster-head performs data aggregation and sends data to the base station.

Phase 1 – Role Determination

The first phase is called the "Role Determination" phase. During this phase, each sensor node in the network sends its current location information and energy level to the base station. Here we assume that all the nodes in the network can directly transmit to the base station. After the base station receives the location information from the nodes, the base station determines the roles of each node in the network for that round using the genetic algorithm described in Section 4. The algorithm is used to find the best combination of cluster-head, cluster member and gateway in wireless sensor networks. After the roles are determined, the base station sends this information to all the nodes in the network and the role determination phase is done.

The genetic algorithm generates an initial population based on a heuristic to start the evolution process. This heuristic acts as a seed to generate the optimal clustering of the nodes. The heuristic generates a possible cluster of nodes and hence the initial population consists of 'k' networks for the given number of nodes, where 'k' is the population size. The fitness of each group in the initial population is evaluated using a fitness function and fitness values are assigned to each group in the population. Based on the fitness values two parent groups are selected and the genetic operators such as crossover and mutation are applied to generate new offspring from the two parent groups. The children are placed in a new population. This process is continued until a new population is generated from the previous population. If the end condition is satisfied then the algorithm terminates. Each component and operation in the proposed genetic algorithm for cluster formation is explained in detail in the following sub-sections.

Chromosomal Representation: The chromosome is represented as a fixed length list, which contains the node number of its cluster-head. The node number can be a positive or a negative number. A negative number indicates that the node is dead. A cluster-head has its own node number, as it is its own cluster-head. For example, given a ten-node network for node numbers from 0 to 9, the following notation is a chromosome that represents a possible wireless sensor network: 5 –1 9 –1 5 5 –1 9 9 5

This notation implies that the nodes 1, 3 and 6 have no energy and hence they are dead. Nodes 0, 4, and 9 belong to the cluster-head 5 in the network. Node 2, 7 and 8 belong to the cluster-head 9. The cluster-head nodes 5 and 9 have their own node numbers as they belong to their cluster.

Initial Population: The initial population is generated using a simple heuristic instead of random generation. The pseudo code of the heuristic is illustrated in Algorithm of Figure 1. Initially in the heuristic, the average node energy is calculated from the current node energies sent by the all the nodes to the base-station. Cluster-heads require more energy as they perform the data aggregation function and are responsible for sending data to the base station. These functions require more energy. An eligible list containing cluster-heads is created which consists of all the nodes that have their current energy greater than that of the calculated average energy. All the nodes in the eligible list are possible cluster-heads for the current round. Depending upon the size of the cluster, x number of cluster-head nodes is randomly selected from the eligible list. This randomness ensures that different networks with different clusters are formed. A member list is also created which consists of all the other nodes that are not cluster-head nodes. For each possible member node in the member list, the distance between the member node and all the x cluster-heads is calculated. The node joins the cluster-head that has the minimum distance so that the node does not require more transmission energy to send data to its cluster-head.

The networks generated by this heuristic might not satisfy all the metrics for efficiency. We pick networks with clusters from their initial state based on their fitness value and they are gradually improved upon by applying the crossover and mutation genetic operators to produce efficient and optimal clusters in the network.

Fitness Function: The fitness of each group of n nodes in the population is evaluated based on the following parameters:

Number of Cluster-head nodes: The number of cluster-head nodes should be minimized to reduce the inter-cluster interference.

Network Distance: The amount of energy the non-cluster-head nodes require to transmit data to the cluster-head should be minimized. The smaller the distance between any two nodes, the less transmit power required to transmit data. Hence, it would be sufficient to minimize the total sum of the distances between all the nodes in each cluster to their cluster-head [9]. Finally, for each cluster in the wireless sensor network, the net distance is calculated as the sum of distances between the nodes and their cluster-head. From the above-mentioned criteria, the fitness function of this algorithm is evaluated using the function F below, where A, B are constants.

$$F = A * \text{Number of Cluster-Heads} + B * \text{Network Distance} \quad (1)$$

The above fitness function is evaluated and a fitness value is assigned to each group in the population. We need to minimize the mentioned criteria; hence the fitness function is a minimizing function. So, the smaller the fitness value the better the group to be selected. To make all the values of the parameters lie in a pre-defined region, taking weights A and B correspondingly normalizes all the parameters. These weights are system dependent and give the flexibility of adjusting each of the parameters in calculating the fitness value. Various applications may require different attributes for cluster formation in a wireless sensor network. As discussed before, this evolutionary approach has the ability to generate clusters with specific desirable attributes. It is also robust and flexible in the sense that different objectives demanded by different applications may be explored by using different fitness functions.

Selection: The whole population is sorted according to their fitness value, and the parent string, which has the minimum fitness value, is selected. To introduce some randomness into the algorithm, the second parent is randomly selected form the population. In this algorithm we would like to minimize the fitness function. The lower the fitness value the better the likelihood of that group being selected.

Crossover: With a crossover probability a single-point crossover is performed on the two parent groups that are selected. A random cross-point value from 0 to n-1 is taken and the string from the beginning of the group to the crossover point is copied from the first parent; the rest is copied from the other parent.

Mutation: The children produced by the crossover process are mutated with a mutation probability. Two random locations in the string are selected and the cluster-heads for both the nodes are swapped.

Elitism: Elitism is also implemented in which some of the best groups are passed on to the next generations so that the subsequent generations do not loose the best characteristics.

The genetic operators such as the crossover and mutation are applied on the two selected parents and the two new children are generated. The children are added to the new population and when the population is completely generated then this replaces the previous population for a further run of the algorithm.

```
Procedure generateClusters()
{
#Calculate avgerage node energy
for i =1 to nn
  tot ← tot + curr_eng(i )
avg_eng ← tot/nn
for i =1 to nn
  if (curr_eng( i) >= avg_eng)
    eligible ← eligible ∪i
Randomly select x, number of cluster -heads from the eligible list
mem_list ← alive_node _list - head_list
for each node in mem_list
  for each cluster -head, i
    Calculate distance, distto(i) between the node and each cluster -head
  min_dist ← MIN{distto (i), distto(i +1)....dist to(x)}
  id ← Node Number of the cluster -head that has minimum distance
  cluster($i d) ← cluster($i d) U node
}
```

Fig. 1. Algorithm to Generate Clusters for Initial Population

End/Terminating Condition: The end condition of this algorithm is used to find out the best role assignment. The algorithm terminates when the specified number of generations is reached. In the last generation the network with the minimum network distance and having balanced clusters is selected. Minimum network distance ensures that the transmission power required by each node is minimized and hence the total energy dissipation in the network decreases. Balanced clusters ensure that the load is evenly distributed among all the clusters and no cluster-head becomes a bottleneck.

Phase 2 – Connection Establishment

The second phase is called the "Connection Establishment" phase. In this phase, connections are established amongst the nodes based on the roles that were assigned during the first phase. The Nodes that are cluster heads create TDMA schedules for all the nodes in their cluster and transmit the schedule to their corresponding cluster members. Nodes that are not cluster heads (i.e., cluster members) determine their TDMA slot for data transmission and go to sleep until it is time for the node to transmit data to the cluster-head. After the nodes in the cluster know their TDMA schedule, the connection establishment phase is done.

Phase 3 – Data Transmission

The final phase is called as the "Data transmission or Steady State" phase. This phase is identical to the steady-state phase proposed in LEACH [9]. The steady state is broken into frames where nodes send their data to the cluster-head at most once per frame during their allocated transmission slot. Each slot in which a node transmits data is constant, so the time for a frame of data transfer depends on the number of nods in the cluster. The radio of each non-cluster-head node is turned off until it is ready to transmit data in its allocated transmission time. As the total bandwidth is fixed and all the nodes need to send data to the cluster-head TDMA schedule is used for efficient us of bandwidth. However, a cluster-head node needs to turn on its receiver to receive data from its cluster members. Once the cluster-head receives all the data, it performs data aggregation and forwards the final data to the base station.

In the first phase, as the base station has the knowledge of the entire network it forms a virtual backbone consisting of all the cluster head nodes in the network. This virtual backbone is formed using the Prim's minimum cost spanning tree [14]. The base station builds a complete graph using the cluster head nodes as the vertices. A cost is assigned to each edge in the network, which is the distance between the connected cluster heads. The base station then uses the Prim's minimum cost spanning tree algorithm that generates a spanning tree that has the minimum distance. Hence this minimizes the overall energy dissipated in the network as the cluster head nodes follow a single path to route the date to the base station which is the minimum distance. The base station also uses the Dijkstra's shortest-path algorithm [14] choosing the base station as the source. Each cluster head has a shortest path to reach the base station.

After determining the route, BS includes the successor and predecessor of each cluster head node to the cluster information that is broadcast in the network. Hence each cluster head will know whether they have predecessors from whom they should get the data signal and then aggregate the data signal. The communication among the cluster head nodes is done using the CSMA method and a unique spreading code for each cluster head node. Let's consider that the cluster head B has a predecessor and successor cluster head, A and C respectively. In this case, B gets the data from the node A and aggregates the signal with that of B's and transmits to its next hop cluster head node C. If node C has the base station as a successor then it transmits the final aggregated signal to the base station.

4 Performance Analysis

We implemented M-GCA and conducted detailed simulations using the MIT uAMPS simulator [11] to evaluate the performance of the cluster-based multi-hop routing protocol. The performance of M-GCA is compared with the performance of the previous single-hop GCA approach [17]. Our evolutionary based genetic cluster formation algorithm assumes the following:

1. The nodes are aware of their location and that of the base station.
2. Devices are stationary during the simulation.
3. The nodes have unlimited data to be sent.
4. The base station has constant supply of energy.

The simulations are performed on random 100-node sensor networks with dimensions 100 meters X 100 meters. The base station was placed 75 meters from the closest node, at (x=50, y=175). For fairness in comparison, the characteristics of the networks used for the simulation are identical to the one used in evaluating LEACH-C. The bandwidth of the channel is set to 1 Mbps. The transmitting and receiving side has a processing delay of $25\mu s$ each. The packet header size is set to 25 bytes and the size of the data is 500 bytes. Each round lasts about 20 seconds based on the analysis.

The population size is taken to be 20. Using simulations we found out the values for the crossover and mutation probability that create good clusters. The crossover probability, CO_PROB is taken as 0.7 and the mutation probability, MT_PROB is taken as 0.001. Each data point plotted in the graph is an average of results obtained through 10 different simulation runs of random networks. Simulation results are taken when all the nodes begin with the same amount of energy and also when there are nodes that have higher energies. All the nodes in the network start with an initial energy of 2J. The performance of the evolutionary cluster-based multi-hop routing protocol is evaluated using the performance indices; the total number of data signals received at the BS over a period of time, the total energy dissipated in the network over a period of time and the total number of nodes that remain alive in the network over a period of time.

4.1 Nodes Start With Equal Energies

In this set of simulation experiments, each node starts with 2J of energy. The total number of sensor nodes is 100. The base station is located at x=50, y=175. The total number of data signals received by the base station, the number of nodes alive over a period of time and the energy expended in the network performance indices of both the M-GCA and GCA protocols are studied.

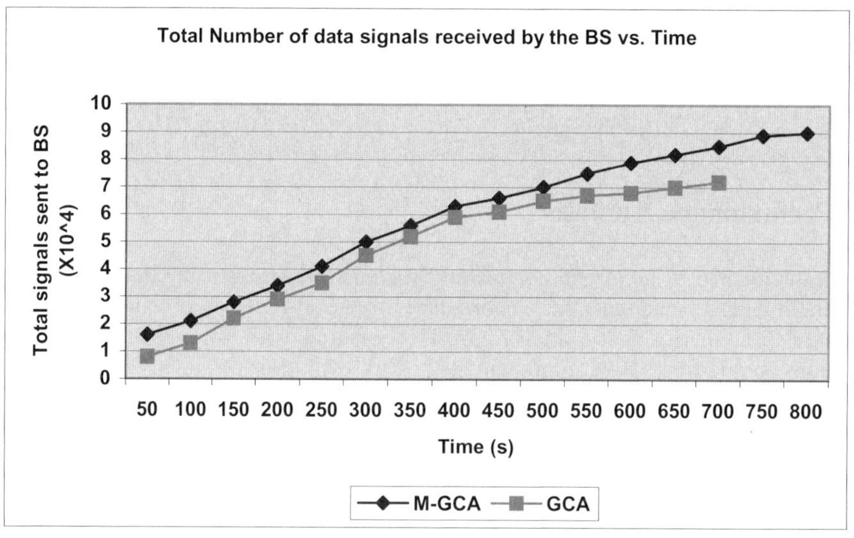

Fig. 2. Total number of data signals received at the BS vs. Time

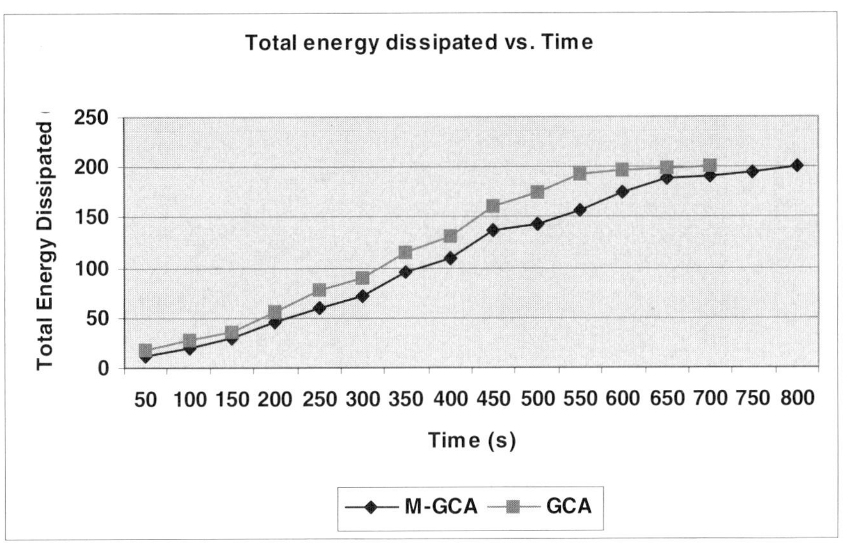

Fig. 3. Total energy dissipated in the network vs. Time

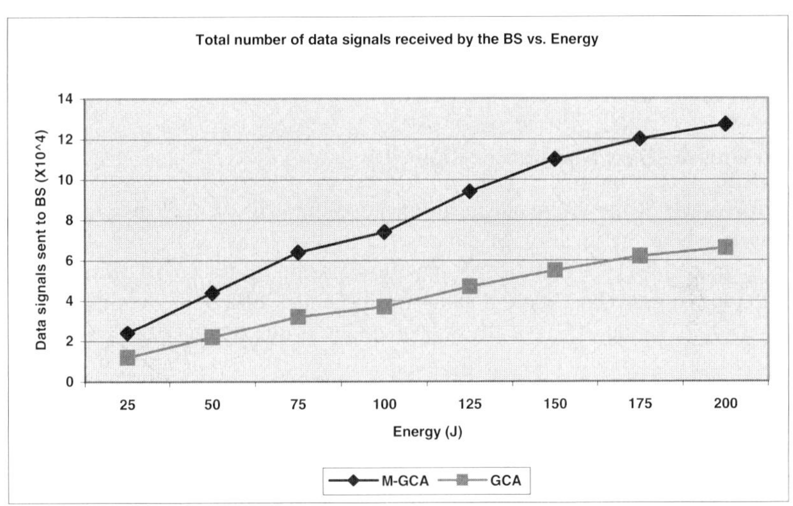

Fig. 4. Total number of signals received at the base station vs. Energy

As shown in Figures 2-5, the multi-hop based genetic clustering algorithm has outperformed the single-hop genetic clustering algorithm in terms of the performance indices studied. This can be attributed to the fact that the backbone created allows us to route more data from each cluster head node to the base station. This in turn will save energy by reducing the long-range transmissions by the far-away cluster heads to the base station. Further increase in the throughput is achieved because of the data aggregation performed by the cluster head nodes along the route until the data is

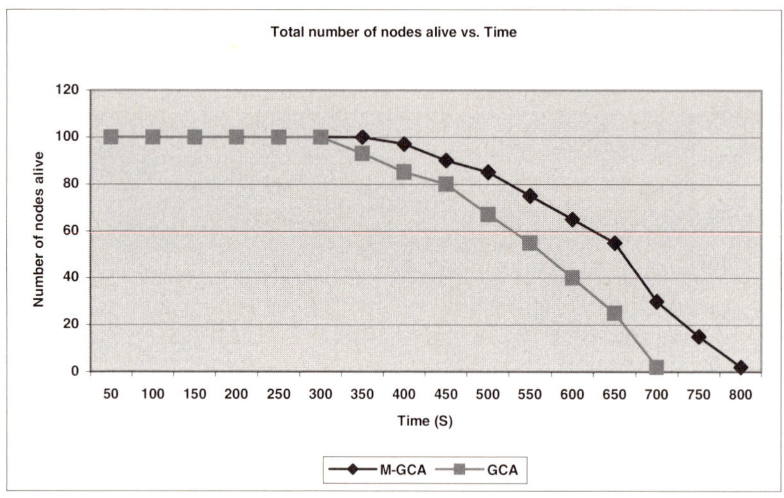

Fig. 5. Total number of nodes alive in the network vs. Time

reached the base station. This second-level data aggregation also decreases the energy dissipation in the network as smaller signals travel lesser distances in M-GCA as compared to larger signals traveling longer distances. Hence, due to the lesser energy dissipation of M-GCA, its nodes live longer than the nodes in GCA. This, in turn, increases the total data sent to the base station per unit energy.

4.2 Varying the Base Station Location

The performance of the GCA clustering protocol and the M-GCA is also studied for the scenario where the location of the base station is varied in the network. The base station is placed in the middle of the network at x=50, y=50. Simulations are performed moving the base station away from the network. The y coordinate is set to 50, 100, 175, 225, and 300. All the sensor nodes in the network start with an initial energy of 2J. All other simulation parameters are the same as mentioned in Section 4.

Figures 6 and 7 compare the total data per unit energy sent to the base station of both GCA and M-GCA. The figures show that the M-GCA outperforms GCA. The reason is that the formed backbone allows routing the data from each cluster head node to the base station in multiple hops. This will save lot of energy by reducing the long-range transmissions by the far-away cluster heads to the base station. The first level of data aggregation is done within the cluster, and the cluster head nodes along the route do the second level of data aggregation until the data reaches the base station. The performance of the multi-hop genetic clustering protocol can be best explained below.

Consider a scenario with two cluster head nodes A and B. Assume that the distance (A, BS) = 350, distance (B, BS) = 300 and the distance (A, B) = 30. In GCA, nodes A and B send data to the base station independently. In this case the total distance traveled is distance (A, BS) + distance (B, BS) = 350+300 = 650. Let the route formed in M-GCA be A, B, BS; i.e., cluster head A sends data to cluster head B, and finally B performs data aggregation and transmits the final data signal to BS. In this

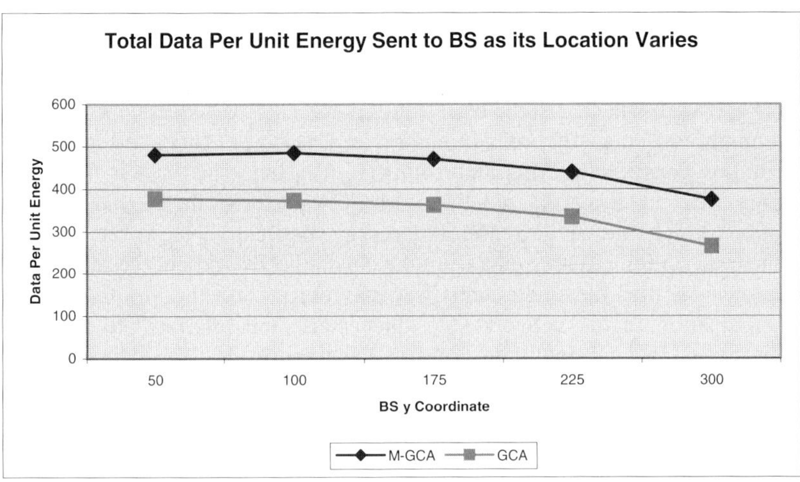

Fig. 6. Av data per unit energy sent to the BS as the location of the BS is varied in the network

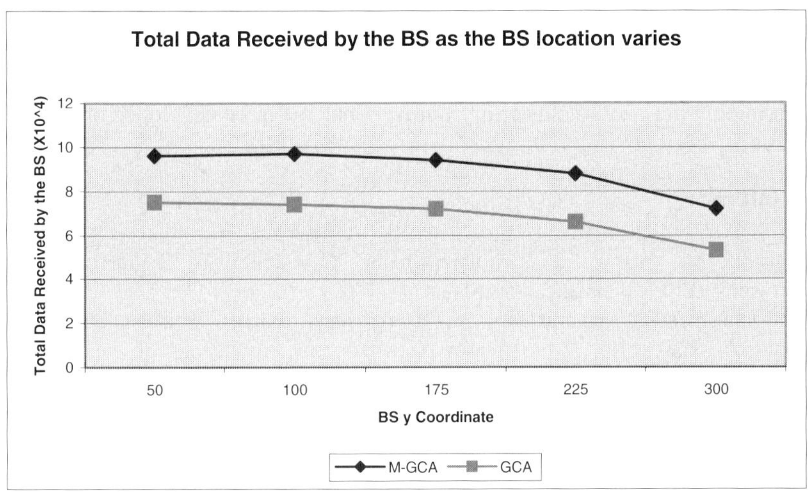

Fig. 7. Total data received by the BS as the location of the BS is varied in the network

case the total distance traveled is distance (A, B) + distance (B, BS) = 30+300 = 330, which is nearly half the distance traveled in the single-hop genetic algorithm. Hence the cluster head A need not dissipate more energy as the total transmission distance is reduced to 30. If any cluster head is near to the base station and joining the multi-hop backbone would increase the distance to reach the base station, then that cluster head sends data directly to the base station. This is taken care of by the genetic algorithm. The reason for M-GCA to outperform GCA across all the performance indices studied is well explained using the above scenario.

5 Conclusions

In summary, the multi-hop genetic clustering protocol (M-GCA) performs well with respect to the total data sent to the base station, total energy dissipated in the network, and the number of nodes that remain alive over a period of time, and it outperforms the single-hop genetic clustering algorithm (GCA). Hence M-GCA is more scalable and energy efficient. It is to be noted that M-GCA performs the second level of data aggregation, which further decreases the energy dissipation. However, in scenarios where the base station requires data from the cluster heads without the second level of data aggregation, then the single-hop GCA may outperform the M-GCA in terms of energy dissipation in the network. This is because the intermediate nodes in the backbone must send data multiple times and the energy is depleted easily in these nodes. One such worst-case scenario is when all the cluster head nodes connect to a single cluster head node and the latter node is a bottleneck node because it must transmit all the data sent by its predecessor cluster heads. This might increase the energy consumption in the bottleneck node, and M-GCA might not be energy-efficient and scalable. In such scenarios, single-hop protocol performs well.

From the above discussion it is evident that application-specific routing protocols should be developed in order to make use of the network efficiently. Some of the parameters to consider while developing the protocols are the type of the application, number of nodes in the network, the type of nodes deployed, the location of the base station and the energy and computation models used. These should be good indicators for determining the type of clustering/routing protocols to be developed or used.

References

1. Akyildiz, M., Su, W., Sankarasubramaniam, Y., Cayirci, E.: A Survey on Sensor Networks. IEEE Communications Magazine (2002)
2. Heinzelman, W., Chandrakasan, A., Balakrishnan: Energy Efficient Communication Protocol for Wireless Micro Sensor Networks. In: Proceedings of the 33rd Hawaii International Conference on System Sciences (2000)
3. Younis, O., Fahmy, S.: Distributed Clustering for Scalable, Long-Lived Sensor Networks. Purdue University, Technical Report, CSD TR-03-026 (2003)
4. Dharia, S.: Thesis: A Resource-Aware Distributed Bluetooth Scatternet Formation Algorithm and Its Application To Wireless Sensor Networks (2003)
5. Amis, A., Prakash, R., Vuong, T., Huynh, D.: Max-Min D-Cluster Formation in Wireless Ad Hoc Networks. In: Proceedings of IEEE INFOCOM, Tel Aviv (2000)
6. Gupta, G., Younis, M.: Load-Balanced Clustering in Wireless Sensor Networks. In: Proceedings of the Int. Conference on Communication, Anchorage, AK (2003)
7. Lindsey, S., Raghavendra, C.: PEGASIS: Power Efficient Gathering in Sensor Information Systems. In: International Conference on Communications (2001)
8. Manjeshwar, A., Agrawal, D.: TEEN: A Routing Protocol for enhanced efficiency in Wireless Sensor Networks. In: Int. Proc. of the 15th Parallel and Dist. Processing Symposium (2001)
9. Basagni, S., Chlamtac, I., Farago, A.: A Generalized Clustering Algorithm for Peer-to-Peer Networks. In: Workshop on Algorithmic Aspects of Com., Bologna, Italy (July 1997)

10. Heinzelman, W.: Application-Specific Protocol Architectures for Wireless Networks. PhD Thesis, Massachusetts Institute of Technology (2000)
11. MIT μAMPS project ns2 code extensions (2007), http://www-mtl.mit.edu/research/icsystems/uamps/research/leach/leach_code.shtml
12. NS2 LEACH Implementation: Jason Pamplin (2004), http://www.internetworkflow.com/downloads/ns2leach/mit.tar.gz
13. Rappaport, T.: Wireless Communications: Principles & Practice. Prentice Hall, Inc., New Jersey (1996)
14. Cormen, T., Leiserson, C., Rivest, R., Stein, C.: Introduction to Algorithms, 2nd edn. McGraw-Hill, New York (2001)
15. Ibriq, J., Mahgoub, I.: Cluster-Based Routing in Wireless Sensor Networks: Issues and Challenges. In: Proceedings of the 2004 Symposium on Performance Evaluation of Computer Telecommunication Systems (2004)
16. Network Simulator (2007), http://www.isi.edu/nsnam/ns
17. Mudundi, S., Ali, H.: A New Robust Genetic Algorithm for Dynamic Cluster Formation in Wireless Sensor Networks. In: Proceedings of Wireless and Optical Communications, Montreal, Quebec, Canada (May 2007)

Qos Provisioning in Mobile Networks Based on Aggregate Bandwidth Reservation

Kelvin L. Dias[1], Stenio F.L. Fernandes[2], and Djamel F.H. Sadok[3]

[1] UFPA, Electrical and Computer Engineering, PO Box 8619,
66.075-900 - Belém, PA, Brazil
kld@ufpa.br

[2] CEFET-AL, Informatics, Barão de Atalaia, S/N
57.020-510, Maceió, AL, Brazil
stenio@cefet-al.br

[3] UFPE, Computer Science, PO Box 7851,
Recife, PE - Brazil
jamel@gprt.ufpe.br

Abstract. This paper proposes a novel resource management framework that integrates Call Admission Control (CAC) and aggregate reservation of bandwidth for mobile networks in a scalable fashion. Our proposal avoids per-user reservation signaling overhead and takes into account the expected bandwidth to be used by calls handed off from neighboring cells within a prediction interval through the Trigg and Leach Method (an adaptive exponential smoothing technique). Our scheme is compared through simulations with the ACR (Adaptive Channel Reservation) scheme, a dynamic reservation-based proposal that uses GPS systems to extrapolate users' movement and to trigger reservations in the next predicted cell. The simulation results show that our proposal provides the best performance in terms of handoff dropping probability and can achieve similar levels of call blocking probability as compared to ACR. In addition, our proposal can grant an upper bound on handoff dropping probability even under very high loads.

1 Introduction

One of the main research challenges for the next generation of mobile systems is the design of efficient resource management frameworks that could avoid application disruption due to handoffs and provide scalable and seamless inteworking with current Internet QoS provisioning schemes.

Handoff in wireless/mobile networks is the mechanism that transfers an ongoing call from the current cell as the mobile station (MS) moves through the coverage area of the system. If the target cell does not have sufficient available bandwidth, the call will be dropped. From the user's point of view handoff dropping is less desirable than the blocking of a new call. Therefore, an important component for mobile/wireless networks is the Call Admission Control (CAC) mechanism. It must be used to address

I. Stojmenovic et al. (Eds.): ISPA 2007, LNCS 4742, pp. 908–919, 2007.

the mobility effects, accepting or rejecting new users in the network. CAC schemes not only have to ensure that the network meets the QoS of newly arriving calls if accepted, but should also guarantee that QoS of existing calls does not deteriorate.

A complementary mechanism used in conjunction with the CAC is the bandwidth reservation. Currently, the majority of proposals use a per-user signaling in order to reserve bandwidth for taking into account the handoff traffic.

On the other hand, Internet frameworks for QoS provisioning rely, basically, on two architectures: Integrated Services (IntServ) [1] and Differentiated Services (DiffServ) [2]. While the IntServ architecture provides strict QoS guarantees through per-user explicit signaling for CAC and reservation using RSVP (Resource Reservation Protocol), it fails in providing the scalability objectives due its reservation based approach. The DiffServ proposal aims at providing less strict QoS guarantees through packet classification at network ingress and differentiation of the treatment according to a set of classes named PHB (Per Hop Behavior), hence offering better network scalability. The Bandwidth Broker (BB) is a network entity proposed for implementing resource management policies in the DiffServ architecture, including the CAC mechanism [3]. In wireless and mobile networks, reservation of resources is more challenging than in wired networks due the scarcity of bandwidth in wireless links. In our opinion, a scalable QoS architecture for wireless/mobile networks should provide CAC schemes that avoid excessive per-user signaling for wireless link reservation purposes.

This paper proposes a novel CAC and bandwidth reservation mechanisms for mobile networks. Our proposal avoids per-user reservation signaling and takes into account the expected bandwidth to be used by calls handed off from neighboring cells within a prediction interval through the Trigg and Leach Method (TL), an adaptive exponential smoothing technique [12]. Our scheme is compared through simulations with the ACR [9] (Adaptive Channel Reservation) scheme, a dynamic reservation-based proposal that uses GPS systems to extrapolate users' movement and to trigger reservations in the next predicted cell. The simulation results show that our proposal provides the best performance in terms of handoff dropping probability and can achieve similar levels of call blocking probability as compared to ACR. In addition, our proposal can grant an upper bound on handoff dropping probability even under very high loads.

The remainder of this paper is organized as follows. In section 2, we describe the related research work. Section 3 gives an overview of the Trigg and Leach Technique for forecasting. We then present the novel CAC and reservation scheme in section 4. Performance results are presented in section 5. Finally, we present our conclusions in section 6.

2 Related Work

Proposals for CAC and bandwidth reservation in wireless/mobile networks present in the literature can be divided into two categories: fixed and dynamic strategies. Fixed strategies, such as the guard channel (GC) [4] scheme, give preferential treatment to handoff calls reserving a fixed number of channels exclusively for them. The advantage of this strategy is its simplicity because there is no need for the exchange of control information between base stations. However, this scheme is not flexible to handle varying traffic loads, since there is no information about current and neighboring cell's load.

Proposed dynamic reservation strategies extend the basic guard channel scheme according to the estimated handoff call rate derived from the number of calls in the neighboring cells and the mobility pattern of these calls to reserve bandwidth in advance in the next cell or in a group of cells. Resource reservation can be problematic, in general, due to the possibility of poor network utilization due to unnecessary blocking of new users and can get even worse if the reservations are made in several adjacent cells. Furthermore, these schemes imply a large amount of signaling overhead.

The scheme proposed in [5] uses the aggregate history of handoffs in each cell to predict the probability a call will be handed off to a certain neighboring cell. Based on handoff prediction, the number of channels is reserved in advance. Each base station records the number of handoff failures and adjusts the reservation by changing the estimation window size. One problem with history-based schemes is the overhead to develop, store and update traffic histories for the different cells. Furthermore, due to short-term changes (e.g., diversion of traffic due to accidents) and medium-term changes (e.g., traffic re-routing during road constructions), these estimates cannot be fully reliable.

In [13] the authors elaborate a handoff prioritization and CAC scheme for an aggregate mobility prediction based on a small mobility cache, which stores the history of handoffs in each base station. Furthermore, the proposal pre-reserves handoff resources aggregately between neighboring cells according to the results obtained from the prediction unit. Despite the scheme's scalability advocated by the authors, depending on the reservation periodicity, the scheme can be ineffective to avoid handoff droppings. The call admission control proposed in [6] takes into consideration the number of calls in adjacent cells, in addition to the number of calls in the admission cell. The authors developed a theoretical model to compute the requirements for handoff requests in order to maintain a target handoff dropping probability. The proposed model assumes that all bandwidth requests are identical, which is not valid if multimedia services with varying bandwidth requirements are to be supported by the network.

In [8] a predictive channel reservation (PCR) scheme based on mobile positioning systems (GPS -Global Positioning System) is proposed. This scheme makes predictive channel reservation for each MS based on its current position and orientation. The reservation is triggered if the MS reaches a certain threshold distance from the next cell. A reservation may be deemed invalid (false reservation) if the MS changes its moving direction. In this case, the cancellation of the reservation must be sent to de-allocate the reserved channel. Furthermore, rather than strictly mapping each reserved bandwidth portion to the MS that made the reservation, all reserved bandwidth is used as a generic pool to serve handoff requests but not new calls. When a MS arrives from a neighboring cell after a handoff, it may use bandwidth from the reserved portion if there is any available. Otherwise, the handoff connection will compete in the free bandwidth portion with other new call attempts.

The ACR (Adaptive Channel Reservation) scheme was proposed in [9] and it is based on the PCR proposal, but it uses a threshold time instead of a threshold distance to trigger the bandwidth reservation in the next predicted cell. The authors argue that using a threshold time permits a better control of the different degrees of mobility to trigger the reservation in the next cell, avoiding waste of bandwidth due to unused reservations. For example, considering a MS located in the overlapping area of two adjacent cells with a very slow moving speed of this MS (close to 0) and requiring a channel for its call. If the PCR scheme is used, two channels (each cell has one channel occupied) will be occupied by this call, one channel is used for communication in the current cell and the other is reserved for this call in the adjacent cell because the threshold distance was reached. Since the MS of this call is almost stationary, the reserved channel may not be used for the lifetime of this call. Consequently, PCR can lead to under-utilization of wireless channels. The PCR as well as the ACR schemes introduce a lot of signaling messages for reservation and cancellation of false reservations. Moreover, the reservations can decrease the dropping probability at the expense of increasing the blocking probability, what may give rise to poor network utilization. The use of GPS for predicting user mobility is also advocated in [10], [11], but as aforesaid problems described for PCR and ACR this proposal suffer from signaling overhead to reserve bandwidth in the next predicted cells.

A similar approach to ours is proposed in [7], [14]. In [7] authors proposed a local predictive resource reservation for handoff based on the Wiener process forecast and a methodology for granting an upper bound on HDP. The limited results obtained for the CBP and HDP metrics were depicted only for the Wiener-based proposal. The lack of performance results in terms of CBP and HDP for their ARIMA-based prediction seems to be justified by the very similar results obtained from the comparative trace analysis with the Wiener-based method conducted in that paper. As shown in paper [15], simple prediction techniques can achieve similar performance results as those decribed in [7]. The proposal in [14] also requires an extensive computational effort to produce the predictions. There is a clear advantage when relying on adaptive exponential smoothing techniques for forecasting the total amount of required bandwidth for future handoff calls. Such techniques are easier to implement than the Linear Time Series (LTS) methods, since there is no need to perform any optimization procedures to parameterize a given model accurately (e.g., ARIMA). Please note that using LTS, one should periodically verify whether a given model is still valid, thus eventually implying in a new model and parameterization. A comprehensive survey on call admission control and resource reservation for mobile/wireless can be found in [16].

In summary, while such dynamic reservation-based schemes have demonstrated significant performance advantages over well-engineered guard channels, the per-user dynamic reservation approach place computation and communication burdens on the network's infrastructure, which increases with the numbers of users and handoffs. Furthermore, proposed solutions based on local predictions require a significant computational effort to be practical. Hence, the scalability and applicability of such solutions to future micro and pico-mobile all-IP networks is not well established.

3 Forecasting Procedures: Exponential Smoothing and Variants

Exponential smoothing methods proved to be optimal for a very general class of state-space models and their correspondent adaptive methods demonstrated to have trustworthy improved forecast accuracy over non-adaptive smoothing [12], [17]. Exponential smoothing techniques have long been the methods of choice for both univariate filtering and forecasting due to their accuracy and ease of use. Researchers from a variety of fields are increasingly utilizing them because of their simplicity and overall good performance. They also suggested their use for short-term prediction.

3.1 Simple Exponential Smoothing

Let Y_t denote a univariate time series. Simple exponential smoothing assumes that the forecast $\hat{Y}$ for period $t+h$ is given by a variable level $\hat{a}$ at period t

$$Y_{t+h} = \hat{a}_t \tag{1}$$

which is recursively estimated by a weighted average of the observed and the predicted value for Y_t.

$$\hat{a}_t = \alpha Y_t + (1-\alpha)\hat{Y}_t \tag{2}$$

$$\hat{a}_t = \alpha Y_t + (1-\alpha)\hat{a}_{t-1} \tag{3}$$

where $0 < \alpha < 1$ is known as the smoothing parameter.

3.2 Adaptive Exponential Smoothing: Trigg and Leach

Although there is no consensus about the most useful adaptive approach, Trigg and Leach is indeed the most widely used procedure. The main advantage for using Trigg & Leach's rule is that it is effortless, does not impose computation overhead, and requires only a small amount of saved data to perform one-step ahead forecasting. In Trigg & Leach's rule, the track signal T^n monitors the estimation process. In the original algorithm, called Trigg's [17], the adaptive stepsize and the track was the same variable. The following equations define Trigg & Leach algorithm:

$$T^n = \frac{S^n}{M^n} \tag{4}$$

$$\alpha^n = \left|T^n\right| \tag{5}$$

where:

$$S^n = (1-\beta)S^{n-1} + \beta\hat{\varepsilon}^n \tag{6}$$

S^n represents the smoothed weighted sum of the observed errors and $\hat{\varepsilon}^n$ is the estimation error at time *n*. M^n represents mean absolute deviation and has the following formulation.

$$M^n = (1-\beta)M^{n-1} + \beta\left|\hat{\varepsilon}^n\right| \tag{7}$$

One can easily show that α^n is between $\left[-1,1\right]$. Values close to zero point out a well-controlled prediction system (smaller prediction errors) whereas values near to the unity indicate an out of control prediction system (huge prediction errors). It is important to emphasize that α^n allow the system to reconcile by not being too reactive to changes. But most importantly, α^n will vary based on variations in the data pattern.

4 The Proposed Call Admission Control and Bandwidth Reservation Scheme

Our novel CAC and bandwidth reservation scheme estimates the total amount of required bandwidth for future handoff calls using TL. The process for predicting the required bandwidth for handoff calls is local, that is, the base station uses only local information (collected bandwidth due to handoffs) that serves as the input for the prediction method without exchange of messages among neighboring cells to this end. Suppose that a base station knows the amount Ω of required resources for handoff calls at the current time t. The amount of resources required for handoffs $E(\Omega)$ at a future time $t+\Delta t$ can be predicted based on the current Ω and its predicted value from the previous time interval $t-\Delta t$. In order to offer statistical guarantees regarding the worst case handoff dropping probability (HDP) for the next time interval, we may use interval prediction based on confidence intervals and confidence levels. This way, we can determine a level L such that $Prob(\Omega \le L) = 1 - HDP$. This level L is called $(1-HDP)*100\%$ upper confidence bound for Ω. This value is given by:

$$\psi = E(\Omega) + Z\gamma\sqrt{\left(\frac{\alpha}{2-\alpha}\sigma^2\right)} \tag{8}$$

where $Z\gamma$ is the q-quartile of the standard Normal distribution of $N(0,1)$, α is the smoothing parameter, and σ^2 the sample variance.

The novel CAC should determines whether the admission cell has sufficient bandwidth to support the user requirements and takes into account the predicted handoff load for that cell. The following condition must be met:

$$\sum^{N} Bi + B + \psi \le C \tag{9}$$

Equation (9) verifies whether the admission cell has sufficient bandwidth to support the new request. N is the number of existing connections, C is the wireless link capacity and Bi is the bandwidth being used by the ith connection in that cell. B is the bandwidth required by the newly requested connection. ψ is the upper confidence bound for the expected bandwidth due to handoff calls $E(\Omega)$ for the next prediction interval. For example, if the network operator has to guarantee a maximum target handoff dropping probability of 5%, ψ will be set to the 95% upper confidence bounds of the predicted bandwidth requirements for handoff calls $E(\Omega)$ for the next prediction interval. At the start of each interval, a new ψ is used to control the admission decision. Upon each handoff arrival in a cell, during a prediction interval, the current ψ is decreased by the MS's bandwidth that has arrived until it reaches 0 or a new prediction interval is initiated.

5 Simulation Results

The metrics of interest in this paper are the handoff dropping probability (HDP) and the call blocking probability (CBP). The simulated model consists of a cellular network with 19 hexagonal cells in a toroidal way to avoid border effects. The unit of bandwidth is called bandwidth unit (BU), which is assumed to be the required bandwidth to support a voice connection as in [5], [11]. Each cell is assumed to have a fixed link capacity of 100 BUs. The traffic model used is similar to the one used in [5], [11]. Call requests are generated according to Poisson distribution with rate λ (call/cell/second) in each cell. The simulated traffic consists of users with bandwidth requirements of 1 BU (voice) and 4 BUs (video) with probabilities Rvo and 1-Rvo, respectively, where Rvo is also called the voice ratio as in [5]. In our simulations Rvo is set to 0.7, that is, 70% of voice traffic and 30% of video traffic. The lifetime of each call is exponentially distributed with mean 180s [8], [9], [11].

We studied two mobility scenarios: In scenario I, the MS chooses a direction and does not change its path while crossing cells during its call lifetime. The time that a call spends in a cell prior to handoff to another cell (residence time) is exponentially distributed with mean 60s, representing high mobility users that execute three handoffs on average considering the call lifetime of 180s. Upon each handoff a new residence time exponentially distributed is obtained. The scenario II uses a probability of 70% to dictate changes in the MS's moving direction, that is, the MS can change its new target handoff cell at any moment in time while crossing a cell with a probability of 70%. If a MS's moving direction is changed, a new path is randomly selected among its six neighboring cells as well as a new residence time is chosen using the exponential distribution with the same mean residence time as that of scenario I. Upon each handoff, a new neighboring cell and residence time are chosen again. The offered load is expressed in terms of call requests generated according to a Poisson distribution in each cell (calls/cell/second).

The evaluation presented below refers to simulations using batch means technique with transient removal at the beginning of the simulation and adopting 10 batches, each for 10^4s. For each simulation run, the metrics were periodically collected and then averaged out. The graphs depict average values for the 10 runs. The bars are plotted for a 95% confidence level. The prediction interval of our proposal (TL) is set to 60s and 10s in the simulated scenarios and the maximum target handoff dropping probability is set to 5%. The ACR's threshold time is set to 60s and 30s as indicated in the labels of the curves. Fig. 1 and Fig. 2 show the scenario I (MS does not change its moving direction while crossing the cells). The best result for the HDP was achieved by our proposal (TL) over the entire range of the offered loads. However, ACR outperforms TL in terms of call blocking probability (CBP) for lower loads. It is important to note that ACR proposal aims at optimizing network utilization by post-poning the reservation of bandwidth resources for handoff in the next predicted cell and, consequently, more users will be admitted into the network. On the other hand, the ACR scheme does not grant an upper bound for HDP in higher load situations as our proposal does. It is also important to note that our proposal achieves better levels of HDP to those of the ACR scheme, without the need for per-user signaling to make advanced reservations of bandwidth in the next predicted cell. With regard to the ACR's HDP, the best result was obtained when the threshold time is set to 60s. Under higher loads, ACR performance can be degraded due to the postponed approach for triggering the reservation in the next predicted cell (as depicted, ACR-30 obtained the worst HDP). This way, it may be too late to request a reservation in the next cell only when the threshold time is reached.

In Fig. 2, our proposal obtained a slightly greater CBP than ACR´s for lower loads, but depending on the mobile operator's objectives, the TL's configuration parameters can be set to benefit the CBP and network utilization at the expense of a greater, but controlled HDP. To this end, Fig. 3 and Fig. 4 depict an experiment for lower loads using the same settings of the scenario I, except by the value of the TL's prediction interval that is set to 10s. The ACR's threshold time is set to 60s (the best setting in Fig. 1 and Fig. 2). As can be seen, for small values of the prediction interval, TL's CBP can be improved.

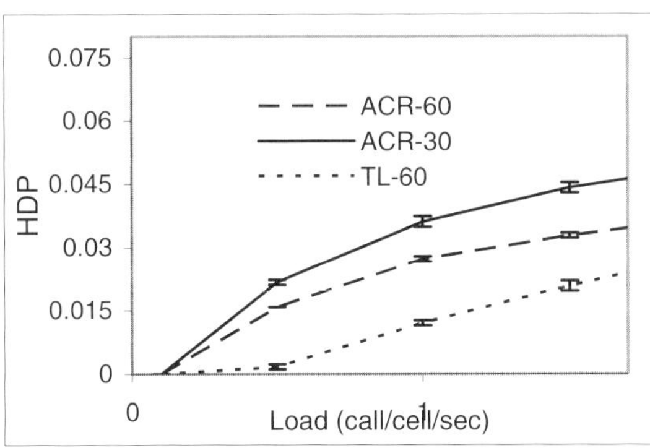

Fig. 1. Handoff dropping probability for scenario I (Deterministic mobility)

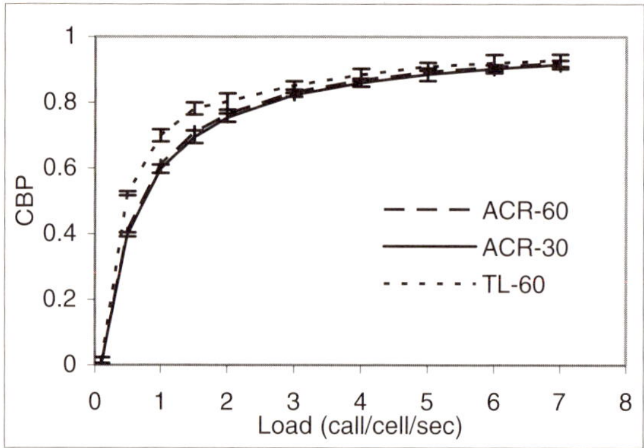

Fig. 2. Call blocking probability for scenario I (Deterministic mobility)

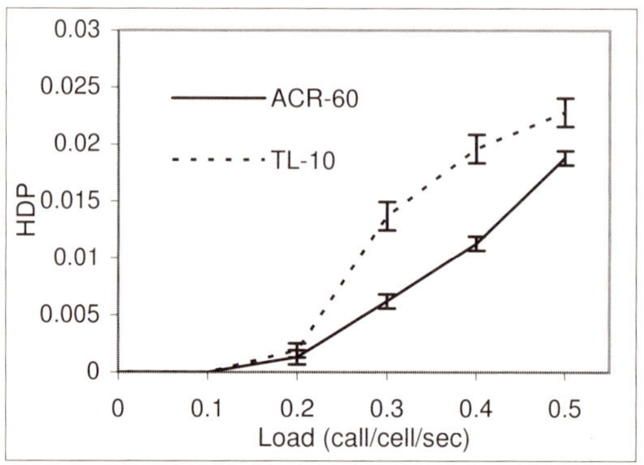

Fig. 3. Handoff dropping probability for scenario I (Deterministic mobility - Lower loads)

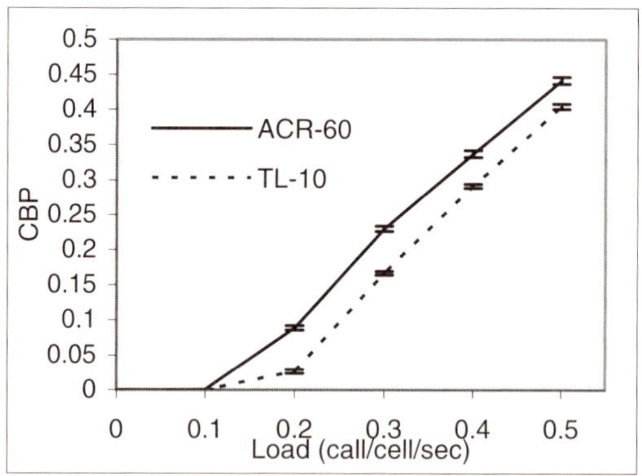

Fig. 4. Call blocking probability for scenario I (Deterministic mobility - Lower Loads)

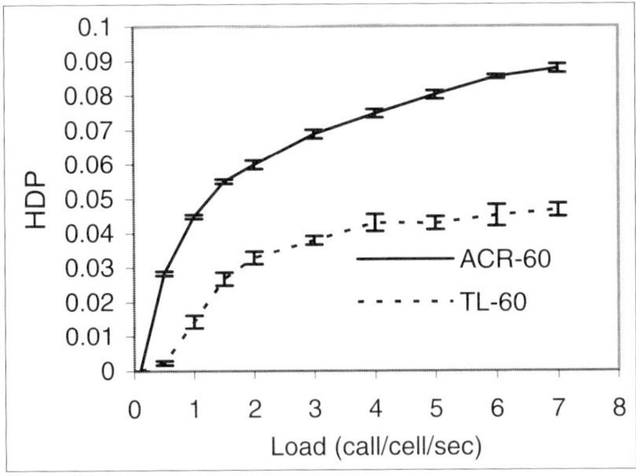

Fig. 5. Handoff dropping probability for scenario II (Random mobility)

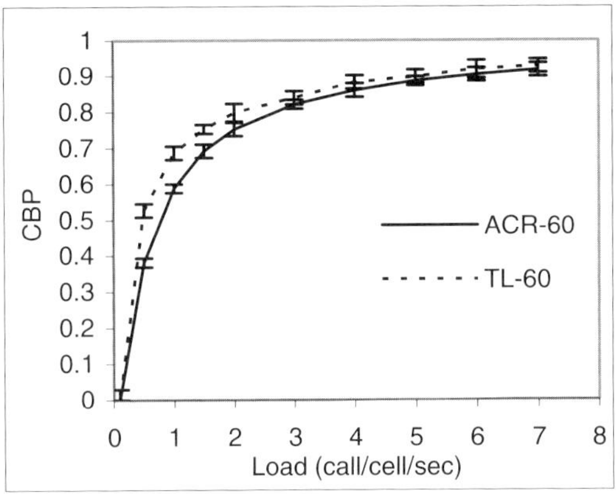

Fig. 6. Call blocking probability for scenario II (Random mobility)

Fig. 5 and Fig 6 depict the simulation results for the scenario II where a MS can change its moving direction while crossing a cell with probability equal to 70% (a new direction is randomly (uniformly distributed) selected among its six neighboring cells). The results are quite similar to scenario I (Fig. 1 and Fig. 2), but ACR obtained an even worst HDP whereas TL's kept below its 5% target. This random mobility scenario deteriorates ACR's HDP mainly due to the changes in MS moving direction that may be followed by the unavailability of sufficient bandwidth in the new cell MS is moving to. It is important to note that ACR signaling increases considerably due to request and cancellation of false reservations. TL scheme can accommodate the fluctuations due to this random mobility without the need for per-user tracking and signaling, providing a good solution without imposing any signaling overhead on the network.

6 Conclusions

In this paper, a novel CAC and bandwidth reservation scheme has been proposed for mobile networks. Our proposal avoids per-user reservation signaling through a predictive technique executed locally by each base-station. In order to predict the expected bandwidth of future handoffs we utilize an adaptive exponential smoothing method, called Trigg and Leach, which is effortless and does not impose computation overhead on the network elements. In addition, this method does not require a huge amount of saved data to perform forecasting. Our approach can also grant an upper bound on the handoff dropping probability even under higher loads. Our future work is concerned with the proposal of an adaptive algorithm to dynamically adjust the TL's prediction interval to optimize the bandwidth utilization depending on the current network load, mobility scenario and HDP objectives.

References

1. Braden, R., et al.: Integrated Services in the Internet Architecture: an Overview. IETF RFC 1633 (June 1994)
2. Blake, S., et al.: An architecture for Differentiated Services. IETF RFC 2475 (December 1998)
3. Nichols, K., et al.: A Two-bit Differentiated Services Architecture for Internet. RFC 2638 (July 1999)
4. Hong, D., Rappaport, S.: Traffic Model and Performance Analysis for Cellular Mobile Radio Telephone Systems with Prioritised and Nonprioritised Handoff Procedures IEEE Tran. Veh Tech. (August 1986)
5. Choi, S., Shin, K.G.: Predictive and Adaptive Bandwidth Reservation for Handoffs in QoS Sensitive Cellular Net-works. In: Proc. ACM SIGCOMM, ACM Press, New York (1998)
6. Naghshineh, M., Schwartz, M.: Distributed Call Admission Control in Mobile/Wireless Networks. IEEE JSAC 14(4), 711–717 (1996)
7. Zhang, T., et al.: Local Predictive Resource Reservation for Handoff in Multimedia Wireless IP Networks. IEEE Journal on Selected Areas in Communications 19(10) (October 2001)
8. Chiu, M.H., Bassiouni, M.A.: Predictive Schemes for Handoff Prioritization in Cellular Networks based on Mobile Positioning. IEEE JSAC 18(3) (March 2000)
9. Xu, Z., et al.: A New Adaptive Channel Reservation Scheme for Handoff Calls in Wireless Cellular Networks. In: Proceedings of IFIP Networking, pp. 672–684 (2002)
10. Soh, W.S., Kim, H.S.: Dynamic Bandwidth Reservation in Cellular Networks Using Road Topology Based Mobility Predictions. In: IEEE INFOCOM, Hong Kong (March 2004)
11. Soh, W.-S., Kim, H.S.: QoS Provisioning in Cellular Networks Based on Mobility Prediction Techniques. IEEE Comm. Mag., 86–92 (January 2003)
12. Trigg, D.W., Leach, D.H.: Exponential Smoothing with an Adaptive Response Rate. Operational Research Quarterly 18, 53–59 (1967)
13. Diederich, J., Zitterbart, M.: A Simple and Scalable Handoff Prioritization Scheme. Elsevier Computer Communications 28, 773–789 (2005)
14. Rozic, N., Kandus, G.: MIMO ARIMA models for handoff resource reservation in multimedia wireless networks. Wiley Wireless Communications and Mobile Computing 4, 497–512 (2004)

15. Dias, K.L., Fernandes, S.F.L., Sadok, D.F.H.: Predictive Call Admission Control for All-IP Wireless and Mobile Networks. In: IFIP/ACM Latin America Networking Conference, pp. 131–139. ACM Press, New York (2003)
16. Ghaderi, M., Boutaba, R.: Call Admission Control in Mobile Cellular Networks: A Comprehensive Survey. Wiley Wireless Communications and Mobile Computing 6(1), 69–93 (2006)
17. Taylor, J.W.: Smooth transition exponential smoothing. Journal of Forecasting 23(6), 385–404 (2004)

A Network Performance Sensitivity Metric for Parallel Applications

Jeffrey J. Evans[1] and Cynthia S. Hood[2]

[1] Purdue University, West Lafayette, IN 47907, USA
jje@purdue.edu
[2] Illinois Institute of Technology, Chicago, IL, 60616, USA
hood@iit.edu

Abstract. Excessive run time variability of parallel application codes on commodity clusters is a significant challenge. To gain insight into this problem our earlier work developed a tools to emulate parallel applications (PACE) by simulating computation and using the cluster's interconnection network for communication, and further study parallel application run time effects (PARSE). This work expands our previous efforts by presenting a metric derived from PARSE test results conducted on several widely used parallel benchmarks and application code fragments. The metric suggests that a parallel application's sensitivity to network performance variation can be quantified relative to its behavior in optimal network performance conditions. Ideas on how this metric can be useful to parallel application development, cluster system performance management and system administration are also presented.

1 Motivation

Interest has grown in clustered Networks of Workstations or NOWs comprised of commodity based machines, interconnects, and systems software [1], and these systems are the fastest growing segment of supercomputing [14]. This evolution is exposing the issue of *systemic performance consistency*, bringing it to the forefront. Systemic performance inconsistency is more common in commodity clusters due to the loosely coupled nature of their subsystems, including the set of applications executing on the machine.

Many factors contribute to the degradation of systemic performance consistency. Changes in applications and high-performance computing platforms manifest into run times of many scientific applications that exceed the mean-time-between-failure of the underlying computing platform. In addition to hard failures, performance degradations, or soft faults are problematic. These performance degradations can manifest into excessive and/or highly variable application run times. Applications designed assuming a certain level of performance from the underlying subsystems can become completely unpredictable when their design assumptions are violated.

Clusters are comprised of several major subsystems, including the communication network and the set of applications executing on the machine. The interactions of these two subsystems is the focus of our work. Network performance

I. Stojmenovic et al. (Eds.): ISPA 2007, LNCS 4742, pp. 920–931, 2007.

degradation due to transmission errors or congestion (soft faults) may violate application performance assumptions. Fine-grained models of communication performance generally do not account for these soft faults, mainly due to the difficulty of describing a) temporal effects, "when" a soft fault event will occur, b) spatial characteristics, "where" it is located in the network, and c) intensity effects, "how long" the event will affect the application in question. Moreover, it is also unclear as to how many such events (or their arrival distribution) are required to significantly affect an application's run time.

Communication Network Elements (NEs - routers and switches) are becoming more sophisticated, adapting the routing of information based on perceived congestion or rising bit error ratios. Subsystem performance degradation is the perception that it is failing to meet its operational objectives. Corrective actions taken by the network subsystem are therefore performed without systemic consideration, which may be counter-productive to maintaining systemic performance consistency.

These issues underscore the importance of scientists and application developers understanding the degree to which their codes are sensitive to communication performance degradation. Simulation of communication performance degradation conditions is challenging to create and difficult to reproduce on an actual HPC machine using real applications. The work in [6], [7], and [9] provides motivation for further analysis into the application's perception of sensitivity to communication cost variability.

The remainder of this paper is organized as follows. Section 2 examines work related to application performance, network performance, communication cost profiling including brief descriptions of the PACE framework, and PARSE functionality. Run time data collection results from benchmark and application evaluations are described in section 3. Section 4 presents our metric that describes a parallel application's run time sensitivity to network performance variation. Finally, we summarize and discuss areas of current and future work in section 5.

2 Related Work

Work related to network performance has traditionally focused on raw bandwidth performance, routing reachability, and adaptability. Routing reachability and adaptability in a hierarchical manner has been explored [2] and [3]. Monitoring high performance networks requires specialized fine-grained techniques such as sophisticated clocks [4] and faster sampling rates [17]. Special nodes to temporarily off-load data during congestion periods [5] or marking of non-uniform traffic prior to entry into the network [13] have been proposed. Both techniques however require additional and modified hardware. Schemes such as overlays [16] and exchanges [18] have also been proposed. These techniques however result in reducing network capacity or adding to the idle time of processes and the application, contributing to run time variability of applications that are more sensitive to these perturbations. Communication performance from the perspective of message passing libraries has been studied. Tools have been developed which focus on measuring maximum performance [11], [12], and [15].

A study on the Intel Paragon [20] is the closest work to our own in characterizing run time sensitivity to network performance. Two approaches were used to degrade network bandwidth. Messages were either exchanged multiple times or synthetic perturbations were applied to communications routines. Both test cases required the introduction of significant application code instrumentation in order to perform the desired measurements and collect the associated data.

The authors have developed a Parallel Application Communication Emulation (PACE) framework to enable controlled and repeatable loading of a cluster network using MPI [10]. This is accomplished by creating and running one or more Emulated Applications (EAs) using MPI communicators, where each EA emulates an independent parallel program execution using similar or dissimilar message sizes, exchanges and patterns. PACE is therefore executed like any other parallel application on a cluster. PACE is allocated a group of processor nodes for a fixed amount of time by the cluster scheduler, then it allocates a subset of its nodes to each EA. Each EA precisely simulates computation, but uses the cluster interconnection network to communicate. The set of EAs form clusters within a cluster.

A necessary condition for using PACE to evaluate a parallel application under test (AUT) is to force concurrent execution while PACE emulates one or more parallel applications. PACE then can be viewed as a communication network "disrupter", providing a controlled and repeatable quantity and temporal dispersion of network traffic, directly competing for network resources with the AUT. Two run time aspects must therefore be addressed to provide flexible integration. The first is the distribution of nodes allocated by the scheduler to accommodate PACE and the AUT. The second is to ensure that the AUT runs only when the PACE EAs are running. In other words, the AUT must not execute while PACE is performing communication cost measurements. The resulting add-on component to the PACE framework described in [8], provides a parallel application run time sensitivity evaluation function, hence the name PARSE.

To perform an application run time sensitivity evaluation, PARSE redistributes the job scheduler's node allocation, then executes PACE and the AUT concurrently while ensuring that the AUT iterations begin after PACE determines communication cost. PARSE interleaves processes among PACE and the AUT according to a user specified "slide" factor, which specifies a modulus for parsing the scheduler allocated "machine file" and re-distributing PACE and AUT nodes into respective machine files. PARSE then executes PACE and the AUT by performing a `fork()` , delaying the AUT execution by the amount of time necessary for PACE to complete its communication cost measurement.

3 Run Time Data Collection

3.1 Cluster Testbed

Parallel application evaluations were performed on the Purdue University recycled Linux cluster, consisting of many 48-node cluster segments. Every PC in a cluster segment is equipped with the same processor, memory, disk capacity, and Fast Ethernet (100Mb/s) NIC. However, not every 48-node cluster segment is identical. Two identical single CPU, 48-node cluster segments were used for this work. Of 96 total nodes, 89 were usable, as one cluster segment had 44 usable nodes and the other 45. Each node in a cluster segment connects to a 48-port switch. Each port is 10/100Mbps Ethernet and switches are connected to a router using a Gigabit Ethernet optical fiber uplink.

Depending on network topology knowledge, the allocation of PACE and AUT nodes and the PACE communication type specified by the user, a "probability of delay" $P[d]$ can be estimated for each AUT communication. To determine a quantifiable ramification of this to the AUT, consider PACE being allocated 38 nodes using `ALL-TO-ALL` communication exchanges. The PARSE node allocation ensures that 19 nodes will be allocated to each switch. Assuming that one half of the communication spans multiple hops and the PACE communication load is set to 90 (percent), the average communication traffic produced by PACE traversing the multiple hops is

$$\frac{19 \text{ nodes/switch} \cdot 100 \times 10^6 \text{bps}}{2} \cdot 0.9 = 855 \times 10^6 \text{ bps},$$

which is equivalent to 85.5% of the capacity of a 1Gbps link. Stated another way, the probability of an AUT message to or from a process located on the other switch being delayed by some amount of time is

$$P[d] = 0.855,$$

which is what the AUT must compete with. The probability of delay does not specify when or how long the delay might be, just the likelihood of one. The $P[d]$ can be adjusted by changing the communication load accordingly.

Tests were performed using three test "scenarios" as described in detail in [8]. The first was a benign network scenario used to establish AUT baseline performance (i.e. $P[d]$ is induced by the AUT itself). The other two scenarios included PARSE, which coordinates the execution of PACE with the AUT. One scenario included all nodes connected to a single switch while the other scenario split nodes between two switches, forcing network communication across a router, from which the probability of delay $P[d]$ could be determined based on the communication pattern and load configuration of PACE. The AUT was executed 100 times in each test scenario.

3.2 NAS Parallel Benchmarks

Version 2.4 of the NAS parallel benchmark suite was used for the work presented in [8], and the run time data acquired from those experiments is used here to develop a mathematical sensitivity metric. The Embarrassingly Parallel (EP), Integer Sort (IS), and MultiGrid (MG) kernel and Lower-Upper diagonal (LU) solver application benchmarks were evaluated.

The EP and IS run time evaluations presented in [8] illustrated that even with a $P[d] = 0.855$ the average run time had not been altered much, if at all. It was also unclear whether either benchmark's run time variability was significantly altered. Conversely, the run time evaluations of MG and LU exhibited visually significant increases in the average value of their respective run times when $P[d] = 0.855$. Additionally, both benchmarks exhibit dramatic increases in their run time variability, and was more pronounced for the MG benchmark. Moreover, this erratic behavior suggests a reason why some cluster users significantly overestimate the run time of their applications when submitting jobs to the machine as exposed in [9].

This finding motivated another set of tests for the MG and LU benchmarks. All variables were identical except the PACE communication load parameter was reduced by a factor of two, from 90 percent to 45 percent. This has the affect of reducing $P[d]$ from 0.855 to 0.4275. A closer examination of this is illustrated in figure 1, clearly showing a definitive increase in the average and variability of the run time.

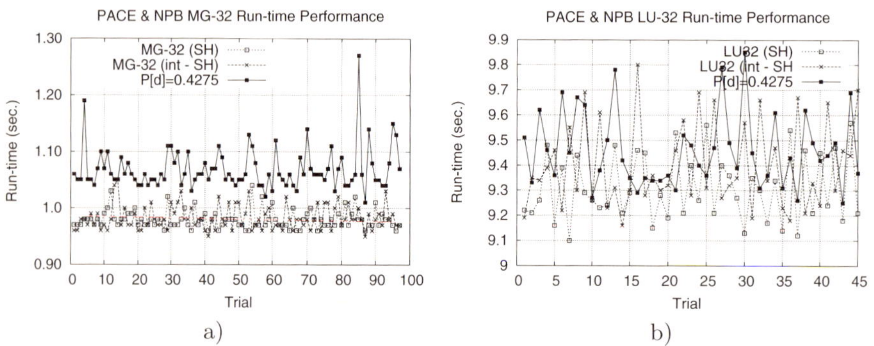

Fig. 1. NAS/PARSE Multihop Performance for a) MG and b) LU

3.3 PSTSWM

The purpose of PACE, PARSE, and the development of a mathematical sensitivity metric is to help facilitate parallel application development and further our understanding of how sets of applications interact with each other and the underlying system. The NAS benchmarks are a useful starting point for gathering run time evaluation data because they are highly portable and easy to use. To further motivate the development of a sensitivity metric a real parallel application was selected as a test case.

The version of the Parallel Spectral Transform Shallow Water Model (PSTSWM) used for the work in [8] was version 6.9 [19]. It was selected due to its similarity with codes used in tight deadline weather forecasting applications and its high ratio of large message communication. The test scenarios used for the NAS benchmarks were repeated for PSTSWM. The baseline run time performance results were as expected, exhibiting minimal run time variation. PSTSWM runs considerably longer than any of the NAS benchmarks so fewer runs (trials) were executed. As with the testing of the NAS benchmarks, the second scenario, PACE and PSTSWM running together on nodes connected to a single switch, produced similar run time results.

Finally, PSTSWM was executed with PACE using PARSE with the node allocation split between two switches, resulting in the same probabilistic scenario for communication delay as created for the NAS benchmarks. As with the other tests only the 32 node PSTSWM scale was tested. Figure 2a shows a dramatic increase in both average the run time and the variability for the runs where $P[d] = 0.855$. It appears there may be some PACE influence in the $P[d] = 0.4275$ case as well, but it is less obvious.

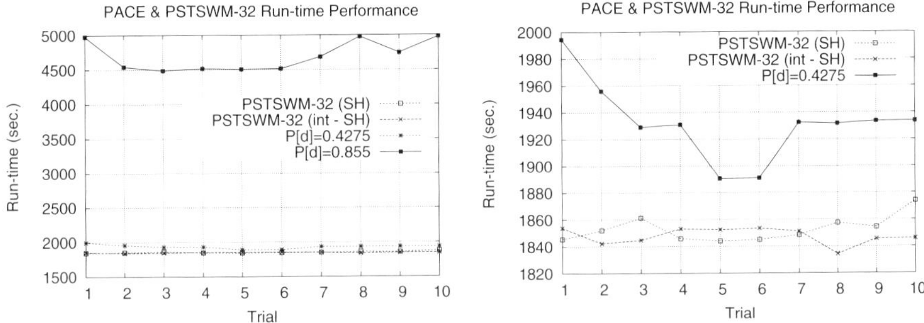

Fig. 2. PSTSWM/PACE a) Multihop Performance b) Bottom Traces Magnified

4 Run Time Sensitivity Metric

Some general observations can be made from the graphical data presented above and in [8]. Some applications, like EP and IS do not exhibit any obvious run time sensitivity to network performance. Conversely, the MG, LU, and PSTSWM applications do exhibit run time sensitivity to network performance. However it is not clear visually whether their sensitivities are related or of similar magnitudes.

Referring back to figure 1a shows the MG application trials, however the maximum network load case is omitted, magnifying the y-axis. The sensitivity of MG clearly becomes more noticeable at this magnification. The mean run time in the $P[d] = 0.4275$ case is clearly higher than the other two (unloaded) cases. The variation in run time is also noticeably greater. The PSTSWM application exhibits a similar qualitative "signature" as shown in figure 2b. Conversely, the LU application exhibits substantially less of an indication of a sensitivity to network performance as illustrated in figure 1b. Yet its run time mean and variation is clearly impacted in the maximum communication load case.

To effectively construct a generally useful sensitivity value or metric the required variables and parameters must be identified. It would be desirable to produce a sensitivity descriptor that can provide insight that is independent of the run time characteristics of a specific application. In other words, such a descriptor should be used equally well suited to applications with run times of seconds, hours, or days. One consideration is whether the sensitivity descriptor should be a continuous quantity or dichotomous.

4.1 Sensitivity Metric Parameters

Each application was run in conditions where the only competing network traffic was that of itself and periodic system monitoring. If the average run time of the baseline is compared to the average run time when perturbed by PACE, a normalized ratio of average run times results. This ratio can be considered a "coefficient of means" (COM) defined as the ratio of the average values of multiple application executions under a given pair of network load operating conditions. Call these operating points i and j. Each operating point exposes the influence of network traffic as produced by the application itself (as in the benign condition) and other applications (emulated by PACE). Stated mathematically,

$$COM_{ij} = \frac{\bar{x_i}}{\bar{x_j}} = \frac{\frac{\sum_1^n T_{run}^i}{n}}{\frac{\sum_1^n T_{run}^j}{n}}, \tag{1}$$

where n is the number of application executions. This approach normalizes the scale of run time independent of application.

In a similar context to the mean, the run time standard deviation σ is an indicator of the predictability (or lack of predictability) of an application's run time. The coefficient of variation is defined as the ratio of the standard deviation of multiple application executions under a given network load operating condition to the mean of those executions, expressed as a percentage,

$$COV = \frac{\sigma_k}{\bar{x_k}} \cdot 100, \tag{2}$$

where k is a network load operating condition. The COV also normalizes differences independent of application.

4.2 Analysis

The coefficients of mean and variation (COM and COV) can now be combined to form a sensitivity factor which is independent of an application's actual run time and standard deviation. Similar to producing the COM value, COV values on points i and j can also be converted into a ratio, representing a relative change in the variability between two operating points. The combination of these two ratios is multiplied to produce a sensitivity factor between two operating points

$$S_{ij} = COM_{ij} \cdot \left(\frac{COV_i}{COV_j}\right). \tag{3}$$

Multiplication of the coefficients is used rather than other operators (such as addition) in order to produce a larger range of continuous values. This tends to more easily distinguish subtle sensitivity differences between applications. Multiplication also forces insensitive applications toward a value of 1. Indeed all applications will yield a sensitivity factor of 1 as the probability of delay (external to itself) goes toward the lower limit (the baseline case)

$$\lim_{P[d]\to 0} S_{i0} = \lim_{i\to 0} S_{00} = COM_{00} \cdot \left(\frac{COV_0}{COV_0}\right) = 1. \tag{4}$$

This simply states that with no network degradation other than that produced by itself, any application will have a run time with its baseline mean and COV. A reasonable question now is how many operational points are sufficient to accurately describe an application's sensitivity? Moreover, what happens if the sensitivity factor changes as a function of the communication load?

Intuitively one might conclude the more operational points available, the better. In our earlier experiments, the mid-point operational scenario ($P[d] = 0.4275$) was selected by intuition, after performing the single hop and $P[d] = 0.855$ tests. Judging from these results, another set of runs at approximately $P[d] = 0.65$ may have provided additional, and perhaps useful information in determining the precise location of the knee corresponding to the abrupt changes in mean and variability observed in some applications.

More operating points present another dilemma, namely, how to handle potentially different, or even non-monotonic sensitivity factor values. It would seem reasonable to expect a sensitive application's sensitivity factor to be proportional to the intensity and/or duration of network degradation. If this were purely an issue of bandwidth reduction there would seemingly be a proportional increase in the mean run time but little or no change in variability. For instance, note that in figure 2b the run time variation is on the order of 20 seconds. This is out of a mean run time of over 33 minutes. Yet for the $P[d] = 0.855$ operating point, run time variation is on the order of 500 seconds (a 25 fold increase) on a mean of about 78 minutes (about a 2.35 fold increase).

Certainly the amount of network degradation is not constant over time, as PACE emulates parallel applications, operating in terms of compute/communicate cycles. When an application desires to communicate but the network blocks the transmission $P[d] = 1.0$. Likewise, it is virtually impossible to predict the duration of the delay in this circumstance. It seems reasonable then to collect run time data on several operational points, then determine the arithmetic mean of the combination of operating point pairs S_{ij}, producing a sensitivity factor for the application

$$S_{app} = \frac{\sum_1^n S_{ij}}{n}. \tag{5}$$

Clearly the availability of more operational points should result in a sensitivity factor that approaches the "true" value. Operational points that only moderately load the network may tend to underestimate the application's true sensitivity while points that severely load the network may have the opposite effect. Conversely, applications that are insensitive may require evaluation at only two points. Furthermore, evaluation of insensitive applications could potentially be minimized by reducing the number of runs required to gather sufficient statistics.

4.3 Sensitivity Factor Calculation

To determine the sensitivity factor for each application, S_{ij} was calculated for each pair of test cases. First the means and standard deviations are used to determine COM and COV values as defined in equations (1) and (2). These are compiled in table 1.

Table 1. AUT Sensitivity Factor Variables

AUT	Load	$\bar{x}$ (sec.)	σ (sec.)	*COV*
EP	1[a]	0.8814	0.0771	8.7526
	2[b]	NA	NA	NA
	3[c]	0.8713	0.0894	10.2607
IS	1	5.9993	2.770	46.1743
	2	NA	NA	NA
	3	4.5669	2.4140	52.9110
LU	1	9.3572	0.1827	1.9529
	2	9.4591	0.1498	1.5838
	3	22.8818	1.0889	4.7588
MG	1	0.9836	0.0202	2.0504
	2	1.06825	0.03683	3.4475
	3	4.5951	1.4138	30.7672
PSTSWM	1	1842.7696	8.8096	0.4781
	2	1932.3100	29.6329	1.5335
	3	4661.0778	199.0537	4.2706

[a] Baseline - $P[d]$ induced by application.
[b] $P[d] = 0.4275$.
[c] $P[d] = 0.855$.

Table 2. AUT Sensitivity Factors

AUT	S_{21}	S_{32}	S_{31}	S_{app}
EP	NA	NA	1.1916	1.1916
IS	NA	NA	0.8723	0.8723
LU	0.8161	7.2683	5.9319	4.6721
MG	1.8261	38.3889	70.1022	36.7724
PSTSWM	3.3637	6.7173	22.5952	10.8921

Inspection of table 1 indirectly reveals the coefficients of the means (COM). Recall from equation 1 that COM is a ratio of means ($\bar{x}$) taken from different operating points. For example, the COM for both EP and IS are calculated based on two operating points, yielding values of 0.988 and 0.761 respectively. As shown in table 1, their means actually decreased slightly with more network traffic. This is counterintuitive, but notice however that the COV values are fairly high for both applications, relative to others such as LU or PSTSWM. This natural variability combined with a number of statistical outliers in the baseline case of IS could be a factor. Inspecting other AUTs and calculating their COM values by using each operating point pair yields coefficients in the range of about 1 to 2.5 for LU and PSTSWM while MG ranges from 1 to nearly 4.5.

Once the sensitivity factor variables have been established, S_{ij} for each test case pair can be determined. Finally, the S_{ij}'s are averaged to produce a final sensitivity factor for each application. This is captured in table 2.

The first observation to be made from table 2 is that EP and IS are essentially insensitive to network degradation, as their S_{app} factors are close to 1.0. The LU application appears to be mildly sensitive, as its S_{app} is just below 4.7 and lies between EP/IS and PSTSWM/MG. PSTSWM and MG seem to be sensitive to network degradation. The sensitivity of PSTSWM is noticeable even in the S_{21} case, having higher sensitivity than even MG. MG on the other hand clearly shows a significant sensitivity, primarily a result of its excessive COV (a factor of 10) and high $\bar{x}$ in load case 3.

In the cases of LU, MG, and PSTSWM a value for S_{32} was calculated. This point represents a ratio between two cases where PACE was used to perturb the network. One might question the usefulness of calculating this data point. Recalculating S_{app} using only S_{21} and S_{31} yields sensitivity factors S_{app} of 3.3740, 35.9642, and 12.9795 respectively. These S_{app} values are close enough to those using S_{32} as to not alter their relative sensitivities to each other. In one case (PSTSWM) the sensitivity does increase from 10.89 to 12.98, over 19%, if S_{32} is not used.

5 Summary and Future Work

In this work the data from earlier PARSE experiments were used to motivate the development of a mathematical metric that quantifies the sensitivity of a parallel application's execution time to network performance variation. The sensitivity factor is a proportional continuous variable, the more sensitive the application is to network performance the higher the sensitivity factor value. The sensitivity factor of a parallel application is computed based on simple coefficients of mean and standard deviation which result from multiple executions of the application on each of several operating points. The coefficient of mean expresses a "shift" or "increase" in the application's run time while the coefficient of variance is a measure of the application's run time predictability (or lack thereof). When analyzed and computed, evaluation results show that applications exhibiting an insensitivity to network performance variation produce sensitivity factor values approximately equal to 1. The more sensitive applications used in this study exhibit sensitivity factors ranging from almost 5.0 to nearly 40.0.

A numeric sensitivity factor can aid scientists and engineers in identifying and localizing sensitive portions of their codes. We are currently investigating other attributes of parallel programs to determine their potential value in the metric. Among these are the number of nodes allocated, their degree of fragmentation, and problem size. We are currently working on generalizing the sensitivity factor evaluation and computation process to be independent of interconnection technology, speed or scale. We are also evaluating the notion of a converse to application sensitivity, namely an application's disruptiveness of network resources. Critical areas of cluster dynamics management, such as job scheduling, network performance management, and application migration can potentially make use of the knowledge of an application's sensitivity and disruptiveness to network performance so the system as a whole can maintain performance consistency.

In systems such as clusters and Grids, central control elements such as schedulers and resource managers know which applications are running and where. Network management systems however do not have this knowledge. The communication performance ramifications of the virtual communication topology created by the scheduler are generally unknown to any of the subsystems. Reactive operations such as application migration or network adaptation can be counter-productive to systemic performance as a whole when the reactive "triggers" lack systemic knowledge. Ultimately we hope to establish simple operating parameters that can be used in a cooperative way among cluster (and Grid) subsystems to maintain systemic operating and performance consistency.

Acknowledgments

This work was supported in part by the U.S. Department of Energy under Contract W-31-109-Eng-38, NSF 0325378 and NSF 9984811. The authors also wish to thank the reviewers for their valuable insights and suggestions for improving the quality of this paper.

References

1. Anderson, T., Culler, D., Patterson, D.: A Case for Networks of Workstations: NOW. IEEE Micro, 54–64 (February 1995)
2. Baik, S., Hood, C.: Decentralized route generation method for adaptive source routing in system area networks. In: The 8th World Multi-Conference on Systemics, Cybernetics and Informatics (July 2004)
3. Baik, S., Hood, C., Gropp, W.: Prototype of AM3: Active Mapper and Monitoring Module for the Myrinet Environment. In: Proceedings of the HSLN Workshop (November 2002)
4. Chakravarthi, S., Pillai, A., Padmanabhan, J., Apte, M., Skjellum, A.: A fine-grain synchronization mechanism for QoS based communication on Myrinet. In: The International Conference on Distributed Computing 2001 (submitted)
5. Coll, S., Flich, J., Malumbres, M.P., Lopez, P., Duato, J., Mora, F.J.: A first implementation of in-transit buffers on myrinet gm software. In: Proceedings of the 15th International Parallel and Distributed Processing Symposium, pp. 1640–1647 (2001)
6. Evans, J.J., Baik, S., Hood, C.S., Gropp, W.: Toward understanding soft faults in high performance cluster networks. In: Proceedings of the 8th IFIP/IEEE International Symposium on Integrated Network Management, pp. 117–120. IEEE Computer Society Press, Los Alamitos (March 2003)
7. Evans, J.J., Baik, S., Kroculick, J., Hood, C.S.: Network Adapability in Clusters and Grids. In: Proceedings from the Conference on Advances in Internet Technologies and Applications (CAITA). IPSI (July 2004) (CDROM)
8. Evans, J.J., Hood, C.S.: PARSE: a tool for parallel application run time sensitivity evaluation. In: ICPADS. Proceedings of the Twelfth International Conference on Parallel and Distributed Systems, pp. 475–484 (July 2006)

9. Evans, J.J., Hood, C.S., Gropp, W.D.: Exploring the relationship between parallel application run-time variability and network performance in clusters. In: Workshop on High Speed Local Networks (HSLN) from the Proceedings of the 28th IEEE Conference on Local Computer Networks (LCN), pp. 538–547. IEEE Computer Society Press, Los Alamitos (October 2003)
10. Evans, J.J., Hood, C.S.: Network performance variability in NOW clusters. In: CCGrid05. Proceedings of the 5th IEEE International Symposium on Cluster Computing and the Grid, IEEE Computer Society Press, Los Alamitos (May 2005) (CDROM)
11. Gropp, W., Lusk, E.: Reproducible measurements of MPI performance characteristics. Technical Report ANL/MCS-P755-0699, Argonne National Laboratory (1999)
12. Grove, D., Coddington, P.: Precise MPI performance measurement using MPIBench. Technical report, Adelaide University, Adelaide SA 5005, Australia (2001)
13. Jurczyk, M.: Traffic control in wormhole-routing multistage interconnection networks. In: Proceedings of the International Conference on Parallel and Distributed Computing and Systems, vol. 1, pp. 157–162 (2000)
14. University of Tennessee: Top500 supercomputer sites (2004), online Document, `http://www.top500.org/`
15. Reussner, R., Sanders, P., Prechelt, L., Muller, M.: SKaMPI: a detailed, accurate MPI benchmark. In: Alexandrov, V.N., Dongarra, J.J. (eds.) Recent Advances in Parallel Virtual Machine and Message Passing Interface. LNCS, vol. 1497, pp. 52–59. Springer, Heidelberg (1998)
16. Petrini, F., Coll, S., Frachtenberg, E., Gurvitts, L., Hoisie, A.: Using multirail networks in high-performance clusters. In: Proceedings of the 2001 IEEE International Conference on Cluster Computing, pp. 15–24. IEEE Computer Society Press, Los Alamitos (2001)
17. Sottile, M.J., Minnich, R.G.: Supermon: A high-speed cluster monitoring system. In: Proceedings of the IEEE International Conference on Cluster Computing, pp. 39–46. IEEE Computer Society Press, Los Alamitos (September 2002)
18. Tam, A.T.C., Wang, C.L.: Contention-free complete exchange algorithm on clusters. In: Proceedings of the IEEE International Conference on Clusters, pp. 57–64. IEEE Computer Society Press, Los Alamitos (November-December 2000)
19. P. H. Worley: Parallel Spectral Transform Shallow Water Model (December 2003), onine Document `http://www.csm.ornl.gov/chammp/pstswm/`
20. Worley, P.H., Robinson, A.C., Mackay, D.R., Barragy, E.J.: A study of application sensitivity to variation in message passing latency and bandwidth. In: Concurrency: Practice and Experience, vol. 10, pp. 387–406. John Wiley & Sons, Chichester (April 1998)

The Influence of Interference Networks in QoS Parameters in a WLAN 802.11g Environment

Jasmine P.L. Araújo[1], Josiane C. Rodrigues[1], Simone G.C. Fraiha[1], Felipe M. Lamarão[1], Nandamudi L. Vijaykumar[2], Gervásio P.S. Cavalcante[1], and Carlos R.L. Francês[1]

[1] Electrical Engineering Faculty, Federal University of Pará (UFPA), 66.075-900, Belém, PA, Brazil
{jasmine,josi,fraiha,gervasio,rfrances}@ufpa.br

[2] National Institute for Space Research (INPE), Computing and Applied Mathematics Laboratory (LAC), P.O. Box 515, 12245-970, São José dos Campos, SP, Brazil
vijay@lac.inpe.br

Abstract. This paper proposes a strategy to determine how much a given network can affect the QoS parameters of another, by interference. In order to achieve this, a measurement campaign was carried out in two stages: firstly with a single AP and later with two APs separated by a distance less than three meters, using the same channel. After the measurement, an analysis of the results and a set of inferences were made by using Bayesian Networks, whose inputs were the experimental data, i.e. QoS metrics such as: throughput, jitter, packet loss, PMOS and physical metrics like power and distance.

1 Introduction

Wireless Local Area Networks (WLAN) IEEE802.11 have been widely used in the recent years due to their mobility and for being practical in configuring them. They have been a very practical and important solution to industries, companies and historical constructions due to their flexibility and low cost benefits during their installation and utilization. These technologies usually support traffic data generated by web browsing and email applications. In the recent past, they have been considered for voice communication especially in offices [1].

VoIP delivers voice packets over the Internet and consequently the costs are drastically reduced when compared with conventional telephone calls (PSTN). However, these applications require that WLAN installed are capable to support very strict QoS specifications for voice transmission. ITU-T (International Telecommunication Union) G.114 defines, for real-time services, a tolerable rate of packet loss is around 1% to 3% and the allowed delay is less than 150 ms but not greater than 400 ms [2]. Due to the sensitivity of the specifications, VoIP has been chosen generally to be evaluated in field tests. With respect to the physical layer, three phenomena exert influence on radio transmission: collisions, radio link quality and interference. Collisions are well known phenomena where several

I. Stojmenovic et al. (Eds.): ISPA 2007, LNCS 4742, pp. 932–945, 2007.

hosts transmit packets to the environment and at the same time it introduces packets with errors that need to be retransmitted. The link quality does not only depend on the noise level but also on the distribution of stations and the topology of the environment (wall positions, furniture density and others). Moreover, the presence of multiple access points may also introduce interference and thus reduce the transmission quality [3]. Such interference lead to receiving packets with errors and at MAC layer, they have to be retransmitted thus affecting the throughput [4]. Added to this fact, the interference may force transmission at lower rates. As already mentioned, the radio environment factors influence the global WLAN performance. But despite this fact very few analyses were conducted to verify this approach.

The main objective of this paper is to use computational intelligence by employing Bayesian Networks to verify, aiming at quantifying and characterizing this influence. This work will study specifically the effect of the interference. This is because in any environment with WLAN, it probably will have to live together with other sources of interferences in the same frequency band, such as, cordless telephones, microwaves ovens and access points using the same channel.

This paper is organized as follows: Section 2 presents some related work; basic concepts on KDD (Knowledge Discovery in Database), Data Mining and Bayesian networks are shown in Section 3, the environment used for obtaining metrics is presented in Section 4 while Section 5 describes the methodology employed in data acquiring; Section 6 presents the results; Section 7 presents the methodology proposal and finally Section 8 concludes the paper.

2 Related Works

This section presents some related works that will be used to compare the results obtained. This also contributes significantly to the research described here. A procedure to design WLAN including VoIP is presented in [5]. It discusses a theoretical model with a suggestion to implement an experimental scenario. An analytical model to plan a WLAN with a guaranteed throughput in an indoor environment is presented in [3]. The algorithm presented explores performance evaluation of the network based on a Markov model of the actual WLAN in which collision and link quality are considered. A cost function was defined as the sum of coverage components, interference and QoS where weights for this function were empirically selected. The objective of [3] is not to choose the least number of access points but keeping the interference at low levels while guaranteeing the throughput.

In [6] it is proposed to integrate radio environment features with an analytical model to evaluate indoor WLAN802.11 performance. An improved Markovian model was proposed by considering signal level, environment topology and geometric distribution of the stations. The model was validated with experiments and suggested as a future work to consider probability of the interference.

The VoIP behavior over 802.11 is discussed in [7] under the perspective of the number of connections that a single access point can support. So, tests are conducted to verify how many VoIP sessions can the network support without any degradation in the quality. Based on the results, it was decided to use, in a metric collection campaign, just one single call which was repeated during the experiment to ensure that the observed effects do not influence in the nominal bandwidth due to other VoIP sessions. Thus, the interfering network is responsible for the variation of the QoS parameters. Optimization problems are not treated in [7]; in the research described here, the influence issue will be addressed.

The references [3] and [7] cite other references where hypotheses to evaluate a network were more simplified by considering an ideal channel and without loss. Therefore, the paper described here compares also researches developed from the cited references. Another major difference is that the experiments are conducted with and without interfering network. In addition,[3] and [7] use Markovian model to evaluate just the throughput and the measurements are conducted at a later stage in order to validate the model. In case of this paper, Bayesian network is used for data analysis as well as to verify the influence of radio environment in QoS parameters (throughput, jitter, packet loss and PMOS).

This paper does not yet address the problem of optimization, but by using Bayesian networks, it is possible to perform a set of inferences and correlations such that a group of possible scenarios that can be analyzed besides optimization parameters. Thus, the generalization provided for Bayesian networks is taken as an advantage for evaluating systems with strong correlation among their random variables.

3 KDD, Data Mining and Bayesian Networks

The process of knowledge discovery in database (KDD) stands as a technology capable of widely cooperating in the search of existing knowledge in the data. Therefore, its main objective is to find valid and potentially useful patterns from the data.

The extraction of knowledge from data can be seen as a process with, at least, the following steps: understanding of the application domain, selection and preparation of the data, data mining, evaluation of the extracted knowledge and consolidation and the use of the extracted knowledge. Once in the data mining stage, considering the core of the KDD process, methods and algorithms are applied for the knowledge extraction from the database. This stage involves the creation of appropriate models representing patterns and relations identified in the data. The results of these models, after the evaluation by the analyst, specialist and/or final user are used to predict the values of attributes defined by the final user based on new data. In this work, the computational intelligence algorithm used for data mining was based on Bayesian networks.

A Bayesian network is composed of several nodes, where each node of the network represents a variable, that is, an attribute of the database; directed arcs connecting them implies in the relation of dependency that the variable can possess over the others; and finally probability tables for each node.

The Bayesian networks can be seen as coding models of the probabilistic relationships between the variables that represent a given domain. These models possess as components a qualitative representation of the dependencies between the nodes and a quantitative (conditional probability tables of these nodes) structure, that can evaluate, in probabilistic terms, these dependencies. These components together provide an efficient representation of the joint probability distribution of the variables of a given domain.

One of the major advantages of the Bayesian networks is their semantics, which facilitates, given the inherent causal representation of these networks, the understanding and the decision making process for the users of these models. Basically, due to the fact that the relations between the variables of the domain can be visualized graphically, besides providing an inference mechanism that allows quantifying, in probabilistic terms, the effect of these relations [8].

4 Scenario and Metrics

The metrics are collected in a two-storey building made of bricks with rooms for Lectures, Computer and Telecommunication Labs and an anechoic camera, whose height occupies both the floors. The building has side glass windows with aluminum frames. The rooms are divided by walls built on bricks. There is a kitchen whose walls are covered with ceramic tiles. At the moment, the building is still unoccupied and with no furniture.

Fig. 1 shows the layouts of both the floors. The network access point under study is shown as a circle at the left side on the ground floor. The interference network, also represented as a circle, is located at the left side on the first floor. The distance that separates the two points is the height of the building.

4.1 Testbed Features

In the experiment, Compaq notebook under Windows XP© was associated with access point 802.11g Linksys© WRT54G Router Speed Booster. This access point was connected to a 100 Mbps Ethernet and one of the LAN ports was connected to the RADCOM© protocol analyzer [9]. The other port of the protocol analyzer was connected to Toshiba Satellite notebook also under Windows XP©. The Compaq notebook was used to make VoIP calls to Toshiba notebook by using CallGen323 (program that makes 1-minute lasting calls) while Openphone [10] was used to receive calls. The metrics obtained in the application layer were monitored through packet loss, jitter, throughput and PMOS by using Performer Media Pro available within the protocol analyzer. A certain number of measurements were collected in an indoor environment. The same process was repeated by adding another network called interfering network. In this interfering network, 2 notebooks and another access point were used. Iperf software [11] was used to generate traffic within this net.

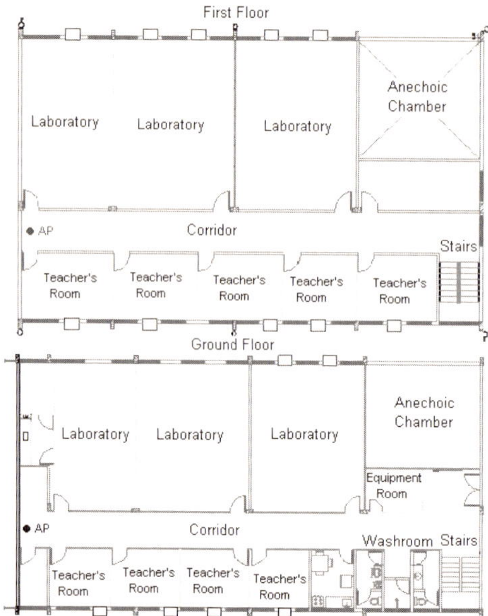

Fig. 1. The Layouts of ground and first floors

5 Methodology and Measurements

In order to take the measurements, the locations were first selected and then were marked with an adhesive tape. Their distances from the walls were also measured. An access point was located at the entrance of the corridor situated in the ground floor. This network is called as network under study and it was programmed to use channel 7 (central frequency under 2.442GHz). In this network, the AP is connected through a network cable to the protocol analyzer which in turn is connected to a receiving notebook. In order to generate VoIP calls, CallGen323, developed by Project OpenH323 [10], was used. The notebook that transmits the packets is positioned on a cart, that is moved to each point where the measurement is taken after remaining for 3 minutes at the previous location. The cart also carries another notebook to measure the power, received by wireless board from several access points, by using Network Stumbler© software [12]. The same notebook was not utilized as the use of Network Stumbler© does not allow the computer in which this software is running to be connected to a network.

During the measurements, the following parameters were stored: power (via software Netstumbler©), distance transmitter-receiver (obtained after treating data through the locations of the measuring points and access point), jitter, packet loss, PMOS and throughput (measured by protocol analyzer).

After this first phase of measurements, and new wireless network was installed called as interfering network using the same channel used by network under study. This new network was placed in the first floor pointing towards the same direction of the network under study Fig.1. Iperf [11] was the program used to generate the traffic as it allows to specify the time at which the traffic can be generated.

After this second phase, data were treated and the measurements were compared. The following section presents the results of this comparison.

6 Some Inferences Based on Bayesian Networks

This section discusses the measurements of the application and physical layers as well as the results obtained by using Bayesian networks. The study involves treating the measured data with and without interference with the Bayesian network technique.

In any process of knowledge discovery, there is a pre-analysis phase of treatment (soft mining) of the data where information that is not going to contribute to the final result are removed. Hence, the input fields for the Bayesian network were obtained from the protocol analyzer after the pre-analysis. They worked as input to the free version Bayesware Discover© (BDD) commercial software [13].

6.1 Bayesian Networks Without Inference

When the Bayesian network is created to analyze the measurements with and without interfering network, each attribute will be turned into a network node as shown in Fig.2(a), Fig.2(b), Fig.3(a) and Fig.3(b).

In this work Bayesian networks were created representing the actual system that is based on the collected data. This network contains joint probability distribution tables of each node. It is based on dependencies, consisting of attributes i.e., possible values that each variable may assume and their respective probabilities. Once these networks are set and verified that they do represent the actual system and database, inferences are conducted on these Bayesian networks so that the verification of the WLAN network behavior as well as the results obtained from this inference is performed.

In Figures 3(a) and 3(b) both PMOS and packet loss are not related with any other measured parameter meaning that they do not vary, for instance, with the distance. This occurred during the measurement, when the network was busy just with one VoIP application which was not using the entire bandwidth. The relationship of QoS and physical layer for networks with and without interference can be identified graphically and it can be pointed that interference has a major impact in the probability relations as observed Fig.2(a), Fig.2(b), Fig.3(a) and Fig.3(b).

Fig.4 and Fig.5 capture the output window from running Bayesware Discoverer© [13]. On the right side, the network is represented as a graph and the left side shows marginal probability distributions determined by Bayesian network, based on the measured data. Each of these probabilities represent Bayesian network's expectation of the WLAN nodes (jitter, PMOS, Packet-Loss, throughput represented as Band, D-Radio, power) [14].

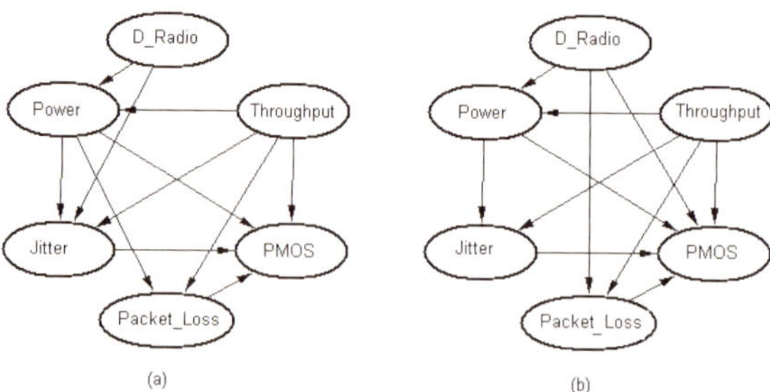

Fig. 2. Bayesian networks results(with interference) to: ground floor(a) and first floor(b)

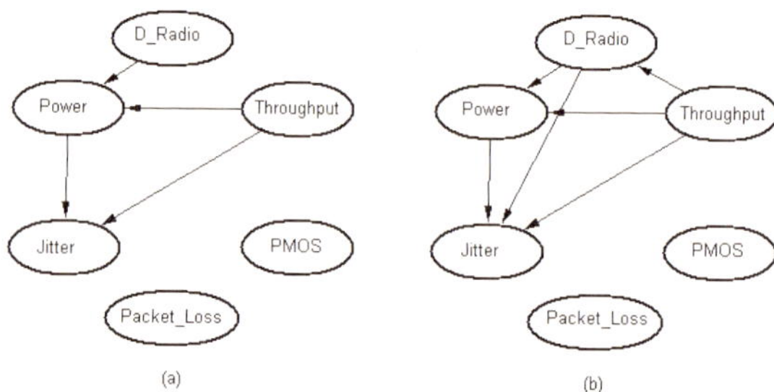

Fig. 3. Bayesian networks results(without interference) to: ground floor(a) and first floor(b)

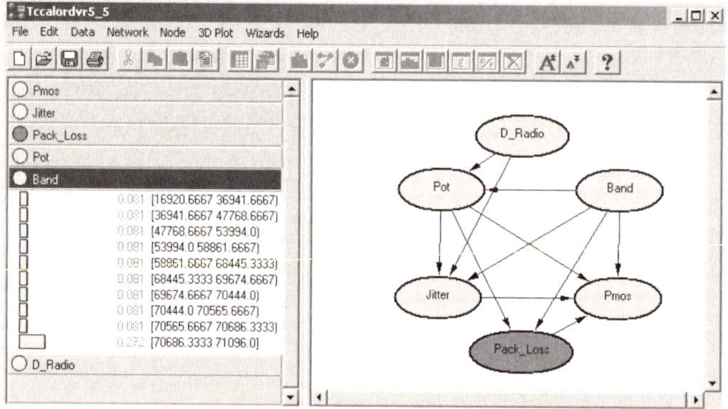

Fig. 4. Bayesian networks without inference with interference to ground floor

6.2 Bayesian Networks with Inference

The most relevant results are shown in Fig.6, Fig.7, Fig.8 and Fig.9 for the two inferences that were conducted. The first inference refers to power with the largest value while the second refers to the worst throughput.

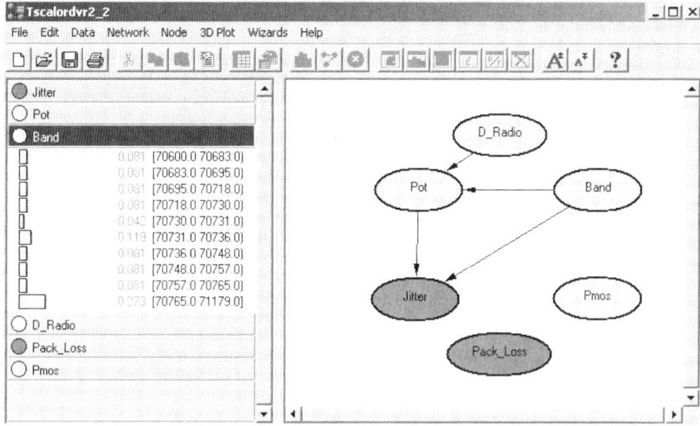

Fig. 5. Bayesian networks without inference without interference to ground floor

One can observe (Fig.6 and Fig.7) that for the larger values assigned to power (ranging from -48.18 to -41.81 dBm), in the first floor considering interference, the probability of throughput lying within 70686.33 and 71096.0 bps is 51.6%. When interference is not considered, the probability of throughput lying within 707650.0 and 711790.0 bps is 37.7%. Therefore, there was a change in the network under study for this specific parameter, the throughput.

Similarly, results are also shown for other metrics. In the case of packet loss, the probability of no loss for network with interference is 55% whereas the value is 88% when interference is not considered. Considering now the jitter, its probability for lying within 4.33 to 6.66 ms is 32.7% for network with interference. This value increases to 84.6% for lying within 0 to 2 ms for network without interference. PMOS was also affected by the interference. Its probability values dropped down from 98.8% for lying within 3.34 to 4.0 (network without interference) to 49.3% for lying within 3.7 to 6.03 (network with interference). Finally, the distance metric had no significant variation as shown in Fig.6 and Fig.7.

Another evidence showing the influence of interference can be shown in the experiment in which the lowest throughput interval of 16920.66 to 36941.66 bps was selected. Fig.8 and Fig.9 show the results.

Bayesian networks that were generated (with and without interference) for the ground floor show that there is an effect from interference into the parameters as shown in Fig.8 and Fig.9. The inference value selected is different for these two situations (with and without interference).

The worst throughput for the network with interference lies within 16920,66 and 36941,66 bps whereas for the network without interference lies within 70600,0 a 70683,0 bps. This demonstrates that the throughput was reduced for the network with interference.

Now, moving to another parameter, the packet loss, the network with interference presented the largest probability (49.9%) in the range 21% to 27%. But in the network without interference presented the largest probability (88%) for the packet loss to be zero.

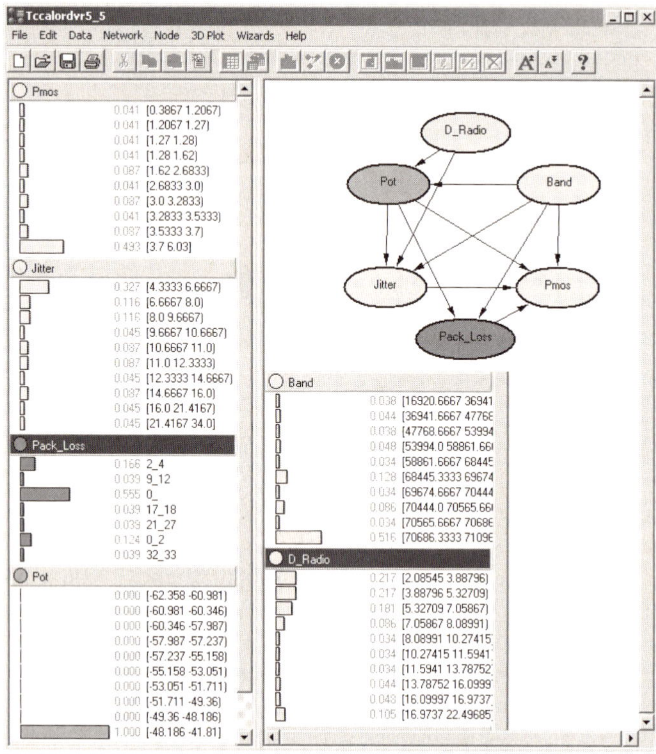

Fig. 6. Bayesian networks with largest power inference with interference applied to ground floor

The probability of jitter to be above 9.66 ms has a probability of 78.3% in case of network with interference and the probability to be below 4 ms is 100% in case of network without interference.

PMOS, in network without interference, has its probability of 98.8% for lying within 3.34 and 4.0. The behavior of this metric in network with interference cannot be well characterized as it presented the same probability of 21% for both ranges of 0.38 to 1.2 and 3.7 and 6.03. However, it can be seen that there is an impact from the interference. Again, distance metric has not variation as shown in Fig.8 and Fig.9. It is worth mentioning that the throughput values used in the inference of the worst throughput in networks with and without interference are different showing once more that interference, in fact, affects QoS parameters.

7 Capacity Planning and Performance Evaluation Issues: A Methodology Proposal

In real building there is a very strong trend to find similar scenarios to the presented ones in this paper, where different networks cohabit and where it is

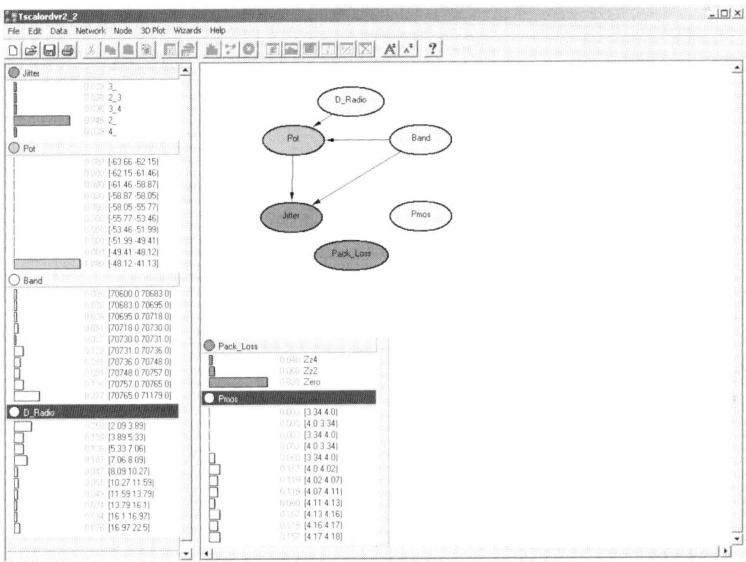

Fig. 7. Bayesian networks with largest power inference without interference applied to ground floor

desirable that applications with rigid parameters of QoS carry out (e.g.: VoIP). To make this possible, the accomplishment of the following stages is necessary, at least, according to the methodology proposed in this paper:

- Characterization of the environment parameters (physical layer) of the WLAN: The presence of obstacles, like walls, environment aspects, among other, on the path of radio transmission attenuates signal power. In this way the reception quality is degraded and the error probability increases The power can vary significantly, since in a short periods, due to mobility and the multipath effect. Consequently retransmissions are produced and WLAN performance is influenced. It must be also considered the signal-to-noise ratio, often written S/N or SNR, which from 10 decibels we can say that we have a suitable signal, from 10 to 15 decibels is enough, from 15 to 20 it is good signal and 20 in ahead is excellent. These numbers are recommendable for data; for voice 25 decibels or more are recommended and not to receive a signal from another access point that is working in the same channel and that is bigger than 10 decibels [5].
- Survey of the interfering networks:
  - Define the spatial distribution of the wireless network;
  - Mark and to obtain the coordinates of access points to be evaluated;
  - Start the application for wireless network to be studied;
  - Use a software for collecting samples of signal level on wireless network;
  - Use an application in the protocol analyzer to store QoS measures;
  - Start application(s) in the interferent wireless network.

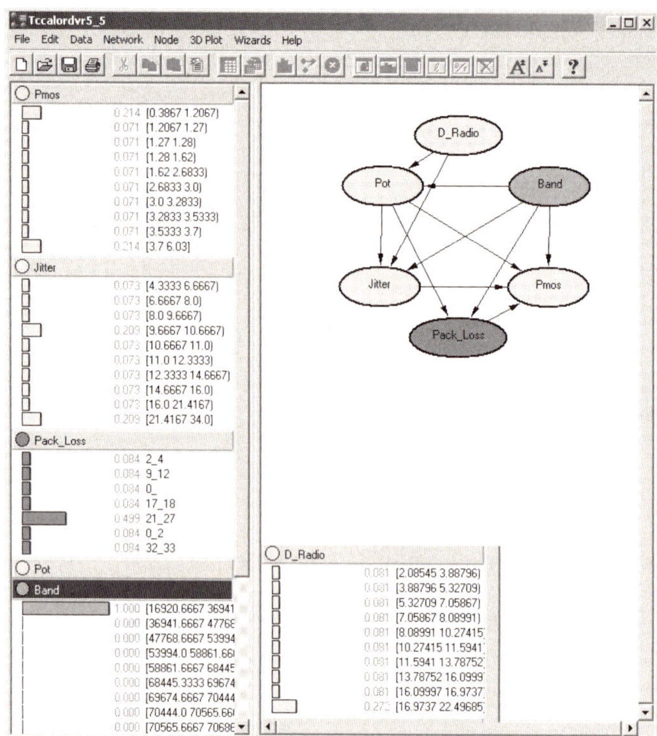

Fig. 8. Bayesian networks with worst throughput inference with interference applied to ground floor

- Definition of QoS requirements of the target application:
  There are several available metrics to measure the quality of a connection, such as packet loss rate, one-way delay, jitter, and throughput. Average one-way delay is probably the most critical parameter for VoIP. If it is too long, conversation flow is compromised and communication may become unnatural. ITU-T guidelines recommend a one-way delay of up to 150 milliseconds [15]. Beyond that, negative consequences gradually accrue. In IEEE 802.11 networks, the one-way delay between client and access point is usually less than 10 milliseconds, and therefore should not be a problem in VoIP. Jitter is the packet-to-packet variation in the one-way delay. Most modern systems will use some type of adaptive playback to smooth out the jitter, but this increases the one-way delay, and can introduce artifacts into the speech. In Wi-Fi networks, jitter is generally small, partially because one-way delay and packet sizes are small, too. However, at this paper showed that there are times when extreme delay variations can occur with significant impact on voice quality. Packet loss rate also affects speech quality, as the decoded speech will present artifacts associated with the lost packets. For VoIP, packet loss rates of up to 1% are generally acceptable [15]. In IEEE 802.11 networks, collisions and

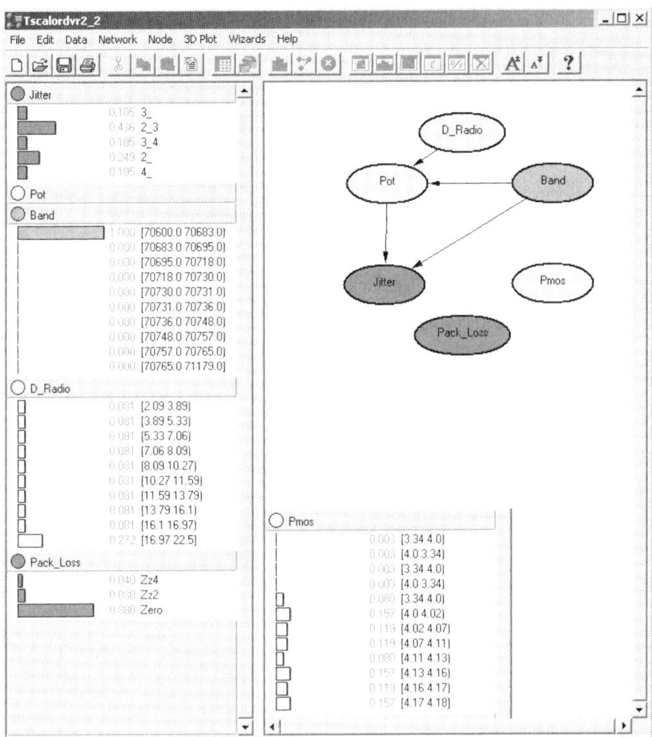

Fig. 9. Bayesian networks with worst throughput inference without interference applied to ground floor

other losses are hidden by an automatic re-transmission strategy. Since these retransmissions are transparent to the application layer, the final packet loss arate is typically less than 1% and, therefore, acceptable for typical VoIP applications. Note, however, that as a mobile terminal gets out of the range, the loss rates increase abruptly; quickly making speech communication impossible. Throughput: the bandwidth required by a single VoIP connection is significantly less than the nominal capacity of IEEE 802.11 networks. Typical speech codecs require no more than 64 Kbps, while 802.11g offers 54 Mbps. However, if the same access point is used to support multiple calls, we may have a capacity problem [15].

It is important to consider if there are WLANs near to our WLAN, where access points channels of our neighbors do not interfere with ours. Technologies that could produce interference are: Bluetooth, microwaves, some cellular phones and others WLANs, among others [5].

- Characterization of traffic for the target application:
  - Running several iterations of the application target observing patterns and typical curves by means of acquisition of samples and utilization of goodness of fit tests;

  - Definition of probability distribution for each performance measure studied, such as: delay, blocking probabilities and throughput;
  - Definition of the measures that must be considered in the computational models (computational intelligence, optimization and simulation).

– Accomplishment of inferences based on simulation, computational intelligence or analytical models/optimization, to verify aspects as: correlation, possible scenarios, scalability, availability and performance.

8 Conclusions

This paper proposes the use of computational intelligence by employing Bayesian Networks to verify the interference influence in QoS parameters. Bayesian analysis showed this influence with precision, pointing out that interference has a major impact in the 802.11 network performance.

As showed in Section 2, the major difference in the work presented here from research cited in [3] and [7] lies in the field experiments with and without interference. A Bayesian network was used to analyze the data to show an evidence, as shown in [7], that there is an influence of the radio environment affecting QoS parameters. However, the work presented in this paper includes investigation of other parameters such as jitter, packet loss and PMOS besides throughput that was the only parameter analyzed in [3] and [7]. The work hasn't included any explicit optimization study but some research is in progress in using Bayesian networks for this purpose.

The sequence of this work is to do new measurement campaign with multiple sources of traffic with and without interference and to draw the roadmap for capacity planning with an optimal number of APs, the cost function will be a Bayesian function and their weights and coefficients will be validated with the use of genetic algorithms and Markov chains for the scenery with and without interference, also proposed in [8] and validate the hypothesis suggested in [8] experimentally.

Only one user in the WLAN was used. One can extend Bayesian network to multiple user scenarios. It is important to mention that Bayesian network offers an approach to select several scenarios of QoS such that it is possible to guarantee a minimum distance to the AP for VoIP application in an indoor WLAN environment.

References

1. Medepalli, K., Gopalakrishnan, P., Famolari, D., Kodama, T.: Voice Capacity of IEEE 80211b 80211a and 80211g Wireless LANs. In: Vehicular Telecommunications Conference (Globecomm 2004), November 29-December 3 2004, vol. 3, pp. 1549–1553. IEEE Communications Society, Los Alamitos (2004)
2. Zhai, H., Wang, J., Fang, Y.: Providing Statistical QoS Guarantee for Voice over IP in the IEEE 802.11 Wireless LANs. IEEE Wireless Communications 3(1), 36–43 (2006)

3. Lu, J.L., Jaffres-Runser, K., Gorce, J.M., Valois, F.: Indoor WLAN Planning with a QoS Constraint Based on a Markovian Performance Evaluation Model. In: WiMob'2006. IEEE International Conference on Wireless and Mobile Computing, Networking and Communications, June 19-21, 2006, pp. 152–158. IEEE Computer Society Press, Los Alamitos (2006)
4. Glisic, S.G.: Advanced Wireless Networks: 4G Technologies. John Wiley and Sons LTDA, Chichester (June 2006)
5. Diaz, L.E.N., Diaz, J.A.P.: A Model for Designing WLAN's 802.11 for VoIP. In: Electronics, Robotics and Automotive Mechanics Conference (CERMA'06). Proceedings of the Electronics, vol. 2, pp. 110–115. IEEE Computer Society, Los Alamitos (September 2006)
6. Lu, J.L., Valois, F.: Performance evaluation of 802.11 WLAN in a real indoor environment. In: WiMob'2006. IEEE International Conference on Wireless and Mobile Computing, Networking and Communications, Montreal-Canada, June 19-21, 2006, pp. 140–147. IEEE Computer Society Press, Los Alamitos (2006)
7. Garg, S., Kappes, M.: Can I add a VoIP call? In: ICC'03. IEEE International Conference on Communications, May 11-15, 2002, vol. 2, pp. 779–783. IEEE Computer Society Press, Los Alamitos (2002)
8. Santana, A.L., et al.: Strategies for improving the modeling and interpretability of Bayesian Networks. Data Knowl. Eng. (2006), doi:10.1016/j.datak.2006.10.005
9. Acessed (January 01, 2007), http://www.radcom.com/
10. Acessed (December 05, 2006), http://www.openh323.org/
11. Accessed (December 19, 2006), http://dast.nlanr.net/Projects/Iperf/
12. Acessed (December 19, 2006), http://www.netstumbler.com/
13. Bayesware Discoverer, Copyright©, Bayesware Limited (2000) (accessed in December 05, 2006), http://www.bayesware.com/
14. Bayesware Discoverer, User Manual, Copyright©, Bayesware Limited (2000) (accessed in January 07, 2007), http://www.bayesware.com/
15. Conceição, A., Lia, J., Florêncio, D., Kon, F.: Is IEEE 802.11 ready for VoIP? In: 8th International Workshop on Multimedia Signal Processing (IEEE MMSP), Victoria, Canada, IEEE Computer Society Press, Los Alamitos (October 2006)

Instruction Selection for Subword Level Parallelism Optimizations for Application Specific Instruction Processors

Miao Wang, Guiming Wu, and Zhiying Wang

School of Computer Science, National University of Defense Technology
Changsha, Hunan, P.R. China, 410073
{wangmiao,wuguiming,zywang}@nudt.edu.cn

Abstract. Application Specific Instruction Processors (or, ASIPs) have the potential to meet the high-performance demands of multimedia applications, such as image processing, audio and video encoding, speech processing, and digital signal processing. To achieve lower cost and efficient energy for high performance embedded systems built by ASIPs, subword parallelism optimization will become an important alternative to accelerate multimedia applications. But one major problem is how to exploit subword parallelism for ASIPs with limited resources. This paper shows that loop transformations such as loop unrolling, variable expansion, etc., can be utilized to create opportunities for subword parallelism, and presents a novel approach to recognize and extract subword parallelism based on Cost Subgragh (or, CSG). This approach is evaluated on Transport Triggered Architecture (TTA), a customizable processor architecture that is particularly suitable for tailoring the hardware resources according to the requirements of the application. In our experiment, 63.58% of loops and 85.64% of instructions in these loops can exploit subword parallelism. The results indicate that significant available subword parallelism would be attained using our method.

1 Introduction

Multimedia processing involves compute-intensive kernels that process long streams of low-precision data and constitutes an increasingly fraction of general-purpose processor's workload. To match the intensive features of multimedia applications, multimedia architectures adopt a single instruction multiple data (SIMD) paradigm, called subword level parallelism, or SLP. Simultaneously, ASIPs, as one important approach to accelerate multimedia applications, has the potential to meet the high-performance demands of embedded systems for multimedia applications.

Subword parallelism is a form of low-cost, small-scale SIMD parallelism [1], it is a technique in which multiple short data elements are packed in a single register and data parallel operations are executed on them in parallel. In order to support and exploit subword parallelism, modern processors extend their Instruction Set Architecture, e.g., Intel's MMX and SSE, AMDs 3DNow!, Suns VIS, and HP's

I. Stojmenovic et al. (Eds.): ISPA 2007, LNCS 4742, pp. 946–957, 2007.

PA-MAX2. Most multimedia extensions provide short SIMD instructions which can operate simultaneously on several subword packed into a word.

While multimedia extensions are popular, the compiler that supports automatically leveraging subword parallelism still faces the challenges of how to identify subword parallelism in sequential descriptions and how to use this information to employ multimedia instructions efficiently. Most prior solutions expect programmers to hand-code their applications in assembly or use library calls. These solutions caused the problems of lack of portability and high cost of software development.

In this paper, we show that traditional parallelization transformations such as loop unrolling, induction variable expansion, etc, can be well suited to exploit subword parallelism for ASIPs. We also build an instruction selector to automatically recognize, evaluate and extract subword parallelism in loop based on Cost Subgragh (CSG). This approach has three distinct phases. First, seed operations are identified in loops. Then potential subgraphs are expanded and enumerated. Finally, each node in a subgraph is assigned a cost value according to a cost function and the CSGs are built. The CSGs that are not suitable to execute subword parallelism could be ignored during code generation.

We have implemented our method on Transport Triggered Architecture (TTA) [4]. We measured the performance of our methods using a set of benchmarks. The results reveal that our subword level parallelism optimization approach produces a reasonable performance improvement over the original generated code. It also shows that can our new instruction selector can effectively extract subword parallelism from loops for ASIPs.

This paper makes the following three contributions:

- It implements SLP optimization approaches for ASIPs on a low-level intermediate representation (IR).
- It presents new algorithms for automatically identifying SLP in loops based on CSG.
- It evaluates effectiveness and performance of these new algorithms on TTA.

2 Related Works

Despite the fact that multimedia extensions have been available in production microprocessors for several years, little has been published on automatic exploitation of the SIMD features of these processors, and most applications that use the multimedia extensions are hand-coded assembly routines for fairly simple multimedia processing algorithms.

Because of architectural similarities between vector processors and multimedia extensions, traditional vectorization was considered to compile programs for multimedia extensions. Vector compilation includes a variety of program transformations that can rearrange and simplify loops so that vector instructions can be used to execute loop body statements [3]. Researches [5,6,7] all applied traditional vectorization to the code generation on commercial compilers. Although vectorization can be used to extract the SLP in certain programs, it is intrinsic complicated and may lead to a performance loss. For examples, when loops contain a mix of vectorizable and non-vectorizable operations, the conventional vetorization techniques distribute a loop into vector and scalar portions, destroying ILP and stifling the processor's ability to provide high performance.

Larsen and Amarasinghe [2] have proposed a non-vectorizing compilation approach for fine-grained SIMD architectures. Instead of vectorizing across loop iterations, this approach identifies isomorphic instructions from the same basic block to pack them into vector instructions. The vectorizer was implemented in SUIF and was targeting AltiVec. Speedups were reported on some floating-point intensive kernels and some of the applications from SPECfp. Leupers has used an approach that builds on the classical tree-based code selection paradigm [8]. This technique is capable of exploiting SIMD instructions without the need for processor-specific code. Other researchers try to provide solutions to the new challenges which arise in vectorizing for multimedia extensions [9,10,11]. However, these approaches are still far from trivial to maximally detect opportunities in the programs where e.g., subword parallelism could be exploited, which causes that most compilers can't fully exploit power of SIMD instructions.

In this work, we proposed an approach based on Cost Subgraph to maximize the use of SIMD instructions across the applications. In contrast to conventional methods, our techniques operate on a low-level intermediate representation, which allows the algorithm to accurately measure the performance trade-offs according to CSG. We describe the compilation process, by which code transformations are used, Cost Subgraphs in loops are identified and instructions in suitable CSCs are selected to generate SIMD instructions. Experiments demonstrate that these techniques could provide high available SLP and effective code to exploit SLP.

3 SLP Pre-optimization

In order to maximally extract subword parallelism on a low-level IR, SLP optimizations are performed. The pre-optimization is divided into three phases. First, strength reduction helps to identify adjacent memory accesses which are well suited for SLP execution. Then, loop unrolling attempts to transform vector parallelism into subword parallelism. Next, variable expansion is applied to eliminate false inter-iteration dependences to expose more SLP for unrolled loops.

3.1 Strength Reduction

In subword parallelism, loads and stores can only be combined if the resulting SIMD load or store is to a contiguous chunk of memory. In order to implement parallel loads and stores, we need to identify adjacent memory accesses within loops. Strength reduction which simplifies the array index computations could be used to realize this goal. On a low-level IR, the memory addresses in loop body are always computed through the value of certain dependent induction variables. Strength reduction could transform these induction variables into basic induction variables and implement the recursion computation of array index. After strength reduction, we determine whether a load or store operation I_i of K-bit value is contiguous within the loop L, if I_i satisfies the following constraints, let a_i be the memory address of I_i :

i)a_i is only defined by instruction I_m containing basic induction variables in L (e.g., I_m is r_i + A -> r_i, A is a loop invariant, a_i is defined by I_m and increments a constant A after each iteration).

ii) The constant increment in I_m equals the increment of the address value of contiguous K-bit load. This ensures that I_i could refer to adjacent memory in each loop iteration (e.g. if I_i is a 8-bit load and A is 1, so a_i increment 1 in each iteration and refer to contiguous 8-bit data in memory).

3.2 Loop Unrolling

In order to exploit subword parallelism, basic blocks in the loops need to contain enough identical operations. Loop unrolling is suitable for the creation of loop bodies with identical operations on different data. After loop unrolling, identical instructions from different loop iterations have the opportunity to be scheduled together to be combined into one SIMD instruction. In order to fully utilize the datapath, the unroll factor must be customized to the data type used within the loop. For example, for a 64-bit datapath, if the operands of the loop body instructions are all 16-bit data types, then the loop can be unrolled 4 times, which means that 4 16-bit data can be packed into one register. In our experiments, we focus on the innermost loops without function calls, early exits and complex control structures.

3.3 Variable Expansion

Variable expansion includes induction variable expansion and accumulator variable expansion. Induction variable expansion is used to eliminate flow, anti-, and output dependences between definitions of induction variables and their uses within an unrolled loop body. Accumulator variable expansion eliminates redefinitions of an accumulator variable within an unrolled loop. If loop L is unrolled N times, we can only expand induction variables in N-1 copies of L. After variable expansion, a higher potential for parallelization of instructions is exposed during scheduling.

4 Instruction Selector

After SLP pre-optimization, identical operations from different iterations in an unrolled loop can be grouped into one SIMD instruction. This parallelization technique can produce a performance improvement. However, packing and unpacking between SIMD instructions and scalar instructions during SIMD code generation may lead to performance degradation. To maximize the use of SIMD instructions across the unrolled loop on a low-level IR, we introduce *Cost Subgraph (CSG)*. CSG is a subset of data flow graph (DFG) of an unrolled loop and each node in CSG contains a cost value. The total cost of a CSG reflects the difference between the speedup gained from subword parallelization and the cost of packing and unpacking.

Operating on data flow graph of an unrolled loop, our instruction selector begins by partitioning instructions in the DFG into unfree and free instructions. Then the algorithm chooses seeds from unfree instructions in original loop body to generate a set of subgraphs. Finally, the subgraphs are evaluated by a cost function and Cost Subgraphs are formed. The total cost of a CSG determines whether instructions in this subgraph and their siblings in unrolled loop can be selected to pack into SIMD instructions. Once a CSG is selected, the loop containing such kind of CSGs is suitable to exploit SLP. Based on CSG, we can maximally detect available instructions to exploit SLP while minimizing the cost produced by packing and unpacking of the instructions. The following sections describe this approach in detail.

4.1 Locating Unfree Instruction

With subword parallelism, we need to pack unrolled versions of the same instructions. However, not all identical instruction groups in loops can be replaced by SIMD instructions. In this section, we classify the instructions in loop body into free and unfree instructions and discuss which kind of instructions can be selected as candidates to generate SIMD instructions.

If a loop L is unrolled N times, N-1 copies of the loop body will be created. Let A_1 represents L's loop body, A_2 to A_n represent A_1's N-1 copies respectively. For any instruction I_{i1} in A_1 , instructions I_{i2} to I_{in} are its siblings in A_2 to A_n, I_{i1} is *unfree* if the execution of I_{i1} and its siblings can't overlap. If I_{i1} is unfree, its duplications I_{i2} to I_{in} are all unfree instructions and can't be freely scheduled to group into one SIMD instruction. Unfree instructions are usually caused by inter-iteration dependences which force instructions from different copies to execute in series. On the contrary, *free* instructions are instructions whose siblings from different copies can be scheduled together to pack into SIMD instructions.

After dependence analysis, all unfree instructions in the loops are identified and marked. Because unfree instructions can't be scheduled to form SIMD instructions, the following works can mainly focus on free instructions and loops containing free instructions that can exploit SLP, called *SLP loops*. To simplify the process of selection, we only consider instructions in original loop body, because once such an instruction is selected, its siblings in unrolled loop will immediately be included.

4.2 Seed Selection

The next step, seed selection, can be performed in several different ways. In order to reduce the initial packing and unpacking cost while covering more candidates, a free instruction I_i in loop L can be chosen as a seed, if I_i satisfies the following conditions:

i)I_i is a contiguous load in L, or
ii)I_i is a load whose address is a loop invariant, or

iii)I_i is an arithmetic instruction and I_i meets any of the three conditions: both of source operands are defined by the instructions outside loop L; or, one source operand is defined by the instruction outside loop L, the other is an immediate; or else, one source operands is defined by the basic induction variables in the loop and the other is an immediate.

The first condition ensures the minimal initial cost because contiguous loads refer to operands pre-packed in memory and require no pack instructions. The last two conditions could enhance the opportunity to cover more instructions to generate subgraphs.

Seed selection is performed by scanning the original loop body to find all initial seeds operations and add them to a set of instructions, called *SeedSet*. The SeedSet will be modified in the next section. An example of initial seed selection is shown in Figure 1, Figure 1A is the C source code of a loop from the kernels and Figure 1B is a DFG of the rolled loop in Figure 1A. In Figure 1B, operation 0 satisfies the condition iii), and can be added to the SeedSet.

4.3 Subgraph Growth

After choosing a seed from initial SeedSet, a subgrpah G consisting only of that operation is formed. Then the algorithm enters the third phase, subgraph growth, trying to expand this subgraph to include more potential SIMD instructions and modify the SeedSet during the expansion. The algorithm in Figure 2 describes this process. Given a seed from the SeedSet of loop L, the seed is first pushed into an instruction set called S and the subgraph G is initialized. After popping an instruction I from S, each instruction I_1 in DUChain(I) and UDChain(I) (DUChain and UDChain refer to Def-Use chain and Use-Def chain, respectively) is examined. Let N_1 be the node representing I_1 in DFG. If I_1 is free and hasn't been identified, the possibility of including N_1 into G depends on whether I_1 is a definition of I or a use of I. If I_1 defines the source operands of I, the algorithm expands N_1 and deletes I_1 from the SeedSet if it is a seed. If I_1 uses the result of I, the procedure NeedNewSeed will be immediately used to test whether I1 is a load or store. If I_1 is a load, N_1 can't be expanded and a new seed representing I_1 is created. Otherwise, N_1 can be added to G. Once N_1 is expanded, I_1 will be added to S. The selection is continued until S becomes empty. Then another seed from SeedSet is selected and the algorithm in Figure 2 is called again to generate another subgraph. The process is repeated until there is no seed in the SeedSet. For illustration, consider the example in Figure 1. Operation 0 is chosen as the initial seed. After popping operation 0 from S, operation 1 (viz. the use of operation 0) can be marked and added to S and subgraph 1. Then, operations 2, 3, 6 and 9 are respectively expanded according to UDChain of operations 1 and 2. After popping operation 3, each instruction in operation 3's DUChain and UDChain is checked. Operations 4 and 5 in UDChain of operation 3 can be added to subgraph 1 and S. However, operations 2 and 13 shouldn't be expanded since operation 2 has been marked before while operation 13 is a load and is excluded by subgraph 1. Because operation 13 satisfies procedure NeedNewSeed, it can be viewed as a new seed and added to the SeedSet. Likewise, subgraph 1 excludes

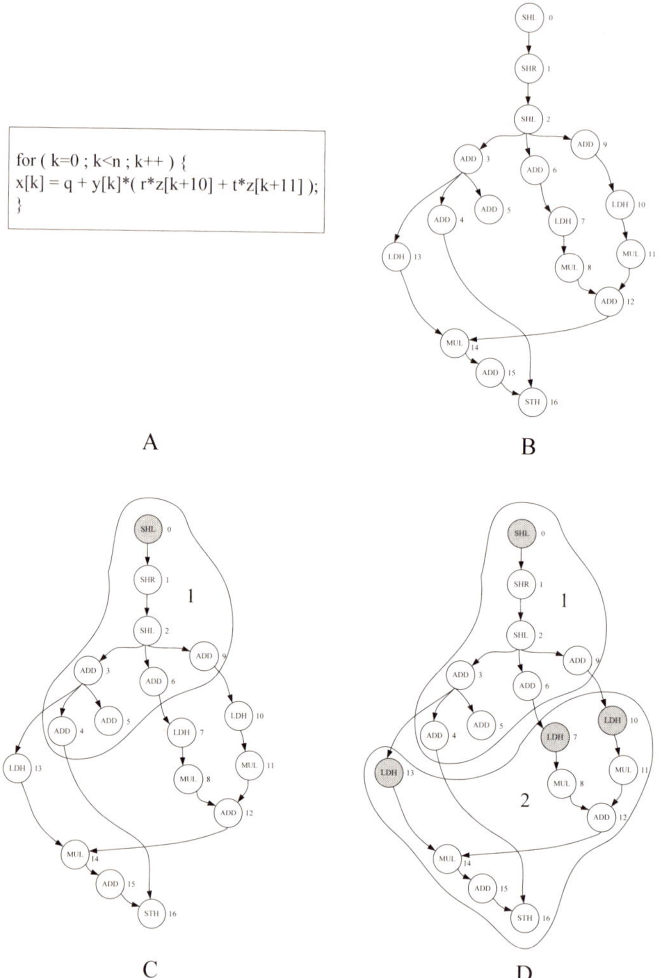

Fig. 1. A. C source code for Hydro fragment from Livermore loops. B. Dataflow graph of the rolled loop. C. Subgraph 1 is identified. D. The final identified subgraphs.

operations 16, 7 and 10 as they are load or store instructions, resulting in the subgraph in Figure 1C. Meanwhile, operations 7 and 10 are included by the SeedSet. Then the process selects operation 13 as a seed node, and the algorithm is repeated to generate subgraph 2 in Figure 1D.

4.4 Subgraph Evaluation

This step builds Cost Subgraph G^{GSC} for each identified subgraph G by assigning a cost to each node in G. Now we define a function F_{COST} to compute the

```
Algorithm SubgraphGrowth:
Initialize S and G
while(S≠Ø)
  Pop an element I from S
    for each I1 ∈ UDChain(I)
      if (I1 and I are in the same copy of L)
        if (I1 is free and unmarked)
          if (NeedNewSeed(I1))
            Add I1 to SeedSet
          else
            Mark I1
            Add I1 to G and S
    for each I1 ∈ DUChain(I)
      if (I1 and I are in the same copy of L)
        if (I1 is free and unmarked)
          Mark I1
          Add I1 to G and S
        if (IsSeed(I1))
          Delete I1 from SeedSet
```

Fig. 2. Subgraph growth algorithm

cost value of subgraph node N_i. Let v_l be the unroll factor, I_i is the instruction that N_i represents. Function F_{COST}: Node -> R is defined as following:

i)N_i is a seed. If I_i is a contiguous load or store, $F_{COST}(N_i)$ = 1- v_l, if I_i is a load or store but not contiguous, $F_{COST}(N_i) = 1$, otherwise, $F_{COST}(N_i)$ = 1- v_l + 2.

ii)N_i is not a seed. If N_i has two predecessors, $F_{COST}(N_i)$ = 1 - v_l, or else if N_i has only one predecessor, $F_{COST}(N_i)$ = 1 - v_l +1. If N_i has no successors, $F_{COST}(N_i) = F_{COST}(N_i) + 1$.

For each node N_i, $F_{COST}(N_i)$ indicates the instruction reduction gained from packing instruction I_i and its siblings in the unrolled loop into one SIMD instruction and the instruction increase caused by introducing pack and unpack instructions during the SIMD code generation. For example, N_i and I_i satisfy condition i) and v_l equals to 4. With SLP, four identical loads referring to adjacent memory data can be grouped together to form a parallel load, by which 4 load instructions will be reduced and one SIMD load will be produced. The total instruction reduction $F_{COST}(N_i)$ is $1 - 4 = -3$.

After cost assignment for each subgraph, CSGs are formed. The total cost of a CSG estimates the instruction reduction of the whole subgraph during SIMD code generation. If the total cost is a negative, the number of the adding pack and unpack instructions is smaller than that of instructions reduced by parallelizing instructions in this subgraph. Therefore, the smaller the total cost, the more suitably the subgraphs to exploit SLP. From F_{COST} definition, we could also conclude that the larger the unroll factor, the smaller the cost value of CSGs. Obviously, if unroll factor equals or is greater than 4, the cost of each CSG node will always be a negative as well as the total value. So that the unrolled loop will definitely reduce its instruction number and get a performance improvement. Using Figure 1D as example, each node in subgraphs 1 and 2 is given a cost value through cost function F_{COST}. Thus, Cost Subgraph 1 and Cost Subgraph 2 in the loop are built. When unroll factor is 4, the total costs of subgraphs 1 and 2 are -11 and -12, respectively. The CSGs' results are all less than zero, which demonstrate that subgraphs 1 and 2 are all suitable to exploit SLP. So that instructions in subgraphs and their siblings can be selected to group into SIMD instructions. Meanwhile, the loop in Figure 1A which contains subgraphs 1 and 2 is a SLP loop.

5 Experiment Results

In this section, several benchmark applications from DSP and multimedia application domains were used to evaluate the SIMD instruction selector for TTAs. We have implemented our instruction selector on the basis of the MOVE C compiler for TTA processors [4]. TTA processor configurations are listed in Table 1. Using the original C code as input, the MOVE C compiler compiled it into sequential assembly code, then, the sequential code was scheduled to exploit the instruction level parallelism. The resulting MOVE executable code was simulated with the MOVE simulator. We added subword operations to the target processor which implements subword functionality in TTA simulator and integrated our algorithms into TTA scheduler.

Table 1. TTA processor configurations

Parameter	Configuration
Move Bus	8 x 32 bits
Register File	128 integer RFs
	128 floating-point RFs
Function Unit	1 load/store FUs
	1 control Unit
	4 integer & logic FUs
	1 floating-point FU

We measured the success of our algorithms on nine kernels (five from Livermore Kernel) and three benchmarks from Mibench, which are often found in multimedia applications. Table 2 describes the characteristics of all programs used in our experiments.

Table 3 lists the experimental results. Columns 1, 2 and 3 give the number of loops, inner loops and inner loops with branches for each benchmark after compilation. Column 4 shows the number of loops which can execute SLP. The unroll factors in Column 5 specify the number of duplications of the loop body, which is necessary to exhibit enough parallelism for exploitation of SIMD instructions. Column 6 presents the percentage of identified loops over the total loops of each benchmark. Table 3 shows that most of the SLP loops can be recognized through our approaches for kernels. All loops in mat, idct, and four livermore kernels can

Table 2. Benchmarks characteristics

Benchmark	Description	Data Width
mat	Matrix multiply	
fir	Finite impulse respond	
iir	Infinite impulse respond	
idct	Inverse discrete cosine transform	
iccg	Incomplete Cholesky Conjugate Gradient	16-bit integer
hydro	Hydro fragment	
tri-diagonal	Tri-diagonal elimination, below diagonal	
linear	General linear recurrence equations	
state	Equation of state fragment	
susan	An image recognition package	8/16-bit integer
bitcount	Count the number of bits in an array	8-bit integer
stringsearch	Search for given words	8/16-bit integer

Table 3. Benchmarks characteristics

Benchmark	#loops	# Inner loops	# Inner loops with branches	# Identified	Unroll factor	# Identified / # nner loops
mat	3	1		1		100%
fir	3	2		1		50%
iir	2	2		1		50%
idct	2	2		2		100%
iccg	2	1	0	1	2	100%
hydro	1	1		1		100%
tri-diagonal	1	1		1		100%
linear	2	2		1		50%
state	1	1		1		100%
susan	137	106	37	3	4/2	2.83%
bitcount	59	50	10	2	4	4%
stringsearch	56	49	11	3	4/2	6.12%

execute subword parallelism, and 50% of loops in fir, iir and linear have the chance to generate SIMD instructions. For benchmarks from Mibench, an average of 4.3% of loops can be identified as SLP loops. The lower identification in these programs is due to most of the loops are excluded by the instruction selector because of their inherent complicated control structures. This also implies that more aggressive approaches (such as hyperblock formation) should be added in the algorithms to extract SLP in more complicated loops.

Figure 3 shows the percentage of unfree, free and identified instructions in each identified SLP loops in benchmarks. Most of the identified loops didn't contain unfree instructions. The unfree instructions in SLP loops in iir, linear

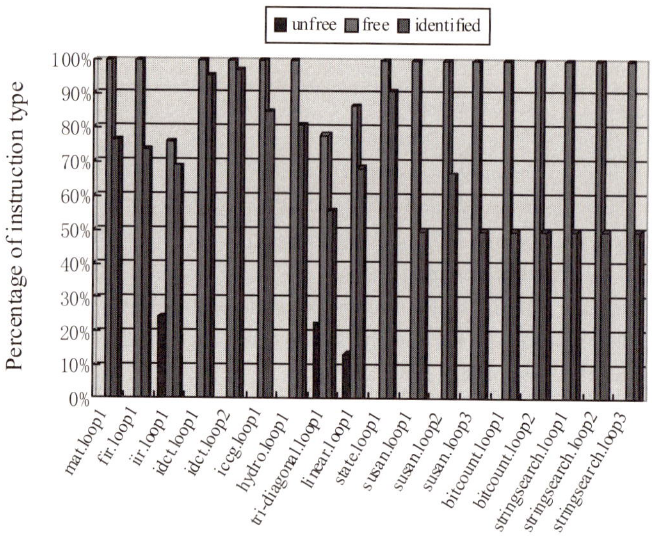

Fig. 3. Percentage of three type instructions in SLP loop

and tri-diagonal are caused by cross-iteration memory dependences. On average, we found that more than 96.45% of instructions in all identified SLP loops were free instructions and 85.64% of free instructions were identified as potential SIMD instructions. As shown for the idct and state instances, more than 90% instructions in their identified loops can be extracted to generate SIMD instructions. In general, Figure 3 clearly shows that our instruction selector could effectively select instruction candidates to exploit SLP.

6 Conclusions

In this work, we first presents that well-known parallelization techniques such as loop unrolling, strength reduction and variable expansion can be used to expose subword parallelism on low-level IR. Then several new algorithms were developed to find subgraph candidates to generate SIMD instructions for ASIPs. The presented instruction selection technique performed subgraph identification and built Cost Subgraphs according to the cost model. The applicability has been demonstrated experimentally by compiling a set of benchmarks on TTA processors designed with the MOVE framework. On average, 63.58% of loops from the benchmarks can exploit SIMD instructions and more than 85.64% of instructions in these identified loops have the opportunity to generate SIMD instructions. In the next step, SIMD code generation would be included and more aggressive techniques would be studied to detect SLP in loops with complicated control structures.

References

1. Lee, R.B., Fiskiran, A.M.: PLX: A Fully Subword-Parallel Instruction Set Architecture for Fast Scalable Multimedia Processing. In: Proceedings of 3rd International Conference on Multimedia and Expo (ICME), Lausanne, Switzerland, pp. 117–120 (2002)
2. Larsen, S., Amarasinghe, S.: Exploiting Superword Level Parallelism with Multimedia Instruction Sets. In: Proceedings of the SIGPLAN'00 Conference on Programming Language Design and Implementation, Vancouver, BC, pp. 145–156 (2000)
3. De Sutter, B., Cristiaens, M., et al.: On the Use of Subword Parallelism in Medical Image Processing. Parallel Computing 24(9-10), 1537–1556 (1998)
4. Corporaal, H., Arnold, M.: Using Transport Triggered Architectures for Embedded Processor Design. Integrated Computer-Aided Eng. 5(1), 19–38 (1998)
5. Cheong, G., Lam, M.S.: An Optimizer for Multimedia Instruction Sets. In: Second SUIF Compiler Workshop, Stanford (1997)
6. Konda, V., Lauer, H., Muroi, K., Tanaka, K., Tsubota, H., Xu, E., Wilson, C.: A SIMDizing C Compiler for the Mitsubishi Electric Neuro4 Processor Array. In: First SUIF Compiler Workshop, Stanford (1996)
7. Krall, A., Lelait, S.: Compilation Techniques for Multimedia Processors. International Journal of Parallel Programming 28(4), 347–361 (2000)
8. Leupers, R.: Code Selection for Media Processors with SIMD Instructions. In: Proceedings of DATE'00, Paris, France, pp. 4–8 (2000)
9. Ren, G., Wu, P., Padua, D.: A Preliminary Study on the Vectorization of Multimedia Applications for Multimedia Extensions. In: Proceedings of the 16th International Workshop on Languages and Compilers for Parallel Computing, Texas A&M University, pp. 420–435 (2003)
10. Ren, G., Wu, P., Padua, D.: An Empirical Study On the Vectorization of Multimedia Applications for Multimedia Extensio. In: Proceedings of the 19th IEEE Int. Parallel and Distributed Processing Symp (IPDPS05), Denver, USA (2005)
11. Larsen, S., Rabbah, R., Aarasinghe, S.: Exploiting Vector Parallelism in Software Pipelined Loops. In: Proceedings of the 38th Annual International Symposium on Microarchitecture, Barcelona, Spain, pp. 119–129 (2005)

High Performance 3D Convolution for Protein Docking on IBM Blue Gene

Akira Nukada[1,2], Yuichiro Hourai[3], Akira Nishida[4,1], and Yutaka Akiyama[3]

[1] Japan Science and Technology Agency, Saitama 332-0012, Japan
[2] The University of Tokyo, Tokyo 113-8685, Japan
nukada@is.s.u-tokyo.ac.jp
[3] Computational Biology Research Center, AIST, Tokyo 135-0064, Japan
{hourai-yuichiro,akiyama-yutaka}@aist.go.jp
[4] Chuo University, Tokyo 112-8551, Japan
nishida@kc.chuo-u.ac.jp

Abstract. We have developed a high performance 3D convolution library for Protein Docking on IBM Blue Gene. The algorithm is designed to exploit slight locality of memory access in 3D-FFT by making full use of a cache memory structure. The 1D-FFT used in the 3D convolution is optimized for PowerPC 440 FP2 processors. The number of SIMOMD instructions is minimized by simultaneous computation of two 1D-FFTs. The high performance 3D convolution library achieves up to 2.16 Gflops (38.6% of peak) per node. The total performance of a shape complementarity search is estimated at 7 Tflops with the 4-rack Blue Gene system (4096 nodes).

1 Introduction

Owing to recent developments in molecular biology, more than 30,000 protein structures have been determined and are available in a public database, Protein Data Bank [1]. Most proteins interact with other proteins to execute specific functions. Many of these protein interactions are being determined, thanks to the growth of experimental technologies like mass spectrometry. However, how proteins or chemical compounds form complexes in 3D space is difficult to determine even with current X-ray or NMR technology. The three-dimensional structures of complexes are essential clues in predicting toxicity or pharmacologic action. It is of practical importance to determine the problem in the earlier stages of the drug-screening process, because experiments by human hands usually involve an immense amount of time and effort, often accompanied by high cost. Therefore, computational solutions are in high demand. There are many computational approaches, from ab initio quantum chemical calculation to empirical machine learning [2,3]. One of the most effective approaches to this problem is a shape complementarity search [4,5,6,7].

Shape complementarity searching is based on the idea that the surfaces of interacting proteins have complementary structures without collision. The surfaces are supposed to be complementary because of hydrophobicity or electrostatic energy. Some empirical scoring schemes have been proposed considering

I. Stojmenovic et al. (Eds.): ISPA 2007, LNCS 4742, pp. 958–969, 2007.

non-structural information [8,9]. The search space of protein orientation is very large and there has been much research aimed at reducing the search space by heuristics or approximation [2,10,11]. However, there is always the possibility of overlooking probable solutions, and accordingly, we are developing an exhaustive search method. FTDock[12] and ZDock[8] utilize Fast Fourier Transform (FFT) for computing shape complementarity exhaustively by translational moves. ZDock has showed particular effectiveness in an open protein-protein docking contest CAPRI[11]. These programs make use of 3D FFT routines in FFTW[13] or vendor-provided FFT libraries for computing convolution (correlation), but they are not optimized for 3D-convolution. We propose a new convolution algorithm to improve the throughput of the shape complementarity search on the IBM Blue Gene system.

FFT is a widely used computational tool in scientific simulation, signal analysis, and many other application areas. Often, FFT provides the computational kernel of such applications, and it has attracted many researchers' interest for its ability to improve performance [14]. There are some previous studies on FFT for the IBM Blue Gene system. Lorenz et al. [15] reported that utilization of a double FPU in 1D-FFT is improved by a vectorization technique. Eleftheriou et al. [16,17] parallelized 3D-FFT with Blue Gene's low-level communication library and the volumetric FFT scale up to more than 512 nodes. Their library was brought into a Molecular Dynamics program, Blue Matter [14], and contributed high parallel efficiency to the molecular simulation. The parallelized version of FFTE by Takahashi [18] marked 2.2-2.3 TFlop/s with 64 racks of Blue Gene/L in HPC Challenge benchmark [19]. The absolute performance appears to be good, but it is far from the peak performance. Unlike previous researchers, our interest is in improving the throughput of many 3D convolutions rather than the latency of a single 3D convolution.

Our ultimate goal is to reveal the protein interaction network by computation. The screening process for a shape complementarity search consists of many tasks that are independent in nature. Therefore, task parallel computation enables high utilization of massive processors. This results in linearly scaling parallel performance without large communication overhead, as in the case of parallelizing small tasks. An actual shape complementarity search within a massive data set will be our next big challenge. This paper describes how we can exploit the potential performance of the Blue Gene system in computing 3D convolutions.

2 Shape Complementarity Search

We are focusing on a protein docking problem where individual 3D structures of proteins are known but the structures of complexes are unknown. The protein structures are assumed to be rigid in this research. As such, the protein docking problem becomes a search for protein orientation. The freedom of docking orientation can be decomposed into translational space and rotational space. Usually, protein structures are represented by coordinates of atoms. Here, they are discretized onto $n \times n \times n$ cubic grids in order to make use of FFT for translational search. Discretized grids for receptor and ligand proteins are superimposed to evaluate docking orientations. Rotational spaces are searched by explicitly rotating ligands and iterating the same procedure for a translational search. After removing the redundancy of rotational angles [8], the numbers of angles to compute translational search space are 3,600 for 15-degree steps (default in ZDock) and 54,000 for 6-degree steps. With the thousands of processors of Blue Gene, we can exploit massive parallelism.

2.1 Scoring Schemes

When a ligand grid at (x_l, y_l, z_l) and a receptor grid at (x_r, y_r, z_r) are superimposed in a translational search, the local matching score for the orientation is computed by $s(x_l, y_l, z_l, x_r, y_r, z_r) = L(x_l, y_l, z_l) \times R(x_r, y_r, z_r)$, where L and R are discretized functions for ligand and receptor structures, respectively. The discrete functions are defined based on biophysical environments or empirical knowledge. The simplest scoring scheme is based only on structural information, such as surface, core, open space, and so on. For example, FTDock[12] defines

$$R(x_r, y_r, z_r) = \begin{cases} 1, & \text{surface} \\ -15, & \text{core} \\ 0, & \text{open space,} \end{cases}$$
$$L(x_l, y_l, z_l) = \begin{cases} 1, & \text{surface or core} \\ 0, & \text{open space,} \end{cases}$$

by default. This gives a penalized score, $-15 \times 1 = -15$, for superimposed cores (collisions) and a favorable score, $1 \times 1 = +1$, for superimposed surface grids. FTDock also computes approximated electrostatic energy by defining $R(x_r, y_r, z_r) = E$, where E is an electrostatic field at (x_r, y_r, z_r) caused from the receptor, and $L(x_l, y_l, z_l) = Q$, where Q is electrostatic charge on the ligand grid at (x_l, y_l, z_l). In the Grid-based Shape Complementarity (GSC) score function of ZDock [8], discrete functions R and L are defined as

$$R(x_r, y_r, z_r) = \begin{cases} 1, & \text{outside of surface} \\ 9i, & \text{inside of molecule} \\ 0, & \text{otherwise,} \end{cases}$$
$$L(x_l, y_l, z_l) = \begin{cases} 1, & \text{surface} \\ 9i, & \text{core} \\ 0, & \text{otherwise,} \end{cases}$$

where $i = \sqrt{-1}$ (See [8] for more details). The Pairwise Shape Complementarity (PSC) score function [9] and other functions in ZDock are slightly more complicated but are defined within the same scoring scheme.

After the discretization of protein structures, the docking orientation score by translational move (x, y, z) $(-n \le x, y, z \le n)$ for a receptor grid is given by *correlation* (*convolution*) form,

$$S(x, y, z) = \sum_i^n \sum_j^n \sum_k^n s(i, j, k, i + x, j + y, k + z)$$

$$= \sum_{i}^{n} \sum_{j}^{n} \sum_{k}^{n} L(i, j, k) \times R(i + x,\ j + y,\ k + z) \qquad (-n \le x, y, z < n),$$

where $R(x, y, z)$ and $L(x, y, z)$ are discretized functions for receptor and ligand grids, respectively. Note that $R(x, y, z)$ and $L(x, y, z)$ are zeros for $\{(x, y, z) \,|\, x < 0,\ y < 0,\ z < 0,\ x \ge n,\ y \ge n, \text{ or } z \ge n\}$ (*linear convolution*). The time complexity to compute all $S(x, y, z)$ directly in the above form is $O(N^6)$ on an $N \times N \times N$ grid, and it takes several days for realistic problems even with a recent processor. The most powerful method to compute convolutions is Fast Fourier Transform (FFT) [20]. The details are described in the next section.

We must note that the scoring function of FTDock is based on real numbers, while the ZDock built-in scoring functions are based on complex numbers. Although the convolution of two real functions can be computed by special FFT algorithms, complex functions can also be computed efficiently using FFT by packing two real functions into real and imaginary parts of a complex function [20]. Therefore, we have only to prepare convolution routines for complex numbers and utilize them for convolution in both complex and real numbers.

2.2 3D Convolution Using 3D-FFT

The 3D convolution can be computed efficiently using 3D-FFT as follows.

Assume that the resolutions of the input data of receptor and ligand are $n \times n \times n$. We consider that n is in the set $\{32, 64, 128\}$.

First, relocate the data into three-dimensional arrays of size $N \times N \times N$ as described below, where $N = 2n$. The space out of the range of input data is filled with zero. The data of the receptor is stored in reverse order.

$$A(x, y, z) = \begin{cases} R(n - x, n - y, n - z)\} & x, y, z \le n \\ 0 & \text{otherwise} \end{cases}$$

$$B(x, y, z) = \begin{cases} L(x, y, z) & x, y, z \le n \\ 0 & \text{otherwise} \end{cases}$$

Second, compute the backward Fourier transform of A and B.

$$A' = IFFT3D(A), \quad B' = IFFT3D(B)$$

Third, compute the element-wise products of A' and B'.

$$C'(x, y, z) = A'(x, y, z) * B'(x, y, z)$$

Finally, compute the forward Fourier transform of C'.

$$C = FFT3D(C')$$

After those steps, the computation of the 3D convolution is completed.

In our implementation, the computation is performed in double precision, but the grid data of receptors and ligands are provided in single precision so as to save memory space.

3 FFT Kernel for SIMOMD Instructions

3D-FFT can be implemented with clusters of 1D-FFTs in each direction [21]. First, we design a high performance 1D-FFT.

PowerPC 440 FP2 processors are installed on the nodes of Blue Gene. The processor has two FPUs that can execute fused multiply-add (FMA) instructions. To use both FPUs, Single Instruction Multiple Operations Multiple Data (SIMOMD) instructions are necessary. The instructions include SIMD-style FMA instructions which execute two FMA operations, and include some additional SIMOMD-style FMA instructions for multiplication of complex numbers [22]. We designed FFT kernels with a minimum number of SIMOMD instructions.

Some FFT kernels for FMA operations have been proposed [23,24], and the numbers of FMA operations of those kernels are smaller than those of the conventional FFT kernels. The operations of those kernels differ from the multiplication of complex numbers, due to aggressive reduction of the number of FMA operations. Therefore they do not match the SIMOMD instructions and additional cross move (or shuffle) instructions are required. As a result, the number of SIMOMD instructions is the same as that of the conventional kernels.

In the case of 1D-FFT as a part of 3D-FFT, many 1D transforms of the same size are performed. In the case of an out-of-place transform, about three times the memory space of input data size is required for an input/output buffer, a temporary buffer and twiddle factor tables. It is possible to compute two transforms of length 256, four transforms of length 128, or eight transforms of length 64 on a 32kB L1 cache. The simultaneous computation of two transforms with FFT kernels for FMA requires only SIMD-style FMA instructions; therefore, FFT kernels with the minimum number of the SIMOMD instructions are easily available.

The computation of multiple transforms also decreases the number of load operations from the twiddle factor tables, although the number of required registers is increased. The PowerPC 440 FP2 processor has 64 FP registers. This number is sufficient to compute two transforms simultaneously. The PowerPC 440 processors can issue only two instructions in each cycle; therefore, decreasing load instruction is very important.

To enable simultaneous computation, a special data arrangement is used on the cache memory. Given two arrays of complex numbers $v_0[]$ and $v_1[]$, the data is stored in an interleaved order described below.

$$Re(v_0[0]), Re(v_1[0]), Im(v_0[0]), Im(v_1[0]), \ldots$$

This arrangement allows efficient load / store operations using parallel load / store instructions. The parallel memory instructions load or store two floating-point numbers at once and simply double the bandwidth of the cache memory.

Table 1 shows the performances of 1D FFT of several libraries available on the Blue Gene system. All of them perform out-of-place, complex-to-complex transforms in double precision. IBM(R) XL C/C++ Advanced Edition V7.0 for Linux(R) and compiler option '-O3 -qansialias' are used in all experiments in this

Table 1. The Performances of 1D FFTs (times in μsec)

	N=64		N=128		N=256	
	Time	Gflops	Time	Gflops	Time	Gflops
New kernel	0.86	2.24	1.90	2.36	4.25	2.41
FFTSS	1.40	1.37	2.89	1.55	5.31	1.93
FFTW2-GEL	0.89	2.15	2.12	2.12	7.17	1.43
FFTW3	2.10	0.92	5.82	0.77	12.02	0.85
FFTW3-SIMOMD	1.58	1.21	2.98	1.50	6.44	1.59
ESSL	1.73	1.10	3.88	1.16	7.57	1.35

paper. The 'new kernel' in the table is our 1D-FFT routine we developed for 3D-FFT. The performances in Gflops are calculated by $5N \log_2 N/\text{elapsed time} \times 10^{-9}$.

Our kernel outperforms all other libraries in our experiments, reaching a maximum performance of 86% of the theoretical peak. That is because all FMA operations of the FFT kernel completely fit the SIMOMD instructions. The decrease of the load operations is also effective.

FFTW3 indicates FFTW library version 3.1.0, which does not support SIMOMD instructions. The secondary FPU does not contribute much to the performance. The original FFTW3 library uses Intel SSE2 instructions [13]. We implemented FFTW3-SIMOMD, which uses SIMOMD instructions. Since both the SSE2 and the SIMOMD instructions support packed double data, it is easy to replace SSE2 instructions with SIMOMD instructions. In the case of FFTW3, the relation between the vector and complex arithmetic operations and SSE2 instructions are defined in the file 'simd/simd-sse2.h'. We replaced them with the SIMOMD instructions. Thus, the FFTW3-SIMOMD could use both FPUs, and the performance of FFTW3-SIMOMD became almost twice as that of FFTW3.

The FFTSS library [25] is a 1D-FFT library that includes FFT kernels tuned for Blue Gene PowerPC 440 FP2 processors. The FFTW2-GEL library is based on FFTW version 2, and is tuned for Blue Gene. FFTW2-GEL and FFTSS are well tuned for Blue Gene, but they have no advantage over the new kernel.

The benchmark results of the ESSL library is provided by IBM, and is still under development. The performance seems to be not very high at present.

4 Elimination of Unnecessary Operations

In the case of our 3D convolution, the input data of the first 3D-FFT includes many zeros padded for convolution. The non-zero data is stored in the range of $x, y, z < N/2$. They occupy only 1/8 of the whole while the other 7/8 are filled with zeros. Since the results of 1D transforms of zeros obviously are zeros, we can eliminate the computation for those ranges.

Assume that the transforms of each direction are computed in the order of X $\rightarrow$ Y $\rightarrow$ Z. The transforms of direction X are only required in the range of $y < N/2, z < N/2$, that is, 1/4 of the whole. The transforms of direction Y are only required in the range of $z < N/2$, that is, half of the whole. The transforms of direction Z are required for all. 3D-FFT requires $15N^3 \log_2 N$ floating-point

Table 2. The performance improvement of 3D convolution by the padding

	N=64		N=128		N=256	
	Time	Gflops	Time	Gflops	Time	Gflops
With padding	46.2ms	1.15	436ms	1.13	4.23s	1.06
Without padding	53.7ms	0.99	742ms	0.67	6.37s	0.70

operations. In the case of our 3D-FFT for convolution, only $8.75N^3 \log_2 N$ floating-point operations are required by eliminating unnecessary operations.

5 Selecting of the Best Padding

If the size of the data is larger than the capacity of the cache memory, the block FFT algorithm [26] is better for efficient memory access. This algorithm is based on the idea of FFT implementation for large hierarchical memory [27], and its implementation consists of 1D-FFT on cache memory, copy-in routine, and copy-out routine. The copy-in routine copies data in a stride array on the main memory into an array on the cache memory, and the copy-out routine copies data in an array on the cache memory into a stride array on the main memory.

For example, the transforms of direction Y are described as follows.

```
do y = 1,N
   v(y) = A(x,y,z)
end do
fft1d(v)
do y = 1,N
   A(x,y,z) = v(y)
end do
```

We describe them as '`fft1d(A(x,:,z))`' for simplicity.

The stride of the memory accesses heavily influences the performance of the main memory. Therefore, we should insert some padding into the 3D arrays to adjust the stride of access along the directions of Y and Z. We examined the performance of the computation of 3D convolution changing the sizes of the padding, independently for the directions Y and Z, in the range of 0, 32, 64, 96, and 128 bytes in consideration of 32 byte line size of the L1 cache. The best performance was achieved with 32 byte padding for both Y and Z.

Table 2 shows the efficacy of inserting the padding. The advancement due to the padding is very large; speedups of 15% to 69% were achieved.

6 Three-Tier Hierarchical Memory

The PowerPC 440 FP2 processor has a 32kB L1 cache, a 4MB L3 cache, and a 512MB main memory. In the range of $64 \leq N \leq 256$, a double complex array of size N fits the L1 cache, and N^2 fits the L3 cache, and N^3 fits the main memory. Therefore, we improved the block FFT algorithm in consideration of three-tier hierarchical memory.

```
do z = 1,N
do y = 1,N
fft1d(A(:,y,z))
end do
end do

do z = 1,N
do x = 1,N
fft1d(A(x,:,z))
end do
end do

do y = 1,N
do x = 1,N
fft1d(A(x,y,:))
end do
end do
```

Fig. 1. Conventional 3D FFT

```
do z = 1,N
do y = 1,N
fft1d(A(:,y,z))
end do
do x = 1,N
fft1d(A(x,:,z)
end do
end do

do y = 1,N
do x = 1,N
fft1d(A(x,y,:))
end do
end do
```

Fig. 2. 3D FFT optimized for multi-level cache

In conventional 3D-FFT, 1D-FFTs for directions X, Y, and Z are performed as described in Fig. 1. In this case, the number of required accesses to the main memory is three, as long as the data of size N^3 exceed the capacity of the L3 cache. To reduce the access to the main memory, we can use a technique of XY-blocking as described in Fig. 2. In this case, the data used in 1D FFTs of direction Y are already available in the L3 cache because they are used by the previous 1D FFTs of direction X. Thus, the number of accesses to the main memory is reduced to two. In addition, the transforms for direction Z are combined with the following element-wise multiplications of the 3D convolution. In the part of inverse 3D-FFT, half of the input data for each 1D-FFT are zeros. We do not need to read those data to the cache memory. Furthermore, we do not need to allocate memory for them. To save memory space, we can place the data of `B(x,y,z)` at `A(x,y,z+N/2)`. Before the inverse transform of direction Z, the data of `A(x,y,1:N/2)` and `A(x,y,N/2+1:N)` are copied to the cache memory. After the transform of direction Z and element-wise multiplication, the results are written back to the area `A(x,y,:)`. Thus, we can compute the 3D convolution with only $N^3 + O(N)$ memory space.

Table 3 shows the performance improvements by XY-blocking. For smaller sizes such as 64, the performance is not improved. That is because the data size fits the capacity of the L3 cache. For larger sizes, speed-ups of about 5% are achieved. The speed-up is sufficiently large considering the small difference between the access speeds of the L3 cache and the main memory[28].

Table 3. The performance improvement of 3D convolution by blocking

	N=64		N=128		N=256	
	Time	Gflops	Time	Gflops	Time	Gflops
With blocking	46.4ms	1.15	414ms	1.19	3.98s	1.13
Without blocking	46.2ms	1.15	436ms	1.13	4.23s	1.06

Table 4. The computation times of the 3D convolution

	N=64	N=128	N=256
Our library	46ms	0.41s	3.98s
FFTW2-GEL	84ms	2.34s	–
FFTW3	115ms	1.84s	–
FFTW3-SIMOMD	90ms	1.55s	–
ESSL	128ms	2.51s	–

Table 4 shows the computation times of the 3D convolution using several FFT libraries. Our library is 80%–270% faster than the other libraries.

7 Dual-Core Parallelization

PowerPC 440 FP2 processors on Blue Gene have two cores. To use both cores for computation, we have two methods. One is a virtual node mode, and the other is thread generation in the co-processor mode.

In the co-processor mode, one core is used as the main computing processor, and the other is usually used as a communication co-processor. In addition, we are able to execute a thread on the co-processor. In that case, the two cores work as a shared memory multiprocessor.

On the other hand, in the virtual node mode, each core acts as a node; that is, two MPI processes run on a PowerPC 440 FP2 processor. This is the simplest way to use both cores for computations. But the system resources of the node become half of those in the co-processor mode. The size of the L3 cache and the amount of available memory become 2MB and 256MB, respectively. Even in co-processor mode, the amount of available memory is only 512MB. The memory size is no longer large and this restricts the size of problems that can be solved.

The computation of the 3-D convolution includes the nested loops described in Fig. 2. The parallelization of the outer loop and inner loop is available. Table 5 shows the performances with those modes. The single-core performance in the virtual node mode is degraded by 10% compared with that in co-processor mode. But the total performance of two virtual nodes is 1.8 times the single-core performance. The size of $256 \times 256 \times 256$ is not available in the virtual node mode, because of the lack of memory space.

The dual-core performance in the co-processor mode becomes higher when the outer loop is parallelized. Since the L1 caches of the cores are not coherent, we

Table 5. The performance with dual-core parallelism

	N=64		N=128		N=256	
	Time	Gflops	Time	Gflops	Time	Gflops
Co-processor mode (parallelize outer loop)	24.7ms	2.16	229ms	2.15	2.37s	1.89
Co-processor mode (parallelize inner loop)	28.4ms	1.87	241ms	2.05	2.51s	1.80
Co-processor mode (single core)	46.4ms	1.15	414ms	1.19	3.98s	1.13
Virtual node mode (single core)	51.8ms	1.03	453ms	1.09	–	–
Virtual node mode (dual core)	–	(2.06)	–	(2.18)	–	–

need to insert synchronizations between the transforms of direction X and Y in case the inner loop is parallelized. In the case of the outer loop, each core accesses an independent part of the data. Therefore, no synchronization is required during the execution of the nested loops. To synchronize the data between the cores, all data in the L1 cache must be evicted. That operation takes many cycles; therefore, parallelization of the outer loop is better.

Compared with the single-core performance in co-processor mode, the dual-core performance is increased by 70% to 90%, and the performance is nearly equal to those in virtual node mode.

8 Performance Estimation of Parallel Shape Complementarity Search

Complementarity scores can be computed using the high performance 3D-convolution. In our design, each node has data of a receptor. The data of a ligand is rotated and discretized on a node, and is distributed to all other nodes via high-speed broadcast network. Then all nodes compute the scores between their own receptor and the same ligand of the same rotation angle. After the computation for all ligands, the data of the next receptor is loaded.

Table 6 shows the broadcast time of the data of a ligand with 4096 nodes. The data size is N^3 bytes. Compared with the computation time of the 3D convolution of corresponding size, the broadcast time is negligible due to the high-speed broadcast network of Blue Gene.

Table 6. The broadcast times of the data of a ligand. The number of nodes is 4096

	N=64	N=128	N=256
Data size	256KB	2MB	16MB
Broadcast time	1.38ms	11.0ms	87.9ms

The complementarity scores of a receptor and multiple ligands are computed. In that case, the results of inverse 3D-FFT of the receptors are reusable. Therefore, the 3D convolution is divided into the inverse 3D-FFT of the receptors and the rest. In addition, the results of the inverse 3D-FFT are previously multiplied by the constant scaling coefficient $1/N^3$. As a result, the number of floating-point operations required for a pair of receptor and ligand is decreased to $23.75N^3 \log_2 N + 6N^3$ whereas the whole 3D-convolution requires $32.5N^3 \log_2 N + 8N^3$.

Table 7 shows the performance of each part. The reuse of the results of the inverse 3D-FFT requires additional memory space to save them. For that reason, the grid size of $256 \times 256 \times 256$ is not available on Blue Gene.

The summation of the times of the inverse 3D-FFT and the rest is longer than the time of 3D-convolution. That is because the division increased the number of accesses to the main memory. But the inverse 3D-FFT of a receptor is computed only once for each receptor, and the performance of the rest is important.

Considering the broadcast time, the performance of a node becomes 1.73 Gflops at $N = 128$. The performance with 4096 nodes will reach 7 Tflops.

Table 7. The performance by reuse of the results of inverse 3D-FFT (in dual-core co-processor mode)

	N=64		N=128		N=256	
	Time	Gflops	Time	Gflops	Time	Gflops
3D convolution	46.4ms	1.15	414ms	1.19	3.98s	1.13
The inverse 3D-FFT only	28.4ms	1.87	241ms	2.05	–	–
The rest	22.7ms	1.71	198ms	1.83	–	–

9 Concluding Remarks

We have developed a high performance 3D convolution so that the throughput of a shape complementarity search by the massive processors of Blue Gene is maximized. The efficient implementation of the 3D convolution has been presented. We have improved the 3D-FFT for three-tier hierarchical memory, and have brought out the high bandwidth of the main memory by adjusting the padding size. We have also developed high performance 1D FFT kernels optimized for Blue Gene PowerPC 440 FP2 processors, and especially for use in the 3D convolution. The high performance 3D convolution library achieves up to 2.16 Gflops (38.6% of peak) per node. The total performance of the complementarity search is estimated at 7 Tflops with the 4-rack Blue Gene system (4096 nodes).

Acknowledgments. This research was partially supported by CREST of JST. We wish to express our gratitude to the people at IBM and NIWS Co., Ltd. who gave us valuable advice and much technical information.

References

1. Sussman, J., et al.: Protein Data Bank (PDB): database of three-dimensional structural information of biological macromolecules. Acta Crystallogr. D. Biol. Crystallogr. D54, 1078–1084 (1998) `http://www.rcsb.org/pdb/`
2. Gardiner, E., Willett, P., Artymiuk, J.: GAPDOCK: A genetic algorithm approach to protein docking in CAPRI round 1. Proteins: Structure, Function, and Genetics 52(1), 10–14 (2003)
3. Chen, H., Zhou, H.: Prediction of Interface Residues in Protein-Protein Complexes by a Consensus Neural Network Method: Test Against NMR Data. PROTEINS 61, 21–35 (2005)
4. Connolly, M.L.: Shape complementarity at the hemoglobin alpha 1 beta 1 subunit interface. Biopolymers 25(7), 1229–1247 (1986)
5. Kuntz, I., et al.: A geometric approach to macromolecule-ligand interactions. Journal of Molecular Biology 161(2), 269–288 (1992)
6. Norel, R., Petrey, D., Wolfson, H.J., Nussinov, R.: Examination of shape complementarity in docking of unbound proteins. Proteins 36(3), 307–317 (1999)
7. Katchalski-Katzir, et al.: Molecular surface recognition: Deterimination of geometric fit between proteins and their ligands by correlation techniques. Proc. Natl. Acad. Sci. 89(6), 2195–2199 (1992)
8. Chen, R., Weng, Z.: Docking Unbound Proteins Using Shape Complementarity, Desolvation, and Electrostatics. Proteins 47, 281–294 (2002)

9. Chen, R., Weng, Z.: A Novel Shape Complementarity Scoring Function for Protein-Protein Docking. PROTEINS 51, 397–408 (2003)
10. Sumikoshi, K., Terada, T., Nakamura, S., Shimizu, K.: A Fast Protein-Protein Docking Algorithm Using Series Expansion in Terms of Spherical Basis Functions. In: Genome Informatics Workshop, vol. 16(2), pp. 161–173 (2005)
11. Janin, J.: CAPRI: A Critical Assessment of PRedicted Interactions. Proteins 52(1), 1–122 (2003)
12. Gabb, H., et al.: Modelling protein docking using shape complementarity, electrostatics and biochemical information. J. Mol. Biol. 272, 106–120 (1997)
13. Frigo, M., Johnson, S.G.: The Design and Implementation of FFTW3. Proceedings of the IEEE 93, 216–231 (2005) special issue on Program Generation, Optimization, and Platform Adaptation.
14. Fitch, B., et al.: Blue Matter: Strong Scaling of Molecular Dynamics on Blue Gene/L. IBM Research Report: RC23688, IBM Research Division (2005)
15. Lorenz, J., et al.: Vectorization techniques for the Blue Gene/L double FPU. IBM Journal of Research and Development 49, 437–446 (2005)
16. Eleftheriou, M., et al.: A Volumetric FFT for BlueGene/L. In: Pinkston, T.M., Prasanna, V.K. (eds.) HiPC 2003. LNCS (LNAI), vol. 2913, pp. 194–203. Springer, Heidelberg (2003)
17. Eleftheriou, M., et al.: Performance Measurements of the 3D FFT on the Blue Gene/L Supercomputer. In: Cunha, J.C., Medeiros, P.D. (eds.) Euro-Par 2005. LNCS, vol. 3648, pp. 795–803. Springer, Heidelberg (2005)
18. FFTE: A Fast Fourier Transform Package, http://www.ffte.jp/
19. Dongarra, J., Luszczek, P.: Introduction to the HPCChallenge Benchmark Suite. ICL Technical Report, ICL-UT-05-01 (2005)
20. Brigham, E.O.: The fast Fourier transform and its applications. Prentice-Hall, Inc., Upper Saddle River, NJ, USA (1988)
21. Loan, C.V.: Computational Frameworks for the Fast Fourier Transform. Society for Industrial and Applied Mathematics (SIAM), Philadelphia (1992)
22. Wait, C.D.: IBM PowerPC 440 FPU with complex-arithmetic extensions. IBM Journal of Research and Development 49, 249–254 (2005)
23. Linzer, E.N., Feig, E.: Implementation of Efficient FFT Algorithms on Fused Multiply-Add Architectures. IEEE Trans. Signal Processing 41, 93–107 (1993)
24. Goedecker, S.: Fast Radix 2,3,4 and 5 Kernels for Fast Fourier Transformations on Computers with Overlapping Multiply-Add Instructions. SIAM J. Sci. Comput. 18, 1605–1611 (1997)
25. Nukada, A.: FFTSS: A High Performance Fast Fourier Transform Library. In: 2006 IEEE International Conference on Acoustics, Speech, and Signal Processing (ICASSP 2006), vol. III, pp. 980–983. IEEE Computer Society Press, Los Alamitos (2006)
26. Takahashi, D.: A Blocking Algorithm for Parallel 1-D FFT on Shared-Memory Parallel Computers. In: Fagerholm, J., Haataja, J., Järvinen, J., Lyly, M., Råback, P., Savolainen, V. (eds.) PARA 2002. LNCS, vol. 2367, pp. 380–389. Springer, Heidelberg (2002)
27. Bailey, D.H.: FFT's in External or Hierarchical Memory. Journal of Supercomputing 4(1), 23–35 (1990)
28. Ohmacht, M., et al.: Blue Gene/L compute chip: Memory and Ethernet subsystem. IBM Journal of Research and Development 49, 255–264 (2005)

KSEQ: A New Scalable Synchronous I/O Multiplexing Mechanism for Event-Driven Applications

Hongtao Xia[1], Weiping Sun[2], Jingli Zhou[2], Yunhua Huang[1], and Jifeng Yu[2]

[1] Zhejiang Electric Power Corp. 310007, Hangzhou, China
hustvag@163.com
[2] Huazhong University of Sci. & Tech., 430074, Wuhan, China
{wpsun,jlzhou,jfyu}@wtwh.com.cn

Abstract. The performance of event-driven network applications, such as Web servers and proxies, was influenced by the scalability and efficiency of synchronous I/O multiplexing mechanism. Research shows that event-based mechanism can ensure the scalability, and using kernel-user shared memory to evade system calls can reduce a lot of system overhead. But these two features can not be combined by any solution till now, because of synchronous problem. This paper attempts to design an event notification mechanism for event-driven network applications, which using kernel-user shared event queues (KSEQ) to achieve both good scalability and low system overhead. The KSEQ works something like double buffer, and both application and kernel can write the shared data structures without the help of synchronization system calls. Experiment shows that the Squid proxy server using this mechanism presents shorter response time than other mechanisms.

1 Introduction

Communication-intensive applications, such as Web servers and proxies, usually handle ten thousands of clients simultaneously. To avoid blocking on network I/O operations, the event-driven architectures are generally used, such as SPED and AMPED [1]. Some research showed that for those event-driven applications under realistic loads, about 50% CPU time was consumed by *select* or *poll* [2], because in most UNIX-like systems, those traditional synchronous I/O multiplexing mechanisms scale poorly with the number of opened sockets

There are two orthogonal approaches to relief this problem: event notification and shared memory. Fig. 1 illustrates the effects of those different approaches. In event notification mechanisms, e.g. *epoll*[3] and AEM[4], each time a socket turns ready, a corresponding event will be generated. The overhead of generating and obtaining events is linear to the actual amount of ready sockets, but to register/deregister an interested socket, additional system call is needed. In *uselect*[5], the shared memory mechanism, kernel sets flags in the shared memory to represent ready sockets, and application scans shared memory directly to find those sockets. Compared with *select/poll*, the overhead has been reduced, because no system call and data copying needed here. But under realistic load, the time for scanning is not negligible, and it

I. Stojmenovic et al. (Eds.): ISPA 2007, LNCS 4742., pp. 970–981, 2007.

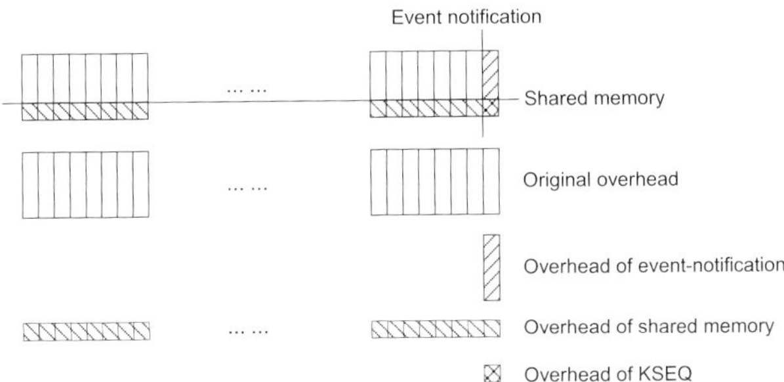

Fig. 1. Two orthogonal approaches to reduce overhead. For the extreme example, only one socket turns ready, event notification mechanism only reports the ready socket, while shared memory mechanism reduces the overhead of scanning all sockets. The KSEQ mechanism represents the ideal low overhead.

delays subsequent processing for all those ready sockets. Worse than that, the scanning time is proportional to the amount of opened sockets but not the amount of ready sockets. We had tested *uselect* on an Intel Pentium III 1000MHz CPU. The delay result from scanning was 45.2ms when application opened 1000 sockets, and was 169.5ms when opened 5000 sockets.

System call overhead can be averted by shared memory approach, and immoderate scanning can be avoided by event notification approach. Combining those two approaches might gain the best performance. But to implement event notification mechanism based on shared memory, application need pick down event and change the shared structures, so some measure must be used to synchronize the access of application and kernel. The synchronization system call is not acceptable, or its overhead will greatly offset the advantage of shared memory, and make the whole method meaningless.

This paper proposes a synchronous I/O multiplexing mechanism using an elaborate data structure: kernel / application shared event queues (KSEQ) to avoid synchronization calls. Exploiting features of event-driven applications, we can maintain its consistency and integrity. Further more, this mechanism provides smart user level APIs, allowing application processes event immediately just after it was found. The KSEQ mechanism is implemented as a Linux loadable kernel module and a user-level library. Experiment shows it is a scalable and high performance mechanism.

The remainder of this paper is organized as follows. Section 2 analyzes some useful features of typical event-driven applications. Section 3 describes the proposed mechanism in detail. Section 4 analyzes its scalability and performance. Section 5 describes the evaluation methodology and presents the results and Section 6 summarizes our contribution.

2 Useful Features of Event-Driven Applications

Experiences with communication-intensive applications demonstrate that restricting the number of kernel threads used by the application is critical to achieving good performance. The most efficient architectures are event-driven [1,6]. An event-driven application typically has a single thread (or process) to manage all opened sockets. This thread is an infinite loop. In each cycle, it gets ready sockets via synchronous I/O multiplexing interface, and then invokes a variety of handlers for corresponding sockets one by one. After that another cycle starts again. If no ready socket found, the thread will be blocked on the synchronous I/O multiplexing interface until some sockets turn to be ready [7].

In multi-processor system, event-driven server might have as many threads as processors. But to avoid data confusion and additional synchronizing work between threads, one opened socket should be processed only by one thread all its lifetime. Here we can conclude following features for typical event-driven applications:

- Thread invokes synchronous I/O multiplexing interface and event handler sequentially;
- Each opened socket will be processed by one thread all its lifetime.

Those features are necessarily true for event-driven applications. Exploiting those features, we can make event-driven application and kernel access the shared event queues harmoniously.

3 Implementation of KSEQ Mechanism

3.1 Software Architecture Overview

KSEQ mechanism is an event-notification mechanism basing on shared memory. It comprises four parts: user-level library, data structures shared by kernel and application, wakeup socket and kernel component. Fig. 2 shows the relationship of those parts.

The user-level library includes: (1) *kseq_create*, a function that initializes the KSEQ mechanism, (2) *kseq_ctl*, a function to register/deregister interested socket, (3) *kseq_next*, a function to get the next ready event, and (4) *kseq_state*, a function to check the state of certain socket instantly. *kseq_ctl* and *kseq_state* execute at user space. *kseq_next* usually just pick down ready event from shared structures. Only if no any socket is ready, it will call *select* to sleep on wakeup socket. Event-driven applications can use those APIs as Fig. 2 shows.

Wakeup socket is a dedicated socket created by *kseq_create*. It was never connected to any client. Kernel component maintains the events and flags in shared structures so that they can represent correct state of each socket. When a socket turns to be ready, say some data arrived, kernel component will generate corresponding event in shared structures according to application's registration, and if application is blocked on wakeup socket, kernel component will wake up it. Besides that, to realize LT (level trigger[1]) as *epoll* already did [8], each time after some system calls were invoked to operate on socket, such as read, kernel component checks current state of the socket, and adds event into shared structures if necessary. The kernel component is implemented as some wrappers of socket callback, *select* and other system calls operating on sockets.

---

[1] Level trigger means if the socket still be ready after last operation on it completed, and application still be interested in its state, an event will be necessary to trigger another operation.

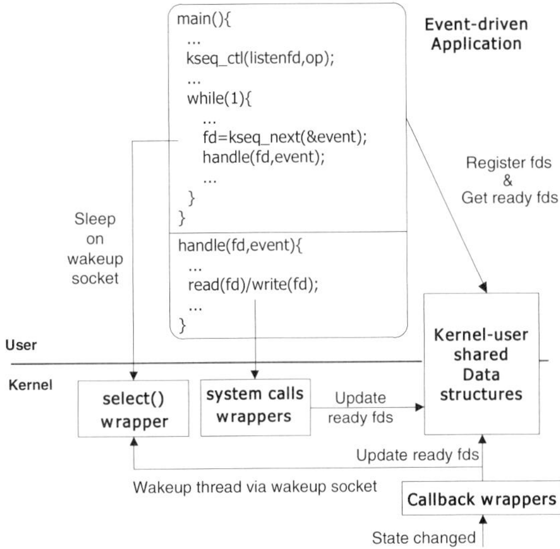

Fig. 2. KSEQ mechanism comprises user APIs, shared data structures, wakeup socket and kernel component. The kernel component consists of callback wrappers, *select* wrapper and wrappers of system calls that operating on fds (file descriptor). In Unix-like system, sockets opened by process are connected to file descriptors.

The shared data structures are the highway for kernel and application to exchange information. Through the highway, application informs kernel about its interested sockets, and kernel notifies application of the ready sockets. Exploiting the features of event-driven application, we can avoid the conflict problem of date sharing.

3.2 Kernel/Application Shared Structures and Synchronization Analysis

The shared structures are created at a piece of kernel / application shared memory. The shared memory will never be swapped out. It only belongs to one application, and just contains information about opened sockets, so the mechanism is safe and secure. There are two event queue sets, a switcher and a flag array in shared memory.

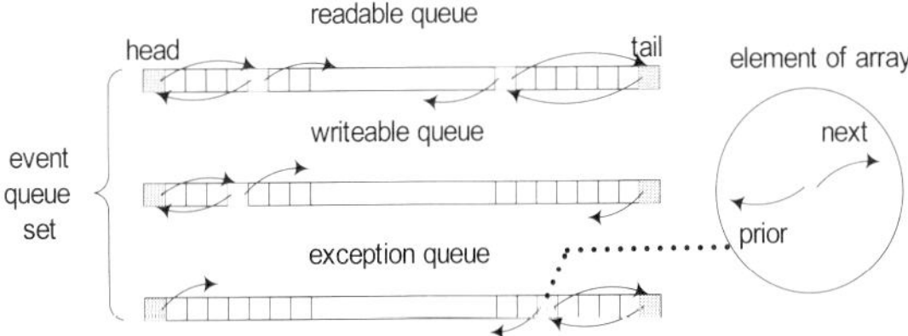

Fig. 3. Structure of event queue set

An event queue set is composed by three parallel queues containing readable events, writable events and exception events respectively. Each event queue is a double linked list based on an array as Fig. 3 shows. The first and the last elements in the array are the list head and tail. Every of other element is associated with a file descriptor, and comprised by two pointers. If an element has been added into the list, those pointers point to its prior and next node respectively, otherwise both of them are zero. Event queue is accessed in FIFO mode via its head and tail, and each node can be deleted directly. One element could not appear in the queue twice, so the length of event queue never exceeds the max number of file descriptors an application can open. That means the event queue will never overflow.

The switcher is a pivotal byte in the shared memory. It indicates which event queue set should be accessed by application. Application obtains event only from this queues set, we call it user event queue set and the other kernel event queue set. If the value of switcher changed, those queue sets will exchange roles and names with each other.

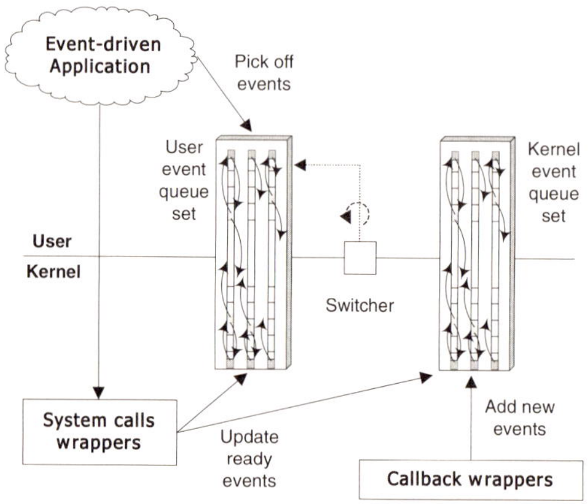

Fig. 4. Event queue sets work as double buffer. Switcher is the pivotal axis

Those two sets work as double buffer, see Fig.4, one for storing and one for picking. Kernel adds new events into kernel event queue set, while application picks off events from user event queue set. When application has picked off all events in user event queue set, it will change the value of switcher. It is safe for application to change switcher directly in uni-processor system. In multi-processor system, the switcher can be protected by a simple spinlock basing on *xchg*[2]. This mechanism never uses any synchronization system call, but there doesn't exist any conflict problem because of following reasons.

Firstly, when the value of switcher is stable, accessing both user and kernel event queues is safe. We have emphasized that in event-driven application only one thread processes an opened socket during its lifetime, so only one thread monitors a fixed set of sockets, and there is only one thread accessing user event queue set. To realize LT, sometimes the system call wrapper, invoked by this thread, also accesses the user

[2] This Intel X86 instruction can be executed both at user-level and kernel-level, and allows the atomic interchange of values between a memory word and a register. It can be used to construct spin lock both for application and kernel [9].

event queues. But the first feature concluded at section 2 tell us that the system all wrapper and the KSEQ API will be called sequentially, so their accessing of user event queues will be sequential. For kernel event queues, only kernel component can access them. So those access operations can be simply synchronized by kernel mechanism such as lock.

Secondly, application can independently decide when to change the value of switcher. The event queue will never overflow, so that kernel never needs additional space for new events. That means kernel never wait for application to release user queue set. Even if application crashed, kernel will always be safe.

Thirdly, changing the value of switcher is safe. In uni-processor system, kernel can't be preempted by application, but the revise is ok. Only after kernel finished its work, application can be continued. According to that, the operation of changing switcher value by application will never disturb kernel's operations on kernel queue set. At the exact time switcher being modified, kernel's operation on kernel queue set must have finished or not started. After switcher changed, kernel and application work on different queue sets respectively. In multi-processor system, application uses the simple spinlock to gain a tiny exclusive time slice and write one byte in the memory. It is also be safe, and the influence on performance is negligible.

In conclusion, kernel and application can exchange events safely via the shared queue sets, without any system call or context switching.

The flag array is an auxiliary memory object. Through it, application registers or deregisters interested sockets. Kernel maintains the state of each socket in this array. Elements in the array also associated with different sockets. One element comprises six bits: IR IW IE and R W E. IR, IW and IE represent if application is interested in the readable, writeable and exception state of corresponding socket. R, W and E represent its current state. User application can write IR IW IE and read R W E, while kernel component dose the reverse. To avoid conflicts, those two sets of bits must be located in two different bytes.

IR, IW and IE bits work as a filter. When a socket turns to be ready, kernel firstly set the R, W or E, and then checks IR, IW or IE to decide if put a new event into the kernel event queue. Application registers its interested socket in a reversed order: It firstly set the IR, IW or IE, then check R, W or E bits to see if the socket is already ready. If ready, puts a corresponding event in the tail of user event queues. These two anti-symmetric algorithms make sure that no event will be missed, even if they run on different processors. Sometimes they all generate an event at respective queues, but system call wrappers will purge redundant event later if necessary.

To deregister an event of socket, application just unsets the IR, IW or IE. *kseq_next* will drop events not registered.

4 Advantage Analysis

KSEQ is a smart event notification mechanism basing on shared memory. It works with practically no system calls, and has the advantages of event notification and shared memory mechanisms, but is better than both of them.

The kernel components of KSEQ, *uselect* and *epoll* almost work in the same way, except that *epoll* only monitors registered sockets, while *uselect* and KSEQ monitor all sockets opened by application. But event-driven applications commonly care most of opened sockets, the difference of their kernel cost is negligible, after all, the whole costs of their kernel components are very small fractions of total CPU utilization. The difference consists in their different user interfaces.

Firstly, KSEQ provides faster and smarter interface for application to register/deregister the events it is interested in.

Because *uselect* reserves the API syntax of *select*, it doesn't have dedicated API to register/deregister events. When *uselect*() is called, it uses the inputted FD_SET structures as filters for all sockets, and modifies those structures to return result, so that those structures can't be reused. Every time application invokes *uselect*(), it has to prepare new FD_SET structures in advance. They should contain all events currently concerned by application. A lot of position computing and bitwise operations are needed. An event occurs only several times during the socket's lifetime in realistic workload, but it is registered in FD_SET structures frequently, and a hot server in WAN is usually interested in a gigantic number of events. This shortage of *uselect* can be solved by reserving a copy of these structures in application, or by changing the API of *uselect*.

epoll provides *epoll_ctl* to register/deregister events, so it doesn't have the shortage of *uselect*, but this interface is a system call. It causes a trap into kernel space, so that at least two times of context switch is necessary to register/deregister events of a socket. KSEQ gives *kseq_ctl* as the dedicated register/deregister interface, but *kseq_ctl* is significantly slim, and only works at user space.

Secondly, through *kseq_next*(), the events retrieving interface of KSEQ, application obtains event more directly and quickly, and has the shortest response time.

Using *uselect* or *epoll*, application should firstly spend a lot of time on *uselect*() or *epoll_wait*() to find all events currently happened, after that it call handlers to process those events. To find events, *uselect*() compares the flag arrays in shared memory with the filter structures, and *epoll_wait*() traps into kernel space, and copies event data out. The time spent on those functions can't be neglected.

kseq_next() works in a totally different way. It usually just picks off one event from user event queues, and application handles this event immediately. The operation of picking off event can be completed in several CPU circles. Its overhead is comparable to that of application parsing the structures returned by *uselect*() or *epoll_wait*() for an event.

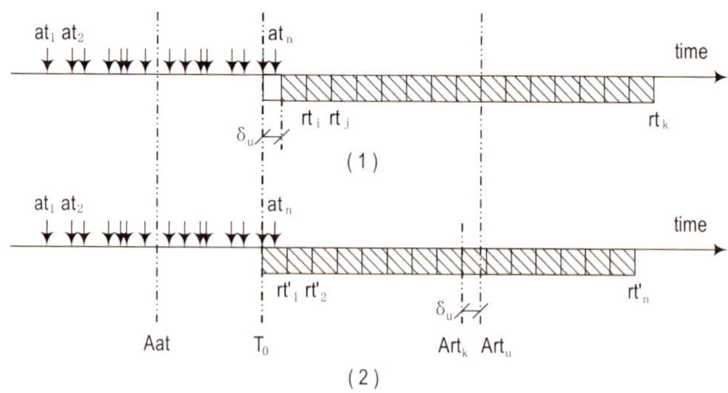

Fig. 5. Simplified models of the application using uselect (1) and KSEQ (2)

Fig 5 depicts simplified models representing the common work pattern of applications using *uselect* and KSEQ. The blocks in shadow represent the process of handling an event. As mentioned above, overhead of *kseq_next*() is comparable to that of parsing FD_SET structures for an event, so that we can simply assume the blocks also contain those operations in respective models, and all those blocks have the same size.

In *uselect* model, application called uselect() at T_0, and the uselect() spent δ_u and found n events that arrived respectively at at_0, at_1, $at_2 \ldots at_n$. The application finished handing those events respectively at rt_i, $rt_j \ldots rt_k$ in the order that they located in FD_SET structures. So the average response time can be calculated as follows:

$$Ar_u = \frac{\sum_{i=1}^{n}(rt_i - at_i)}{n} = \frac{\sum_{i=1}^{n} rt_i}{n} - \frac{\sum_{i=1}^{n} at_i}{n} = Art_u - Aat \quad (1)$$

Aat is the average event arrival time, and Art_u is the average response time of the application using *uselect*.

We assume that the application using KSEQ is subjected to the same workload, and start to call *kseq_next*() also at T_0. The application usually finished handling those events respectively at rt'_0, rt'_1, $rt'_2 \ldots rt'_n$ in the order that they arrived. We can compute the average response time as follows:

$$Ar_k = \frac{\sum_{i=1}^{n}(rt'_i - at_i)}{n} = \frac{\sum_{i=1}^{n} rt'_i}{n} - \frac{\sum_{i=1}^{n} at_i}{n} = Art_k - Aat \quad (2)$$

Art_k is the average response time of the application using KSEQ. The difference of those average response time is:

$$Ar_u - Ar_k = (Art_u - Aat) - (Art_k - Aat) = Art_u - Art_k \quad (3)$$

In our simplified model, we simply has:

$$Art_u - Art_k = \delta_u \quad (4)$$

So that

$$Ar_u - Ar_k = Art_u - Art_k = \delta_u \quad (5)$$

uselect uses shared memory to reduce the kernel/application communication overhead. But it always scans shared flags to find events. δ_u is linear to the max number of registered sockets but not to the number of ready sockets. When application works at WAN environment, δ_u is big enough to affect the performance. The application using KSEQ will have shorter response time.

5 Experimental Evaluation

5.1 Performance of Individual Operations

Measurements of performance were taken on a PC equipped with Intel Pentium III 1000MHz CPU and 512MB memory, running Linux-2.6.3. We raised the file descriptor limit from 1024 to 32768. A program similar to *lmbench* [10] was used to determine the cost associated with these mechanisms: KSEQ, *epoll* and *uselect*. The code under test was executed in a loop, with timing measurements taken outside the loop, and then averaged by the number of loops. Times were measured using the *rdtscl*() facility provided by Linux-2.6.3, which read the Time Stamp Counter (TSC) register. The TSC register has a resolution of 1 nanosecond on the platform under test. Time required to execute the loop itself and calls to *rdtscl*() were measured and the reported values were adjusted to eliminate those overhead. Each test was run 2000 times, with the first test not included in the measurements, in order to eliminate adverse cold cache effects. The mean value of the tests was taken. In all cases, the difference between the mean and median is less than one standard deviation.

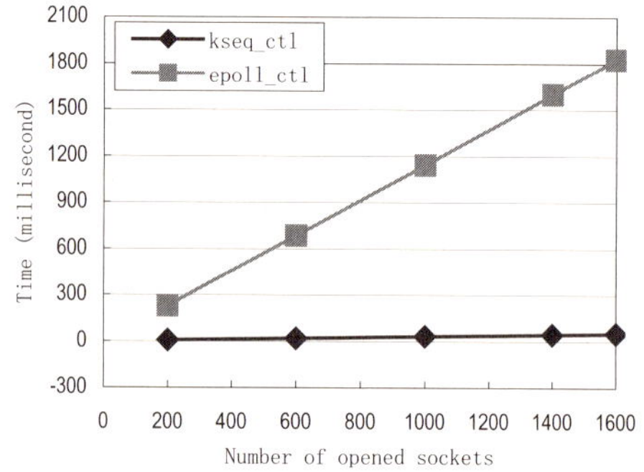

Fig. 6. The time used to register readable events on all opened sockets. Note the *y*-axis origin is shifted in order to better see the results

Firstly, we examined their registering operations. In experiment, application opened a varying number of sockets, and the time required to register readable events of those sockets was recorded. Fig. 6 illustrates that time spent on *epoll_ctl*() is more sensitive to the number of opened sockets. This is because *epoll_ctl*() is a system call, it is much slower than *kseq_ctl*(). Since *uselect* doesn't provide dedicated register/deregister interface, there is no corresponding result.

Another experiment was carried out to examine the time used by their event retrieving interfaces. It's represented as δ_u for *uselect* in section 4, and it affects the response time directly. In experiment, all opened sockets were firstly connected to *svr*, a simple program runs at another machine, and then the readable events of all sockets were registered. *svr* sent back some data through those connections. After that, events retrieving interface was invoked and examined.

srv can be used to control the number of ready sockets. If every single socket is ready, the time spent on *epoll_wait*() would reach the upper bounds. In that case, *epoll_wait*() has to do the maximum amount of work by checking each socket's filter for validity, and returning every event to application. If no socket ready, *epoll_wait*() would return quickly. With real workload, the actual time is somewhere in between. We examined *epoll_wait*() in those two extreme cases. For *uselect*, we did not record the time spent on preparing FD_SET structures.

Table 1. The time spent on event retieving interfaces.(unit:nanosecond)

Socket number	KSEQ	epoll (0 act)	epoll (all act)	uselect
200	31	2,872	128,187	7,737
500	30	2,846	972,362	28,567
1000	31	2,828	2,799,772	45,156
2000	30	2,838	7,122,982	77,527
5000	33	2,874	20,194,242	169,476
10000	31	2,874	41,270,306	343,053

The results are shown in Table 1. We can see that the time spent on *uselect*() increases with the number of registered sockets. Because it must scan the flag bits for all those sockets, no matter what the actual number of ready events will be. The time spent on *epoll_wait*() is constant when no socket ready, and is less then that of *uselect*(), but in the worst case, *epoll_wait*() need much more time. That is due to the overhead of copying events from kernel to application. The time spent on *kseq_next*() is always a very small value, because it only returns one event, and it always works at user space. Using *kseq_next*()□application can get event more immediately.

Table 2. The time spent on *kseq_next*() for all events and the time spent on resolving all events from structures returned by *epoll_wait*() and *uselect*(). We computed the average time in bracket. (unit:nanosecond).

Socket number	KSEQ	Parsing for epoll	Parsing for uselect
200	6,374(31)	1,342(6)	4,773(23)
500	15,470(30)	3,183(6)	10,695(21)
1000	31,019(31)	6,266(6)	21,043(21)
2000	61,237(30)	12,618(6)	46,294(23)
5000	168,060(33)	31,858(6)	112,477(22)
10000	315,872(31)	63,700(6)	224,674(22)

The experiments also shows the total time spent on *kseq_next*() is proportional to the number of events. Table 2 contains the total time spent on *kseq_next*() when all registered events happened. It is less than the time spent on *uselect*() and *epoll_wait*() in the same case.

In Table 2, we also recorded the time spent on resolving all events from structures returned by *epoll_wait*() and *uselect*(). We can see the time spent on *kseq_next*() to obtain all events is just comparable to that of resolving all events for *uselect* or *epoll*.

5.2 Application Level Benchmark

Squid[6,11], a popular web proxy server, was used in this evaluation. It is a typical event-driven application that can manipulate a very large number of communication streams. Squid is originally built around an infinite *select*/*poll* loop. In each cycle, it performs input and output operations on active sockets. The Squid-2.5 STABLE4 was modified to exploit KSEQ interfaces, as well as the interfaces of *uselect* and *epoll* used for comparison. In doing that, we had referred to the Squid-3.0, which is under developing and some effort has been made to exploit *epoll* interface.

Squid runs at the PC used at above evaluation (Intel PentiumIII 1000MHz, 512MB RAM, running Linux-2.6.3). We also increased the upper limit file descriptors to 32768. The client machine was another PC, using a single Intel PentiumIV 1.4GHz processor, 256MB memory. Both machines were equipped with an Intel PRO 1000 MT Gigabit Ethernet card, and connected via a DELL PowerConnect 2508 Gigabit switch. No other traffic was present on the switch at the test time. For the Squid, all files were loaded into the cache memory from web server before starting the test.

In order to generate workload for the web proxy server, the http_load [12] tool was used. It was configured to request URLs from a set of 1000 1KB and 10 1MB cached documents from the proxy, while maintaining 100 parallel connections. The http_load was usually used to test the throughput of web servers, it sent request as quickly as possible through those parallel connections. Another program was used to keep a varying number of idle connections open to the proxy. This approach follows earlier research that shows that web servers have a small set of active connections, and a larger number of inactive connections [2]. The same workload had been used to evaluate *kqueue* mechanism of FreeBSD[13].

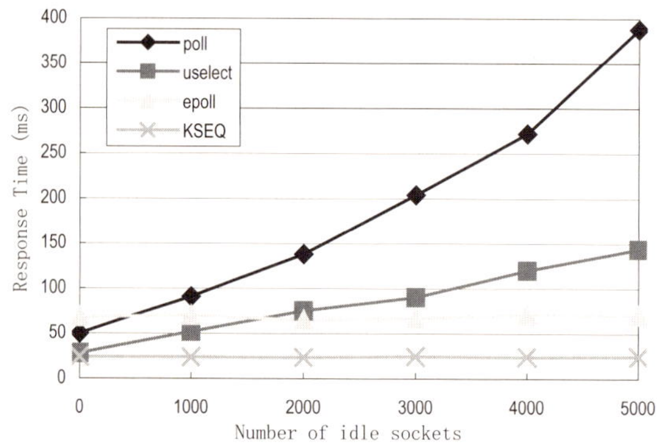

Fig. 7. Response time changes with the number of inactive connections

Fig.7 shows the response time of the proxy as the number of active connections is held at 100, and the number of inactive connections varies. The graph illustrates that the response time of Squid with *epoll* and KSEQ are almost constant regardless of the number of inactive connections. The *epoll* version always has a longer response time than KSEQ version, because both event registering and retrieving interfaces of *epoll* are system calls. For the same reason, the response time of *epoll* version is also longer than those of *uselect* and *poll* versions when there is no inaction connection. The response time of the *uselect* and *poll* versions increase when adding more inactive connections, and when the number of inactive connections is more than about 1700, the uselect version gives a longer response time than *epoll* version. That is because the *uselect*'s overhead of scanning memory increases with the number of registered sockets, and offsets the advantage of shared memory. *uselect* does not scale well with the number of active events, and *poll* also has the same problem. The graph shows Squid with *poll* represents the longest response time when the number of inactive connections is more than about 500. Squid with KSEQ always has the shortest response time.

6 Conclusion

This paper proposed a scalable and fast synchronous I/O multiplexing mechanism for event-driven applications. It is an event notification mechanism, basing on kernel/user shared event queues, which works as a fast event channel between kernel and user application. It provides fast register/deregister interfaces, and allows application obtaining every event directly and processing it as soon as possible. Experiment shows this mechanism provides a reduction in response time for event-driven applications.

References

1. Pai, V., Druschel, P., Zwaenepoel, W.: Flash: An Efficient and Portable Web Server. In: USENIX Annual Technical Conference (1999)
2. Banga, G., Mogul, J.C., Druschel, P.: A scalable and explicit event delivery mechanism for UNIX. In: USENIX Annual Technical Conference (1999)
3. Provos, N., Lever, C.: Scalable network I/O in Linux. Technical Report CITI-TR-00-4, University of Michigan, Center for Information Technology (2000)
4. Rossi, F.: Asynchronous Events on Linux. In: Open Cluster Group Conference (June 25, 2002)
5. Rosu, M.-C., Rosu, D.: Kernel Support for Faster Web Proxies. In: USENIX Annual Technical Conference, pp. 225–238 (2003)
6. NLANR: Squid Web Proxy Cache, http://www.squid-cache.org
7. Banga, G., Mogul, J.C.: Scalable kernel performace for Internet servers under realistic loads. In: USENIX Annual Technical Conference (1998)
8. Linux Programmer's Manual: epoll (2002), http://www.xmailserver.org/linux-patches/epoll.txt
9. Pineda, C., Coyote, H.C., Garcia, J.: User-Kernel Reactive Threads for Linux. In: The 7th World Multiconference on Systemics, Cybernetics and Informatics (SCI 2003) (2003)
10. Mcvoy, L.W., Staelin, C.: lmbench: Portable tools for performance analysis. In: USENIX Annual Technical Conference, pp. 279–294 (1996)
11. Chankhunthod, A., Danzig, P.B., Neerdaels, C., Schwartz, M.F., Worrell, K.J.: A Hierarchial Internet Object Cache. In: Proceedings of the 1996 USENIX Technical Conference, San Diego, CA, pp. 153–163 (1996)
12. Poskanzer, J.: http load, http://www.acme.com/software/http_load/
13. Lemon, J.: Kqueue: A generic and scalable event notification facility. In: FREENIX Track: USENIX Annual Technical Conference (2001)

A Synchronous Mode MPI Implementation on the Cell BE™ Architecture

Murali Krishna[1], Arun Kumar[1], Naresh Jayam[1], Ganapathy Senthilkumar[1], Pallav K. Baruah[1], Raghunath Sharma[1], Shakti Kapoor[2], and Ashok Srinivasan[3]

[1] Dept. of Mathematics and Computer Science, Sri Sathya Sai University, Prashanthi Nilayam, India
{kris.velamati,arunkumar.thondapu, nareshjs,rgskumar1983,baruahpk}@gmail.com, rrs_parthi@rediffmail.com
[2] IBM, Austin
skapoor@us.ibm.com
[3] Dept. of Computer Science, Florida State University
asriniva@cs.fsu.edu

Abstract. The Cell Broadband Engine shows much promise in high performance computing applications. The Cell is a heterogeneous multi-core processor, with the bulk of the computational work load meant to be borne by eight co-processors called SPEs. Each SPE operates on a distinct 256 KB local store, and all the SPEs also have access to a shared 512 MB to 2 GB main memory through DMA. The unconventional architecture of the SPEs, and in particular their small local store, creates some programming challenges. We have provided an implementation of core features of MPI for the Cell to help deal with this. This implementation views each SPE as a node for an MPI process, with the local store used as if it were a cache. In this paper, we describe synchronous mode communication in our implementation, using the rendezvous protocol, which makes MPI communication for long messages efficient. We further present experimental results on the Cell hardware, where it demonstrates good performance, such as throughput up to 6.01 GB/s and latency as low as 0.65 μs on the pingpong test. This demonstrates that it is possible to efficiently implement MPI calls even on the simple SPE cores.

1 Introduction

The Cell is a heterogeneous multi-core processor from Sony, Toshiba and IBM. It consists of a PowerPC core (PPE), which acts as the controller for eight SIMD cores called synergistic processing elements (SPEs). Each SPE has a 256 KB memory called its local store, and access to a shared 512 MB to 2 GB main memory. The SPEs are meant to handle the bulk of the computational load, but have limited functionality and local memory. On the other hand, they are very effective for arithmetic, having a combined peak speed of 204.8 Gflop/s in single precision and 14.64 Gflop/s in double precision.

Even though the Cell was aimed at the Sony PlayStation3, there has been much interest in using it for High Performance Computing, due to the high flop rates it provides. Preliminary studies have demonstrated its effectiveness for important

I. Stojmenovic et al. (Eds.): ISPA 2007, LNCS 4742, pp. 982–991, 2007.

computation kernels [15]. However, a major drawback of the Cell is its unconventional programming model; applications do need significant changes to fully exploit the novel architecture. Since there exists a large code base of MPI applications, and much programming expertise in MPI in the High Performance Computing community, our solution to the programming problem is to provide an *intra-Cell* MPI 1 implementation that uses each SPE as if it were a node for an MPI process [16, 17].

In implementing MPI, it is tempting to view the main memory as the shared memory of an SMP, and hide the local store from the application. This will alleviate the challenges of programming the Cell. However, there are several challenges to overcome. Some of these require new features to the compiler and the Linux implementation on the Cell, which have recently become available. We have addressed the others in [16] and in this paper, related to the MPI implementation. While [16] focuses on buffered mode communication, this paper focuses on synchronous mode communication. These two modes are explained in greater detail below.

In order for an MPI application to be ported to the Cell processor, we need to deal with the small local stores on the SPEs. If the application data is very large, then the local store needs to be used as software-controlled cache and data-on-demand, with the actual data in main memory. These features are available in the latest release of the Cell SDK. These will allow applications to be ported in a generic manner, with minimal changes to the code, when used along with our MPI implementation. Meanwhile, in order to evaluate the performance of our implementation, we hand-coded these transformations for two applications with large data, before the SDK features were made available. We have also developed a version of our MPI implementation for small memory applications, which can be ported directly, maintaining application data in local store. However, we will primarily describe our implementation that uses the local store as a software controlled cache, providing additional information on the small memory implementation occasionally.

Empirical results show that our synchronous mode implementation achieves good performance, with throughput as high as *6.01* GB/s and latency as low as *0.65* μs on the pingpong test. We expect the impact of this work to be broader than just for the Cell processor due to the promise of heterogeneous multicore processors in the future, which will likely consist of large numbers of simple cores as on the Cell.

The outline of the rest of the paper is as follows. In Sect. 2, we describe the architectural features of Cell that are relevant to the MPI implementation. We then describe our implementation in Sect. 3 and evaluate its performance in Sect. 4. We finally summarize our conclusions in Sect. 5.

2 Cell Architecture

Fig. 1 provides an overview of Cell processor. It consists of a cache coherent PowerPC core and eight SPEs running at 3.2 GHz, all of whom execute instructions in-order. It has a 512 MB to 2 GB external main memory, and an XDR memory controller provides access to it at a rate of 25.6 GB/s. The PPE, SPE, DRAM controller, and I/O controllers are all connected via four data rings, collectively known as the EIB. Multiple data transfers can be in process concurrently on each ring, including more than 100 outstanding DMA memory requests between main storage and the SPEs. Simultaneous transfers on the same ring are also possible. The EIB's maximum intra-chip bandwidth is 204.8 GB/s.

Each SPE has its own 256 KB local memory from which it fetches code and reads and writes data. Access latency to and from local store is 6 cycles [6] (page 75, table 3.3). *All loads and stores issued from the SPE can only access the SPE's local memory. Any data needed by the SPE that is present in the main memory must be moved into the local store explicitly, in software, through a DMA operation.* DMA commands may be executed out-of-order.

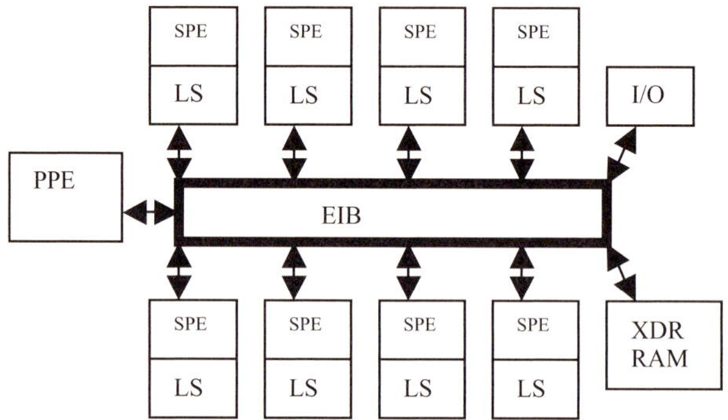

Fig. 1. Overview of cell architecture

In order to use the SPEs, a process running on the PPE can spawn threads that run on the SPEs. A SPE's local store and registers are mapped onto the effective address of the process that spawned a SPE thread. Data can be transferred from the local store or register of one SPE to that of another SPE by obtaining the memory mapped address of the destination SPE, and performing a DMA.

We present some performance results in Fig. 2 for DMA times. We can see that the SPE-SPE DMAs are much faster than SPE-main memory DMAs. The latter attain a maximum bandwidth of around 7 GB/s, in contrast to over 20 GB/s for the former. The latencies are a little higher when multiple SPEs simultaneously access memory.

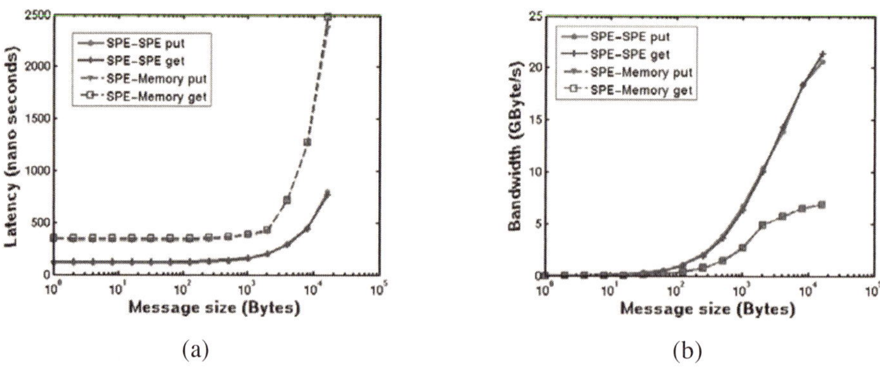

Fig. 2. Latency and bandwidth of DMA operations

3 MPI Design

In this section, we describe our basic design for synchronous mode point-to-point communication. We also describe the application start-up process. We have not described the handling of errors, in order to present a clearer high-level view of our implementation.

3.1 MPI Communication Modes

MPI provides different options for the communication mode chosen for the basic blocking point to point operations, MPI_Send and MPI_Recv. Implementations can use either the buffered mode or the synchronous mode. A safe application should not make any assumption on the choice made by the implementation[1] [13].

In the buffered mode, the message to be sent is copied into a buffer, and then the call can return. Thus, the send operation is local, and can complete before the matching receive operation has been posted. Implementations often use this for small messages [3]. For large messages, they avoid the extra buffer copy overhead by using synchronous mode. Here, the send can complete only after the matching receive has been posted. The rendezvous protocol is typically used, where the receive copies from the send buffer to the receive buffer without an intermediate buffer, and then both operations complete. In this paper, we describe only our synchronous mode implementation, and present experimental results where this mode is used for all message sizes[2].

3.2 MPI Initialization

We first summarize the MPI initialization process presented in [16]. A user can run an MPI application, provided it uses only features that we have currently implemented, by compiling the application for the SPE and executing the following command on the PPE:

```
mpirun -n <N> executable arguments
```

where <*N*> is the number of SPEs on which the code is to be run. The mpirun process spawns the desired number of threads on the SPE. Note that *only one thread can be spawned on an SPE*, and so <*N*> cannot exceed eight on a single processor or sixteen for a blade. We have not considered latencies related to the NUMA aspects of the architecture in the latter case.

Note that the data for each SPE thread is distinct, and not shared, unlike in conventional threads. The MPI operations need some common shared space through which they can communicate, as explained later. This space is allocated by *mpirun*. This information, along with other information, such as the rank in MPI_COMM_WORLD, the effective address of the signal registers on each SPE, and

[1] Other specific send calls are available for applications that desire a particular semantic.

[2] We described the buffered mode in [16]. It has smaller short-message latency but has poorer performance for long messages. The experimental results in [16] show the performance of a hybrid implementation, which switches to synchronous mode for large messages. However, the synchronous mode implementation is not described in [16].

the command line arguments, are passed to the SPE threads by storing them in a structure and sending a mailbox message[3] with the address of this structure. The SPE threads receive this information during their call to MPI_Init. The PPE process is not further involved in the application until the threads terminate, when it cleans up allocated memory and then terminates. It is important to keep the PPE as free as possible for good performance, because it can otherwise become a bottleneck. In fact, an earlier implementation, which used some helper threads on the PPE to assist with communication, showed poor performance.

3.3 Synchronous Mode Point-to-Point Communication

Communication Architecture. Associated with each message is meta-data that contains the following information about the message: Address of the memory location that contains the data[4], sender's rank, tag, message size, datatype ID, MPI communicator ID, and an error field. For each pair of SPE threads, we allocate space for two meta-data entries, one in each of the SPE local stores, for a total of $N(N-1)$ entries, with (N-1) entries in each SPE local store; entry B_{ij} is used to store meta-data for a message from process i to process j, $i \neq j$. Such schemes are used by other implementations too, and it is observed that it is not scalable for large N. However, here N is limited to eight for one processor, and sixteen for a blade (consisting of two processors). Each meta-data entry is *128* bytes, and so the memory used is small. It has the advantage that it is fast.

Send Protocol. We describe the protocol for data in contiguous locations, which is the more common case; data in non-contiguous locations will incur additional overhead. The send operation from P_i to P_j proceeds as follows. The send operation first puts the meta-data entry into buffer B_{ij} through a DMA operation.

The send operation then waits for a signal from P_j notifying that P_j has copied the message. The signal obtained from P_j contains the error value. It is set to MPI_SUCCESS on successful completion of the receive operation and the appropriate error value on failure. In the synchronous mode, an SPE is waiting for acknowledgment for exactly one send, at any given point in time, and so all the bits of the receive signal register can be used. Fig. 3 shows the flow of the send operation.

Receive Protocol. The receive operation has four flavors. (i) It can receive a message with a specific tag from a specific source, (ii) it can receive a message with any tag (MPI_ANY_TAG) from a specific source, (iii) it can receive a message with a specific tag from any source (MPI_ANY_SOURCE), or (iv) it can receive a message with any tag from any source.

The first case above is the most common, and is illustrated in Fig. 3. First, the meta-data entry in B_{ij} is continuously polled, until the flag field is set. The tag value in the meta-data entry is checked. If the application truly did not assume any particular communication mode, then this tag should match, and the check is superfluous. However, correct but unsafe applications may assume buffered mode, and so we perform this check[5]. If the tag matched, then the address of the message is obtained from the meta-data entry.

---

[3] A mailbox message is a communication mechanism for small messages of 32 bits.

[4] The address is an effective address in main memory. In the modification made for small memory applications, it is the effective address of a location in local store.

[5] We do not mention other error checks that are fairly obvious.

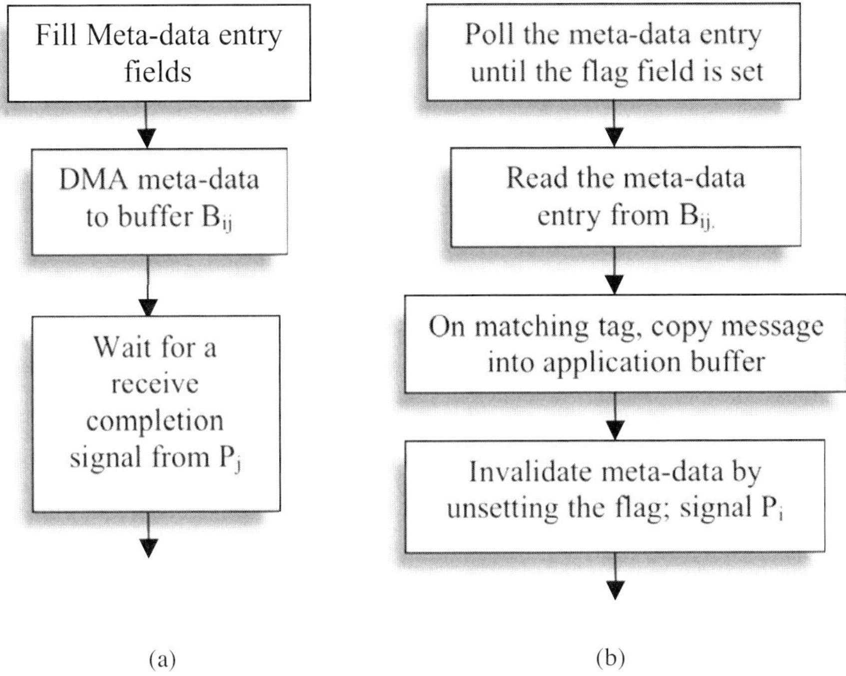

Fig. 3. Execution of (a) send and (b) receive operations from a specific source SPE P_i to P_j

The receive call then transfers data from the source SPE's application buffer to its own buffer and signals P_i's signal register to indicate that the data has been copied. Note that the data transfer is a little complicated, because the SPE cannot perform a *memcpy*, since source and destination buffers are in main memory, and not in its local store. It also cannot DMA from main memory to main memory, because it can only DMA between local store and some effective address. So we DMA the data to local store and then transfer it back to its location in main memory. For large data, this is performed in chunks, with double buffering being used to reduce the latency to a certain extent[6]. After the receiving SPE completes the transfer, it unsets the meta-data flag field, and then signals the sending SPE's signal register.

While the data transfer process described above appears wasteful, a similar situation occurs in traditional cache-based processors too [10]; *memcpy* brings the source and destination to cache from main memory, copies the data, and writes the destination back to cache, incurring three cache misses. Some systems have alternate block copy commands to avoid at least one of these misses. But these cache misses still have a dominant effect on MPI performance on shared memory systems.

The second case is handled in a manner similar to the first, except that any tag matches. The third and fourth cases are similar to the first two respectively, as far as tags are concerned. However, messages from any source can match. So the receive

[6] For small memory applications, both buffers are in local stores. Since a local store address can be mapped to an effective address, a single DMA suffices.

operation checks the meta-data entry flags for each sender, repeatedly, in a round robin fashion, to avoid starvation, even though the MPI standard does not guarantee against starvation. If any of the flags is set, and the tag matches for case (iii), then the rest of the receive operation is performed as above. Note that in case (iii), it is not an error for a tag not to match, because there may be a message from another sender that it should match.

4 Performance Evaluation

The purpose of the performance evaluation is to first show that our MPI implementation achieves performance comparable to good MPI implementations, even though the SPEs are not full-fledged cores. In particular, we will compare with shared memory intra-node MPI implementations, which have low latencies and high throughputs.

We performed our experiments on a 3.2 GHz Rev 2 Cell blade with 1 GB main memory running Linux 2.6.16 at IBM Austin. We had dedicated access to the machine while running our tests.

Fig. 4 shows the latency and bandwidth results using the pingpong test from *mpptest* [9]. It was modified to place its data in main memory, instead of in local store. We determined the wall clock time for these operations by using the decrementer register in hardware, which is decremented at a frequency of 14.318 MHz, or, equivalently, around every 70 ns. Between calls to the timer, we repeated each pingpong test loop 1000 times. For the shortest latencies we obtained (0.65 μs per message), this yields an accuracy of around *0.005%* (observing that each iteration of the loop involves two messages). The accuracy is greater for the larger tests.

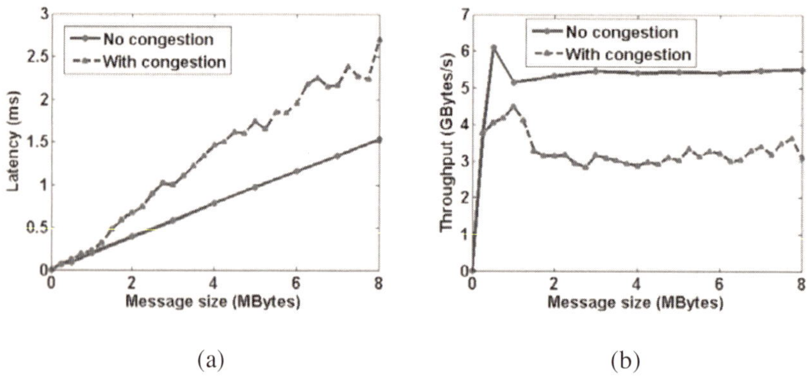

(a) (b)

Fig. 4. Latency and throughput results for point-to-point communication

We performed each test multiple times and took the average. Note that it is sometimes recommended that one take the smallest of the times from multiple experiments to obtain reproducible results [9]. This would give number a little smaller than the average that we report. However, our results were quite close to each other, and so there is not much of a difference between the average and the minimum.

Note that on cache-based processors, one needs to ensure that the tests do not already have their data in cache. However, the SPEs do not have a cache, and so this is not an issue. The implementation transfers data between main memory locations, using the SPE local store as a temporary location (analogous to a cache miss). The small-application tests move data from local store to local store.

Fig. 4 (a) shows the latency results for point to point communication on the pingpong test, in the presence and absence of congestion. The congested test involved dividing the SPEs into pairs, and having each pair exchanging messages. One pair was timed. In the non-congested case, only one pair of SPEs communicated. The smallest latency for the non-congested case is around 0.65 µs. The 0-byte message incurs the following costs: one SPE-SPE DMA, for the meta-data on the sender side, and one SPE_SPE signal on the receive side (the other DMAs, for getting data from main-memory to local store on the receiving side, and once again for sending that data back from local store to main memory, do not occur with a 0-byte message).

Fig. 4 (b) shows the throughput results for the same tests as above for large messages, where the overhead of exchanging meta-data and signals can be expected to be relatively insignificant. The maximum throughput observed is around 6 GB/s. From Fig. 2, we can observe that the maximum bandwidth for blocking SPE to main memory DMAs is around 7 GB/s. Note that though we need to transfer each data twice, once from main memory to SPE and then from SPE to main memory, due to double buffering and the ability to have multiple DMAs simultaneously in transit, the effective time is just half of the round-trip time. This is possible because at 6 GB/s, we have not saturated the bandwidth of 25.6 GB/s available for the main memory. Thus the observed DMA time agrees with what one would expect from the DMA times.

Table 1. Latency and bandwidth comparison

MPI/Platform	Latency (0 Byte)	Maximum throughput
Cell	0.65 µs	6.01 GB/s
Cell Congested	NA	4.48 GB/s
Cell Small	0.65 µs	23.29 GB/s
Nemesis/Xeon	≈ 1.0 µs	≈ 0.65 GB/s
Shm/Xeon	≈ 1.3 µs	≈ 0.5 GB/s
Open MPI/Xeon	≈ 2.1 µs	≈ 0.5 GB/s
Nemesis/Opteron	≈ 0.34 µs	≈ 1.5 GB/s
Open MPI/Opteron	≈ 0.6 µs	≈ 1.0 GB/s
TMPI/Origin 2000	≈ 15.0 µs	≈ 0.115 GB/s

Table 1 compares the latencies and bandwidths with those of some good intra-node implementations on other hardware. We can see that MPI on the Cell has performance comparable to those on processors with full-fledged cores.

In Table 1, *Cell* refers to our implementation on the Cell processor. *Cell Small* refers to our implementation for small applications. *Nemesis* refers to the MPICH using the Nemesis communication subsystem. *Open MPI* refers to the Open MPI implementation. *Shm* refers MPICH using the shared-memory (shm) channel. *TMPI* refers to the Threaded MPI implementation on an SGI Origin 2000 system reported in [14]. *Xeon* refer to timings on a dual-SMP 2 GHz Xeon, reported in [5]. *Opteron* refers to timings on a 2 GHz dual-core Opteron, reported in [3].

5 Conclusions

We have described an efficient implementation of synchronous mode MPI communication on the Cell processor. It is a part of an MPI implementation that demonstrates that an efficient MPI implementation is possible on the Cell processor, using just the SPEs, even though they are not full-featured cores. Small-memory applications using the core features of MPI can use our implementation directly, without any changes to the code being required. Other applications can make relatively small hand-coded changes, along with features provided by the SDK. Thus, our approach eases the programming burden, which is considered a significant obstacle to the use of the Cell processor. Furthermore, our implementation demonstrates that simple cores for future generation heterogeneous multicore processors can run MPI applications efficiently.

Acknowledgment

We thank Darius Buntinas of Argonne National Lab, for referring us to appropriate literature. We also thank several employees at IBM Bangalore for running the performance tests on the Cell hardware. Most of all, we express our gratitude to Bhagavan Sri Sathya Sai Baba, Chancellor of Sri Sathya Sai University, for bringing us all together to perform this work, and for inspiring and helping us toward our goal.

References

1. An Introduction to Compiling for the Cell Broadband Engine Architecture, Part 4: Partitioning Large Tasks (February 2006), http://www-128.ibm.com/developerworks/edu/pa-dw-pa-cbecompile4-i.html
2. An Introduction to Compiling for the Cell Broadband Engine Architecture, Part 5: Managing Memory, Analyzing Calling Frequencies for Maximum SPE Partitioning Optimization (February 2006), http://www-128.ibm.com/developerworks/edu/pa-dw-pa-cbecompile5-i.html
3. Buntinas, D., Mercier, G., Gropp, W.: Implementation and Shared-Memory Evaluation of MPICH2 over the Nemesis Communication Subsystem. In: Proceedings of the Euro PVM/MPI Conference (2006)
4. Buntinas, D., Mercier, G., Gropp, W.: Data Transfers Between Processes in an SMP System: Performance Study and Application to MPI. In: Proceedings of the International Conference on Parallel Processing, pp. 487–496 (2006)
5. Buntinas, D., Mercier, G., Gropp, W.: Design and Evaluation of Nemesis, a Scalable, Low-Latency, Message-Passing Communication Subsystem. In: Proceedings of the International Symposium on Cluster Computing and the Grid (2006)

6. Cell Broadband Engine Programming Handbook, Version 1.0 (April 19, 2006), http://www-306.ibm.com/chips/techlib/techlib.nsf/techdocs/9F820A5FFA3ECE8C8725716A0062585F/$file/BE_Handbook_v1.0_10May2006.pdf
7. Fatahalian, K., Knight, T.J., Houston, M., Erez, M.: Sequoia: Programming the Memory Hierarchy. In: Löwe, W., Südholt, M. (eds.) SC 2006. LNCS, vol. 4089. Springer, Heidelberg (2006)
8. Gropp, W., Lusk, E.: A High Performance MPI Implementation on a Shared Memory Vector Supercomputer. Parallel Computing 22, 1513–1526 (1997)
9. Gropp, W., Lusk, E.: Reproducible Measurements of MPI Performance Characteristics, Argonne National Lab Technical Report ANL/MCS/CP-99345 (1999)
10. Jin, H.-W., Panda, D.K.: LiMIC: Support for High-Performance MPI Intra-Node Communication on Linux Cluster. In: Proceedings of the International Conference on Parallel Processing, pp. 184–191 (2005)
11. MultiCore Framework: Harnessing the Performance of the Cell BE™ Processor, Mercury Computer Systems, Inc. (2006), http://www.mc.com/literature/literature_files/MCF-ds.pdf
12. Ohara, M., Inoue, H., Sohda, Y., Komatsu, H., Nakatani, T.: MPI Microtask for Programming the Cell Broadband EngineTM Processor. IBM Systems Journal 45, 85–102 (2006)
13. Snir, M., Otto, S., Huss-Lederman, S., Walker, D., Dongarra, J.: MPI - The Complete Reference, The MPI Core, 2nd edn. vol. 1. MIT Press, Cambridge (1998)
14. Tang, H., Shen, K., Yang, T.: Program Transformation and Runtime Support for Threaded MPI Execution on Shared-Memory Machines. ACM Transactions on Programming Languages and Systems 22, 673–700 (2000)
15. Williams, S., Shalf, J., Oliker, L., Kamil, S., Husbands, P., Yelick, K.: The Potential of the Cell Processor for Scientific Computing. In: Proceedings of the ACM International Conference on Computing Frontiers (2006)
16. Krishna, M., Kumar, A., Jayam, N., Senthilkumar, G., Baruah, P.K., Sharma, R., Srinivasan, A., Kapoor, S.: A Buffered Mode MPI Implementation for the Cell BE™ Processor. In: Proceedings of the International Conference on Computational Science (ICCS), Lecture Notes in Computer Science (to appear, 2007)
17. Krishna, M., Kumar, A., Jayam, N., Senthilkumar, G., Baruah, P.K., Sharma, R., Srinivasan, A., Kapoor, S.: Brief Announcement: Feasibility Study of MPI Implementation on the Heterogeneous Multi-Core Cell BE™ Architecture. In: Proceedings of the ACM Symposium on Parallelism in Algorithms and Architectures (SPAA) (to appear 2007)

Author Index

Printing: Mercedes-Druck, Berlin
Binding: Stein + Lehmann, Berlin

Lecture Notes in Computer Science

For information about Vols. 1–4583

please contact your bookseller or Springer

Vol. 4743: P. Thulasiraman, X. He, T.L. Xu, M.K. Denko, R.K. Thulasiram, L.T. Yang (Eds.), Frontiers of High Performance Computing and Networking ISPA 2007 Workshops. XXIX, 536 pages. 2007.

Vol. 4742: I. Stojmenovic, R.K. Thulasiram, L.T. Yang, W. Jia, M. Guo, R.F. de Mello (Eds.), Parallel and Distributed Processing and Applications. XX, 995 pages. 2007.

Vol. 4727: P. Pailler, I. Verbauwhede (Eds.), Cryptographic Hardware and Embedded Systems - CHES 2007. XIV, 468 pages. 2007.

Vol. 4720: B. Konev, F. Wolter (Eds.), Frontiers of Combining Systems. X, 2283 pages. 2007. (Sublibrary LNAI).

Vol. 4708: L. Kučera, A. Kučera (Eds.), Mathematical Foundations of Computer Science 2007. XVIII, 764 pages. 2007.

Vol. 4707: O. Gervasi, M.L. Gavrilova (Eds.), Computational Science and Its Applications – ICCSA 2007, Part III. XXIV, 1205 pages. 2007.

Vol. 4706: O. Gervasi, M.L. Gavrilova (Eds.), Computational Science and Its Applications – ICCSA 2007, Part II. XXIII, 1129 pages. 2007.

Vol. 4705: O. Gervasi, M.L. Gavrilova (Eds.), Computational Science and Its Applications – ICCSA 2007, Part I. XLIV, 1169 pages. 2007.

Vol. 4703: L. Caires, V.T. Vasconcelos (Eds.), CONCUR 2007 – Concurrency Theory. XIII, 507 pages. 2007.

Vol. 4697: L. Choi, Y. Paek, S. Cho (Eds.), Advances in Computer Systems Architecture. XIII, 400 pages. 2007.

Vol. 4685: D.J. Veit, J. Altmann (Eds.), Grid Economics and Business Models. XII, 201 pages. 2007.

Vol. 4684: L. Kang, Y. Liu, S. Zeng (Eds.), Evolvable Systems: From Biology to Hardware. XIV, 446 pages. 2007.

Vol. 4683: L. Kang, Y. Liu, S. Zeng (Eds.), Intelligence Computation and Applications. XVII, 663 pages. 2007.

Vol. 4682: D.-S. Huang, L. Heutte, M. Loog (Eds.), Advanced Intelligent Computing Theories and Applications. XXVII, 1373 pages. 2007. (Sublibrary LNAI).

Vol. 4681: D.-S. Huang, L. Heutte, M. Loog (Eds.), Advanced Intelligent Computing Theories and Applications. XXVI, 1379 pages. 2007.

Vol. 4679: A.L. Yuille, S.-C. Zhu, D. Cremers, Y. Wang (Eds.), Energy Minimization Methods in Computer Vision and Pattern Recognition. XII, 494 pages. 2007.

Vol. 4678: J. Blanc-Talon, W. Philips, D. Popescu, P. Scheunders (Eds.), Advanced Concepts for Intelligent Vision Systems. XXIII, 1100 pages. 2007.

Vol. 4673: W.G. Kropatsch, M. Kampel, A. Hanbury (Eds.), Computer Analysis of Images and Patterns. XX, 1006 pages. 2007.

Vol. 4671: V. Malyshkin (Ed.), Parallel Computing Technologies. XIV, 635 pages. 2007.

Vol. 4660: S. Džeroski, J. Todorovski (Eds.), Computational Discovery of Scientific Knowledge. X, 327 pages. 2007. (Sublibrary LNAI).

Vol. 4659: V. Mařík, V. Vyatkin, A.W. Colombo (Eds.), Holonic and Multi-Agent Systems for Manufacturing. VIII, 456 pages. 2007. (Sublibrary LNAI).

Vol. 4658: T. Enokido, L. Barolli, M. Takizawa (Eds.), Network-Based Information Systems. XIII, 544 pages. 2007.

Vol. 4657: C. Lambrinoudakis, G. Pernul, A M. Tjoa (Eds.), Trust and Privacy in Digital Business. XIII, 291 pages. 2007.

Vol. 4656: M.A. Wimmer, J. Scholl, Å. Grönlund (Eds.), Electronic Government. XIV, 450 pages. 2007.

Vol. 4655: G. Psaila, R. Wagner (Eds.), E-Commerce and Web Technologies. VII, 229 pages. 2007.

Vol. 4654: I.Y. Song, J. Eder, T.M. Nguyen (Eds.), Data Warehousing and Knowledge Discovery. XVI, 482 pages. 2007.

Vol. 4653: R. Wagner, N. Revell, G. Pernul (Eds.), Database and Expert Systems Applications. XXII, 907 pages. 2007.

Vol. 4651: F. Azevedo, P. Barahona, F. Fages, F. Rossi (Eds.), Recent Advances in Constraints. VIII, 185 pages. 2007. (Sublibrary LNAI).

Vol. 4649: V. Diekert, M.V. Volkov, A. Voronkov (Eds.), Computer Science – Theory and Applications. XIII, 420 pages. 2007.

Vol. 4647: R. Martin, M. Sabin, J. Winkler (Eds.), Mathematics of Surfaces XII. IX, 509 pages. 2007.

Vol. 4645: R. Giancarlo, S. Hannenhalli (Eds.), Algorithms in Bioinformatics. XIII, 432 pages. 2007. (Sublibrary LNBI).

Vol. 4644: N. Azemard, L. Svensson (Eds.), Integrated Circuit and System Design. XIV, 583 pages. 2007.

Vol. 4643: M.-F. Sagot, M.E.M.T. Walter (Eds.), Advances in Bioinformatics and Computational Biology. XII, 177 pages. 2007. (Sublibrary LNBI).

Vol. 4642: S.-W. Lee, S.Z. Li (Eds.), Advances in Biometrics. XX, 1216 pages. 2007.

Vol. 4641: A.-M. Kermarrec, L. Bougé, T. Priol (Eds.), Euro-Par 2007 Parallel Processing. XXVII, 974 pages. 2007.

Vol. 4639: E. Csuhaj-Varjú, Z. Ésik (Eds.), Fundamentals of Computation Theory. XIV, 508 pages. 2007.

Vol. 4638: T. Stützle, M. Birattari, H.H. Hoos (Eds.), Engineering Stochastic Local Search Algorithms. X, 223 pages. 2007.

Vol. 4637: C. Kruegel, R. Lippmann, A. Clark (Eds.), Recent Advances in Intrusion Detection. XII, 337 pages. 2007.

Vol. 4635: B. Kokinov, D.C. Richardson, T.R. Roth-Berghofer, L. Vieu (Eds.), Modeling and Using Context. XIV, 574 pages. 2007. (Sublibrary LNAI).

Vol. 4634: H.R. Nielson, G. Filé (Eds.), Static Analysis. XI, 469 pages. 2007.

Vol. 4633: M. Kamel, A. Campilho (Eds.), Image Analysis and Recognition. XII, 1312 pages. 2007.

Vol. 4632: R. Alhajj, H. Gao, X. Li, J. Li, O.R. Zaïane (Eds.), Advanced Data Mining and Applications. XV, 634 pages. 2007. (Sublibrary LNAI).

Vol. 4628: L.N. de Castro, F.J. Von Zuben, H. Knidel (Eds.), Artificial Immune Systems. XII, 438 pages. 2007.

Vol. 4627: M. Charikar, K. Jansen, O. Reingold, J.D.P. Rolim (Eds.), Approximation, Randomization, and Combinatorial Optimization. XII, 626 pages. 2007.

Vol. 4626: R.O. Weber, M.M. Richter (Eds.), Case-Based Reasoning Research and Development. XIII, 534 pages. 2007. (Sublibrary LNAI).

Vol. 4624: T. Mossakowski, U. Montanari, M. Haveraaen (Eds.), Algebra and Coalgebra in Computer Science. XI, 463 pages. 2007.

Vol. 4622: A. Menezes (Ed.), Advances in Cryptology - CRYPTO 2007. XIV, 631 pages. 2007.

Vol. 4619: F. Dehne, J.-R. Sack, N. Zeh (Eds.), Algorithms and Data Structures. XVI, 662 pages. 2007.

Vol. 4618: S.G. Akl, C.S. Calude, M.J. Dinneen, G. Rozenberg, H.T. Wareham (Eds.), Unconventional Computation. X, 243 pages. 2007.

Vol. 4617: V. Torra, Y. Narukawa, Y. Yoshida (Eds.), Modeling Decisions for Artificial Intelligence. XII, 502 pages. 2007. (Sublibrary LNAI).

Vol. 4616: A. Dress, Y. Xu, B. Zhu (Eds.), Combinatorial Optimization and Applications. XI, 390 pages. 2007.

Vol. 4615: R. de Lemos, C. Gacek, A. Romanovsky (Eds.), Architecting Dependable Systems IV. XIV, 435 pages. 2007.

Vol. 4613: F.P. Preparata, Q. Fang (Eds.), Frontiers in Algorithmics. XI, 348 pages. 2007.

Vol. 4612: I. Miguel, W. Ruml (Eds.), Abstraction, Reformulation, and Approximation. XI, 418 pages. 2007. (Sublibrary LNAI).

Vol. 4611: J. Indulska, J. Ma, L.T. Yang, T. Ungerer, J. Cao (Eds.), Ubiquitous Intelligence and Computing. XXIII, 1257 pages. 2007.

Vol. 4610: B. Xiao, L.T. Yang, J. Ma, C. Muller-Schloer, Y. Hua (Eds.), Autonomic and Trusted Computing. XVIII, 571 pages. 2007.

Vol. 4609: E. Ernst (Ed.), ECOOP 2007 – Object-Oriented Programming. XIII, 625 pages. 2007.

Vol. 4608: H.W. Schmidt, I. Crnkovic, G.T. Heineman, J.A. Stafford (Eds.), Component-Based Software Engineering. XII, 283 pages. 2007.

Vol. 4607: L. Baresi, P. Fraternali, G.-J. Houben (Eds.), Web Engineering. XVI, 576 pages. 2007.

Vol. 4606: A. Pras, M. van Sinderen (Eds.), Dependable and Adaptable Networks and Services. XIV, 149 pages. 2007.

Vol. 4605: D. Papadias, D. Zhang, G. Kollios (Eds.), Advances in Spatial and Temporal Databases. X, 479 pages. 2007.

Vol. 4604: U. Priss, S. Polovina, R. Hill (Eds.), Conceptual Structures: Knowledge Architectures for Smart Applications. XII, 514 pages. 2007. (Sublibrary LNAI).

Vol. 4603: F. Pfenning (Ed.), Automated Deduction – CADE-21. XII, 522 pages. 2007. (Sublibrary LNAI).

Vol. 4602: S. Barker, G.-J. Ahn (Eds.), Data and Applications Security XXI. X, 291 pages. 2007.

Vol. 4600: H. Comon-Lundh, C. Kirchner, H. Kirchner (Eds.), Rewriting, Computation and Proof. XVI, 273 pages. 2007.

Vol. 4599: S. Vassiliadis, M. Berekovic, T.D. Hämäläinen (Eds.), Embedded Computer Systems: Architectures, Modeling, and Simulation. XVIII, 466 pages. 2007.

Vol. 4598: G. Lin (Ed.), Computing and Combinatorics. XII, 570 pages. 2007.

Vol. 4597: P. Perner (Ed.), Advances in Data Mining. XI, 353 pages. 2007. (Sublibrary LNAI).

Vol. 4596: L. Arge, C. Cachin, T. Jurdziński, A. Tarlecki (Eds.), Automata, Languages and Programming. XVII, 953 pages. 2007.

Vol. 4595: D. Bošnački, S. Edelkamp (Eds.), Model Checking Software. X, 285 pages. 2007.

Vol. 4594: R. Bellazzi, A. Abu-Hanna, J. Hunter (Eds.), Artificial Intelligence in Medicine. XVI, 509 pages. 2007. (Sublibrary LNAI).

Vol. 4593: A. Biryukov (Ed.), Fast Software Encryption. XI, 467 pages. 2007.

Vol. 4592: Z. Kedad, N. Lammari, E. Métais, F. Meziane, Y. Rezgui (Eds.), Natural Language Processing and Information Systems. XIV, 442 pages. 2007.

Vol. 4591: J. Davies, J. Gibbons (Eds.), Integrated Formal Methods. IX, 660 pages. 2007.

Vol. 4590: W. Damm, H. Hermanns (Eds.), Computer Aided Verification. XV, 562 pages. 2007.

Vol. 4589: J. Münch, P. Abrahamsson (Eds.), Product-Focused Software Process Improvement. XII, 414 pages. 2007.

Vol. 4588: T. Harju, J. Karhumäki, A. Lepistö (Eds.), Developments in Language Theory. XI, 423 pages. 2007.

Vol. 4587: R. Cooper, J. Kennedy (Eds.), Data Management. XIII, 259 pages. 2007.

Vol. 4586: J. Pieprzyk, H. Ghodosi, E. Dawson (Eds.), Information Security and Privacy. XIV, 476 pages. 2007.

Vol. 4585: M. Kryszkiewicz, J.F. Peters, H. Rybinski, A. Skowron (Eds.), Rough Sets and Intelligent Systems Paradigms. XIX, 836 pages. 2007. (Sublibrary LNAI).

Vol. 4584: N. Karssemeijer, B. Lelieveldt (Eds.), Information Processing in Medical Imaging. XX, 777 pages. 2007.